The t Distribution

The table entries give values t_a cutting off a right-tail probability of a:

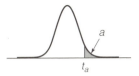

$$\Pr(t > t_a) = a$$

Degrees of freedom	Right-tail probability a				
	0.10	0.05	0.025	0.01	0.005
1	3.078	6.314	12.706	31.821	63.657
2	1.886	2.920	4.303	6.965	9.925
3	1.638	2.353	3.182	4.541	5.841
4	1.533	2.132	2.776	3.747	4.604
5	1.476	2.015	2.571	3.365	4.032
6	1.440	1.943	2.447	3.143	3.707
7	1.415	1.895	2.365	2.998	3.499
8	1.397	1.860	2.306	2.896	3.355
9	1.383	1.833	2.262	2.821	3.250
10	1.372	1.812	2.228	2.764	3.169
11	1.363	1.796	2.201	2.718	3.106
12	1.356	1.782	2.179	2.681	3.055
13	1.350	1.771	2.160	2.650	3.012
14	1.345	1.761	2.145	2.624	2.977
15	1.341	1.753	2.131	2.602	2.947
16	1.337	1.746	2.120	2.583	2.921
17	1.333	1.740	2.110	2.567	2.898
18	1.330	1.734	2.101	2.552	2.878
19	1.328	1.729	2.093	2.539	2.861
20	1.325	1.725	2.086	2.528	2.845
21	1.323	1.721	2.080	2.518	2.831
22	1.321	1.717	2.074	2.508	2.819
23	1.319	1.714	2.069	2.500	2.807
24	1.318	1.711	2.064	2.492	2.797
25	1.316	1.708	2.060	2.485	2.787
26	1.315	1.706	2.056	2.479	2.779
27	1.314	1.703	2.052	2.473	2.771
28	1.313	1.701	2.048	2.467	2.763
29	1.311	1.699	2.045	2.462	2.756
30	1.310	1.697	2.042	2.457	2.750
40	1.303	1.684	2.021	2.423	2.704
60	1.296	1.671	2.000	2.390	2.660
120	1.289	1.658	1.980	2.358	2.617
∞	1.282	1.645	1.960	2.326	2.576

From *Biometrika Tables for Statisticians*, Vol. 1, 3rd ed. (1966), Table 12. Used with permission of the Biometrika Trustees.

Duxbury Titles of Related Interest

Albright & Winston, *Spreadsheet Modeling and Applications*

Albright, Winston, & Zappe, *Data Analysis and Decision Making*

Berger & Maurer, *Experimental Design*

Bowerman & O'Connell, *Linear Statistical Models*

Bowerman, O'Connell, & Koehler, *Forecasting, Time Series and Regression*

Clemen & Reilly, *Making Hard Decisions with Decision Tools*

Davis, *Business Research for Decision Making*

Derr, *Statistical Consulting: A Guide to Effective Communication*

Dielman, *Applied Regression Analysis*

Higgins, *Introduction to Modern Nonparametric Methods*

Hildebrand, Ott, & Gray, *Basic Statistical Ideas for Managers*

Hoerl & Snee, *Statistical Thinking: Improving Business Performance*

Keller & Warrack, *Statistics for Management and Economics*

Kirkwood, *Strategic Decision Making*

Kleinbaum, Kupper, Muller, & Nizam, *Applied Regression Analysis and Multivariable Methods*

Kuchl, *Design of Experiments: Statistical Principles for Research Design and Analysis*

Lattin, Carroll, & Green, *Analyzing Multivariate Data*

Lorh, *Sampling: Design and Analysis*

Lunneborg, *Data Analysis by Resampling*

McClelland, *Seeing Statistics*®

Minh, *Applied Probability Models*

Myerson, *Probability Models for Economic Decisions*

Ott & Longnecker, *An Introduction to Statistical Methods and Data Analysis*

Ramsey & Schafer, *The Statistical Sleuth*

Ryan, Joiner, & Cryer, *Minitab Handbook*

Sall, Creighton, & Lehman, *JMP Start Statistics*

SAS Institute, Inc., *JMP-IN: Statistical Discovery Software*

Schaeffer, Mendenhall, & Ott, *Elementary Survey Sampling*

Seila, Ceric, & Tadikamalla, *Applied Simulation Modeling*

Shapiro, *Modeling the Supply Chain*

Weiers, *Introduction to Business Statistics*

Winston, *Operations Research: Applications and Algorithms*

Winston & Albright, *Practical Management Science*

To order copies, contact your local bookstore or call 1-800-354-9706

For more information, go to www.duxbury.com

DUXBURY

Introduction to Applied Econometrics

Kenneth G. Stewart
University of Victoria

THOMSON
™
BROOKS/COLE

Australia • Canada • Mexico • Singapore • Spain
United Kingdom • United States

THOMSON
BROOKS/COLE

Publisher: *Curt Hinrichs*
Assistant Editor: *Ann Day*
Editorial Assistant: *Katherine Brayton*
Technology Project Manager: *Burke Taft*
Marketing Manager: *Tom Ziolkowski*
Advertising Project Manager:
  Nathaniel Bergson-Michelson
Project Manager, Editorial Production: *Kelsey McGee*
Print/Media Buyer: *Barbara Britton*

Permissions Editor: *Kiely Sexton*
Production Service: *The Book Company*
Illustrator: *Lori Heckelman*
Compositor: *Laserwords*
Cover Designer: *Roy R. Neuhaus*
Cover Image: *Photodisc/Getty Images*
Cover Printing: *Phoenix Color Corp*
Printing and Binding: *QuebecorWorld/*
  Kingsport

For more information about our products,
contact us at:
Thomson Learning Academic Resource Center
1-800-423-0563
For permission to use material from this text,
contact us by:
Phone: 1-800-730-2214 **Fax:** 1-800-730-2215
Web: http://www.thomsonrights.com

Library of Congress Control Number: 2004101383

ISBN 0-534-36916-2

Brooks/Cole Thomson Learning
10 Davis Drive
Belmont, CA 94002
USA

Asia
Thomson Learning
5 Shenton Way #01-01
UIC Building
Singapore 068808

Australia/New Zealand
Thomson Learning
102 Dodds Street
Southbank, Victoria 3006
Australia

Canada
Nelson
1120 Birchmount Road
Toronto, Ontario M1K 5G4
Canada

Europe/Middle East/Africa
Thomson Learning
High Holborn House
50/51 Bedford Row
London WC1R 4LR
United Kingdom

To Rose, Ben, Alex, Ellie, and Andrew

About the Author

Ken Stewart holds an Honours B.A. with a double major in economics and mathematics from Dalhousie University, where he graduated with first class honours and was awarded the University Medal in Economics in his graduating year. He earned an M.Sc. in Economics from the London School of Economics and Political Science, followed by an A.M. in Economics, an A.M. in Statistics, and a Ph.D. in Economics from the University of Michigan. He is an Associate Professor in the Department of Economics at the University of Victoria, where he has taught undergraduate and graduate statistics, econometrics, and empirical finance. He also often teaches courses in macroeconomics and monetary economics. His research is in theoretical and applied econometrics. His theoretical papers deal chiefly with properties of test statistics, while his applied work is primarily in the areas of empirical industrial organization and demand analysis. His most recent papers have appeared in the *Review of Economics and Statistics, Econometric Reviews,* and *Economic Inquiry.* He lives in Victoria, British Columbia, with his wife Rose and their four children.

Brief Contents

Contents

Preface

Nobody believes that he can become a chemist by attending lectures and reading textbooks and journal articles. He should also devote time and energy to the real work in a laboratory.

Henri Theil, Principles of Econometrics, 1971

Any course in econometrics must strike a balance between theory and application. This book adopts Theil's premise that application has a key role to play in motivating the study of econometric theory, particularly at the introductory level. At the same time, applications must be developed in the context of broader theoretical principles and themes that provide a deeper understanding of the foundations on which applied techniques are built.

A second premise of this book is that the principles and themes appropriate to an introductory course have changed somewhat in recent years. The most significant change is certainly in the treatment of time series data. Twenty years ago we had no coherent methodology for studying nonstationary time series and little awareness of the implications of nonstationarity for conventional statistical inference. In what is arguably the greatest ever revolution in econometrics, all that has changed.

The implications of this revolution for the authors of introductory textbooks is as yet unclear; the tendency thus far has been to add a chapter or two on unit roots and cointegration to an otherwise traditional development of econometric theory, an understandable-enough reaction. But upon reflection, it is apparent that the revolution is so fundamental that it has implications for the pedagogy of that traditional theory. This book is my attempt to rethink that pedagogy by reorienting an introduction to econometrics away from the traditional culmination in simultaneous equations and toward time series analysis.

Approach

This reorientation has important implications for the mathematical and statistical tools that an introduction to econometrics should develop. This book makes no attempt to offer a development of either matrix algebra or alternative estimation principles (maximum likelihood and GMM), although students are made aware of the relevance of these methods in appropriate contexts. Instead the emphasis is on the core of econometric techniques that share least squares as a common estimation criterion. The goal is to provide a back-to-basics approach that focuses on building the most elementary analytical skills. This goal is motivated by the belief that, although much may have changed in the teaching of econometrics, much has stayed the same.

Most students beginning their study of econometrics have some fluency with algebraic derivations, but their mathematical and statistical sophistication does not extend a great deal beyond this. Mathematical proofs are still a challenge, the distinction between general results versus special cases hazy, and the use of summation notation unfamiliar. Often cobwebs have formed over even the rudiments of statistical inference. Again and again throughout my teaching career I have encountered students who have had more than one statistics course, yet who are still confused over the distinction between population and sample quantities, the concept of a sampling distribution, the manipulation of expressions involving expected values and variances, the notion of a parameter, the difference between a linear and a nonlinear function, and so on. As so many students find to their dismay, the study of econometrics involves a step up in analytical difficulty from the plug-the-right-number-into-the-right-formula level of most introductory statistics courses. Any first course in econometrics must deal with all the problems of transition that arise.

Introduction to Applied Econometrics is designed from the ground up to do this. This is particularly true of the early chapters and the accompanying Appendices A and B. Chapter 1 sets the stage with some general background on economic data and models. Chapter 2 is designed to refresh students' memories about the key ideas of statistical inference. Because the assumption is that students have already taken an introductory statistics course, the intention is not to offer a perfect substitute for that earlier treatment. Instead the goal in Chapter 2 is to add value to this previous understanding so as to strengthen the foundation on which subsequent material rests. Chapter 3 then provides a bridge between that univariate analysis and the treatment of regression that begins in Chapter 4.

Prerequisites

Most students who take introductory econometrics are third- or fourth-year under-graduates, and this book assumes the training that economics majors usually have at this stage of their studies. The minimal essential background is intermediate micro- and macroeconomic theory, a term or two of probability and statistics, and a term of applied differential calculus. Although this book uses calculus freely, it does so in a fairly kind and gentle manner that, for the most part, requires only the most basic rules of differentiation. The occasional more difficult result—such as Euler's theorem in Section 7.1.1—is explained as we go along. Some integral calculus is used in Appendix B, but in a way that is inessential for the key results of that appendix that are used elsewhere in the book.

Features: Empirical Applications

In addition to its time series orientation and the attempt to organize the analytics in a comprehensive and systematic yet accessible and digestible manner, the other key feature of this book is the empirical applications. My objective has been to provide instructors with a menu of classic data sets. Several criteria have been employed in selecting the applications that appear in this book.

- The applications use economic theory that students are likely to have encountered in their theory courses. This both contributes to the goal of illustrating the interplay of theory and empirics and improves the accessibility of the exercises.

- Applications are important in their own right, so that students gain from studying them in a way that is independent of their value in illustrating econometric technique.

- The applications allow students to replicate published empirical results. For many students, this may be their first exposure to the journal literature that is the primary vehicle by which economics advances. This helps demystify what is otherwise an intimidating and forbidding literature.

- Finally, applications have been chosen with an eye to conveying some appreciation for the historical development of economics as a discipline. Sir Isaac Newton said that if he had seen further, it was by standing on the shoulders of giants. This book tries to give students some acquaintance with the giants on whose shoulders they stand. The hope is that they will come away with an understanding of how economics evolves, and of the strong threads of continuity that underlie empirical inquiry.

One of my most important goals in writing *Introduction to Applied Econometrics* has been to give students a book they can grow with. Instructors of undergraduate econometrics courses are assigned the job of taking students having just a background in introductory statistics and, in one term or perhaps two, giving them the skills to do empirical work and read the empirical work of others. In view of this near-impossible task, it seems to me that one of the most valuable things an instructor can do is introduce students to a book that continues to serve as a resource long after the course is over. Such a book will be one they can come back to time and again to learn new things, things they might not have fully appreciated or understood on their first pass through. It will also be a book that serves as a bridge to other resources, both those dealing with econometric theory and technique and those dealing with applications and empirics.

Organization

There are many kinds of introductory econometrics courses. As well, instructors teach at a range of levels and to student audiences that vary considerably in their background preparation. Some econometrics courses are optional electives intended to appeal to students with fairly basic preparation in statistics, mathematics, and economic theory. Others are required courses in honors programs where students have considerably stronger background in these areas.

No book can meet every need, and it would be a mistake to author a textbook as if that were possible. Nevertheless in writing *Introduction to Applied Econometrics* I have been conscious of this range of teaching contexts. The book is designed to be flexible on several dimensions, and the companion *Instructor's Manual* gives chapter-by-chapter tips on the considerations that bear on this.

- The book as a whole can be used as the text for a full-year development of econometrics in a two-semester or three-quarter course sequence. However many undergraduate programs are not organized in this manner, and so in practice this is perhaps likely to be its least common use.

- Instead many first econometrics courses are essentially a one-semester "applied regression analysis" course for which Chapters 1–10 (with selective use of the applications in Chapters 7 and 9) would be suitable.

- Alternatively, a two-quarter sequence could begin by treating regression using Chapters 1–8, and in the second quarter turn to the more explicitly econometric topics of Chapters 10–14.

- A one-term introduction to time series analysis could be based on Chapters 15–18, regardless of whether this or some other text has been used for prerequisite courses.

- Finally, certain types of courses could make more selective use of material throughout the book. A course in applied production and cost analysis could focus on that material alone. A *Topics in Applied Econometrics* course could emphasize just the empirical applications. A course in empirical finance could use Appendix C jointly with the finance applications.

Many instructors will have chosen this book because they want to include an introduction to time series analysis in their courses, but will nevertheless not have time to cover all of Chapters 15–18. They will find that these chapters are written in a modular manner so that each can be profitably covered on its own. Chapter 15 alone exposes students to many important theoretical and applied ideas that are valuable even if subsequent chapters are not covered.

Many topics in this book are optional in the sense that they can be circumvented by instructors who choose to do so, depending on how they structure their course. However, only a few sections deal with material that sees no significant reference subsequently, and these are indicated with a ★. (Of course, material in the chapter appendices is typically of a supplementary nature, although it may sometimes be helpful elsewhere.)

The exercises span a range of difficulty; some are elementary, others more challenging. Difficult exercises are indicated by a *ϟ* (because some students may find them a shock!).

Software

In researching current instructor teaching practices I have been struck by the range of software used in introductory econometrics courses. Most, of course, use the familiar econometrics packages—EViews, Limdep, Microfit, RATS, Shazam, Stata, TSP—or a statistics package not specifically oriented toward econometrics, such as Minitab, SAS, or SPSS. Often, however, instructors find it convenient to have students do their statistical analysis within a spreadsheet package such as Excel. And in advanced courses software with an explicit programming orientation is sometimes used, such as Fortran, Gauss, Matlab, or S-Plus. Even this list is far from exhaustive.

Consequently, although *Introduction to Applied Econometrics* is heavily applications-oriented, it is intentionally written to be software-independent. However I would have done this even if the range of software use were more limited, because I feel it is the best approach pedagogically. It is important for students to understand that econometric methods are independent of particular software implementations of those methods and that different software may implement estimators and test statistics in different ways and may have different features to offer. These are distinctions that are easily lost on students struggling to understand difficult material for the first time. It is all too easy for them to be left with the belief that a particular software implementation of a method *is* the method and to think that memorization of command syntax is a substitute for genuine understanding of an econometric technique. As well, when students invest time and energy in working through a book, it is important that they continue to be able to use it when they move to different software environments in other courses, or universities, or employment.

Ancillaries and Instructor Aids

1. **The CD packaged with this book** includes two supplements.

   (a) **The data** are given in several proprietary file formats—Stata, EViews, SAS, SPSS, Excel, and Minitab—as well as ASCII (i.e., text) format so that the data can be easily inspected (as students are often asked to do in the exercises). Throughout the book the data files used in the examples and exercises are identified in bold with an accompanying CD symbol, so that it is easy to see the role that the various empirical applications play as they appear and reappear.

(b) **A supplementary Appendix C,** "Application to Portfolio Theory and the Capital Asset Pricing Model," is provided in the file `appendc.pdf`. It shows how the foundations of modern financial theory are essentially just an application of the laws of mathematical expectation and variance in Appendix B, and provides the technical background to the CAPM empirical application in the appendix to Chapter 5.

2. **The companion *Instructor's CD*** has several aids.

(a) **An *Instructor's Manual,*** in pdf format. This includes exercise solutions suitable for hard copy posting and chapter-by-chapter pedagogical tips. Particularly for the early chapters, there are also some supplementary exercises and suggested examination questions.

(b) **Shazam and TSP command files** that generate the results for the empirical examples and exercises. I have used Shazam and TSP because they are among the most widely used packages and because they use a fairly generic self-explanatory command syntax that should be easily translated into equivalent code for other packages.

(c) **Powerpoint files** of figures and tables suitable for classroom projection.

Acknowledgments

Many people have contributed to this book, sometimes knowingly, more often unknowingly. My great intellectual and professional debt is, of course, to my colleagues in my department and to the University of Victoria generally for providing the environment in which this book could be written. In a similar vein, I thank the Beeghly Library of Heidelberg University, Tiffin, Ohio, where portions of this book were written in the summers of 1996 and 2001, for its hospitality and marvelous air conditioning system.

I am indebted to a number of friends and colleagues for generously reading and commenting on specific chapters: Don Ferguson (University of Victoria) on Chapter 11, Will McNally (Wilfred Laurier University) on Appendix C, and Thanasis Stengos (University of Guelph) on Chapters 9 and 13. Donna Wong of the Shazam team caught an error in Chapter 13 that would have confused anyone working through that chapter. Arthur Sweetman (Queen's University) gave me the idea for Section 6.2.4.

I owe a great deal to the reviewers commissioned by my publisher, who offered many excellent suggestions and spurred me to take the book in directions I would not have thought of on my own: Darren Frechette (Penn State), Daniel Gordon (University of Calgary), Wayne Joerding (Washington State University), Alison Kelly (Suffolk University), Daniel Lass (University of Massachusetts, Amherst), David Prescott (University of Guelph), David Ryan (University of Alberta), Pravin Trivedi (Indiana University), Kenneth White (University of British Columbia), and Eric Zivot (University of Washington). I would also like to thank my accuracy checker Francis Vitek (University of British Columbia) who, in addition to offering a number of substantive comments, found several minor errors that had eluded both me and the copy editor.

Despite the efforts of all these individuals, errors and omissions no doubt remain. It goes without saying that responsibility for them lies with me alone. Errata will be made available through my web site:

web.uvic.ca/economics/~kstewart/

In addition to the acknowledgments that appear with copyrighted material, I am grateful to the following individuals for generously providing access to unpublished data sets and permitting their distribution with this book: James Lothian for the data set `ppp.dat` from J.R. Lothian and M.P. Taylor (1996) "Real Exchange Rate Behavior: The Recent Float from the Perspective of the Past Two Centuries," *Journal of Political Economy* 104, 488–509; Charles Nelson for the data set `np.dat` from C.R. Nelson and C.I. Plosser (1982) "Trends and Random Walks in Macroeconomic Time Series," *Journal of Monetary Economics* 10, 139–162; and Mark Watson for the data set `kpsw.dat` from King, R.G., Plosser, C.I., Stock, J.H., and M.W. Watson (1991) "Stochastic Trends and Economic Fluctuations," *American Economic Review* 81, 819–840.

Only an author can know the importance of an editor: first, the willingness to say yes to a project proposal and then support, encouragement, and—not least—patience along the way. I thank Curt Hinrichs for all this and more.

And finally I thank my family—my dear wife Rose and our wonderful children Ben, Alex, Ellie, and Andrew. Little do they know how much this book owes to their willingness to feign indifference to my evening and weekend absences from the glow of the video hearth.

Ken Stewart
2004

1

Economic Data and Economic Models

Truly important and significant hypotheses will be found to have "assumptions" that are wildly inaccurate descriptive representations of reality, and, in general, the more significant the theory the more unrealistic the assumptions. ... The reason is simple. A hypothesis is important if it "explains" much by little, that is, if it abstracts the common and crucial elements from the mass of complex and detailed circumstances surrounding the phenomena to be explained and permits valid predictions on the basis of them alone. To be important, therefore, a hypothesis must be descriptively false in its assumptions; it takes account of, and accounts for, none of the many other attendant circumstances, since its very success show them to be irrelevant for the phenomena to be explained.

—*Milton Friedman, "The Methodology of Positive Economics," 1953*

Econometrics is the application of statistics to economics. In using statistical techniques to study economic phenomena, there is an interplay of theory and observation: Economists use data to illuminate economic theory and use economic theory to illuminate their analysis of data. Such an interplay of theory and observation is the hallmark of all scientific inquiry, and its fruitfulness in advancing human knowledge is difficult to overstate. **Applied econometrics,** the subject of this book, is about this interplay in economics.

In an introduction to applied econometrics, the proper starting point is therefore with the two sides of this coin: economic data and economic models. Only after this, beginning in the next chapter, can we turn to the statistical tools that econometricians use to study them.

1.1 Economic Data

Science is measurement, and economic science relies on measurements of economic phenomena. A group of measurements is called **data.** Economic data are collected from many sources. They may consist of measurements on the activities of individual economic agents such as consumers, workers, and business firms. They may consist of observations on markets: the quantity of some good or service transacted or its price. Financial markets, for example, yield a rich array of price data on primary securities such as stocks and bonds and derivative securities such as futures and options contracts, plus other values such as interest rates and foreign exchange rates. Macroeconomic variables are measurements on economic aggregates such as GDP and other national income-accounting quantities, employment and unemployment, the capital stock, the money stock, the price level, and trade and capital flows between nations.

It is useful to begin our study of econometrics with an appreciation of the wide range of different kinds of data that economists encounter. Perhaps the single most important general point to make is that, in contrast to some other sciences, economists usually work with data from published sources. This means that economists normally have no ability to design the experiments that generate their data; Economic data are almost always **nonexperimental.** The most important implication of this is that it is not possible to hold constant—that is, to control for—the many outside influences that affect economic variables, complicating the study of the relationships of interest.

1.1.1   Types of Economic Data

Here are some of the key terms and distinctions you will encounter in this book.

Quantitative versus Qualitative Data

When we think of economic measurements we usually think first of **quantitative data;** that is, measurements having a **cardinal** meaning so that two values x_1 and x_2 have a difference $x_1 - x_2$ that is itself meaningful. For example, if one employee works $x_1 = 42$ hours per week and another works $x_2 = 39$, the difference $x_1 - x_2 = 3$ hours is meaningful. Often quantitative data take on values in a **continuous** range—value of GDP, duration of employment, and amount of coal can take on any positive values. But quantitative data can also be **discrete. Count data** record incidence of occurrence; for example, the number of automobiles or televisions per household, or the number of accidents at an intersection, take on the values 0, 1, 2, 3, ...

Often, however, information is instead about some **qualitative** characteristic or outcome; the assignment of numerical values to these characteristics or outcomes is a convenient way of recording these data, but the values have no cardinal meaning.

Binary Variables   In applied econometrics the most important qualitative variables are **binary variables,** which take on just two values, typically associated with success/failure or yes/no characteristics, outcomes, or responses; for example, male or female, employed or unemployed, homeowner or renter, married or single. Although in principle these observations could be recorded in many ways, numerically or otherwise, it turns out to be convenient to code them as 0 or 1 (0-1) values.

We see why in Chapter 10, where we also learn that when binary variables are used to explain other variables they are called **dummy variables.**

Categorical Variables   When a variable measures more than two qualitative characteristics, it is said to be **categorical.** There is a distinction between **ordered** and **unordered** categorical data.

> **Ordered response** data assign values in a way that reflects some ranking. For example, educational attainment might be coded 1 for a high school graduate, 2 for some postsecondary education, 3 for one university degree, and so on. Or if survey respondents are asked whether they agree, neither agree nor disagree, or disagree with a statement, these responses might be coded 1, 2, or 3 (1-2-3).

> **Unordered response** data assign values to categories with no implied ranking. In classifying occupations, for example, professions might be coded 1 for teacher, 2 for physician, 3 for dentist, and so on. In the choice of transportation for commuting, automobile might be coded 1, bus 2, subway 3, and so on.

Notice that categorical variables such as these are qualitative, in that the values have no quantitative significance: If one person is coded $x_1 = 3$ and another $x_2 = 1$, the difference $x_1 - x_2$ has no intrinsic meaning.

Stocks and Flows

When a variable measures a quantity, it is either a **stock** or a **flow.** A flow variable is defined with respect to some unit of time: GDP per year, earnings per month, expenditure per week, profits per quarter, hours of labor per day, and so on. Notice that any of these variables would be meaningless without an explicit time dimension. Suppose we are told that someone's income is $10,000. Is this $10,000 per year? Or per month? Or with respect to some other unit of time? The figure means nothing unless the relevant time period is stated. Macroeconomic data such as GDP are often reported quarterly but at annual rates—that is, multiplied by 4 to indicate what the annual GDP would be were that quarterly rate of production maintained for the entire year.

By contrast, stock variables are defined at a point in time and so involve no time dimension. If we are told that the economy has a certain capital stock, that the quantity of money in circulation is such and such, that a firm has a certain stock market capitalization, or that a country has a certain population, these are meaningful statements in their own right. No time dimension is attached to these quantities, although they do of course have dates associated with them.

Rates of return are flow variables. If a bank deposit pays 3% interest, this means that it pays 3 cents for every dollar held on deposit for a year. A 3% annual return is very different from a 3% daily return. When rates of return are quoted, it is normally understood that, unless explicitly stated otherwise, they are annual returns; the yearly time dimension is implicit.

It is important to distinguish between stocks and flows because they are easily confused. Income is a flow, whereas wealth is a stock; investment is a flow, whereas capital (the accumulation of past investment, net of depreciation) is a stock; similarly saving is a flow, whereas *savings* is a stock. A fiscal deficit or surplus is a flow; the national debt (the historical accumulation of past government deficits and surpluses) is a stock. Sometimes the terminology used by economists themselves contributes to the confusion. Usually the terms *supply* and *demand* refer to flow supplies or demands; that is, the supply of or demand for some amount of a good or service per period. An exception is the term *money supply*, which means the same thing as *money stock*: the quantity of money in circulation at a point in time.

The distinction between stocks and flows applies only to quantity variables. (A rate of return is an amount yielded relative to the principle invested, a quantity.) Prices, including exchange rates, are neither stocks nor flows.

Cross-Section versus Time Series Data

One broad distinction between types of economic data is **cross-section data** versus **time series data.** Cross-section data are observed across cases such as households, firms, countries, and so on, at a point in time, whereas time series data are observed over time. The reason this distinction is fundamental relates to what can be assumed about how the data have been generated. The observations in a cross-section data set can usually be treated as having been obtained by a process of **random sampling,** so that each observation can be regarded as a random drawing from the larger **population** of households, firms, or countries, as the case may be. One implication of this is that the ordering of observations in the data set has no special significance. In a data set on 50 households it should not matter which is listed first, which second, and so on. In data on 100 countries it should not matter whether Nepal appears as the 13th observation or the 40th. Consequently the conclusions obtained from studying cross-section data should not depend on the ordering of the observations; findings should be **invariant to sample order.**

Time series data are quite different. Here the ordering of the observations has a significance in addition to that of the values themselves. We do not expect the conclusions drawn from studying the data to be invariant to sample order; quite the contrary, findings presumably depend critically on the time patterns associated with the ordering in time.

How frequently time series data are observed is called the **sampling frequency** of the data. Quarterly data have a higher frequency than annual data, monthly data a higher frequency still. At the extreme of high-frequency economic data are some financial data such as stock prices, which are sometimes available by transaction, perhaps at times occurring at a rate of several per second.

Time Series Components

It is often useful to recognize that an economic time series may be the amalgam of several underlying influences. For example, a macroeconomic variable such as GDP is usually generated in part by a long-term trend associated with the forces of economic growth. Superimposed on this are shorter-term fluctuations due to business cycle, seasonal, and perhaps other effects. If the variable of interest is denoted Y_t, then we might write

$$Y_t = T_t + C_t + S_t, \tag{1.1}$$

where T_t denotes the trend component, S_t the seasonal component, and C_t other short-term fluctuations such as business cycles. These components are not, of course, directly observable; instead it might be one goal of empirical analysis to use the data on Y_t to say something about each of them.

Our ability to do this depends on the sampling interval. Annual data contain no information relevant to studying the seasonal component. If this is our interest, then, at a minimum, quarterly data are needed and monthly data would be better. On the other hand, if our interest is in studying business cycles, then quarterly data may contain all the relevant information and there may be no value to using monthly data. Applied practice appears to confirm this view because virtually all business-cycle research uses quarterly data.

Finally, the forces of economic growth are reflected in the trend component T_t, and to study this there may be no advantage to using quarterly or monthly data over annual data. To put it another way, suppose you are interested in studying economic growth and can have only 100 time series observations to do so. Clearly you will be much better off with 100 annual observations than with 100 quarterly ones covering a 25-year time period. Indeed, you will probably be better off with only 50 annual observations than 100 quarterly ones. That is, for some purposes, the **span** of the data is more important than just the number of observations. It is even conceivable that for studying growth issues it may be a disadvantage to use data of higher than annual frequency because then seasonality must be treated.

Pooled Cross-Section – Time Series Data

Increasingly data sets are available in which cross sections are observed at several points in time, such as data extracted from censuses that have been taken at 5- or 10-year intervals. Such **pooled** data sets having both a time and a cross-section dimension are an especially rich source of information of great interest to economists and other social researchers.

Longitudinal or **panel** data sets are ones in which the same cases are tracked over time: Observations on the same people, firms, or countries are collected in successive periods. Often such data sets are dominated by the cross-section dimension—there are many cases, perhaps hundreds or thousands, but these are observed over a modest number of time periods.

The increasing availability of pooled data, combined with modern computer capabilities for storing, manipulating, and analyzing large data sets, have led to its increasing use by economists. However this is a topic that takes us beyond the methods of this book.

1.1.2 Problems of Flawed Data

Economic data are far from perfect; quite the contrary, invariably they are error-laden. The extent to which this is a problem for empirical analysis and its practical implications for research findings, and whether and how anything can be done about it, are application-specific; it depends on the questions we are seeking to answer. The development of new econometric techniques is often motivated by the desire to overcome deficiencies in the data. Here are some of the more common possibilities.

Data Entry Errors

When working with data that you or others have keyed in manually, it is essential that you be vigilant in correcting data entry errors. Omitted or extraneously introduced digits or digits in reverse order; too many zeros or too few; negative values for variables that must be positive or forgetting the negative sign on a value that should be negative; noninteger values for variables that must be integers; nonfractional values for variables that must be fractional—entry errors such as these are all too easy to make. Always double-check—even triple-check—that your data have been accurately entered; never assume it. One too many zeros inadvertently entered for a single value of a single variable can have the effect of driving empirical results in meaningless ways.

One of the most basic features offered by statistical software is a command for calculating descriptive statistics. This is a simple but invaluable tool for checking data integrity. Entry errors can often be spotted simply by checking the maximum and minimum values that it reports.

Measurement Error

"The Government are very keen on amassing statistics—they collect them, add them, raise them to the nth power, take the cube root and prepare wonderful diagrams. But what you must never forget is that every one of those figures comes in the first instance from the village watchman, who just puts down what he damn pleases" (cited in Stamp 1929, pp. 258–259). This well-known quotation reminds us that even when correctly entered, economic data are bound to be error-ridden.

Even so, measurement error is not necessarily a problem. If an economic model is intended to describe or predict people's behavior and it is the measured variable that they are responding to in making their decisions, the fact that the measurement may be taken with error may not be important.

Missing Observations

It is very common for economic data to have missing observations; for example, nonresponses to some questions on a survey. The importance of this problem depends in part on whether the data are time series or cross section. Clearly, missing observations from a time series impede our ability to study patterns in that time series. In a cross section obtained by random sampling, on the other hand, missing data are not a problem if they are missing randomly; the sample size is just reduced. Often, however, observations are missing systematically. Two important cases can be distinguished.

Sample selectivity occurs when the collection of the data has been influenced systematically by some other variable. For example, suppose a polling firm surveys voting preferences by phone during working hours using residential phone listings. Only people who have telephones and are home during the day will be sampled—a fairly restricted set of the population. This introduces **sample selectivity bias** and the results will not be a good predictor of the population as a whole.

Truncated data occur when observations on a variable are excluded when they fall in a certain range. Examples are studying household automobile expenditures using data on cars costing less than $40,000 and family incomes using data on households earning less than $100,000.

Truncated data should be distinguished from the similar problem of **censored data.** Censoring arises when a quantitative variable has an upper or lower limiting value it can take on and a substantial portion of observations are at that limit. For example, in data on household purchases of major appliances, many households record expenditures of zero in any year. Notice that this is *not* a problem of missing observations, just one in which the concentration of observations at the limiting value must be taken into account when analyzing the variable.

Grouped Data

Instead of being reported in their original, raw, observation-by-observation form, data are often summarized in an aggregated or grouped format. Two possibilities are especially common.

Group means may be used if there is some natural grouping of the data, with variables reported as averages within each group. In Section 8.6 we study data on the demand for electricity that are in this form, with household electricity consumption and income reported as averages within towns—although we do not pay special attention to this particular feature of those data.

Categorized data are aggregated according to imposed categories. For example, firm size as measured by number of employees might be reported as the number of firms with fewer than 10 employees, the number with between 10 and 50, the number with between 50 and 100, and so on.

Although grouped data may be convenient for descriptive interpretation, for statistical analysis an econometrician always prefers the raw data. There is always a loss of information when aggregating data into a grouped format.

1.1.3 Transformations of Data

For data to be useful, economists often transform them in various ways. One simple example is the calculation of percentage changes to measure growth rates. Another is the logarithmic transformation, which is discussed in detail in Chapter 6. Here we consider briefly three other common data transformations: indices, nominal versus real values, and seasonal adjustment.

Indices

It is often useful to express a variable as an **index,** assigning a **base value** (almost always 1 or 100) in a **base period** (in time series data, often the first period), so that other observations are measured relative to this base observation. Although cross-section observations are occasionally presented in this way, by far the most common use of indices is for time series data. This is especially useful when we want to compare how several variables have evolved since a common base period.

An important use of indices is for variables that have no natural units, in particular **aggregate indices** that are computed as a weighted average. The best example is the **consumer price index** (CPI), which measures the price of a basket of goods and services. This is a weighted average of the prices of the individual items, the weights being the shares of each good or service in the total value of the basket. Because it attempts to measure the cost of living, which is what most people—especially the media—are interested in, the CPI is the most commonly cited measure of the price level. It is not, however, the only such measure. Another important aggregate price index is the **GDP deflator,** which is computed as the ratio of nominal to real GDP. The GDP deflator is a broader measure of the price level because it takes into account all goods and services produced, not just those in the consumption basket of households, although it omits imports.

Whenever we use the notation P_t for the price level, as we do throughout this book, we take it to denote some price index such as the GDP deflator or CPI, defined to have base value 1, unless indicated otherwise.

There are many ways of computing aggregate indices, depending on the treatment of the weights in the weighted average. The key distinction is between fixed and variable-weight indices, called **Laspeyres** and **Paasche** indices. A Laspeyres index uses the expenditure weights for some fixed basket, often that for the base period. Let p_{ti}, q_{ti} denote the price-quantity values for good i at time t, and consider a basket of $i = 1, \ldots, n$ goods. If $v_{0i} = p_{0i}q_{0i}$ denotes the value of good i in base period 0, then its weight in total base-period expenditure is $w_{0i} = v_{0i}/\sum_{i=1}^{n} v_{0i}$. The Laspeyres price index at time t is the weighted average of the relative price changes p_{ti}/p_{0i}:

$$\text{Laspeyres index} = \sum_{i=1}^{n} \frac{p_{ti}}{p_{0i}} w_{0i} = \sum_{i=1}^{n} \frac{p_{ti}}{p_{0i}} \frac{v_{0i}}{\sum_i v_{0i}} = \sum_{i=1}^{n} \frac{p_{ti}}{p_{0i}} \frac{p_{0i}q_{0i}}{\sum_i p_{0i}q_{0i}} = \frac{\sum_{i=i}^{n} p_{ti}q_{0i}}{\sum_{i=1}^{n} p_{0i}q_{0i}}.$$

THEORY MEETS APPLICATION   **1.1**

Does the CPI Overstate Cost-of-Living Increases?

As a Laspeyres index based on fixed weights, the CPI tells us what it costs today to purchase some historical consumption basket. It follows that it tends to overstate increases in the cost of living for several reasons. First, it does not take into account the ability of consumers to substitute between goods in response to price changes, shifting to, say, chicken when the relative price of beef increases. Second, it does not take into account changes in the quality of goods. An increase in the price of a TV or VCR may be partially or entirely due to an increase in quality so that it is not the same good that is being purchased. Third, it does not take into account the introduction of new goods. It was not long ago that DVD players and home Internet services had expenditure shares of zero in household budgets; consumption weights from that period do not reflect the introduction of these goods. Finally, the prices that go into the CPI are sampled from specified retail outlets; they do not take into account the lower prices that effectively arise from consumer shifts away from traditional retail outlets such as department and grocery stores in favor of high-volume warehouse-style "stack 'em deep and sell 'em cheap" discount retailers.

The tendency of the CPI to overstate increases in the cost of living is important because many payments are indexed to it. The implications for government budgets are especially important because both revenues and expenditures are affected by price indexing. Government revenues are affected by the indexing of income tax brackets; to the extent that the CPI overstates true inflation, real tax revenues are reduced over time. Expenditures are affected by, among other things, the indexing of publicly funded pensions; overstatement of inflation results in overcompensation of pensioners for cost-of-living increases. Thus overindexation leads, over time, to a reduction in government revenues and an increase in expenditures, exacerbating budget deficits.

These implications prompted the U.S. Senate to appoint a committee of distinguished economists to study the problem; for a summary of their findings, see Boskin et al. (1998). They concluded that the CPI overstates true cost-of-living increases by approximately 1.1% per year, decomposed as follows:

Substitution bias	0.40
New products/quality change	0.60
Outlet substitution	0.10

The committee reported that "This bias might seem small, but when compounded over time, the implications are enormous. Over a dozen years, the cumulative additional national debt from overindexing the budget would amount to more than $1 trillion" (p. 3).

The CPI is a Laspeyres index and is computed in this way:

$$\text{CPI} = \frac{\text{Value of fixed basket at current prices}}{\text{Value of fixed basket at base-period prices}}.$$

Because the CPI is based on a fixed historical consumption bundle it does not take into account people's ability to shift their consumption in response to price changes. For this and other reasons—explored in the accompanying Theory Meets Application 1.1—the CPI tends to overstate increases in the cost of living.

A Paasche index alters the Laspeyres formula by replacing base-period quantities q_{0i} with current-period quantities q_{ti}:

$$\text{Paasche index} = I_t = \frac{\sum_{i=1}^{n} p_{ti} q_{ti}}{\sum_{i=1}^{n} p_{0i} q_{ti}}.$$

The GDP deflator is a Paasche index:

$$\text{GDP deflator} = \frac{\text{Value of current output at current prices}}{\text{Value of current output at base-year prices}}.$$

Notice that in comparing a Paasche index over two periods, say I_t and I_{t-1}, its value changes both because prices change and because the consumption bundle is updated; its change does not measure price changes alone. Because it reflects the simultaneous change in demand, the GDP deflator tends to understate increases in the cost of living; it does not attribute any cost to consumers' having to revise the consumption bundle in response to new prices.

These features of the Laspeyres and Paasche price indices have been contrasted by Schultze (2003, p. 5):

> Because the Laspeyres index neglects the ability of consumers to mitigate the welfare effect of price increases through substitution among goods, it *overstates* the cost of maintaining the consumer's original, or reference period, standard of living. Conversely, because a Paasche index measures how much it would have cost in the past to purchase the basket of goods representing current consumption, it effectively assumes that people had already made the substitution between goods in the past that they have now made in the present, and thus *understates* the cost of maintaining the consumers current, or comparison period, standard of living.

These biases in Laspeyres and Paasche indices illustrate the **index number problem**—no index is perfect. The attempt to aggregate multidimensional changes in prices into a single index value is inherently imperfect in that it inevitably results in a loss of information.

Nominal versus Real Values

A **real** variable q is expressed in physical units: tons of wheat, gallons of gasoline, kilowatt-hours of electricity, number of cars, and so on. Its **nominal** value Q is this real value multiplied by the price per unit p, so $Q = pq$; it is therefore expressed in the same monetary units in which the price is expressed: dollars, pounds, yen, and so on, as the case may be.

These definitions are straightforward enough when the good in question is a narrowly defined homogeneous one such as wheat, gasoline, electricity, or cars of a certain model. But often economists work with variables that are aggregates of many commodities having no common unit of measure. Family food expenditure, for example, is an aggregate over many different units: pounds of meat, gallons of milk, dozens of eggs, and so on. Although its nominal value is easily observed, a corresponding real value is not.

As a practical matter it is, of course, important to distinguish between real and nominal values. If we are told that nominal food expenditure Q_t has increased by 10%, we want to know to what extent this is due to price increases as opposed to an increase in food consumption. Accomplishing this is one important application of price indices. Let P_t denote a price index, such as the GDP deflator or CPI, defined to have base value 1; it can be used to **deflate** the nominal value Q_t to obtain a corresponding real value q_t:

$$q_t = \frac{Q_t}{P_t}. \tag{1.2}$$

This real value is still denominated in monetary units (as opposed to physical units; remember that the variable remains an aggregate over many different physical units), but they are base-period prices. Thus, such deflated or real values are often said to be in **constant dollars,** whereas nominal values are said to be in **current dollars.**

Ideally the price index used for deflating should be one based on the same basket of goods as the nominal aggregate Q_t itself. In practice, however, this is rarely the case. In the absence of a more narrowly defined index, it is not unusual to find a researcher using the CPI—an index that embraces everything from transportation to rent—to deflate food expenditure, a much narrower consumption category. Nevertheless the point should not be forgotten: In deflating nominal variables, try to use the most closely related price index.

The motivation for deflating a nominal variable to obtain a real one is typically because it is the real variable that relates to the economic issues at stake. Economists are usually interested in seeing beyond the veil of monetary values to the more fundamental production and consumption of goods and services.

Just as the transformation of nominal variables by deflating helps to do this, economists use other transformations to abstract from noneconomic forces in order to focus on economic ones. An important example is seasonal adjustment.

Seasonal Adjustment

As our discussion of time series components indicates, it is often useful to think of an economic time series as being the amalgam of trend, cyclical, and—for quarterly or higher-frequency data—seasonal components. Although the trend and cyclical components are generally the outcome of economic activity, the seasonal component is not; it is attributable instead to factors such as social custom or the weather.

It is therefore often desirable to **seasonally adjust** or **deseasonalize** a time series in an attempt to isolate the trend and cyclical components. Do recent fourth-quarter GDP numbers indicate the economy is emerging from a recession or are they higher than the previous quarter merely because of the Christmas season? Do last month's car sales suggest the industry should be expanding (or contracting) production or are they dominated by seasonal effects? To answer questions such as these we must eliminate seasonal variation in the data; to fail to do so might lead to fallacious conclusions arising purely from seasonal influences. For this reason, economic time series are often published in seasonally adjusted form.

In principle, the key elements of deseasonalization are fairly simple; in practice, however, the details are more complicated and the tools of modern time series analysis—including some of the ideas developed in Chapters 15–18—are brought to bear. Consequently, seasonal adjustment is a special topic in its own right, one that cannot be treated in this book.

In any case, the contemporary trend is for more circumspect use of seasonally adjusted data than was once the case. Although deseasonalized variables are valuable for descriptive analysis, when it comes to econometric model building the modern preference is usually to use seasonally unadjusted data, building the treatment of seasonality explicitly into the model. Again, the techniques for doing this are beyond the scope of this book, but we return briefly to some issues of seasonality in Appendix 18B in Chapter 18.

Upper- and Lowercase Notation

It is convenient to conclude our discussion of data transformations with a remark on notation—the distinction between upper- and lowercase symbols.

Upper- and lowercase notation is used for a variety of purposes in statistics and economics. In probability—the theory of random variables, probability distributions, and mathematical expectation—the convention is for an uppercase symbol X to denote a random variable, for the lowercase x to denote a particular value taken on by the random variable. This book uses this convention in the next two chapters and in Appendix B.

In statistics and econometrics, on the other hand, the distinction is often employed for a quite different purpose. If X_i denotes the ith observation on a variable, then x_i denotes the difference between this value and the average,

$$x_i = X_i - \overline{X}.$$

The variable x_i is said to be the **deviation form** of X_i. Deviation form is introduced at the end of Chapter 3 and in Appendix A and is used extensively elsewhere in this book, especially in Chapters 4 and 8 where it serves to simplify the derivation and expression of many formulas.

In economics, upper- and lowercase are used for yet other purposes. It is standard practice to distinguish between real and nominal variables by using lowercase for real and uppercase for nominal—a convention reflected in our notational choices for equation (1.2). Sometimes, on the other hand, upper- and lowercase are used for the quite different purpose of distinguishing between a variable and its logarithm:

$$x = \log X.$$

Another common use is for lowercase to denote **per capita** (per person) values: if Y is GDP and N is population, then $y = Y/N$ is GDP per capita. In the same way, lowercase is sometimes used to denote variables in **labor-intensive form,** meaning relative to the units of labor employed. For example, if Y denotes the amount of output produced using K units of capital and L units of labor, then the capital-labor ratio is denoted by $k = K/L$ and labor productivity, the amount of output per unit of labor, by

$$y = \frac{Y}{L}. \tag{1.3}$$

We make considerable use of this convention, especially in Chapters 7 and 9.

Finally, sometimes the distinction between upper- and lowercase is given no special significance, and lowercase symbols are used for the same thing that uppercase ones are—simply to denote some variable.

Because econometrics is the meeting ground of statistics and economics, econometricians tend to be multifarious in their use of upper- and lowercase. They often skip blithely among alternative uses, allowing the convention to be suggested by the context. In common with the field as a whole, in this book upper- and lowercase symbols are used in all the ways we have indicated. We introduce each usage as we go along, hopefully developing in you the same intuition about notation that all econometricians share.

These comments prompt a general remark on notation in econometrics.

Practitioner's Tip: Notation in econometrics

Because econometrics is the meeting ground of mathematics, statistics, and economic theory, notation is tricky. Econometricians often use the same symbol to mean different things in different contexts. In your own studying, you will find that there is much to be gained by paying meticulous attention to the meaning of symbols and by distinguishing carefully between, for example, upper- and lowercase in your note taking. In addition, be aware that different books often use different notational conventions, even for standard concepts. It is sometimes said facetiously of econometrics that "notation is like a toothbrush—no one uses anyone else's."

1.2   Economic Models

How do economists study the variables that their data measure?

The world is a highly complex place, consisting of many different kinds of economic activity: different economic agents (e.g., consumers, firms, and workers), different markets (e.g., product markets, factor markets, and financial markets), and different levels of aggregation (over members of a household, across firms, or across industries). Economists, like all scientists, recognize that they will never be able to describe the full detail and complexity of reality. Instead our hope is to understand it in some general and approximate way that may be useful. As the opening quotation from Milton Friedman's famous essay "The Methodology of Positive Economics" indicates, this is done by abstracting from the complexity of the real world and telling what you might think of, in the first instance, as stories about how the economy works. Economists call their stories **economic theories** or **hypotheses.**

For these stories to be usefully discussed and applied, they must be rigorously formulated and precisely expressed. Such rigorously formulated theories are called **economic models.** Usually economic models are expressed mathematically, but sometimes an adequately rigorous formulation can be done diagrammatically or, less often, descriptively.

In the same way that a model airplane abstracts from the complexity of a real airplane and yet may capture many of its essentials, including the ability to fly, so too do economists believe that we can learn a great deal about the economy by constructing models. No aircraft manufacturer would dream of putting a new plane into production without a thorough testing of alternative designs in a wind tunnel. Applied econometrics is the economist's wind tunnel, the place where we test our stories about how the economy works.

Because economists tell many stories about the many aspects of the economy that interest them, there are many economic models and they take many forms. Precisely because any model is by definition an abstraction from reality, there will never be just *one* universally applicable model; which details of the real world can be abstracted from will differ depending on the issues to be analyzed. Think of economists' models as being like wrenches in a mechanic's tool chest—intended for different purposes, some more useful than others, some of broad applicability and others for highly specialized tasks.

Because economists use so many different kinds of models, even the most comprehensive taxonomy is bound to be incomplete and, for our purposes, of doubtful value in any case. It is useful, however, to mention some important distinctions that arise in many economic models.

1.2.1 Microeconomic versus Macroeconomic Models

As you know from your other studies, **microeconomics** deals with the decisions of individual economic agents such as households, firms, and workers and their interaction in markets. Agents' decisions are described as the outcome of optimization subject to constraints, for example, a household's maximization of utility subject to a budget constraint or a firm's maximization of profit subject to a production technology. The nature of market interaction and the determination of equilibrium prices depend on the market structure; that is, whether agents behave as perfectly competitive price-takers or imperfect competition creates some scope for strategic interaction involving game-theoretic behavior.

Macroeconomics, by contrast, is concerned with the operation of the economy as a whole, the overall production and consumption of goods and services.

As such, it deals in broad aggregates: total output, employment, unemployment, consumption, saving, investment, imports, exports, the capital stock, and so on. In addition, it attempts to understand the determination of interest rates, exchange rates, and the aggregate price level or its rate of growth, the inflation rate.

The line separating macroeconomics from microeconomics is approximate rather than precise. Macroeconomists often use analytical tools from microeconomics, and microeconomic issues often must be studied in the context of the broader macroeconomic environment.

Econometrics is used to study both microeconomic and macroeconomic questions and draws on the theories offered by both. We illustrate this with many examples throughout this book.

1.2.2 Continuous versus Discrete Time

In both micro- and macroeconomics, it is often useful for theoretical purposes to regard a variable as evolving continuously through time. The capital stock, for example, exists at all points in time and so, in principle, evolves continuously. It changes hour by hour—even second by second—as new investments increase the capital stock and old capital depreciates. It is therefore natural to denote the capital stock K as a **continuous** function of time, $K(t)$. One reason this is useful is that it is then possible to define the derivative

$$\frac{\mathrm{d}K(t)}{\mathrm{d}t}. \tag{1.4}$$

This is a convenient expression for the change in the variable per instantaneous unit of time. Think of $K(t)$ as being like the stock of water in a bathtub, and that the level is being measured continuously. Suppose this level is changing, owing to flows into and out of the bathtub. The derivative $\mathrm{d}K(t)/\mathrm{d}t$ is the change in the water level, measured in appropriate units—gallons per minute, say, or liters per hour. This flow might be constant or might itself vary over time.

Dividing a time-derivative such as (1.4) by the level of the variable gives the instantaneous rate of change, or growth rate. For example the growth rate of the price level (also known as the inflation rate) is denoted

$$\frac{1}{P(t)}\frac{\mathrm{d}P(t)}{\mathrm{d}t}. \tag{1.5}$$

Expressions such as this arise so frequently that it is common to economize the notation by suppressing the argument t, leaving it understood that the variable is a function of time; so an instantaneous growth rate is denoted

$$\frac{1}{P}\frac{\mathrm{d}P}{\mathrm{d}t}.$$

Both stock and flow variables can be treated as continuous functions of time. We occasionally find it useful to do this, beginning in Chapter 6.

Time series *data* are, of course, not observed continuously. Although conceptually the capital stock may evolve continuously through time, measurements of it are taken only at **discrete** time intervals—usually annually or quarterly—and our choice of notation changes to reflect this. Observed time series measurements are denoted with a subscript, for example, K_t, instead of with time as an argument, $K(t)$. The length of the discrete time interval at which measurements are taken (annually, quarterly, monthly, etc.) is called the **sampling interval.** High-frequency data have a short sampling interval, low-frequency data a long sampling interval.

Accordingly, although economic theory is often stated in terms of a continuously evolving variable $K(t)$, expressions that are functions of data are stated in terms of K_t. Depending on the questions of interest, an economic time series is sometimes analyzed in its raw or **level** form, K_t; sometimes in its **first differences,** the absolute changes

$$\Delta K_t = K_t - K_{t-1},$$

and sometimes in its relative changes, the growth rate[1]

$$\frac{1}{K_{t-1}}\Delta K_t = \frac{1}{K_{t-1}}(K_t - K_{t-1}).$$

These are the discrete-time analogs to instantaneous change and growth rate expressions such as (1.4) and (1.5). The delta notation ΔK_t is convenient shorthand for the first difference of a variable. It is the discrete-time analog to the derivative dK/dt.

Growth rates are often multiplied by 100 to express them in percentage terms. For example, from an aggregate price index P_t the percentage rate of inflation is often calculated as

$$\frac{1}{P_{t-1}}\Delta P_t \times 100.$$

Setting aside the factor 100, this is the discrete-time counterpart to expression (1.5).

1.2.3   Ex Post Accounting Identities versus Ex Ante Behavior

Many economic variables are related by **accounting identities.** An accounting identity is a definitional relationship that must hold regardless of the underlying economic forces determining the variables. For example, by definition a firm's assets equal its liabilities because the residual liability net worth is defined to make it so.

[1] In Chapter 6 we learn how to use logarithms as a better way of calculating percentage changes for most purposes.

Perhaps the most famous accounting identity in economics is the macroeconomic definition

$$Y \equiv C + I + G + X - M. \tag{1.6}$$

This says that total production in the economy Y equals the total uses of all goods, comprising consumption C, investment I, government expenditure G, and exports X less imports M. (The symbol $\equiv$ is mathematical notation for an equality that holds definitionally, as opposed to the ordinary equality $=$, which denotes a relationship that must be established to hold and that may only hold under certain circumstances.) This is one of many identities in the **national income accounts,** the system by which economists keep track of a nation's production and uses of goods and services.

Accounting identities can be expressed in either discrete or continuous time and can apply to either stocks or flows. The identity (1.6) deals with flows—a nation's flow of production, consumption, government expenditure, exports, and imports per year, per quarter, or over some other relevant measurement period. The definition that assets equal liabilities, on the other hand, is an identity of stocks of assets and liabilities.

Identities can also mix stocks and flows and may involve variables at different points in time. For example, consider the capital stock at the end of period t, denoted K_t, and its value at the end of the previous period, K_{t-1}. These two stocks are related by the flows of investment I_t (additions to the capital stock) less depreciation D_t (the amount of the beginning-of-period capital stock K_{t-1} that wears out) during period t,

$$K_t = K_{t-1} + I_t - D_t \quad \Leftrightarrow \quad \Delta K_t = I_t - D_t. \tag{1.7}$$

The same identity expressed in continuous time is

$$\frac{dK(t)}{dt} = I(t) - D(t). \tag{1.8}$$

In the terminology of economics, an accounting identity is an **ex post** (Latin for "after the fact") relationship. That is, the definitions according to which data are constructed mean that, looking back at the historical record, identities such as these must be satisfied.

Accounting identities are essential for organizing and keeping track of the information of interest to economists, but their value is limited to that. By themselves, they tell us nothing about the forces causing variables to take on the values they do. However true it may be that a firm's assets equal its liabilities, by itself this tells us nothing about why these assets and liabilities are what they are. Similarly, however true the national income accounting identity (1.6) may be, it tells us nothing about why production Y is what it is or what forces govern its division between the uses on the right-hand side.

Offering such explanations is the purpose of economics; that is, economists are primarily interested in **ex ante** (Latin for "before the fact") behavior. We wish to understand and describe economic forces in a way that allows us to make predictions about their outcome and effect. This is a much more difficult problem than the accounting task of keeping track of the historical record.

The Theory of Supply and Demand

Let us use a simple economic theory to clarify these distinctions. Consider the operation of a market, say the market for apples. One observation we might make about any such market is that, because any purchase by one market participant is a sale by some other, total purchases must equal total sales. Equivalently, the total quantity demanded D must equal the total quantity supplied S:

$$D \equiv S. \tag{1.9}$$

As the notation indicates, this equality of purchases and sales is an ex post definitional accounting identity. It tells us nothing about why the amount of apples exchanged is what it is or how it might be altered if the underlying forces governing the apple market change.

To understand these forces we must tell a story. The story economists are most fond of telling is called the **theory of supply and demand,** and it goes like this. The behavior of the two groups of market participants, the suppliers and demanders of apples, is summarized by supply and demand schedules describing how they respond to various apple prices P. These schedules are shown in Figure 1.1(a). The

FIGURE 1.1

Supply and demand in the market for apples.

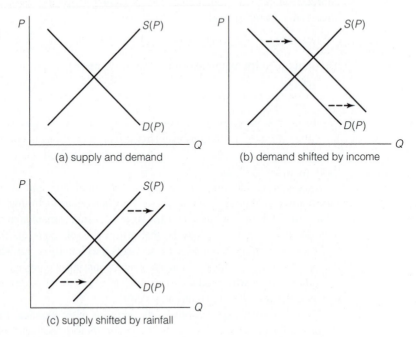

(a) supply and demand

(b) demand shifted by income

(c) supply shifted by rainfall

supply curve $Q^s = S(P)$ is a function describing how farmers vary the amount of apples Q^s they bring to market. It is shown sloping upward, reflecting our belief that higher prices induce farmers to grow more apples. The demand curve $Q^d = D(P)$ is a function describing how consumers respond to different prices. It is shown sloping downward, reflecting our belief that lower prices induce consumers to eat more apples.

These demand and supply schedules describe people's plans, intentions, or desires; that is, they describe ex ante behavior and are therefore called **behavioral relationships.** The key insight of the theory of supply and demand is that, although market participants are a diverse group of people, most of whom will never meet one another, their behavior must nevertheless be consistent in the aggregate. This means that the amount of apples farmers wish to sell must be consistent with the amount consumers wish to buy:

$$Q^d = Q^s.$$

The mechanism by which this occurs is, of course, that price must adjust to cause plans to be consistent:

$$D(P) = S(P). \tag{1.10}$$

If this equality does not hold, all plans of all market participants will not be fulfilled. If price is too high and supply exceeds demand, farmers will be left with unsold apples; if price is too low and demand exceeds supply, consumers will find the grocery shelves bare. These unfulfilled desires will cause prices to be bid up or down until the plans of all market participants are compatible. Because the equality of demand and supply schedules describes a situation in which there is no tendency for change, it is called an **equilibrium condition** and the price that satisfies it (associated with the point of intersection in Figure 1.1(a)) is called the **equilibrium price.**

Notice, then, that an equilibrium condition such as (1.10) concerns ex ante behavior and is quite different in its meaning from the ex post accounting identity (1.9). The accounting identity holds regardless of whether the market is in equilibrium. Suppose that a marketing board is able to impose an artificially high price so that planned supply exceeds demand, $S(p) > D(p)$, and some apples remain unsold. It will nevertheless be the case that, ex post, purchases must equal sales and the accounting identity (1.9) holds. The difference between the accounting identity (1.9) and the equilibrium condition (1.10) is that the latter only holds when the plans of market participants are compatible.

Not all equations are classed as either accounting identities or behavioral relationships. Other equations important in economics include technical relationships, such as a production function, and budget constraints, such as a household's budget constraint that expenditure must not exceed the resources available to it or a government's budget constraint that expenditure must not exceed its sources of finance.

Endogenous versus Exogenous Variables

The theory of supply and demand shows how the interaction of purchasers and sellers in a market yields an equilibrium price P and quantity exchanged Q. These are called the **endogenous** variables of the model, meaning the variables the model seeks to explain. The theory helps to predict how the forces that influence supply and demand affect these endogenous variables.

For example, suppose that the demand schedule depends not only on price P but also on household income Y; for simplicity, let the relationship be linear:

$$Q^d = D(P, Y) = \alpha_1 + \beta_1 P + \gamma Y, \qquad \beta_1 < 0, \ \gamma > 0. \qquad (1.11a)$$

The slope coefficients β_1 and γ are given as negative and positive, respectively, reflecting our belief that apple demand decreases with price and increases with income. Higher incomes will increase the demand for apples at any given price, shifting the demand curve to the right in the price-quantity diagram as shown in Figure 1.1(b).

Similarly, suppose that supply depends not only on price P but also on rainfall R,

$$Q^s = S(P, R) = \alpha_2 + \beta_2 P + \phi R, \qquad \beta_2 > 0, \ \phi > 0. \qquad (1.11b)$$

The slope coefficients β_2 and ϕ are given as positive, reflecting our belief that apple supply increases with both price and rainfall. Higher rainfall increases the supply of apples at any given price, shifting the supply curve to the right in the price-quantity diagram as shown in Figure 1.1(c).

Income Y and rainfall R are examples of **exogenous variables**—variables that affect the endogenous variables of our model but are not themselves explained by the model. The demand and supply equations (1.11) are called the **structural form** of the model. In general, structural equations describe how endogenous variables are determined by other endogenous variables and by exogenous variables. This is what is meant by "a precisely expressed formulation of the theory," in other words, a model.

The values of the endogenous variables that equilibrate the model—corresponding to the point of intersection in Figure 1.1(a)—can be derived by solving the structural equations. The derivation begins by recalling that the equilibrium price is that which equates supply and demand:

$$D(P, Y) = \alpha_1 + \beta_1 P + \gamma Y = \alpha_2 + \beta_2 P + \phi R = S(P, R).$$

Manipulating this, the solutions for equilibrium price and quantity are

$$P = \frac{\alpha_1 - \alpha_2}{\beta_2 - \beta_1} + \frac{\gamma}{\beta_2 - \beta_1} Y - \frac{\phi}{\beta_2 - \beta_1} R,$$
$$Q = \frac{\alpha_1 \beta_2 - \alpha_2 \beta_1}{\beta_2 - \beta_1} + \frac{\gamma \beta_2}{\beta_2 - \beta_1} Y - \frac{\phi \beta_1}{\beta_2 - \beta_1} R. \qquad (1.12)$$

This is called the **reduced form** of the model. In contrast to the structural form, it shows how the equilibrium values of the endogenous variables are determined solely by the exogenous variables (and, of course, the coefficients of the model). This can be emphasized by denoting it as:

$$P = \pi_{10} + \pi_{11}Y + \pi_{12}R,$$
$$Q = \pi_{20} + \pi_{21}Y + \pi_{22}R. \tag{1.13}$$

In specifying income and rainfall as exogenous, we are saying that they can be taken as given for the purpose of studying the apple market—that there is no feedback from the endogenous variables P and Q to the exogenous variables Y and R. The price and quantity of apples are affected by rainfall and household income, but rainfall and household income are not caused by the price and quantity of apples (the incomes of apple growers being a negligible portion of total household income). This is not to suggest that the exogenous variables are not themselves worthy of explanation, only that it is not the goal of this model to explain them. It might well be the goal of some other model to do so; indeed, the determination of people's income is of long-standing interest to labor economists. Similarly, building models to explain rainfall is a perfectly legitimate enterprise, but if this were your interest you would be studying meteorology, not economics. Variables that are exogenous to one model may be endogenous to others.

Comparative Statics

The reduced form of a model is important because it can be used to predict the effect on endogenous variables of changes in the exogenous variables. The effect on equilibrium price and quantity of changes in rainfall or income can be seen qualitatively in Figure 1.1. Consider Figure 1.1(b), which shows apple demand shifting right in response to higher incomes. The result predicted by the model is that more apples are exchanged at a higher equilibrium price. Figure 1.1(c), on the other hand, shows supply shifting in response to higher rainfall. The result predicted by the model is that more apples will be exchanged at a lower equilibrium price.

But how large are these qualitative effects? That depends on the elasticities of the demand and supply curves, which are governed by their coefficients. Taking derivatives of the reduced form yields the expressions for these magnitudes.

$$\frac{\partial P}{\partial Y} = \pi_{11} = \frac{\gamma}{\beta_2 - \beta_1} > 0 \qquad \frac{\partial P}{\partial R} = \pi_{12} = \frac{-\phi}{\beta_2 - \beta_1} < 0$$

$$\frac{\partial Q}{\partial Y} = \pi_{21} = \frac{\gamma\beta_2}{\beta_2 - \beta_1} > 0 \qquad \frac{\partial Q}{\partial R} = \pi_{22} = \frac{-\phi\beta_1}{\beta_2 - \beta_1} > 0$$

If numerical values for the coefficients are available, these formulas can be used to predict the quantitative effects on price and quantity of hypothesized changes in rainfall or income. These derivatives are called **comparative statics** results because they tell us how one static point of equilibrium compares with the new equilibrium that results from a hypothesized change. (Particularly in macroeconomic contexts, comparative statics derivatives are sometimes called **multipliers.**) Notice that our a priori knowledge of the signs of the slope coefficients ($\beta_1 < 0$,

$\gamma > 0$, $\beta_2 > 0$, $\phi > 0$) allows us to determine the sign of these derivatives, and the results are consistent with the qualitative conclusions yielded by the diagrammatic analysis.

Two remarks follow from this framework. First, comparative statics results can only be obtained from the reduced form, not the structural form. In attempting to assess the effect of rainfall on the price and quantity of apples, it is quite meaningless to examine the structural form. A derivative such as $\partial Q^s / \partial R = \phi$ describes only a movement along a curve; it tells us nothing about points of equilibrium.

Second, it is meaningless to ask how one endogenous variable changes with respect to another endogenous variable. It is *not* meaningful to ask, for example, how quantity responds to a change in price because the answer depends on which exogenous change has altered price. In Figure 1.1(b), the increase in quantity accompanies a price increase (these changes arising from higher income); in Figure 1.1(c), the increase in quantity accompanies a price decrease (these changes arising from higher rainfall). That is, we can only usefully consider how changes in endogenous variables arise from hypothesized changes in exogenous variables, not hypothesized changes in other endogenous variables. Again, a derivative such as $\partial Q^s / \partial P = \beta_2$ describes only a movement along a curve; it tells us nothing about the points of equilibrium.

An Example from Macroeconomics

The structure we have just described—of ex post definitions versus ex ante behavior, accounting identities versus equilibrium conditions, endogenous versus exogenous variables, and structural versus reduced forms—is fundamental to economic analysis and therefore to applied econometrics. These basic distinctions underlie virtually all economic models, both microeconomic and macroeconomic.

Consider the national income accounting identity (1.6), which, as we have emphasized, is similar to the definition (1.9) that purchases equal sales in its interpretation as an ex post relationship. There is, however, a parallel equilibrium condition

$$Y = C + I + G + X - M,$$

that is to the accounting identity (1.6) as the equilibrium condition that supply equals demand (1.10) is to the identity (1.9). Just as we can ask what economic forces cause the supply and demand for apples to be equilibrated, we can ask what forces determine a nation's production and the division of that production among its uses.

As an example of a macroeconomic model that seeks to answer these questions, in Chapter 9 we study the Solow-Swan model of economic growth. The Solow-Swan model is one of the simplest macroeconomic models and often the first model studied in a course on macroeconomics. It is a model of a purely closed economy; that is, it does not attempt to explain international trade, and so exports and imports are set to zero, $X = M = 0$. It simplifies further by omitting government, so $G = 0$.

Thus, production Y is viewed as being used for just two purposes, consumption C and investment I:

$$Y = C + I.$$

In addition to this equilibrium condition, the model consists of a production function $Y = f(K, L)$, describing how output is produced from the factors of production capital and labor, and the capital accumulation equation (1.7). Labor L is specified as growing exogenously at rate n, and production is divided between consumption and investment according to an exogenous saving rate s.

In the first instance, the Solow-Swan model seeks to explain a nation's standard of living, measured by output per worker $y = Y/L$, and so this is the key endogenous variable of the model.[2] In its simplest version—the textbook version of the model—living standards are explained by the saving rate s and the population growth rate n. In Chapter 9 we derive the reduced form solution for y as a function of the exogenous variables s and n, an equation of the form

$$y = g(s, n). \tag{1.14}$$

This yields comparative statics results predicting that living standards increase with a nation's saving rate and decrease with its population growth rate:

$$\frac{\partial y}{\partial s} > 0, \qquad \frac{\partial y}{\partial n} < 0. \tag{1.15}$$

In Chapter 9 you will estimate this reduced form and see whether the results are consistent with these theoretical predictions of the model.

1.2.4 Static versus Dynamic Models

Our model of supply and demand is a **static model;** it describes a point of equilibrium, but not the time path by which the endogenous variables reach that equilibrium. Although a different equilibrium can be hypothesized and compared with the original one—which is what the comparative statics results we have derived do—the model does not describe the paths the variables take as they move from one equilibrium to the other.

The Solow-Swan model, on the other hand, is a **dynamic model;** the capital accumulation equation (1.7), or its continuous time version (1.8), describes the evolution of variables over time. As we see in Chapter 9, the model converges to a steady state, the properties of which we will study.

Dynamic versions of the model of supply and demand can be formulated. For example, suppose that in making planting decisions farmers know only last season's price, so the apple harvest for this period depends on lagged rather than current price:

$$Q_t^s = S(P_{t-1}).$$

---

[2] Notice that we are here using the convention (1.3) of lowercase letters denoting per-worker quantities.

Consumers, on the other hand, make consumption decisions on the basis of the current price:

$$Q_t^d = D(P_t).$$

This famous model is called the **cobweb model** because it traces a dynamic path of price–quantity values that look like cobwebs in a supply–demand diagram. For a good treatment of the cobweb model as an example of dynamic economic models generally, see Chiang (1984).

1.2.5   Deterministic versus Stochastic Models

The models we have discussed so far, the model of supply and demand, the Solow-Swan growth model, and the cobweb model, are examples of **deterministic models,** meaning they involve no random elements. Deterministic dynamic models generate smooth (although possibly cyclical) time paths for the variables they describe.

Deterministic models are extremely useful in economics, but are not by themselves a basis for the analysis of data because economic data do not follow smooth time paths. Instead economic data behave erratically, in a way that can only be described through the introduction of random elements. Economic models that involve random elements are called **stochastic models** (*stochastic* means "random"). The view of data as the outcome of randomness is fundamental to statistics and econometrics and so is something that must be developed carefully. The next chapter reviews the key ideas related to this.

1.2.6   Why Do We Need Economic Theory? The Lucas Critique

Applied econometrics studies empirical relationships among variables, and in this chapter we have emphasized the symbiotic interdependence of theory and observation in doing this. You may wonder, however, why we need economic theory as a guide to the study of such relationships. Why not rely on statistical tools alone?

Consider, for example, the reduced form (1.14) that relates living standards y to the national saving rate s and population growth rate n. If statistical methods allow us to uncover and estimate apparently important relationships like this, why not rely on this alone rather than being concerned with any underlying theoretical foundation? After all, the reduced form gives us the comparative statics derivatives that are presumably the focus of interest, so why not limit our interest to establishing statistical relationships among variables, without regard for economic theory?

Econometric Policy Evaluation

Among the most important uses of applied econometrics is **policy evaluation,** assessing the probable effects of policy changes. Consider again our reduced form equation (1.14). The use of econometric methods to estimate the coefficient π_1 suggests we can use this to forecast the effect on living standards of an increase in s. Suppose that a government attempts to increase the nation's saving rate by, say, improving the tax incentives for retirement saving. Will an estimate of π_1 correctly forecast the effect on living standards of this policy?

In a famous paper, the Nobel prize-winning economist Robert Lucas (1976) points out that there is a problem with this approach: The coefficient π_1 may not be stable in the face of the policy change. The reason is that reduced form coefficients such as π_1 are themselves dependent on the underlying structure of the economy, as was explicit in the reduced form (1.13) for our supply–demand model (1.11), in which the parameters π_{ij} are functions of the underlying structural form parameters. These structural parameters typically describe, at least in part, people's behavior, and people's behavior changes in response to the policy change; indeed, the purpose of the policy change is to cause people to behave differently. Thus a reduced-form parameter such as π_1 may itself change in response to the policy change, so that an estimate based on data from the old policy regime may not correctly forecast the effects of the new policy.

The Phillips Curve

Although Lucas's point may seem esoteric, it was prompted by real-world events. In the 1960s, economists documented an apparent inverse relationship between inflation and unemployment known as the *Phillips curve* and interpreted it as representing a usable policy trade-off. Estimated Phillips curves appeared to suggest that unemployment could be lowered at the cost of higher inflation. Macroeconomic policy therefore came to be cast as a cruel choice between the evils of inflation and unemployment. Because moderate inflation was viewed as a lesser evil than unemployment, this doctrine came to justify inflationary policies in the 1970s. In time, however, it was found that the reductions in unemployment that initially seemed to accompany higher inflation were temporary rather than permanent. Unemployment was not permanently reduced.

Why did the prediction of estimated Phillips curves prove false? Lucas argues that the coefficients were unstable because Phillips curves were essentially reduced-form relationships. They failed to take into account that, in response to higher inflation, people would change their behavior.

Lucas's critique indicates that policy evaluation is a much more difficult problem than it might seem; it suggests that to correctly assess policy changes we must use models having coefficients that are invariant to those changes. These policy-invariant coefficients will be ones that describe economic fundamentals such as tastes and technology rather than superficial reduced-form relationships.

At its simplest level, the Lucas critique makes the obvious point that to correctly evaluate policy, economists must understand how the economy works. It is not good enough to rely on seemingly significant statistical relationships among variables. The Lucas critique helps us understand why econometricians need economic theory.

EXERCISES

1.1 Let N_t denote a firm's (or an economy's) end-of-period inventory holdings, Y_t its production, and X_t its sales. These variables are related by

$$N_t - N_{t-1} = Y_t - X_t.$$

This says that inventories accumulate ($N_t - N_{t-1} > 0$) when production exceeds sales and decumulate ($N_t - N_{t-1} < 0$) when sales exceed production.

(a) Which of these variables are stocks and which are flows?

(b) Is this an ex ante or an ex post relationship?

(c) Is it in discrete or continuous time? Whichever you decide, also present it in the alternative form.

1.2 Let $W(t)$ denote a family's wealth, $Y(t)$ its after-tax income, and $C(t)$ its consumption. These variables are related by:

$$\frac{dW(t)}{dt} = Y(t) - C(t).$$

This says that wealth accumulates ($dW(t)/dt > 0$) when consumption is less than after-tax income and decumulates ($dW(t)/dt < 0$) when consumption exceeds after-tax income.

(a) Which of these variables are stocks and which are flows?

(b) Is this an ex ante or an ex post relationship?

(c) Is it in discrete or continuous time? Whichever you decide, also present it in the alternative form.

1.3 Let the national debt of outstanding government bonds be denoted by B_t. The national debt increases or decreases over time according to the government deficit D_t,

$$B_t = B_{t-1} + D_t.$$

The deficit equals government expenditures G_t less tax revenues T_t plus the interest on the preexisting debt $r B_{t-1}$ (where r denotes the interest rate):

$$D_t = G_t - T_t + r B_{t-1}.$$

(*Note*: A negative deficit is a surplus.)

(a) Consider the following variables: the national debt B_t, the deficit D_t, government expenditure G_t, tax revenues T_t, and the interest on the debt $r B_{t-1}$. Which are stocks and which are flows?

(b) Are these relationships ex ante or ex post?

(c) Are these relationships expressed in discrete or continuous time?

1.4 Consider the structural form (1.11) of the model of supply and demand.

(a) Derive the reduced form, showing your steps.

(b) Show how to determine the sign of the comparative statics effects.

1.3   Descriptive Statistics versus Statistical Inference

An important first step in the analysis of data is to summarize it in a form that aids interpretation. Data can be summarized in many ways: graphically, tabularly, and by calculating **summary statistics** such as averages, medians, modes, ranges, and quartiles. The use of these techniques is called **descriptive statistics.**

A great deal can often be learned from descriptive methods, and they are essential in the **exploratory data analysis** stage of an empirical research project. On their own, however, they are rarely adequate for addressing issues of interest to economists or, for that matter, researchers in other disciplines. If trials of a new drug find that the treatment group has a lower incidence of disease than a control group, is this conclusive evidence that the drug is effective or might the difference be due to chance? Questions such as this cannot be answered by descriptive methods. Instead we want to be able to generalize from the available data to conclusions about the larger population from which the data have been drawn—in this example, the population of all patients with the disease. **Statistical inference** is concerned with making such generalizations.

The purpose of this book is to introduce some of the methods of statistical inference that economists have found useful in studying economic problems. In doing this we begin in Chapters 2–14 by phrasing most of our discussion in terms of cross-section data. This is because cross-section data can usually be viewed as having been obtained by random sampling and thus it is, in this clear sense, representative of the larger population. As we see in the next chapter, the structure of random sampling plays an important role in statistical inference.

This is not to say that the ideas of these early chapters are irrelevant to the study of time series data. On the contrary, time series data are sometimes used in these chapters to illustrate the methods we develop, when this can be done in a way that allows us to sidestep issues specific to the analysis of measurements that are ordered in time. We turn to these time-specific issues in Chapters 15–18, in which the ideas of the earlier chapters provide an important foundation for the analysis of economic time series.

In studying these topics it is helpful to proceed by adopting the following strategy. We begin by considering a single variable observed in isolation, asking how a limited amount of data can be used to reach more general conclusions about the behavior of that variable. This is the subject of Chapter 2. Then, beginning in Chapter 3, we turn to the kind of problem that is more often of interest to economists, the study of relationships between variables. When we study time series methods, beginning in Chapter 15, we find that it is valuable to follow the same strategy, focusing initially on the behavior a single variable as it evolves over time and then turning to relationships between variables.

Conclusion

The purpose of this chapter is to instill some appreciation for the range of the different kinds of data with which economists work and for some of the key ideas that underlie the economic models they use to study them. It is useful to begin with this emphasis because our study of statistical inference requires that, at least initially, we abstract from this richness in favor of a focus on the essential elements of inferential analysis. It is these essential elements that are the subject of the next chapter.

Appendix   Internet Data Sources

The World Wide Web provides access to a vast array of economic data. Conveniently, you can find it all through a single gateway, *Resources for Economists on the Internet,* located at http://rfe.org/. This web site is sponsored by the American Economic Association and maintained by Bill Goffe, Department of Economics, State University of New York at Oswego. In addition to data sources, it has links to many other economics-related resources. Ones that are likely to be of most use to students include:

- dictionaries, glossaries, and encyclopedias
- economists, departments, and universities
- announcements of meetings and conferences
- organizations and associations
- software

Data Links

The web site includes links to the following categories of data:

- U.S. macroeconomic and regional data
- other U.S. data
- world and non-U.S. data
- finance and financial-market data
- journal data and program archives

The availability in a single location of links to U.S. data sources is especially valuable. In contrast to many countries, U.S. data collection and dissemination are done by a variety of government agencies rather than being unified under a few authorities. In fact, there is a web site offering not data per se but a guide to the many federal agencies that provide data: www.fedstats.gov.

The links to world and non-U.S. data include national statistical agencies around the world and international organizations. Among the most important of the latter are the following sites:

www.imf.org	International Monetary Fund (IMF) (data for most of the countries of the world)
www.oecd.org	Organization for Economic Cooperation and Development (OECD) (data for the world's wealthiest countries)
www.worldbank.org	World Bank (data related to economic growth and development)

An important problem with international data is that national accounts are kept as nominal values denominated in local currencies, so data may not be comparable internationally. This prompted economists Robert Summers and Alan Heston, University of Pennsylvania, to oversee the gargantuan enterprise of creating internationally comparable real national income accounts statistics. The project, the **Penn World Tables,** is described on their web site. As of writing, the current version of the tables includes data on 168 countries for some or all of the years 1950–2000. In addition to real national income account statistics, it includes other important variables such as population, price indices, and capital stock data. Two universities provide web interfaces for downloading data from the tables:

pwt.econ.upenn.edu   University of Pennsylvania
dc1.chass.utoronto.ca/pwt   University of Toronto

We use data from the Penn World Tables at a couple of points in this book: Population data are used in Chapters 3 and 18, and the data used by Mankiw, Romer, and Weil (1992)—an application studied in Chapter 9—are from this source.

One of the most appealing features of the Penn World Tables is that the entire data set is freely available and is easily downloaded. By contrast, when you follow the links to many web sites, you may be disappointed to find that the data are only available on a commercial basis. In such situations, find out whether your institution subscribes to their data service. For example, much of the OECD and IMF data are obtained on a subscription basis, but many universities subscribe to these services. Check your department's web page: it may have convenient links to the economics data sets and other resources available at your institution.

One web site, WebEc, is specifically devoted to categorizing economics-related sites offering free information, including data: www.helsinki.fi/WebEc. Remember as well that, when web data are proprietary, your library may nevertheless subscribe to the paper documents in which it is published. Tracing web links is an excellent way of finding out what data exist, even if you end up having to access it in traditional form.

2 Statistical Inference

Econometrics is concerned with the statistical analysis of economic data. Econometricians seek to do the following:

- *describe* economic events
- *infer* from the available data broader conclusions about the economy
- *predict* economic behavior and events

To do this, econometrics makes use of the standard concepts of statistical inference, the set of techniques for learning something from data. The purpose of this chapter is to review the most important of these concepts.

The foundation of statistical inference is **distribution theory,** the theory of random variables, probability distributions, and mathematical expectation and variance. Appendix B provides a review of distribution theory. As we begin our study of statistical inference, we will be fairly explicit about the role that distribution theory plays.

2.1 Populations, Samples, and Parameters

As we have seen in the opening chapter, data are simply information in quantitative form; they typically consist of a group of measurements. The reason for studying data, not only in economics but also in the many other fields in which statistical methods are applied, is to try to learn something about the underlying phenomena generating the measurements. Regardless of whether it is associated with the natural world or human social interaction, statisticians call the true underlying phenomenon generating the data the **population model.** The **population** is the set of all measurements that could conceivably have been generated by the population model. A population could be infinite in number; to a geographer interested in the depth of a lake, for example, an infinite number of measurements are in principle relevant.

The problem facing the statistician or econometrician is that, even in the case of a finite population, this set of all relevant measurements is typically unavailable.

(A **census** is an attempt, rarely perfectly successful, to obtain the population.) Instead we have a subset of measurements taken from the larger population; these are the data with which the statistician works. The process of collecting data is called **sampling the population,** and so the resulting observations are sometimes called **sample data.** The task of the statistician or econometrician is to use this limited information to learn or infer something about the underlying phenomenon of interest, the population model. This is the problem of statistical inference.

A fundamental aspect of statistical inference is that the sample data available to the statistician have been generated randomly. In advance of the collection of the data, the researcher does not know what measurements will be obtained. The random nature of the data is determined by the underlying population model. Hence, the population model is most conveniently specified in terms of some probability distribution, which is the key concept in any treatment of uncertainty. The probability distribution generating the population (that is, governing any sample observation drawn from the population) is known as the **population distribution.**

Some examples of actual populations are the incomes of all families this year, the employment status of members of the labor force (unemployment measured by, say, a 1 and employment by 0), and the value of GNP next year. The first two are examples of finite populations, the last of an infinite population. (Of course, when data become available for next year we will have observed just a single sample observation from the infinite number of possible values that could conceivably have been generated by the population model governing GNP.) To illustrate the concept of a population distribution, it is useful to abstract from the real world and consider instead the following very artificial example.

EXAMPLE 1

Consider a population that consists of just the four values 6, 7, 8, and 9. You may find it helpful to think of these as numbered balls in a container. A sample observation is the result of a random drawing from the population. What is the population distribution?

SOLUTION

The population distribution is the probability distribution governing a random drawing from the population. Let the measurement yielded by such a random drawing be denoted by the random variable Y. The possible values y that Y can take on, and their respective probabilities $f(y)$ are:

y	$f(y)$
6	1/4
7	1/4
8	1/4
9	1/4

This probability distribution may also be expressed graphically:

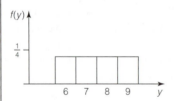

This is an example of a distribution that, for obvious reasons, is known as the uniform distribution. Hence, in this example the population distribution is said to be uniform. This uniform distribution may also be expressed as a formula:

$$f(y) = \frac{1}{4}, \qquad y = 6, 7, 8, 9.$$

Example 1 is artificial in a number of respects. First, the size of the population is very small. In practice, populations are typically much larger. Indeed, perhaps the most important reason why the statistician normally has only a sample of data to work with is that it is not possible, or it is prohibitively expensive, to obtain the entire population. Second, this example is artificial because the population is known. The problem of statistical inference arises precisely because, in practice, populations are unknown. Nevertheless, it is often helpful to illustrate the key concepts of statistical inference with artificial examples in which the population is known. Let us consider another example of a population distribution.

EXAMPLE 2

Consider the population consisting of all members of the labor force, and let the characteristic of interest be employment status. Assign each member of the labor force the value 1 if the individual is unemployed and 0 if employed. Hence, this population may be viewed as a sequence of 0-1 measurements. The unemployment rate, expressed as a proportion of the labor force that is unemployed, is the sum of these 0-1 values (that is, the number of unemployed) divided by the total size of the labor force. Denote this unemployment rate by π. Suppose a census reveals that $\pi = 0.1$, so that 10% of the labor force is unemployed. What is the population distribution?

SOLUTION

The population distribution is the probability distribution governing a random drawing from the population. Let the outcome of this drawing be denoted by the random variable Y. Y can take on just two values: 0 or 1. The observation $y = 1$ is obtained with probability $\pi = 0.1$; $y = 0$ is obtained with probability $1 - \pi = 0.9$. Therefore the population distribution is:

y	$f(y)$
0	$1 - \pi$
1	π

This may also be expressed graphically:

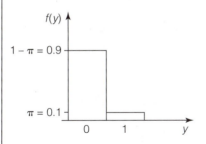

This very simple distribution is called the Bernoulli distribution. The formula for the Bernoulli distribution is:

$$f(y) = \pi^y (1-\pi)^{1-y}, \qquad y = 0, 1. \tag{2.1}$$

You may wish to verify that substitution of the y values into this formula yields the probabilities given in the table.

This example illustrates two important points. First, the concept of a population distribution is important because this is the most convenient may of expressing a population. It is very inconvenient to express this population in terms of the list of 0-1 values; using a probability distribution, expressed as a table, a graph, or a formula, to summarize a population is far more economical and informative than listing the individual measurements constituting the population. Knowledge of the population distribution is equivalent to a listing of the underlying measurements in that there is no significant loss of information in going from the latter to the former.

The second point illustrated by Example 2 is that typically the matter of interest to the econometrician involves some feature of the population. In this case, this is the unemployment rate π. Knowledge of the form of the population distribution, in this case that it is Bernoulli, and the value of π represents all the information about the population that is of interest; it is as good as having the underlying 0-1 values themselves. π is an example of a **population parameter.** Population parameters are key features of the population which, in combination with the specified form of the distribution, fully characterize the population. The Bernoulli distribution is fully characterized by the parameter π. That is, given π, everything that is worth knowing about the distribution is known; it is equivalent to knowing the underlying 0-1 values.

The Bernoulli distribution is fully characterized by a single parameter. Some distributions are more complicated—they are characterized by more than one parameter. An example is the normal distribution, which is fully characterized by two parameters, the mean and variance, commonly denoted by μ and σ^2. If a random variable Y follows a normal distribution this is summarized by:

$$Y \sim \mathrm{N}(\mu, \sigma^2).$$

FIGURE 2.1

The normal dis-
tribution: $Y \sim$
$N(\mu, \sigma^2)$.

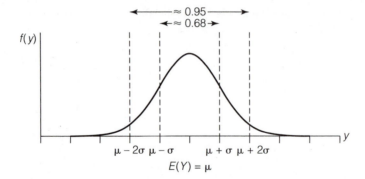

In contrast to the uniform and Bernoulli distributions in Examples 1 and 2, which
are examples of discrete distributions (in that the random variable can take on only
a finite number of values), the normal distribution is a continuous distribution. A
continuous random variable is one taking on an infinite number of values in a
continuous range. Hence, the normal distribution cannot be expressed as a table.
Its formula is:

$$f(y) = \frac{1}{\sqrt{2\pi\sigma^2}} \, e^{-\frac{1}{2\sigma^2}(y - \mu)^2}, \qquad -\infty < y < \infty, \tag{2.2}$$

Here π and e denote the mathematical constants $3.14159\ldots$ and $2.71828\ldots$,
respectively.[1] From this formula it is apparent that, in the same way that the
Bernoulli distribution (2.1) is fully specified by the parameter π, the normal distribution is fully specified by the parameters μ and σ^2.

The normal distribution is shown in Figure 2.1. It was derived by the great
mathematician Carl Gauss (1777–1855), and so is sometimes called the Gaussian
distribution. As the figure indicates, since the parameter σ^2 governs the dispersion
of the distribution it determines the probability that the random variable falls near
its mean. About 68% of the mass of the normal distribution is within one standard deviation of the mean, so there is a 0.68 probability that the variable falls
within the bounds $\mu \pm \sigma$. Similarly, about 95% of the mass of the distribution is
within two standard deviations of the mean.

Even if a population is not normal, the symbols μ and σ^2 are usually used to
denote its mean and variance. Let us state this formally.

Definition 2.1   *The* population mean, *usually denoted by* μ*, is the expected value* $E(Y)$ *of the*
population distribution; the population variance, *usually denoted by* σ^2*, is the*
variance $V(Y)$ *of the population distribution.*

---

[1] Note that in this case π does *not* denote a parameter of the distribution. The slanted symbol π
distinguishes this mathematical constant from the parameter π of the Bernoulli distribution.

The evaluation of population means and variances requires, then, the formulas for the expected value and variance of a random variable. These are developed in Appendix B (mathematical expectation in Section B.2, variance in Section B.4).

EXAMPLE 3 | Find the mean and variance of the uniform population in Example 1.

SOLUTION | Because this population is discrete, it is the formulas for the discrete case that should be used. Applying Definition B.1 (Appendix B, Section B.2), the population mean is

$$\mu = E(Y) = \sum_y yf(y) = 6 \cdot \frac{1}{4} + 7 \cdot \frac{1}{4} + 8 \cdot \frac{1}{4} + 9 \cdot \frac{1}{4} = 7.5.$$

Applying Definition B.2 (Appendix B, Section B.4), the population variance is

$$\sigma^2 = V(Y) = E(Y - EY)^2 = \sum_y (y - \mu)^2 f(y)$$

$$= (6 - 7.5)^2 \frac{1}{4} + (7 - 7.5)^2 \frac{1}{4} + (8 - 7.5)^2 \frac{1}{4} + (9 - 7.5)^2 \frac{1}{4} = \frac{5}{4}.$$

Although the symbols μ and σ^2 are the usual shorthand notation for the population mean and variance, this choice is arbitrary and in some situations other notation might be used. Here is an example.

EXAMPLE 4 | What is the mean of a Bernoulli population?

SOLUTION | The Bernoulli distribution is given by Equation (2.1). In Exercise 2.4a, you are asked to show that its mean is

$$E(Y) = \pi. \tag{2.3}$$

Hence the mean of a Bernoulli population is denoted by π. There is no need to introduce the additional notation μ.

These examples illustrate the general fact that population parameters such as π, μ, and σ^2 are defined in terms of mathematical expectations. (The variance $V(\cdot)$ is, of course, just a particular mathematical expectation—see Appendix B, Section B.4.) The following exercises ask you to use the mathematical expectation and variance formulas found in Appendix B to further your understanding of this.

EXERCISES

2.1 Consider a population consisting of three balls in a container, numbered 1, 2, and 3. Present the population distribution as a table, a formula, and graphically. Find the population mean and variance.

2.2 Consider a population consisting of three balls in a container, numbered 1, 2, and 2. Present the population distribution as a table, a formula, and graphically. Find the population mean and variance.

2.3 For the population in Example 1, use the alternative variance formula (B.10) to verify the variance found in Example 3.

2.4 Consider the Bernoulli distribution (2.1).

(a) Establish the result (2.3). (*Hint:* Read Section B.2.)

(b) Derive $V(Y)$. (*Hint:* Read Section B.4.) Because the Bernoulli distribution is fully characterized by its parameter π, the variance of the distribution should be determined by π. Is it?

2.5 The continuous uniform distribution has the formula

$$f(y) = \frac{1}{\theta_1 - \theta_0}, \qquad \theta_0 < y < \theta_1.$$

Depict this distribution graphically. What are the parameters of a continuous uniform population?

2.6 ⨍ Find the expected value of the continuous uniform distribution. Is this expected value fully determined by the parameters of the distribution?

2.2   Statistics and Sampling Distributions

Statistical inference proceeds by computing quantities from sample data in order to attempt to learn about the underlying population. Such quantities are called **statistics.**

EXAMPLE 5   Consider the example of a uniform distribution given in Example 1. Suppose a sample of size $n = 2$ is drawn: let these drawings be denoted Y_1, Y_2. How is the statistic the **sample mean** computed?

SOLUTION   The sample mean is simply the average of the drawings. Denoting this by $\overline{Y}$, it is computed as

$$\overline{Y} = \frac{Y_1 + Y_2}{2}.$$

In general, for n data observations $Y_1, Y_2, \ldots, Y_n$, the sample mean is computed as:

$$\overline{Y} = \frac{1}{n} \sum_{i=1}^{n} Y_i. \tag{2.4}$$

The calculation of statistics is useful in part because they serve to summarize key features of the sample data. In this respect, they are analogous to parameters, which summarize key features of the population. However, statistics, as sample quantities, are fundamentally different from population quantities such as parameters. This is why we distinguish between the *sample* mean $\overline{Y}$, defined by (2.4), and the *population* mean μ, defined as a mathematical expectation.

Although sample statistics and population parameters are fundamentally different, the fact that statistical inference is concerned with using sample data to learn about populations suggests that the two are linked. In particular, because the population model is fully characterized by its parameters, sample statistics are used to make inferences about these parameters. One important aspect of this is that sample statistics are often used to guess the value of a parameter. A statistic that is intended as a guess of a parameter is called an **estimator.** For example, the sample mean $\overline{Y}$ is often used as an estimator of the population mean μ.

EXAMPLE 6   Let the employment status of members of the labor force be described by a Bernoulli distribution as in Example 2. Given a sample $Y_1, Y_2, \ldots, Y_n$, of 0-1 drawings from the population, propose an estimator $\hat{\pi}$ for the population unemployment rate π.

SOLUTION   The sum of the sample observations $\sum_{i=1}^{n} Y_i$ is simply the total number of people in the sample who are unemployed. A reasonable estimator for the population unemployment rate is the ratio of the number unemployed in the sample to the total sample size:

$$\hat{\pi} = \frac{1}{n} \sum_{i=1}^{n} Y_i. \tag{2.5}$$

This is, of course, just the sample mean. Hence, in this case $\hat{\pi}$ is simply alternative notation for $\overline{Y}$.

Equations (2.4) and (2.5) illustrate that an estimator (or any statistic) is a formula that is applied to the sample. When applied to a particular sample, this formula yields a numerical value. This particular numerical value is called an **estimate.** For instance, suppose in Example 5 that a sample of size $n = 2$ happened to yield the realizations $y_1 = 8$, $y_2 = 6$. Then the statistic $\overline{Y}$ yields the value $\overline{y} = 7$.

The distinction between an estimator and the resulting estimate is emphasized because, although the latter is a numerical value and therefore a fixed constant, an estimator (and, more generally, any statistic) varies in repeated samples. That is, the value yielded by the formula depends on the particular sample that happens to be drawn and will change in successive samples. Consequently a statistic is a random variable. This is simply a restatement of our earlier observation that one does not know what value a statistic will yield until it is applied to the sample. This is another respect in which statistics are fundamentally different from population parameters: $\overline{Y}$ is a random variable; μ, defined as a mathematical expectation, is not.

Given that a statistic is a random variable, it must have a probability distribution. Because this distribution arises from the random nature of the sample data, obtained through a process of random sampling from the population, the probability distribution of a statistic is called a **sampling distribution.**

EXAMPLE 7   Consider a sample of size $n = 2$ drawn from the population of Example 1. Let the drawings be with replacement (by replacing the balls at each turn). Find the sampling distribution of the sample mean $\overline{Y}$. What is the probability that the estimate $\overline{y} = 7$ will be obtained?

SOLUTION   The possible drawings are as follows.

(6,6)   (7,6)   (8,6)   (9,6)
(6,7)   (7,7)   (8,7)   (9,7)
(6,8)   (7,8)   (8,8)   (9,8)
(6,9)   (7,9)   (8,9)   (9,9)

Because each pair has an equal probability of being drawn, this probability is 1/16. Computing the associated values of $\bar{Y}$, it follows that its sampling distribution is:

$\bar{y}$	$f(\bar{y})$
6	1/16
6.5	2/16
7	3/16
7.5	4/16
8	3/16
8.5	2/16
9	1/16

Presented graphically this is:

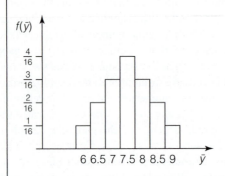

The probability is 3/16 that the estimate $\bar{y} = 7$ will be obtained.

Comparing this sampling distribution with the population distribution in Example 1, notice that a sampling distribution can be rather different from the underlying population distribution, both in the values that can be taken on and the form of the distribution. The form of a sampling distribution depends on, in addition to the population distribution, the sample size n used in calculating the statistic.

EXERCISES

2.7 Consider a sample of size $n = 2$ drawn with replacement from the population in Exercise 2.2. Find the sampling distribution of the sample mean, depicting it both as a table and graphically.

2.3 Properties of Estimators

The most obvious way in which we might attempt to learn about a population model using sample data is to use a sample statistic as an estimator of a parameter of the population. But in any applied context there will be many statistics that can be proposed as estimators for any particular parameter. How can we compare alternative estimators in order to determine which are, in some sense, good, with the hope of choosing the one that is best? The concept of a sampling distribution is important because we choose among estimators on the basis of their properties, and the properties of estimators are defined in terms of features of their sampling distributions.

2.3.1 Unbiasedness

Let us begin thinking about properties of estimators by continuing with our previous examples.

EXAMPLE 8

Consider the population distribution in Example 1, the population mean of $\mu = 7.5$ computed in Example 3, and the sampling distribution for $\overline{Y}$ based on $n = 2$ obtained in Example 7. In this problem, is there any reason why $\overline{Y}$ should be considered a good estimator of μ?

SOLUTION

Figure 2.2 depicts the population distribution in Example 1 and the sampling distribution in Example 7. An obvious feature of $\overline{Y}$ is that its sampling distribution is centered over the population mean. This means that, although the probability of correctly estimating μ on the basis of a particular sample is small (just 1/4), in repeated samples μ is not consistently over- or underestimated. In this respect, $\overline{Y}$ is a good estimator.

Example 8 illustrates the property of **unbiasedness.** In using a statistic (say $\hat{\theta}$) as an estimator of a population parameter θ, it is very unlikely that the resulting estimate will be exactly correct. In Example 8 there is only one chance in four that a random sample will yield $\overline{y} = \mu = 7.5$, and this probability would be much smaller in a larger population. Given the foregone conclusion that we will almost always make mistakes in estimation, it is desirable that estimates yielded by repeated samples be evenly scattered about the population value; that is, that

FIGURE 2.2

An unbiased esti-
mator has a sam-
pling distribution
that is centered
over the popula-
tion parameter. $\overline{Y}$
is unbiased because
its sampling distri-
bution is centered
over μ.

Population distribution:

Sampling distribution:

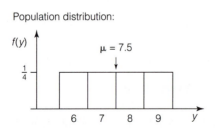

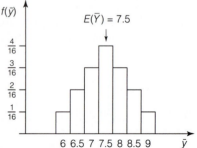

there not be a bias in estimation. This will be the case if the sampling distribution is centered over the parameter value.[2] Because the center of a distribution is given by its expected value, it is possible to use the concept of mathematical expectation to make the property of unbiasedness precise.

Definition 2.2   *A statistic $\hat{\theta}$ is* unbiased *as an estimator for a parameter θ if $E(\hat{\theta}) = \theta$.*

EXAMPLE 9   In Example 8 it was observed that the sampling distribution of $\overline{Y}$ is centered over the population value of μ. Show that the formal definition of unbiasedness is satisfied by showing that $E(\overline{Y}) = 7.5$.

SOLUTION   The evaluation of $E(\overline{Y})$ requires the sampling distribution of $\overline{Y}$. This is given in Example 7 and is a discrete distribution. Applying the formula for the expected value of a discrete random variable[3] yields

$$E(\overline{Y}) = 6 \cdot \frac{1}{16} + 6.5 \cdot \frac{2}{16} + 7 \cdot \frac{3}{16} + 7.5 \cdot \frac{4}{16} + 8 \cdot \frac{3}{16} + 8.5 \cdot \frac{2}{16} + 9 \cdot \frac{1}{16} = 7.5.$$

The difference between an estimator and the true value of the population parameter, $\hat{\theta} - \theta$, is called the **sampling error.** This is the mistake that is made in estimation. Because the estimator $\hat{\theta}$ is a random variable, so too is its sampling error; it will vary in repeated sampling. Some samples happen to yield estimates close to the true parameter value, so the sampling error is small. Other samples yield estimates further away, so the sampling error is larger.

---

[2] The property of unbiasedness is the basis for the following joke about econometricians, although it might more appropriately be told about statisticians generally. Three econometricians go hunting. Upon spotting a moose, one fires, missing the moose 6 feet to the right. The second fires, missing the moose 6 feet to the left. The third shouts, "We got it! We got it!"

[3] See Appendix B, Definition B.1.

The property of unbiasedness says that, although all estimators incur sampling error, it is desirable that, on average in repeated sampling, the sampling error be zero. Thus, an equivalent definition of unbiasedness is that the expected value of the sampling error be zero, or $E(\hat{\theta} - \theta) = 0$.

If an estimator is biased, the expected value of its sampling error is nonzero; this magnitude is known as the **bias** of the estimator.

Definition 2.3   *The* bias *of an estimator $\hat{\theta}$ is the expected value of its sampling error, $E(\hat{\theta} - \theta)$.*

If the bias of an estimator is positive, this means that $E(\hat{\theta}) > \theta$ and the estimator tends to overestimate the population parameter; a negative bias means that the estimator tends to underestimate. The property of unbiasedness simply says that we prefer an estimator that tends to neither overestimate nor underestimate.

Note that the property of unbiasedness is defined in terms of a feature of the sampling distribution. Without the concept of a sampling distribution, it would not be possible in Example 9 to speak of $\overline{Y}$ as being a good estimator in this sense. In general, the behavior of sampling distributions is the key to choosing among alternative estimators.

Although Example 9 is useful in illustrating the property of unbiasedness, it is obviously a very artificial example. In particular, the knowledge of the sampling distribution that allows us to establish unbiasedness is derived from a knowledge of the underlying (very simple) population. The problem of statistical inference arises, however, precisely because the population is unknown. A property such as unbiasedness is only useful if it can be established without knowledge of the underlying population. Is this possible?

A More General Sampling Problem

To consider this question, let us turn from examples based on the very artificial population in Example 1 to a more realistic sampling situation. Consider the much more general problem in which a sample $Y_1, \ldots, Y_n$ is drawn from some population. Nothing in particular is assumed about the nature of this population (it could be normal, Bernoulli, uniform, or some other distribution) except that it has some mean that we label μ and some variance that we label σ^2. (Even the existence of a variance is not essential for establishing Result 2.1.) It is assumed that observations are drawn from the population according to **random sampling,** just as in Example 7, and so successive drawings are statistically independent; that is, the value obtained on one drawing does not affect, nor is it affected by, values obtained on other drawings. These assumptions are summarized by the notation

$$Y_i \sim \text{i.i.d.}(\mu, \sigma^2), \qquad i = 1, \ldots, n, \tag{2.6}$$

where i.i.d. stands for identically and independently distributed; thus, the notation means that the sample observations are identically (because all come from the same population distribution) and independently distributed according to a distribution with parameters μ and σ^2. The summary notation (2.6) is an example of a **statistical model,** which is a joint statement of the population model and the sampling process by which data are obtained from the population. Clearly there is a close relationship between a statistical model and the associated population, in that the population parameters are also parameters of the statistical model. When the meaning is likely to be clear from the context, we often refer to a statistical model as simply the **model.**

Given a sample generated by this model, is an unbiased estimator for the population mean μ available? Our examples suggest that the sample mean $\overline{Y}$ should be considered. Is it possible to establish, in this very general context, that $\overline{Y}$ is unbiased as an estimator for μ?

Result 2.1   *In the context of the model (2.6) in which $Y_i \sim$ i.i.d.(μ, σ^2), the sample mean $\overline{Y}$ is unbiased as an estimator for the population mean μ.*

Proof:

$$E(\overline{Y}) = E\left(\frac{1}{n}\sum_{i=1}^{n} Y_i\right)$$

$$= \frac{1}{n}E\left(\sum_{i=1}^{n} Y_i\right) \qquad \text{by Corollary B.1.1 in Appendix B}$$

$$= \frac{1}{n}\sum_{i=1}^{n} E(Y_i) \qquad \text{by Corollary B.3.1 in Appendix B}$$

$$= \frac{1}{n}\sum_{i=1}^{n} \mu$$

$$= \frac{1}{n}n\mu \qquad\qquad \text{by Law A.2 in Appendix A}$$

$$= \mu \qquad\qquad\qquad\qquad\qquad\qquad \square$$

This result establishes that the useful application of a property such as unbiasedness does not require knowledge of the underlying population. Remarkably, even with only extremely weak assumptions about the population model it is still possible to reach conclusions about important features of sampling distributions. As the proof illustrates, the laws of summation found in Appendix A and the laws of mathematical expectation found in Appendix B are important tools in the study of sampling distributions.

As specified, the model (2.6) has a second parameter σ^2. How is this estimated from the available sample? The estimator commonly used for σ^2 is

$$s^2 = \frac{1}{n-1}\sum_{i=1}^{n}(Y_i - \overline{Y})^2. \tag{2.7}$$

This is known as the **sample variance.** Just as was true of $\overline{Y}$, s^2 is a sample statistic; its value varies in repeated sampling. Hence, like all statistics, it is a random variable and has a sampling distribution. And, again, even on the basis of little knowledge about the population from which the sample is obtained, it is possible to study the features of this sampling distribution. In particular, it is possible to show (although we will not do so here) that:

Result 2.2   *In the context of the model* (2.6) *in which* $Y_i \sim$ i.i.d.(μ, σ^2), *the sample variance* s^2 *is an unbiased estimator for the population variance* σ^2, $E(s^2) = \sigma^2$.

This result explains why formula (2.7) involves division by $n - 1$ rather than n. Given the result that division by $n - 1$ yields an estimator that is unbiased, it follows that anything other than $n - 1$ in the denominator of (2.7) will result in a biased estimator. In particular, consider the following estimator for σ^2 as an alternative to s^2:

$$\hat{\sigma}^2 = \frac{1}{n}\sum_{i=1}^{n}(Y_i - \overline{Y})^2. \tag{2.8}$$

It is apparent that the relationship between the two estimators is

$$\hat{\sigma}^2 = \frac{n-1}{n}s^2. \tag{2.9}$$

Because $(n - 1)/n$ is a fractional value, $\hat{\sigma}^2$ gives a slightly smaller estimate of σ^2 than does s^2. Taking Result 2.2 as given, it follows that

$$E(\hat{\sigma}^2) = \frac{n-1}{n}E(s^2) = \frac{n-1}{n}\sigma^2 \neq \sigma^2. \tag{2.10}$$

The alternative estimator $\hat{\sigma}^2$ is biased; its sampling distribution is not centered over σ^2. Exercise 2.11 asks you to evaluate the bias of $\hat{\sigma}^2$.

It must be emphasized that the validity of results on sampling distributions such as Results 2.1 and 2.2 depends on the specification of—that is, assumptions about—the statistical model. For example, the proof of Result 2.1 uses the assumption that all sample observations Y_i have a common mean μ. If the sample were obtained from some other statistical model (conceivably characterized by parameters other than μ and σ^2), Results 2.1 and 2.2 would not necessarily be meaningful. This point is pursued more fully in Section 2.7.

Asymptotic Unbiasedness

In addition to the fact that $\hat{\sigma}^2$ is biased, the derivation (2.10) reveals another interesting feature of its sampling distribution—the bias becomes smaller as n becomes larger, disappearing entirely in the limit as $n \rightarrow \infty$, because $(n - 1)/n \rightarrow 1$ as $n \rightarrow \infty$. In other words, as the sample size becomes large the sampling distribution of $\hat{\sigma}^2$ becomes centered over σ^2. The position of the sampling distribution changes with the sample size.

FIGURE 2.3

The estimator $\hat{\sigma}^2$ is asymptotically unbiased; its sampling distribution becomes centered over σ^2 as $n \to \infty$.

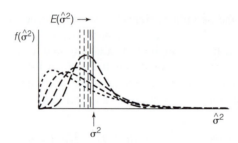

The variance estimators s^2 and $\hat{\sigma}^2$ must take on positive values because they are computed as sums of squares. In addition, their sampling distributions are skewed to the right. The sampling distribution of $\hat{\sigma}^2$ is depicted in Figure 2.3, which illustrates how the sampling distribution shifts as n increases. The shift is to the right because the ratio $(n - 1)/n$, as a fractional value, approaches 1 from below as $n \to \infty$, reflecting the fact that $\hat{\sigma}^2$ underestimates σ^2.

Although not as desirable as unbiasedness, which holds for any value of n, this feature of $\hat{\sigma}^2$ is obviously in its favor. This illustrates the fact that sometimes (in fact, often in econometrics) it is useful to consider the behavior of sampling distributions as the sample size becomes large. Such results are called large-sample or **asymptotic** results. They contrast with results—such as unbiasedness or, in the next section, efficiency and best linear unbiasedness—which apply for any sample size and so are called small-sample or finite-sample results.

If an estimator has a sampling distribution that becomes centered over the population parameter as $n \to \infty$, the estimator is said to be **asymptotically unbiased.** $\hat{\sigma}^2$ is an example of an asymptotically unbiased estimator. Of course, an unbiased estimator has a sampling distribution that is centered over the population value for all n, including infinitely large n, and so is automatically asymptotically unbiased. In Section 2.5.3, we see that the asymptotic behavior of sampling distributions is important not only for properties of estimators, but also for other aspects of statistical inference.

In addition to showing the shifting mean of $\hat{\sigma}^2$, Figure 2.3 indicates another property of sampling distributions: The variance changes as well, typically becoming smaller as n increases. We turn to this feature of sampling distributions next.

EXERCISES

2.8 Consider $\overline{Y}$ computed on the basis of a sample of size $n = 2$ drawn from the population given in Exercise 2.2. Use the sampling distribution you obtained in Exercise 2.7 to show whether $\overline{Y}$ is unbiased as an estimator of the population mean. What is the probability of a zero sampling error?

2.9 Starting with the definition of the bias of an estimator, show that if the estimator is unbiased

it follows that it has a bias of zero. What law of mathematical expectation (from Appendix B) have you used?

2.10 Consider a statistical model in which the Y_i are i.i.d. from a Bernoulli population with parameter π. Use the result (2.3) to show that the estimator $\hat{\pi}$ defined by (2.5) is unbiased. (*Hint:* The Bernoulli distribution is fully characterized by the parameter π. Do not introduce the notation μ or σ^2.)

2.11 Consider as an estimator for σ^2 the statistic $\hat{\sigma}^2$ given by (2.8). Obtain an expression for the bias of $\hat{\sigma}^2$. Does $\hat{\sigma}^2$ tend to over- or under- estimate σ^2; that is, is the bias positive or negative? Show that $\hat{\sigma}^2$ is asymptotically unbiased by showing that its bias goes to zero as $n \to \infty$.

2.3.2 Efficiency

The property of unbiasedness deals with the mean of the sampling distribution of an estimator. Although the mean is one feature of a probability distribution, it is not the only one that is typically of interest. A second important feature of any distribution is its variance. Because an estimator is a random variable, its variance is defined in the same way as that of any random variable:[4]

Definition 2.4   *The* variance $V(\hat{\theta})$ *of an estimator* $\hat{\theta}$ *is* $V(\hat{\theta}) = E(\hat{\theta} - E\hat{\theta})^2$.

The standard deviation of an estimator, the square root of its variance, is given a special name; it is called the **standard error.**

The Variance of the Sample Mean

As with any variance, the variance of a sampling distribution may be evaluated using the usual laws of expectation and variance. Consider, for example, the variance of the sample mean $\overline{Y}$.

Result 2.3   *In the context of the model (2.6) in which* $Y_i \sim$ *i.i.d.*(μ, σ^2), *the sample mean* $\overline{Y}$ *has variance*

$$V(\overline{Y}) = \frac{\sigma^2}{n}.$$

Proof:

$$V(\overline{Y}) = V\left(\frac{1}{n}\sum_{i=1}^{n} Y_i\right)$$

$$= \left(\frac{1}{n}\right)^2 V\left(\sum_{i=1}^{n} Y_i\right) \qquad \text{by Corollary B.2.1 in Appendix B}$$

---

[4] See Appendix B, Definition B.2.

$$= \frac{1}{n^2} \sum_{i=1}^{n} V(Y_i) \qquad \text{by Corollary B.4.1 in Appendix B}$$

$$= \frac{1}{n^2} \sum_{i=1}^{n} \sigma^2$$

$$= \frac{1}{n^2} n\sigma^2 \qquad \text{by Law A.2 in Appendix A}$$

$$= \frac{\sigma^2}{n} \qquad \square$$

This result is illustrated in Figure 2.4, which shows the variance of the sampling distribution becoming smaller as the sample size increases. In the limit as $n \to \infty$, the sampling variance $V(\overline{Y}) = \sigma^2/n$ approaches zero and the sampling distribution collapses at the population mean μ. In general, the shape of a sampling distribution depends on the sample size n, an idea that is illustrated for $\hat{\sigma}^2$ in Figure 2.3. The difference is that in the earlier figure both the mean and variance are changing with n because the bias in $\hat{\sigma}^2$ disappears only asymptotically. By contrast, in Figure 2.4 the mean of the sampling distribution is not shifting because $E(\overline{Y}) = \mu$ for all n.

Because the variance is the dispersion of a random variable about its expected value, as long as an estimator is unbiased (so its expected value equals the population parameter) its variance indicates the precision with which it estimates the parameter. Result 2.3 states that the precision with which $\overline{Y}$ estimates μ depends on two things: σ^2, the variance of the population, and n, the sample size. On the one hand, a large population variance increases $V(\overline{Y})$, making it more difficult to estimate μ precisely; on the other hand, a large sample size n is desirable in that it decreases $V(\overline{Y})$, permitting a more precise estimation of μ. In this respect, Result 2.3 confirms our intuition that it is always better to have more data.

Result 2.3 serves to once again illustrate several things that arise in the study of estimators. First, it is possible to derive important results about sampling distributions with minimal assumptions about the underlying population. Second, doing this requires the repeated application of the laws of summation, mathematical expectation, and variance. Third, our results are conditional on (that is, make use of and

FIGURE 2.4

The variance of $\overline{Y}$ decreases as the sample size increases.

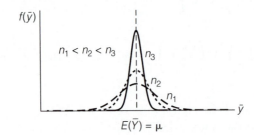

hence are subject to) the statistical model. In particular, the application of Corollary B.4.1 in Appendix B[5] in the preceding proof requires that the Y_i have zero covariance. Thus Result 2.3 relies critically on the assumption of random sampling and would not necessarily hold had the data been obtained by some other sampling process.

Relative Efficiency

The observation that we prefer an estimator that is more precise suggests that another basis on which estimators may be compared is their variance. If two estimators are unbiased, for a given sample size we prefer the one with the smaller variance. It is said to be **more efficient** than the other.

Definition 2.5   *If two estimators $\hat{\theta}_1$ and $\hat{\theta}_2$ are both unbiased and $V(\hat{\theta}_1) < V(\hat{\theta}_2)$, then $\hat{\theta}_1$ is said to be* **more efficient** *than $\hat{\theta}_2$.*

We have seen that the sample mean $\overline{Y}$ is an unbiased estimator of the population mean μ. However, it is not the only estimator that possesses this property. For example, it may be shown that the sample median is also unbiased. Why is $\overline{Y}$ more commonly used than the median? Because, as we see momentarily, for a normal population its variance is smaller; $\overline{Y}$ is the more efficient estimator. As always, such conclusions about the features of sampling distributions are conditional on the statistical model. When we say that the sample mean is more efficient than the sample median, we are speaking with reference to a particular model, specifically, model (2.11) (considered next), although the same conclusion may well hold in the context of other statistical models.

In defining the property of efficiency we limit ourselves to unbiased estimators in order not to compare apples and oranges. Considering Figure 2.5, the estimator $\hat{\theta}_b$ is more efficient than $\hat{\theta}_c$. The estimator $\hat{\theta}_a$ has a smaller variance than either, but is biased. Objectively, however, a researcher might legitimately prefer $\hat{\theta}_a$ over $\hat{\theta}_b$, but this would reflect a personal preference in the trade-off between bias and variance of the estimators.

FIGURE 2.5

The comparative efficiency of three estimators.

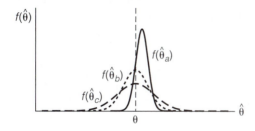

---

[5]   Actually, the application of its more general version given by equation (B.21).

Absolute Efficiency

Although the idea of efficiency in the relative sense of Definition 2.5 is a useful basis for comparing estimators, it is preferable to go further and find the estimator that has the minimum variance among *all* unbiased estimators. Such an estimator is **efficient** in an absolute sense.

Definition 2.6   *An estimator is* efficient *if, in the class of all unbiased estimators, no other estimator has a smaller variance.*

Note that, according to this definition, an efficient estimator is not necessarily unique. It is conceivable that several unbiased estimators could attain the same minimum variance.

Efficiency in this absolute sense is a very powerful property, and we may well ask whether it is ever possible to establish such a strong result. The answer, remarkably, is that it is; however, somewhat stronger assumptions about the statistical model are necessary than we have made so far. Specifically, if we add to model (2.6) the assumption that the common population from which the Y_i are drawn is normally distributed, then we say that the sample is normally independently distributed (n.i.d.):

$$Y_i \sim \text{n.i.d.}(\mu, \sigma^2) \tag{2.11}$$

This is a stronger assumption than the i.i.d. specification that the observations come from some unspecified distribution. Under this stronger assumption, the following result may be established.

Result 2.4   *In the context of model* (2.11) *in which* $Y_i \sim \text{n.i.d.}(\mu, \sigma^2)$, *the sample mean* $\overline{Y}$ *is efficient as an estimator for* μ.

The assumption of a normal distribution as the form of the population is common in statistics and econometrics because, for certain statistical models, it yields important results. The efficiency of an estimator, illustrated by $\overline{Y}$ in Result 2.4, is an example. Just as significantly, later in the chapter Section 2.5 shows that important results in hypothesis testing also hinge critically on the assumption of normality.

The Gauss-Markov Theorem

Even so, requiring the population to be of a particular distributional form is a nontrivial additional assumption and is not to be taken lightly. It is natural to ask whether any conclusions along the lines of Result 2.4 are possible without normality; that is, under the original model (2.6). The answer is "yes," if the form of the estimator is restricted to being a linear function of the data. The famous result that then follows is known as the *Gauss-Markov Theorem*.

Result 2.5	(Gauss-Markov Theorem). *In the context of model (2.6) in which $Y_i \sim$ i.i.d.(μ, σ^2), the sample mean $\overline{Y}$ has the minimum variance in the class of all linear unbiased estimators.*

The Gauss-Markov theorem is a weaker result than Result 2.4 in that it deals with a restricted form for the estimator. An estimator $\hat{\theta}$ is linear as a function of the sample data if it takes the form

$$\hat{\theta} = \sum_{i=1}^{n} a_i Y_i, \tag{2.12}$$

where the a_i are constants. The sample mean $\overline{Y}$ is linear because it is a special case of this formula in which $a_i = 1/n$ for all i. Because $\overline{Y}$ has the minimum variance in the class of all linear unbiased estimators, it is said to be the **best linear unbiased estimator** (BLUE). In other words, the Gauss-Markov theorem says that the BLUE estimator is obtained by setting all $a_i = 1/n$ in this formula and that no other linear unbiased estimator has variance smaller than the expression given by Result 2.3.

The remarkable aspect of the Gauss-Markov theorem is that it is possible to show that $\overline{Y}$ is BLUE without any assumption about the form of the population distribution. The price we pay for this is the requirement of linearity; in the absence of normality, it is possible that there may be some unbiased nonlinear estimator—that is, a statistic that is a function of the sample data of a form different from (2.12)—that has a smaller variance than $\overline{Y}$. Under normality, on the other hand, Result 2.4 states that there is no other such estimator. Obviously linearity is not in and of itself a desirable property; except to the extent that linearity contributes to some other desirable property or facilitates computation, there is no intrinsic value to an estimator being of the form (2.12) as opposed to some other form.

EXERCISES

2.12 Consider the sampling distribution for $\overline{Y}$ based on $n = 2$ that was derived in Example 7. Find the variance of $\overline{Y}$:

(a) by direct evaluation of the sampling distribution (using the appropriate formula for discrete random variables, as developed in Appendix B).

(b) using Result 2.3.

Are the results in (a) and (b) the same?

2.13 Consider the sampling distribution for $\overline{Y}$ based on $n = 2$ that you derived in Exercise 2.7. Find the variance of $\overline{Y}$:

(a) by direct evaluation of the sampling distribution.

(b) using Result 2.3.

Are the results in (a) and (b) the same?

2.14 Consider $\overline{Y}$ based on a sample of size $n = 3$ drawn from the population in Example 1.

(a) What is the mean of the sampling distribution of $\overline{Y}$?

(b) What is the variance of the sampling distribution of $\overline{Y}$?

(c) Do you prefer to have $\overline{Y}$ based on a sample of size 2 or 3? Why?

2.15 Consider a series of Y_i observations obtained by random sampling, where each has mean μ and variance σ_i^2. Note that this statistical model differs from (2.6) in that sample observations are drawn from populations with the same mean but different variances. Derive the expression for $V(\overline{Y})$. How does your expression simplify in the special case in which the population distribution has a constant variance: $\sigma_i^2 = \sigma^2$?

2.3.3   Evaluating Properties Numerically: Monte Carlo Simulation

So far, we have studied properties of estimators *analytically*—that is, by mathematical derivation. A quite different approach is to study properties numerically using computer simulation. These are called **Monte Carlo methods.**

The idea of Monte Carlo methods is that it is possible to simulate the sampling process by computer and in this way investigate the features of the sampling distribution of an estimator. The design of a Monte Carlo study includes the following elements.

Step 1. Specification of the process by which the data are generated. This is called the **data generating process** (DGP). The DGP consists of a chosen statistical model (which, recall, comprises the population distribution and the specification of the sampling process) and assumed values for the population parameters. For example, we might posit a uniform population distribution on the interval $(\theta_0 = 0, \theta_1 = 1)$ and a sample of size $n = 15$ drawn in an i.i.d. manner from this population.

Step 2. Given the specification of the DGP, a computer can be programmed to generate a sample of the specified size. It does this using a random number generator. From such a simulated sample, any statistic of interest can be computed. The generation of such a sample and the computation of the statistic may be repeated many times; this is called the number of **replications.** Each replication yields a different sample and consequently a different value of the statistic. A frequency distribution of these values constitutes a simulated sampling distribution for the statistic. Different statistics may be compared and evaluated on the basis of their simulated sampling distributions.

Figure 2.6 illustrates this. From a uniform distribution on the (0,1) interval, 2000 random samples have been generated. This has been done three times; in the first instance these were samples of size $n = 15$, in the second of $n = 50$, and in the third of $n = 100$.

For each sample two statistics are computed: the mean $\overline{Y}$ and the median. As the figure indicates, the 2000 replications yield simulated sampling distributions for each of these statistics for each of the three sample sizes. These sampling distributions are centered over the population mean of $\mu = (\theta_0 + \theta_1)/2 = 1/2$, reflecting the fact that both the sample mean and median are unbiased estimators of μ.

FIGURE 2.6

Simulated sampling
distributions (uni-
form population).

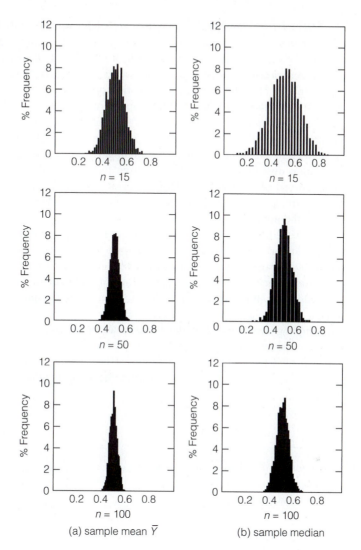

FIGURE 2.6

Simulated sampling distributions (uniform population).

(a) sample mean $\overline{Y}$

(b) sample median

Consider initially the first column of distributions, which are for the sample mean. Note that the simulation experiment confirms the analytical finding of Result 2.3 that the variance of the sample mean declines with the sample size n. In fact, because the population variance σ^2 is known, Result 2.3 tells us the value of $V(\overline{Y})$ for these alternate sample sizes; you are asked to consider this further in Exercise 2.16.

The second column of distributions is for the median. They illustrate that, like the mean, the variance of the median declines as the sample size increases. They also show that, for any given sample size n, the median has a larger dispersion than the mean. This confirms the assertion in the previous section that the sample mean is a more efficient estimator than the median.

Monte Carlo simulation is an extremely useful way of studying the properties of estimators, particularly in complex estimation problems in which it is difficult to derive properties analytically. As a result, it has played an increasingly important role in econometrics. It is apparent, however, that the method is not without its shortcomings. Because computer simulation requires the specification of a complete DGP, including the form of the population distribution and the values of the parameters, the results of the simulation experiment are conditional on these. Take the result that $V(\overline{Y})$ declines with n, for example. From Figure 2.6 alone there is no way of being certain that this finding is not conditional on the choice of population distribution or even the chosen parameter values $\theta_0 = 0$, $\theta_1 = 1$. It is the analytical derivation leading to Result 2.3 that not only yields the formula $V(\overline{Y}) = \sigma^2/n$, but also tells us that this expression is independent of any particular form of the population distribution.

As well, Monte Carlo simulation permits only the evaluation of an estimator relative to particular alternatives; it does not allow us to reach conclusions about the absolute properties of an estimator. Only analytical reasoning can lead to global conclusions such as the Gauss-Markov theorem or absolute efficiency.

Figure 2.6 illustrates another interesting feature of sampling distributions. Even though the population from which the data are drawn is uniform, it is evident that the sampling distributions of the statistics are of a roughly normal form. In fact, it may be shown that the sampling distribution of $\overline{Y}$ is more and more closely approximated by a normal distribution as the sample size becomes larger. This property is an example of a central limit theorem, an idea that is developed in Section 2.5.3.

EXERCISES

2.16 Consider a uniform population distribution on the (0,1) interval, and the sample mean $\overline{Y}$ computed from a sample of size n drawn independently from this population.

(a) What is the value of the population variance σ^2? (*Hint:* Refer to your answer to Exercise B.11 in Appendix B.)

(b) What is $V(\overline{Y})$ for $n = 15$? $n = 50$? $n = 100$?

(c) Suppose that the population distribution is normal instead of uniform, with the same variance σ^2 as in (a). How would you answer (b)?

2.4 Derivation of Estimators

Thus far in our discussion, estimators such as $\overline{Y}$ and s^2 have simply been posited in an ad hoc manner. Where do such formulas come from in the first place? Given a statistical model, is there a systematic way of deriving estimators for its parameters? In fact, statistical theory offers a number of methods for obtaining

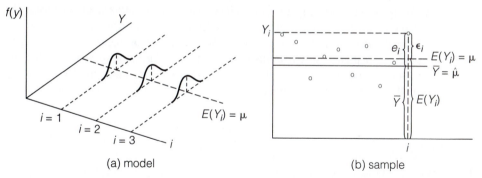

FIGURE 2.7 $Y_i \sim$ i.i.d.(μ, σ^2).

estimators. In this section a particularly simple one is introduced, one that is adequate for the estimation problems we encounter in the chapters ahead: the method of **least squares.**

Let us consider the method of least squares in the context of a model with which we are now well familiar,

$$Y_i \sim \text{i.i.d.}(\mu, \sigma^2) \qquad (i = 1, \ldots, n). \tag{2.13}$$

The objective is to obtain estimators (that is, formulas in terms of the sample data Y_i, $i = 1, \ldots, n$) for the parameters μ and σ^2. Least squares provides us with an estimator for the population mean μ; once this has been obtained it is then possible to turn to the secondary question of an estimator for σ^2.

Figure 2.7 provides a graphical interpretation of this statistical model. Figure 2.7(a) depicts the model and (b) a hypothetical sample of size $n = 10$ generated by it. The dispersion of the Y_i observations about μ is governed, of course, by population variance σ^2. The figure motivates a different means of notating the model (2.13). Consider an artificial random variable ε defined by

$$\varepsilon_i \sim \text{i.i.d.}(0, \sigma^2). \tag{2.14}$$

That is, ε is simply defined to be a random variable with mean 0 and variance σ^2, and the ε_i are just successive independent drawings from this distribution. Then a specification for Y_i completely equivalent to (2.13) is

$$Y_i = \mu + \varepsilon_i \tag{2.15}$$

because, by the laws of mathematical expectation and variance of linear functions,

$$E(Y_i) = E(\mu + \varepsilon_i) = \mu + E(\varepsilon_i) = \mu,$$

$$V(Y_i) = V(\mu + \varepsilon_i) = V(\varepsilon_i) = \sigma^2.$$

Note that ε_i is not observable; that is, data are never available on this random variable. Instead it is artificially defined solely for convenience in specifying model

(2.15). Such an artificially defined random variable is called a **disturbance.** As we have seen, the i.i.d. assumption arises from a very basic sampling process of traditional interest in statistics. Hence, when specified as behaving according to (2.14), ε_i is called a *classical* disturbance. If it is furthermore assumed that the population is normal, so that the model (2.11) applies, then the disturbance is normally independently distributed,

$$\varepsilon_i \sim \text{n.i.d.}(0, \sigma^2).$$

The Least Squares Principle

What is the value of interpreting the process generating Y_i in this way? Returning to the problem of estimating the mean μ, Figure 2.7(b) suggests that a sensible estimator is one that is in the middle of the Y_i observations. How can this notion "in the middle of" be made precise in a way that is usable? An estimator for μ is in the middle of the Y_i if it minimizes the average distance from them. How is distance to be measured? Simply measuring it as the deviation $Y_i - \mu$ is not satisfactory because this quantity is sometimes positive, sometimes negative; any measure of distance should be positive. The method of least squares resolves this by using as a distance measure the squared deviation $(Y_i - \mu)^2$. The average distance is then the sum of squared deviations

$$S \equiv \sum_{i=1}^{n} (Y_i - \mu)^2 \tag{2.16}$$

divided by n. The method of least squares chooses as an estimator $\hat{\mu}$ the value of μ that minimizes the average distance defined in this way; or, equivalently because n is a constant, the value that minimizes the **sum of squares function** S. This is depicted in Figure 2.8.

The value $\hat{\mu}$ is determined by taking the derivative of S with respect to μ, setting this equal to zero, and solving. As a first step, the derivative is

$$\frac{dS}{d\mu} = \sum_{i=1}^{n} 2(Y_i - \mu)(-1). \tag{2.17}$$

FIGURE 2.8

The least squares estimator $\hat{\mu}$ is the value of μ that minimizes the sum of squares function S.

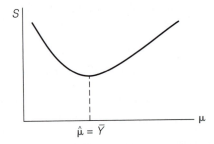

Setting this to zero (and canceling multiplicative constants) defines the particular value of μ, denoted $\hat{\mu}$, that minimizes S:

$$\sum_{i=1}^{n}(Y_i - \hat{\mu}) = 0. \tag{2.18}$$

Note that, in going from the derivative (2.17) to the first-order condition (2.18), the latter defines the particular value of μ that is our estimator and so it is appropriate to replace μ with $\hat{\mu}$. Solving yields

$$\hat{\mu} = \frac{1}{n}\sum_{i=1}^{n} Y_i = \overline{Y}.$$

This is the estimator that is in the middle of the Y_i observations, in the least squares sense. The striking conclusion is that it is the familiar sample mean $\overline{Y}$ that is the least squares estimator for the population mean μ in the model (2.13) or, equivalently, (2.15). Figure 2.7(b) contrasts the sample mean $\hat{\mu} = \overline{Y}$ with the population mean μ.

Least Squares as a Special Case of Minimum Distance Estimation

This derivation of $\overline{Y}$ is based on a particular choice of a distance measure (or, in technical jargon, distance metric). In principle, alternative measures of distance might be considered. Instead of the *squared* deviations $(Y_i - \mu)^2$, consider the *absolute* deviations $|Y_i - \mu|$. An estimator based on minimizing the sum of these absolute deviations could be derived; this would be a **least absolute deviations** (LAD) estimator. The solution turns out to be the sample median.

It is apparent that the method of least squares is just one member of a more general class of **minimum distance estimators.** Why focus on this particular member of this class? In part, at least historically, because of analytical tractability; as the example illustrates, the method of least squares makes it easy to use calculus to obtain estimator formulas for some estimation problems. By contrast, LAD estimators must be obtained numerically.

However in an age of effortless computing capability, this is not in and of itself a consideration of significant weight. More fundamentally, and as Section 2.3 establishes in connection with $\overline{Y}$, least squares estimators often have desirable properties. In particular, we have seen that in the context of the model (2.6) the sample mean is BLUE. With the added assumption of population normality, it is efficient as well. The fact that the method of least squares often yields estimators possessing attractive properties is the most important reason for its use.[6]

---

[6] This is not to say that least squares is without weaknesses. Because it uses *squared* deviations, least squares is relatively strongly influenced by outlying observations.

There is a long-standing, although somewhat peripheral, interest among econometricians and statisticians in alternative minimum distance estimators as a means of **robust estimation**—meaning the use

continued

Estimation of σ^2

Thus far least squares has yielded an estimator for one parameter of the model, μ. There remains a second parameter σ^2, the variance of the Y_i (or, equivalently by the model (2.14) and (2.15), the variance of the disturbance ε_i). How is it to be estimated? The formal definition of σ^2 is, as is true of all population parameters, in terms of a mathematical expectation:

$$\sigma^2 = E(\varepsilon_i^2) = E(Y_i - EY_i)^2 = E(Y_i - \mu)^2.$$

In this sense, then, σ^2 is a certain average of the squares of the ε_i deviations between the Y_i observations and their mean μ. Although these deviations are unobservable, the estimation of μ by $\hat{\mu} = \overline{Y}$ suggests that they may be measured by their sample analogs,

$$e_i \equiv Y_i - \hat{\mu} = Y_i - \overline{Y}. \tag{2.19}$$

Clearly these are computable. The e_i are called **residuals;** they denote the difference between the Y_i observations and their estimated mean $\hat{\mu}$. Computed on the basis of the least squares estimator $\hat{\mu} = \overline{Y}$, the e_i are the *least squares residuals.*

It follows that a natural estimator of the population variance σ^2 is the average of the squared residuals:

$$\hat{\sigma}^2 = \frac{1}{n} \sum_{i=1}^{n} e_i^2 = \frac{1}{n} \sum_{i=1}^{n} (Y_i - \overline{Y})^2.$$

Does this estimator possess any desirable properties? From our previous encounter with it in Section 2.3.1 we know that it is a biased estimator, but is asymptotically unbiased. It is also known, however, that its small sample bias may be removed with a simple modification to the denominator that replaces n with $n - 1$. That is, we have seen previously that

$$s^2 = \frac{1}{n-1} \sum_{i=1}^{n} (Y_i - \overline{Y})^2$$

is an unbiased estimator for σ^2.

---

of estimators that are less strongly influenced by outlying observations than is least squares. It is evident, for example, that the sample median is less influenced by outlying observations than is the sample mean.

One problem with robust estimators is the absence of analytically derivable distributional results for hypothesis testing; by contrast, such results are readily available for least squares, as we see in the next section. Consequently methods of robust estimation make heavy use of bootstrapping—a technique sketched in Section 2.6.2—as a route to hypothesis testing. Unfortunately, it turns out that in the context of robust estimation the performance of bootstrapped tests is rather poor. Recent work on robust estimators has focused on improving the performance of bootstrapped tests; for a survey with some discussion of these points, see Horowitz (2001).

This derivation of s^2 shows that the method of least squares does not yield an estimator for σ^2 directly. That is, s^2 has not been obtained by taking the derivative of any objective function and solving a first-order condition.[7] However, the least squares estimator for the mean does, in combination with more ad hoc reasoning, lead to an estimator for σ^2.

The fact that least squares is primarily useful for deriving estimators associated with the mean of a population distribution rather than higher-order parameters such as the variance is a serious limitation of the method for many estimation problems in econometrics. A second significant deficiency is that, although least squares often yields estimators possessing desirable properties, there is no assurance that this will necessarily be the case. There is no guarantee, for example, that least squares estimators will necessarily be unbiased, asymptotically unbiased, BLUE, or efficient. Instead their properties must be established on a case-by-case basis.

These deficiencies of the method of least squares suggest that it would be useful to have alternative methods of obtaining estimators that both (1) provide a systematic means of deriving estimators for all parameters of the population model, and (2) are guaranteed to yield estimators possessing at least some desirable properties. Two such methods are heavily used in econometrics: the method of **maximum likelihood estimation** and the **generalized method of moments.** The former requires an assumption about the form of the population distribution (most often normality) and yields fairly strong asymptotic properties for the resulting estimators. The latter has the advantage of not requiring an assumed population distribution, but at the cost of yielding estimators with somewhat weaker properties.

A treatment of these methods is important for an understanding of many estimation problems in econometrics. We give some indication of why this is the case in Section 5.3. For the fairly basic econometric models we are studying, on the other hand, the least squares principle yields the appropriate estimators and has the advantage of being easily understood. Purely as a method of estimation, it also requires no assumption about the form of the population distribution. Other considerations, discussed in the next section, will mean that for some of the models we consider it is still advantageous to assume population normality.

EXERCISES

2.17 It has been asserted that "... ε_i is not observable; that is, data are never available on this random variable." Given the model (2.15), why is it not possible to obtain numerical values for the disturbance by computing $Y_i - \mu$?

2.18 Given the definition (2.19) of the least squares residuals, show that they sum to zero: $\sum_{i=1}^{n} e_i = 0$.

2.19 Suppose that, instead of squaring the deviations $Y_i - \mu$ to obtain a positive distance measure,

---

[7]   However, such a derivation is possible for $\hat{\sigma}^2$, based on an appropriate (and somewhat contrived) choice of objective function.

you attempt to derive an estimator for μ by choosing a value that minimizes

$$\sum_{i=1}^{n}(Y_i - \mu).$$

Do you obtain any useful result?

2.20 The estimator $\overline{Y}$ has been derived as the solution to the first-order condition (2.18). Use the second-order condition to confirm that it does indeed correspond to a minimum rather than a maximum of the sum of squares function (2.16).

2.21 Consider a set of observations Y_i ($i = 1, \ldots, n$) that are i.i.d. from a Bernoulli distribution with parameter π. As you are aware from Example 4, $E(Y_i) = \pi$. Derive the least squares estimator for π.

2.5   Hypothesis Testing

Although estimation is an important element of statistical inference, it is just one aspect of the general problem of using sample data to learn about a population. In addition to estimating a population parameter, which yields a **point estimate,** it is sometimes of interest to gauge the precision of our knowledge about a parameter with an **interval estimate,** or **confidence interval,** indicating the probability that, in repeated sampling, certain bounds contain the parameter. Finally, the object of a great deal of applied statistical work, particularly in econometrics, is to determine whether the data support or contradict some hypothesis about the population model; that is, to do **hypothesis testing.** Because the population is fully characterized by its parameters, hypotheses take the form of restrictions on these parameters.

The same distributional results underlie both confidence intervals and hypothesis testing. Because the latter tends to play the more prominent role in applied econometrics, this section focuses on the principles of elementary hypothesis testing procedures. As we shall see, the assumption of normality of the population distribution plays an even more crucial role in these procedures than was true for properties of estimators. It is useful to begin by considering the distributional theory on which hypothesis-testing procedures rest when normality is assumed; we then ask how these procedures change when the population is not normal.

2.5.1   A Normal Population

If data are obtained by random sampling from a normal population, we have seen that the statistical model is

$$Y_i \sim \text{n.i.d.}(\mu, \sigma^2), \tag{2.20}$$

or, equivalently,

$$Y_i = \mu + \varepsilon_i, \quad \varepsilon_i \sim \text{n.i.d.}(0, \sigma^2).$$

If the mean $\overline{Y}$ is computed from a sample generated in this way, we know from Results 2.1 and 2.3 that it has a sampling distribution with mean μ and variance σ^2/n. Is anything else known about the sampling distribution of $\overline{Y}$? Under normality, it turns out that there is—remarkably, we actually know the form of the sampling distribution. This is because of the following very important property of the normal distribution.

Result 2.6   *A linear function of normal random variables is itself normally distributed.*

In particular, in the previous section it was observed that $\overline{Y}$ is a linear function of the Y_i; the sample mean is a special case of the linear form (2.12). Hence, Result 2.6 allows us to conclude that, under the model (2.20), $\overline{Y}$ is normally distributed. Because the mean and variance of this normal distribution have been derived in terms of the mean and variance of the underlying population, the sampling distribution of $\overline{Y}$ is fully determined. It is

$$\overline{Y} \sim \mathrm{N}(\mu, \sigma^2/n). \tag{2.21}$$

It is to be emphasized that Result 2.6 describes a rather special property of the normal distribution that typically does not apply to other distributions. For example, from the sampling distribution derived in Example 7 it is apparent that, although the population distribution was uniform, the distribution of $\overline{Y}$ is not. Therefore linear functions of uniform random variables are not uniform. Similarly, linear functions of Bernoulli random variables are not Bernoulli. That linear functions of normal random variables are normal is a remarkable, and very useful, feature of this distribution.

A **standardizing transformation** of a random variable is one that subtracts the mean and divides by the standard deviation, resulting in a transformed random variable with a mean of zero and a variance of unity. Such a transformation is linear.[8] Consequently, another important implication of Result 2.6 is that a normal random variable so transformed continues to be normally distributed. Applying this to $\overline{Y}$ yields

$$\frac{\overline{Y} - \mu}{\sigma/\sqrt{n}} \sim \mathrm{N}(0, 1). \tag{2.22}$$

This transformation of $\overline{Y}$ is not a computable statistic, of course, because it involves the unknown parameters μ and σ. Suppose that, in place of σ, the estimator s, the square root of s^2 defined by (2.7), is substituted. As is to be expected, the distribution is no longer $\mathrm{N}(0, 1)$; it is the somewhat different t distribution, which depends on a parameter called the degrees of freedom. In the present case, the degrees of freedom are $n - 1$, and the following result holds.

---

[8] Standardizing transformations are treated in Appendix B, Section B.6.

Result 2.7 *Under the model* (2.20),

$$\frac{\overline{Y} - \mu}{s/\sqrt{n}} \sim t(n-1). \tag{2.23}$$

As the sample size becomes large, s^2 estimates σ^2 more and more precisely. For this reason the t distribution, although somewhat different from the standard normal for relatively small values of n, approximates the standard normal more and more closely as $n \to \infty$. You may verify this by examining any table of values for the t distribution, such as those in this book, and observing that they approach the corresponding tabulated values of the standard normal as the degrees of freedom become large.

Hypothesis Testing: Theory and Intuition

The value of the distributional result given by Result 2.7 is that it permits the testing of hypotheses about μ. Consider the **null hypothesis** that μ is equal to some particular numerical value, say μ_0:

$$H_0 : \mu = \mu_0.$$

Let us take the **alternative hypothesis** to be that H_0 is false:

$$H_A : \mu \neq \mu_0.$$

If H_0 is indeed true, then the evaluation of (2.23) under the null hypothesis that $\mu = \mu_0$ yields a t statistic that has the stated t distribution:

$$t = \frac{\overline{Y} - \mu_0}{s/\sqrt{n}} \sim t(n-1).$$

Hence, if the computed value of this t statistic is, roughly speaking, in the center of a t distribution based on $n-1$ degrees of freedom, this is evidence consistent with the null hypothesis. If the null hypothesis were false, so that in reality it was the case that $\mu \neq \mu_0$, then the distribution of the statistic evaluated using $\mu = \mu_0$ would be something different from $t(n-1)$. Consequently the computed value for the statistic would tend to be away from the center of the $t(n-1)$ distribution; a value in the tails of the distribution is therefore interpreted as evidence against the null.

EXAMPLE 10 | A flour mill distributes its product in 10-kilogram bags. In programming its packaging equipment, it wants to ensure that the bags are neither substantially under- or overweight—if they are underweight, customers will be dissatisfied; if they are overweight, the bags may not seal properly. It finds that in a randomly selected shipment of 20 bags, the mean weight is $\overline{Y} = 9.87$ with a standard deviation of $s = 0.35$. Is this clear evidence that the nominal weight is incorrect?

FIGURE 2.9

p-value for
Example 10.

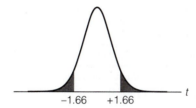

SOLUTION

We wish to judge whether the observed sample mean of $\overline{Y} = 9.87$ is different enough from the hypothesized population mean of $\mu_0 = 10$ that it is unlikely to have been observed were the hypothesis true. The distributional results we have just developed provide the means of making this judgement. Assuming the population to be normally distributed, the sampling experiment is summarized by the model (2.20), and so Result 2.7 provides a test of $H_0: \mu = 10$ versus the alternative of $H_A: \mu \neq 10$. The t statistic computes to

$$t = \frac{\overline{Y} - \mu_0}{s/\sqrt{n}} = \frac{9.87 - 10}{0.35/\sqrt{20}} = -1.66.$$

Is this value far enough out in the tails of the $t(n-1)$ distribution to constitute evidence against the null? Figure 2.9 places it on the horizontal axis under the $t(19)$ distribution (along with the mirror-image value $+1.66$ on the right tail of the distribution). The shaded tail areas beyond these two points are the probability of observing a value of the statistic at least this extreme, were H_0 true. This **probability value,** or **p-value,** conveniently summarizes the weight of the evidence against H_0. In this instance, the finding is that this probability is quite small: The total of these tail areas is about 0.12. Most people would regard this as moderate evidence against H_0 because, were it really true that $\mu = \mu_0 = 10$, there are only approximately 12 chances in 100 that a value of the t statistic this far out in the tails of the distribution would have been observed. If this is the view adopted by the flour mill, it will **reject** H_0 on the basis of this sample evidence and conclude that its packaging equipment needs adjustment.

This example illustrates a number of issues that arise in any hypothesis test. The first is that, in arriving at a decision whether or not to reject the null, we run the risk of making a mistake. The four possible combinations of correct and incorrect decisions are delineated in Table 2.1. There are two types of mistakes. One is the mistake of incorrectly rejecting the null hypothesis when in fact it is true, which is called a Type I error. The probability of a Type I error has a very clear interpretation in Figure 2.9; it is the total of the shaded tail areas. If the quality control staff of the flour mill in Example 10 rejects H_0 on the basis of the sample evidence, there is a 12% chance that this decision is incorrect because there is a 0.12 probability that a t value this extreme could have been generated even if the packaging equipment is not in error.

TABLE 2.1   Possible Hypothesis Test Outcomes

	State of the world	
Test decision	H_0 true	H_A true
Reject H_0	Type I error	Correct decision
Do not reject H_0	Correct decision	Type II error

The opposite mistake is that of incorrectly accepting (or, strictly speaking, failing to reject) the null when it is in fact false; this is called a Type II error. The probability of rejecting the null when it is false (a correct decision) is $1 - \mathrm{Pr}(\text{Type II error})$; this is called the **power** of the test.

The decision whether to reject H_0 implies a choice of **significance level,** which we denote by a; it is also called the **size** of the test. This is the maximum probability of Type I error that the researcher is willing to incur. Conventional choices for a are 0.10, 0.05, and 0.01. The flour mill of Example 10, in deciding to reject H_0, must have had in mind a significance level such as 0.15; had the choice of significance level been $a = 0.10$, a p-value of 0.12 would not have been interpreted as strong enough evidence to reject H_0.

This choice of significance level means that there is an asymmetry in the treatment of Type I and II errors that attaches primacy to controlling the former. The null hypothesis is in the position of a defendant in a court of law who is presumed innocent until proven guilty. Just as the defendant is only found guilty on the basis of clear evidence inconsistent with the presumption of innocence, so too the null hypothesis is only rejected on the basis of compelling evidence against it. A Type I error is analogous to the mistake of convicting an innocent person, and in choosing a significance level we seek to control the probability of making this mistake.

Hypothesis Testing: Formalized Procedure

These comments indicate that any hypothesis test involves essentially four steps, although there are two variations on just how these are presented. Let us summarize them, beginning with the more traditional style of presentation stated in terms of a rejection region for the test statistic. We then turn to a presentation in terms of the p-value.

Step 1. *Specify the null and alternative hypotheses.* The null hypothesis is that some parameter restriction holds; in Example 10 this was $H_0: \mu = 10$. The alternative hypothesis is that this parameter restriction is false; in Example 10 this was $H_A: \mu \neq 10$. The alternative hypothesis may be either **one-sided** or **two-sided:** Example 10 was an example of a two-sided alternative. The most common combinations of null and alternative hypotheses are summarized in

TABLE 2.2   **Null and Alternative Hypotheses, and the Rejection Region**

	a	**b**	**c**
Alternative hypothesis	Two-sided	One-sided	One-sided
H_0	$\mu = \mu_0$	$\mu \leq \mu_0$	$\mu \geq \mu_0$
H_A	$\mu \neq \mu_0$	$\mu > \mu_0$	$\mu < \mu_0$
Rejection region	$\mid t \mid > t_{a/2}(n-1)$	$t > t_a(n-1)$	$t < -t_a(n-1)$

FIGURE 2.10

Rejection regions.

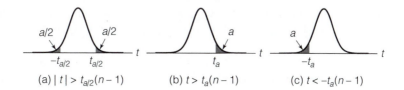

(a) $\mid t \mid > t_{a/2}(n-1)$ (b) $t > t_a(n-1)$ (c) $t < -t_a(n-1)$

Table 2.2. Case a corresponds to Example 10 and is the most common testing situation in economics; as we see in the chapters ahead, economic theory often predicts equality restrictions on parameters (or functions of parameters) that are natural null hypotheses. Cases b and c are one-sided alternatives.

Step 2. *Identify the test statistic and its distribution.* Whether H_0 is rejected or not must be judged on the basis of the data, and the information in the data relevant to this judgement is summarized by the test statistic. For the testing problem of the present discussion, the t statistic and its distribution are given by Result 2.7.

Step 3. *State the rejection region based on a chosen significance level.* What values of the test statistic are to be regarded as evidence inconsistent with the null hypothesis? Intuitively, values that are far out in the tails of the distribution. How far out? This is what is decided by our choice of significance level a. The tabulated values of the distribution associated with this significance level are the **critical values** determining the **rejection region.** The last line of Table 2.2 summarizes the form of the rejection region for the t test under the various hypothesis configurations; these rejection regions are depicted in the corresponding panels of Figure 2.10. The symbol $t_a(n-1)$ denotes the tabulated value of the t distribution with $n-1$ degrees of freedom cutting off a right tail area of a. If the flour mill of Example 10 had used a significance level of $a = 0.20$, then the critical values would be $\pm t_{a/2}(n-1) = \pm t_{0.10}(19) = \pm 1.328$.

    Notice that when the alternative hypothesis is one-sided, the weak inequality is always assigned to the null hypothesis. This is because the test statistic is, at the next step, evaluated under the null and so is evaluated at the equality.

Step 4. *Calculate the test statistic and compare it with the rejection region.* The researcher of Example 10 found that $t = -1.66$. Comparing this with the critical values ± 1.328 associated with the chosen level of significance, the test statistic is in the rejection region. The decision is to reject the null hypothesis in favor of the alternative.

We have noted that as $n \to \infty$ the t distribution converges to the standard normal. In fact, a cursory inspection of a t table shows that tabulated values of the distribution are very close to those for the standard normal even at fairly modest sample sizes, $n > 20$ say. For a two-sided 5% significance test, the critical value is $t_{0.025}(20) = 2.086$, whereas the value for the standard normal is 1.96. This is the basis for the rule of thumb often used by applied researchers when scanning t test results: For a reasonably large number of observations, a t statistic greater than 2 (in absolute value) tends to indicate a statistically significant effect.[9]

Practitioner's Tip: **The t test rule of thumb**

When scanning t test results, keep in mind that for sample sizes larger than approximately 20, t statistics greater than 2 (in absolute value) suggest significant effects.

This rule of thumb holds for t tests in broader contexts—in particular in linear and nonlinear regression, as we see in later chapters.

The p-Value Approach

You may have noticed that steps 3 and 4 of the procedure just outlined are in contrast to the intuition of hypothesis testing as presented in Example 10, in which the researcher was described as obtaining a p-value and using it to reach a decision. In this approach these steps are restated as follows.

Step 3. *Choose a significance level.* For example, the choice of a 20% significance level sets the maximum acceptable probability of Type I error at $a = 0.20$.

Step 4. *Calculate the p-value and compare with the significance level.* In Example 10 we have seen that a test statistic value of $t = -1.66$ corresponds to a p-value of approximately 0.12. Rejection of H_0 on the basis of this evidence, then, implies a probability of Type I error of 0.12. Because this is less than the maximum we have specified as acceptable, H_0 is rejected.

When hypotheses are one-sided, the p-value is half of what it would be for a two-sided alternative. Suppose in Example 10 the concern is only that the bags of flour may be underfilled; overfilling is not a problem. Then the p-value associated with the observed statistic of $t = -1.66$ is just the left tail area shown in Figure 2.9,

---

[9] Of course novice applied econometricians should not trust to rules of thumb—particularly on assignments and examinations.

or approximately 0.06. This implies a rejection of the null hypothesis that the bags are not being underfilled ($H_0: \mu \geq 10$), at a 10% significance level.

Notice that, whereas a *large* value for the test statistic typically leads to a rejection, it is a *small* p-value that constitutes evidence against the null. One way of thinking about the p-value is that it is the smallest significance level that yields a rejection; that is, it is the significance level that is at the margin between acceptance and rejection of the null. For this reason the p-value is sometimes called the **marginal significance level.**

Which style of test reporting is preferable? This is largely a matter of taste, but the p-value approach certainly has much to recommend it because the sample evidence against the null is conveniently summarized in a single number, the p-value. The historical prominence of the rejection region approach was an artifact of the practical difficulty of computing p-values, a difficulty that has largely been overcome by modern software.

The t test is valid for any sample size; under population normality, the t statistic follows a $t(n-1)$ distribution for any value of n. A test that is valid for any sample size is called an **exact test** because it is based on exact knowledge of the form of the sampling distribution of the statistic. This is in contrast to test procedures based on approximations to sampling distributions. There are two broad classes of such approximations—analytical and numerical. Both are introduced in Section 2.5.3. Analytical approximations use the concept of a central limit theorem, an approach that plays a particularly important role in our development of hypothesis testing procedures for models in which exact tests are unavailable.

Statistical Significance versus Practical Significance

The null hypothesis is rejected if the test statistic lands in the rejection region or, equivalently, the p-value is less than the chosen significance level. Whether this happens depends on the estimated standard error $s/\sqrt{n}$ in the denominator of the t statistic; that is, it depends on the precision with which the parameter μ is estimated. This in turn depends in part on the sample size n, which, as we know from Result 2.3, affects our ability to estimate μ precisely. This means that the outcome of significance tests depends on the sample size in a way that must be borne in mind when interpreting test decisions. Specifically, the following comments apply.

Any hypothesis will be rejected on the basis of a large enough sample. A large sample size contributes to a very precise estimate of μ and therefore tends to lead to a rejection of any hypothesis $H_0: \mu = \mu_0$. In our example of 10-kilogram bags of flour, suppose the mean weight turns out to be $\overline{Y} = 9.999$. On the basis of a large enough sample size n and a correspondingly small standard error $s/\sqrt{n}$, the hypothesis $\mu = 10$ will be rejected. Yet although the hypothesis test is *statistically* significant, the difference between 9.999 and 10 kilograms is not *practically* significant. No one cares whether 10-kilogram bags are on average 1 gram underweight. Statistical significance is not always the same thing as practical significance.

We may fail to reject a hypothesis, not because it is true but because of lack of evidence. Consider the other extreme, in which only a few observations are available on which to base a test conclusion. Suppose, for example, that we have the mean and standard deviation $\overline{Y} = 9.87$ and $s = 0.35$ given in Example 10, but that these values have been obtained from weighing just $n = 10$ bags of flour. Then the t statistic is

$$t = \frac{\overline{Y} - \mu_0}{s/\sqrt{n}} = \frac{9.87 - 10}{0.35/\sqrt{10}} = -1.17.$$

For $n - 1 = 9$ degrees of freedom this does not lead to a rejection at conventional significance levels; for example, for a one-sided test at 10% the rejection region is $t < -t_a(n - 1) = -1.383$. Consequently, there is a better than 10% chance that an average weight as low as $\overline{Y} = 9.87$ could have been observed even if the packaging machinery is not systematically underfilling. When only ten bags have been checked, the evidence is not strong enough to conclude otherwise. If the same evidence had been obtained on the basis of 20 bags, it would have been.

This is one reason why we never literally accept a hypothesis, only fail to reject it; and it is why a failure to reject never constitutes proof of the null—the failure to reject may simply arise from a lack of evidence. The fact that, on the basis of checking ten bags of flour, we do not find compelling evidence that they are underweight, does not prove that the packaging equipment is accurate, but only that there is no strong reason to conclude otherwise.

The Power of a Test

Precisely so as to minimize the probability of failing to reject hypotheses for lack of evidence, statisticians prefer statistical tests that have good power properties. Recall that the power of a test is $1 - \Pr(\text{Type II error})$, the probability of correctly rejecting the null when it is in fact false. For given data and a chosen significance level, the preferred statistical test is the one that is the most powerful; that is, has the best chance of correctly rejecting the null. Designing such tests is difficult in practice because the power of a test varies with the value of the parameter. A test that is the most powerful over one range of parameter values may not be most powerful over some other range.

Size Distortions

As we have emphasized, the legitimacy of any inference procedure—in this case a hypothesis test—requires that the statistical model be correctly specified. A mechanical application of a t test may not have the properties described if the model (2.20) is not a correct representation of the manner in which the data were generated because then the "t statistic" may in fact not follow a t distribution at all.

Specifically, in choosing a significance level the researcher intends to set the probability of Type I error; this intended choice is the **nominal size** of the test. However, unless all the assumptions underlying the derivation of the test procedure hold—including the specification of the statistical model—it is possible that the **true size** (also called the **empirical size** or the **actual size**) may differ from the nominal size. In this sense, the mechanical application of a hypothesis-testing procedure may yield unreliable conclusions: The researcher may believe that the probability of Type I error has been set at some small value, but in fact it may be much larger. One famous example of such **size distortions** is encountered in Section 3.2.2 of the next chapter.

Of course there are many respects in which a model may be misspecified. The most obvious possibility in the present context is that the population may be nonnormal. When we study the concept of a central limit theorem in Section 2.5.3 we find that it offers an approximation to the sampling distribution of the t statistic, the quality of which suggests that nonnormality is unlikely to be an important source of size distortions when the sample size is fairly large.

More immediately, however, it is of interest to note that it is sometimes the case that a transformation of the data expands the applicability of exact tests. It is to this that we now turn.

2.5.2 A Lognormal Population

Many population distributions are not normal. Perhaps most obviously, many economic variables take on only positive values. In addition, it is very common for economic variables to have skewed rather than symmetric distributions.

Here is an example having both these features. Hart and Prais (1956) studied the distribution of firm sizes in the United Kingdom, where firm size was measured by stock market capitalization. Their frequency distribution for 1950 is given in Figure 2.11; such a data-based frequency distribution is called an **empirical distribution.** The distribution is skewed to the right, reflecting the fact that most firms are of moderate size, but some are very large. Clearly the size distribution of firms is *not* normal.

In fact many economic variables have distributions that look much like this. Another important example is the distribution of income; no one has a negative income, most people have moderate incomes, and a few have incomes that are very high.

A third example comes from finance. If the price of an asset is denoted P_t so that its **simple rate of return** is

$$R_t \equiv (P_t - P_{t-1})/P_{t-1}, \tag{2.24}$$

FIGURE 2.11

The size distribution of firms in the U.K., 1950, with a fitted lognormal curve.

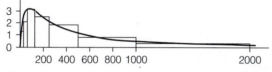

Source: Hart, P.E. and S.J Prais (1956) "The Analysis of Business Concentration: A Statistical Approach," *Journal of the Royal Statistical Society,* Series A, 119, 150–191, Blackwell Publishing. Reprinted with the permission of Blackwell Publishing.

then the **gross simple rate of return** is defined as

$$1 + R_t = 1 + \frac{P_t - P_{t-1}}{P_{t-1}} = \frac{P_t}{P_{t-1}}.$$

This gross simple return is the factor that must be applied to the initial price in order to obtain the new price:

$$(1 + R_t)P_{t-1} = \left(\frac{P_t}{P_{t-1}}\right)P_{t-1} = P_t.$$

For example, if an asset worth $P_{t-1} = \$100$ increases in value by 5%, then the simple return is $R_t = 0.05$ and the new price is

$$P_t = (1 + R_t)P_{t-1} = (1.05)\$100 = \$105.$$

Gross simple returns $1 + R_t$ tend to be distributed in the way we have described. They are positive because under limited liability the largest possible loss is limited to the asset becoming worthless, $P_t = 0$, and so the gross return P_t/P_{t-1} cannot be negative. The distribution is skewed to the right because, although most assets have modest yields, a few generate very high returns.

An interesting feature of many such distributions is that, although the variable itself is clearly nonnormal, its logarithm is approximately normal. Formally, a random variable Y is **lognormally distributed** if its natural logarithm is normal:

$$\ln Y \sim N(\mu, \sigma^2).$$

A sample drawn from a lognormal population is described by

$$\ln Y_i = \mu + \varepsilon_i, \qquad \varepsilon_i \sim \text{n.i.d.}(0, \sigma^2). \tag{2.25}$$

Figure 2.11 superimposes a fitted lognormal curve to Hart and Prais's empirical firm-size distribution, demonstrating the ability of the lognormal distribution to describe their data. Figure 2.12 shows the relationship between the normal and the lognormal distributions.

In the case of rates of return, consider the natural logarithm of a gross simple return,

$$\ln(1 + R_t) = \ln\left(\frac{P_t}{P_{t-1}}\right) = \ln P_t - \ln P_{t-1} = \Delta \ln P_t. \tag{2.26}$$

(Recall the delta notation $\Delta Y_t = Y_t - Y_{t-1}$.) As we study in detail in Chapter 6, this has the interpretation of the **continuously compounded rate of return.** For

FIGURE 2.12

Y is lognormally distributed: $\ln Y \sim N(\mu, \sigma^2)$.

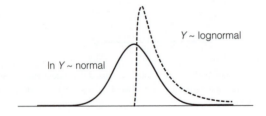

$\ln Y \sim$ normal

$Y \sim$ lognormal

example, if the simple return is 5%, then the corresponding continuously compounded return is $\ln(1 + R_t) = \ln 1.05 \approx 0.04879$. Hence, specifying a gross simple return as lognormal implies that the continuously compounded return is normal.[10]

As these examples illustrate, the distributions of a great many variables in economics and business are closely approximated by the lognormal. They range from firm size—measured not only by market capitalization but also by sales or number of employees—to the size of insurance claims, customer demand for the product of a firm, and the distribution of demand over inventory items. The classic reference on the application of the lognormal to economics is Aitchison and Brown (1957); Lawrence (1988) is a more recent survey. In finance, in the words of Campbell, Lo, and MacKinlay (1997, p. 16), "...the lognormal model has become the workhorse of the financial asset pricing literature."

In many areas of economics, measures of dispersion are important; for example, income inequality and industrial concentration are often measured by Gini coefficients. It turns out that when the populations of interest are lognormal, standard measures of dispersion such as Gini coefficients are often equivalent to the variance of the lognormal; see Hart (1987).

The beauty of the widespread incidence of lognormal populations is that it greatly expands the applicability of exact test procedures such as the t test. The inferential methods that apply to model (2.25)—both estimation and testing—are the same as those for (2.20). The only difference is that logs are taken of the data. For this reason, models involving logarithms are extremely common in applied econometrics, and much of Chapter 6 is devoted to a more detailed examination of their use.

Although the use of logarithms expands the applicability of exact tests, it is nevertheless the case that these procedures rely on a rather special set of circumstances that will not always be satisfied. The alternative to tests based on exact knowledge of sampling distributions are ones that use an approximation to the distribution of the test statistic. We now turn to such approximations.

2.5.3 A Nonnormal Population

The development of Section 2.5.1 makes it clear that the result (2.22) is an important stepping stone in the derivation of the t test procedure and that this stepping stone requires the assumption of a normal population. This suggests that the distributional result (2.23), which says that in this testing problem the t statistic does in fact follow the $t(n - 1)$ distribution under the null, requires normality of the population. If, instead of (2.20), the model is

$$Y_i \sim \text{i.i.d.}(\mu, \sigma^2), \tag{2.27}$$

---

[10] In the finance literature, this description of asset returns goes by the name constant expected return model.

then the assumptions under which (2.23) holds are not satisfied. Consequently, the possibility that the t test may be unreliable—in the sense that size distortions may arise from the failure of the t statistic to follow a $t(n-1)$ distribution exactly—must be addressed.

Given our previous observation that the assumption of any particular form for the population, including normality, is not to be taken lightly, it is natural to ask whether there is any alternative basis for hypothesis testing in the context of the model (2.27). Among the most remarkable results in all of statistics is that there is; it has to do with the asymptotic behavior of the t statistic (2.23).

Although, for any given finite sample size and in the absence of normality of the population, we have seen that this t statistic does not have a t (or, for that matter, any other determinable) distribution, it turns out that as the sample size becomes large its distribution does take on a determinable form. This form is standard normal.

Result 2.8

Under the model (2.27) *the quantity*

$$\frac{\overline{Y} - \mu}{s/\sqrt{n}} \tag{2.28}$$

has a distribution that approaches N(0, 1) *as* $n \to \infty$.

Result 2.8 is an example of a **central limit theorem.** A central limit theorem is another example of an asymptotic result. It describes the distributional behavior of a quantity based on sample data as $n \to \infty$.

Essentially Result 2.8 says that, regardless of the distribution of sample drawings individually, their average is approximately normally distributed for large n. Subtracting the mean μ and dividing by the standard deviation $s/\sqrt{n}$ then standardizes this normal random variable to a N(0, 1). The tendency for averages to be normally distributed is illustrated by the Monte Carlo study in Figure 2.6, where $\overline{Y}$ has a sampling distribution of a roughly normal form despite the fact that the population distribution is uniform, even for the quite small sample size of $n = 15$.

This central limit theorem formalizes the notion that, when a large number of random influences are aggregated, their average or total tends to follow a normal distribution even if the individual influences do not. This in turn helps explain why the normal distribution is so widely encountered in the natural world—many natural phenomena essentially represent the cumulation of a great many underlying random influences. Interestingly, the lognormal distribution results from the multiplicative, rather than additive, aggregation of random influences.[11] Hence the widespread

---

[11] Recall that the logarithm of a product is the sum of the logs. Let a random variable Y be generated as the product of many underlying random influences X_i ($Y = \prod X_i$) and hence be lognormally distributed. Then its logarithm is the sum of many influences ($\ln Y = \sum \ln X_i$) and, by the central limit theorem, is approximately normal. Hence $Y \sim$ lognormal corresponds to $\ln Y \sim$ normal; cf. Figure 2.12.

incidence of lognormal variables in economics and business suggests that they arise as a multiplicative aggregation of many other factors.

To illustrate, consider rates of return aggregated over time. For example, the annual gross simple return $1 + R$ is the product of individual monthly returns,[12]

$$1 + R = (1 + R_1)(1 + R_2) \cdots (1 + R_{12}).$$

This multiplicative relationship is additive in logarithms,

$$\ln(1 + R) = \sum_{i=1}^{12} \ln(1 + R_i),$$

so the annual continuously compounded return is the sum of the monthly continuously compounded returns. The central limit theorem suggests, then, that even if the individual monthly continuously compounded returns are not normal, the annual return tends to be. By implication, the annual gross simple return tends to be lognormal, regardless of the distributions of the monthly rates.

Central limit theorems are extremely useful in statistics because they provide a basis for hypothesis testing in the absence of any assumption about the form of the population distribution, as long as a reasonably large sample size is available. The precision with which the asymptotic result provides an approximation to the sampling distribution of a test statistic depends on the sample size; accordingly, the question always arises of how large a sample is required for the approximation to be satisfactory. Unfortunately, there is no definitive answer to this question because the quality of the approximation will depend on the extent to which the underlying population deviates from normality. If the population is close to normal, the sampling distribution may approach normality in a way that differs little from the convergence of the t distribution to $N(0, 1)$ and the t distribution may provide a quite good approximation to the distribution of the t statistic for even fairly small sample sizes. If the population deviates strongly from normality, this is less likely to be the case.

A Simulation Experiment

How concerned should we be that a mechanical application of the t test may involve significant size distortions in small samples? To consider this question let us return to a Monte Carlo experiment such as that of Section 2.3.3; in fact we shall consider the results of exactly that experiment, which simulated sampling from a uniform population with mean $\mu = (\theta_0 + \theta_1)/2 = \frac{1}{2}$, and of a similar one based on a Bernoulli population with $\mu = \pi = 0.4$. In each case, the sample mean $\overline{Y}$ and sample standard deviation s are computed for 2000 replications; Figure 2.13

---

[12] To satisfy yourself of this, let P_t denote the price of the asset at the end of month t. Then the product of the gross monthly returns is

$$(1 + R_{12})(1 + R_{11}) \cdots (1 + R_1) = \frac{P_{12}}{P_{11}} \cdot \frac{P_{11}}{P_{10}} \cdot \frac{P_{10}}{P_9} \cdots \frac{P_2}{P_1} \cdot \frac{P_1}{P_0} = \frac{P_{12}}{P_0},$$

which is just the annual gross return $1 + R$.

FIGURE 2.13

Simulated sampling distributions for the statistic
$t = \sqrt{n}(\bar{Y} - \mu)/s$
under nonnormality.

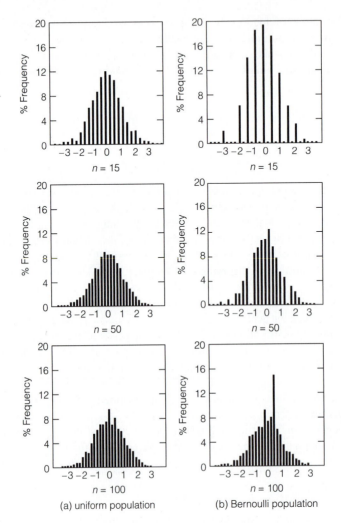

(a) uniform population   (b) Bernoulli population

shows the sampling distributions of the statistic (2.28) based on samples of size $n = 15, 50$, and 100. Note that, although the distributions in the first column of this figure correspond exactly to those in the first column of Figure 2.6, they are now centered over zero and have a roughly common dispersion because they have been standardized with respect to the mean and variance.

Even though the population distributions are nonnormal, it is apparent that the sampling distributions of (2.28) are closely approximated by $t(n-1)$, the distribution that would apply under population normality. Although we know from Result 2.8 that this approximation improves as n increases (both distributions approaching $N(0, 1)$ in the limit), it is remarkably good even for the small sample size of $n = 15$.

These results are somewhat comforting in that they suggest that size distortions arising from nonnormality are likely to be small. Of course, as emphasized in Section 2.3.3, the results of any Monte Carlo experiment are conditional on the assumed population distribution and parameter values, and so these results are merely suggestive.

Conclusion

The practical implication of this finding is that applied econometricians typically proceed with mechanical applications of t tests (or, similarly, other exact tests such as the F test developed in Chapters 8 and 10 in connection with the regression model), implicitly assuming that they are robust to nonnormality.

Practitioner's Tip: Exact tests and normality

Strictly speaking, the derivation of exact tests such as the t test typically requires normality. In practice, however, applied econometricians often use these tests on the implicit assumption that they are robust to nonnormality.

2.5.4 The Role of Linearity

Although our emphasis on the distinction between exact and asymptotic tests may seem something of a fine point, it turns out to be of considerable importance for econometrics. This is because the conditions under which exact tests are available involve more than normality. The development of the t test in Section 2.5.1 indicates that, in addition to normality, linearity of the estimator is a critical ingredient in arriving at the distributional result (2.21). Hence, the linearity of the estimator and normality of the population are both necessary conditions in arriving at the exact test given by Result 2.7: Even if normality is satisfied, an exact test is unavailable if the estimator is a nonlinear function of the data. In this situation, any hypothesis testing procedures have to be based on central limit theorems.

As we shall see, this intuition generalizes to much broader contexts. In relatively simple estimation problems involving linear models, in which estimators possessing desirable properties are linear in the data, the assumption of population normality yields exact tests of hypotheses. The most important example of a model corresponding to this framework is the linear regression model studied in Chapters 4–10. When, beginning in Chapter 13, we turn to more complex estimation problems in which estimators are nonlinear in the data, available test procedures are of necessity asymptotic and there is no value to the assumption of population normality.

2.6   Further Topics in Hypothesis Testing ★

The previous section deals with the aspects of hypothesis testing that are used in the rest of this book. Two supplementary topics follow naturally from that discussion. The first is a subject that occasionally arises in empirical work: testing for normality. This is a topic that turns out not to be particularly important for the applied techniques we are studying, although it is useful to clarify why. The second topic—bootstrap testing—is an exciting recent development in econometrics that is likely to play an increasingly important role in empirical work in the future.

2.6.1   Testing Normality

We have seen that population normality is required for the t statistic to have a t distribution when the sample size is small. Under these circumstances, it is therefore useful to be able to test whether the population is normal. If normality is rejected, this alerts the researcher to the possibility that a mechanical application of a t test may involve significant size distortions.

A number of such tests exist; they proceed by examining the extent to which the shape of the empirical distribution deviates from normality. One way to do this is to compute statistics that describe features of the distribution in addition to its mean and variance (because any mean and variance can be consistent with a normal distribution). The two most important such features are **skewness** and **kurtosis,** which are estimated as follows.

Skewness is the extent to which the distribution is asymmetric: One side of the distribution is not a mirror image of the other. It is estimated by the **coefficient of skewness**

$$S = \frac{\sum (Y_i - \overline{Y})^3 / (n-1)}{s^3}.$$

The denominator is the cube of the standard deviation s, obtained in the usual way from the sample variance s^2 given by the standard formula (2.7). A symmetric distribution such as the normal has a skewness of zero. Positive skewness means that the distribution is right-skewed—it has is a long right-hand tail, like the lognormal distribution. Negative skewness means the opposite—the distribution has a long left-hand tail.

Kurtosis refers to the peakedness of the distribution. It is estimated by the **coefficient of kurtosis**

$$K = \frac{\sum (Y_i - \overline{Y})^4 / (n-1)}{s^4}.$$

FIGURE 2.14

A histogram of the
monthly return
on IBM stock, July
1963–June 1968.

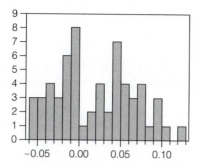

If two distributions have the same variance, the one with more weight in the
center and tails has the larger kurtosis. A normal distribution has a kurtosis
of $K = 3$. Compared with the normal, a distribution with $K > 3$ has a larger
probability of values close to or far away from the mean; it is said to be
leptokurtic. A distribution with $K < 3$ has a larger probability of values
intermediately distant from the mean; it is said to be **platykurtic.**

The Jarque-Bera Test

The test of normality most widely used by econometricians is due to Jarque and
Bera (1980), who showed that under normality the statistic

$$\frac{n}{6}\left(S^2 + \frac{(K-3)^2}{4}\right)$$

has an asymptotic chi-square distribution with 2 degrees of freedom.[13] Notice that
this statistic takes on its smallest possible value of zero under normality, where
the distribution is symmetric (so $S = 0$) and neither leptokurtic nor platykurtic (so
$K = 3$). Values of S and K different from these result in positive values of the
statistic, with suitably extreme values leading to a rejection of normality.

EXAMPLE 11

fama.dat

Fama (1976) presents data on the monthly simple return R_t on IBM stock for the
period July 1963–June 1968. This series is reproduced in Table 5.2; the returns
range from a loss of 5.62% to a gain of 13.58%.
     Our discussion of the lognormality of gross simple returns suggests that it may
be reasonable to treat continuously compounded returns $\ln(1 + R_t)$ as normally
distributed. A histogram of Fama's data, using returns that have been converted
to continuously compounded form, is given in Figure 2.14. The histogram suggests that, at least at a descriptive level, normality is plausible. The coefficients of

---

[13] The 2 degrees of freedom arise from the fact that it is *two* restrictions, $S = 0$ and $K = 3$, that
are being tested. Much later in this book we encounter other tests—the F test of Chapter 10 and
the likelihood ratio test of Chapter 13—in which the degrees of freedom are always the number of
restrictions under test.

skewness and kurtosis are $S = 0.230$ and $K = 2.059$. Is normality supported by a Jarque-Bera test?

SOLUTION

Fama's monthly returns over a 5-year period constitute a sample of $n = 60$ observations. Substituting the coefficients of skewness and kurtosis into the Jarque-Bera statistic yields

$$\frac{n}{6}\left(S^2 + \frac{(K-3)^2}{4}\right) = \frac{60}{6}\left(0.230^2 + \frac{(2.059 - 3)^2}{4}\right) = 2.743.$$

Comparing this against tabulated values of the $\chi^2(2)$ distribution such as those in this book (for example, $\chi^2_{0.10}(2) = 4.61$), the null hypothesis of normality is not rejected at conventional significance levels. The p-value for this statistic turns out to be 0.254.

Notice that, in contrast to a t test, the Jarque-Bera test always uses a one-tailed rejection region. The null hypothesis of normality, in which the joint restrictions $S = 0$ and $K = 3$ hold, is rejected in favor of the alternative that $S > 0$ and/or $K \neq 3$ for values of the statistic in the right tail of the $\chi^2(2)$ distribution.

Exact Tests and Normality Tests

When we are working with a small sample, should we first perform a normality test to see whether t statistics do in fact have t distributions?

The problem with this idea is that normality tests are themselves asymptotic: The distribution of the Jarque-Bera statistic is well approximated as $\chi^2(2)$ only for reasonably large sample sizes. Intuitively, it is easy to understand that on the basis of a small number of observations it will be difficult to judge whether the empirical distribution deviates from normality. When a large sample is available, however, we have seen that central limit theorems such as Result 2.8 provide a sound basis for testing even in the absence of normality. It is when the sample is small that population normality becomes an issue, yet it is in precisely this circumstance that the ability of normality tests to reliably detect departures from normality comes into question.

Furthermore, a number of Monte Carlo studies have established that the small-sample behavior of normality tests is in fact quite poor. Evidence to this effect for the Jarque-Bera statistic has been presented by Jarque and Bera (1987), Anderson (1994), Deb and Sefton (1996), and Urzúa (1996).

Thus there is an almost amusing catch-22 with normality tests: The situations in which we wish to use them are exactly those in which their properties may be poor. Hence, the value of testing normality for the purpose of establishing the legitimacy of exact tests is doubtful. This is not to suggest that normality tests may not be useful in other contexts; for example, to confirm that an application of maximum likelihood estimation based on normality is reasonable. It does explain, however, why researchers do not routinely report normality tests in support of their use of t tests.[14]

---

[14] Or other exact tests that assume normality, such as the F test of Chapter 10.

Rather than trust normality tests to correctly detect failures of the normality assumption, an applied researcher concerned about the sensitivity of test results to assumptions about the population distribution may be best off using a bootstrapped test, our next topic of study.

2.6.2   Bootstrapped Tests

The hypothesis-testing procedures we have developed so far are based on analytical results for the sampling distribution of the test statistic. The exact t test in Section 2.5.1 uses Result 2.7, that, under population normality, the statistic $(\overline{Y} - \mu)/(s/\sqrt{n})$ has a $t(n-1)$ distribution. The asymptotic test of Section 2.5.3 uses the central limit theorem in Result 2.8, that this same t statistic approaches normality for large sample sizes.

Notice that, instead of relying on these analytical results, it is possible to simulate the sampling distribution of the test statistic numerically, much as we have described simulating the sampling distribution of an estimator in our discussion of Monte Carlo simulation. There are two ways of doing this.

Monte Carlo tests proceed exactly as outlined in our discussion of Monte Carlo simulation, simulating the sampling distribution of the test statistic based on some assumed choice of population distribution. We then compare the computed value of the test statistic against this sampling distribution simulated under the null hypothesis and conclude whether the data are consistent with that null. Proceeding in this way, we are performing a **Monte Carlo test.**

Bootstrapped tests use what is, for most purposes, a better way of implementing essentially the same idea. Why sample from an *assumed* population distribution when we have the *empirical distribution* of the data?

Consider treating the sample as a population, taking n random drawings from it (with replacement—drawing without replacement would just yield the original sample), and computing the statistic of interest. This is called **resampling.** Doing this repeatedly yields a simulated sampling distribution for the test statistic based on the empirical distribution of the data. It is possible to modify this idea to generate a simulated sampling distribution with a null hypothesis imposed and in this way to generate a p-value for the observed statistic. This is called **bootstrapping** the test statistic.

The term *bootstrapping* derives from the phrase "pulling oneself up by one's bootstraps"—in this case, using information available in the sample rather than an a priori specification of the population distribution to study the sampling distribution. A novelty at one time, the methodology of bootstrapping has advanced rapidly due to increases in computer power and the accompanying expansion of the use of numerical methods. The advantage of bootstrapping is that it makes analytical results—both exact distributional results such as Result 2.7 and central limit theorems such as Result 2.8—unnecessary as a basis for hypothesis testing. It thus lends itself especially well to complex estimation problems in which such analytical results are difficult or impossible to derive. Consequently bootstrapped tests are increasingly part of the toolkit of the applied econometrician, and the years ahead are bound to see resampling techniques programmed routinely into econometric software.

For an introduction to Monte Carlo methods and bootstrapping, see Johnston and DiNardo (1997, Chap. 11) and Davidson and MacKinnon (1993, Chap. 21). Book-length introductions to bootstrapping, addressed to the applied statistician, are Efron and Tibshirani (1993) and, at a more advanced level, Davison and Hinkley (1997). Surveys oriented toward econometrics include Jeong and Maddala (1993), Veall (1998), Horowitz (2001), and MacKinnon (2002).

EXERCISES

Fama's IBM returns series is available in the file **fama.dat**, along with a similar series for Xerox and the two other series in Table 5.2. This data set is documented in the exercises of the appendix to Chapter 5.

2.22 **fama.dat** Generate the continuously compounded returns series $\ln(1 + R_t)$ for IBM.

(a) Use your software to obtain a frequency histogram of this series similar to Figure 2.14.

(b) Does your software produce the coefficients of skewness and kurtosis reported in Example 11?

2.23 **fama.dat** Generate the continuously compounded returns series $\ln(1 + R_t)$ for Xerox.

(a) Use your software to obtain a frequency histogram of this series similar to Figure 2.14. Does a casual inspection of this histogram lead you to judge these returns to be approximately normal?

(b) Use your software to obtain the coefficients of skewness and kurtosis. Are these returns right-skewed or left-skewed? Leptokurtic or platykurtic?

(c) Perform a Jarque-Bera test for normality, stating it carefully in terms of the four steps in Section 2.5.1.

2.24 In a study of the size distribution of 587 Portuguese firms, where size was measured by the logarithm of employment, Cabral and Mata (2003, p. 1076) found that

> ...the firm size distribution is reasonably symmetric, bell-shaped, and in fact similar in shape to the normal distribution (or, rather, the lognormal distribution, as the x-axis is on a log scale). ... the Jarque-Bera test yields a value of 0.719, based on which one cannot reject normality.

State this Jarque-Bera test explicitly in terms of the four steps of Section 2.5.1. Do you agree with their finding?

2.7 Inference Is Conditional on the Model

This chapter has reviewed a number of concepts in statistical inference that play an important role in econometrics. These have included the importance of distinguishing between sample and population quantities and the role that the important concept of a sampling distribution plays in all aspects of statistical inference: estimation, confidence intervals, and hypothesis testing.

One point that has been emphasized is that the evaluation of features of sampling distributions depends critically on the specification of the statistical model. Properties of estimators and hypothesis-testing procedures are conditional on assumptions about the model; if these assumptions are false, inference procedures derived on the basis of the false model may not be valid.

As a further illustration of this point, recall the model

$$Y_i = \mu + \varepsilon_i, \qquad \varepsilon_i \sim \text{i.i.d.}(0, \sigma^2). \tag{2.29}$$

As we have seen, this is simply an alternative way of specifying model (2.27). If, in addition, the disturbance is normally distributed, the implied population model is

$$Y \sim \text{N}(\mu, \sigma^2). \tag{2.30}$$

Section 2.3 establishes that, in the context of this model, the sample mean $\overline{Y}$ possesses a number of desirable properties as an estimator for μ.

For a variable Y generated in other ways, on the other hand, the statistic $\overline{Y}$ may be of no particular interest. Let us consider some examples.

Regression Models

Suppose the population mean is not a fixed constant. Instead, let the means of the successive Y_i observations vary linearly with some other quantifiable variable X_i:

$$E(Y_i) = \alpha + \beta X_i.$$

The parameters α and β are the intercept and slope of this linear function. If the sample Y_i are drawn randomly from this population, the same disturbance defined in (2.29) may be used to specify the statistical model as

$$Y_i = \alpha + \beta X_i + \varepsilon_i, \qquad \varepsilon_i \sim \text{i.i.d.}(0, \sigma^2). \tag{2.31}$$

If, in addition, the disturbance is normally distributed, the implied population model is[15]

$$Y \sim \text{N}(\alpha + \beta X, \sigma^2),$$

in analogy with (2.30). This model is depicted in Figure 4.1(a).

This model has three parameters: α, β, and σ^2. None of these parameters is interpretable in terms of the parameters of the (false) model (2.29). Consequently, the computation of the estimators $\overline{Y}$ and s^2, and any accompanying hypothesis testing that would have been meaningful in the context of (2.29), is not necessarily meaningful in the context of (2.31). Although as a mechanical matter, we can certainly compute $\overline{Y}$ from data generated by (2.31), this estimator has no obvious interest in connection with this model. Instead we want estimators for α, β, and

---

[15] Strictly speaking, this is the distribution of Y *conditional on* X, as is made explicit in the next chapter.

σ^2 possessing desirable properties, and associated hypothesis-testing procedures. In fact this is exactly what is developed in Chapters 4 and 8, where (2.31), somewhat more fully specified, is studied as the **linear regression model.** Because the appropriate estimators turn out to be linear in the Y_i, the additional assumption of normality yields exact test procedures.

Deterministic Trend Models

As an example of the application of the linear regression model in a particular context, it might be that observations are collected over time and vary randomly around a trend, say,

$$Y_t = \alpha + \beta t + \varepsilon_t, \qquad \varepsilon_t \sim \text{i.i.d.}(0, \sigma^2). \tag{2.32}$$

The explanatory variable is time t; this symbol is used instead of i in order to emphasize that these data are observed over time. This series varies randomly around a mean

$$E(Y_t) = \alpha + \beta t.$$

This is called a **deterministic trend** because it is a deterministic (that is, nonrandom) function of t. The model (2.32) is called a **deterministic trend model** because it treats fluctuations in Y as random variation around this deterministic trend.

An example of a series generated in this way is given in Figure 2.15(a). It is constructed using an intercept of $\alpha = 4.605$, a slope of $\beta = 0.04879$, and a disturbance $\varepsilon_t \sim \text{n.i.d.}(0, 0.25)$ obtained using a random number generator.[16]

Stochastic Trend Models

Another example of a time series model is

$$Y_t = \beta + Y_{t-1} + \varepsilon_t, \qquad \varepsilon_t \sim \text{i.i.d.}(0, \sigma^2). \tag{2.33}$$

This says that this period's value of Y equals the previous period's plus a constant β and a disturbance; β is called a **drift parameter.** A series generated in this way is called a **random walk with drift.** It follows what might be described as a meandering or wandering pattern, as depicted in Figure 2.15(b). If β is positive, the variable tends to drift upward over time, as in the figure; if negative, it tends to drift downward. The choice of the notation β for the drift parameter follows from this fact—that it imparts a trend to the variable and so plays a role similar to the slope coefficient β in the deterministic trend model (2.32). Because the period-by-period changes in Y associated with this trend are due not only to the drift parameter β but also to the random disturbance ε_t, this meandering behavior is an example of what is known more generally as a **stochastic trend.**

---

[16] For the moment, we use these values for α and β without explanation. The basis for this choice will become clear in Section 6.2.1.

FIGURE 2.15

Deterministic and
stochastic trends.

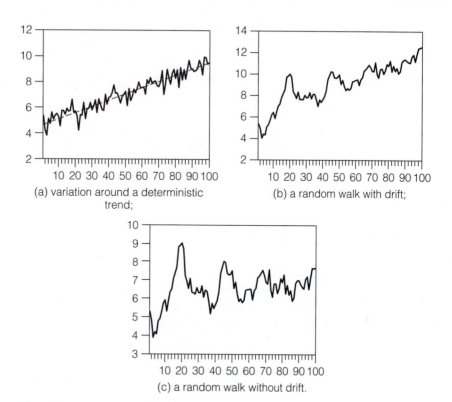

(a) variation around a deterministic
trend;

(b) a random walk with drift;

(c) a random walk without drift.

The series in Figure 2.15(b) is constructed using the same value of $\beta = 0.04879$ that was used for the slope of the deterministic trend in Figure 2.15(a). As well, it begins at the same intercept value of $Y_0 = 4.605$ and uses exactly the same realized series of ε_t shocks. Comparing the two graphs, the conclusion is that two variables can start at the same initial value and trend with the same slope or drift under the influence of the same series of random shocks and yet exhibit quite different patterns of behavior over time, depending on whether they are generated as deterministic or stochastic trends.

To understand better the role of the drift parameter, consider the special case in which $\beta = 0$, a **random walk without drift:**

$$Y_t = Y_{t-1} + \varepsilon_t, \qquad \varepsilon_t \sim \text{i.i.d.}(0, \sigma^2).$$

Such a series is depicted Figure 2.15(c), again using the same shocks and initial value $Y_0 = 4.605$ as the first two graphs. Notice that it exhibits the same meandering behavior as Figure 2.15(b), but not the upward trend. Although it does not possess the predictable trend of the random walk with drift, it is nevertheless the case that over time a random walk without drift can wander arbitrarily far away from any starting point. Hence, even in the absence of drift a random walk series can exhibit trending behavior ex post and so is still said to possess a stochastic trend.

These deterministic and stochastic trend models are additional examples of situations in which the calculation of statistics such as $\overline{Y}$ or s^2 may hold no particular interest because they are not useful estimators of any parameter. In the same way, it is clearly inappropriate to model a stochastic trend series using a deterministic trend, or the converse—a theme we pursue in Chapter 15. These models serve once again to emphasize that the use of any procedure in statistical inference is conditional on the specification of the statistical model.

As we have noted in the previous chapter, time series data are very common in economics. Many economic variables, especially macroeconomic and financial time series, trend in a manner that can be described using deterministic or stochastic trends. Let us consider an example of a stochastic trend.

Application: *The Random Walk Model of Stock Prices*

Perhaps the most important empirical regularity in finance is that the returns on a financial asset tend to be unrelated over time. Because the prices of financial assets are determined by competitive traders, all of whom are trying to anticipate future events, periods of unusually high or low returns do not persist in a predictable way. If they did, there would be an opportunity for traders to act on this predictability in order to take advantage of periods of high returns and avoid periods of low returns.

Consider, for example, the monthly return on IBM stock for the period July 1963–June 1968, studied by Fama (1976). In their continuously compounded form $\ln(1 + R_t)$, these are summarized as the histogram in Figure 2.14. This series is graphed over time in Figure 2.16. On a casual level at least, there is no indication of any predictable cycle in these returns that you could base a profitable trading strategy on.[17]

The implication of this is that returns in financial markets follow a very simple model: They just fluctuate randomly around their mean value. This may be expressed as

$$\ln(1 + R_t) = \beta + \varepsilon_t. \tag{2.34}$$

FIGURE 2.16

The rate of return on IBM stock, July 1963–June 1968.

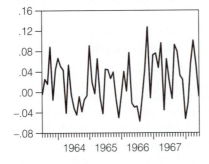

[17] Chapter 15 presents a formal test of whether a series is uncorrelated over time. It is applied to Fama's IBM returns in Example 3 of Section 15.3.3.

Here ε_t denotes an i.i.d. disturbance or, if the return distribution is normal, ε_t is n.i.d. The idea is that, if the return in one month is unrelated to returns in other months, they can be treated like an i.i.d. sample. The parameter β has the interpretation of the expected or mean rate of return:

$$E[\ln(1 + R_t)] = \beta.$$

Because expected returns are positive—otherwise no one would hold the asset—it should be the case that β is positive.

What are the implications of this description of asset *returns* for the evolution of asset *prices* over time?

Recall that, from equation (2.26), continuously compounded returns are the change in the logarithm of the asset price,

$$\ln(1 + R_t) = \Delta \ln P_t = \ln P_t - \ln P_{t-1}.$$

Substituting this into equation (2.34) yields

$$\ln P_t = \beta + \ln P_{t-1} + \varepsilon_t. \tag{2.35}$$

This is just the random walk model. Thus i.i.d. returns imply that the price evolves, in its logarithm, as a random walk with drift. Because stock prices change in response to new information, which, by definition, is an unpredictable surprise, today's price differs from yesterday's in a way that is well described by a disturbance ε. The drift parameter—the rate at which the price would change in the absence of any surprises—is the asset's expected rate of return. Because this expected return β is positive, an asset price tends to drift upward over time so that it appreciates in value. The only way this would turn out not to be the case is if adverse shocks—negative realizations of ε—were so large and sustained as to overcome the positive drift.

These properties explain why the artificially simulated drifting random walk of Figure 2.15(b) looks much like the graph of a stock price that you might see in a newspaper.

We return to the random walk theory of stock prices in Chapter 15, where random walk models are studied in some detail.

Estimating the Drift Parameter as a Sample Mean

Although we have argued that a statistic such as $\overline{Y}$ is not always a useful estimator of parameters of interest, it is nevertheless the case that the basic ideas of this chapter can often be fruitfully applied in more sophisticated contexts. Consider again the random walk model (2.33). As our discussion of stock prices has suggested, another way of looking at the behavior it describes is to rewrite it as

$$\Delta Y_t = \beta + \varepsilon_t. \tag{2.36}$$

Notice that in this form it is nothing more than the model (2.29),

$$Y_i = \mu + \varepsilon_i,$$

with the notation suitably redefined: The changes ΔY_t take the place of Y_i, the drift parameter β plays the role of μ, and the observations are over time t. From our analysis of that model, we know that the least squares estimator of μ is the sample mean of the Y_i, an unbiased estimator of the disturbance variance σ^2 is the sample variance (2.7), and so on.

This suggests that a useful estimator of the drift parameter β is the sample mean of the ΔY_t; because β is the mean change, it makes sense to estimate it as the sample mean of the observed changes in the data. If the data series on Y_t is observed over the sample $t = 1, \ldots, n$, then its differences $\Delta Y_t = Y_t - Y_{t-1}$ are available for the $n - 1$ observations $t = 2, \ldots, n$. The application of the sample mean formula in this context therefore takes the form

$$\frac{1}{n-1} \sum_{t=2}^{n} \Delta Y_t. \tag{2.37}$$

EXAMPLE 12

Suppose the simulated random walk with drift of Figure 2.15(b) is treated as an observed time series, $t = 1, \ldots, 100$. What estimate of the drift does our sample mean formula provide? What is the sampling error of this estimate? How does this relate to the Monte Carlo methodology described in Section 2.3.3?

SOLUTION

Computing the differences ΔY_t $(t = 2, \ldots, 100)$ and averaging, the sample mean formula yields

$$\frac{1}{n-1} \sum_{t=2}^{n} \Delta Y_t = \frac{1}{99} \sum_{t=2}^{n} \Delta Y_t = 0.07305$$

This overestimates the population value of $\beta = 0.04879$ that was used to generate the series by approximately 50%; the sampling error is $0.07305 - 0.04879 = 0.02426$.

In terms of the Monte Carlo methodology of Section 2.3.3, setting $Y_0 = 4.605$, $\beta = 0.04879$, and $\varepsilon_t \sim$ n.i.d.$(0, 0.25)$ in the random walk with drift constitutes the specification of a data-generating process, as described in step 1 in Section 2.3.3. The simulation of this DGP, as presented in Figure 2.15(b), is one replication of the simulation experiment, as described in step 2. Successive artificially generated samples from repeated replications, each time reestimating β, will yield a simulated sampling distribution for the estimator.

Although $\overline{Y}$, the sample mean of Y_t, may be of no particular interest in connection with the random walk model, the sample mean of the changes ΔY_t is of great interest and, in fact, is an estimator that is used when we return to this model in Chapter 6.

EXAMPLE 13

fama.dat

Consider Fama's IBM returns series graphed in Figure 2.16. What methods of statistical inference, as we have developed them in this chapter, apply to this series? What conclusions do these methods yield?

SOLUTION

The random walk model of stock prices says that stock prices behave, in their logarithms, like a drifting random walk (2.35). Equivalently, continuously compounded returns behave like an i.i.d. sample around their mean,

$$\Delta \ln P_t = \beta + \varepsilon_t.$$

This is just the model (2.36) with $Y_t = \ln P_t$. This model has two parameters: the drift β and the return variance σ^2. Following the reasoning we have presented, the drift is estimated by the sample mean of the dependent variable—in this case, the average of the returns $\ln(1 + R_t) = \Delta \ln P_t$. For Fama's IBM returns this sample mean turns out to be $\hat{\beta} = 0.0200$, so that the average monthly continuously compounded return is 2%.

The variance σ^2 is estimated by the sample variance s^2, which turns out to be $s^2 = 0.002132$. This can be used to test hypotheses about the mean return β. For example, is the sample mean return of 0.0200 compelling evidence that the IBM stock price was drifting during this period? Or could it have arisen as the happenstance outcome of a zero-drift random walk? That is, is it possible to reject the null hypothesis $\beta = 0$?

If the returns are normally distributed the exact test in Section 2.5.1 applies. However, even if the returns deviate somewhat from normality, for a sample of size $n = 60$ the central limit theorem in Section 2.5.3 can be assumed to hold.[18] In either case, the t statistic (2.28) can be treated as having a $t(n-1)$ distribution. Under the hypothesis $\beta = 0$ this t statistic evaluates to

$$t = \frac{\hat{\beta} - \beta}{s/\sqrt{n}} = \frac{0.0200 - 0}{0.0462/\sqrt{60}} = 3.36.$$

Comparing this against the tabulated values of the t distribution with $n - 1 = 59$ degrees of freedom, the hypothesis of an absence of drift is rejected at conventional significance levels. The IBM stock price exhibits drift.

EXERCISES

2.25 🔘 **fama.dat** Generate the continuously compounded returns $\ln(1 + R_t)$ for IBM.

(a) Use your software to plot this series. Is it similar to Figure 2.16?

(b) Use your software to obtain the sample mean and variance. Are you able to replicate the values given in Example 13?

(c) As we consider further in Chapter 6, for low rates of return continuously compounded rates are approximately equal to net simple rates:

$$\ln(1 + R_t) \approx R_t.$$

Given this approximate equality, suppose the analysis is performed using Fama's original net simple rate R_t.

[18] Although financial returns are often well approximated by normality, the approximation is not perfect. It is well established that returns are typically leptokurtic; to use the colloquialism of finance, the distributions are **fat-tailed**. This means that extreme returns are more common in the real world than would be suggested by the normal distribution. This feature of returns is discussed by Campbell, Lo, and MacKinlay (1997, Sec. 1.4.2); see also the remarks in Pagan (1996, Sec. 2.4).

(i) Use your software to plot this series. Are these net simple returns very different in appearance from the continuously compounded returns of Figure 2.16?

(ii) What are the sample mean and variance of this series?

(iii) Use these statistics to perform a test of the hypothesis of a zero drift, stating it carefully in terms of the four steps in Section 2.5.1. Is the substantive conclusion of Example 13 affected by how returns are measured?

2.26 💿 **fama.dat** Generate the continuously compounded returns $\ln(1 + R_t)$ for Xerox.

(a) Use your software to obtain the sample mean and variance.

(b) Perform a test of the hypothesis of a zero drift, stating it carefully in terms of the four steps of Section 2.5.1. Is the conclusion similar to that for IBM or different?

(c) Following the reasoning of the previous exercise, redo the analysis using Fama's original net simple returns R_t. Is the substantive finding of the hypothesis test affected by how returns are measured?

2.8 Econometrics and Statistics

This chapter has reviewed some key concepts from statistics that are important in understanding econometrics. Given that econometrics is the application of statistical methods, it is natural to ask whether there is any need for the separate term *econometrics*. What distinguishes econometrics from statistics?

Some argue that the distinction has to do with the nature of economic data. One example, as we have just noted, is that much economic data are observed over time, although economics is certainly not unique in this respect. Another is that, in contrast to the natural sciences and some other areas of the social sciences (notably psychology) in which controlled experimentation by the researcher is possible, most empirical work in economics is based on **nonexperimental data** from published sources. The econometrician has no ability to design the experiment that generates the data and consequently must treat the many outside influences that can be controlled for in laboratory experimentation. This is done by formulating a statistical model intended as a representation of the true way in which the data were generated; accompanying inference procedures—methods of estimation and testing—are then derived. The methodology is therefore one of **model-based inference.** The obvious pitfall of this methodological framework is, as we have emphasized, that findings are contingent on the adequacy of the model.

This suggests, then, that the basis for the specification of the statistical model is the fundamental distinguishing feature of econometrics. What is this basis? The answer is: economic theory. When an econometrician attempts to study empirically some economic issue, this is done by estimating and testing an economic model. It is an economic model that is the basis for the specification of the statistical model.

An economic theory takes the form of hypotheses about a model; because the model is fully characterized by its parameters, these hypotheses are in the form of restrictions on the parameters. A statistical test of the theory is therefore a test of these parameter restrictions and, in essence, follows the testing paradigm of classical statistics as laid out in Section 2.5. The null hypothesis is that the parameter restrictions hold. In the very elementary t testing context of Section 2.5, this is that $\mu = \mu_0$. The econometrician's task is to estimate the model and test these restrictions using an appropriate test statistic. In Section 2.5, the appropriate test statistic was the t statistic given in Result 2.7. In general, econometricians work with a wide range of estimators and test statistics, depending on the statistical model suggested by the economic model. Some test statistics are exact; others are based on central limit theorems and so are asymptotic.

Test statistics follow a variety of distributions, some of which you have encountered in previous studies. In this book, the tests developed in Chapters 4–11 rely exclusively on the t and F distributions. Subsequently in Chapters 12–14 we use tests that, like the Jarque-Bera test, are based on the χ^2 distribution. Finally, in our discussion of time series analysis in Chapters 15–18 we encounter test statistics that, instead of following these standard distributions, require specially tabulated values.

One objective of this book is to give you some sense of the alternative estimators and test statistics that are commonly used in econometrics. Another is to illustrate the role of economic theory in the specification of the statistical model. The following two examples are ones you will meet in the chapters ahead; both are applications of the simple regression model in Chapter 4.

EXAMPLE 14 | The capital asset pricing model (CAPM) is derived in detail in Appendix C. It seeks to explain the rate of return R on an asset in terms of its risk characteristics. The CAPM leads to a statistical model of the form

$$R_t - r_{ft} = \beta(R_{mt} - r_{ft}) + \varepsilon_t.$$

where r_f is the return on a riskless asset, R_m is the return on the market as a whole, and t indexes observations over time. Propose a testable parameter restriction predicted by this theory.

SOLUTION | This equation is in the form of the simple regression model (2.31), where $Y_i = R_t - r_{ft}$ and $X_i = R_{mt} - r_{ft}$, except that the intercept is zero. Hence, the CAPM predicts the parameter restriction $\alpha = 0$.

Estimation and testing procedures for the coefficients of the simple regression model are developed in Chapter 4; you will have an opportunity to estimate and test the CAPM in the appendix to Chapter 5. Interestingly, it turns out that a zero intercept is the prediction of a broad class of linear financial models and so is key to the empirical testing of these models. The statistical methodology for doing this has been intensively developed; an advanced treatment can be found in Campbell, Lo, and MacKinlay (1997, Chap. 5).

EXAMPLE 15

As is developed in detail in Section 7.4, the marginal productivity condition of the constant elasticity of substitution (CES) production function takes the following form:

$$\log(V/L) = \alpha + \beta \log(w). \tag{2.38}$$

Here V/L is output per unit of labor input and w is the wage rate; data are available on both for a number of countries. The Cobb-Douglas production function is a special case of the CES that restricts $\beta = 1$. Is it possible to test statistically whether a Cobb-Douglas form for the production function satisfactorily describes the data?

SOLUTION

Because (2.38) posits a linear relationship between the two variables, as long as the data can be regarded as having been obtained by random sampling the simple regression model (2.31) is an appropriate statistical model. The hypothesis $\beta = 1$ is another example of a restriction that can be tested using the procedures developed in Chapter 4.

2.9 Statistical Methodology and the Philosophy of Science

These examples are ones in which the parameter restriction is, in a sense, the prediction of the theory; a test of the null hypothesis that the restriction holds is, then, a test of the "truth" of the theory. The computation of a test statistic that indicates whether or not we reject this hypothesis reflects the fact that classical statistical inference is founded on the **falsificationist** view of the philosophy of science. According to this view, most closely associated with the philosopher Karl Popper (1902–1994), the objective of scientific inquiry is to seek evidence that is capable of falsifying hypotheses. In the same way that the flour mill of Example 10 either rejected or failed to reject the null hypothesis that its packaging machinery is accurate, researchers either reject or fail to reject theories; our knowledge of the world consists of those theories that have not yet been rejected.

Just as the flour mill should not accept the hypothesis that its packaging machinery is accurate on the basis of a statistical test, a theory is never *accepted*, although this term might be used in casual conversation. For, as we have seen, a statistical test can fail to reject simply through lack of evidence.

Although the goal of scientific inquiry may be to falsify hypotheses, at the same time we do not wish to be overly hasty in rejecting theories; a great deal of work goes into their formulation. Instead, it makes sense that a theory should only be rejected on the basis of compelling evidence against it. This is the rationale for the traditional choice of significance levels such as 10, 5, and 1%, which set the probability of Type I error at a low level, so that the probability of incorrectly rejecting a theory is small. The conventional practice of setting the nominal test size at a small value reflects our reluctance to reject theories prematurely.

In taking the null hypothesis to be that parameter restrictions are satisfied, and using a test statistic to see whether the data are inconsistent with these restrictions, empirical work in economics has largely adhered to this classical paradigm. There is, however, an important body of **Bayesian** methodology within both statistics and econometrics that rejects this paradigm, but this is beyond the scope of this book. Poirier (1995) offers an introduction to econometrics organized around a comparative study of the classical and Bayesian approaches. For a briefer introduction to Bayesian methodology, see Zellner (1987).

3

Relationships between Variables

Chapter 2 concentrates almost exclusively on the principles of statistical inference in situations where data exist on a single variable. But in reality it is rarely the case that an economist's interest focuses on a single variable in isolation. Instead economists are almost always interested in relationships between variables: How does GNP depend on business investment? Investment on interest rates? Interest rates on the money supply? And so on.

Conceptually, the same tools of statistical inference apply when observations on a number of variables are drawn from a population. For example, suppose n families are drawn at random from the population of families; observations on family income X_i and consumption expenditure Y_i are collected. Our interest is in the relationship between these two variables. Is our belief that higher-income households consume more confirmed by the data? How much of an additional dollar of income is consumed? Is this marginal propensity to consume constant across income levels or does it vary? What is the corresponding elasticity? These are the kinds of questions that typically interest the economist.

3.1 Covariance and Correlation

In studying a relationship between variables it continues to be useful to conceive of the population as being generated by a population distribution. Now, this distribution is a joint or bivariate (meaning two-variable) distribution $f(x, y)$ that describes the joint behavior of the two variables X and Y. The univariate or marginal distributions of X and Y individually are derivable from this joint distribution and are characterized by parameters such as the means μ_X and μ_Y and variances σ_X^2 and σ_Y^2, defined as mathematical expectations in the usual way.[1] Thus the parameters of the marginal distributions appear as parameters of the joint distribution. The idea of a bivariate distribution generalizes to a multivariate (meaning many variables) distribution describing the joint behavior of any number of random variables.

---

[1] You may wish to review the development of this material in Appendix B.

In addition to the univariate parameters μ_X, μ_Y, σ_X^2, and σ_Y^2, a bivariate or multivariate distribution is characterized by parameters that relate specifically to the joint behavior of the random variables. Like all parameters, these are defined as mathematical expectations on the underlying probability distribution, in this case the joint distribution. An important example is the **population covariance,** defined as

$$\sigma_{XY} = \text{cov}(X, Y) = E[(X - \mu_X)(Y - \mu_Y)], \qquad -\infty < \sigma_{XY} < \infty. \quad (3.1)$$

Unlike a variance, the covariance may be either positive or negative. A positive covariance means the variables are directly related: When one takes on a large value, the other is likely to do so as well. A negative covariance, on the other hand, indicates that the two vary inversely: When one is large, the other is likely to be small. It is apparent from this definition that the covariance is symmetric: $\text{cov}(X, Y) = \text{cov}(Y, X)$. A deficiency of the covariance as a measure of the relationship between variables is that it depends on the units in which the variables are measured: Measuring the variables in, say, thousands of dollars rather than dollars will change the value of σ_{XY}. Hence, being told that the value of a covariance is, say, 5, tells us nothing about the strength of the relationship between the variables because this value can be changed arbitrarily by altering the units in which the variables are measured.

A parameter that does not have this deficiency is the **population correlation**

$$\rho_{XY} = \frac{\sigma_{XY}}{\sigma_X \sigma_Y}, \qquad -1 \le \rho_{XY} \le 1. \quad (3.2)$$

This transforms the covariance so it is independent of the units of measure. This feature of the correlation means that the magnitude of ρ_{XY} provides a useful indication of the strength of the relationship between the two random variables. A value of ρ_{XY} close to 1 indicates a strong direct relationship between the variables, a value close to -1 indicates a strong inverse relationship, and a value close to 0 indicates a weak relationship. If two random variables are statistically independent their covariance and correlation are zero. Because the covariance is symmetric, so too is the correlation; the correlation between X and Y is the same as that between Y and X.

EXAMPLE 1

You are already familiar with the univariate normal distribution, which is given in the previous chapter as equation (2.2). The formula for the bivariate normal distribution is given in Appendix B, equation (B.19). What are the parameters of the bivariate normal distribution? How many parameters characterize a multivariate normal distribution relating three random variables?

SOLUTION

An inspection of the bivariate formula (B.19) reveals that the distribution is fully characterized by five parameters. These are the four univariate parameters, the means μ_X and μ_Y and the standard deviations σ_X and σ_Y (or, equivalently, the variances σ_X^2 and σ_Y^2), plus a fifth parameter governing the joint behavior of the variables. As expressed in the formula, this fifth parameter is the correlation ρ_{XY}, although it could have equivalently been written in terms of the covariance σ_{XY}

by substituting in the formula (3.2). Thus, either the covariance or the correlation may be viewed as the fifth parameter of the bivariate normal. As in the case of the univariate normal, the symbols π and e denote numerical constants, not parameters.

A multivariate normal distribution relating three random variables is characterized by three means (say, μ_1, μ_2, and μ_3), three variances (say, σ_1^2, σ_2^2, and σ_3^2), and three correlations (say, ρ_{12}, ρ_{13}, and ρ_{23}) describing the pairwise interaction of the variables. This is a total of nine parameters. Notice that the symmetry of the correlation means that it is not necessary to list ρ_{21}, ρ_{31}, and ρ_{32} as distinct parameters.

Because the covariance or correlation describes the pairwise relationship between variables and the number of pairs grows exponentially as the number of variables increases, studying the interaction among a large number of variables by studying their pairwise correlations turns out not to be very useful. We return to this point in Section 3.2 (and in Exercise 3.2, where you will see just how quickly the number of correlations increases as we consider more variables). For the moment, however, let us consider the estimation of these parameters.

EXERCISES

3.1 ƒ Two random variables are statistically independent if their bivariate distribution is the product of their marginal distributions,[2]

$$f(x, y) = f_X(x) f_Y(y).$$

In the case of normally distributed random variables, for example, the marginal distribution is given by the formula (2.2) and the bivariate distribution is given by the formula (B.19). The definition of independence is not satisfied because (B.19) allows the two variables to be dependent.

For random variables generally, statistical independence implies zero correlation, but zero correlation does not necessarily imply statistical independence. Show, however, that in the case of normal random variables $\rho = 0$ does imply statistical independence.

3.2 How many parameters characterize a multivariate normal distribution relating four random variables? Five random variables? Present a formula for the number of covariances that will, in general, relate K variables. (*Hint:* You may find the appendix to this chapter or Section B.11 in Appendix B helpful.)

3.1.1 Estimation

Just as estimation and hypothesis testing with respect to the parameters of univariate distributions are the keys to studying a single variable in isolation, so too is statistical inference with respect to joint distributions the key to studying relationships between variables. The methods of Chapter 2 still apply to the univariate

[2] See Appendix B, Definition B.3, equation (B.17).

parameters; what is needed is the extension of these procedures to multivariate parameters such as σ_{XY} and ρ_{XY}.

Consider, for example, a sample X_i, Y_i that is i.i.d. from some population. It may be shown that an unbiased estimator of σ_{XY} is the **sample covariance**

$$s_{XY} = \frac{1}{n-1} \sum_{i=1}^{n} (X_i - \overline{X})(Y_i - \overline{Y}). \tag{3.3}$$

This estimator is unbiased in exactly the same sense that is defined in Chapter 2: Its sampling distribution is centered over the population value σ_{XY}, so that $E(s_{XY}) = \sigma_{XY}$. (This would not be true if the denominator of (3.3) were anything but $n-1$.) If, in addition, the population distribution is bivariate normal, then s_{XY} is efficient as well; no other unbiased estimator has a smaller variance.

An estimator for ρ_{XY} may be obtained by substituting into (3.2) the estimators we now have for σ_{XY}, σ_X, and σ_Y; it is the **sample correlation**

$$r_{XY} = \frac{s_{XY}}{\sqrt{s_X^2 s_Y^2}} = \frac{\sum(X_i - \overline{X})(Y_i - \overline{Y})}{\sqrt{\sum(X_i - \overline{X})^2 \sum(Y_i - \overline{Y})^2}}. \tag{3.4}$$

The estimators s_{XY} and r_{XY} possess a number of features that parallel those of their population analogs. First, they satisfy $-\infty < s_{XY} < \infty$ and $-1 \leq r_{XY} \leq 1$. Second, both are symmetric: $s_{XY} = s_{YX}$ and $r_{XY} = r_{YX}$. Third, as Exercise 3.7 asks you to confirm, r_{XY} is independent of the units of measure.

Another property of r_{XY} that parallels that of ρ_{XY} is that it measures only the strength of the linear relationship between variables.[3] A value of $|r_{XY}|$ close to 1 indicates a strong linear relationship. In fact, just as is true of ρ_{XY}, a deterministic linear relationship between variables always results in $|r_{XY}| = 1$, a fact that you are asked to establish in Exercise 3.8. A correlation of 0 indicates the absence of a linear relationship. Two variables could be nonlinearly related, yet show little correlation. In this sense it might be said that "causality does not imply correlation." A low correlation does not necessarily indicate the absence of *any* relationship between variables, only the absence of a linear one.[4]

That linearity underlies the use of the statistic r_{XY} suggests that the functional relationship between random variables merits further discussion. We turn to this in Section 3.2.

3.1.2 Examples of Using the Correlation

Let us use the sample correlation in a preliminary examination of some of the applications and examples that appear in the chapters ahead. These examples are taken from three areas: production economics, consumer demand, and macroeconomics. They include examples of positive correlations, negative correlations, and

---

[3] See Appendix B, Section B.10.4 for a discussion of this feature of ρ.

[4] Appendix B, Example 19 gives a numerical example of this feature of ρ. Two random variables are exactly related as $Y = X^2$, yet have a correlation of 0.

FIGURE 3.1

Production costs
and output are pos-
itively correlated.

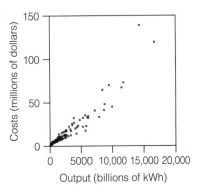

an absence of correlation. In addition to illustrating the use of the sample correlation, these examples serve to indicate some of the limitations of using correlations
to study relationships between variables.

Production Economics: Production Costs and Output

Total production costs increase with output; It costs more to produce more. This
suggests that there should be a positive association between costs and output.

The dependence of production costs on output and factor prices is called a **cost
function.** Cost functions are one of the most important concepts in analyzing firm
behavior, as we investigate in detail in Chapter 11. In a landmark study of cost
functions, Marc Nerlove (1963) analyzed data from 145 electric power generation
companies. We work with his complete data set, including information on factor
prices, in Chapter 11. For the moment let us concentrate on how production costs
vary with output.

These variables are plotted for Nerlove's 145 firms in Figure 3.1. Notice
that there is indeed a clear positive association between costs and output. This
is reflected in the sample correlation, which is positive and close to 1:

$$r = 0.9525.$$

Exercise 3.6 at the end of this chapter asks you to calculate a sample correlation
using data for just five firms taken from Nerlove's data.

Production Economics: Labor Productivity and Capital per Worker

In any production process, output is produced by employing factors of production
such as capital and labor. Let us denote the quantity of output by Q, the capital
stock by K, and labor by L. **Labor productivity** may be thought of as the ratio
Q/L, the amount of output produced by each unit of labor. It stands to reason that
this should depend on the amount of capital each worker has, the ratio K/L—as the
typical worker is given more machinery and equipment to use, it should be possible
to produce more. This suggests a positive correlation between labor productivity
and capital per worker.

FIGURE 3.2

Labor productivity and capital per worker are positively correlated.

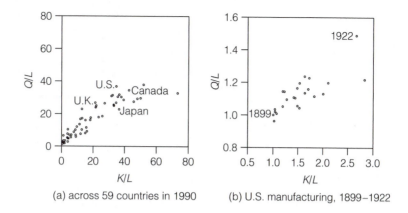

(a) across 59 countries in 1990   (b) U.S. manufacturing, 1899–1922

Several types of data sets could be used to investigate this hypothesis. Across firms in an industry we expect that firms that give their workers more capital are able to achieve higher levels of output per worker. Across industries in an economy, those using more capital per worker should have higher labor productivity. Similarly, countries with large capital stocks relative to their workforce should be more productive.

Figure 3.2(a) presents data of this latter type. It plots GDP per worker and capital per worker for 59 countries in 1990. The data are from the Penn World Tables and are in thousands of 1985 U.S. dollars. Notice the strong positive association between the two variables. This is reflected in the sample correlation, which is

$r = 0.904.$

Instead of a cross-sectional data set, consider an economy over time. Because most economies accumulate more capital per worker as they develop, it should be the case that labor becomes more productive. This was the approach taken by Charles Cobb and Paul Douglas, who in the 1920s studied annual data on output, employment, and the capital stock for the U.S. manufacturing sector from 1899 to 1922. We consider their work in Chapter 7, where their data are presented in Table 7.1. The ratios Q/L and K/L for each of the 24 years are plotted in Figure 3.2(b). Notice that the positive association between the two variables is clearly revealed. The sample correlation is

$r = 0.779.$

These correlations confirm our belief that, both over time and at any point in time, greater capital intensity of production results in greater labor productivity.

As we see when we study their work in Sections 6.1 and 7.2, Cobb and Douglas's contribution was to propose a model for the relationship between output and factor inputs—the **Cobb-Douglas production function**—that, among other nice properties, may be estimated as a linear regression. One way this can be done is in terms of the variables in the form we have just studied them: labor

FIGURE 3.3

Electricity consumption, household income, and price.

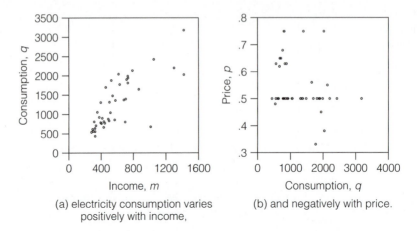

(a) electricity consumption varies
positively with income,

(b) and negatively with price.

productivity Q/L and capital per worker K/L. The advantage of their approach over just examining the correlation is that it yields estimates of parameters having a direct economic interpretation in terms of the properties of the production process. In addition, their approach suggests that a better way of interpreting the data is by studying the variables in logarithmic form as $\log(Q/L)$ and $\log(K/L)$.

Consumer Demand: Electricity Consumption, Income, and Price

Consumer demand for a commodity depends on, among other things, consumer incomes and the price of the commodity. For most goods, higher incomes lead consumers to purchase more of the good. This suggests that there should be a positive correlation between income and quantity consumed. With respect to price, a higher price normally leads consumers to purchase less. This is the "law of demand"—demand curves slope downward. This inverse relationship between price and quantity should show up as a negative correlation between the two variables.

In an early examination of these relationships, Hendrick Houthakker (1951) studied the demand for electricity. He collected data for 42 British towns in the late 1930s on average household income m and electricity consumption q and the price of electricity p. These data are presented in Table 3.1. Detailed variable definitions and units of measure are given in Section 8.6.

Figure 3.3 gives scatter plots of the relationship between q and m and between p and q. Just as our understanding of consumer demand predicts, the plots indicate that consumption is related positively to income and negatively to price, although the positive relationship to income is clearly stronger than the negative one to price. These patterns are confirmed by the sample correlations. Applying the formula (3.4), the correlation between consumption and income is

$$r_{qm} = 0.767,$$

TABLE 3.1   Electricity Consumption, Income, and Price

Town	Electricity consumption, q	Income, m	Price, p
Aberdeen	1772	629	0.33
Barnsley	532	279	0.48
Bath	2133	788	0.55
Birmingham	874	486	0.63
Blackburn	758	403	0.68
Blackpool	1989	730	0.50
Bolton	550	324	0.50
Bristol	1478	539	0.50
Bury	431	325	0.50
Cardiff	1647	868	0.56
Coventry	828	497	0.63
Darlington	1358	575	0.50
Dewsbury	1041	513	0.50
Dundee	661	431	0.62
Exeter	1370	681	0.50
Halifax	1052	352	0.50
Hove	2205	1301	0.50
Huddersfield	804	313	0.50
Ipswich	1939	733	0.45
Leeds	896	413	0.50
Leicester	1697	455	0.50
Lincoln	808	432	0.75
Liverpool and Bootle	1900	715	0.50
Manchester	1314	501	0.50
Motherwell and Wishaw	608	293	0.50
Newport	2026	1422	0.75
Paisley	555	300	0.63
Plymouth	1811	731	0.50
Reading	2427	1055	0.50
Rochdale	1304	394	0.50
Salford	704	335	0.65
South Shields	798	698	0.75
Stockport	853	566	0.50
Stockton-on-Tees	1394	705	0.75
Stoke-on-Trent	2040	614	0.38
Sunderland	920	375	0.50
Tynemouth	673	1017	0.65
Wakefield	782	393	0.50
Wallasey	3183	1422	0.50
West Bromwich	632	323	0.50
West Hartlepool	767	444	0.50
Wolverhampton	1877	524	0.50

Source: Houthakker, H.S. (1951) "Some Calculations on Electricity Consumption in Great Britain," *Journal of the Royal Statistical Society*, Series A, 114, 359–371, Blackwell Publishing. Reprinted with the permission of Blackwell Publishing.

FIGURE 3.4

U.S. unemployment and inflation rates. Open circles, 1953–1970; triangles, 1971–1983; solid circles, 1984–1996.

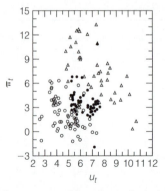

Source: Reprinted from the *Handbook of Macroeconomics*, Vol. IA, J.H. Stock and M.W. Watson, "Business Cycle Fluctuations in US Macroeconomic Time Series," p. 47, ©1999, with permission from Elsevier.

whereas the correlation between consumption and price is

$$r_{qp} = -0.274.$$

In Section 6.5, we study the relationship between consumption and income as an application of simple regression. Subsequently, in Section 8.6 we use multiple regression to estimate a fully specified demand equation that describes the joint dependence of consumption on income, price, and other variables, replicating Houthakker's early work. A limitation of correlations is that they measure only pairwise bivariate relationships taken in isolation. Multiple regression allows us to study the joint dependence of one variable on others in a way that, in measuring any one effect, controls for the other influences. As well, multiple regression estimates parameters that are usually more directly interpretable in terms of economic theory than are correlations. For example, in estimating Houthakker's electricity demand equation we will see that we can obtain estimates of and test hypotheses about the income and price elasticities of demand.

Macroeconomics: The Phillips Curve

For almost half a century, macroeconomists have been intrigued by an apparent negative correlation between inflation and unemployment. This relationship is the famous **Phillips curve,** named after the economist A. W. Phillips, who was the first to document the phenomenon econometrically. We return to the Phillips curve in Chapter 6. For the moment, let us examine the correlation in which he was interested.

The Phillips curve has been investigated using a great many data sets for different countries and time periods. As one example, Stock and Watson (1999) examined U.S. data for the period 1953–1996. Figure 3.4 reproduces their scatter plot of the inflation (π_t) and unemployment (u_t) rates for these years. It depicts the observations in a way that distinguishes among the subperiods 1953–1970, 1971–1983, and 1984–1996.

Focusing on the individual subsamples, it is evident that in at least some periods there is indeed an inverse relationship between the variables: Years of high inflation often tend to be ones of low unemployment. Stock and Watson verified this by calculating the following sample correlations.

Period	Correlation r
1953–70	−0.4
1971–83	−0.4
1984–96	−0.3

Economists have often found negative correlations like these for many countries and time periods. It is easy to understand how this could have led them to believe that there was a usable policy trade-off between inflation and unemployment, as was discussed in our treatment of the Lucas critique in Section 1.2.6.

The problem with the Phillips curve phenomenon is that this empirical finding does not stand up to alterations in the sample period, especially for longer historical time periods. In the terminology of the Phillips curve debate, empirical Phillips curve trade-offs are unstable. This is apparent when we look at Figure 3.4 overall, without focusing on the individual subsamples. All that we see is a cloud of points, with no obvious tendency for years of high inflation to be ones in which unemployment is low. Indeed, Stock and Watson found that over the full 1953–1996 sample the correlation turns out to be

$$r = 0.16.$$

Hence, not only is the relationship very weak, in the long run it is actually *positive*. To the extent that there is any relationship at all, in the long run it may be that higher inflation tends to be associated with higher, not lower, unemployment.

Macroeconomics: Living Standards, Saving, and Population Growth

The standard of living varies enormously across countries. Some countries are desperately poor, whereas others are, by comparison, enormously rich. In Chapter 9, we study data on living standards, measured by output per adult, for 75 countries. These are presented in Table 9.1. The figures reveal that in 1985 some countries had an output per adult of less than $1000 per year—and this sample omits many of the world's poorest countries. Others, by contrast, had an output per adult closer to $20,000.

What factors account for this enormous disparity in living standards? In Chapter 9, we study a model—the Solow-Swan model of economic growth—that tries to answer this question. The Solow-Swan model was discussed briefly in Section 1.2.3, where we mentioned that in its simplest textbook version it yields a reduced-form solution (1.14) for living standards y as a function of national saving rates s and population growth rates n,

$$y = g(s, n).$$

FIGURE 3.5

National living standards are related positively to saving rates and negatively to population growth rates.

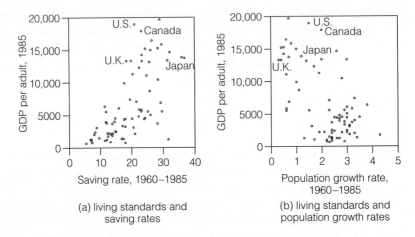

(a) living standards and saving rates

(b) living standards and population growth rates

This in turn yields the comparative statics results (1.15), suggesting that living standards y are related *positively* to saving rates s and *negatively* to population growth rates n.

Are these predictions of the Solow-Swan model borne out in the data? Figure 3.5 shows how output per adult in 1985 was related to the rates of saving and population growth during the previous 25 years. Figure 3.5(a) shows that output per adult is indeed directly related to saving rates; the sample correlation is

$$r_{ys} = 0.666.$$

Figure 3.5(b) shows that output per adult is inversely related to population growth rates; the sample correlation is

$$r_{yn} = -0.607.$$

In Chapter 9 we study these data further by estimating this reduced-form relationship.

Macroeconomics: Mobility in National Living Standards

One way of thinking about international disparities in living standards is that there is a cross-country income distribution that is analogous to the income distribution of households within a country. It is natural to ask the same questions about the cross-country income distribution that we might ask about household income distribution. In the case of the income distribution of households, one issue that has traditionally been of interest is social mobility—that is, the ability to move within the distribution. Is it the case, for example, that the rich tend to remain rich and the poor remain poor? Or is it instead the case that countries, like people, move within the distribution over time? That poor countries can, with good economic policies, gradually become rich, or that bad economic policies (or perhaps other factors) can drive a once-rich country into poverty?

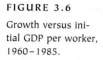

FIGURE 3.6

Growth versus ini-
tial GDP per worker,
1960–1985.

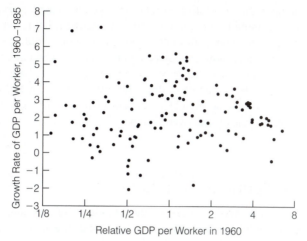

Source: Reprinted from the *Handbook of Macroeconomics*, Vol. IA, E.R. McGrattan and J.A. Schmitz, Jr.
"Explaining Cross-Country Income Differences," p. 676, ©1999, with permission from Elsevier.

At a casual level, it is easy to think of examples of both cases. Table 9.1 provides a comparison of output per adult in 1960 and 1985. Some countries (growth
miracles) had astonishingly high growth rates over this period. The best-known
examples are the Asian economies of Hong Kong, Japan, Korea, and Singapore,
all of which grew in excess of 5% per year. This enabled these economies to
move from being poor to rich during this period. A few countries (growth dis-
asters) had negative growth rates; they were actually worse off in 1985 than 25
years before.

It is, of course, just as easy to think of countries whose position in the income
distribution changes little over time: rich countries that stay rich and poor countries
that stay poor. Not all nations that start out poor necessarily grow quickly and end
up relatively better off.

Figure 3.6 is a simple way of illustrating this pattern of social mobility among
nations. It is reproduced from McGrattan and Schmitz (1999), although similar
scatter plots have been presented by many authors. It plots the growth rate of
living standards, measured by GDP per worker, over the 1960–1985 period against
relative GDP per worker in 1960 for 125 countries. (A relative GDP per worker
of 1 means that the country had an average level of living standards.) The scatter
plot is a cloud of points, with no obvious association between the two variables.
This was confirmed by McGrattan and Schmitz, who found the correlation to be
essentially zero:

$$r = 0.01.$$

This absence of correlation is of great interest. It means that how quickly a
country grows has nothing to do with whether it starts off rich or poor. It is not,
for example, the case that "the rich get richer and the poor get poorer," which

would imply a larger positive correlation. The absence of correlation suggests that there is some mobility in national living standards; it holds out the hope that good economic policies may contribute to helping a country out of poverty.

Just what these policies may be and how best to implement them is, of course, a difficult question, one that is of central interest to development economists. The absence of correlation indicates that mobility within the world income distribution is modest; it would be greater if the correlation were negative. Although some countries grow quickly and overcome poverty, others grow slowly and remain poor.

3.1.3 Spurious Correlation

These examples serve to illustrate the usefulness of the sample correlation. Nevertheless correlations can sometimes be misleading in what they suggest about the relationship between variables. The most important reason for this is that the correlation coefficient r_{XY} does not control for other influences. This means that a problem sometimes exists in interpreting correlations; a correlation can fail to reveal a relationship between variables or may suggest a relationship in a way that is misleading. Let us say more about both possibilities.

Causality does not imply correlation. A correlation can fail to indicate a relationship between variables when in fact one does exist. We have already noted one way in which this can happen: Since the correlation measures only the strength of the linear relationship between variables, variables can be related nonlinearly in a way that is not revealed by their correlation. The failure to control for other influences can be a second source of this problem. A formal investigation of this must await our development of regression; we return to it in Section 8.9.1.

Correlation does not imply causality. Conversely, the correlation can appear to indicate a relationship between variables that does not in fact exist. This is said to be a **spurious** or **nonsense correlation.** Again, the reason this can happen has to do with the role of other influences.

The second case can be illustrated as follows. We know that if two variables are exactly linearly related then their correlation is $|r| = 1$. Suppose that our interest is in two variables X and Y, but that each is an exact linear function of a third variable Z:

$$Y_i = \alpha + \beta Z_i$$
$$X_i = \gamma + \delta Z_i.$$

Then X and Y are themselves linearly related by

$$Y_i = \alpha + \beta \frac{X_i - \gamma}{\delta} = \alpha - \beta \frac{\gamma}{\delta} + \frac{\beta}{\delta} X_i$$

and so have a correlation of 1.

More realistically, suppose the relationships between X, Y, and Z are stochastic:

$$Y_i = \alpha + \beta Z_i + \varepsilon_{1i} \tag{3.5a}$$
$$X_i = \gamma + \delta Z_i + \varepsilon_{2i}. \tag{3.5b}$$

Here ε_{1i} and ε_{2i} are i.i.d. disturbances. Although both X and Y are determined by the common influence Z they are otherwise unrelated, in the sense that ε_{1i} and ε_{2i} are assumed to be independent of one another. Nevertheless it is apparent that the sample correlation between X and Y may be quite large owing to the common influence of Z. The true relationships, however, are between Y and Z and between X and Z. In this sense the large correlation between X and Y is spurious; instead of reflecting a true direct relationship between X and Y it merely reflects the role of the common influence Z. It is instructive to consider an example of this situation.

Do the Poor Have More Children?

We occasionally encounter the popular prejudice that the poor have a greater proclivity to reproduce. Is there any statistical evidence that the poor have larger families?

As background to this question, it is useful to recall what at first may seem an unrelated matter—the life cycle of the typical family. Families have their first child when the parents are young, the second child when the parents are somewhat older, and so on. Hence, family size grows with age, peaking in middle age when the children begin to leave home. Family income follows a similar pattern. Young adults are in the process of acquiring education, skills, and experience. They earn relatively low incomes, but those incomes increase steadily throughout their working lives as those investments pay off.

In a study of Canadian family data, Sarlo (1998, p. 24) pointed out the following implication of this family life cycle.

> Overall, there is a positive relationship between family size and income. The higher the level of reported income, the more people in the family. However there is no causal connection between income and family size. No one would suggest, for example, that you can increase your income by having more children or that higher incomes promote fecundity. The fact is that age is the key "third" variable that is strongly correlated to both income and family size ...

Consequently the correlation between family size and income is the opposite of what popular prejudice might suggest and, in any case, cannot be interpreted as reflecting the childbearing propensities of the poor versus the nonpoor.

To draw any inference about these childbearing propensities, it is essential to control for this third variable. Sarlo did this by comparing the number of children of poor and nonpoor families across different age categories. His data are summarized in Table 3.2.

TABLE 3.2   Number of Children by Age of Household Head and Poverty Status

Age of head of household	Poor	Nonpoor
20–24	1.25	1.15
25–29	1.51	1.55
30–34	1.74	1.90
35–39	1.71	2.01

Source: Sarlo, C., "Do the Poor Have More Children?" *Fraser Forum*, February 1998. Used with permission.

Notice that, focusing on either poor or nonpoor families, the life-cycle pattern of family size is as we have described: Older families tend to be larger, at least until middle age.

Controlling for age, poor families in which the age of the household head is in the range 20–24 years have an average of 1.25 children, slightly more than the 1.15 children of nonpoor families in the same category. However, for the other age categories the poor actually have slightly fewer children than the nonpoor.

The conclusion is that family income and childbearing decisions appear to be unrelated. The positive correlation between income and family size is a spurious correlation. To be more precise, it is not so much the correlation itself that is spurious. A positive correlation correctly indicates that higher-income families also tend to be larger families.[5] What is spurious is the inference that this reflects a causal relationship, that higher incomes *lead* people to have more children. Instead, the positive correlation just reflects the fact that higher-income families also tend to be in their peak earning years, when the largest number of children are living at home.

Solving the Spurious Correlation Problem

The sample correlation r_{XY} estimates the population correlation ρ_{XY}. Irrespective of issues of spurious correlation, ρ_{XY} continues to be defined as in (3.2),

$$\rho_{XY} = \frac{\sigma_{XY}}{\sigma_X \sigma_Y},$$

where σ_X, σ_Y, and σ_{XY} are defined by the usual mathematical expectations, the last as in (3.1). The problem of spurious correlation is that these sample and population correlations fail to represent the true effects of interest. The true effects are ones that control for other influences, just as Sarlo controlled for age in his analysis. The solution to the spurious correlation problem is to specify a model in terms of alternative parameters that represent the ceterus paribus effects.

---

[5]   There is, of course, the issue of whether a nonzero correlation is statistically significant or just reflects sampling error. Hypothesis testing for correlations is a topic we have not treated.

There are a couple of approaches to doing this. One is to define alternative population correlations—called **partial correlation coefficients**—and analogous sample correlations that control for other variables. The problem with this approach is that it does not address the other deficiency of correlations, that studying the interaction of even a modest number of variables involves examining an unmanageably large number of correlations.

A more useful way of controlling for other influences is to use multiple regression, which is introduced in Chapter 8. The regression approach accomplishes two things. First, as we see when we study multiple regression, the regression model is in terms of parameters that represent ceteris paribus effects. As long as the model is correctly specified, the role of other influences is controlled for. Second, the regression model involves fewer parameters than would be the case were correlations used. The relationship to the correlation approach is examined in Section 3.2. First, however, it is useful to consider the problem of spurious correlation in the context of time series variables.

Common Trends

In recent decades, econometricians have come to appreciate that one of the most important situations in which a spurious correlation arises is when two variables are observed over time and the third influence is time itself. Suppose two variables follow deterministic trend models such as equation (2.32) of the previous chapter:

$$Y_t = \alpha + \beta t + \varepsilon_{1t} \tag{3.6a}$$
$$X_t = \gamma + \delta t + \varepsilon_{2t}. \tag{3.6b}$$

Each consists of random variation around a trend, like the series depicted in Figure 2.15(a). This is just our model (3.5) of spurious correlation, with Z replaced by t. As we see later in Chapter 6, many time series variables grow in a way that is well approximated by a deterministic trend. This common influence of time means that these variables are often highly correlated, despite the fact that they are otherwise unrelated.

Although a full appreciation of this problem is recent, the recognition of its existence is not. The first to study it systematically was George Yule (1871–1951) in a famous 1926 paper entitled "Why Do We Sometimes Get Nonsense-Correlations between Time Series?" As an example, Yule considered data on the mortality rate in England and Wales between 1866 and 1911, and the proportion of Church of England marriages relative to all marriages for the same years. Both series tend to decline over this period. Yule found a sample correlation of $r_{XY} = 0.95$ between them.

> Now I suppose it is possible, given a little ingenuity and goodwill, to rationalize very nearly anything. And I can imagine some enthusiast arguing that the fall in the proportion of Church of England marriages is simply due to the Spread of Scientific Thinking since 1866, and the fall in mortality is also clearly to be ascribed to the

FIGURE 3.7

Population in
Canada, the United
Kingdom, and
the United States,
1950–1992.

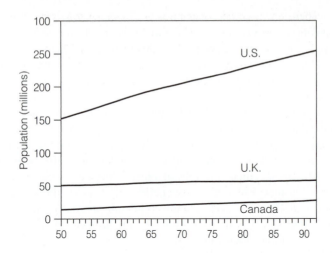

Progress of Science; hence both variables are largely or mainly influenced by a common factor and consequently ought to be highly correlated. But most people would,
I think, agree with me that the correlation is simply sheer nonsense; that it has no
meaning whatsoever; that it is absurd to suppose that the two variables in question
are in any sort of way, however indirect, causally related to one another. (Yule,
1926, p. 2)

Population Growth across Countries

Let us make the same point with another example. Table 3.3 presents data on the
populations of Canada, the United Kingdom, and the United States for the years
1950–1992. These data are from the Penn World Tables.[6] The plot of these series
in Figure 3.7 indicates that all three are well approximated by linear trends such
as equations (3.6).

Figure 3.8 presents pairwise scatter plots of these variables. They indicate a
strong positive association among the three variables: When population is high in
one country, it is also high in the other two. This positive association is captured
by the correlation coefficients, which are as follows.

Countries	Correlation r
Canada–United Kingdom	0.977
Canada–United States	0.998
United Kingdom–United States	0.966

Now suppose you are asked by a friend who has no knowledge of economics
or statistics to help her understand why the population in the United States evolves

---

[6]   Alan Heston, Robert Summers and Bettina Aten, Penn World Table Version 6.1, Center for International Comparisons at the University of Pennsylvania (CICUP), October 2002.

TABLE 3.3

Population in Canada, the United Kingdom, and the United States (thousand)

Year	Canada	U.K.	U.S.
1950	13,737	50,614	152,273
1951	14,138	50,730	155,000
1952	14,537	50,847	157,727
1953	14,937	50,964	160,475
1954	15,336	51,080	163,202
1955	15,735	51,197	165,929
1956	16,170	51,469	168,882
1957	16,605	51,741	171,835
1958	17,040	52,013	174,767
1959	17,475	52,285	177,720
1960	17,910	52,557	180,673
1961	18,270	52,951	183,687
1962	18,614	53,412	186,537
1963	18,963	53,690	189,244
1964	19,326	54,034	191,889
1965	19,678	54,378	194,309
1966	20,049	54,650	196,564
1967	20,411	54,933	198,717
1968	20,744	55,156	200,706
1969	21,028	55,372	202,675
1970	21,324	55,632	205,052
1971	21,592	55,928	207,661
1972	21,822	56,097	209,896
1973	22,072	56,223	211,909
1974	22,364	56,236	213,854
1975	22,697	56,226	215,973
1976	22,993	56,216	218,035
1977	23,273	56,190	220,239
1978	23,517	56,178	222,585
1979	23,747	56,242	225,055
1980	24,043	56,330	227,757
1981	24,342	56,352	230,138
1982	24,583	56,306	232,520
1983	24,787	56,347	234,799
1984	24,978	56,460	237,001
1985	25,165	56,618	239,279
1986	25,353	56,763	241,625
1987	25,625	56,930	243,942
1988	25,950	57,065	246,307
1989	26,219	57,236	248,231
1990	26,522	57,411	250,372
1991	27,300	57,564	252,688
1992	27,445	57,848	255,000

Source: Penn World Tables in Heston, Summers, and Aten (2002).

FIGURE 3.8

Population in
Canada, the U.K.,
and the U.S.,
1950–1992.

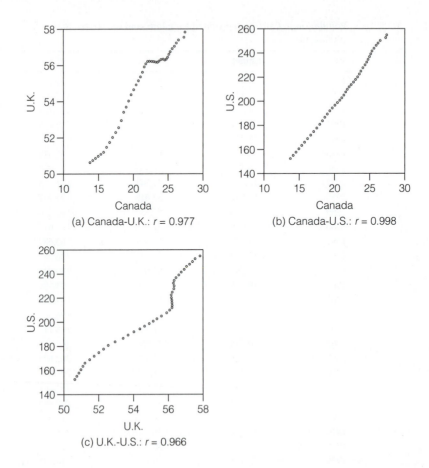

(a) Canada-U.K.: $r = 0.977$

(b) Canada-U.S.: $r = 0.998$

(c) U.K.-U.S.: $r = 0.966$

over time in the way it does. You could explain that population is determined by rates of fertility and mortality and by in- and out-migration. These are, in turn, affected by other factors, economic and otherwise: fertility by household childbearing decisions, which are in turn related to decisions about female labor force participation, mortality by the quality of health care, and so on. Your friend would likely find this explanation quite helpful and illuminating.

Suppose instead that you offer your friend the following explanation of the U.S. population. After explaining the concept of statistical correlation, you point out the high correlations between the population of the United States and those of Canada and the United Kingdom. You then assert that these high correlations indicate that the population of the United States is determined by the populations of Canada and the United Kingdom and can only be understood by understanding the populations of these other countries. Your friend would no doubt thank you politely for your advice, but would be unlikely to seek your opinion in the future on matters of substance. Instead, she would turn away in dismay, certain that the fields of economics and statistics must be of no practical value. Her common sense would tell her that it is preposterous to suggest that the U.S. population is determined by the populations of other countries, that if, for example, population growth were to cease in Canada, it would also cease in the United States.

The reason your second explanation is wrong is that the high correlations are spurious. To put it more precisely, the correlations are real enough: There is indeed a positive association between these variables. What is spurious is the inference that these high correlations reflect causal dependencies between the variables.

Because economic time series so often follow trends, distinguishing genuine relationships from spurious ones is a fundamental problem in the analysis of time series data, and it is only in recent decades that this problem has been solved by econometricians. The techniques that permit this form the culmination of our treatment of time series methods in Chapters 15–18.

EXERCISES

3.3 A newspaper item entitled "TV Dooms Kids to Gloom" (*Hartford Courant*) reported the results of university research into depression.

> Comparing the growth of television and depression, "our conclusion is that the rise of television corresponds with the rise in major depression almost exactly, ..."

> [The researcher] compared the rates of major depression in people up to age 24 with 10-year averages of the number of televisions in use, the number of households with televisions and the number of families with more than one TV set. "As things turn out, they're exactly the same curve," he says. "As television grows, so does the rate of major depression."

Explain in your own words why this should not necessarily be interpreted as evidence that television causes depression.

3.2   Regression

Estimation is, as Chapter 2 emphasizes, just one aspect of statistical inference, and we could at this point consider procedures for computing confidence intervals and doing hypothesis testing with respect to σ_{XY} and ρ_{XY}. But precisely because the questions with which economists are typically concerned involve the interaction of many variables, the study of covariances and correlations is not the most useful way to proceed. We therefore turn instead to a different framework.

This simpler framework (simpler because it involves fewer parameters) is based on the observation that, in economics as well as in other disciplines, theories about the interaction of variables are often phrased in terms of causal links between the variables. For example, in the case of data on household income X and consumption expenditure Y, it is natural to phrase hypotheses about household consumption behavior in terms of consumption expenditure being determined by income. We do not, after all, think of income as being determined by expenditure. One, although not the only, reason for thinking in these terms is that the ultimate objective of empirical analysis is often to obtain an estimated model that allows us to predict or forecast one variable conditional on (that is, on the basis of hypothetical values for) others.

3.2.1   The Conditional Normal Distribution

Therefore, instead of working in terms of the joint probability distribution of the variables, it is more natural to think in terms of the conditional distribution of one given the others. In general the conditional distribution depends on exactly the same parameters as the joint distribution. For example, in the case of the bivariate normal, the conditional distribution of Y given X is itself normal with a mean and variance that depend on the five parameters of the bivariate distribution:

$$f(y|x) = N(\underbrace{\mu_Y - \mu_X \rho_{XY} \frac{\sigma_Y}{\sigma_X}}_{\alpha} + \underbrace{\rho_{XY} \frac{\sigma_Y}{\sigma_X}}_{\beta} x, \; \underbrace{\sigma_Y^2(1 - \rho_{XY}^2)}_{\sigma^2})). \tag{3.7}$$

As the braces emphasize, this mean and variance are of a form that bears closer scrutiny. We have defined the new parameters

$$\alpha = \mu_Y - \mu_X \rho_{XY} \frac{\sigma_Y}{\sigma_X}, \tag{3.8a}$$

$$\beta = \rho_{XY} \frac{\sigma_Y}{\sigma_X}, \tag{3.8b}$$

$$\sigma^2 = \sigma_Y^2(1 - \rho_{XY}^2). \tag{3.8c}$$

Most notably, the mean is linear in X. The conditional distribution of Y given X may be expressed as

$$Y \sim N(\alpha + \beta X, \sigma^2).$$

You will recall that this is one way of expressing the linear regression model introduced in Section 2.7. Alternatively, the statistical model governing data generated by random sampling from this population may be expressed in terms of a disturbance:

$$Y_i = \alpha + \beta X_i + \varepsilon_i, \qquad \varepsilon_i \sim \text{n.i.d.}(0, \sigma^2). \tag{3.9}$$

This shows that the bivariate normal distribution (B.19) in Appendix B and the regression model (3.9) with a normal disturbance are essentially the same model. The difference is simply in how the parameters are defined. Working in terms of the conditional distribution in which one variable is regarded as being determined by the other permits us to make use of the relabeling of parameters given by (3.8). Such a relabeling is called **reparameterizing** the model, which means nothing more than redefining parameters in a way that happens to be more convenient for the task at hand.

The Curse of Dimensionality

Why is this reparameterization useful? Because it reduces the number of parameters to be studied. In the simple (i.e., two-variable) regression model, this reduction is modest—from the five-parameter bivariate normal to the three-parameter regression model. But, as the number of variables increases, the use of the regression model, rather than working directly with the joint distribution, results in a more and more significant economy in the number of parameters to be studied.

EXAMPLE 2

Consider five random variables X_1, X_2, X_3, X_4, and X_5 that are jointly distributed according to a multivariate normal. If X_1 is regarded as being determined by the others and in consequence is relabeled Y, then the conditional distribution of Y given X_2, X_3, X_4, and X_5 gives rise to a multiple regression model:

$$Y_i = \beta_1 + \beta_2 X_{i2} + \beta_3 X_{i3} + \beta_4 X_{i4} + \beta_5 X_{i5} + \varepsilon_i, \quad \varepsilon_i \sim \text{n.i.d.}(0, \sigma^2). \quad (3.10)$$

What reduction in the number of parameters occurs as a result of this reparameterization?

SOLUTION

In Exercise 3.2 you found that 20 parameters characterize a multivariate normal relating five variables. The model (3.10), on the other hand, has only six parameters. Thus, the reparameterization results in a reduction of 14 parameters.

The tendency for the number of parameters needed to study relationships between variables to increase faster than the number of variables is called the **curse of dimensionality.** This is a generic problem in statistics and econometrics, affecting diverse areas of study. For example, in studying the interrelated demand for several goods—Chapter 11 touches on both factors of production and consumer goods—the curse of dimensionality limits the number of goods that can be considered. In studying the joint determination of asset prices, the number of correlations increases faster than the number of assets—a problem tackled by the capital asset pricing model in Appendix C. In studying the joint evolution of variables over time—introduced in Chapter 18—the curse of dimensionality limits the number of time series that can be considered. In the present context in which we are thinking primarily of cross-sectional data, the regression model offers a solution to the curse of dimensionality.

Normality and Linearity

The fact that the conditional distribution (3.7) has a mean that is linear in X is another remarkable feature of the normal distribution because, as is now evident, it leads to regression models such as (3.9) and (3.10), in which the variables are related linearly. This is extremely useful because, of course, linear relationships are easy to work with mathematically and, as the discussion of Chapter 2 indicates, they tend to lead to estimators linear in the data and thus to the availability of exact test procedures.

In turn, this means that our use of linear statistical models rests on more than convenience because it is known that the normal distribution is by far the most common distribution to arise in the study of natural and social phenomena. Furthermore, Section 2.5.3 suggests why this is the case. Recall that, in essence, a central limit theorem expresses the notion that an aggregation of a large number of random influences is normally distributed, even when the individual influences are not. Both natural phenomena and human behavior reflect, to a very great extent, the influence of many random factors; consequently, it is not really surprising to find that data from both the physical world and the world of human social interaction are often normally (or, in the case of multiplicative interactions, lognormally) distributed. Because, presumably for these reasons, so many variables are in practice normally distributed, it is reasonable to expect that linear models will be adequate for the analysis of many applied problems.

Having said this, it is nevertheless the case that some problems do involve fundamentally nonlinear functional relationships between variables. Chapter 13 develops the relevant inferential procedures. Because least squares estimators for nonlinear models are nonlinear in the data, we find that asymptotic testing principles apply.

For the moment, however, linear regression models of the form (3.9) and (3.10) are the focus of our interest. Although multivariate normality implies a linear relationship between variables in which the disturbance is normally distributed, it is possible to have linearly related variables without the disturbance necessarily being normal. In our treatment of the regression model, we are careful to indicate the role that normality of the disturbance plays in the analysis.

EXERCISES

3.4 If X and Y are bivariate normal, their marginal distributions are univariate normal: $X \sim N(\mu_X, \sigma_X^2)$ and $Y \sim N(\mu_Y, \sigma_Y^2)$. Show that if X and Y are uncorrelated ($\rho = 0$), the conditional distribution of Y given X, given by equation (3.7), reduces to the marginal distribution of Y.

3.5 In Exercise 3.2 you obtained a formula for the number of covariances as a function of the number of variables K being studied. For $K = 2$ through $K = 10$, graph (a) the total number of parameters (means, variances, and covariances) of the multivariate normal distribution and (b) the number of parameters of the regression model. (c) Compare the two.

3.2.2 Spurious Regression

The problem of spurious correlation is one in which the failure to treat omitted influences leads to a spurious finding of a relationship between variables. This can happen in regression analysis just as it can in correlation analysis. And again, one of the most common sources of spurious relationships is when time series variables follow trends.

To make this point, Hendry (1980) presented a regression equation "explaining" the U.K. price level for the period 1964–1975 as a function of a variable C:

> ... the fit is spectacular, the parameters are "highly significant", ... but, alas, the whole exercise is futile as well as deceitful since C is simply *cumulative rainfall* in the U.K. It is meaningless to talk about "confirming" theories when spurious results are so easily obtained. (Hendry, 1980, pp. 394–395)

In a regression context the existence of nonsense correlations between time series variables is called **spurious regression,** a term coined by Granger and Newbold (1974). Thus far we have spoken of such nonsense correlations in terms of deterministic trend models such as

$$Y_t = \alpha + \beta t + \varepsilon_t. \tag{3.11}$$

Granger and Newbold provide the seminal demonstration that the phenomenon is not limited to variables that fluctuate around deterministic trends but can arise with stochastic trends as well. Recall that we gave as an example of a stochastic trend the random walk model (2.33),

$$Y_t = \beta + Y_{t-1} + \varepsilon_t. \tag{3.12}$$

The meandering evolution of such a variable is depicted in Figure 2.15(b), based on a drift parameter of $\beta = 0.04879$. A positive value for β means that the variable tends to drift upward over time.

As we remark in our examination of Figure 2.15, the drift parameter imparts a trend to the variable that bears some analogy to the role of the slope parameter in imparting a deterministic trend. Consequently, it is to be expected that stochastically trending variables with drift may exhibit spurious correlation, just as variables with underlying deterministic trends may. For example, if the stock prices of IBM and General Motors both follow upward-drifting random walks they may well exhibit some positive correlation, even if the fortunes of the two firms are completely unrelated.

What is more surprising is that, as Granger and Newbold show, stochastically trending variables can exhibit spurious correlation even when their drifts are zero. Setting $\beta = 0$ in (3.12), a random walk without drift is

$$Y_t = Y_{t-1} + \varepsilon_t.$$

As the example of such a series in Figure 2.15(c) illustrated, zero-drift random walks often trend ex post as they wander away from their starting points. These ex post trends, although not arising from any predictable drift, can nevertheless generate spurious correlations.

Granger and Newbold demonstrate how easily this can happen. They performed a Monte Carlo study in which two variables X_t and Y_t were generated as independent nondrifting random walks. They were independent in the sense that the disturbances were simulated as statistically independent sequences of random numbers, and so the two series were unrelated. The sample correlation r_{XY} was computed. The experiment was repeated for 100 replications. The average value of r_{XY} was 0.52 and in five cases exceeded 0.84! Furthermore a t test of the hypothesis of no relationship between the series ($H_0{:}\rho = 0$) using a 5% significance level led to a *rejection* of this restriction in 76 of the 100 replications; in the terminology of the previous chapter, a test procedure having a nominal size of 5% had an empirical size of 76%! This is an example of the size distortions mentioned in Section 2.5; a researcher naively applying a mechanical t test in this context might think there was only a 5% chance of mistakenly finding a significant relationship, when in fact there was a 76% chance of incorrectly rejecting $\rho = 0$. The conclusion of the Granger-Newbold analysis is that even nondrifting stochastic trends can give rise to apparent relationships between variables when in fact none exists.

The appropriate way of dealing with this is to specify a statistical model that describes the stochastic trend in the data explicitly. This is our approach in Chapters 15–18, in which methods for analyzing time series data are studied. For the moment, our study of the regression model in Chapters 4–14 assumes that the data are generated by random sampling, and thus do not possess trends—deterministic or stochastic.

3.3   Deviation-Form Notation

Thus far we have found it useful to adopt the convention in probability of using uppercase symbols (e.g., Y) to indicate a random variable and lowercase symbols (e.g., y) to indicate a particular realization of that random variable. Although useful for the purposes of Chapters 2 and 3 and Appendix B, it now becomes valuable to adopt an entirely different notational convention. We shall no longer distinguish between random variables and their realizations. Instead, in statistical expressions we use lowercase symbols to indicate a deviation from the sample mean:

$$y_i \equiv Y_i - \overline{Y}. \tag{3.13}$$

This is valuable because a great many formulas may be expressed most economically using this notation. For example, the sample variance (2.7), covariance (3.3), and correlation (3.4) may now be written

$$s_Y^2 = \frac{\sum y_i^2}{n-1}, \tag{3.14a}$$

$$s_{XY} = \frac{\sum x_i y_i}{n-1}, \tag{3.14b}$$

$$r_{XY} = \frac{\sum x_i y_i}{\sqrt{\sum x_i^2 \sum y_i^2}}. \tag{3.14c}$$

Appendix A presents two laws that are used in the manipulation of algebraic expressions involving deviation form. We make extensive use of these laws, and of deviation form generally, in our study of the regression model.

3.4   Conclusions

In contrast to some other sciences, econometric analysis is typically based on nonexperimental data. Nonexperimental data, because they are generated in the real world instead of a laboratory, are subject to many influences.

A correlation measures the strength of the linear relationship between two variables. Regression provides an alternative means of investigating relationships between variables, one that both controls for the role of other influences and uses fewer parameters than the correlation approach.

In the use of either correlation or regression, the failure to treat omitted influences can result in the spurious finding of a relationship between variables. This is just another manifestation of the conclusion of the last chapter: The legitimacy of inferential methods is conditional on the specification of the statistical model. Just as this was true for a variable studied in isolation, so too is it true for relationships between variables.

When the role of other influences is minor, the correlation ρ is a useful parameter to estimate, and so the sample correlation r has important interpretive value. When, on the other hand, the population relationship is a more complicated one involving interrelationships among several variables or a dependence on time, ρ may not be a parameter of an appropriately specified model—any more than μ is a parameter of the regression model. Consequently, the sample correlation r may not be a useful statistic to compute—any more than $\overline{Y}$ is a useful statistic to compute in connection with a regression model.

For data obtained by random sampling the key tool in controlling for other influences is multiple regression, the subject of Chapters 8–14. Simple regression, in which we study the bivariate relationship between a dependent variable and a single explanatory variable, is an important first step in understanding multiple regression, and so the chapters immediately ahead focus on this special case. For time series data, the key to addressing the problem of spurious regressions is to specify models that treat deterministic and stochastic trends. This is the subject of Chapters 15–18.

In using regression to study relationships between variables, we are not abandoning the population distribution framework that we introduced in Chapter 2. Quite the contrary, a population distribution continues to lie under the surface of regression analysis. In estimating a regression model, we are indirectly estimating the parameters of a joint normal distribution—or at least a certain transformation of those parameters that overcomes the curse of dimensionality. Consequently, the methodology of statistical inference as we developed it in Chapter 2 continues to apply. In particular, the sampling distributions of estimators and test statistics continue to be the focus of interest.

EXERCISES

3.6 The following data on output X and production costs Y were collected for five electric power companies in 1955.[7]

	Production costs (thousands of dollars)	Output (billions of kWh)
Bangor Hydro-electric Co.	501	43
Tucson Gas, Electric, Light and Power Co.	2382	338
Montana Electric Co.	7185	1109
Florida Power Corp.	16674	2226
Alabama Power Co.	22828	5819

(a) Drawing on your background knowledge of economics (or just common sense), do you expect costs and output to be directly or inversely related? Translate your hypothesis into a restriction on a population parameter. Does a cursory examination of the data seem to confirm your hypothesis?

(b) Compute the sample covariance and correlation by proceeding as follows.

i. Compute the exact values of the following quantities (do not round):

$$\sum_{i=1}^{n} X_i, \quad \sum_{i=1}^{n} Y_i, \quad \sum_{i=1}^{n} X_i^2, \quad \sum_{i=1}^{n} Y_i^2, \quad \sum_{i=1}^{n} X_i Y_i.$$

ii. Use these and the results of Appendix A, Exercises A.6 and A.7 to compute

$$\sum_{i=1}^{n} x_i^2, \quad \sum_{i=1}^{n} y_i^2, \quad \sum_{i=1}^{n} x_i y_i.$$

iii. Now use these quantities to compute s_{XY} and r_{XY}.

(c) How will the sample covariance and correlation change if costs are measured in millions rather than thousands of dollars? (*Hint:* The easiest way to answer this is to do Exercise 3.7.)

Appendix   Laws of Sample Means and Variances

In this chapter and the previous one, we have seen that populations are characterized by the parameters of their distributions, parameters such as the means $\mu_X \equiv E(X)$ and $\mu_Y \equiv E(Y)$, the variances $\sigma_X^2 \equiv V(X)$ and $\sigma_Y^2 \equiv V(Y)$, and the covariance $\sigma_{XY} \equiv E[(X-\mu_X)(Y-\mu_Y)]$ or correlation $\rho_{XY} \equiv \sigma_{XY}/\sigma_X\sigma_Y$. In the general case of K variables $X_1, X_2, \ldots, X_K$, the number of such parameters expands accordingly, with means $\mu_1, \mu_2, \ldots, \mu_K$, variances σ_k^2 $(k = 1, \ldots, K)$, and covariances σ_{jk} (or, equivalently, correlations ρ_{jk}). The variances and covariances may be listed in a triangle:

$$\begin{matrix} \sigma_1^2 & \sigma_{12} & \sigma_{13} & \cdots & \sigma_{1K} \\ & \sigma_2^2 & \sigma_{23} & \cdots & \sigma_{2K} \\ & & \sigma_3^2 & \cdots & \sigma_{3K} \\ & & & \ddots & \vdots \\ & & & & \sigma_K^2 \end{matrix}$$

There is no need to list the lower triangle, below the diagonal, because by the symmetry property of covariances $\sigma_{jk} = \sigma_{kj}$.

[7] You will encounter these firms again in Chapter 11.

Consider the simplest case of just two variables, X and Y, that are characterized by their means, variances, and covariance (or correlation). When data X_i, Y_i ($i = 1, \ldots, n$) are drawn from the population, these parameters may be estimated using the analogous statistics, the sample means $\overline{X}$ and $\overline{Y}$, the sample variances s_X^2 and s_Y^2, and the sample covariance s_{XY} or correlation r_{XY}. These population and sample quantities are summarized as follows.

	Population parameters	*Sample statistics*
Means	μ_X, μ_Y	$\overline{X}$, $\overline{Y}$
Variances	σ_X^2, σ_Y^2	s_X^2, s_Y^2
Covariance	σ_{XY}	s_{XY}
Correlation	ρ_{XY}	r_{XY}

The properties of *population* means and variances are derived in Appendix B; the resulting laws of expectation and variance are summarized in Table B.2. It turns out that *sample* means and variances have analogous properties, and these are the subject of this appendix; they are established using the laws of summation in Appendix A, and the exercises in Appendix A provide a framework for deriving them.

The Sample Mean of a Linear Function

Law 3.1   *Consider a variable Z_i that is a linear function of X_i:*

$$Z_i = a + bX_i.$$

Then

$$\overline{Z} = a + b\overline{X}.$$

In other words, the sample mean of a linear function is the linear function of the sample mean.

Proof:

See Appendix A, Exercise A.1.   □

The constants a and b may take on any numerical values. Two useful special cases are $a = 0$ and $b = 1$. First, setting $a = 0$ yields the following result.

COROLLARY 3.1.1. *If $Z_i = bX_i$, then*

$$\overline{Z} = b\overline{X}.$$

In other words, the sample mean of a multiple of a variable is the constant times the sample mean.

EXAMPLE 3

Consider a change in the units of measure of a variable X_i. As is described in more detail in Section 4.8, this involves the application of a multiplicative **scaling factor.** Denoting the rescaled variable in boldface, the change in units of measure can be represented as

$$\mathbf{X}_i = v X_i.$$

What is the effect of this rescaling on the deviation form of the variable?

SOLUTION

By Corollary 3.1.1, the sample mean is transformed by the same scaling factor:

$$\overline{\mathbf{X}} = v\overline{X}.$$

The deviation form of the rescaled variable is therefore

$$\mathbf{x}_i = \mathbf{X}_i - \overline{\mathbf{X}} = v X_i - v\overline{X} = v(X_i - \overline{X}) = v x_i.$$

Thus, the deviation form is transformed by the same scaling factor as the raw variable.

Exercise 3.7 asks you to use this result to study the effects of changes in units of measure on the covariance and correlation. We also use it in the next chapter to study the effect of units changes on regression analysis.

Turning to the other useful special case of Law 3.1, consider setting $b = 1$.

COROLLARY 3.1.2. *If $Z_i = a + X_i$, then*

$$\overline{Z} = a + \overline{X}.$$

In other words, the sample mean of a constant plus a variable is the constant plus the sample mean.

The Sample Variance of a Linear Function

Law 3.2

Consider a variable Z_i that is a linear function of X_i:

$$Z_i = a + b X_i.$$

Then

$$s_Z^2 = b^2 s_X^2.$$

In other words, in obtaining the sample variance of a linear function of a variable, additive constants are irrelevant and multiplicative constants must be squared.

Proof:

See Appendix A, Exercise A.4. □

As before, the constants a and b may take on any numerical values; two useful special cases are $a = 0$ and $b = 1$. First, setting $a = 0$ yields the following result.

COROLLARY 3.2.1. *If $Z_i = bX_i$, then*

$$s_Z^2 = b^2 s_X^2.$$

In other words, in obtaining the sample variance of a multiple of a variable, the multiplicative constant must be squared.

Second, setting $b = 1$ yields the following result.

COROLLARY 3.2.2. *If $Z_i = a + X_i$, then*

$$s_Z^2 = s_X^2.$$

In other words, additive constants are irrelevant to the sample variance of a variable.

Linear Combinations

Having considered the laws that apply to a linear function of a single variable, $Z_i = a + bX_i$, let us turn to the more general case of functions of more than one variable, say

$$Z_i = aX_i + bY_i. \tag{3.15}$$

Such a function is called a **linear combination** of variables. In its most general form, a linear combination could include an arbitrary number of variables $X_{1i}, X_{2i}, \ldots, X_{Ki}$. Using summation notation, this is expressed as

$$Z_i = a_1 X_{1i} + a_2 X_{2i} + \cdots + a_K X_{Ki} = \sum_{k=1}^{K} a_k X_{ki}. \tag{3.16}$$

In what circumstances might such a linear combination be of interest? Here is an example.

EXAMPLE 4

Suppose that you have investments in two assets, so that proportion a of your wealth is invested in asset 2 and proportion $(1 - a)$ is invested in asset 1. Such a combination of assets is called a **portfolio.** Let the rates of return on the two assets be denoted R_1 and R_2. Show that the rate of return R_P on the portfolio as a whole is a linear combination like (3.15); specifically, show that

$$R_P = (1 - a)R_1 + aR_2.$$

SOLUTION

For any asset of value A, its simple rate of return R is the relative change in its value:

$$R_t = \frac{A_t - A_{t-1}}{A_{t-1}}.$$

This is just the definition (2.24) of a simple return, given in the previous chapter.

Consider a portfolio A_P that, at any point in time t, is the total of two assets having values A_1 and A_2:

$$A_{Pt} = A_{1t} + A_{2t}.$$

Because this is true at all points in time, it holds at $t-1$:

$$A_{P,t-1} = A_{1,t-1} + A_{2,t-1}.$$

Now consider subtracting the latter from the former:

$$A_{Pt} - A_{P,t-1} = (A_{1t} - A_{1,t-1}) + (A_{2t} - A_{2,t-1}).$$

Divide by the lagged total wealth $A_{P,t-1}$:

$$\frac{A_{Pt} - A_{P,t-1}}{A_{P,t-1}} = \frac{A_{1t} - A_{1,t-1}}{A_{P,t-1}} + \frac{A_{2t} - A_{2,t-1}}{A_{P,t-1}}.$$

This can equivalently be written in terms of the respective rates of return:

$$\underbrace{\frac{A_{Pt} - A_{P,t-1}}{A_{P,t-1}}}_{R_{Pt}} = \frac{A_{1,t-1}}{A_{P,t-1}} \cdot \underbrace{\frac{A_{1t} - A_{1,t-1}}{A_{1,t-1}}}_{R_{1t}} + \frac{A_{2,t-1}}{A_{P,t-1}} \cdot \underbrace{\frac{A_{2t} - A_{2,t-1}}{A_{2,t-1}}}_{R_{2t}}.$$

The ratios $A_{1,t-1}/A_{P,t-1}$ and $A_{2,t-1}/A_{P,t-1}$ are the shares of each asset in total wealth; using the notation given, these are the portfolio weights $1-a$ and a.[8] Hence, the last equation can be written

$$R_{Pt} = (1-a)R_{1t} + aR_{2t}. \tag{3.17}$$

This establishes the desired result. The return on a portfolio is a weighted average of the returns on the individual assets, the weights being the shares of each asset in the portfolio.

This result generalizes to an arbitrary number of returns. In a portfolio comprising K assets having returns $R_{1t}, R_{2t}, \ldots, R_{Kt}$, the return on the portfolio is the linear combination of the individual returns:

$$R_{Pt} = \sum_{k=1}^{K} a_k R_{kt}. \tag{3.18}$$

---

[8]   Notice that the asset shares sum to 1:

$$\frac{A_{1t}}{A_{Pt}} + \frac{A_{2t}}{A_{Pt}} = \frac{A_{1t} + A_{2t}}{A_{Pt}} = 1.$$

This is an example of the general linear combination (3.16). The portfolio weights a_k are, again, the asset shares. Because asset shares must sum to 1, it is understood that $\sum_{k=1}^{K} a_k = 1$.

That portfolio returns are a weighted average of individual asset returns is the foundation of modern portfolio theory. Appendix C provides an introduction to this theory; it uses the laws of mathematical expectation and variance of Appendix B to study the expected return and risk of portfolios.

Our interest here is not in mathematical expectations and variances but in sample means and variances.

The Sample Mean of a Linear Combination

Law 3.3

Consider the linear combination (3.15),

$$Z_i = aX_i + bY_i.$$

Then

$$\overline{Z} = a\overline{X} + b\overline{Y}.$$

In other words, the sample mean of a linear combination is the linear combination of the sample means.

Proof:

See Appendix A, Exercise A.2.   □

One useful application of this result is to portfolio returns.

EXAMPLE 5

fama.dat

Consider the IBM and Xerox returns in Chapter 2. The averages of the monthly simple returns over the period were $\overline{R}_1 = 0.0212$ for IBM and $\overline{R}_2 = 0.0400$ for Xerox.[9] Suppose that during this period you had invested 40% of your wealth in IBM and 60% in Xerox. What would you have obtained as an average monthly return on your portfolio?

SOLUTION

Applying Law 3.3 to the linear combination (3.17),

$$\overline{R}_{\mathrm{P}} = (1 - a)\overline{R}_1 + a\overline{R}_2 = 0.4 \times 0.0212 + 0.6 \times 0.0400 = 0.0325.$$

The average monthly return on the portfolio would have been 3.25%. You are asked to verify this in Exercise 3.11.

Consider the general linear combination (3.16). The generalization of Law 3.3 is

$$\overline{Z}_i = \sum_{k=1}^{K} a_k \overline{X}_k.$$

This may be applied to portfolios of more than two assets.

[9]   These average returns are calculated in Exercises 2.25 and 2.26.

EXAMPLE 6

fama.dat

Returning to Fama's data, the average return on treasury bills during this period was $\overline{R}_3 = 0.0034$. Suppose you had divided your wealth between IBM, Xerox, and treasury bills in a 20/30/50 split. What would the average return on your portfolio have been?

SOLUTION

Applying Law 3.3 to the portfolio return (3.18),

$$\overline{R}_P = \sum_{k=1}^{K} a_k \overline{R}_k.$$

In the special case of the $K = 3$ assets IBM, Xerox, and treasury bills,

$$\overline{R}_P = a_1 \overline{R}_1 + a_2 \overline{R}_2 + a_3 \overline{R}_3$$
$$= 0.2 \times 0.0212 + 0.3 \times 0.0400 + 0.5 \times 0.0034 = 0.0179.$$

This portfolio would have yielded an average monthly return of 1.79%.

Law 3.3 holds for any values of the constants a and b. An important special case is when $a = b = 1$, so the linear combination is just a sum of variables.

COROLLARY 3.3.1. *Consider a variable Z_i that is a sum of other variables:*

$$Z_i = X_i + Y_i.$$

Then

$$\overline{Z} = \overline{X} + \overline{Y}.$$

In other words, the sample mean of a sum is the sum of the sample means.

The Sample Variance of a Linear Combination

Just as we have considered the sample mean of a linear combination, we can also consider its sample variance.

Law 3.4

Consider the linear combination (3.15),

$$Z_i = aX_i + bY_i.$$

Its sample variance is related to the individual variances of X_i and Y_i by

$$s_Z^2 = a^2 s_X^2 + b^2 s_Y^2 + 2ab s_{XY}.$$

Proof:

See Appendix A, Exercise A.5

Consider the variance of a portfolio return.

THEORY MEETS APPLICATION 3.1

Decomposing the Variability of Changes in GNP

When GNP fluctuates over the business cycle, how does this variability break down among its various components?

Total production in an economy is used for a number of purposes: consumption, investment, government expenditure, and net exports (exports less imports). A standard national income accounting identity expresses this as

$$Y = C + I + G + XM.$$

Each of these broad categories of expenditure may in turn be broken down in various ways. For example, investment I is the total of residential construction (because the housing stock is one component of society's capital stock), business fixed investment (investment in plant and equipment), and inventory investment (because inventory holdings count as part of the capital stock). Consider expanding the accounting identity to separate out inventory investment I_i from remaining fixed (residential and business) investment I_f:

$$Y = C + I_i + I_f + G + XM.$$

What is the relative importance of these components over the business cycle?

In absolute magnitude, inventory investment I_i is a tiny component of GNP, typically less than 1%. By contrast, consumption accounts for approximately two-thirds of GNP. Nevertheless, as was first carefully documented by Abramovitz (1950), its variability over the business cycle is greatly out of proportion to its size. Abramovitz showed that in periods of economic boom firms build up

their inventories, so that production exceeds sales, whereas in periods of recession firms let their inventories run down, so that sales exceed production. To put it slightly differently, the boom in production is associated with firms' willingness to accumulate inventories, the recession with their desire to liquidate them. Thus inventory investment is **procyclical,** amplifying fluctuations in production relative to sales. To a large extent, then, business cycles are inventory cycles, and understanding the business cycle hinges on understanding firms' inventory investment behavior.

The relative variability of inventory investment was illustrated by Blinder (1981), who studied the changes in the components of GNP:

$$\Delta Y = \Delta C + \Delta I_i + \Delta I_f + \Delta G + \Delta XM.$$

Blinder applied the variance of a linear combination formula (3.20) to this, decomposing the variance in GNP changes as follows:

$$\text{var}(\Delta Y) = \text{var}(\Delta C) + \text{var}(\Delta I_i) + \text{var}(\Delta I_f)$$
$$+ \text{var}(\Delta G) + \text{var}(\Delta XM) + \text{covariance terms.}$$

His decomposition is given in Table 3.4. The variances are given in bold down the diagonal of the table; covariances are given above the diagonal, correlations below. Notice that changes in inventory investment account for almost one-third of the total variability of changes in GNP—more than any single component. Notice as well that changes in inventory investment and GNP are positively correlated, illustrating Abramovitz's point that inventory investment is procyclical.

EXAMPLE 7

fama.dat

The returns on IBM and Xerox have sample variances $s_1^2 = 0.002246$ and $s_2^2 = 0.010621$; the sample covariance turns out to be $s_{12} = 0.002612$. Consider a 40/60 portfolio of IBM and Xerox. What is the sample variance of this portfolio?

SOLUTION

Applying Law 3.4 to the portfolio return (3.17) yields

$$s_P^2 = (1-a)^2 s_1^2 + a^2 s_2^2 + 2(1-a)a s_{12}$$
$$= 0.4^2 \times 0.002246 + 0.6^2 \times 0.010621 + 2(0.4)(0.6)0.002612 = 0.00544.$$

A sample variance such as this is of interest because it serves as a measure of the risk of the portfolio.

In the case of the general linear combination (3.16) the variance depends on all the individual variances and covariances,

$$s_Z^2 = \sum_{k=1}^{K} a_k^2 s_k^2 + 2 \sum_{j=1}^{K-1} \sum_{k=j+1}^{K} a_j a_k s_{jk}. \tag{3.19}$$

This may be usefully compared with the population formula (B.20) in Appendix B. It may be applied to portfolios of any number of assets; here is an application for $K = 3$.

EXAMPLE 8

fama.dat

The return on treasury bills has a sample variance of $s_3^2 = 0.000000294$; its sample covariances with IBM and Xerox are $s_{13} = 0.00000271$ and $s_{23} = -0.0000105$. Consider a 20/30/50 portfolio of IBM, Xerox, and treasury bills. What is the sample variance of the portfolio return?

SOLUTION

Applying Law 3.4 to the portfolio return (3.18) yields:

$$s_P^2 = a_1^2 s_1^2 + a_2^2 s_2^2 + a_3^2 s_3^2 + 2a_1 a_2 s_{12} + 2a_1 a_3 s_{13} + 2a_2 a_3 s_{23}$$
$$= 0.2^2 \times 0.002246 + 0.3^2 \times 0.010621 + 0.5^2 \times 0.000000294$$
$$+ 2(0.2)(0.3)0.002612 + 2(0.2)(0.5)0.00000271 - 2(0.3)(0.5)0.0000105$$
$$= 0.00136.$$

This law holds for any values of the constants in the linear combination. As with Law 3.3, an important special case is when the linear combination is just a sum of variables.

COROLLARY 3.4.1. *Consider a variable* Z_i *that is a sum of other variables:*

$$Z_i = X_i + Y_i.$$

Then

$$s_Z^2 = s_X^2 + s_Y^2 + 2s_{XY}.$$

TABLE 3.4   Decomposition of the Variance of Changes in GNP, March 1947–January 1981[a]

	ΔGNP	ΔI_i	ΔC	ΔI_f	ΔG	ΔXM
ΔGNP	**111. 5**	29. 6	43. 2	32. 9	5. 3	0. 5
ΔInventory investment	0. 49	**33. 1**	−2. 4	4. 4	−1. 9	−3. 4
ΔConsumption expenditure	0. 71	−0. 07	**32. 9**	15. 9	−1. 5	−1. 7
ΔFixed investment	0. 76	0. 19	0. 68	**16. 7**	−2. 2	−1. 9
ΔGovernment purchases	0. 15	−0. 10	−0. 08	−0. 17	**10. 6**	0. 3
ΔNet exports	0. 02	−0. 22	−0. 11	−0. 17	0. 04	**7. 1**

Source: Blinder, A.S. (1981) "Retail Inventory Behavior and Business Fluctuations," *Brookings Papers on Economic Activity*, 443–505. Reprinted with permission.

[a] Variances are on the diagonal, with covariances above and correlations below.

Specializing the general formula (3.19) in the same way, this corollary can be stated more generally in terms of K variables:

$$s_Z^2 = \sum_{k=1}^{K} s_k^2 + 2 \sum_{j=1}^{K-1} \sum_{k=j+1}^{K} s_{jk}. \tag{3.20}$$

An application of this version of the variance law is described in Theory Meets Application 3.1 and illustrated in Table 3.4.

The laws of sample means and variances are summarized in Table 3.5 on page 126. A comparison of this table with Appendix B Table B.2 reveals how the laws of sample means and variances of this appendix parallel the analogous laws of mathematical expectation and variance of Appendix B.[10]

EXERCISES

3.7 Suppose that the units of measure of X_i and Y_i are changed through the application of scaling constants vX_i and wY_i. How will this affect

(a) the sample covariance s_{XY}?

(b) the sample correlation r_{XY}?

3.8 Show that if X_i and Y_i are exactly linearly related so that $Y_i = a + bX_i$, then $|r_{XY}| = 1$. What determines whether $r_{XY} = 1$ or -1? (*Hint:* Use the result in Appendix A, Exercise A.3.)

3.9 Suppose you had invested 70% of your wealth in IBM and 30% in treasury bills.

(a) What average monthly rate of return would have been yielded by this portfolio?

(b) What would the sample variance of this portfolio have been?

3.10 Suppose you had invested in IBM, Xerox, and treasury bills in the proportion 30/50/20.

(a) What average monthly rate of return would have been yielded by this portfolio?

(b) What would the sample variance of this portfolio have been?

[10] Table 3.5 does not list special cases of Law 3.4 in which the covariance is 0, analogous to those of Appendix B in which $\sigma_{XY} = 0$, because even when variables are unrelated in the population their sample covariance s_{XY} is typically not exactly 0.

TABLE 3.5   Laws of Sample Means and Variances

Law	Corollary
If $Z_i = a + bX_i$, then	
3.1 $\overline{Z} = a + b\overline{X}$	**3.1.1** If $Z_i = bX_i$, then $\overline{Z} = b\overline{X}$
	3.1.2 If $Z_i = a + X_i$, then $\overline{Z} = a + \overline{X}$
3.2 $s_Z^2 = b^2 s_X^2$	**3.2.1** If $Z_i = bX_i$, then $s_Z^2 = b^2 s_X^2$
	3.2.2 If $Z_i = a + X_i$, then $s_Z^2 = s_X^2$
If $Z_i = aX_i + bY_i$, then	
3.3 $\overline{Z} = a\overline{X} + b\overline{Y}$	**3.3.1** If $Z_i = X_i + Y_i$, then $\overline{Z} = \overline{X} + \overline{Y}$
3.4 $s_Z^2 = a^2 s_X^2 + b^2 s_Y^2 + 2abs_{XY}$	**3.4.1** If $Z_i = X_i + Y_i$, then $s_Z^2 = s_X^2 + s_Y^2 + 2s_{XY}$

3.11 ⊙ **fama.dat** Use the IBM and Xerox returns series to do the following.

(a) Compute

i.   the sample means of the simple returns.

ii. the sample variances of the simple returns.

iii. the sample covariance.

iv. the sample correlation.

(b) Consider a portfolio consisting of 40% IBM and 60% Xerox.

i.   Generate a series for the monthly simple returns on this portfolio, R_{Pt}, for the period July 1963 through June 1968.

ii. Compute the sample mean of this series, $\overline{R}_P$. Is this the same as the value obtained in Example 5?

iii. Compute the sample variance of this series, s_P^2. Is this the same as the value obtained in Example 7?

3.12 ⊙ **fama.dat** Use the IBM, Xerox, and treasury bill returns series to do the following.

(a) Compute

i.   the sample means of the simple returns.

ii. the sample variances of the simple returns.

iii. the sample covariances.

iv. the sample correlations.

(b) Consider a portfolio consisting of a 20/30/50 split among IBM, Xerox, and treasury bills.

i.   Generate a series for the monthly simple returns on this portfolio, R_{Pt}, for the period July 1963 through June 1968.

ii. Compute the sample mean of this series, $\overline{R}_P$. Is this the same as the value obtained in Example 6?

iii. Compute the sample variance of this series, s_P^2. Is this the same as the value obtained in Example 8?

3.13 Consider Blinder's decomposition of the variability of GNP changes given in Table 3.4. The entries above the diagonal are covariances, and those below are correlations.

(a) Correlations must be fractional: $-1 < r_{XY} < 1$. Is this satisfied by all the below-diagonal entries?

(b) Because a covariance and correlation must have the same sign, any covariance above the diagonal should have the same sign as its corresponding correlation below. Is this satisfied throughout the table?

(c) Show how the numbers in the table are consistent with the decomposition-of-variance formula (3.20).

4

Simple Regression

Our preliminary treatment of statistical relationships between variables has suggested that linear models are a natural starting point for the study of these relationships. We begin our consideration of linear statistical models in this chapter by focusing in some detail on the simple regression model

$$Y_i = \alpha + \beta X_i + \varepsilon_i, \qquad \varepsilon_i \sim \text{n.i.d.}(0, \sigma^2). \tag{4.1}$$

The adjective *simple* refers to the specification of Y as depending on just a single variable X; the generalization of this model to one involving multiple right-hand-side variables is considered beginning in Chapter 8. The model (4.1), or its multiple regression generalization, is known as the **classical normal linear regression model.**

The present chapter proceeds along the following lines. First, although the discussion of Chapter 3 has served to motivate this model, it is important to comment more fully on the assumptions underlying it. This is the subject of Section 4.1. The objective is to provide deeper insight into the basis for the model and the empirical phenomena it can realistically be used to study and, hence, something of an appreciation for its limitations. These limitations in turn motivate the econometric models introduced in later chapters.

Having developed a better understanding of the model specification, it is possible to turn to the standard question of statistical inference: How can sample data be used to learn about the model parameters? Section 4.2 applies the method of least squares to obtain estimators for α, β, and σ^2. Section 4.3 shows that these are optimal estimators in the sense of possessing the desirable properties discussed in Chapter 2. Subsequent sections develop hypothesis tests and related matters. A major theme of this chapter is that the analysis of the regression model is largely an application of the statistical principles highlighted in Chapter 2.

With the essentials of regression covered in the present chapter, Chapter 5 turns to some supplementary topics: forecasting, regression through the origin, and a preliminary indication of some important situations in which least squares regression can be misleading or inappropriate. Because our goal in these two chapters is to develop the key elements of statistical inference in simple regression, the discussion of empirical applications is limited to a few illustrative examples. Section 4.10 applies simple regression to study the relationship between output and production costs in electricity generation. For a topic requiring more theoretical background, the appendix to Chapter 5 considers an important application of simple regression in financial economics—the estimation of the capital asset pricing model.

More extensive applications are contained in the two chapters that follow Chapter 5. Chapter 6 treats a number of issues that tend to arise in applied work, and in particular shows how linear regression can often be used to study nonlinear relationships between variables. Chapter 7 illustrates this with applications to production economics.

4.1   Model Specification

The classical normal linear regression model (4.1) specifies that the left-hand-side (or **dependent**) variable Y (also called the **regressand**) is determined by two components. The first is the **systematic component** $\alpha + \beta X$ determining the mean of Y as a linear function of the right-hand-side (or **explanatory** or **independent**) variable X (also called the **regressor**); the coefficients of this linear function are the parameters α and β. The second component is the disturbance ε, which determines the variance of the Y_i observations about their systematic component. The disturbance is **unsystematic** in that it is purely random; it is not a function of observable variables, nor is it in any sense predictable. The model involves three parameters: the coefficients α and β, associated with the systematic mean, and the variance σ^2, associated with the unsystematic component. Figure 4.1(a) (in Section 4.2) portrays the determination of the Y_i values as the random outcome of a distribution with variance σ^2, the mean of this distribution changing with X_i according to the systematic component.

4.1.1   The Classical Disturbance

The model is classical in several senses. First, it makes use of the classical disturbance specification $\varepsilon_i \sim \text{i.i.d.}(0, \sigma^2)$ introduced in the previous chapters, supplementing this with the additional assumption of a normal form for the population distribution. As we have seen in those chapters, the fundamental basis for the assumption that the ε_i are identically and independently distributed is the presumption that the sample data are drawn from a common population distribution according to a process of random sampling.

Although this is a natural starting point for our study of statistical relationships between variables, it is far from the only means by which the data could have been generated. Another possibility is that the variance of Y_i may not be constant across all observations, so that the disturbance is **heteroskedastic:** $\varepsilon_i \sim \text{n.i.d.}(0, \sigma_i^2)$. A classical disturbance is the special case of a common variance $\sigma_i^2 = \sigma^2$ across all observations $i = 1, \ldots, n$ and is said to be **homoskedastic.** The implications of heteroskedasticity for the use of the linear regression model are considered in Chapter 14.

Another example in which the classical disturbance of (4.1) may not necessarily correspond with the true process by which data are generated is with respect to the assumed sampling procedure. As was noted in Chapter 2, if the data are collected by sampling randomly from the population it follows that successive observations will be statistically independent. For cross-section data (data collected across cases—individuals, households, firms, countries, etc.) this is often a realistic assumption, and a statistical model such as (4.1) that assumes independence is a plausible model specification. For other types of data, however—particularly time series data—it is unlikely to hold. A time series variable that involves a temporal dependence between observations is said to be **autocorrelated,** and so the assumption of independence captured in the i.i.d./n.i.d. notation is sometimes referred to as the assumption of **nonautocorrelation.** Because autocorrelation is bound up with other issues in the study of time series data, there is little point attempting to consider it prior to our study of time series analysis in Chapters 15–18.

4.1.2 The Explanatory Variable

In order to proceed with our analysis of the regression model it is necessary to make two assumptions about the explanatory variable. The first is for convenience in working with the model, deriving estimators and test statistics, and analyzing their properties. The second is necessary in order to estimate the model.

Nonstochastic Explanatory Variable

A second respect in which the classical normal linear regression model (4.1) hails from a long tradition in statistics and so is classical has to do with what is assumed about the X_i. In contrast to the previous chapter in which X and Y are both treated explicitly as random variables, it turns out to be useful to view the explanatory variable as **nonstochastic.** That is, X is not regarded as a random variable. Instead the X_i values are just taken to be a series of numerical constants.

This is a realistic assumption in situations in which the explanatory variable is under the control of the researcher. Consider an experiment that studies the response of crop yield to fertilizer application. The amount of fertilizer applied to different fields is set by the researcher. It is not a random variable. Crop yield Y is then generated, in part, as a result of the amount of fertilizer—the systematic influence—but also due to purely random factors captured by the disturbance ε. These unsystematic influences might include variations in soil quality, rainfall, drainage of the fields, and so on. It was in connection with applications such as this in the experimental sciences that regression analysis and other statistical methods were first developed; the treatment of the explanatory variable as nonstochastic is thus part of a long-standing tradition, and in this sense is classical. Indeed, it is because, in this tradition, the explanatory variable is under the independent control of the researcher that it is often called the independent variable.

Although this conception of the determination of X may be appropriate for the experimental sciences, it is obviously not accurate for most problems in economics, where data are nonexperimental and observations on explanatory variables are the outcome of a process of random sampling just as is true of the dependent variable. Despite this, it is helpful to proceed with our analysis of the regression model using the classical assumption that the explanatory variable is nonstochastic. This is sometimes expressed by saying that the X_i values are assumed to be **fixed in repeated sampling.** The notion is that a given series of n values for the explanatory variable X yield randomly generated values for the dependent variable Y and that a second set of sample data would consist of a somewhat different set of n randomly generated values for Y resulting from the same series of X_i values. For example, if in another year the same amounts of fertilizer are applied to the same fields, random factors will result in different crop yields from those initially observed.

The advantage of proceeding according to this assumption is that it simplifies our analysis of the model. Given a fixed (that is, nonstochastic) value of X_i, the model (4.1) indicates that any Y_i is generated as a function of the single random disturbance ε_i and the nonrandom term $\alpha + \beta X_i$; the latter is an additive constant for any i. Because, under this specification, Y_i is a function of one rather than two random variables, its expected value and variance are particularly simple to evaluate. By the laws of mathematical expectation and variance applied to linear functions, they are

$$E(Y_i) = \alpha + \beta X_i + E(\varepsilon_i) = \alpha + \beta X_i,$$
$$V(Y_i) = V(\varepsilon_i) = \sigma^2.$$

Furthermore, the fact that Y is a linear function of the normal random variable ε allows us to summarize the population model generating any Y_i as the unconditional distribution

$$Y_i \sim N(\alpha + \beta X_i, \sigma^2). \tag{4.2}$$

The alternative of treating X as random would require instead that this expectation and variance be evaluated conditional on X. Although it would be possible to proceed in this more complicated way, for the applied issues considered in our use of the regression model it offers no advantage. For an advanced book on econometric theory that studies the regression model treating the explanatory variables explicitly as stochastic, see Davidson (2000).

There are, of course, certain issues for which it *is* important to recognize explicitly that X may be stochastic. This is particularly the case in situations in which the population model implies that X and ε may be correlated; that is, when the condition[1]

$$E(X_i \varepsilon_i) = 0 \tag{4.3}$$

---

[1]   From Appendix B, Result B.8, if one random variable has zero mean then the covariance is the expected value of the product: $cov(X_i, \varepsilon_i) = E(X_i \varepsilon_i)$. Thus the random variables are uncorrelated if $E(X_i \varepsilon_i) = 0$.

is not satisfied. One example of such a situation, it may be shown, is when X is measured with error. Another is when the variables of interest are generated as a result of the simultaneous interaction of more than one behavioral relationship, as in the supply–demand example of Section 1.2.3. This is an especially important problem in econometrics and more will be said about it in the next chapter. However, it turns out that the solution is to turn away from least squares in favor of alternative estimators, and so this class of econometric problems is beyond the scope of this book. Thus, our study of the regression model will proceed on the basis of the assumption of a nonstochastic explanatory variable.

The Explanatory Variable Must Exhibit Variation

As a final assumption, it is necessary to require that the observations on the explanatory variable exhibit some variation. It is not acceptable for the X_i to take on just a single value for all $i = 1, \ldots, n$. Obviously if exactly the same amount of fertilizer is applied to every field it will be impossible to learn anything about the relationship between fertilizer application and crop yield. A study of the link between these variables requires that the amount of fertilizer used be varied across fields. Because the expression $\sum (X_i - \overline{X})^2$ is a measure of the dispersion of the X_i, a natural way of specifying the requirement that the explanatory variable exhibit variation is to assume that

$$\sum_{i=1}^{n} (X_i - \overline{X})^2 \neq 0. \tag{4.4}$$

Intuitively it is clear that the amount of variation exhibited by X will have an effect on our ability to study the relationship between X and Y. Exactly in what sense this is true is revealed by the analysis in Section 4.2.

To summarize, in addition to the formal statement (4.1), the classical normal linear regression model assumes that the explanatory variable is nonstochastic and that it exhibits variation so that (4.4) is satisfied.

4.1.3 Normality and Linearity

As we have seen in Section 3.2, *normality* and *linearity* play related roles in the classical normal linear regression model. For if X is stochastic and jointly normally distributed with Y, (4.1) is the corresponding statistical model. Hence, the assumption of a linear relationship linking the two variables rests on more than just wishful thinking. Because in practice it is known that a great many variables are normally distributed, it is in turn likely that linear relationships will often be adequate for studying the interaction of variables.

It is possible to consider a linear relationship of the form (4.1) without the assumption of a normal disturbance. In this case, in which the weaker specification

$$\varepsilon_i \sim \text{i.i.d.}(0, \sigma^2) \tag{4.5}$$

applies, we are studying the **classical linear regression model.** Indeed, as we argue in Chapter 2, there is something to be said for this approach because the assumption of a particular form for the population distribution is always a strong one. As was suggested by the analysis in that chapter, the result is that it becomes necessary to rely on central limit theorems for the distributional results on which to base hypothesis testing procedures; that is, only asymptotic test procedures are available.

Chapter 2 also shows that when the model is such that the optimal estimators are linear functions of the random data, the assumption of population normality yields exact test procedures. Recall that the example given in Chapter 2 is the t test of the population mean μ for a normal population, which is valid even in small samples.

The estimators for α and β in the classical linear regression model derived in the next section are, as we shall see, linear in the Y_i (or, equivalently, the ε_i). Consequently, this is another situation in which the assumption of population normality yields exact rather than asymptotic test procedures. Hence, the regression model is another context in which the assumption of population normality turns out to have very useful consequences, and this is the reason for making it. At the same time, it is natural to ask how our conclusions about the analysis of the model would change if (4.5) were assumed instead. The primary consequence, it is now possible to anticipate, is that only asymptotic test procedures based on central limit theorems would become available.

Although models based on a linear functional relationship between variables are a compelling starting point for any study of econometrics, it is of course the case that in some situations the relationship between variables may be fundamentally nonlinear. If the disturbance is additive (and it is an open question whether this may the case) a more general relationship between X and Y may be denoted

$$Y_i = f(X_i) + \varepsilon_i, \tag{4.6}$$

where $f(\cdot)$ is some specified function involving parameters to be estimated. The linear simple regression model is, of course, the special case in which the functional form is

$$f(X_i) = \alpha + \beta X_i. \tag{4.7}$$

The nonlinear regression model (4.6) is the subject of Chapter 13, where estimators of the parameters of $f(\cdot)$ are derived through the application of the same least squares principle applied in this chapter to the special case (4.7). In contrast to the results of the next section, in which the least squares estimators are linear functions of the Y_i, however, these **nonlinear least squares** estimators are nonlinear functions of the dependent variable. Consequently, again following the intuition of Chapter 2, the assumption of population normality is of no benefit in this context: It does not follow that the estimators are normally distributed because only linear functions of normals are normal. For this reason we find in Chapter 13 that statistical inference in nonlinear models such as (4.6) must be built entirely on a foundation of asymptotic results; this being the case, there is no value to assumptions of particular forms for the population distribution, normal or otherwise. Instead, all that is needed for the relevant central limit theorems to hold is that the disturbance behave according to (4.5), and so it is on this specification that we proceed in our study of the nonlinear regression model (4.6).

For the linear regression model, on the other hand, the fact that the least squares estimators are linear in the Y_i means that the assumption of normality yields exact test procedures, as we see in Sections 4.5 and 4.6.2. Consequently, throughout our discussion of the linear regression model up through Chapter 12, we employ this assumption. When we come to nonlinear regression in Chapter 13, the normality assumption will have outlived its usefulness.

4.1.4   Completeness of the Model

In this chapter, we proceed with our analysis of the classical normal linear regression model on the assumption that (4.1) is a complete statement of the model. That is, we assume there is no other knowledge about the behavior of these variables that can be exploited in analyzing them. Under this assumption, we find, for example, that least squares is efficient.

If additional information becomes available, on the other hand, then it makes intuitive sense that it should be used and, indeed, it can be shown that if it is not used then least squares loses its efficiency. But what additional information do we have in mind? Here are the two most important possibilities.

Knowledge about the parameters. Suppose we have a priori knowledge that, say, a coefficient must equal some numerical value, or that α and β must satisfy some functional relationship. In other words, the coefficients must satisfy certain restrictions. In Section 10.2.1 we use some simple examples to show that the use of such restrictions contributes to efficiency in estimation.

The regression is part of a larger system. If the regression is one relationship in a larger system of relationships, then this should—and in some respects *must*—be used in estimation to achieve efficiency and for other purposes as well. The intuition for this should be clear from our discussion of structural and reduced forms in Chapter 1. The need to estimate some equations as part of a system is something we say more about in Sections 5.3.3 and 12.5.

In this chapter, both of these possibilities are neglected and the classical normal linear regression model is analyzed on the assumption that our specification of it is complete.

EXERCISES

4.1 Consider the regression model (4.1).

(a) Under the classical assumptions,

i.   what is the appropriate expression for $E(Y_i)$?

ii. what is the appropriate expression for $V(Y_i)$?

(b) In contrast to the classical assumptions, suppose that X_i is a random variable with $E(X_i) = \mu_X$

and $V(X_i) = \sigma_X^2$, and that it covaries with the disturbance: $E(X_i \varepsilon_i) = \sigma_{X\varepsilon}$.

i.   What is the appropriate expression for $E(Y_i)$?

ii. What is the appropriate expression for $V(Y_i)$?

Indicate which laws from Appendix B are relevant to your answer.

4.2 Show that if $X_i = X$, a given numerical value, for all $i = 1, \ldots, n$, then (4.4) is not satisfied.

4.2   Least Squares Estimation

In studying statistical inference in the classical normal linear regression model (4.1), our first task is to estimate the parameters. The application of the least squares estimation principle to this model—in either its simple or multiple regression forms—yields **ordinary least squares** (OLS) estimators. This term distinguishes the least squares estimation of classical linear regressions from the application of the principle to other types of regression models. The two most important variants are nonlinear least squares (NLS), which we study in Chapter 13, and generalized least squares (GLS), which we encounter in Chapter 14.

4.2.1   Estimating α and β

As Figure 4.1 emphasizes, the simple regression model specifies the Y_i observations as being generated randomly around a mean

$$E(Y_i) = \alpha + \beta X_i. \tag{4.8}$$

This is called the **population regression line** or **population regression function.**

The Sample Regression Line

Let us begin by focusing on the coefficients α and β of this population regression line, for which we wish to obtain estimators $\hat{\alpha}$ and $\hat{\beta}$. As is always true of estimators, these must be functions of the sample data X_i, Y_i $(i = 1, \ldots, n)$. They will define a **sample regression line**

$$\hat{Y}_i = \hat{\alpha} + \hat{\beta} X_i, \tag{4.9}$$

where $\hat{Y}_i$ denotes **fitted** or **predicted** values obtained by evaluating the right-hand side of (4.9) on the basis of the X_i observations. This equation is called the sample regression line because all its elements are computable on the basis of sample data. This is in contrast to the population regression line (4.8), which is unobservable; it is unobservable because α, β, and $E(Y_i)$ are associated with the population and are therefore unknown, as is always true of population quantities.

Figure 4.1(b) contrasts the population and sample regression lines. They differ because $\hat{\alpha}$ and $\hat{\beta}$ are imperfect estimators of α and β (imperfect in the sense that

FIGURE 4.1

The population and
sample regression
lines.

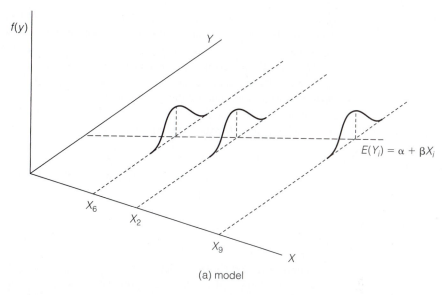

(a) model

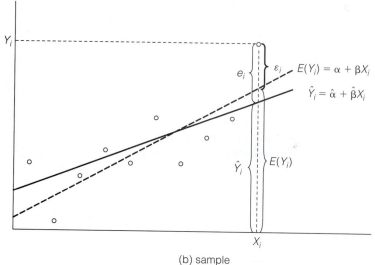

(b) sample

estimators always involve sampling error). Another way of expressing this is to note that for a given X_i the associated $E(Y_i)$ and $\hat{Y}_i$ are different.

It is also clear from Figure 4.1(b) that the fitted values $\hat{Y}_i$ differ from the original data observations Y_i. The difference is

$$e_i \equiv Y_i - \hat{Y}_i = Y_i - \hat{\alpha} - \hat{\beta}X_i. \tag{4.10}$$

Paralleling the terminology established in Chapter 2, these are called the **residuals.** As indicated in Figure 4.1(b), a residual is the vertical distance by which an observation Y_i differs from the sample regression line. The e_i are residual in the sense that they are associated with the variation in the Y_i observations that is not accounted for by the estimation of the systematic component of the model. Some of the residuals are positive, others negative. They are sample quantities that can be computed given an estimated regression line; they differ from the unobservable disturbances ε_i associated with the population.

Figure 4.1(b) also makes it clear that the relationship between the observed Y_i's, the sample regression line, and the residuals is

$$Y_i = \hat{\alpha} + \hat{\beta} X_i + e_i, \tag{4.11}$$

which may usefully be contrasted with the model (4.1). A comparison of Figure 4.1 with Figure 2.7 is instructive.[2]

The Sum of Squares Function

Estimating the regression model involves choosing a sample regression line that best fits the sample data. The derivation of estimators $\hat{\alpha}$ and $\hat{\beta}$ defining such a sample regression line requires that the notion of "best fit" be made precise. In analogy with the logic of Section 2.4, the method of least squares suggests that $\hat{\alpha}$ and $\hat{\beta}$ be chosen to be those values of α and β that minimize the sum of squares function

$$S = \sum_{i=1}^{n}(Y_i - EY_i)^2 = \sum_{i=1}^{n}(Y_i - \alpha - \beta X_i)^2. \tag{4.12}$$

Just as in that earlier application of the method, least squares is a minimum distance estimator that uses as its distance metric the square of the vertical distance between the Y_i values and the systematic component of the model. The only difference is that the earlier application was to the somewhat simpler model

$$Y_i = \mu + \varepsilon_i \tag{4.13}$$

in which the sum of squares function takes the form (2.16),

$$S = \sum_{i=1}^{n}(Y_i - EY_i)^2 = \sum_{i=1}^{n}(Y_i - \mu)^2.$$

In fact, it is apparent that this earlier model (4.13) is nothing more than the special case of the regression model in which $\beta = 0$ and the symbol α is relabeled μ. In this respect, then, the regression model is simply an extension of a model previously studied, and it should come as no surprise that essentially the same estimation methodology applies.

---

[2]   Although the two figures are similar, there are some important differences. In particular, as Figure 4.1(b) makes explicit, there is no reason why the X_i drawings would be ordered in magnitude or be equidistant from one another.

Of course, just as was true in that earlier discussion, minimum distance estimators based on alternative distance metrics can be defined. It would be possible to consider, for example, LAD estimators or an objective function defined in terms of the horizontal or perpendicular distances. Again, our focus on the least squares metric arises from the fact that it happens to yield estimators possessing desirable properties, as we shall see.

The Least Squares Normal Equations

An important difference from the earlier estimation problem is that now, instead of just a single coefficient μ, the sum of squares function (4.12) involves two coefficients. Minimizing S requires that partial derivatives be taken with respect to α and β:

$$\frac{\partial S}{\partial \alpha} = \sum_{i=1}^{n} 2(Y_i - \alpha - \beta X_i)(-1), \tag{4.14a}$$

$$\frac{\partial S}{\partial \beta} = \sum_{i=1}^{n} 2(Y_i - \alpha - \beta X_i)(-X_i). \tag{4.14b}$$

Setting these equal to zero and cancelling multiplicative constants, the associated first-order conditions may be expressed as

$$\sum_{i=1}^{n} (Y_i - \hat{\alpha} - \hat{\beta} X_i) = 0, \tag{4.15a}$$

$$\sum_{i=1}^{n} (Y_i - \hat{\alpha} - \hat{\beta} X_i) X_i = 0. \tag{4.15b}$$

Note that the parameters α and β in (4.14) have been replaced by the estimators $\hat{\alpha}$ and $\hat{\beta}$ because the first-order conditions (4.15) define the estimators. The importance of these first-order conditions is such that they are given a special name—they are called the **normal equations.**

One reason the normal equations are important is that it is possible to see directly from them two interesting features of the least squares sample regression line, even before solving for $\hat{\alpha}$ and $\hat{\beta}$. Using the definition of the residuals (4.10) the normal equations may be reexpressed as:

$$\sum_{i=1}^{n} e_i = 0, \tag{4.16a}$$

$$\sum_{i=1}^{n} X_i e_i = 0. \tag{4.16b}$$

These establish two remarkable properties of the least squares residuals. First, recall in connection with Figure 4.1(b) that the sample regression line passes through the data in such a way that some residuals are positive, others negative. In summing the residuals over the full sample $i = 1, \ldots, n$, it stands to reason that positive residuals will tend to cancel with negative ones. The first normal equation (4.16a) indicates that this cancellation is *exact*: The least squares estimators yield a sample regression line having the property that the residuals sum exactly to zero.

The second normal equation (4.16b) indicates that when the pairwise products of the X_i and e_i are summed over the full sample $i = 1, \ldots, n$, they total to zero. In the terminology of linear algebra, the two vectors $[X_1 \cdots X_n]$ and $[e_1 \cdots e_n]$ are said to be **orthogonal.** Hence, the second normal equation (4.16b) is sometimes called the orthogonality condition of least squares. Notice that least squares imposes on the sample data an orthogonality condition analogous to the population orthogonality condition (4.3), suggesting that least squares is a valuable estimation principle in situations in which the latter is satisfied. Although it is not possible to pursue this point in any detail, it is perhaps worth remarking that the analogy between population and sample orthogonality conditions illustrated by (4.3) and (4.16b) is the basis for the generalized method of moments estimation principle mentioned in Section 2.4, an estimation principle that can be used to obtain estimators in situations in which (4.3) is not satisfied. Because it makes use of the analogy between population and sample orthogonality conditions, the generalized method of moments sometimes goes by the name **analog estimation.**

The fact that, as indicated by the normal equations, the least squares residuals sum to zero and are orthogonal to the explanatory variable, is an interesting feature of least squares that generalizes to the multiple regression model studied in Chapter 8. They are examples of what might be termed **numerical properties** of least squares, properties that must be satisfied exactly in any sample of data and that are capable of direct verification.

Solving the Normal Equations

Although these numerical properties of the least squares sample regression line are noteworthy, the immediate task at hand is to obtain solutions for $\hat{\alpha}$ and $\hat{\beta}$. The manipulation of the first-order conditions (4.15) yields as an algebraically equivalent statement of the normal equations the relations

$$\sum_{i=1}^{n} Y_i = n\hat{\alpha} + \hat{\beta} \sum_{i=1}^{n} X_i, \tag{4.17a}$$

$$\sum_{i=1}^{n} X_i Y_i = \hat{\alpha} \sum_{i=1}^{n} X_i + \hat{\beta} \sum_{i=1}^{n} X_i^2. \tag{4.17b}$$

These are convenient because they indicate clearly that the first-order conditions represent two simultaneous linear equations in the two unknowns $\hat{\alpha}$ and $\hat{\beta}$ and so may be solved. Furthermore, an examination of (4.17a) reveals another interesting feature of the least squares sample regression line—multiplying by $1/n$ yields

$$\overline{Y} = \hat{\alpha} + \hat{\beta}\overline{X}. \tag{4.18}$$

That is, the sample regression line passes through the point $(\overline{X}, \overline{Y})$ of variable means. This provides a particularly easy way of computing $\hat{\alpha}$ given $\hat{\beta}$ because rearranging yields

$$\hat{\alpha} = \overline{Y} - \hat{\beta}\overline{X}. \tag{4.19}$$

With this as the most convenient expression for $\hat{\alpha}$, it may be substituted into the second normal equation (4.17b) to yield, after some manipulation,

$$\hat{\beta} = \frac{\sum X_i Y_i - n\overline{X}\,\overline{Y}}{\sum X_i^2 - n\overline{X}^2} \tag{4.20}$$

as a solution for $\hat{\beta}$. Given the computation of the slope estimator by this formula, it is then possible to return to (4.19) for the computation of $\hat{\alpha}$.

A more convenient expression for $\hat{\beta}$ is available through the use of the deviation form notation introduced in Section 3.3. Defining $x_i = X_i - \overline{X}$ and $y_i = Y_i - \overline{Y}$, the least squares slope estimator may be expressed as

$$\hat{\beta} = \frac{\sum x_i y_i}{\sum x_i^2}. \tag{4.21}$$

Note that the numerator $\sum x_i y_i$ is the same as the numerator of the sample covariance s_{XY} or correlation r_{XY} given by (3.14b) or (3.14c); hence, all three have the same sign. For example, an inverse relationship between the variables, as measured by a negative sample covariance or correlation, will also be reflected in a negatively sloped sample regression line.

It is also noteworthy that the denominator of (4.21) is $\sum x_i^2 = \sum (X_i - \overline{X})^2$, a measure of the dispersion of the explanatory variable that is required by condition (4.4) to be nonzero. If this condition is violated, then the denominator of (4.21) is zero and $\hat{\beta}$ is not uniquely defined. It is in this sense that variation in X_i is required for it to be possible to study the relationship between X and Y.

EXAMPLE 1

 nerlove1.dat

Figure 3.1 of the previous chapter plots production costs against output for 145 electric power companies. As a first approximation to this cost function relationship, use least squares to estimate a linear regression between these two variables.

SOLUTION

The least squares coefficient estimates are $\hat{\alpha} = -0.741$ and $\hat{\beta} = 0.00643$.[3] The sample regression line may be expressed as

$$\hat{Y}_i = -0.741 + 0.00643 X_i$$

---

[3] The units of measure of the variables are those of Figure 3.1.

THEORY MEETS APPLICATION   **4.1**

Mincer's Statistical Earnings Function

A large body of research in labor economics studies the returns to education. In an early example, Jacob Mincer (1974) estimated the relationship between earnings Y and years of schooling X using a sample of 31,093 white, nonfarm, nonstudent males drawn from 1960 census data. The dependent variable Y was expressed in logarithmic form. Mincer obtained an intercept estimate of $\hat{\alpha} = 7.58$ and a slope estimate of $\hat{\beta} = 0.070$, so that the sample regression line may be expressed as

$$\widehat{\log Y_i} = 7.58 + 0.070 X_i,$$

or, avoiding the awkward carat notation,

$$\log Y_i = 7.58 + 0.070 X_i + e_i.$$

By selecting white, nonfarm, nonstudent males Mincer controlled for influences that would otherwise have to be treated using multiple regression.

The dependent variable is expressed in logarithmic form because earnings are approximately lognormally distributed, as we note in our discussion of the lognormal distribution in Section 2.5.2. If earnings were being studied in isolation, it would be natural to use the lognormal model (2.25),

$$\log Y_i = \mu + \varepsilon_i, \qquad \varepsilon_i \sim \text{n.i.d.}(0, \sigma^2).$$

The regression model with the dependent variable in log form continues to specify Y as lognormally distributed, but with a mean that depends on years of schooling.

Regression models like Mincer's, in which earnings appear in log form, are called **statistical earnings functions** and are the workhorse models of much of empirical labor economics. In Chapter 6 we say more about the economic theory underlying statistical earnings functions. Most important, it turns out that the slope coefficient β has the interpretation of the percentage increase in earnings yielded by each additional year of schooling. Mincer's estimate of $\hat{\beta} = 0.070$ is the now-classic finding that a year of education yields approximately a 7% return.

This return is in excess of a base income that would be earned by a (perhaps hypothetical) person having no education. Setting $X = 0$ in the sample regression line yields the predicted value

$$\widehat{\log Y} = 7.58.$$

Mincer used natural logarithms, so the implied value of Y is 1958.6. A typical uneducated white, nonfarm, nonstudent male earned just under $2000 per year in 1960.

or, equivalently,

$$Y_i = -0.741 + 0.00643 X_i + e_i.$$

Notice that it would be incorrect to express the sample regression line as

$$Y_i = -0.741 + 0.00643 X_i,$$

because the observed Y_i sample values do not lie on the line.

Having successfully derived the least squares estimators, it is perhaps useful to pause and reemphasize the important distinction between an estimator and a parameter: $\hat{\alpha}$ and $\hat{\beta}$ are estimators, α and β parameters. The former are sample quantities computable from data, the latter unknown population quantities. In using $\hat{\beta}$ to estimate β, it is very unlikely that the parameter will be correctly estimated; that is, the sampling error $\hat{\beta} - \beta$ will almost certainly be nonzero.

Because the residuals e_i are defined by minimizing the sum of squares function (4.12), the least squares estimators minimize $\sum e_i^2$. No other coefficient estimators will yield a smaller value for the sum of squared residuals. This is what it means for the sample regression line to best fit the data in the least squares sense. This is of interest, in part, because the sum of squared residuals $\sum_i e_i^2$ plays an important role in the estimation of the third parameter of the model σ^2, a matter to which we turn next.

EXERCISES

4.3 Show how (4.20) is obtained from (4.17b).

4.4 Starting with (4.21), show that it is equivalent to (4.20).

4.5 Consider the special case of the model (4.1) in which $\beta = 0$:

$$Y_i = \alpha + \varepsilon_i.$$

(a) Derive the least squares estimator for α.

(b) In this context, what is the definition of the least squares residuals e_i?

(c) What property of the residuals is apparent from the first-order condition?

4.6 Consider the special case of the model (4.1) in which $\alpha = 0$:

$$Y_i = \beta X_i + \varepsilon_i.$$

(a) Derive the least squares estimator for β.

(b) In this context, what is the definition of the least squares residuals e_i?

(c) What property of the residuals is apparent from the first-order condition?

4.7 Using deviation-form notation, an alternative expression for the least squares residuals is

$$e_i = y_i - \hat{\beta} x_i. \qquad (4.22)$$

Beginning with this expression, use (4.19) to establish its equivalence with (4.10).

4.8 Use (4.22) and the properties of deviation form to confirm (4.16a).

4.9 Use (4.22) and the properties of deviation form to confirm (4.16b).

4.10 Use (4.22) to show that the sum of squared residuals $\sum e_i^2$ can be computed solely on the basis of the quantities $\sum y_i^2$, $\sum x_i^2$, and $\sum x_i y_i$.

4.2.2 Estimating σ^2

Having derived estimators for the parameters associated with the mean of Y, our attention now turns to the third parameter of the model, the variance σ^2. The formal definition of σ^2 is, as is true for all population parameters, in terms of a mathematical expectation:

$$\sigma^2 = E(\varepsilon_i^2) = E(Y_i - EY_i)^2 = E(Y_i - \alpha - \beta X_i)^2.$$

In this sense, then, σ^2 is a certain average of the squares of the ε_i, which are deviations between the Y_i observations and their mean $\alpha + \beta X_i$. Entirely in analogy with our earlier discussion in Section 2.4 of the estimation of σ^2 in the context of the simpler model (4.13), these deviations may be measured by their sample analogs

$$e_i = Y_i - \hat{Y}_i = Y_i - \hat{\alpha} - \hat{\beta}X_i,$$

the least squares residuals. It follows that a natural estimator of the population variance σ^2 is an average involving, in the numerator, the sum of squared residuals $\sum e_i^2$. This statistic is called the **sum of squared errors** (SSE):

$$\text{SSE} = \sum e_i^2.$$

Experience indicates that the denominator of this average will be critical in determining whether the resulting estimator is unbiased. It turns out that in this case the appropriate denominator is $n - 2$. That is,

$$s^2 = \frac{1}{n-2}\sum_{i=1}^{n} e_i^2 = \frac{1}{n-2}\sum_{i=1}^{n}(Y_i - \hat{\alpha} - \hat{\beta}X_i)^2 \tag{4.23}$$

is an unbiased estimator for σ^2: it may be shown that $E(s^2) = \sigma^2$. The statistic (2.7) that the symbol s^2 previously denoted was, it is now clear, the appropriate estimator for σ^2 in the special case of the model when $\beta = 0$.

As always when a variance is defined as a measure of dispersion, it is for some purposes convenient to use its square root, the standard deviation. In the context of regression analysis, the estimated standard deviation defined by

$$s = \sqrt{s^2}$$

is called the **standard error of the estimate** because it is associated with the sample (i.e., estimated) regression line. This is reported by the acronym SEE on the output of many regression packages.

EXAMPLE 2

nerlove1.dat

Using Nerlove's data in Figure 3.1, the estimated variance for the regression of Example 1 is $s^2 = 36.591$. What is the standard error of the estimate?

SOLUTION   The SEE is $s = \sqrt{s^2} = 6.049$.

EXERCISES _____

4.11 ∮ Consider as an alternative to least squares the following rather different approach to estimating the parameters of the regression model. As we have seen in Chapter 3, the simple regression model can be regarded as a reparameterization of the bivariate normal distribution. The equations (3.8) express this reparameterization, where the parameters of the

regression model have been placed on the left of the equalities and those of the bivariate normal on the right. Recall as well that statistics are available for the estimation of all the parameters of the bivariate normal. Specifically, the parameters μ_X, μ_Y, σ_X^2, and σ_Y^2 may be estimated by the usual sample means and variances $\overline{X}$, $\overline{Y}$, s_X^2, and s_Y^2, and the parameter ρ_{XY} may be estimated by the sample correlation r_{XY}. Drawing on this background knowledge and working as much as possible in deviation form:

(a) Propose an estimator for β, say $\tilde{\beta}$. Establish any relationship with the least squares estimator $\hat{\beta}$.

(b) Propose an estimator for α, say $\tilde{\alpha}$. Establish any relationship with the least squares estimator $\hat{\alpha}$.

(c) Propose an estimator for σ^2, say $\tilde{\sigma}^2$. Establish any relationship with s^2. (*Hint*: Use your solution to Exercise 4.10.)

4.3 Sampling Properties of the Least Squares Estimators

Does the method of least squares yield estimators having sampling distributions with attractive features? We saw in Chapter 2 that it often does, but that there is no guarantee of this. The properties of least squares estimators must be evaluated on a case-by-case basis.

Unbiasedness

Consider first the property of unbiasedness. Formally, the meaning of *unbiasedness* is exactly the same as in Chapter 2: The estimator $\hat{\beta}$ is unbiased if its sampling distribution is centered over the population value β. The mathematical expression of this property is $E(\hat{\beta}) = \beta$.

The least squares estimators of the coefficients of the linear regression model *are* unbiased. As in the past, establishing this involves using the laws of summation, deviation form, and mathematical expectation. The population regression line (4.8) is also used. The proof of the unbiasedness of $\hat{\beta}$ is as follows.

$$E(\hat{\beta}) = E\left(\frac{\sum x_i y_i}{\sum x_i^2}\right)$$

$$= \frac{1}{\sum x_i^2} E\left(\sum x_i y_i\right) \qquad \text{by Corollary B.1.1 in Appendix B}$$

$$= \frac{1}{\sum x_i^2} E\left(\sum x_i Y_i\right) \qquad \text{by Law A.5 in Appendix A}$$

$$= \frac{1}{\sum x_i^2} \sum x_i E(Y_i) \qquad \text{by Law B.3 in Appendix B}$$

$$= \frac{1}{\sum x_i^2} \sum x_i (\alpha + \beta X_i) \qquad \text{using the population regression line (4.8)}$$

$$= \frac{1}{\sum x_i^2} \left(\alpha \sum x_i + \beta \sum x_i^2\right)$$

$$= \beta$$

The last step uses Law A.4: The sum of any deviation-form variable is zero.

Equivalently, although in using $\hat{\beta}$ to estimate β a sampling error is incurred, the expected value of this sampling error is zero. In repeated sampling, $\hat{\beta}$ does not systematically under- or overestimate β. Exercise 4.13 asks you to show that $\hat{\alpha}$ is also unbiased.

Efficiency and Best Linear Unbiasedness

Turning to the second key feature of sampling distributions, the properties of $\hat{\alpha}$ and $\hat{\beta}$ associated with their variances are entirely in analogy with our findings in the simpler context of Chapter 2. Unbiasedness means, of course, that both $\hat{\alpha}$ and $\hat{\beta}$ are candidates for the properties of efficiency and best linear unbiasedness. It may be shown that under the assumptions of the model (4.1), in which normality holds, the least squares estimators are efficient; they have the smallest possible variance among all unbiased estimators. In the absence of normality, on the other hand, a version of the Gauss-Markov theorem holds.

Result 4.1   **(Gauss-Markov Theorem).** *In the context of the classical linear regression model*

$$Y_i = \alpha + \beta X_i + \varepsilon_i, \qquad \varepsilon_i \sim \text{i.i.d.}(0, \sigma^2), \tag{4.24}$$

the least squares estimators $\hat{\alpha}$ and $\hat{\beta}$ have the smallest variances in the class of all linear unbiased estimators.

That is, least squares is BLUE. Note that $\hat{\beta}$ is indeed linear in the Y_i values because it is of the form

$$\hat{\beta} = \frac{\sum x_i Y_i}{\sum x_i^2} = \sum \left(\frac{x_i}{\sum x_i^2} \right) Y_i. \tag{4.25}$$

This corresponds to the linear expression (2.12) with $a_i = x_i / \sum x_i^2$. Because $\hat{\alpha} = \overline{Y} - \hat{\beta}\overline{X}$ and each of $\overline{Y}$ and $\hat{\beta}$ are linear in the Y_i, it follows that $\hat{\alpha}$ is also linear. You are asked to investigate this in more detail in Exercise 4.14.

The fact that $\hat{\alpha}$ and $\hat{\beta}$ are linear estimators is important for reasons beyond the establishment of the Gauss-Markov theorem. In combination with normality, linearity allows us to establish the exact form of the sampling distributions. This in turn makes possible the derivation of exact hypothesis-testing procedures.

EXERCISES

4.12 Consider the estimator that you derived in Exercise 4.6. Establish whether it is unbiased.

4.13 Show that $\hat{\alpha}$ is an unbiased estimator of α.

4.14 Beginning with the formula (4.19), show that $\hat{\alpha}$ is a linear combination of the form $\sum a_i Y_i$, where the constants a_i are

$$a_i = \frac{1}{n} - \frac{\overline{X}x_i}{\sum x_i^2}.$$

4.15 What is the relationship between the version of the Gauss-Markov theorem just presented and that of Chapter 2?

4.4   The Sampling Distributions of $\hat{\alpha}$ and $\hat{\beta}$

Our investigation of the properties of the least squares estimators has yielded knowledge of several important features of their sampling distributions. First, the fact that both $\hat{\alpha}$ and $\hat{\beta}$ are linear functions of normally distributed Y_i means that they are, in turn, normally distributed. Second, we have established the means of these normal sampling distributions because the property of unbiasedness tells us that $E(\hat{\alpha}) = \alpha$ and $E(\hat{\beta}) = \beta$. Consequently, it may be concluded that $\hat{\alpha} \sim N(\alpha, \cdot)$ and $\hat{\beta} \sim N(\beta, \cdot)$. Because a normally distributed random variable is fully characterized by its mean and variance, the only missing piece of information is the variances.

The Variances of the Least Squares Estimators

The variances of $\hat{\alpha}$ and $\hat{\beta}$ are easily derived using the laws of the variance applied to linear functions. Beginning with $\hat{\beta}$, we have

$$V(\hat{\beta}) = V\left(\frac{\sum x_i y_i}{\sum x_i^2}\right)$$

$$= \left(\frac{1}{\sum x_i^2}\right)^2 V\left(\sum x_i y_i\right) \qquad \text{by Corollary B.2.1 in Appendix B}$$

$$= \left(\frac{1}{\sum x_i^2}\right)^2 V\left(\sum x_i Y_i\right) \qquad \text{by Law A.5 in Appendix A}$$

$$= \frac{1}{\left(\sum x_i^2\right)^2} \sum x_i^2 V(Y_i) \qquad \text{by Corollary B.4.1 in Appendix B}$$

$$= \frac{1}{\left(\sum x_i^2\right)^2} \sigma^2 \sum x_i^2$$

$$= \frac{\sigma^2}{\sum x_i^2}. \qquad (4.26)$$

Just as in the earlier derivation of $V(\overline{Y})$ in Result 2.3, the application of Corollary B.4.1, [actually the generalization of this corollary given by equation (B.21)], uses the fact that the Y_i have covariances of zero because they are statistically independent due to random sampling.

FIGURE 4.2

Implications of variation in X.

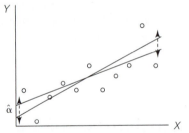
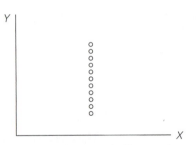

(a) a broad range of experience in X contributes to precise estimation of α and β

(b) absence of variation in X means the sample regression line is not uniquely determined

An inspection of this variance expression reveals that the precision with which $\hat{\beta}$ estimates β depends on just two factors. The first is the disturbance variance σ^2: A large variance of the unsystematic component makes it difficult to obtain a good estimate of the parameters of the systematic component. The second is that $V(\hat{\beta})$ is inversely related to $\sum x_i^2 = \sum(X_i - \overline{X})^2$. Recall that this is a measure of the dispersion of the explanatory variable. Values of the explanatory variable over a large range help to yield a precise estimate of the slope. In estimating the effect of fertilizer application on crop yield, for example, a range of fertilizer quantities is desirable. If exactly the same amount of fertilizer were applied to every field, then the X_i would exhibit no variation, the condition (4.4) would be violated, and, in addition to $\hat{\beta}$ not being uniquely defined, its sampling variance (4.26) would be undefined. These two situations are contrasted in Figure 4.2.

By a similar derivation, it is possible to use the linearity of $\hat{\alpha}$ to derive

$$V(\hat{\alpha}) = \sigma^2 \left(\frac{1}{n} + \frac{\overline{X}^2}{\sum x_i^2} \right) \tag{4.27}$$

as the variance of the sampling distribution of $\hat{\alpha}$. This indicates that the precision with which $\hat{\alpha}$ estimates α depends on much the same factors as was true for $\hat{\beta}$, and in much the same way. In addition, n enters the formula directly: $V(\hat{\alpha})$ is inversely related to the sample size, so that a large sample contributes to the precise estimation of the intercept. Again, the notion that "more information is good" is clearly manifested. This effect enters $V(\hat{\beta})$ through the denominator of (4.26), $\sum_{i=1}^{n} x_i^2$, which can only become larger as n increases. Finally, (4.27) indicates that $V(\hat{\alpha})$ is minimized at $\overline{X} = 0$. The intuition is that, for a given dispersion of the explanatory variable $\sum x_i^2$, the sampling variability of the intercept estimator increases as the mean of the explanatory variable moves away from the origin. The further the center of the data is from the origin, the more difficult it is to estimate the intercept precisely.

In conclusion, the sampling distributions of the least squares estimators may be summarized as

$$\hat{\alpha} \sim N\left[\alpha, \sigma^2 \left(\frac{1}{n} + \frac{\overline{X}^2}{\sum x_i^2} \right) \right], \qquad \hat{\beta} \sim N\left[\beta, \frac{\sigma^2}{\sum x_i^2} \right]. \tag{4.28}$$

This knowledge is clearly of a theoretical nature; the sampling variances (4.26) and (4.27) are not computable on the basis of sample data because they depend on the unknown population variance σ^2.

Estimating the Sampling Variances

Nevertheless, given the availability of the unbiased estimator s^2 for σ^2 developed in Section 4.2.2, a natural means of estimating $V(\hat{\alpha})$ and $V(\hat{\beta})$ is apparent. Simply substituting s^2 for σ^2 in (4.27) and (4.26) yields the estimated variances

$$s_{\hat{\alpha}}^2 = s^2 \left(\frac{1}{n} + \frac{\overline{X}^2}{\sum x_i^2} \right), \tag{4.29a}$$

$$s_{\hat{\beta}}^2 = \frac{s^2}{\sum x_i^2}. \tag{4.29b}$$

These *are* computable on the basis of sample data. The unbiasedness of s^2 implies automatically that these estimated sampling variances are in turn unbiased for the true sampling variances $V(\hat{\alpha})$ and $V(\hat{\beta})$. In the case of $\hat{\beta}$, for example,

$$E(s_{\hat{\beta}}^2) = E \left(\frac{s^2}{\sum x_i^2} \right) = \frac{1}{\sum x_i^2} E(s^2) = \frac{1}{\sum x_i^2} \sigma^2 = V(\hat{\beta}),$$

and similarly for $\hat{\alpha}$.

Thus, $s_{\hat{\alpha}}^2$ and $s_{\hat{\beta}}^2$ may be used as measures of the precision with which $\hat{\alpha}$ and $\hat{\beta}$ estimate the regression coefficients. An alternative measure is the corresponding **estimated standard errors**

$$s_{\hat{\alpha}} = \sqrt{s_{\hat{\alpha}}^2} = s \sqrt{\frac{1}{n} + \frac{\overline{X}^2}{\sum x_i^2}}, \qquad s_{\hat{\beta}} = \sqrt{s_{\hat{\beta}}^2} = \frac{s}{\sqrt{\sum x_i^2}}. \tag{4.30}$$

Their computed values are often simply called **standard errors** when no confusion with population values is likely.

EXAMPLE 3

 nerlove1.dat

Applying these formulas to Nerlove's output and production cost data, regression output reports estimated standard errors of $s_{\hat{\alpha}} = 0.622$ and $s_{\hat{\beta}} = 0.0001719$. What are the corresponding estimated variances?

SOLUTION

The estimated variances are the squares of the standard errors, $s_{\hat{\alpha}}^2 = 0.387$ and $s_{\hat{\beta}}^2 = 0.00000002955$.

Estimated standard errors play a central role in hypothesis testing and confidence intervals, our next topic of study.

EXERCISES

4.16 Derive the formula for $V(\hat{\alpha})$ given in equation (4.27).

4.17 Show that $s_{\hat{\alpha}}^2$ is an unbiased estimator for $V(\hat{\alpha})$.

4.18 (Continuation of Exercise 4.6.) Derive $V(\hat{\beta})$ when $\hat{\beta}$ is the least squares estimator you derived in Exercise 4.6.

4.5   Hypothesis Testing

The sampling distributions (4.28) provide the basis for hypothesis tests and confidence intervals on α and β, in a way that parallels the logic of Section 2.5.1.

Transforming $\hat{\beta}$ by subtracting its mean and dividing by its standard deviation yields the standard normal random variable

$$\frac{\hat{\beta} - \beta}{\sigma \big/ \sqrt{\sum x_i^2}} \sim N(0, 1).$$

This transformation of $\hat{\beta}$ is not a computable statistic, of course, because it involves the unknown parameters β and σ. Suppose that, in place of σ, the standard error of the estimate s is substituted. Equivalently, suppose the denominator is replaced by the estimated standard error $s_{\hat{\beta}}$ defined in (4.30). As is to be expected, the variability associated with $s_{\hat{\beta}}$ means that the distribution is no longer N(0, 1). Instead the following result holds, which may fruitfully be compared with Result 2.7 of Chapter 2.

Result 4.2   *In the context of the classical normal linear regression model* (4.1),

$$\frac{\hat{\alpha} - \alpha}{s_{\hat{\alpha}}} \sim t(n - 2) \quad and \quad \frac{\hat{\beta} - \beta}{s_{\hat{\beta}}} \sim t(n - 2). \tag{4.31}$$

The value of this result is that confidence interval formulas and hypothesis-testing procedures follow from it.

Confidence Intervals

Consider a confidence interval on β. The distributional result (4.31) means that there is, for example, a 95% probability that the statistic will fall between bounds cutting off tail areas of 0.025 of the $t(n - 2)$ distribution. More formally, the following probability statement may be made:

$$\Pr\left(-t_{a/2}(n - 2) < \frac{\hat{\beta} - \beta}{s_{\hat{\beta}}} < t_{a/2}(n - 2) \right) = 1 - a, \tag{4.32}$$

where $t_{a/2}(n - 2)$ indicates a tabulated value of the t distribution with $n - 2$

degrees of freedom cutting off a right-tail area of $a/2$. After we manipulate the inequality inside the parentheses, an equivalent statement is

$$\Pr\left(\hat{\beta} - s_{\hat{\beta}}t_{a/2}(n-2) < \beta < \hat{\beta} + s_{\hat{\beta}}t_{a/2}(n-2)\right) = 1 - a. \tag{4.33}$$

This means that, in repeated sampling, bounds computed as

$$\hat{\beta} \pm s_{\hat{\beta}}t_{a/2}(n-2) \tag{4.34}$$

will include the true population value of β a proportion $(1-a)$ of the time. These bounds are called a $(1-a)100\%$ confidence interval for β. Considering the significance level $a = 0.05$, when the sample size is greater than about $n = 20$ the tabulated value of $t(n-2)$ is approximately 2; this tabulated value approaches 1.96, the corresponding value of the standard normal distribution, as $n \to \infty$. This is the basis for the rule of thumb that a coefficient lies within two standard errors of its estimate with 95% confidence. By a similar derivation analogous bounds are available for α.

Practitioner's Tip: **The confidence interval rule of thumb**

For sample sizes larger than about twenty, a regression coefficient lies within two standard errors of its estimate with 95% confidence.

This is, of course, just the confidence-interval analog of the t test rule of thumb given in the Practitioner's Tip in Section 2.5.1.

EXAMPLE 4

In Jacob Mincer's statistical earnings function discussed in Theory Meets Application 4.1, the rate of return to a year of education was estimated to be $\hat{\beta} = 0.070$. Mincer obtained an estimated standard error of

$$s_{\hat{\beta}} = 0.00160.$$

How precise is his estimate of the returns to education?

SOLUTION

Mincer's estimate was based on a very large sample of size $n = 31,093$, and so the tabulated values of the t distribution are those of the standard normal. For a tail area of $a/2 = 0.025$, the tabulated value of the t distribution is $t_{a/2} = 1.96$. Consequently, the bounds

$$\hat{\beta} \pm s_{\hat{\beta}}t_{a/2} = 0.070 \pm 0.00160 \times 1.96 = (0.0669, 0.0731)$$

should contain the true value of β approximately 95% of the time in repeated sampling. In this sense, Mincer's estimate is quite precise; we can be very confident that the true rate of return is roughly in the range 6.7 to 7.3%.

Hypothesis Tests

Although the ability to construct confidence intervals is important in statistics generally and serves to illustrate the value of a distributional result such as Result 4.2, interval estimation tends to play a minor role in applied econometrics. Economists are most often interested in whether a posited theoretical explanation for economic events is consistent with what has been observed, and so hypothesis testing is the most heavily used application of results such as (4.31).

Consider the null hypothesis that β is equal to some particular numerical value, say β_0:

$$H_0: \beta = \beta_0. \tag{4.35}$$

The alternative hypothesis is that H_0 is false:

$$H_A: \beta \neq \beta_0.$$

If H_0 is indeed true, then the evaluation of (4.31) under the null hypothesis that $\beta = \beta_0$ yields a t statistic that has the t distribution given by Result 4.2:

$$t = \frac{\hat{\beta} - \beta_0}{s_{\hat{\beta}}} \sim t(n - 2). \tag{4.36}$$

Hence, if the computed value of this t statistic is, loosely speaking, in the center of a t distribution based on $n - 2$ degrees of freedom, this is evidence consistent with the null hypothesis. If the null hypothesis is false, so that in reality it is the case that $\beta \neq \beta_0$, then the distribution of the statistic evaluated using $\beta = \beta_0$ is something different from $t(n - 2)$. Consequently, the computed value for the statistic tends to be away from the center of the $t(n - 2)$ distribution, and this is interpreted as evidence against the null hypothesis.

The mechanics of applying these ideas were summarized in Section 2.5.1. Let us restate these steps, this time cast in terms of a test on β.

Step 1. *Specify the null and alternative hypotheses.* As we have emphasized repeatedly, a population is characterized by its parameters. Hypotheses about the population therefore take the form of restrictions on these parameters. The null hypothesis is that some parameter restriction holds; hypothesis (4.35) is an example. The alternative hypothesis is that this restriction is false; it may be one-sided or two-sided. Table 4.1 lists the most common combinations of null and alternative hypotheses on a single parameter such as β: case a is of a two-sided alternative, cases b and c are of one-sided alternatives. Although our focus at present is on restrictions involving just a single parameter, in Chapter 10 you will learn how to test much more general restrictions involving more than one parameter.

Step 2. *Identify the test statistic and its distribution.* Whether H_0 should be rejected or not must be judged on the basis of the data, and the information in the data relevant to this judgement is summarized by the test statistic. For the testing problem we are considering, the t statistic and its distribution are given in Result 4.2.

Step 3. *Statement of the rejection region based on a chosen significance level.* What values of the test statistic will be regarded as evidence inconsistent with the null hypothesis? Intuitively, values that are far out in the tails of the distribution. How

TABLE 4.1   **Null and Alternative Hypotheses and the Rejection Region**

	a	b	c
Alternative hypothesis	Two-sided	One-sided	One-sided
H_0	$\beta = \beta_0$	$\beta \leq \beta_0$	$\beta \geq \beta_0$
H_A	$\beta \neq \beta_0$	$\beta > \beta_0$	$\beta < \beta_0$
Rejection region	$|t| > t_{a/2}(n-2)$	$t > t_a(n-2)$	$t < -t_a(n-2)$

far out? This is decided by our choice of significance level a. The tabulated values of the distribution associated with this significance level are the critical values determining the rejection region. The last line of Table 4.1 summarizes the form of the rejection region for the t test under the various hypothesis configurations. The symbol $t_a(n-2)$ denotes the tabulated value of the t distribution with $n-2$ degrees of freedom cutting off a right tail area of a.

Step 4. Calculate the test statistic and compare it with the rejection region. The calculation of the t statistic (4.36) and comparison of it with the rejection region allow us to conclude whether we are led to reject H_0 in favor of H_A on the basis of the data.

EXAMPLE 5   Does Mincer's earnings function constitute compelling evidence that there is an economic return to education, or might the positive slope estimate simply be due to sampling error?

SOLUTION   It is natural to take as a null hypothesis the absence of a return to education: H_0: $\beta \leq 0$. It will only be concluded that there is a positive return if this can be rejected in favor of the alternative, H_A: $\beta > 0$.

The test statistic is the t statistic (4.36). The rejection region is one-sided; the null hypothesis is rejected if $t > t_a(n-2)$. For, say, a 1% level of significance, the critical value is $t_{0.01}(n-2) = 2.326$. This is a tabulated value from the standard normal distribution because the sample size $n = 31,093$ is very large.

Using Mincer's slope estimate and standard error, the test statistic evaluates to

$$t = \frac{\hat{\beta} - \beta_0}{s_{\hat{\beta}}} = \frac{0.070 - 0}{0.00160} = 43.75.$$

This greatly exceeds the critical value, and so the null hypothesis is rejected. Diagrammatically, the computed value of the test statistic relative to its distribution is as follows:

0

43.75

The conclusion is that Mincer's data offer strong evidence of a positive return to education.

Notice that when hypotheses are one-sided, the weak inequality is always assigned to the null hypothesis and the strong inequality to the alternative. This is because the test statistic is evaluated under the null and so is evaluated at this equality, as this example illustrates.

When we choose to test at a significance level of 1%, we are setting the probability of Type I error to be no greater than 0.01. Recall that a Type I error is the mistake of incorrectly rejecting the null hypothesis—of finding a significant effect purely as a result of sampling error. For Mincer's regression, the t statistic is so large it would reject at a significance level considerably lower than 0.01; in other words, the p-value is much smaller than 0.01. Another way of expressing this is that if it were really true that $\beta = 0$, it is extremely unlikely that an estimate as large as $\hat{\beta} = 0.070$ would be obtained from his data. The chance of finding such a value as a result of sampling error is remote.

EXAMPLE 6

 nerlove1.dat

In Nerlove's electricity generation data, do production costs depend on the level of output?

SOLUTION

If costs do not depend on output, the implication is that $\beta = 0$ in the simple regression model of Example 1. The alternative hypothesis is that $\beta \neq 0$.[4]

The test statistic is the t statistic (4.36). The rejection region is two-sided; the null hypothesis will be rejected if $|t| > t_{a/2}(n - 2)$. For a sample of size $n = 145$, the t distribution is closely approximated by the standard normal; at, say, a 1% level of significance, the critical value is $t_{0.005}(n - 2) = 2.576$.

Using the previously reported slope estimate and standard error, the test statistic evaluates to

$$t = \frac{\hat{\beta} - \beta_0}{s_{\hat{\beta}}} = \frac{0.00643 - 0}{0.0001719} = 37.40.$$

This greatly exceeds the critical value, and so the null hypothesis is rejected. The conclusion is that Nerlove's data offer strong evidence that production costs depend on the level of output.

As in the discussion of Chapter 2, the last two steps of the testing procedure may be restated using the p-value approach. In both these examples, the test statistic is so large that the p-value is close to zero.

---

[4] Had the question been posed as one of whether costs *increase* with output, the hypotheses would have been formulated as one-sided. The null would be $\beta \leq 0$ (costs do not increase with output), the alternative that $\beta > 0$ (costs do increase with output).

EXERCISES

4.19 Show the series of steps that lead from the inequality inside the parentheses of (4.32) to that of (4.33).

4.20 Consider the data on output X and production costs Y for the five electric power companies that are given in Exercise 3.6. Use the intermediate quantities you computed in part (b) of that exercise to do the following.

(a) Compute $\hat{\beta}$ and $\hat{\alpha}$.

(b) Compute SSE and s^2. (*Hint:* Use your solution to Exercise 4.10.)

(c) Compute $s_{\hat{\beta}}^2$ and $s_{\hat{\alpha}}^2$.

(d) Is the level of output an important determinant of production costs? Assuming population normality, carry out an appropriate test of H_0: $\beta = 0$ against H_A: $\beta \neq 0$.

(e) Do you expect that electric power generation involves significant fixed costs? Check your conjecture formally by testing H_0: $\alpha = 0$ against H_A: $\alpha > 0$. Be careful in indicating how this one-sided alternative hypothesis affects your selection of a rejection region for your test.

4.6   Decomposition of Sample Variation

We note in the introduction that a regression model

$$Y_i = \alpha + \beta X_i + \varepsilon_i \tag{4.37}$$

describes the determination of Y_i as the total of a systematic component associated with the explanatory variable and an unsystematic component associated with ε_i. Given our estimation of the sample regression line (4.9), one expression of which is

$$Y_i = \hat{Y}_i + e_i = \hat{\alpha} + \hat{\beta} X_i + e_i, \tag{4.38}$$

it is natural to ask what portion of the variation in Y_i is attributed to each of these two components by the estimated model. By *the variation in Y_i* we mean its variation about its sample mean,

$$\text{SST} = \sum_{i=1}^{n}(Y_i - \overline{Y})^2 = \sum_{i=1}^{n} y_i^2. \tag{4.39}$$

The acronym SST stands for **sum of squares (total)**; this statistic is also called the **sample variation** of Y. It is the numerator of the sample variance (2.7), the variance estimator that would be computed if Y_i was being studied in isolation.

A Simpler Model

In the context of the earlier simpler model in Chapter 2,

$$Y_i = \mu + \varepsilon_i, \tag{4.40}$$

the decomposition of sample variation is simple. Recall that the least squares estimator of μ is the sample mean: $\hat{\mu} = \overline{Y}$. The sample (i.e., estimated) version of the model is therefore

$$Y_i = \hat{\mu} + e_i = \overline{Y} + e_i. \tag{4.41}$$

This is to the model (4.40) as the sample regression line (4.38) is to the population regression model (4.37). In this context, the fitted values of the model are simply the values of Y that lie on the horizontal line determined by $\hat{\mu}$, so $\hat{Y}_i = \hat{\mu} = \overline{Y}$, and the least squares residuals are therefore the deviation forms of the dependent variable, $e_i = Y_i - \hat{Y}_i = Y_i - \overline{Y} = y_i$. Consequently, this model attributes the sample variation of Y entirely to the unsystematic component, the disturbance: $\sum y_i^2 = \sum e_i^2$.

The Regression Model

In the case of the regression model, on the other hand, the sample variation of the dependent variable SST is due to both the systematic and unsystematic influences on the right-hand side of the model. The natural measure of the unsystematic influence continues to be the sum of squared errors

$$\text{SSE} = \sum_{i=1}^{n} e_i^2 = \sum_{i=1}^{n} (Y_i - \hat{Y}_i)^2,$$

as defined in Section 4.2.2. Note, incidentally, the distinction between the SSE and the sum of squares function S defined by (4.12). The latter is a *function* of the regression coefficients; the least squares estimators are those that minimize this function. SSE denotes the value of the function at this minimum.

To isolate the component of SST attributable to the systematic influence—the explanatory variable—note that, for a particular observation i,

$$Y_i - \overline{Y} = (Y_i - \hat{Y}_i) + (\hat{Y}_i - \overline{Y}) = e_i + (\hat{Y}_i - \overline{Y}).$$

This decomposition is illustrated in Figure 4.3. Therefore,

$$\text{SST} = \sum_{i=1}^{n} [(\hat{Y}_i - \overline{Y}) + e_i]^2$$

$$= \sum_{i=1}^{n} (\hat{Y}_i - \overline{Y})^2 + \sum_{i=1}^{n} e_i^2 + 2\sum_{i=1}^{n} (\hat{Y}_i - \overline{Y}) e_i$$

$$= \text{SSR} + \text{SSE} + 0.$$

The notation SSR stands for **sum of squares of the regression.** It represents the variation in Y_i associated with the systematic component.[5]

---

[5] Unfortunately the SSR, SSE notation is not standardized across textbooks. In fact some texts use SSE (or ESS) to denote the component *explained* by variation in the explanatory variable, and SSR (or RSS) for the sum of squared *residuals*. The convention adopted here seems at least as common as the others.

FIGURE 4.3

Decomposition of
the sample variation
about $\bar{Y}$.

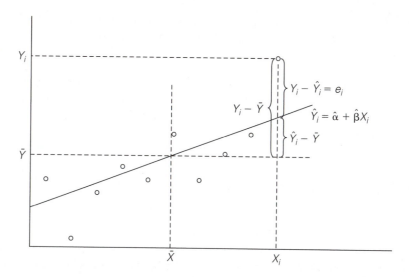

What establishes that the cross-product term is zero? Multiplying out that third
term, note first that

$$\sum_{i=1}^{n} \bar{Y} e_i = \bar{Y} \sum_{i=1}^{n} e_i = \bar{Y} \cdot 0 = 0.$$

This result follows from the fact that the least squares residuals sum to zero, the
first property (4.16a) of the least squares normal equations. Turning to the other
component of the cross-product term,

$$\sum_{i=1}^{n} \hat{Y}_i e_i = \sum_{i=1}^{n} (\hat{\alpha} + \hat{\beta} X_i) e_i = \hat{\alpha} \sum_{i=1}^{n} e_i + \hat{\beta} \sum_{i=1}^{n} X_i e_i = \hat{\alpha} \cdot 0 + \hat{\beta} \cdot 0 = 0.$$

The penultimate step uses the properties (4.16a) and (4.16b) of the normal equations.

4.6.1 R^2

This decomposition of the sample variation of Y_i suggests a convenient summary
measure of the proportion of the total variation in the dependent variable that is
explained by X_i. This is the **coefficient of determination** defined as[6]

$$R^2 = \frac{\text{SSR}}{\text{SST}} = 1 - \frac{\text{SSE}}{\text{SST}}, \qquad 0 \le R^2 \le 1. \tag{4.42}$$

The second expression follows from the first, given that SSR = SST − SSE.

Note that because SST, SSR, and SSE are all sums of squares they must be
positive. Further, because SST is the total of SSR and SSE, it follows that R^2 is a

---

[6] An important caveat to this definition is that this is not an appropriate goodness-of-fit measure when
the intercept is set equal to zero: $\alpha = 0$. This is the case of regression through the origin, considered
in Section 5.2.

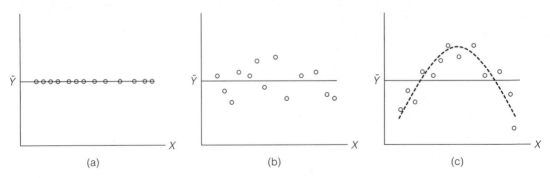

FIGURE 4.4 A horizontal sample regression line and zero R^2.

positive fraction. In the extreme $R^2 = 1$ if the (X_i, Y_i) data values lie exactly on the sample regression line, so that there is no unsystematic component involved in the generation of Y. In this case, the functional relationship between the two variables is deterministic rather than stochastic.

A convenient alternative formula for SSR may be obtained by using the sample regression line (4.9) and the fact (4.18) that it passes through the point of variable means. Subtracting (4.18) from (4.9) yields

$$\hat{Y}_i - \overline{Y} = \hat{\beta}(X_i - \overline{X}) = \hat{\beta}x_i, \tag{4.43}$$

so that SSR is

$$\text{SSR} = \sum_{i=1}^{n}(\hat{Y}_i - \overline{Y})^2 = \hat{\beta}^2 \sum_{i=1}^{n} x_i^2. \tag{4.44}$$

Hence, an alternative formula for R^2 that relates it directly to the slope estimator is

$$R^2 = \frac{\text{SSR}}{\text{SST}} = \frac{\hat{\beta}^2 \sum x_i^2}{\sum y_i^2}. \tag{4.45}$$

This indicates that $R^2 = 0$ when the sample regression line is horizontal, $\hat{\beta} = 0$.

Figure 4.4 shows that there are several ways in which this situation can arise. Figure 4.4(a) depicts a situation in which, irrespective of whatever the population value of β may be, the sampling procedure has for some reason not yielded observations on Y exhibiting variation. Consequently—at least in terms of the available data—there is no variation in Y for the regression model (or any other model) to explain. The R^2 formula (4.45) is actually undefined in this case because the denominator $\sum y_i^2$ is zero.

Contrast this with Figure 4.4(b), which depicts the case in which the data exhibit variation in Y, but in such a way that $\hat{\beta} = 0$ has been obtained. If this is because the population regression line is horizontal, so $\beta = 0$, then the model (4.40) is appropriate. In this instance, the explanatory variable X does not explain any of the variation in Y about its mean; this variation instead arises entirely from the disturbance ε_i.

Finally, Figure 4.4(c) depicts the case in which the linear regression model is misspecified: It is an incorrect representation of the data, which are in fact related nonlinearly in a way that has yielded $\hat{\beta} = 0$.

The R^2 and Statistical Significance

The positive relationship between R^2 and $|\hat{\beta}|$ described by (4.45) is of interest because it confirms our intuition that a low value for one will tend to be associated with a low value for the other. However, it is important not to make the mistake of inferring from a low R^2 that the explanatory variable is unimportant in determining Y. A test of the hypothesis H_0: $\beta = 0$ is the appropriate means of judging this. It is perfectly possible for X to be a statistically significant determinant of Y and yet explain a fairly small portion of its total variation. In fact, this situation is rather common in econometrics, where much of the variation in variables of interest may be due to unobservable or unquantifiable influences captured by ε_i. A classic example is statistical earnings functions such as the Mincer regression. In general, statistical earnings functions seek to understand the determination of wages or earnings as a function of personal characteristics such as age, education, gender, race, and so on. Although there is no difficulty finding variables that are important determinants of earnings—each of the four mentioned certainly is—the variation in earnings explained by quantifiable influences such as these is quite modest. In Mincer's simple regression of the log of earnings on years of schooling the R^2 turned out to be

$$R^2 = 0.067,$$

so education explains less than 7% of the variation in earnings among white, non-farm, nonstudent males. Nevertheless, as we have seen in Example 5, the hypothesis $\beta = 0$ is rejected very strongly by this data, so education is clearly a highly significant determinant of earnings. When Mincer proceeded to a multiple regression analysis in which work experience and its square were included as additional explanatory variables, these too were highly significant, yet the R^2 only increased to a still modest 0.285.

Practitioner's Tip: The R^2 and statistical significance

Never use the R^2 to judge the statistical significance of a regressor. The proper way to judge statistical significance is with a hypothesis test.

Relationship to the Correlation Coefficient

The R^2 is not the first summary measure of the strength of the linear relationship between two variables that we have studied. In Chapter 3, the sample correlation coefficient

$$r_{XY} = \frac{\sum x_i y_i}{\sqrt{\sum x_i^2 \sum y_i^2}} \tag{4.46}$$

was defined. The formula (4.45) makes it easy to see the link between the two because, substituting in the estimator formula $\hat{\beta} = \sum x_i y_i / \sum x_i^2$,

$$R^2 = \left(\frac{\sum x_i y_i}{\sum x_i^2}\right)^2 \frac{\sum x_i^2}{\sum y_i^2} = \frac{(\sum x_i y_i)^2}{\sum x_i^2 \sum y_i^2} = r_{XY}^2.$$

Hence, the coefficient of determination R^2, defined in connection with the decomposition of sample variation of the simple regression model, is in fact nothing more than the square of the correlation coefficient r_{XY}, which is defined independent of that model.

EXAMPLE 7

 nerlove1.dat

For the simple regression in Example 1 estimated using Nerlove's cost and output data, the decomposition of sample variation is

$$SST = 56422.86, \qquad SSR = 51190.39, \qquad SSE = 5232.47.$$

What is the R^2 and how does it relate to the sample correlation for these data given in Chapter 3?

SOLUTION

The R^2 is

$$R^2 = \frac{SSR}{SST} = \frac{51190.39}{56422.86} = 0.9073.$$

In our inspection of Nerlove's data set in Figure 3.1, the correlation between these variables is given as $r_{XY} = 0.9525$. Note that

$$r_{XY}^2 = (0.9525)^2 = 0.9073 = R^2.$$

Because the R^2 is just the square of the correlation coefficient, the caveats of the previous chapter concerning the interpretation of sample correlations apply equally to the R^2, and it is useful to reiterate them.

Causality does not imply correlation. Variables may be related in a way that is not revealed by the R^2. Because the R^2 is defined in connection with the linear regression model, it only indicates the strength of the linear relationship between the variables, just as we have seen is true of the correlation. A low R^2 may mask a strong nonlinear relationship, as in Figure 4.4(c). Furthermore, even when the true relationship is linear, a low R^2 can result from the failure to use multiple regression to control for omitted variables. Finally, a low R^2 is not the same thing as an absence of statistical significance. The Mincer example illustrates that one variable can be a highly significant determinant of another, yet explain only a very small portion of its variation.

Correlation does not imply causality. Just as in the example of family income and child-bearing propensities given in the previous chapter, a high R^2 can arise from the common effect of some unrecognized third influence. This is especially true of time series data, for which common trends can lead to spurious regressions.

EXERCISES

4.21 Given the definitions SST$= \sum y_i^2$ and SSE$= \sum e_i^2$, start with (4.42) and use your result from Exercise 4.10 to present an alternative proof that $R^2 = r_{XY}^2$.

4.22 Another interpretation of the R^2 is that it is the square of the correlation between the observed Y_i values and the fitted values. Establish this as follows.

(a) To begin, use the definition of the fitted values (4.9) to show that their sample mean $\sum \hat{Y}_i/n$ must be the same as the sample mean of the observed dependent variable, $\overline{Y}$.

(b) Given the result in (a), the sample correlation between the observed and fitted values is, applying the standard formula (4.46),

$$\frac{\sum (Y_i - \overline{Y})(\hat{Y}_i - \overline{Y})}{\sqrt{\sum (Y_i - \overline{Y})^2 \sum (\hat{Y}_i - \overline{Y})^2}}.$$

Use (4.43) to show that this is equal to r_{XY}, the sample correlation between the dependent and explanatory variables.

4.23 (Continuation of Exercise 4.20.) Use the intermediate quantities computed in Exercise 3.6b from the data on the five electric power companies to answer the following questions. Compute all intermediate quantities to the full internal accuracy of your calculator.

(a) Use equation (4.44) to compute SSR.

(b) In Exercise 3.6b, you have computed SST$= \sum y_i^2$ and in Exercise 4.20b you have computed SSE. Do your values satisfy SST $=$ SSR $+$ SSE?

(c) Use your decomposition of sample variation to compute the R^2. How is it related to the value for the sample correlation coefficient r_{XY} that you obtained in Exercise 3.6b?

4.6.2   Analysis of Variance and the F Test

The decomposition of sample variation leads to an alternative approach to testing the hypothesis H_0: $\beta = 0$ against H_A: $\beta \neq 0$ from the t test of Section 4.5. These hypotheses essentially ask whether the null hypothesis (4.40) of variation around a constant mean μ is rejected in favor of the regression model (4.37). This amounts to asking whether the systematic component measured by SSR is significantly large in relation to the unsystematic component measured by SSE. This may be tested formally with an F statistic of the form

$$F = \frac{\text{SSR}}{\text{SSE}/(n-2)} \sim F(1, n-2). \tag{4.47}$$

FIGURE 4.5

The F distribution,
with tabulated value
cutting off a tail
area of a.

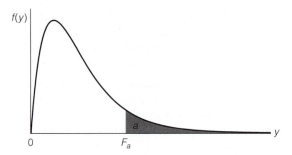

Because we are effectively asking whether the regression model (4.37) does a better job of explaining the behavior of Y than the simpler model (4.40), this is called the **F test of the regression model.**

The F distribution is shown in Figure 4.5. Under the null hypothesis $\beta = 0$, the value of SSR will be small in relation to SSE and the computed value of the statistic should fall in the center of the distribution. A value in the right tail of the distribution arises when SSR is large relative to SSE and is evidence against the null hypothesis. H_0 is rejected at significance level a if $F > F_a(1, n - 2)$. Notice that, although the alternative hypothesis $\beta \neq 0$ is two-sided, the rejection region is one-tailed. It would not make sense to reject H_0 on the basis of a value of the statistic in the *left* tail of the distribution. A small value of SSR relative to SSE is evidence consistent with $\beta = 0$, not $\beta \neq 0$.

What is the relationship between this test procedure and the t test in Section 4.5? For the null hypothesis $\beta = 0$, the t test is based on the computed statistic $t = \hat{\beta}/s_{\hat{\beta}}$. Using previously established results and notation,

$$F = \frac{\text{SSR}}{\text{SSE}/(n - 2)} = \frac{\hat{\beta}^2 \sum x_i^2}{s^2} = \frac{\hat{\beta}^2}{s^2/\sum x_i^2} = \left(\frac{\hat{\beta}}{s_{\hat{\beta}}}\right)^2 = t^2.$$

Thus the F statistic is nothing more than the square of the t statistic. Furthermore, a similar relationship exists between the tabulated values of the two distributions: For v degrees of freedom it is always the case that $F(1, v) = t^2(v)$. This means that the outcomes of the two test procedures are always consistent; given a chosen level of significance, it is not possible to reject using one procedure and fail to reject using the other.

The calculations linking the decomposition of sample variation to the F statistic are often summarized in the **analysis of variance** (ANOVA) table presented in Table 4.2. The total variation in the dependent variable SST is decomposed into its two components SSR and SSE. These sums of squares are statistics having sampling distributions; each can be shown to have a chi-square distribution, which is characterized by a degrees-of-freedom parameter. The degrees of freedom that apply in the present context of simple regression are given in the third column. The mean square is SSR and SSE divided by their respective degrees of freedom. (Note, incidentally, that SSE/$(n - 2)$ corresponds to the variance estimator s^2.)

TABLE 4.2

Analysis of Variance for Simple Regression

Source of variation	Sum of squares	Degrees of freedom	Mean square	F
Regression	$SSR = \hat{\beta}^2 \sum x_i^2$	1	SSR	$\dfrac{SSR}{SSE/(n-2)}$
Error	$SSE = \sum e_i^2$	$n-2$	$\dfrac{SSE}{n-2}$	
Total	$SST = \sum y_i^2$	$n-1$		

It can be shown that SSR and SSE are statistically independent. Hence, the F statistic, computed by dividing the mean squares, is the ratio of two independent chi-square random variables, each divided by its respective degrees of freedom. This is the definition of an F random variable.

EXAMPLE 8

 nerlove1.dat

Present the ANOVA table for the cost function regression using Nerlove's data. Perform an F test of the hypothesis $\beta = 0$. How does it compare with the t test of Example 6?

SOLUTION

The ANOVA for the regression in Example 1 is as follows.

Source of variation	Sum of squares	Degrees of freedom	Mean square	F
Regression	51190.39	1	51190.39	1399.0
Error	5232.47	143	36.591	
Total	56422.86	144		

This table shows that the computed value of the F statistic is

$$F = \frac{SSR}{SSE/(n-2)} = \frac{51190.39}{5232.47/143} = 1399.0.$$

Comparing this against a tabulated value of the distribution for, say, $a = 0.01$, we find that $F > F_{0.01}(1, 143) \approx 6.63$, so H_0 is easily rejected even at this high level of significance. The conclusion is that production costs depend very strongly on the level of output.

Compare this test procedure with the t test of Example 6; notice that the F statistic is the square of the t statistic,

$$F = 1399.0 = 37.40^2 = t^2,$$

and that the same relationship applies to the tabulated values:

$$F_{0.01}(1, 143) \approx 6.63 = 2.567^2 \approx t_{0.005}^2(143).$$

Consequently the outcomes of the two test procedures must be consistent: At a chosen level of significance, we can reject with one only if we reject with the other.

This equivalence of the two procedures means that, in the context of the simple regression model, the F test offers no advantage over the t test for testing hypotheses about β.[7] In fact the t test is the more useful of the two because it permits tests of the general hypothesis H_0: $\beta = \beta_0$ and is not limited to the special case $\beta = 0$; the t test also permits one-sided alternatives, whereas the alternative hypothesis of the F test is always $\beta \neq 0$. A consideration of the F test is primarily useful at this point because it anticipates a more general, and extremely useful, version of the test that arises in multiple regression.

Practitioner's Tip: The F test in simple regression

In simple regression, the F test of the regression model offers no information that is not available from a t test.

EXERCISES

4.24 (Continuation of Exercise 4.23.) Use the values for the decomposition of sample variation obtained in Exercise 4.23 to compute the F statistic, presenting your calculations in the form of an ANOVA table. Use this to apply the F test procedure, indicating carefully the relevant hypotheses, the value of the test statistic, the rejection region, and your decision. Indicate how each of these test components relates to or compares with the analogous components of the test you performed in Exercise 4.20d.

4.25 Because the R^2 and the F statistic are both

based on the decomposition of sample variation, we suspect they are related.

(a) Show that they are in fact very directly related by obtaining an expression for the F statistic alternative to (4.47) that can be computed solely from knowledge of R^2 and n. (*Hint:* Use (4.42).)

(b) A simple regression is to be estimated between two variables having a correlation of 0.92, based on 54 observations. Will the restriction $\beta = 0$ be rejected?

4.7   Presentation of Regression Results

We have now developed many formulas in connection with the regression model. Which of these yield values that are important to report for the purposes of an applied regression analysis?

The key regression results can be presented very briefly. They consist of the coefficient estimators $\hat\alpha$ and $\hat\beta$, their estimated standard errors $s_{\hat\alpha}$ and $s_{\hat\beta}$, and the R^2. In addition, determining the appropriate degrees of freedom for the t test requires

---

[7] This statement does not apply to a more general version of the F test that permits tests of joint hypotheses on α and β. Discussion of this more general test is deferred to Chapter 10, where it is most conveniently developed in the context of multiple regression.

knowledge of the sample size. A conventional way of summarizing this information is as follows.

$$Y_i = \underset{(s_{\hat{\alpha}})}{\hat{\alpha}} + \underset{(s_{\hat{\beta}})}{\hat{\beta}} X_i + e_i \qquad \begin{aligned} R^2 &= \\ n &= \end{aligned}$$

For example, the estimation results for the cost-output regression using Nerlove's data may be summarized in the following way.

$$Y_i = \underset{(0.622)}{-0.741} + \underset{(0.000172)}{0.00643} X_i + e_i \qquad \begin{aligned} R^2 &= 0.907 \\ n &= 145 \end{aligned}$$

When the only restrictions likely to be of interest are $\alpha = 0$ or $\beta = 0$, researchers sometimes report the values of the t ratios $\hat{\alpha}/s_{\hat{\alpha}}$ and $\hat{\beta}/s_{\hat{\beta}}$ in parentheses under the coefficients, rather than the estimated standard errors. In this way the reader can observe immediately whether the t ratio exceeds the critical value corresponding to some chosen significance level. When other hypotheses may be of interest, the more common convention is to report the estimated standard errors and leave the calculation of t statistics to the reader.

EXERCISES

4.26 Reporting the four values $\hat{\beta}$, $s_{\hat{\beta}}$, R^2, and n, although useful for completeness, involves some redundancy in that any one of the four can be deduced from the other three.

(a) Establish the functional relationship among them that will permit this. That is, find an equation that involves all four quantities, so that any one of them can be solved for. (*Hint:* Use your answer to Exercise 4.25.)

(b) The regression described in Exercise 4.25b yields the estimate $\hat{\beta} = 37.5$. What is its standard error?

4.8   Scaling and Units of Measure

The essential elements of an applied regression analysis are, then, very simple. It is worth examining how they are affected by one aspect of the analysis that involves some arbitrariness: the units of measure of the variables X and Y. Units of measure are arbitrary in that there are typically a number of ways in which a variable may be measured: millions instead of billions, meters instead of feet, liters instead of gallons, and so on. Transforming a variable from one unit of measure to another involves a **scaling factor.** For example, if X_i is GNP measured in billions of dollars (say, $12.345 billion) and X_i denotes the same variable measured in millions ($12,345 million), the two are related by $X_i = v X_i$, where $v = 1000$ is the scaling factor. Similarly, measuring in quarts rather than gallons involves a scaling factor of 4.

Scale Invariance

Given that in any data analysis the units of measure are to some degree arbitrary, it is often useful to work in terms of quantities that are not affected by variable scalings. Such quantities are said to be **scale invariant.**

An elementary example of a scale-invariant quantity is a percentage change. When we work in terms of percentages, we do so because we want to express changes in a way that is independent of the absolute magnitude of the variable. This is just another way of saying that it is more convenient to work in terms of scale-invariant quantities.

EXAMPLE 9

The percentage change in a variable is the relative change

$$\frac{\Delta X_t}{X_{t-1}} = \frac{X_t - X_{t-1}}{X_{t-1}}$$

times 100. Show that such changes are scale invariant.

SOLUTION

Consider the relative change of the rescaled variable:

$$\frac{X_t - X_{t-1}}{X_{t-1}} = \frac{v X_t - v X_{t-1}}{v X_{t-1}} = \frac{v(X_t - X_{t-1})}{v X_{t-1}} = \frac{X_t - X_{t-1}}{X_{t-1}}.$$

Thus the scaling factor v cancels out of the expression. The relative or percentage change in a variable is the same regardless of how it is measured.

Another good illustration of a scale-invariant quantity is an index. Consider the Laspeyres index in Section 1.1.3,

$$\text{Laspeyres index} = \frac{\sum_{i=i}^{n} p_{ti} q_{0i}}{\sum_{i=1}^{n} p_{0i} q_{0i}}.$$

The point of computing an index is to measure the relative values a variable takes on, abstracting from its absolute level. Suppose that the amount of each commodity in the CPI market basket is doubled, so that the quantities are scaled by the factor $v = 2$. The index remains unchanged:

$$\frac{\sum_{i=i}^{n} p_{ti} 2q_{0i}}{\sum_{i=1}^{n} p_{0i} 2q_{0i}} = \frac{2 \sum_{i=i}^{n} p_{ti} q_{0i}}{2 \sum_{i=1}^{n} p_{0i} q_{0i}} = \frac{\sum_{i=i}^{n} p_{ti} q_{0i}}{\sum_{i=1}^{n} p_{0i} q_{0i}}.$$

Similarly, suppose that both base period prices p_{0i} and current period prices p_{ti} are ten times as high, perhaps because we choose to measure in dimes instead of dollars. The common factors in the numerator and denominator will cancel, leaving the index unchanged. An index is scale invariant.

Regression and Scale Invariance

How are the results of regression analysis affected by variable scalings? It stands to reason that some of the values obtained, such as the estimated coefficients, may be dependent on the units of measure. Because $\hat{\beta}$ represents the typical response in Y to a one unit change in X, it makes sense that it be defined with respect to the chosen units of measure. The response of consumption expenditure to a unit change in income, for example, will differ depending on whether that unit is \$1 or \$1000. On the other hand, we hope that other aspects of the analysis will be invariant to scaling of the data. An important example is a test of the hypothesis $\beta = 0$. Because this is the hypothesis that X is unimportant as a determinant of Y, it is to be hoped that the answer to this question does not depend on the manner in which the variables happen to be measured. Another example is the coefficient of determination: To be a useful measure of the proportion of the sample variation in Y explained by X, the R^2 should not be affected by variable scalings.

The effect of data scaling on least squares regression analysis may be examined fairly easily using the deviation-form expressions for the statistics. Consider the scaling factors v and w applied to X and Y,

$$X_i = vX_i, \qquad Y_i = wY_i.$$

By Example 3 of Chapter 3, the same scalings will apply to the deviation forms of the variables:

$$x_i = X_i - \overline{X} = vX_i - v\overline{X} = v(X_i - \overline{X}) = vx_i,$$

and similarly for Y. The sample covariance and correlation are convenient examples to use in illustrating the effect on sample statistics of changes in units of measure.

EXAMPLE 10

In Chapter 3, the sample covariance relating X and Y is defined as:

$$s_{xy} = \frac{1}{n-1} \sum_{i=1}^{n} x_i y_i.$$

It is asserted there that one disadvantage of the sample covariance as a measure of the strength of the relationship between variables is that it is dependent on the units of measure. This then motivates the introduction of the sample correlation coefficient

$$r_{XY} = \frac{\sum x_i y_i}{\sqrt{\sum x_i^2 \sum y_i^2}},$$

which is asserted to be invariant to the units of measure. Show that the covariance is affected by units of measure but the correlation is not.

SOLUTION

Computed on the basis of scaled variables, the numerator of the covariance is

$$\sum_{i=1}^{n} x_i y_i = \sum_{i=1}^{n} vx_i wy_i = vw \sum_{i=1}^{n} x_i y_i,$$

and so the covariance is affected by the units of measure. The correlation, on the other hand, is

$$r_{XY} = \frac{\sum x_i y_i}{\sqrt{\sum x_i^2 \sum y_i^2}} = \frac{\sum v x_i w y_i}{\sqrt{\sum v^2 x_i^2 \sum w^2 y_i^2}} = \frac{vw \sum x_i y_i}{\sqrt{v^2 w^2 \sum x_i^2 \sum y_i^2}}$$

$$= \frac{vw \sum x_i y_i}{vw \sqrt{\sum x_i^2 \sum y_i^2}} = \frac{\sum x_i y_i}{\sqrt{\sum x_i^2 \sum y_i^2}} = r_{XY},$$

which is not.

Thus the correlation is an example of a scale-invariant quantity. Appendix B, Section B.10.4 shows that this is true of a population correlation just as it is of the sample correlation.

EXAMPLE 11   Suppose initially two variables X and Y are measured in gallons and meters, respectively. Subsequently the variables are measured in quarts and centimeters. How are the covariance and correlation affected?

SOLUTION   In this case, the scale factors are $v = 4$ and $w = 100$, so the covariance increases by a factor of 400. The correlation is unaffected.

Scale-invariant quantities are also called **dimensionless.** The dimensionless quantity best known to economists is an elasticity.

Scale Invariance of Regression Coefficients

With this background, let us return to regression analysis. Because we have shown that the coefficient of determination is just the square of the correlation, $R^2 = r_{XY}^2$, it follows immediately that it must be scale invariant. The following results with respect to the estimated coefficients and standard errors are obtainable by derivations similar to that of Example 10. (Exercises 4.27 and 4.28 guide you through the steps leading to the results for $\hat{\beta}$.)

$$\hat{\alpha} = w\hat{\alpha} \qquad\qquad \hat{\beta} = \frac{w}{v}\hat{\beta}$$

$$s_{\hat{\alpha}} = w s_{\hat{\alpha}} \qquad\qquad s_{\hat{\beta}} = \frac{w}{v} s_{\hat{\beta}}$$

These results indicate that both the estimated coefficients and their standard errors are, in general, affected by units of measure. The values associated with the slope are affected by scalings applied to both the explanatory and dependent variables; however, note that if $v = w$ so that the *same* measurement change is applied to both variables, the effects cancel. The values of $\hat{\alpha}$ and $s_{\hat{\alpha}}$ are affected only by the scaling of the dependent variable.

Scale Invariance of Test Statistics

What do these effects on the coefficients and standard errors mean for hypothesis tests? For the hypotheses $\alpha = 0$ or $\beta = 0$ the relevant test statistics are the t ratios, which are unaffected:

$$t = \frac{w\hat{\alpha}}{ws_{\hat{\alpha}}} = \frac{\hat{\alpha}}{s_{\hat{\alpha}}}, \qquad t = \frac{(w/v)\hat{\beta}}{(w/v)s_{\hat{\beta}}} = \frac{\hat{\beta}}{s_{\hat{\beta}}}.$$

Hence, for these hypotheses, t statistics are another example of dimensionless quantities. The invariance of these test statistics to data scaling means that, reassuringly, our decisions with respect to these hypotheses will not be affected by arbitrary choices of units of measure. Note, however, that for the more general hypotheses $\alpha = \alpha_0$ or $\beta = \beta_0$ the cancellation of the factors in the numerator and denominator of the t statistics does not take place, and so these test results *will* be affected by scaling. This is as it should be: When the dependent and explanatory variables are scaled by different factors (so that $v \neq w$) the magnitudes of the coefficients relating them change; hypotheses have to be reformulated accordingly, scaled by the appropriate factor. The exception is the slope coefficient when $v = w$, so the same scaling applies to both variables. In this case, we have already seen that $\hat{\beta}$ and $s_{\hat{\beta}}$ are unaffected and, consequently, so too is the t statistic even for the general hypothesis $\beta = \beta_0$.

In conclusion, some aspects of least squares regression analysis are affected by changes in the units of measure, others are invariant to such changes. It makes sense that this should be the case. Most important, the R^2 and the t statistics for the hypotheses of zero coefficients are all scale invariant.

Scale invariance of test statistics is an important property. If a test statistic is not scale invariant, then different test conclusions can be reached simply by changing the units in which variables are measured. It happens that in certain estimation problems applied econometricians sometimes unwittingly use test statistics that are not scale invariant, a point to which we return in Section 13.8.6.

Invariance to Sample Order

Scale invariance is an example of an **invariance property.** It is one aspect of the general consideration that statistical analysis should not depend on what might be termed *arbitrary incidentals.* In addition to units of measure, another example of an arbitrary incidental is the sample ordering of cross-section data (or, for that matter, any data obtained by i.i.d. sampling). In the analysis of Nerlove's 145 electricity generating plants, our conclusions should not depend on which plant happens to be labeled observation 1, which is labeled observation 2, and so on. Estimators, test statistics, and other statistics such as the R^2 should be **invariant to sample order.**

It is easy to see that least squares regression analysis is invariant to sample order. Upon inspecting the various formulas we have derived in this chapter, it is apparent that the results of simple regression depend only on the sums $\sum X_i$, $\sum Y_i$, $\sum X_i^2$, $\sum Y_i^2$, and $\sum X_i Y_i$, not on the ordering of the individual observations that make up those sums.[8] Invariance to sample order is another appealing invariance property possessed by least squares regression.

EXERCISES

In the first four of the following exercises, assume that the units of measure of both the dependent and explanatory variables have been changed by scaling factors.

4.27 Use the deviation form expression (4.21) for $\hat{\beta}$ to show that $\hat{\beta} = (w/v)\hat{\beta}$.

4.28 Proceed through the following steps to examine the effect of scaling on the estimated standard error of $\hat{\beta}$, which, you recall, is computed as the square root of

$$s_{\hat{\beta}}^2 = \frac{s^2}{\sum x_i^2} = \frac{1}{\sum x_i^2} \frac{\sum e_i^2}{n-2}.$$

(a) In Exercise 4.7 you show that the least squares residuals may be expressed as $e_i = y_i - \hat{\beta}x_i$. Show that $e_i = we_i$.

(b) Using the definition $s^2 = \sum e_i^2/(n-2)$, show that $s^2 = w^2 s^2$.

(c) Using the definition $s_{\hat{\beta}}^2 = s^2/\sum x_i^2$, show that $s_{\hat{\beta}}^2 = (w/v)^2 s_{\hat{\beta}}^2$.

4.29 It has been concluded that, because the R^2 is the square of the correlation coefficient r_{XY} and the latter is scale invariant, so too must be the R^2. Let us consider this issue directly by examining the R^2 in terms of the decomposition of sample variation.

(a) How is SST affected by variable scalings?

(b) How is SSE affected by variable scalings? (*Hint:* You may take as given the results of the previous exercise, in particular the result that $e_i = we_i$.)

(c) Given your conclusions about SST and SSE, by implication how must SSR be affected by variable scalings?

(d) How, then, is the R^2 affected?

4.30 The F test provides an alternative approach to testing whether $\beta = 0$. Is the value of the F statistic invariant to scaling of the data? Explain your answer.

4.31 Consider your estimation of the relationship between production costs Y and output X in Exercises 4.20, 4.23, and 4.24, which are based on data provided in Exercise 3.6. Suppose costs were measured in millions rather than thousands of dollars. Indicate how the following aspects of your regression analysis would be affected.

(a) The estimated coefficients $\hat{\alpha}$ and $\hat{\beta}$.

(b) Their estimated standard errors $s_{\hat{\alpha}}$ and $s_{\hat{\beta}}$.

(c) The R^2.

(d) Your test of the hypothesis that $\beta = 0$.

(e) Your test of the hypothesis that $\alpha = 0$.

4.32 The following estimation results are obtained for an equation relating household consumption Y to income X, both variables being measured in thousands of dollars.

$$\hat{Y}_i = 14.17 + 0.776\ X_i \qquad R^2 = 0.66$$
$$\quad (4.32) \quad (0.0290) \qquad\quad n = 372$$

(a) What unit change in consumption expenditure is associated with a one-unit change in income?

(b) What is the value of the t statistic for a test of the hypothesis that income is not an important determinant of consumption?

(c) What is the value of the t statistic for a test of the hypothesis that the marginal propensity to consume is 0.8?

---

[8] For example, consider the hand calculator Exercise 3.6 and the regression exercises in this chapter that follow from it. Had you simply been given the numerical values of the sums in Exercise 3.6b, you could have proceeded with the rest of the analysis.

(d) Suppose that the equation is reestimated with consumption measured in dollars and income in hundreds of dollars.

i. What unit change in consumption expenditure will now be found to be associated with a unit change in income?

ii. What is the value of the t statistic for a test of the hypothesis that income is not an important determinant of consumption?

iii. What is the value of the t statistic for a test of the hypothesis that $\beta = 0.8$ in the newly estimated model?

iv. What is the value of the t statistic for a test of the hypothesis that the marginal propensity to consume is 0.8?

4.9   Summary: Sampling, Numerical, and Invariance Properties

We have now discussed so many properties of least squares that it may be useful to conclude this chapter by noting that these properties fall into three distinct groups.

Sampling Properties What we have most often referred to as *properties of estimators* are in fact their sampling properties—properties such as unbiasedness, efficiency, and best linear unbiasedness that relate to features of the sampling distribution of the estimator. As we have taken some care to emphasize, sampling properties are conditional on the assumed underlying population model—in other words, they depend on how the data have been generated. Because features of a sampling distribution can only be established on the basis of an assumed population model, sampling properties may not hold if this assumed model does not accurately describe the generation of the data.

Numerical Properties Sampling properties contrast with what we have called the numerical properties of least squares. These are properties that hold for least squares as a mechanical or descriptive curve-fitting device and that have nothing to do with how the sample was generated. Specifically, we have seen that the normal equations imply two numerical properties of the least squares residuals: (1) the residuals sum to zero and (2) the residuals are orthogonal to the explanatory variable. As a corollary of the first property, the least squares sample regression line passes through the point of variable means. We have shown algebraically that these properties must always hold and that they can be verified numerically. If the least squares sample regression line and its associated residuals do not satisfy these properties, a mistake has been made in the calculations.

Invariance Properties Finally, we have seen that least squares regression analysis has desirable invariance properties. The least squares estimators and related quantities such as test statistics and R^2 are invariant to arbitrary incidentals such as units of measure and sample order.

Numerical and invariance properties can be established by direct inspection of the relevant statistics, as we have done in this chapter. By contrast, sampling properties are derived on the basis of an assumed population distribution, but cannot be verified to hold for any particular sample of data because we can never know whether that assumed population model is a correct representation of how the data were generated. It is, however, possible in some situations to test statistically the population assumptions on which sampling properties depend, as we see in Chapters 12 and 14.

4.10   Application: Output and Production Costs

Beginning with Exercise 3.6 of the previous chapter, a series of hand-calculator exercises has guided you through the elements of correlation and simple regression analysis. The five observations of output and production costs used in those exercises are taken from Nerlove's complete data set on 145 electricity generating companies that we initially inspected in Figure 3.1. All 145 observations are available in the file **nerlove1.dat**.

Use econometric software to answer the following questions. Begin by inspecting the data file, noting the order of the variables and the fact that the first two lines of the file are occupied by variable names and a blank line. The variable definitions are as follows.

costs   Total production costs (millions of dollars).

kwh   Electricity generation (billions of kilowatt-hours).

EXERCISES

4.33 (a) 💿 **nerlove1.dat** Produce a plot of the data, with output on the horizontal axis and costs on the vertical axis. Does your plot reproduce Figure 3.1?

(b) As a new variable, generate average cost per unit of output, often called simply **unit cost.** Produce a plot of this variable against output. In generating this variable, scale by a factor of 1000 (implicitly changing the unit of measure of costs to thousands of dollars rather than millions) in order to avoid very small values on the vertical axis. Unit costs are usually thought to decline with the level of output. Is this the pattern revealed by these data?

4.34 💿 **nerlove1.dat** Returning to the original variables, obtain the sample correlation between costs and output. Does it check with the value given in Chapter 3 in connection with Figure 3.1?

4.35 💿 **nerlove1.dat** Estimate a least squares regression of costs on output. The key elements of this regression analysis have been presented in a series of examples in this chapter.

EXAMPLE 1   The coefficient estimates $\hat{\alpha}$ and $\hat{\beta}$.

EXAMPLE 2   The estimated variance s^2 and its square root, the standard error of the estimate s.

EXAMPLE 3   The estimated standard errors $s_{\hat{\alpha}}$ and $s_{\hat{\beta}}$.

EXAMPLE 6   The t statistic for the hypothesis $\beta = 0$.

EXAMPLE 7   The decomposition of sample variation, and the R^2.

EXAMPLE 8   The F statistic.

(a) i. Identify as many of these values on your output as possible.

ii. In this data set, costs are measured in millions of dollars, whereas in the hand-calculator exercises beginning with Exercise 3.6 they are expressed in thousands of dollars. Suppose this data set has also now been so expressed. Which of the quantities you have identified is invariant to this change?

(b) We have seen that certain relationships should hold among the statistics of a regression analysis.
i. What relationship should hold between the R^2 and the sample correlation of Exercise 4.34? Is this satisfied on your output?

ii. What relationship should hold between the t statistic for the hypothesis $\beta = 0$ and the F statistic? Is this satisfied on your output? Highlight both values, drawing a line between them to emphasize this link. If your software produces p-values for these statistics, they should be the same because the two tests are equivalent. Are they?

(c) Does your software allow you to conveniently plot the sample regression line against the data? If so, does this suggest any deficiency in the way this regression model describes this cost function?

5

Supplementary Topics in Regression

This chapter considers some natural extensions and qualifications to the regression analysis of the preceding chapter: forecasting, regression through the origin, and an acknowledgement of some important limitations to the applicability of least squares regression. Finally, the appendix studies an empirical application of simple regression that is a natural follow-up to our treatment of regression through the origin, the capital asset pricing model.

Our coverage of these topics anticipates their occasional reappearance in later chapters. The results on forecasting provide some intuition that will be important in our treatment of time series analysis in Chapters 15–18. Regression through the origin plays a role in Chapters 10 and 14. And the capital asset pricing model is one of the empirical models cited in Section 12.5.2, as well as having as its foundation the portfolio analysis of Appendix C.

Although these topics could as easily be presented in connection with multiple regression, and thus postponed until after Chapter 8, it turns out to be convenient to develop them using the elementary notation and formulas of simple regression.

5.1 Forecasting

In the introduction to Chapter 2 we remark that statistics uses data to describe, to infer, and to predict. We have now seen how it *describes* by estimating model parameters and how it *infers* by using hypothesis tests and confidence intervals to reach conclusions about the broader population. But how does statistics *predict*? The simple regression model can be used to illustrate some of the considerations that bear on this.

Consider using a simple regression to forecast. We continue to work in terms of the simple regression model of the previous chapter:

$$Y_i = \alpha + \beta X_i + \varepsilon_i, \qquad \varepsilon_i \sim \text{n.i.d.}(0, \sigma^2). \tag{5.1}$$

The estimated model is the sample regression line

$$\hat{Y}_i = \hat{\alpha} + \hat{\beta} X_i. \tag{5.2}$$

Suppose we want to make our best guess of the value Y_0 that is most likely to be associated with a hypothesized X_0. If the model is a correct description of how the dependent variable is in fact determined, Y_0 will be generated as

$$Y_0 = \alpha + \beta X_0 + \varepsilon_0. \tag{5.3}$$

The disturbance ε_0, being one realization of an i.i.d. random variable, is not predictable. The forecast must instead be based on the systematic component of the model using the best guesses of α and β; these are, of course, the least squares estimators. Thus the obvious forecast is given by the sample regression line:

$$\hat{Y}_0 = \hat{\alpha} + \hat{\beta} X_0.$$

EXAMPLE 1

 nerlove1.dat

In Chapter 4 we studied Nerlove's data on the production costs of electricity generation, estimating (in Example 1) the linear cost function

$$\hat{Y}_i = -0.741 + 0.00643 X_i.$$

As Figure 3.1 indicates, Nerlove's sample included a wide range of plant sizes, with output ranging from 2 billion kWh to over 15 trillion.

Suppose an electric power utility is considering building a new plant with a generating capacity of 6 trillion kWh. Predict its likely operating costs at capacity.

SOLUTION

Using the units on the basis of which the regression was estimated, substitute $X_0 = 6000$ into the cost function:

$$\hat{Y}_0 = -0.741 + 0.00643 \times 6000 = 37.839.$$

The predicted operating costs are \$37.839 million.

By coincidence there is, within the observed sample, a plant that happens to have this production level: the Duquesne Light Company. Its observed operating costs were \$33.154 million, well below the prediction of the model. Why not use this observed value as the forecast? The problem with doing so is that the Duquesne Light Company's costs are in part idiosyncratic to it, perhaps due to the plant's particular location, local regulatory or pollution restrictions, local labor and fuel costs, and so on. It is these idiosyncratic factors that are represented by its disturbance ε_i. A forecast should abstract from these plant-specific factors and be based on factors common to all firms. Thus, the forecast should use the information in the cost-output figures of other plants—even ones operating at quite different output levels—in making the prediction for the new plant. This is what the regression model does.

Unbiasedness of the Least Squares Forecast

Thus the regression model combines the information in all the sample observations in making forecasts. But in principle there are many ways of doing this. Is the least squares forecast in any sense an optimal one?

The mistake made in forecasting is the difference between the value we would like to forecast, Y_0, and the forecast provided by the model, $\hat{Y}_0$. This difference is called the **forecast error:**

$$\text{Forecast error} = Y_0 - \hat{Y}_0. \tag{5.4}$$

Assuming the model to be correctly specified, this forecast error has two sources.[1] This can be seen as follows.

$$\underbrace{Y_0 - \hat{Y}_0}_{\text{forecast error}} = (Y_0 - E(Y_0)) + (E(Y_0) - \hat{Y}_0)$$

$$= \underbrace{\varepsilon_0}_{\text{disturbance}} + \underbrace{(\alpha - \hat{\alpha}) + (\beta - \hat{\beta})X_0}_{\text{sampling error}}. \tag{5.5}$$

This shows that mistakes are made in forecasting for two reasons. First, even if the population regression line were known, forecasts would be made with error because the disturbance ε_0 is unknown. And second, the population regression line is *not* known; instead it must be estimated, and the mistakes made in estimation—sampling error—contribute further to the forecast error.

This expression can be used to show that the expected forecast error is zero:

$$E(Y_0 - \hat{Y}_0) = E(\varepsilon_0) - E(\hat{\alpha} - \alpha) - X_0 E(\hat{\beta} - \beta) = 0.$$

This uses the zero-mean property of the disturbance, $E(\varepsilon_0) = 0$, and the unbiasedness of the least squares estimators.

In this sense, then, the forecast is unbiased. Although mistakes are made in forecasting, these forecast errors are nevertheless evenly scattered around the true value Y_0; it is not being systematically over- or underpredicted.

Forecast Intervals

In addition to knowing that the least squares forecast is unbiased, it is useful to be able to gauge its accuracy. This can be done with a **forecast interval,** which is similar to a confidence interval. Whereas a confidence interval is a bound on a parameter value, a forecast interval is a bound on the value we are seeking to forecast, Y_0. Analogous to the $(1-a)100\%$ confidence interval (4.34) for β derived in the previous chapter, a **forecast interval** takes the form

$$\hat{Y}_0 \pm s_F t_{a/2}. \tag{5.6}$$

Here s_F denotes the estimated standard deviation of the forecast error, something we make precise below.

---

[1] If the model might not be correctly specified, specification uncertainty constitutes another source of forecast error. In what follows, the expressions for the forecast error variance s_F^2 would have to be modified accordingly. Model misspecification is considered in Chapter 12, although that chapter does not attempt to address its relevance to forecasting.

This forecast interval is an economical way of expressing the following probability statement:

$$\Pr\left(\hat{Y}_0 - s_F t_{a/2} < Y_0 < \hat{Y}_0 + s_F t_{a/2}\right) = 1 - a. \tag{5.7}$$

The underlying basis for the forecast interval is, therefore, a distributional result that allows us to make this probability statement. To understand the derivation of this distributional result, it is instructive to begin with the special case of known coefficients.

5.1.1   Forecast Intervals: No Coefficient Uncertainty

Consider the situation in which the coefficients α and β are known and hence need not be estimated. We can then forecast using the population regression line so that, in contrast to (5.2), the prediction is

$$\hat{Y}_i = \alpha + \beta X_i.$$

Because both the sample Y_i observations generated by the model (5.1) and the population regression line are known, the implication of this artificial setup is that the ε_i disturbances are known. In this context, there is no distinction between the residuals e_i and the disturbances ε_i; they are the same:

$$e_i = Y_i - \hat{Y}_i = \alpha + \beta X_i + \varepsilon_i - (\alpha + \beta X_i) = \varepsilon_i.$$

Although these disturbance realizations, $i = 1, \ldots, n$, are known, the variance σ^2 generating them is nevertheless unknown and still has to be estimated. The natural estimator continues to the sample variance s^2 given by (4.23).[2]

We do not, however, observe the disturbance ε_0 generating the value Y_0 that is to be forecasted. For example, if we want to predict the production costs of an electricity-generating plant with capacity $X_0 = 6000$, its idiosyncratic disturbance ε_0 is unpredictable. (After all, if ε_0 was known then equation (5.3) could be used to predict Y_0 exactly, and there would be no forecasting problem.)

Thus Y_0, the value we are seeking to forecast, is generated randomly by the regression model (5.3). The forecast is obtained from the population regression line:

$$\hat{Y}_0 = \alpha + \beta X_0.$$

The mistake made in forecasting is now due entirely to the fact that the disturbance ε_0 is unknown:

$$\text{Forecast error} = Y_0 - \hat{Y}_0 = \alpha + \beta X_0 + \varepsilon_0 - (\alpha + \beta X_0) = \varepsilon_0.$$

Compared with the general expression (5.5), this is the special case in which there is no sampling error component to the forecast error.

---

[2]   Although now the denominator should be n instead of $n - 2$ to have an unbiased estimator because no coefficients are being estimated.

In this formulation of the forecasting problem, it easy to obtain the distribution for the forecast error because we know the distribution of ε_0—it is given by the specification of the disturbance in the model (5.1),

$$\text{Forecast error} = Y_0 - \hat{Y}_0 = \varepsilon_0 \sim \mathrm{N}(0, \sigma^2).$$

If the true variance σ^2 was known, it could be used to standardize this normal random variable:

$$\frac{Y_0 - \hat{Y}_0}{\sigma} \sim \mathrm{N}(0, 1).$$

This would become the basis for our needed probability statement. But in fact the population variance σ^2 is unknown and must instead be replaced with its estimator s^2. As usual, the effect of this is that the relevant distribution is the t distribution:

$$\frac{Y_0 - \hat{Y}_0}{s} \sim t.$$

This permits the probability statement

$$\mathrm{Pr}\left(-t_{a/2} < \frac{Y_0 - \hat{Y}_0}{s} < t_{a/2}\right) = 1 - a,$$

which can be rearranged in the form (5.6),

$$\hat{Y}_0 \pm s\, t_{a/2}.$$

This is the desired forecast interval.

Figure 5.1 shows this forecast interval around the regression line. It shows that, because the standard deviation s is constant, the interval takes the form of parallel bounds. These parallel bounds have some implausible implications, which are best explained by thinking in terms of a time series forecasting problem.

Application to a Deterministic Trend Model

So far we have phrased the forecasting problem in terms of a **within-sample** prediction; that is, forecasting within the range of the observed data. But, especially in a time series context, economists are often interested in **out-of-sample** forecasting.

FIGURE 5.1

Forecast interval without coefficient uncertainty.

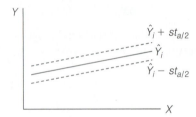

To make this point, let us restate the previous forecasting problem as one of predicting the future. Consider a variable observed over time, Y_t $(t = 1, \dots, n)$. Suppose it follows the deterministic trend model (2.32) introduced in Section 2.7,

$$Y_t = \alpha + \beta t + \varepsilon_t. \tag{5.8}$$

Remember that this is called a deterministic trend model because it describes Y_t as evolving randomly around a population regression line that is a deterministic trend: $E(Y_t) = \alpha + \beta t$.

Because this is just a change of notation from the simple regression specification (5.1), the previous forecast interval applies.

Result 5.1   *In the absence of coefficient uncertainty, a deterministic trend model with an i.i.d. disturbance has fixed-width forecast intervals.*

In forecasting beyond the most recently observed period n, a τ-period-ahead forecast is given by

$$\hat{Y}_{n+\tau} = \alpha + \beta(n + \tau).$$

Result 5.1 says that forecast uncertainty does not increase with the forecast horizon τ. We can forecast 100 years into the future with as much certainty we can forecast 1 year hence! This implication is, of course, quite implausible; no one believes the long term can be predicted as accurately as the short term.

There are two ways of resolving this unsatisfactory implication of deterministic trend models. One is to consider other ways of describing trends, something we do in Chapters 15–18. The other is to take into account coefficient uncertainty.

5.1.2   Forecast Intervals: Coefficient Uncertainty

In the more realistic situation in which the regression coefficients are unknown and so must be estimated, much the same ideas apply to the derivation of a forecast interval. The primary difference is that now the appropriate expression for the forecast error variance is more complicated because it must account for sampling error.

Returning to the forecast (5.3) given by the sample regression line, the appropriate expression for the forecast error is the more complex one (5.5). Now that coefficient uncertainty contributes to this forecast error, the appropriate expression for the forecast error variance turns out to be

$$\sigma_F^2 = V(Y_0 - \hat{Y}_0) = \sigma^2 \left[1 + \frac{1}{n} + \frac{(X_0 - \overline{X})^2}{\sum x_i^2} \right]. \tag{5.9}$$

Exercise 5.3 gives some hints for how to derive this. The last two terms inside the brackets arise from sampling error; in their absence the expression reduces to the previous one, $\sigma_F^2 = \sigma^2$, of the no-coefficient-uncertainty case.

Determinants of Forecast Accuracy

This expression helps us understand which factors contribute to forecast precision. First, σ_F^2 is directly related to the disturbance variance σ^2; a larger disturbance variance makes it harder to forecast accurately. Second, σ_F^2 is inversely related to the sample size n and the range of experience on the explanatory variable (as measured by its sample variation $\sum x_i^2$); larger values for these contribute to forecast accuracy.

Not coincidentally, these are the same factors that, in the previous chapter, we see contributing to estimator precision. It stands to reason that when the model coefficients can be estimated accurately, it makes it easier to forecast accurately.

As well, there is now an additional element in the formula—the difference $X_0 - \overline{X}$, the distance between the value X_0 on the basis of which the forecast is being made and the sample mean $\overline{X}$. The variance σ_F^2 is minimized when $X_0 = \overline{X}$, in which case the last term disappears. That is, forecasts are most accurate when we are at the center of our range of experience with the explanatory variable. The further we move away from this, the less accurate forecasts become.

The Forecast Interval

With this background, let us return to the derivation of a forecast interval. The forecast error (5.5) is still normally distributed because it is a linear function of the disturbance ε_0 and the estimators $\hat{\alpha}$ and $\hat{\beta}$, all of which are normal. As we established previously, it has mean zero. With the previous variance expression, therefore, the forecast error can be standardized to obtain the following distributional result:

$$\frac{Y_0 - \hat{Y}_0}{\sigma_F} \sim N(0, 1).$$

Of course, σ_F^2 is unknown because σ^2 is unknown. However, the latter can be estimated with the usual estimator s^2 given by (4.23); substituting this into the formula for σ_F^2 yields the estimator

$$s_F^2 = s^2 \left[1 + \frac{1}{n} + \frac{(X_0 - \overline{X})^2}{\sum x_i^2} \right].$$

The square root of this, s_F, is called the **standard error of the forecast.**

Using this estimate s_F in place of the standard deviation σ_F, the distribution becomes $t(n - 2)$ instead of $N(0, 1)$:

$$\frac{Y_0 - \hat{Y}_0}{s_F} \sim t(n - 2).$$

This permits a probability statement that can be arranged in the form (5.7), or, equivalently, the forecast interval

$$\hat{Y}_0 \pm s_F t_{a/2}(n - 2).$$

EXAMPLE 2

nerlove1.dat

Compute a 95% forecast interval for the forecast of Example 1.

SOLUTION

The average output of Nerlove's $n = 145$ plants was $\overline{X} = 2133.1$ billion kWh, with $\sum x_i^2 = 1,237,864,991$. The estimated disturbance variance is, from Example 2 of the previous chapter, $s^2 = 36.591$. The estimated forecast error variance for $X_0 = 6000$ is, therefore,

$$s_F^2 = s^2 \left[1 + \frac{1}{n} + \frac{(X_0 - \overline{X})^2}{\sum x_i^2} \right]$$

$$= 36.591 \times \left[1 + \frac{1}{145} + \frac{(6000 - 2133.1)^2}{1,237,864,991} \right]$$

$$= 37.285.$$

For this sample size, the tabulated values of the t distribution are those of the standard normal, and so a 95% forecast interval is

$$\hat{Y}_0 \pm s_F t_{a/2}(n - 2) = 37.839 \pm 6.106 \times 1.96 = (25.9, 49.8).$$

This suggests that a new generating plant with a 6 trillion kWh capacity will have operating costs in the range of $25.9 to $49.8 million, with 95% confidence. Notice, incidentally, that the operating costs of the firm in the sample with this output, the Duquesne Light Company with costs of $33.154 million, easily fall within these bounds.

Because the forecast error variance σ_F^2 depends on the distance $X_0 - \overline{X}$, it changes with X_0. This means that the forecast interval is not of constant width. Instead it varies with the location on the sample regression line, being minimized at $X_0 = \overline{X}$. This is emphasized in Figure 5.2, which, in contrast to Figure 5.1, shows bounds that are not parallel. Instead the bounds diverge as we move further from $\overline{X}$, indicating that forecasts become less reliable as we attempt to forecast outside the range of our experience.

FIGURE 5.2

Forecast interval with coefficient uncertainty.

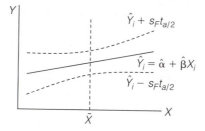

Application to a Deterministic Trend Model

As our numerical example illustrates, for within-sample forecasts the forecast error variance s_F^2 is typically dominated by the disturbance variance s^2. For out-of-sample forecasts, on the other hand, this may not be the case.

Consider the deterministic trend model (5.8) and the τ-period-ahead forecast

$$\hat{Y}_{n+\tau} = \hat{\alpha} + \hat{\beta}(n + \tau).$$

In this context, $X_0 = n+\tau$, and so the forecast horizon τ enters the forecast interval via the third term of the expression for s_F^2. As the forecast horizon lengthens—that is, as we forecast further and further into the future—it is the third term of s_F^2 that dominates the expression, the other two terms being negligible in comparison. Thus, it is approximately the case that, for large τ,

$$s_F^2 \text{ is proportional to } \frac{(n + \tau - \overline{X})^2}{\sum x_i^2}.$$

Here $\overline{X} = \sum_{t=1}^{n} t$ and, similarly, $\sum x_i^2$ is some fixed numerical value. Thus, taking square roots on both sides in order to express things in terms of the standard error of the forecast, we can go further and say that

$$s_F \text{ is proportional to the forecast horizon } \tau.$$

Because the width of the forecast interval is, in turn, proportional to s_F, the forecast interval is proportional to τ. This conclusion is in striking contrast to the parallel forecast bounds of the no-coefficient-uncertainty case, and it is useful to state it formally.

Result 5.2   *In deterministic trend models with coefficient uncertainty, the forecast interval grows in proportion to the forecast horizon τ.*

One implication of this is that the width of the forecast interval is unbounded—it does not approach some fixed width as $\tau \to \infty$ but instead continues to grow. Thus, forecasts are increasingly unreliable as we consider longer and longer forecast horizons, as common sense tells us they should be.

5.1.3 Conclusions

This section has used the simple regression model to derive some important results on forecasting. These results extend naturally to multiple regression, and the same intuition continues to hold: In the absence of coefficient uncertainty the forecast interval takes the form of parallel bounds, whereas the introduction of coefficient uncertainty yields curved bounds.

This means that our conclusions about the forecast intervals for deterministic trends apply to more than just a linear trend. Consider, for example, a more complex deterministic trend model that is quadratic in time,

$$Y_t = \alpha + \beta t + \delta t^2 + \varepsilon_t.$$

It continues to be the case that, with known coefficients, the forecast interval is fixed-width.

This is a troubling implication of deterministic trend models. We have seen that it can be resolved by the introduction of coefficient uncertainty. But even so, this may not be an entirely satisfactory resolution. Consider the thought experiment of an imaginary known-coefficient world with stochastic shocks. Is it plausible to think that in such a world it would be possible to forecast into the indefinite future with a fixed degree of reliability? Some would argue no, that even in these circumstances forecast intervals would be unbounded as the forecast horizon lengthens. This is one consideration that motivates interest in alternatives to deterministic trend models for describing trending variables, in particular the stochastic trend models introduced in Section 2.7. The contrasting forecasting properties of deterministic and stochastic trends are emphasized in our development of these models in Chapters 15–18.

EXERCISES

5.1 Consider a plant with a capacity of 1 trillion kWh.

(a) Compute a 90% forecast interval for its projected operating costs at capacity.

(b) The South Carolina Electricity and Gas Company generated this amount of electricity at a cost of $6,388,000. Is this within your forecast bounds?

5.2 Beginning with the definition of the forecast error (5.4), derive expression (5.5).

5.3 Beginning with the forecast error expression (5.5), use the laws of variance in Appendix B, Table B.2, to derive the forecast error variance (5.9). [*Hint*: Use the following facts. (1) The disturbance ε_0 is independent of the within-sample disturbances that determine $\hat{\alpha}$ and $\hat{\beta}$. (2) The covariance between $\hat{\alpha}$ and $\hat{\beta}$ is $\text{cov}(\hat{\alpha}, \hat{\beta}) = -\sigma^2 \overline{X} / \sum x_i^2$. (This is derived in the appendix to Chapter 8.)]

5.2   Regression through the Origin

Much of Chapter 2 is concerned with the univariate model $Y_i \sim \text{n.i.d.}(\mu, \sigma^2)$. As we have emphasized at a number of points in the present chapter, this univariate model may be viewed as a special case of the simple regression model in which $\beta = 0$ and α is relabeled μ. Consequently many of the results of Chapter 2 have been found merely to be special cases of more general results in Chapter 4.

It is useful to consider a different special case of simple regression—that in which $\alpha = 0$, so that the model becomes

$$Y_i = \beta X_i + \varepsilon_i. \tag{5.10}$$

Because this implies that the population regression line passes through the origin, it is known as the case of **regression through the origin.** The implication is that a value of zero for X_i is associated with a mean of zero for Y_i, a rather special circumstance that only applies in particular situations. Nevertheless, the relevant analysis may usefully be contrasted with that of the general model in which $\alpha \neq 0$.

5.2.1 Estimation and Hypothesis Testing

The method of least squares suggests that β be estimated by minimizing the sum of squares function $S = \sum (Y_i - EY_i)^2$. In this context, where $E(Y_i) = \beta X_i$, this is

$$S = \sum (Y_i - \beta X_i)^2.$$

Taking the derivative, the relevant first-order condition is

$$\sum_{i=1}^{n} (Y_i - \hat{\beta} X_i) X_i = 0. \tag{5.11}$$

Solving for $\hat{\beta}$ yields the least squares estimator

$$\hat{\beta} = \frac{\sum X_i Y_i}{\sum X_i^2}. \tag{5.12}$$

The striking feature of this formula is that it is of the same form as the slope estimator (4.21) in the general model, but with variables in raw rather than deviation form. A simple derivation establishes that the variance of the sampling distribution is

$$V(\hat{\beta}) = \frac{\sigma^2}{\sum X_i^2}, \tag{5.13}$$

which bears a similar resemblance to the earlier expression (4.26).

The predicted values of the model are $\hat{Y}_i = \hat{\beta} X_i$, and so the residuals are

$$e_i = Y_i - \hat{Y}_i = Y_i - \hat{\beta} X_i.$$

As previously, these residuals provide the basis for estimating σ^2. In this case an unbiased estimator is

$$s^2 = \frac{1}{n-1} \sum_{i=1}^{n} e_i^2, \tag{5.14}$$

which is analogous to the previous formula (4.23). (Note, however, the change in the denominator.) An unbiased estimator of (5.13) is, in turn,

$$s_{\hat{\beta}}^2 = \frac{s^2}{\sum X_i^2},$$

analogous with the earlier formula (4.29b).

Most regression packages have options that apply these formulas to estimate the regression model under the restriction that $\alpha = 0$. Hypothesis tests and confidence intervals on β proceed much as before, where the relevant distributional result is

$$\frac{\hat{\beta} - \beta}{s_{\hat{\beta}}} \sim t(n-1).$$

Note the change in the appropriate degrees of freedom from (4.31).

5.2.2 Goodness-of-Fit Measures

Although, for the most part, the analysis of a regression through the origin is very similar to regressions with an intercept, goodness-of-fit measures are an important exception.

Let us begin by noting that the first-order condition (5.11) represents an orthogonality condition of the form

$$\sum_{i=1}^{n} X_i e_i = 0. \tag{5.15}$$

This is analogous to the earlier normal equation (4.15b). Interestingly, however, no parallel condition with respect to $\sum e_i$ has been obtained; in fact, for a regression through the origin the least squares residuals do not necessarily sum to zero, as we know they must when the regression includes an intercept. The most important implication of this fact is that the decomposition of sample variation of Section 4.6 does not hold, a point you are asked to examine more closely in Exercise 5.10.

For this reason, although as a mechanical matter it is still possible to define a coefficient of determination as

$$R^2 = 1 - \frac{\sum e_i^2}{\sum y_i^2}, \tag{5.16}$$

this measure no longer has the properties established in Section 4.6.1. In particular, it is no longer the square of the correlation coefficient: $R^2 \neq r_{XY}^2$, where the latter continues to be defined as (3.14c). In fact, because the decomposition of sample variation no longer applies, it is actually possible for $\sum e_i^2 > \sum y_i^2$ so that the goodness-of-fit statistic defined by (5.16) is negative.

There is an alternative decomposition of sample variation that can form the basis for a different goodness-of-fit measure. An expression for the sample regression line is

$$Y_i = \hat{\beta} X_i + e_i. \tag{5.17}$$

Starting with this and using the orthogonality condition (5.15), it is easy to derive the decomposition

$$\sum_{i=1}^{n} Y_i^2 = \hat{\beta}^2 \sum_{i=1}^{n} X_i^2 + \sum_{i=1}^{n} e_i^2. \tag{5.18}$$

A goodness-of-fit measure presented by some regression packages is thus

$$1 - \frac{\sum e_i^2}{\sum Y_i^2}.$$

This is called the **uncentered** R^2 because it is based on the raw Y_i values instead of the centered deviation-form y_i. Because each of the terms in the decomposition must be positive, the uncentered R^2 must be a positive fraction. However, it too has no particular relationship to the sample correlation coefficient r_{XY}.

This is just one of several goodness-of-fit measures that may be proposed, none of which has been universally adopted. For this reason some econometric packages do not report a goodness-of-fit measure when a regression is through the origin. When such a measure is reported by software, it is important to understand just how it is defined and what interpretation can legitimately be assigned to it. Aigner (1971, pp. 85–90) discusses the issues surrounding R^2 measures for regression through the origin. See also Poirier (1995, Sec. 9.12).

Practitioner's Tip: R^2 **in regression through the origin**

In presenting estimation results for a regression through the origin, only report a goodness-of-fit measure such as an R^2 if you define which measure is being used.

5.2.3 Application: The Great Ratios of Macroeconomics

When is regression through the origin appropriate? One example of an economic model that gives rise to a statistical model of this form is the capital asset pricing model (CAPM), discussed in the appendix to this chapter. The CAPM is usually estimated with an intercept in order to test the restriction $\alpha = 0$, the primary testable implication of the model. Here we consider another example of regression through the origin.

Great Ratios

Many macroeconomic variables grow over time. Examples are real gross national product Q, aggregate saving S, the capital stock K, employment L, the money stock M, and the price level P. An important feature of this growth is that

FIGURE 5.3

U.S. private output, consumption, and investment, 1949:1–1988:4.

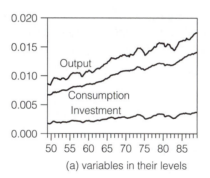

(a) variables in their levels

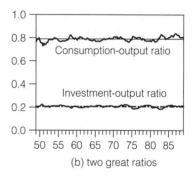

(b) two great ratios

it occurs in such a way that certain variables tend to remain in balance with one another; that is, their *ratios* are relatively stable and do not follow growth trends.

Consider aggregate output Q and two of its principal uses: saving/investment S, the component of Q used as an addition to the capital stock to enhance society's productive capacity in the future, and consumption C, the component used to meet households' consumption needs. As these three variables grow over time, it should not be the case that, say, saving disappears and all production comes to be consumed, because then the capital stock could not be maintained or expanded. Similarly it should not be the case that saving comes to fully absorb all production because the implication would be that households are left with nothing to meet their consumption needs. In other words, output and its components should grow in such a way that ratios such as C/Q and S/Q are fairly stable over time. Although the variables follow growth trends, their ratios should not.

To illustrate, consider quarterly per capita data on U.S. real private output, consumption, and investment over the period 1949:1–1988:4 studied by King, Plosser, Stock, and Watson (KPSW) (1991). These series are plotted in Figure 5.3(a) and their ratios in Figure 5.3(b). Figure 5.3(a) shows that, as we expect, all three series trend upward over time, reflecting their long-term growth trends. Superimposed on these trends is a considerable degree of short-term fluctuation, although the variables differ in this respect. Consumption fluctuates less than output because people act—as individuals and therefore also in the aggregate—to smooth consumption relative to income. This difference is picked up by the other key category of aggregate expenditure, investment, which is more volatile relative to its level than the other two variables.

Notice that although these series trend in their levels, their ratios given in Figure 5.3(b) do not. The ratio of consumption to output fluctuates around an average value of 0.791, so that as these variables grow it continues to be the case that approximately 80% of output is used for consumption. The ratio of investment to output fluctuates around an average value of 0.206, so that approximately 20% of output is used to supplement the capital stock.

The relative stability of ratios such as these is a key feature of the macroe-conomy. Klein and Kosobud (1961) and Klein (1962) identify several such "great ratios of economics," three of which are:

- The saving-income ratio S/Q.
- The capital-output ratio K/Q.
- Labor's share of nominal income wL/PQ, where w denotes the average wage rate.

The stability of a great ratio means that it can be viewed as fluctuating over time around a constant. For example, the consumption-output ratio might be described by

$$(C/Q)_t = \mu + \varepsilon_t.$$

This is, of course, nothing more than our model of Chapter 2, for which we know that the least squares estimator of μ is the sample mean. For the KPSW data, for example, we have said that the sample mean of the consumption-output ratio is $\hat{\mu} = 0.791$.

Suppose, on the other hand, that our interest is in describing the relationship between the numerator and denominator of the ratio. An alternative statistical model for the great ratio phenomenon is a regression through the origin,

$$C_t = \beta Q_t + \varepsilon_t.$$

Here β denotes the population value of the great ratio. The regression says that consumption varies in proportion to income, plus random variation. In this consump-tion-income context, β represents both the marginal effect on consumption of an additional dollar of income—the **marginal propensity to consume** (MPC)—and the great ratio of consumption to income—the **average propensity to consume** (APC).

Long-Run versus Short-Run Consumption Functions

The long-term stability of great ratios is an important empirical regularity that guides the formulation of macroeconomic models of long-term phenomena, as we see when we study a model of economic growth in Chapter 9. At the same time, economic events in the short run can be quite different from, and sometimes seemingly inconsistent with, what must be true in the long run. It happens that the behavior of the consumption-income ratio is an important illustration of this point and, for this reason, has been of special interest historically in the development of macroeconomics.

Consider describing the relationship between aggregate consumption and natio-nal income by a regression with an intercept,

$$C_t = \alpha + \beta Q_t + \varepsilon_t.$$

Such a relationship is portrayed in Figure 5.4, which emphasizes that the ratio of consumption to income—the slope of a line from the origin to the consumption

FIGURE 5.4

A regression with
an intercept implies
an APC that is
greater than the
MPC and that
declines with
income.

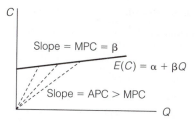

function—changes as we move along the regression line, declining as income increases. That is, when an intercept is included the APC is not constant and so is not a parameter of the model. The coefficient β represents only the MPC, not the APC.

An equation with an intercept is more typical of the behavior of consumption spending over relatively short periods such as business cycles. That is, in the short run the APC tends to decline with income: As national income increases so too does aggregate consumption, but in such a way that consumption falls as a proportion of income. It is also typical of consumption behavior in cross-sectional household data; higher-income households consume more than lower-income ones (that is, the MPC out of additional income is positive), but they consume a smaller proportion of their incomes (their saving rates are higher).

This short-term and cross-sectional behavior of consumption is so pervasive that it was at one time doubted whether the APC could reasonably be treated as a stable ratio in the long run. The first to document carefully that the APC does not fall in the long run—with the implication that long-term consumption behavior can be described by a regression through the origin—was Simon Kuznets in a celebrated study published in 1946. Kuznets constructed decade averages of U.S. national income and consumption expenditure in the century prior to World War II. His data, which are reproduced in Table 5.1, show that over this long historical period the APC did not fall. Acceptance of this finding was the basis for the inclusion of the consumption-income ratio in Klein and Kosobud's list of great ratios.

But how is it possible for consumption spending to behave in one way in the short run and across households and in another way in the long run? Kuznets's findings provided the impetus for the development of theories of consumption behavior that could reconcile these seemingly contradictory patterns in the data. The best known of these theories are the permanent income hypothesis of Milton Friedman (1957) and the life-cycle model associated with the names of A. Ando, F. Modigliani, and R. Brumberg. The latter explains the finding that MPC<APC across households by noting that high-income households tend to be those in the peak earning years of their life cycles, people who are saving for retirement and who consequently have high saving rates. Low-income households, on the other hand, tend to be young families or the retired, both of whom have low saving rates. Consequently cross-sectional regressions find an APC that declines with income. For the economy as a whole, however, the age structure of the population remains stable over time, and so the aggregate APC tends to be constant in the long run.

TABLE 5.1   Kuznets's Data (in millions of 1929 dollars)

Decade	National income, Q_t	Consumption expenditure, C_t	APC, C_t/Q_t
1869–1878	9,340	8,056	0.862
1874–1883	13,601	11,649	0.856
1879–1885	17,875	15,260	0.853
1884–1893	21,042	17,660	0.839
1889–1898	24,170	20,248	0.837
1894–1903	29,751	25,356	0.852
1899–1908	37,324	32,265	0.864
1904–1913	44,992	39,114	0.869
1909–1918	50,560	43,970	0.869
1914–1923	57,269	50,719	0.885
1919–1928	69,047	62,031	0.898
1924–1933	73,265	68,900	0.940
1929–1938	72,045	71,002	0.985

Source: Kuznets (1946, Table II).

This life-cycle view of household behavior continues to play a central role in many macroeconomic models; most macroeconomics texts have chapters surveying the history and theory of the consumption function.

As a final comment, it is perhaps wise to remark that none of this is to suggest that the long-term APC is an immutable constant. Different countries may well be governed by different values of β in long-term consumption functions taking a regression-through-the-origin form. Indeed the saving rate $s \equiv 1 - \beta$ is known to vary among countries, and this is one reason why living standards differ internationally, as we have seen in the scatter plot of Figure 3.5a. Similarly, it is possible that an economy could undergo a structural change in the APC that shifts the long-term consumption function due to a change in the national taste for consumption versus saving. Indeed, much has been made of an apparent decline in the saving rate during the 1980s in a number of countries.

EXERCISES

The first two of the following exercises ask you to estimate the average propensity to consume using two very different data sets: the KPSW quarterly data for the period 1949:1–1988:4 and Kuznets's decade averages in the century prior to World War II. Each exercise asks you to estimate the average propensity to consume using three alternative estimators. Exercise 5.8 asks you to compare these estimators analytically.

Because these data sets consist of time series that trend and have not been obtained by random sampling, the hypothesis-testing procedures we have derived are not necessarily valid. Consequently, our focus in these two empirical exercises is solely on alternative point estimates of the average propensity to consume rather than on other aspects of inference. We return to the study of the KPSW data in Chapter 18 as an application of the time series methods developed there.

For empirical exercises that include hypothesis testing of the appropriateness of a regression through the origin, see the capital asset pricing model application in the appendix to this chapter. Although this too is estimated with time series data, the rates of return that are used do not trend and can be taken to be more akin to data obtained by random sampling.

5.4 💿 **kpsw.dat** The KPSW data on output, consumption, and investment are available in the file **kpsw.dat**. The first two lines of the file contain variable names. The variable definitions are as follows.

quarter   Quarterly period, January 1947–April
          1988.
output   Real private GNP per capita.
consump   Real consumption expenditure per
          capita.
invest   Real private investment per capita.

The following questions ask you to analyze only the output and consumption series; the investment series is used when we return to this data set in Chapter 18. As in Figure 5.3, KPSW limited their analysis to the sample 1949:1–1988:4; the earlier observations are used in Chapter 18 to treat lagged effects. Consequently you should answer the following questions using the 160 observations that begin in 1949.

(a) Begin by plotting consumption C against output Q. From this plot, do you judge a regression through the origin to be a reasonable model?

(b) Generate as an additional variable the ratio of consumption to output, C/Q. Then compute the

average of these ratios. Are you able to reproduce the value for the sample mean cited in connection with Figure 5.3(b)?

(c) Estimate a regression through the origin.
i.   What estimated APC do you obtain?

ii. Does your software produce a goodness-of-fit measure? If so, how is it defined?

(d) Obtain yet another estimator of the APC, the ratio of the averages $\overline{C}/\overline{Q}$.

(e) Comparing your three estimators, are they fairly similar or radically different?

5.5 💿 **kuznets.dat** Kuznets's data on income and consumption are available in the file **kuznets.dat**. The first two lines of the file contain the following variable names.

income   Decade averages of annual national
          income.
consump   Decade averages of annual consump-
          tion expenditure.

(a) Begin by plotting consumption C against income Q. From this plot, do you judge a regression through the origin to be a reasonable model?

(b) Generate as an additional variable the ratio of consumption to income C/Q. Then compute the average of these ratios.

(c) Estimate a regression through the origin.
i.   What estimated APC do you obtain?

ii. Does your software produce a goodness-of-fit measure? If so, how is it defined?

(d) Obtain yet another estimator of the APC, the ratio of the averages $\overline{C}/\overline{Q}$.

(e) Comparing your three estimators, are they fairly similar or radically different?

5.6 Establish whether $\hat{\beta}$ given by (5.12) is unbiased.

5.7 Derive the expression (5.13) for the variance of $\hat{\beta}$.

5.8 ⨍ Another respect in which the results of least squares estimation differ from those for the model that includes an intercept is that the sample regression line does *not* pass through the point of variable means. That is, when $\hat{\beta}$ is defined by (5.12), it is not the case that $\overline{Y} = \hat{\beta}\overline{X}$. It is, however, possible to define an estimator $\tilde{\beta}$ that does have this property: $\overline{Y} = \tilde{\beta}\overline{X}$.

(a) What is the formula for $\tilde{\beta}$?

(b) i. Establish whether $\tilde{\beta}$ is an unbiased estimator.

ii. Derive the variance of $\tilde{\beta}$.

(c) Given your conclusions about the unbiasedness of $\tilde{\beta}$ and (from Exercise 5.6) of $\hat{\beta}$, is there any reason to prefer one estimator over the other? (*Hint:* Use your result from Appendix A, Exercise A.8a.)

(d) Yet another approach to estimating β is to take the ratios Y_i / X_i and average them. The estimator is

$$\ddot{\beta} = \frac{1}{n}\sum_{i=1}^{n}\frac{Y_i}{X_i}.$$

i. Is $\ddot{\beta}$ unbiased?

ii. Is there any basis for preferring $\hat{\beta}$? (*Hint:* Confirm that $\ddot{\beta}$ is a linear estimator and use the Gauss-Markov theorem.)

5.9 Suppose instead of the variance estimator (5.14) we use $n - 2$ in the denominator. Obtain an expression for the bias of this alternative estimator. Does this bias represent a systematic over- or underestimation of σ^2? Is the estimator asymptotically unbiased?

5.10 Beginning with the decomposition

$$Y_i - \overline{Y} = (Y_i - \hat{Y}_i) + (\hat{Y}_i - \overline{Y})$$

attempt to reproduce the derivation of the decomposition of sample variation given in Section 4.6. At what point does this derivation break down?

5.11 Starting with the sample regression line (5.17), derive the decomposition (5.18).

5.3   When Regression Goes Wrong ★

Regression is a powerful tool, more widely used than any other statistical technique. Precisely because it is so powerful and widely used, there can be a danger of applying it mechanically in the belief that the results are infallible. The newly minted applied econometrician, still basking in the glow of a hard-won mastery of regression analysis, must beware of the adage "To a man with a hammer, the world looks like a nail." It is important to be aware that there are situations in which a mechanical application of least squares regression yields incorrect or misleading results and to have a healthy respect for the limitations of the technique.

We have already discussed one such limitation: spurious correlation and regression. Spurious correlation and regression can arise in cross-section contexts due to the failure to control for omitted influences or in time series contexts due to the presence of trends.

Spurious correlation and regression are themes to which we return from time to time throughout this book, specifically in Section 8.9.1, where we analyze formally the consequences of omitting a relevant regressor from a multiple regression, and in Chapters 15–18 where the distinction between deterministic and stochastic trends is developed rigorously.

This section focuses on three other important situations in which least squares regression is inappropriate. The first, Galton's fallacy, involves no violation of the assumptions of the classical normal linear regression model and so relates not to the formal properties of the least squares estimators but to their interpretation. By contrast, the other two situations—qualitative and limited dependent variables and simultaneous equations—do represent violations of the classical assumptions and so it is useful to relate them to our discussion of those assumptions in the previous chapter.

There are, of course, many ways in which the assumptions of the classical normal linear regression model may be violated in real-world data; the topics considered here are just two important examples. Beginning in Chapter 12, the later chapters of this book are largely concerned with other kinds of violations.

Why consider qualitative and limited dependent variables and simultaneous equations here? First, they are very important classes of problems in applied econometric work, and you may as well become aware of them sooner rather than later. Yet despite their importance, they cannot be fully addressed in this book because they require estimation principles other than least squares. Thus, they serve as important illustrations of situations in which least squares is an inadequate estimation principle and help explain why other estimation principles are sometimes needed—in particular, the method of maximum likelihood and the generalized method of moments that are mentioned in Section 2.4.

5.3.1   Galton's Fallacy

Applied econometricians are often in the position of wanting to say something about behavior over time, but of having only cross-section data available to do so. The most important lesson of Galton's fallacy is of the pitfalls inherent in doing this.

In the 19th century, Sir Francis Galton studied the relationship between the heights of fathers and sons. Because unusually tall or short fathers are in the tails of the height distribution, purely as a matter of probability it is likely that a son will be closer to the mean height than is his father. That is, there is a tendency for sons to "regress toward the mean." Hence, as a matter of probability rather than genetics, there is a negative correlation between the heights of fathers and sons; equivalently, a regression of one on the other will have a negative slope. Galton initially inferred that this represented a tendency toward mediocrity in human evolution, that male heights would over time converge toward the mean. But, in fact, the negative correlation he observed is consistent with an unchanging distribution of heights, a distribution characterized by continued dispersion over time. Galton's fallacy of regression toward the mean is where regression originally got its name and is the classic example of the danger of attempting to draw inferences about time series behavior from cross-sectional regressions.

Because the temptation to draw inferences about behavior over time from cross-sectional regressions is so strong, variants of Galton's fallacy arise from time to time in empirical work. Consider Figure 3.6, which shows the absence of correlation between initial living standards and subsequent growth rates among countries in the world income distribution. Some researchers have argued that this apparent absence of a relationship is due to the failure to control for other factors and have addressed this by estimating multiple regression models of the form

$$\Delta q_i = \alpha + \beta(\text{initial } q_i) + \text{other factors} + \varepsilon_i.$$

Here q denotes some measure of living standards such as output per adult; Δq_i is its growth rate over some period (the variable on the vertical axis of Figure 3.6), and the explanatory variable is its value at the beginning of the period (the variable on the horizontal axis of the figure). Such regressions sometimes yield estimates of β that are negative and statistically significant.

What should we make of this finding? In our discussion of Figure 3.6 we argue that an inverse relationship between these variables indicates strong mobility within the cross-country income distribution, stronger than the mobility that exists in the absence of a relationship. Some researchers have gone further and argued that it indicates a **convergence of living standards**—a reduction in the variance of the distribution over time. After all, if poor countries grow more quickly than rich ones, does this not mean that all countries are converging to a common standard of living? The answer is no: Just as an inverse relationship between the heights of fathers and sons does not imply a reduction in the variance of the height distribution over time, so too an inverse relationship between country incomes and growth rates does not imply a reduction in the income distribution over time.

Friedman (1992) and Quah (1993) were the first to point out that this misinterpretation of a negative value for β in this regression is an example of Galton's fallacy. Sala-i-Martin (1996) emphasized that the proper interpretation is of mobility within the distribution rather than a reduction in the variance of the distribution over time.

Practitioner's Tip: **Time series inferences from cross-section data**

In general in empirical research, be wary of making inferences about behavior over time from models estimated with cross-section data.

EXERCISES

5.12 The Department of Highways sponsors an aggressive campaign of speed limit enforcement. It finds that, of the sections of highway that had the highest accident rates immediately prior to the program, most are now no longer in this category. Should you interpret this as evidence that the campaign has been effective? Explain your answer.

5.3.2 Qualitative and Limited Dependent Variables

Our development of regression in the previous chapter assumes that the disturbance is normally distributed. For example, we have seen that the statistical theory underlying t and F tests uses this assumption.

Often, of course, data come from populations that are not strictly normal. This is usually not a problem because central limit theorems establish that t and F tests are still approximately valid, especially for larger sample sizes. As well, sometimes a transformation of the dependent variable can improve the validity of the normality assumption; Section 2.5.2 shows that the logarithm of a lognormally distributed variable is normal. The use of logarithmic transformations in regression is explored in detail in the next chapter.

There are, however, situations in which data are nonnormal in ways that should be explicitly treated; specifically, when the nature of the data suggests a form for the population distribution that can be exploited in estimation. Here we consider what is probably the most important category of such problems: qualitative and limited dependent variables, and some closely related problems—count data, sample selectivity, and duration data. Our goal is not to develop the estimation techniques for these models because this is best done as part of a systematic development of maximum likelihood estimation and could easily occupy a book in its own right; see, for example, Maddala (1983), Long (1997), or Wooldridge (2001) or, for count data, Cameron and Trivedi (1998) or Winkelmann (2000). Instead, the objective is to give you some insight into why least squares regression is not the appropriate tool for such problems.

Qualitative Dependent Variables

As we describe in Section 1.1.1, qualitative variables are ones that represent some limited number of categories, choices, or responses. The key issues in the analysis of such data are illustrated by the simplest case of binary responses.

Binary Responses Consider a variable Y that represents an either/or decision or categorization. There are many such variables in economics, for example, a bank's decision whether to approve a loan or a woman's decision whether to join the labor force, or a high school graduate's decision to work or continue with education.

As we have seen in Chapter 2, binary variables are governed by the Bernoulli distribution (2.1),

$$f(y) = \pi^y (1 - \pi)^{1-y}, \qquad y = 0, 1.$$

In the case of female labor force participation, for example, we might define

$$Y = \begin{cases} 1 & \text{if a woman belongs to the labor force,} \\ 0 & \text{if a woman does not belong to the labor force.} \end{cases}$$

From the analysis of this distribution in Chapter 2, we know that the parameter π has the interpretation the female labor force participation rate. Equivalently, it is the probability that a randomly drawn woman belongs to the labor force: $\pi = \Pr(Y = 1)$. It is also the expected value of Y,

$$E(Y) = \pi. \tag{5.19}$$

The parameter π also determines the variance of Y,[3]

$$V(Y) = \pi(1 - \pi). \tag{5.20}$$

If we are interested solely in this variable taken in isolation, we know how to study it. With data on n women drawn from the population, the estimator $\hat{\pi}$ can be computed, the proportion of women in the sample who are members of the labor force. As well, an estimate $\hat{\pi}(1 - \hat{\pi})$ of its variance can be obtained for use in constructing a confidence interval or doing a hypothesis test. This is, of course, analogous to using data from a normal population to do inference with respect to the mean μ and variance σ^2, the parameters of interest in that context.

But as we emphasize beginning in Chapter 3, an economist's interest rarely lies in studying a variable in isolation. Instead we are interested in relationships between variables. How, for example, is female labor force participation affected by having preschool-age children? Being married? The availability of subsidized day care?

When two variables X and Y are bivariately normally distributed, we know that the classical regression model is the appropriate empirical framework. We have seen in Section 3.2.1 that it offers a convenient reparameterization of the bivariate normal distribution.

Clearly, however, when X and Y are related but Y is Bernoulli, the bivariate normal—and thus the regression model—is no longer the appropriate empirical framework. Instead, we need an alternative empirical model that is based on the Bernoulli distribution. As is to be expected, the key parameter of interest will continue to be π, the probability that a randomly observed female belongs to the labor force. The issue of interest is how X—or, in general, some list of explanatory variables—affects this key parameter.

The Linear Probability Model From this perspective, simply mechanically running the regression

$$Y_i = \alpha + \beta X_i + \varepsilon_i \tag{5.21}$$

is not a proper formulation of the problem because it fails to draw on the structure offered by the Bernoulli distribution.

At the same time, it is not completely without justification. Recall from our analysis of the simple regression model that the expected value of Y is the systematic component of the model:

$$E(Y_i) = \alpha + \beta X_i.$$

---

[3] This is the solution to Exercise 2.4b.

Combining this with (5.19), we have

$$\pi = \alpha + \beta X_i. \tag{5.22}$$

That is, the implication of running this regression is that the probability π is being explained as a linear function of X. Thus, in this context, the regression (5.21) is called the **linear probability model.** And clearly the linear probability model makes some sense because it seeks to explain what we have said needs to be explained—the parameter π.

The problem is that the way in which the linear probability model explains π is not very satisfactory. There are several ways of seeing this.

Predicted values not in the range 0–1. Because it is a probability, π must be between zero and one; yet nothing in least squares regression ensures that the predicted values of the regression (5.21) lie in this range. The linear probability model can predict probabilities that are negative or greater than one.

Constant marginal effects. According to (5.22), the marginal effect of X on the participation rate π is β,

$$\frac{d\pi}{dX} = \beta,$$

which is constant at all levels of X and π. But this is not the most plausible form of behavior. Suppose X is government day-care subsidies and consider a randomly drawn woman whose probability of being a member of the labor force is $\pi = \frac{1}{2}$. Because she is, in a sense, on the margin of whether to belong to the labor force, the effect of increased subsidies on her probability of belonging should presumably be much higher than for a woman whose value of π is closer to 0 or 1–that is, someone who almost certainly is, or is not, a member of the labor force. In other words, it makes more sense to allow a *nonlinear* relationship between π and X that permits large marginal effects at intermediate values of π.

Heteroskedasticity. Finally, combining (5.20) and (5.22), the variance of Y_i is

$$V(Y_i) = \pi(1 - \pi) = (\alpha + \beta X_i)[1 - (\alpha + \beta X_i)].$$

That is, the variance of Y_i depends on X_i and thus changes with the data. In other words, the disturbance of the linear probability model (5.21) must be heteroskedastic. The linear probability model is not a classical regression.

Probit and Logit   There are two widely used ways of handling these problems: the probit and logit models. Both can be stated in the form

$$Y_i = g(X_i) + \varepsilon_i,$$

where the function $g(\cdot)$ is a nonlinear functional form that resolves the deficiencies of the linear probability model: It limits the dependent variable to the range 0–1 and allows for nonlinear marginal effects.

Probit and logit differ in the functional forms used for $g(\cdot)$. Both use cumulative distribution functions (CDFs); because a CDF yields cumulative probabilities, it must generate values between 0 and 1.[4] The probit model uses the CDF of the normal distribution, whereas the logit model uses the CDF of the logistic distribution. Because

$$E(Y_i) = \pi = g(X_i),$$

both models can still be interpreted as explaining the probability π.

The probit and logit models are estimated by the method of maximum likelihood, which uses the structure of the Bernoulli distribution, thus treating the heteroskedasticity in ε_i. The nonlinear forms for $g(\cdot)$ used by the probit and logit models are quite close and so in practice usually yield fairly similar estimation results.

Categorical Responses The probit and logit models generalize to more than two discrete choices. Recall that in Section 1.1.1 we distinguish between ordered and unordered categorical responses. The most common model for ordered responses is the **ordered probit** model and for unordered responses the **multinomial logit** model.

Count Data

Section 1.1.1 describes count data as recording the incidence of occurrence of some event; it takes on the values $0, 1, 2, 3, \ldots$. As examples, Cameron and Trivedi (2001) cite studies of the number of childbirths for mothers, the number of accidents for airlines, the number of trips by people to recreational sites, and the number of physician visits or days in the hospital per year for people. Although a count variable is quantitative rather than qualitative, it is obviously similar to a qualitative variable because it takes on only integer values. As well, the presumption is that it usually takes on small values; we do not normally find families making hundreds of visits a year to their doctors, for example. If we did, then it would most likely be treated as a conventional quantitative variable rather than as count data. At the same time, no upper bound is placed a priori on the number of possible occurrences of the event.

Just as the Bernoulli distribution describes binary responses, here we need to ask: What distribution governs the number of occurrences of a moderately rare event? You may recall from your first statistics course that the distribution usually

---

[4]   A CDF, denoted by $F(y)$, yields the probability that a random variable Y takes on a value less than or equal to a particular y: $F(y) = \Pr(Y \le y)$. In the notation of Appendix B,

$$F(y) = \begin{cases} \displaystyle\sum_{t \le y} f_Y(t) & \text{if } Y \text{ is discrete,} \\[2ex] \displaystyle\int_{-\infty}^{y} f_Y(t)\,dt & \text{if } Y \text{ is continuous.} \end{cases}$$

used to describe such situations is the **Poisson distribution.** And in fact the most popular model for studying count data is the **Poisson regression model.** Because it makes use of the structure given by the Poisson distribution, just as probit and logit use the Bernoulli distribution, the Poisson regression model must be estimated by maximum likelihood.

Limited Dependent Variables

Similar considerations apply to the study of censored or truncated data. These types of variables are introduced in Section 1.1.2 under the topic flawed data.

Censored Data These arise when a quantitative variable has an upper or lower limit on the value it can take on and a substantial portion of observations are at that limit. Sometimes this occurs because the variable is artificially limited in the range that is observable. For example, suppose that people with high incomes are simply recorded as earning "$100,000 or more." Then the data do not allow us to distinguish those earning exactly $100,000 from those earning far more. The data thus have an artificial concentration of observations at that arbitrary limit, which biases the usual regression estimates.

The standard model for censored data is the **tobit model** (Tobin 1958a). James Tobin (1918–2002) is best known for his contributions to macroeconomics and monetary economics, for which he was awarded the 1981 Nobel prize in economics, but earlier in his career he also made this seminal contribution to econometrics. He gave as one example of the censoring phenomenon rationed goods, in which many people will buy the limit of their ration. As another example he cited data on household consumption of certain goods, where—especially for luxuries—many households may have expenditures of zero. Again, the concentration of values at this limit will bias standard regression estimates of the effect of other variables on the consumption of the good. The tobit model makes use of the distributional structure implied by the censoring and so is estimated by maximum likelihood.

Truncated Data A sample of data is truncated if some observations are omitted because of the values they take on. In contrast to censoring, this is a problem of missing observations, in which the observations are missing systematically rather than randomly. The systematic omission of observations is something that can be treated using **truncated regression models,** which, again, are estimated by maximum likelihood.

Sample Selection

In truncated data, observations on a variable are missing when that variable takes on values in some range. Often, however, data are missing in a way that is systematically related to other variables. This is the problem of **sample selection** and is especially common in data studied by labor economists.

Consider, for example, statistical earnings functions such as that described in Theory Meets Application 4.1, which seek to explain the determination of earnings. The data available to estimate such regressions are only on employed workers, not on those who happen to be unemployed at the time. Furthermore, characteristics such as education that determine earnings probably also influence the probability of being unemployed. Thus, the omission of observations from the sample is related to the variable under study.

The labor econometrician James Heckman developed innovative techniques for handling sample selection problems like this and was awarded the 2000 Nobel prize in economics for his contributions. He shared the prize with another econometrician, Daniel McFadden, who has developed methods for the analysis of discrete choice data.

Duration Models

Economists are often interested in how long it takes for something to happen: how long a spell of unemployment lasts, how long until an insurance claim is made, the duration of a strike, or the duration of marriage. Such length-of-time variables are called **duration data.** Sometimes interest lies not just in the duration, but also in what happens afterward; for example, whether a hospital stay results in release or death. These are called **transition data** because they concern the transition to a new state at the termination of the duration.

The reason durations are interesting is, of course, that they are random, and we would like to understand what influences them. As with the other models we have discussed, their distribution is typically nonnormal in a way that can be exploited by maximum likelihood estimation.

Consider a duration Y, which is a continuously distributed random variable that, because it is a length of time, is nonnegative. Consistent with the notation used elsewhere in this book, let its probability density function be denoted $f_Y(y)$ and its CDF be $F(y)$. A key concept in the analysis of duration data is the **survivor function**

$$S(y) \equiv 1 - F(y).$$

This gives the probability that a condition that began at time 0 still persists at time y; for example, the probability that someone is still unemployed after y weeks.

An important related concept is the **hazard function**

$$h(y) \equiv \frac{f_Y(y)}{S(y)}.$$

This has the interpretation of the exit rate from the condition at time y; for example, the probability of finding a job after y periods of unemployment, of dying after y years of life, of going bankrupt after y years in business, and so on.

It is evident that the probability density $f_Y(y)$, the distribution function $F(y)$, the survivor function $S(y)$, and the hazard function $h(y)$ are just different ways of looking at the same thing: if one is known, any of the others can be derived. Nevertheless, depending on the nature of the problem, it is sometimes more natural to work in terms of one rather than another. In many applied contexts, the hazard function is the preferred framework of analysis.

It is also evident that different probability distributions $f_Y(y)$ yield different hazard functions, and applied econometricians work with a variety of distributions for this purpose. Hazard functions derived from the exponential distribution, the gamma distribution, the Weibull distribution, and the lognormal distribution are all commonly used in empirical work. The appropriate choice depends, of course, on the nature of the problem, but all are implemented using the method of maximum likelihood.

Conclusions

In this section we have considered some important examples of situations in which the population distribution of the variable of interest is nonnormal in a way that can be specified. This provides a basis for the implementation of the maximum likelihood method of estimation, so that least squares regression is not the appropriate tool for studying the variable.

5.3.3 Simultaneous Equations

Many economic variables are determined simultaneously through the interaction of several behavioral relationships. This creates a special set of problems for econometricians, problems that have been central to the development of the field.

The simplest example is the simultaneous determination of price and quantity in a market through the interaction of supply and demand. We used such an example in Section 1.2.3 to illustrate the distinction between structural and reduced forms. Recall the structural form (1.11), modified to include disturbances:

$$
\begin{aligned}
Q_i^{d} &= \alpha_1 + \beta_1 P_i + \gamma Y_i + \varepsilon_{1i} \quad \text{(demand)} \\
Q_i^{s} &= \alpha_2 + \beta_2 P_i + \phi R_i + \varepsilon_{2i} \quad \text{(supply)}.
\end{aligned}
\tag{5.23}
$$

The demand curve is shifted by the exogenous variable Y_i, household income, as well as by random factors captured by the disturbance ε_{1i}. The supply curve is shifted by the exogenous variable R_i, rainfall, as well as by random factors captured by the disturbance ε_{2i}.

The shifting of the two curves by these systematic and random factors is shown in Figure 5.5(a). The changing point of intersection creates a cloud of observed equilibrium price-quantity pairs, shown in Figure 5.5(b), which are the data available to the econometrician.

Notice that the cloud of data points traces out neither the supply curve nor the demand curve; a simple regression of quantity on price (or price on quantity) estimates neither of these curves. For the same reason, a multiple regression of quantity Q on price P and income Y will not estimate the demand function, nor will a regression of quantity Q on price P and rainfall R estimate the supply function.

FIGURE 5.5

Price and quantity are determined by supply and demand.

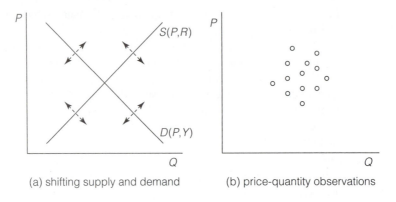

(a) shifting supply and demand   (b) price-quantity observations

Although as a purely mechanical matter these regressions can be estimated, they have no useful interpretation of any kind.

The Reduced Form

Are there any relationships involving these variables that *can* be usefully estimated by least squares? Consider the reduced form (1.12), rederived to account for the inclusion of disturbances in the structural form:

$$P_i = \frac{\alpha_1 - \alpha_2}{\beta_2 - \beta_1} + \frac{\gamma}{\beta_2 - \beta_1}Y_i - \frac{\phi}{\beta_2 - \beta_1}R_i + \frac{\varepsilon_{1i} - \varepsilon_{2i}}{\beta_2 - \beta_1}$$

$$Q_i = \frac{\alpha_1\beta_2 - \alpha_2\beta_1}{\beta_2 - \beta_1} + \frac{\gamma\beta_2}{\beta_2 - \beta_1}Y_i - \frac{\phi\beta_1}{\beta_2 - \beta_1}R_i + \frac{\beta_2\varepsilon_{1i} - \beta_1\varepsilon_{2i}}{\beta_2 - \beta_1}.$$

(5.24)

Similar to the notation (1.13), this reduced form may be denoted

$$P_i = \pi_{10} + \pi_{11}Y_i + \pi_{12}R_i + v_{1i}$$
$$Q_i = \pi_{20} + \pi_{21}Y_i + \pi_{22}R_i + v_{2i},$$

where v_{1i} and v_{2i} denote the composite disturbances

$$v_{1i} = \frac{\varepsilon_{1i} - \varepsilon_{2i}}{\beta_2 - \beta_1}, \qquad v_{2i} = \frac{\beta_2\varepsilon_{1i} - \beta_1\varepsilon_{2i}}{\beta_2 - \beta_1}.$$

A **composite disturbance** is one that is a function of several other underlying disturbances. Composite disturbances are not necessarily problematic. Notice that, because v_{1i} and v_{2i} are just linear combinations of ε_{1i} and ε_{2i}, they inherit their properties. Specifically, if ε_{1i} and ε_{2i} are n.i.d., then so too are v_{1i} and v_{2i}.

In light of this conclusion about the disturbances, these reduced-form equations are just multiple regressions of each of the endogenous variables P and Q on the exogenous variables Y and R; there is no violation of the classical assumptions, and reduced-form equations *can* be meaningfully estimated by least squares. Recall that, as we have seen in Section 1.2.3, the slope coefficients π_{ij} are comparative statics derivatives. Thus least squares estimation of the reduced form yields estimates of these derivatives.[5]

Properties of Least Squares Applied to the Structural Form

Why does least squares yield meaningful estimates of the reduced form, but not of the structural form?

If least squares estimates of the structural form coefficients are not meaningful, this must mean that they lack desirable properties. If they lack desirable properties, it must be because the structural-form equations fail to satisfy the assumptions of the classical normal linear regression model. In what respect is this true?

The fundamental difference between the structural and reduced forms is that the former includes endogenous variables on the right-hand side, whereas the latter includes only exogenous variables. This is of critical importance because the reduced form (5.24) makes it clear that each endogenous variable (1) must be stochastic because each is generated by the system disturbances ε_{1i} and ε_{2i} and, more to the point, (2) these stochastic regressors must therefore be correlated with these disturbances. That the endogenous variables must be stochastic is intuitively clear from the diagrammatic interpretation in Figure 5.5(a), where the randomly shifting supply and demand curves produce what must in turn be randomly generated equilibrium values of price and quantity.

We argue in Section 4.1.2 that stochastic explanatory variables are not by themselves a problem as long as they are not correlated with the regression disturbance. This was our justification for the artificial but analytically convenient strategy of assuming a nonstochastic regressor in our formal analysis of the simple regression model. But with simultaneous equations we have a case in which endogenous variables must be stochastic and must, by the logic of the model, be correlated with the disturbances. A positive shock ε_{1i} to the demand curve tends to generate higher prices P_i and quantities Q_i, whereas a positive shock ε_{2i} to the supply curve tends to generate lower prices P_i and higher quantities Q_i. It is in this respect that structural equations containing endogenous explanatory variables violate the classical assumptions, and consequently the desirable properties of least squares are lost. This violation is called **simultaneity** because it arises from the simultaneous determination of the endogenous variables.

By contrast, reduced-form equations include only exogenous variables as regressors. Even if these are viewed as stochastic they are nevertheless uncorrelated with the disturbances because, by definition, exogenous variables are determined outside the system. Rainfall and household incomes are not the outcome of shocks to the apple market. Thus, the desirable properties of least squares hold when applied to reduced-form equations.

---

[5]   Although, as we have pointed out, these may be subject to the Lucas critique.

Solutions to the Simultaneity Problem

Were our interest solely in estimating comparative statics derivatives, we could work exclusively with the reduced form, estimating it by least squares. But usually econometricians are interested in the underlying structure of the economy—as the Lucas critique tells us they should be.

One idea that might occur to you for estimating the structural form is to first estimate the reduced form by least squares and then deduce the implied estimates of the structural form coefficients using their relationship to the π_{ij}, as given by (5.24). This idea is known as **indirect least squares.** Unfortunately, it only works under rather special circumstances, when there is a one-to-one correspondence between the two sets of parameters—which in Chapter 10 we call a situation of exact identification. In practice, this situation rarely applies and more generally applicable ways of estimating the structural form directly are needed.

This problem was solved by econometricians in the 1940s and 1950s. It is one of the great triumphs of econometrics and one of the field's greatest contributions to statistics. The solution lies in using additional information in the form of instrumental variables to disentangle the respective shiftings of the equations of the system. An **instrumental variable** is one that is *correlated* with the right-hand-side endogenous variables—the source of the simultaneity problem—but *uncorrelated* with the disturbances; that is, a legitimate instrument must be correlated with the dependent variable only via its effect on the endogenous explanatory variables. It turns out that exogenous variables that do not appear in the structural equation to be estimated have these properties and so are legitimate instruments.

Section 2.4 mentions two important estimation principles that are often used by econometricians as alternatives to least squares: the generalized method of moments (GMM) and the method of maximum likelihood (ML). GMM with instrumental variables yields an **instrumental variables estimator;** its application to a single equation from a simultaneous system has an interpretation known as **two-stage least squares** (2SLS), whereas its application to the joint estimation of all the equations of the system is known as **three-stage least squares** (3SLS).[6] On the other hand, ML applied to a single equation is called **limited-information maximum likelihood** (LIML); applied to the system as a whole it is known as **full-information maximum likelihood** (FIML).

In addition to being based on more sophisticated estimation principles than least squares, these methods as applied to simultaneous equations are best formulated using matrix algebra and so are beyond the scope of this book. Even so, as this brief introduction has indicated, the topic of simultaneous equations is central to applied econometrics. After all, what could be more fundamental to economics than supply and demand? Even if it is not possible to show you the details of how to solve the simultaneity problem, it is essential that you be aware of it and the inapplicability of least squares in this context.

---

[6]   This statement paints with a broad brush. For a systematic development of the relationship among GMM, 2SLS, and 3SLS, see Hayashi (2000).

THEORY MEETS APPLICATION

5.1

Education, Earnings, and Ability

In Theory Meets Application 4.1 we studied Jacob Mincer's statistical earnings function, which estimated that an additional year of schooling yields a 7% return to earnings. But is education exogenous? Suppose that people's earnings and education are both the outcome of other factors, perhaps largely unmeasurable, that we might think of as *ability.* Under this interpretation it is ability that is exogenous, whereas education and earnings are jointly endogenously determined by people's decisions based on their ability.

In this view, a Mincerian statistical earnings function may be subject to the simultaneity problem: Education may be an endogenous explanatory variable. If so, conventional least squares estimates of the return to education lose their usual desirable properties, including unbiasedness.

This potential bias has long been of interest to labor econometricians; see, for example, Griliches (1977). It could be investigated if an instrument were available to treat the simultaneity. But is there a variable that is correlated with education, but not with earnings except via its effect on education?

In a novel analysis, Angrist and Krueger (1991, p. 979) argued that *season of birth* satisfies these criteria and used this to obtain an instrumental variables estimate of the return to education.

> We establish that season of birth is related to educational attainment because of the school start age policy and compulsory school attendance laws. Individuals

born in the beginning of the year start school at an older age, and can therefore drop out after completing less schooling than individuals born near the end of the year. Roughly 25 percent of potential dropouts remain in school because of compulsory schooling laws. We estimate the impact of compulsory schooling on earnings by using quarter of birth as an instrument for education. The instrumental variables estimate of the return to education is close to the ordinary least squares estimate, suggesting that there is little bias in conventional estimates.

Angrist and Krueger estimated statistical earnings functions using census data on U.S. men, so that very large samples were available. The dependent variable is the logarithm of weekly earnings. Their estimates of the rate of return to education are as follows.

Decade of birth	Census	Sample size	Estimator Least squares	Estimator Instrumental variables
1920–29	1970	247,199	0.0802	0.0769
1930–39	1980	329,509	0.0711	0.0891
1940–49	1980	486,926	0.0573	0.0553

The values yielded by the two estimators are qualitatively similar. Angrist and Krueger find that in none of the three cases is the difference statistically significant. For a survey comparing least squares and instrumental variables estimates across several studies, see Card (1999, Sec. 4).

You should also be aware that instrumental variables estimators are not necessarily a panacea. They require, first of all, that equations be **identified.** The concept of identification is introduced in Section 10.3, although in a context different from simultaneous equations.

Weak Instruments

A second reason why instrumental variables techniques are not a panacea is that their efficacy as a solution to the simultaneity problem depends on the availability of good instruments. A good instrument is one that is strongly correlated with endogenous explanatory variables in the equation to be estimated. It is not always easy to find a variable satisfying both this criterion and the requirement that it be uncorrelated with the disturbance. Indeed, there has been much recent interest in the problem of **weak instruments;** see the surveys by Stock, Wright, and Yogo (2002) and Dufour (2003).

In a striking demonstration of this problem, Bound, Jaeger, and Baker (1995) consider the Angrist and Krueger (1991) analysis discussed in Theory Meets Application 5.1. Angrist and Krueger use season of birth as an instrument for education in the estimation of statistical earnings functions. Remarkably, Bound, Jaeger, and Baker show that the Angrist-Krueger results are little changed if this instrumental variable is replaced by random numbers! They go on to conclude that "...the use of instruments that ... explain little of the variation in the endogenous variables can do more harm than good" (1995, p. 449).

Conclusions

Because economic variables are often determined through the equilibration of a number of simultaneous relationships, simultaneity is a fundamental problem for econometrics. The relevant econometric techniques are developed in many books, especially more advanced books in which matrix algebra is used.

This important body of material is, however, beyond the scope of this book. In part the justification for this omission lies in our desire to concentrate on some of the simpler estimation problems that interest econometricians, problems that are amenable to least squares. There is, however, a better reason for neglecting the simultaneous equations problem in an introductory treatment of econometrics. As a practical matter, simultaneous equations models are often estimated with time series data. In the supply–demand example of Figure 5.5, it is natural to think of the price-quantity data as being observed over successive time periods, rather than across some cross-sectional unit. As we have already had occasion to remark, the dominant feature of economic time series is that they often involve trends. It turns out that, important as the simultaneity problem may be, it is a secondary problem relative to the primary one of treating trends in economic time series. Consequently, the orientation here is toward the latter task, an orientation that culminates in Chapters 15–18.

EXERCISES

5.13 Beginning with the structural form (5.23), derive the reduced form (5.24).

5.14 Consider the following formulation of the education-earnings-ability relationship. Suppose that log earnings Y depends on both schooling

S and ability A and that schooling also depends on ability:

$$Y_i = \beta_1 + \beta_2 S_i + \beta_3 A_i$$
$$S_i = \alpha + \beta A_i.$$

Answer the following questions.

(a) Which of these variables do you identify as endogenous and which as exogenous?

(b) Is this model a structural or reduced form? Whichever you decide, derive the other form.

(c) Use the reduced form to obtain all possible comparative statics derivatives. Assuming that all slope coefficients in the model are positive, can you sign these comparative statics derivatives? Do the signs make sense?

Appendix Application to the Capital Asset Pricing Model

The field of finance is an important branch of economics. One prominent area within finance is the theory of asset pricing, which is concerned with understanding the determinants of asset prices and yields.[7]

The most important respect in which assets differ is in their risk. Riskier assets tend to yield, on average, higher returns; this is the inducement for investors to hold those riskier assets. Formally, this relationship between the expected return on an asset j and its risk may be expressed as

$$E(R_j) = f(\text{risk}_j). \tag{5.25}$$

The **capital asset pricing model** (CAPM) formalizes this relationship by providing both a specification for the function $f(\cdot)$ and a measure of risk.

Appendix C provides a detailed derivation of the CAPM. This involves treating returns on risky assets explicitly as random variables and applying the laws of expectation and variance of Appendix B to study the implications of combining assets into portfolios.

Systematic and Nonsystematic Risk

The most important of these implications is that pooling assets results in a **diversification of risk:** The risk of a portfolio is typically less than the risk of any of the assets individually. Some of the risk associated with any one asset may, then, be eliminated by combining it with others. However, not all risk can be diversified. Even if an investor's wealth is spread among all available assets and so is fully diversified (by, say, buying an index mutual fund that replicates the market as a whole), there remains the risk of the market. This is called **market risk.** Market risk is the risk that cannot be diversified away by combining assets into portfolios; it is therefore also called **nondiversifiable risk.** Because it is associated with the systematic variation in the return on the market—as opposed to the **nonsystematic** or **idiosyncratic** factors specific to individual assets—it also goes by the name of **systematic risk.**

---

[7] For a brief survey of finance that locates the CAPM in the context of the field as a whole, see Ross (1987).

The risk of any single asset consists, then, of two components. One is nonsystematic or idiosyncratic risk, which can be eliminated through diversification. This is also called **diversifiable** risk. The other component is systematic risk, which cannot be eliminated through diversification. This is the risk associated with the market as a whole.

Diversification is inexpensive; a competitive mutual fund industry offers diversified portfolios at modest management expense. Therefore, in equilibrium investors should not be rewarded for bearing diversifiable risk. Instead they should only be rewarded—in terms of a higher expected return $E(R_j)$—for the component of an asset's return associated with variation in the market as a whole, the systematic risk that cannot be eliminated through random diversification. It follows that the appropriate measure of an asset's risk (at least, that component of risk that is relevant for economic decisions) is a measure of its systematic risk because this is the only component of risk that the market should reward. Idiosyncratic risk can be eliminated through diversification and so should be irrelevant to the pricing of the asset.

This is the basic intuition of the CAPM. It is an extension to the theory of asset pricing of the standard economic logic that the pricing of any good depends on marginal effects rather than total or average effects. What is relevant for economic decisions is not an asset's total risk taken in isolation (as measured by, say, its variance or standard deviation) but its marginal effect on the risk of a portfolio—specifically, the market portfolio.

Consider the random return R_j on asset j, the random return R_m on the market as a whole, and a risk-free rate of return r_f. (Because r_f is a guaranteed return it is not a random variable.) An asset's **risk premium** is the excess of its return over the risk-free rate: the risk premium of asset j is $R_j - r_f$. To say that investors are usually rewarded for bearing risk is to say that the expected value of this risk premium is positive:

$$E(R_j - r_f) = E(R_j) - r_f > 0. \tag{5.26}$$

Why do different assets have different expected risk premia? According to the CAPM, because they have differing degrees of systematic risk. In terms of data on rates of return observed over time t, the CAPM may be expressed as

$$R_{jt} - r_{ft} = \beta_j(R_{mt} - r_{ft}) + \varepsilon_t. \tag{5.27}$$

The equation relates the risk premium on asset j to the risk premium on the market; this relationship is governed by the parameter beta. Assets having risk premia that fluctuate less than one-for-one with the market ($\beta_j < 1$) are called **defensive** assets; they offer a means of escaping from the systematic risk of the market as a whole. Being attractive to investors in this respect, they command a relatively low expected return over the riskless asset. Assets having risk premia that fluctuate more than one-for-one with the market ($\beta_j > 1$) are called **aggressive** assets; investors must receive a higher expected return to induce them to take on this additional risk. Assets that fluctuate one-for-one with the market ($\beta_j = 1$) are said to be **neutral;** over- or underweighting the market portfolio by a neutral asset does not affect the

FIGURE 5.6

The characteristic line shows how the risk premium on an asset responds to the risk premium on the market. It predicts a regression through the origin.

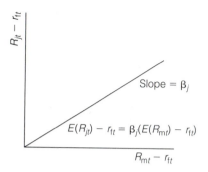

risk of the portfolio, and so neutral assets receive the same expected risk premium as the market.

These observations suggest that β_j is a measure of the risk of asset j relative to the market. The estimation of (5.27) as a simple regression model yields an estimate of beta. Inclusion of an intercept α_j in the estimation offers a test of the model because a rejection of the hypothesis $\alpha_j = 0$ suggests that the returns earned by investors are not commensurate with the systematic risk they have borne.

In addition, the decomposition of sample variation offers a decomposition of the total variability of the asset's risk premium (SST) into its systematic (SSR) and nonsystematic (SSE) components. Thus the R^2 measures the proportion of the total variability in the asset's risk premium that is attributable to market risk.

The CAPM equation (5.27) has two diagrammatic interpretations. The first is the usual interpretation of any population regression line. Taking the mathematical expectation of the CAPM regression (5.27), the expected risk premium (5.26) is[8]

$$E(R_{jt}) - r_{ft} = \beta_j(E(R_{mt}) - r_{ft}).$$

This population regression line is shown in Figure 5.6. In the finance literature, it is called the **characteristic line.** Like any population regression line, the characteristic line indicates how successive observations on the variables—in this case, the risk premium of asset j and that of the market—are associated. The slope of the characteristic line is, of course, β_j; we have noted that the key testable implication of the CAPM is that the intercept is zero, so that the characteristic line passes through the origin.

The Security Market Line

A more interesting diagrammatic interpretation of the CAPM depicts not the relationship governing successive observations t on a given asset j but the implications of the model for different assets. What determines the expected return of asset j, $E(R_j)$, as opposed to the expected return of some other asset i? Taking expecta-

---

[8]   Because it is the fact that the returns R_j and R_m are random that is the central focus of our discussion, this is recognized explicitly by carrying the expected value through the right-hand side and applying it to R_m. The simplifying assumption of a nonstochastic regressor used in Chapter 4 is not invoked.

FIGURE 5.7

The security mar-
ket line shows how
the expected return
$E(R_j)$ on a risky
asset is a markup
over the risk-free
rate.

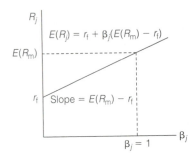

tions of (5.27) (and suppressing the time subscript t), the CAPM predicts that the expected returns on different assets are linearly related to their betas:

$$E(R_j) = r_f + \beta_j(E(R_m) - r_f). \tag{5.28}$$

That is, $E(R_j)$ differs from $E(R_i)$ to the extent that the two have different betas— different amounts of systematic risk. This equation is our sought-after relationship (5.25): The appropriate measure of risk is β_j, and the nature of the functional relationship between $E(R_j)$ and risk β_j is a linear one with intercept r_f and slope $E(R_m) - r_f$.

This linear relationship is shown in Figure 5.7; it is called the **security market line** (SML). Note that, whereas the characteristic line depicted the relationship between the risk premium $E(R_j) - r_f$ of a given asset and that of the market—a relationship in which β_j was the slope—the SML depicts the relationship between expected return $E(R_j)$ and risk β_j across different assets indexed by j. Thus in the SML diagram β_j is on the horizontal axis and $E(R_m) - r_f$ is the slope.

The SML emphasizes the prediction of the CAPM that the betas of different assets should lie on a straight line that passes through two points. One point is the intercept corresponding to the risk-free rate of return and $\beta_j = 0$. If an asset's return is uncorrelated with the market then its risk is entirely idiosyncratic. But this idiosyncratic risk can be easily diversified away; consequently, it should offer no expected return in excess of the risk-free rate.

The second point through which the SML passes is that corresponding to $\beta_j = 1$ and the expected return on the market $E(R_m)$. A neutral asset has a return that varies one-for-one with the market; overweighting the market portfolio in favor of it does not change the risk of the portfolio. The forces of demand and supply should therefore result in that asset having an expected return $E(R_j)$ equal to $E(R_m)$. If, for example, it is the case that $E(R_j) > E(R_m)$ then asset j represents an unusually attractive investment opportunity: By starting with a market portfolio and overweighting in favor of j, investors can increase their expected return without changing their risk. Attempts by investors to do this will drive down $E(R_j)$ into conformity with $E(R_m)$.

Given that it passes through these two points, the geometry of the diagram confirms that the slope of the SML is $(E(R_m) - r_f)/1$. Different assets represent trade-offs along this line; the more systematic risk an investor is willing to bear,

TABLE 5.2   Monthly Returns for Four Assets[a]

Month	IBM	Xerox	NYSE	T-Bills	Month	IBM	Xerox	NYSE	T-Bills
63.7	−0.0040	0.2471	−0.0095	0.0025	66.1	−0.0060	0.0755	0.0435	0.0037
63.8	0.0259	0.1653	0.0506	0.0027	66.2	0.0413	0.0834	0.0109	0.0038
63.9	0.0163	−0.0075	−0.0134	0.0027	66.3	0.0019	0.0454	−0.0219	0.0037
63.10	0.0929	0.2954	0.0163	0.0028	66.4	0.0804	0.0269	0.0337	0.0037
63.11	−0.0152	0.0274	−0.0068	0.0028	66.5	−0.0220	−0.0406	−0.0724	0.0037
63.12	0.0448	0.1389	0.0075	0.0028	66.6	−0.0296	0.0155	−0.0046	0.0037
64.1	0.0690	−0.0772	0.0201	0.0028	66.7	−0.0278	−0.0738	−0.0127	0.0039
64.2	0.0521	0.0095	0.0270	0.0028	66.8	−0.0562	−0.2191	−0.0931	0.0040
64.3	0.0444	0.0784	0.0314	0.0029	66.9	−0.0094	−0.0148	−0.0143	0.0043
64.4	−0.0404	0.1141	−0.0031	0.0028	66.10	0.0457	−0.0736	0.0127	0.0043
64.5	0.0549	0.2228	0.0116	0.0028	66.11	0.1358	0.2670	0.0382	0.0043
64.6	−0.0063	−0.0013	0.0154	0.0028	66.12	−0.0120	−0.0366	0.0162	0.0040
64.7	−0.0314	−0.0935	0.0277	0.0028	67.1	0.0754	0.1703	0.1428	0.0038
64.8	−0.0438	−0.0420	−0.0090	0.0028	67.2	0.0791	0.0784	0.0209	0.0037
64.9	−0.0091	0.2213	0.0370	0.0028	67.3	0.0488	0.1250	0.0320	0.0035
64.10	−0.0378	−0.1221	0.0170	0.0029	67.4	0.1009	0.0228	0.0365	0.0031
64.11	−0.0149	−0.1168	0.0007	0.0029	67.5	−0.0352	−0.0506	−0.0179	0.0029
64.12	−0.0073	0.0450	−0.0069	0.0031	67.6	0.0670	0.0055	0.0516	0.0028
65.1	0.0952	0.1255	0.0537	0.0031	67.7	0.0206	−0.0183	0.0709	0.0035
65.2	0.0195	0.1239	0.0278	0.0032	67.8	−0.0136	−0.0173	0.0028	0.0034
65.3	−0.0033	−0.0311	0.0053	0.0032	67.9	0.0970	0.0551	0.0378	0.0036
65.4	0.0677	0.1253	0.0359	0.0032	67.10	0.0825	0.0531	−0.0359	0.0037
65.5	−0.0113	0.0791	−0.0079	0.0031	67.11	0.0330	−0.0022	0.0067	0.0038
65.6	−0.0418	−0.0358	−0.0743	0.0031	67.12	0.0245	0.0395	0.0554	0.0040
65.7	0.0459	0.0947	0.0291	0.0031	68.1	−0.0518	−0.1650	−0.0035	0.0041
65.8	0.0449	0.1022	0.0451	0.0031	68.2	−0.0222	−0.0253	−0.0416	0.0040
65.9	0.0271	−0.0088	0.0308	0.0032	68.3	0.0560	−0.0183	−0.0045	0.0041
65.10	0.0400	0.0356	0.0474	0.0032	68.4	0.1061	0.1489	0.1164	0.0043
65.11	−0.0122	0.1219	0.0300	0.0033	68.5	0.0558	0.0904	0.0586	0.0045
65.12	−0.0495	0.0313	0.0327	0.0035	68.6	−0.0091	−0.0182	0.0192	0.0045

[a]NYSE, New York Stock Exchange; T-Bills, treasury bills.

the higher the expected return over the risk-free rate. Aggressive assets with $\beta_j >$ 1 offer expected returns greater than the market because their returns magnify fluctuations in the market as a whole. Defensive assets with $\beta_j < 1$ offer expected returns less than the market because they offer a refuge from the volatility of the market. In the extreme, an investor can escape completely from the volatility of the market by investing entirely in the risk-free asset (or, equivalently, in assets having a beta of zero); the cost of doing this is, of course, that the investor earns only the risk-free rate.

Like any economic model, the CAPM represents hypotheses about ex ante behavior—the world as we imagine it works. This is reflected in the fact that equation (5.28) tells us how expected returns should be determined. But of course the econometrician does not observe expectations: the data on the basis of which the CAPM regression equation (5.27) must be estimated are ex post realizations—the world as it is. Consequently *estimated* betas and *realized* returns will not lie exactly on the security market line. Nevertheless, if the reasoning underlying the CAPM is valid, there should be a tendency for these values to lie around the SML: Assets exhibiting estimated betas greater than 1 should usually also exhibit higher realized returns than the market, and vice versa.

The exercises ask you to investigate these aspects of the CAPM using the data in Table 5.2. Following a preliminary inspection of these yields, you will estimate the CAPM, obtaining an estimated beta and testing the hypothesis that the characteristic line passes through the origin for that security. You will then see whether the estimated beta and realized return seem consistent with the security market line. For another data set and extensive empirical exercises see Berndt (1991, Chap. 2).

Historical Notes

The theory of portfolio diversification was developed in the 1950s by Harry Markowitz. Markowitz's portfolio theory provided the foundation for the CAPM, which was developed independently by several economists in the early 1960s, notably Sharpe (1964) and Lintner (1965). The regression (5.27)—with or without an intercept—is known as the Sharpe-Lintner form of the CAPM. Markowitz, Sharpe, and a third financial economist Merton Miller were jointly awarded the 1990 Nobel prize in economics for their contributions.

EXERCISES

The data of Table 5.2 are available in the file **fama.dat**, which is organized as follows.

month   Month, July 1963–June 1968.

ibm   Monthly rate of return on IBM stock.

xerox   Monthly rate of return on Xerox stock.

nyse   Monthly rate of return on the market portfolio of New York Stock Exchange common stock.

tbills   Monthly rate of return on U.S. 91-day treasury bills.

The last series is given to a greater degree of accuracy than is presented in Table 5.2. The first three series are from Fama (1976), who interpreted NYSE common stock as "the market portfolio."

Begin by inspecting the file, satisfying yourself that the data are the same as those presented in Table 5.2, and noting that the first two rows are occupied by variable names and a blank line.

5.15 (a) 💿 **fama.dat** Compute the sample mean of each of the four returns series.

(b) If one of these average monthly returns is denoted $\overline{R}$, an approximate[9] annualized rate may be computed as

$$R_{\text{annual}} = (1 + \overline{R})^{12} - 1.$$

Use a hand calculator to compute such approximate annualized rates of return for each asset. Do your answers seem plausible?

(c) Risky assets should enjoy positive risk premia $R_j - r_f$, on average. That is, they should on average yield higher returns than a riskless asset. Taking treasury bills to be riskless, compute series for the risk premia on each of Xerox, IBM, and the market.

i. Compute the sample means of each of these risk premia series. Are they in fact positive?

ii. Although risky assets may yield returns higher than a riskless asset on average, there will of course be times when it is better to hold the riskless asset. For each of the three risky assets, what is the largest negative risk premium that was experienced and with which time period was it associated?

5.16 💿 **fama.dat** Estimate the CAPM (5.27) for Xerox, including an intercept.

(a) Consider your estimate of beta.
i. Is Xerox best described as a defensive, neutral, or aggressive stock?

ii. To the extent that your point estimate of beta differs from 1, this could be due to sampling error.

Is your conclusion in (i) statistically significant? That is, are you able to reject the null hypothesis that Xerox is a neutral stock in favor of the alternative that $\beta_{jm} \neq 1$?

iii. The CAPM suggests that securities having more systematic risk than the market should typically also earn a higher risk premium than the market, and vice versa. Considering your estimate of beta and the average risk premia computed in Exercise 5.15, is this true of Xerox? Locate Xerox in a security market diagram like Figure 5.7, placing the annualized returns you computed in Exercise 5.15b on the vertical axis.

(b) Do your results for the intercept α support the theory behind the CAPM? Specifically, does a hypothesis test lead you to reject the null that $\alpha = 0$ in favor of the alternative that $\alpha \neq 0$?

(c) From your regression results, what proportion of the total variability of the Xerox risk premium is attributable to systematic risk?

5.17 💿 **fama.dat** Repeat the Exercise 5.16 for IBM.

5.18 💿 **fama.dat** (Continuation of Exercise 3.11.) Consider a portfolio in which 40% of your wealth is invested in IBM and 60% in Xerox. Generate a series for the return on this portfolio.

(a) Compute the mean return. How is it related to the mean returns on Xerox and IBM individually that you computed in Exercise 5.15a?

(b) Generate a series for the risk premium on the portfolio. Use it to estimate the CAPM for the portfolio.

i. Is the portfolio best described as defensive, neutral, or aggressive?

ii. How does the beta of the portfolio relate to the betas of Xerox and IBM individually?

---

[9] We study the calculation of exact annualized rates in the next chapter.

6

Matters of Functional Form

We have seen that the link between normality and linearity implies that linear functional forms are likely to have wide applicability in studying relationships between variables. This motivated our focus, in the previous two chapters, on the linear regression model

$$Y_i = \alpha + \beta X_i + \varepsilon_i, \qquad \varepsilon_i \sim \text{n.i.d.}(0, \sigma^2). \tag{6.1}$$

It is important to emphasize that, from the point of view of the methods of statistical inference developed in these chapters, the critical sense in which this model is linear is with respect to the *coefficients*. It is perfectly possible for the *variables* to enter nonlinearly. Consider, for example, a model in which Y depends on the square of a variable Z:

$$Y_i = \alpha + \beta Z_i^2 + \varepsilon_i. \tag{6.2}$$

Because the observations on Z_i^2 are just a series of numerical values, we may define $X_i = Z_i^2$ and the linear regression model (6.1) applies. Other powers are possible, of course—even fractional or negative ones. For example, our least squares methodology applies equally to the model

$$Y_i = \alpha + \beta \sqrt{X_i} + \varepsilon_i.$$

In Section 6.4 later in this chapter the case of a power of -1 is considered in some detail, which yields the reciprocal model

$$Y_i = \alpha + \beta \frac{1}{X_i} + \varepsilon_i.$$

That the linear regression model permits variables to enter nonlinearly as long as the model remains linear in its coefficients means that it is much more flexible and widely applicable than may initially be apparent. Such models are termed **intrinsically linear.** They contrast with **intrinsically nonlinear** models, which, as a result of being nonlinear in at least some of their coefficients, require the nonlinear estimation methods of Chapter 13.

The objective of this chapter is to introduce you to some of the more important intrinsically linear regression models that applied econometricians have found useful in studying nonlinear relationships between variables. These are as follows.

The consideration of one important class of intrinsically linear models is deferred to Section 8.8. Models such as (6.2), in which the explanatory variables are known positive-integer powers of other variables, are examples of **polynomial regression.** Polynomial regressions typically involve several powers of a variable and so are best treated in the context of multiple regression.

6.1   Loglinear Models

Perhaps the most important group of intrinsically linear models uses logarithms to convert multiplicative relationships into additive ones.[1] A good example of such a multiplicative relationship is the Cobb-Douglas production function

$$Q = \gamma K^\beta L^\alpha. \tag{6.3}$$

Here Q denotes the output from some production process; K and L are capital and labor inputs; and γ, α, and β are parameters. Taking logarithms yields the linear relationship

$$\log Q = \log \gamma + \beta \log K + \alpha \log L. \tag{6.4}$$

For data series $Q_i^* = \log Q_i$, $K_i^* = \log K_i$, and $L_i^* = \log L_i$, and redefining the intercept as $\gamma^* = \log \gamma$, this may be estimated as

$$Q_i^* = \gamma^* + \beta K_i^* + \alpha L_i^* + \varepsilon_i.$$

This is just an application of the linear multiple regression model we study in Chapter 8.

Alternatively, if constant returns to scale hold so that $\alpha + \beta = 1$, it is possible to divide through (6.3) by L and obtain the **labor-intensive** form

$$q = \frac{Q}{L} = \gamma \frac{K^\beta L^{1-\beta}}{L} = \gamma \frac{K^\beta}{L^\beta} = \gamma k^\beta. \tag{6.5}$$

Here $q \equiv Q/L$ is output per unit of labor input (labor productivity) and $k \equiv K/L$ is the capital-labor ratio.[2] Applying a logarithmic transformation to both sides

---

[1] Recall that it is a basic property of logarithms that $\log(ab) = \log a + \log b$. An excellent exposition of material related to exponential and logarithmic functions is provided by Chiang (1984, Chap. 10).

[2] Note that in this context lowercase is being used to denote labor-intensive quantities, *not* deviation form.

FIGURE 6.1

The log-log model.

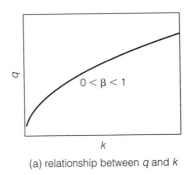
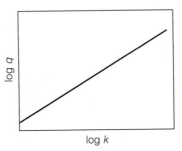

(a) relationship between q and k (b) relationship between $\log q$ and $\log k$

and introducing a disturbance to reflect the random nature of the data yields the statistical model

$$\log q_i = \log \gamma + \beta \log k_i + \varepsilon_i = \gamma^* + \beta \log k_i + \varepsilon_i. \qquad (6.6)$$

With variables suitably redefined, this is of the simple regression form (6.1). Figure 6.1(a) depicts the nonlinear relationship (6.5) between q and k for $\beta > 0$;[3] Figure 6.1(b) depicts the corresponding linear relationship between the logarithms of these variables.

This model is intrinsically linear in the parameters γ^* and β. However, note that it is intrinsically nonlinear in γ. Nevertheless, typically β is the coefficient of economic interest, and the fact that least squares yields a direct estimate of γ^* rather than γ is of no particular consequence. An indirect point estimate of γ may of course be deduced from $\hat{\gamma}^*$ using the relationship $\gamma = \text{antilog}(\gamma^*)$, and a hypothesis about γ translates into a corresponding hypothesis about γ^*.

This example illustrates that the use of the logarithmic transformation in this way is to some extent dependent on the specification of the disturbance in the model. Specifically, defining the transformed disturbance $u_i = e^{\varepsilon_i}$, our derivation of the regression model (6.6) implicitly assumes that the intensive form of the production function involved a **multiplicative disturbance:**[4]

$$q_i = \gamma k_i^{\beta} u_i = \gamma k_i^{\beta} e^{\varepsilon_i}.$$

Taking logarithms yields (6.6),

$$\log q_i = \log \gamma + \beta \log k_i + \log u_i = \gamma^* + \beta \log k_i + \varepsilon_i.$$

The relationship between the two disturbances is

$$\log u_i = \varepsilon_i.$$

---

[3]   As we see when the Cobb-Douglas production function is considered in more detail in the next chapter, economic theory suggests that $0 < \beta < 1$.

[4]   The symbol e denotes the irrational number $2.71828\ldots$, the base of the natural logarithm. The use of natural logarithms is standard but not essential. The transformation of the data using logarithms of some other base, say a, would just imply a disturbance of the form a^{ε_i}.

The estimation of this model as a classical normal linear regression specifies ε_i as normally distributed. Comparing the relationship between u_i and ε_i with equation (2.25) in our discussion of the lognormal distribution in Section 2.5.2, the implication is that u_i is lognormal.[5] (Remember that the definition of a lognormal random variable is one whose logarithm is normal.)

Suppose that instead the stochastic relationship between the intensive forms of the variables is specified using an **additive disturbance:**

$$q_i = \gamma k_i^\beta + \varepsilon_i. \tag{6.7}$$

This cannot be converted to the form of a linear regression. Instead, it is an example of an intrinsically nonlinear model, equation (4.6).

Which specification is more plausible, the intrinsically linear model based on a multiplicative disturbance or the intrinsically nonlinear one based on an additive disturbance? From Section 2.5.2 we know that the lognormal distribution arises from the multiplicative interaction of random factors. Because the Cobb-Douglas production function specifies output as being generated by the multiplicative interaction of factor inputs, a lognormal distribution for q_i (and thus a normal distribution for $\log q_i$ as implied by one for ε_i) seems to be the most natural assumption. This is the basis for the belief that the intrinsically linear model (6.6)—the additive-in-logs model with a normal disturbance—is the more plausible specification.

Indeed from this perspective the intrinsically nonlinear model (6.7) is a rather peculiar formulation. It suggests that although output is generated as the multiplicative interaction of factor inputs, q_i is nevertheless normally distributed. This is contrary to what we know is the usual distribution arising from multiplicative interactions.

Although the intrinsically nonlinear model (6.7) may be the less plausible one, it still serves as a useful example of nonlinear regression that we revisit in Chapter 13.

6.1.1 The Coefficient Is the Elasticity

Regression models that are linear in the logarithms of their variables are called **loglinear, log-log,** or **double-log** specifications. They have the attractive feature that the slope coefficient is the elasticity. To understand this, let X_i and Y_i be related loglinearly:

$$\log Y_i = \alpha + \beta \log X_i + \varepsilon_i. \tag{6.8}$$

As we have seen, this is equivalent to specifying the underlying functional relationship between the two variables as

$$Y = e^\alpha X^\beta e^\varepsilon. \tag{6.9}$$

---

[5] In terms of the notation of equation (2.25), Y_i takes the role of u_i and μ is zero.

The elasticity of Y with respect to X, defined as the percentage change in Y associated with a 1% change in X, is

$$\frac{X}{Y}\frac{dY}{dX} = \frac{X}{Y}e^{\alpha}\beta X^{\beta-1}e^{\varepsilon} = \beta.$$

The last step has been obtained by substituting (6.9) for Y in the middle expression. Although (6.9) was presented in terms of logarithms of base e, the same derivation holds for any base. In conclusion, $\hat{\beta}$ yielded by the estimation of (6.8) is an estimate of the elasticity of Y with respect to X.

Practitioner's Tip: Elasticities in log-log models

In a log-log regression model, a slope coefficient has the interpretation as the percentage response in the dependent variable to a 1% change in the independent variable; that is, as the *elasticity* relating the variables.

Another way of arriving at this result is to use the property that, mathematically, an elasticity is a logarithmic derivative. We use this fact many times in the chapters ahead, and so it is useful to state it formally.

Result 6.1   *If Y and X are related functionally by $Y = f(X)$ then*[6]

$$\frac{d\ln Y}{d\ln X} = \frac{X}{Y}\frac{dY}{dX}. \qquad (6.10)$$

Proof:

See Chiang (1984, pp. 292–293).   □

Applying this to the log-log model (6.8) verifies immediately that β is the elasticity. Here is another application of this result.

EXAMPLE 1   Show that in the Cobb-Douglas production function (6.3) the exponents β and α are the elasticities of output with respect to capital and labor, respectively.

SOLUTION   Taking logarithms of the Cobb-Douglas production function yields the loglinear form (6.4). Applying Result 6.1, the elasticities of output with respect to capital and labor are

$$\frac{K}{Q}\frac{\partial Q}{\partial K} = \frac{\partial \log Q}{\partial \log K} = \beta, \qquad \frac{L}{Q}\frac{\partial Q}{\partial L} = \frac{\partial \log Q}{\partial \log L} = \alpha.$$

It is to be emphasized that the result (6.10) does not require the function $f(\cdot)$ to be loglinear; but, as the notation makes explicit, in this most general form

[6] Technically, $f(X)$ must be a differentiable function. However, this is not normally an important limitation in economic applications.

requires the use of natural logarithms.[7] This is important because it means that this result can be used to obtain elasticity expressions even for nonlinear functions. But in the special case in which the function is loglinear—such as equation (6.8) or the Cobb-Douglas production function in Example 1—the slope coefficient is the elasticity regardless of the base used.

Because an elasticity is a dimensionless quantity—it is independent of units of measure—it should be the case that $\hat{\beta}$ obtained from a loglinear model is invariant to data scalings. Exercise 6.1 asks you to verify this. This contrasts with what, in Section 4.8, we have seen is true of the slope estimator in a nonlog model—its value is affected when different scalings ($v \neq w$) are applied to X and Y.

If a model is *not* loglinear, what is the elasticity? If X and Y are related linearly in their levels, as in (6.1), the elasticity is:

$$\frac{X}{Y}\frac{dY}{dX} = \frac{X}{Y}\beta. \tag{6.11}$$

That is, the elasticity must be evaluated on the basis of particular values for X and Y in addition to an estimate of β. It is different at different points on the sample regression line. One possibility is to evaluate (6.11) at the point of variable means $(\overline{X}, \overline{Y})$ because the sample regression line is known to lie on this point; but in principle the elasticity may be evaluated at any $(X, \hat{Y})$ point. In contrast, a loglinear model implies a constant elasticity at all points on the sample regression line.

That a loglinear model yields a direct estimate of the elasticity is particularly useful in studying demand relationships. If the relationship between the quantity demanded of a good q and its price p is of the form

$$\log q_i = \alpha + \beta \log p_i + \varepsilon_i,$$

then $\hat{\beta}$ is an estimate of the price elasticity of demand. Hypothesis tests can be used to investigate whether the demand curve is downward sloping ($\beta < 0$) and, if so, whether demand is price elastic ($\beta < -1$) or inelastic ($-1 < \beta < 0$).

If the relationship between the logarithms of q and p is linear, what does this imply about their relationship in terms of their original units of measure? Figure 6.2 shows that a linear relationship between $\log p$ and $\log q$ translates into a nonlinear relationship between p and q that is more plausible as a demand relationship than a strict linear specification of the form (6.1) would be. In particular, it allows quantity demanded to approach infinity or zero in an asymptotic manner as price varies between zero and infinity. In contrast, a model linear in the *levels* of the variables rather than their logarithms has two implausible implications: First, at some finite price, demand is completely choked off; and second, no matter how low price may get, demand will never expand beyond some limit.

This discussion illustrates that a priori theoretical considerations can be important in choosing a model specification. As well, a graphical examination of the data is often useful. In the example of a demand function, a plot of the price-quantity points may tell us a great deal about whether a linear or loglinear model is likely

---

[7] Because only the natural logarithm has the property that $d \log x / dx = 1/x$.

FIGURE 6.2

The log-log model
($\beta < 0$).

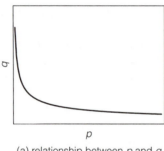

(a) relationship between p and q

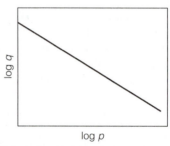

(b) relationship between $\log p$ and $\log q$

to be the most reasonable. Unfortunately, graphical methods become less useful in the study of relationships among a number of variables. As well, in many areas of application, economic theory may offer little guidance on the appropriate functional form. Instead it is preferable to have a more objective statistical basis for model selection and to be able to test formally whether a particular model specification seems satisfactory. The topics of model choice and specification testing are covered in Chapter 12.

The widespread use of loglinear models in applied econometrics is illustrated in the next chapter, where we consider in detail their application to production functions. Subsequently you will encounter a loglinear demand equation in Section 8.6 and a loglinear cost function in Chapter 11.

What Kind of Logarithm?

Our use of logarithms has assumed some general background knowledge on your part; in particular, recall from your earlier studies that a logarithm is defined with respect to a **base.** The logarithm of a number x is the exponent to which the base b must be raised to obtain x: $\log_b x$ is y such that $x = b^y$.

In the early empirical work of decades ago, applied econometricians often used base 10 or **common logarithms.** We encounter examples of this in our study of some of those classic applications. Today, however, there is no reason to use anything but **natural logarithms**—logarithms to the base $e = 2.71828\ldots$. Consequently, for most purposes we need not distinguish between natural and common logarithms; in using the notation *log* it is understood that natural logarithms are meant. In the occasional situation where reference is made to common logarithms—as in examples in which older empirical work is cited, or Exercise 6.3 in which the effects of different logarithms on regression analysis are investigated—this will be made explicit with the notation $\log_{10}$.

Practitioner's Tip: Use natural logs

In your own empirical work, there is no reason to use anything other than natural logarithms.

In any case, many of the properties of logarithms hold regardless of the base used. For example, in a linear relationship such as (6.8) the slope coefficient is the elasticity regardless of the base of the logarithm, as we mentioned. Occasionally, however, results are true only for natural logarithms, usually because they rely on the unique property of natural logs that the derivative of the logarithm is the reciprocal of the variable: $d \log x / dx = 1/x$. An example is Result 6.1: the elasticity is the logarithmic derivative for any functional relationship as long as natural logs are used. When we wish to emphasize that a result depends specifically on the use of natural logarithms, as in Result 6.1, we do so by using the notation *ln*.

EXERCISES

We have claimed that an elasticity is a dimensionless quantity. Consequently, it should be independent of both the base of the logarithm and the units of measure. The first three of these exercises ask you to investigate this.

6.1 ✍ Consider a loglinear regression model (6.8) yielding the least squares slope estimator $\hat{\beta}$. Now suppose units of measure are changed, so that the model is reestimated on the basis of $X_i = vX_i$, $Y_i = wY_i$: let the new estimator be denoted $\hat{\beta}$.

(a) Is $\hat{\beta} = \hat{\beta}$, even when $v \neq w$? Justify your answer.

(b) How is the intercept estimate affected?

6.2 Considering a conventional linear model (6.1), suppose the units of measure are changed: $X_i = vX_i$, $Y_i = wY_i$. In Section 4.8, the effect on $\hat{\alpha}$ and $\hat{\beta}$ is determined. What is the effect on the elasticity (6.11) if it is evaluated

(a) at an arbitrary point (X_i, Y_i).

(b) at the point of variable means $(\overline{X}, \overline{Y})$.

6.3 Consider estimating the loglinear model (6.8), first using common (base 10) logarithms

$$\log_{10} Y_i = \alpha + \beta \log_{10} X_i + \varepsilon_i,$$

and then using natural logs:

$$\ln Y_i = \alpha + \beta \ln X_i + \varepsilon_i.$$

Let us denote the results of the former estimation $\hat{\alpha}$ and $\hat{\beta}$ and the results of the latter $\hat{\boldsymbol{\alpha}}$ and $\hat{\boldsymbol{\beta}}$. It can be shown (Chiang 1984, p. 286) that the relationship between the two types of logarithms is

$$\ln x = \ln 10 \log_{10} x = 2.3026 \log_{10} x, \quad (6.12)$$

so that use of one rather than another is essentially a matter of a scaling constant. Use the results on the effects of scaling factors in Section 4.8 to establish

(a) the relationship between $\hat{\boldsymbol{\beta}}$ and $\hat{\beta}$.

(b) the relationship between their standard errors $s_{\hat{\boldsymbol{\beta}}}$ and $s_{\hat{\beta}}$.

(c) the relationship between their t statistics for the general hypothesis $H_0 \colon \beta = \beta_0$.

(d) the relationship between $\hat{\boldsymbol{\alpha}}$ and $\hat{\alpha}$.

6.4 Consider the labor-intensive form of the Cobb-Douglas production function (6.5),

$$q = \gamma k^{\beta}.$$

Show that β has the interpretation as the elasticity of labor productivity q with respect to capital per worker k.

6.2 Log-Lin Models

The loglinear models we have just discussed are linear in the logarithms of both the dependent and explanatory variables and serve to transform multiplicative relationships into linear ones. Models in which only one of the variables is transformed by logarithms have somewhat different interpretations and are called **semilogarithmic models.**

In this section we consider in detail semilog models in which the dependent variable has been transformed by a logarithm, called **log-lin models:**

$$\log Y_i = \alpha + \beta X_i + \varepsilon_i. \tag{6.13}$$

In fact, we have already encountered a simpler version of this model in Section 2.5.2:

$$\log Y_i = \mu + \varepsilon_i.$$

We have seen that, in combination with a normal disturbance, the implication is that Y is lognormally distributed. The only difference now is that, instead of the constant mean μ, the mean of that lognormal distribution is linear in X: $E(\log Y_i) = \alpha + \beta X_i$.

One example that has been cited of a distribution that is approximately lognormal is the distribution of income. Instead of specifying people's incomes as lognormal around a fixed mean μ, the log-lin model (6.13) permits mean income to vary systematically with some characteristic X. There are many possibilities for X, and much of empirical labor economics is concerned with estimating multiple regressions that attempt to explain the log of earnings[8] as a function of variables describing education, experience, and other characteristics such as age, race, gender, and family background. We have encountered a simple example of such a statistical earnings function in the Mincer wage equation discussed in Theory Meets Application 4.1. By estimating his equation only for white nonfarm nonstudent males Mincer was able to control for some of the influences, such as race and gender, that would otherwise have to be included as variables in a multiple regression. Consequently he was able to use a simple regression to isolate the effect of education on earnings. Berndt (1991, Chap. 5) provides a useful introduction to statistical earnings functions.

The lognormality of earnings means that statistical earnings functions are one important application of the log-lin model. However, let us turn to what, at least at first glance, appears to be a quite different interpretation of the model.

---

[8] There is an important distinction between income and earnings. Earnings are income from employment. By contrast, total income includes both earnings and income from sources other than employment, such as investment income. In most research in labor economics, it is earnings that are the natural focus of interest.

6.2.1 The Constant Growth Model

Consider a variable Y_t evolving over time so that it grows annually at rate g. In period t its value changes from that in the previous period $t-1$ according to

$$Y_t = (1+g)Y_{t-1}. \tag{6.14}$$

This might roughly describe the growth of a country's population, GNP, capital stock, or price level. Or it might describe the value of some asset: the price of a stock, the capitalization of a firm, or the value of real estate. For concreteness, let us think of it as a bank account balance in which interest is credited annually.

As an illustration, for the interest rate $g = 0.05$ and Y_t starting at an initial value of $Y_0 = \$100$, some values for Y_t are calculated in Table 6.1. This time path is plotted in Figure 6.3(a).

As the final line of Table 6.1 indicates, at any point in time the variable may be expressed in terms of its initial value Y_0 and the growth rate g:

$$Y_t = (1+g)^t Y_0.$$

TABLE 6.1

Constant Growth Model in Discrete Time with $g = 0.05$

Period	Y_t	$\Delta Y_t = Y_t - Y_{t-1}$
0	$Y_0 = 100$	
1	$Y_1 = (1+g)Y_0 = (1.05)100 = 105$	5
2	$Y_2 = (1+g)Y_1 = (1+g)^2 Y_0 = (1.05)^2 100 = 110.25$	5.25
3	$Y_3 = (1+g)Y_2 = (1+g)^3 Y_0 = (1.05)^3 100 = 115.7625$	5.5125
4	$Y_4 = (1+g)Y_3 = (1+g)^4 Y_0 = (1.05)^4 100 = 121.550625$	5.788125
$\vdots$	$\vdots$	$\vdots$
t	$Y_t = (1+g)^t Y_0$	gY_{t-1}

FIGURE 6.3

The constant growth model in discrete time ($Y_0 = 100$, $g = 0.05$).

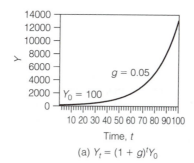

(a) $Y_t = (1+g)^t Y_0$

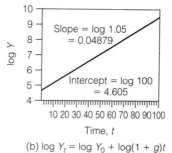

(b) $\log Y_t = \log Y_0 + \log(1+g)t$

The table indicates how this is derived. First, the one-period relationship (6.14) holds for all periods going back to period 0.

$$Y_t = (1+g)Y_{t-1}$$
$$Y_{t-1} = (1+g)Y_{t-2}$$
$$Y_{t-2} = (1+g)Y_{t-3}$$
$$\vdots$$

Substituting these successively into the first equation yields:

$$Y_t = (1+g)Y_{t-1}$$
$$= (1+g)^2 Y_{t-2}$$
$$= (1+g)^3 Y_{t-3}$$
$$\vdots$$
$$= (1+g)^t Y_0.$$

The last expression is the final line of Table 6.1. The method by which this has been derived is called the **method of recursive substitution.**

The final column of Table 6.1 shows the change in Y_t from its value in the previous period, $Y_t - Y_{t-1}$ (recall that the delta notation ΔY_t was introduced in Chapter 1). These changes are, of course, in the amount of 5% every year. For example, the percentage increase in Y_t between $t = 2$ and $t = 3$ is

$$\frac{Y_3 - Y_2}{Y_2} \times 100 = \frac{5.5125}{110.25} \times 100 = 0.05 \times 100 = 5\%.$$

In general the percentage growth in Y_t from the previous year is always

$$\frac{\Delta Y_t}{Y_{t-1}} = \frac{Y_t - Y_{t-1}}{Y_{t-1}} = \frac{(1+g)Y_{t-1} - Y_{t-1}}{Y_{t-1}} = \frac{gY_{t-1}}{Y_{t-1}} = g \tag{6.15}$$

multiplied by 100. This confirms that $100g$ is indeed the annual percentage growth rate.

As the last column of Table 6.1 and Figure 6.3(a) make clear, compound growth at a constant rate results in larger and larger absolute increases in the variable. Five percent of 1000 is larger than 5% of 100; 5% of a million is larger still. The time path

$$Y_t = Y_0(1+g)^t, \qquad t = 0, 1, 2, \ldots, \tag{6.16}$$

is said to be one of exponential growth because the variable of which Y is a function, t, appears as an exponent on the right-hand side. The larger and larger absolute increases in the variable mean that exponential growth is nonlinear.

Notice, however, that the right-hand side of this model is a multiplicative relationship. Our experience using logarithms to convert multiplicative relationships to additive ones suggests that we apply a log transformation to (6.16):

$$\log Y_t = \underbrace{\log Y_0}_{\alpha} + \underbrace{\log(1+g)}_{\beta} t. \tag{6.17}$$

FIGURE 6.4

U.S. GDP per
capita, 1880–1987.

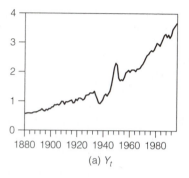

(a) Y_t

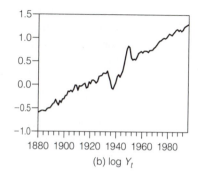

(b) $\log Y_t$

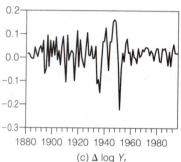

(c) $\Delta \log Y_t$

This is of the log-lin form (6.13) with intercept $\alpha = \log Y_0$, slope $\beta = \log(1 + g)$, and explanatory variable time t. Figure 6.3(b) depicts this linear relationship for the numerical values of Table 6.1 using natural logarithms: $\log Y_0 = \ln 100 \approx 4.605$ and $\log(1 + g) = \ln 1.05 \approx 0.04879$.

The conclusion is that taking logs converts an exponential growth path into a linear one. This is why economic time series exhibiting exponential growth are often plotted in log form: The log transformation converts increasing absolute changes in the variable into roughly constant changes in its logarithm, reflecting the underlying roughly constant percentage growth rate. As an example, Figure 6.4 plots a series on U.S. GDP per capita, 1880–1987, studied by Jones (1995). Figure 6.4(a) plots the raw series and (b) its natural logarithm. Figure 6.4(a) clearly exhibits the nonlinear path associated with exponential growth in the level of the variable arising from, over long periods, sustained growth in living standards. Figure 6.4(b) shows that this secular growth takes the form of, again on average over long periods, constant increases in the log of the variable. That these increases are constant in the long term is emphasized by Figure 6.4(c), which shows that, although the changes in the logarithms vary from year to year, they do not trend systematically upward or downward. The exercises at the end of this section ask you to investigate these aspects of Jones's series.

The model (6.16) (or, equivalently, (6.17)) is called the **constant growth model in discrete time.** It is in discrete time in that interest on the bank balance is only credited annually, so compounding is annual. That is, the formula (6.16) is only defined for integer values of time: $t = 0, 1, 2, \ldots$ For noninteger values, the formula does not give the correct answer. For example, setting $t = 1/2$ (a 6-month time period) in (6.16) yields $Y_{1/2} = (1 + g)^{1/2} Y_0 = \sqrt{1.05} \cdot 100 \approx 102.47$. But after 6 months the bank balance will not be \$102.47; it will still only be \$100 because interest is credited only at the end of the year.

That a log transformation converts an exponential growth path into a linear one does not depend on the base of the logarithm. The use of a different base would change the numerical values of the intercept and slope of the log-lin trend line (6.17), but not the linearity of the functional relationship. Figure 6.3(b) uses the base $e \approx 2.718$; as we have seen, the slope is therefore $\log(1 + g) = \ln 1.05 \approx 0.04879$. But is there any reason to prefer this base? It turns out that the natural logarithm—in our numerical example with $g = 0.05$, the value 0.04879—has an interesting economic interpretation. Let us investigate this.

Continuous Evolution through Time

A bank balance of \$100, compounded annually at 5%, grows as calculated in Table 6.1. But suppose that instead interest is compounded semi-annually; every 6 months accrued interest is credited to the account and earns interest thereafter. Then, obviously, the value of the principal will grow slightly more quickly than is indicated in Table 6.1. What if the compounding takes place quarterly? The principal grows still more quickly. How about monthly? Weekly? Daily? Hourly? In the limit—that is, under **continuous compounding**—the principal grows most quickly. Equivalently, a slightly lower continuously compounded rate of interest will achieve the same results as a discretely compounded rate of 5%. What is this slightly lower continuously compounded rate? It is 0.04879.

Many economic processes evolve in a manner that is best thought of as continuous. A nation's population, output, and capital stock all evolve continuously through time (although the timing of our data observations, the **sampling interval,** is of course discrete). Recall from Section 1.2.2 that when a variable is a continuous function of time this is denoted $Y(t)$, in contrast to the notation Y_t, which denotes a value at the discrete time point t.

Because it is a continuous function of time, we may consider the derivative of $Y(t)$ with respect to t. This is something we will use with some frequency, and so it is convenient to denote the **time-derivative** of a variable by the dot notation

$$\dot{Y} \equiv \frac{dY(t)}{dt}.$$

This is the instantaneous analog to the discrete-time change ΔY_t. Similarly, the instantaneous analog to the discrete relative change $\Delta Y_t / Y_{t-1}$ is the **instantaneous growth rate**

$$\frac{\dot{Y}}{Y} \equiv \frac{1}{Y} \frac{dY(t)}{dt}.$$

Multiplied by 100, this becomes an instantaneous percentage rate of change.

The following result is an important property of such instantaneous growth rates.

Result 6.2	*The instantaneous growth rate of a variable is the time-derivative of its (natural) logarithm:*

$$\frac{\dot{Y}}{Y} = \frac{d\ln Y}{dt}.$$

Proof:

$$\frac{d\ln Y}{dt} = \frac{d\ln Y}{dY}\frac{dY}{dt} = \frac{1}{Y}\frac{dY}{dt} = \frac{\dot{Y}}{Y}.$$

The first step is the chain rule of calculus; the second uses the derivative property of the natural logarithm that $d\ln Y/dt = 1/Y$. □

That instantaneous growth rates may be obtained as the time-derivative of the logarithm turns out to be extremely useful in deriving relationships between growth rates, something that is pursued in detail in Appendix 6B at the end of the chapter.

Constant Growth in Continuous Time

Suppose that a continuously evolving variable is growing at a constant rate, as in our bank balance example. How is this described mathematically? The continuous growth in a variable at rate β is described by

$$Y(t) = Y(0)e^{\beta t}, \qquad t \geq 0. \tag{6.18}$$

This is the **constant growth model in continuous time;** it describes growth at the continuously compounded rate β, in contrast with the discrete-time model (6.16), which describes growth at discrete rate g.

In Table 6.2 some values are calculated for the continuous-time constant growth model, using $Y(0) = 100$ and $\beta = \ln 1.05 = 0.04879$. The calculations reproduce the values for Y_t of Table 6.1, confirming that under continuous compounding the slightly lower growth rate of $\beta = 0.04879$ is needed to achieve what the higher rate of $g = 0.05$ does under discrete compounding. Although Table 6.2 presents values of $Y(t)$ only for integer values of t, the model may legitimately be evaluated for noninteger values—in contrast to the discrete-time model. For example, after 6 months of continuous compounding a \$100 bank balance will be worth $Y(\frac{1}{2}) = e^{0.04879(1/2)}100 = \$102.47$.

In analogy with its discrete-time counterpart, taking logarithms converts the nonlinear model (6.18) into a linear one:

$$\log Y(t) = \log Y(0) + \beta t. \tag{6.19}$$

It follows that β has the interpretation of an instantaneous growth rate because, as long as natural logarithms have been used, applying Result 6.2 establishes that

$$\frac{d\log Y}{dt} = \beta = \frac{\dot{Y}}{Y}. \tag{6.20}$$

TABLE 6.2

Constant Growth Model in Continuous Time with $\beta = \log 1.05 = 0.04879$

Period	$Y(t)$	$\Delta \log Y(t)$
0	$Y(0) = 100$	
1	$Y(1) = e^\beta Y(0) = e^\beta 100 = 105$	0.04879
2	$Y(2) = e^\beta Y(1) = (e^\beta)^2 Y(0) = e^{2\beta} 100 = 110.25$	0.04879
3	$Y(3) = e^\beta Y(2) = (e^\beta)^3 Y(0) = e^{3\beta} 100 = 115.7625$	0.04879
4	$Y(4) = e^\beta Y(3) = (e^\beta)^4 Y(0) = e^{4\beta} 100 = 121.550625$	0.04879
$\vdots$	$\vdots$	
t	$Y(t) = e^{\beta t} Y(0)$	

The key parameter of interest in the constant growth model is the instantaneous growth rate β. This is the parameter that we want to estimate for any series having an underlying trend that is thought to be well described by the constant growth model. For example, in the case of the growth of the price level, β is the inflation rate; in the case of the growth in the value of an asset over time, β is the rate of return, or interest rate.

6.2.2 Estimating the Growth Rate

Given data observations Y_t, $t = 1, \ldots, n$, on a variable $Y(t)$ that we regard as growing in a constant-growth manner, our objective is to estimate the growth rate β. There are two approaches to doing this. They involve different ways of introducing a disturbance into the constant growth model.

The Deterministic Trend Approach

Although an observed variable may follow a trend that seems to be well approximated as one of constant growth, economic data are also determined by random factors. Accordingly, observed time series fluctuate around their trends; Jones's GDP per capita series is an example. One way of expressing this is to add a disturbance to the deterministic trend,

$$\log Y_t = \alpha + \beta t + \varepsilon_t. \tag{6.21}$$

Figure 2.15(a) presents a simulated series generated according to such a deterministic trend model. It is based on the intercept and slope values $\alpha = 4.605$ and $\beta = 0.04879$, which correspond to the initial value $Y_0 = 100$ and 5% discrete growth rate in this chapter. Consequently, the linear deterministic trend of Figure 6.3(b) is the one underlying Figure 2.15(a).

Least squares can be applied in standard fashion to this log-lin model. The resulting estimate of α is an estimate of $\log Y(0)$—indirectly, an estimate of the initial value of the series associated with time point zero. Note that in going from the mathematical model (6.19) to the statistical model (6.21) we shift notation from $Y(t)$ to Y_t because the statistical model is a statement about the generation of data, and data are observed at a discrete sampling interval.

EXAMPLE 2

 jones.dat

Estimate the constant growth model for Jones's series on GDP per capita.

SOLUTION

Running the log-lin regression yields

$$\log Y_t = -0.817 + 0.01773t + e_t, \qquad R^2 = 0.964.$$

The conclusion is that over the period 1880–1987 U.S. GDP per capita grew at a rate of approximately 1.8% annually.

This example illustrates that, multiplied by 100 and for small changes in the variables, β may be interpreted as the percentage change in the dependent variable associated with a small change in the explanatory variable. This percentage change is, as we now understand, in terms of continuous compounding. In the present context, the explanatory variable is time t. As we see shortly, however, the same interpretation applies to applications of the log-lin model in broader contexts.

Estimating the constant growth model as a log-lin regression in this way is called the **deterministic trend** approach to modeling the time series because it simply involves adding a disturbance to the deterministic trend (6.19). It contrasts with an alternative approach to describing economic time series, to which we now turn.

The Stochastic Trend Approach

As always in statistics and econometrics, many estimators can be proposed for a population parameter. The estimate of β yielded by the deterministic trend approach is not the only estimator that might be considered. In fact, an alternative estimator of the instantaneous growth rate is often used, one that does not require the estimation of a regression model. Consider lagging the relationship (6.19) one period and subtracting:

$$\log Y_t - \log Y_{t-1} = \Delta \log Y_t = \beta t - \beta(t - 1) = \beta. \qquad (6.22)$$

That is, when a variable grows at a constant rate, the continuously compounded growth rate is the time-difference of its logarithms. The series $\Delta \log Y_t$ is often called the **log-difference,** for short;[9] because it measures the continuously compounded growth rate over the period, we often refer to log-differences as **continuous growth rates.** Notice that in the last column of Table 6.2 the log-differences

[9] Note that this term is slightly confusing: The log-difference is the difference of the logarithms, not the logarithm of the difference. The latter is not defined for zero or negative changes.

are always 0.04879, consistent with the fact that the series was constructed based on this instantaneous growth rate.[10]

The random nature of observed data can be recognized by adding a disturbance to this relationship,

$$\Delta \log Y_t = \beta + \varepsilon_t \qquad (t = 2, \ldots, n). \tag{6.23}$$

Notice the sample range over which the statistical model is defined. If the data on a variable are over the n observations $t = 1, \ldots, n$ then, because no Y_0 is observed, its differences are available for the $n - 1$ observations $t = 2, \ldots, n$. It is often said that in differencing a variable, we lose an observation from the series: Differencing a series of n observations yields $n - 1$ differenced values.

This is a quite different way of introducing a disturbance into the constant growth model from the deterministic trend approach. It is called a **stochastic trend** model, a term that is introduced in Section 2.7. Figure 2.15(b) presents a simulated series that is generated in this way, contrasting it with one generated by a deterministic trend model. As we point out in that discussion, instead of being in the form of a regression model the stochastic trend model is in the form of model (2.15) of Chapter 2, in which the dependent variable is now $\Delta \log Y_t$ and β plays the role of μ. This says that although Y grows, it does so in such a way that its percentage changes fluctuate around a constant mean, the growth rate β.

Figure 6.4(c) shows that the log-differences of Jones's GDP per capita series behave in this way. On a period-by-period basis, the growth rate of per capita GDP is not constant—far from it. In some years it is large, in others small, and in others negative. Nevertheless, these percentage changes do not become systematically larger or smaller over time. Consequently, they can reasonably be viewed as fluctuating around a mean growth rate β. The model (6.23) is just the mathematical expression of this common sense.

Recall that for a model of this form the least squares estimator of β is just the sample mean of the dependent variable. In this case, this is

$$\frac{1}{n-1} \sum_{t=2}^{n} \Delta \log Y_t. \tag{6.24}$$

Because the log-differences of a variable are its continuous growth rates period by period, it makes sense to estimate the mean growth rate β as the average of these

---

[10] One way of recognizing that log-differences are continuously compounded growth rates is by starting with the identity

$$\frac{Y_t}{Y_{t-1}} = \exp\left(\log \frac{Y_t}{Y_{t-1}}\right)$$

and restating it as

$$Y_t = Y_{t-1} \exp(\log Y_t - \log Y_{t-1}).$$

Thus the log-difference $\Delta \log Y_t$ plays the role of the exponent in the continuous-time constant growth model (6.18) and hence is the continuously compounded one-period growth rate by which Y_{t-1} evolves into Y_t.

log-differences. This is just the formula (2.37) with Y_t in log form. It is a different estimator from that yielded by the log-lin regression model (6.21).

EXAMPLE 3

jones.dat

Apply this estimator to Jones's data.

SOLUTION

The sample mean of the log-differences of Jones's series—the log-differences plotted in Figure 6.4(c)—is 0.01776. This is very close, but not identical, to the estimate of 0.01773 obtained in the previous example from the deterministic trend approach.

Upon inspection, it is apparent that this estimator has one especially convenient feature: The formula (6.24) simplifies as follows.

$$\frac{1}{n-1} \sum_{t=2}^{n} \Delta \log Y_t$$

$$= \frac{1}{n-1} \left[(\log Y_n - \log Y_{n-1}) + (\log Y_{n-1} - \log Y_{n-2}) + \cdots \right.$$
$$\left. + (\log Y_3 - \log Y_2) + (\log Y_2 - \log Y_1) \right]$$
$$= \frac{\log Y_n - \log Y_1}{n-1} \tag{6.25}$$

That is, in computing the mean of a differenced series, all but the first and last values of the original series cancel. To compute the average growth rate of a series all we need are its initial and terminal values. By contrast, the estimation of the deterministic trend model (6.21) requires the complete time series.

EXAMPLE 4

Jones's values for GDP per capita in 1880 and 1987, the initial and terminal values plotted in Figure 6.4(a), are 0.5511 and 3.6841. Using only this information, estimate the growth rate.

SOLUTION

The period 1880 to 1987 includes 108 years, so $n - 1 = 107$. Applying formula (6.25),

$$\frac{\log Y_n - \log Y_1}{n-1} = \frac{\log 3.6841 - \log 0.551}{107} = 0.01776.$$

This is the same value obtained by averaging the complete series of log-differences in Example 3, as the derivation indicates it should be.

It is useful to check that when this formula is applied to a series generated as a deterministic growth trend it yields the correct answer.

EXAMPLE 5

Suppose the variable Y_t has the observed values $Y_1 = 105.00$ and $Y_4 = 121.55$. What is its average growth rate?

SOLUTION

Because the complete series is not given, the regression approach is not an option. Instead we apply the formula (6.25):

$$\frac{\log Y_n - \log Y_1}{n-1} = \frac{\log 121.55 - \log 105.0}{3} = 0.04879.$$

The average growth rate is 4.879%, continuously compounded. The correct interpretation is one of continuous compounding because, by working in log-differences, we have computed a continuous growth rate. Of course we knew in advance that this would turn out to be the answer because the values given for Y_1 and Y_4 are just those from Table 6.2, values that by construction grew at the continuous rate of 0.04879.

We could instead have computed the average *discrete* growth rate. However, the calculation is not as simple. Discretely compounded growth at rate g from $Y_1 = 105.00$ to $Y_4 = 121.55$ takes the form

$$(1+g)^3 Y_1 = Y_4.$$

Solving for g yields

$$g = \left(\frac{Y_4}{Y_1}\right)^{\frac{1}{3}} - 1 = \left(\frac{121.55}{105.00}\right)^{\frac{1}{3}} - 1 = 0.05,$$

so the average discrete growth rate is 5%. Of course we knew in advance that this would turn out to be the answer because the values given for Y_1 and Y_4 are just those from Table 6.1, values that by construction grew at the discrete rate of 0.05.

In general, for a time series $Y_t, t = 1, \ldots, n$, calculation of the average discrete growth rate involves taking a $(n-1)$th root:

$$g = \left(\frac{Y_n}{Y_1}\right)^{1/(n-1)} - 1. \tag{6.26}$$

This is a less convenient calculation than the simple division by $n-1$ involved in calculating the continuous growth rate (6.25).

In Example 5, the $(n-1)$th root or average is appropriate because there are $n-1$ growth rates linking the values $Y_1, \ldots, Y_n$. When, on the other hand, n growth rates are being averaged, it is the nth root or average that is appropriate. Here is an example of discrete growth rates in which the nth root is relevant.

EXAMPLE 6

Fama's data given in Table 5.2 indicate that in July, August, and September of 1963 the monthly return on IBM stock was -0.0040, 0.0259, and 0.0163, respectively. In the terminology of Chapter 2, these are simple returns. What was the rate of return over the quarter? At an annual rate? What was the average monthly return?

SOLUTION

Let these monthly returns be denoted R_1, R_2, R_3. The rate of return on an asset is the growth rate of its price.[11] If the price is denoted P_t, then the discrete rate of return is

$$R_t = \frac{P_t - P_{t-1}}{P_{t-1}}. \tag{6.27}$$

Thus a simple return is a discrete growth rate. Such discrete growth rates are related by

$$1 + R_{\text{quarterly}} = (1 + R_1)(1 + R_2)(1 + R_3).$$

Thus the gross quarterly rate is

$$1 + R_{\text{quarterly}} = (0.9960)(1.0259)(1.0163) = 1.0385,$$

so over the quarter the price increased at the net rate of 3.85%. This is a gross annual rate of return of

$$1 + R_{\text{annual}} = (1 + R_{\text{quarterly}})^4 = 1.0385^4 = 1.1629,$$

or a net rate of 16.29%. The average gross monthly rate is

$$(1 + R_{\text{quarterly}})^{\frac{1}{3}} = 1.0385^{\frac{1}{3}} = 1.01267,$$

or a net rate of 1.27%. This gross monthly rate could have been obtained equivalently as

$$(1 + R_{\text{annual}})^{\frac{1}{12}}.$$

As Example 5 illustrates, there are a number of respects in which continuous growth rates are very convenient to work with. Some other nice properties of continuous growth rates are developed in Appendix 6B at the end of this chapter.

Which Estimator Is Better?

Although the ease of calculating the average growth rate is appealing, we know that computational considerations are not the primary basis on which we choose one estimator over another. Instead we choose estimators according to their sampling properties, such as unbiasedness and efficiency, and our initial inclination might be to attempt to compare the deterministic and stochastic trend approaches to estimating β in this way.

However, this would be misguided. It only makes sense to compare the sampling properties of estimators when they are alternative estimators for a parameter in a *common* statistical model. Comparing different estimators in different models is like comparing apples and oranges.

---

[11] This simplifies by assuming that the return arises purely from capital gains. If the asset earns dividends, rent, or other non–capital gains income, the rate of return will have to be redefined appropriately.

Remember that the legitimacy of any inference procedure is contingent on the proper specification of the model. To show that an estimator has certain desirable properties in the context of a particular model is of little interest if that model is a poor description of how the data are generated.

The deterministic and stochastic trend approaches to estimating β yield different estimators because they are different models of how the data are generated. The real question is therefore not so much which one is the better estimator, but which one is the better model.

It turns out that this seemingly esoteric question has been the target of an enormous amount of intellectual firepower in econometric theory in recent decades. There are two reasons for this. First, although both deterministic and stochastic trends have the constant growth model as their common starting point, the alternative ways of introducing the disturbance into the model turn out to have quite different implications for the underlying behavior of economic variables, implications that are important for our understanding of economic phenomena and the analysis of time series data. Some suggestion of this is provided in Section 2.7 in our comparison of the simulated deterministic and stochastic trends in Figure 2.15(a) and (b). Both simulated series are based on the same intercept/initial value of $\alpha = 4.605$ or $Y_0 = 100$ and the same slope or drift of $\beta = 0.04879$. Both are based on exactly the same series of random shocks. Yet the two models generate quite different patterns of behavior in the simulated series—Figure 2.15(a) looks very different from (b).

The second reason for the interest in deterministic and stochastic trends is that, as we have presented them, they are actually special cases of much more general models, models that are not limited to either linear trends or i.i.d. fluctuations. These more general models are the subject of Chapters 15 and 17.

The outcome of the debate over the two types of models is that many econometricians now believe that growing economic variables are often best described by stochastic trends such as (6.23). Consider Jones's series for GDP per capita shown in Figure 6.4. Is it better described by a deterministic or stochastic trend model? Comparing this series with the simulated series of Figure 2.15, inspection suggests that per capita GDP evolves in a way that looks more like the stochastic trend in Figure 2.15(b) than the deterministic trend in (a). That economic variables are often best described by stochastic trends has important implications for the study of relationships between time series variables, as we see in Chapter 18.

The Statistical Earnings Function Revisited

So far our discussion of log-lin regressions has focused on the deterministic trend implementation of the constant growth model. But as our introductory remarks indicate, time series variables are not the only possible application of the log-lin model. We have noted that another important application is statistical earnings functions such as

$$\log Y_i = \alpha + \beta X_i + \varepsilon_i. \tag{6.28}$$

Here, Y_i is the earnings of individual i and X_i is, say, education. What insights does the constant growth interpretation of the log-lin model give into the earnings function?

Just as the value of a capital asset may grow in a manner described by the constant growth model, so may the returns to investments in human capital. Suppose that people with no education ($X = 0$) earn some base income $Y = Y_0$ and that each year of schooling raises this income by the continuously compounded rate β. Someone with 1 year of schooling ($X = 1$) earns $Y = Y_0 e^{\beta}$, someone with 2 years of schooling earns $Y = Y_0 e^{2\beta}$, and so on. In general, then, an individual having X years of schooling earns

$$Y = Y_0 e^{\beta X}.$$

This is, of course, just the continuously compounded constant growth model (6.18). Taking logarithms yields a log-lin equation of the form (6.28) in which $\alpha = \log Y_0$. Different individuals, indexed by i, have different earnings Y_i and levels of education X_i. The estimation of (6.28) yields an estimate of β that, analogous to (6.20), has the interpretation of the percentage increase in earnings associated with an additional year of schooling:

$$\beta = \frac{d \log Y}{dX} = \frac{1}{Y}\frac{dY}{dX}.$$

Recall, for example, that Jacob Mincer's earnings equation on p. 140 is the form (6.13). He obtained the estimate $\hat{\beta} = 0.07$. The implication is that, for the representative white, nonfarm, nonstudent male, an additional year of schooling results in a 7% increase in annual earnings. This interpretation was simply asserted in Theory Meets Application 4.1, but the underlying basis for it is now apparent.

In a log-lin model, the slope coefficient indicates the *relative* change in Y associated with a small *absolute* change in X. Multiplied by 100, the slope coefficient may therefore be interpreted as the percentage change in Y associated with a unit change in X. In the example of an earnings equation, this is the percentage change in earnings due to an additional year of schooling. Note that β is *not* the elasticity of Y with respect to X, which is instead

$$\frac{X}{Y}\frac{dY}{dX} = X\beta.$$

An elasticity relates relative changes to relative changes. This formula shows that in the log-lin model it must be evaluated on the basis of both an estimate of β and a value for X. In most applications of the log-lin model, however, it is β that has the most immediate interpretive value and the elasticity is of no particular interest. The earnings function and the deterministic trend implementation of the constant growth model are examples. Because coefficients in semilog models are, like β, not literally elasticities but are closely related to elasticities, they are sometimes called **semielasticities.**

THEORY MEETS APPLICATION   6.1

Returns to Education across Countries

Psacharopoulos (1994) has surveyed the inter-national evidence on returns to education. Considering earnings functions estimated separately for males and females, he found that women on average receive 12.4% higher earnings for each additional year of schooling and men 11.1% (Psacharopoulos 1994, Table 7). Distinguishing between types of education, he found that academic training yields a return of 11.7% whereas technical/vocational training yields 10.5% (1994, Table 9).

Grouping countries into four income categories, the typical value of the coefficient on years of schooling (multiplied by 100) is given in the last column of the following table (information from Psacharopoulos 1994, Table 3).

The pattern, as Psacharopoulos notes, is that returns to education "...decline by the level of the country's per capita income. This is another reflection of the law of diminishing returns to the formation of human capital at the margin" (p. 1327).

Overall, then, Psacharopoulos concludes that "...educating females is marginally more

Income category	Mean per capita income (dollars)	Mean years of schooling	Coefficient (%)
Low income ($610 or less)	301	6.4	11.2
Lower middle income (to $2,449)	1,383	8.4	11.7
Upper middle income (to $7,619)	4,522	9.9	7.8
High income ($7,620 or more)	13,699	10.9	6.6
World	3,665	8.7	10.1

profitable than educating males, the academic secondary school curriculum is a better investment than the technical/vocational track, and the returns to education obey the same rules as investment in conventional capital, i.e. they decline as investment is expanded" (1994, p. 1335).

Practitioner's Tip: **Semielasticities in log-lin models**

In a log-lin regression, a slope coefficient (multiplied by 100) has the interpretation of the percentage response in the dependent variable to a (small) one-unit change in the independent variable.

This Practitioner's Tip has been qualified by the requirement that the unit change in the independent variable be a *small* one. The reason for this caveat is clarified in Section 6.2.4.

An enormous theoretical and empirical literature in labor economics deals with aspects of the statistical earnings function. The theoretical underpinnings of the equation relate to the concept of human capital; again, see Berndt (1991, Chap. 5). In particular, note that the multiplicative compounding of returns to education leads to a model in which the lognormal is the natural specification for the distribution of earnings, consistent with what, from Section 2.5.2, we know is true of income distribution.

6.2.3 Interpreting Discrete versus Continuous Rates

As we have seen, the estimation of the log-lin continuous growth model (6.21) yields an estimate of the continuous growth rate β. There is, of course, an implied value for the associated discrete growth rate g; because the two are linked by

$$\beta = \log(1 + g)$$

we may solve for an estimate of g by inverting:

$$g = \text{antilog}(\beta) - 1.$$

Because it takes a slightly higher discrete rate to achieve the same growth that continuous compounding does, g will be slightly larger than β.

However, in most applications there is no reason to do this. As long as it is understood that the proper interpretation of the slope in a log-lin model is as a continuously compounded growth rate, there is no interest in obtaining the associated discrete rate. In any case, the two values are usually very close, at least for small growth rates. This has been illustrated in our numerical example in which the continuously compounded rate of $\beta = 0.04879$ is so close to 5% that few of us would spend much time emphasizing the distinction from the discrete rate $g = 0.05$. Similarly, although we could start with Mincer's estimate $\hat{\beta} = 0.07$ and compute

$$\hat{g} = \text{antilog}(\hat{\beta}) - 1 = \text{antilog}(0.07) - 1 = 0.0725$$

as the corresponding discretely compounded rate of return, in most applications there is no point in doing this.

That the continuously and discretely compounded rates β and g are usually very close reflects the general property of logarithms that, for small values of g,

$$\log(1 + g) \approx g. \tag{6.29}$$

That is, the log of 1 plus a small number is approximately equal to that small number. The reason for this is as follows. As shown in Figure 6.5, the logarithmic function intersects the horizontal axis at the value 1; $y = \log x = \log 1 = 0$ because $e^0 = 1$. The slope at this point is 1:

$$\left.\frac{dy}{dx}\right|_{x=1} = \left.\frac{d\log x}{dx}\right|_{x=1} = \left.\frac{1}{x}\right|_{x=1} = 1.$$

By inspection of the curvature of the function relative to this slope, a basic property of logarithms is that the left-hand side of the approximate equality (6.29) must be less than the right-hand side:

$$\log(1 + g) < g. \tag{6.30}$$

FIGURE 6.5

The natural log-
arithmic function
$y = \log x$.

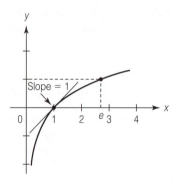

One way of thinking about why this must be true is that a lower continuously compounded growth rate is needed to achieve what a higher discretely compounded rate would.

Applying this property of logarithms to the period-by-period changes in a variable shows that this same approximate equality of discrete and continuous growth rates will also apply on a period-by-period basis. Recall from (6.22) that the continuous growth of Y_t from its previous value is at the rate given by its log-difference:

$$\Delta \log Y_t = \log Y_t - \log Y_{t-1} = \log \left(\frac{Y_t}{Y_{t-1}} \right).$$

The ratio in parentheses on the right-hand side of this equality may be manipulated as follows:

$$\frac{Y_t}{Y_{t-1}} = \frac{Y_{t-1} + Y_t - Y_{t-1}}{Y_{t-1}} = \frac{Y_{t-1}}{Y_{t-1}} + \frac{Y_t - Y_{t-1}}{Y_{t-1}} = 1 + \frac{\Delta Y_t}{Y_{t-1}}.$$

For low growth rates, $\Delta Y / Y$ is a small number, and the log of 1 plus a small number is approximately that small number:

$$\log \left(\frac{Y_t}{Y_{t-1}} \right) = \log \left(1 + \frac{\Delta Y_t}{Y_{t-1}} \right) \approx \frac{\Delta Y_t}{Y_{t-1}}.$$

This verifies that, even on a period-by-period basis, continuous and discrete growth rates are approximately equal:

$$\text{Continuous growth rate} = \Delta \log Y_t \approx \frac{\Delta Y_t}{Y_{t-1}} = \text{Discrete growth rate.}$$

Again, because continuous compounding achieves the value that a slightly higher discretely compounded rate does, the left-hand side is slightly less than the right-hand side.

EXAMPLE 7

Consider Fama's monthly simple returns of $R_1 = -0.0040$, $R_2 = 0.0259$, and $R_3 = 0.0163$ and the quarterly and annual returns of $R_{\text{quarterly}} = 0.0385$ and $R_{\text{annual}} = 0.1629$ that are computed in Example 6. What are the analogous continuous rates?

SOLUTION

From equation (6.27), Fama's discrete returns are the relative price changes

$$R_t = \frac{P_t - P_{t-1}}{P_{t-1}}.$$

The continuous rate of return is

$$\Delta \log P_t = \log\left(\frac{P_t}{P_{t-1}}\right) = \log(1 + R_t).$$

Hence, the monthly returns, expressed as continuously compounded rates, are

$$\log(1 + R_1) = \log 0.9960 = -0.0040,$$
$$\log(1 + R_2) = \log 1.0259 = 0.0256,$$
$$\log(1 + R_3) = \log 1.0163 = 0.0162.$$

The quarterly rate is the sum of these monthly rates,

$$-0.0040 + 0.0256 + 0.0162 = 0.0377,$$

or may be obtained from the discrete quarterly rate,

$$\log(1 + R_{\text{quarterly}}) = \log(1.0385) = 0.0377.$$

The average monthly rate is this quarterly rate divided by 3:

$$\frac{-0.0040 + 0.0256 + 0.0162}{3} = \frac{0.0377}{3} = 0.0126.$$

Equivalently, this may be obtained from the discrete average monthly rate,

$$\log(1 + R_{\text{monthly}}) = \log(1.0127) = 0.0126.$$

Similarly, the annual rate may be obtained by multiplying the quarterly rate by 4:

$$0.0377 \times 4 = 0.1509,$$

or from the discrete annual rate,

$$\log(1 + R_{\text{annual}}) = \log(1.1629) = 0.1509.$$

Notice that in all cases the continuous rates are slightly less than the discrete ones.

The relationships between these quarterly and annual discrete and continuous rates may be summarized as follows. Notice that any one value can be obtained from any other by traveling around the diagram in either of two directions.

$$R_{\text{quarterly}} = 0.0385 \longrightarrow \log(1 + R_{\text{quarterly}}) = 0.0377$$

$$\Big\downarrow 1 + R_{\text{annual}} = (1 + R_{\text{quarterly}})^4 \qquad \Big\downarrow \log(1 + R_{\text{annual}}) = 4 \times \log(1 + R_{\text{quarterly}})$$

$$R_{\text{annual}} = 0.1629 \longrightarrow \log(1 + R_{\text{annual}}) = 0.1509$$

To summarize, in the context of rates of return, discrete growth rates are called simple returns and continuous rates are called continuously compounded returns; these terms are used in Chapter 2. For a more extensive development of simple and continuously compounded returns than is possible here, see Campbell, Lo, and MacKinlay (1997, Sec. 1.4).

The approximate equality of discrete and continuous rates holds when the change in question is small, and in most economic applications this is the case. Situations sometimes arise, however, when the change is large enough that it is important to distinguish between discrete and continuous rates. Here is an example.

EXAMPLE 8

In a famous study of money demand under hyperinflation, Phillip Cagan (1956) presented data for a number of European hyperinflations. For the Hungarian hyperinflation of 1945–1946, Cagan presented the following values for the monthly log-differences of the price level during the final year of the hyperinflation.[12]

Month		$\Delta \log P_t$
1945	July	0.3113
	Aug.	0.4876
	Sept.	0.7957
	Oct.	1.8581
	Nov.	1.6769
	Dec.	1.1607
1946	Jan.	0.5551
	Feb.	1.7969
	Mar.	1.4559
	Apr.	2.9521
	May	5.7546
	June	11.3434
	July	33.6698

In discussing historical episodes of hyperinflation Cagan (1987) comments, "The world's record occurred in Hungary after World War II when an index of prices rose an average 19,800 per cent per month from August 1945 to July 1946 and 4.2×10^{16} per cent in the peak month of July." How can these percentages be reconciled with the given log-differences?

SOLUTION

Suppose you began July of 1946 with 100 kronen. During the month, the price level increased according to

$$33.6698 = \Delta \log P_t = \log P_t - \log P_{t-1} = \log P_t - \log 100.$$

Solving for P_t, it then required $P_t = 4.2 \times 10^{16}$ kronen to purchase what $P_{t-1} = 100$ kronen purchased at the beginning of the month. Common parlance expresses this as a $(4.2 \times 10^{16})\%$ increase in prices (not 3366.98% continuously compounded), the figure cited by Cagan.

Similarly, summing the inflation rates for August 1945 through July 1946 and dividing by 12, the average of these monthly rates is 5.2922. Suppose you began a

---

[12] In the original source, Cagan (1956, Table B9) expressed his log-differences using common logarithms. These have been reexpressed in terms of natural logs by multiplying by $\log 10 = 2.3026$.

representative month with 100 kronen. During the month, the price level increased according to

$$5.2922 = \Delta \log P_t = \log P_t - \log P_{t-1} = \log P_t - \log 100.$$

Solving for P_t, it then required $P_t = 19{,}880$ kronen to purchase what 100 kronen purchased at the beginning of the month. Common parlance expresses this as a $(19{,}880 - 100) = 19{,}780\%$ increase in prices (not 529.22% continuously compounded). This is roughly the 19,800% figure cited by Cagan.

Thus, when changes in a variable are large the numerical values of the discretely and continuously compounded growth rates are quite different, and it is the former that has the standard interpretive value. Notice that the relationship between the two kinds of rates continues to be that the continuously compounded rates are less than the discretely compounded ones.

Exactly this same issue of interpretation sometimes arises in certain kinds of log-lin regressions. This situation occurs often enough in applied work that it warrants a brief digression.

EXERCISES

Table 5.2 shows monthly returns for Xerox. Use these to answer the following questions.

6.5 Consider the returns on Xerox for the months July–September 1963.

(a) What was the quarterly return over this period?

(b) What was the average monthly return?

(c) What were these rates of return on an annual basis?

In each case give both the discrete and continuous rates, indicating clearly the relationship between the two.

6.6 Consider the returns on Xerox for the months July–December 1963.

(a) What was the semi-annual return over this period?

(b) What was the average monthly return?

(c) What were these rates of return on an annual basis?

In each case give both the discrete and continuous rates, indicating clearly the relationship between the two.

6.2.4 Pitfalls of Interpreting Dummy Variables ★

We have said that in most applications of the log-lin model it is the continuously compounded return β that is of the most natural economic interest and, in any case, at low growth rates it is typically little different from the associated discrete rate g. Are there any applications in which this is not true—that is, where the two *are* substantially different and where the discrete rate is the natural focus of interest?

The Practitioner's Tip in Section 6.2.2 summarizes the conclusion that the slope coefficient in a log-lin model has the interpretation of the percentage response to a unit change in the independent variable. It qualifies this conclusion with the caveat that the unit change in the independent variable be a *small* one. Let us investigate this qualification.

Dummy Variables in Log-Lin Models

Consider a situation in which a *large* relative change in Y is associated with a *large* absolute change in X. For example, consider an earnings equation in which X measures, not years of schooling but whether or not the individual has a university degree:

$$X_i = \begin{cases} 0 & \text{if individual } i \text{ is not a university graduate,} \\ 1 & \text{if individual } i \text{ is a university graduate.} \end{cases}$$

Hence, X can take on just two values, 0 or 1. It is an example of a binary variable, introduced in Chapter 1. In Section 5.3.2 we discuss models in which the dependent variable is binary. Here, in contrast, we consider it as an explanatory variable, in which case it is called a **dummy variable.** We say much more about dummy variables in Chapter 10. For the moment, you need only be aware that when qualitative variables are used as regressors, there is no violation of the classical assumptions and so conventional least squares regression analysis is perfectly legitimate. What does require some clarification is the appropriate interpretation of the slope estimate.

Whereas using years of schooling to measure education does so in such a way that a small change in X is associated with a small relative change in Y, this may not be the case when X is a dummy variable. The difference between 12 years of education and 11 is a fairly small percentage change in earnings; the difference between having a university degree and not having one may be much larger. As just one of an almost infinite number of examples that can be taken from the labor economics literature, Hanushek and Quigley (1978, Table 2) reported estimation results for a regression explaining the wages of American black males. The coefficient on a dummy variable indicating a graduate degree is 0.6443. Does this mean that a graduate degree increases the wages of a black male by 64%—that, for example, someone earning $50,000 without a graduate degree would earn $82,000 with one? No, because this coefficient now measures a large effect associated with a discrete change in X, not a small effect associated with a tiny one. It is therefore important to distinguish between continuously and discretely compounded rates of return, and it is the discrete return that is appropriate here:

$$\hat{g} = \text{antilog}(\hat{\beta}) - 1 = \text{antilog}(0.6443) - 1 = 0.9047. \tag{6.31}$$

Hence, the correct inference is that a graduate degree increases the wages of black males by more like 90%—from, say, $50,000 to $95,000.

Note that if changes in the variable were explicitly stated in terms of log-differences then there would be nothing wrong with expressing these in terms of the continuous rate β. Continuously compounded growth of 64.43% in a salary of $50,000 is

$$\log \$50,000 + 0.6443 = \log \$95,233,$$

the correct answer. But common parlance expresses percentage changes in discrete terms such as (6.15), not in log-differences. If we mean to say that a graduate degree will increase someone's salary from $50,000 to $95,000, we express this as a 90% increase, not a 64% increase continuously compounded.

Improved Estimates of the Semielasticity

Halvorsen and Palmquist (1980) were the first to note this common error in the interpretation of coefficients on dummy variables in log-lin regressions. Subsequently, Kennedy (1981) pointed out that, due to the nonlinear relationship between $\hat{g}$ and $\hat{\beta}$ in (6.31), $\hat{g}$ is a biased estimator. He suggested as an alternative

$$\tilde{g} = \text{antilog}\left(\hat{\beta} - \frac{1}{2}s_{\hat{\beta}}^2\right) - 1,$$

which, although still not unbiased, has a smaller bias than $\hat{g}$. For example, in their study in which $\hat{\beta} = 0.6443$ Hanushek and Quigley obtained the estimated standard error $s_{\hat{\beta}} = 0.1308$. Kennedy's estimate of g is therefore

$$\tilde{g} = \text{antilog}\left(0.6443 - \frac{1}{2}0.01711\right) - 1 = 0.8884,$$

suggesting that a graduate degree increases the wages of black males by approximately 89%. Although in this case the conclusion is little different from that yielded by $\hat{g}$, this is because β happens to be estimated precisely ($s_{\hat{\beta}}$ is small). In other circumstances this might well not be the case and Kennedy's formula could yield a substantially different estimate.

Kennedy's estimator has been endorsed by Giles (1982), who presents a much more complicated unbiased estimator for g, but shows that it yields estimates that are numerically very close to $\tilde{g}$.

6.2.5   Limitations of the Constant Growth Model

In light of our emphasis on the usefulness of the constant growth model, it is perhaps important to conclude with a recognition of some of its limitations.

Not All Growing Variables Are Adequately Described by the Constant Growth Model

Example 8 presents Phillip Cagan's data for the Hungarian hyperinflation of 1945–1946. This series can be used to make another important point: Not all growing variables are adequately described by the constant growth model.

FIGURE 6.6

Prices during
the Hungarian
hyperinflation of
1945–1946.

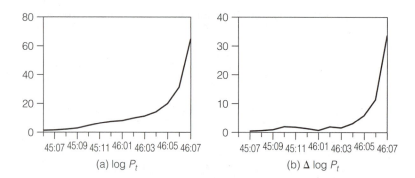

(a) log P_t (b) Δ log P_t

Figure 6.6 plots this series. Figure 6.6(b) plots the log-differences given in Example 8, and Figure 6.6(a) plots the implied log of the price level, constructed as an index that sets log $P_0 = 1$ in June 1945. This figure is analogous to Figure 6.4(b) and (c) for Jones's per capita GDP series, and a comparison of the two figures is instructive. (We do not attempt to plot the untransformed level of prices, analogous to Figure 6.4(a), because the explosive nature of hyperinflationary prices makes this impractical.)

Whereas taking logarithms transformed the nonlinear trend in per capita GDP into a linear one, clearly this is not the case for the Hungarian price level. Even in logarithms, this series continues to trend nonlinearly. The reason is that it is not characterized by constant growth. Indeed, the salient feature of hyperinflations is an acceleration of inflation over time, so that the growth rate of the price level steadily increases.

This is just what we see in examining the log-differences of the price level in Figure 6.6(b). In contrast to Figure 6.4(c), in which the log-differences of per capita GDP do not trend, Figure 6.6(b) shows that the Hungarian inflation rate trends upward. This cannot be described as variation around a constant mean growth rate; instead, this is a situation in which the growth rate is itself growing.

It follows that it is not appropriate to use the constant growth model—in either its deterministic or stochastic trend versions—as a description of these data. Although Example 8 calculates the average continuously compounded monthly rate of 5.2922 as the sample mean of the log-differences, this is best seen merely as a descriptive statistic rather than as an estimate of β in the stochastic trend model (6.23). The calculation of this descriptive statistic, although fine for the purpose of casual summary, fails to reveal the most interesting feature of the data: The inflation rate accelerates in the course of the hyperinflation.

It is evident that the econometric modeling of variables with trending growth rates is a topic of some interest. However, it is one that is best postponed for our systematic development of time series methods in Chapters 15–18. We return to it in Section 17.4. At the same time, it is important not to overstate the likely incidence of this behavior in economic data. Hyperinflations are extraordinary economic events, not ordinary ones. As the fairly short-lived nature of hyperinflations illustrates, growing growth rates are usually not sustainable in the economic world. This suggests that the constant growth model will often be satisfactory in providing a reasonable approximation to the long-term trend of growing economic variables.

Growth Rates Can Undergo Structural Changes

Even if a growth rate does not trend over time, it can undergo one-time shifts. The destruction of much of Japan's and Europe's capital stock during World War II presumably implies a structural change in their growth rates at that time. Similarly, many Western industrialized countries appear to have experienced a structural decline in their growth rates around 1970, the reasons for which have been a topic of contemporary interest to macroeconomists. As another example, a structural shift in central bank policies with respect to the control of money supply growth has led to a marked decline in the average rate of inflation since the early 1980s in many countries.

These are all examples in which a **structural change** has taken place so that the parameters of the model, in this case the growth rate β, have changed. It is obviously inappropriate to estimate a model that assumes that the parameters have remained constant over the full sample period. An estimate of β obtained from a simple-minded estimation of the constant growth model—in either its deterministic or stochastic trend versions—is misleading. Instead we want distinct estimates of the different values of β that prevailed during the two subsamples. Methods for treating structural shifts in the coefficients of regression models are studied in Chapter 10.

Despite these caveats, the phenomenon of economic growth—at rates that, historically, may not have altered dramatically—so dominates macroeconomic aggregates that the constant growth model sometimes provides a surprisingly good description of the long-term behavior of these time series. Jones's per capita GDP series plotted in Figure 6.4 illustrates this.

Descriptive Fit versus Economic Understanding

This leads to our final qualification. It is one thing for a statistical model such as the constant growth model to offer a good descriptive portrayal of the behavior of a variable; it is another matter entirely for the model to represent a genuine understanding of the underlying economic forces determining that variable. The constant growth model may fit a variable such as per capita GDP well and provide, in the sense we study shortly, fairly accurate forecasts. Yet it obviously reflects *no* understanding of the fundamental forces of capital accumulation and technical progress that drive economic growth. Indeed, as we see when time series data are considered in more detail in Chapters 15–18, it is quite easy to find statistical models that appear to offer a good descriptive picture of a time series variable, yet are actually inconsistent with (and very misleading about) the true process generating the variable.

Attempting to formulate portrayals of such true processes is the task of economic theory. In the case of economic growth, in Chapter 9 we study the theory and empirics of the basic model that is the starting point for all analyses of growth.

6.2.6 Application: The Growth of Per Capita GDP

A natural measure of a nation's living standards is its real gross domestic product per capita. As the series plotted in Figure 6.4(a) reveals, economic growth has meant that living standards have increased over time, although in fits and starts around the long-term trend. Abstracting from these fits and starts, how well does a simple constant growth model describe this long-term trend? Jones (1995) considered this question.

> Consider the following simple exercise. An economist living in the year 1929 (who has miraculous access to historical per capita GDP data) fits a simple linear trend to the natural log of per capita GDP for the United States from 1880 to 1929 in an attempt to forecast per capita GDP today, say in 1987. How far off would the prediction be?
>
> ... the somewhat surprising result of this exercise ... [is that] the prediction is off by only about 5 percent of GDP! Furthermore, the prediction *overestimates* per capita GDP rather than underestimates it, indicating that the average growth rate between 1880 and 1929 (1.81 percent annually) was actually slightly larger than that between 1929 and 1987... (Jones 1995, pp. 497–498)

The exercises that follow ask you to take the deterministic and stochastic trend approaches to analyzing per capita GDP. Our purpose is to illustrate the estimation and interpretation of regression coefficients in a log-lin constant growth model and related matters such as the use of lagged variables, as well as to examine descriptive features of discrete and continuous growth rates. Another application in Section 6.5 considers broader aspects of inference such as hypothesis testing.

For an application of the log-lin model to a topic requiring more background in economic theory, see the application to the monetary dynamics of hyperinflation in Appendix 6A at the end of this chapter.

EXERCISES

The data on GDP and population used to generate the per capita GDP series plotted in Figure 6.4 are presented in Table 6.3 and are available in the file **jones.dat**. The variables are

year   Year, 1880–1987.

gdp   Index of U.S. gross domestic product, 1913 = 100.

population   U.S. population, in thousands.

6.7 Use a hand calculator to do this exercise. Consider the values for GDP and population in 1880 and 1987.

(a) Calculate per capita GDP for each of these two years. (To avoid very small values for this variable, scale the GDP index by 1000.)

(b) Calculate the average annual continuous growth rate over this period for each of GDP, population,

TABLE 6.3   Data on U.S. GDP and Population, 1880–1987[a]

Year	GDP	Population	Year	GDP	Population	Year	GDP	Population
1880	27.7	50,262	1916	108.0	101,966	1952	317.2	157,553
1881	28.9	51,542	1917	105.3	103,414	1953	330.1	160,184
1882	30.1	52,821	1918	114.8	104,550	1954	325.6	163,026
1883	30.9	54,100	1919	115.8	105,063	1955	343.6	165,931
1884	31.5	55,379	1920	114.7	106,466	1956	350.4	168,903
1885	32.1	56,658	1921	112.1	108,541	1957	356.1	171,984
1886	34.3	57,938	1922	118.3	110,055	1958	353.8	174,882
1887	35.7	59,217	1923	133.9	111,950	1959	374.5	177,830
1888	36.6	60,496	1924	138.0	114,113	1960	381.5	180,671
1889	38.7	61,775	1925	141.2	115,832	1961	391.8	183,691
1890	41.5	63,056	1926	150.4	117,399	1962	412.6	186,538
1891	43.3	64,361	1927	151.9	119,038	1963	430.2	189,242
1892	47.5	65,666	1928	153.6	120,501	1964	455.5	191,889
1893	45.2	66,970	1929	163.0	121,770	1965	482.5	194,303
1894	43.9	68,275	1930	147.5	123,188	1966	507.1	196,560
1895	49.2	69,580	1931	135.2	124,149	1967	518.5	198,712
1896	48.2	70,885	1932	117.1	124,949	1968	540.2	200,706
1897	52.8	72,189	1933	114.7	125,690	1969	555.8	202,677
1898	53.9	73,494	1934	123.7	126,485	1970	555.3	204,879
1899	58.8	74,799	1935	133.6	127,362	1971	573.5	207,053
1900	60.4	76,094	1936	152.7	128,181	1972	602.9	208,846
1901	67.2	77,585	1937	160.2	128,961	1973	631.9	210,410
1902	67.9	79,160	1938	152.9	129,969	1974	627.3	211,901
1903	71.2	80,632	1939	165.0	131,028	1975	621.1	213,559
1904	70.3	82,165	1940	178.2	132,122	1976	651.5	215,152
1905	75.5	83,820	1941	209.6	133,402	1977	680.7	216,880
1906	84.2	85,437	1942	249.2	134,860	1978	715.8	218,717
1907	85.5	87,000	1943	294.6	136,739	1979	730.3	220,584
1908	78.5	88,709	1944	318.7	138,397	1980	730.3	227,757
1909	88.1	90,492	1945	312.8	139,928	1981	757.4	230,138
1910	89.0	92,407	1946	252.9	141,389	1982	738.7	232,520
1911	91.9	93,868	1947	245.6	144,126	1983	768.5	234,799
1912	96.2	95,331	1948	255.0	146,631	1984	822.4	237,011
1913	100.0	97,227	1949	255.2	149,188	1985	848.1	239,279
1914	92.3	99,118	1950	277.0	152,271	1986	873.3	241,625
1915	94.9	100,549	1951	305.4	154,878	1987	898.7	243,942

Source: Maddison (1982, 1989), as described in Jones (1995). Parts of tables A6 and B2 from *Phases of Capitalist Development* by Maddison, A. (1982) reprinted by permission of Oxford University Press.

[a] For U.S. GDP, 1913 = 100. Population is in thousands.

and per capita GDP. Are these three values related by any equality?

(c) Calculate the average annual discrete growth rate over this period for each of GDP, population, and per capita GDP. Are these values related by the same identity as the continuous rates?

6.8 ● jones.dat Using software, generate a complete series for per capita GDP. (To avoid very small values for this series, scale the GDP index by 1000).

(a) Plot per capita GDP against the year. Does your plot appear to reproduce Figure 6.4(a)?

(b) Plot the logarithm of per capita GDP against the year. Does your plot appear to reproduce Figure 6.4(b)? Do you judge the log-lin model (6.21) to be suitable for describing the long-term behavior of this series?

6.9 ● jones.dat We have seen that the relative changes (6.15) are discretely compounded growth rates, whereas the log-differences (6.22) are continuously compounded rates. (Remember that in differencing you lose an observation from the series.)

(a) Generate the log-differences for each of the variables GDP, population, and per capita GDP. Eyeballing these series, do you think that on an observation-by-observation basis they are related by any equality? If so, what?

(b) Next, generate the relative changes $\Delta Y_t / Y_{t-1}$ for each of the variables. On an observation-by-observation basis, are they related by the same identity as the continuous rates?

(c) Focus now on a comparison of the alternative growth rates for one of the variables, say GDP per capita.

i.   Eyeballing the series, do you think there is a dependable relationship between the magnitudes of the discrete and continuous rates on an observation-by-observation basis? Is this as it should be?

ii.   In what year did the highest growth take place? Do you reach the same conclusion based on either discrete or continuous rates?

iii.   Sometimes growth is negative. In what year

did the largest percentage decline occur? Do you reach the same conclusion based on either discrete or continuous rates?

(d) Compute the sample means of the discrete and continuous growth rates for GDP per capita.

i.   What is the relationship between the magnitudes of the two mean growth rates? Is this as it should be?

ii.   To what formula in the chapter does your mean continuously compounded growth rate correspond? How does it compare with the average continuous growth rate you obtained in Exercise 6.7b?

iii.   By contrast, how does the mean discrete rate compare with the average rate you found in Exercise 6.7c?

(e) Plot the log-differenced series. Does your plot reproduce Figure 6.4(c)?

6.10 ● jones.dat Estimate the constant growth model (6.21) for per capita GDP, over the following sample periods. Begin by letting time t be measured by year.

(a) 1880–1987. How close is your value of $\hat{\beta}$ to the alternative estimate computed in the Exercise 6.9?

(b) 1880–1929.

i.   How close is your value of $\hat{\beta}$ to Jones's estimate of 1.81%?

ii.   Use your estimated model to obtain a predicted value of per capita GDP for 1987, $\hat{Y}_t$. According to the data in Table 6.3, what was the observed value of per capita GDP in 1987? (Do not forget to scale the index value by 1000, as you have done in your estimation.) Jones found that his predicted value overestimated the observed value by approximately 5%. What do you find? (The data you have been given are slightly different from those used by Jones.)

(c) Does it matter how time is measured? Define a new variable time that takes the values $t = 1, 2, \ldots, 108$. Reestimate the 1880–1929 regression using this variable.

i.   Is the estimate $\hat{\beta}$ affected?

ii.   Is the forecast for 1987 affected?

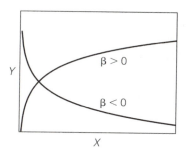

6.3 Lin-Log Models

The other type of semilog model is the **lin-log model**:

$$Y_i = \alpha + \beta \log X_i + \varepsilon_i. \qquad (6.32)$$

Just as the log-lin model effectively relates relative (i.e., percentage) changes in Y to absolute changes in X, the lin-log model relates *absolute* changes in Y to *relative* changes in X. The implied nonlinear relationship between the levels of X and Y is depicted in Figure 6.7 for alternative values of β.

A good example of an application in which the lin-log model has been successfully employed by many researchers is in the estimation of Engel curves. An **Engel curve** is the name given to the relationship between household consumption of a particular commodity and household income or total expenditure. It is named after Ernst Engel (1821–1896), a 19th-century German statistician who was a pioneer in the study of consumer behavior. On the basis of a study of Belgian working-class families he concluded that "the poorer a family, the greater the proportion of its total expenditure that must be devoted to the provision of food," a proposition that came to be known as **Engel's law.** It turns out that Engel's law is equivalent to the income elasticity of food being less than 1, so that food is a necessity. You are asked to establish the equivalence of the two propositions in Exercise 6.15. Whether Engel's law holds for a particular group of households is, of course, an empirical matter to be determined on the basis of econometric evidence.

The lin-log model is an appealing specification for Engel curves because typically the relationship between household income and consumption of a particular commodity is nonlinear. At low income levels, additional income results in relatively large increases in expenditure, at high income levels somewhat smaller ones. This is exactly the nature of the relationship depicted in Figure 6.7 for $\beta > 0$.

Of course, household expenditure on any good depends on more than income. Most obviously this will include prices, both of the good itself and of substitutable or complementary commodities. However, as long as the Engel curve is estimated using observations *across households* collected at a *single point in time*

FIGURE 6.8

Prais and
Houthakker's Engel
curve for meat con-
sumption, based on
a lin-log regression
model.

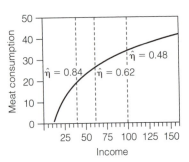

all households will normally face the same prices. Hence, these need not be included
as additional explanatory variables and the simple regression model

$$q_i = \alpha + \beta \log m_i + \varepsilon_i \tag{6.33}$$

adequately describes the ceteris paribus effect of income on expenditure; multiple
regression is unnecessary.[13] Here q_i denotes the consumption of the commodity of interest, m denotes income (or total household expenditure), and i indexes
households.

Let the income elasticity of demand be denoted by η. Note that this is *not*
equal to β, because only in a log-log model is the slope coefficient the elasticity.
Instead, assuming natural logarithms so that $d \log m / dm = 1/m$,

$$\eta = \frac{m}{q} \frac{dq}{dm} = \frac{m}{q} \frac{1}{m} \beta = \frac{1}{q} \beta. \tag{6.34}$$

Given an estimate of β, this must be evaluated at a particular level of consumption q.

EXAMPLE 9

One particularly thorough early study of Engel curves is that of Prais and Houthakker (1955), who studied British household data from the late 1930s using a
variety of functional forms. For example, for meat consumption by working-class
households the lin-log form yielded (1955, Table 21):

$$\hat{q}_i = -40.8 + 37.5 \log m_i. \tag{6.35}$$

The implied Engel curve is shown in Figure 6.8.

Annual income m was measured in pounds sterling, consumption q in shillings
(£1 = 20 shillings). In accordance with the conventions of their day, Prais and
Houthakker used common logarithms. Obtain the income elasticities of the demand
for meat for the income levels £40, £62.2, and £100. (The middle value is the mean
of Prais and Houthakker's sample; £40 and £100 correspond roughly to the lower
and upper quartiles.) Are these income elasticities consistent with Engel's law?

---

[13] In Section 8.6 you will estimate a demand function in which prices vary across observations. Therefore, multiple regression is required.

SOLUTION

The predicted meat consumptions associated with the given income levels are 19.28, 26.47, and 34.20 shillings, respectively.

Had Prais and Houthakker estimated their equation using natural logarithms, the elasticity formula could be evaluated simply by substituting in these alternative predicted values and the coefficient estimate $\hat{\beta} = 37.5$. However, their use of common logarithms necessitates a slight modification to the elasticity expression. Prais and Houthakker estimated

$$q_i = \alpha + \beta \log_{10} m_i + \varepsilon_i.$$

By the relationship (6.12) that $\ln x = 2.3026 \log_{10} x$, this may be reexpressed as

$$q_i = \alpha + \beta \frac{1}{2.3026} \ln m_i + \varepsilon_i.$$

Hence, the elasticity must be evaluated as

$$\eta = \frac{m}{q} \frac{dq}{dm} = \frac{m}{q} \beta \frac{1}{2.3026} \frac{1}{m} = \frac{1}{q} \frac{1}{2.3026} \beta. \tag{6.36}$$

Evaluating this expression on the basis of the predicted $\hat{q}$ values and $\hat{\beta} = 37.5$, the elasticities are as follows (values from Prais and Houthakker 1955, Table 11).

Income, m (£)	Meat consumption, $\hat{q}$ (shillings)	Elasticity, $\hat{\eta}$
40.0	19.28	0.84
62.2	26.47	0.62
100.0	34.20	0.48

These elasticities are shown in Figure 6.8. Consistent with Engel's law, they indicate that meat appears to be a necessity. As well, they illustrate that a lin-log Engel curve permits elasticities to decline with income. By contrast, a log-log functional form yields a constant elasticity of 0.69.

A variation on this lin-log Engel curve defines the dependent variable not as the absolute expenditure on the good but as its share of the consumer's budget:

$$\frac{q_i}{m_i} = \alpha + \beta \log m_i + \varepsilon_i. \tag{6.37}$$

This was first estimated by Working (1943) and subsequently endorsed by Leser (1963). The Working-Leser Engel curve is the form that is perhaps of the greatest contemporary interest, for reasons that become apparent in Section 11.6.1.

EXERCISES

6.11 For vegetables, Prais and Houthakker (1955) presented the estimated Engel curve

$$\hat{q}_i = -11.6 + 11.2 \log m_i.$$

Compute the income elasticities associated with the same income levels as in Example 9. Are they consistent with Engel's law? Do they decline with

income? Is vegetable consumption more or less income elastic than meat consumption?

6.12 ✦ Often interest focuses on testing hypotheses with respect to the elasticity η rather than β. For example, we might be interested in whether the data clearly support Engel's law. It would be natural to specify the null hypothesis as $H_0: \eta \geq 1$ (Engel's law is false) and ask whether the data allow us to reject this in favor of $H_A: \eta < 1$. Consider two approaches to doing this.

(a) Hypotheses on η may be restated as hypotheses on β. The relationship (6.34) between η and β is of the form

$$\eta = b\beta, \tag{6.38}$$

where $b = 1/q$, and a value for one implies a corresponding value for the other. In the case of (6.36) in Example 9, for instance, $b = 1/(q \cdot 2.3026)$, and at the mean of the sample where $\hat{q} = 26.47$ the correspondence is

$$\eta \geq 1 \Leftrightarrow \beta \geq 60.95,$$
$$\eta < 1 \Leftrightarrow \beta < 60.95.$$

The regression (6.35) is based on $n = 54$ households and yields an estimated standard error of $s_{\hat{\beta}} = 2.215$. Use this to test whether Engel's law is supported.

(b) If the relationship between $\hat{\eta}$ and $\hat{\beta}$ is linear, an implied standard error for $\hat{\eta}$ may be obtained and used in a direct test on η.
i. Treating b in (6.38) as a numerical constant, what is the relationship between $V(\hat{\eta})$ and $V(\hat{\beta})$? Use this to obtain an estimated standard error for $\hat{\eta}$, $s_{\hat{\eta}}$.
ii. Use your value for $s_{\hat{\eta}}$ to test whether Engel's law is supported.

(c) What is the relationship between your test statistics in parts a and b?

6.13 ✦ Suppose two parameters η and β are related by an *unknown* multiplicative constant a: $\eta = a\beta$. (For example η might be an elasticity and β a regression coefficient, as in Exercise 6.12, but this is just one possible interpretation.) You wish to test

the hypothesis $\eta = 0$ but have available only an estimate $\hat{\beta}$ and its standard error $s_{\hat{\beta}}$.

(a) Can an estimate $\hat{\eta}$ and its standard error $s_{\hat{\eta}}$ be deduced?

(b) Show that, despite your answer to part a, the t ratio for $\beta = 0$ may be used to test the hypothesis of interest.

6.14 The Engel curve (6.33) is specified as determining the quantity purchased q_i. In practice, though, this quantity is normally measured by expenditure on the good; this may be notated explicitly by denoting expenditure on good i by pq_i, where p is price. Consumption is measured by expenditure rather than quantity because household budget surveys typically collect data on broad commodity categories (such as "food") that aggregate goods over a number of units of measure, rather than more narrowly defined goods categories ("flour") to which a single unit of measure would apply.

In obtaining an income elasticity from an estimated Engel curve, therefore, we are in practice typically obtaining the quantity

$$\frac{m}{pq} \frac{d(pq)}{dm}.$$

Because the formal definition of an income elasticity is with respect to the response of quantity demanded q rather than expenditure pq,

$$\eta = \frac{m}{q} \frac{dq}{dm},$$

it is natural to ask whether this is important for results like those of Prais and Houthakker. Note that because the implicit price p of the aggregate is constant across the observations i it plays the role of a scale factor applied to the dependent variable. The effects of such scale factors are explored in Section 4.8. Use those results to answer the following. Imagine that Prais and Houthakker's expenditure series is based on $p = 2$ and that their equation (6.35) is reestimated using q_i rather than pq_i as the dependent variable.

(a) How is the resulting $\hat{\beta}$ affected?

(b) How is the resulting value of the income elasticity affected? Why?

6.15 ✗ Consider an Engel curve of the general form $Y = f(X)$, where X is income and Y is expenditure on some food category. We have defined Engel's law to be the assertion that the income elasticity is less than 1:

$$\frac{X}{Y}\frac{dY}{dX} < 1.$$

An alternative statement of Engel's law is that the share of food in income (Y/X) declines as income increases:

$$\frac{d(Y/X)}{dX} < 0.$$

Starting with the latter, show that the two definitions are equivalent.

6.4   Reciprocal Models

The use of logarithms is not the only way in which intrinsically linear models may be used to capture nonlinear relationships between variables. Another example is the reciprocal model

$$Y_i = \alpha + \beta\frac{1}{X_i} + \varepsilon_i, \tag{6.39}$$

which yields relationships of the type shown in Figure 6.9.

Note first that, for $\beta < 0$, the reciprocal model implies a curve similar to the lin-log model for Engel curves. In fact, the reciprocal model has been used by some researchers for this purpose.

EXAMPLE 10

Using the same data employed in the lin-log Engel curve in Example 9, Prais and Houthakker (1955) estimated the reciprocal model

$$\hat{q}_i = 41.0 - 801\frac{1}{m_i}.$$

The implied Engel curve is shown in Figure 6.10. Find the elasticities associated with the income levels in Example 9.

FIGURE 6.9

The reciprocal model: $Y = \alpha + \beta\frac{1}{X}$.

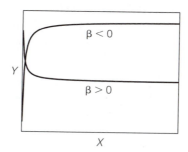

$\beta < 0$

Y

$\beta > 0$

X

FIGURE 6.10

Prais and
Houthakker's Engel
curve for meat con-
sumption, based on
a reciprocal regres-
sion model.

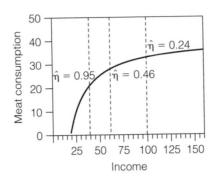

SOLUTION

The appropriate elasticity expression for the reciprocal model (6.39) is

$$\frac{X}{Y}\frac{dY}{dX} = \frac{X}{Y}\beta(-1)X^{-2} = -\frac{1}{XY}\beta.$$

Evaluating this at the income levels £40, £62.2, and £100 (and the corresponding predicted values $\hat{q}$ of 20.975, 28.12, and 32.99 shillings), using $\hat{\beta} = -801$, yields the following elasticities.

Income, m (£)	Meat consumption, $\hat{q}$ (shillings)	Elasticity, $\hat{\eta}$
40.0	20.975	0.95
62.2	28.120	0.46
100.0	32.990	0.24

These values are shown in Figure 6.10. Although the reciprocal functional form yields elasticity values that differ from those obtained from the lin-log form in Example 9, they follow the same pattern of both declining with income and being consistent with Engel's law.

6.4.1 The Phillips Curve

Perhaps the classic application of the reciprocal model, however, is to the Phillips curve. In the late 1950s, A. W. Phillips (1914–1975) studied U.K. data on the rate of change of wage rates (Y) and the unemployment rate (X) from the period 1861–1913. He reasoned that the relationship between the two should be nonlinear because of the asymmetry that probably exists with respect to nominal wage changes.

> When the demand for labour is high and there are very few unemployed we should expect employers to bid wage rates up quite rapidly, each firm and each industry being continually tempted to offer a little above the prevailing rates to attract the most suitable labour from other firms and industries. On the other hand it appears that workers are reluctant to offer their services at less than the prevailing rates when

FIGURE 6.11

The Phillips curve.
Source: Phillips, A.W.
(1958) "The Relation
Between Unemploy-
ment and the Rate
of Change of Money
Wate Rates in the
United Kingdom,
1861–1957," *Eco-
nomica* 25, 283–299,
Blackwell Publishing.

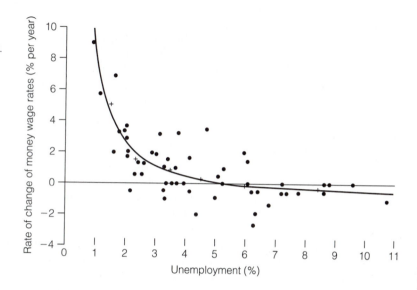

the demand for labour is low and unemployment is high so that wage rates fall only
very slowly. The relation between unemployment and the rate of change of wage
rates is therefore likely to be highly non-linear. (Phillips, 1958, p. 283)

On this basis Phillips estimated the intrinsically nonlinear model

$$Y_i = \alpha + \beta X_i^\gamma + \varepsilon_i,$$

obtaining the result

$$\hat{Y}_i = -0.900 + 9.638 X_i^{-1.394}. \tag{6.40}$$

Because the estimate $\hat{\gamma} = -1.394$ was quite close to -1, the simpler reciprocal
model (6.39), readily estimable by least squares, came to be widely adopted in
subsequent work.

Phillips's fitted relationship is graphed against his data in Figure 6.11 and confirms his conjecture of a nonlinear inverse relationship between wage inflation and
unemployment. That is, periods of rapid increases in wages tended to be associated
with low unemployment, and vice versa. On the face of it this result is, of course,
entirely plausible. It makes perfect sense that periods of economic boom would
exhibit both low unemployment and a comparatively rapid escalation in wages
and periods of recession the opposite. This finding was particularly intriguing to
macroeconomists at the time, however, because it was interpreted as supporting
Keynesian theories of the labor market that predicted lower unemployment arising
from fiscal and monetary policies that increased the nominal price level. Phillips's
study spawned 2 decades of intensive theoretical and empirical work into the linkages underlying these relationships. As part of this, the empirical phenomenon of
the Phillips curve evolved into the doctrine that the curve represented a usable
policy trade-off, and that government fiscal and monetary policies were largely

concerned with choosing a particular combination of inflation and unemployment on the curve. This doctrine in turn came to be the basis for the inflationary policies pursued by many countries in the 1960s and 1970s in the hope that the result would be a reduction in unemployment and a concomitant increase in national product.

That this interpretation came to be attached to the Phillips curve may be seen, in retrospect, to be a rather remarkable example of the confusion of correlation and causality. For, as we emphasize in Section 4.6, just because two variables are correlated does not necessarily imply that one causes the other. In the case of the Phillips curve, although historical data may at times exhibit an inverse correlation between unemployment and inflation, it does not necessarily follow that the adoption of inflationary policies will result in a permanent decline in unemployment. In fact, the opposite was precisely the experience of the 1970s. In country after country it was observed that, although higher inflation tended initially to result in lower unemployment, this was a transitory rather than a permanent effect. In this sense, Phillips curve trade-offs were found to be unstable, as we have seen in our inspection of the Stock-Watson data in Figure 3.4. Among the first to predict that this would be the case was economist Milton Friedman in his famous 1968 address as president of the American Economic Association.

The experience with the Phillips curve indicates that the confusion between correlation and causality can appear in sophisticated guises. Robert E. Lucas, Jr. expressed the matter as follows:

> The fact that nominal prices and wages tend to rise more rapidly at the peak of the business cycle than they do in the trough has been well recognized from the time when the cycle was first perceived as a distinct phenomenon. The inference that permanent inflation will therefore induce a permanent economic high is no doubt equally ancient, yet it is only recently that this notion has undergone the mysterious transformation from obvious fallacy to cornerstone of the theory of economic policy. (Lucas, 1976, p. 19)

That virtually an entire generation of macroeconomists, including many of the most brilliant of that generation, could come to subscribe to a fundamentally fallacious doctrine was a humbling realization that has had a profound effect on both empirical and theoretical research in macroeconomics. With respect to empirical work, the 1980s saw widespread disillusionment with policy analysis based on large-scale macroeconometric models incorporating empirical Phillips curve trade-offs. In terms of macroeconomic theory, both technical aspects of modeling and more substantive views of how the economy works have been affected. Because Phillips curve theories relied on treatments of expectations formation that presumed that individuals would repeatedly make systematic mistakes in forecasting the future, macroeconomists instead now use the methodology of rational expectations, which does not carry this implication.[14] Macroeconomists in the Keynesian tradition (the New Keynesian school) continue to base their models on some notion

---

[14] The relationship between rational expectations and mathematical expectation is explained in Appendix B, Section B.2.2.

of nonclearing of the labor market involving "sticky prices" so that unemployment includes an involuntary component and typically with some role for fiscal and monetary stabilization policy. They do this, however, using rational expectations and in a way that does not involve the now-discredited implication of a permanent Phillips curve policy trade-off. Other macroeconomists (the New Classical school) seek instead to understand the macroeconomy entirely in market-clearing, equilibrium terms.

Although the doctrine of the Phillips curve as a usable long-term policy trade-off has long since been laid to rest, the notion of a short-term trade-off has enjoyed a remarkable resurgence in the New Phillips Curve literature typified by the work of Gali, Gertler, and López-Salido (2001). This reflects the fact that the short-term response of output and prices to monetary policy is among the most enduring of macroeconomic questions. An increase in the money supply ultimately increases prices, but in the short run has a stimulative effect on investment, output, and employment. Thus the dynamics of the interaction between output and prices is at the center of the transmissions mechanism for a monetary impulse, and many macroeconomists of both the New Classical and Keynesian schools find it useful to formulate this interaction in terms of some concept of a short-run Phillips curve.

A useful summary of the current status of the Phillips curve is provided by Stock and Watson (1999, Sec. 4.1). Parkin (1998) assesses contemporary macroeconomic theory and policy in light of the Phillips curve experience.

EXERCISES

6.16 For vegetables, Prais and Houthakker (1955) presented the estimated Engel curve

$$\hat{q}_i = 12.7 - 231\frac{1}{m_i}.$$

Compute the income elasticities associated with the same income levels as in Example 10. Are they consistent with Engel's law? Do they decline with income?

6.17 At what point does the estimated Phillips curve (6.40) cross the horizontal axis? That is, what unemployment rate does the model predict will be associated with a zero rate of wage inflation? (Answer algebraically, not by simple inspection of Figure 6.11.)

6.18 For $\beta > 0$, the reciprocal model yields a curve similar to a log-log model. Why did Phillips not consider a loglinear specification for his curve?

6.5   Application: Engel Curves

We have used Engel curves to illustrate the use of lin-log and reciprocal functional forms. As we have seen, in both cases the income elasticity of demand η must be evaluated at a point on the curve and varies as we move along the

TABLE 6.4 The Income Elasticity of Demand

$$\eta = \frac{m}{q}\frac{\partial q}{\partial m}$$

$1 < \eta$	Income elastic
$0 < \eta < 1$	Income inelastic
$\eta < 0$	Inferior

curve. At any such point, demand is characterized as income elastic, inelastic, or inferior, according to the value of η. These possibilities are summarized in Table 6.4.

The following exercises ask you to study the income elasticity of demand for electricity using data from an early demand study by Hendrick Houthakker (1951). The data are given in Table 3.1 and plotted in Figure 3.3(a). The positive relationship revealed by that scatter plot is reflected in the sample correlation, which is computed to be 0.767.

Our use of Houthakker's data to estimate an Engel curve is a first step toward the estimation of more fully specified demand equations for electricity using multiple regression, something considered in Section 8.6. In terms of those more fully specified demand equations, the Engel curves estimated here by simple regression will be seen to be *misspecified*—to anticipate terminology introduced in Chapter 8; this is investigated in Exercise 8.18.

EXERCISES

Houthakker's data are available in the file **houthak1.dat**; the first two lines contain variable names and a blank line. This is an abbreviated version of a data set that is described in more detail in Section 8.6. The variables are as follows.

income   Household income (£ per year).
consump   Household electricity consumption (kilowatt-hours).

The following exercises ask you to estimate three functional forms for an Engel curve for electricity consumption:

log-log	$\log q_i = \alpha + \beta \log m_i + \varepsilon_i$
lin-log	$q_i = \alpha + \beta \log m_i + \varepsilon_i$
reciprocal	$q_i = \alpha + \beta(1/m_i) + \varepsilon_i$

Figure 6.12 shows the fitted Engel curves against the data. For functional forms involving logarithmic transformations, be sure to use natural logs.

As the Prais-Houthakker examples have illustrated, it is important to evaluate elasticities at a point on the curve; that is, based on predicted values of the dependent variable rather than observed values. It only makes sense to evaluate the elasticity at a point that is actually on the estimated Engel curve. Keep this in mind in evaluating the elasticities that follow.

6.19 **houthak1.dat** Inspect the data file to verify that these data are the same as those given for these two variables in Table 3.1. Obtain a scatter plot between the variables, with income m on the horizontal axis and consumption q on the vertical axis. Are you able to reproduce Figure 3.3(a)? Obtain the sample correlation between the variables. Are you able to reproduce the value given in connection with that figure?

FIGURE 6.12

Alternative functional forms for an Engel curve fitted to Houthakker's electricity demand data.

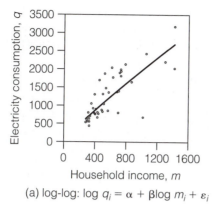

(a) log-log: log $q_i = \alpha + \beta \log m_i + \varepsilon_i$

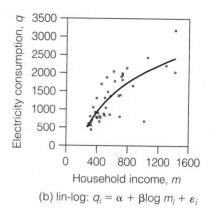

(b) lin-log: $q_i = \alpha + \beta \log m_i + \varepsilon_i$

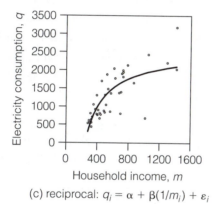

(c) reciprocal: $q_i = \alpha + \beta(1/m_i) + \varepsilon_i$

6.20 🖸 **houthak1.dat** Estimate a log-log Engel curve.

(a) According to these estimation results, what is the income elasticity? Is electricity demand elastic, inelastic, or inferior?

(b) Is the evidence in the estimated elasticity strong enough to establish clearly that electricity demand is income inelastic, or might this finding be due to chance? Examine this by testing the null hypothesis that $\eta \geq 1$ against the alternative that $\eta < 1$. Are you able to reject this null?

6.21 🖸 **houthak1.dat** Estimate a lin-log Engel curve.

(a) For this model specification, what is the formula for the income elasticity of demand?

(b) Evaluate the income elasticity at the following points.

i. Compute the mean household income $\overline{m}$. What is the income elasticity at this income level?

ii. Your least squares sample regression line passes through the point of variable means. For this sample regression line, what are these variable means? What is the income elasticity at this point?

iii. Inspecting Table 3.1, which town has the highest average household income? Which the lowest? What is the income elasticity of demand for electricity at each of these household incomes?

Locate these four income elasticities in a sketch similar to Figure 6.12(b). We have seen that, for the lin-log functional form, Prais and Houthakker found that the income elasticity of meat consumption declines with income. Is the income elasticity of electricity consumption similar in this respect?

(c) Regression analysis permits the testing of hypotheses on regression coefficients such as β. However, hypotheses of interest often concern related quantities such as elasticities rather than the coefficients themselves. For example, you have evaluated the income elasticity at the point of variable means to be

$$\hat{\eta} = \frac{1}{\bar{q}}\hat{\beta} = \frac{1}{1271.2}1165.2 = 0.9166.$$

This point estimate suggests that electricity demand is income inelastic at this income level. However, it is possible that this finding has occurred by chance and that a different sample drawn from the same population will indicate an elastic effect. How can we know whether this point estimate indicates clearly that demand is income inelastic? It would be interesting to see whether the information in this point estimate is strong enough to allow us to reject the null hypothesis that demand is income elastic, $H_0: \eta \geq 1$, in favor of the alternative that demand is income inelastic, $H_A: \eta < 1$. Consider two approaches to doing this.

i. Hypotheses on η may be restated as hypotheses on β. The relationship between η and β is of the form

$$\eta = b\beta,$$

so a value for one implies a corresponding value for the other. In this instance in which the elasticity is being evaluated at the point of variable means, $b = 1/\bar{q} = 1/1271.2$, the correspondence is

$$\eta \geq 1 \quad \Leftrightarrow \quad \beta \geq 1271.2, \tag{6.41}$$

$$\eta < 1 \quad \Leftrightarrow \quad \beta < 1271.2. \tag{6.42}$$

Use this correspondence to test these hypotheses about η by recasting the test as one on β. Do the data establish clearly that, at the point of variable means, electricity demand is income inelastic?

ii. If the relationship between $\hat{\eta}$ and $\hat{\beta}$ is linear, an implied standard error for $\hat{\eta}$ may be obtained and used in a direct test on η.

A. Treating $b = 1/\bar{q} = 1/1271.2$ as a numerical constant, what is the relationship between $V(\hat{\eta})$ and $V(\hat{\beta})$? Use this to obtain an estimated standard error $s_{\hat{\eta}}$ for $\hat{\eta}$.

B. Use your value for $s_{\hat{\eta}}$ to construct a t statistic that allows you to test the hypotheses of interest, cast directly in terms of restrictions on η.

iii. What is the relationship between your test statistics in parts i and ii?

6.22 💿 **houthak1.dat** Estimate a reciprocal form for the Engel curve.

(a) For this model specification, what is the formula for the income elasticity of demand?

(b) Evaluate the income elasticity

i. at mean household income $\bar{m}$.

ii. at the highest and lowest household incomes in Houthakker's sample.

Locate these three income elasticities in a sketch similar to Figure 6.12(c). We have seen that, for the reciprocal functional form, Prais and Houthakker found that the income elasticity of meat consumption declines with income. Is the income elasticity of electricity consumption similar in this respect?

(c) You have found that the elasticity evaluated at $\bar{m}$ is $\hat{\eta} = 0.7096$. Does this point estimate indicate clearly that electricity demand is income inelastic, or might it have been obtained by chance? Examine this question by following the two methods sketched in Exercise 6.21.

i. Test the null hypothesis $\eta \geq 1$ against the alternative $\eta < 1$ by recasting these hypotheses as restrictions on β.

ii. Test these hypotheses directly by obtaining an implied standard error for $\hat{\eta}$ and using this to construct a t statistic for η.

iii. What is the relationship between your test statistics in parts i and ii?

6.23 Why not consider a log-lin specification for this Engel curve?

6.6 Conclusions

Regression models linear in coefficients and estimable by least squares can be used to study a wide range of nonlinear relationships between variables. Elasticities typically must be evaluated at a point, as indeed is the case even in a standard linear-in-levels regression. The one exception is a log-log model in which the coefficient is the elasticity. Table 6.5 summarizes the most important intrinsically linear functional forms and the corresponding elasticity formulas.

Practitioner's Tip: Evaluate elasticities at a point on the curve

For most functional relationships—the log-log being the exception—the elasticity varies as we move along the curve. Accordingly, the elasticity must be evaluated at a point on the curve. For elasticity formulas that are a function of the dependent variable, as in linear, lin-log, or reciprocal functional forms, the elasticity should therefore be evaluated using the predicted value of the dependent variable.

A particularly important class of intrinsically linear models employs the logarithmic transformation. A log-log model relates *relative* changes to *relative* changes; it is because the slope coefficient therefore indicates the percentage response in Y to a 1% change in X that it is interpretable as an elasticity. Semilogarithmic models, on the other hand, mix relative and absolute changes. The log-lin model relates *relative* changes in Y to *absolute* changes in X, such as the growth in Y over a year or the percentage effect on earnings of an additional year of schooling. The lin-log model relates *absolute* changes in Y to *relative* changes in X. For example, a lin-log form for an Engel curve specifies that a 1% increase in income results in a constant absolute increase in the consumption of that good, regardless of the income level. For many commodities, this appears to be a fairly accurate portrayal of actual demand patterns.

The use of logarithms of different bases is equivalent to a rescaling of variables, and consequently the implications for empirical analysis are as we have indicated in Section 4.8. In any case, there is no reason for any modern researcher to use

TABLE 6.5 Some Intrinsically Linear Functional Forms

Model	Function	Elasticity
Linear	$Y = \alpha + \beta X$	$\beta \frac{X}{Y}$
Log-log	$\log Y = \alpha + \beta \log X$	β
Log-lin	$\log Y = \alpha + \beta X$	βX
Lin-log	$Y = \alpha + \beta \log X$	$\beta \frac{1}{Y}$
Reciprocal	$Y = \alpha + \beta \frac{1}{X}$	$-\beta \frac{1}{XY}$

anything but natural logarithms; the use of common logarithms in some older econometric work is an artifact of an earlier age.

The ability of intrinsically linear models to describe nonlinear relationships is enormously useful and widely exploited in applied work. However, often there is little a priori basis for the choice of one functional form over another. For example, in terms of the underlying theory of consumer demand there is no objective basis for choosing between a lin-log and a reciprocal form for an Engel curve. We might hope instead for a statistical basis for the choice between alternative model specifications; that is, for guidance from the data as to which functional form may be most appropriate. In this vein, the topics of specification testing and model choice are ones we pursue in Chapter 12. Notwithstanding the availability of these methods, it is often the case that simple graphical techniques can be helpful in choosing among model specifications. The exercise below is intended to give you some sense of this.

Regardless of how a model specification may have been arrived at, the choice of *any* particular functional form constrains the description of the economic behavior under study in a way that is unrelated to the intrinsic nature of that behavior. For example, although economic theory may offer no objective basis for choosing between a lin-log and a reciprocal form for an Engel curve, this choice may well affect the outcome of tests of hypotheses such as Engel's law. Another example, which we study in some detail in the next chapter, is that the Cobb-Douglas functional form turns out to restrict the nature of substitution possibilities between factors of production.

Thus tests of economic hypotheses are in fact joint tests of those hypotheses and the empirical model. It is always possible that statistical rejections of hypotheses may occur, not because the economic theory predicting the parameter restrictions under test is false, but because the empirical model representing that theory is in some respect deficient. We would prefer to work with an empirical model that imposes as little a priori structure on the nature of economic relationships as possible, beyond that suggested by economic theory. This problem is tackled head-on in Chapter 11, where the use of flexible functional forms to approximate arbitrary production technologies or consumer preferences is introduced.

EXERCISES

6.24 **nerlove1.dat** Marc Nerlove's data on production costs and output for 145 electricity generating plants is available in the file **nerlove1.dat**. This data set is documented in Section 4.10.

(a) Generate a series for unit costs, scaling by 1000 to avoid very small values for the variable. Produce a scatter plot of unit costs against output. What do economists believe should be true of the

relationship between unit costs and output? Is this pattern exhibited by this data? Is the relationship exhibited by these data linear or nonlinear?

(b) Consider attempting to model the relationship between unit costs and output using the intrinsically linear models we have studied. Estimate the following, with unit costs as the dependent variable: a standard linear model, a loglinear model, a log-lin model, a lin-log model, and a reciprocal model.

i. In each case, does the sign of the slope coefficient of your estimated model make sense?

ii. Purely on the basis of the estimation results, do you judge any of these models to be clearly unsatisfactory in describing the relationship between average costs and output? Why?

iii. Each of your estimated models implies predicted values for unit costs. (For models in which the dependent variable is in log form, these will be the antilogs of the OLS fitted values.) For each of the five models, plot these predicted values against output. On the basis of these plots, can any of the models be discarded as providing a poor fit to the relationship between unit costs and output?

6.25 Consider the quadratic-in-logs functional relationship

$$\log Y = \alpha + \beta \log X + \delta (\log X)^2.$$

Find the elasticity of Y with respect to X. Does this elasticity take on the same value at all points of the function or must it be evaluated at a particular point?

Appendix 6A Application to Hyperinflation

As our study of statistical earnings functions illustrates, not all log-lin models are regressions on a time trend. Hence, not all log-lin regressions represent the estimation of a constant growth model, although an understanding of the underlying constant growth interpretation of the regression is sometimes helpful.

This appendix considers another application of log-lin regression: Phillip Cagan's (1956) model of money demand under hyperinflation. Cagan's model is another example of an application in which, although the constant growth interpretation lies under the surface, it is not the only, or even the best, way of understanding the regression. The economic theory behind Cagan's model is developed in the sections ahead. Much later we revisit Cagan's model and data as an application of the tools of time series analysis developed in Chapters 17–18.

The Quantity Theory of Money

In most countries, the price level has tended to increase during the last half-century. The rate of increase of the price level—its growth rate—is called the inflation rate. Expressed instantaneously, this is $\dot{P}/P$. As a continuous rate calculated from data, it may be denoted

$$\pi_t \equiv \log P_t - \log P_{t-1}. \tag{6.43}$$

The inflation rate has varied historically. During the 1970s and early 1980s many countries experienced fairly high inflation rates. Since then rates have tended to fall, so that many countries now have very low inflation rates.

What determines the price level? The classical view is that the price level is determined by the quantity of money in circulation relative to people's willingness to hold it. This classical view is called the **quantity theory of money.**

FIGURE 6.13

Money and prices during the German hyperinflation, September 1920–November 1923 (Sept. 1920 = 1.0).

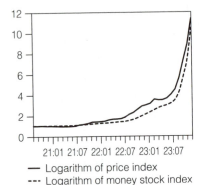

— Logarithm of price index
--- Logarithm of money stock index

FIGURE 6.14

Money and prices during the Polish hyperinflation, April 1922–November 1923 (April 1922 = 1.0).

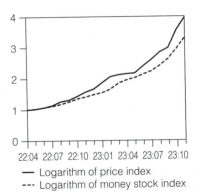

— Logarithm of price index
--- Logarithm of money stock index

The empirical basis for the quantity theory lies in historical experiences of inflation. In 16th- and 17th-century Europe, for example, the value of gold and silver coinage—the money of those times—steadily depreciated. Why? Because of the enormous importation of these metals following the discovery of the New World. The increased supply of money lowered its value in relation to that of other goods; equivalently, the price of goods increased relative to the value of money—there was inflation.

When money takes the form, not of gold and silver which must be mined, but of paper currency that is easily printed, the discovery of new continents ceases to be a precondition to inflation. Very high rates of inflation are called **hyperinflation.** Figures 6.13 and 6.14 show the growth of the price level and money stock during the German and Polish hyperinflations that followed World War I. The data are from Cagan (1956). The curves for the price level are analogous to Figure 6.6(a) for the Hungarian hyperinflation of 1945–1946 that we have inspected previously. As in that earlier figure, the fact that in their logarithms these variables are trending nonlinearly indicates that growth rates are accelerating. Consequently, it would not be appropriate to describe them using the constant growth model. As a purely descriptive calculation, Table 6.6 indicates that the average monthly inflation rate

TABLE 6.6   Percentage Monthly Growth Rates of Money and Prices

Hyperinflationary episode		Currency M	Prices P
Austria	1921–22	30.9	47.1
Germany	1922–23	314.0	322.0
Greece	1943–44	220.0	365.0
Hungary	1923–24	32.7	46.0
Hungary	1945–46	12,200	19,800
Poland	1923–24	72.2	81.4
Russia	1921–24	49.3	57.0

Source: Cagan, P. (1956) "The Monetary Dynamics of
Hyperinflation," in *Studies in the Quantity Theory of
Money*, ed. by M. Friedman, table 1, pp. 26. © 1956 by
the University of Chicago. Reprinted with permission.
Taylor (1991, Table 3, p. 334).

during the German hyperinflation was 322%, whereas for the Polish hyperinflation
it was 81.4%. Although well below the stunning experience of the Hungarian
hyperinflation, these are still very high inflation rates. That the Polish hyperinflation
was the least severe of the three is consistent with the fact that the logarithmic
transformation comes closest to transforming its price and money stock indices to
a linear trend.

In contrast to the earlier figure for the Hungarian hyperinflation, these diagrams
plot the logarithm of the money stock as well as that of the price level. Both the
German and Polish hyperinflations are dramatic demonstrations of the basic fact
motivating the quantity theory: Historically, rapid expansions of the money stock
have accompanied rapid increases in the price level.

We have said that the quantity theory explains the price level in terms of
the amount of money in circulation relative to people's willingness to hold it. In
his study, Cagan was interested in a particular aspect of people's willingness to
hold money—their response to hyperinflation. He reasoned that, because inflation
represents a loss in the purchasing power of money, people's willingness to hold
money should decline during hyperinflationary times. He proposed a log-lin model
to describe this effect.

At first Cagan's conjecture may seem puzzling. If hyperinflation is caused by
rapid increases in money, how can people be holding less of it? To sort this out it
is useful to begin with a summary of the quantity theory of money.[15] We then turn

[15] Most books on macroeconomics have discussions of the quantity theory of money. You may find it
helpful to compare the sketch that follows with the more complete treatment you are likely to find in
your macroeconomics text. However, even macroeconomics texts usually cannot do full justice to the
fascinating historical pedigree of the quantity theory of money. For an especially thorough treatment of
the theory with an emphasis on its historical development, see Makinen (1977). Poole (1978, Chap. 2)
offers a briefer introduction that complements the treatment here by motivating the quantity theory in
terms of historical episodes of hyperinflation. The survey by Friedman (1987) is more advanced.

For given money-holding practices and the level of production in the economy, a doubling of the money stock results in a doubling of the price level. In Milton Friedman's famous phrase, "inflation is always and everywhere a monetary phenomenon."

The Endogeneity of k

Instead of phrasing the quantity theory of money in terms of the supply and demand for nominal (i.e., dollar) quantities, it can be expressed in terms of a real demand for money as a proportion of the real volume of goods being bought and sold. Reexpressed in real terms, the equilibrium condition is

$$\frac{M}{P} = kQ. \tag{6.46}$$

For given money-holding practices and the level of production in the economy, the proportionality of money and prices means that the real quantity of money in circulation will be constant.

Regardless of whether we think of people's behavior in nominal or real terms, k will be affected by anything that influences this behavior. One example of such an influence is interest rates—the opportunity cost of holding wealth in the form of money. Hence, k is implicitly a function of interest rates,

$$k = k(i).$$

The relationship is inverse. Higher interest rates increase the opportunity cost of holding money, causing people to trade their money for assets that pay interest instead of using the money to buy goods. The attempt by everyone to do this, in the face of a given quantity of money in circulation, reduces the price level, reequilibrating the supply and demand for money.

Although k (and consequently P) may be affected by other factors in this way, the specification of money demand explicitly as a proportion of Q reflects the belief that it is the volume of transactions that is the primary determinant of money demand and therefore the price level. The quantity theory of money tends to view other factors as being of secondary importance, at least in normal times.

Economists have differing views about the relative importance of the various determinants of money demand. The tendency in recent decades has been toward a stronger recognition of the role of factors in addition to Q in affecting real money demand. Accordingly, a modern monetary economist will specify the real demand for money as some general function of variables such as interest rates, real gross national income, and so on, so that monetary equilibrium is expressed as

$$\frac{M}{P} = f(i, Q, \dots).$$

If this function is to be estimated it is necessary to choose a functional form. Because it is a demand relationship, loglinear functional forms have been popular trade 5.61 times. By 1970, velocity had fallen to 1.73, so that dollars were turning over less rapidly. Phrasing this in terms of k, the reciprocal of velocity, in 1970 people were holding more money relative to the volume of transactions in which they were engaging compared with practices in 1869.

Friedman and Schwartz (1963, p. 639) conjectured that one possible explanation for this decline in velocity was that the growth in living standards over the century made people willing to enjoy the luxury of holding more money in relation to their transactions needs.

> We are inclined to attribute the secular decline to the associated rise in per capita real income, that is, to view the services rendered by money balances as a "luxury" of which the amount demanded rises more than in proportion to the rise in income.

We return to the Nelson-Plosser velocity series and say more about the Friedman-Schwartz conjecture in our study of time series analysis in Chapter 15.

Money Demand under Hyperinflation

In his classic study, Phillip Cagan focused on a determinant of real money demand different from those we have mentioned so far—the expected rate of inflation. His interest was in the following phenomenon. Inflation reduces the purchasing power of money, so that those who hold money during a period of inflation find that the quantity of real goods and services it purchases is reduced. The greater the quantity of money held, the greater the loss. Consequently, if people expect inflation to occur, they will respond by attempting to reduce their money holdings. In other words, expected inflation is one of the determinants of the behavioral factor k.

Investigating this effect empirically is not possible under ordinary circumstances because at modest rates of inflation this influence on money demand is minor relative to the other determinants we have described, such as i and Q, and so is not detectable. Cagan argued that to study this effect it would be necessary to consider extraordinary circumstances, ones in which expectations of future inflation were the dominant determinant of money demand, with other variables playing a minor role in comparison. These extraordinary circumstances are ones of hyperinflation. As Cagan (1956, p. 25) expresses it,

> Hyperinflations provide a unique opportunity to study monetary phenomena. The astronomical increases in prices and money dwarf the changes in real income and other real factors. Even a substantial fall in real income, which generally has not occurred in hyperinflations, would be small compared with the typical rise in prices. Relations between monetary factors can be studied, therefore, in what almost amounts to isolation from the real sector of the economy.

In studying the effect of inflation on money demand, it is important to note that it is real money demand that is at issue. Because inflation, and especially hyperinflation, is always and everywhere a monetary phenomenon, the hyperinflation is caused in the first place by an expansion in the nominal quantity of money M. Thus it is not their *nominal* money demand that people reduce; nominal money in circulation is expanding, typically very rapidly, and must be held by someone. Instead, the reduced willingness to hold money is reflected in the *real* quantity of money M/P; people reduce not their nominal money holdings but their money holdings measured in terms of the real goods and services that money buys. Instead of people holding, say, money equal to a week's purchases, they are willing to hold only a few days or a few hours worth instead. The implication is that it is real money demand under hyperinflation that is of interest rather than nominal demand.

If both nominal money M and the price level P are increasing but in such a way that the ratio M/P is falling, this must mean that P is increasing faster than M.[16] Consequently, the proportionality (6.45) between M and P that the quantity theory suggests should hold in normal times ("a doubling of money leads to a doubling of prices") is altered. Why is this? Under hyperinflation people reduce their real demand for money because they are seeking to avoid holding money that is depreciating in value. Money is like a hot potato that people are trying to get rid of as quickly as possible. This is why, paradoxically, those who live through periods of hyperinflation often perceive them to be times in which there is a shortage of money. To again quote Poole (1978, p. 22),

> When prices are rising, as shown especially clearly by episodes of hyperinflation, it becomes costly to hold money because the money held buys less and less every day. Consequently, when prices are rising people tend to hold a smaller amount of money measured in terms of command over goods. In extreme cases, a severe scarcity of money adjusted for prices occurs because it is so very expensive to hold a reserve of purchasing power in money form. The greater the rate of expansion of nominal money, the lower will be the quantity of real money; stopping the printing presses will *increase* the real quantity of money in circulation.

The attempt by everyone to spend their money as soon as they get it, instead of holding it for more extended periods as they would in normal times, drives up prices faster than would be the case were the increasing money supply by itself the only factor at work. The hyperinflation is, then, to some extent self-generating.

Cagan illustrated this phenomenon by examining data from seven European hyperinflations that occurred in the years following the first and second world wars. His figures for the average monthly inflation rates and the average percentage increases in currency are reproduced in Table 6.6.[17] The key point to note is that the growth rate of prices is always greater than the growth rate of currency, often substantially so. This is reflected in Figures 6.13 and 6.14, in which the growth path of the money stock remains below that of the price level. Although both money and prices grow during a hyperinflation, prices grow more rapidly.

---

[16] If this is unclear, see Example 14 in Appendix 6B.

[17] The average inflation rate of 19,800% for the Hungarian hyperinflation of 1945–1946 is verified in Example 8.

FIGURE 6.16

Real money hold-ings $\log(M_t/P_t)$ decline during a hyperinflation.

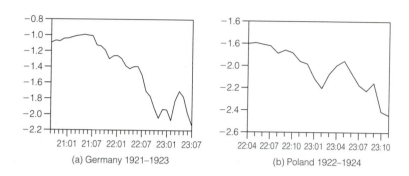

(a) Germany 1921–1923

(b) Poland 1922–1924

Another way of seeing the same phenomenon is by plotting real money hold-ings. Figure 6.16 does this for the German and Polish data. Notice that real money demand declined over the course of the hyperinflation. It declined more strongly in Germany than in Poland, reflecting the greater severity of the German hyper-inflation. (Recall that, according to the inflation rates in Table 6.6, the Polish hyperinflation was mild relative to the German one.)

Cagan's Money Demand Function

Cagan's descriptive statistics reveal a considerable range of hyperinflationary expe-rience in terms of the various rates of change of money and prices that occurred. Do these historical episodes display any underlying uniformity of human behavior?

Cagan investigated this by specifying real money demand as a function of expected inflation—a relationship such as (6.47), but in which expected inflation is the explanatory variable—using a log-lin functional form:

$$\log M_t - \log P_t = \alpha + \beta\pi^e_{t+1}. \tag{6.48}$$

The expected rate of inflation is defined as

$$\pi^e_{t+1} = \log P^e_{t+1} - \log P_t,$$

where P^e_{t+1} is the price level expected to prevail in the next period.

From our discussion of the log-lin functional form, β is the semielasticity of real money demand with respect to expected inflation. It describes the response by people in their real money holding behavior, to expectations of inflation. Our reasoning suggests that higher expected inflation should reduce real money holding, so β should be negative. In normal times when expected inflation is not an important determinant of money demand the implication is that $\beta = 0$ and the function should reduce to

$$\log\left(\frac{M_t}{P_t}\right) = \alpha. \tag{6.49}$$

This just says that real money holdings are constant, a restatement of the stan-dard expression (6.46) of the quantity theory of money. During hyperinflationary times, on the other hand, if Cagan is correct that inflationary expectations are the

TABLE 6.7   Estimation Results for the Cagan Model

Hyperinflationary episode		Cagan Semielasticity	Taylor Semielasticity	R^2
Austria	1921–22	−8.55	−1.407	0.58
Germany	1922–23	−5.46	−2.211	0.60
Hungary	1923–24	−8.70	−1.368	0.46
Poland	1923–24	−2.30	−1.219	0.75

Source: Cagan, P. (1956) "The Monetary Dynamics of Hyperinflation," in Studies in the Quantity Theory of Money, ed. by M. Friedman, Table 3, p. 334. © 1956 by the University of Chicago. Reprinted with permission.

primary determinant of money-holding behavior and that other factors are relatively unimportant, the R^2 of a regression based on (6.48) should be fairly high.

Treating Expectations

The main issue that arises in the estimation of this equation is that we do not observe people's expectations. Instead, expectations must be modeled in some way. Over the years, economists have tried many ways of treating expectations formation in economic models. Indeed, the Cagan model has been one of the most important guinea pigs for applying alternative approaches to handling expectations formation.

Taylor (1991) used what is certainly the simplest treatment. He simply replaced the expected inflation rate π_{t+1}^e with the currently observed rate π_t. Repeating equation (6.43), the currently observed rate is

$$\pi_t = \log P_t - \log P_{t-1}.$$

The implicit assumption is that the inflation rate that people have experienced most recently is a pretty good measure of what they expect will prevail in the next period.[18] Thus Taylor estimated the log-lin simple regression

$$\log M_t - \log P_t = \alpha + \beta \pi_t + \varepsilon_t.$$

Because the explanatory variable is $\pi_t = \log P_t - \log P_{t-1} = \log(P_t/P_{t-1})$, you might wonder whether this is better characterized as a log-log regression rather than a log-lin one. The key point is that the appropriate interpretation of β is as the semielasticity of real money demand with respect to expected inflation rather than as the elasticity.

Taylor estimated this equation using Cagan's data for four of the European hyperinflations. His results are summarized in Table 6.7. Cagan estimated his model using a different way of treating expectations formation—the method of **adaptive expectations**—and his estimates of the semielasticity are provided for comparison.

The different approaches to treating expectations formation used by Cagan and Taylor yield rather different semielasticities, with Cagan's approach indicating the

---

[18] In Chapter 18 we see that there is a more sophisticated justification for Taylor's practice.

stronger response. Nevertheless all are negative, as they should be, and Taylor's R^2 values indicate that during hyperinflations real money holding is substantially determined as a response to expected inflation. Furthermore, for a given expectations treatment the semielasticities are of similar magnitude, suggesting an underlying uniformity of human behavior in responding to hyperinflation.

Implications for Price Level Determination

Cagan's money demand model and the estimated value of β turn out to have important implications for the determination of the price level under hyperinflation. To develop this, let us return to the original specification of Cagan's money demand function in terms of expected inflation, equation (6.48), with the definition for π^e_{t+1} substituted in:

$$\log M_t - \log P_t = \alpha + \beta(\log P^e_{t+1} - \log P_t).$$

Recall that, as stated, no assumption about how expectations are formed has been made. Let us consider a treatment of expectations different from both the Taylor or Cagan methods—the hypothesis of **perfect foresight.** Perfect foresight treats expectations by simply assuming that people correctly foresee the future; the price level expected to prevail next period is that which actually occurs:

$$P^e_{t+1} = P_{t+1}.$$

You may find this assumption implausible—after all, people do not know the future—and indeed this implausibility is why we did not attempt to base the estimation of the model on this assumption. Nevertheless, perfect foresight provides a useful benchmark and some interesting insights.

In developing these insights, it is helpful to minimize the amount of notation in the derivations that follow by using lowercase symbols to denote variables in log form,

$$m_t = \log M_t \qquad p_t = \log P_t.$$

As well, because we know that β should and does turn out to be negative, let γ denote its absolute value: $\gamma = -\beta$. With the assumption of perfect foresight and these notational changes Cagan's money demand function is

$$m_t - p_t = \alpha - \gamma(p_{t+1} - p_t).$$

Like our original statement of the quantity theory, this equation constitutes a theory of price level determination, a theory intended to apply to hyperinflationary circumstances. Let us therefore consider the implications for prices of the equation. Solving for the price level at time t yields

$$p_t = \frac{-\alpha}{1+\gamma} + \frac{1}{1+\gamma}m_t + \frac{\gamma}{1+\gamma}p_{t+1}.$$

Because this relationship holds at all points in time, the next period's price level will be determined in the same way:

$$p_{t+1} = \frac{-\alpha}{1+\gamma} + \frac{1}{1+\gamma} m_{t+1} + \frac{\gamma}{1+\gamma} p_{t+2}.$$

Now consider substituting the second equation into the first:

$$p_t = \frac{-\alpha}{1+\gamma}\left[1 + \left(\frac{\gamma}{1+\gamma}\right)\right] + \frac{1}{1+\gamma} m_t + \frac{\gamma}{(1+\gamma)^2} m_{t+1} + \frac{\gamma^2}{(1+\gamma)^2} p_{t+2}.$$

Again, the price level in period $t+2$ is determined by another forward-shifting of the equation:

$$p_{t+2} = \frac{-\alpha}{1+\gamma} + \frac{1}{1+\gamma} m_{t+2} + \frac{\gamma}{1+\gamma} p_{t+3}.$$

This can, in turn, be substituted back into the previous equation:

$$p_t = \frac{-\alpha}{1+\gamma}\left[1 + \left(\frac{\gamma}{1+\gamma}\right) + \left(\frac{\gamma}{1+\gamma}\right)^2\right]$$

$$+ \frac{1}{1+\gamma} m_t + \frac{\gamma}{(1+\gamma)^2} m_{t+1} + \frac{\gamma^2}{(1+\gamma)^3} m_{t+2} + \frac{\gamma^3}{(1+\gamma)^3} p_{t+3}.$$

At this point, the pattern is evident. We can continue to substitute in this way indefinitely, so that today's price level may be seen to be determined as

$$p_t = \frac{-\alpha}{1+\gamma}\left[1 + \left(\frac{\gamma}{1+\gamma}\right) + \left(\frac{\gamma}{1+\gamma}\right)^2 + \left(\frac{\gamma}{1+\gamma}\right)^3 + \cdots\right] + \frac{1}{1+\gamma}$$

$$\left[m_t + \left(\frac{\gamma}{1+\gamma}\right) m_{t+1} + \left(\frac{\gamma}{1+\gamma}\right)^2 m_{t+2} + \left(\frac{\gamma}{1+\gamma}\right)^3 m_{t+3} + \cdots\right].$$

Although this equation for the price level is complicated, the first term simplifies nicely. This simplification uses the fact that the ratio $\gamma/(1+\gamma)$ must be a fractional value. Let this fraction be denoted b:

$$b = \frac{\gamma}{1+\gamma}.$$

Using this notation, the expression inside the square parentheses of the first term is of the form

$$1 + b + b^2 + b^3 + \cdots.$$

The terms in this sum are called a **geometric series**. The sum has the property that, as long as $-1 < b < 1$, it converges to the value $1/(1-b)$:

$$1 + b + b^2 + b^3 + \cdots = \frac{1}{1-b} \quad \text{for } -1 < b < 1.$$

As a numerical example, consider $b = \frac{1}{2}$. The infinite series result says that

$$1 + \frac{1}{2} + \left(\frac{1}{2}\right)^2 + \left(\frac{1}{2}\right)^3 + \cdots = 1 + \frac{1}{2} + \frac{1}{4} + \frac{1}{8} + \cdots = \frac{1}{1 - \frac{1}{2}} = 2$$

Consider applying this to the first term in the equation for the price level. The expression inside the square parentheses is

$$1 + \left(\frac{\gamma}{1+\gamma}\right) + \left(\frac{\gamma}{1+\gamma}\right)^2 + \left(\frac{\gamma}{1+\gamma}\right)^3 + \cdots$$

$$= \frac{1}{1 - \gamma/(1+\gamma)} = \frac{1}{1/(1+\gamma)} = 1 + \gamma.$$

Hence, the first term reduces to $-\alpha$, and the solution for the price level is

$$p_t = -\alpha + \frac{1}{1+\gamma}\left[m_t + \left(\frac{\gamma}{1+\gamma}\right)m_{t+1} + \left(\frac{\gamma}{1+\gamma}\right)^2 m_{t+2} + \left(\frac{\gamma}{1+\gamma}\right)^3 m_{t+3} + \cdots\right].$$

This equation has an interesting interpretation. It says that when money demand depends on the expected future price level, which in turn will depend on the future money supply, the price level today depends not only on the current money supply m_t but also on all future money stocks. This dependence is governed by weights that are powers of the fraction $\gamma/(1+\gamma)$. If γ is large—so that current money holdings are strongly affected by expected future inflation, as in periods of extreme hyperinflation—then this fraction will be close to 1 and the weights will decline slowly. The implication is that the current price level is heavily determined by future money. On the other hand, if γ is small, then the fraction $\gamma/(1+\gamma)$ will be small and the weights will decline rapidly.

Consider the largest and smallest estimates of γ obtained by Taylor, those for Germany and Poland. Table 6.8 shows the geometrically declining weights in each case. For Germany, where $\hat{\gamma} = 2.211$, the weights decline slowly. For Poland, where $\hat{\gamma} = 1.219$, they decline more quickly.

TABLE 6.8

Geometrically Declining Weights in the Cagan Model

Periods ahead	Weight	Germany, 1922–1923 $\hat{\gamma} = 2.211$	Poland, 1922–1924 $\hat{\gamma} = 1.219$
1	$\gamma/(1+\gamma)$	0.689	0.549
2	$[\gamma/(1+\gamma)]^2$	0.474	0.302
3	$[\gamma/(1+\gamma)]^3$	0.326	0.166
4	$[\gamma/(1+\gamma)]^4$	0.225	0.091
5	$[\gamma/(1+\gamma)]^5$	0.155	0.050
6	$[\gamma/(1+\gamma)]^6$	0.107	0.027
$\vdots$	$\vdots$	$\vdots$	$\vdots$

In the extreme case of $\gamma = 0$ where current money holdings are not affected at all by expected future inflation—the circumstance we expect to hold in ordinary times—the equation reduces to

$$p_t = -\alpha + m_t$$

or

$$\log M_t - \log P_t = \alpha,$$

which just returns us to the quantity theory of money (6.49) or, equivalently, equation (6.46).

The Rational Expectations Solution

These conclusions have been premised on the assumption of perfect foresight, which we began by noting may be implausible. It is therefore interesting to remark that the perfect foresight solution is very closely related to the solution that arises from a more realistic way of modeling expectations formation—rational expectations.[19] Rational expectations recognizes that the value a variable will take in the future is, from the perspective of today, a random variable. It therefore assumes that people's expectation of that future value is its mathematical expectation,

$$p_{t+1}^e = E(p_{t+1}).$$

Cagan's money demand function can be written

$$m_t - p_t = \alpha - \gamma(E p_{t+1} - p_t).$$

By a chain of logic that, although technically more difficult, parallels the perfect foresight solution, it can be shown that the current price level depends on the expected future money stock in a manner exactly analogous to the perfect foresight solution:

$$p_t = -\alpha$$
$$+ \frac{1}{1+\gamma}\left[m_t + \left(\frac{\gamma}{1+\gamma}\right)E m_{t+1} + \left(\frac{\gamma}{1+\gamma}\right)^2 E m_{t+2} + \left(\frac{\gamma}{1+\gamma}\right)^3 E m_{t+3} + \cdots\right].$$

This makes explicit the intuition that, when money demand depends on expected future inflation, the price level today is determined not only by the money currently in circulation but also by the expected future money supply.

EXERCISES

Cagan's data for Germany and Poland are available in the files **germany.dat** and **poland.dat**. Each file contains three variables.

month Month of the hyperinflation.

money $\log_{10}(P_t/M_t)$, the negative of the logarithm of real money holdings.

inflation $\log_{10}(P_t/P_{t-1})$, the inflation rate expressed as log-differences.

---

[19] Rational expectations is discussed in Appendix B, Section B.2.3.

The German data run from September 1920 through November 1923 and those for Poland from April 1922 through November 1923. The first two lines of each file contain variable names and a blank line.

In using these data sets, two points should be noted. First, money is the negative of the required dependent variable in the money demand function, so before using it be sure to generate $\log(M_t/P_t)$ as $-\log(P_t/M_t)$. It is this that is plotted in Figure 6.16.

Second, in keeping with the conventions of his time Cagan used common rather than natural logarithms, and so the third series is not directly interpretable as a continuously compounded monthly inflation rate. (To do so, it is only necessary to multiply by the constant $\log 10 = 2.3026$ that links the two kinds of logarithms, as indicated by equation (6.12).) This is not important for Exercise 6.27; because both the dependent and explanatory variables are in log form, the OLS slope coefficient results are invariant to the base of the logarithm.[20]

6.26 germany.dat Cagan's average percentage monthly growth rate of prices for Germany of 322%, reported in Table 6.6, is for the months August 1922 through November 1923. Show how (rounded to the nearest 100%, as in Example 8) this figure derives from the data.

6.27 germany.dat poland.dat Use the data for one of these countries to estimate Taylor's log-lin regression. If you use the German data, be aware that Taylor used the subsample ending with July 1923.

(a) Are you able to reproduce his estimate of the semielasticity and value of the R^2?

(b) Suppose you throw caution to the winds and take the implausible perfect foresight approach to treating expectations formation.

i. Does the magnitude of the slope estimate indicate a stronger or weaker response of money holding to expected inflation, relative to that yielded by Taylor's regression?

ii. Use this estimate to recompute the geometrically declining weights of Table 6.8. Is the dependence of the price level on future money stronger or weaker than before?

iii. Does the R^2 indicate a better or worse fit?

6.28 One important interpretation of the quantity theory of money is as a theory of aggregate demand. Consider rearranging the quantity theory equation as

$$Q = \frac{1}{k}\frac{M}{P}.$$

This may be interpreted as an **aggregate demand curve** that indicates the amount of goods Q that people can afford to buy at any prevailing price level P, given the amount of money in circulation M and money-holding habits k. However, this theory of aggregate demand assumes something rather special about the elasticity of demand for goods Q with respect to prices P.

(a) What is the value of this elasticity of demand?

(b) We usually think of demand curves as downward sloping: that is, as having an elasticity of demand that is negative. Is this true of this aggregate demand curve?

Appendix 6B More on Logarithms and Growth Rates

Our treatment of the constant growth model has shown that logarithms have a natural use in describing the growth of variables. This appendix develops this idea further. The first section considers the use of logarithms in establishing relationships

---

[20] This is the finding in Exercise 6.3.

between instantaneous growth rates. The second considers parallel relationships between continuous growth rates—that is, log-differences—of variables.

Properties of Instantaneous Growth Rates

The rate of growth of a variable is its change per unit of time relative to its value. In this chapter, we have seen that it is often convenient mathematically to use growth rates defined with respect to an instantaneous unit of time. Such an **instantaneous growth rate** is denoted

$$\frac{\dot{Y}}{Y} = \frac{1}{Y}\frac{dY}{dt}.$$

In the continuous-time constant growth model (6.18) the parameter β describes this instantaneous growth rate.

A useful trick in working with instantaneous growth rates is given by Result 6.2: The instantaneous growth rate of a variable is the time-derivative of its natural logarithm:

$$\frac{\dot{Y}}{Y} = \frac{d\log Y}{dt}.$$

This may be used to establish a number of basic relationships between growth rates.

1. *The instantaneous growth rate of a product is the sum of the growth rates.* Consider a variable Z that is the product of two other variables X and Y: $Z = XY$. Then, because the logarithm of a product is the sum of the logs, the trick of taking logs and time-derivatives establishes that

$$\log Z = \log X + \log Y,$$
$$\frac{d\log Z}{dt} = \frac{d\log X}{dt} + \frac{d\log Y}{dt},$$
$$\frac{\dot{Z}}{Z} = \frac{\dot{X}}{X} + \frac{\dot{Y}}{Y}.$$

EXAMPLE 11 In a well-known monograph on economic growth Robert Solow (1970, p. 2) remarks, "Since output is the product of labour input and output per unit of labour input, the rate of growth of output will be the sum of the rates of growth of labour input and of productivity." Express this idea mathematically.

SOLUTION Let Q denote output, L labor, and $q = Q/L$ labor productivity, output per unit of labor input. Then these variables are related definitionally in their levels by

$$Q = L \cdot q$$

and, by rule 1, in their growth rates by

$$\frac{\dot{Q}}{Q} = \frac{\dot{L}}{L} + \frac{\dot{q}}{q}.$$

The rate of growth of output is the sum of the rates of growth of labor input and of productivity.

2. *The instantaneous growth rate of a ratio is the difference of the growth rates.* Consider a variable Z that is the ratio of two other variables X and Y: $Z = X/Y$. Then, because the logarithm of a ratio is the difference of the logs, the trick of taking logs and time-derivatives establishes that

$$\log Z = \log X - \log Y,$$
$$\frac{d \log Z}{dt} = \frac{d \log X}{dt} - \frac{d \log Y}{dt},$$
$$\frac{\dot{Z}}{Z} = \frac{\dot{X}}{X} - \frac{\dot{Y}}{Y}.$$

EXAMPLE 12

In our study of the Cobb-Douglas production function in Section 6.1 we have seen that it is often useful to express variables in labor-intensive form. The examples we encounter there are labor productivity $q = Q/L$ and the capital-labor ratio $k = K/L$. Given these definitions, how are the growth rates of labor-intensive and non-labor-intensive variables related?

SOLUTION

By rule 2, the growth rates of labor-intensive and nonintensive variables are related by

$$\frac{\dot{q}}{q} = \frac{\dot{Q}}{Q} - \frac{\dot{L}}{L}, \tag{6.50a}$$

$$\frac{\dot{k}}{k} = \frac{\dot{K}}{K} - \frac{\dot{L}}{L}. \tag{6.50b}$$

The first of these is, of course, just a rearrangement of the growth identity in the previous example. It says that the growth rate of labor productivity is the growth rate of output less that of labor. If labor productivity is increasing (so that its growth rate is positive), it must be that output is growing faster than labor input. The second says that the growth rate of the capital-labor ratio is the growth rate of capital less that of labor. If the capital-labor ratio is decreasing (so that its growth rate is negative), it must be that the capital stock is growing more slowly than labor.

These simple rules can often be used to draw more interesting conclusions about relationships between growth rates.

EXAMPLE 13

In summarizing the "stylized facts" of economic growth Robert Solow (1970, p. 2) remarks "The stock of real capital, crudely measured, grows at a more or less constant rate exceeding the rate of growth of labour input. So capital per man can also be said to grow at a more or less steady rate. ..." Express this idea mathematically.

THEORY MEETS APPLICATION   **6.2**

The Fisher Identity

Economists make an important distinction between *real* and *nominal* values. As we have seen in Chapter 1 (recall equation (1.2)), a real value q is a nominal value Q divided by the price level P: $q = Q/P$. We have seen as well (recall equation (1.5)) that the inflation rate is the growth rate of the price level; in continuous time this is

$$\text{Inflation rate} = \frac{\dot{P}}{P}.$$

Consider the application of these definitions to asset prices. Suppose there is an asset (such as a house or a stock) of value $V(t)$. Let the growth rate of this dollar value be denoted i,

$$i = \frac{\dot{V}}{V}.$$

This is called the asset's **nominal rate of return.**

The real value $v(t)$ of the asset is obtained by deflating the nominal value:

$$v = \frac{V}{P}.$$

The growth rate of this real value, denoted r,

$$r = \frac{\dot{v}}{v},$$

is called the real (or after inflation) rate of return.

Notice that, as an application of our rules of growth rates, the growth rate of the real value is the growth rate of the nominal value less the growth rate of the price level:

$$\frac{\dot{v}}{v} = \frac{\dot{V}}{V} - \frac{\dot{P}}{P}.$$

Equivalently, the real rate of return is the nominal rate less the inflation rate:

Real rate of return r = Nominal rate of

return i − Inflation rate.

This is called the **Fisher identity** between real and nominal interest rates and inflation, after the economist Irving Fisher (1867–1947), who was among the first to study the relationship between interest rates and inflation.

SOLUTION | Let K denote the stock of real capital and L labor; "capital per man" is the capital-labor ratio $k = K/L$. From Example 12, the relationship between the growth rates of these variables is given by equation (6.50b). Now if the growth rate of capital exceeds that of labor, this is expressed as

$$\frac{\dot{K}}{K} > \frac{\dot{L}}{L}.$$

The implication is that

$$\frac{\dot{k}}{k} = \frac{\dot{K}}{K} - \frac{\dot{L}}{L} > 0.$$

In conclusion, the capital-labor ratio must be growing—its growth rate is positive.

EXAMPLE 14 | In our discussion of the monetary dynamics of hyperinflation in Appendix 6A we have seen that in times of hyperinflation prices P and nominal money in circulation M increase, but in such a way that the real quantity of money falls. Show that the rate of inflation must be greater than the growth rate of the money stock.

SOLUTION

The relationship between prices and the real and nominal quantities of money is

$$\text{Real money stock} = \frac{M}{P}.$$

Taking logs and derivatives,

$$\text{Growth rate of real money stock} = \frac{\dot{M}}{M} - \frac{\dot{P}}{P}.$$

If the real money stock is falling, its growth rate is negative:

$$\frac{\dot{M}}{M} - \frac{\dot{P}}{P} < 0.$$

Therefore, the growth rate of the nominal money stock must be less than the inflation rate:

$$\frac{\dot{M}}{M} < \frac{\dot{P}}{P}.$$

3. *If a ratio is constant, the two variables are growing at the same rate.* As a special case of rule 2, suppose a variable Z is constant and so its growth rate is zero:

$$\frac{\dot{Z}}{Z} = 0.$$

If Z is the ratio of two variables X and Y then, from rule 2,

$$0 = \frac{\dot{X}}{X} - \frac{\dot{Y}}{Y},$$

or, equivalently,

$$\frac{\dot{X}}{X} = \frac{\dot{Y}}{Y}.$$

The two variables in the ratio have the same growth rate. If labor productivity Q/L is constant, output Q must be growing at the same rate as labor L. If the capital-labor ratio is constant, capital and labor must be growing at the same rate.

EXAMPLE 15

Among his stylized facts of economic growth Robert Solow (1970, p. 2) notes, "...the rates of growth of real output and the stock of capital goods tend to be about the same, so that the ratio of capital to output shows no systematic trend." Express this idea mathematically.

SOLUTION

Denote the ratio of capital to output by K/Q. If the growth rates of K and Q "tend to be about the same," then

$$\text{Growth rate of } K/Q = \frac{\dot{K}}{K} - \frac{\dot{Q}}{Q} = 0.$$

In conclusion, K/Q must be constant—it shows no systematic trend.

Our three rules of growth rates may be combined in obvious ways.

THEORY MEETS APPLICATION   6.3

The Friedman Rule for Monetary Policy

Money demand is part of people's more general decisions about asset holding. When people choose to hold a portion of their wealth in the form of money, they do so on the basis of the costs and benefits of doing so relative to holding their wealth in other forms: bonds, stocks, a house, a car, and so on.

Thus there is an opportunity cost to holding money, this being the benefit that could be obtained by holding wealth in an alternative form that yields a return. The nominal interest rate i is this opportunity cost. Strictly speaking, this opportunity cost i is defined to be the return that would be paid on a hypothetical bond that has the same risk and liquidity characteristics as money. In practice, this hypothetical return would probably be little different from the yield on government treasury bills. This opportunity cost leads people, in some degree, to economize on their money holdings.

By the Fisher identity in Theory Meets Application 6.2, the nominal return i is the sum of the real return and the inflation rate:

$$i = r + \frac{\dot{P}}{P}.$$

Thus, the opportunity cost of holding money can be thought of as having two components: the real return that an alternative asset would yield and the depreciation in the purchasing power of money that arises from inflation. For example, in Appendix 6A we saw that during hyperinflations people economize on their money holdings in extreme fashion because the second of these components is very high.

In a famous essay, Milton Friedman (1969) observed that money is costless to produce:

Central banks can print money (or, more typically, create new bank deposits) at virtually zero cost. Yet people economize on their money holdings because nominal interest rates are positive. It must be suboptimal for people to economize in their use of something that is costless to produce. This led Friedman to advocate that monetary policy should be conducted so as to have the effect that the nominal interest rate is zero, so that there would be no opportunity cost to holding money:

$$i = 0 = r + \text{Inflation rate.}$$

In other words, the **Friedman rule** would set the inflation rate equal to the negative of the real rate of return:

$$\text{Inflation rate} = -r.$$

Because real asset returns are positive, the implication is that inflation should be negative. That is, monetary policy should be conducted to result in *deflation,* so that money appreciates in value. This appreciation would mean that there would be no disincentive to holding money (relative to a hypothetical asset with money's liquidity and risk characteristics; assets with liquidity and risk characteristics different from money would yield returns that would compensate investors accordingly).

Although central banks do not literally follow the Friedman rule, many come close to it. Many central banks pursue monetary policies consistent with very low rates of inflation, the money-holding implications of which are probably little different from a literal adoption of the Friedman rule.

THEORY MEETS APPLICATION

6.4

Balanced Growth and the Great Ratios of Macroeconomics

In Section 5.2.3 we cite what Klein and Kosobud (1961) call the "great ratios of economics." They observed that macroeconomic variables such as real gross national product Q, saving S, the capital stock K, and employment L all tend to grow over time, but that this growth occurs in such a way that certain ratios are relatively stable and do not follow growth trends. They identified the following "celebrated ratios of economics" as being relatively constant over time:

- The saving-income ratio S/Q.
- The capital-output ratio K/Q.
- Labor's share of nominal income wL/PQ, where w denotes the average wage rate and P is the price level.

If these ratios are fairly constant, the numerator and denominator must be growing at about the same rate. For example, the second of these ratios is Solow's capital-output ratio K/Q from Example 15. If the ratio K/Q is constant, it must be that

$$\frac{\dot{K}}{K} = \frac{\dot{Q}}{Q},$$

so that K and Q are growing at a common rate.

The stability of the great ratios means that economic growth takes place in such a way that numerators and denominators remain in balance. The implication that key variables share common growth rates is therefore called the property of **balanced growth.** Clearly this property is one we should look for in any theory that purports to explain economic growth, something we in fact do when we turn to such a theory in Chapter 9.

EXAMPLE 16

Appendix 6A describes the quantity theory of money, which is summarized by the equation

$$M = kPQ.$$

The quantity of money in circulation M is determined by the policies of the central bank, output Q is determined by the real side of the economy, and k is a behavioral parameter that describes people's money-holding practices. With these variables predetermined in this way, the equation indicates how the price level P is determined in relation to them.

Show that if the quantity theory of money holds and k may be treated as constant, the inflation rate will be the rate of money growth less the growth rate of output. Show further that, if output is not growing, the inflation rate will simply equal the growth rate of the money stock.

SOLUTION

Taking the logs and derivatives of the quantity theory equation yields

$$\frac{\dot{M}}{M} = \frac{\dot{k}}{k} + \frac{\dot{P}}{P} + \frac{\dot{Q}}{Q}.$$

If k is constant, then $\dot{k} = 0$. Rearranging the remaining terms, we have

$$\frac{\dot{P}}{P} = \frac{\dot{M}}{M} - \frac{\dot{Q}}{Q}.$$

This says that the inflation rate equals the rate of money growth less the growth rate of output, our first property. The interpretation is that prices grow at a rate determined by the growth of the money supply less the need for increased money to facilitate a growing volume of transactions.

If the volume of transactions is not growing and so is constant, then $\dot{Q} = 0$ and we are left with

$$\frac{\dot{P}}{P} = \frac{\dot{M}}{M}.$$

The inflation rate is just equal to the growth rate of the money stock, our second property.

4. *Instantaneous growth rates of exponential functions.* Suppose Z is related exponentially to X,

$$Z = X^{\beta},$$

where β is a parameter that is not changing through time. The relationship between the growth rates of Z and X may be found by taking logs and derivatives:

$$\log Z = \beta \log X,$$
$$\frac{d \log Z}{dt} = \beta \frac{d \log X}{dt},$$
$$\frac{\dot{Z}}{Z} = \beta \frac{\dot{X}}{X}.$$

As an example, consider the Cobb-Douglas production function in labor-intensive form (6.5):

$$q = \gamma k^{\beta}.$$

If the relationship between the levels of output per worker q and capital per worker k is governed by this equation, what is the relationship between their growth rates? Taking logs and derivatives, γ is eliminated because, like β, it is a constant parameter and so its growth rate is zero. The result is

$$\frac{\dot{q}}{q} = \beta \frac{\dot{k}}{k}. \tag{6.51}$$

The growth rate of output per worker depends on the growth of capital per worker, but in a way that depends on β.

These are the most basic rules governing instantaneous growth rates. They may be combined to establish more complicated results. For example, consider the Cobb-Douglas production function (6.3):

$$Q = \gamma K^{\beta} L^{\alpha}.$$

What does this imply about the relationship between the growth rates of the variables? Taking logarithms yields

$$\log Q = \log \gamma + \beta \log K + \alpha \log L.$$

Next take time-derivatives. Again, because γ is a constant, the time-derivative of $\log \gamma$ is zero and that term disappears, leaving

$$\frac{\dot{Q}}{Q} = \beta \frac{\dot{K}}{K} + \alpha \frac{\dot{L}}{L}. \tag{6.52}$$

This equation may be interpreted as decomposing output growth into components attributable to growth in the factor inputs.

We use these properties of instantaneous growth rates many times in the chapters ahead. In particular, equation (6.52) is a special case of a more general **growth accounting equation** that is developed in the next chapter.

Properties of Continuous Growth Rates

Instantaneous growth rates are defined in terms of time-derivatives. Their properties, as we have developed them in the preceding pages, stand independent of anything that might be said about the analysis of data.

In considering an observed data series Y_t, $t = 1, \ldots, n$, we have seen in this chapter that the log-differences of the series

$$\Delta \log Y_t = \log Y_t - \log Y_{t-1} \qquad (t = 2, \ldots, n)$$

have the interpretation as continuously compounded growth rates. We have therefore referred to these log-differences as continuous growth rates. Like discrete growth rates, multiplied by 100 they have the interpretation as percentage changes—just in continuously compounded form.

Working in terms of percentage changes is convenient because it abstracts from absolute magnitudes. In Example 9 of Chapter 4 we verify this for discrete relative changes—quantities of the form $\Delta Y_t / Y_{t-1}$—by showing that they are scale invariant. In the same way, continuous growth rates also have the advantage of scale invariance.

EXAMPLE 17 | Show that continuous growth rates are independent of units of measure.

SOLUTION | Consider a variable rescaling: $\mathbf{Y} = w Y$. The continuous growth rate is the log-difference

$$\log \mathbf{Y}_t - \log \mathbf{Y}_{t-1} = \log(w Y_t) - \log(w Y_{t-1})$$
$$= (\log w + \log Y_t) - (\log w + \log Y_{t-1})$$
$$= \log Y_t - \log Y_{t-1}.$$

Hence, like discrete rates, continuous growth rates are scale invariant.

One reason it is useful to work in terms of continuous growth rates when analyzing data—instead of conventional discrete percentage changes—is that they possess properties that parallel those we have just derived for instantaneous growth rates.

1. *The continuous growth rate of a product is the sum of the growth rates.* Consider a time series Z_t that is the product of two other series X_t and Y_t, all observed over $t = 1, \ldots, n$: $Z_t = X_t Y_t$. The logarithms are related by

$$\log Z_t = \log X_t + \log Y_t$$

for all $t = 1, \ldots, n$, including $t - 1$:

$$\log Z_{t-1} = \log X_{t-1} + \log Y_{t-1} \qquad (t = 2, \ldots, n).$$

Subtracting the latter from the former yields a relationship in log-differences:

$$\Delta \log Z_t = \Delta \log X_t + \Delta \log Y_t \qquad (t = 2, \ldots, n).$$

Because these log-differences are continuous growth rates, we have established that, period by period, the growth rate of Z_t will be the sum of the growth rates of X_t and Y_t. In fact not only is this true period by period, it is also true of the average growth rates, as can be seen by summing and dividing by $n - 1$:

$$\frac{1}{n-1} \sum_{t=2}^{n} \Delta \log Z_t = \frac{1}{n-1} \sum_{t=2}^{n} \Delta \log X_t + \frac{1}{n-1} \sum_{t=2}^{n} \Delta \log Y_t.$$

Of course each of these average growth rates simplifies according to (6.25) and so can be calculated from just the initial and terminal values of the series.

2. *The continuous growth rate of a ratio is the difference of the growth rates.* Consider a time series Z_t that is the ratio of two other series X_t and Y_t: $Z_t = X_t / Y_t$. The logarithms are related by

$$\log Z_t = \log X_t - \log Y_t$$

for all $t = 1, \ldots, n$. Taking log-differences similar to rule 1 yields

$$\Delta \log Z_t = \Delta \log X_t - \Delta \log Y_t \qquad (t = 2, \ldots, n).$$

Hence, the continuous growth rate of Z_t will be the difference of the growth rates of X_t and Y_t, not only period by period but on average:

$$\frac{1}{n-1} \sum_{t=2}^{n} \Delta \log Z_t = \frac{1}{n-1} \sum_{t=2}^{n} \Delta \log X_t - \frac{1}{n-1} \sum_{t=2}^{n} \Delta \log Y_t.$$

EXAMPLE 18 In Exercise 6.7 we study Jones's series on GDP, population, and GDP per capita, obtaining growth rates for each. Do these computed growth rates satisfy rule 2?

SOLUTION The calculations of Exercise 6.7 are summarized in Table 6.9. The continuous growth rates are computed using equation (6.25), the discrete rates using (6.26). In this context X_t is GDP, Y_t is population, and Z_t is their ratio, GDP per capita.

TABLE 6.9   Average Growth Rates for Jones's Time Series

	GDP	Population	1000 × GDP per capita
1880	27.7	50262	0.551112
1987	898.7	243942	3.684072
Continuous growth rate	0.03252	0.01476	0.01776
Discrete growth rate	0.03305	0.01487	0.01791

Rule 2 says that the continuous growth rates should be related as

$$0.01776 = 0.03252 - 0.01476,$$

which does in fact hold. Hence, the rule is verified. Alternatively, the values may be rearranged as

$$0.03252 = 0.01776 + 0.01476,$$

with the interpretation that the growth rate of GDP is the sum of the growth rates of GDP per capita and population. In this form, the values verify rule 1, that the continuous growth rate of a product is the sum of the individual rates. Notice that no such properties are satisfied exactly by the discrete growth rates in Table 6.9, illustrating the appeal of working in terms of continuous rates.

Let us consider as another example the continuous growth rate version of the Fisher identity discussed in Theory Meets Application 6.2.

EXAMPLE 19

Suppose that at the end of last year you purchased an asset of value $V_{t-1} = \$1000$. At the end of this year it is worth $V_t = \$1083.29$. However over the course of the year inflation has reduced your purchasing power; a basket of goods and services that previously cost $P_{t-1} = \$100$ now costs $P_t = \$103.05$. What is: (a) your nominal rate of return; (b) the rate of inflation; and (c) your real rate of return. Establish that these are related by a continuous growth rate version of the Fisher identity.

SOLUTION

Working in terms of log-differences, the annual nominal rate of return on the asset is

$$i_t = \log V_t - \log V_{t-1} = \log 1083.29 - \log 1000 = 0.08,$$

or 8% continuously compounded.

Similarly, the rate of inflation is the growth rate of the price level:

$$\text{Inflation rate} = \log P_t - \log P_{t-1} = \log 103.05 - \log 100 = 0.03,$$

or 3% continuously compounded.

What is the real return on this investment after inflation has taken its toll? Treating the price level P_t as a price index, it can be used to deflate nominal values to obtain real ones. As measured by this price index, the real purchasing power of your initial $1000 investment was

$$v_{t-1} = \frac{V_{t-1}}{P_{t-1}/100} = \frac{\$1000}{1.00} = \$1000,$$

whereas your real purchasing power at the end of the year is

$$v_t = \frac{V_t}{P_t/100} = \frac{\$1083.29}{1.0305} = \$1051.23.$$

In terms of beginning-of-the-year units of purchasing power you have received $51.23 as a reward for abstaining from the consumption of your initial $1000. As a rate of return this is

$$r_t = \log v_t - \log v_{t-1} = \log \$1051.23 - \log \$1000 = 0.05,$$

or 5% continuously compounded. Notice that these rates of return satisfy the Fisher identity in Theory Meets Application 6.2:

5% real rate of return = 8% nominal rate of return − 3% inflation rate.

The reason for this equality is now apparent; in general

$$
\begin{aligned}
r_t &= \log v_t - \log v_{t-1} \\
&= \log \left(\frac{V_t}{P_t/100} \right) - \log \left(\frac{V_{t-1}}{P_{t-1}/100} \right) \\
&= (\log V_t - \log P_t) - (\log V_{t-1} - \log P_{t-1}) \\
&= (\log V_t - \log V_{t-1}) - (\log P_t - \log P_{t-1}) \\
&= i_t - \text{Inflation rate.}
\end{aligned}
$$

Thus the Fisher identity can be expressed in terms of either instantaneous rates, as in Theory Meets Application 6.2, or continuous ones.

Of course it follows as a corollary of rule 2 that if observed time series have a constant ratio they have the same growth rate.

3. *Continuous growth rates aggregate easily over time.* If a variable grows at continuous rate β each quarter, what is its annual growth rate? If we think of Table 6.2 as representing quarterly values, the answer is easy: 4β. So, for example, a 5% quarterly growth rate aggregates to a 20% annual rate, as long as rates are expressed in terms of continuous compounding. Similarly, a monthly growth rate of β aggregates to an annual rate of 12β.

If the continuous rates vary period by period, they can be aggregated by summing. Consider continuous growth rates in May, June, and July:

July: $\Delta \log Y_t = \log Y_t - \log Y_{t-1}$

June: $\Delta \log Y_{t-1} = \log Y_{t-1} - \log Y_{t-2}$

May: $\Delta \log Y_{t-2} = \log Y_{t-2} - \log Y_{t-3}$

Then the growth rate over the quarter is the sum of the three monthly rates:

$$\Delta \log Y_t + \Delta \log Y_{t-1} + \Delta \log Y_{t-2} = \log Y_t - \log Y_{t-3}.$$

The average monthly rate is obtained by dividing by 3.

No such convenient properties hold for discretely compounded rates. For example, the figures in Table 6.1 show that discrete growth of 5% per quarter translates into annual growth of 21.55%, not 20%. Starting with the annual rate of 21.55, we cannot derive the quarterly rate by dividing by 4.

Instantaneous Rates Have a Discrete Time Dimension

In light of these observations about the aggregation over time of growth rates, it is natural to add one further remark about instantaneous rates. Suppose we are told that a variable grows at instantaneous rate 0.02:

$$\frac{\dot{Y}}{Y} = 0.02.$$

This means that if this variable grows throughout the period at this instantaneous rate, over the period it will have changed by the factor $e^{0.02}$—that is, at the continuously compounded rate of 2%. The key point to note is that, for the statement about the growth of the variable to be complete, the length of the period must be specified. Instantaneous growth of 2% per month is an entirely different matter—indeed, as rule 3 tells us, 12 times as rapid—than 2% per year. Hence, although a growth rate $\dot{Y}/Y$ is expressed instantaneously, it is always defined with respect to some discrete time period.

Application: Changes in Poverty Intensity

Many costly social programs are, in one way or another, aimed at the alleviation of poverty. Gauging the success of these programs requires that poverty be measured.

Most measures of poverty begin with the concept of a **poverty line,** a level of income below which the normal necessities of life are thought to be unattainable. A common international standard is to define the poverty line as one-half of median income. The **poverty rate** (Rate, for short), the most commonly cited measure of poverty in the popular press, is the percentage of the population whose incomes fall below the poverty line. One limitation of the poverty rate as a measure of poverty, pointed out by Sen (1976), is that it does not reflect the depth of poverty: The poverty rate would be the same regardless of whether many of the poor had incomes close to the line or far below it.

An alternative, albeit less widely encountered, measure that addresses this is the **average poverty gap ratio** (Gap, for short). A poor person's **poverty gap** is the amount by which their income falls below the poverty line; their **poverty gap ratio** is the poverty gap relative to the poverty line. The average poverty gap ratio is, then, the average percentage by which the incomes of the poor fall below the poverty line. This measure has the deficiency that it is insensitive to the number of the poor: It does not distinguish between whether there are only a few poor people or a great many.

Another dimension of poverty is the degree of inequality among the poor themselves. Great inequality might be taken to indicate that the problem of poverty is more severe, in the sense that if inequality is increased by transferring income from a poor person to a less poor one, presumably poverty has been made worse. Inequality among the poor may be measured using a **Gini coefficient** of poverty gap ratios, which we denote by the symbol G.[21] However, clearly the Gini coefficient is not by itself a suitable measure of poverty. In addition to being purely a measure of inequality, it too is unaffected by either the depth of poverty or the number of the poor.

Considered independently, then, none of these concepts is by itself a satisfactory measure of poverty. A measure that attempts to overcome these and other problems is the Sen-Shorrocks-Thon (SShT) index of **poverty intensity.** Among its most interesting properties is that it has been shown by Osberg and Xu (2000) to be directly related to the other measures by

SShT = Rate $\times$ Gap $\times$ (1 + G).

The properties of logarithms and growth rates tell us that this multiplicative relationship translates into an additive relationship between growth rates. Taking log-differences yields

$$\Delta \log \text{SShT}_t = \Delta \log \text{Rate}_t + \Delta \log \text{Gap}_t + \Delta \log(1 + G_t). \tag{6.53}$$

Thus, as Osberg and Xu (2000, pp. 55–56) remark, "Poverty intensity may be increasing because more people are becoming poor, or because the average income shortfall below the poverty line is increasing, or because income shortfalls have become more unequal, or some combination. . . ."

These equations appear as equations (2) and (3) in Osberg (2000) and as equations (8) and (9) in Osberg and Xu (2000).[22] It turns out that in most countries

---

[21] A Gini coefficient is defined in terms of areas above and below a Lorenz curve. A larger value indicates greater inequality. Most introductory economics texts have discussions of Lorenz curves and Gini coefficients. Gini coefficients are used by economists to measure inequality in a variety of areas, including also income and wealth.

[22] Although note the typographical error in the latter reference.

TABLE 6.10   Decomposition of the Sen-Shorrocks-Thon Index of Poverty Intensity

		SShT index	Decomposition		
			Rate	Gap	1 + G
Canada	1971	0.102	0.149	0.359	1.914
	1997	0.070	0.118	0.306	1.932
	Log-difference:	−0.376	−0.233	−0.160	0.009
United States	1974	0.099	0.146	0.355	1.913
	1997	0.106	0.168	0.333	1.901
	Log-difference:	0.068	0.140	−0.064	−0.006

Source: Osberg, L. (2000) "Poverty in Canada and the United States: Measurement, Trends, and Implications," *Canadian Journal of Economics* 33, 847–877, Blackwell Publishing. Reprinted with the permission of Blackwell Publishing. Osberg and Xu (2000, Table 2, pp. 70–71).

the degree of inequality among the poor changes little over time, so that the last term is close to zero. Accordingly, in practice

$$\Delta \log \text{SShT}_t \approx \Delta \log \text{Rate}_t + \Delta \log \text{Gap}_t.$$

In Osberg's (2000, p. 852) words, "...changes over time (or differences between countries...) in the inequality of poverty gaps ... are empirically very small, especially when compared with differences in the poverty rate and average poverty gap. Hence, the percentage change in poverty intensity can be approximated as the sum of the percentage changes of the poverty rate and the average poverty gap ratio."

These relationships are illustrated in Table 6.10, which gives figures for the SShT index and its decomposition for Canada and the United States.[23] Notice that in the early 1970s the pattern of poverty was virtually identical in the two countries, both overall, as measured by the SShT index, and in terms of the components of the decomposition. By 1997, however, the pattern of poverty had diverged. The SShT index indicates that poverty had fallen in Canada but increased in the United States.

Although, on a national basis, Canada has less poverty than the United States, differences in national poverty intensity between the two countries emerged only within the last thirty years. Poverty intensity in Canada was virtually indistinguishable from that of the United States in the early 1970s.... (Osberg 2000, p. 856)

Table 6.10 shows that the decline in poverty in Canada was the result of declines in both the poverty rate and the average poverty gap ratio.[24] The poor were fewer in number (relative to the population as a whole), and the typical income shortfall was smaller. This occurred despite a slight increase in inequality among the poor.

By contrast, the increase in poverty in the United States was due entirely to an increase in the poverty rate; the proportion of the population living below the

[23] See Osberg and Xu (2000) for similar figures for 17 other countries.

[24] The log-differences do not satisfy equation (6.53) exactly due to rounding error.

poverty line was larger. This effect was strong enough to swamp a decline in the average income shortfall (the gap)—similar to but not as large as what occurred in Canada—and a decline in inequality among the poor.

EXERCISES

6.29 Consider the following variables.

N	adult population
L	labor force
E	employment

From these variables the following may be defined: unemployment is $U = L - E$, the unemployment rate is $u = U/L$, and the labor force participation rate is $l = L/N$. Applying the rules of instantaneous growth rates that we have derived, show that

(a) the growth rate of the unemployment rate is the growth rate of unemployment less the growth rate of the labor force.

(b) if the labor force participation rate is constant, the labor force must be growing at the same rate as the adult population.

(c) if the unemployment rate is constant, the growth rate of employment is the same as the growth rate of the labor force.

(d) if the participation rate and the unemployment rate are both constant, unemployment must be growing at the same rate as the adult population.

(e) the growth rates of the unemployment rate and the participation rate must sum to the growth rate of unemployment less the growth rate of the adult population.

6.30 Consider the following variables.

N	adult population
L	labor force
Q	output

From these variables the following may be defined: labor productivity (output per worker) is $q = Q/L$, the living standard (output per adult) is $y = Q/N$, and the labor force participation rate is $l = L/N$. Show that if the participation rate is constant, living standards y and labor productivity q have the same growth rate.

6.31 Consider the following variables.

N	adult population
L	labor force
E	employment
Q	output

From these variables the following may be defined: unemployment is $U = L - E$, the unemployment rate is $u = U/L$, the labor force participation rate is $l = L/N$, labor productivity (output per employed person) is Q/E, and the living standard (output per adult) is Q/N. Show that if the unemployment rate is constant, the growth rate of living standards is the sum of the growth rates of labor productivity and the participation rate.

6.32 Suppose that the labor force L is split between two uses: workers used in production L_Y and workers used in research L_R; so $L = L_Y + L_R$. Let the proportion of the labor force used in research be denoted $s_R = L_R/L$. Show that if s_R is constant, then L_Y and L_R both grow at the same rate as L.

6.33 Letting Q denote GDP and B total outstanding government bonds, the debt-to-GDP ratio can be defined as

$$b = \frac{B}{Q}.$$

It is sometimes suggested that even in the face of continued deficit spending, so that the national debt B increases over time, the burden of the debt can be reduced through economic growth.

(a) Is it possible for the debt-to-GDP ratio to decrease even if the total national debt is increasing? If so, what must be true of the growth rate of GDP relative to that of the national debt?

(b) Government expenditures consist of spending on goods and services G and interest payments on the debt rB. The government's deficit D is its excess of expenditures over tax revenues,

$$D = G + rB - T.$$

This deficit must be financed through new bond issuance, so

$$D = \frac{dB}{dt}.$$

Suppose that the government decides to operate on a pay-as-you-go basis, so that current spending G is financed entirely through taxation. Under this policy the primary deficit $G - T$ is zero and new debt is issued only to cover the interest on the outstanding debt. Treating the interest rate r as constant, how does the growth rate of the national debt depend on the interest rate?

(c) What condition must be satisfied for the burden of the debt to be reduced through economic growth under a fiscal policy that sets the primary deficit to zero? Combine your answers from parts a and b to establish such a condition involving the interest rate and the growth of output.

6.34 In international economics there is an important distinction between *nominal* and *real* exchange rates. A nominal exchange rate e_n is the rate at which currencies are traded. This is the exchange rate that is quoted in the newspaper and that applies when you buy foreign currency to travel abroad. For example, if 1 dollar buys 0.5 pound sterling then the nominal exchange rate is $e_n = 0.5$ pounds per dollar. This is of course equivalent to taking the reciprocal and quoting the rate as $2 per pound. As defined, so that we are looking at the exchange rate from the point of view of dollars being the domestic currency, if e_n increases we say that the domestic currency has appreciated in value: Each dollar buys more pounds. If the nominal exchange rate decreases, the domestic currency is said to have depreciated in value.

By contrast, the real exchange rate e_r is the rate at which goods are exchanged. It is also known

as the terms of trade. This is not quoted in the newspaper but is the exchange rate that is usually of most interest to economists because it governs the demands for imports and exports. The real exchange rate is defined as

$$e_r = e_n \times \frac{P_d}{P_f}.$$

Here P_d denotes the domestic price level (the domestic price of a bundle of goods in dollars) and P_f denotes the foreign price level (the price of the same bundle of goods in Britain, in pounds). The real exchange rate tells us the rate at which domestic goods can be traded for foreign goods.

Show that if the terms of trade are constant and the foreign inflation rate exceeds the domestic rate, the domestic currency appreciates.

6.35 Real variables are obtained from nominal variables by deflating using a price index. If Y denotes the nominal variable, y the variable measured in real terms, and P the price index defined using a base of 100, then the relationship is

$$y = \frac{Y}{P/100}. \tag{6.54}$$

(a) What is the relationship between the growth rate of the real variable $\dot{y}/y$, the growth rate of the nominal variable $\dot{Y}/Y$, and the inflation rate $\dot{P}/P$?

(b) Nelson and Plosser (1982) studied a U.S. data set that included two such relationships.
i. Their data set included annual data on real and nominal GNP and the price index that relates them, the GNP deflator, for the years 1909–1970. The initial and terminal values in these series are as follows. (Because the 1909 values are reported to only an accuracy of a small number of digits, they satisfy (6.54) only approximately.)

Year	Real GNP	Nominal GNP	GNP deflator
1909	116.8	33.400	29.1
1970	720.0	974.126	135.3

Compute the average continuous growth rate for each of these variables over this period. What is the relationship between these growth rates?

ii. Their data set included annual data on the real wage, the nominal wage, and the consumer price index, for the years 1900–1970. The initial and terminal values in these series are as follows.

Year	Real wage	Nominal wage	CPI
1900	1948	487	25.0
1970	7008	8150	116.3

Compute the average continuous growth rate for each of these variables over this period. What is the relationship between these growth rates?

6.36 The decomposition of the Sen-Shorrocks-Thon index of poverty intensity shows that the pattern of poverty in Canada and the United States diverged between the 1970s and the 1990s. Poverty intensity fell in Canada but increased in the U.S. Nevertheless, during the 1990s this trend may have reversed. Osberg (2000) presents the following figures for 1994.

	SShT index	Decomposition		
		Rate	Gap	$1 + G$
Canada	0.05891	0.11136	0.273	1.935
United States	0.12594	0.18526	0.360	1.888

(a) Referring to Table 6.10, compute the percentage changes of the decomposition (6.53) for the period 1994–1997. Is the equality of the decomposition satisfied approximately?

(b) Osberg (2000, p. 858) states,

> ... between 1994 and 1997 poverty rose in Canada and fell in the United States. ... In Canada, two-thirds of the increasing poverty was due to a larger poverty gap among the poor, but in the United States most of the improvement came from a fall in the poverty rate. On a national basis, poverty in Canada remained significantly less than that in the United States ...

Are these conclusions consistent with the data?

7

Applications to Production Functions

In Section 6.1 we see that the Cobb-Douglas production function is an example of a relationship between variables that can be converted to a linear regression using a logarithmic transformation. This chapter considers the use of loglinear models to study a variety of issues related to production functions. To do this, we begin by reviewing the economic theory of production functions.

7.1   General Features of Production Functions

A production function is a technical relation describing the use of factor inputs to produce output. Because this activity is a basic function of both individual firms and the economy as a whole, the concept of a production function is a key building block in both microeconomic and macroeconomic models. Consider the case of a single output Q and two factor inputs, capital K and labor L. A production process that converts K and L into Q may be described by the function

$$Q = f(K, L). \tag{7.1}$$

What properties might such a function be expected to exhibit? First, presumably more factor inputs always produce more output. That is, $f(\cdot)$ is increasing in both K and L. This should be true regardless of whether K and L are increased simultaneously or individually. In the latter case, the function should exhibit **diminishing marginal returns:** Increasing one factor while the other is held fixed should increase output, but by amounts that decline at each step as the variable factor is increased.

This property of diminishing returns is illustrated in Figure 7.1. It shows that although output Q is increasing in L, this occurs in such a way that the marginal product $f_L = \partial Q / \partial L$ is declining. Why does it make sense that additional amounts of labor employed should generate smaller and smaller increases in output? The idea is that factor inputs are employed first where their marginal product is the greatest; this should be true regardless of whether we are speaking of a single firm, an entire industry, or the economy as a whole. As additional units of labor are introduced they will at each stage be used in their next most productive employment. The same is true if capital is varied holding labor fixed.

FIGURE 7.1

Diminishing
marginal returns.

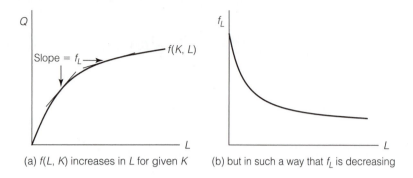

(a) $f(L, K)$ increases in L for given K (b) but in such a way that f_L is decreasing

7.1.1   Returns to Scale

It is to be emphasized that diminishing returns refers specifically to the effect of changing one factor while others are held constant. The result of varying all factors simultaneously is a somewhat different matter and relates to the **returns-to-scale** properties of the production function. The appropriate measure of the returns to scale is the **elasticity of scale** ϵ, which denotes the percentage change in output arising from a 1% change in all factor inputs.

Considering factors individually, the effect on output of increasing the jth factor x_j is summarized by the **elasticity of output** with respect to factor j:

$$\epsilon_j \equiv \frac{x_j}{Q}\frac{\partial Q}{\partial x_j}. \tag{7.2}$$

It may be shown that the elasticity of scale is the sum of these output elasticities over all factors:

$$\epsilon = \sum_j \epsilon_j. \tag{7.3}$$

We say that there are

increasing returns to scale (or economies of scale)   if $\epsilon > 1$,
constant returns to scale   if $\epsilon = 1$,
decreasing returns to scale (or diseconomies of scale)   if $\epsilon < 1$.

In practical situations, the elasticity of scale typically varies over different ranges of output. A common pattern that is thought to apply to many firms and industries is for returns to be increasing at low output levels, then constant in some range, and perhaps decreasing at high levels of output.

Homogeneous Functions

Beyond these general considerations, it is often the case that particular specifications for production functions have special returns-to-scale features. Several popular choices for production functions—including the Cobb-Douglas and CES forms discussed in this chapter—are examples of **homogeneous functions.** In general, a function $f(x_1, x_2, \ldots, x_n)$ is said to be homogeneous of degree v if it has the property that

$$f(\lambda x_1, \lambda x_2, \ldots, \lambda x_n) = \lambda^v f(x_1, x_2, \ldots, x_n). \tag{7.4}$$

In terms of a production function, the implication is that multiplying all inputs by a factor λ results in a λ^v-fold increase in output,

$$\lambda^v Q = f(\lambda K, \lambda L).$$

The symbol v is called the **degree of homogeneity** of the function; when the function in question is a production function, it is also called the **degree of returns to scale.** For example, if $v = 1$, then a doubling ($\lambda = 2$) or tripling ($\lambda = 3$) of each of the inputs results in a doubling or tripling of output and the function exhibits constant returns. If a doubling of inputs results in less than a doubling of output, then $v < 1$ and the technology exhibits decreasing returns. Finally, increasing returns to scale corresponds to $v > 1$.

This background suggests that, if a production function is homogeneous, the elasticity of scale ϵ should be the same as its degree of homogeneity v. To verify that this is in fact the case, we consider Euler's theorem.

Euler's Theorem

Homogeneous functions tend to arise with some frequency in economics, and so the following theorem from calculus is very useful.

EULER'S THEOREM. *If a function $f(x_1, x_2, \ldots, x_n) = f(\cdot)$ is homogeneous of degree v, then*

$$vf(\cdot) = f_1 x_1 + \cdots + f_n x_n = \sum_j f_j x_j, \tag{7.5}$$

where the first partial derivatives of the function are denoted by

$$f_j \equiv \frac{\partial f(\cdot)}{\partial x_j}. \tag{7.6}$$

Proof:

Euler's theorem may be established by starting with the definition of a homogeneous function, differentiating with respect to λ, and evaluating at $\lambda = 1$. The derivative of (7.4) is

$$v\lambda^{v-1} f(\cdot) = \frac{\partial f}{\partial(\lambda x_1)} \frac{\partial \lambda x_1}{\partial \lambda} + \cdots + \frac{\partial f}{\partial(\lambda x_n)} \frac{\partial \lambda x_n}{\partial \lambda}.$$

Because the definition of homogeneity (7.4) holds for all values of λ, so does this relationship. Evaluating at $\lambda = 1$ (and noting that $\partial(\lambda x_j)/\partial \lambda = x_j$) yields (7.5). $\square$

For example, if the two-factor production function (7.1) is homogeneous, Euler's theorem states that

$$v f(K, L) = f_K K + f_L L, \tag{7.7}$$

where the symbols f_K and f_L denote the marginal products (7.6):

$$f_K = \frac{\partial Q}{\partial K}, \qquad f_L = \frac{\partial Q}{\partial L}.$$

Euler's theorem can be used to establish that, if a production function is homogeneous, its elasticity of scale ϵ equals its degree of homogeneity v. Dividing through (7.5) by $Q = f(\cdot)$, the terms in the sum are recognized as the output elasticities (7.2):

$$v = f_1 \frac{x_1}{Q} + \cdots + f_n \frac{x_n}{Q} = \sum_j \frac{\partial Q}{\partial x_j} \frac{x_j}{Q} = \sum_j \epsilon_j = \epsilon.$$

7.1.2 Revenue, Costs, and Market Structure

Euler's theorem has other interesting implications. Consider the relationship between a firm's revenue and its costs of production. If the firm pays a rental rate r on capital and a wage w, then its production costs are

$$C = rK + wL. \tag{7.8}$$

Letting p denote its product price, the profit earned by employing factors K and L to produce output Q is

$$\text{Profit} = pQ - C = pf(K, L) - rK - wL.$$

Taking derivatives with respect to each of K and L reminds us that the choices of K and L that maximize this profit are determined by the marginal productivity conditions

$$r = pf_K, \qquad w = pf_L. \tag{7.9}$$

That is, factors are hired up to the point at which the value of the marginal product of each factor equals its factor price. This is the famous marginal productivity theory of income distribution: Factors are paid the value of their marginal product. Substituting these back into the cost expression (7.8) yields

$$C = pf_K K + pf_L L = p(f_K K + f_L L).$$

If the production function is homogeneous of degree v then, by Euler's theorem (7.7),

$$C = pv f(K, L) = vpQ.$$

The implications of this result are striking. Under decreasing returns ($v < 1$) costs are less than the value of output and the firm earns a pure economic profit. Under constant returns ($v = 1$) factor payments exactly exhaust total revenue and profits are zero:

$$pQ = C = rK + wL. \tag{7.10}$$

Finally, a firm operating in a region of its technology characterized by increasing returns ($\nu > 1$) incurs losses; it must pay out more in factor payments than it earns in revenue. A firm might be willing to do this on a temporary basis while attempting to expand its operations to a point of constant or decreasing returns. If the extent of the market does not permit expanding output to this point, the firm would have to be offered subsidies—perhaps in the form of being allowed to operate as a regulated monopoly—to induce it to remain in business.

Market Structure

This last point leads us to observe that, in taking derivatives of the profit function to obtain the marginal productivity conditions (7.9), we have implicitly assumed that the firm is operating competitively in both its output and factor markets. The firm is therefore a price taker with respect to its output and factor prices; taking these as given, its only decision is how much K and L to hire (and, by implication, how much output Q to produce) in order to maximize profits. It is this assumption about market structure that has led to the conclusion that increasing returns result in losses.

By contrast, a firm operating in a range of output characterized by increasing returns can earn profits if does not face a perfectly competitive environment in, say, its output market and so can charge a price p higher than would be determined under perfect competition. Indeed, this may be the normal circumstance in new industries, which typically arise from the invention of new ideas and technologies. The early recognition and exploitation of the new technology by a very small number of firms gives them, at least temporarily, a degree of market power in their product market, allowing them to make profits even though they may be experiencing increasing returns. The early developers of word processing and spreadsheet software, for example, were not price takers in their product markets. Indeed, it is the early chase for these **monopoly rents** that is the incentive for the invention of new ideas and products, as society recognizes by the conferring of patent and copyright protection on their developers. (An economic rent is a payment to a fixed factor of production—in this case, the new idea.)

These observations have important implications for the dynamic evolution of industry structure over time. In a young industry, we typically find a few firms operating on a small scale at which increasing returns are present but imperfect competition makes profits possible. Over time, these profits draw in new industry entrants; as well, the industry expands and average costs fall. The increasingly competitive environment and falling average costs drive down the price of the product—just as has occurred with word processing and spreadsheet software.

An excessive number of new industry entrants, in advance of firms growing to a size at which constant returns to scale are present, will result in losses and exits from the industry. This enables the remaining firms to expand to a scale characterized by constant returns at which, even under perfect competition, they are able to fully cover their costs of production.

In the longer term, of course, firms will attempt to expand their operations beyond the range of constant returns into that characterized by scale diseconomies in order to earn a pure economic profit. However, competition among all firms to do this—and the new industry entrants that any pure economic profits will encourage—will tend to keep firm sizes in the range of constant returns.

The conclusion of this reasoning is rather profound, and to emphasize this it is useful to state it in its purest form: even if the production *technology* exhibits scale economies at low output levels and diseconomies at higher ones, *firms* in a mature competitive industry will only be observed operating at output levels characterized by constant returns. It would therefore not be surprising if a typical finding is that data from mature competitive industries fail to reject the hypothesis of constant returns to scale.

In Chapter 11 we find that the story we have just told seems to fit the U.S. electric power generation industry as it evolved between 1955 and 1970. In 1955 this industry was still fairly young; analyzing data from that time, you will find that many firms were operating at output levels characterized by increasing returns.[1] However, by 1970 average firm sizes had increased to the point at which scale economies had been fully exploited.

Output Elasticities Are Factor Shares

Let us focus on circumstances in which firms are competitive price takers, so that marginal productivity conditions such as (7.9) hold. Returning to the definition of the output elasticities (7.2), consider the output elasticities of capital and labor:

$$\epsilon_K = \frac{K}{Q}\frac{\partial Q}{\partial K} = \frac{K}{Q}\frac{r}{p} = \frac{rK}{pQ}, \tag{7.11a}$$

$$\epsilon_L = \frac{L}{Q}\frac{\partial Q}{\partial L} = \frac{L}{Q}\frac{w}{p} = \frac{wL}{pQ}. \tag{7.11b}$$

The numerators of the final expressions are the factor payments to capital and labor, respectively (the components of total cost (7.8)); the denominators are total revenue from the sale of output pQ.

These expressions are, then, the ratios of these factor payments to the total value of output. The revenue of a firm flows through as factor payments to the various factors of production; as we have seen, under constant returns these factor payments exactly exhaust total revenue and profits are zero.

The proportion that each factor payment takes of the value of output pQ is called that factor's share of output. Labor's share of output is wL/pQ; capital's share is rK/pQ. These **factor shares** may, of course, be defined purely as an accounting matter, independent of any concept of a production function or any assumptions about market structure. What the derivation shows, however, is that under the marginal productivity theory of income distribution (i.e., assuming the marginal productivity conditions (7.9) hold), output elasticities are factor shares.

---

[1] You will take a first run at this issue in Exercise 8.12 of the next chapter.

One reason the concept of factor shares is important is that empirical features of factor shares have played an important role in motivating choices for functional forms for production functions. Let us consider one such choice.

EXERCISES

7.1 Show that if a production function $Q = f(K, L)$ is homogeneous of degree 1, it may always be rewritten in the **intensive form**

$$q = f(k)$$

where $q = Q/L$ and $k = K/L$.

7.2   The Cobb-Douglas Production Function

The previous section identified some of the most basic considerations relevant to the specification of production functions. Particular areas of application, however, might call for the function to possess additional features. In the 1920s, economist Paul Douglas (1892–1976) was interested in estimating a production function describing the U.S. manufacturing sector. In seeking a parameterized functional form for $f(\cdot)$, he noticed that his data exhibited the remarkable regularity that the factor payments to capital and labor were stable shares of output over time.

In view of these considerations, Douglas asked a mathematician colleague Charles Cobb to suggest a functional form that would exhibit both diminishing marginal returns and constant factor shares. Cobb suggested

$$Q = \gamma K^\beta L^\alpha, \qquad 0 < \alpha < 1, \quad 0 < \beta < 1, \qquad (7.12)$$

a function that had been proposed even earlier by Philip Wicksteed (1844–1927). Cobb and Douglas were, however, the first to employ it in empirical work.

Let us examine the features of the Cobb-Douglas production function. Consider first the parameter γ, which is called the efficiency parameter. If two firms are operating using the same production technology and quantities of factor inputs, they might still produce different levels of output if one firm is more efficiently managed than the other; γ captures this. If Wal-Mart develops a more efficient retail distribution system or McDonald's finds a better way to run a restaurant, this would imply a higher value of γ for these firms relative to others in their industry. For the economy as a whole, technological innovations and improved management practices might mean that over time more can be produced with the same factor inputs. Again, this would be represented as a change in γ. In fact, in the next section this possibility is considered explicitly and a method for deducing a measure of γ over time (suitably relabeled $A(t)$) is developed. For the moment, however, let us treat γ as a fixed parameter.

Turning to the role of the factor inputs K and L, note the parameter restrictions $0 < \alpha < 1$ and $0 < \beta < 1$. That both parameters are required to be positive simply ensures that output is increasing in K and L.

The restrictions $\alpha < 1$ and $\beta < 1$, on the other hand, impose diminishing marginal returns. To see this, take derivatives of (7.12) to obtain the marginal product expressions

$$f_K = \frac{\partial Q}{\partial K} = \gamma\beta K^{\beta-1}L^{\alpha} = \beta\gamma\frac{L^{\alpha}}{K^{1-\beta}} \tag{7.13a}$$

$$= \beta\frac{\gamma K^{\beta}L^{\alpha}}{K} = \beta\frac{Q}{K}, \tag{7.13b}$$

$$f_L = \frac{\partial Q}{\partial L} = \gamma K^{\beta}\alpha L^{\alpha-1} = \alpha\gamma\frac{K^{\beta}}{L^{1-\alpha}} \tag{7.14a}$$

$$= \alpha\frac{\gamma K^{\beta}L^{\alpha}}{L} = \alpha\frac{Q}{L}. \tag{7.14b}$$

Let us focus initially on (7.13a) and (7.14a), which express each of the marginal products in terms of the factor inputs. Both marginal products are positive (more of the input yields more output) but, because the respective factor input is in the denominator of the expression, this positive marginal product is inversely related to the absolute amount of the factor employed (as long as $\alpha < 1$, $\beta < 1$). In the case of (7.14a), for example, higher L lowers its marginal product f_L given a fixed level of K, exactly the pattern described in Figure 7.1. It is apparent that diminishing returns requires the restrictions $\alpha < 1$ and $\beta < 1$.[2]

The alternative expressions (7.13b) and (7.14b) have also been derived for the marginal products. They make it easy to see that the output elasticities (7.2) are the coefficients β and α,

$$\epsilon_K = \frac{K}{Q}\frac{\partial Q}{\partial K} = \frac{K}{Q}\beta\frac{Q}{K} = \beta, \qquad \epsilon_L = \frac{L}{Q}\frac{\partial Q}{\partial L} = \frac{L}{Q}\alpha\frac{Q}{L} = \alpha.$$

This is just an alternative derivation of this feature of the Cobb-Douglas production function; it was derived previously in Example 1 of Chapter 6 as an application of Result 6.1 that elasticities are logarithmic derivatives.

Using (7.3), it follows that the elasticity of scale of the Cobb-Douglas production function is

$$\epsilon = \epsilon_L + \epsilon_K = \alpha + \beta. \tag{7.15}$$

A 1% increase in all factor inputs yields an $(\alpha + \beta)\%$ increase in output.

Part of the original motivation for Douglas's interest in this functional form was his empirical observation that factor shares appeared to be fairly constant over time. Because output elasticities are factor shares, it follows automatically that α and β have the interpretations as factor shares of labor and capital. To derive this from first principles, recall from (7.9) that in competitive factor markets firms employ factors of production up to the point at which the real factor price equals

---

[2]   Mathematically, diminishing returns hold as long as the second derivatives f_{LL} and f_{KK} are negative. For the Cobb-Douglas function, starting with (7.13a), $f_{KK} = \partial^2 Q/\partial K^2 = \gamma\beta(\beta-1)K^{\beta-2}L^{\alpha}$, which is negative as long as $\beta < 1$. Similarly for f_{LL} as long as $\alpha < 1$.

the marginal physical product. Using (7.13b) and (7.14b), this means that these marginal productivity conditions may be expressed as

$$\frac{r}{p} = f_K = \beta\frac{Q}{K}, \qquad \frac{w}{p} = f_L = \alpha\frac{Q}{L}, \tag{7.16}$$

which in turn implies

$$\beta = \frac{rK}{pQ}, \qquad \alpha = \frac{wL}{pQ}. \tag{7.17}$$

Hence, the parameters α and β have the interpretations not only of output elasticities but also of factor shares. If, for example, $\beta = 0.3$, this implies that 30% of production is paid out as a return to capital. This verifies that the general conclusion of the previous section—that, under the marginal productivity theory of income distribution, output elasticities are factor shares—holds in the particular context of a Cobb-Douglas function.

Finally, the Cobb-Douglas functional form is an example of a homogeneous function. If inputs are increased by a factor λ, then

$$\gamma(\lambda K)^\beta(\lambda L)^\alpha = \lambda^{\alpha+\beta}\gamma K^\beta L^\alpha = \lambda^{\alpha+\beta}Q.$$

It is evident, then, that the degree of returns to scale is $\nu = \alpha + \beta$. Given the result (7.15) that the elasticity of scale is $\epsilon = \alpha + \beta$, this confirms the general result of the previous section that, if a function is homogeneous, its elasticity of scale is the degree of homogeneity.

At the level of the firm, it is an open question which assumption about returns to scale might be most accurate. A particular production technology might well exhibit varying returns-to-scale properties at different levels of output—increasing at low levels, constant at intermediate levels, and decreasing at high levels. (Although, as we have noted in the previous section, we would not normally expect to find competitive price-taking firms operating indefinitely at output levels characterized by increasing returns because this implies losses.) Which case best describes the circumstances of a particular firm is an empirical matter, and Chapters 8 and 10 discuss methods for estimating α and β and for testing hypotheses about returns to scale.

At the level of a large industry or the economy as a whole, on the other hand, most macroeconomists regard the assumption of constant returns to scale as not only plausible, but compelling. For recall that we have seen from (7.10) that, by Euler's theorem, constant returns implies that factor payments exhaust the total value of output; equivalently, dividing through (7.10) by pQ, factor shares sum to 1:

$$1 = \frac{rK}{pQ} + \frac{wL}{pQ}.$$

This is in fact what has been observed historically in national income accounting data. As economist Robert Solow once expressed it,[3]

---

[3] For a brief contemporary treatment of the constant returns assumption in macroeconomic models, see Romer (2001, p. 10).

... if all factor inputs are classified either as K or L, then the available figures always show [the factor shares] adding up to one. Since we have assumed that factors are paid their marginal products, this amounts to assuming the hypotheses of Euler's theorem. The calculus being what it is, we might just as well assume the conclusion, namely that f is homogeneous of degree one. (Solow 1957, p. 313)

In the particular context of the Cobb-Douglas production function, this implies that $\alpha + \beta = 1$, and the function may be written

$$Q = \gamma K^\beta L^{1-\beta}. \tag{7.18}$$

As we have seen in Section 6.1, this in turn means that the function may be rewritten in its labor-intensive form[4]

$$q = \gamma k^\beta, \tag{7.19}$$

where $q = Q/L$ and $k = K/L$. Introducing a multiplicative disturbance and taking logarithms in the way described there, the Cobb-Douglas production function with constant returns to scale may be estimated as the simple regression

$$\log q_i = \log \gamma + \beta \log k_i + \varepsilon_i. \tag{7.20}$$

Exercise 7.2 asks you to estimate this model using the original data on the U.S. manufacturing sector employed by Cobb and Douglas in their classic 1928 article; their data is reproduced in Table 7.1. In doing this, you are fitting a loglinear functional form to the series on q and k that we originally inspected in Figure 3.2. This fitted loglinear model is shown in Figure 7.2. As you will see, the slope estimate in this loglinear regression is $\hat{\beta} = 0.254$, suggesting that approximately one-quarter of total output is paid out as a return to capital and the remaining three-quarters to labor.

Douglas's observation that, in the data available to him, factor shares were roughly constant, still holds today. Figure 7.3 shows capital's share of output, 1970–2001, for three countries: Canada, the United Kingdom, and the United States. This factor share is remarkably stable in all three, in addition to being remarkably similar at around one-third.

For this reason the Cobb-Douglas production function continues to be a favored specification in macroeconomic research, in addition to being widely used in the

---

[4] This is simply a special case of the more general result of Exercise 7.1 that any production function that is homogeneous of degree 1 may be rewritten in intensive form.

[5] Prescott's point about an increasing real wage in the face of a constant rental price of capital relates to a feature of the Cobb-Douglas production function that lies beyond the scope of what we have been able to develop. Specifically, when the function is incorporated into the neoclassical model of economic growth it may be shown that the real wage grows at the rate of technical progress while the rental price of capital remains fixed. See the appendix to Chapter 9.

TABLE 7.1   Indices of Real Output and Capital and Labor Inputs, U.S.
Manufacturing, 1899–1922

Year	Q	K	L	Year	Q	K	L
1899	100	100	100	1911	153	216	145
1900	101	107	105	1912	177	226	152
1901	112	114	110	1913	184	236	154
1902	122	122	118	1914	169	244	149
1903	124	131	123	1915	189	266	154
1904	122	138	116	1916	225	298	182
1905	143	149	125	1917	227	335	196
1906	152	163	133	1918	223	366	200
1907	151	176	138	1919	218	387	193
1908	126	185	121	1920	231	407	193
1909	155	198	140	1921	179	417	147
1910	159	208	144	1922	240	431	161

Source: Cobb, C.W., and P.H. Douglas (1928) "A Theory of
Production," *American Economic Review* 18 (Supplement).
Reprinted with permission.

FIGURE 7.2

The Cobb-Douglas
production function
fitted to their data.

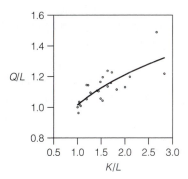

microeconomic analysis of the firm. As one prominent contemporary business cycle
researcher has put it:

> Secularly in the United States, capital and labor shares of output have been approxi-
> mately constant, as has r, the rental price of capital. However the nation's real wage
> has increased greatly—more than 100 percent since the Korean War.[5] For these
> results to hold, the model's production function must be approximately Cobb-Douglas
> ... (Prescott, 1986a, p. 14)

No doubt Cobb and Douglas (not to mention Wicksteed) would be gratified to
know their functional form has withstood the test of time. George Stigler (1987,
p. 153) notes sardonically, "It is now customary practice in economics to deny its
validity and then to use it as an excellent approximation."

FIGURE 7.3

Capital's share of
output, 1970–2001.
Source: OECD, ratio of
gross operating sur-
plus and mixed income
to GDP (income
approach).

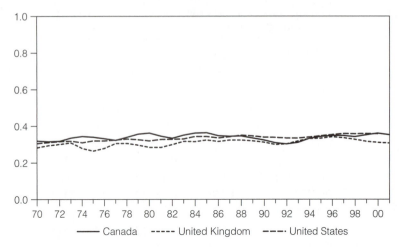

EXERCISES

7.2 cobbdoug.dat Consider Cobb and Douglas's
data presented in Table 7.1, which is available in
the file cobbdoug.dat.

(a) Begin by generating the series $q = Q/L$ and
$k = K/L$.
i. Plot each series against time. What is happening
to labor productivity and the capital-labor ratio over
time? Is this what you expect?

ii. Produce a scatter plot of q against k. Does it
appear to reproduce Figure 3.2(b)?

iii. Obtain the correlation between q and k. Do
you obtain the value reported in connection with
Figure 3.2(b)?

(b) Estimate the regression model (7.20).

i. What is the economic significance of the
requirement that $\beta > 0$? Does your point estimate
satisfy this restriction?

ii. What is the economic significance of the
requirement that $\beta < 1$? Does your point estimate
satisfy this restriction?

iii. What economic interpretation is associated with
the value $\hat{\beta}$? Does your estimate make sense in these
terms?

iv. Cobb and Douglas expressed their data in
index form, using 1899 as the base year. Hence,

their variables are not directly interpretable in
terms of physical units—worker-hours of labor,
for example. Suppose that they had instead chosen
to present their data in physical units. Would $\hat{\beta}$ be
affected? Why? (*Hint:* Reflect on your answer to
Exercise 6.1.)

7.3 cobbdoug.dat Suppose your interest is in
$\alpha = 1 - \beta$. From the results of Exercise 7.2:
(a) Deduce an estimate $\hat{\alpha}$ from $\hat{\beta}$.
(b) Deduce an estimated standard error $s_{\hat{\alpha}}$ from $s_{\hat{\beta}}$.
(*Hint:* What do the laws of variance of Appendix
B allow you to conclude about the relationship
between $V(\hat{\alpha})$ and $V(\hat{\beta})$?)

7.4 cobbdoug.dat Consider another approach to
estimating α. The intensive form (7.19) relates the
productivity of labor Q/L to the capital-labor ratio
K/L and was derived by dividing (7.18) through
by L.

(a) Derive an alternative intensive form that relates
the productivity of capital Q/K to the labor-capital
ratio.

(b) Present a loglinear model based on this
alternative intensive form, in which the slope coefficient is α.

(c) Use the Cobb-Douglas data to estimate this alternative intensive form. How do $\hat{\alpha}$ and $s_{\hat{\alpha}}$ compare to those obtained in Exercise 7.3?

(d) How does your estimate of $\log \gamma$ and its standard error compare with those you obtained in Exercise 7.2?

(e) How does the SSE of the capital intensive form compare with that for the labor-intensive form? By this measure, does one model fit the data better than the other?

(f) In conclusion, do the substantive results of an empirical analysis depend on which intensive form we choose?

(g) Now examine the R^2s for the two intensive forms. How do they compare? Are the R^2 values a useful basis for comparing your two sets of estimation results—for, say, arguing that one intensive form is "better" than the other?

7.5 ✝ Starting with the algebraic formulas by which $\hat{\beta}$ in Exercise 7.3 and $\hat{\alpha}$ in Exercise 7.4 are computed, show algebraically that in general $\hat{\alpha} = 1 - \hat{\beta}$. (*Hint:* In the course of your derivation recall that $\log x^{-1} = -\log x$.)

7.6 ✝ (Continuation of Exercise 5.8) Estimating α and β by the direct estimation of the production function has the advantage of requiring data only on Q, K, and L. Were data also available on prices p, r, and w, however, a quite different approach is available. The interpretation (7.17) of α and β as factor shares suggests that they could be estimated as the factor shares evaluated at, say, the mean of the sample:

$$\tilde{\beta} = \frac{\overline{rK}}{\overline{pQ}}, \qquad \tilde{\alpha} = \frac{\overline{wL}}{\overline{pQ}},$$

where $\overline{pQ} = \sum p_i Q_i / n$ and similarly for $\overline{rK}$ and $\overline{wL}$. (One difference in this approach to estimation is that it does not assume constant returns to scale.) In this approach $\tilde{\beta}$ may be regarded as an estimator of β in the model

$$r_i K_i = \beta p_i Q_i + \varepsilon_i,$$

and similarly for $\tilde{\alpha}$. This is in the form of the regression through the origin

$$Y_i = \beta X_i + \varepsilon_i,$$

where $Y_i = r_i K_i$ and $X_i = p_i Q_i$.

Answer the following questions as an application of your previous analysis in Exercise 5.8.

(a) From the analysis of regression through the origin given in Section 5.2, what is the least squares estimator $\hat{\beta}$?

(b) Compare $\hat{\beta}$ and $\tilde{\beta}$. Which is the preferred estimator? Why?

(c) Yet another approach to estimating β is to take the ratios Y_i / X_i and average them. The estimator is

$$\ddot{\beta} = \frac{1}{n} \sum_{i=1}^{n} \frac{Y_i}{X_i}.$$

(This is in fact the estimator you are implicitly using when you eyeball Figure 7.3 and judge that β is approximately 0.3.)

i. Is $\ddot{\beta}$ unbiased?

ii. Is there any basis for preferring $\hat{\beta}$? (*Hint:* Is $\ddot{\beta}$ a linear estimator?)

7.3 Technical Change

Let us consider another data set, one studied by Robert Solow (1957). It is presented in Table 7.2; the observations are over the period 1909–1949, almost twice as many years as the Cobb-Douglas data.

TABLE 7.2   Solow's Data for the Calculation of A_t

Year	Share of property in income	GNP per worker-hour	Capital per worker-hour	A_t
1909	0.335	0.623	2.06	1.000
1910	0.330	0.616	2.10	0.983
1911	0.335	0.647	2.17	1.021
1912	0.330	0.652	2.21	1.023
1913	0.334	0.680	2.23	1.064
1914	0.325	0.682	2.20	1.071
1915	0.344	0.669	2.26	1.041
1916	0.358	0.700	2.34	1.076
1917	0.370	0.679	2.21	1.065
1918	0.342	0.729	2.22	1.142
1919	0.354	0.767	2.47	1.157
1920	0.319	0.721	2.58	1.069
1921	0.369	0.770	2.55	1.146
1922	0.339	0.788	2.49	1.183
1923	0.337	0.809	2.61	1.196
1924	0.330	0.836	2.74	1.215
1925	0.336	0.872	2.81	1.254
1926	0.327	0.869	2.87	1.241
1927	0.323	0.871	2.93	1.235
1928	0.338	0.874	3.02	1.226
1929	0.332	0.895	3.06	1.251
1930	0.347	0.880	3.30	1.197
1931	0.325	0.904	3.33	1.226
1932	0.397	0.879	3.28	1.198
1933	0.362	0.869	3.10	1.211
1934	0.355	0.921	3.00	1.298
1935	0.351	0.943	2.87	1.349
1936	0.357	0.982	2.72	1.429
1937	0.340	0.971	2.71	1.415
1938	0.331	1.000	2.78	1.445
1939	0.347	1.034	2.66	1.514
1940	0.357	1.082	2.63	1.590
1941	0.377	1.122	2.58	1.660
1942	0.356	1.136	2.64	1.665
1943	0.342	1.180	2.62	1.733
1944	0.332	1.265	2.63	1.856
1945	0.314	1.296	2.66	1.895
1946	0.312	1.215	2.50	1.812
1947	0.327	1.194	2.50	1.781
1948	0.332	1.221	2.55	1.810
1949	0.326	1.275	2.70	1.853

Source: Adapter from Solow (1957, Table 1). Values for A_t for 1943–1949 are the corrected ones computed by Hogan (1958).

FIGURE 7.4

Solow's data on the factor share of capital, 1909–1949.

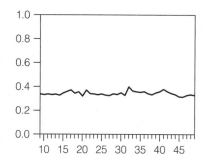

FIGURE 7.5

Solow's data on labor productivity and capital per worker, 1909–1949.

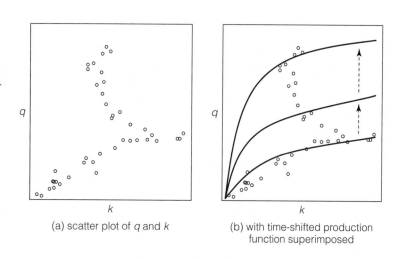

(a) scatter plot of q and k (b) with time-shifted production function superimposed

The first variable is the "share of property in income"—in other words, the factor share of capital ϵ_K. This is plotted in Figure 7.4 and confirms that factor shares are relatively stable over time. Its sample mean is $\bar{\epsilon}_K = 0.34$, which is in the same ballpark as the estimate $\hat{\beta} = 0.254$ that we obtained with the Cobb-Douglas data from a different sample period.

The next two variables are GNP per worker-hour and capital per worker-hour; that is, these are observations on labor productivity q and the capital-labor ratio k analogous to the variables we used to estimate the Cobb-Douglas production function. However, when these variables are plotted, as in Figure 7.5(a), it is apparent that the relationship between them is not as clean as is true of the Cobb-Douglas data.

An inspection of the series in Table 7.2 reveals the reason for this. GNP per worker-hour tends to increase steadily throughout this period. However, the same is not true for capital per worker-hour, which tends to increase during the first 2 decades of the sample but then falls during the Great Depression, remaining at a relatively low level throughout the 1940s. That Solow's data, as plotted in Figure 7.5, fail to exhibit the clear association that the Cobb-Douglas data do, reflects the puzzle that labor productivity continued to increase in the face of declining or constant capital per worker.

This surprising feature of Solow's data has important implications for the estimation of a production function. Suppose we estimate a Cobb-Douglas production function by running a loglinear regression using these data. As you will find in Exercise 7.11, the slope estimate turns out to be $\hat{\beta} = 0.845$, suggesting that approximately 85% of output is paid as a return to capital. This figure is both inconsistent with the mean factor share of 0.34 and quite implausible: No one believes that labor receives only 15% of output as a factor payment.

7.3.1 Technical Change and the Production Function

Solow's contribution was to propose an explanation for this perplexing feature of his data and to use it in the estimation of a production function. His idea was this. Whereas the Cobb-Douglas data were for the relatively short time span of 1899–1922, over more extended periods it may be that the measured capital stock does not accurately represent the true productivity of capital. The reason for this is that **technical change** improves the productivity of capital in a way that is not captured by reported capital stock data.

To give a concrete example, personal computers and word processing software have made an hour of a secretary's time far more productive today than was the case a quarter century ago. This is true for two reasons. First, the quality of capital is greatly improved; resources that twenty-five years ago would have bought a good quality typewriter now buy word processing equipment. Technical change of this sort that increases the productivity of capital is fundamentally distinguished from simple increases in the quantity of capital of a given quality. The secretary could be given any number of additional 1980-vintage typewriters and still not be as productive as the word processing equipment makes possible. Changes in the quality of capital are not reflected in capital stock data. Five hundred 1980 dollars of 21st-century capital is much more productive than $500 of capital was in 1980. Thus data that indicate, say, a doubling of the measured capital stock may in fact represent a manyfold increase in what can be produced.

Second, the changing quality of capital is not the only reason the secretary is more productive. The use of word processing software requires a higher level of training, so that the quality of labor has also increased. An hour of work by someone skilled in the use of word processing software is far more productive than an hour of work by someone who is merely able to type quickly.

One approach to describing these changes might be to attempt to define measures of factor inputs that reflect improvements in their quality due to technical change. Unfortunately, there is no direct way of doing this. An hour of a secretary's time is something that is readily measured; its quality as affected by technical change is not.

Instead, Solow observed that one way of thinking about changes in the quality of capital and labor is to imagine that the production function is shifting over time in its arguments, the measured factor inputs. This can be represented by introducing time t as an argument of the function:

$$Q = F(K, L; t). \tag{7.21}$$

Figure 7.5(b) illustrates this by superimposing successive levels of the production function on Solow's data. The function is plotted in intensive form by assuming constant returns to scale, so that it may be treated as homogeneous of degree 1 in K and L. Multiplying each of Q, K, and L by the common factor $1/L$ yields the labor-intensive form

$$q = \frac{Q}{L} = F(K/L, 1; t) = F(k; t). \tag{7.22}$$

An inspection of the figure shows that it may well be possible to rationalize the seemingly peculiar behavior of Solow's data in terms of a shifting production function.

We can now understand why a mechanical application of a log-log Cobb-Douglas regression to this data yields the misleadingly high estimate of $\hat{\beta} = 0.845$. In estimating a production function, it is necessary to take into account that the sample observations q_t, k_t in successive years are effectively on different production functions, each one dependent on the technology that prevailed in that year. A simple loglinear regression fitted to the data fails to do this and yields a curve with an artificially high slope. In other words, the omission of technical change from the analysis leads to a biased estimate of the factor share β, and that bias is positive.

Starting with this promising set of ideas, Solow proposed a way of deriving a measure of the level of technology and showed how to use it to correct the estimation of the production function. His method has been enormously influential in macroeconomics and is still used today.[6] He began by assuming that technology can be factored out of the production function in the following way:

$$Q = A(t) f(K, L). \tag{7.23}$$

In this case technical change is said to be **Hicks neutral.** The implication of this separable form is, as Solow (1957, p. 316) put it, that shifts in the function are "... pure scale changes, leaving marginal rates of substitution unchanged at given capital/labor ratios." This means that, for given relative factor prices, technical progress leaves the K/L ratio unchanged. In terms of our example of a secretary, the presumption is that the introduction of word processing software improves the quality of both capital and labor in such a way that there is no systematic effect on a firm's optimal ratio of measured capital to labor. The implication is that changes in the K/L ratio should be unrelated to the rate of technical change.

The factor $A(t)$ is called **multifactor productivity** or **total factor productivity** (TFP). Our notation makes explicit that it varies with time; this is implicitly also the case for the other variables, which can be written explicitly as $Q(t)$, $K(t)$, and $L(t)$. Solow observed that if a measure of $A(t)$ could be derived it would be

---

[6] For a brief discussion of Solow's analysis in the context of contemporary macroeconomic theory, see Blanchard and Fischer (1989, Chap. 1).

possible to compute $Q/A(t)$ as a transformed dependent variable and estimate the production function as

$$\frac{Q}{A(t)} = f(K, L). \tag{7.24}$$

The substantive questions are, therefore, two: Is technical change reasonably approximated as being Hicks neutral, and can a measure of $A(t)$ be obtained?

As we have argued, if technical change is Hicks neutral it should be the case that the K/L ratio is unrelated to the rate of technical change. Let us therefore focus initially on the second matter of obtaining a measure of $A(t)$. We will then be in a position to examine whether this measure is uncorrelated with K/L.

7.3.2 Growth Accounting

To understand the derivation of Solow's measure of $A(t)$ let us begin by considering the following question. Given that the production function (7.23) describes output as the product of capital, labor, and the level of technology, is it possible to decompose a change in output into the components due to each of these three elements? To understand this, it may be helpful to think in terms of the following numerical example.

EXAMPLE 1

Consider the Cobb-Douglas production function

$$Q = AK^{0.3}L^{0.7}.$$

Suppose that at the beginning of the year technology A is at level 50, capital K is at level 200, and labor L is at level 100. The variables then grow steadily over the year at the following instantaneous rates:

$$\frac{\dot{A}}{A} = 0.02, \qquad \frac{\dot{K}}{K} = 0.03, \qquad \frac{\dot{L}}{L} = 0.01.$$

What is the resulting increase in output?

SOLUTION

At the initial levels of technology and factor inputs, output is

$$Q = 50 \cdot 200^{0.3} 100^{0.7} = 6155.722.$$

The variables then grow according to the continuous-time constant growth model of Section 6.2.1, so that their new levels may be calculated using log-differences:

$$\frac{\dot{A}}{A} = 0.02 = \Delta \log A_t = \log A_t - \log(50),$$

$$\frac{\dot{K}}{K} = 0.03 = \Delta \log K_t = \log K_t - \log(200),$$

$$\frac{\dot{L}}{L} = 0.01 = \Delta \log L_t = \log L_t - \log(100).$$

Solving for the implied end-of-year levels of the variables, we obtain approximately $A_t = 51.010$, $K_t = 206.091$, and $L_t = 101.005$. The new level of output will be

$$Q = 51.010 \cdot 206.091^{0.3} 101.005^{0.7} = 6381.357.$$

Output has increased over the year at the instantaneous rate of 3.6%:

$$\Delta \log Q_t = \log(6381.357) - \log(6155.722) = 0.036 = \frac{\dot{Q}}{Q}.$$

The question we are posing is this: Can this 3.6% growth rate be decomposed into components attributable to the individual percentage changes in technology, capital, and labor? If so, it is possible to account for the sources of growth.

The Growth Accounting Equation

To do this it is necessary to derive the implications of a production function such as (7.23)—which is in terms of the levels of the variables—for the linkages between their percentage changes. Let us begin by taking the derivative of the production function with respect to t, remembering that Q, A, K, and L all evolve through time and so are implicitly functions of t. Using the chain rule of differentiation, the result is:

$$\frac{dQ}{dt} = \frac{dA}{dt} f(K, L) + A \frac{\partial f}{\partial K} \frac{dK}{dt} + A \frac{\partial f}{\partial L} \frac{dL}{dt}.$$

To go from time-derivatives to growth rates, divide through by Q using the production function (7.23):

$$\frac{\dot{Q}}{Q} = \frac{\dot{A}}{A} + A \frac{\partial f}{\partial K} \frac{\dot{K}}{Q} + A \frac{\partial f}{\partial L} \frac{\dot{L}}{Q}. \tag{7.25}$$

In terms of the present form of the production function that includes the TFP factor $A(t)$, the output elasticities (7.11) are

$$\epsilon_K = \frac{\partial Q}{\partial K} \frac{K}{Q} = A \frac{\partial f}{\partial K} \frac{K}{Q} = \frac{rK}{pQ}, \tag{7.26a}$$

$$\epsilon_L = \frac{\partial Q}{\partial L} \frac{L}{Q} = A \frac{\partial f}{\partial L} \frac{L}{Q} = \frac{wL}{pQ}. \tag{7.26b}$$

The last equality in each line uses what we learned in Section 7.1: If factors are paid their marginal products, these elasticities are also the factor shares.

Returning to (7.25), it may be expanded as

$$\frac{\dot{Q}}{Q} = \frac{\dot{A}}{A} + \underbrace{A \frac{\partial f}{\partial K} \frac{K}{Q}}_{\epsilon_K} \frac{\dot{K}}{K} + \underbrace{A \frac{\partial f}{\partial L} \frac{L}{Q}}_{\epsilon_L} \frac{\dot{L}}{L}.$$

As the braces emphasize, this may be rewritten as

$$\frac{\dot{Q}}{Q} = \frac{\dot{A}}{A} + \epsilon_K \frac{\dot{K}}{K} + \epsilon_L \frac{\dot{L}}{L}. \tag{7.27}$$

This is our sought-after decomposition, the **growth accounting equation.** It decomposes output growth into three components: technological progress, growth of capital, and growth of labor. Note that, whereas a 1% increase in technology translates into a 1% increase in output, this is not true of capital and labor. Instead, the extent to which growth in a factor input contributes to growth in output depends on its output elasticity.

We have derived a general version of the growth accounting equation that is not dependent on any particular functional form for the production function. Special cases of it apply to particular functional forms.

EXAMPLE 2   Consider the Cobb-Douglas production function

$$Q = \gamma K^\beta L^\alpha.$$

How is growth in output related to growth in the factor inputs?

SOLUTION   It is a property of the Cobb-Douglas production function that the exponents are the output elasticities: $\epsilon_K = \beta$ and $\epsilon_L = \alpha$. Applying the growth accounting equation with $\dot{A} = 0$ (as specified there is no technological progress in this production function, and so the growth rate of technology is zero), the relationship between growth rates is

$$\frac{\dot{Q}}{Q} = \beta \frac{\dot{K}}{K} + \alpha \frac{\dot{L}}{L}.$$

This is equation (6.52) of the previous chapter, a special case of the growth accounting equation (7.27).

Although the growth accounting equation has been derived in the particular context of production functions, it tells us how to translate any functional relationship between the levels of variables into a companion relationship between growth rates. Example 2 shows how this applies in the case of the Cobb-Douglas function. Next is an example that has nothing to do with production functions.

EXAMPLE 3   Consider a portfolio A_P that is the total of two assets having values A_1 and A_2:

$$A_P = A_1 + A_2.$$

An asset's continuously compounded rate of return is the growth rate of its value; for example,

$$\text{Rate of return on the portfolio} = \frac{\dot{A}_P}{A_P}.$$

What is the relationship between the rate of return on the portfolio and the returns on the individual assets?

SOLUTION

In this context the growth accounting equation (7.27) is

$$\frac{\dot{A}_P}{A_P} = \epsilon_1 \frac{\dot{A}_1}{A_1} + \epsilon_2 \frac{\dot{A}_2}{A_2}.$$

The elasticities are

$$\epsilon_1 = \frac{A_1}{A_P} \frac{\partial A_P}{\partial A_1} = \frac{A_1}{A_P} \equiv 1 - a, \qquad \epsilon_2 = \frac{A_2}{A_P} \frac{\partial A_P}{\partial A_2} = \frac{A_2}{A_P} \equiv a.$$

That is, the elasticities are just the asset shares. (Recall that a and $1 - a$ are the notations for the asset shares, introduced in Example 4 in the appendix to Chapter 3. This notation reflects the fact that asset shares must sum to 1.) Substituting these elasticities into the growth accounting equation yields

$$\frac{\dot{A}_P}{A_P} = (1 - a)\frac{\dot{A}_1}{A_1} + a\frac{\dot{A}_2}{A_2}.$$

The conclusion is that the rate of return on the portfolio is a weighted average of the individual asset returns, the weights being the asset shares. This is the continuous-time analog of the portfolio return equation (3.17), returns here being expressed instantaneously.

Let us return to growth accounting and the numerical illustration in Example 1.

EXAMPLE 4

Show that the percentage changes of Example 1 are related according to the growth accounting equation (7.27).

SOLUTION

Example 1 hypothesized the growth rates

$$\frac{\dot{A}}{A} = 0.02, \qquad \frac{\dot{K}}{K} = 0.03, \qquad \frac{\dot{L}}{L} = 0.01.$$

For a Cobb-Douglas production function, the factor shares are the exponents in the function; in Example 1, therefore,

$$\epsilon_K = 0.3, \qquad \epsilon_L = 0.7.$$

Substituting these values into the right-hand side of (7.27) yields

$$\frac{\dot{Q}}{Q} = 0.02 + 0.3 \cdot 0.03 + 0.7 \cdot 0.01 = 0.036.$$

This is the same 3.6% change in output we find in Example 1.

Measuring Technical Change

This numerical example has been phrased in terms of computing output growth given values for the right-hand side of (7.27). The practical problem motivating this discussion is instead the desire to obtain a measure of technology $A(t)$. But this is now easy! Equation (7.27) can be rearranged to solve for $\dot{A}/A$:

$$\frac{\dot{A}}{A} = \frac{\dot{Q}}{Q} - \epsilon_K \frac{\dot{K}}{K} - \epsilon_L \frac{\dot{L}}{L}.$$

Data are available for everything on the right-hand side: the growth of output and factor inputs and the factor shares. Once the implied rate of technical progress $\dot{A}/A$ is computed, an implied index of technology $A(t)$ can be deduced. Because Solow's measure of TFP growth is computed as a residual in this way[7]—that is, as output growth less the components attributable to growth in factor inputs—it is often called the **Solow residual.**

Solow's method for measuring total factor productivity has had a great impact on macroeconomics. First, it is the basis for a large literature on **growth accounting** that attempts to quantify the sources of economic growth. One interesting finding of this research is that the slowdown in economic growth that began to affect many industrialized countries in the early 1970s was largely due to a slowing of TFP growth rather than, say, a fall in the rate of capital accumulation. This finding has in turn spawned many attempts to explain this phenomenon, none entirely convincing. Most macroeconomics texts have discussions of growth accounting and these contemporary controversies; you are encouraged to read the relevant sections of your macroeconomics textbook.

Second, an important class of quantitative models of the macroeconomy, called **real business cycle** (RBC) models, hypothesizes that business cycle fluctuations have their origins in random shocks to the real side of the economy—as opposed to the nominal (i.e., monetary) side. In particular, these real shocks are thought to be associated with technological innovation—exactly what is measured by the Solow residual. In fact, simulated RBC models use the time series behavior of the Solow residual to specify the shocks used in the computer simulations. For a discussion of this point, see Prescott (1986a, p. 15), the classic introduction to the RBC research agenda.

Third, the fact that technological progress is an important source of economic growth has led economists to attempt to explain it as the endogenous outcome of economic decisions. This is the basis for the large literature on **endogenous growth** that has emerged in the last 2 decades. To say more about this, however, we first return to Solow's original application.

Because of its importance, the properties of the Solow residual have been intensively studied; Hall (1990) is a notable contribution. Especially intriguing is the work of Basu and Fernald (1997, 2002). Instead of the traditional derivation of the Solow residual that we have presented, which is based on the marginal

---

[7] This is a different use of the term *residual* than we have defined it in connection with the regression model.

productivity theory of income distribution (and thus assumes competitive pricing) and an aggregate production function with constant returns to scale, they model the economy as an aggregation of heterogeneous firms that are not necessarily perfectly competitive and may not have constant returns.

7.3.3   Solow's Application

It is convenient to reexpress the growth accounting equation (7.27) in terms of the labor-intensive quantities $q = Q/L$ and $k = K/L$. From (6.50) of the previous chapter, the growth rates of intensive and nonintensive variables are related in the following way:

$$\frac{\dot{q}}{q} = \frac{\dot{Q}}{Q} - \frac{\dot{L}}{L},\tag{7.28}$$

and similarly for $\dot{k}$. Let us also assume what we know to be true for aggregate data: Factor shares sum to 1. (Recall that, from Euler's theorem, this is formally equivalent to assuming constant returns to scale.) In terms of the growth accounting equation, from (7.26) this allows us to impose $\epsilon_L = 1 - \epsilon_K$. Putting all this together, the growth accounting equation (7.27) may be restated as

$$\frac{\dot{q}}{q} = \frac{\dot{A}}{A} + \epsilon_K \frac{\dot{k}}{k}.\tag{7.29}$$

Hence, the rate of technical change may be deduced from data on output per worker-hour, capital per worker-hour, and the share of capital in national income—exactly the data given in Table 7.2. Like the earlier growth accounting equation, this is a general relationship that does not depend on any choice of a functional form for the production function.

   The results of Solow's calculations are given in Figure 7.6. Figure 7.6(a) plots the rate of technical change, and (b) plots a corresponding index A_t of TFP obtained using a base of $A_t = 1$ in the initial year $t = 1909$.[8] The latter series is also given

FIGURE 7.6

Solow's calculations.

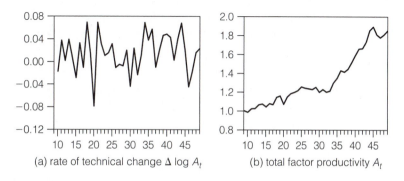

(a) rate of technical change $\Delta \log A_t$

(b) total factor productivity A_t

---

[8]   These are similar to Solow (1957, Charts 2 and 3).

in the last column of Table 7.2. Figure 7.6(a) indicates that, as we expect, the rate of technical change fluctuates considerably over time. In some years, it is actually negative, which may reflect factors other than technical change. Note in particular that the two largest negative shifts are associated with the ends of the two world wars. In reality, Solow's procedure picks up *any* factor shifting the production function and labels it technical change; the presumption is simply that other factors play a minor role and consequently that technical change is the primary influence being captured.[9] As is suggested by Figure 7.6(a) and confirmed by (b), the rate of technical change is on average positive. Solow noted further that this rate appears to be somewhat higher in the later half of the period than in the earlier half, a conjecture that we examine more closely in Exercise 7.9.

Although this development has assumed that technical change is Hicks neutral, as specified by (7.23), an appealing feature of Solow's procedure is that it may be shown to be independent of the form of the production function. Applying the same series of steps to the general function $Q = F(K, L; t)$ of equation (7.21) as we have applied to the separable form $Q = A(t)f(K, L)$ of equation (7.23), the following generalization of the intensive-form growth accounting equation (7.29) can be obtained:

$$\frac{\dot{q}}{q} = \frac{1}{F(\cdot)} \frac{\partial F(\cdot)}{\partial t} + \epsilon_K \frac{\dot{k}}{k}. \tag{7.30}$$

The first term on the right-hand side is analogous to $\dot{A}/A$ in that it represents the rate of technical change; as previously, the equation can be rearranged to solve for it. Hence, Solow's procedure yields an index of TFP even if technical progress is not Hicks neutral. However, the use of the index so obtained to estimate $f(\cdot)$ according to (7.24) still requires Hicks neutrality, and so the legitimacy of the form (7.23) continues to be of interest.

Exercises 7.9 and 7.10 guide you through Solow's original application of this methodology. As we have argued, if the rate of technical progress $\dot{F}/F$ is uncorrelated with the capital-labor ratio k then Hicks neutrality holds. You will find in Exercise 7.10, as Solow did, that in fact this condition appears to be satisfied for his data. Consequently, it is legitimate to take the form of the production function to be (7.23) and to make use of this in the estimation of $f(\cdot)$.

Because we have found the assumption of constant returns to scale to be inherent in the analysis, the estimation of $f(\cdot)$ may as well be done in intensive form:

$$q = \frac{Q}{L} = A(t)f(K/L, 1) = A(t)f(k). \tag{7.31}$$

In terms of the transformed dependent variable, this is

$$\frac{q}{A(t)} = f(k). \tag{7.32}$$

---

[9] This presumption can, of course, be challenged. Some analysts question whether the Solow residual usefully measures technical change. For a detailed exposition of this view, see Lipsey and Carlaw (2000).

FIGURE 7.7

Solow found
that productivity
increases are pri-
marily due to tech-
nical change rather
than capital accu-
mulation — shifts
upward in the pro-
duction function
rather than move-
ments along it.

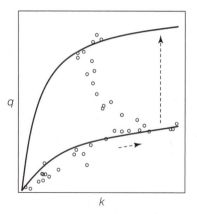

The only remaining issue is the choice of a functional form for $f(\cdot)$. Solow estimated several alternatives including the obvious one, a Cobb-Douglas function.
Exercise 7.10 provides you with an opportunity to replicate his results.

Technical Change versus Capital Accumulation

Equation (7.31) describes labor productivity q, measured by Solow as private nonfarm GNP per worker-hour, as being determined by two forces. One is k, the amount
of capital available to each worker. The other is the level of technology $A(t)$, for
which we now have a measure. Hence, productivity improvements can arise in two
ways. First, increases in k move the economy along the production function at a
given level of technology. Even if there were no technological progress, greater
capital per worker would increase output per worker. Second, technical change
shifts the production function upward. Even if measured k did not increase, productivity q would increase because technological progress improves the quality of
capital.

Figure 7.7 shows how productivity improvements arise from the combination
of these two forces: productivity increases both because capital accumulation moves
us along the production function *and* because technical change shifts the function
upward. What is the relative importance of these two influences?

Solow's figures provided the seminal, and at the time controversial, demonstration that the primary source of productivity growth is technical progress, not
capital accumulation.

> . . . over the 40 year period output per man hour approximately doubled. At the
> same time, according to [Figure 7.6(b)], the cumulative upward shift in the produc-
> tion function was about 80 percent. It is possible to argue that about one-eighth of
> the total increase is traceable to increased capital per man hour, and the remaining
> seven-eighths to technical change. The reasoning is this: real GNP per man hour
> increased from $0.623 to $1.275. Divide the latter figure by 1.809, which is the 1949
> value for $A(t)$, and therefore the full shift factor for the 40 years. The result is a

"corrected" GNP per man hour, net of technical change, of $0.705. Thus about 8 cents of the 65 cent increase can be imputed to increased capital intensity, and the remainder to increased productivity [associated with technical change].[10] (Solow, 1957, p. 316)

Another way of reaching the same conclusion is to consider the average growth rates of productivity and TFP. The log-differences of Solow's productivity and TFP series in Table 7.2 average to $\Delta \log q = 0.0179$ and $\Delta \log A = 0.0154$, so that the 1.79% average growth in GNP per man-hour was approximately 86% attributable to technical change and only approximately 14% due to capital accumulation.

Just as providing a secretary with additional 1980-vintage typewriters would result in only modest (if any) productivity gains, so too providing society with additional 1909-vintage carriages and oil lamps could not have generated the increases in output per worker that had taken place by 1949. Instead, these productivity improvements were largely due to the vast technical progress, and the accompanying accumulation of knowledge, that occurred during the period—electrification; the production line; the automobile, airplane, and telephone; and the great number of other innovations that we today take for granted.

Concluding Comments

In Section 1.2.3 we discuss the difference between ex post accounting identities and ex ante behavior. Interesting and useful as growth accounting may be, it is, as its name indicates, nevertheless purely an *accounting* exercise. By itself it tells us nothing about ex ante behavior—the economic forces that generate the numbers yielded by these accounting decompositions. We turn to an ex ante theory of economic growth in Chapter 9.

For 30 years following Solow's analysis, the technical progress measured by the Solow residual was taken as given (that is, as exogenous) in economic models. This was rather unsatisfactory in that it meant that the lion's share of the forces underlying economic growth were taken as not being amenable to economic analysis. In recent decades, a large literature on **endogenous growth** has developed in an attempt to explain technical progress as the outcome of economic decisions. Several advanced texts treat these developments, notably Aghion and Howitt (1998), Barro and Sala-i-Martin (1995), and Romer (2001, Chap. 3). A textbook introduction suitable for undergraduates is Jones (2002). For an applied orientation with much discussion of the economics of technical change, see Ruttan (2001).

A key concept in this literature is the distinction between human and physical capital, which we say more about in Chapter 9. Topel (1999) is an excellent and relatively accessible survey of human capital in endogenous growth. It includes

---

[10] More recent evidence suggests that Solow's conclusion that approximately seven-eighths of GNP growth is due to technical progress is an overestimate. Most economists now put the proportion at closer to two-thirds. See Cooley and Prescott (1995, p. 11).

THEORY MEETS APPLICATION

7.1

Growth Accounting and the East Asian Tigers

Robert Solow's analysis showed that, for the United States in the period he studied, the increase in living standards arose primarily from technical change rather than an increase in the capital-labor ratio.

This finding would not necessarily hold for all historical episodes in all countries. Young (1995) used growth accounting to study the sources of growth in the East Asian tiger economies of Hong Kong, Singapore, South Korea, and Taiwan for the period 1966–1990, when these economies were experiencing remarkable growth. He found the following growth rates for total output and TFP.

	Output(%)	*TFP(%)*
Hong Kong	7.3	2.3
Singapore	8.7	0.2
South Korea	10.3	1.7
Taiwan	9.4	2.6

Notice that, although these output growth rates are exceptionally high, the TFP growth rates are not. The TFP growth rates are not greatly

different from Solow's average rate of 1.54% for the U.S. economy in 1909–1949. The implication is that output growth in the East Asian tigers was largely due to growth in the conventional factor inputs labor and physical and human capital, and only to a small extent to technical change. For these economies to grow rapidly, it was not necessary to develop new technologies, only to adopt existing technologies and grow through the accumulation of conventional factors of production.

Although such growth is possible for a time, it is not possible indefinitely. Chapter 9 introduces the most important model of economic growth, also due to Solow. As we see in the appendix to that chapter, an important conclusion of that model is that in the long run sustained growth in living standards can only come from technical change. Only in the short run is it possible for productivity growth to arise from increases in the capital-labor ratio, the apparent source of the East Asian miracle.

an insightful discussion of the relationship between ex post growth accounting exercises and ex ante theories of endogenous growth, including a thorough assessment of Young's analysis of the East Asian tigers described in Theory Meets Application 7.1.

EXERCISES

7.7 Starting with (7.27) and the assumption of constant returns to scale, use (7.28) (and the analogous relation arising from the definition $k = K/L$) to derive (7.29).

7.8 Starting with (7.21), derive (7.30).

7.9 💿 **solow.dat** Solow's data for the years 1909–1949 on the share of property in income

ϵ_{Kt}, private nonfarm GNP per worker-hour q_t, and employed capital per worker-hour k_t are presented in Table 7.2 and are available in the file **solow.dat**.

(a) In Section 6.2.1 of the previous chapter we see that an instantaneous growth rate such as $\dot{q}/q$ is measured by the log-difference

$$\Delta \log q_t = \log q_t - \log q_{t-1}. \qquad (7.33)$$

Compute log-differences of Solow's series on q and k. (Remember that in defining the lagged variable you lose an observation from the series, and so the growth rates are defined for $t = 1910$–1949.) Plot both growth rate series. What is the average growth rate of GNP per worker-hour? Of capital per worker-hour?

(b) Use (7.29) to obtain a series for $\Delta \log A_t$. Plot this series. Does your plot reproduce Figure 7.6(a)? Compute the average rate of technical progress. Solow (1957, p. 316) concluded that "The over-all result for the whole 40 years is an average upward shift of about 1.5 per cent per year." Does this correspond with your finding?

(c) Solow (1957, p. 316) further noted that

> There is some evidence that the average rate of progress in the years 1909–29 was smaller than that from 1930–49. The first 21 relative shifts average about 9/10 of one per cent per year, while the last 19 average $2\frac{1}{4}$ per cent per year.

Split up your sample in the way suggested by Solow and compute the subsample means. In terms of growth rates notated as in (7.33), the first 21 relative shifts should correspond to $t = 1910$–1930 and the last 19 to $t = 1931$–1949. Are you able to verify Solow's figures? For future use (in Exercise 10.1) compute the subsample variances as well.

(d) An index of technical progress A_t may be obtained by choosing the base $A_t = 1$ at $t = 1909$ and computing successive values of A_t using your series for $\Delta \log A_t$. Use a hand calculator to do this for $t = 1910, 1911, 1912$. Show your work. How close do you come to reproducing Solow's values for this index given in Table 7.2?

(e) Technical progress is Hicks neutral, so that the production function takes on the separable form (7.23), if the rate of technical change is unrelated to the capital-labor ratio. Examine whether this

seems to hold for Solow's data by running the regression

$$\Delta \log A_t = \alpha + \beta k_t + \varepsilon_t.$$

How is the hypothesis of Hicks neutrality expressed as a coefficient restriction? What is the test outcome? What is your conclusion regarding the legitimacy of proceeding with the analysis on the basis of the separable form (7.23)?

7.10 solow.dat Solow's values for the index A_t are provided in the fourth column of Table 7.2.

(a) Compute the transformed dependent variable q_t/A_t. Produce a scatter plot of this against the explanatory variable k_t. Does your plot reveal a systematic relationship between these two variables worthy of investigation by regression analysis?

(b) Using the complete 1909–1949 sample, estimate (7.32) using a Cobb-Douglas (intensive) form for $f(\cdot)$. Solow obtained[11] $\hat{\beta} = 0.353$, an intercept of -0.729, and an R^2 of 0.999. How close do you come to replicating these values?

(c) One interpretation of your estimate of β is as capital's share of output. But of course historical data on this variable are available in the second column of Table 7.2. What is the average of these values? How does it compare with the estimate $\hat{\beta}$?

7.11 solow.dat An examination of Figure 7.5 suggested that a failure to recognize that technical progress shifts the aggregate production function will result in the overestimation of β.

(a) Suppose you fail to use the total factor productivity index A_t and, instead of (7.32), estimate the unmodified Cobb-Douglas intensive form (7.20). What is your estimate of β?

(b) Comparing your estimate with that obtained in Exercise 7.10, do you find that it does in fact overestimate? If so, by how much?

[11] Using the subsample 1909–1942.

7.4 Testing Marginal Productivity Conditions

In Section 7.2 we have seen how to estimate the Cobb-Douglas production function under constant returns to scale as a loglinear simple regression. However, beyond confirming that $0 < \hat{\beta} < 1$, so that output is increasing in the factor inputs in a manner that is characterized by diminishing marginal returns, at no point have we tested whether the Cobb-Douglas specification is a reasonable one. It would be preferable if the theory embodied some prediction that was potentially falsifiable by the data, so estimation results could be used to judge whether the model was actually supported empirically. Is there any way of doing this?

7.4.1 The Cobb-Douglas Production Function

Instead of focusing on the production function directly, as we have done so far, note that the analysis of Section 7.2 has provided a number of subsidiary relationships that potentially fill this role. Consider, for example, the marginal productivity condition for labor (7.16):

$$\frac{w}{p} = f_L = \alpha \frac{Q}{L}. \tag{7.34}$$

In terms of nominal (i.e., money) wages and the value of output $V \equiv pQ$, this may equivalently be written as

$$\frac{V}{L} = \frac{1}{\alpha} w,$$

or, using logarithms to convert this multiplicative relationship to an additive one and introducing a disturbance in the usual manner,

$$\log(V/L)_i = -\log \alpha + \log w_i + \varepsilon_i. \tag{7.35}$$

Why is this marginal productivity condition of interest? Because it predicts a relationship between variables that may be either confirmed or rejected by the data and in this sense offers a test of whether the underlying theory that has led to (7.35) is reasonable. Note that V/L, output per worker, and w, the wage rate, are readily measurable variables, and (7.35) predicts something very specific about the relationship between them: The slope coefficient β in a regression of $\log(V/L)$ on $\log w$ should equal 1. The hypothesis $H_0: \beta = 1$ is, of course, testable against the alternative $H_A: \beta \neq 1$ using a t test.

In a classic study Arrow, Chenery, Minhas, and Solow (1961) (henceforth ACMS) did exactly this. On the premise that in mature industries essentially the same production technology is available everywhere, they collected cross-country data on output per worker and wages and estimated simple regressions of the form[12]

$$\log(V/L)_i = \text{intercept} + \beta \log w_i + \varepsilon_i \tag{7.36}$$

---

[12] At this point we return to the standard simple regression notation in which β denotes the slope coefficient rather than a parameter of the production function.

TABLE 7.3   Data for the Dairy Products Industry

Country	L/V	w
United States (1954)	0.1256	3833
Canada (1954)	0.1860	2751
New Zealand (1955/56)	0.2003	2053
Australia (1955/56)	0.2638	1886
Denmark (1954)	0.3758	1314
Norway (1954)	0.3170	1228
United Kingdom (1951)	0.5077	972
Ireland (1953)	0.5019	910
Puerto Rico (1952)	0.3180	1234
Colombia (1953)	0.3480	937
Mexico (1951)	0.6188	495
Argentina (1950)	0.7437	396
El Salvador (1951)	0.5388	501
Southern Rhodesia (1952)	0.7294	536
Ceylon (1952)	0.5960	412
Japan (1953)	0.5920	501

Source: Arrow, K.J., Chenery, H.B., Minhas, B.S., and R.M. Solow "Capital-Labor Substitution and Economic Efficiency," *Review of Economics and Statistics* 43, 225–250, © 1961 MIT Press Journals. Reprinted with permission from MIT Press Journals.

for 24 industries. The variables were measured in the following ways:

V annual value added in thousands of U.S. dollars.

L labor input in man-years.

w money wage rate (total labor cost divided by L) in dollars per man-year.

The data for one industry, dairy products, are shown in Table 7.3. For example, for Canada $L/V = 0.1860$, so that the average Canadian dairy products worker produced $5376 in 1954, in current U.S. dollars. Similarly $w = 2751$, indicating that the same worker had an annual income of $2751.

EXAMPLE 5

 dairy.dat

Estimate the ACMS marginal productivity condition using the data of Table 7.3. Is the restriction $\beta = 1$ supported?

SOLUTION

An estimation of (7.36) for the dairy products industry yields

$$\log(V/L)_i = -4.01 + \underset{(0.0552)}{0.719} \ \log w_i + e_i, \qquad \text{SSE} = 0.31557.$$

(The SSE is reported for future reference in Chapter 10.) The t statistic for the hypothesis $\beta = 1$ is $t = (0.719 - 1)/0.0552 = -5.09$, which for $n - 2 = 14$ degrees of freedom rejects at conventional significance levels. (The p-value is 0.00016.) Hence, the data do not support this restriction.

TABLE 7.4   Results of ACMS Study

Industry	Intercept	$\hat{\beta}$	$\overline{R}^2$	n	p-value for H_0: $\beta = 1$
Dairy products	0.419	0.721	0.921	16	0.00016
Fruit and vegetable canning	0.355	0.855	0.910	14	0.07304
Grain and mill products	0.429	0.909	0.855	16	0.36306
Bakery products	0.304	0.900	0.927	16	0.16159
Sugar	0.431	0.781	0.790	13	0.08288
Tobacco	0.564	0.753	0.629	15	0.12758
Textiles	0.296	0.809	0.892	18	0.01033
Knitting mills	0.270	0.785	0.915	15	0.00511
Lumber and wood	0.279	0.860	0.910	18	0.04767
Furniture	0.226	0.894	0.952	16	0.06856
Pulp and paper	0.478	0.965	0.858	16	0.72931
Printing and publishing	0.284	0.868	0.940	16	0.03622
Leather finishing	0.292	0.857	0.921	14	0.03506
Basic chemicals	0.460	0.831	0.898	16	0.03360
Fats and oils	0.515	0.839	0.869	14	0.09814
Miscellaneous chemicals	0.483	0.895	0.938	16	0.09914
Clay products	0.273	0.919	0.878	13	0.42899
Glass	0.285	0.999	0.921	13	0.98973
Ceramics	0.210	0.901	0.974	12	0.19661
Cement	0.560	0.920	0.770	12	0.60343
Iron and steel	0.363	0.811	0.936	13	0.00983
Non-ferrous metals	0.370	1.011	0.886	10	0.93732
Metal products	0.301	0.902	0.897	13	0.29037
Electric machinery	0.344	0.870	0.804	14	0.29092

Source: Adapted from Arrow, K.J., Chenery, H.B., Minhas, B.S., and R.M. Solow "Capital-Labor Substitution and Economic Efficiency," *Review of Economics and Statistics* 43, 225–250. © 1961 MIT Press Journals. Reprinted with permission from MIT Press Journals.

It turns out that this finding for the dairy products industry is fairly typical of the ACMS results. These are summarized in Table 7.4, which is adapted from their journal article.[13] For most industries they found that the hypothesis of a unitary slope coefficient was rejected, suggesting that the Cobb-Douglas production function does not adequately describe the production process. Why might this be?

[13] The results are taken from Table 2 of the ACMS article, with the exception of the p-values, which have been obtained independently. The $\overline{R}^2$ is the adjusted R^2 defined in Chapter 8. The estimate of β reported by ACMS for the dairy products industry is slightly different from that obtained in Example 5, reflecting the fact that the ACMS results were obtained using mechanical calculators. Their intercept estimate is, on the other hand, dramatically different to an extent not attributable to calculation precision. You are asked to investigate why in Exercise 7.14.

As our discussion of functional forms for demand relationships in Section 6.1 reveals, any choice of a particular parametric specification for a functional relationship involves certain (typically implicit) restrictions on the nature of the underlying behavior that is being described. The Cobb-Douglas production function is attractive because it allows for diminishing returns and alternative returns-to-scale possibilities while having the plausible implication of constant factor shares. But are there any respects in which this parametric form might be regarded as unduly limiting? One important feature of any production process that we have not yet considered is the nature of substitution possibilities between factors. Let us investigate the implications of the Cobb-Douglas form for factor substitutability.

7.4.2 Factor Substitutability

The substitution possibilities permitted by any production technology are described by the curvature of its **production isoquants.** An isoquant, such as the one depicted by the solid line in Figure 7.8(a), is simply a plot of the alternative (K, L) combinations that could be used to produce a particular level of output Q. Higher levels of Q are associated with isoquants further from the origin.

FIGURE 7.8

Alternative substitution possibilities. MRTS, marginal rate of technical substitution.

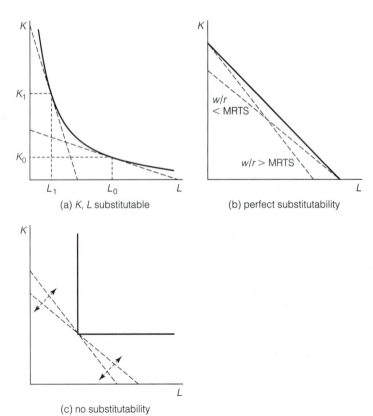

(a) K, L substitutable

(b) perfect substitutability

(c) no substitutability

It is apparent in Figure 7.8(a) that K and L are substitutable; this level of output may be produced with an infinite number of combinations of the two inputs. Starting at a particular combination such as (K_0, L_0), it is possible to reduce the amount of labor to L_1 as long as we substitute for it an increased quantity of capital K_1. However, the rates at which the two may be substituted vary; for example, at a low level of labor such as L_1 a great deal of additional capital must be employed to compensate for any additional reduction in L. Starting at (K_0, L_0), on the other hand, the same reduction in L could be accomplished by substituting a much smaller amount of capital. It makes sense that most production technologies are likely to be of this type, and this is the nature of the isoquants implied by the Cobb-Douglas production function.

Because the rate at which the factors may be substituted is described by the slope of the isoquant, it can be characterized mathematically. The absolute value of this slope is given by

$$\text{MRTS} = \frac{f_L}{f_K},$$

which is called the **marginal rate of technical substitution** (MRTS).

Substitution Possibilities

Although in general the MRTS varies with the capital-labor ratio (that is, it changes as we move along an isoquant such as that pictured in Figure 7.8(a)), there are two special cases in which the rate at which the two inputs may be substituted is fixed. One is when the isoquants are linear, as depicted in Figure 7.8(b). In this case the inputs are said to be **perfectly substitutable,** in the sense that the rate at which they can be substituted is constant regardless of the capital-labor ratio.

At the other extreme there may be no substitutability at all between inputs. Instead production may require that the factors be combined in fixed proportions. The associated isoquants are shown in Figure 7.8(c) and indicate that a reduction in one factor input cannot be compensated for by an increase in the other. In this case, MRTS $= 0$. Such a production process is called a Leontief technology, after the Nobel prize-winning economist Wassily Leontief (1906–1999), who was the first to study fixed-proportions technologies in detail.

Given that, with the exception of Leontief technologies, output may be produced using an infinite number of capital-labor combinations, how does a firm choose a particular capital-labor ratio with which to operate? As we suggest in Section 7.2, by minimizing costs. In the long run, all costs are variable and total production costs are

$$C = rK + wL. \tag{7.37}$$

Hence, the capital-labor combinations associated with a particular level of costs C are described by the **isocost line**

$$K = \frac{C}{r} - \frac{w}{r}L.$$

These are shown by dashed lines in each of the three panels of Figure 7.8. The slope of the line is $-w/r$ and describes the rate at which the firm may trade units of one input for the other, this rate depending on the relative prices.

In choosing the least-cost combination of inputs, a firm seeks to attain the lowest isocost line consistent with the level of output it wishes to produce. The result is that the point at which the isocost line is tangent to the isoquant determines a unique choice of capital and labor, as depicted in Figure 7.8(a). Equivalently, the firm operates so that the MRTS equals the ratio of factor prices:

$$\frac{f_L}{f_K} = \frac{w}{r}. \tag{7.38}$$

A firm responds to a change in factor prices by choosing an alternative least-cost combination of factor inputs. This is depicted in Figure 7.8(a). An increase in the price of labor w in relation to that of capital r, for example, increases the ratio of factor prices w/r and therefore results in a more steeply sloped isocost line. The new point of tangency is associated with a higher level of K and a lower level of L. Hence, when labor becomes relatively more expensive the firm substitutes away from labor toward capital, increasing the capital-labor ratio.

An extreme form of this substitution is shown in Figure 7.8(b), in which the isoquant is linear. In this case, depending on the relative slopes of the isocost line and the isoquant, the firm produces entirely using labor or capital. A change in factor prices from $w/r < $ MRTS to $w/r > $ MRTS would cause the firm to shift entirely out of labor and into capital. The only circumstance under which both might be used would be if $w/r = $ MRTS and the two lines happen to coincide, in which case the firm would be indifferent among the infinite number of (K, L) combinations on the line.

Finally, Figure 7.8(c) shows that for a Leontief technology the absence of substitution possibilities means that a change in factor prices does not affect the least-cost combination of inputs. The fixed-proportions nature of the production technology means that the firm is obliged to employ a fixed capital-labor ratio regardless of the relative costs of the factors.

The Elasticity of Substitution

Given the importance of the substitution possibilities embodied in the curvature of production isoquants, it is useful to have a measure of this curvature. Notice that the MRTS is *not* such a measure: It describes the slope of the isoquants at a point, not their curvature. For example, the isoquant in Figure 7.8(a) has, at the appropriate point, the same MRTS as the linear isoquant in Figure 7.8(b), yet the substitution possibilities are entirely different. A measure of the curvature should indicate the change in the capital-labor ratio that will take place as we move along the isoquant—that is, in response to changes in the slope of the isocost line, the absolute value of which is w/r. Furthermore, as is always preferable in economics, such a measure of substitutability should be in the form of an elasticity so that it is dimensionless. This is the basis for the definition of the **elasticity of substitution:**[14]

$$\sigma \equiv \frac{(w/r)}{(K/L)} \frac{\mathrm{d}(K/L)}{\mathrm{d}(w/r)} = \frac{(f_L/f_K)}{(K/L)} \frac{\mathrm{d}(K/L)}{\mathrm{d}(f_L/f_K)}.$$

This is the percentage change in the K/L ratio associated with a 1% change in the ratio of factor prices. The final expression arises from the knowledge (7.38) that the MRTS equals the ratio of factor prices and makes it possible to evaluate the elasticity of substitution entirely on the basis of a chosen production function and without reference to factor prices at all.

Using the interpretation of an elasticity in terms of natural logarithms presented in equation (6.10), the elasticity of substitution can be defined equivalently as

$$\sigma \equiv \frac{\mathrm{d}\ln(K/L)}{\mathrm{d}\ln(w/r)} = \frac{\mathrm{d}\ln(K/L)}{\mathrm{d}\ln(f_L/f_K)}. \tag{7.39}$$

The Cobb-Douglas Case

Let us evaluate this for the Cobb-Douglas production function. Note first that, for a Leontief technology such as that shown in Figure 7.8(c), the elasticity of substitution is zero: A change in factor prices does not change K/L. For a linear isoquant such as that in Figure 7.8(b), on the other hand, the elasticity of substitution is infinite: An appropriate change in w/r shifts the firm entirely away from the exclusive use of one factor and entirely into the other. Hence, in general, $0 \le \sigma < \infty$, and it is to be expected that the Cobb-Douglas function with isoquants such as those in Figure 7.8(a) will yield a value for σ in this range.

From (7.13b) and (7.14b) note that, in the Cobb-Douglas case, the ratio of the marginal products is

$$\frac{f_L}{f_K} = \frac{\alpha Q/L}{\beta Q/K} = \frac{\alpha}{\beta} \frac{K}{L}. \tag{7.40}$$

The capital-labor ratio can therefore be written as

$$\frac{K}{L} = \frac{\beta}{\alpha} \frac{f_L}{f_K}. \tag{7.41}$$

Taking the logarithms of both sides and applying the elasticity definition (7.39), it is apparent that the elasticity of substitution of the Cobb-Douglas production function is

$$\sigma = \frac{\mathrm{d}\ln(K/L)}{\mathrm{d}\ln(f_L/f_K)} = 1.$$

---

[14] The use of the Greek letter sigma to denote an elasticity of substitution is conventional in microeconomics. We use the slanted symbol σ to distinguish it from a standard deviation σ; the two are not to be confused.

This means that, despite all the attractive features we have discussed, the Cobb-Douglas production function presumes something very specific, and potentially unduly restrictive, about the nature of factor substitutability. It assumes that a 1% decline in one factor can always be compensated for by a 1% increase in the other and that this is true at all points on the production isoquant. It is, of course, perfectly conceivable that in the real world this is not an acceptable approximation to reality. In turn, this restrictive feature of the function may account for its rejection in an empirical context, just as occurred in the ACMS analysis.

Why Focus on the Marginal Productivity Condition for Labor?

As a final empirical point, recall that equation (7.35) is derived from the expression (7.14b) for the marginal product of labor. Our focus on this particular expression may seem, and to some extent is, arbitrary. We could as easily transform (7.13b) in an analogous manner into an equation that could be estimated given data on V/K and r. Equation (7.41) is another example of a relationship between variables predicted by the Cobb-Douglas function that, in combination with (7.38), could in principle provide the basis for estimation and testing.

Why did ACMS choose to base their empirical work on (7.35)? The answer has to do with data issues rather than any theoretical consideration. Comparing (7.35) with the other possibilities suggested, note that it is the only relationship that requires data on neither the capital stock K nor the rental price of capital r. It can be estimated solely with data on output V and labor-related variables—the wage w and labor input L. The measurement of these variables is relatively straightforward and so comparatively good data exist on them, even in less-developed economies. In contrast, although the rental price of capital r is conceptually well defined (as the price that must be paid to hire a representative unit of capital for one period), in terms of measurable quantities it is somewhat amorphous because most firms own most of their capital. Similarly, the measurement of the capital stock involves subjective judgements that may lead to variations in both its definition and the quality of the measurements internationally. In order to avoid these data problems, it makes sense to estimate a relationship involving variables on which the highest quality data are likely to be available.

7.4.3   The Constant Elasticity of Substitution Production Function

Is there an alternative production function that permits more general substitution possibilities? Their empirical findings led ACMS to propose the **constant elasticity of substitution** (CES) production function:

$$Q = f(K, L) = \gamma[\delta K^{-\rho} + (1 - \delta)L^{-\rho}]^{-\nu/\rho}. \tag{7.42}$$

As its name suggests, this function implies a value for σ that is constant at all points on the isoquant, but that may differ from unity. The parameters of the function govern the essential features of the production technology in much the same way that the parameters of the Cobb-Douglas function did and must satisfy certain restrictions. The parameters are:

γ,	the efficiency parameter:	$\gamma > 0.$
ν,	the degree of homogeneity:	$\nu > 0.$
δ,	the distribution parameter:	$0 < \delta < 1.$
ρ,	the substitution parameter:	$-1 < \rho < \infty, \rho \neq 0.$

Let us consider some of the features of this function and the basis for these restrictions by investigating the role of each parameter.

The efficiency parameter γ plays the same role that it did in the Cobb-Douglas function: It permits shifts in production efficiencies across firms or over time. Because this is not important for the issues that presently concern us, it is useful to simplify the derivations that follow by setting $\gamma = 1$. In situations in which γ is to be estimated, it should be that $\gamma > 0$ so that increases in factor inputs yield increased output.

The degree of homogeneity ν governs returns to scale, as may be confirmed by multiplying both K and L by a factor λ and noting that the result is a λ^{ν}-fold increase in Q:

$$\gamma[\delta(\lambda K)^{-\rho}+(1-\delta)(\lambda L)^{-\rho}]^{-\nu/\rho} = \gamma(\lambda^{-\rho})^{-\nu/\rho}[\delta K^{-\rho}+(1-\delta)L^{-\rho}]^{-\nu/\rho} = \lambda^{\nu}Q.$$

Constant returns to scale, then, correspond to the case $\nu = 1$, and for simplicity in the derivations that follow we limit ourselves to this case. Because an elasticity of scale should not be negative—again, increases in all factor inputs should yield increased output—it must be that $\nu > 0$.

The distribution parameter δ is so called because it plays a role in determining the distribution of output into factor shares. This can be seen by examining the marginal product expressions, something that is most easily done by deriving these for the special case of $\nu = 1$. The marginal products of capital and labor are

$$f_K = \frac{\partial Q}{\partial K} = \delta \left(\frac{Q}{K}\right)^{1+\rho}, \tag{7.43a}$$

$$f_L = \frac{\partial Q}{\partial L} = (1-\delta)\left(\frac{Q}{L}\right)^{1+\rho}. \tag{7.43b}$$

These may usefully be compared with the analogous expressions (7.13b) and (7.14b) for the Cobb-Douglas function. The ratio of these marginal products is

$$\frac{f_L}{f_K} = \frac{1-\delta}{\delta}\left(\frac{K}{L}\right)^{1+\rho}, \tag{7.44}$$

which may be compared with equation (7.40) of the Cobb-Douglas derivation. An inspection of the marginal products (7.43) reveals that, for them to be positive (as marginal products should normally be), it must be that $0 < \delta < 1$. Hence, this is the restriction given for this parameter.

Because δ influences the marginal products that, under the marginal productivity theory of distribution, equal factor prices and thus help determine factor shares, it is apparent that δ governs the distribution of output as factor payments. Another way of seeing this is by using the condition (7.38) characterizing cost minimization and, multiplying through by L/K, noting that the ratio of factor payments is

$$\frac{wL}{rK} = \frac{f_L}{f_K}\frac{L}{K} = \frac{1-\delta}{\delta}\left(\frac{K}{L}\right)^\rho.$$

Thus, the distribution of output into relative factor payments is governed by δ, as well as being affected by the capital-labor ratio and the parameter ρ. Within the range $0 < \delta < 1$, an increase in δ toward 1 shifts factor payments in favor of capital, whereas a decrease toward 0 shifts them in favor of labor.

The substitution parameter ρ governs the degree of factor substitutability. Let us examine this by deriving the elasticity of substitution of the CES production function using the definition (7.39). This is easily done because, rearranging (7.44), an expression for the capital-labor ratio is

$$\frac{K}{L} = \left(\frac{\delta}{1-\delta}\right)^{1/(1+\rho)}\left(\frac{f_L}{f_K}\right)^{1/(1+\rho)}.$$

Taking logarithms of both sides, it follows that

$$\sigma = \frac{d\ln(K/L)}{d\ln(f_L/f_K)} = \frac{1}{1+\rho}.$$

This confirms that ρ governs the curvature of the isoquants of the CES production function.

The relationship between ρ and the elasticity of substitution σ is summarized in Table 7.5. As $\rho \to -1$ clearly $\sigma \to \infty$, so this is the limiting case of perfect substitution. At the other extreme, as $\rho \to \infty$ it is the case that $\sigma \to 0$, corresponding to the limiting case of a fixed-proportions production process. Because σ must fall in this range, this explains the restriction $-1 < \rho < \infty$ specified in (7.42). Finally, although it is not legitimate to set $\rho = 0$ because this would lead to division by zero in (7.42), ACMS were able to show that as $\rho \to 0$ the CES production function reduces to the Cobb-Douglas form as a special case. In this instance, the appropriate value for the elasticity of substitution is, therefore, unity.

Hence, the CES production function is more general than the Cobb-Douglas. It possesses many of the same attractive features, providing for diminishing marginal returns and alternative returns to scale possibilities, and it permits as well more general substitution possibilities between factors. Although the CES isoquants have

TABLE 7.5   Relationship between ρ and σ

	Limiting value of	
Technology	ρ	σ
Leontief	∞	0
Cobb-Douglas	0	1
Perfect substitution	-1	∞

a constant elasticity of substitution at all points, σ may take on values in the full range $0 < \sigma < \infty$ between the extremes of perfect substitutability and a complete absence of substitutability.

Estimating the Marginal Productivity Condition

What are the implications of these considerations for empirical work; in particular, the interpretation of a regression such as (7.36)? Note first that the CES production function is an example of a model that is intrinsically nonlinear in parameters. It cannot be converted to a linear regression model by taking logarithms.[15] The obvious alternative route to examining the function empirically (and the only one that was available to ACMS at the time) is to estimate subsidiary relationships that can be converted to a linear form.

This was done previously for the Cobb-Douglas function by considering its marginal productivity condition for labor (7.34) and transforming this into the regression model (7.35). Let us proceed in the same way to examine the marginal productivity condition for labor of the CES function. Using the marginal product expression (7.43b) and the implication of profit maximization that $f_L = w/p$, this is

$$\frac{w}{p} = f_L = (1-\delta)\left(\frac{Q}{L}\right)^{1+\rho}, \tag{7.45}$$

which is analogous to (7.34). For convenience, define $p = 1$ so that output $Q = V$ is measured in value terms. This can be inverted as

$$\frac{V}{L} = \left(\frac{1}{1-\delta}w\right)^{1/(1+\rho)}.$$

Finally, taking logarithms and introducing a disturbance in the usual manner yields

$$\log(V/L)_i = -\frac{1}{1+\rho}\log(1-\delta) + \frac{1}{1+\rho}\log w_i + \varepsilon_i. \tag{7.46}$$

This is a loglinear regression model of the same form as (7.36). Consequently, although the regressions of $\log(V/L)$ on $\log w$ run by ACMS were presented in Section 7.2 as estimations of the marginal productivity condition of the Cobb-Douglas function, they may now be seen to represent the estimation of the analogous condition for the CES function.

Note further that the CES marginal productivity condition (7.46) possesses as its slope the expression

$$\sigma = \frac{1}{1+\rho},$$

which is the elasticity of substitution! Hence, the slope estimates presented by ACMS are estimates of the elasticity of substitution. Their finding that the restriction $\sigma = 1$ is often rejected is evidence that the Cobb-Douglas assumption of a

---

[15] In fact, in Chapter 13 the CES function is used as an application of nonlinear regression.

unitary elasticity of substitution is not satisfied in these industries. This suggests that the less restrictive CES function offers a better description of the production technology in these industries.

EXERCISES

7.12 Considering the CES form (7.42) under constant returns to scale, derive the marginal product expressions (7.43a) and (7.43b).

7.13 ♪ The marginal product expressions (7.43a) and (7.43b) are special cases based on $\gamma = \nu = 1$. The more general expressions are

$$f_K = \frac{\partial Q}{\partial K} = \nu \gamma^{-\rho/\nu} \delta \frac{Q^{1+(\rho/\nu)}}{K^{1+\rho}},$$

$$f_L = \frac{\partial Q}{\partial L} = \nu \gamma^{-\rho/\nu} (1 - \delta) \frac{Q^{1+(\rho/\nu)}}{L^{1+\rho}}.$$

Use these to show that even in this more general case the elasticity of substitution is still $1/(1 + \rho)$.

7.14 💿 **marginal productivity conditions** Choose one of the industries considered by ACMS and use their data to estimate the marginal productivity condition (7.36). (Data for two industries, dairy products and basic chemicals, are contained in the files **dairy.dat** and **basichem.dat**; you may want to use the former to verify the results of Example 5.) In generating the dependent variable do not forget to invert their L/V series. Because data on all industries were not available in all countries, not all industries have the same number of observations.

(a) Compare your results with those of ACMS, reproduced in Table 7.4.

i. Is your $\hat{\beta}$ the same as (or very close to) the value reported by ACMS?

ii. Is your R^2 close to the coefficient of determination that they report? (Their $\overline{R}^2$ is the "adjusted coefficient of determination" discussed in the next chapter.)

iii. Is your intercept the same?

(b) ♪ What accounts for the difference in the estimated intercept? That is, what would you have to do differently to reproduce the ACMS intercept estimate? (*Hint*: Reflect on your answers to Exercises 6.1 and 6.3.)

(c) The analysis of this chapter has made you aware that, under the assumption of a CES production function, β has the interpretation of the elasticity of substitution σ.

i.   Test the hypothesis $\beta = 0$. Because an elasticity of substitution must be positive, note that the appropriate alternative hypothesis is one-sided. Can your industry be described satisfactorily by a Leontief technology?

ii. If your software permits the calculation of a p-value for the hypothesis $\beta = 1$, do this. Are you able to reproduce the p-value reported in Table 7.4?

iii. Test the hypothesis $\beta = 1$. Can your industry be described satisfactorily by a Cobb-Douglas technology?

7.15 ACMS estimated (7.46), which is derived from (7.45). Consider the alternative of simply taking logarithms of (7.45) directly and estimating

$$\log w_i = \log(1 - \delta) + (1 + \rho) \log(V/L)_i + \varepsilon_i.$$

(a) As a purely mechanical matter, would it have been possible to proceed in this way?

(b) If so, why did they not?

7.16 From the CES production function we have seen that it is possible to derive the marginal product of capital (7.43a):

$$f_K = \delta \left(\frac{Q}{K} \right)^{1+\rho}.$$

(a) How can this be rearranged in the form of a regression equation in which the slope coefficient is the elasticity of substitution?
(b) How can f_K be measured (at least in principle)?

(c) Why did ACMS choose the marginal productivity condition for labor as the basis for their empirical work rather than the analogous condition for capital?

7.5   Conclusions

The CES production function provides a useful illustration of the means by which economics, and science generally, advances. Initially researchers work with a theory or model, in this case the Cobb-Douglas production function, that has been found useful in the study of particular issues or problems. In time the theory or model, as it is employed repeatedly in alternative empirical contexts, is found to be unsatisfactory in certain respects, in this instance in the treatment of factor substitutability. This motivates researchers to develop an alternative or more general understanding of the phenomenon under study.

This paradigm of scientific inquiry suggests three comments. First, the earlier theory may still be useful for certain purposes. Indeed, we have seen that the Cobb-Douglas production function continues to be widely employed in theoretical and empirical work by both micro- and macroeconomists. The **principle of parsimony** in model building suggests that, ceteris paribus, a simpler model is preferred to a more complex one.[16] Additional complexity is only useful if it helps us understand the phenomenon of interest. All models, and certainly economic models, are, after all, abstractions from reality and in this respect are ultimately "wrong." The question is whether they are "right" in the sense of providing some useful insight into the world we observe. As Robert Solow (1970, pp. 1–2) has argued,

> ... we are dealing with a drastically simplified story, a "parable" ... You ask of a parable not if it is literally true, but if it is well told. Even a well-told parable has limited applicability. There are always tacit or explicit assumptions underlying a simplified story. They may not matter for the point the parable is trying to make; that is what makes parables possible. When they do matter, the parable may mislead. There are always aspects of economic life that are left out of any simplified model. There will therefore be problems on which it throws no light at all; worse yet, there may

---

[16] The principle of parsimony is also called **Occam's razor.** William of Occam was a 14th-century English philosopher.

> Occam is best known for a maxim which is not to be found in his works, but has acquired the name of "Occam's razor." This maxim says: "Entities are not to be multiplied without necessity." Although he did not say this, he said something which has much the same effect, namely: "It is vain to do with more what can be done with fewer." That is to say, if everything in some science can be interpreted without assuming this or that hypothetical entity, there is no ground for assuming it. I have myself found this a most fruitful principle in logical analysis. (Russell 1945, p. 472)

be problems on which it appears to throw light, but on which it actually propagates error. It is sometimes difficult to tell one kind of situation from the other.

For many questions of interest it may not be important that the Cobb-Douglas production function makes a particular assumption about the degree of factor substitutability. The fact that Newtonian mechanics may be "wrong" from the perspective of relativity theory does not mean that it is useless; only that it may not be adequate to address all of the questions of physics.

Second, the new model will, in time, no doubt itself be found to be wanting in certain respects. In the case of the CES function, for some purposes it may not be acceptable to impose a constant elasticity on the production isoquants, even if this can take on any value. Instead it may be desirable to permit varying degrees of factor substitutability. The flexible functional form techniques mentioned in Section 6.6 and considered in more detail in Chapter 11 are, when applied to production economics, in part an attempt to accomplish this.

Finally, empirical methods are a key ingredient in scientific inquiry. Theorizing without reference to measured phenomena is meaningless because the ultimate objective of theory is to understand the world we observe. The role of econometrics is the exciting one of asking whether an economic model does this.

8 Multiple Regression

Our study of simple regression has been useful as an introduction to the study of relationships between variables. However, it is rarely the case that economists find it satisfactory to consider two variables in isolation; instead bivariate relationships must be studied in a way that controls for other influences or, in the language of economics, considers ceterus paribus effects. This is accomplished through multiple regression.

One reason for our emphasis on the analysis of the simple regression model is that to a large extent its extension to multiple regression is straightforward. This is true for the specification of the model, the derivation of the least squares estimators, the analysis of their properties, and further inference procedures.

8.1 Model Specification

The multiple regression model specifies that the mean of the dependent variable $E(Y_i)$ is a linear function, not of one but of a number of explanatory variables:

$$Y_i = \beta_1 + \beta_2 X_{2i} + \beta_3 X_{3i} + \cdots + \beta_K X_{Ki} + \varepsilon_i, \quad \varepsilon_i \sim \text{n.i.d.}(0, \sigma^2). \quad (8.1)$$

In this notation there are $K - 1$ explanatory variables $X_{2i}, \ldots, X_{Ki}$, each having observations $i = 1, \ldots, n$. Hence, X_{ki} denotes the ith observation on variable k $(k = 2, \ldots, K)$. In contrast to the notation of simple regression, it is now convenient to denote the intercept by β_1.

In Chapter 3 we see that this model can be obtained as a reparameterization of a multivariate normal distribution for the K variables $Y_i, X_{2i}, \ldots, X_{Ki}$, a reparameterization that afforded an economy of parameters that became greater as K increased. By this reasoning we have concluded that a linear relationship such as (8.1) follows if the variables are jointly normally distributed, and this continues to be a useful way to motivate our interest in linear models. Nevertheless, just as was true for simple regression, it is preferable to proceed with the analysis of the model assuming **nonstochastic regressors:** The X_{ki} will be taken to be nonrandom in the sense of being fixed in repeated sampling. The role of this assumption in the analysis of the model is exactly what it was in the case of simple regression—it greatly simplifies derivations without materially affecting the appropriate inference procedures, as long as in application stochastic regressors are uncorrelated with the model disturbance,

$$E(X_{ki}\varepsilon_i) = 0 \qquad (k = 2, \ldots, K).$$ (8.2)

The limitations of this assumption are discussed in Section 4.1.2. In addition, and again in analogy with the specification of the simple regression model, it is assumed that all the X_{ki} exhibit variation across their observations i; that is, condition (4.4) applies to each of the explanatory variables. As well, we continue to assume that the model is complete, in the sense discussed in Section 4.1.4.

Beyond this, only two further assumptions need be introduced. Both concern the explanatory variables, which is not surprising because this is the only respect in which multiple regression differs from simple regression. They are as follows.

Absence of perfect multicollinearity. No regressor may be an exact linear function of others. For example, it is not permitted that

$$X_{3i} = a + bX_{2i}.$$ (8.3)

If such an equality holds, then the information in one variable is essentially duplicated in the other; both are measuring the same underlying influence, similar to a change in units of measure, and it will not be possible to distinguish separate effects on Y_i. The formal implications of a violation of this assumption for the least squares estimators are considered in Section 8.7.1.

Adequate degrees of freedom. It is assumed that the number of coefficients K is less than the number of observations n on the basis of which they are to be estimated: $K < n$. The reason for this is most easily explained with reference to the simple regression model

$$Y_i = \alpha + \beta X_i + \varepsilon_i,$$

where $K = 2$. Suppose in this case that only $n = K = 2$ observations on each of X_i and Y_i are available. Then these two (X_i, Y_i) data points uniquely determine a line running through them that fits perfectly. There are no residuals, the third parameter σ^2 cannot be estimated, and so nothing can be learned about the variances of the sampling distributions of the coefficient estimators; in turn, there is no scope for hypothesis testing. This illustrates the general principle in statistics that a model is only estimable if there are at least as many observations as parameters. In simple regression, at least $n = 3$ observations are needed to estimate the three parameters α, β, and σ^2; in multiple regression, at least $n = K + 1$ observations are needed to estimate $\beta_1, \beta_2, \ldots, \beta_K$ and σ^2.

With these assumptions concerning the explanatory variables, we continue to refer to the model (8.1) as the **classical normal linear regression model;** the simple regression model is seen to be just a special case. The classical disturbance $\varepsilon_i \sim$ n.i.d.$(0, \sigma^2)$ is, of course, identical to that on which the analysis in Chapter 4 was based. It follows from the same underlying assumption of random sampling from a normal population distribution. The assumptions of homoskedasticity and nonautocorrelation imply the same limitations for the inference procedures developed in this chapter as are true for simple regression, limitations that are explored in later chapters.

The model specification (8.1), along with the assumption of nonstochastic regressors, means that the rules of mathematical expectation and variance may be applied to evaluate the mean and variance of Y_i as

$$E(Y_i) = \beta_1 + \beta_2 X_{2i} + \cdots + \beta_K X_{Ki} + E(\varepsilon_i)$$
$$= \beta_1 + \beta_2 X_{2i} + \cdots + \beta_K X_{Ki},$$
$$V(Y_i) = V(\varepsilon_i) = \sigma^2. \tag{8.4}$$

Furthermore, the fact that Y is a linear function of the normal random variable ε allows us to summarize the population distribution generating any Y_i as

$$Y_i \sim N(\beta_1 + \beta_2 X_{2i} + \cdots + \beta_K X_{Ki}, \sigma^2).$$

This is, of course, just a generalization of the simple regression model (4.2).

8.2 Least Squares Estimation

Let us now turn to the estimation of the multiple regression model (8.1), beginning with the coefficients. Coefficient estimators $\hat{\beta}_1, \hat{\beta}_2, \ldots, \hat{\beta}_K$ define fitted values $\hat{Y}_i$ lying on the sample regression line

$$\hat{Y}_i = \hat{\beta}_1 + \hat{\beta}_2 X_{2i} + \cdots + \hat{\beta}_K X_{Ki}, \tag{8.5}$$

and the residuals

$$e_i = Y_i - \hat{Y}_i = Y_i - \hat{\beta}_1 - \hat{\beta}_2 X_{2i} - \cdots - \hat{\beta}_K X_{Ki}. \tag{8.6}$$

Just as is the case in previous applications of the method in Chapters 2 and 4, the method of least squares chooses the $\hat{\beta}_k$ to be those values that minimize the sum of squares function

$$S = \sum_{i=1}^{n} (Y_i - EY_i)^2 = \sum_{i=1}^{n} (Y_i - \beta_1 - \beta_2 X_{2i} - \cdots - \beta_K X_{Ki})^2. \tag{8.7}$$

The difference is that now the solution to this minimization problem will involve K first-order conditions arising from the following derivatives:

$$\frac{\partial S}{\partial \beta_1} = \sum_{i=1}^{n} 2(Y_i - \beta_1 - \beta_2 X_{2i} - \cdots - \beta_K X_{Ki})(-1)$$

$$\frac{\partial S}{\partial \beta_2} = \sum_{i=1}^{n} 2(Y_i - \beta_1 - \beta_2 X_{2i} - \cdots - \beta_K X_{Ki})(-X_{2i})$$

$$\vdots$$

$$\frac{\partial S}{\partial \beta_K} = \sum_{i=1}^{n} 2(Y_i - \beta_1 - \beta_2 X_{2i} - \cdots - \beta_K X_{Ki})(-X_{Ki}).$$

Setting these equal to zero and canceling multiplicative constants yields the first-order conditions

$$\sum_{i=1}^{n}(Y_i - \hat{\beta}_1 - \hat{\beta}_2 X_{2i} - \cdots - \hat{\beta}_K X_{Ki}) = 0 \tag{8.8}$$

$$\sum_{i=1}^{n}(Y_i - \hat{\beta}_1 - \hat{\beta}_2 X_{2i} - \cdots - \hat{\beta}_K X_{Ki})X_{ki} = 0 \qquad (k = 2, \ldots, K).$$

These are a set of normal equations implicitly defining the least squares coefficient estimators; the carat notation is introduced to reflect this. Because the normal equations constitute K linear equations in the K unknown $\hat{\beta}_k$, they may be solved uniquely for closed form expressions for the estimators.

Properties of the Normal Equations

Several properties of the least squares sample regression line (8.5) can be recognized immediately from these first-order conditions. First, using the definition of the residuals (8.6), we have

$$\sum_{i=1}^{n} e_i = 0 \tag{8.9a}$$

$$\sum_{i=1}^{n} X_{ki} e_i = 0 \qquad (k = 2, \ldots, K). \tag{8.9b}$$

Both of these generalize properties of the least squares residuals established in simple regression. In the first instance, the residuals sum exactly to zero. In the second, the residuals e_i are orthogonal to each of the explanatory variables X_{ki} ($k = 2, \ldots, n$). The latter property is a sample analog of the population orthogonality conditions (8.2), suggesting that least squares is an estimation principle that is valuable in circumstances in which that population condition is satisfied.

Finally, applying the summation in (8.8) to each of the terms and multiplying through the equation by $1/n$, yields

$$\overline{Y} = \hat{\beta}_1 + \hat{\beta}_2 \overline{X}_2 + \cdots + \hat{\beta}_K \overline{X}_K. \tag{8.10}$$

The least squares sample regression line passes through the point of variable means $(\overline{Y}, \overline{X}_2, \ldots, \overline{X}_K)$, again generalizing this feature from the case of simple regression.

Although in principle it is possible to solve the K first-order conditions for closed-form solutions for the $\hat{\beta}_k$, in practice this is only conveniently done using matrix notation. This most general solution to the least squares estimation problem may be found in the appendix to this chapter. For present purposes it is more useful to note first that, rearranging (8.10), the intercept estimator may be expressed as

$$\hat{\beta}_1 = \overline{Y} - \hat{\beta}_2 \overline{X}_2 - \cdots - \hat{\beta}_K \overline{X}_K. \tag{8.11}$$

That is, given the slope estimators, the intercept can always be deduced by using the fact that the least squares sample regression line passes through the point of variable means.

Solution in the Special Case of $K = 3$

In the case of the slope coefficients, the nature of the solutions for the least squares estimators is usefully illustrated by considering the special case of $K = 3$, so that the regression model is

$$Y_i = \beta_1 + \beta_2 X_{2i} + \beta_3 X_{3i} + \varepsilon_i.$$

In this case of just two explanatory variables the least squares solutions are:

$$\hat{\beta}_2 = \frac{\sum x_{3i}^2 \sum x_{2i} y_i - \sum x_{2i} x_{3i} \sum x_{3i} y_i}{\sum x_{2i}^2 \sum x_{3i}^2 - (\sum x_{2i} x_{3i})^2}, \tag{8.12a}$$

$$\hat{\beta}_3 = \frac{\sum x_{2i}^2 \sum x_{3i} y_i - \sum x_{2i} x_{3i} \sum x_{2i} y_i}{\sum x_{2i}^2 \sum x_{3i}^2 - (\sum x_{2i} x_{3i})^2}. \tag{8.12b}$$

Note that each estimator is a function of all three variables Y_i, X_{2i}, and X_{3i}. The estimate of the effect of X_2 on Y depends not only on those two variables but also on X_3. In general, the least squares estimate of the effect of X_k on Y takes into account the behavior of all other explanatory variables. It is in this sense that least squares estimation of the slope coefficients seeks to measure the ceterus paribus effect of each regressor on the dependent variable by controlling for the influence of all other explanatory variables.

Examples

Let us consider two examples of least squares estimates of the coefficients of multiple regression models. The first is a case in which $K = 3$, so that the slopes are calculated according to the formulas (8.12).

EXAMPLE 1

cobbdoug.dat

In Section 6.1 we see that the Cobb-Douglas production function may be written as the multiple regression

$$\log Q_i = \log \gamma + \beta \log K_i + \alpha \log L_i + \varepsilon_i.$$

The slope coefficients α and β have the interpretations as the factor shares of labor and capital. Using the Cobb-Douglas data in Table 7.1, how close do the least squares estimates of these coefficients come to satisfying the constant returns to scale restriction $\alpha + \beta = 1$?

SOLUTION

Least squares yields the sample regression line

$$\log Q_i = -0.177 + 0.233 \log K_i + 0.807 \log L_i + e_i.$$

The slope coefficients are calculated according to (8.12), the intercept by (8.11). The slopes indicate that approximately 23% of output goes as a factor payment to capital and approximately 81% to labor. These coefficients sum to $\hat{\alpha} + \hat{\beta} = 1.04$, and so come remarkably close to satisfying constant returns to scale.

This example indicates that it is of interest to have a formal test of whether $\hat{\alpha} + \hat{\beta}$ is significantly different from 1, something that we develop in Chapter 10. Our next example is of three explanatory variables, so $K = 4$.

EXAMPLE 2

Theory Meets Application 4.1 discusses Jacob Mincer's work with statistical earnings functions. The version of his regression considered there was of the log of earnings Y on years of schooling X,

$$\log Y_i = 7.58 + 0.070X_i + e_i, \qquad R^2 = 0.067.$$

The interpretation of this slope coefficient was that an additional year of schooling increases income by 7%.

Mincer expanded this regression to include work experience Z. He obtained

$$\log Y_i = 6.20 + 0.107X_i + 0.081Z_i - 0.0012Z_i^2 + e_i, \qquad R^2 = 0.285.$$

The motivation for allowing experience to enter quadratically is that it permits a nonlinear pattern in the lifetime earnings profile. This is illustrated in Figure 8.1. Earnings tend to increase with experience, but only up to a point in mid-life when they peak. The quadratic specification permits this parabolic shape for the earnings profile. The return to an additional year of experience is

$$\frac{\partial \log Y}{\partial Z} = 0.081 - 2(0.0012)Z.$$

Whereas the analogous effect for education is a constant return, now estimated to be 10.7%, this return to experience depends on the level of experience itself. It declines in that level, so that there are diminishing returns to experience. Even at $Z = 0$ years of experience when the marginal return to experience is greatest—yielding an 8.1% increase in income—the return to a year of experience is still less than the return to a year of education.

The parabolic shape of the earnings profile that is permitted by this quadratic specification means that these diminishing returns eventually turn negative. This

FIGURE 8.1

Earnings peak in mid-life.

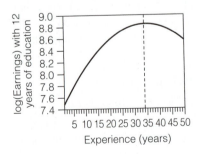

pattern only arises if the coefficient on Z_i is positive while that on Z_i^2 is negative, and so it is of interest that this is in fact the empirical finding.

According to Mincer's estimates, at what level of experience do earnings peak?

SOLUTION

The peak of earnings is also the peak of log earnings. Setting the derivative to zero and solving for Z, the parabola has its peak at $Z^* = 33.75$ years of experience. For Mincer's sample of white, nonfarm, nonstudent males, the earnings of the typical high school graduate peak in his early 50s.

Mincer's finding that the log of earnings is well described as linear in education and quadratic in experience is arguably the single most important empirical regularity in labor economics. Having illustrated the use of least squares multiple regression estimates, let us return to our formal analysis of the multiple regression model.

Estimating σ^2

Turning to the last parameter of the model, σ^2, our reasoning parallels exactly that of the simple regression case. The formal definition of σ^2 is

$$\sigma^2 = E(\varepsilon_i^2) = E(Y_i - EY_i)^2 = E(Y_i - \beta_1 - \beta_2 X_{2i} - \cdots - \beta_K X_{Ki})^2.$$

Although a function of population quantities and therefore unobservable, the ε_i disturbances are measured by the residuals (8.6). It follows that a natural estimator of the population variance σ^2 is an average involving the sum of squared residuals $\sum e_i^2$. Experience indicates that the denominator of this average will be critical in determining whether the resulting estimator is unbiased. It turns out that in this case the appropriate denominator is $n - K$. That is,

$$s^2 = \frac{1}{n-K} \sum_{i=1}^{n} e_i^2 = \frac{1}{n-K} \sum_{i=1}^{n} (Y_i - \hat{\beta}_1 - \hat{\beta}_2 X_{2i} - \cdots - \hat{\beta}_K X_{Ki})^2 \quad (8.13)$$

is an unbiased estimator for σ^2; it may be shown that $E(s^2) = \sigma^2$. Of course this reduces to the earlier formula (4.23) in simple regression where $K = 2$.

8.3 Properties of the Least Squares Estimators

What are the properties of the least squares coefficient estimators? Just as is true in the case of simple regression, they may be shown to be unbiased:

$$E(\hat{\beta}_k) = \beta_k \qquad \text{for all } k.$$

As well, under the assumption of a normal population distribution they are efficient: For the model (8.1) the $\hat{\beta}_k$ possess the minimum variance attainable by unbiased estimators.

What is this minimum variance? Just as for general K the coefficient estimators $\hat{\beta}_k$ are only conveniently expressed in matrix form, so too this is the case for their variance expressions. Once again, however, a great deal of insight can be obtained by considering the formulas that apply in the special case of $K = 3$. Variance expressions for (8.12a) and (8.12b) are:

$$\sigma_{\hat{\beta}_2}^2 = V(\hat{\beta}_2) = \frac{\sigma^2}{\sum x_{2i}^2 (1 - r_{23}^2)} \tag{8.14a}$$

$$\sigma_{\hat{\beta}_3}^2 = V(\hat{\beta}_3) = \frac{\sigma^2}{\sum x_{3i}^2 (1 - r_{23}^2)}, \tag{8.14b}$$

where r_{23} denotes the sample correlation (3.14c) between X_{2i} and X_{3i}:

$$r_{23} = \frac{\sum x_{2i} x_{3i}}{\sqrt{\sum x_{2i}^2 \sum x_{3i}^2}}. \tag{8.15}$$

In general we shall find it convenient to use the symbol $\sigma_{\hat{\beta}_k}^2$ to denote the sampling variance of $\hat{\beta}_k$. These formulas indicate that the variance of the sampling distribution of $\hat{\beta}_k$ depends on much the same factors as in the case of simple regression. $V(\hat{\beta}_k)$ is directly related to the disturbance variance σ^2 and inversely related to the sample variation $\sum x_{ki}^2$. In addition, the precision with which any single β_k can be estimated depends on the manner in which that explanatory variable X_k interacts with the other regressors, captured in (8.14) by r_{23}. In the special case in which $r_{23} = 0$, both (8.14a) and (8.14b) reduce to the variance expression (4.26) that applies in the simple regression case—a point that is pursued further in Section 8.7.2.

As before, the proof that the variance expressions (8.14) are the minimum attainable requires population normality. Although in the absence of normality it is therefore not possible to establish efficiency, it is nevertheless still possible to establish best linear unbiasedness.

Result 8.1   **Gauss-Markov Theorem.** *In the context of the classical linear multiple regression model*

$$Y_i = \beta_1 + \beta_2 X_{2i} + \beta_3 X_{3i} + \cdots + \beta_K X_{Ki} + \varepsilon_i, \qquad \varepsilon_i \sim \text{i.i.d.}(0, \sigma^2),$$

the least squares estimators $\hat{\beta}_k$ have the smallest variances in the class of all linear unbiased estimators.

One of the prerequisites for least squares to be BLUE is linearity of the estimator. Exercise 8.1 asks you to verify linearity by manipulating (8.12a) in order to confirm that it is linear in the Y_i.

That the $\hat{\beta}_k$ are linear estimators is important for more than the Gauss-Markov theorem. In combination with normality, linearity allows us to establish the exact form of the sampling distributions. Specifically, because (1) the coefficient estimators are linear functions of the Y_i, (2) the Y_i are normally distributed via the

ε_i in the model (8.1), and (3) linear functions of normals are normal, it follows that the $\hat{\beta}_k$ are normally distributed. The complete specification of their sampling distribution is therefore

$$\hat{\beta}_k \sim N(\beta_k, \sigma^2_{\hat{\beta}_k}). \tag{8.16}$$

The mean of this distribution is, of course, given to us by the property of unbiasedness, and the variances are given by the formulas (8.14) when $K = 3$. As with simple regression, this knowledge of the form of the sampling distributions provides the foundation for exact hypothesis tests.

EXERCISES

8.1 Show that (8.12a) may be written in the linear form

$$\hat{\beta}_2 = \sum a_i Y_i$$

by finding the appropriate expression for a_i.

(*Hint:* Begin by using the deviation-form property that $\sum x_{ki} y_i = \sum x_{ki} Y_i$.)

8.2 Starting with (8.12a), derive (8.14a).

8.4 Hypothesis Testing

The distributional result (8.16) provides the basis for hypothesis tests and confidence intervals. The chain of logic by which these are derived is essentially that of Sections 2.5.1 and 4.5.

First, any normally distributed random variable can be standardized by subtracting its mean and dividing by its standard deviation:

$$\frac{\hat{\beta}_k - \beta_k}{\sigma_{\hat{\beta}_k}} \sim N(0, 1). \tag{8.17}$$

This transformation of $\hat{\beta}_k$ is not a computable statistic, even on the basis of a hypothesized value of β_k, because $\sigma^2_{\hat{\beta}_k}$ depends on the unknown disturbance variance σ^2, as is apparent from (8.14). A natural means of obtaining an unbiased estimator $s^2_{\hat{\beta}_k}$ is to substitute s^2 for σ^2; in the case of (8.14), for example, this is

$$s^2_{\hat{\beta}_k} = \frac{s^2}{\sum x^2_{ki}(1 - r^2_{23})}. \tag{8.18}$$

Replacing the true standard error $\sigma_{\hat{\beta}_k}$ in the denominator of (8.17) with its estimated counterpart $s_{\hat{\beta}_k} = \sqrt{s^2_{\hat{\beta}_k}}$, the distribution is no longer $N(0, 1)$. Instead the following proposition holds.

Result 8.2 *In the context of the classical normal linear regression model (8.1),*

$$\frac{\hat{\beta}_k - \beta_k}{s_{\hat{\beta}_k}} \sim t(n - K). \tag{8.19}$$

The importance of this result is that it provides the basis for confidence interval formulas and hypothesis-testing procedures. For example, duplicating the reasoning in Section 4.5, a $(1 - a)100\%$ confidence interval for β_k is

$$\hat{\beta}_k \pm s_{\hat{\beta}_k} t_{a/2}(n - K). \tag{8.20}$$

Similarly, hypotheses of the form

$$H_0: \beta_k = \beta_0 \tag{8.21}$$

may be tested with the t statistic (8.19). This is, of course, a straightforward extension of the earlier t test procedure developed in Chapters 2 and 4.

EXAMPLE 3

With standard errors reported for the slope coefficients, Mincer's earnings function in Example 2 is

$$\log Y_i = 6.20 + \underset{(0.00148)}{0.107} \; X_i + \underset{(0.00107)}{0.081} \; Z_i - \underset{(0.0000215)}{0.0012} \; Z_i^2 + e_i.$$

Recall that X is schooling and Z is experience, and the equation is estimated using data on 31,093 men. Obtain a 90% confidence interval for the rate of return to education. Is the quadratic term on experience statistically significant?

SOLUTION

For such a large sample size the tabulated values of the t distribution are those of the standard normal: For a tail area of $a/2 = 0.05$ the tabulated value is $t_{a/2} = 1.645$. Consequently the bounds

$$\hat{\beta}_2 \pm s_{\hat{\beta}_2} t_{a/2} = 0.107 \pm 0.00148 \times 1.645 = (0.105, 0.109)$$

should contain the true value of β_2 approximately 90% of the time in repeated sampling. We can be 90% confident that an additional year of education yields an increase in earnings in the range of 10.5 to 10.9%.

It is interesting to compare this with the earlier conclusion of Example 4 in Chapter 4, where the simple regression version of the earnings function suggests a 95% confidence interval of (6.7, 7.3)% for the return to education. This interval is well outside the interval of (10.5, 10.9) that we have now calculated, illustrating that confidence intervals and hypothesis tests are always conditional on a chosen regression specification. To the extent that there is uncertainty about that specification, the precision suggested by a confidence interval can be illusory.

Turning to the quadratic term, the null hypothesis $\beta_4 = 0$ is tested with the t statistic

$$t = \frac{\hat{\beta}_4 - 0}{s_{\hat{\beta}_4}} = \frac{-0.0012}{0.0000215} = -55.8.$$

Comparing this against two-sided critical values $\pm t_{a/2}(n - K)$ such as ± 1.645 $(a = 0.10)$ or ± 1.96 $(a = 0.05)$, this easily rejects at conventional significance levels. The data support very strongly a quadratic effect of experience on earnings, so earnings peak in mid-life.

In using the t statistic, the usual variations involving one-sided hypotheses are possible. As well, the p-value approach is always available as an alternative style for presenting test results.

EXAMPLE 4

cobbdoug.dat

With standard errors included, the Cobb-Douglas production function of Example 1 is

$$\log Q_i = -0.177 + \underset{(0.0635)}{0.233} \ \log K_i + \underset{(0.145)}{0.807} \ \log L_i + e_i.$$

Do these estimation results clearly indicate that (a) the effect of factor inputs on output is positive, and (b) factors exhibit diminishing marginal returns?

SOLUTION

Let us begin with the first question. In asking whether the effect of factor inputs on output is clearly positive, we are asking whether the null hypotheses $\alpha \leq 0$ and $\beta \leq 0$ can be rejected in favor of the alternatives that $\alpha > 0$ and $\beta > 0$. The relevant t statistics are

$$\text{Capital:} \quad t = \frac{\hat{\beta} - 0}{s_{\hat{\beta}}} = \frac{0.233}{0.0635} = 3.67$$

$$\text{Labor:} \quad t = \frac{\hat{\alpha} - 0}{s_{\hat{\alpha}}} = \frac{0.807}{0.145} = 5.57.$$

For these one-sided hypotheses, the rejection region is of the form $t > t_a(n - K)$, where $n - K = 24 - 3 = 21$. These t statistics easily reject the null hypothesis at conventional significance levels, so the data clearly indicate that more of each factor input yields more output.

Turning to the second question, the factors exhibit diminishing marginal returns if $\alpha < 1$ and $\beta < 1$; the question is whether the data reject the null hypotheses of $\alpha \geq 1$ and $\beta \geq 1$ in favor of these alternatives. The relevant t statistics are

$$\text{Capital:} \quad t = \frac{\hat{\beta} - 1}{s_{\hat{\beta}}} = \frac{0.233 - 1}{0.0635} = -12.1$$

$$\text{Labor:} \quad t = \frac{\hat{\alpha} - 1}{s_{\hat{\alpha}}} = \frac{0.807 - 1}{0.145} = -1.33.$$

For these one-sided hypotheses the rejection region is of the form $t < -t_a(n - K)$, where $n - K = 24 - 3 = 21$. The null hypothesis of an absence of diminishing returns is easily rejected at conventional significance levels for capital. (For example, $-t_{0.01}(21) = -2.518$.) The case is less compelling for labor: $t = -1.33$ corresponds to a p-value of 0.099 when the rejection region is one-sided.[1] The hypothesis of an absence of diminishing returns is just barely rejected at a 10% significance level.

---

[1]   If the null were $\alpha = 1$ and the alternative $\alpha \neq 1$, then the p-value would be 0.198. This must be divided by 2 to obtain the p-value appropriate to one-sided hypotheses.

Hypotheses about the point values of individual coefficients are an important class of testable parameter restrictions. They are, however, just one example of restrictions that may be of interest. An economic theory might, for example, predict not that a coefficient takes on a particular numerical value (which is the nature of the hypothesis (8.21) tested in these examples), but that a group of coefficients satisfy some functional relationship. For example, recall in connection with Example 4 that Section 6.1 shows that the hypothesis of constant returns to scale takes the form of the restriction $\alpha + \beta = 1$ on the parameters of the Cobb-Douglas production function. In Chapter 10 methods for testing more general linear coefficient restrictions such as this are developed. Chapter 13 covers methods for testing nonlinear restrictions.

8.5   Decomposition of Sample Variation

Is it possible to obtain a decomposition of sample variation for multiple regression analogous to that which exists in simple regression? Obviously we can continue to define the statistics

$$\text{SST} = \sum_{i=1}^{n} y_i^2 = \sum_{i=1}^{n} (Y_i - \overline{Y})^2, \qquad \text{SSE} = \sum_{i=1}^{n} e_i^2. \tag{8.22}$$

The question is whether there continues to be a statistic

$$\text{SSR} = \sum_{i=1}^{n} (\hat{Y}_i - \overline{Y})^2$$

for the component of SST explained by the sample regression line, which satisfies $\text{SST} = \text{SSR} + \text{SSE}$.

To examine this, note that it continues to be possible to decompose $y_i = Y_i - \overline{Y}$ as

$$Y_i - \overline{Y} = (Y_i - \hat{Y}_i) + (\hat{Y}_i - \overline{Y}) = e_i + (\hat{Y}_i - \overline{Y}).$$

Therefore

$$\text{SST} = \sum_{i=1}^{n} [(\hat{Y}_i - \overline{Y}) + e_i]^2$$

$$= \sum_{i=1}^{n} (\hat{Y}_i - \overline{Y})^2 + \sum_{i=1}^{n} e_i^2 + 2 \sum_{i=1}^{n} (\hat{Y}_i - \overline{Y}) e_i$$

$$= \text{SSR} + \text{SSE} + 0.$$

This is the required decomposition as long as the third term can be confirmed as zero. Note first that, by the first least squares normal equation (8.9a),

$$\sum_{i=1}^{n} \overline{Y} e_i = \overline{Y} \sum_{i=1}^{n} e_i = \overline{Y} \cdot 0 = 0.$$

Turning to the other element of the third term,

$$\sum_{i=1}^{n} \hat{Y}_i e_i = \sum_{i=1}^{n} (\hat{\beta}_1 + \hat{\beta}_2 X_{2i} + \cdots + \hat{\beta}_K X_{Ki}) e_i$$

$$= \hat{\beta}_1 \sum_{i=1}^{n} e_i + \hat{\beta}_2 \sum_{i=1}^{n} X_{2i} e_i + \cdots + \hat{\beta}_K \sum_{i=1}^{n} X_{Ki} e_i$$

$$= \hat{\beta}_1 \cdot 0 + \hat{\beta}_2 \cdot 0 + \cdots + \hat{\beta}_K \cdot 0 = 0,$$

by properties (8.9a) and (8.9b) of the least squares normal equations.

This establishes that the decomposition of sample variation does generalize to multiple regression.

8.5.1 R^2

We can do the same things with this decomposition of variation that we did in simple regression, in particular define an R^2 goodness-of-fit measure and an F test.

A **coefficient of multiple determination** may be defined as

$$R^2 = \frac{\text{SSR}}{\text{SST}} = 1 - \frac{\text{SSE}}{\text{SST}}, \qquad 0 \le R^2 \le 1.$$

It is according to this formula that the R^2 values for Mincer's earnings functions in Example 2 were computed. In the special case of simple regression this formula is, of course, the same one we defined in Chapter 4.

EXAMPLE 5

cobbdoug.dat

What are the decomposition of sample variation and the R^2 for the Cobb-Douglas production function of previous examples?

SOLUTION

The decomposition of sample variation is

$$\text{SST} = 1.6672, \qquad \text{SSR} = 1.5962, \qquad \text{SSE} = 0.07098.$$

This yields

$$R^2 = \frac{\text{SSR}}{\text{SST}} = \frac{1.5962}{1.6672} = 0.957,$$

indicating that in the Cobb-Douglas data the variation in $\log K$ and $\log L$ explains approximately 95.7% of the variation in $\log Q$.

Deficiency of the R^2

A deficiency of this goodness-of-fit measure in the multiple regression context relates to the fact that it must always increase as additional regressors are introduced into the model. Consequently a model with more explanatory variables will always, according to the R^2, appear to explain the behavior of the dependent variable better than one with fewer. Why is this? Consider the original sum of squares function (8.7) compared with one that includes an additional regressor X_{K+1}:

$$S^* = \sum_{i=1}^{n} (Y_i - \beta_1 - \beta_2 X_{2i} - \cdots - \beta_{K+1} X_{K+1,i})^2.$$

The minimization problem min S, which yields our previous least squares estimators and SSE $= \sum e_i^2$, is equivalent to the minimization of S^* subject to the restriction that $\beta_{K+1} = 0$; that is, it is equivalent to the constrained minimization problem

min S^* subject to $\beta_{K+1} = 0$.

Comparing this to the *unconstrained* minimization problem min S^* yielding SSE*, the unconstrained minimization must always attain at least as low a minimum as the constrained problem:

SSE* $\leq$ SSE.

The equality will only hold if the restriction is satisfied exactly in the sample; that is, $\hat{\beta}_{K+1} = 0$. This illustrates that, in general, an unconstrained optimization problem must attain at least as extreme a value of the objective function as a constrained version of the same optimization problem.

Hence, additional regressors will always yield an estimated model that "fits the data" better (or at least as well), as indicated by the SSE, regardless of the nature of the regressors themselves. Equivalently, comparing the R^2s,

$$1 - \frac{\text{SSE*}}{\text{SST}} \geq 1 - \frac{\text{SSE}}{\text{SST}},$$

so the equation with additional regressors always has at least as great an R^2.

8.5.2 $\overline{R}^2$

This feature of the standard definition of the R^2 motivates an alternative goodness-of-fit measure that does not have this undesirable property. The **adjusted coefficient of determination** is

$$\overline{R}^2 = 1 - \frac{\text{SSE}/(n-K)}{\text{SST}/(n-1)} = 1 - \frac{\text{SSE}}{\text{SST}} \cdot \frac{n-1}{n-K}.$$

It is apparent that its relationship to R^2 is

$$\overline{R}^2 = 1 - (1 - R^2) \frac{n-1}{n-K},$$

which in turn implies that

$$\overline{R}^2 < R^2 \qquad (K > 1).$$

Indeed, it is possible for $\overline{R}^2$ to be negative, although this typically occurs only for a very low value of R^2.

EXAMPLE 6

cobbdoug.dat

Compute the $\overline{R}^2$ for the Cobb-Douglas production function of previous examples.

SOLUTION

The Cobb-Douglas production function in its multiple regression form has $K = 3$ coefficients; it was estimated using $n = 24$ observations. Using the values for the decomposition of sample variation given in Example 5,

$$\overline{R}^2 = 1 - \frac{\text{SSE}}{\text{SST}} \cdot \frac{n-1}{n-K} = 1 - \frac{0.07098}{1.6672} \cdot \frac{23}{21} = 0.953.$$

Comparing this with the R^2 value of 0.957, the relationship $\overline{R}^2 < R^2$ is verified.

$\overline{R}^2$ and Model Choice

Under what circumstances will the $\overline{R}^2$ increase when an additional regressor is introduced? This happens when the t ratio associated with the new regressor exceeds 1 (in absolute value). Establishing this result requires the material of Chapter 10, and we return to it in Section 10.2.4. The implication is that selecting the regression with the higher $\overline{R}^2$ is a weaker—that is, less demanding—criterion for adding regressors than is hypothesis testing at conventional significance levels. Equivalently, if we decide to add a regressor because it increases the $\overline{R}^2$, we are effectively performing a hypothesis test using a less-stringent than conventional significance level. Thus, although $\overline{R}^2$ offers some protection against the temptation to introduce additional regressors, it still tends to lead to the overparameterization of the regression relative to what would result from hypothesis testing at conventional significance levels.

To the extent that we wish to use $\overline{R}^2$ as a basis for selecting from among several regression specifications, the same qualification applies as it does to R^2: It is only useful for comparing models with a common dependent variable.[2] We comment further on $\overline{R}^2$ as a basis for model choice in Section 12.4.

> **Practitioner's Tip:** **Goodness-of-fit statistics and model choice**
>
> Only use goodness-of-fit statistics such as R^2 and $\overline{R}^2$ to compare regressions with a *common* dependent variable, not regressions with different dependent variables.

Of course the value 1 is of no special importance on the t distribution, and in this respect the definition of $\overline{R}^2$ is somewhat arbitrary. It does nevertheless have an objective basis, which we now consider.

---

[2] A dramatic illustration of this is given in Exercises 7.2–7.4, in which the Cobb-Douglas production function is estimated in its labor- and capital-intensive forms. Although the two estimated models are empirically equivalent, they have very different R^2s.

Where Does $\overline{R}^2$ Come From?

The $\overline{R}^2$ modifies the formula for R^2 by introducing the factor $(n-1)/(n-K)$. But where does this factor come from?

The purpose of $\overline{R}^2$ is to permit the comparison of regressions with different sets of explanatory variables in a way that introduces a penalty for additional coefficients. The $\overline{R}^2$ will only increase if the smaller SSE that arises from adding variables is worth the introduction of the new coefficients that must be estimated.

Consider two regressions: an *unrestricted* one having K_U coefficients and a *restricted* one having K_R coefficients that are fewer in number, so $K_R < K_U$. The adjusted coefficients of determination are

$$\overline{R}_U^2 = 1 - \frac{\text{SSE}_U/(n-K_U)}{\text{SST}/(n-1)}, \qquad \overline{R}_R^2 = 1 - \frac{\text{SSE}_R/(n-K_R)}{\text{SST}/(n-1)}.$$

(Both formulas have the same SST because the regressions have the same dependent variable.) What are the implications of choosing the regression with the higher $\overline{R}^2$?

Consider for a moment a seemingly different criterion for model selection: Choose the regression that "fits the data best," in the sense of yielding the smallest estimate for the variance σ^2. Applying formula (8.13), in each case the unbiased estimator for σ^2 is

$$s_U^2 = \frac{\text{SSE}_U}{n-K_U}, \qquad s_R^2 = \frac{\text{SSE}_R}{n-K_R}.$$

Comparing these expressions with the respective $\overline{R}^2$s, it is evident that $\overline{R}^2$ is defined so that selecting the regression with the larger $\overline{R}^2$ is the same as selecting the regression with the smaller variance s^2, something that is not true of R^2.

This explains the factor $(n-K)$, but how about the factor $(n-1)$? Note as an incidental matter that the denominator $\text{SST}/(n-1)$ is familiar as the unbiased estimator (2.7) for the disturbance variance in the model (2.6) in Chapter 2. Consider the special case of $K = 1$ in which there are no explanatory variables and the regression reduces to that model:

$$Y_i = \mu + \varepsilon_i.$$

From our discussion of the decomposition of sample variation in simple regression in Section 4.6, we know that in this special case the model attributes the variation in the dependent variable entirely to the disturbance ε_i, so that $\text{SSR} = 0$ and $\text{SSE} = \text{SST}$. In this case, therefore, the systematic component of the model explains *none* of the variation in the dependent variable, and the formula for $\overline{R}^2$ reduces to

$$\overline{R}^2 = 1 - \frac{\text{SSE}/(n-K)}{\text{SST}/(n-1)} = 1 - \frac{\text{SST}/(n-1)}{\text{SST}/(n-1)} = 0,$$

which is as it should be.

8.5.3   *F* Test of the Regression Model

The multiple regression model explains the variation in Y_i in terms of the explanatory variables X_{ki}—the systematic component—and the disturbance ε_i—the unsystematic component. The decomposition of sample variation quantifies the relative contributions of these two components.

Just as is true in the case of simple regression, it is of interest to ask whether the regression model does a better job of explaining the behavior of Y_i than the earlier model in Chapter 2,

$$Y_i = \mu + \varepsilon_i.$$

This simple model describes Y_i as varying around the constant mean μ, so its variation is entirely unsystematic. As in simple regression, answering this question requires the decomposition of sample variation.

In simple regression, the hypothesis that the regression model is no better at explaining Y_i than the model just presented is the hypothesis that the slope is zero, $\beta = 0$, so that the explanatory variable is not an important determinant of Y_i. In multiple regression, the corresponding hypothesis is that *all* the slopes are zero,

$$H_0: \beta_2 = \beta_3 = \cdots = \beta_K = 0. \tag{8.23}$$

This is the hypothesis that the explanatory variables are jointly not important determinants of Y_i. (Note that the intercept β_1 is not included, so under this hypothesis the regression model reduces to the previous model with $\beta_1 = \mu$.) The alternative hypothesis is that this H_0 is false, so that at least one of the slope coefficients is nonzero.

The decomposition of sample variation permits a test of this hypothesis with the *F* statistic

$$F = \frac{\mathrm{SSR}/(K-1)}{\mathrm{SSE}/(n-K)} \sim F(K-1, n-K). \tag{8.24}$$

This is a generalization of the simple regression *F* statistic (4.47), which may be obtained by setting $K = 2$. Just as in that earlier discussion, H_0 is rejected at significance level a if, in comparing the computed value of the statistic against tabulated values of the distribution, it is found that $F > F_a(K-1, n-K)$.

EXAMPLE 7

 cobbdoug.dat

The Cobb-Douglas production function in its multiple regression form is

$$\log Q_i = \log \gamma + \beta \log K_i + \alpha \log L_i + \varepsilon_i.$$

Perform an *F* test using the Cobb-Douglas data.

SOLUTION

An *F* test is a test of the null hypothesis that $\alpha = \beta = 0$—that neither capital nor labor is a significant determinant of output—against the alternative that at least one is, so that $\alpha \neq 0$ and/or $\beta \neq 0$. Using the decomposition of sample variation given in Example 5, the *F* statistic evaluates to

$$F = \frac{\mathrm{SSR}/(K-1)}{\mathrm{SSE}/(n-K)} = \frac{1.5962/2}{0.07098/21} = 236.12.$$

Comparing with tabulated values of the F distribution (for example, $F_{0.01}(2, 21)$ = 5.78), this easily rejects at conventional significance levels. Not surprisingly, the data provide strong evidence that factor inputs are important in determining output.

Relationship of the F Test to t Tests

This test procedure is very similar to the F test in simple regression. There is, however, an important difference. The test presented in Section 4.6.2 is shown to be equivalent to a simple t test on the slope coefficient; in contrast, the test offered by (8.24) of the hypothesis (8.23) has no necessary relationship to t tests of the hypotheses $\beta_k = 0$ ($k = 2, \ldots, K$) on the individual slope coefficients. In principle, for a chosen level of significance, any of the following cases is possible.

Case 1: The F test is significant; all of the t tests are significant.
Case 2: The F test is significant; some of the t tests are significant.
Case 3: The F test is significant; none of the t tests is significant.
Case 4: The F test is insignificant; all of the t tests are significant.
Case 5: The F test is insignificant; some of the t tests are significant.
Case 6: The F test is insignificant; none of the t tests is significant.

Cases 1 and 6 are ones in which the two sets of test outcomes are fully consistent. In case 1, if the F test rejects (8.23) it makes perfect sense that individual t tests will also uniformly reject $\beta_k = 0$ ($k = 2, \ldots, K$). Our Cobb-Douglas production function example illustrates this situation; as we have just seen, the F test rejects the joint hypotheses $\alpha = 0$ and $\beta = 0$, fully consistent with their individual rejections by the t statistics in Example 4. Case 6 is the similar but opposite situation: If the F test fails to reject (8.23), it is not difficult to understand that t tests will find each of the explanatory variables to be unimportant in determining Y.

What is perhaps surprising is that these are not the only possibilities and that there is scope for seemingly inconsistent t and F test outcomes. The most perverse is case 4, which is extremely unusual but in principle possible. Cases 2 and 3 tend to be associated with multicollinearity, a topic treated in the next section.

How is it possible that such apparent inconsistencies can arise? Intuitively, the answer is that they are not really inconsistencies at all, in the sense of being inconsistent answers to a given question. Instead the joint hypothesis (8.23) asks about the importance of the explanatory variables *jointly*—that is, as a group; t tests, on the other hand, ask about the role of variables *individually*. It is possible, for example, that variables, as a group, are important in determining a dependent variable, but that a particular one, taken individually, is not. This is case 2. Similarly, it is possible that one variable may be important individually in determining Y, as judged by a t test, yet in combination with other variables not explain a large enough portion of the variation in Y to generate a significant F statistic. This is case 5. In conclusion, t and F tests can yield different conclusions about the role of explanatory variables because they are addressing somewhat different questions.

FIGURE 8.2

Rejection regions of
t and *F* tests.

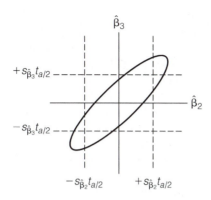

Practitioner's Tip: *t* **tests and the** *F* **test of the regression model**

Individual *t* tests need not be—and often will not be—what you might think of as
fully consistent with the *F* test of the regression model.

A Diagrammatic Interpretation

This can be understood more formally by considering a diagrammatic interpretation
of the rejection regions for the two types of tests, as provided in Figure 8.2. The
figure applies to the special case of the regression model with just two explanatory
variables:

$$Y_i = \beta_1 + \beta_2 X_{2i} + \beta_3 X_{3i} + \varepsilon_i.$$

It portrays the rejection regions for hypotheses about β_2 and β_3. The individual
hypotheses $\beta_2 = 0$ and $\beta_3 = 0$ are, as we have seen in Section 8.4, tested with t
ratios of the form

$$\frac{\hat{\beta}_k}{s_{\hat{\beta}_k}} \sim t(n-3).$$

Such a t test rejects when $|\hat{\beta}_k / s_{\hat{\beta}_k}| > t_{a/2}(n-3)$ or, equivalently, when $\hat{\beta}_k$ is
suitably different from zero:

$$|\hat{\beta}_k| > s_{\hat{\beta}_k} t_{a/2}(n-3).$$

Because $\hat{\beta}_2$ is measured on the horizontal axis in the diagram, the critical values
$\pm s_{\hat{\beta}_2} t_{a/2}(n-3)$ are portrayed as the vertical lines equidistant from the origin.
Values of $\hat{\beta}_2$ beyond these lines correspond to a rejection of the hypothesis $\beta_2 = 0$.
Similarly, for $\hat{\beta}_3$ the critical values $\pm s_{\hat{\beta}_3} t_{a/2}(n-3)$ are shown as the horizontal
lines equidistant from the origin. Hence, the diagram indicates the rejection status
of each of the hypotheses $\beta_2 = 0$ and $\beta_3 = 0$ for any pair of estimates $(\hat{\beta}_2, \hat{\beta}_3)$,
on the basis of individual t tests.

The rejection region for the F test of the joint hypothesis $\beta_2 = \beta_3 = 0$ is, on the other hand, of a quite different form. As indicated in Figure 8.2, it is an ellipse:[3] The interpretation is that estimated $(\hat{\beta}_2, \hat{\beta}_3)$ values outside the ellipse correspond to a rejection of the joint hypothesis. Considering alternative $(\hat{\beta}_2, \hat{\beta}_3)$ pairs, an examination of the diagram indicates how all six of the enumerated cases may arise.

It can be shown that the shape of the ellipse depends on the relationship between the two explanatory variables; it is positively sloped if $r_{23} > 0$ and negatively sloped if $r_{23} < 0$. As $|r_{23}| \to 1$, the ellipse becomes more narrow and elongated. Hence, a high degree of correlation between the explanatory variables contributes to the likelihood of seeming inconsistencies—such as case 3—between t and F test results.

This observation motivates a closer examination of the implications of relationships between the explanatory variables for statistical analysis of the multiple regression model. This is the subject of Section 8.7.

EXERCISES

8.3 Because the R^2 and the F statistic are both based on the decomposition of sample variation, it follows that they are related.

(a) Show that they are in fact very directly related by obtaining an expression for the F statistic alternative to (8.24) that can be computed solely from

knowledge of R^2, n, and K.

(b) Mincer's expanded earnings function in Example 2 has an R^2 of 0.285. Perform an F test of the regression model, specifying clearly all parts of your test procedure.

8.6   Application: Electricity Demand

Consumer demand for a commodity is one of the most common economic relationships of interest to applied econometricians. Economists—and others, for example, market researchers—are often interested in what factors are important in determining the consumption of a good and in estimating its own- and cross-price elasticities and its income elasticity. Sometimes these are of intrinsic interest to the economist; in other cases, they serve as inputs to subsequent analyses such as the social welfare effects of tax changes.

In the exercises that follow you will replicate the results of a classic early study by Hendrick Houthakker (1951) of electricity consumption in Britain. Houthakker's data consist of observations from 42 towns in the late 1930s. This data set has two interesting features.

The first is that it is a cross-sectional data set in which electricity was priced differently in different towns. Very often in demand studies prices are constant across consumers at a point in time, and so the demand relation must be estimated with data observed over time in order to get variation in the price series. This in

[3] For a more detailed discussion see Kmenta (1986, pp. 413–414).

turn raises issues in the analysis of time series data and the question of whether preferences can reasonably be treated as fixed over time. The fact that Houthakker's data exhibit price variation across towns allowed him to circumvent the issues that would have arisen in connection with a time series data set.

The second interesting feature of Houthakker's data is that the manner in which electricity was priced in the United Kingdom at this time was somewhat different from the pricing of most commodities. His data are for residential (in his terminology, "domestic") consumers who had elected to be billed according to a two-part pricing structure, which Houthakker called a "two-part tariff," which includes both a fixed charge and a "running charge." The fixed charge is a fixed cost to the household of receiving electrical service, and so does not vary with the amount of electricity used. The running charge is the variable cost associated with a price per kilowatt-hour of consumption; this price is the marginal cost of additional electricity consumption. The existence of these two components of total cost means that average cost will differ from marginal cost; it is the latter, of course, that is relevant to any economic decision and on which any estimated demand relation should be based. In Houthakker's words,

> Under a two-part tariff the *own price* variable has two components: the fixed charge and the running charge. Once the choice of tariff has been made ... the marginal price will be chiefly relevant. The fixed charge has to be paid irrespective of consumption and will therefore have only an insignificant income effect on consumption. The amount consumed will be determined by ... the running charge of one kWh. This argument, obvious though it may seem to the economist, has been overlooked in many ... of the demand studies occurring in the electrical literature. (Houthakker 1951, p. 360)

The component of Houthakker's data set that you will need is available in the file **houthak.dat**. The variables are defined as follows; the last variable is not used here, but is used in Chapter 14.

income Average income of two-part consumers (pounds per year).

p36 Running charge on domestic two-part tariffs in 1935–1936 (pence per kWh).

p38 Running charge on domestic two-part tariffs in 1937–1938 (pence per kWh).

gas36 Marginal price of gas in 1935–1936.

equip Average holding of heavy electric equipment by domestic two-part consumers in 1937–1938 (kW).

consump Consumption on domestic two-part tariffs per consumer in 1937–1938 (kWh).

expend Average total expenditure on electricity by two-part customers in 1937–1938 (in pounds).

num Number of two-part consumers in the town in 1937–1938 (thousands).

Incidentally, in the estimation exercises that follow you will *not* be able to reproduce the published results found in Houthakker's article, for reasons that become apparent in Section 14.3.

Further Reading

The study of consumer demand is a large and fascinating area within applied econometrics. For further reading on empirical studies of the demand for electricity, including more discussion of Houthakker's work and additional empirical exercises, see Berndt (1991, Chap. 7). The interaction between electricity demand and holdings of durable electric appliances, treated by Houthakker through his use of the variable equip, continues to be of interest to contemporary researchers; see Dubin (1985) and Dubin and McFadden (1984). For the econometrics of consumer demand more generally, an excellent introduction is Thomas (1987).

EXERCISES

8.4 houthak.dat Houthakker's preferred specification for the systematic component of his demand relation was of the form

$$q = f(m, p_1, p_2, h), \qquad (8.25)$$

where q is the quantity of electricity consumed per household, m is household income, p_1 is the price (marginal cost) of electricity, p_2 is the price of a substitutable or complementary good, and h is any other variable that may be relevant. This specification was based on his reasoning that

> In any demand analysis the principal explanatory variables will be income, the price of the commodity under consideration, and the prices of such complementary or competing goods as are considered sufficiently closely related to exercise a noticeable influence. In addition it may be necessary to introduce extra-economic factors to account for differences in preferences between consumers; for the rest preferences are assumed to be affected only by random disturbances. (Houthakker 1951, p. 359)

(a) Indicate which of the variables in this data set is appropriate as a measure for each these variables. (Ignore the dates associated with the variables for the moment.) Explain in particular the rationale for your choice of h.

(b) Print the variables you have identified as appropriate measures of own-price p_1 and other price p_2. Use the series for 1935–1936. Do they indeed exhibit variation across observations, as is required if it is to be possible to estimate own-price and cross-price effects on consumption from this data set?

(c) Produce a scatter plot of the relationship between consumption q and the own-price p_1. Does it seem to reproduce Figure 3.3(b)? Obtain the correlation between these two variables. Is it the value reported in connection with Figure 3.3(b)?

(d) Print the variables you have identified as appropriate measures of household income m and electricity consumption q.

i. Does household income vary considerably across municipalities?

ii. Scanning these two series, is it your impression that they are correlated? Produce a scatter plot between the two variables. Does it seem to reproduce Figure 3.3(a)? Obtain the sample correlation. Is it the value reported in connection with Figure 3.3(a)?

iii. What are the implications of these features of the data set for the estimation of the income elasticity of demand? In particular, do you expect that it is possible to obtain a good (i.e., precise) estimate of the income elasticity of electricity consumption from these data?

TABLE 8.1 Demand Elasticities

Own-price elasticity $\epsilon = \dfrac{p}{q}\dfrac{\partial q}{\partial p}$		Income elasticity $\eta = \dfrac{m}{q}\dfrac{\partial q}{\partial m}$	
$\epsilon < -1$	Price elastic	$1 < \eta$	Income elastic
$-1 < \epsilon < 0$	Price inelastic	$0 < \eta < 1$	Income inelastic
$0 < \epsilon$	Giffen	$\eta < 0$	Inferior

8.5 houthak.dat Your data set includes a series on total expenditure on electricity by the average consumer in 1937–1938 and on the running charge during the same period. Use these to answer the following questions.

(a) A commodity's budget share is the proportion it represents in the consumer's budget. Divide electricity expenditure into household income to generate a series of observations on the budget share of electricity. Average this across the municipalities to obtain a typical household budget share. Does this number seem plausible?

(b) Divide electricity expenditure into consumption to generate the unit price of electricity per kilowatt-hour. (*Hint:* Electricity expenditure is measured in pounds sterling. Compute a unit price in pence by making use of the fact that, at this time in Britain, £1 equalled 20 shillings and there were 12 pence per shilling.)

i. As described, the cost of electrical service is the total of a fixed cost and a variable cost; in Houthakker's terminology,

Total cost = Fixed charge + Total running charge.

From your understanding of the arithmetic of average costs, should average total cost be more or less than average variable cost?

ii. The total running charge is quantity times price, the latter being the running charge given by the variable p38. In light of your reasoning, how should the unit price you have generated and the running charge compare in magnitude? Print out both series. Is the relationship you have conjectured borne out in your numbers?

8.6 houthak.dat In his estimation of the model (8.25) Houthakker used prices for 1935–1936. Replicate his analysis by doing your own least squares estimation of a loglinear form for the model,

$$\log q_i = \beta_1 + \beta_2 \log m_i + \beta_3 \log p_{1i} + \beta_4 \log p_{2i} + \beta_5 \log h_i + \varepsilon_i. \quad (8.26)$$

Recall that, in a log-log model, the coefficients are elasticities. Using the summary in Table 8.1, consider the following elasticities.[4]

(a) *The own-price elasticity.*
i. Is the demand curve for electricity downward sloping?

ii. Is the demand for electricity price elastic or inelastic? Or is it a Giffen good?

iii. Is the own-price effect on electricity demand statistically significant at conventional significance levels?

[4] Table 8.1 uses the most common terminology for demand elasticities. Other terms are used differently by different authors. Income inelastic goods are sometimes called *necessities* and income elastic ones *luxuries*; however, some microeconomists object to this use of these terms. Goods with a positive income elasticity (i.e., those that are not inferior) are usually called *normal goods*; the term *superior good* is usually (although not universally) used as a synonym. However, a few authors use the term *normal good* to refer instead to goods having a negative own-price elasticity (a downward-sloping demand curve).

(b) *The cross-price elasticity.*

i.   What percentage change in electricity consumption will arise from a 1% increase in the price of residential gas? Does this suggest that electricity and gas are substitutes or complements? Is this what you expect?

ii.   Is this cross-price elasticity statistically significant at conventional significance levels?

(c) *The income elasticity.*

i.   What is the income elasticity of demand for electricity?

ii.   Is the demand for electricity income elastic, inelastic, or inferior?

iii.   Is the evidence contained in your point estimate strong enough to enable you to reject the null hypothesis that electricity is *not* income elastic? State all parts of your test procedure carefully, including the specification of your hypotheses.

(d) Perform an *F* test of the significance of your regression model. State all parts of your test procedure carefully, including (i) the null and alternative hypothesis, (ii) the relevant test statistic and its computed value, and (iii) your rejection region and conclusion. Comparing the result of the *F* test to those of the individual *t* tests, which of the six cases in Section 8.5.3 applies?

8.7 💿 **houthak.dat** In addition to the loglinear model, Houthakker studied the following linear-reciprocal functional form:

$$q_i = \beta_1 + \beta_2 m_i + \beta_3 \frac{1}{p_{1i}} + \beta_4 p_{2i}$$
$$+ \beta_5 h_i + \varepsilon_i. \tag{8.27}$$

This specification, although linear in parameters, provides for a nonlinear relationship between consumption and price of the type that we typically assume characterizes a demand schedule by having the own-price enter in reciprocal form.

(a) From your understanding of reciprocal relationships (you may wish to review Section 6.4), do you expect β_3 to be positive or negative? Taking this conjecture as a one-sided alternative hypothesis, is it supported by a hypothesis test?

(b) Because this model is not loglinear, elasticities will differ at different points on the demand schedule. Therefore, elasticities must be evaluated conditional on particular values for the variables entering into the demand equation. The income elasticity of demand, for example, is

$$\eta = \frac{m}{q} \frac{\partial q}{\partial m} = \frac{m}{q} \beta_2, \tag{8.28}$$

which must be evaluated on the basis not only of an estimate $\hat{\beta}_2$ but also on values for m and q. Note, however, that it only makes sense to evaluate the elasticity at a point that is actually on the estimated demand curve. If the elasticity is to be evaluated at a point of the data set, this should be done using the corresponding *predicted* value $\hat{q}$ rather than the *observed* value of the dependent variable because the latter is not actually on the estimated curve. Bearing this consideration in mind, evaluate the income elasticity of demand at the point $m = 500$, $p_1 = 0.50$, $p_2 = 8.0$, $h = 0.50$. Houthakker's result for this elasticity was 1.01. How close do you come to reproducing this?

(c) Obtain an expression analogous to (8.28) for the own-price elasticity. (*Hint:* You will have to recall some basic calculus concerning the differentiation of reciprocal functions.) Evaluate this elasticity at the data point given in part b. Houthakker reported a value of -1.04 for this elasticity. How does yours compare?

(d) A common practice is to evaluate elasticities in nonloglinear models at the variable means. Begin by computing the sample means of m, p_1, p_2, and h and the associated predicted value $\hat{q}$. Evaluate your income and own-price elasticities at this point.

(e) Consider the income elasticity η, evaluated at the variable means. How should you test the hypothesis $H_0: \eta \geq 1$, at conventional levels of significance? Indicate clearly all parts of your test procedure. (*Hint:* You may find it helpful to review your approach to a similar problem in Exercise 6.12.)

8.7   Multicollinearity

The formulas for the least squares coefficient estimators (8.12) indicate that each $\hat{\beta}_k$ is calculated using not only its regressor X_k but all the other explanatory variables of the model as well. This reflects the fact that each slope coefficient β_k has the interpretation of "holding all other influences constant":

$$\beta_k = \frac{\partial Y_i}{\partial X_{ki}} \qquad (k = 2, \ldots, K).$$

That is, β_k represents the ceterus paribus effect on Y of a one unit change in X_k. Any procedure for estimating the β_k, least squares or otherwise, must do so in a way that controls for the effects of other factors, and this is why it makes sense that the other explanatory variables should play a role in the formula for each $\hat{\beta}_k$. The estimation of a regression model is an attempt to disentangle the influences of the various explanatory variables on Y.

Accomplishing this is often a demanding task, certainly in economics, because typically the explanatory variables themselves are to some degree interrelated. These interrelationships are called **multicollinearity.** As an example, consider a multiple regression generalization of an Engel curve, like the ones in Chapter 6. Let expenditure on some commodity, say clothing, be a function of education and income; for simplicity, assume a linear specification:

$$Y_i = \beta_1 + \beta_2 X_{2i} + \beta_3 X_{3i} + \varepsilon_i.$$

Here Y_i is clothing expenditure, X_{2i} is years of education, X_{3i} is income, and i indexes individuals. Note that, in any sample collected, the two explanatory variables will almost certainly be correlated: $r_{23} > 0$. It will therefore be difficult to gauge the independent effect of each on the dependent variable. If individuals with high levels of education tend to have high clothing expenditure, is this because education increases one's preference for clothing or is it because high education generates high income and it is the latter that directly affects clothing expenditure?

Let us examine how this consideration enters formally into the analysis of the regression model. In the special case of $K = 3$, we know that a useful measure of the linear relationship between the explanatory variables X_{2i} and X_{3i} is the sample correlation r_{23} given by (8.15). It is instructive to examine three possibilities: (1) the case of perfect multicollinearity in which $|r_{23}| = 1$, (2) the case of a complete absence of multicollinearity in which $r_{23} = 0$, and (3) the normal circumstance of a degree of multicollinearity in which $0 < |r_{23}| < 1$. We consider each of these in the sections that follow.

8.7.1   Perfect Multicollinearity

When $|r_{23}| = 1$, this means that there is an exact linear dependence between the variables:

$$X_{3i} = a + b X_{2i}.$$

This violates assumption (8.3) that no such linear relationships exist. Exact linear relationships between the variables mean that it will be impossible to disentangle their individual influences because effectively they are measuring the same influence. One variable is essentially just a change in units of measure of the other, like the units changes in Section 4.8. In terms of the calculation of $\hat{\beta}_2$ and $\hat{\beta}_3$ note that, rearranging the definition (8.15), $|r_{23}| = 1$ implies that

$$\left(\sum x_{2i} x_{3i}\right)^2 = \left(\sqrt{\sum x_{2i}^2 \sum x_{3i}^2}\right)^2.$$

It then follows that the denominators of (8.12) are equal to zero and the least squares slope estimators are not uniquely defined. An infinite number of alternative $\hat{\beta}_2, \hat{\beta}_3$ values correspond to the same minimum of the sum-of-squares function.

In general when $K > 3$ and the regression model involves an arbitrary number of explanatory variables, the assumption of no exact linear relationship among the variables is the assumption that there is no set of numerical constants a_k for which

$$a_2 X_{2i} + \cdots + a_K X_{Ki} = a_1 \qquad (i = 1, \ldots, n). \tag{8.29}$$

In the terminology of linear algebra, this is the requirement that the explanatory variables be **linearly independent.** It is equivalent to requiring that it not be possible to write one explanatory variable as a linear function of others. For example, if in the $K = 3$ case constants a_1, a_2, and a_3 exist such that (8.29) is satisfied, note that it can be arranged as (8.3). In such a circumstance, the variables are **linearly dependent** (or are said to be **exactly collinear**) and the least squares estimators are not uniquely defined—this is the case of **perfect multicollinearity.**

Although explanatory variables are typically correlated to some degree, as discussed in Section 8.7.3, this does not normally take the extreme form of an exact linear dependence. An exception is when variables happen to be defined in such a way that a linear dependence exists by construction. Let us consider some examples of how this can happen.

Variables Related by Identities

As we remark in Chapter 1, many economic variables are related by identities, especially in macroeconomics. Often this takes the form of linear dependencies. Here are some examples.

National Income Accounting Identities. Variables in the national income accounts are constructed according to certain accounting identities. For example, GNP is by definition the total of consumption spending, investment, government expenditure, and exports less imports; using standard notation,

$$Y = C + I + G + X - M.$$

Because these variables are related by this accounting identity, it would not make sense to include all of them as explanatory variables in a multiple regression; they are not independent influences. To do so would result in perfect multicollinearity.

Multiplicative Identities Are Additive in Logarithms. Because multiplicative relationships between variables are linear in logarithms, variables that are defined multiplicatively are related by identities in their logarithms. We give three examples.

Per-unit variables. Economists often work with variables defined as ratios: unit production costs, income per household, output per worker, the capital-labor ratio, and so on. As a concrete example, consider total output Q, labor input L, and labor productivity q; the last is defined as

$$q = \frac{Q}{L}.$$

Taking logarithms, the variables are related by

$$\log q = \log Q - \log L. \tag{8.30}$$

This linear dependence means that it is inappropriate to include all three as explanatory variables in a multiple regression. To do so would result in perfect multicollinearity.

Notice that, in their original nonlogarithmic form, all three—q, Q, and L—could be used as regressors; because they are related multiplicatively rather than additively they would not result in perfect multicollinearity. Nevertheless we must ask why it would make sense to include all three given the redundancy among them.

Our remaining two examples are manifestations of this same idea, and much the same comments apply.

Nominal and real quantities. Nominal and real quantities are related definitionally by a price index. Consider a variable Y measured in nominal (dollar) terms and some price index P having base 100. Then, a real variable y is obtained by using the price index to deflate the nominal variable:

$$y = \frac{Y}{P/100}. \tag{8.31}$$

In their logarithms these variables are related by

$$\log y = \log Y - \log P + \log 100. \tag{8.32}$$

This linear dependence[5] means that it would be inappropriate to include all three—$\log y$, $\log Y$, and $\log P$—as explanatory variables in a multiple regression. To do so would result in perfect multicollinearity.

Money, national income, and the velocity of circulation of money. In Appendix 6A we discuss the quantity theory of money, which is sometimes expressed in terms of the equation of exchange

$$MV = PQ.$$

---

[5] The constant $\log 100$ plays the role of a_1 in equation (8.29).

Here M is the quantity of money in circulation, PQ is nominal gross national income (the product of the price level P and real gross national income Q), and V is the velocity of circulation of money. Because money M and gross national income PQ are both observable variables, a measure of V can be calculated as

$$V = \frac{PQ}{M}.$$

That is, the velocity of circulation of money is the value of transactions supported by each dollar in circulation. If $V = 10$ this means that $10 of transactions take place each year for every dollar in circulation. Equivalently, each dollar in the money stock is exchanged, or turns over, ten times a year on average, in facilitating trades among agents.

Taking logarithms of this relationship yields

$$\log V = \log(PQ) - \log M. \tag{8.33}$$

This linear dependence means that it is inappropriate to include all three—$\log V$, $\log(PQ)$, and $\log M$—as explanatory variables in a multiple regression. To do so would result in perfect multicollinearity.

Identities between Growth Rates

A similar but less obvious linear dependence can arise when using growth rates. In Appendix 6B we see that the growth rates of products and ratios are related linearly. For a product $Z = XY$ the growth rate of Z is the sum of the growth rates of X and Y:

$$\frac{\dot{Z}}{Z} = \frac{\dot{X}}{X} + \frac{\dot{Y}}{Y}.$$

For a ratio $Z = X/Y$ the growth rate of Z is the difference of the growth rates:

$$\frac{\dot{Z}}{Z} = \frac{\dot{X}}{X} - \frac{\dot{Y}}{Y}.$$

To illustrate, let us return to the example of labor productivity $q = Q/L$. In Example 12 of Appendix 6B we apply the last rule to observe that the growth rates of these variables are related by

$$\frac{\dot{q}}{q} = \frac{\dot{Q}}{Q} - \frac{\dot{L}}{L}. \tag{8.34}$$

Not only do identities such as this relate instantaneous growth rates defined in terms of derivatives, we also have seen that they relate continuous growth rates computed as log-differences. Suppose that a researcher has data on output Q_t, labor L_t, and productivity q_t. The last has been computed as $q_t = Q_t/L_t$, either by the researcher or by the agency from which the data were obtained. The researcher calculates continuous growth rates as log-differences,

$$\Delta \log q_t, \quad \Delta \log Q_t, \quad \Delta \log L_t.$$

As we have seen in Appendix 6B, continuous growth rates satisfy the same relationships as instantaneous ones, and so these log-differences are related by the growth identity (8.34):

$$\Delta \log q_t = \Delta \log Q_t - \Delta \log L_t. \tag{8.35}$$

This parallels the linear dependence between the log-levels of these variables given in equation (8.30).

In exactly the same way, an identity must relate the growth rates of nominal and real variables and the price level,

$$\Delta \log y_t = \Delta \log Y_t - \Delta \log P_t,$$

in parallel with the linear dependence between their log-levels given by equation (8.32).[6] Similarly, an identity relates the growth rates of velocity, nominal income, and the money stock,

$$\Delta \log V_t = \Delta \log(P Q_t) - \Delta \log M_t,$$

in parallel with the linear dependence between their log-levels given by equation (8.33).

Returning to the example of labor productivity, perhaps unaware that the exact linear dependence (8.35) must hold, suppose the researcher now proceeds to a regression analysis. A model is specified that seeks to explain some dependent variable as a function of these three growth rates and perhaps other variables. The researcher will find that this regression cannot be estimated because the explanatory variables exhibit perfect multicollinearity. This will be true regardless of whether the regression is a time series regression in which the data observations are growth rates over successive time periods, or a cross-section regression in which the observations are growth rates observed across industries or countries. The solution is to reformulate the regression model to ensure that the explanatory variables are independent influences.

The Near Perfect Multicollinearity of Discrete Growth Rates

An especially pernicious variant of this problem arises when growth rates are computed as conventional discrete percentage changes rather than log-differences. Suppose once again that our hypothetical researcher has obtained data on productivity, output, and labor, not realizing that the statistical agency has simply constructed q_t as Q_t / L_t. This time, however, instead of computing continuous growth rates the researcher computes the discrete rates

$$\frac{\Delta q_t}{q_t}, \quad \frac{\Delta Q_t}{Q_t}, \quad \frac{\Delta L_t}{L_t}.$$

As we have seen in Appendix 6B, although these discrete rates come close to satisfying the growth identity (8.34), unlike continuous rates they do not satisfy

---

[6]   The growth rate of the numerical constant $\log 100$ in equation (8.32) is, of course, zero.

it exactly. Hence, now when the researcher runs the regression it may appear to estimate correctly—the regressors exhibit a **near perfect multicollinearity,** but not an exact linear dependence that makes it impossible to solve uniquely for the OLS estimators. The consequences for the estimation results are an extreme form of case 3, a degree of multicollinearity (Section 8.7.3). Nevertheless, the fact that it may be possible to compute the least squares estimators can hardly be viewed as satisfactory; perfect multicollinearity has been avoided only as an artifact of how growth rates are calculated. The correct approach is to respecify the regression model so that it does not involve a redundancy among the regressors.

Indeed, this is one more argument for always[7] computing growth rates as log-differences: Any redundancies will be manifested as perfect multicollinearity, as they should be.

Constructed Relationships between Variables

Much the same problem arises in other contexts. Often in empirical analysis one variable is constructed from others, and the inadvertent use of variables related by construction can give rise to perfect or near perfect multicollinearity.

For example, consider the calculation of ex post real rates of return from nominal interest rates and inflation. A nominal interest rate is the one you are used to thinking about—an observed rate of return that is calculated using nominal values, without any adjustment for losses of purchasing power due to inflation. For a riskless asset such as a bank balance covered by deposit insurance or a government treasury bill, this is the rate published in the newspaper. For a risky asset it is the ex post rate of return earned when the asset is sold. In any case, let us denote this nominal rate of return by i_t.

By contrast, denote the real—that is, after inflation—rate of return by r_t. This is not something we read in the newspaper. Instead, it is typically calculated as

$$\text{Real rate of return } r_t = \text{Nominal rate of return } i_t - \text{Inflation rate.} \qquad (8.36)$$

This is the *Fisher identity* between real and nominal interest rates and inflation. It was derived for instantaneous rates in Theory Meets Application 6.2 and—of more relevance to the present context—for continuous rates in Example 19 of Chapter 6.

It would be a very naive researcher who would take some nominal interest rate, subtract from it an inflation rate to obtain a real rate of return, and then

---

[7]   Well, almost always. Portfolio calculations are usually done with simple returns because, as we establish in Example 4 in the appendix to Chapter 3, the simple return on a portfolio is the weighted average of the individual simple returns. It turns out that this is not true of continuously compounded returns obtained as log-differences, which is perhaps surprising because it does hold for instantaneous returns (as we have seen in Example 3 of Chapter 7). The portfolio weighted average property would of course hold *approximately* for continuous returns at low rates, because then the log-differences are close to the simple returns.

run a regression with all three included as regressors. Fortunately, such a naive researcher would be saved from this mistake by the fact that the regression cannot be estimated; the regressors exhibit perfect multicollinearity.

The more serious problem arises when a not-quite-so-naive researcher obtains measures of these variables from independent sources: a nominal interest rate series from one source (and there are many from which to choose), an inflation rate from a second source (and again there are several price indices on which an inflation rate can be based), and some measure of real rates of return from a third source. The real rate of return must have been computed in the way we have described, but no doubt from nominal interest rate and inflation series different from those that happen to have been selected by the researcher. Consequently, the variables will exhibit a near-perfect multicollinearity, but not an exact linear dependence that prevents the regression from being estimated. Again, however, the problem is not so much that the regressors exhibit near perfect multicollinearity—their construction dictates that this must be the case—but instead the flawed logic that has led to the specification of a regression model involving a redundancy among the regressors.

Conclusions

In conclusion, perfect or near-perfect multicollinearity arises when a mistake has been made in specifying the explanatory variables. Instead of specifying variables that are genuinely distinct determinants of the dependent variable, the researcher has inadvertently used regressors that involve a redundancy. Such a redundancy can arise because the variables are related by an identity or by construction. The solution is to respecify the regression model so that there is no redundancy.

Practitioner's Tip: **Perfect and near-perfect multicollinearity**

Avoid perfect and near-perfect multicollinearity by ensuring that your variables involve no redundancies; that is, that they are not related by definition or construction. Regressors must be genuinely distinct influences.

In addition to the examples we have considered, there is another common situation in which a mistake in the specification of the regressors introduces a linear dependence. This has to do with the use of dummy variables—called the **dummy variable trap**—and it is considered in Chapter 10.

8.7.2 Absence of Multicollinearity

Let us turn to the other extreme of $r_{23} = 0$. Examining the correlation expression (8.15), it is apparent that this can only occur if its numerator is zero: $\sum x_{2i} x_{3i} = 0$. Equivalently, the sample observations on the explanatory variables are, in their deviation forms, orthogonal. The effect on the least squares coefficient estimators is, examining the formulas (8.12), that they simplify:

$$\hat{\beta}_2 = \frac{\sum x_{3i}^2 \sum x_{2i} y_i - \sum x_{2i} x_{3i} \sum x_{3i} y_i}{\sum x_{2i}^2 \sum x_{3i}^2 - (\sum x_{2i} x_{3i})^2} = \frac{\sum x_{2i} y_i}{\sum x_{2i}^2}, \qquad \text{when } r_{23} = 0;$$

$$\hat{\beta}_3 = \frac{\sum x_{2i}^2 \sum x_{3i} y_i - \sum x_{2i} x_{3i} \sum x_{2i} y_i}{\sum x_{2i}^2 \sum x_{3i}^2 - (\sum x_{2i} x_{3i})^2} = \frac{\sum x_{3i} y_i}{\sum x_{3i}^2}, \qquad \text{when } r_{23} = 0.$$

The final expressions are recognizable as the slope estimators in two simple regressions of Y_i on each of X_{2i} and X_{3i}, respectively. Hence, when explanatory variables are unrelated (in the sense of being uncorrelated), the estimated slope coefficients yielded by multiple regression are identical to those that would be obtained from $K - 1$ simple regressions! The lack of any interrelationship among the variables means that it is not necessary to control for the effects of the other variables in estimating the relationship between Y and a particular X_k; a simple regression correctly estimates the ceterus paribus effect.

Although this result is striking, we hasten to add that the same conclusion does not apply to the estimated standard errors $s_{\hat{\beta}_k}$. Even with orthogonal regressors these will differ between multiple regression and a series of simple regressions. The reason is that, although the sampling variances (8.14) reduce to the simple regression expressions of the form (4.26) when $r_{23} = 0$, the appropriate way of estimating σ^2 continues to be s^2 given by the multiple regression formula (8.13). Consequently, if statistical inference beyond point estimation is of interest, we do not want to substitute a series of simple regressions for a single multiple regression.

Because the sampling variances (8.14) are minimized for $r_{23} = 0$, researchers in disciplines in which there is scope for **experimental design** sometimes find it useful to design the experiments that generate their data in such a way that, by construction, explanatory variables are orthogonal. For example, in studying the effects of fertilizer X_2 and insecticide X_3 on crop yield Y you might vary their application across fields in such a way that X_2 and X_3 are uncorrelated. This is possible because in the experimental sciences explanatory variables are under the control of the researchers. Unfortunately such opportunities are rare in the social sciences (with the notable exception of psychology, in which controlled experimentation on subjects plays a large role). Because economists almost always work with nonexperimental data, the case of orthogonal regressors is largely of theoretical rather than practical interest in econometrics. Instead, in practice economic variables are virtually always correlated to some degree, and it is this that we have termed multicollinearity.

8.7.3 A Degree of Multicollinearity

We have emphasized that a degree of correlation between the explanatory variables makes it difficult to disentangle their individual influences on the dependent variable. This is apparent from the variance expressions (8.14), which indicate that the sampling variances $V(\hat{\beta}_2)$ and $V(\hat{\beta}_3)$ are directly related to $|r_{23}|$; as $|r_{23}| \to 1$ the denominators of these expressions approach zero. In general, multicollinearity increases the sampling variances of the least squares estimators. It is in this very precise sense that the accuracy with which the ceterus paribus effects can be estimated is reduced.

This explains why some of the seeming inconsistencies between t and F tests discussed in the previous section can so easily arise, particularly cases 2 and 3, some (or all) insignificant t tests simultaneously with a significant F test. Large variances of the least squares estimators, because the corresponding estimated standard errors are in the denominators of the t ratios, will give rise to low t statistics. Hence, an insignificant t test does not necessarily mean that the explanatory variable in question is unimportant as a determinant of Y; only that the available sample data do not allow us to estimate the coefficient precisely enough to justify the conclusion that it clearly *is* important. At the same time, an F test may well indicate that the explanatory variables are jointly important. Seeming inconsistencies of this sort between t and F tests become more likely as the degree of multicollinearity increases, exactly as is evident from Figure 8.2 when we consider the effect of $|r_{23}| \to 1$ on the rejection region of the F test.

Several points follow from these observations. First, note that, despite these consequences of multicollinearity, there is no violation of any of the classical assumptions of the model specification (8.1). All our conclusions concerning the properties of the least squares estimators continue to hold: they are unbiased, efficient, and BLUE. Multicollinearity simply means that, although the least squares estimators have the smallest variance among all unbiased estimators (or, in the absence of normality, the smallest variance among all linear unbiased estimators), this minimum variance is still relatively large. Nevertheless, no other unbiased (or linear unbiased) estimator does better.

In using least squares to estimate the ceterus paribus effects, then, we have done our best; it is just that our best is not very good. However, this is unavoidable in that it arises, ultimately, from the nature of the data, which do not provide the information needed to more clearly disentangle the separate effects of the explanatory variables.

Measuring Multicollinearity

A second point is that, as Kmenta (1986, p. 431) has put it, "Multicollinearity is a question of degree and not of kind. The meaningful distinction is not between the presence and the absence of multicollinearity, but between its various degrees." This is related to the fact that multicollinearity " ... is a feature of the sample and not of the population." That is, our model specification (8.1) involves no parameters that we might regard as being associated with multicollinearity; instead, the problem is that the particular sample of data that we are using to estimate the model has low informational content. On this logic, it is not possible to test for multicollinearity because it is not manifested in the form of testable parameter restrictions.

THEORY MEETS APPLICATION   8.1

Does Ridge Regression Resolve Multicollinearity?

An approach to multicollinearity that gained some interest among econometricians at one time is **ridge regression.** Although it has since fallen out of favor, it is worth mentioning here because it relates to our discussion of properties of estimators in Chapter 2.

The basic problem of multicollinearity is that it results in the least squares estimators $\hat{\beta}_k$ having large sampling variances, despite the Gauss-Markov theorem that these are the smallest variances attainable by any linear unbiased estimator. Ridge regression provides alternative estimators $\tilde{\beta}_k$ that are biased (and therefore are neither efficient nor BLUE), but that have smaller variances than least squares. The idea is illustrated by the following figure, in which the biased estimator $\tilde{\beta}$ may be preferred to the unbiased one $\hat{\beta}$.

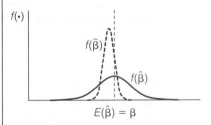

$f(\cdot)$

$f(\tilde{\beta})$

$f(\hat{\beta})$

$E(\hat{\beta}) = \beta$

A researcher might be willing to trade the unbiasedness of the least squares estimator for the smaller variance of the ridge estimator. Ridge regression introduces bias by shrinking the mean of the sampling distribution toward zero and falls under the general topic of **shrinkage estimation;** discussions of this method are also encountered under the title of **biased estimation.** It illustrates that the property of unbiasedness is not necessarily sacrosanct.

Ridge regression makes use of outside information in a way that is rather ill-defined, and this is one reason for the decline in its use since the method enjoyed a flurry of application in the 1970s. The underlying theory, and the sense in which outside information is employed, can only properly be developed in the context of Bayesian statistics. Another issue in the application of the technique is that the use of biased estimators in hypothesis testing is problematic. For all these reasons, ridge regression is no longer favored by econometricians. It continues to enjoy some interest among statisticians, as evidenced by the comprehensive book by Gruber (1998).

Ultimately multicollinearity is best seen as a state of the world in which the data are uninformative about some hypotheses of interest, such as those tested with t statistics (but perhaps not about others, such as that tested with the F statistic). Its existence is properly and accurately manifest through large standard errors. Any merits of ridge regression have little to do with these considerations.

This perspective is, however, premised on the convenient fiction that the regressors are nonstochastic. Although a useful assumption, it is an artificial one. If this premise is abandoned, then a test for multicollinearity in principle becomes possible. Judge et al. (1985, pp. 926–927) provide a brief survey of work in this area. However, the usefulness of such a test is questionable because it is known in advance that most sets of explanatory variables will exhibit some degree of multicollinearity; a test that confirms that this is the case does not get us very far.

A more common approach is to compute descriptive measures of the degree of multicollinearity. In the case of just two explanatory variables, the obvious measure is, of course, the correlation r_{23} (or, to have a positive measure, $|r_{23}|$ or r_{23}^2). For $K > 3$ we might be tempted to extend this idea by examining pairwise correlations between variables. One difficulty of this approach is that, as we have seen in Chapter 3, the number of pairwise correlations grows exponentially as K increases, so that for even a moderate number of regressors many correlations have to be examined. A single statistic would be preferred. More fundamentally, however, the examination of pairwise correlations is simply not a reliable means of gauging the degree of multicollinearity. Kmenta (1986, pp. 433–434) presents a striking example of just $K - 1 = 3$ explanatory variables that are linearly dependent (that is, exhibit *perfect* multicollinearity so that the least squares estimators are not uniquely defined) and yet for which no pairwise correlation exceeds 0.5.

Perhaps the most common measure of multicollinearity reported by econometrics software packages is the **condition number** advocated by Belsley, Kuh, and Welsch (1980), an understanding of which requires concepts from matrix algebra. However, no one statistic has been universally adopted as an entirely satisfactory indicator. At least as useful as descriptive measures in judging whether multicollinearity may be a problem are its classic symptoms. One is, as we have seen, a significant F statistic accompanied by many insignificant t statistics. Because multicollinearity generates large sampling variabilities, another symptom is a sensitivity of estimation results to minor changes in the sample or the model specification. If coefficient magnitudes or signs change dramatically when a few observations are deleted from the sample or an additional explanatory variable is introduced, we should suspect that multicollinearity may be present to an extent that compromises what can be learned from the analysis.

Ultimately, however, interest in indicators of multicollinearity is mitigated by the fact that the remedies are very few. Because the fundamental problem is a lack of informational content in the sample data, any remedy must be in the form of additional information of some sort. Although in principle this additional information can take a variety of forms, in practice the feasibility of doing this is both very limited and highly application-specific and so little in general can be said. An example of the application-specific nature of multicollinearity is given in the next section.

The Similarity between Multicollinearity and Variation in the Data

"Everyone talks about the weather, but no one does anything about it." If Mark Twain had been an econometrician he might have said much the same about multicollinearity.

Formally, the implications of multicollinearity for regression analysis are similar to those of an absence of variation in the data. Recall that in our specification of the classical regression model we require that the data exhibit variation, just as we require an absence of perfect multicollinearity. A complete absence of variation in the data means that the regression cannot be estimated—the least squares esti-

370 CHAPTER 8 Multiple Regression

mators are not uniquely defined, just as is true under perfect multicollinearity. Low variation in the data means that coefficients are estimated imprecisely, estimated variances are large, and t statistics are low, just as is true when there is a degree of multicollinearity. Yet given a sample of data and model to be estimated, both are a fact of life about which nothing can be done; researchers can no more do something about "the multicollinearity problem" than they can do something about "the lack-of-variation problem."

Practitioner's Tip: Multicollinearity

Multicollinearity is a bit like the weather: Although much can be said about it, in the end not much can be done about it. Given a model specification and an available sample of data, multicollinearity is a fact of life, like the degree of variation in the sample.

EXERCISES

8.8 The Fisher identity (8.36) is established in Chapter 6 for both instantaneous and continuous rates. Suppose that, employing the notation of Example 19 in Chapter 6, there is a price level P_t and nominal and real values V_t and v_t that are related definitionally by $v_t = V_t/P_t$. Instead of instantaneous or continuous rates, consider the discrete rates,

$$\text{Inflation rate} \equiv \frac{\Delta P_t}{P_{t-1}}, \text{Nominal rate } i_t \equiv \frac{\Delta V_t}{V_{t-1}},$$

$$\text{Real rate } r_t \equiv \frac{\Delta v_t}{v_{t-1}}.$$

(a) Does the equality (8.36) still hold? If you conclude it does not, does any definitional relationship hold among these discrete rates? If so, what?

(b) Suppose a researcher includes all three of these discrete rates as explanatory variables. Is this best described as a situation of perfect multicollinearity, near-perfect multicollinearity, a degree of multicollinearity, or an absence of multicollinearity?

8.9 In international economics there is an important distinction between *nominal* and *real* exchange rates. A nominal exchange rate e^n is the rate at which currencies are traded. This is the exchange rate that is quoted in the newspaper. By contrast, the real exchange rate e^r is the rate at which goods are exchanged. It is also known as the terms of trade. This is not observed directly, but can be constructed from available data as

$$e^r = e^n \times \frac{P^d}{P^f}.$$

Here P^d denotes the domestic price level (the domestic price of a bundle of goods) and P^f denotes the foreign price level (the price of the same bundle of goods in the other country, in the foreign currency). The real exchange rate tells us the rate at which domestic goods can be traded for foreign goods.

(a) Suppose you have a friend who is considering estimating a regression equation that uses these variables as regressors. What are the consequences for estimation of using as regressors

i. the logs of the variables: $\log e^r$, $\log e^n$, $\log P^d$, and $\log P^f$.

ii. the continuous percentage changes in the variables: $\Delta \log e_t^r$, $\Delta \log e_t^n$, $\Delta \log P_t^d$, and $\Delta \log P_t^f$;

iii. the discrete percentage changes in the variables: $\Delta e_t^r/e_{t-1}^r$, $\Delta e_t^n/e_{t-1}^n$, $\Delta P_t^d/P_{t-1}^d$, and $\Delta P_t^f/P_{t-1}^f$;

iv. the variables untransformed: e^r, e^n, P^d, and P^f.

In each case, what would your advice be to your friend regarding the desirability of estimating a regression of the proposed form?

(b) Does your advice depend on whether the regression is estimated using time series data (observations over time for a single pair of countries) or cross-section data (observations at a point in time over many country pairs)?

8.8   Application: The Quadratic Cost Function

As a firm increases its output by employing more factor inputs, costs rise. The typical pattern of costs C as they vary with output Q is portrayed in Figure 8.3. Although costs always increase with output (it never costs less to produce more), they do so in a way that relates to the returns-to-scale properties of the production process. At low levels of output at which returns to scale are increasing, a doubling of output can be achieved with a less than doubling of costs. At high levels of output governed by decreasing returns, an increase in output requires a more than proportional increase in costs. This gives rise to the typical reverse-S-shape pattern of the cost function and the accompanying $\cup$ shape of the average and marginal cost curves.[8]

How might this nonlinear relationship between C and Q be modeled empirically? Chapter 6 studied several ways of using the linear regression model to treat nonlinear relationships between variables, which we call intrinsically linear functional forms. However, none produced a reverse-S-shape curve like the total cost

FIGURE 8.3

Total, average, and marginal costs.

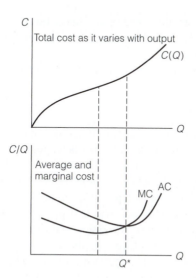

---

[8]   This is a very superficial sketch of the relationship between costs and returns to scale. Section 11.1 offers a more thorough treatment.

FIGURE 8.4

Alternative intrinsically linear cost functions.

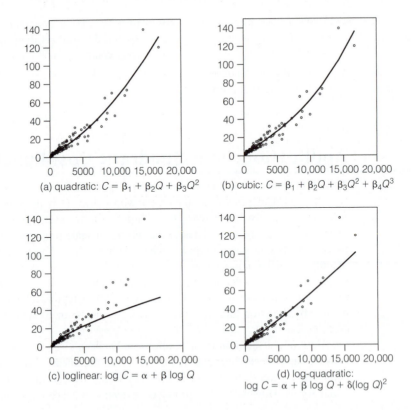

(a) quadratic: $C = \beta_1 + \beta_2 Q + \beta_3 Q^2$

(b) cubic: $C = \beta_1 + \beta_2 Q + \beta_3 Q^2 + \beta_4 Q^3$

(c) loglinear: $\log C = \alpha + \beta \log Q$

(d) log-quadratic:
$\log C = \alpha + \beta \log Q + \delta(\log Q)^2$

function. Here we consider another intrinsically linear functional form, **polynomial regression.** (It would have been premature to introduce this in Chapter 6 because it requires multiple regression).

Consider first a regression model that specifies C to be a quadratic function of Q:

$$C_i = \beta_1 + \beta_2 Q_i + \beta_3 Q_i^2 + \varepsilon_i. \tag{8.37}$$

This is an intrinsically linear model because it can be estimated as a conventional least squares multiple regression (using the constructed regressor Q_i^2). Nevertheless, it permits a nonlinear relationship between C and Q, one with a single bump that would be suitable if we were modeling not total cost C but average or marginal costs. This quadratic cost function is depicted in Figure 8.4(a) for Nerlove's cost-output data on electricity generation that was first presented in Figure 3.1.

A special case of this quadratic regression sets $\beta_3 = 0$, which just yields a simple regression. In this case, of course, the curve has no bump at all—it is just a straight line. This simple regression is the subject of many of the examples of Chapter 4, culminating in the exercises of Section 4.10. You found in Exercise 4.34c that this linear specification fails to capture the curvature in these data.

A quadratic function is a polynomial of degree 2; a linear function is a polynomial of degree 1. Note that a polynomial of degree 1 has no bump, and a polynomial of degree 2 has one bump. This suggests that, in general, a polynomial of degree k has $k - 1$ bumps, and that a curve with two bumps, such as the total cost curve, may be described by a polynomial of degree 3:

$$C_i = \beta_1 + \beta_2 Q_i + \beta_3 Q_i^2 + \beta_4 Q_i^3 + \varepsilon_i. \tag{8.38}$$

Exercise 8.11 asks you to estimate this cubic cost function; the result is shown in Figure 8.4(b). Although in principle it has the desirable feature of permitting a point of inflection, a comparison with Figure 8.4(a) indicates that this turns out not to be particularly important for modeling Nerlove's data; inspection suggests that the cubic specification yields only a slightly different estimated cost function from the quadratic. You are asked to test this formally in Exercise 8.11b.

Multicollinearity

A practical problem with polynomial regression that is important for some applications is that, because the regressors Q_i, Q_i^2, and Q_i^3 are just successive powers of the same variable, they are often strongly correlated. That is, they exhibit multicollinearity. (Because the relationship between these regressors is nonlinear, the assumption of linear independence is not violated.) The implication, as we have seen in the previous section, is that at least some of the coefficients in the polynomial regression may be estimated imprecisely.

Is there any way around this multicollinearity problem? As we have emphasized, because multicollinearity relates fundamentally to the informational content of the sample data, there is no general means of treating multicollinearity. What we can do, however, is ask less of the data. In the present context, is there any way of describing the reverse-S-shape of the total cost curve that does not require the estimation of as many coefficients as appear in the cubic cost function?

Let us first consider the simpler problem of a curve with one bump, such as the left half of the cost curve in Figure 8.3(a), the region in which returns are increasing. Although this could be modeled with a quadratic function, an alternative that we have studied in Chapter 6 is to use a logarithmic model, say

$$\log C_i = \alpha + \beta \log Q_i + \varepsilon_i.$$

However, in capturing the increasing returns portion of the cost function, this specification fails utterly to describe the rest of the function, as Figure 8.4(c) reveals.

To resolve this, let us reason by analogy that a curve with two bumps—that is, one that describes both the increasing and decreasing returns portions of the cost function—may be obtained with a quadratic-in-logs regression:

$$\log C_i = \alpha + \beta \log Q_i + \delta(\log Q_i)^2 + \varepsilon_i. \tag{8.39}$$

This has one fewer coefficient than the alternative of the cubic-in-levels regression (8.38). Exercise 8.12 asks you to use Nerlove's data to estimate and interpret this log-quadratic model. It is shown in Figure 8.4(d).

The Minimum Efficient Scale of Production

For what purposes might it be important to obtain precise estimates of the parameters of the cost curve? A concept that has some importance in applied production analysis is the **minimum efficient scale** of production. This is the level of output at which the minimum of the average cost curve is reached, denoted by Q^* in Figure 8.3. Average cost AC is, of course, total cost C divided by output Q:

$$AC = \frac{C}{Q}.$$

The minimum of the AC curve is the same as the minimum of the logarithm of that curve[9] and so, if the quadratic-in-logs cost curve (8.39) is the chosen empirical model, we may equivalently consider

$$\log AC = \log C - \log Q = \alpha + (\beta - 1) \log Q + \delta (\log Q)^2.$$

The derivative is

$$\frac{d \log AC}{dQ} = \frac{\beta - 1}{Q} + \frac{2\delta \log Q}{Q}. \tag{8.40}$$

Setting this equal zero and solving for Q yields a minimum efficient scale of

$$Q^* = \exp\left(\frac{1 - \beta}{2\delta}\right). \tag{8.41}$$

Naturally the minimum efficient scale depends on the parameters of the cost function, in this case β and δ. Our ability to estimate Q^* precisely depends on the precision with which those parameters can be estimated.

Further Comments

This treatment of the cost function has been overly simplistic: we have focused only on how costs vary with output, neglecting to recognize that they vary with factor prices as well. This more general conception of the cost function is developed in Chapter 11. In Section 11.5 we find that the quadratic-in-logs cost curve (8.39) is the basis for the famous **translog cost function** that dominates empirical work in production analysis.

It is interesting to consider the special case of $\delta = 0$, the linear-in-logs function

$$\log C = \alpha + \beta \log Q.$$

This may be interpreted as the application of a Cobb-Douglas functional form to the cost curve,

$$C = \gamma Q^\beta,$$

where we have defined $\alpha = \log \gamma$. In Chapter 11 we study a generalization of this Cobb-Douglas cost function that includes factor prices. Although we find that it

---

[9] Because the logarithm is a monotonic transformation. Monotonic transformations do not change the extrema of a function.

has many appealing features, ultimately we reject it as an adequate specification, in part because it fails to permit a reverse-S-shape for the cost curve—just as Figure 8.4(c) indicates.

We have acknowledged that factor prices as well as output should appear on the right-hand side of the cost function. It is therefore natural to inquire into the implications for a regression analysis of failing to include relevant explanatory variables. This is one of the topics of the next section.

EXERCISES

Marc Nerlove's data on production costs and output for 145 electricity generating plants is available in the file **nerlove1.dat**. This data set is documented in Section 4.10.

8.10 nerlove1.dat Estimate the quadratic cost function (8.37). An inspection of Figure 8.4(a) suggests that this model captures a nonlinearity in the data that is missed by the simple linear cost function in Chapter 4, which sets $\beta_3 = 0$. Is the quadratic term in (8.37) statistically significant?

8.11 nerlove1.dat Estimate the cubic cost function (8.38).

(a) Have the coefficients of this model been estimated fairly precisely? How are you able to judge?

(b) A comparison of Figure 8.4(a) and 8.4(b) suggests that the cubic function may not add that much to the description of the nonlinear relation-

ship between costs and output, over and above the quadratic. Perform a test of this.

8.12 nerlove1.dat Estimate the log-quadratic cost function (8.39).

(a) Have the coefficients of this model been estimated fairly precisely? How are you able to judge?

(b) A comparison of Figure 8.4(c) and 8.4(d) suggests that the quadratic term contributes in an important way to describing this data. Perform a test of this.

(c) Compute an estimate of the minimum efficient scale of production. Examining his data set, how many of Nerlove's 145 firms were operating below this level?

8.13 Show how the minimum efficient scale expression (8.41) is derived from the derivative (8.40).

8.9   Model Misspecification

Our analysis of the regression model has assumed that the model is correctly specified; that is, that a model such as (8.1) is an accurate description of the population. Although the derivation of properties of estimators and test procedures must be done on the basis of an assumed population model, models are abstractions from reality and so ultimately there is no "true" model. It is therefore important to have an understanding of the implications of model misspecification—the use of an incorrectly specified model—for applied econometric analysis.

There are, of course, many respects in which a model might be incorrectly specified; several were alluded to in our discussion of the specification of the regression model in Sections 4.1 and 8.9. With respect to the disturbance, the assumptions of homoskedasticity and nonautocorrelation may not be satisfied in some circumstances. With respect to the functional form of the model, some relationships between economic variables may be intrinsically nonlinear.

In the present context of the classical linear regression model, the most useful type of specification error to discuss is the possibility that the set of explanatory variables has been misspecified. There are two possible cases. One is when a relevant explanatory variable has been omitted from the estimated model; the other is when an irrelevant variable has mistakenly been included. Let us consider each in turn.

8.9.1 Omission of a Relevant Regressor

To examine the consequences of omitting a relevant explanatory variable from a linear regression, imagine that the true model is

$$Y_i = \beta_1 + \beta_2 X_{2i} + \beta_3 X_{3i} + \varepsilon_i. \tag{8.42}$$

For example, this might be a regression explaining clothing expenditure Y_i as a function of education X_{2i} and income X_{3i}. A least squares estimation of this true model yields the coefficient estimators $\hat{\beta}_1$, $\hat{\beta}_2$, and $\hat{\beta}_3$ given by the formulas (8.11) and (8.12).

Suppose, however, that the researcher is unaware of the role of X_3 in determining Y and mistakenly estimates a simple regression of Y on X_2. The resulting sample regression line may be denoted

$$Y_i = b_1 + b_2 X_{2i} + e_i. \tag{8.43}$$

Here b_1 and b_2 denote the least squares estimators for the intercept and slope of the simple regression model, and are given by the usual formulas

$$b_1 = \overline{Y} - b_2 \overline{X}_2, \qquad b_2 = \frac{\sum x_{2i} y_i}{\sum x_{2i}^2}.$$

Obviously these differ from $\hat{\beta}_1$ and $\hat{\beta}_2$. Because, for example, b_2 does not make use of X_3 in estimating the effect of X_2 on Y, our intuition tells us that it cannot, in general, correctly capture the ceterus paribus relationship between the two. This intuition may be made precise by studying the properties of b_1 and b_2.

Omitted Variable Bias

Let us focus on b_2. Is it unbiased? Using the laws of summation, deviation form, mathematical expectation, and the fact that the true model generating Y_i is the regression (8.42), we have:

$$E(b_2) = E\left(\frac{\sum x_{2i} y_i}{\sum x_{2i}^2}\right)$$

$$= E\left(\frac{1}{\sum x_{2i}^2} \sum x_{2i} Y_i\right)$$

$$= \frac{1}{\sum x_{2i}^2} \sum x_{2i} E(Y_i)$$

$$= \frac{1}{\sum x_{2i}^2} \sum x_{2i} (\beta_1 + \beta_2 X_{2i} + \beta_3 X_{3i})$$

$$= \frac{1}{\sum x_{2i}^2} \left(\beta_1 \sum x_{2i} + \beta_2 \sum x_{2i}^2 + \beta_3 \sum x_{2i} x_{3i} \right)$$

$$= \beta_2 + \beta_3 \frac{\sum x_{2i} x_{3i}}{\sum x_{2i}^2}$$

$$= \beta_2 + \beta_3 b_{23} \tag{8.44}$$

$$\neq \beta_2.$$

The penultimate line introduces the notation

$$b_{23} = \frac{\sum x_{2i} x_{3i}}{\sum x_{2i}^2},$$

the slope estimator in a simple regression of X_3 on X_2.

This derivation shows that b_2 is a biased estimator; in repeated sampling it systematically under- or overestimates the true ceteris paribus effect. By how much does it under- or overestimate? The **omitted variable bias** is in the amount of

$$E(b_2) - \beta_2 = \beta_3 b_{23}. \tag{8.45}$$

What is the interpretation of this expression? Consider our example in which we mistakenly estimate a simple regression of clothing expenditure Y on education X_2, ignoring the role of income X_3. The omission of income means that b_2 is a biased estimate of the true effect of education on clothing expenditure. Expression (8.45) indicates that this bias has two elements. The expression b_{23} is the slope estimator in a simple regression of income on education, which should be positive; these two explanatory variables are directly related. The coefficient β_3 is the true effect of income on clothing expenditure, which should also be positive. Hence, the omitted variable bias (8.45) describes how education affects income and then, indirectly via income, clothing expenditure. It says that by failing to control for income, the estimator b_2 tends to *overestimate*—because we have reasoned that in this example the bias should be positive—the true effect of education on clothing expenditure. The misspecified simple regression will suggest a misleadingly large effect of education on clothing expenditure because it fails to control for the indirect effect of education on income and, in turn, income on clothing expenditure.

Omitted variable bias does not disappear asymptotically: There is nothing in the bias expression (8.45) causing it to go to zero as $n \to \infty$. Not only is b_2 biased, it is also *not* asymptotically unbiased.

In general, the bias expression (8.45) may be positive or negative, depending on the signs of β_3 and b_{23}. Although the latter is a sample quantity and therefore computable, the former is an unknown population value. Consequently, it is not possible to compute the magnitude of this bias and any belief we may have even about its sign is conjectural. In some situations, however, it may be possible to make plausible conjectures. Here is an example.

EXAMPLE 8

Consider a statistical earnings function in which a correctly specified model would explain the logarithm of earnings Y using both schooling S and ability A:

$$\log Y_i = \beta_1 + \beta_2 S_i + \beta_3 A_i + \varepsilon_i.$$

Ability is unobserved and so the regression is estimated using schooling alone:

$$\log Y_i = b_1 + b_2 S_i + e_i.$$

This is the regression originally estimated by Jacob Mincer (1974). As we describe in Theory Meets Application 4.1, he obtained an estimate of the rate of return to education of $b_2 = 0.07$.

Suppose we can be confident that both earnings and education are positively related to ability. In what direction is Mincer's estimate biased?

SOLUTION

This falls into the framework of omitted variable bias, where β_3 is the effect of ability on earnings and b_{23} is the slope in a regression of ability on education. If both are assumed to be positive, then the bias expression (8.45) is positive in total, so that $E(b_2) - \beta_2 > 0$ or, equivalently,

$$E(b_2) > \beta_2.$$

That is, Mincer's estimate most likely *overstates* the true return to education.

How large is this **ability bias?** This is something we can never know, precisely because ability is unobservable. If it were observable we could just estimate the correctly specified multiple regression. Nevertheless there have been many attempts to use various measures of ability to gauge the size of the bias. One of these attempts is described in Theory Meets Application 8.2.

Correlation and Causality Revisited

In Chapter 3 we see that causality does not imply correlation and correlation does not imply causality. The main reason for this is that the failure to control for outside influences can mean that an estimated correlation—or, in the present context, an estimated regression coefficient—can give a misleading indication of the relationship between two variables. Our bias result makes it possible to understand this formally because the omission of the relevant regressor X_3 from the estimated model (8.43) constitutes a failure to control for an outside influence.

Correlation does not imply causality. The estimated effect b_2 could be substantial in magnitude, even if the true effect β_2 is zero. In our example, it is conceivable that in the population there is *no* ceteris paribus effect of education on clothing expenditure ($\beta_2 = 0$), but that the estimated effect b_2 is substantial owing to the omitted variable bias, the indirect effect of education on income and income on clothing expenditure.

THEORY MEETS APPLICATION

8.2

Ability Bias in Estimating the Return to Education

As Example 8 shows, the omission of ability from a statistical earnings function will bias the estimate of the return to education upward. Is there any way to gauge the size of this ability bias?

Although ability is not observable, it can be measured in various ways—admittedly all highly imperfect. Griliches (1976, 1977) studied the returns to education of young men for whom IQ data were available. Using IQ as a proxy for ability, Griliches (1976, equations B1 and B3 in Table 2; 1977, equations 4 and 5 in Table 1) estimated earnings functions with and without this proxy.

	Earnings functions	
Variable	IQ omitted	IQ included
Schooling	0.065	0.059
IQ	. . .	0.0019

The idea of a **proxy variable** is as follows. Although we do not take it seriously as a measure of the variable we would ideally like to have—no one believes that IQ measures ability—it may nevertheless be *correlated* with the unobservable variable. Hence, when the proxy is included as a regressor, its coefficient is not to be interpreted as equivalent to the coefficient on the true variable; we would not attempt to use the estimation results for the coefficient on IQ to make inferences about

the effect of ability on earnings (or at least would be extremely cautious about doing so). Instead, the value of the proxy variable is that its presence may serve to mitigate the omitted variable bias in the other coefficients of the regression.

How did this work in Griliches's application? Notice that the introduction of IQ does indeed reduce the estimated rate of return to education by approximately 10%, from 0.065 to 0.059. This is consistent with the prediction that the omission of ability will result in an artificially high estimate.

On the basis of results such as these Griliches concluded that ability bias is fairly small, and this finding has stood the test of time. In a survey of more recent work Card (1999, p. 1855) concludes that the return to education

> . . . is not much below the estimate that emerges from a simple cross-sectional regression of earnings on education. The "best available" evidence from the latest studies . . . suggests a small upward bias (on the order of 10%) in the simple OLS estimates.

One reason ability bias may be fairly small is that it may be offset by a different source of bias—the simultaneity bias discussed in Theory Meets Application 5.1. For a textbook treatment of Griliches's work that both considers omitted variable bias and treats IQ as an error-ridden measure of ability—a problem similar in its econometric implications to simultaneity—see Hayashi (2000, Sec. 3.9).

As another illustration, consider the example from Chapter 3 of the correlation between family income and number of children, in which we see that it is important to control for parental age as a third variable. In terms of our present notation, let Y denote number of children, X_2 denote family income, and X_3 denote the age of the household head. We have seen that Y is positively correlated with X_2, so that a simple regression yields a slope b_2 that suggests that higher incomes "cause" more children. But this positive effect is due to omitted variable bias. The variables Y and X_2 are spuriously correlated because of the failure to take into account the fact that parental age X_3 is positively correlated with both.

Causality does not imply correlation. Omitted variable bias can as easily understate effects as overstate them. The true effect β_2 of X_2 on Y could be a strong one, yet the estimated effect b_2 could be small owing to the bias.

Under What Circumstances Is the Bias Zero?

Returning to the bias expression (8.45), it is instructive to note that there are two special cases in which it is zero: $\beta_3 = 0$ or $b_{23} = 0$. Let us consider the meaning of each.

1. **A zero coefficient on the omitted regressor.** If $\beta_3 = 0$, then X_3 does not belong in the model (8.42) and the regression (8.43) constitutes the estimation of the true model. There is no model misspecification, and so it makes perfect sense that the omitted variable bias is zero.

2. $b_{23} = 0$. If $b_{23} = 0$, then this can only be because $\sum x_{2i} x_{3i} = 0$ (because the denominator $\sum x_{2i}^2$ is some positive value, given the assumption of variation in X_{2i}). There are two ways in which this numerator can be zero: uncorrelated regressors and an absence of variation in X_{3i}. Let us consider each possibility.

    (a) **Uncorrelated regressors:** $r_{23} = 0$. In our discussion of an absence of multicollinearity in Section 8.7.2, this was described as the case of orthogonal regressors. We have seen that in this circumstance a series of simple regressions yields the same coefficient estimates as a single multiple regression. By this result, in the special case when regressors are uncorrelated the misspecified simple regression (8.43) will yield the same slope estimate as the correctly specified multiple regression: $b_2 = \hat{\beta}_2$. It follows that in this special case the omitted variable bias is zero.

    This should not be interpreted as saying that there is no cost to the misspecification, only that the cost does not take the form of a coefficient bias. We have seen in earlier discussion that a simple regression does not correctly estimate the standard errors, and so even with orthogonal regressors we would still want to estimate the multiple regression.

    (b) **Absence of variation in X_{3i}.** Suppose that in the available sample of data the variable X_3 does not vary across observations, so that the common value $X_{3i} = X_3$ holds over all i. In this case, the sample mean also equals this common value, $\overline{X}_3 = X_3$, the deviation forms $x_{3i} = X_{3i} - \overline{X}_3$ are zero, and therefore so is the expression $\sum x_{2i} x_{3i}$. The intuition is as follows. Because the variation in the dependent variable Y is not due to variation in X_3 (because there is no such variation), X_3 is not a variable that must be controlled for in correctly estimating β_2, and the omitted variable bias is zero. Indeed, the absence of variation in X_3 means that it is not even possible to estimate the true model (8.42) with the available sample.

Consider the following example of situation 2b.

EXAMPLE 9

Consider the regression model

$$Y_i = \beta_1 + \beta_2 X_{2i} + \beta_3 X_{3i} + \varepsilon_i,$$

in which Y_i is crop yield, X_{2i} is fertilizer application (which is under the control of the researcher), and X_{3i} is rainfall. All are observed across fields indexed by i. Suppose, however, that once the data are collected we find that all fields have experienced exactly the same rainfall, so that $X_{3i} = X_3$. What are the implications for the estimation of this regression model and the study of the effect of fertilizer on crop yield?

SOLUTION

Because we do not observe differential rainfall across fields, it is obviously not possible to learn anything about the link between rainfall and crop yield from these data. That is, the true model is not estimable.

Note, however, that it is the effect of fertilizer application, not rainfall, that is the researcher's interest, and for this purpose the lack of variation in X_3 is actually a simplification—an advantage rather than a liability. There are no negative implications for β_2, which is estimable in the usual way (as the slope coefficient in a simple regression). Although this regression is the misspecified model (8.43), by the previous reasoning the omitted variable bias is zero. Because rainfall is constant across observations, its influence has already been controlled for; it is unnecessary to use multiple regression to accomplish this.

What Determines the Size of the Bias?

Outside these special cases, the bias (8.45) is nonzero. The magnitude of this bias relates naturally to our discussion of multicollinearity; the bias is larger the larger is the sample covariation $\sum x_{2i} x_{3i}$ (in absolute value). The stronger the correlation between the explanatory variables—that is, the greater the degree of multicollinearity—the greater the role the other variables play in correctly estimating any one ceteris paribus effect and hence the greater the bias introduced by failing to control for them.

EXAMPLE 10

In Section 7.3 we study Robert Solow's method for obtaining an index of multifactor productivity A_t. Estimation of an aggregate production function in a way that controls for technical change makes use of the intensive form

$$\frac{q_t}{A_t} = f(k_t),$$

which is equation (7.32). In Exercise 7.10 you do this using a Cobb-Douglas form for $f(\cdot)$, estimating

$$\log q_t - \log A_t = \log \gamma + \beta \log k_t + \varepsilon_t. \tag{8.46}$$

Suppose you are unaware of the role of technical change in economic growth and naively obtain as an estimated aggregate production function the least squares regression

$$\log q_t = b_1 + b_2 \log k_t + e_t. \tag{8.47}$$

What are the implications for b_2 as an estimator of β?

SOLUTION

This is essentially the setup of the preceding discussion, in which the estimated model (8.47) corresponds to (8.43) with $Y = \log q$ and $X_2 = \log k$ and the correctly specified model (8.46) corresponds to (8.42) with $X_3 = \log A$, $\beta_2 = \beta$, and $\beta_3 = 1$. Hence, by (8.44), b_2 as an estimator of β has the property that

$$E(b_2) = \beta + \frac{\sum x_{2i} x_{3i}}{\sum x_{2i}^2} \neq \beta. \tag{8.48}$$

That is, it is biased. Furthermore, in contrast to the more general situation described by (8.45) in which the bias depends on the unknown parameter β_3, in this instance the value of the bias may be determined; you are asked to compute it in Exercise 8.17. Most notably, an inspection of Solow's series on the capital-labor ratio k and technical progress A_t in Table 7.2 indicates that they are positively correlated: Historically, technical progress has accompanied greater capital-intensity of production. Hence, the bias expression in (8.48) is positive because it takes the same sign as the correlation. The implication is that b_2 overestimates the true value of β. This is consistent with the reasoning of Section 7.3, in which the examination of Figure 7.5 suggests that the failure to treat technical change will lead to an artificially high estimate of β.

Omitted Variable Bias and Multicollinearity

The finding that the omission of relevant regressors biases the remaining coefficients provides some insight into one aspect of our discussion of multicollinearity. We have seen that correlations among regressors make it difficult to disentangle their respective ceteris paribus effects on the dependent variable. One "solution" to multicollinearity that we did *not* propose is the dropping of regressors. Our result from omitted variable bias explains why. However regrettable multicollinearity may be, we have seen that nevertheless least squares does the best that can be done under the circumstances, including retaining the property of unbiasedness. To drop relevant regressors is to introduce what most would view as the greater evil of biasing the remaining coefficient estimates. Our inspection of the bias expression has revealed that the stronger the correlation with the remaining regressors, the greater this bias will be. If variables are strongly interrelated it is all the more important to control for them in attempting to estimate ceteris paribus effects,

FIGURE 8.5

The ceterus paribus and indirect effects of X_2 on Y.

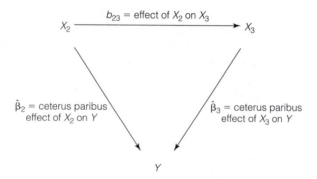

even if the best that can be done is to obtain estimated effects that are relatively imprecise.

A Sample Analog to the Bias Result

Because it is a bias result, (8.44) is largely in terms of population quantities. Exercise 8.15 asks you to establish the analogous sample relationship

$$b_2 = \hat{\beta}_2 + \hat{\beta}_3 b_{23}. \tag{8.49}$$

This says that the misleading simple regression slope estimator b_2 is the correctly estimated ceterus paribus effect $\hat{\beta}_2$ plus the indirect effect of X_2 on Y via the relationship between X_2 and X_3. In summary,

Gross effect of X_2 on Y = Ceterus paribus effect + Indirect effect.

The indirect effect of X_2 on Y is the product of the effect of X_2 on X_3 (measured by b_{23}) and the effect of X_3 on Y (measured by $\hat{\beta}_3$). The two components of the misleading gross effect, the ceterus paribus effect and the indirect effect, are portrayed in Figure 8.5.

Conclusions

The fact that least squares estimators are, in general, biased when relevant regressors are omitted means that the consequences of this type of model misspecification are extremely serious. For it follows immediately that least squares is neither efficient nor BLUE because unbiasedness is a prerequisite for both properties. It implies as well that the usual hypothesis testing procedures are meaningless, as unbiasedness lies behind the validity of distributional results such as (8.19). In what sense are they meaningless? Given some chosen nominal significance level a, in proceeding mechanically with the usual steps of a t or F test we may in fact be incurring a probability of Type I error very different from a. In the terminology of Section 2.5.1, the true test size may depart from its nominal size. Similarly, a constructed $(1 - a)100\%$ confidence interval may in reality bound the true parameter value a proportion of the time very different from $(1 - a)$ in repeated sampling.

These findings provide some insight into the importance of the assumption (8.2) that the explanatory variables of a regression model be uncorrelated with the disturbance. Because the omission of a regressor effectively means that this influence is factored into the disturbance, any correlation between the omitted and included variables implies a violation of condition (8.2). As is now apparent, biased estimators are the result.

That the desirable properties of least squares disappear so completely in the face of what is, in practice, likely to be a common specification error, can only be humbling to the applied econometrician. Of course, as the expression (8.44) makes clear, the magnitude of the bias and hence the importance of the consequences that flow from it depend on the particular application under study. In some cases these consequences may be severe, in others less so, and we have seen examples of both cases. In going from Engel curves estimated using Houthakker's electricity demand data in Section 6.5 to the fully specified demand functions of Section 8.6, we have found that the estimated income elasticities were not greatly altered. Similarly, Griliches's findings suggest that the ability bias in statistical earnings functions is probably small. On the other hand, as Exercise 8.17 demonstrates, the Solow application is a dramatic illustration of just how severe omitted variable bias can be.

EXERCISES

8.14 Show that b_1 is biased as an estimator for β_1. Provide an expression for the bias.

8.15 Use the appropriate estimator expressions for b_2, $\hat{\beta}_2$, $\hat{\beta}_3$, and b_{23} to establish the sample relationship (8.49).

8.16 ⊙ **nerlove1.dat** Section 8.8 proposes the log-quadratic cost function

$$\log C_i = \beta_1 + \beta_2 \log Q_i + \beta_3 (\log Q_i)^2 + \varepsilon_i.$$

Suppose that instead a loglinear cost function is estimated,

$$\log C_i = b_1 + b_2 \log Q_i + e_i.$$

Use Nerlove's data on output and production costs in the file **nerlove1.dat** to compute the statistics b_2, $\hat{\beta}_2$, $\hat{\beta}_3$, and b_{23}. Do they satisfy the relationship (8.49)?

8.17 ⊙ **solow.dat** Returning to Robert Solow's data as presented in Table 7.2 (available in the file **solow.dat**), run the appropriate simple regression to compute b_{23}, the bias term in (8.48).

(a) Is this bias positive, as the reasoning of Example 10 suggests it should be?

(b) How does its value compare with your answer to Exercise 7.11b?

(c) What special case of the sample relationship (8.49) applies in this context? Indicate how your equation applies to the numerical values of the Solow application.

8.18 ⊙ **houthak.dat** In Exercise 8.6 you replicate Hendrick Houthakker's estimation of a loglinear model for electricity demand:

$$\log q_i = \beta_1 + \beta_2 \log m_i + \beta_3 \log p_{1i}$$
$$+ \beta_4 \log p_{2i} + \beta_5 \log h_i + \varepsilon_i. \quad (8.50)$$

Let us denote the least squares estimators you obtain in that exercise $\hat{\beta}_1$ through $\hat{\beta}_5$. Suppose you are unaware of the variation in p_1, p_2, and h across municipalities and use just the data on electricity consumption q and income m to estimate a loglinear Engel curve. Let the resulting least squares sample regression line be denoted

$$\log q_i = b_1 + b_2 \log m_i + e_i.$$

This misspecified model is estimated in Exercise 6.20.

(a) From your estimation of this Engel curve, what is the income elasticity of demand for electricity? Is electricity an inferior good? If not, is it income elastic or inelastic? How does this compare with your conclusion in Exercise 8.6 based on the correctly specified model (8.50)?

(b) The generalization of (8.49) that applies in this case (because three relevant explanatory variables have been omitted instead of just one) may be shown to be

$$b_2 = \hat{\beta}_2 + \hat{\beta}_3 b_{23} + \hat{\beta}_4 b_{24} + \hat{\beta}_5 b_{25}. \qquad (8.51)$$

This indicates that the gross effect of $\log m$ on $\log q$ given by the misspecified model differs from the ceterus paribus effect $\hat{\beta}_2$ due to indirect effects involving the relationships between $\log m$ and each of the other regressors in (8.50). If $\log m$ were uncorrelated with these other regressors ($r_{23} = r_{24} = r_{25} = 0$), the two effects would be the same—that is, the simple regression would yield the same income elasticity as the multiple regression: $b_2 = \hat{\beta}_2$. But because the regressors are correlated they differ.

i. Perform the three simple regressions of each of $\log p_1$, $\log p_2$, and $\log h$ on $\log m$ to obtain b_{23}, b_{24}, and b_{25}, respectively.

ii. Use the least squares estimates $\hat{\beta}_k$ obtained in Exercise 8.6 to verify (8.51).

8.19 ⨍ Suppose the true process generating the data is the simple regression model

$$Y_i = \alpha + \beta X_i + \varepsilon_i,$$

but that you omit X_i and estimate instead

$$Y_i = a + e_i.$$

(a) What is the formula for your least squares estimator a? (It is not necessary to present a derivation.)

(b) Establish whether your estimator is unbiased. If you find that it is biased,

i. present an expression for the bias.

ii. examine the behavior of this expression as $n \to \infty$ in order to determine whether your estimator is asymptotically unbiased.

8.20 ⨍ Suppose the true process generating the data is the simple regression model

$$Y_i = \alpha + \beta X_i + \varepsilon_i,$$

but that you omit the intercept and estimate instead a regression through the origin:

$$Y_i = b X_i + e_i.$$

(a) What is the formula for your least squares estimator b? (It is not necessary to present a derivation.)

(b) Establish whether your estimator is unbiased.

8.9.2 Inclusion of an Irrelevant Regressor

Let us turn to a specification error the opposite of the one just considered, the case of mistakenly including in a multiple regression an explanatory variable that does not in fact belong there. Suppose, for example, that the true model is

$$Y_i = \beta_1 + \beta_2 X_{2i} + \varepsilon_i, \qquad (8.52)$$

but that a sample regression denoted by

$$Y_i = b_1 + b_2 X_{2i} + b_3 X_{3i} + e_i$$

is estimated. What are the properties of b_1 and b_2 as estimators of β_1 and β_2?

The estimators b_1, b_2, and b_3 are computed according to (8.11), (8.12a), and (8.12b). Focusing on b_2, the properties of deviation form and the laws of mathematical expectation imply that

$$E(b_2) = \frac{\sum x_{3i}^2 \sum x_{2i} E(Y_i) - \sum x_{2i} x_{3i} \sum x_{3i} E(Y_i)}{\sum x_{2i}^2 \sum x_{3i}^2 - (\sum x_{2i} x_{3i})^2}.$$

Focusing just on the components of this expression involving expectations, and using the population regression line $E(Y_i) = \beta_1 + \beta_2 X_{2i}$ implied by the true model (8.52), note that

$$\sum x_{2i} E(Y_i) = \sum x_{2i}(\beta_1 + \beta_2 X_{2i}) = \beta_1 \sum x_{2i} + \beta_2 \sum x_{2i} X_{2i} = \beta_2 \sum x_{2i}^2,$$

$$\sum x_{3i} E(Y_i) = \sum x_{3i}(\beta_1 + \beta_2 X_{2i}) = \beta_1 \sum x_{3i} + \beta_2 \sum x_{3i} X_{2i} = \beta_2 \sum x_{2i} x_{3i}.$$

Substituting these intermediate findings into the derivation, we have

$$E(b_2) = \frac{\beta_2[\sum x_{2i}^2 \sum x_{3i}^2 - (\sum x_{2i} x_{3i})^2]}{\sum x_{2i}^2 \sum x_{3i}^2 - (\sum x_{2i} x_{3i})^2} = \beta_2.$$

The remarkable conclusion is that least squares yields unbiased estimators even in the presence of an irrelevant explanatory variable. Exercise 8.22 asks you to confirm this for the intercept estimator b_1. It may be shown as well that the estimated variances $s_{\beta_k}^2$ computed according to the usual formulas are unbiased and hence provide a legitimate basis for the usual hypothesis-testing procedures.

Is there, then, no cost whatsoever to model misspecification of this type? There is, but it appears in a subtler form than as an estimator bias, a form that relates to the efficiency of the estimators. Note first that, for the correctly specified model (8.52), the usual least squares simple regression estimators $\hat{\beta}_1$ and $\hat{\beta}_2$ are known to be efficient and BLUE. Thus, the minimum variance attainable by any unbiased estimator for β_2 is

$$\frac{\sigma^2}{\sum x_{2i}}, \qquad (8.53)$$

which is simply the variance formula (4.26) applied to (8.52). What is the variance of the estimator b_2 arising from estimation of the misspecified model? It is, reproducing (8.14a),

$$V(b_2) = \frac{\sigma^2}{\sum x_{2i}^2 (1 - r_{23}^2)},$$

which exceeds (8.53) any time the explanatory variables are correlated. If, on the other hand, the explanatory variables are uncorrelated, then multiple regression yields estimated slopes identical to those obtained by a series of simple regressions; they must therefore be equally efficient. Typically, however, irrelevant regressors will be correlated in some degree with relevant ones and will therefore compromise the precision with which the effects of the latter on the dependent variable can be estimated. This is the loss associated with specification error of this type.

Although this efficiency loss is of some concern, clearly the consequences of this type of misspecification are relatively benign compared with those of omitting a relevant variable. For this reason, the applied researcher uncertain as to the correct set of explanatory variables (a common circumstance) much prefers to err on the side of including too many regressors than too few. This is called **overfitting** the regression equation. Because t tests remain valid, they may then be used to judge whether individual regressors are irrelevant.

Practitioner's Tip: Overfitting a regression

When you are unsure about a model specification, you are better off erring on the side of including too many variables than too few.

This practical advice is offered on the understanding that it be tempered by an awareness of the inappropriateness of going too far in the other direction—of estimating **kitchen-sink regressions** in which everything but the kitchen sink is thrown in.

A common means of selecting a favored model choice is to proceed in this way, beginning with an overfitted regression and engaging in successive estimations based on increasingly parsimonious specifications. Applied econometric work is permeated with **specification searches** of this sort. It is important to be aware, however, that such a search strategy involves certain perils, which we consider next.

EXERCISES

8.21 Prove that $E(b_3) = 0$ under the specification error of this section.

8.22 Prove that $E(b_1) = \beta_1$ under the specification error of this section. (You may use the result from Exercise 8.21 in your derivation.)

8.23 ∮ Suppose the true model generating the data is

$$Y_i = \alpha + \varepsilon_i, \qquad (8.54)$$

but that you mistakenly include an explanatory variable, obtaining an estimated model denoted by

$$Y_i = a + bX_i + e_i.$$

(a) Derive $E(b)$.

(b) Consider your least squares estimator a.
i. Establish whether it is unbiased as an estimator for α.

ii. Derive $V(a)$. (*Hint:* Establish that the variance expression (4.27) still applies.)

(c) Consider the true model (8.54).
i. What is the least squares estimator $\hat{\alpha}$? (No derivation is necessary.)

ii. Present the expression for $V(\hat{\alpha})$.

iii. Compare $V(a)$ with $V(\hat{\alpha})$. Which is the more efficient estimator?

8.24 ∮ Suppose the true model generating the data is

$$Y_i = \beta X_i + \varepsilon_i, \qquad (8.55)$$

but that you mistakenly include an intercept, obtaining an estimated model denoted by

$$Y_i = a + bX_i + e_i.$$

(a) Consider your least squares slope estimator b.

i.   Establish whether it is unbiased.

ii.   Derive $V(b)$.

iii.   Present the expression for $V(\hat{\beta})$, where $\hat{\beta}$ is the least squares slope estimator in the correctly specified model (8.55).

iv.   Compare $V(b)$ with $V(\hat{\beta})$. Which is the more efficient estimator? (*Hint:* Use your answer to Appendix A, Exercise A.8b.)

(b) Derive $E(a)$.

8.10   Pre-Test Estimation ★

Consider a situation in which a researcher is confident that X_2 is an appropriate regressor, but is uncertain about the role of X_3. The question is therefore whether (8.42) or (8.52) is the true model. Using the search strategy just described, the researcher begins by overfitting; that is, estimating (8.42). If $\hat{\beta}_3$ is significant ($|t| = |\hat{\beta}_3|/s_{\hat{\beta}_3} \geq 2$, say) then (8.42) is judged to be the correct model and $\hat{\beta}_2$ is used as the estimator of β_2. Alternatively, if $\hat{\beta}_3$ is insignificant X_3 is dropped from the equation, (8.52) is estimated, and b_2 in (8.43) is used as the estimator of β_2.

This is an example of a **sequential estimator,** one that involves a **preliminary test,** or **pre-test.** Denoting this **pre-test estimator** by $\tilde{\beta}_2$, it may be summarized as

$$\tilde{\beta}_2 = \begin{cases} \hat{\beta}_2 & \text{if } |t| \geq 2 \\ b_2 & \text{if } |t| < 2. \end{cases}$$

The problem with the pre-test estimator is that the t test on which it depends involves, as does any hypothesis test, some nonzero probability of Type I error. When $\beta_3 \neq 0$, it is possible that we may be incorrectly led to believe the contrary and thus to use b_2 when the true model is (8.42), in which case b_2 is biased.

To put it slightly more formally, the sampling distribution of the pre-test estimator depends not only on the fact that the estimators $\hat{\beta}_2$ and b_2 are random variables, but also on the randomness of the t statistic. The mean of this sampling distribution is

$$E(\tilde{\beta}_2) = E(\hat{\beta}_2)\Pr(|t| \geq 2) + E(b_2)\Pr(|t| < 2),$$

a weighted average of the means of the two estimators. The only circumstance under which the pre-test estimator is unbiased is if $\beta_3 = 0$ and the true model is (8.52) because in this situation both $\hat{\beta}_2$ and b_2 are unbiased. Otherwise, it is a biased estimator because it attaches a nonzero weight (equal to the nonzero probability of Type I error) to the biased estimator b_2.

Pre-testing issues arise in a great many contexts because virtually all empirical work involves proceeding in a sequential manner that depends at each step on some test outcome; the choice of explanatory variables is merely one illustration. Although its consequences are important, there is, regrettably, little systematic or coherent methodology for dealing with the implications of pre-testing in applied work. For an introduction to pre-testing with references, see Kennedy (1998, Chap. 12). The preceding example illustrates the conventional wisdom that the implications of pre-testing are negative; however there are situations in which this is not necessarily the case, a point emphasized in the more advanced survey by Giles and Giles (1993).

Specification searches and pre-testing have implications for the properties not only of estimators but also of hypothesis tests. The latter are considered in Chapter 12 under the topic of data mining.

Appendix Multiple Regression in Matrix Form

For those familiar with elementary matrix operations such as matrix multiplication, inversion, and transposition, it is useful to formulate the least squares estimation of the multiple regression model in general terms.

The Regression Model in Matrix Form

Let us begin by specifying the model in matrix form. Let **y** denote the column vector of observations on the dependent variable, **X** a similarly stacked matrix of observations on the explanatory variables, $\boldsymbol{\beta}$ the column vector of the regression coefficients, and ε the column vector of disturbances:

$$\mathbf{y} = \begin{bmatrix} Y_1 \\ Y_2 \\ \vdots \\ Y_n \end{bmatrix}, \ \mathbf{X} = \begin{bmatrix} 1 & X_{21} & X_{31} & \cdots & X_{K1} \\ 1 & X_{22} & X_{32} & \cdots & X_{K2} \\ \vdots & \vdots & \vdots & & \vdots \\ 1 & X_{2n} & X_{3n} & \cdots & X_{Kn} \end{bmatrix}, \ \boldsymbol{\beta} = \begin{bmatrix} \beta_1 \\ \beta_2 \\ \vdots \\ \beta_K \end{bmatrix}, \ \varepsilon = \begin{bmatrix} \varepsilon_1 \\ \varepsilon_2 \\ \vdots \\ \varepsilon_n \end{bmatrix}.$$

$$(n \times 1) \qquad\qquad (n \times K) \qquad\qquad (K \times 1) \qquad (n \times 1)$$

Then the multiple regression model (8.1) may be expressed compactly as

$$\mathbf{y} = \mathbf{X}\boldsymbol{\beta} + \varepsilon. \tag{8.56}$$

Note that the orders of these vectors and matrices are such that they are conformable with respect to matrix multiplication and addition. It is by specifying the first column of **X** as a series of 1s that the coefficient β_1 is given the role of an intercept.

The specification of the disturbance continues to be what it has always been:

$$\varepsilon_i \sim \text{n.i.d.}(0, \sigma^2). \tag{8.57}$$

In terms of the vector ε, this may be reexpressed as follows. First, because its components ε_i are normally distributed, the vector ε formally has a multivariate normal distribution.[10] This multivariate normal distribution is characterized by two sets of parameters: those associated with the mean of ε and those associated with its variance.

The mean of ε is just a vector of 0s:

$$E(\varepsilon) = \mathbf{0}. \tag{8.58}$$

---

[10] The concept of a multivariate distribution is defined in Appendix B, Section B.11.

The variance properties of ε are described by an $n \times n$ covariance matrix, the formal definition of which is (as a generalization of the scalar variance Definition B.2 in Appendix B):

$$V(\varepsilon) = E[(\varepsilon - E\varepsilon)(\varepsilon - E\varepsilon)']. \tag{8.59}$$

The diagonal components of this covariance matrix list the n variances of the ε_i, which are all σ^2; the off-diagonal elements list their covariances, which, by the statistical independence of the ε_i, are all 0. Using (8.58) to simplify the definition (8.59), this may all be conveniently summarized with the matrix notation

$$V(\varepsilon) = E(\varepsilon\varepsilon') = \sigma^2 \mathbf{I}, \tag{8.60}$$

where $\mathbf{I}$ denotes an $n \times n$ identity matrix. (An identity matrix is a square matrix having 1s down the diagonal and 0s off-diagonal.)

The behavior of the random vector ε is, then, fully specified by

$$\varepsilon \sim N(\mathbf{0}, \sigma^2 \mathbf{I}),$$

which is the vector equivalent of the scalar disturbance specification (8.57).

Least Squares Estimation

The formal logic of obtaining the least squares estimators proceeds much as before. Any estimator vector $\hat{\boldsymbol{\beta}}$ defines a vector of fitted values

$$\hat{\mathbf{y}} = \mathbf{X}\hat{\boldsymbol{\beta}}$$

and an associated residual vector

$$\mathbf{e} = \mathbf{y} - \hat{\mathbf{y}} = \mathbf{y} - \mathbf{X}\hat{\boldsymbol{\beta}}.$$

Given the notation we have established, both of these are $n \times 1$ column vectors. The resulting sum of squared residuals is $\text{SSE} = \mathbf{e}'\mathbf{e}$, a scalar quantity (that is, of order 1×1).

The least squares estimators are those that yield the minimum value for this SSE; that is, they are the value of the coefficient vector $\boldsymbol{\beta}$ that minimizes the sum of squares function

$$S = (\mathbf{y} - \mathbf{X}\boldsymbol{\beta})'(\mathbf{y} - \mathbf{X}\boldsymbol{\beta}) = \mathbf{y}'\mathbf{y} - \mathbf{y}'\mathbf{X}\boldsymbol{\beta} - \boldsymbol{\beta}'\mathbf{X}'\mathbf{y} + \boldsymbol{\beta}'\mathbf{X}'\mathbf{X}\boldsymbol{\beta},$$

which is the matrix form of (8.7).

The derivative of this sum of squares function with respect to $\boldsymbol{\beta}$ may be obtained by vector differentiation. The result is

$$\frac{\partial S}{\partial \boldsymbol{\beta}} = -2\mathbf{X}'\mathbf{y} + 2\mathbf{X}'\mathbf{X}\boldsymbol{\beta}.$$

Letting $\hat{\boldsymbol{\beta}}$ denote the value of $\boldsymbol{\beta}$ that sets this vector of derivatives to zero, the set of first-order conditions may be expressed as

$$\mathbf{X}'\mathbf{y} - \mathbf{X}'\mathbf{X}\hat{\boldsymbol{\beta}} = \mathbf{X}'(\mathbf{y} - \mathbf{X}\hat{\boldsymbol{\beta}}) = 0. \tag{8.61}$$

Using the definition of the residuals, these may be interpreted as a set of orthogonality conditions

$$\mathbf{X}'\mathbf{e} = \mathbf{0} \tag{8.62}$$

analogous to (8.9).

The normal equations (8.61) involve the square $K \times K$ matrix $\mathbf{X}'\mathbf{X}$, which may be inverted. The solution for the least squares estimators may therefore be expressed generally as

$$\hat{\boldsymbol{\beta}} = (\mathbf{X}'\mathbf{X})^{-1}\mathbf{X}'\mathbf{y}. \tag{8.63}$$

To take a special case, when $K = 3$ the matrix $\mathbf{X}'\mathbf{X}$ is 3×3, $\mathbf{X}'$ is $3 \times n$, and $\mathbf{y}$ is $n \times 1$. These multiply together to give the 3×1 estimator vector $\hat{\boldsymbol{\beta}} = [\hat{\beta}_1 \ \hat{\beta}_2 \ \hat{\beta}_3]'$. The slope estimators $\hat{\beta}_2$ and $\hat{\beta}_3$ are, in their scalar expressions, given by (8.12).

Special Case of $K = 2$

Let us consider the special case of simple regression in detail. Reverting to the notation in Chapter 4, we may suppress the subscript 2 and denote the single explanatory variable as $X_{2i} = X_i$. The matrices $\mathbf{X}'\mathbf{X}$ and $\mathbf{X}'\mathbf{y}$ are then

$$\mathbf{X}'\mathbf{X} = \begin{bmatrix} 1 & 1 & \cdots & 1 \\ X_1 & X_2 & \cdots & X_n \end{bmatrix} \begin{bmatrix} 1 & X_1 \\ 1 & X_2 \\ \vdots & \vdots \\ 1 & X_n \end{bmatrix} = \begin{bmatrix} n & \sum X_i \\ \sum X_i & \sum X_i^2 \end{bmatrix}, \tag{8.64}$$

$$\mathbf{X}'\mathbf{y} = \begin{bmatrix} 1 & 1 & \cdots & 1 \\ X_1 & X_2 & \cdots & X_n \end{bmatrix} \begin{bmatrix} Y_1 \\ Y_2 \\ \vdots \\ Y_n \end{bmatrix} = \begin{bmatrix} \sum Y_i \\ \sum X_i Y_i \end{bmatrix}.$$

Inverting the $\mathbf{X}'\mathbf{X}$ matrix, the least squares estimator vector is

$$\hat{\boldsymbol{\beta}} = (\mathbf{X}'\mathbf{X})^{-1}\mathbf{X}'\mathbf{y} = \frac{1}{n\sum X_i^2 - (\sum X_i)^2} \begin{bmatrix} \sum X_i^2 & -\sum X_i \\ -\sum X_i & n \end{bmatrix} \begin{bmatrix} \sum Y_i \\ \sum X_i Y_i \end{bmatrix}$$

or

$$\begin{bmatrix} \hat{\beta}_1 \\ \hat{\beta}_2 \end{bmatrix} = \begin{bmatrix} \dfrac{\sum X_i^2 \sum Y_i - \sum X_i \sum X_i Y_i}{n \sum X_i^2 - (\sum X_i)^2} \\[4mm] \dfrac{-\sum X_i \sum Y_i + n \sum X_i Y_i}{n \sum X_i^2 - (\sum X_i)^2} \end{bmatrix}. \tag{8.65}$$

It is easy to see that $\hat{\beta}_2$ is equivalent to the simple regression slope estimator (4.20) in Chapter 4. Less obvious is that $\hat{\beta}_1$ is equivalent to the intercept estimator (4.19), a result you are asked to establish in Exercise 8.25.

The Sampling Distribution of $\hat{\boldsymbol{\beta}}$

The estimator $\hat{\boldsymbol{\beta}}$ is, like all estimators, random, and so has a probability distribution. Because $\hat{\boldsymbol{\beta}}$ is a vector, this distribution is a multivariate distribution. What can we say about this distribution?

First, the least squares formula (8.63) indicates that $\hat{\boldsymbol{\beta}}$ is computed by applying the matrix expression $(\mathbf{X}'\mathbf{X})^{-1}\mathbf{X}'$—ultimately just some matrix of numerical constants—to $\mathbf{y}$. Because matrix multiplication effectively involves taking a linear combination (in mathematical terminology, it is a linear operator), $\hat{\boldsymbol{\beta}}$ is a linear function of the components of $\mathbf{y}$. These are in turn specified by the model to be, via ε, normally distributed. Hence, $\hat{\boldsymbol{\beta}}$ is a linear function of normal random variables and so must itself be normally distributed.

This multivariate normal distribution is fully characterized by a mean vector and a covariance matrix. The result is

$$\hat{\boldsymbol{\beta}} \sim \mathrm{N}(\boldsymbol{\beta}, \sigma^2(\mathbf{X}'\mathbf{X})^{-1}). \tag{8.66}$$

The rest of this section is devoted to establishing that these are the appropriate expressions for the mean and covariance matrix.

The result for the mean merely restates what we already know from Section 8.3 to be true—that $\hat{\boldsymbol{\beta}}$ is an unbiased estimator and so $E(\hat{\boldsymbol{\beta}}) = \boldsymbol{\beta}$. However, we may now establish this rigorously, something that was not done there. Taking the expected value of $\hat{\boldsymbol{\beta}}$ (and using the fact that, from the model (8.56), $E(\mathbf{y}) = \mathbf{X}\boldsymbol{\beta} + E(\varepsilon) = \mathbf{X}\boldsymbol{\beta}$), we have

$$E(\hat{\boldsymbol{\beta}}) = (\mathbf{X}'\mathbf{X})^{-1}\mathbf{X}'E(\mathbf{y}) = (\mathbf{X}'\mathbf{X})^{-1}\mathbf{X}'\mathbf{X}\boldsymbol{\beta} = \boldsymbol{\beta}. \tag{8.67}$$

Notice that, because matrix operations involve linear transformations, an expected value $E(\cdot)$ can always be taken through the parts of the expression that involve matrices of constants (in this case $\mathbf{X}$) and applied just to the part that is random. This is just a matrix generalization of Law B.3 (in Appendix B) that the expected value of a linear function of random variables is the linear function of the expected values.

It is instructive to note the analogy this derivation bears to the proof of the unbiasedness of the least squares slope estimator in simple regression, as given in Section 4.3.

Turning to the derivation of the covariance matrix, a useful intermediate result is that $\hat{\boldsymbol{\beta}}$ may be expressed as

$$\begin{aligned} \hat{\boldsymbol{\beta}} &= (\mathbf{X}'\mathbf{X})^{-1}\mathbf{X}'\mathbf{y} \\ &= (\mathbf{X}'\mathbf{X})^{-1}\mathbf{X}'(\mathbf{X}\boldsymbol{\beta} + \varepsilon) \\ &= \boldsymbol{\beta} + (\mathbf{X}'\mathbf{X})^{-1}\mathbf{X}'\varepsilon. \end{aligned} \tag{8.68}$$

This is, incidentally, another way of seeing that $\hat{\boldsymbol{\beta}}$ is a linear combination of the normally distributed disturbance and so must itself be normal.

The formal definition of the covariance matrix of the random vector $\hat{\boldsymbol{\beta}}$ is, in analogy with (8.59),

$$V(\hat{\boldsymbol{\beta}}) = E[(\hat{\boldsymbol{\beta}} - E\hat{\boldsymbol{\beta}})(\hat{\boldsymbol{\beta}} - E\hat{\boldsymbol{\beta}})'].$$

By the unbiasedness of $\hat{\boldsymbol{\beta}}$, just established by (8.67), this is

$$V(\hat{\boldsymbol{\beta}}) = E[(\hat{\boldsymbol{\beta}} - \boldsymbol{\beta})(\hat{\boldsymbol{\beta}} - \boldsymbol{\beta})'].$$

An expression for $\hat{\boldsymbol{\beta}} - \boldsymbol{\beta}$ is provided by (8.68), and so the derivation of $V(\hat{\boldsymbol{\beta}})$ may be completed as follows.

$$\begin{aligned}
V(\hat{\boldsymbol{\beta}}) &= E[\left((\mathbf{X'X})^{-1}\mathbf{X'}\varepsilon\right)\left((\mathbf{X'X})^{-1}\mathbf{X'}\varepsilon\right)'] \\
&= E[(\mathbf{X'X})^{-1}\mathbf{X'}\varepsilon\varepsilon'\mathbf{X'}(\mathbf{X'X})^{-1}] \\
&= (\mathbf{X'X})^{-1}\mathbf{X'}E(\varepsilon\varepsilon')\mathbf{X'}(\mathbf{X'X})^{-1} &&\text{because only } \varepsilon\varepsilon' \text{ is random} \\
&= (\mathbf{X'X})^{-1}\mathbf{X'}(\sigma^2\mathbf{I})\mathbf{X'}(\mathbf{X'X})^{-1} &&\text{by (8.60)} \\
&= \sigma^2(\mathbf{X'X})^{-1}
\end{aligned}$$

The last step uses the fact that a scalar appearing inside a matrix expression, in this case σ^2, may be taken outside.

This establishes the covariance matrix expression $V(\hat{\boldsymbol{\beta}}) = \sigma^2(\mathbf{X'X})^{-1}$ asserted in (8.66). In general, this is a $K \times K$ matrix with variances down the diagonal that we have denoted by $\sigma^2_{\hat{\beta}_k} = V(\hat{\beta}_k)$ $(k = 1, \ldots, K)$ and covariances off-diagonal. In the special case of $K = 3$, the (2,2) and (3,3) elements of this 3×3 matrix correspond to the variance expressions (8.14) of Section 8.3.

The covariance matrix $V(\hat{\boldsymbol{\beta}}) = \sigma^2(\mathbf{X'X})^{-1}$ may be estimated by replacing σ^2 with its estimator s^2 given by (8.13). Because s^2 is unbiased it follows that this covariance matrix estimator is unbiased:

$$E(s^2(\mathbf{X'X})^{-1}) = E(s^2)(\mathbf{X'X})^{-1} = \sigma^2(\mathbf{X'X})^{-1} = V(\hat{\boldsymbol{\beta}}).$$

The diagonal components of this covariance matrix estimator are the estimated variances that we have denoted $s^2_{\hat{\beta}_k}$.

Special Case of $K = 2$

Let us return to the special case of simple regression. Inverting the $\mathbf{X'X}$ matrix (8.64), the covariance matrix $\sigma^2(\mathbf{X'X})^{-1}$ is

$$V(\hat{\boldsymbol{\beta}}) = \frac{\sigma^2}{n\sum_i X_i^2 - (\sum X_i)^2}\begin{bmatrix} \sum X_i^2 & -\sum X_i \\ -\sum X_i & n \end{bmatrix}.$$

The diagonal components of this are

$$\sigma^2_{\hat{\beta}_1} = \frac{\sigma^2\sum X_i^2}{n\sum X_i^2 - (\sum X_i)^2}, \tag{8.69a}$$

$$\sigma^2_{\hat{\beta}_2} = \frac{n\sigma^2}{n\sum X_i^2 - (\sum X_i)^2}. \tag{8.69b}$$

These are equivalent to the variance expressions (4.27) and (4.26) for the least squares intercept and slope estimators in the simple regression model. You are asked to verify this in Exercise 8.27.

The off-diagonal component of the matrix is the covariance between the two coefficient estimators:

$$\text{cov}(\hat{\beta}_1, \hat{\beta}_2) = \frac{-\sigma^2 \sum X_i}{n \sum X_i^2 - (\sum X_i)^2}.$$

This expression is used in deriving the forecast error variance (5.9); see Exercise 5.3.

EXERCISES

8.25 Starting with the intercept estimator (4.19), show that it is equivalent to the solution for $\hat{\beta}_1$ given in (8.65). (You may use the slope estimator given in (8.65) in your derivation.)

8.26 Confirm that the first of the K orthogonality conditions represented by (8.62) corresponds to (8.9a), and that this in turn implies the intercept estimator (8.11).

8.27 Show that the variance expressions derived for the $K = 2$ case are equivalent to those presented in Chapter 4.

(a) Show that (8.69b) is equivalent to (4.26). (*Hint:* Use the result of Exercise A.7.)

(b) Show that (8.69a) is equivalent to (4.27).

9

Application to Economic Growth

As we have now seen in a range of applications, econometricians look to economic theory as the basis for specifying an econometric model. However, the strength of the link between the underlying theory and a regression specification varies widely. Several applications we have studied have been ones in which the relationship is very direct. For example, the CAPM regression in the appendix to Chapter 5 may be derived rigorously from the theory of portfolio choice in finance, as is done in Appendix C. The production function applications in Chapter 7 also involve regression models directly linked to economic theory.

Often in applied econometric work, the link is weaker. For example Houthakker's electricity demand equation in Section 8.6 involves no explicit derivation from the microeconomic theory of consumer demand. Instead, it is just reasoned more informally that the quantity of electricity consumed should depend on its price, the price of substitute commodities, income, and other factors likely to shift the demand curve, and that the nature of demand relationships make a loglinear functional form one plausible choice. In Section 11.6, we see that modern developments in consumer demand analysis provide econometric demand models that are explicitly derived from microeconomic theory, an enormous advance over the methodology available to Houthakker.

The advantages of a strong link to economic theory go beyond the choice of variables and a functional form. Economic theory often suggests **testable parameter restrictions** on the econometric model. This chapter studies an application that helps make this point—a test of the **neoclassical model of economic growth** performed by Mankiw, Romer, and Weil (1992) (henceforth MRW). This in turn helps motivate the development of general methods for testing broad classes of restrictions, something we begin to consider in the next chapter.

A second reason for studying the MRW analysis is that it illustrates the coefficient biases that arise from omitting relevant explanatory variables. Chapter 8 shows that when a relevant variable is omitted from a regression the coefficient estimates on the remaining variables are biased; they over- or underestimate the true effects. We begin, as MRW did, by considering the simplest textbook version of the neoclassical growth model as an explanation for differing living standards across countries. Although the model leads to estimation results that show some promise, the coefficient estimates are implausible. This leads us to ask: What is wrong with the model? The answer offered by MRW is that the textbook neoclassical model fails to recognize the importance of human capital—education and skills, as distinct from conventional physical capital—in contributing to economic growth. Estimating an augmented version of the model that includes this omitted variable leads to much more plausible coefficient estimates.

The body of this chapter focuses on the cross-sectional implications of growth theory, examining how the neoclassical model explains differences in living standards across countries. Growth models also seek to explain the evolution over time in key macroeconomic aggregates such as output and the capital stock. The appendix to this chapter offers some comments on this aspect of the theory of economic growth.

9.1 Introduction

Macroeconomic variables such as a country's output, capital stock, and employment exhibit two key features as they evolve through time. First, they grow. Because this growth is often at percentage rates that are fairly stable over long periods, we have seen in Chapter 6 that the constant growth model often provides a good description of the long-term growth trend of such series.

Second, this growth is not smooth. Around these secular trends, macroeconomic series fluctuate due to seasonal, business cycle, and purely random effects. Much of macroeconomics seeks to understand these short-term fluctuations, with some schools of thought advocating that governments attempt to mitigate them with countercyclical fiscal and monetary policies.

In the longer run, however, the effects of compounding over extended periods mean that even a tiny increase in the average growth rate of output will lead to improvements in the standard of living that dwarf any benefits that might arise from countercyclical policies.[1] The effects of the compounding of higher growth rates is easy to see. Examining economies internationally, the most notable way in which they differ is that some have experienced high growth rates historically and so enjoy high living standards today, whereas others have not.

Indeed, among the most remarkable of economic phenomena is the vast disparity in living standards among the peoples of the world. Table 9.1 presents data on living standards in 1960 and 1985, measured by output per adult in 1985 U.S. dollars, for 75 countries. The data are from MRW. Focusing on 1985 living standards, the poorest country in the group is Ethiopia with GDP per adult of just $608; the richest is Norway at $19,723, more than 32 times as much. In less than two weeks, a Norwegian produces what it takes an entire year for an Ethiopian to produce.

---

[1] Lucas (2003) argues that the welfare cost of the business cycle amounts to only approximately one-twentieth of 1% of consumption, far less than the potential "...gains from providing people with better incentives to work and to save...."

TABLE 9.1   Output per Adult, 1960–1985

	1960	1985	Growth rate		1960	1985	Growth rate
Algeria	2485	4371	2.258	Greece	2257	6868	4.451
Botswana	959	3671	5.369	Ireland	4411	8675	2.705
Cameroon	889	2190	3.606	Italy	4913	11,082	3.253
Ethiopia	533	608	0.526	Netherlands	7689	13,177	2.154
Ivory Coast	1386	1704	0.826	Norway	7938	19,723	3.640
Kenya	944	1329	1.368	Portugal	2272	5827	3.767
Madagascar	1194	975	−0.810	Spain	3766	9903	3.867
Malawi	455	823	2.370	Sweden	7802	15,237	2.677
Mali	737	710	−0.149	Switzerland	10,308	15,881	1.728
Morocco	1030	2348	3.296	Turkey	2274	4444	2.680
Nigeria	1055	1186	0.468	United Kingdom	7634	13,331	2.229
Senegal	1392	1450	0.163	Canada	10,286	17,935	2.223
South Africa	4768	7064	1.572	Costa Rica	3360	4492	1.161
Tanzania	383	710	2.468	Dominican Rep.	1939	3308	2.136
Tunisia	1623	3661	3.253	El Salvador	2042	1997	−0.089
Zambia	1410	1217	−0.588	Guatemala	2481	3034	0.804
Zimbabwe	1187	2107	2.295	Haiti	1096	1237	0.484
Bangladesh	846	1221	1.467	Honduras	1430	1822	0.969
Burma	517	1031	2.760	Jamaica	2726	3080	0.488
Hong Kong	3085	13,372	5.866	Mexico	4229	7380	2.227
India	978	1339	1.256	Nicaragua	3195	3978	0.876
Israel	4802	10,450	3.110	Panama	2423	5021	2.914
Japan	3493	13,893	5.522	Trinidad & Tobago	9253	11,285	0.794
Jordan	2183	4312	2.722	United States	12,362	18,988	1.716
Korea	1285	4775	5.250	Argentina	4852	5533	0.525
Malaysia	2154	5788	3.953	Bolivia	1618	2055	0.956
Pakistan	1077	2175	2.811	Brazil	1842	5563	4.421
Philippines	1668	2430	1.505	Chile	5189	5533	0.256
Singapore	2793	14,678	6.636	Colombia	2672	4405	1.999
Sri Lanka	1794	2482	1.298	Ecuador	2198	4504	2.869
Syrian Arab Rep.	2382	6042	3.723	Paraguay	1951	3914	2.784
Thailand	1308	3220	3.603	Peru	3310	3775	0.525
Austria	5939	13,327	3.233	Uruguay	5119	5495	0.283
Belgium	6789	14,290	2.977	Venezuela	10,367	6336	−1.969
Denmark	8551	16,491	2.627	Australia	8440	13,409	1.851
Finland	6527	13,779	2.988	Indonesia	879	2159	3.594
France	7215	15,027	2.934	New Zealand	9523	12,308	1.026
Germany, Fed. Rep.	7695	15,297	2.748				

Source: Mankiw, M.G., D. Romer, and D.M. Weil "A Contribution to the Empirics of Economic Growth," *Quarterly Journal of Economics* 107, 407–43. © 1992 MIT Press Journals. Reprinted with permission from MIT Press Journals. Growth rate calculated by author.

To be sure, output per adult or per worker is not necessarily the same thing as happiness or quality of life. Scitovsky (1976, Chap. 7) has noted that economic growth does not seem to change the distribution of happiness in society. We do not know with certainty that Norwegians are a happier or more fulfilled people than Ethiopians. We do, however, observe a strong demand by people in underdeveloped countries to emigrate to developed ones, suggesting they prefer high material living standards.

In the same vein, growth does not correlate perfectly with other development measures. The country with the highest labor productivity may not have the highest literacy rate, the greatest life expectancy, or the lowest rate of infant mortality. But these measures of well-being do tend to be linked. The ability to work productively enables a society to provide a whole range of benefits to its citizens, including education and health care.[2]

It follows that an understanding of the determinants of economic growth and how best to foster it ranks among the foremost of economists' concerns.

> I do not see how one can look at figures like these without seeing them as represent-
> ing *possibilities*. Is there some action a government of India could take that would
> lead the Indian economy to grow like Indonesia's or Egypt's? If so, *what* exactly?
> If not, what is it about the "nature of India" that makes it so? The consequences for
> human welfare involved in questions like these are simply staggering: Once one starts
> to think about them, it is hard to think about anything else. (Lucas 1988, p. 5)

We have already touched on two topics that relate peripherally to these questions. First, in Chapter 6 we have found that the constant growth model often provides a good descriptive portrayal of the secular trends of economic time series. However, we have also emphasized in Section 6.2.5 that this is an entirely different matter from offering an economic explanation of these growth patterns. What are the underlying factors that lead to such vast differences in living standards across countries?

Second, in Section 7.3.2 we have studied the growth accounting equation. This decomposed output growth into components attributable to growth in factor inputs and technical progress. The latter we term total factor productivity, and it is measured by the Solow residual. As the name suggests, this is purely an accounting exercise. It offers no explanation for why these growth rates are what they are or why different economies experience radically different patterns of growth.

It is such an explanation that we now seek. The next section begins by reviewing a model of economic growth developed by Solow (1956) and Swan (1956) that attempts to isolate the key factors determining labor productivity. The Solow-Swan model is the starting point for all analyses of growth. We then turn to the

---

[2] The relationship between per capita output and quality of life is of particular interest to development economists. If the link between the two is weak, say because of inequitable income distribution, then policies designed to foster economic growth—defined conventionally in terms of per capita output—may do little to improve the lives of much of an underdeveloped country's population. Chakraborty (1999) surveys the empirical work on this question.

econometric implementation of this theory by MRW. It turns out that, although the underlying economic theory is sophisticated, understanding their analysis involves little more than replicating a couple of least squares regressions. Section 9.4 offers a brief guide to these essentials and can be read largely independently of the deeper treatment of the Solow-Swan model in the next two sections.

EXERCISES

9.1 Consider the data on the level and growth rate of output per adult given in Table 9.1.

(a) How is the growth rate calculated from the levels? Show that you understand this by reproducing the growth rates for India and Indonesia. Is Robert

Lucas's statement about the relative growth rates of these countries correct?

(b) What would Indian GDP per adult have been in 1985 if that economy had grown at the same rate as Indonesia's?

9.2   The Textbook Solow-Swan Model

Distilling matters down to their essence, we seek an economic theory that explains the variation in living standards exhibited by the data of Table 9.1. At an empirical level, we would like this economic theory to provide the basis for an econometric model—one that can be estimated and tested—in which, say, the more recent data for 1985 are the dependent variable. In terms of the notation that we bring with us from earlier chapters, this dependent variable is output per worker—labor productivity—denoted $q = Q/L$.[3]

We have already said a great deal in this book about the modeling of total output Q. Let us assume that output is produced according to the Cobb-Douglas production function in Chapter 7:

$$Q = \gamma K^{\alpha} L^{1-\alpha}. \tag{9.1}$$

(In contrast to the notation in Chapter 7, we follow MRW in letting α denote the exponent on capital.)

As we discuss there, because this is intended to describe the production of output for an economy as a whole, constant returns to scale is a natural assumption.

All three variables evolve through time. Data on variables such as these is available discretely—annually, quarterly, or monthly, say—and these data observations are denoted by Q_t, K_t, and L_t. For the purpose of developing an economic theory, however, it is convenient to make use of some of the tools and notation we have introduced in Chapter 6 to recognize that in reality these variables evolve continuously and so are implicitly continuous functions of time: $Q(t)$, $K(t)$, and $L(t)$.

---

[3] The data in Table 9.1 are for output per adult rather than per worker. Nevertheless, to the extent that labor force participation rates do not vary greatly across countries, an explanation for one is an explanation for the other.

The Evolution of Capital and Labor

The evolution of total output Q depends on the evolution of the capital stock K and labor L. What can be said about these?

The evolution of an economy's labor force depends on the fertility and mortality rates of the population and on in- and out-migration. These are factors that economists typically take as exogenous (although the field of demography has important links to economics). Hence, it is for our purposes acceptable to take the growth of the labor force as exogenous, proceeding at a constant growth rate n.[4] This can be described with the constant growth model in Chapter 6. Because the labor force evolves continuously, we use the constant growth model in continuous time:

$$L(t) = L(0)e^{nt} \tag{9.2}$$

As we have seen in Section 6.2.1, we can confirm that n represents the instantaneous growth rate of the labor force by noting that

$$\log L(t) = \log L(0) + nt$$

and so

$$n = \frac{d \log L}{dt} = \frac{d \log L}{dL}\frac{dL}{dt} = \frac{1}{L}\frac{dL}{dt} = \frac{\dot{L}}{L}. \tag{9.3}$$

(Compare this with equation (6.20).) For example, using the numerical values from that earlier treatment, discrete growth of 5% per year corresponds to continuously compounded growth of $n = 0.04879$.

What about the other variable determining output, the capital stock K? The capital stock evolves over time in a way that depends on society's willingness to direct resources to enhancing the economy's productive capacity in the form of additional machinery, plants, buildings, roads, and so on. Resources so directed are called **gross investment.** Total output Q is allocated between gross investment and consumption: As a society, we either consume the goods we produce or use them to add to the capital stock so as to improve our ability to produce in the future. The proportion of total output used for gross investment is called the **saving rate;** let us denote this by s. Gross investment is therefore in the amount sQ. To summarize,

$$\text{Gross investment} = sQ, \tag{9.4}$$

$$\text{Consumption} = (1 - s)Q. \tag{9.5}$$

The sum of the two is total output Q.

This is, to be sure, a very simple description of consumption and saving. No doubt in the real world these decisions are influenced by other factors not captured in this model, such as interest rates and economic conditions generally. Is it possible that a treatment as simple as this can be satisfactory? Notice that, in specifying

---

[4] This is the standard notation for the growth rate of labor. Do not confuse it with a sample size.

consumption and saving as being constant proportions of output, we are using the great ratios property of these variables that we discuss in Section 5.2.3. We have seen there that historically the ratios of consumption and saving to income have tended to remain fairly stable. Hence, it makes perfect sense to use this in a model intended to describe the economy in the long run.[5]

The change in K over a period such as a year can be represented using the delta notation of Section 6.2.1 and is called **net investment:**

$$\text{Net investment} = \Delta K_t = K_t - K_{t-1}. \tag{9.6}$$

The distinction between gross and net investment arises because not all gross investment ends up as a net addition to the capital stock. Some must be used to replace older capital that has worn out, called **capital depreciation.** It is reasonable to assume that some fixed proportion δ of the preexisting capital stock wears out each period, so depreciation may be represented as δK_{t-1}; δ is called the **depreciation rate.**

Net investment is the portion of gross investment not used to replace worn-out capital:

$$\text{Net investment} = \text{Gross investment} - \text{Depreciation}.$$

In terms of the notation we have established, over a discrete time period such as a year this is expressed as

$$\Delta K_t = s Q_t - \delta K_{t-1}.$$

In continuous time, the same idea is

$$\dot{K} = s Q - \delta K, \tag{9.7}$$

which is called the **capital accumulation equation.** As we have noted in Section 1.2.2 and more recently in Chapter 6, the time-derivative $\dot{K} = dK/dt$ is just the continuous-time analog of the discrete-time difference ΔK_t.

Notice that we now have three equations that jointly constitute a complete model of the economy. The production function (9.1) describes the transformation of factor inputs K and L into output. According to (9.2), labor L grows exogenously at rate n. Finally, the capital accumulation equation says that output is divided between consumption and investment according to the saving rate s and that, after covering depreciation, this governs the accumulation of capital.

9.2.1   Solution of the Model

The model has so far been expressed in terms of aggregate rather than per-worker variables. Recall, however, that our interest is in understanding the determination of living standards, represented here by output per worker $q = Q/L$. Recall as

---

[5] In Section 5.2.3, the great ratio of consumption to income—the average propensity to consume—is denoted β. In the notation we have now established, the APC is $1 - s$.

well that the Cobb-Douglas production function with constant returns to scale can easily be rewritten in per-worker terms:

$$q = \frac{Q}{L} = \frac{\gamma K^\alpha L^{1-\alpha}}{L^\alpha L^{1-\alpha}} = \gamma \frac{K^\alpha}{L^\alpha} = \gamma k^\alpha. \tag{9.8}$$

This serves to emphasize that living standards depend on the capital-labor ratio. As each worker has more machinery and equipment to work with, each is able to produce more.

According to this, growth in living standards depends on growth in the capital-labor ratio, and so let us focus on the forces determining k. Because $k = K/L$, the rules of instantaneous growth[6] tell us that the growth rates are related by

$$\frac{\dot{k}}{k} = \frac{\dot{K}}{K} - \frac{\dot{L}}{L}. \tag{9.9}$$

Both right-hand-side growth rates are given by the processes governing the two factors of production. From (9.3), L grows at the exogenously specified rate n. By the capital accumulation equation (9.7),

$$\frac{\dot{K}}{K} = s\frac{Q}{K} - \delta. \tag{9.10}$$

Substituting these into (9.9), the capital-labor ratio grows according to

$$\frac{\dot{k}}{k} = s\frac{Q}{K} - \delta - n.$$

Multiplying through by k and using the fact that

$$q = \frac{Q}{L} = \frac{Q}{K}\frac{K}{L},$$

tells us that the capital-labor ratio changes through time according to

$$\dot{k} = sq - (\delta + n)k. \tag{9.11}$$

This is an important equation, worth examining in detail. Consider the meaning of each part of the right-hand side. The expression

$$sq = s\frac{Q}{L}$$

is gross investment per worker, the total amount of output directed to supplementing the capital stock on a per worker basis. But not all gross investment serves as a net addition to the capital stock. As we have seen, depreciated capital must be replaced. In addition, when the population is growing ($n > 0$) new workers must be provided with capital. These two considerations are captured in the expression

$$(\delta + n)k, \tag{9.12}$$

which is called the **capital-widening level of investment** per worker. It indicates

---

[6]   Recall Appendix 6B, in particular Example 12 and equation (6.50b).

FIGURE 9.1

The steady state
of the Solow-Swan
model.

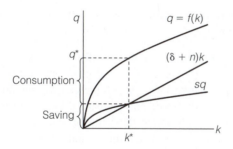

the amount of investment needed, on a per worker basis, to both replace worn-out capital and provide newly born workers with the same capital as existing workers.

If gross investment is only just enough to meet these two needs, then the capital-labor ratio will not change:

$$\text{If } sq = (\delta + n)k, \quad \text{then } \dot{k} = 0.$$

Although the aggregate capital stock K is increasing (gross investment exceeds depreciation), all net investment is going to equip new workers. This situation is called **capital widening.**

If capital per worker is to increase, gross investment must exceed the capital widening level:

$$\text{If } sq > (\delta + n)k, \quad \text{then } \dot{k} > 0.$$

This is called **capital deepening.**

Figure 9.1 presents a diagrammatic interpretation of these forces—the most famous diagram in all of growth theory. The upper curve is the labor-intensive production function (9.8). It tells us the output per worker q produced for each level of capital per worker k. Its curvature reflects the diminishing marginal returns property associated with the restriction $\alpha < 1$ that is discussed in detail in Section 7.2. As capital per worker k increases so does output per worker q, but by successively diminishing increments.

Society allocates any quantity of output q between two uses: consumption and gross investment. This division is portrayed by the lower curve $sq = s\gamma k^{\alpha}$, which just shifts the production function down by the saving rate s. We call this curve the **saving curve.** It indicates the gross investment per worker that takes place for any level of k. The vertical distance between the two curves is the difference between output and saving—consumption per worker.

Finally, the straight line from the origin is the capital-widening level of investment per worker (9.12). It indicates the amount of investment that must take place for the capital-labor ratio to be maintained.

The intersection of the capital-widening line with the saving curve has an important interpretation. Only at this point is the level of saving in the economy just enough to maintain the capital-labor ratio. That is, k^* is that level of k that perpetuates itself, so that k does not change: $\dot{k} = 0$.

Furthermore, there are dynamic forces at work driving the economy toward k^*. These are as follows:

when $k < k^*$ gross investment exceeds the capital-widening level,
$sq > (\delta + n)k$, and the capital-labor ratio increases: $\dot{k} > 0$.

when $k = k^*$ gross investment equals the capital-widening level,
$sq = (\delta + n)k$, and the capital-labor ratio is constant: $\dot{k} = 0$.

when $k > k^*$ gross investment falls short of the capital-widening level,
$sq < (\delta + n)k$, and the capital-labor ratio decreases: $\dot{k} < 0$.

Because k^* is a stable value toward which the economy gravitates, it is called the **steady-state** capital-labor ratio.

The Steady State and Balanced Growth

In a steady state, the capital-labor ratio k is constant. Because all other per-worker quantities are determined by k, they too must be constant. This includes labor productivity $q = \gamma k^\alpha$, gross investment per worker sq, and consumption per worker $(1 - s)q$.

Recall that if a ratio is constant, its numerator and denominator must grow at the same rate. For example, for the capital-labor ratio $k = K/L$ the growth identity (9.9) holds:

$$\frac{\dot{k}}{k} = \frac{\dot{K}}{K} - \frac{\dot{L}}{L} = \frac{\dot{K}}{K} - n.$$

Now, if $\dot{k}/k$ is zero, as it is in a steady state, then the aggregate capital stock must be growing at the rate of population growth:

$$\frac{\dot{K}}{K} = n.$$

By the same logic, this must be true of other per-worker quantities and their associated aggregates. It follows that in the steady state of the Solow-Swan growth model all aggregate variables—capital K, output Q, and aggregate investment and consumption—grow at the rate of population growth. When variables share a common growth rate in this way, they are said to exhibit **balanced growth.**

As we have seen in Theory Meets Application 6.4, the notion of balanced growth goes hand-in-hand with the conclusion that ratios are constant in a steady state. In Section 5.2 on regression through the origin and again in Appendix 6B on logarithms and growth rates, we discuss the view of Klein and Kosobud (1961) that the macroeconomy is characterized by a relative stability of certain ratios. Included in their list of great ratios are—restated using the Solow-Swan notation—the saving-income ratio sQ/Q, the capital-output ratio K/Q, and labor's share of income $1 - \alpha$.

Notice that these great ratios all appear in the Solow-Swan model, and that the balanced growth property of the model predicts that they will be constant in a steady state. Admittedly, in some cases this is by assumption: The saving rate s was taken to be constant in the specification of the model, as were the factor shares of α and $1-\alpha$ for capital and labor. Indeed, it is the historical stability of the great ratios that makes these assumptions reasonable. Nevertheless, it is reassuring to verify that the steady state of the Solow model is consistent with the observed stability of the great ratios.

Steady State and Equilibrium

It is perhaps useful to emphasize the distinction between the concept of a steady state and the concept of economic equilibrium. The most common concept of equilibrium is of a system at rest. However this is not a particularly useful definition in a growth context because, even in a steady state, it is only per-worker variables such as k and q that are constant. Aggregate variables continue to grow: aggregate capital K, labor L, and output Q all grow at the rate of population growth n, as we have seen.

An alternative meaning of equilibrium is that the plans of all economic agents are consistent with one another, so that there is no incentive for anyone to behave differently. This is what we mean when we say that a market is in equilibrium when supply equals demand: Price is such that the total brought to market by those seeking to sell the good is consistent with what purchasers wish to buy.

In this sense, the Solow-Swan model is always in equilibrium—even when it is out of a steady state—in that the plans of all economic agents are by definition consistent with one another. Here the plans of agents relate to their saving and investment behavior. Because the model sets gross investment equal to saving by definition, there is no distinction between the plans of savers versus those of investors and no market in which an interest rate adjusts to reconcile these plans. This simplification means that there is no possibility of the model being out of equilibrium: Investment is always, by definition, equal to saving. A steady state is simply an equilibrium in which per-worker quantities perpetuate themselves.

These remarks suggest that a useful extension to the Solow-Swan model would be to introduce a more sophisticated description of households. This would model households as utility maximizers so that their consumption-saving behavior is determined endogenously, instead of simply being imposed by the exogenous saving rate s. There would then be a market in which an interest rate adjusts to equilibrate the willingness of households to save with the demand for investment by the production sector.

In fact, there are two versions of this extension to the Solow-Swan model that differ in the way they model households. One uses the Ramsey (1928) model of the household as an infinitely lived representative consumer; this was incorporated into the Solow-Swan model by Cass (1965) and Koopmans (1965). The other, due to Diamond (1965) and following work by Allais (1947) and Samuelson (1958), treats households as having finite lifetimes in overlapping generations.[7]

---

[7]   Barro (1974) showed that if one generation leaves bequests to the next, then the two versions are equivalent, because then a household with a finite lifetime behaves as if it is infinitely lived. If, on the other hand, one generation does not care about the next or bequests are otherwise precluded, the two

continued

These important classes of models are treated in advanced macroeconomics texts, notably Romer (2001, Chap. 2) and, at a more advanced level, Blanchard and Fischer (1989, Chaps. 2–3). Barro and Sala-i-Martin (1995, Chap. 2) focus on the Ramsey-Cass-Koopmans model, with less emphasis on the overlapping-generations form. Simplified versions of the Diamond model have appeared in some undergraduate texts, notably Miller and Upton (1974) and, more recently, Auerbach and Kotlikoff (1998).

Although these models yield important insights for many issues in macroeconomics,[8] economic growth is not one of them. It turns out that we can understand the basic determinants of living standards without endogenizing saving and the interest rate. Let us therefore return to our development of the textbook Solow-Swan model based on the exogenous saving rate s.

Solving for the Steady State

What are the fundamental factors determining steady state k and the associated level of living standards q? We can solve for steady state k by substituting the production function (9.8) into equation (9.11) and setting $\dot{k} = 0$:

$$s\gamma k^\alpha - (\delta + n)k = 0. \tag{9.13}$$

The particular value of k that satisfies this equality can be solved for:

$$k^* = \left(\frac{\gamma s}{\delta + n}\right)^{1/(1-\alpha)}.$$

Substituting this steady-state capital-labor ratio back into the production function (9.8) yields the corresponding steady-state level of living standards:

$$q^* = \gamma \left(\frac{\gamma s}{\delta + n}\right)^{\alpha/(1-\alpha)} = \gamma^{1/(1-\alpha)} s^{\alpha/(1-\alpha)} (\delta + n)^{-\alpha/(1-\alpha)}. \tag{9.14}$$

versions of model are not equivalent and have different predictions about some important policy issues. The most important example concerns fiscal policy, in particular the effect of debt-versus tax-financed government spending. When households are infinitely lived the consequences of government spending are independent of the means of finance so, for example, a debt-financed tax cut has no effect. This is called the **Ricardian equivalence theorem,** after the 19th century economist David Ricardo who was the first to formulate it. By contrast, when households have finite lives and there are no bequests, a debt-financed tax cut gives rise to a wealth effect that can have real effects, violating Ricardian equivalence.

[8]   As just one example of a substantive economic issue whose analysis is affected fundamentally by the treatment of saving, consider the taxation of capital. The traditional view in the public finance literature is that income from capital—corporate profits, capital gains, dividend and interest income, and so on—should be taxed. However, this conclusion has come from models in which the saving rate is exogenous, as in the Solow-Swan model. When saving is modeled as the endogenous outcome of household decisions, the taxation of capital reduces saving and therefore capital accumulation. Recognition of this leads to the conclusion that capital should not be taxed. See Atkeson, Chari, and Kehoe (1999).

This solution for the steady-state capital-labor ratio and standard of living indicates that they depend on a number of factors. One set of factors has to do with aspects of the production technology and the nature of capital, specifically capital's share of output α and the depreciation rate δ. But even if these are roughly the same across economies, other factors that almost certainly do differ across economies will lead those economies to gravitate toward different steady-state capital-labor ratios and living standards. In particular, it is apparent that k^* and q^* depend on the saving rate s and the rate of population growth n. Let us examine the effect of changes in these.

A Change in the Saving Rate

Changes in the determinants of the saving curve or the capital-widening line shift those curves and so affect the steady-state capital-labor ratio and standard of living. Consider an increase in the saving rate s to s'. This shifts the saving curve up as shown in Figure 9.2, indicating that, at any level of k, the division of output into consumption versus saving has shifted in favor of the latter.

This change initiates a set of forces moving the economy from the initial steady state k^* to the new one k_1^*. At k^*, it is no longer the case that the amount being saved is just enough to maintain the capital-labor ratio. Instead, saving exceeds the capital-widening level, and so the capital-labor ratio increases over time. These forces continue to operate until the new steady state k_1^* is attained, at which point per capita saving is just enough to cover depreciation and provide new workers with the same capital as older ones.

An interesting implication of the Solow-Swan model is that a country's steady-state growth rate is *not* affected by its saving rate. In the new steady state, the capital-labor ratio k and standard of living q are both constant, just as was true in the initial steady state: Their growth rates are zero. Because these per-worker quantities are constant, we have seen that it follows that aggregate variables such as capital K and output Q grow at the rate of population growth n.

A higher saving rate does not, therefore, permanently raise the growth rates of either per-worker quantities such as the standard of living q or aggregate quantities such as total output Q. In a steady state, these growth rates are 0 and n, respectively. It does however, raise these growth rates temporarily during the transition from the

FIGURE 9.2

An increase in the saving rate.

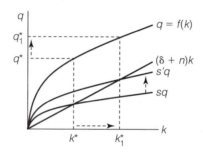

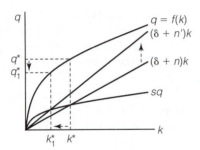

initial steady state to the new one. What the higher saving rate does do is lead to a
higher *level* of living standards—q_1^* in the diagram instead of q^*. Ceteris paribus,
then, the Solow-Swan model predicts that countries with higher saving rates will
enjoy higher living standards.

A Change in the Population Growth Rate

Just as a shift in the saving curve affects the steady-state capital-labor ratio and
living standards, so does a shift in the capital-widening line. As we have seen, the
capital-widening line depends on two factors, the population growth rate n and the
depreciation rate δ. There is no strong reason to expect that the depreciation rate
differs greatly among countries; presumably machinery and bridges wear out about
as quickly in India as they do in Canada. Population growth rates, on the other
hand, do vary significantly internationally. What is the effect on the steady state of
a change in population growth?

An increase in n to n' shifts the capital-widening line upward, as shown in
Figure 9.3. At the initial capital-labor ratio k^* the new capital-widening line is
above the saving curve. Saving is not in the amount needed to maintain the capital-
labor ratio because it is not adequate to equip the now-faster-growing generations
of newly born workers with the same amount of capital as previous generations.
Capital per worker declines. These forces continue to operate until the capital-
labor ratio reaches the new steady value k_1^* associated with the lower standard of
living q_1^*.

Ceteris paribus, then, the Solow-Swan model predicts that countries with high
population growth rates will have low living standards.

9.2.2 Understanding Variations in Living Standards

The Solow-Swan growth model predicts that the standard of living across countries
will be directly related to their saving rates and inversely related to their rates of
population growth. In the terminology of Chapter 1, the steady-state equation (9.14)
is the reduced-form relationship (1.14), and the effects we have described are the
comparative statics effects (1.15).

FIGURE 9.4

Different rates of saving and population growth yield different steady-state living standards.

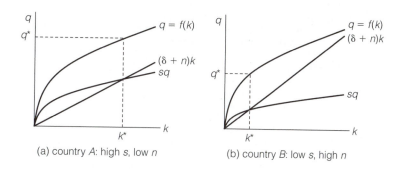

(a) country A: high s, low n   (b) country B: low s, high n

Consider the two countries A and B in Figure 9.4. Both have the same production function with common parameters α and γ. They differ in that country A has a relatively high saving rate and relatively low rate of population growth. As a result, it enjoys a relatively high steady-state capital-labor ratio and standard of living. In contrast, country B has a relatively low saving rate and high rate of population growth. Its steady-state capital-labor ratio and standard of living are relatively low. The Solow-Swan model suggests that the differences in living standards we observe internationally are much like the differences in countries A and B.

Does this explanation of living standards stand up empirically? We know that, descriptively, these predictions of the Solow-Swan model are consistent with the data. We have seen in Figure 3.5 that living standards are correlated positively with saving rates, negatively with population growth rates. But can the model be tested more formally?

Let us return to the formal solution for living standards provided by the model, equation (9.14). In essence, this is a multiplicative relationship that can be converted to a linear one by taking logarithms:

$$\log q = \frac{\log \gamma}{1 - \alpha} + \frac{\alpha}{1 - \alpha} \log s - \frac{\alpha}{1 - \alpha} \log(\delta + n). \tag{9.15}$$

For all the usual reasons, we do not expect that data on output per worker q_i, the saving rate s_i, and population growth n_i will satisfy this linear relationship exactly. Like all economic models, the Solow-Swan model involves gross abstractions from reality; it does not capture a great many factors influencing the world. Even if the model were literally correct (which it obviously is not), at any point in time economies may not be in a steady state. Any economy is continually influenced by a variety of random shocks affecting production, household saving behavior, population growth, and the depreciation of capital. For any economy, then, the saving curve and capital-widening line are continually shifting. The economy tends to gravitate toward the continually shifting steady state, perhaps never actually attaining it.

Despite all these caveats, if the basic explanation of living standards provided by the Solow-Swan model has any validity, the data should bear some relation to the pattern predicted by the model. Restated as a regression equation, the loglinear solution (9.15) is

$$\log q_i = \beta_1 + \beta_2 \log s_i + \beta_3 \log(\delta + n_i) + \varepsilon_i. \tag{9.16}$$

TABLE 9.2

Estimation of the Textbook Solow-Swan Model[a]

Dependent variable = $\log q_{1985}$		
Intercept	β_1	5.36
		(1.55)
$\log s$	β_2	1.31
		(0.17)
$\log(\delta + n)$	β_3	−2.01
		(0.53)
$\overline{R}^2$		0.59
SSE		26.848

[a] Standard errors are in parentheses.

Source: Mankiw, M.G., D. Romer, and D.W. Weil "A Contribution to the Empirics of Economic Growth," *Quarterly Journal of Economics* 107, 407–43. © 1992 MIT Press Journals. Reprinted with permission from MIT Press Journals.

This can be estimated using data on q_i, s_i, and n_i across countries, assuming some plausible value for the rate of depreciation δ. What do we expect to find from these estimation results?

First, β_2 should be positive and β_3 negative. As we have seen, the theory predicts that living standards are related positively to the saving rate and related negatively to population growth. Second, except for the sign difference these coefficients should be about the same because in absolute value both are $\alpha/(1 - \alpha)$. In fact, our background knowledge of α gives us a fairly good idea of what this magnitude should be. Recall from Section 7.2 that α, the exponent on capital in the Cobb-Douglas production function (9.1), has the interpretation as capital's share of output. We have seen that factor shares are quite stable over time, and for many economies capital's share has historically been approximately $\frac{1}{3}$. Hence, both β_2 and β_3 should have a magnitude of approximately

$$\frac{\alpha}{1 - \alpha} = \frac{\frac{1}{3}}{1 - \frac{1}{3}} = \frac{1}{2}. \tag{9.17}$$

Finally, if the Solow-Swan model is correct in identifying the rates of saving and population growth as the key determinants of living standards, their effects should be statistically significant and the equation should explain a substantial portion of the variation in the dependent variable.

How do these predictions of the Solow-Swan growth model stand up? Table 9.2 presents the estimation results for equation (9.16) obtained by MRW using their sample of 75 countries. The dependent variable is the logarithm of output per adult in 1985 given in Table 9.1. The saving rate s is measured by the average annual share of real investment in GDP over the 1960–1985 period. Population growth n is measured as the average annual growth rate of the working-age population during this period. Finally, depreciation is assumed to occur at a rate of 5% per year for all countries: $\delta = 0.05$.[9] In estimating (9.16), then, we are asking whether the saving and population growth rates that prevailed on average in these countries during 1960–1985 explain the living standards that they enjoyed at the end of that period.

The regression has an $\overline{R}^2$ of 0.59, indicating that variation in saving and population growth rates *does* explain much of the variation in living standards. As well, the signs on the two explanatory variables are as predicted: Living standards are directly related to saving rates and inversely related to population growth. Furthermore these coefficients are highly statistically significant (*t* tests easily reject the hypotheses $\beta_2 = 0$ and $\beta_3 = 0$), so that these explanatory variables are each important determinants of living standards. Finally, the two slope coefficients are of roughly the same magnitude, $\hat{\beta}_2 = 1.31$ and $\hat{\beta}_3 = -2.01$, so that the restriction $\hat{\beta}_2 + \hat{\beta}_3 = 0$ implicit in (9.15) is roughly satisfied. In these respects, then, the results are strongly supportive of the Solow-Swan model.

Nevertheless one aspect of these estimation results is puzzling: The magnitudes of $\hat{\beta}_2$ and $\hat{\beta}_3$ are inconsistent with (9.17). Equivalently, the value of α implied by these coefficient estimates is implausible. For example, consider the estimate $\hat{\beta}_2 = 1.31$. The implied estimate of α is 0.567. Yet we know from our study of factor shares in Section 7.2 that historically capital's share of output has been nowhere near 60%; indeed, it has typically been little more than half that.

The α estimate of 0.567 implied by $\hat{\beta}_2 = 1.31$ is one of two estimates implied by the regression results in Table 9.2. A different estimate is implied by $\hat{\beta}_3 = -2.01$. This is an important enough point that it is worth summarizing formally.

EXAMPLE 1 What is the relationship between the coefficients of the regression equation (9.16) and the parameters γ and α of the Solow-Swan growth model? What is the implication for estimating γ and α?

SOLUTION Comparing (9.16) and (9.15), the relationship is

$$\beta_1 = \frac{\log \gamma}{1 - \alpha},$$
$$\beta_2 = \frac{\alpha}{1 - \alpha},$$
$$\beta_3 = \frac{-\alpha}{1 - \alpha}.$$

[9] Actually, MRW work in terms of a slightly more sophisticated version of the Solow-Swan model that incorporates technical change, so the value 0.05 is the total of the depreciation rate and the rate of technical change. This complication is not important for our purposes. The version of the model with technical change is developed in the appendix to this chapter.

The implication is that the regression estimates imply multiple rather than unique estimates of γ and α. For example, the expression for β_2 may be rearranged as

$$\alpha = \frac{\beta_2}{1 + \beta_2}$$

and, using this, that for β_1 as

$$\log \gamma = \beta_1 (1 - \alpha) = \frac{\beta_1}{1 + \beta_2}.$$

Based on the regression results in Table 9.2, the implied estimates are $\hat{\alpha} = 0.567$ and $\hat{\gamma} = 10.2$. However, a second pair of estimates is implied by the estimate of β_3. You are asked to calculate these in Exercise 9.7b.

This is a situation we consider in much more detail in the next chapter, one that we call a case of overidentifying restrictions. It is evident that it would be useful to be able to estimate the model in such a way that unique estimates of γ and α are obtained and also to be able to perform a statistical test of the implied restriction that $\beta_3 = -\beta_2$. The next chapter develops methods for both.

How can it be that in so many respects these estimation results for the Solow-Swan model are encouraging, and yet the coefficient magnitudes are implausible? One possibility suggested by the previous chapter is model misspecification. In Section 8.9.1 we have seen that the omission of relevant influences from a regression model biases estimates of the remaining coefficients. It is natural to ask, therefore, whether our formulation of the textbook Solow-Swan model may have failed to include some important determinant of economic growth.

EXERCISES

9.2 Consider a country that has the following production function:

$$Q = K^{1/2} L^{1/2}.$$

The economy behaves according to the Solow-Swan growth model.

(a) Does this production function have constant returns to scale? Justify your answer.

(b) What is the per-worker production function $q = f(k)$?

(c) Suppose that the country saves 10% of output each year, its population grows at a rate of 2%, and capital depreciates by 3% per year. In a steady state what is

i. the capital-labor ratio?

ii. labor productivity?

iii. consumption per worker?

iv. the wage rate?

v. the interest rate?

vi. the growth rate of labor productivity?

vii. the growth rate of aggregate output?

9.3 An increase in the saving rate in the Solow-Swan model leads to an increase in the level of living standards q. But this concept of living standards may be misleading because it is not so much their output that is the ultimate interest of agents as what they are able to consume: $(1 - s)q$.

(a) In the Solow-Swan diagram, indicate the amount of consumption per worker associated with the steady state k^*.

(b) Does an increase in the saving rate necessarily result in higher consumption per worker? Is it possible for an economy to save too much, in the sense that a reduction in the saving rate would result in an *increase* in steady-state consumption per worker?

(c) Suppose you could set the saving rate in the Solow-Swan model. Present a diagrammatic analysis showing how you would set it to maximize steady-state consumption per worker.

Comment: If you were a central planner in charge of this economy, agents would want you to set the saving rate to maximize their consumption. In doing this, you would be following the golden rule of doing unto others as you would have them do unto you. For this reason, the saving rate that maximizes steady-state consumption per worker is called the **golden rule saving rate.** An interesting implication of models of economic growth is that there are no market forces driving an economy toward the golden rule saving rate.

9.3   Human Capital in the Solow-Swan Model

The Solow-Swan model focuses on the role of capital accumulation in economic growth; in fact, it often goes by the name **neoclassical model of capital accumulation.** People produce using the available capital stock, consuming a portion of what they produce and saving the rest. This saving supplements the capital stock and increases society's future productive capacity. The essence of saving is, then, forgone consumption: We are willing to give up the pleasure of consumption today in return for the promise of higher productivity and consumption tomorrow.

Although capital plays this key role in the model, we have so far given only passing thought to what is meant by this concept. Our discussion has been phrased in terms of the national income accounting definition of capital as that which takes a physical tangible form: machinery, production plants, buildings, highways, ports, and so on. But in its pure economic sense capital is created whenever we forgo consumption today in order to increase our ability to produce in the future. Most notably, during their period of education students forgo production and consumption. The incentive to do this is that the **human capital** so acquired raises their productivity and so yields a return in the future. As we know from our discussion of the log-lin earnings function in Section 6.2, the empirical evidence shows that the accumulation of human capital *is* rewarded. From Theory Meets Application 6.1, in developed countries an additional year of schooling yields approximately a 7% increase in annual income; the return is slightly higher in less-developed countries.

Brief reflection indicates that society makes enormous investments in human capital. A substantial portion of government budgets is devoted to education at all levels: primary, secondary, and postsecondary. Students pursuing postsecondary education make substantial sacrifices to do so, both directly and in terms of forgone earnings, as any undergraduate will testify. Furthermore, the acquisition of human capital is not limited to formal education—a great deal of skill acquisition takes the form of on-the-job training. Viewed in these broad terms, it is conceivable that the accumulation of human capital rivals physical capital in the demand it places on society's resources.

In light of the empirical deficiencies of the textbook Solow-Swan model that we have seen, MRW reformulated the model to recognize this distinctive role of human capital. In this section, we study their reformulation. This requires revisiting each of the steps we have gone through in our study of the textbook model: formulating the model, deriving an expression for steady-state living standards, and estimating a regression equation based on this steady-state solution.

Setup of the Model

Let us begin, as we have previously, with the production function. We wish to recognize the existence of three factors of production: labor L and two categories of capital, physical capital K and human capital H. The generalization of the Cobb-Douglas production function to three factors is

$$Q = \gamma K^\alpha H^\beta L^{1-\alpha-\beta},$$

where constant returns to scale continues to be imposed by the requirement that the exponents add to 1. Just as in the previous model, this may be expressed in labor-intensive form:

$$q = \frac{Q}{L} = \frac{\gamma K^\alpha H^\beta L^{1-\alpha-\beta}}{L^\alpha L^\beta L^{1-\alpha-\beta}} = \gamma k^\alpha h^\beta. \tag{9.18}$$

As before, the goal is to explain the variation in output per worker q across countries. According to the labor-intensive form of the production function, this depends on physical capital per worker $k = K/L$ and human capital per worker $h = H/L$. The labor force continues to be specified as growing exogenously at rate n.

Both physical capital and human capital are treated as growing in the same way that physical capital did in the textbook model. Society devotes a proportion s_k of total output to the accumulation of physical capital and a proportion s_h to the provision of education and training. Both categories of capital depreciate over time, and so both grow when gross investment exceeds depreciation:

$$\dot{K} = s_k Q - \delta K, \tag{9.19a}$$
$$\dot{H} = s_h Q - \delta H. \tag{9.19b}$$

The first of these just repeats (9.7). For simplicity, it is assumed that a common depreciation rate applies to both types of capital: Skills become obsolete at about the same rate that physical capital wears out.

This treatment of the production function and physical and human capital accumulation completes the respecification of the Solow-Swan model to incorporate human capital.

Solving for Steady-State Living Standards

With this respecification, we can ask the same questions as in the earlier version of the model. Does the model gravitate toward a steady-state level of living standards? What are the fundamental forces determining this steady state? These questions are addressed by the same series of steps that we have gone through previously.

First let us derive the implications of the capital accumulation equations for the growth of physical and human capital per worker. Equation (9.9) provides a definitional relationship among the growth rates of k, K, and L. The analogous identity relating the growth rates of h, H, and L is

$$\frac{\dot{h}}{h} = \frac{\dot{H}}{H} - \frac{\dot{L}}{L} = \frac{\dot{H}}{H} - n. \tag{9.20}$$

The capital accumulation equations (9.19) imply the growth rates

$$\frac{\dot{K}}{K} = s_k \frac{Q}{K} - \delta,$$

$$\frac{\dot{H}}{H} = s_h \frac{Q}{H} - \delta,$$

the first of which just repeats (9.10). Substituting these into the growth identities (9.9) and (9.20) yields

$$\frac{\dot{k}}{k} = s_k \frac{Q}{K} - \delta - n,$$

$$\frac{\dot{h}}{h} = s_h \frac{Q}{H} - \delta - n.$$

Finally, multiplying through by k and h, respectively, yields equations analogous to (9.11) for each of our two categories of capital:

$$\dot{k} = s_k q - (\delta + n)k,$$

$$\dot{h} = s_h q - (\delta + n)h.$$

These are the fundamental equations describing the evolution of each type of capital.

Just as in the textbook Solow-Swan model, the economy reaches a steady state when per worker capital stocks cease to grow. Substituting the labor-intensive production function (9.18) into these dynamic equations, these steady-state conditions are:

$$\dot{k} = s_k \gamma k^\alpha h^\beta - (\delta + n)k = 0, \tag{9.21a}$$

$$\dot{h} = s_h \gamma k^\alpha h^\beta - (\delta + n)h = 0. \tag{9.21b}$$

These must be solved for the steady-state levels of k and h, just as in the textbook model the steady-state condition is solved for k. However, doing this is more complicated than it is for the textbook model because the two steady-state conditions both involve k and h and so must be solved simultaneously for the steady-state values of these variables. The solutions are

$$k^* = \left(\frac{\gamma s_k^{1-\beta} s_h^{\beta}}{\delta + n}\right)^{1/(1-\alpha-\beta)}, \tag{9.22a}$$

$$h^* = \left(\frac{\gamma s_k^{\alpha} s_h^{1-\alpha}}{\delta + n}\right)^{1/(1-\alpha-\beta)}. \tag{9.22b}$$

Substituting these into the production function (9.18) yields a solution for steady-state living standards. Taking logarithms, this solution may be expressed in loglinear form as

$$\log q^* = \frac{\log \gamma}{1-\alpha-\beta} + \frac{\alpha}{1-\alpha-\beta}\log s_k - \frac{\alpha+\beta}{1-\alpha-\beta}\log(\delta+n) + \frac{\beta}{1-\alpha-\beta}\log s_h. \tag{9.23}$$

As a regression model, this is

$$\log q_i = \beta_1 + \beta_2 \log s_{ki} + \beta_3 \log(\delta + n_i) + \beta_4 \log s_{hi} + \varepsilon_i. \tag{9.24}$$

In spite of the involved derivation leading to it, this is nothing more than the regression (9.16) of the textbook model augmented to include one additional explanatory variable—the saving rate for human capital s_h. The interpretation of the coefficients has changed somewhat; they are now functions of both α and β, the shares in national income of physical and human capital, respectively. It is still the case that the income share of physical capital should be approximately $\frac{1}{3}$. The income share of human capital is less clear-cut. Because human capital is not directly observable in the way that physical capital is, it is not possible to decompose total labor income into components attributable to raw (i.e., unskilled) labor versus acquired skills. For the sake of the argument, however, let us suppose that human capital is important enough that it earns a share of national income equal to that of physical capital: $\beta = \alpha = \frac{1}{3}$. National income is therefore divided equally into payments to physical capital K, human capital H, and unskilled labor L. Then the estimates we expect to find for the slope coefficients in regression (9.24) are roughly

$$\beta_2 = \frac{\alpha}{1-\alpha-\beta} = \frac{\frac{1}{3}}{1-\frac{1}{3}-\frac{1}{3}} = 1,$$

$$\beta_3 = -\frac{\alpha+\beta}{1-\alpha-\beta} = -\frac{\frac{1}{3}+\frac{1}{3}}{1-\frac{1}{3}-\frac{1}{3}} = -2,$$

$$\beta_4 = \frac{\beta}{1-\alpha-\beta} = \frac{\frac{1}{3}}{1-\frac{1}{3}-\frac{1}{3}} = 1.$$

The estimation results obtained by MRW for this augmented regression are presented in Table 9.3. They used data on the percentage of the working-age population in secondary school, on average over the years 1960–1985, as a measure

THEORY MEETS APPLICATION   **9.1**

Public Capital and Living Standards

Any economy relies on **public capital**—the infrastructure of roads, bridges, airports, schools, medical facilities, public utilities and communications networks, and other government-provided capital that the private sector depends on to function. There has been some concern in recent decades that we have failed to adequately maintain and renew our stock of public capital, a concern that has spawned a considerable body of research by economists on infrastructure investment.

The MRW analysis emphasizes the distinction between physical and human capital and studies their separate roles in determining living standards. In principle, however, capital can be decomposed in many ways, and a number of studies have extended the MRW framework to consider alternative decompositions.

In one study, Milbourne, Otto, and Voss (2003) retained the MRW distinction between physical and human capital, but decomposed physical capital into its private and public components.

They reformulated the MRW analysis by beginning with a production function that permits distinct roles for private capital K_p and public (or government) capital K_g,

$$Q = \gamma K_p^{\alpha_1} K_g^{\alpha_2} H^\beta L^{1-\alpha_1-\alpha_2-\beta}.$$

This leads to a regression equation for living standards of the form

$$\log q_i = \beta_1 + \beta_2 \log s_{pi} + \beta_3 \log(\delta + n_i)$$
$$+ \beta_4 \log s_{hi} + \beta_5 \log s_{gi} + \varepsilon_i,$$

where s_{pi} and s_{gi} denote the saving rates on private and public capital.

In estimating this equation they found that the saving rate on public capital is statistically insignificant. Important as public capital may be to the functioning of an economy, different saving rates for public capital do not appear to be an important source of variation in living standards across countries.

TABLE 9.3   Estimation of the Augmented Solow-Swan Model[a]

Dependent variable = $\log q_{1985}$		
Intercept	β_1	7.81
		(1.19)
$\log s_k$	β_2	0.70
		(0.15)
$\log(\delta + n)$	β_3	−1.50
		(0.40)
$\log s_h$	β_4	0.73
		(0.10)
$\overline{R}^2$		0.77
SSE		14.680

[a] Standard errors are in parentheses.

Source: Mankiw, M.G., D. Romer, and D.W. Weil "A Contribution to the Empirics of Economic Growth," *Quarterly Journal of Economics* 107, 407–43. © 1992 MIT Press Journals. Reprinted with permission from MIT Press Journals.

of s_h. It is apparent that this variable does contribute usefully to the model; a t test shows β_4 to be statistically significant, and the $\overline{R}^2$ is now 0.77 instead of the previous 0.59 obtained for the textbook model. In terms of coefficient magnitudes, the estimates $\hat{\beta}_2 = 0.70$, $\hat{\beta}_3 = -1.50$, and $\hat{\beta}_4 = 0.73$ are in the ballpark we conjectured; certainly these estimates are consistent with a plausible income share for human capital. As in the textbook model, there are multiple implied estimates for γ, α, and β, and again it is worth stating this example of overidentifying restrictions explicitly.

EXAMPLE 2

What is the relationship between the coefficients of the regression equation (9.24) and the parameters γ, α, and β of the augmented Solow-Swan growth model? What is the implication for estimating γ, α, and β?

SOLUTION

Comparing (9.24) and (9.23), the relationship is

$$\beta_1 = \frac{\log \gamma}{1 - \alpha - \beta},$$
$$\beta_2 = \frac{\alpha}{1 - \alpha - \beta},$$
$$\beta_3 = \frac{-(\alpha + \beta)}{1 - \alpha - \beta},$$
$$\beta_4 = \frac{\beta}{1 - \alpha - \beta}.$$

Similar to Example 1, multiple solutions are implied for γ, α, and β. For example, the expressions for β_2 and β_3 may be solved as

$$\alpha = \frac{\beta_2}{1 - \beta_3},$$
$$\beta = \frac{\beta_2 + \beta_3}{\beta_3 - 1}.$$

From the regression results in Table 9.3, these formulas imply the estimates $\hat{\alpha} = 0.28$ and $\hat{\beta} = 0.32$. But this is just one of three distinct pairs of estimates for α and β. You are asked to compute the other two in Exercise 9.8b.

Finally, similar to the textbook model these overidentifying restrictions between the two sets of parameters imply a restriction on the regression coefficients: $\beta_2 + \beta_4 = -\beta_3$. It is remarkable just how close the estimates come to satisfying this restriction.

EXERCISES

9.4 Starting with the steady-state conditions (9.21), derive the solutions (9.22).

9.5 Starting with the solutions (9.22), derive the loglinear equation (9.23).

9.4

Summary: Mankiw, Romer, and Weil in a Nutshell

At this point, it is useful to step back from the details of the two versions of the Solow-Swan model we have derived and summarize the essentials of the MRW analysis.

The Solow-Swan model of economic growth seeks to explain the determination of living standards. In its textbook form, it leads to the regression equation (9.16),

$$\log q_i = \beta_1 + \beta_2 \log s_i + \beta_3 \log(\delta + n_i) + \varepsilon_i.$$

This says that output per capita q is determined fundamentally by the saving rate s and the population growth rate n. The underlying theory suggests that q should depend positively on s, so $\beta_2 > 0$, and negatively on n, so $\beta_3 < 0$. With data on these variables and a specified value for the depreciation rate δ, this regression can be estimated by least squares. Doing this yields the estimation results of Table 9.2, in which the explanatory variables are statistically significant and have the anticipated signs.

The regression coefficients have an interpretation in terms of the parameters γ and α of the underlying constant-returns-to-scale Cobb-Douglas production function (9.1):

$$\beta_1 = \frac{\log \gamma}{1 - \alpha},$$

$$\beta_2 = \frac{\alpha}{1 - \alpha},$$

$$\beta_3 = \frac{-\alpha}{1 - \alpha}.$$

The implication is that the estimated slopes should roughly satisfy the restriction $\beta_2 + \beta_3 = 0$, which does in fact come fairly close to holding for the estimates of Table 9.2.

These relationships may be used to solve for implied estimates of γ and α. The parameter α has the interpretation as the factor share of capital and so should be in the neighborhood of $\frac{1}{3}$. The nature of these relationships means that there are two solutions for these parameters and so the implied estimates are not unique. One set of implied estimates is obtained in Example 1. Because α and γ are overdetermined in this way, the restrictions are said to be overidentifying. However, regardless of which set of implied estimates we consider, the estimate of α is implausibly large.

This led MRW to formulate an augmented version of the Solow-Swan model that distinguishes between physical and human capital. It leads to a regression equation of the form (9.24),

$$\log q_i = \beta_1 + \beta_2 \log s_{ki} + \beta_3 \log(\delta + n_i) + \beta_4 \log s_{hi} + \varepsilon_i.$$

This is similar to the first regression except that it includes an additional explanatory variable s_h, the proportion of output devoted to investments in human capital. The notation s_k and s_h is used to distinguish between the saving rates for physical and human capital; s_k has the same meaning and is measured in the same way as the previous s.

The relationship among the coefficients of this regression and the underlying parameters of the production function is

$$\beta_1 = \frac{\log \gamma}{1 - \alpha - \beta},$$

$$\beta_2 = \frac{\alpha}{1 - \alpha - \beta},$$

$$\beta_3 = \frac{-(\alpha + \beta)}{1 - \alpha - \beta},$$

$$\beta_4 = \frac{\beta}{1 - \alpha - \beta}.$$

Here α and β are the factor shares of physical and human capital. As before, these are overidentifying relationships in that they imply multiple solutions for α, β, and γ.

The estimation of the augmented regression, as reported in Table 9.3, shows all three variables to be important determinants of living standards. Furthermore, the coefficient estimates are consistent with the implied restriction $\beta_2 + \beta_4 = -\beta_3$. Most important, the implied estimates of the factor shares, although again not unique, are nevertheless reasonable. An illustration is provided in Example 2, in which one set of implied estimates is derived.

In conclusion, whereas the point estimates in the textbook model do not make sense in terms of our prior knowledge of factor shares, those for the augmented model do. This suggests that the regression equation derived from the textbook model is subject to the omitted variable bias analyzed in Section 8.9.1. The failure to include a relevant explanatory variable—the saving rate for human capital—results in biased coefficient estimators and implausible estimates; including this relevant explanatory variable corrects this.

EXERCISES

The MRW data for their 75-country sample are available in the file **mrw.dat**. The variable definitions are as follows.

country   Country number assigned by MRW. The countries are in the same order as in Table 9.1.

gdp60   GDP per adult in 1960.

gdp85   GDP per adult in 1985.

pop   Average annual percentage growth rate of the working-age population, 1960–1985. (100 × the population growth rate n.)

Igdp   Gross investment as a percentage of GDP, on average over the period 1960–1985. (100 × the saving rate s.)

school   Percentage of the working-age population in secondary school, on average over the period 1960–1985.

Examine the file, satisfying yourself that the figures on GDP per adult are the same as those reported in Table 9.1.

9.6 💿 **mrw.dat** Produce scatter plots of the relationship between gdp85 and each of Igdp and pop.

(a) Are they similar to the plots of Figure 3.5?

(b) Are you able to reproduce the correlations reported in Chapter 3?

9.7 💿 **mrw.dat** Estimate the regression (9.16) assuming $\delta = 0.05$.

(a) How close do you come to replicating the results reported in Table 9.2?

(b) Consider the estimates $\hat{\beta}_3 = -2.01$ and $\hat{\beta}_1 = 5.36$. What are the implied estimates of α and γ? Is this estimate of α plausible?

9.8 💿 **mrw.dat** Now proceed to the estimation of the augmented regression (9.24), again assuming $\delta = 0.05$.

(a) How close do you come to replicating the results reported in Table 9.3?

(b) The estimates of α and β implied by $\hat{\beta}_2 = 0.70$ and $\hat{\beta}_3 = -1.50$ are calculated in Example 2.
i. What estimates are implied by $\hat{\beta}_3 = -1.50$ and $\hat{\beta}_4 = 0.73$?

ii. What estimates are implied by $\hat{\beta}_2 = 0.70$ and $\hat{\beta}_4 = 0.73$?

iii. You have found that there are three distinct pairs of estimates implied for α and β. How many distinct estimates of γ are there? What are they?

9.9 One difficulty in introducing human capital into the model is that it is not as easily measured as physical capital. In particular, the saving rate for human capital s_h is intended to represent the proportion of GDP devoted to human capital accumulation, just as s_k is the proportion devoted to physical capital. However, the best measure of s_h that MRW could come up with is their variable school, the proportion of the working-age population enrolled in secondary school. It may well be that this is not a very good measure of s_h.

Suppose that s_h and school are not the same thing, but that the two are proportional: $s_h = \phi \cdot$ school, say. (The proportionality factor ϕ is unknown; otherwise we would be able to use it to obtain s_h.) What are the implications for the coefficient estimates of the augmented regression?

9.5 Conclusions

In this chapter, we have used the Solow-Swan model of economic growth to illustrate two econometric principles. One is the idea of omitted variable bias that was studied in the previous chapter: When a relevant regressor is omitted from a regression model, the remaining coefficient estimates are biased. Here we have seen that estimating an equation based on the textbook Solow-Swan model results in coefficient estimates that are inconsistent with our prior knowledge of factor shares. Adding an additional regressor for human capital resolves this, yielding estimates consistent with plausible factor shares.

The second econometric principle illustrated by the Solow-Swan model is that economic theory gives rise to testable parameter restrictions. We have encountered testable restrictions in previous chapters, but they usually[10] have taken the elementary form of a parameter being equal to some hypothesized value, for example,

---

[10] A more general restriction is tested by the F test of the regression model discussed in Section 8.5.3; the null hypothesis is the joint restriction that all slope coefficients are zero.

$\beta_k = \beta_0$ in a regression model or, in Chapter 2, $\mu = \mu_0$. In Chapter 10 we call these **fixed value restrictions.** It is now apparent that testable parameter restrictions can take more interesting forms. In the textbook Solow-Swan model, the underlying theory from which the regression equation is derived predicts the restriction $\beta_2 = -\beta_3$. In the augmented model, it is $\beta_2 + \beta_4 = -\beta_3$. Both are examples of linear restrictions on the regression coefficients, something that arises in a great many contexts and that is defined more systematically in the next chapter.

The existence of linear restrictions such as these raises a couple of interesting questions. First, we have seen that the coefficient estimates obtained for the Solow-Swan model are roughly consistent with these restrictions, almost exactly so in the case of the augmented model. This suggests that it would be useful to have a formal statistical test of the null hypothesis that these restrictions hold, just as we already have tests for fixed-value restrictions. Such a general test procedure is developed in Section 10.2.2.

Second, the Solow-Swan model has illustrated that these coefficient restrictions are typically associated with an overdetermination of the underlying parameters of the economic model, such as γ, α, and β in the augmented model, so that multiple rather than unique estimates of these parameters are implied. This is investigated in some detail in Example 1 for the textbook Solow-Swan model and in Example 2 for the augmented model. If the coefficient restrictions can be imposed in estimation (so that the estimated coefficients satisfy the restrictions exactly), then unique estimates can be obtained. Section 10.2.1 shows how to do this.

Finally, another purpose of this chapter has been to introduce you to the theory of economic growth and the influential empirical work of MRW. Other researchers have since extended their analysis in a number of directions. Our summary of the MRW estimation results has focused on their 75-country sample. They found, however, that the model performs less well when applied to just the OECD nations. Nonneman and Vanhoudt (1996) address this by distinguishing among physical capital, human capital, and technological know-how, measuring the saving rate on the last by the proportion of research and development (R&D) expenditures to GDP. They find that this improves the ability of the model to explain variations in living standards among the OECD nations. Other authors have considered other extensions. Knowles and Owen (1995, 1997) allow for distinct roles for education and health in the production function and find that health is a significant determinant of productivity. Temple (1998) separates physical capital into equipment and structures and finds that the implied returns to equipment investment are very high in developing countries. As discussed in Theory Meets Application 9.1, Milbourne, Otto, and Voss (2003) separate physical capital into its private and public components and find that investment in public capital does not appear to be an important source of variation in living standards.

An assessment of the MRW contribution in relation to subsequent developments in the growth literature can be found in Aghion and Howitt (1998, pp. 34–35); see also Foley and Michl (1999, pp. 173–174). The MRW analysis also figures prominently in the survey of growth empirics by Durlauf and Quah (1999).

Appendix   Technical Change

The MRW analysis studies the ability of the Solow-Swan model to explain the diversity of living standards across countries and so focuses on the cross-sectional implications of the model. What are the implications of the model for the time series behavior of variables? The answer to this question turns out not to depend on the role of human capital, and so we revert to the textbook version of the Solow-Swan model to consider it.

Time Series Implications of the Model without Technical Change

In our discussion of the steady state of the textbook version of the Solow-Swan model, we established the steady-state growth rates of variables. To summarize, in a steady state per-worker variables such as the capital-labor ratio $k = K/L$ and labor productivity $q = Q/L$ are constant; their growth rates are therefore zero. Because when a ratio is constant the numerator and denominator of that ratio must grow at the same rate, it follows that aggregate variables such as capital K and output Q grow at the rate of population growth n. That aggregate variables grow at a common rate so that they remain in balance—their ratios are constant—is called the property of balanced growth.

   In terms of relating the Solow-Swan model to observed phenomena, the conclusion that the economy gravitates toward a steady state in which labor productivity q is constant is not a very satisfactory one. Historical data reveal no tendency for economies to converge toward some stagnant level of living standards. On the contrary, perhaps the most remarkable feature of the economic history of the last few centuries is the sustained growth in living standards that has taken place; there is no apparent tendency for growth in living standards to peter out.

   To illustrate, consider Jones's data for GDP per capita from 1880 to 1987 in Figure 6.4. As we have found in our discussion of the constant growth model in connection with our study of that data, the fact that the series is linear in its logarithms—as portrayed in Figure 6.4(b)—reflects an underlying process of approximately constant growth. This is indicated even more clearly in Figure 6.4(c) in which the log-differences of the series are plotted. These period-by-period percentage changes, although they fluctuate considerably, show no systematic tendency to decline.

Implications for Factor Prices

The perverse prediction of the basic Solow-Swan model that the economy converges toward stagnant living standards also has some unsatisfactory implications for factor prices. Remember that the marginal productivity theory of income distribution says that under competitive conditions the prices of factors are determined by their marginal products. Recall the derivations (7.13) and (7.14) in our treatment of the Cobb-Douglas production function in Section 7.2; in our present notation, the marginal products of capital and labor are

$$\text{Rental rate on capital} = r = \frac{\partial Q}{\partial K} = \alpha \frac{Q}{K} = \alpha \frac{Q/L}{K/L} = \alpha \frac{q}{k}, \tag{9.25a}$$

$$\text{Real wage} = w = \frac{\partial Q}{\partial L} = (1-\alpha)\frac{Q}{L} = (1-\alpha)q. \tag{9.25b}$$

Now consider the behavior of these factor prices in a steady state. Because the per-worker quantities q and k are constant, these marginal product expressions make it easy to see that factor prices must also be constant.

How does this compare with the world we observe? The constancy of the rental rate on capital is a reasonable enough implication of the model; real interest rates today are little different from what they were 100, or even 1000, years ago. But the same is not true of the real wage. Hand in hand with sustained increases in living standards, real wages have tended to increase historically, reflecting increased productivity. The real payment for 1 hour of labor today is considerably higher than it was a century ago, much higher still than in the Stone Age.

In conclusion, contrary to the implications of the Solow-Swan model as we have so far presented it, historical data reveal an asymmetric behavior of factor prices. A model of economic growth should be able to explain this, along with the sustained growth in living standards that has been observed historically.

Time Series Implications of the Model with Technical Change

These unsatisfactory time series implications of the most basic version of the Solow-Swan model can be resolved by introducing technical change.

Technical Change in the Solow-Swan Model

Recall that Section 7.3 studied Robert Solow's (1957) method for calculating an index of technology—alternately known as total factor productivity, multifactor productivity, or the Solow residual. We use it there to treat technical change in the estimation of a Cobb-Douglas production function. The notion is that technological progress changes the productivity of measured capital and labor inputs in a way that has the effect of shifting the production function upward over time.

It turns out that introducing this idea into the Solow-Swan growth model has important implications for the steady state of the model. Suppose the level of technology $A(t)$ grows continuously at rate β, so that it may be described by the constant growth model in continuous time

$$A(t) = A(0)e^{\beta t}.$$

This is the simplest possible treatment of technological progress; technology is just being taken as exogenous, no different from the treatment of labor $L(t)$ in equation (9.2). As in equation (9.3), the properties of logarithms and time-derivatives may be used to verify that β has the interpretation as the instantaneous growth rate of technology:

$$\beta = \frac{d \log A}{dt} = \frac{d \log A}{dA} \frac{dA}{dt} = \frac{1}{A} \frac{dA}{dt} = \frac{\dot{A}}{A}.$$

Now suppose that technology shifts the production function of the Solow-Swan model in the following way:

$$Q = \gamma K^{\alpha} (AL)^{1-\alpha}. \tag{9.26}$$

In this formulation, technology is said to be labor augmenting. The idea is that although new technology is typically embodied in the quality of physical capital, its effect is to enhance the productivity of labor.[11] The input AL is labor in **effective labor units,** so that it is not so much physical worker-hours of labor L that are productive in use but their effectiveness as determined by the level of technology.

It turns out that with this respecification of the production function, some key features of the steady state of the Solow-Swan model are altered. In particular, per-capita variables such as k and q grow at rate β in a steady state:

$$\frac{\dot{q}}{q} = \beta.$$

Aggregate variables such as output $Q = qL$ grow at rate

$$\frac{\dot{Q}}{Q} = \frac{\dot{q}}{q} + \frac{\dot{L}}{L} = \beta + n.$$

That is, total production in the economy grows both because the number of workers is growing and because technical change enables output per worker to grow. Notice that, because aggregate variables such as Q and K grow at the common rate $\beta + n$, their ratios are constant in a steady state; that is, even with technical change the model continues to exhibit balanced growth. Recall that the capital-output ratio K/Q is one of Klein and Kosobud's great ratios. Even with technical change, the Solow-Swan model continues to predict the long-term stability of this great ratio.

---

[11] Section 7.3 uses instead the assumption of Hicks neutrality in its formulation of growth accounting. As we have noted, however, Hicks neutrality is not a prerequisite for growth accounting. It only plays a crucial role at the stage when the Solow residual is used to estimate the technology-corrected production function, which is not our interest here.

In any case, when the production function is Cobb-Douglas the distinction between Hicks-neutral and labor-augmenting technological progress is not important. As may be seen through a suitable redefinition of the technology factor, labor-augmenting technical change is also Hicks neutral,

$$Q = \gamma K^{\alpha} (AL)^{1-\alpha} = A^{1-\alpha} \gamma K^{\alpha} L^{1-\alpha} = A^* \gamma K^{\alpha} L^{1-\alpha}.$$

Here $A^* = A^{1-\alpha}$ denotes Hicks-neutral technological progress.

In general, so that the production function is not necessarily Cobb-Douglas, it may be shown that the existence of a steady state requires that technological progress be labor augmenting. For a proof, see Barro and Sala-i-Martin (1995, pp. 54–55).

The conclusion is that, in contrast to the basic form of the model in which q converges to a stagnant level, technical change gives rise to continued growth in living standards. This finding is one of the most important insights of the Solow-Swan model. The accumulation of more of a given kind of capital—the force generating convergence to the steady state in the model without technical change—cannot give rise to sustained growth in living standards. Only the creation of capital of improved quality that incorporates new ideas and technology can do this. In this sense, new ideas and technologies are the "engine of growth"—they are the fundamental driving force behind sustained growth in living standards.

A limitation of the Solow-Swan model is that this engine of growth is taken as exogenous: There is no explanation for why technical change is what it is. The Solow-Swan model is therefore one of **exogenous growth;** it offers no suggestion as to what economic policies might serve to foster more rapid growth. As we remark at the end of Section 7.3, it is the goal of contemporary **endogenous growth** theory to do better than this by saying something about the economic forces underlying the creation of new ideas and technologies.

Implications for Factor Prices

In addition to yielding sustained growth in living standards, the introduction of technical change resolves the puzzle of the asymmetric behavior of factor prices. Let us return to the marginal productivity conditions (9.25):

$$\text{Rental rate on capital} = \frac{\partial Q}{\partial K} = \alpha \frac{q}{k},$$

$$\text{Real wage} = \frac{\partial Q}{\partial L} = (1 - \alpha)q.$$

Exercise 9.10 asks you to verify that these expressions for the marginal products continue to be the appropriate ones for the production function (9.26) in which labor-augmenting technical change is present.

Notice that if the per-worker variables k and q both grow at rate β, the implication is that the rental rate on capital is constant while the real wage grows at rate β. Hence, technical change introduces an asymmetric behavior of factor prices consistent with what we observe in the real world—interest rates do not trend, but real wages trend upward at the rate of technical change.

Implications for the Time Series Behavior of Living Standards

If living standards q grow at constant rate β, they may be described by the constant growth model. As we know from our study of the constant growth model in Chapter 6, this means that the variable is linear in its logarithms,

$$\log q_t = \alpha + \beta t.$$

This is, of course, exactly the model we use in Section 6.2 to study Jones's (1995) series on per capita GDP plotted in Figure 6.4. Hence, the Solow-Swan model with technical change leads to a prediction about the time series evolution of living standards that is fully consistent with our use of the constant growth model to describe the long-term trend in per capita GDP, albeit one that ultimately begs the question of the underlying determinants of the growth rate.

In this interpretation, the slope β of the logarithmic trend line is the rate of technical change. In Section 6.2.2 we have seen that there are two ways to estimate β, depending on how a disturbance is introduced into the model. The deterministic trend approach models q_t as varying randomly around this loglinear trend,

$$\log q_t = \alpha + \beta t + \varepsilon_t.$$

In Example 2 of Chapter 6 we find that the estimation of this as a least squares simple regression using Jones's data yields the estimate $\hat{\beta} = 0.01773$.

This contrasts with the stochastic trend approach, which models the percentage changes in q_t as varying randomly around β,

$$\Delta \log q_t = \beta + \varepsilon_t.$$

Under this approach, the natural estimator of β is the sample mean of the log-differences. As we have seen in Example 3 of Chapter 6, this yields the estimate 0.01776. Hence, for Jones's data the deterministic and stochastic trend approaches both suggest that technical change has proceeded at a rate of slightly less that 1.8% per year.

Although the estimates yielded by Jones's data are almost identical, we know that deterministic and stochastic trends are rather different descriptions of the time series behavior of a variable. This is illustrated in Section 2.7 in our comparison of the simulated deterministic and stochastic trends in Figure 2.15(a) and (b). Both simulated series are based on the same intercept/initial value of $\alpha = 4.605$ or $Y_0 = 100$ and the same slope or drift of $\beta = 0.04879$. Both are based on exactly the same series of random shocks. Yet the two models generate quite different patterns of behavior in the simulated series; the variation around a deterministic trend of Figure 2.15(a) looks very different from the stochastic trend of (b).

Which of these models best describes economic growth? Is growth in living standards best thought of as proceeding around a deterministic trend, as in Figure 2.15(a), or as a stochastic trend, as in (b)? The Solow-Swan model as we have presented it gives no answer to this question because it incorporates no stochastic elements. That is, we have studied only a deterministic version of the model, without considering the possibility of random shocks to technology, the saving rate, or other parts of the model.

Recent developments in growth theory have provided important insights into this question. Lau (1997, 1999) and Fatás (2000) studied the consequences of introducing stochastic shocks into various types of growth models. They show that, depending on the nature of the shocks, exogenous growth models such as the Solow-Swan model can generate either deterministic or stochastic trends. Endogenous growth models, on the other hand, necessarily generate stochastic trends in growing variables. Because ultimately growth must be endogenous—new ideas and technologies arise from economic behavior as a response to economic incentives—this suggests that economic growth is probably best thought of as following a stochastic trend such as in Figure 2.15(b).

EXERCISES

9.10 Consider the marginal product expressions (9.25).

(a) Starting with the production function (9.1), show how they are derived.

(b) Show that the same marginal product expressions (9.25) apply for the production function (9.26) with labor-augmenting technical change.

9.11 Consider the textbook Solow-Swan model.

(a) For the model *without* technical change, what is the steady-state growth rate of
i.   the capital-labor ratio K/L?
ii. the capital-output ratio K/Q?

(b) For the model *with* technical change, what is the steady-state growth rate of
i.   the capital-labor ratio K/L?
ii. the capital-output ratio K/Q?

(c) In a well-known monograph Robert Solow (1970, p. 2) summarizes the "stylized facts" of economic growth. He remarks that

> The stock of real capital, crudely measured, grows at a more or less constant rate exceeding the rate of growth of labour input. So capital per man can also be said to grow at a more or less steady rate...

and that

> ...the rates of growth of real output and the stock of capital goods tend to be about the same, so that the ratio of capital to output shows no systematic trend.

Is the Solow-Swan model consistent with these stylized facts
i.   without technical change in the model?
ii. with technical change in the model?

9.12 Our initial discussion of the great ratios of macroeconomics has been in connection with

regression through the origin in Section 5.2. There the ratio of aggregate consumption to income is cited as an example of a stable great ratio, which in turn provides the basis for modeling long-run consumption using a regression through the origin.

Let us denote aggregate consumption by C, so that the proportion of output used for consumption is C/Q. We refer to this proportion as the **consumption rate.**

(a) In terms of the notation we have developed for the Solow-Swan model, what is the consumption rate? Is it constant (i) in a steady state? (ii) out of a steady state? Does your answer depend on whether or not the model includes technical change? Is the Solow-Swan model consistent with regarding the consumption rate as a stable great ratio?

(b) What is the growth rate of consumption per worker C/L in a steady state
i.   in the model without technical change?
ii. in the model with technical change?

(c) What is the growth rate of aggregate consumption C in a steady state
i.   in the model without technical change?
ii. in the model with technical change?

9.13 Because living standards q grow in the steady state of the Solow-Swan model with technical change, the question arises of what exactly is constant. The answer is called the **output-technology ratio** $q/A = Q/AL$ (actually the ratio of output per worker to technology), also known as **output per effective worker,** which can be shown to have the steady-state value

$$\frac{q}{A} = \gamma \left(\frac{\gamma s}{n + \beta + \delta} \right)^{\alpha/(1-\alpha)}.$$

Notice that this is only a slight modification of the steady-state solution (9.14) for the model without technical change; the expression on the right-hand side differs from the former solution only through the introduction of the rate of technical change β in the denominator.

(a) Inspecting this expression, how do we know it is constant?

(b) Taking the constancy of this expression as given, how does it follow that output per worker q grows at the rate of technical change β?

10 Dummy Variables and Restricted Coefficients

As the empirical examples we have studied demonstrate, the methodology of statistical inference formulates hypotheses as restrictions on the parameters of a model. This chapter develops this idea more systematically. We show how to estimate a regression model subject to any set of linear restrictions on the coefficients, and how to perform a test of those restrictions. We illustrate these ideas by continuing to draw on some of the examples from previous chapters.

For reasons that become apparent as we proceed, it is natural to develop this jointly with another important topic in applied regression analysis—dummy variables. Recall from Chapter 1 that a dummy variable is a binary variable used as a regressor.

Section 5.3.2 studies binary variables as the dependent variable of the regression, so that it is the binary variable that the model seeks to explain. We have seen that an appropriate econometric model, such as probit or logit, uses the structure of the Bernoulli distribution, so that maximum likelihood is the relevant estimation principle—which is typical of qualitative and limited dependent variables generally.

By contrast, qualitative variables used as regressors involve no violation of the classical assumptions, and least squares regression is perfectly legitimate. The relevant inference procedures are, therefore, those derived in Chapter 8. Nevertheless, dummy variables and their coefficients have special interpretations that make them among the most valuable tools of the applied econometrician and that require detailed explanation.

10.1 Dummy Variables

The best way to understand how dummy variables work is to study a series of successively more complicated examples, and that is how we proceed in the sections ahead. For the student encountering dummy variables for the first time, valuable insights are gained by digressing briefly and recalling a familiar problem from preregression statistical inference.

10.1.1 Test for the Equality of Population Means

The following inference problem is dealt with in virtually all introductory statistics texts.[1] Consider a series of observations $Y_1, \ldots, Y_n$ drawn from normal populations with a common variance σ^2. The first n_1 observations have mean μ_A, the remaining n_2 observations have mean μ_B; the total sample size is $n = n_1 + n_2$. The data, and the associated subsample means and variances, may be summarized as follows.

$$\underbrace{Y_1, Y_2, \ldots, Y_{n_1}}_{n_1 \text{ observations}}, \underbrace{Y_{n_1+1}, \ldots, Y_n}_{n_2 \text{ observations}}$$

$$\Downarrow \qquad\qquad \Downarrow$$
$$\overline{Y}_A, s_A^2 \qquad\qquad \overline{Y}_B, s_B^2$$

This sampling problem may be denoted

> Subsample A: $Y_i \sim \text{n.i.d.}(\mu_A, \sigma^2)$ $(i = 1, \ldots, n_1)$
>
> Subsample B: $Y_i \sim \text{n.i.d.}(\mu_B, \sigma^2)$ $(i = n_1 + 1, \ldots, n)$.

(10.1)

To be explicit, the subsample means and variances are computed as follows.

> Subsample A: $\overline{Y}_A = \dfrac{1}{n_1}\displaystyle\sum_{i=1}^{n_1} Y_i, \quad s_A^2 = \dfrac{1}{n_1 - 1}\displaystyle\sum_{i=1}^{n_1}(Y_i - \overline{Y}_A)^2$
>
> Subsample B: $\overline{Y}_B = \dfrac{1}{n_2}\displaystyle\sum_{i=n_1+1}^{n} Y_i, \quad s_B^2 = \dfrac{1}{n_2 - 1}\displaystyle\sum_{i=n_1+1}^{n}(Y_i - \overline{Y}_B)^2$.

These are, of course, just the usual formulas of Chapter 2 that would be computed if the subsamples were being analyzed separately.

To make this more concrete, it may be helpful to think of the two samples as daily observations on the output of two production processes. The natural question of interest is whether the mean outputs of the processes differ; that is, whether $\mu_A = \mu_B$. In order to test the hypothesis H_0: $\mu_A = \mu_B$ against the alternative H_A: $\mu_A \neq \mu_B$ it is necessary to compute an additional statistic that combines the information from both samples. This is typically presented as the pooled variance

$$s_P^2 = \frac{(n_1 - 1)s_A^2 + (n_2 - 1)s_B^2}{n - 2}.$$

The standard test of H_0 is then based on the distributional result

$$t = \frac{\overline{Y}_B - \overline{Y}_A}{s_P\sqrt{n/n_1 n_2}} \sim t(n - 2).$$

(10.2)

---

[1] You may find it helpful to locate its treatment in your first statistics text and compare that presentation with what follows.

FIGURE 10.1

Solow's total factor productivity (TFP) growth rates: Are the subsample means significantly different?

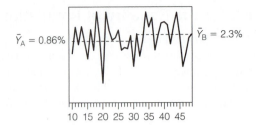

$\bar{Y}_A = 0.86\%$ $\bar{Y}_B = 2.3\%$

10 15 20 25 30 35 40 45

As usual, the computed value of this t statistic is interpreted as representing evidence against the null if, at a level of significance a, $|t| > t_{a/2}(n-2)$.

EXAMPLE 1

solow.dat

In Section 7.3, Robert Solow's method for obtaining an index of multifactor productivity A_t was studied. In examining the relative changes in his index Solow observed that:

> There is some evidence that the average rate of progress in the years 1909–29 was smaller than that from 1930–49. The first 21 relative shifts average about 9/10 of one per cent per year, while the last 19 average $2\frac{1}{4}$ per cent per year. (Solow 1957, p. 316)

Does a hypothesis test confirm Solow's conjecture that these two subperiods experienced different rates of technological progress?

SOLUTION

Solow's index (given in the last column of Table 7.2) may be used to compute its growth rate by taking the log-differences

$$\Delta \log A_t = \log A_t - \log A_{t-1}.$$

This series, which we denote by Y_i, is plotted in Figure 10.1 (which simply reproduces Figure 7.6(a)).[2] Let us denote the first $n_1 = 21$ relative shifts as subsample A, the remaining $n_2 = 19$ as subsample B. The subsample means are $\bar{Y}_A = 0.0085628$ and $\bar{Y}_B = 0.022999$; these are approximately the average growth rates cited by Solow and are shown in the figure. The subsample variances are $s_A^2 = 0.0012422$ and $s_B^2 = 0.00097889$. The numerator and denominator of the t statistic (10.2) are $\bar{Y}_B - \bar{Y}_A = 0.0144362$ and $s_P\sqrt{n/n_1 n_2} = 0.01058$, and so it evaluates to $t = 1.364$; for $n - 2 = 38$ degrees of freedom this corresponds to a p-value of 0.181. In conclusion, the data do not lead to a rejection of the hypothesis of equal growth rates at conventional significance levels, say $a = 0.10$. The data could be regarded as supporting Solow's conjecture at a larger test size such as $a = 0.2$, however.

---

[2] The figure suggests that, although this series is observed over time, a model such as (10.1) describing data obtained by random sampling may not be unreasonable. Essentially, technological innovations occur as random unpredictable shocks and so may be treated as behaving in an i.i.d. manner. It would of course be of interest to perform a formal test of whether it is reasonable to treat the series in this way. This is done in Section 15.3.4.

EXERCISES

10.1 **solow.dat** In Exercise 7.9c you compute the subsample statistics $\overline{Y}_A$, $\overline{Y}_B$, s_A^2, and s_B^2 using *your* series for $\Delta \log A_t$ (which differs slightly from Solow's). Use these to perform the test for the equality of means.

10.1.2 One Dummy Variable

It is instructive to contrast this test procedure with a computationally simpler alternative that avoids the calculation of the pooled variance s_P^2 and instead involves running just a single least squares simple regression. Consider defining the dummy variable D_i as

$$D_i = \begin{cases} 0 & \text{if output is from process A} \\ 1 & \text{if output is from process B} \end{cases} \tag{10.3}$$

and estimating the simple regression

$$Y_i = \alpha + \beta D_i + \varepsilon_i, \qquad \varepsilon_i \sim \text{n.i.d.}(0, \sigma^2) \tag{10.4}$$

over the full sample $i = 1, \ldots, n$. Notice that, in relation to the notation of the previous section,

$$E(Y_i) = \alpha + \beta D_i = \begin{cases} \alpha & = \mu_A & \text{when } D_i = 0 \\ \alpha + \beta = \mu_B & \text{when } D_i = 1. \end{cases} \tag{10.5}$$

Hence, the distributions implied for the Y_i values by the regression model (10.4) are identical to (10.1).

It follows that the null and alternative hypotheses of interest may equivalently be expressed as

$$H_0: \mu_A = \mu_B \quad \Leftrightarrow \quad H_0: \beta = 0$$
$$H_A: \mu_A \neq \mu_B \quad \Leftrightarrow \quad H_A: \beta \neq 0. \tag{10.6}$$

That is, the equality of the mean outputs of the two processes may be tested using a standard t test of the regression slope:

$$t = \frac{\hat{\beta}}{s_{\hat{\beta}}} \sim t(n-2). \tag{10.7}$$

What is the relationship between these two test procedures?

EXAMPLE 2

 solow.dat

Defining a dummy variable appropriately, implement the regression-based test of the equality of population means for Solow's productivity growth series. How does the result compare with that of Example 1?

SOLUTION

The dummy variable would be defined as:

$$D_i = \begin{cases} 0 & \text{for the first 21 values of the series } \Delta \log A_t \\ 1 & \text{for the last 19 values of the series } \Delta \log A_t. \end{cases}$$

Estimating the regression model (10.4) yields

$$\hat{Y}_i = 0.0085628 + 0.014437\, D_i.$$
$$(0.01058)$$

Notice the correspondence between the coefficient estimates $\hat{\alpha}$ and $\hat{\beta}$ and the sample means $\overline{Y}_A$ and $\overline{Y}_B$ of Example 1.

$$(0.0085628 =) \quad \overline{Y}_A = \hat{\alpha} \qquad (= 0.0085628)$$
$$(0.022999 \;=) \quad \overline{Y}_B = \hat{\alpha} + \hat{\beta} \quad (= 0.0085628 + 0.014437)$$

This is analogous to the relationship (10.5) between the corresponding parameters. It is therefore evident that $\hat{\beta} = 0.014437 = \overline{Y}_B - \overline{Y}_A$, so that the numerators of the t statistics (10.2) and (10.7) are the same. Similarly, the denominators are $s_{\hat{\beta}} = 0.01058 = s_P\sqrt{n/n_1 n_2}$. Hence, the t statistic for the hypothesis $\beta = 0$ evaluates to $t = \hat{\beta}/s_{\hat{\beta}} = 1.364$, the same as the t value in Example 1.

This example illustrates that the two test procedures yield identical values for the t statistic and consequently yield the same conclusion. Exercise 10.3 asks you to show that this is always the case by showing that the two test statistics (10.2) and (10.7) are algebraically equivalent.

The Behrens-Fisher Problem

A noteworthy feature of this test is that, regardless of the version employed, it presumes a constant variance σ^2 for the full sample. Because it is the possibility that the two populations may differ in their means that is being tested, the assumption that they have the same variance seems somewhat artificial. It would be more natural to test (10.6) permitting different population variances σ_A^2 and σ_B^2; the procedure instead imposes $\sigma_A^2 = \sigma_B^2$ as a maintained hypothesis. (A **maintained hypothesis** is a parameter restriction that is imposed a priori in estimation rather than being subject to test.)

A test of the equality of means allowing for distinct population variances is a somewhat different testing problem from the one we have considered; it is known as the **Behrens-Fisher problem.** The Behrens-Fisher problem has been of some interest historically in statistics because, in contrast to the case of equal variances and despite the fact that some tests have been developed, no one definitive solution exists. Perhaps for this reason it is common for applied econometricians to employ, somewhat cavalierly, dummy variable tests of the type we have outlined without questioning the implicit assumption of a constant variance across subsamples. In the course of this chapter, we find that this observation applies to considerably more general contexts.

EXERCISES

10.2 (a) solow.dat Using your series for $\Delta \log A_t$ obtained in Exercise 7.9 and defining a dummy variable appropriately, perform the regression-based test for the equality of population means. How does the value of your test statistic compare with that in Exercise 10.1?

(b) Does the definition of the dummy variable matter? How is the value of your test statistic affected by

i. reversing the assignment of the 0-1 values in the definition of the dummy?

ii. choosing any two values other than 0 and 1 in defining the dummy?

10.3 ∮ Establish the algebraic equivalence of the test statistics (10.2) and (10.7) by showing that, in general,

(a) $\hat{\beta} = \bar{Y}_B - \bar{Y}_A$.

(b) $\hat{\alpha} = \bar{Y}_A$.

(c) $s_{\hat{\beta}}^2 = s_p^2 n / n_1 n_2$.

10.4 The coding of a dummy variable as taking on 0-1 values is, of course, arbitrary. Suppose that, in a model such as (10.4), the dummy were redefined using some other value v in place of 1:

$$D_i = \begin{cases} 0 & \text{if } D_i = 0 \\ v & \text{if } D_i = 1. \end{cases}$$

Use your knowledge of the effects of variable scaling to determine the resulting

(a) effect on the slope estimator.

(b) effect on the estimated standard error for the slope.

(c) effect on the t statistic (10.7).

In conclusion, is the arbitrary definition of the dummy variable important for the outcome of the regression-based test of $\mu_A = \mu_B$?

10.1.3 Two Dummy Variables

Consider a problem similar to the one just studied, but in which there exist three production processes having mean outputs μ_A, μ_B, and μ_C. It is possible to distinguish among them using the regression model

$$Y_i = \beta_1 + \beta_2 D_{2i} + \beta_3 D_{3i} + \varepsilon_i, \qquad \varepsilon_i \sim \text{n.i.d.}(0, \sigma^2) \tag{10.8}$$

and the dummy variables

$$D_{2i} = \begin{cases} 1 & \text{if output is from process B} \\ 0 & \text{otherwise} \end{cases} \tag{10.9}$$

$$D_{3i} = \begin{cases} 1 & \text{if output is from process C} \\ 0 & \text{otherwise.} \end{cases} \tag{10.10}$$

It follows that the relationship between the regression coefficients and the mean outputs is:

$$E(Y_i) = \beta_1 + \beta_2 D_{2i} + \beta_3 D_{3i} = \begin{cases} \beta_1 & = \mu_A \text{ when } D_{2i} = 0 \ D_{3i} = 0 \\ \beta_1 + \beta_2 = \mu_B \text{ when } D_{2i} = 1 \ D_{3i} = 0 \\ \beta_1 + \beta_3 = \mu_C \text{ when } D_{2i} = 0 \ D_{3i} = 1. \end{cases}$$

Notice that there are several hypotheses concerning the relationship among the production processes that are potentially of interest, some of which are:

$$\begin{aligned}
\mu_A = \mu_B && \Leftrightarrow && \beta_2 = 0 \\
\mu_A = \mu_C && \Leftrightarrow && \beta_3 = 0 \\
\mu_A = \mu_B = \mu_C && \Leftrightarrow && \beta_2 = \beta_3 = 0.
\end{aligned}$$

The first is the hypothesis that processes A and B have the same mean output, but that this is not necessarily the same as that of process C; the second is that A and C are the same, but that B may differ; and the third is that all three are the same. All these are testable using the methods in Chapter 8, the first two by t tests on each of β_2 and β_3 and the last by the F test in Section 8.5.3. The remaining hypothesis that B and C are the same is

$$\mu_B = \mu_C \Leftrightarrow \beta_2 = \beta_3. \tag{10.11}$$

Note that in the context of the estimated model (10.8), this is not testable by the methods in Chapter 8. It is, however, testable as an application of the F test of linear restrictions that we develop in Section 10.2.2.

That the hypothesis $\mu_B = \mu_C$ does not translate into a restriction of the form $\beta_k = 0$ on the regression (10.8) is, however, an artifact of the particular setup of the dummy variables that has been chosen. For suppose that D_3 continues to be defined by (10.10) and D_2 is redefined as

$$D_{2i} = \begin{cases} 1 & \text{if output is from process A} \\ 0 & \text{otherwise.} \end{cases}$$

In this case,

$$E(Y_i) = \beta_1 + \beta_2 D_{2i} + \beta_3 D_{3i} = \begin{cases} \beta_1 & = \mu_B \text{ when } D_{2i} = 0 \ D_{3i} = 0 \\ \beta_1 + \beta_2 = \mu_A \text{ when } D_{2i} = 1 \ D_{3i} = 0 \\ \beta_1 + \beta_3 = \mu_C \text{ when } D_{2i} = 0 \ D_{3i} = 1, \end{cases}$$

and it is apparent that the hypothesis $\mu_B = \mu_C$ is the restriction $\beta_3 = 0$, which is testable with a t test.

This illustrates that there is an element of arbitrariness in the definition of dummy variables, so there is some scope for defining them in a manner that is most suitable for the task at hand. The basic rule that applies is that, for a regression containing an intercept in which we wish to distinguish among a number of categories, one fewer dummy variable should be defined than the number of categories. To distinguish between two production processes it is necessary to define one dummy variable, three production processes require two dummy variables, and so on.

Practitioner's Tip: **The dummy variable rule**

To distinguish among several characteristics in a regression with an intercept, use one fewer dummy variable than the number of characteristics.

The Dummy Variable Trap

In contrast, suppose that the same number of dummy variables as categories is defined. For example, suppose that in the model of two production processes we define, in addition to (10.3) which we now call D_{2i}, the second dummy variable

$$D_{3i} = \begin{cases} 1 & \text{if output is from process A} \\ 0 & \text{if output is from process B.} \end{cases} \qquad (10.12)$$

What is the consequence of attempting to include both as regressors in a model of the form (10.8)? The consequence is that the model cannot be estimated because there is an exact linear dependence between the regressors. Specifically, a linear relationship exists between D_2 and D_3 of the form (8.3) in which we set $a = 1$ and $b = -1$:

$$D_{3i} = 1 - D_{2i}.$$

Hence, the assumption that precludes such linear dependencies between regressors has been violated. In the terminology of Section 8.7, an attempt to include in a regression model the same number of dummy variables as there are categories among which we seek to distinguish results in perfect multicollinearity. The **dummy variable trap** is the mistake (into which novice applied econometricians sometimes fall) of inadvertently defining dummy variables in a way that such an exact linear dependency is introduced.

It is, on the other hand, possible to use as many dummies as there are categories, if this is done in a model *without* an intercept. For example, in the case of two production processes with D_2 and D_3 defined by (10.3) and (10.12), it is possible to estimate a regression through the origin of the form

$$Y_i = \beta_2 D_{2i} + \beta_3 D_{3i} + \varepsilon_i.$$

In this case, the relationship of the coefficients to the output means is

$$E(Y_i) = \beta_2 D_{2i} + \beta_3 D_{3i} = \begin{cases} \beta_2 = \mu_B & \text{when } D_{2i} = 1 \ D_{3i} = 0 \\ \beta_3 = \mu_A & \text{when } D_{2i} = 0 \ D_{3i} = 1, \end{cases}$$

so that the hypothesis $\mu_A = \mu_B$ is the restriction $\beta_2 = \beta_3$. However, this is unlikely to be the preferred version of the model for estimation because this hypothesis is more conveniently tested as $\beta = 0$ in the simple regression with an intercept (10.4).

A Categorical Variable versus Multiple Dummies

Finally, it must be emphasized that using two dummies to distinguish among three categories, as in model (10.8), is *not* equivalent to defining a single categorical variable, say

$$X_i = \begin{cases} 0 & \text{if output is from process A} \\ 1 & \text{if output is from process B} \\ 2 & \text{if output is from process C.} \end{cases}$$

and estimating a simple regression

$$Y_i = \alpha + \beta X_i + \varepsilon_i.$$

The relationship of these coefficients to the output means is

$$E(Y_i) = \alpha + \beta X_i = \begin{cases} \alpha & = \mu_A \text{ when } X_i = 0 \\ \alpha + \beta & = \mu_B \text{ when } X_i = 1 \\ \alpha + 2\beta & = \mu_C \text{ when } X_i = 2 \end{cases}$$

The estimation of this model imposes the implication that μ_A differs from μ_B if and only if μ_C differs from μ_A and, if so, then μ_C differs from μ_A by exactly twice the amount that μ_B differs from μ_A. These implications are, obviously, quite inappropriate. They explain why it is usually preferable to distinguish among categories using a set of dummy variables rather than a single categorical explanatory variable.

Dummy Variables and Seasonality

A common application of dummy variables is to control for seasonal effects. Consider quarterly data and dummy variables for spring, summer, fall, and winter:

$$D_{ki} = \begin{cases} 1 & \text{for season } k \ (k = 1, 2, 3, 4) \\ 0 & \text{otherwise.} \end{cases}$$

One approach is to estimate a model that omits one of the dummies:

$$Y_i = \beta_1 + \beta_2 D_{2i} + \beta_3 D_{3i} + \beta_4 D_{4i} + \varepsilon_i. \tag{10.13}$$

Equivalently, we could include all four dummies but omit the intercept:

$$Y_i = \alpha_1 D_{1i} + \alpha_2 D_{2i} + \alpha_3 D_{3i} + \alpha_4 D_{4i} + \varepsilon_i. \tag{10.14}$$

We return to the use of dummy variables for this purpose when we discuss seasonality further in the appendix to Chapter 18.

EXERCISES

10.5 For the model of three production processes, consider defining in addition to (10.9) and (10.10) the third dummy variable

$$D_{1i} = \begin{cases} 1 & \text{if output is from process A} \\ 0 & \text{otherwise} \end{cases}$$

and estimating a regression through the origin of the form

$$Y_i = \beta_1 D_{1i} + \beta_2 D_{2i} + \beta_3 D_{3i} + \varepsilon_i.$$

(a) Establish the relationship between the regression coefficients and the output means.

(b) Do the t statistics yielded by the estimation of this model test $\mu_A = \mu_B$? $\mu_B = \mu_C$? $\mu_A = \mu_C$?

10.6 What is the relationship between the coefficients of the two seasonal regressions (10.13) and (10.14).

10.7 Inference problems of the type considered in this section are usually presented by statisticians in terms of a one-way analysis of variance. In the case of three groups—in this instance, three production processes—the model is specified as

$$\begin{aligned} Y_i &= \mu + \alpha_1 + \varepsilon_i && \text{for observations from group 1.} \\ Y_i &= \mu + \alpha_2 + \varepsilon_i && \text{for observations from group 2.} \\ Y_i &= \mu + \alpha_3 + \varepsilon_i && \text{for observations from group 3.} \end{aligned}$$

Here μ is termed the grand mean and the α_g have the interpretation as the deviation of the mean of the gth group from that grand mean.

(a) What is the relationship between this parameterization of the model and that of equation (10.8)?

(b) What parameter restriction corresponds to the hypothesis of equal group means?

10.8 A researcher is using bond ratings as an explanatory variable, the ratings being of the form AAA, AA, A, and so on. The researcher is considering two ways of treating this variable. One is to express the information in a single variable coded 1 for AAA, 2 for AA, 3 for A, and so on. The other is to construct a set of dummy explanatory variables D_{ki} coded as follows:

$$D_{2i} = \begin{cases} 1 & \text{if the bond is rated AAA} \\ 0 & \text{otherwise} \end{cases}$$

$$D_{3i} = \begin{cases} 1 & \text{if the bond is rated AA} \\ 0 & \text{otherwise} \end{cases}$$

and so on. Which of these approaches do you recommend to the researcher? Why?

10.1.4 Dummy Variables and Quantitative Variables

In contrast to the examples considered thus far, econometricians almost always use dummy variables in combination with conventional quantitative regressors. To understand the implications and usefulness of this practice, begin by considering a simple regression model with a quantitative explanatory variable X:

$$Y_i = \alpha + \beta X_i + \varepsilon_i \tag{10.15}$$

For example, this might be an aggregate consumption function in which Y denotes annual consumption expenditure, X denotes disposable income, and β denotes the marginal propensity to consume. Suppose this is estimated over two distinct sample periods A and B, say a period of peace and a period of war, so that the possibility exists that consumption behavior may differ between the two periods. The dummy variable

$$D_i = \begin{cases} 0 & \text{in peacetime (period A)} \\ 1 & \text{in wartime   (period B)} \end{cases} \tag{10.16}$$

may be defined and included as an additional regressor, in which case the model becomes

$$Y_i = \alpha + \beta X_i + \alpha^* D_i + \varepsilon_i.$$

This is a multiple regression equation that can be estimated by least squares.

What meaning is to be attached to the results of this estimation? The mean of Y_i is

$$E(Y_i) = \alpha + \beta X_i + \alpha^* D_i = \begin{cases} \alpha & + \beta X_i \text{ in peacetime when } D_i = 0 \\ \alpha + \alpha^* & + \beta X_i \text{ in wartime when } D_i = 1. \end{cases}$$

This shows that the effect of the dummy variable is to permit different intercepts to apply to each of the two subsamples, as depicted in Figure 10.2(b). In this example, it is presumably the case that consumption in wartime is lower than it would be in peacetime due to rationing and other policies; hence, it is to be expected that $\alpha^* < 0$. This is a hypothesis that can be tested.

Using dummy variables to shift the intercept across subsamples is not the only way in which they can be employed. Suppose it is the possibility of a different

FIGURE 10.2

A dummy variable shifts the intercept and slope: $\alpha^* < 0$, $\beta^* < 0$.

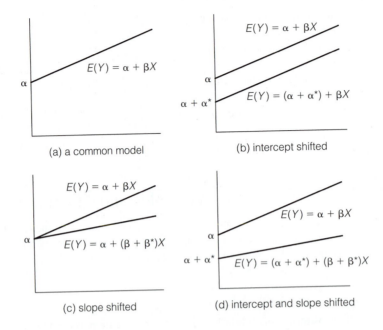

(a) a common model

(b) intercept shifted

(c) slope shifted

(d) intercept and slope shifted

slope rather than intercept that we wish to introduce. This can be done by using the dummy in the following way:

$$Y_i = \alpha + \beta X_i + \beta^* D_i X_i + \varepsilon_i$$

That is, a new variable $D_i X_i$ is defined that is the product of X_i with the dummy, and this is added as a regressor. The interpretation of the coefficients is now

$$E(Y_i) = \alpha + \beta X_i + \beta^* D_i X_i = \begin{cases} \alpha + \beta X_i & \text{in peacetime when } D_i = 0 \\ \alpha + (\beta + \beta^*) X_i & \text{in wartime when } D_i = 1. \end{cases}$$

It is apparent that the effect is to allow for different marginal propensities to consume (MPC) between wartime and peacetime while requiring a common intercept. This is depicted in Figure 10.2(c).

Finally, suppose that our desire is to allow all the coefficients to vary across the subsamples. Then the dummy variable may be used to shift both the intercept and slope by estimating

$$Y_i = \alpha + \beta X_i + \alpha^* D_i + \beta^* D_i X_i + \varepsilon_i, \tag{10.17}$$

because it follows that

$$
\begin{aligned}
E(Y_i) &= \alpha + \beta X_i + \alpha^* D_i + \beta^* D_i X_i \\
&= \begin{cases} \alpha \qquad\quad + \beta X_i & \text{in peacetime when } D_i = 0 \\ \alpha + \alpha^* + (\beta + \beta^*) X_i & \text{in wartime when } D_i = 1. \end{cases}
\end{aligned}
\tag{10.18}
$$

Figure 10.2(d) depicts the two consumption functions under the assumption that both the intercept and MPC are shifted downward in wartime: $\alpha^* < 0$ and $\beta^* < 0$.

Separate Subsample Regressions

That a dummy variable may be used in this way to shift the coefficients of a regression leads us to wonder how this compares with another way of accomplishing the same thing—estimating separate equations for each of the subsamples. To estimate two consumption functions, one for each subsample, yields distinct estimates of the intercept and MPC for each period. Let us denote these subsample regressions by

$$
\begin{aligned}
Y_i &= \alpha_1 + \beta_1 X_i + \varepsilon_i \quad \text{in peacetime,} \\
Y_i &= \alpha_2 + \beta_2 X_i + \varepsilon_i \quad \text{in wartime.}
\end{aligned}
\tag{10.19}
$$

How do these coefficients relate to those of (10.17)? The subsample regressions imply

$$
E(Y_i) = \begin{cases} \alpha_1 + \beta_1 X_i & \text{in peacetime} \\ \alpha_2 + \beta_2 X_i & \text{in wartime.} \end{cases}
$$

Comparing with (10.18), the two sets of coefficients are related by:

$$
\begin{aligned}
\alpha_1 &= \alpha, & \alpha_2 &= \alpha + \alpha^*, \\
\beta_1 &= \beta, & \beta_2 &= \beta + \beta^*.
\end{aligned}
\tag{10.20}
$$

In Exercise 10.11 you learn that this correspondence applies not only to the population coefficients but also to their least squares estimates. This correspondence between the estimates plays a role in Section 10.2.3 in testing for structural change.

10.1.5 Application: Marginal Productivity Conditions

Section 7.4 reviews the work of Arrow, Chenery, Minhas, and Solow (1961), who estimated marginal productivity conditions of the form

$$
\log(V/L)_i = \alpha + \beta \log w_i + \varepsilon_i.
\tag{10.21}
$$

Recall that V/L is labor productivity and w is the annual wage. They estimated equations of this type for a number of industries, using data observed across countries. We have seen that β has the interpretation as the elasticity of substitution of the CES production function. The finding of ACMS (summarized previously in Table 7.4) was that, for most industries, the point estimate of β was far enough below unity that the restriction $\beta = 1$ was rejected. For example, Example 5 of Chapter 7 shows that estimation of (10.21) using data for the dairy products industry yields

$$
\log(V/L)_i = -4.01 + \underset{(0.0552)}{0.719} \log w_i + e_i \qquad \text{SSE} = 0.31557.
\tag{10.22}
$$

The resulting t statistic of $t = (0.719 - 1)/0.0552 = -5.09$ rejects the hypothesis H_0: $\beta = 1$ at conventional significance levels. ACMS concluded that the production technologies employed by these industries could not be satisfactorily described by a Cobb-Douglas production function, which implies an elasticity of substitution equal to one.

It was subsequently pointed out by Victor Fuchs (1963) that the ACMS regressions were estimated over essentially two groups of countries: developed and

TABLE 10.1

Fuchs's Country Groupings

Developed	Underdeveloped
United States	Colombia
Canada	Brazil
New Zealand	Mexico
Australia	Argentina
Denmark	El Salvador
Norway	Southern Rhodesia
United Kingdom	Iraq
Ireland	Ceylon
Puerto Rico	Japan
	India

underdeveloped. His categorization is given in Table 10.1.[3] Fuchs suggested that it may not be accurate to assume that developed and underdeveloped countries have the same production technology; the estimation of a marginal productivity condition such as (10.21) should take this into account.

Fuchs accomplished this by using a dummy variable:

$$D_i = \begin{cases} 0 & \text{for developed countries} \\ 1 & \text{for underdeveloped countries.} \end{cases} \tag{10.23}$$

He reestimated the marginal productivity conditions as

$$\log(V/L)_i = \alpha + \beta \log w_i + \alpha^* D_i + \varepsilon_i. \tag{10.24}$$

By permitting developed and underdeveloped countries to have different intercepts in this way, Fuchs found that the ACMS results were reversed: For most industries the restriction $\beta = 1$ is now *not* rejected. His point estimates of β are reported in Table 10.2. Comparing these with the original ACMS estimates presented in Table 7.4, it is apparent that most are now considerably closer to 1.

EXAMPLE 3

dairy.dat

Estimate Fuchs's version of the marginal productivity condition for dairy products using the data in Table 7.3, and test the hypothesis $\beta = 1$. How does the new estimate of the elasticity of substitution compare with the earlier one?

SOLUTION

Introduction of a dummy variable yields[4]

$$\log(V/L)_i = -5.39 + \underset{(0.0806)}{0.901} \log w_i + \underset{(0.110)}{0.302} D_i + e_i \qquad \text{SSE} = 0.20036.$$

[3] Remember that Fuchs was using the ACMS data from the mid-1950s. Obviously the categorization would be somewhat different today.

[4] Just as we have found in Chapter 7 in replicating the original ACMS regressions, the reestimation of these equations using modern software may yield numerical results slightly different from those published.

TABLE 10.2   Elasticity of Substitution when a Dummy Variable Is Included in the Marginal Productivity Condition

Industry	$\hat{\beta}$
Dairy products	0.902
Fruit and vegetable canning	1.086
Grain and mill products	1.324
Bakery products	1.065
Sugar	0.898
Tobacco	1.215
Textiles	0.976
Knitting mills	0.948
Lumber and wood	1.083
Furniture	1.043
Pulp and paper	0.912
Printing and publishing	1.021
Leather finishing	0.975
Basic chemicals	1.113
Fats and oils	1.058
Miscellaneous chemicals	1.060
Clay products	0.658
Glass	1.269
Ceramics	1.078
Cement	1.308
Iron and steel	0.756
Nonferrous metals	0.935
Metal products	1.006
Electric machinery	1.026

Source: Fuchs, V.R. "Capital-Labor Substitution: A Note," *Review of Economics and Statistics* 45, 436–438. © 1963 MIT Press Journals. Reprinted with permission from MIT Press Journals.

The t statistic for H_0: $\beta = 1$ is $t = (0.901 - 1)/0.0806 = -1.23$, which does not reject at conventional significance levels. (The p-value is 0.23985.) The distinct sample regression lines are

$$\log(V/L)_i = \begin{cases} -5.39 + 0.901 \log w_i + e_i & \text{for developed countries} \\ -5.09 + 0.901 \log w_i + e_i & \text{for underdeveloped countries.} \end{cases}$$

The new estimate of the elasticity of substitution is $\hat{\beta} = 0.901$, considerably closer to 1 than the ACMS estimate of 0.719.

Why should the introduction of the dummy variable have this effect on the estimated elasticity of substitution? Fuchs explained the difference using a diagram like

FIGURE 10.3

Marginal productivity conditions with a shifted intercept.

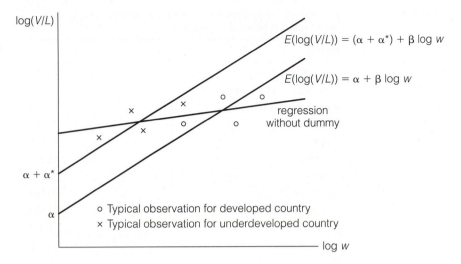

Figure 10.3. When the marginal productivity condition is estimated with a common intercept applying to both groups, the result is an artificially low value for the elasticity of substitution. The introduction of the dummy variable into the equation permits separate intercepts, resulting in a higher estimated slope. Fuchs argued that the failure of ACMS to allow for a difference between the two groups resulted in a biased estimate of the elasticity of substitution. This is simply an example of the general result of Section 8.9.1 that the omission of relevant regressors—in this case a dummy variable—leads to biased estimators.

Fuchs's work established that, for most industries, permitting different production technologies for developed versus underdeveloped countries leads to estimated elasticities of substitution that are *not* significantly different from 1. Ironically, the empirical finding that led ACMS to develop the CES production function as a generalization of the Cobb-Douglas may have been an artifact of a misspecified regression model. It may be that, allowing for differences in production methods across country groups, the Cobb-Douglas production function and its implication of a unitary elasticity of substitution constitute a perfectly satisfactory description of these data.

EXERCISES

The following exercises ask you to reestimate the ACMS marginal productivity condition you have studied previously in Exercise 7.14, using a dummy variable to shift the intercept and slope.

10.9 💿 **marginal productivity conditions** Obtain the data for one of the ACMS industries. Using the

country groupings given in Table 10.1, add to your data set the dummy variable defined by (10.23).

(a) Estimate Fuchs's equation (10.24).

(b) Test the hypothesis $\alpha^* = 0$. For your industry, do the data support Fuchs's hypothesis that developed and underdeveloped countries may have different production technologies?

(c) Test the hypothesis $\beta = 1$. Do the data suggest that your industry may be adequately described by a Cobb-Douglas production function?

10.10 marginal productivity conditions   Construct the new variable $D_i \log w_i$ and reestimate the marginal productivity condition in a way that permits both the intercept and elasticity of substitution to differ between the country groups.

(a) What are the estimated intercept and elasticity of substitution for developed countries?

(b) What are the estimated intercept and elasticity of substitution for underdeveloped countries?

(c) Is the elasticity of substitution for developed countries significantly different from that for underdeveloped countries?

10.11 marginal productivity conditions   Partition your sample into subsamples associated with the two country groups. Estimate separate marginal productivity conditions for each, analogous to (10.19).

(a) Denoting the developed country estimates by $\hat{\alpha}_1$ and $\hat{\beta}_1$, how do they compare with the values of the previous exercise?

(b) Denoting the underdeveloped country estimates by $\hat{\alpha}_2$ and $\hat{\beta}_2$, how do they compare with the values of the previous exercise?

10.2   Restricted Coefficients

We now turn to the second major topic of this chapter: linear restrictions on the regression coefficients. As with dummy variables, it is best to proceed by considering a series of examples. We find that it is typically possible to estimate a regression model subject to linear restrictions and that these linear restrictions can be tested.

10.2.1   Linear Restrictions

Consider a multiple regression with coefficients β_k ($k = 1, \ldots, K$). A linear restriction on the coefficients is of the form

$$\sum_{k=1}^{K} a_k \beta_k = a_0, \tag{10.25}$$

where the a_k ($k = 0, 1, \ldots, K$) are known numerical constants. Let us illustrate this by a series of examples for the model with $K = 4$:

$$Y_i = \beta_1 + \beta_2 X_{2i} + \beta_3 X_{3i} + \beta_4 X_{4i} + \varepsilon_i, \tag{10.26}$$

where (10.25) is

$$a_1 \beta_1 + a_2 \beta_2 + a_3 \beta_3 + a_4 \beta_4 = a_0. \tag{10.27}$$

The examples are summarized in Table 10.3, which indicates the values of the a_k in each case. Let us consider each example in turn.

TABLE 10.3   Examples of Linear Restrictions

Example number	Restriction(s)	Number of restrictions (g)	a_1	a_2	a_3	a_4	a_0
1	$\beta_1 = 0$	1	1	0	0	0	0
2	$\beta_1 = a_0$	1	1	0	0	0	a_0
3	$\beta_2 = 0$	1	0	1	0	0	0
4	$\beta_2 = a_0$	1	0	1	0	0	a_0
5	$\beta_2 = \beta_3 = \beta_4 = 0$	3	0	1	0	0	0
			0	0	1	0	0
			0	0	0	1	0
6	$\beta_3 = \beta_4 = 0$	2	0	0	1	0	0
			0	0	0	1	0
7	$\beta_3 = \beta_4$	1	0	0	1	-1	0
8	$\beta_2 + \beta_3 = 1$	1	0	1	1	0	1

1. *Zero intercept.* The first example is the restriction $\beta_1 = 0$; that is, that the intercept is zero, so the model is a regression through the origin. In terms of the general linear restriction (10.27), this is the special case in which $a_1 = 1$ and the other a_k equal zero. As noted in our treatment of regression through the origin in Section 5.2, it is possible to impose this restriction in estimation (that is, estimate subject to the restriction) by using the appropriate option of the least squares estimation routine provided by regression software. If our interest is in testing the hypothesis that the restriction is true, this is easily done with a t test using the estimation results for the unrestricted model.

2. *Intercept equal to a constant.* As a minor extension of the previous case, consider the restriction $\beta_1 = a_0$, where, again, a_0 is a known numerical constant. To impose this restriction in estimation we need only estimate the model

    $$Y_i - a_0 = \beta_2 X_{2i} + \beta_3 X_{3i} + \beta_4 X_{4i} + \varepsilon_i.$$

    This involves generating the constructed dependent variable $Y_i - a_0$ and estimating a regression through the origin. As in the previous example, a test of H_0: $\beta_1 = a_0$ is easily performed as a t test using the estimation results for the unrestricted model.

3. *Zero slope.* Similarly, a test of $\beta_2 = 0$ is a t test on (10.26). Estimation subject to this restriction involves dropping X_2 as a regressor, so the estimated model is

    $$Y_i = \beta_1 + \beta_3 X_{3i} + \beta_4 X_{4i} + \varepsilon_i.$$

Note that, if the restriction is true, then not making use of it has consequences that are easy to understand in light of our discussion of specification error in Chapter 8. As we have seen in Section 8.9.2, the estimation of the unrestricted model (10.26) constitutes the inclusion of an irrelevant regressor, implying that the resulting estimators are inefficient. This illustrates a general feature of statistical problems: The use of outside information, in this case a coefficient restriction, contributes to efficiency of estimation (as long, of course, as that outside information is true). This conclusion is anticipated in the discussion of Section 4.1.4.

Notwithstanding this, we have seen in Section 8.5 that imposition of this restriction results in a larger SSE and hence a smaller R^2 (although not necessarily a smaller $\overline{R}^2$). Hence, paradoxically, it could easily be the case that more efficient estimators are associated with a poorer fitting model.

4. *Slope equal to a constant.* The restriction $\beta_2 = a_0$ may be imposed in estimation by rewriting the model as

$$Y_i - a_0 X_{2i} = \beta_1 + \beta_3 X_{3i} + \beta_4 X_{4i} + \varepsilon_i,$$

and generating the constructed dependent variable. The hypothesis that the restriction holds is testable by a t test on the estimated unrestricted model.

For example, Fuchs's marginal productivity condition (10.24) is

$$\log(V/L)_i = \alpha + \beta \log w_i + \alpha^* D_i + \varepsilon_i.$$

Suppose we want to estimate this subject to the restriction of a unitary elasticity of substitution: $\beta = 1$. Substituting this into the equation, it is estimated as

$$\log(V/L)_i - \log w_i = \alpha + \alpha^* D_i + \varepsilon_i. \tag{10.28}$$

A test of the restriction requires only the estimation results for the unrestricted model, just as in Example 3.

A closely related restriction is one of the form $a_k \beta_k = a_0$ which, because it can be reexpressed as $\beta_k = a_0/a_k$, can be imposed and tested in the same way.

5. *All zero slopes.* The restriction $\beta_2 = \beta_3 = \beta_4 = 0$ is in fact three linear restrictions; a test of this restriction is the F test of the regression model developed in Section 8.5.3. The estimation of the model subject to this restriction reduces it to $Y_i = \beta_1 + \varepsilon_i$, which is the model (2.15) of Chapter 2.

6. *Some zero slopes.* By contrast, consider the two restrictions $\beta_3 = \beta_4 = 0$. Estimation subject to these restrictions is straightforward; it involves simply dropping X_3 and X_4 from (10.26). However, we have, at this point, developed no means of testing this joint restriction.

As an example of a case like this, consider the regression model (10.17) in which the dummy terms permit the intercept and slope to shift between wartime and peacetime. The hypothesis that there is no such shift—that the same intercept and slope apply to both subsamples—is the restriction that $\alpha^* = \beta^* = 0$. It would obviously be of interest to be able to test this hypothesis.

7. *Equal coefficients.* Another useful contrast to the earlier examples is the restriction $\beta_3 = \beta_4$, a single linear restriction that sets $a_3 = 1$, $a_4 = -1$, and the remaining a_k to zero. The imposition of this restriction implies the restricted model

$$Y_i = \beta_1 + \beta_2 X_{2i} + \beta_3(X_{3i} + X_{4i}) + \varepsilon_i,$$

the estimation of which simply requires generating the constructed regressor $X_3 + X_4$. In contrast to example 6, which restricts the coefficients to the unique numerical values $\beta_3 = 0$ and $\beta_4 = 0$, this restriction constrains the coefficients to satisfy a certain relationship to one another; it can be satisfied for an infinite number of values of the coefficients. Like the previous example, the methods in Chapter 8 do not provide a means of testing the restriction.

8. *Coefficients sum to 1.* Our final example is the restriction $\beta_2 + \beta_3 = 1$, which sets $a_2 = a_3 = a_0 = 1$. This is the form of the hypothesis of constant returns to scale in a Cobb-Douglas production function, as we have seen in Chapter 7. The restriction may be reexpressed as $\beta_3 = 1 - \beta_2$; substituting this into (10.26) and rearranging, the restricted form of the model may be written

$$Y_i - X_{3i} = \beta_1 + \beta_2(X_{2i} - X_{3i}) + \beta_4 X_{4i} + \varepsilon_i.$$

Hence the generation of a constructed dependent variable and regressor are necessary. This restricted model yields a direct estimate $\hat{\beta}_2$ and the implied estimate $\hat{\beta}_3 = 1 - \hat{\beta}_2$. In what amounts to the same thing, the restriction may instead be expressed as $\beta_2 = 1 - \beta_3$ and the restricted model written

$$Y_i - X_{2i} = \beta_1 + \beta_3(X_{3i} - X_{2i}) + \beta_4 X_{4i} + \varepsilon_i.$$

In this case a direct estimate of β_3 is obtained, implying the estimate $\hat{\beta}_2 = 1 - \hat{\beta}_3$. Because the estimation of either restricted model involves simply minimizing the SSE of (10.26) subject to the given restriction $\beta_2 + \beta_3 = 1$, both yield the same estimated coefficients and value of the SSE.

As in the previous two examples, the t and F tests in Chapter 8 do not provide a means of testing this restriction.

These examples are instructive in several respects. It is apparent that it is always possible to rewrite a regression model so as to incorporate a set of linear restrictions. These restrictions may be in the nature of fixed-value restrictions that set the coefficients to particular numerical values, as in examples 1–6, or they may have the coefficients satisfy some functional relationship, as in examples 7 and 8. An example of an economic theory that imposes the latter type of restriction is the Solow-Swan growth model in the previous chapter.

EXAMPLE 4

 mrw.dat

In Section 9.2 the textbook version of the Solow-Swan growth model leads to the regression (9.16):

$$\log q_i = \beta_1 + \beta_2 \log s_i + \beta_3 \log(\delta + n_i) + \varepsilon_i. \tag{10.29}$$

In terms of the underlying model from which this is derived, these coefficients have the following interpretations:

$$\beta_1 = \frac{\log \gamma}{1 - \alpha}, \tag{10.30a}$$

$$\beta_2 = \frac{\alpha}{1 - \alpha}, \tag{10.30b}$$

$$\beta_3 = \frac{-\alpha}{1 - \alpha}. \tag{10.30c}$$

What restriction on the regression coefficients is implied? Is it linear? How would the regression be estimated subject to this restriction?

SOLUTION

Because the expressions on the right-hand sides of (10.30b) and (10.30c) are the same except for a sign change, they imply the restriction

$$\beta_2 + \beta_3 = 0.$$

This is linear. (The link to the Solow-Swan growth model does not restrict the intercept β_1.) Table 9.2 reports the estimation results obtained by Mankiw, Romer, and Weil for the unrestricted regression. Their estimates $\hat{\beta}_2 = 1.31$ and $\hat{\beta}_3 = -2.01$ are roughly consistent with the restriction.

We now know how to impose the restriction in estimation. Mankiw, Romer, and Weil did this by setting $\beta_3 = -\beta_2$ and rewriting the regression as

$$\log q_i = \beta_1 + \beta_2(\log s_i - \log(\delta + n_i)) + \varepsilon_i.$$

This yields $\hat{\beta}_2 = 1.43$ (and therefore an implied $\hat{\beta}_3 = -\hat{\beta}_2 = -1.43$) and SSE = 27.330.

In contrast, the augmented Solow-Swan model leads to a modified regression equation and so to a somewhat different coefficient restriction.

EXAMPLE 5

 mrw.dat

In Section 9.3 we study an augmented version of the Solow-Swan growth model that includes human capital. This model leads to the regression equation (9.24):

$$\log q_i = \beta_1 + \beta_2 \log s_{ki} + \beta_3 \log(\delta + n_i) + \beta_4 \log s_{hi} + \varepsilon_i.$$

The coefficients have the following interpretations in terms of the parameters of the augmented Solow-Swan model:

$$\beta_1 = \frac{\log \gamma}{1 - \alpha - \beta},$$ (10.31a)

$$\beta_2 = \frac{\alpha}{1 - \alpha - \beta},$$ (10.31b)

$$\beta_3 = \frac{-(\alpha + \beta)}{1 - \alpha - \beta},$$ (10.31c)

$$\beta_4 = \frac{\beta}{1 - \alpha - \beta}.$$ (10.31d)

What restriction on the regression coefficients is implied? Is it linear? How would the regression be estimated subject to this restriction?

SOLUTION

The expressions for the slopes imply the restriction

$$\beta_2 + \beta_3 + \beta_4 = 0,$$

which is linear. Table 9.3 reports the estimation results obtained by Mankiw, Romer, and Weil for the unrestricted regression. Their estimates $\hat{\beta}_2 = 0.70$, $\hat{\beta}_3 = -1.50$, and $\hat{\beta}_4 = 0.73$ are roughly consistent with the restriction.

We now know how to impose the restriction in estimation. Mankiw, Romer, and Weil did this by setting $\beta_3 = -(\beta_2 + \beta_4)$ and rewriting the regression as

$$\log q_i = \beta_1 + \beta_2(\log s_{ki} - \log(\delta + n_i)) + \beta_4(\log s_{hi} - \log(\delta + n_i)) + \varepsilon_i.$$

They obtained $\hat{\beta}_2 = 0.71$ and $\hat{\beta}_4 = 0.74$ (and therefore an implied $\hat{\beta}_3 = -(\hat{\beta}_2 + \hat{\beta}_4) = -1.45$) and SSE $= 14.684$.

Restrictions such as these that have the coefficients satisfy some functional relationship can be imposed on the regression in more than one way. For example, the textbook model could have been restricted by setting $\beta_2 = -\beta_3$ and rewriting the regression (10.29) as

$$\log q_i = \beta_1 + \beta_3(\log(\delta + n_i) - \log s_i) + \varepsilon_i.$$

However the resulting least squares estimates and value of the SSE are invariant to these alternative restricted forms, as the next example illustrates.

EXAMPLE 6

 cobbdoug.dat

In Section 6.1 we have seen that the Cobb-Douglas production function may be written as the multiple regression

$$\log Q_i = \log \gamma + \beta \log K_i + \alpha \log L_i + \varepsilon_i,$$ (10.32)

and that constant returns to scale implies the parameter restriction $\alpha + \beta = 1$. How would the model be estimated in restricted form?

SOLUTION

Rewriting the model to incorporate the restriction $\alpha = 1 - \beta$, the restricted model is

$$\log Q_i = \log \gamma + \beta \log K_i + (1 - \beta) \log L_i + \varepsilon_i$$

or

$$\log Q_i - \log L_i = \log \gamma + \beta(\log K_i - \log L_i) + \varepsilon_i$$

or

$$\log q_i = \log \gamma + \beta \log k_i + \varepsilon_i,$$

where $q = Q/L$ and $k = K/L$ are labor-intensive quantities. That is, the restricted model is simply the production function in intensive form, as we have seen previously in Section 6.1. In Exercise 7.2, the estimation of this labor-intensive form using the original Cobb-Douglas data yields $\hat{\beta} = 0.25413$ (and thus an implied $\hat{\alpha} = 1 - \hat{\beta} = 0.74587$) and SSE $= 0.071643$.

Equivalently, the restriction $\beta = 1 - \alpha$ can imposed on (10.32) by rewriting it as

$$\log Q_i = \log \gamma + (1 - \alpha) \log K_i + \alpha \log L_i + \varepsilon_i$$

or

$$\log Q_i - \log K_i = \log \gamma + \alpha(\log L_i - \log K_i) + \varepsilon_i$$

or

$$\log(Q_i/K_i) = \log \gamma + \alpha \log(L_i/K_i) + \varepsilon_i.$$

In Exercise 7.4 the estimation of this capital-intensive form yields $\hat{\alpha} = 0.74587$ (and thus an implied $\hat{\beta} = 1 - \hat{\alpha} = 0.25413$) and SSE $= 0.071643$. The same standard errors and estimate of $\log \gamma$ as for the labor-intensive form are also obtained.

In summary, the imposition of restrictions gives rise to the distinction between a restricted and an unrestricted model, the latter being the original multiple regression. We already know how to test some of these restrictions. Specifically, the t and F tests of Chapter 8 provide a means of testing some types of fixed-value restrictions, such as those of examples 1–5 in Table 10.3. These procedures are based on the estimation results for the unrestricted model; it is not necessary to estimate the restricted model in order to test these hypotheses.

Our examples also motivate interest in developing a general means of testing arbitrary linear restrictions. We would like, for example, to be able to test whether the restrictions of the Solow-Swan growth model are formally rejected by the data, instead of just examining the point estimates of the unrestricted regression and arguing that they seem to be roughly consistent with the restriction. Similarly, we would like to be able to test constant returns to scale in the Cobb-Douglas production function. Because the t and F tests of Chapter 8 apply to a particular class of linear restrictions, any such general test procedure should encompass them as special cases.

EXERCISES

10.12 💿 **mrw.dat** Use the Mankiw, Romer, and Weil data set **mrw.dat** of Chapter 9 to do the following.

(a) Estimate the restricted regressions of Examples 4 and 5 in order to verify the results reported there.

(b) Estimate alternative restricted models to those in Examples 4 and 5, showing that you get the same SSE value and coefficient estimates (direct or implied).

10.13 💿 **marginal productivity conditions** Consider the regression model (10.24), Fuchs's marginal productivity condition with an intercept dummy, which you estimate in Exercise 10.10. Reestimate it imposing the restriction $\beta = 1$.

10.14 Consider the regression model

$$Y_i = \beta_1 + \beta_2 X_{2i} + \beta_3 X_{3i} + \varepsilon_i.$$

In each of the following cases indicate whether the restrictions are linear and, if so, (i) the number of restrictions specified and (ii) how the regression could be rewritten to incorporate them.

(a) $2\beta_3 = 6$

(b) $\beta_2/2 + \beta_3 = 1$

(c) $\beta_1 = \beta_3/(-3)$

(d) $\beta_2^2 = 3.7$

(e) $\beta_2/\beta_3 = 2$

(f) $\beta_2\beta_3 = 1$

(g) $\beta_2^2 = \beta_3$

(h) $\beta_2 = \gamma$, $\beta_3 = \gamma$, where γ is a parameter to be estimated

(i) $\beta_1 = \beta_3/(-3) = 1$

(j) $\beta_1 = \beta_2$, $\beta_2 = \beta_3$, $\beta_3 = \beta_1$

10.15 Theory Meets Application 9.1 describes the extension of the Mankiw-Romer-Weil model by Milbourne, Otto, and Voss to distinguish between private and public capital. They began with a Cobb-Douglas production function of the form

$$Q = \gamma K_p^{\alpha_1} K_g^{\alpha_2} H^\beta L^{1-\alpha_1-\alpha_2-\beta}.$$

This led to the following regression equation for living standards:

$$\log q_i = \beta_1 + \beta_2 \log s_{pi} + \beta_3 \log(\delta + n_i)$$
$$+ \beta_4 \log s_{hi} + \beta_5 \log s_{gi} + \varepsilon_i.$$

The interpretation of the regression coefficients in terms of the parameters of the production function is

$$\beta_1 = \frac{\log \gamma}{1 - \alpha_1 - \alpha_2 - \beta},$$

$$\beta_2 = \frac{\alpha_1}{1 - \alpha_1 - \alpha_2 - \beta},$$

$$\beta_3 = \frac{-(\alpha_1 + \alpha_2 + \beta)}{1 - \alpha_1 - \alpha_2 - \beta},$$

$$\beta_4 = \frac{\beta}{1 - \alpha_1 - \alpha_2 - \beta},$$

$$\beta_5 = \frac{\alpha_2}{1 - \alpha_1 - \alpha_2 - \beta}.$$

What restriction on the regression coefficients is implied? Is it linear?

10.2.2 *F* Test of Linear Restrictions

A general test of linear restrictions is available through a comparison of the restricted and unrestricted models. In particular, consider the SSEs arising from the estimation of the two models; let that for the unrestricted model be denoted SSE_U, that for the restricted model be SSE_R. As an extension of the reasoning in Section 8.5, least squares estimation of the regression model subject to constraints must yield an estimated model that fits the data less well than if the estimation is unconstrained. Specifically, it must be that $SSE_R \geq SSE_U$ or, equivalently,

$$SSE_R - SSE_U \geq 0. \tag{10.33}$$

The equality will hold only if the restrictions are exactly satisfied in the sample.

Intuitively, if the data are consistent with the parameter restrictions then the imposition of these restrictions should not make much difference in the ability of the model to fit the data; the difference (10.33) should be relatively small. If, on the other hand, imposition of the restrictions has a dramatic effect on the ability of the model to fit the data, this suggests that the restrictions are inconsistent with the data. Formalizing this intuition, the following distributional result may be established:

$$\frac{(SSE_R - SSE_U)/g}{SSE_U/(n - K)} \sim F(g, n - K). \tag{10.34}$$

That is, under the null hypothesis that the restrictions hold, this statistic has the indicated distribution. A large value for the statistic (*large* meaning, as usual, a value exceeding some critical value based on a chosen level of significance) is therefore evidence against the null. Hence, (10.34) provides a general test for arbitrary linear restrictions. As in Table 10.3, g denotes the number of restrictions under test. Let us begin with examples of $g = 1$ restriction.

EXAMPLE 7

mrw.dat

(Continuation of EXAMPLES 4 and 5) Use the Mankiw, Romer, and Weil regressions to test the restriction of the Solow-Swan growth model in both its textbook and augmented forms.

SOLUTION

As we recall in Example 4, the textbook form of the Solow-Swan model leads to the unrestricted regression (10.29):

$$\log q_i = \beta_1 + \beta_2 \log s_i + \beta_3 \log(\delta + n_i) + \varepsilon_i.$$

The estimation of this in Section 9.2 yields $SSE_U = 26.848$. We see in Example 4 that the underlying theory of the Solow-Swan model predicts the parameter restriction $\beta_2 + \beta_3 = 0$. Imposing this leads to a restricted regression with $SSE_R = 27.330$. (Note that the relationship (10.33) is satisfied.) Hence, the hypothesis H_0: $\beta_2 + \beta_3 = 0$ can be tested against H_A: $\beta_2 + \beta_3 \neq 0$ by computing the statistic

$$F = \frac{(SSE_R - SSE_U)/g}{SSE_U/(n - K)} = \frac{(27.330 - 26.848)/1}{26.848/(75 - 3)} = 1.293.$$

(The value of K is always that for the unrestricted model.) Comparing this against tabulated values of the $F(1, 72)$ distribution (for example, $F(1, 72) \approx 4.0$ for a 0.05 level of significance), the hypothesis is not rejected.

Turning to the augmented model in Example 5, the unrestricted regression is

$$\log q_i = \beta_1 + \beta_2 \log s_{ki} + \beta_3 \log(\delta + n_i) + \beta_4 \log s_{hi} + \varepsilon_i.$$

Estimation of this in Section 9.3 yields $SSE_U = 14.680$. We see in Example 5 that the underlying theory of the Solow-Swan model predicts the parameter restriction

$\beta_2 + \beta_3 + \beta_4 = 0$. Imposing this leads to a restricted regression with $\text{SSE}_R = 14.684$. (Note that the relationship (10.33) is satisfied.) Hence, the hypothesis H_0: $\beta_2 + \beta_3 + \beta_4 = 0$ can be tested against H_A: $\beta_2 + \beta_3 + \beta_4 \neq 0$ by computing the statistic

$$F = \frac{(\text{SSE}_R - \text{SSE}_U)/g}{\text{SSE}_U/(n-K)} = \frac{(14.684 - 14.680)/1}{14.680/(75-4)} = 0.0219.$$

Comparing this against tabulated values of the $F(1, 71)$ distribution ($F(1, 71) \approx 4.0$ for a 0.05 level of significance), the hypothesis is not rejected.

Recall that both versions of the Solow-Swan model are instances in which the unrestricted coefficient estimates are roughly consistent with the hypothesized restriction. Unrestricted estimates that are approximately consistent with the restriction will yield an F test that does not reject it. The F test provides a way of rigorously formalizing the decision-making process by which the conclusion is reached of whether the restriction is consistent with the data.

EXAMPLE 8

cobbdoug.dat

(Continuation of EXAMPLE 6) Use Cobb and Douglas's data to test constant returns to scale in their production function.

SOLUTION

As we see in Example 6, the restricted model (in either its labor- or capital-intensive form) yields $\text{SSE}_R = 0.071643$. The estimation of the unrestricted model (10.32), on the other hand, yields $\text{SSE}_U = 0.070982$. (Note that the relationship (10.33) is satisfied.) Hence, the hypothesis H_0: $\alpha + \beta = 1$ may be tested against H_A: $\alpha + \beta \neq 1$ by computing the statistic

$$F = \frac{(\text{SSE}_R - \text{SSE}_U)/g}{\text{SSE}_U/(n-K)} = \frac{(0.071643 - 0.070982)/1}{0.070982/(24-3)} = 0.196.$$

Comparing this against tabulated values of the $F(1, 21)$ distribution (for example, $F(1, 21) = 4.32$ for a 0.05 level of significance), the hypothesis of constant returns to scale is not rejected. Our treatment of this as a maintained hypothesis in Chapter 7 appears to have been justified.

These have been examples of tests of a single linear restriction; the next example involves more than one restriction.

EXAMPLE 9

dairy.dat

Exercise 10.10 deals with the estimation of the model

$$\log(V/L)_i = \alpha + \beta \log w_i + \alpha^* D_i + \beta^* D_i \log w_i + \varepsilon_i. \tag{10.35}$$

Test the hypothesis that, for the dairy products industry, the same marginal productivity condition applies to both developed and underdeveloped countries.

SOLUTION

This hypothesis is the restriction H_0: $\alpha^* = \beta^* = 0$. Imposing this just yields the original ACMS model (10.21) and the estimated simple regression (10.22), so

$SSE_R = 0.31557$. The unrestricted model (10.35) yields $SSE_U = 0.18957$. Hence, the computed value of the F statistic is

$$F = \frac{(SSE_R - SSE_U)/g}{SSE_U/(n - K)} = \frac{(0.31557 - 0.18957)/2}{0.18957/(16 - 4)} = 3.99.$$

Based on the tabulated critical value $F(2, 12) = 3.89$ for a 5% level of significance, the restriction is rejected. The empirical evidence suggests that the two country groups are governed by different marginal productivity conditions.

These examples illustrate the general F test of linear restrictions. As the examples in Table 1 show, fixed-value restrictions on individual coefficients, as well as the joint hypothesis $\beta_2 = \cdots = \beta_K = 0$, are also examples of linear restrictions. They are testable by the t and F tests in Chapter 8. These tests should, therefore, be interpretable as special cases of (10.34). Exercise 10.21 asks you to investigate this for the F test in Chapter 8. That t tests are just a special case of the general F test of this chapter is the subject of Section 10.2.4, in which we find that in situations of $g = 1$ restriction the F statistic is always the square of the t statistic.

The distinction between a restricted and an unrestricted model is very important in econometrics and has much greater applicability than in the present context of linear restrictions on the single-equation linear regression model. It is partly for this reason that we have chosen to express the statistic (10.34) explicitly in terms of SSE_R and SSE_U. It turns out, however, that the F statistic may be computed solely from the estimation of the *unrestricted* model; Exercise 10.20 gives some idea of how this can be possible. The least squares estimation routines of most econometric software packages offer options that allow the testing of restrictions. Exercise 10.19 asks you to use this feature of your software to reproduce the F test in Example 8.

EXERCISES

10.16 💿 **mrw.dat** Mankiw, Romer, and Weil (1992) presented estimation results for their models based on an expanded sample of 98 countries.

(a) For the textbook model, this expanded sample yields $SSE_U = 45.108$ and $SSE_R = 45.504$. Test the restriction of the model, indicating clearly all parts of your test procedure.

(b) For the augmented model, this expanded sample yields $SSE_U = 24.226$ and $SSE_R = 24.418$. Test the restriction of the model, indicating clearly all parts of your test procedure.

10.17 💿 **marginal productivity conditions** Consider the versions of the ACMS marginal productivity condi-

tions that you estimate in Exercises 7.14 and 10.10. Use these to test the joint hypothesis $\alpha^* = \beta^* = 0$. Do the data indicate that it is appropriate to apply a common marginal productivity condition to the two country groups?

10.18 💿 **marginal productivity conditions** Consider the marginal productivity condition (10.35) in which both the intercept and slope are permitted to shift across the subsamples.

(a) Indicate the parameter restriction(s) that correspond to the hypothesis that developed and underdeveloped countries are both governed by Cobb-Douglas production functions (although not necessarily the *same* Cobb-Douglas production function). How many restrictions on the general model (10.35) is this? Are these restrictions linear? Have you estimated the restricted model previously?

(b) Test this hypothesis.

10.19 ⊙ **cobbdoug.dat** Use the original Cobb-Douglas data given in Table 7.1 to estimate the unrestricted model (10.32), confirming the value for SSE$_U$ reported in Example 8.

(a) What values for $\hat{\alpha}$ and $\hat{\beta}$ do you obtain? How close do they come to satisfying $\alpha + \beta = 1$?

(b) Use the appropriate option of the least squares command to test the constant-returns-to-scale restriction. How does the F value compare with that of Example 8?

10.20 ƒ ⊙ **cobbdoug.dat** In the special case of just $g = 1$ linear restriction, another approach to testing is sometimes presented. Note that the linear combination of coefficients on the left-hand side of (10.25) may be thought of as a parameter in its own right: $v = \sum a_k \beta_k$, say, with estimator $\hat{v} = \sum a_k \hat{\beta}_k$. For example, for the constant-returns-to-scale restriction $\alpha + \beta = 1$ we may define $v = \alpha + \beta$ with estimator $\hat{v} = \hat{\alpha} + \hat{\beta}$.

(a) From your estimation results in Exercise 10.19a, what is your estimate of v?

(b) In general, the variance of a linear combination of K random variables is given by a formula such as (B.20) in Appendix A; it depends on their K variances and $K(K-1)/2$ distinct covariances. In the case of your estimator $\hat{v} = \hat{\alpha} + \hat{\beta}$, this simplifies to

$$V(\hat{v}) = V(\hat{\alpha}) + V(\hat{\beta}) + 2\,\mathrm{cov}(\hat{\alpha}, \hat{\beta}),$$

which is merely an application of Corollary B.4.2 in Appendix B.
i. Does your econometric software report an estimate of $\mathrm{cov}(\hat{\alpha}, \hat{\beta})$? (You may have to rerun your regression for Exercise 10.19, requesting supplementary output, to obtain this.)

ii. Use this to obtain an estimate of $V(\hat{v})$. Let us denote this by $s_{\hat{v}}^2$.

(c) Use your estimate $\hat{v}$ and its standard error $s_{\hat{v}}$ to test the restriction $H_0: v = 1$. State clearly all parts of your test procedure.

(d) Is your test conclusion consistent with that obtained from the F test in Exercise 10.19? Is there any relationship between the value of that F statistic and your t statistic?

(e) What do you identify as the primary advantages of the F test procedure over this t test, for testing linear restrictions generally?

10.21 ƒ ⊙ **cobbdoug.dat** Consider the F test of the regression model as treated in Section 8.5.3, which tests the hypothesis that all slope coefficients are jointly equal to zero. For the Cobb-Douglas production function (10.32), this is the hypothesis that $\alpha = \beta = 0$.

(a) Use your estimation results for (10.32) to perform this test using the statistic (8.24),

$$F = \frac{(\mathrm{SST} - \mathrm{SSE})/(K-1)}{\mathrm{SSE}/(n-K)}$$
$$\sim F(K-1, n-K). \qquad (10.36)$$

(b) The hypothesis in question involves a certain set of linear restrictions.
i. In the Cobb-Douglas example, what is the number of restrictions? What is it for general K?

ii. What is the restricted form of the model?

iii. What is the relationship between SSE$_R$ and the SST of (10.36)? (*Hint:* You may find it helpful to reread the opening paragraphs of Section 4.6.)

iv. For the Cobb-Douglas data, what is the value of SSE$_R$? (*Hint:* Use the relationship you identify in part iii to deduce SSE$_R$ from your estimation results for the unrestricted model. It should not be necessary to estimate the restricted model.) Is the relationship (10.33) satisfied?

v. Given that you have SSEs for the restricted and unrestricted models, test the restrictions by applying the statistic (10.34).

vi. What in general can be said about the relationship between an F test of the regression model based on (10.36) versus one based on the F test of linear restrictions (10.34)?

10.2.3 Chow Test for Structural Change

The problem often arises of whether a common regression model adequately describes both subsamples of a data set. For example, in Section 10.1.4 we consider estimating the model (10.15) over a full sample of data,

$$Y_i = \alpha + \beta X_i + \varepsilon_i \qquad (i = 1, \ldots, n, \text{ yielding } SSE_R), \tag{10.37}$$

versus estimating separate models (10.19) over two subsamples, say A and B, which constitute the full sample,

$$Y_i = \alpha_1 + \beta_1 X_i + \varepsilon_i \text{ (subsample A yielding } SSE_1)$$
$$Y_i = \alpha_2 + \beta_2 X_i + \varepsilon_i \text{ (subsample B yielding } SSE_2). \tag{10.38}$$

In the context of that earlier discussion, the two subsamples were peacetime and wartime. Clearly, however, the idea of a sample potentially involving distinct subsample-specific features is much more general.

The restrictions $\alpha_1 = \alpha_2$ and $\beta_1 = \beta_2$ are the hypothesis that both subsamples have been generated by the common model (10.37). One approach to testing this hypothesis, as we have seen, is to define a dummy variable that distinguishes between the two subsamples and introduce it into (10.37) in such a way that all the coefficients of the model are permitted to shift across the subsamples; this was model (10.17). It is then possible to test whether the dummy terms are jointly significant: $\alpha^* = \beta^* = 0$. Such a test is illustrated in Example 9 in which, in the context of Fuchs's reestimation of the ACMS regressions, these restrictions are rejected and it is concluded that different marginal productivity conditions hold for developed and underdeveloped countries. This is a test for **parameter constancy** or the absence of structural change in the regression coefficients.

An alternative but, as we shall see, ultimately equivalent means of implementing the same test was suggested by Gregory Chow (1960). Instead of using the estimation results for the model with dummy terms, Chow's procedure uses the estimation results for the three regressions (10.37) and (10.38). The restricted model is the full sample regression (10.37) that imposes H_0: $\alpha_1 = \alpha_2$, $\beta_1 = \beta_2$ and yields SSE_R. Note that the null hypothesis involves, in general, K linear restrictions—one for each of the K coefficients. The unrestricted model consists of the two subsample regressions (10.38). Their estimation yields an SSE_1 and SSE_2; let us therefore denote the SSE of the unrestricted model as $SSE_U = SSE_1 + SSE_2$. Chow was able to establish that, under the null hypothesis,

$$F = \frac{(SSE_R - SSE_U)/K}{SSE_U/(n - 2K)} = \frac{(SSE_R - (SSE_1 + SSE_2))/K}{(SSE_1 + SSE_2)/(n - 2K)}$$
$$\sim F(K, n - 2K). \tag{10.39}$$

EXAMPLE 10

dairy.dat

(Continuation of EXAMPLE 9) Use a Chow test to examine whether the same marginal productivity condition applies to developed and underdeveloped countries. How do the calculations relate to those in Example 9?

SOLUTION

The ACMS marginal productivity condition for dairy products, estimated over the full sample of all countries, is (10.22), and so $SSE_R = 0.31557$. Note that this is the same value of SSE_R as in the dummy variable test in Example 9 because in both cases the restricted model is the same, (10.21). Estimated over the subsamples the model yields $SSE_1 = 0.08662$ and $SSE_2 = 0.10295$, for a total of $SSE_U = 0.18957$. (Note that this is the same value as in Example 9, in which the unrestricted model is that with dummy variables.) Hence, for $K = 2$ restrictions, Chow's F statistic (10.39) evaluates to

$$F = \frac{(0.31557 - (0.08662 + 0.10295))/2}{(0.08662 + 0.10295)/(16 - 4)} = 3.99,$$

the same value as in Example 9. Because the degrees of freedom and thus the appropriate rejection region are the same, we reach the same conclusion: The hypothesis of a common marginal productivity condition for the two country groups should be rejected.

This example illustrates that the Chow test and the dummy-based test will always give the same result. Why is this? The correspondence between most elements of the two test statistics (10.34) and (10.39) is easy to see. SSE_R is the same in both statistics because the restricted model is (10.37) in both cases, regardless of whether we view it as the result of imposing the restriction $\alpha^* = \beta^* = 0$ in (10.17) or of imposing $\alpha_1 = \alpha_2$ and $\beta_1 = \beta_2$ in (10.38). Similarly, K in the dummy-based test (10.34) is the number of coefficients in a model with a full set of shift dummies, such as (10.17); this is always twice the value of K in the Chow test (10.39), in which no dummies appear. Finally, the number of restrictions (dummy terms) g in (10.34) is always equal to the number of coefficients K in the regressions on which the Chow test is based.

Less obviously, it must be that $SSE_U = SSE_1 + SSE_2$ in the Chow test is the same as SSE_U in the dummy-based test statistic. To see this, start with the definition of the latter as $\sum e_i^2 = \sum (Y_i - \hat{Y}_i)^2$ and use the definition of the dummy variable (10.16):

$$SSE_U = \sum_{i=1}^{n}(Y_i - \hat{\alpha} - \hat{\beta}X_i - \hat{\alpha}^* D_i - \hat{\beta}^* D_i X_i)^2$$
$$= \underbrace{\sum(Y_i - \hat{\alpha} - \hat{\beta}X_i)^2}_{A} + \underbrace{\sum(Y_i - (\hat{\alpha} + \hat{\alpha}^*) - (\hat{\beta} + \hat{\beta}^*)X_i)^2}_{B}$$
$$= \underbrace{\sum(Y_i - \hat{\alpha}_1 - \hat{\beta}_1 X_i)^2}_{A} + \underbrace{\sum(Y_i - \hat{\alpha}_2 - \hat{\beta}_2 X_i)^2}_{B}$$
$$= SSE_1 + SSE_2.$$

The notation $\sum_A$ denotes a summation over all observations associated with subsample A, and $\sum_B$ denotes the same for B. The penultimate step uses the correspondence (10.20) between the coefficients of the two approaches, a correspondence that applies both to the population values and to the least squares estimators, as is illustrated in Exercise 10.11.

The numerical equivalence of the two tests for structural change means that the choice between them is purely a matter of convenience. The Chow test requires three least squares estimations rather than the two of the dummy variable test; however, this is often easier than setting up the required dummy variables, unless these have already been generated as part of other analysis. Both procedures are easily extended to situations with more than two subsamples.

The Behrens-Fisher Problem Revisited

The equivalence of the two procedures is analogous to the earlier equivalence that we have established between the test for the equality of population means in Section 10.1.1 and the use in Section 10.1.2 of a single dummy variable to shift the intercept of a simple regression. Indeed, these can now be viewed as a particularly simple example of a test for structural change. Just as we have seen is true in that earlier discussion, the Chow test implicitly assumes a constant variance across all subsamples. Testing for structural change in the absence of this maintained hypothesis is thus a generalization of the Behrens-Fisher problem, and the same issues arise. Specifically, although some tests for structural change have been developed that permit distinct variances for the different subsamples, no definitive solution to this testing problem exists.

In light of this, how is the applied econometrician to proceed? Almost certainly the most useful approach in practice is to note that distinct subsample variances are just a special case of heteroskedasticity. Our goal then becomes one of testing linear restrictions (in this case, the restrictions associated with an absence of structural change) in a way that is robust to (i.e., valid in the presence of) heteroskedasticity. Heteroskedasticity-robust test procedures are developed in Chapter 14.

EXERCISES _____

10.22 💿 **marginal productivity conditions**   Use your estimation results for the ACMS marginal productivity condition in Exercises 7.14 and 10.11 to perform a Chow test for structural change. How does your result compare with that in Exercise 10.17?

10.2.4 t Tests as a Special Case of the F Test of Linear Restrictions

The F test developed in this chapter permits the testing of *any* set of linear restrictions on the coefficients of a multiple regression. A particularly simple subset of such hypotheses are fixed-value restrictions such as $\beta_k = a_0$; that is, the hypothesis that a coefficient equals some numerical value. This class of restrictions is, of course, testable using t tests. It follows that t tests must be interpretable as a special case of the general F test. Let us clarify this interpretation.

As is so often the case, it is most helpful to proceed by considering some examples. For this purpose let us return to Fuchs's version (10.24) of the ACMS marginal productivity condition, which is

$$\log(V/L)_i = \alpha + \beta \log w_i + \alpha^* D_i + \varepsilon_i.$$

Example 3 reports the estimation results for this equation for the dairy products industry, which it is useful to repeat here:

$$\log(V/L)_i = -5.39 + \underset{(0.0806)}{0.901} \ \log w_i + \underset{(0.110)}{0.302} \ D_i + e_i \quad \text{SSE} = 0.20036. \quad (10.40)$$

Let us consider two linear restrictions on this model. The first is the restriction $\alpha^* = 0$, which is the hypothesis that developed and underdeveloped countries have the same marginal productivity condition.

EXAMPLE 11

 dairy.dat

Test the hypothesis H_0: $\alpha^* = 0$ using, first, a t test, and, second, an F test. What is the relationship between the two test procedures?

SOLUTION

Using the estimation results for the unrestricted model (10.40), the t statistic for this hypothesis is $t = 0.302/0.110 = 2.75$. This rejects at, say, a 5% significance level ($t_{0.025}(13) = 2.16$).

An F test of the same hypothesis involves a comparison of the SSEs of the restricted and unrestricted models. From (10.40), $\text{SSE}_U = 0.20036$. Imposing the restriction $\alpha^* = 0$ just yields the original ACMS model (10.21); from (10.22), $\text{SSE}_R = 0.31557$. The computed value of the F statistic is therefore

$$F = \frac{(\text{SSE}_R - \text{SSE}_U)/g}{\text{SSE}_U/(n - K)} = \frac{(0.31557 - 0.20036)/1}{0.20036/(16 - 13)} = 7.475.$$

Comparing this with a tabulated value of the F distribution with 1 and 13 degrees of freedom ($F_{0.05}(1, 13) = 4.67$), the restriction is rejected at a 5% level of significance.

What is the relationship between the two tests? It is apparent that the F statistic is the square of the t: $F = 7.475 = 2.75^2 = t^2$. We know as well that, for $g = 1$ degrees of freedom in the numerator, the same relationship holds between the tabulated values of the distributions: $F_{0.05}(1, 13) = 4.67 = 2.16^2 = t_{0.025}(13)^2$. Hence, the two test procedures must always yield the same conclusion.

As a second example, consider the unitary elasticity of substitution restriction $\beta = 1$.

EXAMPLE 12

 dairy.dat

Test the hypothesis H_0: $\beta = 1$ using, first, a t test, and, second, an F test. What is the relationship between the two test procedures?

SOLUTION

As we have seen in Example 3, the estimation results for the unrestricted model (10.40) yield a t statistic for this hypothesis of $t = (0.901 - 1)/0.0806 = -1.23$. This fails to reject at, say, a 5% significance level (as in the previous example, $t_{0.025}(13) = 2.16$).

An F test of the same hypothesis involves a comparison of the SSEs of the restricted and unrestricted models. The unrestricted model continues to be (10.40) with $SSE_U = 0.20036$. The restricted model we have encountered previously as equation (10.28), the estimation of which yields $SSE_R = 0.22375$. The computed value of the F statistic is therefore

$$F = \frac{(SSE_R - SSE_U)/g}{SSE_U/(n - K)} = \frac{(0.22375 - 0.20036)/1}{0.20036/(16 - 3)} = 1.518.$$

Comparing this with the same tabulated value of the F distribution given in the previous example, the hypothesis of a unitary elasticity of substitution is not rejected.

Again it is evident that the relationship between these two test procedures is that the F statistic is the square of the t: $F = 1.518 = (-1.23)^2 = t^2$. Hence, they are equivalent.

These examples illustrate that, for $g = 1$ restriction, the F statistic is always interpretable as the square of a t statistic.[5] It turns out that, from this fact, it is a short step to establishing an assertion made in Chapter 8 about the adjusted R^2.

$\overline{R}^2$ Revisited

In Section 8.5.1 the adjusted R^2 is introduced as a goodness-of-fit measure that does not necessarily increase with the inclusion of additional regressors. It is defined as

$$\overline{R}^2 = 1 - \frac{SSE/(n - K)}{SST/(n - 1)}. \tag{10.41}$$

This is proposed as an alternative to the ordinary R^2, which has the unattractive feature that it can only increase with additional regressors. As we have seen, this feature arises fundamentally from the fact that constraining a least squares estimation must result in a larger SSE. In adding new regressors, if the restricted and unrestricted regressions have K_R and K_U regressors with $K_R < K_U$, then it must be that

$$SSE_U \le SSE_R.$$

Under what circumstances will $\overline{R}^2$ increase with an additional regressor? It has been asserted this will happen when the t statistic associated with the new regressor exceeds 1 in absolute value. We are now in a position to establish this result, using the fact that for $g = 1$ restriction the F statistic is the square of the t statistic. It is useful, however, to begin by stating the result somewhat more generally.

Result 10.1 *When additional regressors are included in a regression, the $\overline{R}^2$ will increase if and only if the F statistic on those additional regressors is greater than 1.*

---

[5] Exercise 10.20 is another illustration.

Proof:

If $\overline{R}^2$ increases with additional regressors then

$$\overline{R}_R^2 < \overline{R}_U^2, \tag{10.42}$$

or, from the definition (10.41),

$$1 - \frac{\text{SSE}_R/(n - K_R)}{\text{SST}/(n - 1)} < 1 - \frac{\text{SSE}_U/(n - K_U)}{\text{SST}/(n - 1)}.$$

(SST is the same for both the restricted and unrestricted regressions because they have the same dependent variable.) Manipulating this, $\overline{R}^2$ increases if

$$\frac{\text{SSE}_R}{\text{SSE}_U} > \frac{n - K_R}{n - K_U}. \tag{10.43}$$

This may be transformed to

$$F = \frac{(\text{SSE}_R - \text{SSE}_U)/(K_U - K_R)}{\text{SSE}_U/(n - K_U)} > 1. \tag{10.44}$$

This expression is recognizable as the F statistic for the hypothesis that the added regressors have zero coefficients; the numerator degrees of freedom is the number of zero-restrictions $g = K_U - K_R$. Consequently, this condition is equivalent to the condition (10.42), and $\overline{R}^2$ increases if and only if the F statistic on the additional regressors exceeds 1. □

As a corollary to this result, consider the special case in which just a single regressor is being added. Then we know that the F statistic on that additional regressor is the square of the t statistic. Setting $K_R = K$ and $K_U = K + 1$ in the F statistic, we have that the $\overline{R}^2$ increases if and only if

$$t^2 = F = \frac{\text{SSE}_R - \text{SSE}_U}{\text{SSE}_U/(n - K_U)} > 1.$$

This is equivalent to the t statistic exceeding 1 in absolute value:

$$|t| = \frac{|\hat{\beta}_{K+1}|}{s_{\hat{\beta}_{K+1}}} > 1. \tag{10.45}$$

Thus a new regressor increases $\overline{R}^2$ if and only if its t statistic exceeds 1 in absolute value.

A value of 1 for the t statistic is, of course, of no special importance, and so the property that $\overline{R}^2$ increases when $|t| > 1$ is somewhat arbitrary. The basic issue is how to capture the trade-off between model fit and model parsimony in a single number. A more complicated model can always fit the data better than a simpler one, yet we value simplicity for its own sake. There are many ways of making this trade-off, and therefore many ways of adjusting the fit of the model—as indicated by, say, the SSE—for the loss of degrees of freedom that accompanies a more complex model. We say more about various approaches to this trade-off in our discussion of model choice in Chapter 12.

E X E R C I S E S

10.23 ● marginal productivity conditions

(a) In Exercise 10.9 you perform t tests of the hypotheses $\alpha^* = 0$ and $\beta = 1$. For the restriction $\alpha^* = 0$, what is SSE_R?

i. Perform an F test of this restriction. How does it compare with your earlier t test?

ii. Compare the $\overline{R}^2$s of your restricted and unrestricted models. Does $\overline{R}^2$ increase when the additional regressor is included? Is this consistent with the magnitude of the t statistic?

(b) In Exercise 10.13 you estimate the model subject to the restriction $\beta = 1$.

i. What is SSE_R?

ii. Perform an F test of this restriction. How does it compare with your earlier t test?

10.24 ● marginal productivity conditions   Consider the models you have estimated in Exercises 10.9 and 10.10.

(a) Which of the two is the restricted model and which the unrestricted?

(b) State the hypothesis embodied in the restricted model (i) as a parameter restriction and (ii) interpreted in terms of its economic meaning.

(c) Perform an F test of the hypothesis you have described. How does the value of your statistic compare with that in Exercise 10.10c?

(d) What happens to the $\overline{R}^2$ in going from the restricted to the unrestricted model? What is the value of the t statistic associated with the added variable? Is this consistent with the result of this section?

10.25 Show that (10.44) may be manipulated into the condition (10.43).

10.2.5 Nested Testing Structures

As our discussion of F testing of linear restrictions has illustrated, when we test a parameter restriction on an econometric model we are testing whether the data reject some special case of that model relative to some more general case. Often economic theory predicts a number of restrictions that give rise to a sequence of successively more restrictive special cases of the model. Such a sequence is called a **nested testing structure.**

The marginal productivity conditions we have worked with in this chapter provide a simple example of a nested testing structure. The most general of these allows developed and underdeveloped countries to have different CES production functions, by allowing both the intercept and slope of the marginal productivity condition to shift:

$$F1: \quad \log(V/L)_i = \alpha + \beta \log w_i + \alpha^* D_i + \beta^* D_i \log w_i + \varepsilon_i.$$

In considering the various versions of this equation that might describe the ACMS industries, we have studied various combinations of the restrictions $\beta = 1$, $\alpha^* = 0$, and $\beta^* = 0$. These are summarized in Table 10.4, which includes SSEs for these regressions estimated with the ACMS data for the dairy products industry.

The regression $F1$ is the most general marginal productivity condition under consideration. It is the maintained hypothesis, in the sense that it is not itself subject

TABLE 10.4   Alternative Marginal Productivity Conditions

Function	Regression	Restrictions	SSE (dairy products)
F1	$\log(V/L)_i = \alpha + \beta \log w_i + \alpha^* D_i + \beta^* D_i \log w_i + \varepsilon_i$ (developed and underdeveloped countries have different CES production functions)	Maintained hypothesis	0.18957
F2	$\log(V/L)_i = \alpha + \beta \log w_i + \alpha^* D_i + \varepsilon_i$ (Fuchs's model; different CES production functions, but a common elasticity of substitution)	$\beta^* = 0$	0.20036
F3	$\log(V/L)_i - \log w_i = \alpha + \alpha^* D_i + \varepsilon_i$ (developed and underdeveloped countries have different Cobb-Douglas production functions)	$\beta^* = 0, \beta = 1$	0.22375
F4	$\log(V/L)_i = \alpha + \beta \log w_i + \varepsilon_i$ (the ACMS regression; developed and underdeveloped countries have the same CES production function)	$\alpha^* = \beta^* = 0$	0.31557
F5	$\log(V/L)_i - \log w_i = \alpha + \varepsilon_i$ (developed and underdeveloped countries have the same Cobb-Douglas production function)	$\alpha^* = \beta^* = 0, \beta = 1$	0.90037

to test as a special case of any yet more general model. This is not to say that this model is necessarily correct or that no more general model exists; we can never know with any certainty whether this is the case for any model. But we must start somewhere, and the maintained hypothesis—the most general model under consideration—is the model we adopt as our initial premise.

Within $F1$, the first restriction of interest is whether $\beta^* = 0$. This yields the special case $F2$, the regression estimated by Fuchs. It allows developed and underdeveloped countries to have different CES production functions (because the intercept is permitted to shift), but with a common elasticity of substitution (because β does not shift). Being a special case of the general model, $F2$ is said to be **nested** within $F1$.

Within Fuchs's regression $F2$ we have studied two special cases: $\beta = 1$, which is denoted $F3$, and $\alpha^* = 0$, denoted $F4$. The function $F3$ imposes the special case of a Cobb-Douglas production function (because $\beta = 1$ restricts the elasticity of substitution to unity), but allows different Cobb-Douglas production functions to apply to developed and underdeveloped countries (because the dummy variable allows the intercept to shift). The function $F4$ in which $\alpha^* = \beta^* = 0$ is just the original ACMS regression in which the same CES production function applies to both developed and underdeveloped countries.

Notice that the restrictions $\beta = 1$ and $\alpha^* = 0$ that give rise to the functions $F3$ and $F4$ are imposed only within Fuchs's regression $F2$. They are not imposed directly on $F1$ in the absence of Fuchs's restriction $\beta^* = 0$ because the models that would result have no clear economic interpretation.

Finally, the restrictions $\beta = 1$ and $\alpha^* = 0$ may be imposed jointly rather than individually. This yields the function $F5$, which has the interpretation that all countries have the same Cobb-Douglas production function. $F5$ is a special case of all the preceding models.

Nested Hypothesis Testing

These relationships are depicted in Table 10.5, which makes it easy to see that there are two **ordered nests** of successively more restricted models: nest $N1$ consisting of the sequence $F1 \rightarrow F2 \rightarrow F3 \rightarrow F5$, and nest $N2$ consisting of $F1 \rightarrow F2 \rightarrow F4 \rightarrow F5$. Within each nest, each function is a special case of those that precede it, obtained by imposing the associated restrictions. As such, the SSEs must increase as we proceed through the ordered nest because successively more restricted models must fit the data less well. The SSEs of Table 10.4 confirm this for the dairy products data.

Because in this example these restrictions are linear restrictions on linear models, the t and F tests we have developed provide a means of testing any function against those that precede it in the ordered nest. For example, testing the null hypothesis of $F3$ against the alternative of $F2$ is a t test of $\beta = 1$ in $F2$; testing $F3$ against $F1$ is an F test of the $g = 2$ restrictions $\beta^* = 0$, $\beta = 1$ in $F1$. The various possibilities are summarized in Table 10.6 on page 467, which gives the SSEs of the restricted and unrestricted models and the p-values of the resulting tests.

As the table indicates, several of these tests are ones we have encountered in the examples and exercises of this chapter; for example, a test of the null of $F4$ against the alternative of $F1$ is the Chow test for structural change. The table uses parentheses to enclose references to exercises as a reminder that you may have completed those exercises with data for an industry other than dairy products, in which case you will have obtained p-values for that industry.

Considering the test results as a whole, on balance they suggest that the most restricted form of the model that is not rejected by the data is $F3$, the marginal productivity condition that implies different Cobb-Douglas production functions for developed and underdeveloped countries. This supports Fuchs's conjecture that the Cobb-Douglas production function adequately describes the production technology for these data, as long as we do not attempt to impose the *same* Cobb-Douglas function on all countries. Of course, this conclusion is for the dairy products industry.

TABLE 10.5   Marginal Productivity Conditions: Paths of Ordered Nests for Functions $F1$–$F5$

Nest	Functions
$N1$	$F1$, $F2$, $F3$, $F5$
$N2$	$F1$, $F2$, $F4$, $F5$

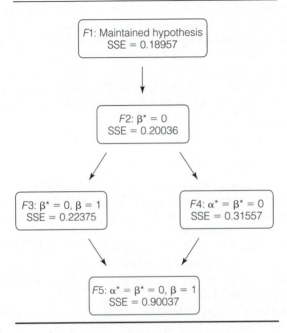

$F1$: Maintained hypothesis
SSE = 0.18957

$F2$: $\beta^* = 0$
SSE = 0.20036

$F3$: $\beta^* = 0$, $\beta = 1$
SSE = 0.22375

$F4$: $\alpha^* = \beta^* = 0$
SSE = 0.31557

$F5$: $\alpha^* = \beta^* = 0$, $\beta = 1$
SSE = 0.90037

Different conclusions might apply to other industries, and Exercise 10.26 asks you to assess the evidence for your industry.

Nonnested Models

The nests $N1$ and $N2$ differ because of the roles of the models $F3$ and $F4$. Both $F3$ and $F4$ are nested within $F2$. But neither is a special case of the other—neither $F3$ nor $F4$ can be obtained by imposing restrictions on the other function—thus, neither is nested within the other. $F3$ and $F4$ are said to be **nonnested** models.

The t and F tests we have developed allow us to test nested hypotheses—the restrictions associated with one model as a special case of another. They do not, however, provide a way of testing nonnested hypotheses, such as $F3$ versus $F4$, directly in relation to one another. We cannot, for example, call one of these functions the restricted model and the other the unrestricted and apply the F statistic (10.34), because neither model is a restricted version of the other.

This is not particularly important in contexts like the present one in which the nonnested models are both special cases of a more general model, because

TABLE 10.6   Hypothesis Tests within a Nested Structure: Marginal Productivity Condition for Dairy Products

Unrestricted model		Restricted model			Restrictions under test			
H_0	SSE	H_A	SSE	p-value	$\beta = 1$	$\alpha^* = 0$	$\beta^* = 0$	Comments
$F1$	0.18957	$F2$	0.20036	0.4246			✓	Test of the Fuchs specification: [Exercises 10.10c, 10.24]
		$F3$	0.22375	0.3699	✓		✓	[Exercise 10.18]
		$F4$	0.31557	0.0470		✓	✓	Chow test: Examples 9, 10 [Exercises 10.17, 10.22]
		$F5$	0.90037	0.0002	✓	✓	✓	
$F2$	0.20036	$F3$	0.22375	0.2398	✓			Examples 3, 12 [Exercises 10.9c, 10.23b]
		$F4$	0.31557	0.0171		✓		Example 11 [Exercises 10.9b, 10.23a]
		$F5$	0.90037	0.0001	✓	✓		
$F3$	0.22375	$F5$	0.90037	0.0000		✓		
$F4$	0.31557	$F5$	0.90037	0.0002	✓			from Table 7.4 [Exercise 7.14c]

they can be tested as restrictions on that general model. It is common, however, for competing economic theories to yield nonnested econometric models that are *not* simply special cases of some more general model that encompasses them both. Because one of the goals of econometrics is to distinguish empirically between theories, it is of interest to be able to test the nonnested models directly against one another. This is a topic that we return to in Chapter 12, in which nonnested tests are most naturally developed as a topic in model evaluation.

Mizon's Nested Testing Structure

As a more complicated example of a nested testing structure, Mizon (1977) tested a variety of production function specifications. These are summarized in Table 10.7; the first three are labeled with the name of the economist most closely associated with them.

TABLE 10.7   Production Functions Estimated by Mizon

$F1$	$Q = [\alpha^2 N^{\rho_1} + \beta^2 K^{\rho_2} + \gamma^2 H^{\rho_3}]^{\rho_4}$	(Mukerji)
$F2$	$Q = \{[\alpha^2 N^\rho + \beta^2 K^\rho]^{\mu/\rho} + \gamma^2 H^\mu\}^{\nu/\mu}$	(Sato)
$F3$	$Q = [\alpha^2 N^\rho + \beta^2 K^\rho + \gamma^2 H^\rho]^{\nu/\rho}$	(Uzawa)
$F4$	$Q = H^\gamma [\alpha^2 N^\rho + \beta^2 K^\rho]^{\nu/\rho}$	
$F5$	$Q = [\alpha^2 N^\rho + \beta^2 K^\rho]^{\nu/\rho}$	
$F6$	$Q = [\alpha^2 (NH)^\rho + \beta^2 K^\rho]^{\nu/\rho}$	(Simple)
$F7$	$Q = A N^{\alpha^*} K^{\beta^*} H^{\gamma^*}$	
$F8$	$Q = A(NH)^{\alpha^*} K^{\beta^*}$	
$F9$	$Q = A N^{\alpha^*} K^{\beta^*}$	

Source: Mizon, G.E. (1977) "Inferential Procedures in Nonlinear Models: An Application in a UK Industrial Cross Section Study of Factor Substitution and Returns to Scale," *Econometrica* 45, 1221–1242. Reprinted with permission.

Some of the more general of these production functions are three-factor CES-type forms in which labor is decomposed into the number of workers N and hours per worker H. (Here H does *not* denote human capital, as it did in the Mankiw-Romer-Weil analysis.) Workers and hours are allowed to enter as separate factors of production because employers may be able to substitute between them, choosing between over-time versus new hiring. Some of the more restrictive specifications aggregate labor into the single factor worker-hours NH or use number of workers N alone.

One respect in which this is a more complicated example of a nested testing structure than our marginal productivity conditions is that there are three alternative maintained hypotheses; that is, three most general models that cannot be tested as special cases of one another (they are nonnested). These are $F1$, $F2$, and $F6$. The remaining functions are special cases of these. The relationships are delineated in Table 10.8, which reveals an elegant nested testing structure. The ordered nests are summarized as $N1$ through $N8$.

Many of Mizon's production functions are intrinsically nonlinear, and so the t and F tests we have studied do not apply to testing the nested hypotheses. Instead, Mizon used nonlinear methods to study these ordered nests. In Chapter 13, we use a small part of Mizon's structure—the two-factor CES and Cobb-Douglas functions $F6$ and $F8$—to illustrate the principles of nonlinear estimation and testing.

The General-to-Specific Testing Principle

Within a nested testing structure, it stands to reason that the preferred way to proceed is to begin with the most general model—the maintained hypothesis—and *test down* through the ordered nest. In testing successive restrictions on the maintained hypothesis, we ultimately arrive at a special case that is supported by the data; that is, a restricted model whose restrictions are not rejected. By this means, we have concluded that $F3$ is the most restrictive marginal productivity condition suitable for the dairy products industry. And indeed the optimality of such a **general-to-specific testing strategy** can be established formally; it is one point of Mizon's (1977) analysis.

TABLE 10.8   Mizon's Production Functions: Paths of Ordered Nests for Functions $F1-F9$

Maintained hypothesis	Nest	Functions
Simple	$N1$	$F6, F8$
Sato	$N2$	$F2, F3, F7, F8$
	$N3$	$F2, F3, F7, F9$
	$N4$	$F2, F4, F7, F8$
	$N5$	$F2, F4, F7, F9$
	$N6$	$F2, F4, F5, F9$
Mukerji	$N7$	$F1, F3, F7, F9$
	$N8$	$F1, F3, F7, F8$

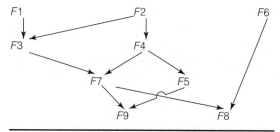

Source: Mizon, G.E. (1977) "Inferential Procedures in Nonlinear Models: An Application in a UK Industrial Cross Section Study of Factor Substitution and Returns to Scale," *Econometrica* 45, 1221–1242. Reprinted with permission.

Perhaps the most important lesson of the **LSE methodology**—named after Mizon, David Hendry, Denis Sargan, and other influential econometricians who have been associated with the London School of Economics—is that the desirability of proceeding in a general-to-specific manner is a principle that should govern all econometric modeling. This lesson is an important one because much empirical research unwittingly adopts exactly the opposite strategy of **specific-to-general** testing. A typical piece of empirical analysis begins with some conjectured model, estimates it, and then asks whether it stands up to alteration in a number of directions: functional form, properties of the disturbance, and so on. When such tests fail, the model is extended accordingly. Thus, instead of proceeding in a general-to-specific manner, such research begins with a specific model and *tests up* to some more general one.

Practitioner's Tip: **General-to-specific testing**

When testing ordered nests, try to test in a general-to-specific manner.

The spirit of the LSE methodology is represented in Hendry (2000). For a favorable evaluation of the LSE methodology see Hoover and Perez (1999), who construct an intriguing horse race between competing empirical methodologies.

EXERCISES

10.26 ⊙ **marginal productivity conditions** If your econometric software produces p-values, construct a table similar to Table 10.6 for the industry you have been analyzing in the exercises in this chapter.

Considering this evidence as a whole, what do you judge is the most restricted version of the model that is not rejected by your data?

10.3   Identification

Overidentifying Restrictions

As we have now seen in a range of examples, restrictions on the parameters of a model give rise to the distinction between a restricted and an unrestricted model. In the case of the Cobb-Douglas production function we have seen that the unrestricted model (10.32) is estimated as the multiple regression

$$\log Q_i = \beta_1 + \beta_2 \log K_i + \beta_3 \log L_i + \varepsilon_i \tag{10.46}$$

whereas the model restricted to satisfy constant returns to scale can be denoted

$$\log Q_i = \gamma^* + \beta \log K_i + (1 - \beta) \log L_i + \varepsilon_i.$$

The relationship between the two sets of coefficients is

$$\beta_1 = \gamma^*, \tag{10.47a}$$
$$\beta_2 = \beta, \tag{10.47b}$$
$$\beta_3 = 1 - \beta. \tag{10.47c}$$

The restricted-form coefficients are overdetermined as functions of the unrestricted form coefficients. That is, attempting to solve for the restricted-form coefficients yields the multiple solutions $\beta = \beta_2$ and $\beta = 1 - \beta_3$ rather than a unique solution for β. This is, of course, nothing more than saying that estimation of the unrestricted model (10.46) does not yield a unique estimate of β because it does not impose the restriction of constant returns to scale. To obtain such a unique estimate, the model must be estimated subject to this restriction—that is, in intensive form.

EXAMPLE 13   The textbook version of the Solow-Swan growth model leads to the restricted equation

$$\log q_i = \frac{\gamma}{1 - \alpha} + \frac{\alpha}{1 - \alpha} \log s_i - \frac{\alpha}{1 - \alpha} \log(\delta + n_i) + \varepsilon_i.$$

This has been expressed as the unrestricted regression (10.29):

$$\log q_i = \beta_1 + \beta_2 \log s_i + \beta_3 \log(\delta + n_i) + \varepsilon_i. \tag{10.48}$$

What is the relationship between these two sets of parameters?

SOLUTION

The relationship is summarized in Example 4 as

$$\beta_1 = \frac{\log \gamma}{1 - \alpha}, \tag{10.49a}$$

$$\beta_2 = \frac{\alpha}{1 - \alpha}, \tag{10.49b}$$

$$\beta_3 = \frac{-\alpha}{1 - \alpha}. \tag{10.49c}$$

The two restricted-form parameters γ and α are overdetermined in terms of the unrestricted parameters β_1, β_2, and β_3. Mankiw, Romer, and Weil obtained the unrestricted estimates $\hat{\beta}_1 = 5.36$, $\hat{\beta}_2 = 1.31$, and $\hat{\beta}_3 = -2.01$. Attempting to solve for implied estimates of γ and α yields multiple solutions; equation (10.49b) yields $\hat{\alpha} = 0.567$ (and then, from (10.49a), $\hat{\gamma} = 10.2$), whereas equation (10.49c) yields $\hat{\alpha} = 0.668$ (and therefore $\hat{\gamma} = 5.93$).

To obtain unique estimates of the restricted-form parameters, the regression (10.48) must be estimated subject to the implied restriction $\beta_2 + \beta_3 = 0$, as we discuss in Example 4. The result is the estimates $\hat{\beta}_1 = 7.10$ and $\hat{\beta}_2 = 1.43$ and therefore the unique implied estimates $\hat{\alpha} = 0.588$ and $\hat{\gamma} = 18.5$.

When restrictions overdetermine the parameters of the model to be estimated they are said to be **overidentifying.** As the Cobb-Douglas example shows, constant returns to scale is an overidentifying restriction in the Cobb-Douglas production function; β is said to be overidentified in relation to the parameters of the unrestricted model. Similarly, the restrictions of the Solow-Swan growth model are overidentifying on the regression (10.48). The examples in Table 10.3 are all cases of overidentifying restrictions. As all these examples illustrate, overidentifying restrictions constrain the ability of a model to fit the data. This, in turn, means that it is possible to test overidentifying restrictions. In this chapter, we have learned how to do this for linear restrictions on the linear regression model. The F test of Section 10.2.2 does this by comparing the estimation results for the restricted and unrestricted models and making use of the fact that the former must fit the data less well than the latter: $SSE_R > SSE_U$.

Exactly Identifying Restrictions

Relationships between parameters are not necessarily overidentifying. Consider the intercept of (10.46), which has alternatively been expressed as

$$\beta_1 = \gamma^* = \log \gamma.$$

The functional relationship (10.47a) between β_1 and γ^* (or, equivalently, γ) is what mathematicians call a one-to-one correspondence: Either is uniquely determined in relation to the other. One-to-one correspondences between parameters are said to be **exactly identifying;** γ^* (or γ) is uniquely determined or exactly identified in relation to the parameters of the unrestricted model. The restrictions (10.47) are, as a whole, overidentifying because (10.47b) and (10.47c) overdetermine β.

Exactly identifying restrictions are not testable. Rewriting the intercept of (10.46) as γ^* or $\log \gamma$ is just a change of notation—it does not affect the ability of the model to fit the data. As another example of exactly identifying restrictions, consider the association (10.20) between the two sets of parameters of the Chow and dummy-variable versions of the F test for structural change. It was precisely because this one-to-one correspondence also holds for the coefficient estimates that the two versions of the test turn out to be equivalent. Although the test for structural change is a test of overidentifying restrictions (for example, that $\alpha^* = \beta^* = 0$ in the dummy-variable version or, equivalently, that $\alpha_1 = \alpha_2$ and $\beta_1 = \beta_2$ in (10.38)), the one-to-one correspondence (10.20) between these two sets of coefficients constitutes an exactly identifying relationship that is not itself testable.

As another example, consider the model of two production processes with dummy variables defined as

$$D_{2i} = \begin{cases} 0 & \text{if output is from process A} \\ 1 & \text{if output is from process B} \end{cases}$$

$$D_{3i} = \begin{cases} 1 & \text{if output is from process A} \\ 0 & \text{if output is from process B.} \end{cases}$$

In distinguishing between the two mean outputs, contrast the model (10.4) involving just one dummy variable,

$$Y_i = \alpha + \beta D_{2i} + \varepsilon_i, \tag{10.50}$$

with the alternative of using two dummies but omitting the intercept:

$$Y_i = \beta_2 D_{2i} + \beta_3 D_{3i} + \varepsilon_i. \tag{10.51}$$

The relationship between the two sets of coefficients is

$$\beta_2 = \alpha + \beta,$$
$$\beta_3 = \alpha.$$

This is exactly identifying. Note that if we substitute these "restrictions" into the "unrestricted" model (10.51) we obtain as the "restricted" model

$$Y_i = (\alpha + \beta) D_{2i} + \alpha D_{3i} + \varepsilon_i = \alpha(D_{2i} + D_{3i}) + \beta D_{2i} + \varepsilon_i$$
$$= \alpha \cdot 1 + \beta D_{2i} + \varepsilon_i,$$

which is just (10.50). Although we can in this sense estimate the model subject to the restrictions, they do not constrain the ability of the model to fit the data; the estimation of (10.50) and (10.51) will yield identical SSEs. Indeed, it is apparent that when restrictions are exactly identifying it is arbitrary which of the models is regarded as restricted and which as unrestricted.

Underidentifying Restrictions

In some cases relationships between parameters are such that some are **underidentified:** They cannot be estimated. As an example, consider the simple regression model

$$Y_i = \alpha + \beta X_i + \varepsilon_i, \qquad \varepsilon_i \sim \text{n.i.d.}(\mu, \sigma^2). \tag{10.52}$$

This is in all respects the classical model of Chapter 4 *except* that the disturbance is specified as having a nonzero mean μ. Why do we not consider this possibility in our original analysis of that model? Because it implies that

$$E(Y_i) = \alpha + \beta X_i + E(\varepsilon_i) = (\alpha + \mu) + \beta X_i.$$

That is, the model is equivalent to

$$Y_i = (\alpha + \mu) + \beta X_i + \varepsilon_i = \alpha^* + \beta X_i + \varepsilon_i, \qquad \varepsilon_i \sim \text{n.i.d.}(0, \sigma^2), \quad (10.53)$$

and the parameters α and μ are not separately estimable. We can, of course, estimate α^* by the usual least squares formula, but the relationship

$$\alpha^* = \alpha + \mu$$

means that α and μ are underdetermined in terms of it and cannot be solved for uniquely. For any estimate of α^* that might be obtained, there are an infinite number of values for α and μ that are consistent with it. There is no sense in which the model can be estimated subject to this restriction in order to obtain separate estimates of α and μ. Any nonzero mean of the disturbance is not separately identifiable from the intercept of a linear regression—in estimation, it is effectively factored into the intercept estimate.

As another example, consider the requirement (4.4) that regressors exhibit variation: $\sum x_i^2 \neq 0$. If this is not satisfied then the implication is that the variable takes on just a single value $X_i = X$ over all observations, and we have seen that the least squares estimator of its coefficient is not uniquely defined. Another way of looking at this is in terms of identification. The simple regression model reduces to

$$Y_i = (\alpha + \beta X) + \varepsilon_i = \mu + \varepsilon_i.$$

Although μ is estimable (the least squares estimator being, as we know from Section 2.4, the sample mean $\overline{Y}$) the restriction

$$\mu = \alpha + \beta X$$

does not separately identify α and β. Hence, the requirement that regressors exhibit variation is said to be an identifying condition that must be satisfied if slope coefficients are to be separately identifiable from the intercept.

This observation allows us to interpret aspects of our discussion of omitted variable bias in Section 8.9.1 in terms of identification. Consider the following reinterpretation of Example 9 of Chapter 8.

EXAMPLE 14 | Consider the regression model

$$Y_i = \beta_1 + \beta_2 X_{2i} + \beta_3 X_{3i} + \varepsilon_i,$$

in which Y_i is crop yield, X_{2i} is fertilizer application (which is under the control of the researcher), and X_{3i} is rainfall. All are observed across fields indexed by i. Suppose, however, that once the data are collected we find that all fields have experienced exactly the same rainfall, so that $X_{3i} = X_3$ and the identifying condition $\sum x_i^2 \neq 0$ is not satisfied for this variable. What are the implications for the estimation of this regression model and the study of the effect of fertilizer on crop yield?

SOLUTION

Because we do not observe differential rainfall across fields, it is obviously not possible to learn anything about the link between rainfall and crop yield from these data. This is reflected in the fact that the model reduces to

$$Y_i = (\beta_1 + \beta_3 X_3) + \beta_2 X_{2i} + \varepsilon_i = \alpha + \beta_2 X_{2i} + \varepsilon_i.$$

Although α is estimable, β_1 and β_3 are not separately identified.

Note, however, that it is the effect of fertilizer application, not rainfall, that is the researcher's interest, and for this purpose the lack of variation in X_3 is actually a simplification. There are no negative implications for β_2, which is identified and estimable in the usual way (as the slope coefficient in a simple regression). Because rainfall is constant across observations, its influence has already been controlled for; it is unnecessary to use multiple regression to accomplish this.

Model Identification

A regression model is said to be **identified** if unique coefficient estimates are associated with the minimum of the sum of squares function S. For example, the regression model (10.52) having a disturbance with a nonzero mean is not identified because, as we have seen, an infinite number of possible values of α and μ are consistent with the least squares SSE. Minimizing the sum of squares function—or, for that matter, the application of any other estimation principle—provides no means of selecting from among this infinite number of (α, μ) pairs. Note that this example is one in which the lack of identification is a feature of the model and has nothing to do with the nature of the data. In other situations, on the other hand, a model may be identified for some data sets but not for others. In Example 14, the coefficient β_3 is identified for data sets in which rainfall exhibits variation, but is not for those in which it does not.

Perfect Multicollinearity as an Identification Problem

As another example in which the nature of the sample data has implications for identification, it is useful to note that perfect multicollinearity may be interpreted as an absence of model identification. In our discussion of perfect multicollinearity in Section 8.7.1 we see that this is a situation in which the regressors are linearly dependent. In the special case of two explanatory variables where the model is

$$Y_i = \beta_1 + \beta_2 X_{2i} + \beta_3 X_{3i} + \varepsilon_i,$$

perfect multicollinearity means that one regressor is an exact linear function of the other, say

$$X_{3i} = a + b X_{2i}.$$

The fundamental problem is that one variable is essentially just a change of units of measure of the other; they are not genuinely distinct influences. This can be seen by substituting this rescaling into the model:

$$Y_i = \beta_1 + \beta_2 X_{2i} + \beta_3 (a + b X_{2i}) + \varepsilon_i$$
$$= \underbrace{(\beta_1 + a\beta_3)}_{\alpha} + \underbrace{(\beta_2 + b\beta_3)}_{\beta} X_{2i} + \varepsilon_i.$$

What is really just data on a single variable permits only the estimation of the intercept and slope of a simple regression, here denoted α and β. Although unique estimates of α and β are associated with the minimum of the sum of squares function of this simple regression, there are an infinite number of estimates of β_1, β_2, and β_3 associated with that same minimum. The multiple regression is not identified in the absence of independent variation in the explanatory variables.

At the end of Section 8.7, we remark on the formal similarity between multicollinearity and a lack of variation in the data in their implications for regression analysis. Identification is one interpretation of this similarity: The assumption of the regression model that regressors are linearly independent is, like the assumption that they exhibit variation, an identifying condition on the model.

Further Comments

These examples illustrate that an absence of identification reflects, in a sense, a lack of information, and that this information may take several forms. In Example 14, the information that leads to identification is in the form of variation of the explanatory variable. However, identification may also be achieved with information on parameters. The standard specification of the regression model in terms of a zero-mean disturbance imposes the identifying restriction $\mu = 0$ on the model (10.52). But in principle other restrictions can serve to identify the model. Suppose, for example, that the restriction $\alpha - \mu = a_0$ is known to hold, where a_0 is some known constant. Then (10.53) can be estimated subject to this restriction as, say,

$$Y_i - a_0 = 2\mu + \beta X_i + \varepsilon_i.$$

This yields estimates of α and μ (the implied estimate of α being $\hat{\alpha} = a_0 + \hat{\mu}$). The additional information, in this case in the form of a parameter restriction, serves to exactly identify parameters that, in the absence of this information, are not identified. Because the restriction is exactly identifying, it is not testable.

Returning to the model of two production processes, note that the dummy variable trap of estimating the model

$$Y_i = \beta_1 + \beta_2 D_{2i} + \beta_3 D_{3i} + \varepsilon_i \tag{10.54}$$

is, as just one instance of perfect multicollinearity more generally, essentially one of lack of identification. The failure of the explanatory variables to be linearly independent means that the coefficients are not separately identified. However, additional information in the form of parameter restrictions may result in identification. The

TABLE 10.9   Identification and Testing

Can the restriction be:	Type of Restriction		
	Over-identifying	Exactly identifying	Under-identifying
Imposed in estimation?	Yes	Yes	No
Tested?	Yes	No	No

model (10.50) imposes the restriction $\beta_3 = 0$; the model (10.51), on the other hand, achieves identification by imposing $\beta_1 = 0$. The choice of identifying restriction is a matter of convenience, depending on the nature of the particular application at hand. Because the result of these restrictions is to convert an underidentified model into an exactly identified one, they are not testable.

Daniel Suits (1984) has pointed out that, for some purposes, yet other identifying restrictions on (10.54) may be convenient and that in general any linear restriction on the β_k will serve to identify them. In particular, he points out that the model may be rewritten in terms of a new set of coefficients $\beta_2^* = \beta_2 + \gamma$ and $\beta_3^* = \beta_3 + \gamma$ with γ chosen so that they average to zero: $\sum_k \beta_k^* = \sum_k (\beta_k + \gamma) = 0$. This restriction identifies the β_k^* in such a way that they are interpretable as representing deviations of the output of each production process from an aggregate mean output measured by the intercept.[6]

In conclusion, overidentifying restrictions may be both imposed in estimation and tested. Exactly identifying restrictions may be imposed in estimation but not tested. And underidentifying restrictions may be neither imposed nor tested. These conclusions are summarized in Table 10.9.

EXERCISES

10.27 Mankiw, Romer, and Weil estimated the augmented Solow-Swan model in restricted form. Their coefficient estimates are reported in Example 5 to be $\hat{\beta}_2 = 0.71$ and $\hat{\beta}_4 = 0.74$. What are the implied estimates of α and β? Are they unique?

10.28 Consider a demand function of the form

$$q_i = \beta_1 + \beta_2 p_{1i} + \beta_3 p_{2i} + \beta_4 m_i + \varepsilon_i, \quad (10.55)$$

where q_i is quantity of the good purchased, p_{1i} is its price, p_{2i} is the price of some complementary or substitutable commodity, and m_i is income. All are observed across households indexed by i. Suppose, however, that all households face the same

prices $p_{1i} = p_1$ and $p_{2i} = p_2$. What are the implications for

(a) the study of own- and cross-price elasticities?

(b) the study of the income elasticity of demand?

10.29 Consider the following argument, which is occasionally encountered in applied econometric discussions.

In a cross-sectional regression it may be that at the point in time at which the data were collected, all observations were subject to a common shock. (For example, it might be that a demand function such as (10.55) in Exercise 10.28 is being estimated with

---

[6] For some subtleties of interpretation of this mean, see the subsequent comment by Kennedy (1985).

household data collected during wartime, reflected in unusually extreme values for ε_i for all households.) It is asserted that this implies that the disturbance is correlated across households, so that the classical assumption that the ε_i are i.i.d. is violated. Consequently, the assumptions of the classical normal linear regression model are no longer fully satisfied, and alternative methods of estimation must be applied that treat the correlation across observations.

What do you think of this argument? Answer using the tools of this section.

10.30 Suppose that in Example 14 the common rainfall $X_{3i} = X_3$ experienced by all fields is known. Does this additional information serve to identify β_1 and β_3?

10.31 Consider the relationship between the two sets of seasonal coefficients that you establish in Exercise 10.6. Is this relationship over-, exactly, or underidentifying?

10.32 Consider the estimation of the model (10.54) in which identification is achieved through the imposition of the restriction $\beta_2 + \beta_3 = 0$.

(a) Write down a restricted form of the model that will yield a direct estimate of β_2.

(b) Describe the nature of the explanatory variable of your restricted model.

(c) What correspondence exists between β_1 and β_2 and the coefficients α and β of the model (10.4)? Is this correspondence over-, exactly, or underidentifying?

10.33 In Exercise 10.7, you consider the one-way analysis of variance parameterization of the inference problem treated in Section 10.1.3.

(a) In terms of the correspondence you identified in Exercise 10.7a, are the parameters of the one-way analysis of variance model over-, exactly, or underidentified?

(b) In their specification of the one-way analysis of variance model, statisticians add the requirement that $\sum \alpha_g = 0$. Why?

11 Applications to Cost Functions

The quantitative study of production data has a long history dating from the earliest empirical inquiries in economics. The analysis of production has also always had a central position in economic theory, as a cursory examination of any microeconomics text will reveal. Although not unique in spanning theory and application—the same is true of, say, work on consumer demand—the strong theoretical and empirical traditions in production analysis offer a natural training ground for the applied econometrician.

The purpose of this chapter is to provide this training ground. For reasons that become apparent as we proceed, doing so requires that we begin by introducing the concept of the cost function. Although the bulk of this chapter is concerned with production analysis, it is natural to conclude by sketching parallel developments in the study of consumer demand.

We find that the empirical analysis of cost involves many of the ideas of the preceding chapters: the derivation of an empirically implementable model from economic theory, the estimation of that model as a multiple regression, coefficient restrictions as the embodiment of theoretical hypotheses, identification, the use of the F statistic to test linear overidentifying restrictions, and multicollinearity.

11.1 The Cost Function

A key element governing the operations of a firm is its **cost function.** A cost function describes the minimum cost of producing a certain level of output Q given the prevailing prices the firm must pay for its factor inputs. In the case of two factors of production x_1 and x_2 having prices p_1 and p_2, the cost function is denoted

$$C = c(p_1, p_2, Q). \tag{11.1}$$

In contrast to a production function, which is a purely technical relation, the cost function embodies a certain behavioral hypothesis—that firms act so as to minimize costs.

As an accounting matter, the cost of employing x_1 and x_2 is

$$C = p_1 x_1 + p_2 x_2. \tag{11.2}$$

The behavioral hypothesis embodied in (11.1) says that the firm chooses x_1 and x_2 so as to minimize this total cost. These choices are described by the **conditional factor demand functions**

$$x_1(p_1, p_2, Q), \tag{11.3a}$$
$$x_2(p_1, p_2, Q). \tag{11.3b}$$

When substituted into the definition (11.2) these yield the cost function (11.1). The cost function so defined is a long-run cost function in that the firm is assumed to be able to vary all factor inputs freely. In the short run, by contrast, some factor inputs may be fixed, giving rise to a fixed component of total cost and the distinction between fixed and variable costs.

The demand functions (11.3) are called *conditional* factor demands because they describe the cost-minimizing choice of factor inputs conditional on a given level of output. From them may be derived demand elasticities such as the own-price elasticity of demand for factor i, defined by

$$\epsilon_{ii} \equiv \frac{p_i}{x_i} \frac{\partial x_i}{\partial p_i}. \tag{11.4}$$

The belief that factor demands are downward sloping is the hypothesis that this elasticity is negative.

Another accounting quantity related to the identity (11.2) that tends to show up in many aspects of cost analysis is the **share of factor i in total costs,** denoted by

$$S_i \equiv \frac{p_i x_i}{C}. \tag{11.5}$$

Given the definition of total costs (11.2), it follows, again purely as an accounting matter, that the cost shares of all factors must sum to 1:

$$\sum_i S_i = \sum_i \frac{p_i x_i}{C} = \frac{1}{C} \sum_i p_i x_i = \frac{1}{C} C = 1. \tag{11.6}$$

Although one is a technical relation whereas the other embodies a behavioral hypothesis, there is nevertheless a very close relationship between the cost function and the production function that has been summarized by Varian (1992, p. 84): "the cost function of a firm summarizes all of the economically relevant aspects of its technology." This relationship is referred to as the **duality** of production and cost. One purpose of this chapter is to develop this idea of duality and demonstrate its usefulness in empirical analysis.

The role that the factor prices p_i play in the cost function is very important in its empirical application, as we see in Section 11.3. In investigating the features of the function, however, it is useful to begin by concentrating on how costs vary with output.

FIGURE 11.1

Long- and short-run
average costs and
long run marginal
cost.

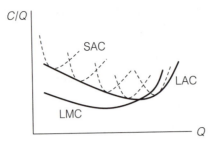

11.1.1 Average Costs and Returns to Scale

Elementary treatments of the cost function often focus on the relationship between C and Q, implicitly holding the factor prices p_1 and p_2 fixed. The long-run average cost curve given by

$$\frac{C}{Q} = \frac{c(p_1, p_2, Q)}{Q} \tag{11.7}$$

is normally thought to have the appearance of the curve LAC in Figure 11.1. As the figure indicates, the long-run curve is the outer envelope of a series of short-run average cost curves; the latter are defined by successive levels of some fixed factor. At any point in time, an individual firm may be subject to some degree of fixed costs and so may be operating at a point on its short-run average cost curve. However, empirical cost analysis typically estimates a cost function using data across firms in an industry, firms employing very different levels of the factors that, for any one of them in the short run, may be fixed. Hence, firm data are typically thought to trace out the industry's long-run cost function, and so it is this that is normally thought to be the appropriate construct for the empirical study of costs.[1]

Figure 11.1 also depicts long-run marginal costs, denoted LMC. This is the minimum additional cost of increasing output, assuming all factors are freely variable. The arithmetic of costs implies that as long as marginal cost is below average cost, average cost must be falling. Conversely, if marginal cost is above average cost, average cost must be increasing. It follows that LMC must pierce the minimum of the LAC curve, as shown in the figure.

Short-run average cost curves take their classic $\cup$ shape precisely because of the role of fixed factors. At low levels of output, costs tend to be dominated by the decline in average fixed costs, so that SAC initially falls. At higher levels of output, on the other hand, fixed factors imply capacity constraints and a cost function dominated by increasing average variable costs.

In the long run, average costs still follow a $\cup$ shape, but for quite different reasons involving returns to scale. Although, as we have seen in Chapter 7, returns

---

[1] Although see Berndt (1991, pp. 482–484) for references to the literature on short-run cost functions.

to scale are formally a property of the production function, they translate into parallel properties of the cost function. Intuitively, the reasons for this are easy to see. The same technological factors and the specialization and division of labor that give rise to economies of scale equivalently allow producers to reduce unit costs by expanding the scale of operation. Similarly, the same coordination problems and limits to efficient management that imply diseconomies of scale at some level of output equivalently imply increasing average costs in the long run.

More formally, recall from Section 7.1.1 that the most general characterization of the returns-to-scale properties of the production function is the elasticity of scale ϵ, which is defined as the percentage increase in output arising from a 1% increase in all factor inputs. Now consider the elasticity of total cost with respect to output, which is derivable from the cost function:

$$\frac{Q}{C}\frac{\partial C}{\partial Q} = \frac{\partial C/\partial Q}{C/Q} = \frac{\text{Marginal cost}}{\text{Average cost}}. \qquad (11.8)$$

It may be shown that this elasticity of cost is the reciprocal of the elasticity of scale:

$$\frac{Q}{C}\frac{\partial C}{\partial Q} = \frac{1}{\epsilon}. \qquad (11.9)$$

Hence, the elasticity of scale has a very direct relationship to average and marginal costs:

$$\epsilon = \frac{\text{Average cost}}{\text{Marginal cost}}.$$

It follows that

returns are increasing   if $\epsilon > 1$, LAC > LMC, and LAC is falling.
returns are constant   if $\epsilon = 1$, LAC = LMC, and LAC is constant.
returns are decreasing   if $\epsilon < 1$, LAC < LMC, and LAC is rising.

Costs When the Production Function Is Homogeneous

An even more direct relationship exists between the production and cost functions when the production function is homogeneous. Recall from Section 7.1.1 that a production function $Q = f(x_1, x_2)$ is homogeneous of degree ν if

$$\lambda^{\nu} Q = f(\lambda x_1, \lambda x_2);$$

ν is the degree of returns to scale.

It may be shown that in this circumstance the cost function specializes to the multiplicatively separable form

$$C = c(p_1, p_2)Q^{1/\nu}. \qquad (11.10)$$

Using the properties of logarithmic derivatives (that is, recalling the result (6.10)), the elasticity of cost is

$$\frac{Q}{C}\frac{\partial C}{\partial Q} = \frac{\partial \log C}{\partial \log Q} = \frac{1}{\nu}. \qquad (11.11)$$

Because we know from Section 7.1.1 that $\epsilon = \nu$ when a production function is homogeneous, the relationship (11.9) between the elasticity of cost and the elasticity of scale is verified.

This separable form for the cost function is particularly intuitive in the case of constant returns. Consider the cost of producing just one unit of output, which by (11.1) is $c(p_1, p_2, 1)$. As a notational matter, let us redefine this unit cost as $c(p_1, p_2)$. Then, under constant returns it should be possible to produce Q units by simply replicating the production of one unit Q times; the total cost would be

$$C = c(p_1, p_2)Q. \tag{11.12}$$

This is, of course, just the special case of (11.10) when $\nu = 1$.

This offers another way of seeing the link between average costs and returns to scale. If a firm has a production function that is homogeneous of degree 1 so that the cost function is of the form (11.12), average costs are:

$$\frac{C}{Q} = \frac{c(p_1, p_2, Q)}{Q} = \frac{c(p_1, p_2)Q}{Q} = c(p_1, p_2).$$

That is, average costs do not depend on the level of output; the average cost curve is horizontal.

Linear Homogeneity of the Cost Function

In contrast to features of the cost function that may or may not hold—such as particular returns-to-scale properties—it is useful to consider whether there are any more fundamental properties that the cost function should satisfy as a matter of logical consistency. Although there are several,[2] the one it is useful to focus on for the present discussion is that the cost function should be homogeneous of degree 1 in input prices. That is, it should have the property that

$$\lambda C = c(\lambda p_1, \lambda p_2, Q).$$

Thus a doubling of factor prices ($\lambda = 2$) should result in an exact doubling of the cost of producing some given level of output Q.

That this should be the case is easily seen from the accounting definition (11.2), because

$$\lambda p_1 x_1 + \lambda p_2 x_2 = \lambda(p_1 x_1 + p_2 x_2) = \lambda C.$$

Note in particular that a doubling of factor prices should not affect the cost-minimizing choice of factor inputs x_1 and x_2. Factor demands should depend on relative, not absolute, prices.[3]

---

[2] The others are, first, that cross-price effects should be symmetric and, second, that the function should be concave in input prices.

[3] You are asked to verify that this is true of Cobb-Douglas factor demands in Exercise 11.3 in the next section.

Functions that are homogeneous of degree 1 are often said to be **linear homogeneous,** and this is the term we use here in referring to this property of the cost function. It is of course different from—and unrelated to—any homogeneity of the production function.

Section 7.1.1 showed how Euler's theorem may be applied to homogeneous functions. The linear homogeneity of the cost function suggests that Euler's theorem may be fruitfully applied to it. Pursuing this idea requires, however, that a variety of preliminary topics be dealt with. We return to Euler's theorem in Section 11.3.

EXERCISES

11.1 Show how the result (11.11) is derived from (11.10).

11.2 A technology's **efficient scale** is the level of output at which its average cost curve reaches its minimum. Show that the minimum of the average cost curve (11.7) occurs at the value of Q for which the elasticity (11.8) equals 1.

11.2 | Deriving the Cost Function

These observations suggest there is a fairly strong link between a firm's production function and its cost function; it stands to reason that the cost of producing something will depend on the available production technology. To clarify this link, let us begin by considering the firm's most general objective—profit maximization. We then focus on the subsidiary goal of cost minimization.

11.2.1 Profit Maximization

It is assumed that a firm's ultimate objective is to maximize profits. Profits are revenues minus costs. For a firm employing two factors to produce a single output that sells for price p this is:

$$\text{Profits} = pQ - c(p_1, p_2, Q). \tag{11.13}$$

If a firm is a price taker in its product and factor markets, its problem is to choose the profit-maximizing level of output Q and the associated factor inputs x_1 and x_2, given the prices p_1, p_2, and p.

The profit-maximizing choice of factor inputs is described by the firm's (unconditional) factor demand functions

$$x_1^*(p_1, p_2, p), \tag{11.14a}$$
$$x_2^*(p_1, p_2, p). \tag{11.14b}$$

Note that these contrast with the conditional factor demands defined previously by (11.3). The difference between the two sets of demands is perhaps best explained by examining the elasticities that arise from each. Let us therefore take a brief detour into an examination of these elasticities.

FIGURE 11.2

Output and substi-
tution effects on the
demand for x_1 aris-
ing from a fall in its
price.

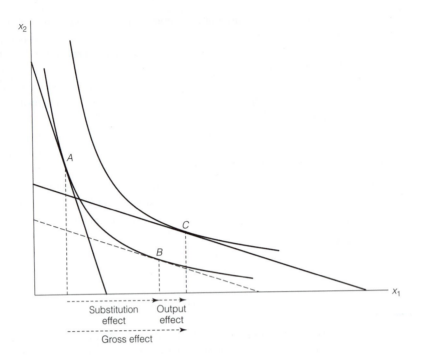

Gross versus Output-Constant Elasticities

The own-price elasticity of demand arising from these unconditional demands is

$$\epsilon_{ii}^* \equiv \frac{p_i}{x_i^*} \frac{\partial x_i^*}{\partial p_i}.$$

It describes the change in the firm's use of factor i arising from a 1% increase in its factor price p_i, when the firm is allowed to vary the employment of all factor inputs and the level of output produced.

   This decision is portrayed in Figure 11.2, which shows that a change in relative factor prices (described by a tilting of the isocost line) may result not only in a substitution between factors but also in operating on a different production isoquant (i.e., at a different level of output). A fall in p_1 results in a shift from point A to point C, which represents both an increase in output and a change in factor proportions. The **gross effect** on the employment of x_1 is the total of two effects. The **output effect** is the increased employment of x_1 arising from the fact that more output can now be produced at the same total cost as previously. The **substitution effect** is the change in the employment of x_1 arising from the fact that it is now relatively less expensive. This decomposition is portrayed by constructing an isocost line having the same slope as the new one, but tangent to the original isoquant. Point B is this point of tangency. The movement from A to B is the substitution effect and that from B to C is the output effect. In summary,

$$\text{Gross effect} = \text{Output effect} + \text{Substitution effect.} \tag{11.15}$$

In terms of elasticities, because ϵ_{ii}^* allows output to adjust to a new profit-maximizing level, it is this that measures the gross effect. The output-constant elasticity ϵ_{ii} defined earlier by (11.4) in terms of the conditional demand functions (11.3) measures only the substitution effect because these factor demands hold output fixed. It can be shown[4] that the relationship between the two corresponding to (11.15) is

$$\epsilon_{ii}^* = S_i \eta + \epsilon_{ii}, \tag{11.16}$$

where η denotes the elasticity of demand in the product market. Note that the output effect depends on just two things: product demand and the cost share. The difference between ϵ_{ii}^* and ϵ_{ii} is small if the firm faces an inelastic demand curve in its product market and if factor i accounts for a small share of total cost.

We emphasize this distinction between the two types of elasticities because our use of the cost function allows us to compute only output-constant elasticities such as ϵ_{ii}, as we see in Section 11.3. That analyses based on the cost function permit the calculation only of pure substitution effects rather than gross effects is a point that is often obscured in empirical applications of the cost function. These pure substitution effects are, however, the appropriate measure of factor demand elasticity in circumstances in which the firm is operating in an output-constant mode; that is, when the firm is expected to service an exogenously given demand for its product. An example is regulated utilities, in which a regulatory authority typically sets rates and the firm must then supply its product (telephone services, water, electricity, natural gas, etc.) to meet demand by consumers. In these circumstances, the firm has no ability to trade off output against product price by moving along the consumer demand curve it faces in its product market and similarly cannot adjust output in response to changing factor prices.

11.2.2 Cost Minimization

Returning to the problem of maximizing profit (11.13), it is apparent that it can be thought of as decomposing into two steps. The first is to chose a profit-maximizing level of output Q; the second is to produce this output at the lowest possible cost. It is this minimum cost that is given by the cost function.

To examine the nature of the cost function, then, let us focus on the second step of minimizing production cost. The firm's problem is to choose its factor inputs x_1 and x_2 so as to minimize the cost (11.2) of producing some level of output Q, given the available production technology. Formally,

$$\min \; p_1 x_1 + p_2 x_2 \quad \text{subject to} \quad f(x_1, x_2) = Q.$$

---

[4] The relationship between conditional and unconditional demands is the bread and butter of the microeconomic theory of factor demand, and there are many textbook treatments. One that is at about the same level of technical difficulty as the present discussion and that develops the intuition behind elasticity relationships such as (11.16) in some detail is Layard and Walters (1978). Equation (11.16) is found on p. 270 of that book (with some notational changes).

In Section 7.4.2, this problem is considered informally by using the diagrammatic interpretation given in Figure 7.8. That diagrammatic interpretation shows that the least-cost combination of factor inputs is associated with a point of tangency between the isocost line and the production isoquant. The substitution possibilities available to the firm are dependent on the nature of the production technology and are described by the elasticity of substitution.

The time has come to consider this problem more formally. To do so, however, we need to work in terms a particular choice of production technology. It is useful to emphasize that the Cobb-Douglas case is just one of several possible choices by presenting the derivation as an example.

EXAMPLE 1

The Cobb-Douglas production function is of the form

$$Q = \alpha_0 x_1^{\alpha_1} x_2^{\alpha_2}, \tag{11.17}$$

where returns to scale are governed by the degree of homogeneity

$$v = \alpha_1 + \alpha_2. \tag{11.18}$$

Derive the cost function.

SOLUTION

This is a constrained optimization problem that is most easily solved using the method of Lagrange multipliers.[5] The general form of the Lagrangian function is

$$L = p_1 x_1 + p_2 x_2 - \lambda(f(x_1, x_2) - Q).$$

Differentiating with respect to the choice variables x_1 and x_2 and the Lagrange multiplier λ yields the following first-order conditions, the last of which simply reproduces the constraint.

$$p_1 - \lambda \frac{\partial f(x_1, x_2)}{\partial x_1} = 0, \tag{11.19a}$$

$$p_2 - \lambda \frac{\partial f(x_1, x_2)}{\partial x_1} = 0, \tag{11.19b}$$

$$f(x_1, x_2) - Q = 0 \tag{11.19c}$$

As an interesting aside, note that the first two conditions may be rearranged as

$$p_1 = \lambda f_1,$$
$$p_2 = \lambda f_2,$$

where f_1 and f_2 are shorthand notation for the respective derivatives, the marginal products. Then the ratio of these two conditions is, after canceling λ,

$$\frac{p_1}{p_2} = \frac{f_1}{f_2}. \tag{11.20}$$

---

[5] Constrained optimization is a somewhat advanced technique with which you may not be familiar. If not, just scan the derivation to get a rough idea of how it proceeds. The important thing is the result—the Cobb-Douglas cost function.

This is simply the tangency condition (7.38) indicating that, at the optimum, the factor price ratio equals the marginal rate of technical substitution.

Pursuing our primary objective of deriving the cost function, when applied to the Cobb-Douglas production function the first-order conditions (11.19a) and (11.19b) may be written

$$p_1 = \lambda \alpha_0 \alpha_1 x_1^{\alpha_1 - 1} x_2^{\alpha_2},$$

$$p_2 = \lambda \alpha_0 \alpha_2 x_1^{\alpha_1} x_2^{\alpha_2 - 1}.$$

Multiplying these by x_1 and x_2, respectively, yields

$$p_1 x_1 = \lambda \alpha_1 \alpha_0 x_1^{\alpha_1} x_2^{\alpha_2} = \lambda \alpha_1 Q,$$

$$p_2 x_2 = \lambda \alpha_2 \alpha_0 x_1^{\alpha_1} x_2^{\alpha_2} = \lambda \alpha_2 Q.$$

Dividing by p_1 and p_2, respectively, shows that the optimal factor inputs may be expressed as

$$x_1 = \lambda \frac{\alpha_1}{p_1} Q, \tag{11.21a}$$

$$x_2 = \lambda \frac{\alpha_2}{p_2} Q. \tag{11.21b}$$

Substituting both of these into the production function (11.17):

$$\alpha_0 \left(\lambda \frac{\alpha_1}{p_1} Q \right)^{\alpha_1} \left(\lambda \frac{\alpha_2}{p_2} Q \right)^{\alpha_2} = Q.$$

It is now possible to solve for λ:

$$\lambda = \left[\frac{1}{\alpha_0} \left(\frac{p_1}{\alpha_1} \right)^{\alpha_1} \left(\frac{p_2}{\alpha_2} \right)^{\alpha_2} Q^{1-\nu} \right]^{1/\nu}.$$

(Recall the notation (11.18).) This may be used to reexpress the optimal factor inputs (11.21) as

$$x_1(p_1, p_2, Q) = (\alpha_0 \alpha_1^{\alpha_1} \alpha_2^{\alpha_2})^{-1/\nu} \alpha_1 p_1^{(\alpha_1/\nu)-1} p_2^{\alpha_2/\nu} Q^{1/\nu}, \tag{11.22a}$$

$$x_2(p_1, p_2, Q) = (\alpha_0 \alpha_1^{\alpha_1} \alpha_2^{\alpha_2})^{-1/\nu} \alpha_2 p_1^{\alpha_1/\nu} p_2^{(\alpha_2/\nu)-1} Q^{1/\nu}, \tag{11.22b}$$

which are the conditional factor demand functions (11.3).

Substituting these into the cost identity (11.2), it must be that the minimum cost of producing Q is

$$c(p_1, p_2, Q) = p_1 x_1(p_1, p_2, Q) + p_2 x_2(p_1, p_2, Q).$$

Defining the summary notation

$$\psi \equiv \nu(\alpha_0 \alpha_1^{\alpha_1} \alpha_2^{\alpha_2})^{-1/\nu}, \tag{11.23}$$

the most convenient expression to which this cost function reduces is

$$c(p_1, p_2, Q) = \psi p_1^{\alpha_1/\nu} p_2^{\alpha_2/\nu} Q^{1/\nu}. \tag{11.24}$$

This is the Cobb-Douglas cost function.

11.2.3 Features of the Cobb-Douglas Cost Function

Although the derivation is a long one and the result (11.24) perhaps somewhat intimidating, inspection reveals that this cost function has several fascinating features.

Returns to Scale and Average Costs

Note first that it is of the separable form (11.10):

$$c(p_1, p_2, Q) = \psi p_1^{\alpha_1/\nu} p_2^{\alpha_2/\nu} Q^{1/\nu} = c(p_1, p_2) Q^{1/\nu},$$

confirming this feature of cost functions that are dual to homogeneous production functions. In the special case of constant returns to scale in which $\nu = \alpha_1 + \alpha_2 = 1$, (11.24) reduces to

$$c(p_1, p_2, Q) = \psi p_1^{\alpha_1} p_2^{\alpha_2} Q = c(p_1, p_2) Q,$$

which is of the separable form (11.12).

The Cobb-Douglas cost function (11.24) has, using (11.11), an elasticity of scale of

$$\left(\frac{\partial \log C}{\partial \log Q} \right)^{-1} = \left(\frac{1}{\nu} \right)^{-1} = \nu.$$

This confirms what, on the basis of our derivation of the Cobb-Douglas cost function, we already know: $\nu = \alpha_1 + \alpha_2$ is the degree of homogeneity of the production function.

The average cost curve (11.7) takes the form

$$\frac{C}{Q} = \frac{\psi p_1^{\alpha_1/\nu} p_2^{\alpha_2/\nu} Q^{1/\nu}}{Q} = c(p_1, p_2) Q^{(1-\nu)/\nu}.$$

As we have just noted, in the presence of constant returns ($\nu = 1$ so that Q vanishes) this reduces to the horizontal AC curve $c(p_1, p_2)$. Under increasing returns it is the case that $\nu > 1$, the exponent $(1-\nu)/\nu$ is negative, and average costs are decreasing in output. Finally, if there are decreasing returns, then $\nu < 1$, the exponent $(1-\nu)/\nu$ is positive, and average costs increase with Q.

Loglinearity and Linear Homogeneity

Another remarkable feature of the Cobb-Douglas cost function is that it is worthy of its name; not only has it been derived from its namesake production function, but in addition it possesses the same characteristic functional form. One implication of this, as we know from Chapter 6, is loglinearity; (11.24) may be transformed to

$$\log C = \log \psi + \frac{1}{\nu} \log Q + \frac{\alpha_1}{\nu} \log p_1 + \frac{\alpha_2}{\nu} \log p_2. \tag{11.25}$$

Because this linear equation is estimable as a regression model, it is natural to relabel the coefficients:

$$\log C = \alpha + \beta \log Q + \gamma_1 \log p_1 + \gamma_2 \log p_2. \qquad (11.26)$$

This reparameterization defines the new set of parameters α, β, γ_1, and γ_2, the parameters of the loglinear cost function. Their relationship to the parameters of the original production function (11.17) is

$$\alpha = \log[(\alpha_1 + \alpha_2)(\alpha_0 \alpha_1^{\alpha_1} \alpha_2^{\alpha_2})^{-1/(\alpha_1 + \alpha_2)}], \qquad (11.27a)$$

$$\beta = \frac{1}{\alpha_1 + \alpha_2}, \qquad (11.27b)$$

$$\gamma_1 = \frac{\alpha_1}{\alpha_1 + \alpha_2}, \qquad (11.27c)$$

$$\gamma_2 = \frac{\alpha_2}{\alpha_1 + \alpha_2}. \qquad (11.27d)$$

However, note that γ_1 and γ_2 are not really independent parameters: by (11.27c) and (11.27d), they must add to 1:

$$\gamma_1 + \gamma_2 = 1. \qquad (11.28)$$

What is the economic meaning of this restriction? Consider multiplying factor prices by some constant λ in the cost function (11.24):

$$\psi(\lambda p_1)^{\gamma_1} (\lambda p_2)^{\gamma_2} Q^\beta = \lambda^{\gamma_1 + \gamma_2} \psi p_1^{\gamma_1} p_2^{\gamma_2} Q^\beta = \lambda^{\gamma_1 + \gamma_2} c(p_1, p_2, Q) = \lambda^{\gamma_1 + \gamma_2} C.$$

Evidently the restriction $\gamma_1 + \gamma_2 = 1$ requires that total cost be factored by the same multiple. But this is simply the property of linear homogeneity discussed in Section 11.1.1.

Although linear homogeneity is built into the Cobb-Douglas cost function (11.24), it must be imposed on its reparameterized loglinear version (11.26). In the terminology of Section 10.3, the parameter correspondence (11.27) is overidentifying; the restricted-form parameters of (11.25) are overdetermined in terms of the unrestricted form (11.26). This overidentification is embodied in the homogeneity restriction, which may be imposed on (11.26) by rewriting it as, say,

$$\log C = \alpha + \beta \log Q + \gamma_1 \log p_1 + (1 - \gamma_1) \log p_2$$

$$\Leftrightarrow \quad \log C - \log p_2 = \alpha + \beta \log Q + \gamma_1 (\log p_1 - \log p_2). \qquad (11.29)$$

Comparing the parameters of this restricted model with those of (11.25), the relationship is simply (11.27a)–(11.27c). This relationship is exactly identifying—the parameters of the production function $(\alpha_0, \alpha_1, \alpha_2)$ are uniquely determined in relation to the parameters $(\alpha, \beta, \gamma_1)$ of the homogeneity-constrained cost function.

Because the linear homogeneity restriction is an overidentifying restriction it may be tested. It thus serves as a check on the legitimacy of the empirical exercise; something is seriously wrong with any estimated cost function that fails to satisfy this fundamental prediction of microeconomic theory. This is in contrast to other features of the cost function—such as constant returns to scale—that might or might not hold.

Cost Shares

Finally, the conditional demand functions (11.22) may be used to show that the γ_i parameters of the cost function have an interpretation as the cost shares. Recall from (11.5) that the share of factor i in total cost C is defined to be

$$S_i = \frac{p_i x_i}{C} = \frac{p_i x_i (p_1, p_2, Q)}{c(p_1, p_2, Q)}. \tag{11.30}$$

Substituting in the conditional factor demands (11.22) and the cost function (11.24), in the Cobb-Douglas case these cost shares reduce to

$$S_i = \gamma_i. \tag{11.31}$$

Another way of interpreting the linear homogeneity restriction $\sum_i \gamma_i = 1$ is, then, that it requires that the estimated model be consistent with the accounting identity (11.6) that the cost shares sum to 1.

This interpretation of the γ_i parameters suggests a way of estimating them that is an alternative to using the cost function. Given a series of observations on the cost share of a factor i (across firms in an industry, say), these data may be viewed as being generated by the statistical model

$$S_i = \gamma_i + \varepsilon_i, \tag{11.32}$$

which simply adds a disturbance to (11.31). But this is just the model (2.15) in Chapter 2, where γ_i corresponds to μ.[6] As we know from our discussion of that very simple statistical model, the least squares estimator of γ_i is just the sample mean $\bar{S}_i$ of the observed cost share series.

The desirability of proceeding in this way depends on two considerations: the available data and the economic questions that are ultimately of interest. By the definition (11.30), obtaining cost share series requires data on factor inputs x_i (but avoids the need for output Q required in the estimation of the cost function). Thus, the data requirements for estimating (11.32) are somewhat different from those of the cost function.

With respect to the economic issues at stake, we find in Section 11.3 that the primary interest of the estimated γ_i is that they yield demand elasticities. If this is the ultimate purpose of the analysis, then estimation of the cost share equations (11.32) is all that is needed. But note that knowledge of the γ_i does not allow us to solve for the parameters of the production function, which are underidentified in the absence of (11.27b). (Although estimates of the γ_i tell us the ratios α_i / ν, from these alone it is not possible to deduce estimates of ν or the individual α_i.) Furthermore, without an estimate of ν it is not possible to say anything about returns to scale. Because returns to scale relate fundamentally to how costs vary as output varies, learning about the returns-to-scale properties of

---

[6] Note that our use of the subscript i has changed. In all other chapters of this book, i indexes observations in the sample, whereas in this chapter the indexing of sample observations is suppressed and left implicit. Instead here i indexes different factors of production (or, in Section 11.6, consumer goods), which is the standard notation in all analyses of factor inputs.

the production technology requires that we have data on output and work directly with the cost function.

The Duality of Cost and Production

The one-to-one correspondence between the cost and production functions is a remarkable result. It means that, given values for the parameters of the cost function, we may work backward and obtain the parameters of the production function. Equally remarkable is that microeconomists have established that this correspondence exists for *any* production technology—the Cobb-Douglas case is merely one illustration.

> Given a cost function we can "solve for" a technology that could have generated that cost function. This means that the cost function contains essentially the same information that the production function contains. Any concept defined in terms of the properties of the production function has a "dual" definition in terms of the properties of the cost function and vice versa. (Varian 1992, p. 81)

The problem of minimizing cost is said to be dual to the primal problem of maximizing profit.

This duality of cost and production was first studied systematically by Shephard (1953); the associated theory was subsequently developed by a number of microeconomists, notably Diewert (1971, 1974). Although production analysis was the first area in economics in which the existence of a dual relationship was recognized, it has since been found that the concept of duality has much broader applicability.

> The duality between seemingly different ways of representing economic behavior is useful in the study of consumer theory, welfare economics, and many other areas in economics. Many relationships that are difficult to understand when looked at directly become simple, or even trivial, when looked at using the tools of duality. (Varian 1992, p. 81)

Although duality is of enormous interest purely from the perspective of microeconomic theory, it is particularly important for the empirical implementation of that theory. Indeed, the development of duality was to a large extent motivated by empirical considerations. In the next section we see how to use an estimated Cobb-Douglas cost function to recover not only estimates of the parameters of the production function, but also the returns-to-scale properties of that production function and factor demand elasticities.

EXERCISES

11.3 In the discussion of linear homogeneity in Section 11.1.1, it is asserted that factor demands should depend only on relative prices. Show that the Cobb-Douglas factor demands (11.22) do in fact depend on p_1 and p_2 only through their ratio p_1/p_2.

11.4 Show how (11.30) reduces to (11.31).

11.5 In our discussion of the estimation of the share equations (11.32) it is noted that the indexing of sample observations is left implicit. Let us now make it explicit by supposing that cost shares are observed across firms indexed by $t = 1, \ldots, n$, so that S_{it} denotes the share of factor i in the costs of firm t. (As always, n denotes the sample size and there are $i = 1, \ldots, k$ factors of production.) The share equation (11.32) can therefore be written as

$$S_{it} = \gamma_i + \varepsilon_{it},$$

which, as we have noted, is just the familiar model (2.15) of Chapter 2. The least squares estimator of γ_i is the sample mean $\overline{S}_i$, which may now be written explicitly as

$$\hat{\gamma}_i = \overline{S}_i = \frac{1}{n} \sum_{t=1}^{n} S_{it}.$$

Show that these $\hat{\gamma}_i$ $(i = 1, \ldots, k)$ must satisfy the linear homogeneity restriction; that is, show that

$$\sum_{i=1}^{k} \hat{\gamma}_i = 1.$$

11.3   Using the Cost Function

Because all economically relevant aspects of the firm's technology are embodied in the cost function, it may be used to investigate the same questions that are associated with a production function.

Consider the estimation of the homogeneity-constrained Cobb-Douglas cost function (11.29) as a linear regression. The estimation results may be used to study the following aspects of the production process.

Returns to Scale and Output Elasticities

One example is returns to scale. Comparing the estimable Cobb-Douglas cost function (11.26) with the restricted form (11.25), the relevant parameter correspondence is (11.27):

$$\beta = \frac{1}{\nu} = \frac{1}{\alpha_1 + \alpha_2}.$$

It is evident that the constant-returns restriction $\nu = \alpha_1 + \alpha_2 = 1$ translates into the hypothesis $\beta = 1$. Increasing returns to scale implies $\beta < 1$, decreasing returns the opposite.

Going further, the correspondence (11.27) may be used to solve for the parameters of the production function. As we know from Chapter 7, the exponents in the Cobb-Douglas production function (11.17) have the interpretation as output elasticities. Recall that this is easy to see from the loglinearity of the function and the result (6.10) that elasticities are logarithmic derivatives:

$$\frac{\partial \log Q}{\partial \log x_i} = \alpha_i.$$

Demand Elasticities

So far we have focused on the role of output Q in the cost function. However, in the empirical study of production very often interest focuses on aspects of factor use—specifically, the price responsiveness of the demand for factors and the degree of substitutability between them. If a construction trades union is able to negotiate artificially high wages, how will this affect the employment of its members? The answer depends on the own-price elasticity of demand. How about the employment of non-union trades? This depends on the cross-price elasticity.

Answering these questions requires knowledge of factor demand equations such as (11.3). One reason the cost function is so important is that it turns out that these can be derived directly from it. In most practical contexts, firms employ more than just two factors of production. It is now useful to recognize this explicitly and specify the cost function as

$$C = c(p_1, p_2, \ldots, p_k, Q).$$ (11.33)

That factor demands can be derived directly from the cost function is a result known as Shephard's lemma.

SHEPHARD'S LEMMA. *The conditional demand for a factor x_i is given by*

$$x_i(p_1, \ldots, p_k, Q) = \frac{\partial C}{\partial p_i} \equiv C_i.$$

A lemma is the mathematical term for a result that is primarily useful as a stepping-stone to the derivation of other results. This is the role of Shephard's lemma, which is the single most important tool in using the cost function to study factor usage. It tells us that the derived demand for a factor, which is in general a function of its own price and the price of other factors and is conditional on the level of output Q, may be obtained simply as the derivative of the cost function with respect to the price of that factor. The notation C_i serves as convenient shorthand for this derivative.

EXAMPLE 2 | Derive the conditional factor demands for the Cobb-Douglas cost function (11.24).

SOLUTION | Applying Shephard's lemma,

$$x_1(p_1, p_2, Q) = \frac{\partial C}{\partial p_1} = \psi \frac{\alpha_1}{v} p_1^{(\alpha_1/v)-1} p_2^{\alpha_2/v} Q^{1/v},$$

$$x_2(p_1, p_2, Q) = \frac{\partial C}{\partial p_2} = \psi \frac{\alpha_2}{v} p_1^{\alpha_1/v} p_2^{(\alpha_2/v)-1} Q^{1/v}.$$

These are the conditional demands derived previously as equations (11.22).

Having obtained the factor demands from the cost function using Shephard's lemma in this way, it is now possible to derive the elasticities that characterize the price responsiveness of factor usage. The own-price elasticity of demand for factor i is defined to be

$$\epsilon_{ii} \equiv \frac{p_i}{x_i} \frac{\partial x_i}{\partial p_i}.$$

Downward-sloping factor demands imply that this should be negative; if demand is inelastic it is less than 1 in absolute value. The cross-price elasticity describing the change in demand for factor i arising from a 1% change in the price of factor j is

$$\epsilon_{ij} \equiv \frac{p_j}{x_i} \frac{\partial x_i}{\partial p_j}.$$

Factors are described as substitutes or complements according to the sign of their cross-price elasticity:[7]

$$i \text{ and } j \text{ are substitutes} \quad \text{if } \epsilon_{ij} > 0.$$
$$i \text{ and } j \text{ are complements} \quad \text{if } \epsilon_{ij} < 0.$$

EXAMPLE 3 | Derive the own- and cross-price elasticities for the Cobb-Douglas factor demands of Example 2.

SOLUTION | Although the formal elasticity expressions are as just given, it is convenient to use their equivalence to the logarithmic derivative (6.10). This allows us to exploit the loglinearity of the Cobb-Douglas factor demands and see easily that the own-price elasticities are

$$\epsilon_{11} = \frac{\partial \log x_1}{\partial \log p_1} = \frac{\alpha_1}{v} - 1 = \gamma_1 - 1, \tag{11.34a}$$

$$\epsilon_{22} = \frac{\partial \log x_2}{\partial \log p_2} = \frac{\alpha_2}{v} - 1 = \gamma_2 - 1. \tag{11.34b}$$

Similarly, the cross-price elasticities are

$$\epsilon_{12} = \frac{\partial \log x_1}{\partial \log p_2} = \frac{\alpha_2}{v} = \gamma_2, \tag{11.35a}$$

$$\epsilon_{21} = \frac{\partial \log x_2}{\partial \log p_1} = \frac{\alpha_1}{v} = \gamma_1. \tag{11.35b}$$

[7] The distinction between gross and output-constant elasticities emphasized in Section 11.2 means that these definitions of substitutability and complementarity—or, for that matter, whether ϵ_{ii} is elastic or inelastic—are somewhat arbitrary. Anticipating terminology to be introduced in the next section, the definitions offered here are of **Allen** substitutability or complementarity. Analogous definitions in terms of gross demand elasticities would be of *gross* substitutability or complementarity. The two definitions are, of course, not equivalent. For example, a large enough (negative) output effect could mean that Allen substitutes are gross complements.

These results imply several important features of the Cobb-Douglas elasticities. Recall first that the α_i exponents in the Cobb-Douglas production function (11.17) must be positive. Hence, $\gamma_i = \alpha_i/v = \alpha_i/(\alpha_1 + \alpha_2)$ must be a positive fraction. It follows that, first, the own-price elasticities are negative fractions, so that Cobb-Douglas factor demands must be downward sloping and price inelastic. Second, the cross-price elasticities are positive, so that the two factors are substitutes; as we know from our study of factor substitution in Chapter 7, this is as it should be when there are just two factors of production.

Note that cross-price elasticities are *not* symmetric:

$$\epsilon_{ij} \neq \epsilon_{ji}.$$

There is no reason why the percentage change in capital employed in response to a 1% change in the wage would be the same as the change in labor employed as a result of a 1% change in the rental price of capital. This is reflected in our Cobb-Douglas results in which, in terms of the version of the cost function (11.29) to be estimated, there is no reason for γ_1 and γ_2 to be the same. What *is* true is that, because of their association with the cost function via Shephard's lemma, the associated partial derivatives are symmetric:

$$\frac{\partial x_i}{\partial p_j} = \frac{\partial C_i}{\partial p_j} = C_{ij} = \frac{\partial^2 C}{\partial p_i \partial p_j} = \frac{\partial^2 C}{\partial p_j \partial p_i} = C_{ji} = \frac{\partial C_j}{\partial p_i} = \frac{\partial x_j}{\partial p_i}.$$

The middle equality is the standard result in calculus that the order of differentiation is irrelevant (Young's theorem).

Consequently, although the cross-price elasticities are not symmetric, they are related by

$$\epsilon_{ij}\frac{x_i}{p_j} = \epsilon_{ji}\frac{x_j}{p_i}.$$

Rearranging and dividing both sides by total costs C yields the relationship

$$\epsilon_{ij}\frac{x_i p_i}{C} = \epsilon_{ij} S_i = \epsilon_{ji} S_j = \epsilon_{ji}\frac{x_j p_j}{C}, \tag{11.36}$$

so that cross-price elasticities are related symmetrically by their cost shares. Because cost shares must be positive, it follows that ϵ_{ij} and ϵ_{ji}, although not equal, must have the same sign. If capital is a substitute for labor, then labor cannot be a complement to capital.

Consider factor i's own-price elasticity ϵ_{ii} and its cross-price elasticities with all other goods, ϵ_{ij} $(j \neq i)$. It turns out that a certain dependency exists between these elasticities. We have noted that a cost function must be homogeneous of degree 1 in factor prices (the linear homogeneity property of Section 11.1.1) and, from Section 7.1.1, that Euler's theorem applies to homogeneous functions. Let us apply Euler's theorem to the cost function in order to establish the following result.

Result 11.1 *A factor's own- and cross-price elasticities sum to 0:*

$$\sum_j \epsilon_{ij} = 0. \tag{11.37}$$

Proof:

Because the cost function is homogeneous of degree 1 in factor prices, Euler's theorem tells us that

$$C = p_1 C_1 + p_2 C_2 + \cdots + p_k C_k = \sum_j p_j C_j. \tag{11.38}$$

Dividing through by C and using Shephard's lemma shows that

$$\sum_j \frac{p_j x_j}{C} = \sum_j S_j = 1,$$

which merely reproduces the accounting identity (11.6) that the cost shares must sum to 1. Consider, however, differentiating (11.38) again with respect to p_i:

$$C_i = \sum_{j \neq i} p_j C_{ij} + C_i + p_i C_{ii}.$$

This may be rewritten

$$\sum_j p_j C_{ij} = \sum_j p_j \frac{\partial x_i}{\partial p_j} = 0.$$

Dividing through by x_i yields (11.37). ☐

EXAMPLE 4 Show that the Cobb-Douglas elasticities derived in Example 3 for the two-factor case satisfy the dependency (11.37).

SOLUTION For factor 1

$$\sum_j \epsilon_{1j} = \epsilon_{11} + \epsilon_{12} = (\gamma_1 - 1) + \gamma_2 = 0,$$

and for factor 2

$$\sum_j \epsilon_{2j} = \epsilon_{21} + \epsilon_{22} = \gamma_1 + (\gamma_2 - 1) = 0,$$

both by linear homogeneity (11.28).

Hence, yet another interpretation of linear homogeneity is that it requires the dependency (11.37) to hold.

This dependency among a factor's own- and cross-price elasticities has some important implications. Because the own-price elasticity ϵ_{ii} must be negative (demand curves slope downward), in the two-factor case it follows that the cross-price elasticity must be positive: the factors must be substitutes. For more than two factors, however, not all of them need be substitutes; it is possible to have some negative cross-price elasticities and still have (11.37) hold. At the same time, not all factors can be complements. At least two must be substitutes—that is, at least one of the ϵ_{ij} must be positive for (11.37) to be satisfied.

Deficiencies of the Cobb-Douglas Cost Function

The features of the Cobb-Douglas cost function are, then, quite remarkable. From the estimation of the homogeneity-constrained regression model (11.29) we may (1) solve uniquely for the parameters of the companion production function, (2) investigate the returns-to-scale properties of the production technology by obtaining an estimate of the elasticity of scale and testing hypotheses about returns to scale, and (3) obtain estimated own- and cross-price elasticities of demand. All this is possible by merely estimating one multiple regression. In addition, the restriction of linear homogeneity is testable.

However, what from one perspective is a strength is from another a weakness. Because the Cobb-Douglas cost function accomplishes all this with just a few parameters, the result is that it must impose restrictions on economic behavior unrelated to optimizing activity or inherently plausible features of technology. We already know this to be the case for the Cobb-Douglas production function: It imposes a unitary elasticity of substitution between factors.

In the same way, the Cobb-Douglas cost function imposes restrictions that may not be appropriate. Although it has a parameter capturing returns to scale, it imposes a common elasticity of scale at all output levels. The average cost curve must be either falling ($\epsilon > 1$), horizontal ($\epsilon = 1$), or rising ($\epsilon < 1$), but not all three; that is, a $\cup$-shaped LAC curve is not permitted.

Patterns of factor demand and substitutability are also limited. Own-price effects require that factor demands be price inelastic. (Recall that according to (11.27c) and (11.27d) the elasticities (11.34) must be fractional.) Cross-price elasticities must be positive, so factors must be substitutes. Although not objectionable in the case of two factors where this should be the case, for three or more factors there is no basis for precluding some factors from being complements.

Another way of seeing that the Cobb-Douglas cost function imposes a somewhat artificial pattern of factor demand and substitution is to recall the cost share equations (11.31):

$$S_i = \frac{p_i x_i}{C} = \gamma_i .$$

These say that the Cobb-Douglas model treats the share of factor i in total costs as a fixed value, regardless of its price. If wages increase, then the employment of labor will decline as firms substitute toward capital, but in such a way that this more expensive labor continues to account for exactly the same proportion of total costs as previously. Although the Cobb-Douglas cost function imposes this particular pattern of substitutability, there is no reason to believe that this correctly describes actual substitution possibilities.

EXERCISES

11.6 In general the cost function is $C = c(p_1, \ldots, p_k, Q)$. Show that

$$\frac{\partial \log C}{\partial \log p_j} = S_j.$$

11.7 In the next section the Hicks-Allen partial elasticity of substitution is defined as

$$\sigma_{ij} = \frac{1}{S_j} \epsilon_{ij}.$$

Another frequently encountered expression for this elasticity is

$$\sigma_{ij} = \frac{C_{ij} C}{C_i C_j}.$$

Establish the equivalence of the two expressions.

11.4   Application: Returns to Scale in Electricity Generation

In a study using cost data from electric power generation, Marc Nerlove (1963) was the first to use the dual approach to investigating a production technology. Nerlove's data were on steam generation plants where, in addition to capital and labor, fuel is an important component of costs. Hence, three factors of production apply in this industry, and the variables may be summarized as follows.

C Production costs

Q Output of electricity

x_1 Labor input
x_2 Capital input

x_3 Fuel input

p_1 Wage rate

p_2 Price of capital

p_3 Price of fuel

Let us quickly recapitulate the essentials of our analysis of the cost function, generalizing it to the three-factor case. The Cobb-Douglas production function is

$$Q = \alpha_0 x_1^{\alpha_1} x_2^{\alpha_2} x_3^{\alpha_3}, \tag{11.39}$$

where the returns to scale are governed by the degree of homogeneity

$$v = \alpha_1 + \alpha_2 + \alpha_3.$$

From the general discussion of homogeneous production functions in Section 7.1.1, we know that this degree of homogeneity is also the elasticity of scale: $\epsilon = v$.

The companion cost function is

$$c(p_1, p_2, p_3, Q) = \psi p_1^{\alpha_1/v} p_2^{\alpha_2/v} p_3^{\alpha_3/v} Q^{1/v},$$

which is loglinear:

$$\log C = \log \psi + \frac{1}{\nu} \log Q + \frac{\alpha_1}{\nu} \log p_1 + \frac{\alpha_2}{\nu} \log p_2 + \frac{\alpha_3}{\nu} \log p_3. \qquad (11.40)$$

Reparameterizing in the form that may be estimated as a multiple regression, this is

$$\log C = \alpha + \beta \log Q + \gamma_1 \log p_1 + \gamma_2 \log p_2 + \gamma_3 \log p_3. \qquad (11.41)$$

The correspondence between the slopes of the two models is[8]

$$\beta = \frac{1}{\alpha_1 + \alpha_2 + \alpha_3}, \qquad (11.42a)$$

$$\gamma_1 = \frac{\alpha_1}{\alpha_1 + \alpha_2 + \alpha_3}, \qquad (11.42b)$$

$$\gamma_2 = \frac{\alpha_2}{\alpha_1 + \alpha_2 + \alpha_3}, \qquad (11.42c)$$

$$\gamma_3 = \frac{\alpha_3}{\alpha_1 + \alpha_2 + \alpha_3}. \qquad (11.42d)$$

As stated, these are overidentifying: Estimates of the unrestricted-form coefficients β, γ_1, γ_2, γ_3 yield multiple implied estimates of the α_i. An exactly identifying relationship between the coefficients of the unrestricted cost function (11.41) and the production function requires that we impose the restriction implicit in (11.42b)–(11.42d),

$$\gamma_1 + \gamma_2 + \gamma_3 = 1,$$

which is the linear homogeneity restriction.

Returns to Scale

The parameter of the estimable cost function (11.41) that recovers the returns-to-scale properties of the production function is

$$\beta = \frac{1}{\nu}.$$

Because $\epsilon = \nu$, an estimate of the elasticity of scale may be obtained as the reciprocal of the estimate of β. Similarly, hypotheses about ϵ translate into testable hypotheses on β; for example, the hypothesis of decreasing returns, $\epsilon < 1$, corresponds to $\beta > 1$.

Demand Elasticities

Paralleling the results in Example 3, the own-price elasticities of demand are

$$\epsilon_{ii} = \gamma_i - 1$$

and the cross-price elasticities are

$$\epsilon_{ij} = \gamma_j \qquad (i \neq j).$$

---

[8]   The correspondence between the intercepts simply represents an exactly identifying relationship between α and the parameter α_0 of the production function, analogous to (11.27a).

Note that these satisfy the dependency (11.37): For each factor i

$$\sum_j \epsilon_{ij} = \gamma_1 + \gamma_2 + \gamma_3 - 1 = 0,$$

by linear homogeneity.

Elasticities of Substitution

In Section 7.4.2 the elasticity of substitution σ was introduced in the context of two factors of production, there described as capital and labor. For factors x_1 and x_2 having marginal products f_1 and f_2 and prices p_1 and p_2, σ is defined by

$$\sigma = \frac{f_2/f_1}{x_1/x_2} \frac{\mathrm{d}(x_1/x_2)}{\mathrm{d}(f_2/f_1)} = \frac{p_2/p_1}{x_1/x_2} \frac{\mathrm{d}(x_1/x_2)}{\mathrm{d}(p_2/p_1)}. \tag{11.43}$$

This is just equation (7.39).

Although this is a natural measure of substitutability when there are just two factors of production, it is problematic in the case of more than two factors. The problem is that it measures the ability to substitute x_1 for x_2, implicitly holding all other factors fixed. But the ability to substitute capital for labor in the face of an increase in relative wages may well depend on the extent to which other factors can also be substituted for labor.

A solution to this problem lies closer at hand than might be apparent; for this broader concept of substitutability has already been captured in the cross-price elasticity ϵ_{ij}, which describes the effect on x_i of an increase in p_j by a firm that is simultaneously adjusting its employment of all other factors, consistent with cost minimization. Hence, an elasticity of substitution alternative to (11.43) may be defined as a transformation of ϵ_{ij}. The Hicks-Allen partial elasticity of substitution, often simply called the **Allen elasticity,** does just this, transforming ϵ_{ij} by the reciprocal of j's cost share:

$$\sigma_{ij} = \frac{1}{S_j} \epsilon_{ij} \qquad (i \neq j).$$

Notice that, rearranging (11.36), these are symmetric:

$$\sigma_{ij} = \sigma_{ji}.$$

This is in contrast to what we have seen is true of the cross-price elasticities themselves. In the case of just two factors of production, it may be shown that the Allen elasticity reduces to σ defined by (11.43).

In the special case of Cobb-Douglas technologies, we know from Chapter 7 that substitution possibilities are restricted. Recall first that we have found that $\epsilon_{ij} = \gamma_j$ and the cost shares have the interpretation that $S_j = \gamma_j$. Consequently, the Allen elasticities are

$$\sigma_{ij} = \frac{1}{S_j} \epsilon_{ij} = \frac{1}{\gamma_j} \gamma_j = 1,$$

consistent with what we found to be true in Section 7.4.2 in the case of just two factors.

EXERCISES

Nerlove's data set is available in the file **nerlove.dat**. It consists of observations on 145 steam-driven electricity generation plants in 1955. The variables are as follows.

plant	Plant number.
costs	Total production costs (millions of dollars).
kwh	Electricity generation (billions of kilowatt-hours).
pl	Wage rate (dollars per hour).
pk	Capital price (index).
pf	Fuel price (cents per million BTU).

The variables costs and kwh were first examined in Figure 3.1 and have been studied previously in Sections 4.10, 6.6, and 8.8, in the file **nerlove1.dat**.

11.8 **nerlove.dat** Estimate Nerlove's cost function (11.41) unrestricted and then restricted to satisfy linear homogeneity.

(a) Nerlove reported an R^2 of 0.931 for the restricted model. How close do you come to replicating this?

(b) Use your results to test the linear homogeneity hypothesis. Do you judge the data to be consistent with this restriction?

11.9 **nerlove.dat** Use your estimation results for the homogeneity-constrained cost function to investigate the following features of the U.S. electric power generation industry in 1955.

(a) *Returns to scale.*
i.   Nerlove deduced an estimate of the degree of returns to scale of $\hat{v} = 1.39$. How does yours compare? Do returns to scale appear to be increasing, constant, or decreasing?

ii. Perform a test of the hypothesis of constant returns to scale. Is this hypothesis rejected by the data?

(b) *Elasticities of output.* Use the parameter correspondence (11.42) to solve for estimates of α_1, α_2, and α_3. The values Nerlove presented for these elasticities were 0.78, −0.00, and 0.61. How close do you come to replicating his figures? Is there any aspect of these results that you find unsatisfactory?

(c) *Own-price demand elasticities.* What are the own-price elasticities of demand ϵ_{ii} for each of the three factors? Do these suggest that the factor demand curves are downward sloping? Is there any aspect of these results that you find unsatisfactory?

(d) *Cross-price demand elasticities.* What are the cross-price elasticities of demand ϵ_{ij}? Present them, along with the own-price elasticities, in a matrix of the following form.

$$\begin{bmatrix} \epsilon_{LL} & \epsilon_{LK} & \epsilon_{LF} \\ \epsilon_{KL} & \epsilon_{KK} & \epsilon_{KF} \\ \epsilon_{FL} & \epsilon_{FK} & \epsilon_{FF} \end{bmatrix} \qquad (11.44)$$

i.   According to your results, which factors are substitutes and which are complements? Are any of these conclusions ones that you would not necessarily be willing to accept at face value? Why?

ii. What is the meaning of the condition (11.37) in terms of the entries in your matrix?

11.10 **nerlove.dat** Given the troublesome nature of the capital variable you have noted, we should ask why it seems problematic. Recall first the discussion at the end of Section 7.4.2 in which it is observed that data on stock variables such as capital are often more difficult to obtain reliably than that on flow variables such as labor and fuel. This is particularly true in the case of capital because most firms own most of their capital stock; hence, there is no directly observable "price" of capital services, as there would be if capital were rented. These considerations call into question the quality of Nerlove's capital price index. The best measure of a firm's cost of capital may be the interest rate at which it can borrow; in the case of electric utilities, all may face very close to the same borrowing rate.

(a) Suppose, then, that it is in fact the case that all firms face the same p_2 in the cost function (11.41).

i. Considering just the cost function (11.41) in isolation, what does this imply about the identification status of γ_2? (*Hint:* You may find it helpful to review Example 14 of Chapter 10.)

ii. Can the linear homogeneity restriction be imposed in estimation? Does it affect the ability of the model to fit the data? Is it testable?

(b) In light of these conclusions, estimate the model

$$\log C = \alpha + \beta \log Q + \gamma_1 \log p_1 + \gamma_3 \log p_3.$$

i. Suppose that, in addition to the model itself, we are aware of the additional information of the linear homogeneity restriction. How does this additional information affect the identification status of γ_2?

ii. Are the parameters of the production function (11.39) exactly, over-, or underidentified?

iii. Solve for estimates of α_1, α_2, and α_3. Do they seem more plausible than those you obtained in Exercise 11.9?

11.11 💿 **nerlove.dat** Having engaged in these preliminary estimations, let us return to a more elementary examination of Nerlove's data. In particular, consider firm size, measured by output.

(a) What is the smallest firm in Nerlove's sample? The largest? How many times larger is the largest firm than the smallest?

(b) Thinking in terms of Figure 11.1, do these values suggest that firm costs in this industry are measured over a fairly broad range of output or over a fairly narrow range?

(c) Generate average costs C/Q and plot the average cost curve. Does the pattern of average costs make sense? From your understanding of the relationship between average costs and returns to scale, do you expect a model that imposes a fixed degree of returns to scale on all firms to offer a satisfactory description of this industry?

Nerlove addressed this matter by modifying the estimation of the cost function so as to permit returns to scale to vary with output. He took three approaches to doing this. The first was to separate the data into five subsamples, ordered by firm size,

and to use dummy variables to allow α and β to shift across the subsamples. The second was to estimate separate cost functions for each of the subsamples. The third was to modify the functional form of the cost function in a way that allows returns to scale to vary. The following questions ask you to consider each of these in turn.

11.12 💿 **nerlove.dat** Define a set of four dummy variables that distinguish among five 29-firm subsamples, ordered by output. (The first subsample consists of observations 1–29, the second of observations 30–58, and so on.) Introduce these into your homogeneity-constrained version of (11.26) so as to permit both α and β to shift across the subsamples.

(a) Use your estimation results to obtain an estimate of the degree of returns to scale ν for each of the subsamples. Nerlove's values are presented in the second column of Table 11.1. How do yours compare? Do these findings make sense in terms of your understanding of the link between returns to scale and the shape of the average cost curve?

(b) Perform a joint test of whether all of the subsamples have the same returns-to-scale characteristics. State all components of your test procedure carefully. (*Hint:* The null hypothesis under test concerns only β; α should still be permitted to vary across the subsamples.) Is your conclusion what you expected?

11.13 💿 **nerlove.dat** Estimate a separate homogeneity-constrained cost function for each of the five subsamples.

(a) From your estimation results, compute the degree of returns to scale ν for each of the five subsamples. Nerlove's values are presented in the third column of Table 11.1. How do yours compare?

(b) Do the data formally reject the application of a single cost function to the entire sample? Generalize the Chow test procedure in Section 10.2.3 to the present context of five subsamples. State carefully all aspects of your test procedure, including the null and alternative hypotheses and the test statistic.

(c) Check your Chow test by implementing a dummy-variable version of the same test.

TABLE 11.1   Returns to Scale Estimated by Nerlove

Subsample observations	Shifted using dummies	Subsample regressions
1–29	2.52	2.52
30–58	1.53	1.50
59–87	1.14	1.08
88–116	1.10	1.09
117–145	0.94	0.96

Source: Nerlove (1963, Table 4).

11.14 nerlove.dat In an ad hoc[9] attempt to allow the returns-to-scale properties of the function to vary with output, Nerlove introduced a quadratic term into the model:

$$\log C = \alpha + \beta \log Q + \delta(\log Q)^2 + \gamma_1 \log p_1$$
$$+ \gamma_2 \log p_2 + \gamma_3 \log p_3.$$

Estimate the homogeneity-constrained version of this cost function over the full sample of data.

(a) Is δ statistically significant?

(b) Show that for this functional form the elasticity (11.11) is[10]

$$\frac{\partial \log C}{\partial \log Q} = \beta + 2\delta \log Q.$$

(c) The elasticity of scale for this cost function is therefore

$$\frac{1}{\beta + 2\delta \log Q}.$$

Evaluate this for each of the subsamples (at the mean value of Q for the subsample). Do your values depict a similar returns-to-scale pattern as those of Table 11.1?

(d) A technology's efficient scale is the level of output at which its average cost curve reaches its minimum. In Exercise 11.2 you show that the condition characterizing this efficient scale is

$$\frac{\partial \log C}{\partial \log Q} = 1.$$

i. Show that for this cost function the efficient scale level of output is

$$Q = \exp\left(\frac{1 - \beta}{2\delta}\right).$$

ii. Based on your estimation results, what was the efficient scale level of output in the U.S. electric power generation industry in 1955? How many of the firms in your sample were operating below this level?

11.5   The Translog Cost Function

We have found that the Cobb-Douglas cost function is unduly restrictive in its description of cost-minimizing behavior. One approach to dealing with this is to specify yet more general functional forms; we can, for example, specify a CES

---

[9] In the sense that the cost function has not been derived from any companion production function.

[10] You have encountered this problem previously as Exercise 6.25.

production function and derive the associated cost function. But this will typically just push the problem back one step. In the CES case, although the elasticity of substitution may differ from 1, it must still be constant. Is it possible to study the economics of cost and production in a way that avoids this problem? That is, is it possible to specify an estimable functional form that uses the structure implied by optimizing behavior but, beyond this, places minimal prior restrictions on the nature of technology or agent behavior?

To consider this, recall the general k-factor cost function (11.33):

$$C = c(p_1, p_2, \ldots, p_k, Q). \tag{11.45}$$

In estimating some representation for this function, what are its essential characteristics that we seek to describe? These include, first, the value of the function (that is, the level of costs); this corresponds, in a linear model, to the intercept parameter. Also included are its $k+1$ first derivatives; the first k of these correspond (by Shephard's lemma) to the factor demands $x_i = C_i$, and the last to the elasticity of scale. Included as well are the k^2 second derivatives C_{ij} associated with the demand elasticities. In rough terms, then, we have counted $k^2 + k + 2$ effects;[11] to have any hope of adequately describing these, an estimated cost model must have a comparable number of parameters. The fundamental problem with the Cobb-Douglas cost function (11.26) is that, with just $k+2$ parameters, it can never hope to do this.

These observations suggest, however, a quite different approach to formulating an estimable cost model that captures these first- and second-order effects. This is to use methods for approximating mathematical functions to take, at the minimum, a second-order approximation to the arbitrary cost function (11.45). Because mathematics offers many ways of approximating a function and because for some purposes it is conceivable that we may want an even higher-order approximation, a number of such approximations have been developed. However, one has emerged as the empirical model of choice among applied econometricians. It is the transcendental logarithmic,[12] or **translog**, cost function introduced by Christensen, Jorgenson, and Lau (1973); this parameterizes the cost function (11.45) in the form

$$\log C = \alpha + \beta \log Q + \frac{1}{2}\delta(\log Q)^2 + \sum_i \gamma_i \log p_i$$

$$+ \frac{1}{2}\sum_i \sum_j \gamma_{ij} \log p_i \log p_j + \sum_i \gamma_{Qi} \log Q \log p_i. \tag{11.46}$$

An econometric model such as this that offers at least a second-order approximation to the function of interest is called a **flexible functional form.** The translog

---

[11] This discussion is suggestive rather than definitive. To some extent we have overstated the problem because not all of these effects are independent. Linear homogeneity reduces the number of independent first derivatives by one. Similarly, as we see shortly, the symmetry of cross-substitution effects reduces the number of independent second derivatives.

[12] A transcendental function is one that cannot be expressed in terms of powers of polynomials. The logarithmic function is one example of a transcendental function.

cost function may be derived as a second-order Taylor series approximation to the logarithm of (11.45). Its popularity arises from the fact that it is linear in its coefficients and, although it has considerably more parameters than the Cobb-Douglas model, these are still fairly modest in number. There is no corresponding parametric form for the production function to which this cost function is dual.

Parameter Restrictions

Note first that the translog is a generalization of the Cobb-Douglas cost function, in that the Cobb-Douglas is the special case in which[13]

$$\delta = 0, \tag{11.47a}$$

$$\gamma_{ij} = 0, \tag{11.47b}$$

$$\gamma_{Qi} = 0. \tag{11.47c}$$

Because these are just restrictions on the coefficients of the translog model, it is possible to test whether the specialization to the Cobb-Douglas model is supported by the data.

Just as is true of the Cobb-Douglas cost function, linear homogeneity must be imposed on the translog model and, because it involves overidentifying parameter restrictions, is a hypothesis that may be tested. It turns out that the restrictions

$$\sum_i \gamma_i = 1, \tag{11.48a}$$

$$\sum_i \gamma_{Qi} = 0, \tag{11.48b}$$

$$\sum_i \gamma_{ij} = 0 \qquad \text{for all } j, \tag{11.48c}$$

$$\sum_j \gamma_{ij} = 0 \qquad \text{for all } i \tag{11.48d}$$

will ensure a translog cost function that is homogeneous of degree 1 in factor prices.

However, in contrast to the simpler Cobb-Douglas model, it turns out that linear homogeneity is not the only set of restrictions implied by the microeconomic theory of the firm. Symmetry of cross-price effects requires the **symmetry restrictions**

$$\gamma_{ij} = \gamma_{ji} \qquad (i \neq j). \tag{11.49}$$

In the context of the estimation of the cost function (11.46) in isolation, the γ_{ij} coefficients are underidentified.[14] The imposition of these symmetry restrictions serves to exactly identify them.

---

[13] Which of these restrictions yields Nerlove's ad hoc model that you considered in Exercise 11.14?

[14] You are asked to explain why in Exercise 11.15.

Returns to Scale

Because the translog cost function is not of a separable form like (11.10), it does not have a fixed degree of returns to scale. The elasticity of cost with respect to output is

$$\frac{\partial \log C}{\partial \log Q} = \beta + \delta \log Q + \sum_i \gamma_{Qi} \log p_i. \tag{11.50}$$

The elasticity of scale is the reciprocal of this. It is evident that the restrictions $\delta = \gamma_{Qi} = 0$ would imply a fixed elasticity of scale at all output levels, in the amount $\epsilon = 1/\beta$. Constant returns would require the additional restriction $\beta = 1$. These are linear restrictions that may be imposed on the cost function (11.46) and tested.

Factor Demands

In deriving the conditional factor demands, the logarithmic form of the cost function means that Shephard's lemma is most readily applied as

$$x_i = \frac{\partial C}{\partial p_i} = \frac{C}{p_i} \frac{\partial \log C}{\partial \log p_i} = \frac{C}{p_i} \left(\gamma_i + \sum_j \gamma_{ij} \log p_j + \gamma_{Qi} \log Q \right).$$

Rearranging and adding a disturbance, these factor demands are most naturally estimated in the form:

$$S_i = \gamma_i + \sum_{j=1}^{k} \gamma_{ij} \log p_j + \gamma_{Qi} \log Q + \varepsilon_i \qquad (i = 1, \ldots, k). \tag{11.51}$$

Note that these cost share equations are a generalization of the Cobb-Douglas share equations (11.32), in that the Cobb-Douglas equations correspond to the special case in which the restrictions (11.47b) and (11.47c) are imposed. These share equations show that the translog model allows cost shares to vary with factor prices and output, in contrast to the fixed cost shares implied by the Cobb-Douglas model.

Demand Elasticities

As always, elasticities usefully characterize the nature of factor demand. However, instead of having fixed values over all ranges of prices and output, as the Cobb-Douglas model does, demand elasticities now vary with the data.

Result 11.2   *For the translog cost function the own-price elasticities of demand are*

$$\epsilon_{ii} = \frac{\gamma_{ii} + S_i(S_i - 1)}{S_i} \tag{11.52}$$

and the cross-price elasticities are

$$\epsilon_{ij} = \frac{\gamma_{ij} + S_i S_j}{S_i}, \qquad i \neq j. \tag{11.53}$$

Proof:

Fundamentally these elasticities must be derived from the factor demand functions, the most useful expression of which takes the share-equation form (11.51). As a first step, note that it is an implication of these share equations that

$$\frac{\partial \log S_i}{\partial \log p_j} = \frac{\partial \log S_i}{\partial S_i} \frac{\partial S_i}{\partial \log p_j} = \frac{1}{S_i} \gamma_{ij} \qquad \text{for all } i, j. \tag{11.54}$$

As a second step, note that the logarithm of the cost share definition (11.30) is:

$$\log S_i = \log x_i + \log p_i - \log C.$$

The derivative of this with respect to the own-price p_i is

$$\frac{\partial \log S_i}{\partial \log p_i} = \frac{\partial \log x_i}{\partial \log p_i} + 1 - \frac{\partial \log C}{\partial \log p_i} = \epsilon_{ii} + 1 - S_i,$$

and the derivative with respect to the cross-price p_j is[15]

$$\frac{\partial \log S_i}{\partial \log p_j} = \frac{\partial \log x_i}{\partial \log p_j} - \frac{\partial \log C}{\partial \log p_j} = \epsilon_{ij} - S_j.$$

Equating these expressions with (11.54), they may be solved for ϵ_{ii} and ϵ_{ij}.   □

The expressions for the Allen elasticities are

$$\sigma_{ij} = \frac{1}{S_j} \epsilon_{ij} = \frac{\gamma_{ij} + S_i S_j}{S_i S_j}, \qquad i \neq j, \tag{11.55}$$

which are clearly symmetric in i, j as long as the symmetry restrictions $\gamma_{ij} = \gamma_{ji}$ are satisfied.

Estimation

The translog cost function (11.46) is linear in its coefficients; in the terminology of Chapter 6 it is an intrinsically linear model. It is therefore estimable as a linear multiple regression, and the exercises that follow guide you through this using Nerlove's data.

This approach is not without its problems, however. The last two terms of (11.46) involve all possible cross-products of $\log Q$ and the $\log p_i$, variables that appear by themselves in the earlier terms. Consequently, the explanatory variables of the translog cost function tend to exhibit considerable multicollinearity, with the classic result (as you will see) that coefficients tend to be estimated very imprecisely. Is there a better way?

There is. Entirely in analogy with our discussion of the pros and cons of estimating the Cobb-Douglas cost function (11.26) directly versus the share equations (11.32), in the translog case the share equations (11.51) may be estimated. The data requirements are, again, somewhat different from those of the cost function itself; the cost shares S_i imply knowledge of the input quantities x_i in addition

---

[15] We have used the result of Exercise 11.6.

TABLE 11.2   **Christensen and Greene's Estimation of the Translog Model Using Nerlove's Data**

Coefficient	Estimate	Standard Error
α	8.841	0.2376
β	0.252	0.0581
δ	0.079	0.0099
γ_L	0.365	0.0737
γ_K	0.076	0.0835
γ_F	0.559	0.0592
γ_{LL}	0.040	0.0171
γ_{LK}	−0.024	0.0159
γ_{LF}	−0.016	0.0082
γ_{KK}	0.175	0.0277
γ_{KF}	−0.151	0.0235
γ_{FF}	0.167	0.0240
γ_{QL}	−0.017	0.0015
γ_{QK}	−0.008	0.0047
γ_{QF}	0.025	0.0045

Source: Christensen, L.R., and W.H. Greene (1976) "Economies of Scale in U.S. Electric Power Generation," Journal of Political Economy 84, 655–676. © 1956 by the University of Chicago. Used with permission. Also Jorgenson (1986, Table 2).

to their prices. It is exactly this additional information that makes it possible to overcome the multicollinearity that tends to characterize the regressors of the cost function.[16]

Note that not all of the parameters of the cost function appear in the share equations (11.51). Most important, the parameters β and δ are missing; by (11.50), these relate to returns to scale. The estimation of the share equations (11.51) alone, therefore, does not allow us to learn anything about returns to scale, exactly as we conclude in our earlier discussion of the Cobb-Douglas share equations (11.32).

Whether this is important depends on the economic issues at stake. As we see momentarily, the γ_{ij} coefficients govern the demand elasticities; if these are all that are of interest then the estimation of the system of factor demands (11.51) is all that is required.

If the returns-to-scale properties of the underlying production function are of interest, on the other hand, then the cost function (11.46) must be included in the estimation of the system. This was the approach of the study by Christensen and Greene (1976), who began by doing this for Nerlove's 1955 data. Their estimation results are presented in Table 11.2. They then repeated the exercise for an updated

[16] Another advantage of the share-equation approach to estimation is that in this context the symmetry restrictions (11.49) are testable.

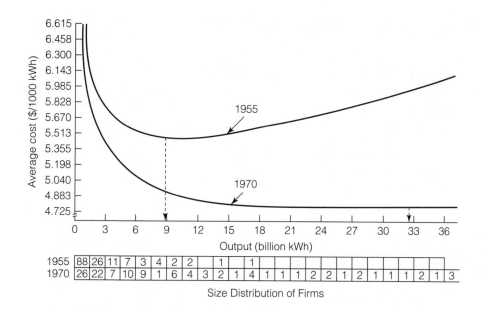

1955	88	26	11	7	3	4	2	2		1		1													
1970	26	22	7	10	9	1	6	4	3	2	1	4	1	1	1	2	2	1	2	1	1	1	2	1	3

Size Distribution of Firms

FIGURE 11.3 Average cost curves of Christensen and Greene's translog models. (*Source:* Christensen, L.R., and W.H. Greene (1976) "Economies of Scale in U.S. Electric Power Generation," *Journal of Political Economy* 84, 655–676. © 1976 by the University of Chicago. Used with permission.)

data set for 1970; their interest was in investigating whether the returns-to-scale properties of the U.S. electric power industry had changed during this 15-year period. Their finding was that

> ... the U.S. electric power industry can be characterized by substantial scale economies at low levels of output. But the implied decreases in average cost diminish in importance for larger firms, resulting in an average cost curve that is very flat for a broad range of output. In 1955 most firms were producing on the low side of this range. By 1970, however, the bulk of U.S. electricity generation was by firms operating in the essentially flat area of the average cost curve. (Christensen and Greene 1976, p. 656)

The average cost curves for 1955 and 1970 implied by Christensen and Greene's estimates are shown in Figure 11.3; the size distribution of firms is also indicated. (The dotted lines show minimum average costs.) The figure shows that, although the average firm size increased between 1955 and 1970, the primary source of decreased average costs of electricity generation was *not* economies of scale resulting from moving along an essentially stable average cost curve. Instead the entire cost curve underwent a substantial downward shift during this period. "This implies that technical change unrelated to increases in scale deserves the primary attribution for declines in the cost of production" (Christensen and Greene 1976, p. 674).

Recall the discussion at the end of Section 7.1.1 on the implications of returns to scale for industry structure. Christensen and Greene's evidence that the nature

Do Baseball Teams Substitute among Player Skills?

The field of sports economics views professional sports teams as firms in an industry, hiring inputs in order to produce output so as to maximize profits.

But what are the factor inputs of teams? Stewart and Jones (1998) hypothesized that teams' inputs are best thought of as the skills of players. In a study of major league baseball, they considered four skill categories: experience, hitting ability, pitching ability, and star status. They used data on these skills and player salaries to estimate the prices implicitly paid by teams for these skills. (Such estimated prices are called **hedonic prices.**)

Using these estimated hedonic prices p_i and skills x_i observed across major league baseball teams over the six seasons 1986–1991, Stewart and Jones estimated an otherwise standard translog factor demand system. They considered as measures of output both attendance at home games and the proportion of wins over the season. For each of these output measures they obtained the following Allen elasticities.

Notice that the pattern of factor substitutability revealed by these results is not sensitive to the choice of output measure. The own-price effects given by the diagonal entries are all negative, indicating that an increase in the price of any player skill causes teams to demand less of it. The cross-price effects,

	Experience	Hitting	Pitching	Stars
Output = Attendance				
Experience	−1.051	0.365	0.647	0.569
Hitting		−0.408	0.362	0.304
Pitching			−2.390	0.659
Stars				−6.691
Output = Wins				
Experience	−1.053	0.371	0.645	0.533
Hitting		−0.413	0.370	0.291
Pitching			−2.385	0.591
Stars				−6.240

given by the off-diagonal entries, are all positive, so that an increase in the price of one skill leads teams to employ more of the others. For example, when output is measured by attendance the Allen elasticity relating pitching and hitting is 0.362. This means that a 1% increase in the price of one of these skills leads teams to substitute away from it and increase their demand for the other by 0.362%. Thus, teams substitute among player skills in much the same way that any firm might substitute among its factor inputs.

of power generation costs is such that minimum average costs are attainable at relatively modest levels of output suggests that there is no basis for permitting monopolistic practices.

We conclude that a small number of extremely large firms are not required for efficient production and that policies to promote competition in electric power generation cannot be faulted in terms of sacrificing economies of scale. (Christensen and Greene 1976, p. 656)

EXERCISES

11.15 Consider the translog cost function (11.46) for the case of three factors.

(a) Write the cost function out explicitly. (*Hint:* In the three-factor case, prior to the imposition of the homogeneity or symmetry restrictions the cost function has a total of 18 coefficients.)

(b) Consider the matrix of coefficients associated with the double summation term in (11.46).

$$\begin{bmatrix} \gamma_{11} & \gamma_{12} & \gamma_{13} \\ \gamma_{21} & \gamma_{22} & \gamma_{23} \\ \gamma_{31} & \gamma_{32} & \gamma_{33} \end{bmatrix} \qquad (11.56)$$

i. Write the symmetry restrictions (11.49) out explicitly. What is their meaning in terms of this matrix?

ii. In the context of the cost function you've written out in part a, what is the identification status of the coefficients involved in the symmetry restrictions? What are the implications of the symmetry restrictions for this identification status?

iii. Show how the symmetry restrictions are imposed in estimation. Are they testable?

(c) Write the linear homogeneity restrictions (11.48) out explicitly. What is the meaning of the restrictions (11.48c) in terms of the matrix (11.56)? What about (11.48d)?

(d) Christensen and Greene (1976) estimated this cost function using Nerlove's data. Their results are reported in Table 11.2.

i. In what sense do their estimates satisfy symmetry?

ii. Establish whether their estimates satisfy linear homogeneity.

11.16 ● **nerlove.dat** Use Nerlove's data to do the following.

(a) Estimate the cost function you present in Exercise 11.15a, imposing the symmetry restrictions you consider in 11.15b. (*Hint:* Do not forget to include the multiplicative constant $\frac{1}{2}$ in your generation of the explanatory variables, where appropriate.)

(b) What parameter restrictions correspond to the special case of the Cobb-Douglas cost function?

Estimate this restricted form of the model. Using your estimation results for the restricted and unrestricted models, perform a test of whether the data support the specialization of the translog model to the Cobb-Douglas. Are your findings surprising in light of your understanding of Nerlove's Cobb-Douglas analysis from Section 11.4?

(c) Consider linear homogeneity.

i. Show how the translog model in part a may be rewritten to incorporate linear homogeneity. (*Hint:* Once the symmetry restrictions are used to eliminate, say, γ_{21}, γ_{31}, and γ_{32} from the model, linear homogeneity implies just five additional restrictions. Use these to eliminate γ_3, γ_{13}, γ_{23}, γ_{33}, and γ_{Q3}.)

ii. Estimate your restricted cost function. Using your estimation results for the restricted and unrestricted models, test the hypothesis of linear homogeneity.

(d) Compare your estimation results for the homogeneity and symmetry-constrained model with those of Christensen and Greene, as reported in Table 11.2. Generally speaking, how do your coefficient estimates compare? How about the standard errors? How do you explain this?

(e) Consider the restrictions implied by constant returns to scale.

i. Show how your homogeneity and symmetry-constrained model in part c can be restricted further to satisfy constant returns.

ii. Estimate this restricted model. Use these results for this restricted model and those for the unrestricted model in part c (so that homogeneity and symmetry are treated as maintained hypotheses) to test the hypothesis of constant returns. Does your conclusion make sense in terms of your broader understanding of the problem you are studying?

Answer the following questions using the Christensen-Greene results presented in Table 11.2.

11.17 *Returns to scale.* The cost-output elasticity (11.50) may be evaluated at any point of the data. Christensen and Greene chose to evaluate it for the median firm of each of Nerlove's five sub-

TABLE 11.3   Median Firms of Nerlove's Five Subsamples

Firm	C	Q	PL	PK	PF	$\dfrac{Q}{C}\dfrac{\partial C}{\partial Q}$
Bangor Hydro-electric Co.	0.501	43	1.75	170	42.8	0.592
Tucson Gas, Elec., Light and Power Co.	2.382	338	1.85	163	24.6	0.742
Montana Electric Co.	7.185	1109	2.05	177	35.1	0.843
Florida Power Corp.	16.674	2226	2.00	217	34.3	0.896
Alabama Power Co.	22.828	5819	1.79	196	18.5	0.960

TABLE 11.4   Translog Cost Function Estimated Using Nerlove's Data:
Own-Price and Allen Elasticities

	Labor	**Capital**	**Fuel**
Labor	$\epsilon_{LL} = -0.499$	$\sigma_{LK} = 0.411$	$\sigma_{LF} = 0.650$
Capital		$\epsilon_{KK} = -0.159$	$\sigma_{KF} = 0.223$
Fuel			$\epsilon_{FF} = -0.170$

Source: Christensen, L.R., and W.H. Greene (1976) "Economies of Scale in U.S. Electric Power Generation," *Journal of Political Economy* 84, 655–676. © 1976 by the University of Chicago. Used with permission.

samples. The data for these five median firms is given in Table 11.3.

(a) Evaluate this elasticity for each of these five median firms. Christensen and Greene's values are presented in the last column of Table 11.3.[17] How do yours compare?

(b) Take the reciprocal of your elasticities to obtain an estimate of ϵ for each of the five firms. How do these estimates of ϵ obtained from the translog cost function compare with those obtained by Nerlove using the (modified) Cobb-Douglas, as presented in Table 11.1? Does essentially the same pattern of returns to scale emerge from the two analyses?

11.18 *Cost shares.* Demand elasticities must be evaluated at a point on the demand curve. In the case of the translog model, as we have seen, the most convenient expressions for the factor demands are the share equations (11.51).

(a) Let us choose as a point in the data the median firm of Nerlove's sample, which is the Montana Electric Company. Using the data given in Table 11.3 and Christensen and Greene's coefficient estimates, obtain predicted cost shares $\hat{S}_i$ for each of labor, capital, and fuel. Are your values plausible? In particular, are they positive fractions?

(b) Do your predicted cost shares sum to 1?

11.19 *Own-price elasticities.* Using your predicted cost shares from Exercise 11.18, evaluate the own-price elasticities (11.52). How do these compare with

(a) Christensen and Greene's own-price elasticities, as presented in Table 11.4? (Theirs are the average elasticities over all firms.)

(b) the own-price elasticities yielded by the Cobb-Douglas model, as you report them in Exercise 11.9?

---

[17] Christensen and Greene (1976, Table 7) actually presented 1 minus this elasticity as a measure of economies of scale.

11.20 *Allen elasticities.* Evaluate the Allen elasticities of substitution (11.55). How do they compare with

(a) Christensen and Greene's Allen elasticities, as presented in Table 11.4? (Theirs are the average elasticities over all firms.)

(b) the Allen elasticities implicit in the use of the Cobb-Douglas cost function? In particular, for these data does it seem to be important to allow the data to determine the pattern of substitutability among factors rather than imposing a certain pattern a priori as the Cobb-Douglas cost function does?

11.21 *Cross-price elasticities.* Evaluate the cross-price elasticities (11.53).

(a) Which factor pairs are substitutes and which are complements?

(b) How do your elasticities compare with those yielded by the Cobb-Douglas model, as you report them in Exercise 11.9? In particular, is the pattern of substitutability or complementarity consistent across the two models?

(c) Summarize your own- and cross-price elasticities in a matrix like (11.44). Does it satisfy the property (11.37)?

11.6 Consumer Demand

This chapter has been devoted to introducing the modern flexible functional-form approach to production analysis. We have noted that duality theory has a much broader applicability than just to production. It is natural to conclude the chapter by sketching parallel developments in consumer demand analysis.

Formally the consumer's optimization problem is in many respects similar to a firm's. Whereas a firm chooses inputs and output to maximize profits subject to its technology, a consumer chooses consumption levels q_i to maximize a utility function

$$u(q_1, \ldots, q_k) \tag{11.57}$$

subject to a budget constraint. The budget constraint says that total expenditure cannot exceed income; denoting this total expenditure by m, as an accounting matter it is defined by

$$m = p_1 q_1 + \cdots + p_k q_k, \tag{11.58}$$

where the p_i are the commodity prices. This is analogous to the definition (11.2) of the costs of the firm.

One approach to deriving consumer commodity demands q_i is to ask what consumption amounts maximize utility for a given level of expenditure m. The solution is a set of demand functions

$$q_i(p_1, \ldots, p_k, m), \qquad (i = 1, \ldots, k). \tag{11.59}$$

There is, however, an alternative but completely equivalent way of viewing the consumer's optimization problem. Asking which commodity demands maximize utility at given expenditure is exactly the same as asking which demands minimize expenditure for given utility. The minimum expenditure required to attain utility u at prevailing goods prices p_i is described by the **expenditure function,** denoted

$$e(p_1, \ldots, p_k, u). \tag{11.60}$$

The expenditure function of the consumer is exactly analogous to the cost function of the firm:[18] Whereas the cost function describes the minimum cost of producing a certain level of output in the face of given factor prices, the expenditure function describes the minimum expenditure required to achieve a certain level of utility in the face of given commodity prices.

Given this analogy between the two functions, it is not surprising that the expenditure function plays much the same role in consumer analysis that the cost function plays in production analysis. Just as the cost function is dual to the production function, it may be shown that the expenditure function is dual to the utility function—it embodies the economically relevant aspects of consumer preferences. Furthermore, just as conditional factor demands may be easily derived from the cost function, so too may the consumer demands (11.59) be derived from the expenditure function.

Just as the cost function gives rise to the distinction between conditional and unconditional factor demands, consumer theory involves an analogous distinction between **Hicksian** (or **income-compensated**) and **Marshallian** consumer demands. It is the Marshallian demands that are represented by (11.59).

11.6.1 The Almost Ideal Demand System

Although in microeconomic theory there is an exact analogy between the cost and expenditure functions, for the purposes of empirical implementation this is not entirely the case. In particular note that, whereas the cost function can be estimated directly, this is not true of the expenditure function (11.60) because it depends on utility u, which is unobservable. (Whereas the output of the firm is observable, we never have data on people's utility). Instead, the only way to estimate parameters associated with consumer behavior is to work directly with the consumer demand equations. To derive these, we need to start by specifying a parametric form for the expenditure function. Our discussion of flexible functional forms suggests that we do this with a second-order approximation. Just as we discussed previously, there are in principle many ways of doing this. And again, one model has emerged as the empirical model of choice among applied econometricians—the **Almost Ideal Demand System** (AIDS)[19] of Deaton and Muellbauer (1980a), which is of the form

$$S_i = \alpha_i + \sum_{j=1}^{k} \gamma_{ij} \log p_j + \beta_i \log \frac{m}{P} \qquad (i = 1, \ldots, k). \tag{11.61}$$

Here S_i is the share of good i in total expenditure, k is the number of goods (and thus the number of equations in the system), m denotes total expenditure,

---

[18] Indeed the analogy is so complete that some microeconomists refer to the expenditure function as the cost function, because it represents the cost of attaining utility u.

[19] Publishing in 1980, Deaton and Muellbauer had no way of anticipating what an unfortunate choice the acronym AIDS would prove to be.

and P is an aggregate price index defined in terms of the individual commodity prices p_i. Note the formal similarity of the AIDS to the translog system of factor demands (11.51) and the equally transparent intuition that the share of good i in the consumer's budget depends on individual commodity prices and, effectively, real income.

This highlights the fact that, despite its rigorous theoretical underpinnings, the intuition of any one of the equations in the AIDS model is little different from naive single-equation demand regressions such as Houthakker's model of electricity demand in Section 8.6. For recall that, if we let good i be electricity, Houthakker's loglinear regression (8.26) expresses quantity demanded q as a function of the own-price p_1, the price p_2 of gas as a substitute good, and income m. So although the flexible functional form approach offers the many advantages we have discussed, the essential functional relationships in question are the same.

The income elasticities for the AIDS model are

$$\eta_i = \frac{m}{q_i} \frac{\partial q_i}{\partial m} = 1 + \frac{\beta_i}{S_i}.$$

The appropriate means of computing own- and cross-price elasticities has been the subject of some discussion in the literature; see Alston, Foster, and Green (1994) and Buse (1994). The preferred formulas seem to be those of Chalfant (1987). A convenient economy of notation is afforded by defining

$$\delta_{ij} = \begin{cases} 0 & \text{for} \quad i = j \quad \text{(own-price elasticities)} \\ 1 & \text{for} \quad i \neq j \quad \text{(cross-price elasticities)} \end{cases}$$

Then Marshallian price elasticities are given by

$$\frac{\gamma_{ij} - \beta_i S_j}{S_i} - \delta_{ij},$$

and Hicksian price elasticities by

$$\frac{\gamma_{ij}}{S_i} + S_j - \delta_{ij}.$$

AIDS Engel Curves

Consider a cross-sectional data set in which all consumers face the same commodity prices p_j. Then the γ_{ij} coefficients are not identified, the middle term in (11.61) is absorbed into the intercept, and the demand system reduces to

$$S_i = \alpha_i + \beta_i \log \frac{m}{P}.$$

This is just the Working-Leser Engel curve (6.37) encountered in our earlier discussion of lin-log Engel curves.

In some applications, Engel curves that are merely loglinear in expenditure are thought to be something of a limitation, and some extensions to the AIDS model relax this to permit quadratic Engel curves (see the references in Ryan and Wales 1999).

Recent Developments

Like production analysis, the literature on consumer demand is enormous, and the following section contains some suggested readings for those interested in pursuing advanced topics. One stream of contemporary research follows so immediately from our discussion of the expenditure function that it is natural to mention it.

Although it makes sense that consumer demand equations must fundamentally represent relationships between quantities demanded (in the case of the AIDS, in budget-share form), prices, and income, common sense tells us that other factors must also be relevant; for example, demographic variables or household characteristics. As well, presumably current consumption decisions are often conditional on other decisions taken in the past: in Houthakker's model, electricity consumption depended on the consumer's holdings of heavy electric equipment h (i.e., durable appliances). Finally, a household's consumption decisions are made jointly with decisions about labor supply; a spell of unemployment or a move from part-time to full-time work almost certainly has implications for consumption. How can these considerations be introduced into an empirical demand model such as the AIDS?

These observations suggest that the notion that a consumer maximizes a utility function (11.57) that depends on just a set of consumption goods is a rather simplistic portrayal of consumer behavior. Many other considerations also affect utility; these include the quantity of labor supplied l; demographic variables or household characteristics, which may be denoted by z; and what might be called conditioning goods, which, following Houthakker, we denote by h. Conditioning goods are ones for which consumption levels are exogenously given in relation to the consumer's current decisions regarding the endogenous consumption levels q_i.

A more realistic definition of the expenditure function is, then, that the consumer seeks to minimize the cost (11.58) of acquiring the goods q_i needed to achieve a level of utility given by a utility function of the form $u(q_1, \ldots, q_k, l, z, h)$. The solution is the **conditional expenditure function**

$$e(p_1, \ldots, p_k, l, z, h, u),$$

which is just a generalization of (11.60). The microeconomic theory of the conditional expenditure function was developed by Pollak (1969) and Browning (1983). The corresponding generalization of the AIDS model, termed the quadratic almost ideal system, has been developed by Lewbel (1991) and applied by Banks, Blundell, and Lewbel (1997).

11.7   Further Reading

One motivation for this chapter is that other expositions of the econometrics of production tend to be at a level slightly out of reach of undergraduates. As we have seen, there is no intrinsic reason why this need be so. For those with a graduate background in microeconomics, a thorough one-volume treatment of production analysis that integrates theory and application is Chambers (1988). For a more explicitly econometric orientation see Jorgenson (1986).

For consumer demand analysis the best starting point is Thomas (1987). Deaton and Muellbauer (1980b) offer a comprehensive presentation of the microeconomic theory of consumer behavior, with some coverage of empirical issues. For the reverse emphasis, the masterly survey by Deaton (1986) has not been surpassed. An advanced discussion of the econometric implications of duality can be found in Varian (1992, Chap. 12).

This chapter has not provided exercises in the estimation of systems of demand equations such as (11.51) and (11.61) because the relevant econometric methods take us slightly beyond the scope of this book. Berndt (1991, Chap. 9) provides such exercises for factor demands. Berndt (1991, Chap. 3) has exercises that use Christensen and Greene's 1970 data to estimate the Cobb-Douglas cost function and compare the results with Nerlove's findings.

12 Model Discovery

All models are wrong, but some are useful.

George Box (1976)

Any model—in economics or in any other discipline—is an approximation to reality. Well done, this is a strength, not a weakness. The purpose of a model is to abstract from the complexity of the real world in a way that isolates, and therefore allows us to think clearly about, the key forces at work.

As we emphasize in our introductory survey of the principles of statistical inference in Chapter 2, the derivation of the sampling properties of estimators and test statistics can only be done on the basis of an assumed population model. Consequently, inference is conditional on the model. Accordingly, the derivation of the sampling properties of least squares regression in Chapters 4 and 8 proceeds on the assumption that it was the "true" population model—a classical normal linear regression—that was being estimated, although in Section 8.9 we explore the implications of omitting relevant explanatory variables or including irrelevant ones.

Although the derivation of sampling properties necessitates the assumption of some population model, the fact that all models are approximations to reality—and are therefore, in this sense, false—means that the notion that it is the "true" model that is being estimated can never be anything but a convenient fiction. In practice, any empirical modeling exercise involves uncertainty about an appropriate model specification. The econometrician must be concerned not just with statistical inference in a postulated model, but with whether that model is a good approximation to reality.

This fact of life has important implications for estimation and testing. Typically, empirical researchers reach the conclusions of their analysis following a **specification search** over various model formulations. The implications of this are considered in Section 12.1.

In proceeding with a specification search, we typically wish to assess the adequacy of any model under study. This is the problem of **model evaluation,** of which there are several dimensions. We may be attempting to assess the chosen model in isolation, without evaluating it directly against some competing model, and to consider whether it may be unsatisfactory in some respect. This is the problem of **specification testing,** sometimes called **misspecification testing** or **diagnostic testing,** and is considered in Section 12.2.

Other times several competing models are available and we want to choose among them. One approach to doing this is to use hypothesis tests to test one model against another. When the competing models lie within a nested testing structure, we have seen in Section 10.2.5 that the conventional methods of statistical inference apply. When, on the other hand, models are nonnested, new methods are needed; the most common nonnested tests are discussed in Section 12.3.

An alternative, and conceptually quite different, approach to evaluating competing models is to ask which does the best job of explaining the data. This is the problem of model choice, and is considered in Section 12.4.

We will find that there is no definitive solution to the model evaluation problem. It is a cliché of economics—indeed, of empirical modeling in all disciplines—that model building is as much an art as a science. Economic modeling, both theoretical and empirical, can be likened to baking a cake. Just as two chefs starting with the same ingredients might bake quite different cakes, two economists starting with the same data may build quite different models. Although we might hope that econometrics would help us choose between these competing models, in some cases the data may be uninformative in this regard. Arguing over which is the better model may end up being almost as vacuous as arguing over which is the better cake.

Because there is no definitive solution to the model evaluation problem, the goals of this chapter are more modest. They are, first, to develop the implications of specification searches for conventional inference; second, to introduce some of the techniques econometricians have found useful in guiding model formulation; and third, to develop some appreciation of how regression fits into the broader classes of models that econometricians use. To further this last objective, the final section of this chapter discusses some important examples of systems of equations.

12.1   Data Mining

Applied empirical modeling proceeds quite differently from the estimation-of-a-known-population-model paradigm of classical statistics. The researcher begins with a set of variables that may be related, sometimes with several alternative measures of these variables, and proceeds to estimate a variety of models using subsets of the variables. Ultimately some preferred model specification is arrived at, and these are the results that are presented. Readers of the research typically see only the final results and have at best only a vague impression of the specification search that led to it.

Such specification searches have implications for the properties of estimators and test statistics. The former is considered under the topic of pre-test estimation in Section 8.10. It is shown there that in general pre-test estimators—estimators that are the outcome of some sequence of hypothesis tests—are biased.

Specification searches also affect the correct interpretation of hypothesis tests. As a dramatic illustration, Freedman (1983) constructed an artificial example of a specification search. He began by using a computer to generate 51 variables of 100 random numbers each. Because the numbers are random, the variables are unrelated by design. He then ran a regression of one of the variables on the other 50. Regressors not significant at the 25% level were dropped, and the regression was rerun with the remaining significant variables. In ten replications of this simulation experiment, Freedman found that in the second regression as many as nine regressors were significant at 5%, with an R^2 as high as 0.48. The point of Freedman's analysis is that a specification search can easily lead a researcher to find seemingly significant relationships among variables that are unrelated. These "significant" regressions look much like those found in a great deal of published research.

This tendency is compounded when researchers can search not only over regressors but also over functional forms. Consider repeating Freedman's exercise and estimating not just linear regressions but also loglinear ones as well. Then there will be an even greater tendency to find "significant" regressions. This tendency increases further if we consider in addition semilog or polynomial forms. In considering many variables and functional forms, we are in a sense mining the data for significant relationships—hence the term **data mining.** Data mining has facetiously been described as "torturing the data until they confess."

Specification Searches and Significance Levels

Technically, the basic problem that gives rise to the data mining phenomenon is that specification searches change the relevant significance levels, causing true test sizes to deviate from nominal ones. This was investigated formally by Lovell (1983); Table 12.1 reproduces his calculations for the probability of finding significant regression results with random data when selecting the two best regressors from some larger group of candidate explanatory variables, all of which are in fact unrelated to the dependent variable.[1]

Consider first the classical benchmark in which a known two-regressor population model is being estimated, so that there are only $c = 2$ candidate explanatory variables. Using t tests at a significance level of $a = 0.05$, the probability of finding a particular regressor to be insignificant (the correct decision) is

$$1 - \text{Pr(Type I error)} = 1 - a = 1 - 0.05 = 0.95.$$

The probability of finding *both* regressors to be insignificant is therefore $(1-a)^2 = (0.95)^2 = 0.9025$. Thus, there is a better than 90% chance that the researcher will

---

[1] Lovell simplified his probability calculations by assuming a known disturbance variance and orthogonal candidate explanatory variables.

TABLE 12.1   Probability of Finding "Significant" Results from Random Data When Selecting the Two Best Regressors Using a 5% Significance Level

	Number of candidate explanatory variables				
	$c = 2$	$c = 5$	$c = 10$	$c = 20$	$c = 100$
Number of significant coefficients reported					
None significant	0.903	0.774	0.599	0.358	0.006
One significant	0.095	0.204	0.315	0.377	0.031
Two significant	0.0025	0.023	0.086	0.264	0.962
True significance level	5.0%	12.0%	22.6%	40.1%	92.3%

Source: Adapted from Lovell, M.C. "Data Mining," *Review of Economics and Statistics* 65, 1–12. © 1983 MIT Press Journals. Reprinted with permission from MIT Press Journals.

correctly conclude that neither of the variables is an important determinant of the dependent variable. The probability of finding exactly one to be significant is $2a(1 - a) = 0.095$. And the probability of finding both to be significant is $a^2 = 0.0025$. These probabilities are summarized in the first column of Table 12.1. In this classical case, the actual or true significance level is the same as the nominal one.

Contrast this with a specification search in which the best two regressors are chosen from, say, $c = 5$ candidate regressors. The probability that all are found to be insignificant (the correct decision) now falls to $(1 - a)^5 = (0.95)^5 = 0.774$. The probability that exactly one of the five is significant is given by the binomial distribution (one success in $c = 5$ trials when the probability of success on any trial is $a = 0.05$); it is $(c!/(1!(c-1)!))a(1-a)^{c-1} = (5!/(1!4!))(0.05)(0.95)^4 = 0.204$. And the probability that at least two are significant is 1 minus the other two probabilities: $1 - 0.204 - 0.774 = 0.023$. These probabilities are summarized in the second column of Table 12.1.

Notice that the specification search lowers the probability of reaching the correct decision (that no variables are significant) and increases the probability of finding one or more significant regressors. Another way of saying the same thing is that the nominal significance level of 5% at which the t tests are performed understates the true probability of Type I error. In fact, the following question can be posed: In the classical framework of a known two-regressor population model, at what significance level a would the t tests have to be performed to yield the true rejection probabilities we have derived? The answer for $c = 5$ candidate regressors is given by solving $(1 - a)^2 = (1 - 0.05)^c = 0.95^5$, which yields $a = 0.120$ or 12.0%. This is the true significance level given in the last line of Table 12.1. In this sense, when a researcher engages in a specification search, the true significance level is larger than the nominal level at which tests are performed.

The remaining columns of Table 12.1 repeat these calculations for $c = 10, 20,$ and 100 candidate regressors. In the last case of choosing the best two regressors from 100 candidates, there is an overwhelming likelihood of finding two significant

THEORY MEETS APPLICATION   12.1

Publication Bias

The consequences of data mining can arise even in the absence of model uncertainty and specification searches.

The objective of much research, in economics and in other fields, is to uncover systematic relationships between variables. Research that fails to uncover such relationships—that is, that finds no statistically significant effects—will typically be viewed as uninteresting, just as the absence of any relationship between random numbers is uninteresting. Being uninteresting, it will probably not be accepted for publication in research journals. By contrast, research that does uncover statistically significant effects will be published.

Now consider ten researchers using a common statistical model, so that there is no uncertainty over the appropriate model specification. Working independently, each samples data from the relevant population, estimates the common

model, and tests the hypothesis of interest at a 10% significance level. A significance level of 10% means that there is a probability of Type I error of 0.1; that is, in any one application of the test, there is one chance in ten that the data will misleadingly suggest a significant effect when in fact none exists. On average, then, one researcher of the ten will find a significant effect.

The nine researchers who failed to find a statistically significant effect will not have their research accepted for publication because the absence of significant effects is uninteresting. The study that will be published is the one in ten that found a significant effect.

Thus, even though none of the researchers individually is engaged in data mining, the process of research publication has the same effect as if they were.

regressors and only a tiny chance of reaching the correct conclusion that no regressors are important. Instead of a nominal significance level of 5%, the probabilities are equivalent to performing t tests at an actual level of 92.3% under classical conditions—and thereby incurring a very high probability of Type I error.

Confidence Intervals When the Specification Is Uncertain

These results on hypothesis testing are essentially the same phenomenon that we have noted for confidence intervals in earlier chapters. When analysis proceeds on the assumption of a known population model, without recognizing the uncertainty surrounding model specification, the precision with which parameters are estimated is overstated. This is illustrated in Chapters 4 and 8 with Mincer's statistical earnings function. In Example 4 of Chapter 4 we have found that, on the basis of a simple regression in which years of schooling is the explanatory variable, the estimated rate of return to education of 7.0% has a 95% confidence interval of (6.7%, 7.3%). This suggests that the return of 7.0% has been quite precisely estimated. Yet when, in Examples 2 and 3 of Chapter 8, we consider an alternative model specification that introduces experience as an additional explanatory influence, the return to education is reestimated as 10.7% with 90% confidence bounds of (10.5%, 10.9%). Hence, as we remark at the time, the apparent precision of the

THEORY MEETS APPLICATION   **12.2**

Data Mining and Investment Filter Rules

The study of historical data on financial markets sometimes reveals apparent patterns in price movements. For example, in studying the history of a stock, you might find that if only you had bought the stock every time its price increased by 5% and sold when it next fell by 5%, you would have made money. Or perhaps if you had bought at the beginning of every January and sold at the end of that month, profits would have been earned. Such mechanical investing strategies are called **filter rules** because the rule by which trading decisions are made is like a filter that picks out an apparent pattern in the historical record.

Exhaustive statistical analysis of filter rules has shown that, after trading costs, they do not yield returns in excess of a simple buy-and-hold strategy. (For some of the filter rules researchers have studied, see Malkiel 2003.) Although ex post we can find seemingly profitable filter rules by searching among enough of them, this is no different from finding seemingly significant regressions

by searching among enough variables. The apparent statistical significance of the filter rule is illusory, precisely because it has been found through an ex post searching over historical realizations. Just as a seemingly significant regression obtained through data mining will typically not stand up to out-of-sample data, filter rules that appear to be profitable on the basis of historical data typically fail to yield profits when used subsequently. This is reflected in the commonsense saying of the trading floor that "the problem with trading on the basis of historical price anomalies is that, as soon as you try to use them, the anomalies disappear."

The failure of filter-rule investment strategies illustrates the idea that financial markets are efficient—securities prices fully reflect all available information, including the history of price movements. Consequently, historical information cannot be used to profitably forecast future prices. We say more about the theory of **efficient markets** in Chapter 15.

---

initial analysis is illusory—as, indeed, is that of the subsequent one because that specification is itself uncertain.

In conclusion, the premise of classical statistics that the researcher is working with a known population model leads to an overstatement of the precision with which parameters are estimated.[2] Our finding that uncertainty over model specification introduces a divergence between nominal and true significance levels is just the other side of this coin.

Practitioner's Tip: **Data mining**

In your own empirical work, be aware that specification searches over alternative model formulations tend to lead to an overstatement of statistical significance, causing you to find "significant" effects and relationships where none exist.

---

[2]   Similarly, conventional forecast intervals that take into account sampling error but not model uncertainty overstate forecast accuracy, as we note in Section 5.1.

Stepwise Regression

Some statistics and econometrics packages include routines for what is called stepwise regression. They allow the researcher to begin with an overfitted regression—one that includes a number of regressors that may or may not belong. The routine then automatically drops variables with low t ratios step by step as the regression is successively reestimated, until a specification with all significant regressors is reached.

Our observations about data mining explain why stepwise regression is frowned on—for it automates the process of data mining. It is bad enough that, in trying to find a good model to explain some variable, researchers may inadvertently be engaged in data mining; automating the practice is all the more likely to lead to unsound research findings.

Can the Data Mining Problem be Addressed?

In view of its practical importance for applied work, can anything be done about the data mining problem?

Data mining is one aspect of the pre-testing problem that we first discuss in Section 8.10. There has been a great deal of formal theoretical analysis of pre-test estimation and testing; for a survey see Giles and Giles (1993). However, it seems safe to say that this theoretical literature has had little impact on applied work.

The alternative of avoiding specification searches entirely and estimating just a single model specification is clearly unrealistic. Exploring alternative model formulations is part of the process of scientific discovery, from which there is a great deal to be learned. Indeed, one of the more substantive conclusions to emerge from the theoretical pre-testing literature is that the implications of pre-testing can be positive as well as negative; again, see Giles and Giles (1993). This supports the commonsense idea that specification searches are to some extent necessary and desirable.

Because specification searches typically result in an overstatement of statistical significance, one suggestion is that significance levels be adjusted to reflect this. Lovell (1983) provides a rule of thumb for doing this that is often cited in textbooks, but is rarely used in practice. The informality and complexity of specification searches across so many aspects of model specification makes it difficult to say what adjustment should be made.

Another common prescription that is rarely adopted in practice is that a subset of the data be reserved to check that the model successfully predicts out-of-sample behavior. This would give some confidence that the model is more than just a good ex post fit to the particular realization of the data that happens to have been observed. A more realistic empirical strategy that is in this spirit is for the researcher to demonstrate, insofar as it is possible to do so, that the substantive conclusions of the analysis are robust to plausible variations in the model specification, the measurement of variables, and the sample.

A promising recent development is the contribution of White (2000), who formulates a test of the null hypothesis that the best model encountered during a specification search has no predictive superiority over a benchmark model. If this null is not rejected, the implication is that this seemingly "best" model yielded by the specification search is just the outcome of data mining. As White (2000, p. 1098) remarks, "This permits data snooping/mining to be undertaken with some degree of confidence that one will not mistake results that could have been generated by chance for genuinely good results." However, White's test involves numerical simulation and so is beyond the scope of this book.

In practice, the approach to addressing the data mining problem that has had the biggest impact on applied work is the philosophy of the LSE methodology mentioned in Section 10.2.5, which may be summarized as: test, test, test! That is, we develop confidence in a model by testing it against alternatives. A few of the tests that econometricians have found useful for this purpose are discussed in the sections that follow.

12.2   Specification Testing

Once a model has been estimated—and regardless of how its specification has been arrived at, whether by a specification search or simple a priori conjecture—we wish to confirm that it offers a good description of the phenomenon it is intended to explain. That is, we wish to check whether the model may in some respects be inconsistent with the data. This is the purpose of **specification testing,** a term that encompasses many different kinds of tests.

Tests of Restrictions Suggested by Economic Theory

The restrictions most prized by econometricians are those that come to us from economic theory because it is these that offer the most direct test of that theory. Recent chapters have provided some examples.

> **The Mankiw-Romer-Weil equation for living standards.** In Chapter 9, we have seen that the textbook and augmented versions of the Solow-Swan model imply restrictions on their respective steady-state solutions for living standards that are not rejected by the data.

> **Linear homogeneity of cost functions.** In Chapter 11, we have seen that a cost function should be homogeneous of degree 1 in prices, so that a doubling of factor prices doubles cost. This property takes the form of a linear restriction on the coefficients of the Cobb-Douglas cost function and is testable by an F test. Nerlove's data do not reject this restriction.[3]

When restrictions such as these are not rejected, it helps give us confidence that the model has some validity. It does not, of course, prove that the model is correct;

---

[3] This should be your finding if you answered Exercise 11.8.

failure to reject a hypothesis never proves the hypothesis. Mankiw, Romer, and Weil found that, despite the failure to reject the restriction of the textbook model, the model was nevertheless unsatisfactory in other respects—coefficient estimates were inconsistent with plausible factor shares. This led them to formulate the augmented version of the model by introducing human capital. Similarly, despite the absence of a rejection of linear homogeneity in Nerlove's work, we have seen that the Cobb-Douglas cost function is in other respects unsatisfactory. This motivated the development of more sophisticated functional forms such as the translog.

Of course, sometimes the restrictions of economic theory *are* rejected, as we have seen in the following example.

Marginal productivity conditions. Section 7.4 shows that a marginal productivity condition derived from a Cobb-Douglas production function implies a slope coefficient of 1, reflecting the underlying assumption of a unitary elasticity of factor substitution embodied in the Cobb-Douglas function. In estimated marginal productivity conditions, however, this restriction is rejected, which led Arrow, Chenery, Minhas, and Solow to develop the more general CES production function.

In Section 10.1.5 we have seen that this is just one interpretation of this empirical finding. Victor Fuchs argued that the simple regression form of the marginal productivity condition may be misspecified. He showed that when a dummy variable is included to distinguish between developed and underdeveloped countries, the restriction of a unitary elasticity of substitution is not rejected.

These examples are ones in which a model is predicted to satisfy a certain parameter restriction; the rejection of that restriction falsifies the model without, in and of itself, suggesting any alternative model. Rejections do, however, spur the development of alternative or more general theories. Arrow, Chenery, Minhas, and Solow responded to the apparent failure of the Cobb-Douglas marginal productivity condition in one way and Fuchs in quite another. Mankiw, Romer, and Weil modified the textbook Solow-Swan model by incorporating human capital, but their insight was just one of many possibilities that might have been pursued. Similarly, a rejection of linear homogeneity falsifies that cost function without suggesting what alternative might be appropriate; the translog is just one possibility.

In some applications, on the other hand, the restrictions given to us by economic theory are ones that distinguish competing models. In the terminology of Section 10.2.5, the models are part of a nested testing structure. Chapter 11 gives us the following example.

Does the translog cost function reduce to the Cobb-Douglas? In using factor demand data to estimate a cost function or system of demand equations, the translog and Cobb-Douglas models are just two of many cost functions that might be considered. How can we choose among these competing models? Often one model is nested within another, and so the simpler model can be tested as a special case of the more complex one. We have seen, for example, that the Cobb-Douglas cost function is a special case of the translog and that the coefficient restrictions that reduce the translog to the Cobb-Douglas are testable. If the cost function is being estimated directly, the restrictions (11.47) reduce the translog (11.46) to the Cobb-Douglas; if it is the factor demands that are being estimated, the restrictions $\gamma_{ij} = \gamma_{Qi} = 0$ reduce the translog share equations (11.51) to those of the Cobb-Douglas (11.32). A rejection of the restrictions is a rejection of the Cobb-Douglas cost function.

Often the predictions of economic theory are less formal than in these examples. They may include coefficient signs (whether an effect is positive or negative) or magnitudes (e.g., the size of certain elasticities or multipliers). But the consequences of a falsification of the predictions are the same. Estimation results that do not conform with our a priori understanding, as embodied in the model that has been estimated, lead us to ask: What is wrong with that understanding?

Diagnostic Testing

Whether or not a model has been derived in such a way that economic theory yields testable restrictions—and especially when it has not—it is of interest to be able to test other aspects of its econometric specification.

There are many ways in which an econometric model may be misspecified. The assumptions underlying the classical normal linear regression model are discussed in Chapters 4 and 8. The implications of relaxing them are dealt with elsewhere in this book. For example, the next chapter considers intrinsically nonlinear functional forms, Chapter 14 a heteroskedastic disturbance, and Chapters 15–18 the implications of observing data over time rather than as the outcome of random sampling.

Testing the assumptions on which a model is based is called **diagnostic testing.** Let us consider an example of a diagnostic test that is an application of the F test and that is most naturally discussed here rather than in the violations of the classical assumptions dealt with in the chapters that follow.

12.2.1 Regression Specification Error Test for Functional Form

When we estimate a regression model, we do so on the basis of a chosen functional form. But how can we check whether this choice is a reasonable approximation of the pattern in the data? If we have a specific alternative model in mind, then the two specifications can be tested directly against one another using conventional nested testing methods, or perhaps the nonnested tests in Section 12.3, or compared using the model selection criteria in Section 12.4. But suppose there is no specific alternative model that suggests itself?

As an example, consider Nerlove's data on the cost of electricity generation. In our earliest examination of these data we focus on the relationship between generation costs and output, neglecting a fully specified cost function that includes

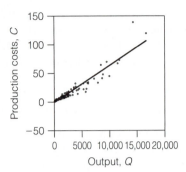

factor prices (as studied in Chapter 11). Initially, in Section 4.10, we fit a simple linear regression to these cost-output data:

$$C_i = \beta_1 + \beta_2 Q_i + \varepsilon_i.$$

The sample regression line is shown in Figure 12.1; notice that the data reproduce our earliest plot of these data in Figure 3.1. In Section 8.8, we explore quadratic and cubic extensions of this regression.

It is evident from the figure that there is a nonlinearity in the data that is not captured by this simple linear regression. Although in this instance this is revealed graphically, in more complex econometric problems graphical methods may be less useful in identifying model misspecifications like this. Is it possible to test statistically for such specification inadequacies?

Because the problem is that the specified functional form fails to capture nonlinearities in the data, the obvious approach is to add nonlinear terms to the regression and see whether they are significant. The easiest way to do this is to add powers of the explanatory variables, creating a polynomial regression. Consider adding quadratic and cubic terms to the function:

$$C_i = \beta_1 + \beta_2 Q_i + \beta_3 Q_i^2 + \beta_4 Q_i^3 + \varepsilon_i.$$

One justification for this is the mathematical fact that a nonlinear function can be approximated arbitrarily closely by a polynomial of adequate order.

EXAMPLE 1

nerlove1.dat

Using Nerlove's data, are the polynomial terms in this cost function jointly statistically significant?

SOLUTION

The two models have been estimated previously in the exercises in Sections 4.10 and 8.8. The joint significance of the polynomial terms can be tested with an F test. This yields $F = 34.91$ which, for $g = 2$ and $n - K = 141$ degrees of freedom, rejects at conventional significance levels (the p-value is zero to several decimal places). The statistical significance of the polynomial terms confirms the graphical conclusion that the simple linear regression is unsatisfactory as a functional form for Nerlove's data.

This polynomial regression is the cubic cost function that was estimated in Section 8.8. Although this is used as the basis for the test, there is no suggestion that it is the correct alternative model. On the contrary, Section 8.8 proposed the log-quadratic model as one that offers similar theoretical properties to a cubic polynomial (permitting a reverse-S-shaped cost function), but with one fewer parameters. Rejection of the null in the above test means only that the null is unsatisfactory; it leaves open the question of what alternative might be better.

The Regression Specification Error Test

So what might be better? In the case of cost data, economic theory tells us that a properly specified cost function includes factor prices. The Cobb-Douglas cost function (11.41) in Chapter 11 modeled nonlinearities in the data with a loglinear functional form:

$$\log C_i = \alpha + \beta \log Q_i + \gamma_1 \log p_{1i} + \gamma_2 \log p_{2i} + \gamma_3 \log p_{3i} + \varepsilon_i.$$

Suppose we want to test the adequacy of this specification. To add squares and cubes of all the explanatory variables is in principle possible, but this would expand a $K = 5$ regression to $K = 13$. In more complex models with more limited data sets, this would quickly use up degrees of freedom. Ramsey (1969) proposed as a solution to this problem that, instead of powers of the explanatory variables, powers of the predicted values of the regression be tested. Letting $\hat{c}_i$ denote the predicted values of the regression, Ramsey's **regression specification error test** (RESET) estimates an augmented regression such as

$$\log C_i = \alpha + \beta \log Q_i + \gamma_1 \log p_{1i} + \gamma_2 \log p_{2i} + \gamma_3 \log p_{3i}$$
$$+ \phi_1 \hat{c}_i^2 + \phi_2 \hat{c}_i^3 + \varepsilon_i$$

and tests the joint significance of the $\hat{c}_i$ terms, in this case the hypothesis $\phi_1 = \phi_2 = 0$. Of course the choice to include second and third powers of $\hat{c}_i$ is somewhat arbitrary. Occasionally a fourth power is used as well; Davidson and MacKinnon (2004, p. 655) recommend that only the squared term be used, so that the RESET becomes a t test on that coefficient. Note that the $\hat{c}_i$ variable itself cannot be included among the set of **test variables** because it is a linear combination of the original explanatory variables and is therefore perfectly collinear with them.

EXAMPLE 2

nerlove.dat

Does a RESET indicate that the Cobb-Douglas cost function fails to capture any nonlinearity in Nerlove's data?

SOLUTION

An F test of the restrictions $\phi_1 = \phi_2 = 0$ yields $F = 47.63$ which, for $g = 2$ and $n - K = 138$ degrees of freedom, rejects at conventional significance levels. The conclusion is that, whatever its other merits may be, the Cobb-Douglas cost function does not adequately describe Nerlove's cost data.

This conclusion is not very surprising because we have seen in Section 8.8 that a simple loglinear relationship between costs and output provides a poor description of the relationship between these variables; recall Figure 8.4(c). This fundamental deficiency is unlikely to be overcome merely by the inclusion of factor prices. As we have seen in Exercise 11.14, Nerlove himself recognized this and attempted to address it with the ad hoc introduction of a quadratic term on $\log Q$:

$$\log C_i = \alpha + \beta \log Q_i + \delta (\log Q_i)^2 + \gamma_1 \log p_{1i} + \gamma_2 \log p_{2i} + \gamma_3 \log p_{3i} + \varepsilon_i.$$

In doing this, he anticipated the log-quadratic formulation of the cost-output relationship in the translog functional form (11.46). How satisfactory is Nerlove's modification?

EXAMPLE 3

nerlove.dat

Perform a RESET of Nerlove's log-quadratic extension to the Cobb-Douglas cost function.

SOLUTION

Obtaining the predicted values of the cost function and reestimating it introducing their squares and cubes, yields a RESET statistic of $F = 1.482$; for $g = 2$ and $n - K = 137$ degrees of freedom, the p-value is 0.231. Consequently, the null hypothesis of an absence of functional form misspecification is not rejected at conventional significance levels.

Conclusions

The RESET is a test of the absence of functional form misspecification; the null hypothesis is that the model is correctly specified, the alternative hypothesis that it is not. The test proceeds by adding a set of test variables to the model and testing their joint significance. Typical choices for these test variables are powers of the explanatory variables or, in Ramsey's version, powers of the predicted values.

When a RESET rejects the null of an absence of misspecification, by itself this does not suggest an alternative specification. An appropriate alternative may be some other intrinsically linear functional form that permits a different functional relationship between the variables through the use of logarithmic, reciprocal, or polynomial (or some other) transformations; or it may be some intrinsically nonlinear form.

EXERCISES

12.1 nerlove.dat Replicate the results of the preceding examples by proceeding as follows.

(a) Estimate the cubic cost function and do a joint test on the significance of the polynomial terms. How close do you come to replicating the F statistic reported in Example 1?

(b) Estimate the Cobb-Douglas cost function, and then use the predicted values to perform a RESET. How close do you come to replicating the F statistic reported in Example 2?

(c) Estimate the log-quadratic Cobb-Douglas cost function, and then use the predicted values to perform a RESET. How close do you come to replicating the F statistic reported in Example 3?

12.2 houthak.dat Consider Houthakker's demand equation for electricity consumption, as developed in Section 8.6.

(a) The primary specification used by Houthakker was a loglinear one, equation (8.26). Perform a RESET of this functional form. What are your conclusions regarding the adequacy of this specification?

(b) Suppose that a linear (not loglinear) regression had been used. What does a RESET have to say about the adequacy of this specification?

12.3 Nonnested Testing

Diagnostic testing asks whether the econometric specification is consistent with the data. As the RESET illustrates, we do not necessarily have any alternative candidate model in mind.

In some circumstances, however, alternative model specifications may be available, and we may want to test a chosen specification directly against a competitor. When the testing structure is nested, we already have the statistical tools to do this. (Nested testing structures are discussed in Section 10.2.5.)

It is common in applied work, however, that the models under consideration are not special cases of one another and so do not fall within a nested testing structure. Thus, they cannot be tested directly against one another using standard tests for overidentifying restrictions.

We first encounter such **nonnested models** in Chapter 10 in which, in Tables 10.4 and 10.5, the restricted marginal productivity conditions $F3$ and $F4$ were nonnested. They were, however, separately testable as restricted versions of the general ACMS marginal productivity condition with dummy terms $F1$ and so could be tested as special cases of that general model.

In contrast, in many economic problems, theory suggests nonnested models that are not special cases of any more general model, and so it is desirable to be able to test them directly against one another. As an example of such a situation, consider our use in Chapter 6 of alternative intrinsically linear functional forms to study Engel curves. In the exercises in Section 6.5, we used Houthakker's electricity demand data to estimate, among other specifications, the following lin-log and reciprocal Engel curves.

$$H_1: \quad q_i = \alpha + \beta \log m_i + \varepsilon_i \quad \text{(lin-log)}$$

$$H_2: \quad q_i = \alpha + \beta \frac{1}{m_i} + \varepsilon_i \quad \text{(reciprocal)}$$

These functions are denoted H_1 and H_2 to indicate that they are different hypotheses about how electricity consumption depends on income. Their sample regression lines are shown fitted to Houthakker's data in Figure 6.12(b) and (c). They are *nonnested hypotheses* in that neither can be obtained as a restricted (and therefore testable) special case of the other.

Here economic theory suggests no more general Engel curve specification within which H_1 and H_2 can be tested as restricted regressions. The obvious approach to nonnested testing is to create an artificial compound model that includes both as special cases and is thus amenable to the use of conventional nested testing methods. There are two approaches to doing this that are widely used in applied econometrics: the **encompassing test** and a class of tests typified by the **J test.**

Many-Degrees-of-Freedom Tests: The Encompassing Test

The most obvious way to combine H_1 and H_2 into a single general model is to include all the potential regressors on the right-hand side:

$$q_i = \alpha + \beta_1 \log m_i + \beta_2 \frac{1}{m_i} + \varepsilon_i.$$

We can then test as follows:

a test of the null of H_1 against the alternative of H_2 is a test of $\beta_2 = 0$.
a test of the null of H_2 against the alternative of H_1 is a test of $\beta_1 = 0$.

This approach to nonnested testing can be interpreted as an application of the "encompassing principle" of Mizon and Richard (1986); see also Mizon (1984). Hence, it is called the encompassing test.

EXAMPLE 4

houthak.dat

Consider the lin-log and reciprocal Engel curves estimated using Houthakker's electricity demand data. What is the outcome of encompassing tests?

SOLUTION

The results for the respective t tests on the slopes β_1 and β_2 of the encompassing regression are as follows.

	t statistic	*p-value*	
H_1: $\beta_2 = 0$	−0.105	0.917	(lin-log null)
H_2: $\beta_1 = 0$	1.729	0.092	(reciprocal null)

The very large p-value for H_1 lends support to the lin-log formulation; the reciprocal model, by contrast, is rejected at a 10% significance level.

In general, regression models may be nonnested with respect to several explanatory variables, and the encompassing test is an F test on several coefficients; it is therefore called a many-degrees-of-freedom test. Here is an example.

EXAMPLE 5

houthak.dat

The following electricity demand equations are variations on Houthakker's specifications in Section 8.6.

$$H_1: q_i = \beta_1 + \beta_2 \log m_i + \beta_3 \log p_{1i} + \beta_4 p_{2i} + \beta_5 h_i + \varepsilon_i \quad \text{(lin-log)} \quad (12.1a)$$

$$H_2: q_i = \beta_1 + \beta_2 \frac{1}{m_i} + \beta_3 \frac{1}{p_{1i}} + \beta_4 p_{2i} + \beta_5 h_i + \varepsilon_i \quad \text{(reciprocal)} \quad (12.1b)$$

These regressions differ according to whether income m and own-price p_1 enter in logarithmic or reciprocal form; the cross-price of gas p_2 and household holdings of heavy electric equipment h appear linearly in both specifications. Test the two formulations against one another.

SOLUTION

The encompassing model may be denoted

$$q_i = \beta_1 + \beta_{11} \log m_i + \beta_{12} \log p_{1i} + \beta_{21} \frac{1}{m_i} + \beta_{22} \frac{1}{p_{1i}} + \beta_4 p_{2i} + \beta_5 h_i + \varepsilon_i.$$

Using Houthakker's data, the results for the respective F tests are as follows.

	F statistic	*p-value*	
$H_1: \beta_{21} = \beta_{22} = 0$	0.011	0.989	(lin-log null)
$H_2: \beta_{11} = \beta_{12} = 0$	4.580	0.017	(reciprocal null)

Once again the very large p-value for H_1 lends support to the lin-log formulation, whereas the reciprocal model is rejected at a 5% significance level.

Single-Degree-of-Freedom Tests: The J Test

Although the encompassing test is perhaps the natural one for intrinsically linear regressions, it turns out that it does not always generalize to more complex situations such as the nonlinear regression models we study in Chapter 13. Consequently, some nonnested tests are based on an alternative approach to creating an artificial compound model; these tests are often applied even to linear regressions.

Consider the electricity demand equations in Example 5 and an artificial nesting of the form

$$q_i = \beta_1 + \theta(\beta_{11} \log m_i + \beta_{12} \log p_{1i}) + (1 - \theta)\left(\beta_{21} \frac{1}{m_i} + \beta_{22} \frac{1}{p_{1i}}\right)$$
$$+ \beta_4 p_{2i} + \beta_5 h_i + \varepsilon_i.$$

The parameter θ acts like a switch that selects between the two specifications, and the hypotheses of interest may be stated as restrictions on this switch:

$H_1: \theta = 1$ (lin-log null),

$H_2: \theta = 0$ (reciprocal null).

Thus, if these restrictions on θ could be tested, it would be possible to distinguish between the two models.

Unfortunately, θ cannot be tested directly because, as stated, the regression is not identified and therefore cannot be estimated—θ is not separately identifiable from β_{11}, β_{12}, β_{21}, β_{22}. Nevertheless Davidson and MacKinnon (1981) showed that a test based on this artificial compound model can be implemented in two steps, as follows.

Step 1. Estimate the separate regressions under H_1 and H_2 (in our example, the original lin-log and reciprocal models (12.1)), and obtain the respective predicted values (denoted, say, $\hat{q}_{1i}$ and $\hat{q}_{2i}$).

Step 2. Include these predicted values in augmented versions of H_1 and H_2, respectively. A test of the null of H_1 against the alternative of H_2 is a test of $\theta_2 = 0$ in the following regression:

$$q_i = \beta_1 + \beta_2 \log m_i + \beta_3 \log p_{1i} + \beta_4 p_{2i} + \beta_5 h_i + \theta_2 \hat{q}_{2i} + \varepsilon_i \quad \text{(lin-log null)}.$$

THEORY MEETS APPLICATION   12.3

Private and Public Capital in the Mankiw-Romer-Weil Model

Chapter 9 discusses the Mankiw-Romer-Weil reformulation of the Solow-Swan growth model to incorporate human capital. MRW derived the following steady-state equation for living standards, equation (9.24), which we call here hypothesis H_1.

$$H_1: \log q_i = \beta_1 + \beta_2 \log s_{ki} + \beta_3 \log(\delta + n_i)$$
$$+ \beta_4 \log s_{hi} + \varepsilon_i$$

As described in Theory Meets Application 9.1, Milbourne, Otto, and Voss extended the MRW analysis to distinguish between private and public capital. Denoting the respective saving rates s_p and s_g, they called this hypothesis H_2.

$$H_2: \log q_i = \beta_1 + \beta_2 \log s_{pi} + \beta_3 \log(\delta + n_i)$$
$$+ \beta_4 \log s_{hi} + \beta_5 \log s_{gi} + \varepsilon_i$$

We have reported that the saving rate on public capital s_g turns out to be statistically insignificant, implying that only private capital is important for living standards. Let us call this hypothesis H_3.

$$H_3: \log q_i = \beta_1 + \beta_2 \log s_{pi} + \beta_3 \log(\delta + n_i)$$
$$+ \beta_4 \log s_{hi} + \varepsilon_i$$

The restriction $\beta_5 = 0$ is an example of nested testing; that is, H_3 is nested within H_2.

Relative to H_1, however, H_2 and H_3 are nonnested models; both include variables that do not appear in H_1, and H_1 includes the variable $\log s_k$ that does not appear in either H_2 or H_3. Milbourne, Otto, and Voss estimated these regressions over two country samples: a group of 74 non-oil-producing countries and another intermediate group of 57 countries. For each sample, they performed J tests of these nonnested hypotheses, reporting the following p-values.

	Hypotheses H_1 and H_2		Hypotheses H_1 and H_3	
Sample	Null: H_1	Null: H_2	Null: H_1	Null: H_3
Non-oil-producing	0.16	0.00	0.12	0.06
Intermediate	0.02	0.21	0.02	0.25

These test results are mixed. At a 10% significance level, any one model is rejected against some other for one of the samples, although at a 5% significance level H_3 is not rejected against H_1 for either sample, to some extent favoring this model. In the next section we throw more light on this by taking a different approach to comparing these models.

The idea is that, if H_1 is the correct model, then the component of q explained by H_2 should not be statistically significant over and above the regressors in H_1. Similarly, a test of the reciprocal null H_2 against the lin-log alternative H_1 is a test of $\theta_1 = 0$ in

$$q_i = \beta_1 + \beta_2 \frac{1}{m_i} + \beta_3 \frac{1}{p_{1i}} + \beta_4 p_{2i} + \beta_5 h_i + \theta_1 \hat{q}_{1i} + \varepsilon_i \quad \text{(reciprocal null)}.$$

Davidson and MacKinnon called this the J test because effectively these regressions constitute the *joint* estimation of the switch parameter θ_1 or θ_2 and the coefficients of the original models H_1 or H_2.

TABLE 12.2   Electricity Demand: *p*-Values for Nonnested Tests

| Test | Null hypothesis | |
	H_1 (lin-log)	H_2 (reciprocal)
J test	0.915	0.004
Encompassing test	0.989	0.017

The *p*-values for the *t* tests of H_1: $\theta_2 = 0$ and H_2: $\theta_1 = 0$ are given in Table 12.2; for comparison, the results of the encompassing test from Example 5 are also reported. In this example, the outcomes of the two tests are very similar, both clearly favoring the logarithmic over the reciprocal formulation. Notice that, whereas the encompassing test is in general an *F* test, the *J* test is always a *t* test on the single parameter θ. The *J* test, and the variations on it that derive from this approach to artificial nesting, are therefore called single-degree-of-freedom tests. In the special case in which the nonnested regressions differ by only a single variable so that the encompassing test is a single-degree-of-freedom test, as in Example 4, the two tests turn out to be identical; you confirm this for the lin-log and reciprocal Engel curves in Exercise 12.3c.

Inconclusive Test Outcomes

In our examples of the nonnested testing of lin-log (H_1) versus reciprocal (H_2) Engel curves and demand equations, each test yields consistent decisions, rejecting H_2 in favor of H_1 and failing to reject H_1 against H_2. This was the basis for our overall conclusion that, of the two functional forms, the data clearly favor the lin-log specification.

In general, however, nonnested tests need not lead to a conclusive model choice; for a chosen level of significance, a nonnested test may reject both models or may fail to reject both. The possibilities are summarized in Table 12.3.

It is often said that the possibility of such inconclusive test outcomes—rejecting both models or failing to reject them—is a problem with nonnested testing. However, this "problem" is inherent in the choice of hypothesis testing as a tool in model evaluation. By design, hypothesis tests always treat hypotheses asymmetrically, rejecting the null only on the basis of compelling evidence. When a nonnested test is used to test H_1 against H_2, a primacy has been attached to H_1 a priori such that it will only be rejected on strong grounds; similarly for H_2

TABLE 12.3   Possible Outcomes of Nonnested Testing

| Test of H_2 against H_1 | Test of H_1 against H_2 | |
	Reject	Fail to reject
Reject	Both models rejected	H_2 rejected in favor of H_1
Fail to reject	H_1 rejected in favor of H_2	Neither model rejected

against H_1. When nonnested tests reject both hypotheses, the data are indicating that both models are unsatisfactory and the researcher should consider yet other models. When nonnested tests fail to reject both hypotheses, the data are indicating that the evidence is not strong enough to conclude that either model is clearly unsatisfactory.

If an applied econometrician finds such inconclusive outcomes unsatisfactory, it is the choice of nonnested testing as a framework for model evaluation that is at fault, not the framework itself. Nonnested tests are not intended to find the one "best" model. If this is the objective, then the researcher is concerned with model choice, a conceptually distinct approach to model evaluation that is considered in the next section.

In the same spirit, all the usual qualifications about the correct interpretation of hypothesis tests apply. If a nonnested test rejects H_1 in favor of H_2 this does not prove that H_2 is the correct model; the rejection of a null hypothesis never implies acceptance of the alternative. There could be many reasons why H_1 is false; the model H_2 is just one possibility. Similarly, a failure to reject H_1 does not prove that it is the correct model; failure to reject a hypothesis never implies its acceptance.

Further Comments

As we have presented them, the encompassing and J tests apply only to nonnested models having a common dependent variable. They do not, for example, offer a means of testing linear versus loglinear regression specifications, a testing problem that in practice would often be of interest. Although nonnested tests have been developed for such situations, they are more difficult to apply than the fairly straightforward tests we have considered here and are less frequently encountered in applied work. In such cases empirical researchers may prefer to turn to model choice as a framework for model evaluation.

EXERCISES

12.3 ⊙ **houthak.dat** Use Houthakker's data as documented in Section 8.6 to answer the following questions.

(a) How close can you come to replicating the encompassing test results in Examples 4 and 5?

(b) How close can you come to replicating the J test results in Table 12.2?

(c) Perform J tests of log-lin versus reciprocal Engel curves. How do the results compare to your encompassing tests of the same models?

12.4 Consider regressions H_1 and H_2 in the Milbourne, Otto, and Voss analysis. For one set of measures available to them, the saving rate on physical capital s_k was the total of the saving rates on private and public capital: $s_k = s_p + s_g$. Does this imply a testable restriction on the coefficients of H_2?

12.4   Model Choice

Suppose we are considering several alternative models. Instead of asking which are or are not rejected in favor of others, another approach to model discovery is to ask which is the best model. Finding the best model from among several competing ones is the problem of **model choice** or **model selection.** This is a fundamentally different approach from nonnested testing because it treats models *symmetrically*; by contrast, in adopting the framework of hypothesis testing, nonnested tests treat alternative models *asymmetrically* by taking one as the null hypothesis, to be rejected only on the basis of compelling evidence.

But what do we mean by *best*? The purpose of any model is to explain observable phenomena; in the case of a regression model, to explain the dependent variable. Thus, the problem of model selection is inherently related to predictive ability. Models that do a good job of explaining the variables they are intended to explain, and therefore generate accurate predictions, are good models; the best model is the one that has the best predictive ability. This idea applies in both cross-sectional and time series contexts.

12.4.1   Selection of Regressors

How can we judge how well a model explains its dependent variable? One approach is to consider the correlation between the dependent variable Y_i and the predicted values $\hat{Y}_i$ generated by the estimated model; in a regression model, this is equivalent to the R^2.[4] Given the definition of the R^2 as $1 - \text{SSE}/\text{SST}$, for a given dependent variable this is the same as choosing the model that minimizes the SSE or, equivalently, the disturbance variance estimator $\hat{\sigma}^2 = \text{SSE}/n$.

R^2 and $\overline{R}^2$ Revisited

The problem with this approach as stated is that, as we have seen in Chapter 8, the R^2 can always be increased (or, equivalently, the SSE reduced) by adding more variables and parameters. This motivates the definition of the $\overline{R}^2$, which introduces a penalty for additional parameters in such a way that choosing the model to maximize $\overline{R}^2$ is equivalent to minimizing the unbiased disturbance variance estimator $s^2 = \text{SSE}/(n - K)$ (recall Section 8.5.2). The motivation for this penalty is that it is always possible to explain the data better by constructing a more complicated model; importance should be attached as well to model simplicity. As we argue in our discussion of the principle of parsimony in Section 7.5, it is only worth adopting a more complex model if that model does a substantially better job of explaining the data than some simpler model.

---

[4]   See Exercise 4.22. The derivation generalizes to multiple regression.

There is, however, no objective basis for making the trade-off between predictive ability and model parsimony. Ultimately, the particular penalty used by $\overline{R}^2$ is arbitrary, and others could be considered. Indeed, we have seen in Section 8.5.2 that the penalty implicit in $\overline{R}^2$ is slight: $\overline{R}^2$ can increase when a variable is added even when a hypothesis test finds it insignificant. Thus, when $\overline{R}^2$ is used as a selection criterion it is fairly easy to make the mistake of including irrelevant variables. In a comprehensive study of model selection criteria Mills and Prasad (1992, p. 221) found $\overline{R}^2$ to be "...clearly the worst, with a serious tendency towards overparametrization."

The Loglikelihood Function

After the $\overline{R}^2$, the most widely used criteria for model selection can be interpreted as transformations of the **loglikelihood function,** which we denote by $\mathscr{L}$. The value of the loglikelihood function of an estimated model is usually printed by econometric software. For regression models, it is just a transformation of $\hat{\sigma}^2$:

$$\mathscr{L} = -\frac{n}{2}\left(1 + \log(2\pi) + \log\hat{\sigma}^2\right). \tag{12.2}$$

The nature of this transformation—involving as it does the negative sign in front— is such that the maximum of $\mathscr{L}$ is the minimum of $\hat{\sigma}^2$. Consequently, choosing the model that maximizes $\mathscr{L}$ is the same as choosing one that minimizes $\hat{\sigma}^2$ or, equivalently in light of our previous discussion, minimizes SSE or maximizes the R^2. The loglikelihood function by itself involves no penalty for additional parameters—K does not appear in the formula—and so as a basis for model choice suffers from the same deficiency as R^2.

Information Criteria

Some of the most popular selection criteria essentially modify $\mathscr{L}$ or, equivalently, $\hat{\sigma}^2$, by introducing such a penalty. The one that is perhaps most often encountered in applied work, other than the $\overline{R}^2$, is the **Akaike information criterion** (AIC) (Akaike 1974), the original expression for which is

Original AIC $= \hat{\sigma}^2 e^{2K/n}$.

Another is the **Bayesian information criterion** (BIC) of Schwartz (1978), also known as the **Schwartz criterion:**

Original BIC $= \hat{\sigma}^2 n^{K/n}$.

These are the formulas implemented by some software.[5] Notice that, defined in this way as transformations of $\hat{\sigma}^2$, smaller values of the AIC or BIC indicate a better fitting model. The multiplicative factors applied to $\hat{\sigma}^2$ are penalty terms that,

---

[5] Notably the econometrics package Shazam.

it may be shown, are a more severe constraint on additional parameters than is the penalty implicit in $\overline{R}^2$.

To see how these formulas compare and how they relate to $\mathcal{L}$, consider taking their logarithms and introducing the additive constants of the loglikelihood function so as to define:

$$\text{Alternative AIC} = -\frac{2\mathcal{L}}{n} + \frac{2K}{n}$$

$$\text{Alternative BIC} = -\frac{2\mathcal{L}}{n} + \frac{K \log n}{n}.$$

The negative sign in front of the first term in these expressions has the effect that *larger* values of $\mathcal{L}$ correspond to *smaller* values of the criteria, so that smaller values continue to indicate a better fitting model.

The numerical values produced by these alternative formulas will, of course, differ from those of the original formulas. Nevertheless, a given criterion such as the AIC yields the same ranking of alternative models, regardless of whether the original or alternative form is used. This is because the different versions of the formula arise merely from the application of the logarithmic transformation and the introduction of additive constants.[6] Many software packages use these alternative versions of the statistics.[7] Some use yet other variants, often because they omit some of the additive constants from the definition of the loglikelihood (12.2) for reasons that become clearer in the next chapter.

It is evident that the AIC and BIC differ in the penalties they impose on additional coefficients. Comparing the two penalty terms, the BIC's is larger than the AIC's as long as $\log n > 2$, or $n > e^2 = 7.389$, establishing that for realistic sample sizes the BIC incorporates a larger penalty for additional parameters than does the AIC. In their study Mills and Prasad (1992, p. 222) concluded that on balance the BIC "... should probably be the first choice of applied researchers."

EXAMPLE 6

houthak1.dat

Consider the lin-log and reciprocal Engel curves that were estimated with Houthakker's electricity demand data. Do the various model selection criteria we have considered suggest a preferred model? How does this compare with the outcome of nonnested testing?

SOLUTION

Because the lin-log and reciprocal Engel curves have the same number of explanatory variables—both are simple regressions—the different penalties for additional parameters imposed by the different selection criteria will not be important for the decision. All will suggest the same preferred model because they are all just transformations of the SSE.

---

[6] To use mathematical terminology, the alternative formulas are just monotonic transformations of the original ones.

[7] Notably EViews and, in the case of the BIC, TSP. A given software package may even change its definition of these statistics across releases.

Selection criterion	Model		
	Lin-log		Reciprocal
SSE	6352600	<	6837300
R^2	0.6247	>	0.5961
$\overline{R}^2$	0.6153	>	0.5860
$\mathscr{L}$	−310.056	>	−311.600
AIC	14.860	<	14.933
BIC	14.943	<	15.016

These AIC and BIC values are those yielded by the alternative formulas. Notice that for each model the value of the BIC is similar to but larger than that for the AIC, reflecting the larger penalty assigned to any given number of parameters.

These selection criteria indicate that the lin-log model provides a better description of these data than does the reciprocal model, a conclusion consistent with the nonnested tests in the previous section (as discussed in Example 4).

Further Comments

Different model selection criteria essentially strike slightly different balances between the benefits of including additional information in a model versus the costs of estimating additional parameters. Information criteria such as the AIC and BIC (and the many other model selection criteria that have been proposed) are derived from **loss functions** that formalize this trade-off between predictive ability and model parsimony.

Ultimately, however, there is no objective basis for this trade-off, even when it is formalized in this way. This led Amemiya (1980, p. 352) to conclude "...the general picture that has emerged...is that all of the criteria considered are based on a somewhat arbitrary assumption which cannot be fully justified, and that by slightly varying the loss function and the decision strategy one can indefinitely go on inventing new criteria. This is what one would expect, for there is no simple solution to a complex problem."

This arbitrariness is not by itself an objection to the use of these criteria as a basis for model choice. As our discussion of $\overline{R}^2$ in Section 8.5.2 illustrates, the seeming arbitrariness in the trade-off between fit and parsimony really just mirrors the arbitrariness in the choice of significance level in hypothesis testing. The choice of a particular penalty for additional parameters is no more arbitrary than the choice of significance level.

This is not to suggest that the model selection approach is by itself entirely satisfactory. Even the "best" model, however judged, may be rejected by the data, and if this is the case we would certainly want to know it. Model selection criteria are best viewed as one useful tool in the applied econometrician's toolbox, a complement to rather than a substitute for hypothesis testing. In Theory Meets Application 12.3 and 12.4, we illustrate the joint use of nonnested tests and model selection criteria as interactive tools of model evaluation, by applying them to

THEORY MEETS APPLICATION   12.4

Private and Public Capital Revisited

In Theory Meets Application 12.3 we show how Milbourne, Otto, and Voss used nonnested testing to distinguish among alternative versions of the Mankiw-Romer-Weil regression based on different decompositions of capital. Do model selection criteria shed any additional light on this?

Recall that three regressions were estimated, using the saving rates s_p, s_g, and s_h for private, public, and human capital, respectively, and s_k for the aggregate of private and public physical capital:

$$H_1: s_k, s_h \quad H_2: s_p, s_h, s_g \quad H_3: s_p, s_h.$$

Milbourne, Otto, and Voss reported the following $\overline{R}^2$s for the non-oil-producing and intermediate samples.

| | $\overline{R}^2$ | | |
Sample	H_1	H_2	H_3
Non-oil-producing	0.71	0.71	0.72
Intermediate	0.68	0.70	0.71

The similarity of these $\overline{R}^2$s indicates that there is no strong basis for preferring one model over another—the same conclusion that came out of nonnested testing. Nevertheless the following observations can be made.

H_1 versus H_3. A comparison of the $\overline{R}^2$s indicates that, for both samples, H_3 is preferred over H_1. Furthermore, this conclusion is not contingent on the use of $\overline{R}^2$ as the selection criterion; because these two models have the same number of coefficients, penalties for additional parameters are irrelevant and all the model choice criteria we have studied will yield the same decision.

H_1 versus H_2. The similarity of the $\overline{R}^2$s for these models indicates that the additional coefficient of H_2 roughly balances a smaller SSE. A heavier penalty for the additional coefficient, such as that imposed by the AIC or BIC, could easily favor of the more parsimonious model H_1.

H_2 versus H_3. These models are nested: H_2 involves the additional regressor s_g. As we report in Theory Meets Application 9.1, this variable is statistically insignificant—so insignificant, in fact, that introducing it actually causes the $\overline{R}^2$ to fall, implying that its t statistic must be less than 1. (In fact, the t ratio on this variable is 0.41 for the non-oil-producing sample and 0.18 for the intermediate sample.)

On balance, then, the model selection approach gives the edge to H_3. This reinforces our previous conclusion that public capital is unimportant in explaining variations in living standards across countries, either as an aggregate with private capital (s_k in H_1) or on its own (s_g in H_2).

---

the alternative versions of the Mankiw-Romer-Weil regression estimated by Milbourne, Otto, and Voss (2003). As we note in Chapter 16, information criteria such as the AIC and BIC are especially popular as a guide to the specification of time series models, a use endorsed by, for example, Granger, King, and White (1995). For an introduction to their use in this context, see Diebold (2004, Chap. 4).

> Practitioner's Tip: **Model selection**
>
> All model selection criteria make a trade-off between goodness-of-fit and model parsimony. Alternative selection criteria differ according to the penalty they impose for additional parameters. For models with the same number of parameters, model selection criteria are equivalent to simply comparing SSEs, as illustrated by Example 6.

12.4.2 Transformed Dependent Variables

Our discussion has been phrased in terms of regressions with a common dependent variable. But, of course, it is very common to wish to compare models with different dependent variables. The most common such situation is when the dependent variable may or may not be in log form. Consider, for example, lin-log versus log-log Engel curves:

$$q_i = \alpha + \beta \log m_i + \varepsilon_i \quad \text{(lin-log: } \mathcal{L}_1\text{)}$$

$$\log q_i = \alpha + \beta \log m_i + \varepsilon_i \quad \text{(log-log: } \mathcal{L}_2\text{)}$$

In such situations the selection criteria we have discussed do not apply for the same reason that the R^2 or $\overline{R}^2$ cannot be used to compare regressions with different dependent variables. Specifically, $\mathcal{L}_1$ is the loglikelihood function value of a model for q_i, whereas $\mathcal{L}_2$ is the loglikelihood function value of a model for $\log q_i$; as loglikelihood function values for *different* dependent variables, the two are not directly comparable.

It turns out, however, that a fairly minor modification makes them comparable and so provides the basis for a selection criterion. Consider the following modification of $\mathcal{L}_2$:

$$\mathcal{L}_2 - \sum_{i=1}^{n} \log q_i.$$

The second term, the sum of the log-dependent variable, is called the **Jacobian term;** it converts $\mathcal{L}_2$, the loglikelihood function value for the model with the log-dependent variable, into an implied loglikelihood function value for q_i that can be compared with $\mathcal{L}_1$.

E X A M P L E   7

houthak1.dat

Use this modification to compare log-log versus lin-log Engel curves for Houthakker's electricity demand data.

SOLUTION The loglikelihood function value for the log-log regression is $\mathcal{L}_2 = -11.2307$ and the sum of its dependent variable is $\sum_{i=1}^{n} \log q_i = 295.029$. Comparing this with $\mathcal{L}_1$ from Example 6, we have

$$\text{(log-log)} \quad \mathcal{L}_2 - \sum_{i=1}^{n} \log q_i = -306.260 > -310.056 = \mathcal{L}_1 \quad \text{(lin-log)}.$$

Because it has the higher value, the log-log specification is preferred to the lin-log.

The derivation of the Jacobian term requires an understanding of maximum likelihood estimation. The same idea applies to other types of transformations of the dependent variable, and the Jacobian term has to be derived appropriate to the case; see Davidson and MacKinnon (2004, Sec. 10.8).

Notice that the comparison of models in this way involves no penalty for additional parameters. This is not an issue in models with the same number of parameters, like Example 7, but it is for models with different numbers of parameters. In such applications we could use the comparable loglikelihood function values as a basis for the calculation of comparable AICs or BICs, and all the same issues surrounding alternative penalties would apply.

Practitioner's Tip: Model selection with different dependent variables

As a rule, do not use model selection criteria to compare models with different dependent variables. The exception is when one dependent variable is a transformation of the other, in which case the loglikelihood function values can be compared (with some chosen penalty for additional parameters) as long as the appropriate Jacobian term is used.

EXERCISES

12.5 houthak1.dat Use Houthakker's data to estimate the lin-log, reciprocal, and log-log Engel curves.

(a) Are you able to verify the numerical values of Examples 6 and 7? In particular, does your software produce the correct loglikelihood function values?

(b) If your software reports the AIC and BIC, are they computed according to the original or alternative, or some other, formula?

12.6 houthak.dat The exercises in Section 8.6 consider two specifications of electricity demand that were estimated by Houthakker (1951), a log-linear model (8.26) and a reciprocal model (8.27). Which specification is best? Does your answer depend on the choice of penalty for additional parameters?

12.5

Should the Equation Be Part of a System? ★

Thus far in this chapter our concern has been with model discovery in a single-equation context. Sometimes, however, the equation of interest is one of several that are related. That is, it is one of a system of equations, and estimation can exploit this. We have discussed systems of equations briefly at a few points in earlier chapters, and now is a good time to reassert that relationships of interest must sometimes be analyzed as part of a larger system.

As we have seen in Section 5.3.3, the estimation of systems of equations requires the appropriate application of the GMM or maximum likelihood principles. Because these are beyond the scope of this book, our goal in what follows is not to discuss the specifics of the estimation of such systems; there are many excellent treatments of systems estimation in more advanced books that use matrix algebra. Instead, our goal is to give you some awareness of when systems estimation is appropriate and the benefits it offers. The best way to do this is to study some examples.

12.5.1 Systems of Simultaneous Equations

We have already seen one important class of economic systems—the simultaneous equations model. As a simple example of a simultaneous system, we have considered in Section 5.3.3 the supply–demand model (5.23):

$$Q_i^d = \alpha_1 + \beta_1 P_i + \gamma Y_i + \varepsilon_{1i},$$
$$Q_i^s = \alpha_2 + \beta_2 P_i + \phi R_i + \varepsilon_{2i}.$$

This structural form of the model is distinguished from its reduced form (5.24),

$$P_i = \pi_{10} + \pi_{11} Y_i + \pi_{12} R_i + v_{1i},$$
$$Q_i = \pi_{20} + \pi_{21} Y_i + \pi_{22} R_i + v_{2i}. \tag{12.3}$$

The hallmark of such a simultaneous system is that, in its structural form, there are endogenous explanatory variables. As we have explained in some detail, the result is that least squares applied to the structural form loses its desirable properties and we must turn to alternative estimators. These alternative estimators can be single-equation estimators, such as two-stage least squares or limited information maximum likelihood, or they can be systems estimators such as three-stage least squares or full information maximum likelihood. Even single-equation estimators use information from the system as a whole, in the form of knowledge of exogenous variables to use as instruments.

12.5.2 Systems of Regression Equations

Not all systems of equations are necessarily simultaneous ones. Econometricians often work with systems of conventional regression equations—regressions that, except for being part of a system, otherwise satisfy the classical assumptions. In particular, all explanatory variables are exogenous.

The benefits of systems estimation depend on the nature of the system and the economic issues under study. Usually—but not always, as we shall see momentarily—estimation as part of a system contributes to the efficiency of estimators. As well—and to some extent, more important—systems estimation makes possible the testing of **across-equation restrictions** that cannot be tested in a single-equation context.

There are two closely related categories of regression systems: multivariate regression (MR) systems and systems of seemingly unrelated regressions (SUR).

Multivariate Regression

The multivariate regression model is a system of regression equations having a common set of explanatory variables. We have already encountered one prominent example of this structure, the reduced form of a simultaneous equations model. Notice that, as illustrated by (12.3), the equations of a reduced form explain each of the endogenous variables as a function of *all* the exogenous variables. Hence, all equations of the system have the same set of regressors.[8]

This may seem like a rather special structure, and to some extent it is: In what circumstances are a group of endogenous variables explained by an identical set of exogenous ones? The MR model is a key model in statistics, where it is the framework for the field of **multivariate analysis.** Among econometricians, however, it is less well known because its applicability to economics is limited; only a few econometric problems have this structure. Those that do are, however, quite important. In addition to the reduced form of a simultaneous equations model, two prominent categories of econometric models fall under this framework: systems of demand equations and systems of asset pricing equations.

Systems of Demand Equations   Households demand consumer goods in product markets, and firms demand inputs to their production processes in factor markets. In Chapter 11 we have seen how to derive a firm's conditional factor demands from its cost function using Shephard's lemma. In Section 11.6, we have seen that similar ideas apply to the derivation of consumer demands from a consumer's expenditure function. It turns out that many cost and expenditure functions yield systems of factor and consumer demands that take the form of the MR model. Here are some examples.

Factor Demands: The Translog System.   Consider a firm's demands for its factors of production. In the case of a translog cost function, these take the form of

---

[8]   Unfortunately the term *multivariate regression* is sometimes used for multiple regression. This regrettable choice of terminology is especially common for simple regression, which is often called *bivariate regression* because it involves two variables. Consistency in terminology would require that the term **bivariate regression** be reserved for the special case of a MR model having two equations. Without loss of confusion, the classic econometrics text by Malinvaud (1970) entitles its chapter on the MR model "Multiple Regressions."

equation (11.51). Imagine a firm that produces its output Q using three factor inputs x_1, x_2, and x_3, for which it pays prices p_1, p_2, and p_3, so that total production costs are

$$C = p_1 x_1 + p_2 x_2 + p_3 x_3$$

and the cost shares are

$$S_1 \equiv \frac{p_1 x_1}{C}, \qquad S_2 \equiv \frac{p_2 x_2}{C}, \qquad S_3 \equiv \frac{p_3 x_3}{C}.$$

Let the sample of data on these variables be indexed by $i = 1, \ldots, n$; the unit of observation i might be firms in an industry, plants within a firm, observations over time for a single firm, or something else. From (11.51), the interrelated factor demands are described by the following three-equation system:

$$S_{1i} = \gamma_1 + \gamma_{11} \log p_{1i} + \gamma_{12} \log p_{2i} + \gamma_{13} \log p_{3i} + \gamma_{Q1} \log Q_i + \varepsilon_{1i},$$
$$S_{2i} = \gamma_2 + \gamma_{21} \log p_{1i} + \gamma_{22} \log p_{2i} + \gamma_{23} \log p_{3i} + \gamma_{Q2} \log Q_i + \varepsilon_{2i},$$
$$S_{3i} = \gamma_3 + \gamma_{31} \log p_{1i} + \gamma_{32} \log p_{2i} + \gamma_{33} \log p_{3i} + \gamma_{Q3} \log Q_i + \varepsilon_{3i}.$$

Each equation has a common set of explanatory variables because the demand for each factor depends on all three factor prices—its own price and those of the other substitutable or complementary factors—and the firm's output Q. Hence, the system of factor demands is of an MR form.

The estimation as an MR model rather than a simultaneous equations model requires that all the explanatory variables be exogenous. In what circumstances might this be a reasonable assumption? As long as the firm is a price taker in its factor markets, the factor prices p_1, p_2, and p_3 are exogenous. The exogeneity of output Q is more problematic. In what contexts is a firm's level of production not determined simultaneously with its choice of factor inputs? The best example is a regulated industry in which the firm is obliged to service whatever consumers demand at prices set by the regulator. This was the logic behind Nerlove's and Christensen and Greene's use of electricity generation as their industry of study.[9]

Because the explanatory variables are exogenous, these equations could be estimated individually by least squares. However, they do not satisfy all the classical assumptions because the assumption that the model is complete (discussed in Section 4.1.4) is violated when any one equation is considered in isolation. Despite this, it turns out that least squares does *not* lose its efficiency properties, a remarkable feature of the very special MR structure. Consequently, if our sole interest is in obtaining coefficient point estimates or testing **within-equation restrictions,** there is nothing wrong with using equation-by-equation least squares.

By a *within-equation restriction*, we mean a restriction that involves coefficients from just that equation. An example is the restriction (11.48d) associated with

[9]   In practice it is not unusual to find researchers applying the MR model to the estimation of factor demands even when the exogeneity of Q is more questionable, presumably because this is a context in which it can be difficult to find good instruments. (Recall the weak instruments problem discussed in Section 5.3.3.)

linear homogeneity of the cost function, which requires that each factor demand be homogeneous of degree 0 in factor prices. For the three-factor system, these restrictions are as follows.

First equation: $\gamma_{11} + \gamma_{12} + \gamma_{13} = 0$ (12.4a)

Second equation: $\gamma_{21} + \gamma_{22} + \gamma_{23} = 0$ (12.4b)

Third equation: $\gamma_{31} + \gamma_{32} + \gamma_{33} = 0$ (12.4c)

Because these are within-equation linear restrictions, there is no difficulty in imposing them in estimation if the demand equations are estimated individually as OLS regressions. Similarly, they can be tested equation-by-equation with F tests.

Often, however, hypotheses are not of a within-equation form. Consider the hypothesis of symmetry (11.49), which in this system consists of the three restrictions

$$\gamma_{12} = \gamma_{21}, \qquad \gamma_{13} = \gamma_{31}, \qquad \gamma_{23} = \gamma_{32}. \qquad (12.5)$$

Because these restrictions involve coefficients in different equations they cannot be imposed or tested on an equation-by-equation basis. The imposition and testing of such across-equation restrictions can only be done on a systems basis, and so equation-by-equation OLS is inadequate.

Notice that it is often essential to be able to impose restrictions such as these in estimation; the estimates are typically used in subsequent policy or welfare analysis and must satisfy the theoretical properties of those models. For example, Theory Meets Application 11.1 reports Allen elasticities for baseball player skills; they are computed from the coefficients of a homogeneity- and symmetry-constrained translog system. It would not make much sense to try to compute these elasticities from a system without symmetry imposed because we know a priori that Allen elasticities must be symmetric.

A systems analysis also permits the joint testing of equation-by-equation restrictions such as homogeneity (12.4), which is often preferable to equation-by-equation testing. That is, if the demand equations are treated as a system, it is possible to compute a single test statistic indicating whether the restrictions (12.4) are jointly rejected by the data. This is preferable to having to interpret the three separate F statistics that would be obtained from equation-by-equation homogeneity tests, which might well yield mixed test decisions.

Consumer Demands: The Almost Ideal Demand System.   Just as factor demands can be derived from a cost function, a household's consumption demands can be derived from its expenditure function. Consider a household that obtains its utility by consuming three goods q_1, q_2, and q_3, for which it pays prices p_1, p_2, and p_3, so that total expenditure is

$$m = p_1 q_1 + p_2 q_2 + p_3 q_3$$

and the expenditure shares are

$$S_1 \equiv \frac{p_1 q_1}{m}, \qquad S_2 \equiv \frac{p_2 q_2}{m}, \qquad S_3 \equiv \frac{p_3 q_3}{m}.$$

Consider a sample of data over $i = 1, \ldots, n$ (i might index households or observations over time for a representative household). The almost ideal demand system (11.61) takes the following three-equation form.

$$S_{1i} = \alpha_1 + \gamma_{11} \log p_{1i} + \gamma_{12} \log p_{2i} + \gamma_{13} \log p_{3i} + \beta_1 \log(m_i/P_i) + \varepsilon_{1i} \quad (12.6a)$$
$$S_{2i} = \alpha_2 + \gamma_{21} \log p_{1i} + \gamma_{22} \log p_{2i} + \gamma_{23} \log p_{3i} + \beta_2 \log(m_i/P_i) + \varepsilon_{2i} \quad (12.6b)$$
$$S_{3i} = \alpha_3 + \gamma_{31} \log p_{1i} + \gamma_{32} \log p_{2i} + \gamma_{33} \log p_{3i} + \beta_3 \log(m_i/P_i) + \varepsilon_{3i} \quad (12.6c)$$

Recall that P_i denotes an aggregate price index, so that m_i/P_i is real expenditure.

Similar to a translog factor demand system, this system of consumer demands is a MR model, as long as goods prices and real total expenditure can be treated as exogenous. The restrictions of homogeneity (12.4)—so that consumer demands are homogeneous of degree 0 in goods prices—and symmetry (12.5) continue to be of interest in this context, and the same estimation and testing considerations apply.

Systems of Asset Pricing Equations The appendix to Chapter 5 discusses the estimation of the capital asset pricing model (CAPM). As we develop it there, the Sharpe-Lintner version of the CAPM is the simple regression (5.27),

$$R_t - r_{ft} = \alpha + \beta(R_{mt} - r_{ft}) + \varepsilon_t.$$

Here R_t denotes the return on an asset during period t, r_{ft} the return on a risk-free asset, and R_{mt} the return on the market as a whole. The regression is estimated over a sample of time periods indexed by t. As we have discussed, in this form the primary testable implication of the CAPM is that $\alpha = 0$, so that the equation is a regression through the origin.

This regression seeks to explain the excess return $R_t - r_{ft}$ (the return in excess of the riskless rate) of a single asset. Similar equations apply to each of any number of different assets that might be considered, for example, different stocks. A group of asset returns would, then, be described by a system of such equations. There are two important variants of this CAPM system: One based on the Sharpe-Lintner regression, and a second based on an alternative version of the CAPM due to Black (1972).

The Sharpe-Lintner CAPM. Consider the returns on n assets, each described by a CAPM regression of the Sharpe-Lintner form:

$$R_{1t} - r_{ft} = \alpha_1 + \beta_1(R_{mt} - r_{ft}) + \varepsilon_{1t}$$
$$R_{2t} - r_{ft} = \alpha_2 + \beta_2(R_{mt} - r_{ft}) + \varepsilon_{2t}$$
$$\vdots$$
$$R_{nt} - r_{ft} = \alpha_n + \beta_n(R_{mt} - r_{ft}) + \varepsilon_{nt}.$$

Because all equations have as a common explanatory variable the excess return on the market $R_{mt} - r_{ft}$, which is viewed as exogenous from the point of view of the return on any individual asset, the system is of an MR form. The hypothesis of interest is the regression-through-the-origin restriction that the intercepts jointly equal zero:

$$\alpha_1 = \alpha_2 = \cdots = \alpha_n = 0. \tag{12.7}$$

The considerations relevant to testing these zero-intercept restrictions are entirely analogous to the linear homogeneity restrictions (12.4) of demand analysis. They could be tested individually on an equation-by-equation basis with t tests, and in fact this was the approach of early financial econometricians, notably Black, Jensen, and Scholes (1972). But the modern approach is the preferable one of testing them jointly with a statistic computed from the system as a whole.

To be estimable the Sharpe-Lintner CAPM requires that data be available on the riskless return r_{ft}. But is it reasonable to assume that such a thing exists? The usual choice for a risk-free rate is the return on government treasury bills. But even if it is accepted that these have no practical risk of default, they may at times have a nonnegligible inflation risk. Is it possible to formulate a version of the CAPM that does not require an observable risk-free return?

Black's Zero-Beta CAPM.   The financial economist Fischer Black (1938–1995) formulated the zero-beta version of the CAPM, which does not assume the existence of a riskless return. The equations describing the returns on n assets again take an MR form:

$$R_{1t} = \alpha_1 + \beta_1 R_{mt} + \varepsilon_{1t}$$
$$R_{2t} = \alpha_2 + \beta_2 R_{mt} + \varepsilon_{2t}$$
$$\vdots$$
$$R_{nt} = \alpha_n + \beta_n R_{mt} + \varepsilon_{nt}.$$

The testable implication of Black's zero-beta CAPM is *not* a set of zero-intercept restrictions like (12.7). Instead it is the following set of restrictions:

$$\alpha_i = \gamma(1 - \beta_i) \qquad (i = 1, \ldots, n). \tag{12.8}$$

That is, the model predicts a linear relationship between the intercepts and slopes of each equation; the factor of proportionality γ is unknown but common across all n restrictions. This is another example in which a joint test of the restrictions must be based on the system as a whole.

The restrictions of the Sharpe-Lintner and Black versions of the CAPM are classic testing problems in financial econometrics and are the subject of Campbell, Lo, and MacKinlay (1997, Chap. 5).

Further Comments on Testing in Multivariate Regression   The move from OLS regressions to a systems analysis has important implications for the distribution theory that applies to test statistics. As the chapters on single-equation regression have emphasized, under the classical assumptions—including normality—t and F statistics possess their namesake distributions even in small samples. Such finite sample results are not usually available in systems contexts, and inference must rely instead on asymptotic results; that is, approximations to the distributions of test statistics that hold in large samples. Chapter 13 introduces the most important asymptotic testing methods: the Wald, likelihood ratio, and Lagrange multiplier principles.

The availability of exact tests is, then, a very special feature of the classical normal linear regression model that does not usually extend to more general contexts. In simultaneous equations models and in SUR systems, as we discuss next, only asymptotic test criteria apply.

A remarkable feature of the MR model is that it happens to be a more general context in which exact tests *are* sometimes available. This is not true of all restrictions, but is true for a certain class of linear restrictions—called uniform mixed linear (UML) restrictions—that are often encountered in applied work. Within-equation linear restrictions are of this class, even when they are considered jointly across the equations of the system. For example, in demand analysis the hypothesis of joint homogeneity (12.4) is of the UML class; the availability of an exact test was first pointed out by Latinen (1978) in the context of consumer demands. The symmetry restrictions (12.5), on the other hand, are not of this class, and only asymptotic tests are available. The Sharpe-Lintner CAPM restrictions (12.7) are of the UML class; the availability of an exact test appears to have first been recognized by MacKinlay (1987) and Gibbons, Ross, and Shanken (1989). The Black zero-beta restrictions (12.8), on the other hand, are not of the UML form, and only asymptotic test criteria apply. The scope for exact testing in the MR model is discussed in Stewart (1997).

Conclusions To summarize, in multivariate regression the motivation for systems analysis comes from the ability to impose across-equation restrictions in estimation, and the availability of systemwide tests of joint and across-equation restrictions. Examples are demand homogeneity and symmetry and the restrictions implied by the Sharpe-Lintner and Black versions of the CAPM.

This contrasts with SUR systems, in which estimator efficiency is also a consideration. Let us investigate this.

Seemingly Unrelated Regressions

A SUR model is a system of regression equations that do not share an identical set of regressors. Here are two examples, both taken from demand analysis.

Factor Demands: The Generalized Leontief System. The translog model is just one of many flexible functional form parameterizations of a cost function. A predecessor model—the first modern flexible functional form—was the **generalized Leontief** (GL) cost function of Diewert (1971). In the three-input case it yields the following factor demand system:

$$(x_{1i}/Q_i) = \gamma_{11} \qquad\qquad + \gamma_{12}(p_{2i}/p_{1i})^{1/2} + \gamma_{13}(p_{3i}/p_{1i})^{1/2} + \varepsilon_{1i} \qquad (12.9a)$$

$$(x_{2i}/Q_i) = \gamma_{21}(p_{1i}/p_{2i})^{1/2} + \gamma_{22} \qquad\qquad + \gamma_{23}(p_{3i}/p_{2i})^{1/2} + \varepsilon_{2i} \qquad (12.9b)$$

$$(x_{3i}/Q_i) = \gamma_{31}(p_{1i}/p_{3i})^{1/2} + \gamma_{32}(p_{2i}/p_{3i})^{1/2} + \gamma_{33} \qquad\qquad + \varepsilon_{3i}. \qquad (12.9c)$$

This has been presented with the intercepts γ_{11}, γ_{22}, and γ_{33} down the diagonal, in order to emphasize the symmetric role of prices on the right-hand side.

This system differs in a number of respects from the translog model (12.6). One difference is that the dependent variables are the input–output ratios x_j/Q instead of cost shares S_j. Another is that, because factor prices appear as ratios, linear homogeneity holds automatically; a doubling of factor prices leaves factor demands unchanged. This means that linear homogeneity is imposed as a maintained hypothesis and is not testable. Symmetry, on the other hand, continues to be testable; it still consists of the restrictions (12.5).

Most important for our purposes, the GL model differs from the translog by *not* having a common set of explanatory variables. Indeed, the equations share no common regressors at all (although the six different regressors are constructed from various ratios of the three prices p_1, p_2, and p_3). Because it does not share a common regressor set, the GL system is not a MR model. Instead, it is a set of **seemingly unrelated regressions.**

Joint Estimation of the Translog System with Its Cost Function. Returning to the translog demand system (12.6), recall that we note in Chapter 11 that not all the parameters of the cost function appear in the factor demands. Thus, although there is a duality of cost and production, not all features of the production technology can be recovered from the demand system alone.[10]

The translog cost function (11.46) is, in the three-factor case,

$$\log C_i = \alpha + \beta \log Q_i + \tfrac{1}{2}\delta(\log Q_i)^2 + \gamma_1 \log p_{1i} + \gamma_2 \log p_{2i} + \gamma_3 \log p_{3i}$$

$$+ \tfrac{1}{2}\,[\quad \gamma_{11}(\log p_{1i})^2 \qquad + \gamma_{12} \log p_{1i} \log p_{2i} + \gamma_{13} \log p_{1i} \log p_{3i}$$
$$+ \gamma_{21} \log p_{2i} \log p_{1i} + \gamma_{22}(\log p_{2i})^2 \qquad + \gamma_{23} \log p_{2i} \log p_{3i}$$
$$+ \gamma_{31} \log p_{3i} \log p_{1i} + \gamma_{32} \log p_{3i} \log p_{2i} + \gamma_{33}(\log p_{3i})^2 \qquad]$$

$$+ \gamma_{Q1} \log Q_i \log p_{1i} + \gamma_{Q2} \log Q_i \log p_{2i} + \gamma_{Q3} \log Q_i \log p_{3i}.$$

Comparing this with the demand system (12.6), the coefficients missing from the factor demands are those governing returns to scale: α, β, and δ. If it is an objective of the analysis to study the returns-to-scale properties of the technology, it is therefore necessary to estimate the cost function directly. Although this could be done by estimating it as a single equation, we have seen in Chapter 11 that the strong multicollinearity that typically characterizes the regressors results in very imprecise estimates. For this reason, the normal practice in studying returns to scale is to estimate the cost function joint with the factor demands (12.6). Although the latter constitute an MR system, once the cost function is added this is no longer the case because all equations no longer share a common set of regressors. Instead the model is a SUR system.

---

[10] This is a problem with the translog model; it is not generic to factor demand analysis generally. For example, the symmetric generalized McFadden cost function of Diewert and Wales (1987) permits the recovery of all features of the production technology from the factor demand system alone, including the parameters governing returns to scale.

Estimation and Testing in SUR Systems   SUR systems consist of equations that, except for being part of a system, otherwise satisfy the classical assumptions and so could be estimated individually as OLS regressions. In particular, all regressors must be exogenous, as would be true of these models when applied to a regulated industry. Not only do the equations of a SUR system not share a common set of regressors, they need not share *any* regressors, as is the case for the GL system (12.9) in which each demand equation has distinct explanatory variables.

But if, like the GL system, equations have distinct dependent and explanatory variables, in what sense are they related at all in a way that is important for estimation and testing? In what sense does any one equation considered in isolation not make use of information available in the rest of the system?

The linkages among the equations of a SUR system are subtle ones that involve the disturbances. Although each equation of, say, the GL system (12.9) is assumed to have a classical disturbance,

$$\varepsilon_{1i} \sim \text{n.i.d.}(0, \sigma_1^2),$$
$$\varepsilon_{2i} \sim \text{n.i.d.}(0, \sigma_2^2),$$
$$\varepsilon_{3i} \sim \text{n.i.d.}(0, \sigma_3^2),$$

it is nevertheless the case that these will typically be correlated:

$$\text{cov}(\varepsilon_{1i}, \varepsilon_{2i}) = \sigma_{12}, \qquad \text{cov}(\varepsilon_{1i}, \varepsilon_{3i}) = \sigma_{13}, \qquad \text{cov}(\varepsilon_{2i}, \varepsilon_{3i}) = \sigma_{23}.$$

These correlations arise because the equations of a SUR system describe some joint or related set of economic activities, and so the disturbances must be generated to some extent by the same random factors. In the case of a factor demand system such as the generalized Leontief, for example, the factor demands are presumably all affected by some of the same shocks to the firm or industry; hence, the disturbances must be correlated. It is because of the subtle nature of this linkage, in contrast to any more obvious sharing of regressors, that these equations are said to be *seemingly* unrelated.[11]

These correlations can be exploited in estimation and testing, and it is this information that would be lost if the equations were estimated individually as OLS regressions. This is why OLS loses its efficiency properties in this context and why efficiency in estimation requires systems estimation, just as is true of a simultaneous equations system. And also like simultaneous equations—but in contrast to multivariate regression—only asymptotic test criteria are available.[12]

---

[11] It should be emphasized that these disturbance correlations are not unique to the SUR model; the same covariance structure is also assumed for simultaneous equations and MR models. It just happens that the special nature of the MR model means that these covariances are not relevant to obtaining efficient estimators.

[12] This statement is something of an oversimplification. The availability of exact distributional results for UML restrictions in the MR model can be exploited in the testing of non-UML restrictions in MR and SUR models with bounds tests procedures; see Dufour and Khalaf (2003). A notable example

continued

Conclusions

We have discussed two classes of regression systems, the MR and SUR models. In the MR model, equation-by-equation least squares yields efficient estimators and there is some scope for exact testing even with joint and across-equation restrictions. In the SUR model, on the other hand, systems estimation is required to make use of all the information in the data and only asymptotic test criteria are available.

These important differences are surprising because the models are so similar. The MR model is often described as the special case of a SUR model having identical regressors. This description is slightly misleading because usually when one model is said to be a special case of another this means that it is nested within the general model; that is, the special case can be obtained by imposing parameter restrictions on the general case. But the MR model is not a restricted version of the SUR model; just the opposite, in fact. Consider taking a SUR model such as the GL system (12.9) and creating a companion MR model in which each equation includes all the regressors of the system. In the GL example, these would be the six regressors appearing in all three equations,

$$(p_{2i}/p_{1i})^{1/2}, \quad (p_{3i}/p_{1i})^{1/2}, \quad (p_{1i}/p_{2i})^{1/2}, \quad (p_{3i}/p_{2i})^{1/2}, \quad (p_{1i}/p_{3i})^{1/2}, \quad (p_{2i}/p_{3i})^{1/2}.$$

Then the SUR system could be obtained as a restricted version of the MR system, restrictions that could be tested.[13] In this sense, it is the SUR model that is the restricted version of the MR.

Model Misspecification in Equation Systems

In simultaneous equations systems and systems of regression equations, the possibility of specification error arises just as it does in single-equation regression. Much of the intuition extends naturally; for example, overparametrization typically leads to an efficiency loss, whereas underparameterization introduces bias. Many of the tools of model evaluation have been extended to systems contexts.

A key result is that, when equations are estimated as a system, specification error in one equation introduces bias and/or efficiency losses in all the estimators of the model, not just those for the parameters of that equation. Thus specification error is transmitted throughout the system. This consideration mitigates the value of moving from single equation to systems estimation in the hope of achieving efficiency gains alone. It reiterates that in practice the strongest motivation for systems estimation is often the desire to impose and test joint or across-equation restrictions.

is Beaulieu, Dufour, and Khalaf (2003), who take this approach to testing the Black CAPM. But these techniques are simulation-based, and the latter paper is on the frontier of contemporary financial econometrics.

[13] Typically these tests will not be exact; these restrictions are not in general of the UML form.

12.6   Conclusions

This chapter has introduced some of the ideas and tools of model discovery. Because these issues arise in any area of empirical modeling, our treatment has been selective and suggestive rather than exhaustive or definitive. Indeed, an exhaustive treatment of model evaluation would not be possible; the methods of specification testing and model choice in time series models alone could easily command their own book.

Because there are many specification tests that arise in many different kinds of models, they are often best developed as part of the discussion of those models. For example, in our treatment of the F testing of linear restrictions in Chapter 10 we have studied the Chow test, which can now be seen as a specification test for parameter constancy. Another example is heteroskedasticity as a specification error; Chapter 14 presents a test of the null hypothesis of homoskedasticity against the alternative of heteroskedasticity (the Breusch-Pagan test developed in Section 14.4.1).

One by-product of our treatment of systems of equations has been to reiterate the distinction between exact and asymptotic tests that is first emphasized in Chapter 2. This serves to motivate the need for a more systematic development of asymptotic testing methods. The best way to provide such a development is to return to the single-equation context and consider nonlinear models. This is the subject of the next chapter.

Another respect in which this chapter is not exhaustive is in our treatment of systems of equations, which has focused on the most important classes of systems that apply when the random sampling assumption goes unchallenged. However, systems of equations are also used in time series analysis. The most important example is vector autoregressive (VAR) models, which are introduced in Chapter 18.

13 *Nonlinear Regression*

Our focus so far has been exclusively on *linear* regression models, in which testable parameter restrictions are also linear. As the applications we have studied demonstrate, many interesting empirical problems fall within this framework. Nevertheless it can easily be the case that economic theory leads to a regression model, or parameter restrictions, or both, that are nonlinear. In this chapter, we consider this possibility.

The **nonlinear regression model** is notated as

$$Y_i = f_i(\boldsymbol{\beta}) + \varepsilon_i, \qquad \varepsilon_i \sim \text{i.i.d.}(0, \sigma^2). \tag{13.1}$$

The population regression function $f_i(\boldsymbol{\beta})$ is a specified function of coefficients represented by $\boldsymbol{\beta}$ and, implicitly, explanatory variables; $\boldsymbol{\beta}$ denotes a **vector** of K coefficients to be estimated. (A vector is a list; the items in the list, in this case the K coefficients, are called its **components.**) The subscript i on the function $f_i(\boldsymbol{\beta})$ reflects the fact that the sample data on the explanatory variables vary across the observations $i = 1, \dots, n$.

The linear regression model of Chapter 8 is the special case in which the population regression function is linear:

$$f_i(\boldsymbol{\beta}) = \beta_1 + \beta_2 X_{2i} + \cdots + \beta_K X_{Ki}. \tag{13.2}$$

The coefficient vector is $\boldsymbol{\beta} = [\beta_1\, \beta_2 \cdots \beta_K]$. In Chapter 6 we have seen that the key respect in which this functional form is linear is in its coefficients. As we emphasize there, a model linear in its coefficients may be used to study a wide range of nonlinear relationships between variables. Examples were loglinear and semilog models, reciprocal models, and, in Section 8.8, polynomial regression. Models describing nonlinear relationships between variables that are nevertheless linear in their coefficients, and thus estimable by ordinary least squares, we termed intrinsically linear.

This chapter considers situations in which the nonlinear relationship between variables is such that it is not adequately described by a model linear in its coefficients: $f_i(\boldsymbol{\beta})$ is intrinsically nonlinear. The consequence is that OLS as we have developed it in connection with intrinsically linear models is not applicable. It is nevertheless the case that the least squares estimation principle applies as a method of deriving estimators, ones that are called **nonlinear least squares** (NLS) estimators. This chapter develops the methods of statistical inference—estimation and hypothesis testing—associated with NLS.

Although the focus of this chapter is on using NLS to estimate and test intrinsically nonlinear regressions, the relevance of these techniques goes well beyond this. Essentially the same issues arise with other important classes of econometric problems, such as the qualitative and limited dependent variable models sketched in Section 5.3.2, and some time series models, such as the moving average processes described in Chapter 16. Thus, although these estimation problems are not considered here, much of what you learn in this chapter is relevant to them.

13.1   Introduction

We have already encountered several examples of intrinsically nonlinear functional forms. The simplest example, involving just two coefficients, is the Cobb-Douglas production function in intensive form with an additive disturbance, equation (6.6):

$$q_i = \gamma k_i^{\beta} + \varepsilon_i. \tag{13.3}$$

Here the coefficient vector is $\boldsymbol{\beta} = [\gamma\,\beta]$. A slightly more complicated example, because it involves the $K = 3$ coefficients $\boldsymbol{\beta} = [\gamma\,\beta\,\alpha]$, is the Cobb-Douglas production function without constant returns to scale imposed, again with an additive disturbance:

$$Q_i = \gamma K_i^{\beta} L_i^{\alpha} + \varepsilon_i. \tag{13.4}$$

The versions of these production functions that you estimate in Chapters 7 and 10 assumed multiplicative rather than additive disturbances and so were intrinsically linear because they could be transformed into linear regressions using logarithms. In contrast, assuming an additive disturbance means that no such transformation is possible and the models are intrinsically nonlinear. As we argue in Section 6.1, on a priori grounds a multiplicative disturbance is probably the more plausible specification, and so estimation of the Cobb-Douglas production function in its loglinear form is the natural way to proceed. Nevertheless these alternative forms with additive disturbances provide a useful illustration of nonlinear regression models that you will have some opportunity to estimate in this chapter.

A more interesting example of nonlinear regression, in that there is no version of the model that is intrinsically linear, is the CES production function in Section 7.4.3:

$$Q = \gamma[\delta K^{-\rho} + (1 - \delta)L^{-\rho}]^{-\nu/\rho}. \tag{13.5}$$

Although as a mechanical matter logarithms may be taken of this function,

$$\log Q = \log \gamma - \frac{\nu}{\rho} \log[\delta K^{-\rho} + (1 - \delta)L^{-\rho}], \tag{13.6}$$

it remains intrinsically nonlinear. We have seen in Section 7.4 that the CES production function may be investigated indirectly by estimating an associated marginal productivity condition, as Arrow, Chenery, Minhas, and Solow did in their pioneering work. However, this only yields an estimate of the elasticity of substitution—indirectly, an estimate of the substitution parameter ρ.[1] It would obviously be of interest to obtain estimates of all four parameters $\boldsymbol{\beta} = [\gamma \nu \delta \rho]$ by estimating the function directly, something you will do in this chapter using nonlinear regression. Arrow, Chenery, Minhas, and Solow were not able to do this because the limitations in computing technology that existed at the time they were doing their work meant that nonlinear least squares was unavailable.

Models Linear in One Form, Nonlinear in Another

Turning to other examples, a class of models that is of some importance in applied work is one in which variables appear linearly, so that in one form the equation is estimable as a linear regression, but in which parameters of economic interest enter in a manner that is intrinsically nonlinear. Two examples of this appeared in earlier chapters.

The Mankiw-Romer-Weil Regression for Living Standards
In Chapter 9 we have studied the Solow-Swan model of economic growth, which in its textbook form leads to the loglinear regression (9.16):

$$\log q_i = \beta_1 + \beta_2 \log s_i + \beta_3 \log(\delta + n_i) + \varepsilon_i. \tag{13.7}$$

The variables are output per adult q_i, a measure of living standards across countries; the saving rate s_i; and the population growth rate n_i. (Recall that δ denotes the rate of depreciation; rather than being a parameter to be estimated, this was taken to be 0.05 for all countries.) In terms of the parameters of the Solow-Swan model, this regression took the form (9.15):

$$\log q_i = \frac{\log \gamma}{1 - \alpha} + \frac{\alpha}{1 - \alpha} \log s_i - \frac{\alpha}{1 - \alpha} \log(\delta + n_i) + \varepsilon_i. \tag{13.8}$$

Here γ and α are the parameters of the underlying Cobb-Douglas production function, with α representing capital's share of output. Although linear in the variables $\log s_i$ and $\log(\delta + n_i)$, in this form the equation is a nonlinear regression model because it is intrinsically nonlinear in the parameters $\boldsymbol{\beta} = [\gamma \alpha]$.

If our interest is solely in obtaining point estimates of γ and α, then we already know how to do this. As we have seen in Chapter 10, the relationship between the two regressions is that the restricted-form parameters γ and α are overidentified in terms of the unrestricted coefficients β_1, β_2, and β_3. Unique implied estimates of γ and α may be deduced from the estimation of (13.7) by imposing the restriction $\beta_3 = -\beta_2$. In Example 13 of Chapter 10 we have seen that doing this with the Mankiw, Romer, and Weil data set for 75 countries yields the implied estimates $\hat{\alpha} = 0.588$ and $\hat{\gamma} = 18.5$.

---

[1]   An indirect estimate of δ can also be deduced from the intercept of the marginal productivity condition, although we have not exploited that feature of the ACMS regressions.

Purely for the purpose of obtaining estimates of the underlying parameters, then, it is not necessary to estimate the model in its intrinsically nonlinear form (13.8). But often our interest extends beyond point estimation—we want estimated standard errors as well, for the usual purposes of hypothesis testing or the construction of confidence intervals. One approach to doing this is to estimate the intrinsically nonlinear model (13.8) directly using nonlinear least squares. Although in principle possible, we find in this chapter that it is often easier to use methods of nonlinear inference to obtain estimated standard errors by exploiting the relationship between the two sets of parameters of (13.7) and (13.8).

The Cobb-Douglas Cost Function Similar points apply to a second example we have seen of this type of econometric problem. In Chapter 11 we derive the two-factor Cobb-Douglas cost function and see that it can be estimated as a loglinear regression model of the form (11.26):

$$\log C_i = \alpha + \beta \log Q_i + \gamma_1 \log p_{1i} + \gamma_2 \log p_{2i} + \varepsilon_i. \tag{13.9}$$

Here C_i denotes the production costs of firm i, Q_i its level of output, and p_{1i} and p_{2i} its factor prices. In terms of the underlying parameters of the production function this takes the form (11.25):[2]

$$\log C_i = \alpha + \frac{1}{\alpha_1 + \alpha_2} \log Q_i + \frac{\alpha_1}{\alpha_1 + \alpha_2} \log p_{1i} + \frac{\alpha_2}{\alpha_1 + \alpha_2} \log p_{2i} + \varepsilon_i. \tag{13.10}$$

Although linear in the variables $\log Q_i$, $\log p_{1i}$, and $\log p_{2i}$, in this form the equation is a nonlinear regression model because it is intrinsically nonlinear in the parameters α_1 and α_2.

If our interest is solely in obtaining point estimates of α_1 and α_2, then we already know how to do this. As we have seen in Chapter 11, the relationship between the two regressions is that the restricted form parameters α_1 and α_2 are overidentified in terms of the unrestricted coefficients β, γ_1, and γ_2. Unique implied estimates of α_1 and α_2 may be deduced from the estimation of (13.9) by imposing the linear homogeneity restriction $\gamma_1 + \gamma_2 = 1$, equation (11.28). In Exercise 11.9, you do this for the three-factor case using Nerlove's electricity generation data.

Purely for the purpose of obtaining estimates of the underlying parameters of economic interest, then, it is not necessary to estimate the model in its intrinsically nonlinear form (13.10). But if we want to perform hypothesis testing or construct confidence intervals, then we need standard errors as well. One approach to doing this is to estimate the intrinsically nonlinear model (13.8) directly using nonlinear least squares. Although in principle possible, it is often easier to use methods of

---

[2] As we have seen in the derivation of the cost function, α takes a complicated nonlinear form in terms of the underlying parameters α_0, α_1, and α_2 of the production function. However, this is of no particular interest because, given identification of α_1 and α_2, there is a one-to-one correspondence between α and α_0. Effectively, the intercepts of the production and cost functions are linked by an exactly identifying relationship. Hence, it is a matter of indifference whether we regard the coefficient vector of interest to be $\beta = [\alpha_0 \, \alpha_1 \, \alpha_2]$ or $\beta = [\alpha \, \alpha_1 \, \alpha_2]$, and we do not bother to write out the intercept α of (13.10) explicitly in terms of the underlying parameters of the production function.

nonlinear inference to obtain estimated standard errors by exploiting the relationship between the two sets of parameters of (13.9) and (13.10).

These examples illustrate that statistical inference in nonlinear regression models is of natural interest in economics. Let us therefore turn to the methods of inference associated with nonlinear least squares.

13.2   Nonlinear Least Squares

We begin our treatment of statistical inference in nonlinear regression models by considering the application of the least squares principle to intrinsically nonlinear regressions of the form (13.1). Once the use of nonlinear least squares to obtain coefficient point estimators is developed we will be in a position, in Section 13.8, to treat hypothesis testing.

The application of the least squares principle proceeds, at least initially, much as it has done in our earlier applications of the method to linear models in Sections 2.4, 4.2, and 8.2. The goal is, of course, to obtain coefficient estimators, the vector of which may be denoted $\hat{\boldsymbol{\beta}}$. Any such estimators yield predicted values denoted by

$$\hat{Y}_i = f_i(\hat{\boldsymbol{\beta}}),$$

and the associated least squares residuals

$$e_i = Y_i - \hat{Y}_i = Y_i - f_i(\hat{\boldsymbol{\beta}}). \tag{13.11}$$

The least squares principle suggests that these estimators be chosen to minimize the sum of squares function

$$S(\boldsymbol{\beta}) = \sum_{i=1}^{n}(Y_i - EY_i)^2 = \sum_{i=1}^{n}(Y_i - f_i(\boldsymbol{\beta}))^2. \tag{13.12}$$

The second equality holds because it follows from the original model specification (13.1) that

$$E(Y_i) = f_i(\boldsymbol{\beta}) + E(\varepsilon_i) = f_i(\boldsymbol{\beta}).$$

Recall that $f_i(\boldsymbol{\beta})$ is nonrandom, depending as it does only on coefficients and nonstochastic explanatory variables.

The notation $S(\boldsymbol{\beta})$ recognizes explicitly that the sum of squares function has the regression coefficients as its arguments. In our application of least squares to the linear regression model in Chapter 8 we solve this minimization problem by taking the derivatives of S with respect to each of the K arguments $\boldsymbol{\beta} = [\beta_1 \cdots \beta_K]$. The resulting first-order conditions are then solved for expressions for the least squares estimators, such as equations (8.12) or, in matrix form, (8.63). The best way to see that solving in this way is not possible for intrinsically nonlinear models is to examine the first-order conditions that apply in the nonlinear case.

13.2.1 The Normal Equations for Nonlinear Regression

Suppose we attempt to minimize $S(\boldsymbol{\beta})$ by following the usual practice of taking the derivatives with respect to each of the coefficients. These K derivatives are

$$\frac{\partial S(\boldsymbol{\beta})}{\partial \beta_1} = \sum_{i=1}^{n} -2(Y_i - f_i(\boldsymbol{\beta}))\frac{\partial f_i(\boldsymbol{\beta})}{\partial \beta_1}$$

$$\frac{\partial S(\boldsymbol{\beta})}{\partial \beta_2} = \sum_{i=1}^{n} -2(Y_i - f_i(\boldsymbol{\beta}))\frac{\partial f_i(\boldsymbol{\beta})}{\partial \beta_2}$$

$$\vdots$$

$$\frac{\partial S(\boldsymbol{\beta})}{\partial \beta_K} = \sum_{i=1}^{n} -2(Y_i - f_i(\boldsymbol{\beta}))\frac{\partial f_i(\boldsymbol{\beta})}{\partial \beta_K}.$$

Setting these equal to zero and canceling multiplicative constants yields the first-order conditions

$$\sum_{i=1}^{n}(Y_i - f_i(\hat{\boldsymbol{\beta}}))\frac{\partial f_i(\hat{\boldsymbol{\beta}})}{\partial \hat{\beta}_k} = 0 \qquad (k = 1, \ldots, K), \tag{13.13}$$

which are a set of K normal equations defining the least squares coefficient estimators $\hat{\boldsymbol{\beta}}$. Employing the notation (13.11) for the least squares residuals, these may be expressed more economically as

$$\sum_{i=1}^{n}\frac{\partial f_i(\hat{\boldsymbol{\beta}})}{\partial \hat{\beta}_k}e_i = 0 \qquad (k = 1, \ldots, K).$$

This makes it clear that, entirely in analogy with the conditions (8.9) that applied for the linear regression model, the normal equations may be interpreted as a set of K orthogonality conditions on the least squares residuals.

In fact, in the special case of the linear regression function (13.2) the derivatives are simply

$$\frac{\partial f_i(\boldsymbol{\beta})}{\partial \beta_1} = 1,$$

$$\frac{\partial f_i(\boldsymbol{\beta})}{\partial \beta_k} = X_{ki} \qquad (k = 2, \ldots, K)$$

and it is evident that these orthogonality conditions reduce to the conditions (8.9).

Note in particular that if the nonlinear regression model has an intercept, it follows that the residuals will sum to zero, just as is true in the linear case. A model without an intercept does not possess this property, something we first encountered in our discussion of regression through the origin in Section 5.2.

EXAMPLE 1

Derive the first-order conditions for the Cobb-Douglas production function (13.4). Do the least squares residuals sum to zero for this model?

SOLUTION

The derivatives of the regression function $f_i(\boldsymbol{\beta}) = \gamma K_i^\beta L_i^\alpha$ are:

$$\frac{\partial f_i(\boldsymbol{\beta})}{\partial \gamma} = K_i^\beta L_i^\alpha,$$

$$\frac{\partial f_i(\boldsymbol{\beta})}{\partial \beta} = \gamma \beta K_i^{\beta-1} L_i^\alpha,$$

$$\frac{\partial f_i(\boldsymbol{\beta})}{\partial \alpha} = \gamma \alpha K_i^\beta L_i^{\alpha-1}.$$

The associated normal equations (13.13) defining the least squares estimators are therefore

$$\sum_{i=1}^n (Y_i - \hat{\gamma} K_i^{\hat{\beta}} L_i^{\hat{\alpha}}) K_i^{\hat{\beta}} L_i^{\hat{\alpha}} = 0, \tag{13.14a}$$

$$\sum_{i=1}^n (Y_i - \hat{\gamma} K_i^{\hat{\beta}} L_i^{\hat{\alpha}}) \hat{\gamma} \hat{\beta} K_i^{\hat{\beta}-1} L_i^{\hat{\alpha}} = 0, \tag{13.14b}$$

$$\sum_{i=1}^n (Y_i - \hat{\gamma} K_i^{\hat{\beta}} L_i^{\hat{\alpha}}) \hat{\gamma} \hat{\alpha} K_i^{\hat{\beta}} L_i^{\hat{\alpha}-1} = 0. \tag{13.14c}$$

Because this model does not have an intercept, none of these normal equations corresponds to the condition that

$$\sum_{i=1}^n e_i = \sum_{i=1}^n (Y_i - \hat{Y}_i) = \sum_{i=1}^n (Y_i - \hat{\gamma} K_i^{\hat{\beta}} L_i^{\hat{\alpha}})$$

equals zero. Hence, the residuals do not necessarily sum to zero.

The intuition of the normal equations for nonlinear regression is, then, in many respects similar to that for linear regression. However, there are important differences. In the linear regression model, the K normal equations are linear in the K coefficients. In general, a system of linear equations in which there are as many equations as unknowns yields a unique solution (as long as, as we have seen in Chapter 8, certain identifying conditions such as variation in the data and an absence of perfect multicollinearity are satisfied). Furthermore, this unique solution may be obtained analytically (that is, by mathematical derivation) as closed-form expressions. (A closed-form expression is one that is solely in terms of known quantities—in the case of estimators, in terms of the sample data. For example, in the $K = 3$ case these are the equations (8.12).) In contrast, the normal equations for a nonlinear regression model, such as those for the Cobb-Douglas production function, are nonlinear in the coefficients and cannot be solved analytically. It is not possible to rearrange the normal equations (13.14)—or, in general, (13.13)—to obtain closed-form solutions for the coefficient estimators.

13.1 Consider the Cobb-Douglas production function in labor-intensive form with an additive disturbance, model (13.3). Derive the normal equations for least squares. Is it possible to solve these analytically for closed-form estimators $\hat{\gamma}$ and $\hat{\beta}$? Must the NLS residuals sum to zero for this model?

13.2 If a nonlinear regression model has an intercept, will the sample regression line pass through the point of variable means?

13.2.2 Numerical Solution for Nonlinear Least Squares Estimators

Although, unlike OLS estimators, NLS estimators cannot be obtained analytically as closed-form algebraic expressions, the minimization of the sum of squares function $S(\boldsymbol{\beta})$ is nevertheless a well-defined optimization problem that can be solved numerically by computer. The value of $S(\boldsymbol{\beta})$ at its minimum we continue to denote by SSE:

$$\text{SSE} = S(\hat{\boldsymbol{\beta}}) = \sum_{i=1}^{n} e_i^2.$$

There are many algorithms by which a computer can be programmed to solve a system of nonlinear equations such as the first-order conditions (13.13)—or, equivalently, to seek the coefficient vector $\hat{\boldsymbol{\beta}}$ that minimizes the sum of squares function $S(\boldsymbol{\beta})$. The way in which econometric software typically does this involves **iterating on a solution.** Beginning with some initial set of guesses for the coefficients called **starting values,** the algorithm proceeds by a series of steps that seek to zero in on estimates that minimize the sum of squares function for that data set. If the algorithm is successful at zeroing-in on a minimum, it is said to have **converged.** It stops iterating when, at successive iterations, the coefficient estimates no longer change by more than some tiny amount, called the **convergence tolerance.** If the algorithm is unable to zero in on a minimum, it has **failed to converge.** There are many excellent references on the algorithms commonly used for econometric estimators. Textbook introductions include Griffiths, Hill, and Judge (1993, Chap. 22); Pindyck and Rubinfeld (1991, Chap. 9); and, in more detail, Greene (2003, Chap. 9) and Judge, Hill, Griffiths, Lütkepohl, and Lee (1988, Chap. 12). Advanced references are Amemiya (1983) and Quandt (1983).

Even if you are not familiar with the details of how these iterative procedures work, there are two aspects of their implementation that you should be aware of. The first is that NLS is much more computationally intensive than OLS. This means that issues of computer numerics are critical in using NLS. This point is pursued in the next section.

The second issue is that, whereas a system of K linear equations in K unknowns has a unique solution, this is not necessarily the case if the system of equations is nonlinear. Instead, when the system of first-order conditions is nonlinear it may have

FIGURE 13.1

In nonlinear regression, the sum of squares function may have multiple minima.

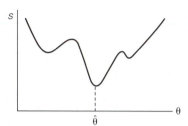

more than one solution; that is, the sum of squares function may have more than one minimum. This situation is depicted in Figure 13.1, which shows the sum of squares function varying with a single parameter θ. It has several minima. The lowest of these minima, at $\hat{\theta}$, is called the **global minimum.** The others are called **local minima.**

The starting values used by a nonlinear least squares estimation routine can be user-set; if you do not specify them, the routine uses arbitrarily chosen **default starting values,** usually just the value 0 or 1 for all coefficients. As the routine iterates on a solution, it may converge to a local rather than a global minimum.

The best way to prevent this is to provide the routine with starting values that are better guesses of the coefficients than the default values. You can almost always do this. First, as a researcher you have typically engaged in related empirical analyses, or know of related analyses, that give you some idea of which coefficient values are consistent with the data. Second, you have knowledge of the nature of the economic problem being studied, and this usually suggests plausible coefficient values. Let us consider examples of both these sources of starting values.

Related Empirical Analyses as a Source of Starting Values

Suppose you are asked to estimate the Cobb-Douglas production function with an additive disturbance, model (13.4). How do you choose sensible starting values for the coefficients? One possibility is your background knowledge of economics. You know, for example, that β has the interpretation as capital's share of output and α as labor's share. As Cobb and Douglas observed so long ago, in aggregate data—that is, for the economy as a whole—there has historically been approximately a one-third/two-thirds division between these factor shares. Of course, these might not be such good guesses at the microeconomic level, say across firms in an industry. Nevertheless, in the absence of other information these are reasonable starting values.

But you can do even better than this. You already know how to estimate by OLS a closely related model having the same coefficients—the Cobb-Douglas production function with a multiplicative disturbance. This may be estimated as a loglinear regression, as we first describe in Section 6.1; these estimates can then be used as starting values in the nonlinear least squares estimation of the model with an additive disturbance.

Although this can be illustrated with the same Cobb-Douglas data in Table 7.1 that we use in earlier examples, it is useful to turn to a different data set. Throughout

TABLE 13.1   Mizon's 1957 Data

Industry	Q	K	LF	U	H
Food processing	405	335	605	9	47
Drink and tobacco	245	130	202	2	46
Coke ovens	31	100	19	0	48
Mineral oil refining	37	191	37	0	48
Chemicals	526	615	459	4	47
Iron and steel (melting, rolling, and casting)	430	504	404	4	48
Iron and steel (tinplate and tubes)	88	63	70	1	47
Nonferrous metals	130	98	133	1	47
Engineering and electrical goods	1558	758	1940	16	47
Shipbuilding and marine engineering	221	58	318	6	48
Motors and cycles	365	270	411	6	46
Aircraft	273	140	303	1	47
Railway locomotives and rolling stock	94	44	160	0	48
Metal goods	404	197	517	6	45
Textiles	605	589	1015	15	44
Leather, clothing, footwear	308	82	681	10	41
Building materials	184	105	195	2	50
Pottery and glass	91	48	147	3	45
Timber and furniture	184	54	289	5	45
Paper, printing, publishing	503	356	571	4	45
Other manufacturing	189	133	282	4	46
Construction	1124	252	1466	39	49
Gas	127	309	142	1	47
Electricity	290	1810	211	1	48

Source: Pyatt and Stone (1964).

this chapter we will develop examples based on an important article by Mizon (1977) on statistical inference in nonlinear regression. Mizon estimated and tested a variety of specifications for production functions, including the Cobb-Douglas and CES functions having both additive and multiplicative disturbances. His analysis is cited in Tables 10.7 and 10.8 as an example of a nested testing structure.

Mizon used data from Pyatt and Stone (1964) on capital, labor, and output across 24 industries, in the years 1954, 1957, and 1960.[3] These data are described in more detail in the exercises at the end of this section. The 1957 data used in the examples of this chapter are presented in Table 13.1.

---

[3] These data had been used earlier by Feldstein (1967).

EXAMPLE 2

mizon57.dat

Use Mizon's 1957 data to estimate the Cobb-Douglas production function without constant returns to scale, first assuming a multiplicative disturbance and then in its intrinsically nonlinear form. Use the first set of estimates as starting values in the second estimation.

SOLUTION

A multiplicative disturbance. The Cobb-Douglas production function is

$$Q_i = \gamma K_i^\beta L_i^\alpha e^{\varepsilon_i}.$$

As we first describe in Chapter 6, this may be estimated as a loglinear regression of the form:

$$\log Q_i = \log \gamma + \beta \log K_i + \alpha \log L_i + \varepsilon_i.$$

OLS estimation of this equation using Mizon's 1957 data yields[4]

$$\log Q_i = 0.655 + 0.190 \log K_i + 0.788 \log L_i + e_i.$$

The implied estimate of γ is 1.925. For future reference, the estimation yields SSE = 0.743489 and a loglikelihood function value of $\mathcal{L} = 7.63894$.

An additive disturbance. The intrinsically nonlinear form (13.4) of the Cobb-Douglas production function is

$$Q_i = \gamma K_i^\beta L_i^\alpha + \varepsilon_i.$$

The starting values suggested by the loglinear regression are $\gamma = 1.925$, $\beta = 0.190$, $\alpha = 0.788$. NLS converges to a minimum of the sum of squares function of SSE = 85002.1, a loglikelihood function value of $\mathcal{L} = -132.123$, and the following estimates.

Parameter	Estimate	Standard error
γ	1.6212	0.452371
β	0.1476	0.046187
α	0.8631	0.046524

We have remarked in the past that coefficient estimators such as $\hat{\alpha}$ and $\hat{\beta}$ are jointly distributed random variables related by a nonzero covariance. Although this covariance is not normally reported as part of the presentation of regression results, it can usually be obtained by an appropriate option of the estimation software. For future reference in our discussion of Wald tests in Section 13.8.3, the estimated covariance of $\hat{\alpha}$ and $\hat{\beta}$ is $s_{\hat{\alpha},\hat{\beta}} = -0.0011365$.

All econometrics packages should reproduce the results of this example, with the possible exception of a few of the statistics. First, some NLS routines may report slightly different values of the standard errors and the covariance $s_{\hat{\alpha},\hat{\beta}}$, for reasons to be discussed in Section 13.7.

---

[4] See the end-of-section exercises for the definition of labor input L.

Second, although for a given model and data all software packages should report the same value for the SSE, some may yield different values for the loglikelihood function. In the previous chapter we have seen that, for regression models, the loglikelihood function is a transformation of the SSE:

$$\mathscr{L} = -\frac{n}{2}(1 + \log 2\pi - \log n) - \frac{n}{2}\log \text{SSE}. \qquad (13.15)$$

(Recall equation (12.2).) Although this is presented there for the linear regression model, it also holds for nonlinear regression. You should verify that it is satisfied by the values of Example 2. Notice that, given a sample size n, the first term in this expression is just an additive constant. Some software packages omit all or part of this constant in reporting $\mathscr{L}$ because it is irrelevant for the practical purpose for which the loglikelihood value is most often used—performing likelihood ratio tests. As will become apparent in Section 13.8.4, additive constants cancel in the computation of the likelihood ratio statistic. As well, when a model selection criterion is computed as a transformation of $\mathscr{L}$, the omission of the additive constant will not change the ranking of alternative models yielded by the criterion.

In using the Cobb-Douglas production function as an example of nonlinear regression, we have exploited a special feature of that example. That an intrinsically linear version of the model is available that can be estimated by OLS to obtain starting values is not typical of nonlinear estimation problems. Nevertheless, it serves to illustrate the more general point that related empirical analyses can be a useful source of starting values.

Economic Theory as a Source of Starting Values

Another useful source of starting values is your background knowledge of economics. After all, the parameters of an econometric model normally have some meaning in terms of the underlying economic phenomenon of interest.

Consider the CES production function. From Section 7.4, its parameters have certain interpretations in terms of the underlying production technology and consequently should take on values in certain ranges. These are

γ,   the efficiency parameter: $\gamma > 0$
v,   the degree of homogeneity: $v > 0$
δ,   the distribution parameter: $0 < \delta < 1$
ρ,   the substitution parameter: $-1 < \rho < \infty, \rho \neq 0$

We have very good a priori knowledge of plausible values for some of these parameters. The degree of homogeneity v is the degree of returns to scale. The obvious benchmark is constant returns, $v = 1$. From Table 7.5, the substitution parameter ρ, when set equal to zero, yields an elasticity of substitution of unity, and the CES production function specializes to the Cobb-Douglas. However, we should not use $\rho = 0$ as a starting value because it results in division by zero in the exponent $-v/\rho$ in (13.5); instead it makes sense to set it to some small value fairly close to zero, say $\rho = -0.2$. Finally, the distribution parameter δ influences factor shares. As we discuss in Section 7.4.3, it should be in the range $0 < \delta < 1$, and a sensible starting value is $\delta = 0.5$.

The only parameter for which a natural starting value is not suggested by prior knowledge of this sort is γ. There is a reason for this. The manner in which γ enters the CES function means that it corresponds to, in a sense, the intercept of the model—as, indeed, is explicit in its logarithmic version (13.6). The estimate of γ yielded by a data set will be scaled by the units of measure of the variables. Because the magnitude of any estimate of γ depends on the magnitudes of the dependent and explanatory variables, theory alone cannot suggest a good starting value for this coefficient. However, we already have a good data-based guess for γ—the estimate obtained from the Cobb-Douglas functional form in Example 2.

EXAMPLE 3

 mizon57.dat

Use Mizon's 1957 data to estimate the CES production function, assuming both multiplicative and additive disturbances. In both cases, use the guidelines just discussed to specify starting values.

SOLUTION

An additive disturbance. The CES production function is estimated as

$$Q_i = \gamma[\delta K_i^{-\rho} + (1-\delta)L_i^{-\rho}]^{-\nu/\rho} + \varepsilon_i. \tag{13.16}$$

We use the starting values $\nu = 1$, $\rho = -0.2$, $\delta = 0.5$, and, from the results of estimating the Cobb-Douglas function with an additive disturbance in Example 2, $\gamma = 1.621$. NLS yields SSE = 81397.1, a loglikelihood function value of $\mathcal{L} = -131.603$ and the following estimates.

Parameter	Estimate	Standard error
γ	1.5049	0.437850
ν	1.0208	0.046455
δ	0.8656	0.046470
ρ	−0.3441	0.355903

A multiplicative disturbance. This enters the CES function as

$$Q_i = \gamma[\delta K_i^{-\rho} + (1-\delta)L_i^{-\rho}]^{-\nu/\rho}e^{\varepsilon_i},$$

so it should be estimated as

$$\log Q_i = \log \gamma - \frac{\nu}{\rho}\log[\delta K_i^{-\rho} + (1-\delta)L_i^{-\rho}] + \varepsilon_i. \tag{13.17}$$

This is just the logarithmic form (13.6) with an additive disturbance. We use the starting values $\nu = 1$, $\rho = -0.2$, $\delta = 0.5$, and, from the results of estimating the Cobb-Douglas function with a multiplicative disturbance in Example 2, $\log \gamma = 0.655$. NLS yields SSE = 0.698454, a loglikelihood value of $\mathcal{L} = 8.38876$, and the following estimates.

Parameter	Estimate	Standard error
$\log \gamma$	0.7073	0.238277
ν	0.9723	0.045588
δ	0.7602	0.055617
ρ	0.4269	0.407196

For simplicity in estimation, we have chosen to regard $\log \gamma$ rather than γ as the parameter to be estimated, similar to the Cobb-Douglas case. The implied estimate of γ is 2.028. Had it been important to obtain an estimated standard error for γ rather than $\log \gamma$, this could have been done by writing the NLS estimation code explicitly as $\log(\gamma)$.

Comparing the two estimations, notice that they yield similar estimates of γ, ν, and δ. The substitution parameter ρ, on the other hand, is estimated rather imprecisely by this data set; this is reflected in the quite different estimates obtained from the two functional forms and in their relatively large standard errors. The implied elasticities of substitution are in turn rather different. For the model with an additive disturbance, the implied estimate of $1/(1+\rho)$ is 1.525, suggesting fairly substantial capital-labor substitutability: a 1% change in relative factor prices results in a 1.525% change in the capital-labor ratio. For the model with a multiplicative disturbance, on the other hand, the implied estimate of $1/(1+\rho)$ is 0.701, suggesting that capital-labor substitution is more inelastic: a 1% change in relative factor prices results in only a 0.701% change in the capital-labor ratio.

In addition to using related empirical analyses and economic theory as a source of starting values, it is useful to experiment with alternative sets of starting values to ensure that your NLS estimation routine has located a global minimum.

EXERCISES

Mizon's data sets for the years 1954, 1957, and 1960 are provided in the files mizon54.dat, mizon57.dat, and mizon60.dat. Each data set consists of observations for $n = 24$ industries in the United Kingdom, on the following variables.

Q   Gross value added at factor cost (millions of pounds).

K   Value of the stock of plant and machinery (millions of pounds).

LF   Labor force available for work in the industry (thousands).

U   Number of workers unemployed in the industry (thousands).

H   Average hours per week worked by those employed.

From the last three variables the following measure of worker-hours of labor input may be generated:

$$L = (LF - U) \times H/100.$$

The variable is divided by 100 so that it is consistent in magnitude with Q and K, in anticipation of considerations developed in the next section.

13.3 mizon54.dat mizon60.dat Use Mizon's data for 1954 or 1960 to estimate the Cobb-Douglas production function,

(a) assuming a multiplicative disturbance.

(b) assuming an additive disturbance.

Explain your choice of starting values in part b.

13.4 mizon54.dat mizon60.dat Use Mizon's data for 1954 or 1960 to estimate the CES production function,

(a) assuming an additive disturbance.

(b) assuming a multiplicative disturbance.

In each case, explain your choice of starting values. How do the implied elasticities of substitution compare?

13.3 | Computer Numerics

We have seen that NLS estimation routines proceed by iterating on a solution. Even with good starting values, this is much more computationally demanding than computing closed-form OLS estimators, where an analytical solution to the least squares minimization problem is available. This in turn leads to certain issues in the application of NLS that you must have some appreciation of, even if you have no understanding of the numerical algorithms used by econometric software. These issues relate to the way in which digital computers represent numbers and the resulting approximation errors that can arise from the cumulation of a great many calculations.[5]

Computers store numerical values as approximations using **floating-point numbers,** which in high school you probably studied as **scientific notation.** The idea is that a number such as 3141.592654 can be written as

$$0.3141592654 \times 10^4,$$

whereas the number 0.003141592654 can be written

$$0.3141592654 \times 10^{-2}.$$

Thus, very large and very small numbers are represented internally in the computer in the same way and to the same number of digits accuracy. In the **single-precision** accuracy that, unless programmed otherwise, is the default for calculations, most computers store base 10 numbers to approximately six-digit accuracy. Hence, even if you keyed them in as data, the last four digits in these examples would not be used in calculation; the numbers would be stored as

$$0.314159 \times 10^4 \quad \text{and} \quad 0.314159 \times 10^{-2}.$$

Purely from the point of view of data accuracy, this rounding is of no great concern because economic data are only rarely accurate to six digits anyway. The real problem arises when a computer does calculations involving large and small numbers, because then errors are introduced that accumulate over many computations. Consider the following example given by Davidson and MacKinnon (1993, pp. 26–27). Suppose we wish to evaluate

$$2,393,121 - 1.0235 - 2,393,120.$$

This is equal to -0.0235. Suppose, however, that the expression is evaluated by a computer that stores numbers to six-digit accuracy, so that the three numbers are stored as

$$0.239312 \times 10^7, \quad 0.10235 \times 10^1, \quad \text{and} \quad 0.239312 \times 10^7.$$

Evaluated in the order given, the first two terms in the expression compute as

$$2,393,120 - 1.0235 = 2,393,118.9765.$$

This intermediate answer is stored internally in the computer to six-digit accuracy as

$$0.239312 \times 10^7,$$

---

[5] This section is inspired by, and follows very closely, Davidson and MacKinnon (1993, Sec. 1.5).

and so the final step in evaluating the original expression is

$$0.239312 \times 10^7 - 0.239312 \times 10^7 = 0.000000.$$

This is, of course, wrong: We know that the correct answer is -0.0235.

You might think that it would be possible to mitigate this problem by doing calculations involving large magnitudes first, but this is not the case. Suppose we reorder the calculation as

$$0.239312 \times 10^7 - 0.239312 \times 10^7 - 0.102350 \times 10^1.$$

The first subtraction is zero, leaving as the answer -1.0235. This is even further from the correct answer than the previous one.

These inaccuracies can, of course, be reduced by increasing the degree of precision to which numbers are stored, using **double precision** to store numbers to approximately 12 digits accuracy instead 6. But this just pushes the problem back one step; it cannot be eliminated entirely.

This limitation of floating-point arithmetic is of fundamental concern to the numerical analysts who design the algorithms used in statistical and other software. Donald Knuth (1997, p. 229) has drawn the following caricature of two groups of computer users.

> Floating point computation is by nature inexact. ... There's a credibility gap: We don't know how much of the computer's answers to believe. Novice computer users solve this problem by implicitly trusting in the computer as an infallible authority; they tend to believe that all digits of a printed answer are significant. Disillusioned computer users have just the opposite approach; they are constantly afraid that their answers are almost meaningless.

Applied econometricians should probably aim for a balance between these extremes.

The approximation errors intrinsic to floating-point arithmetic have important implications for the programming of econometric software. To illustrate, consider the computation of the sample variance of Chapter 2, formula (2.7):

$$s^2 = \frac{1}{n-1} \sum_{i=1}^{n} (Y_i - \overline{Y})^2. \tag{13.18}$$

Using this formula with a hand calculator is a lot of work because it requires calculating each of the n deviations $Y_i - \overline{Y}$. Statistics textbooks often suggest instead the shortcut formula

$$s^2 = \frac{1}{n-1} \left(\sum_{i=1}^{n} Y_i^2 - n\overline{Y}^2 \right). \tag{13.19}$$

It is a standard exercise in introductory courses to have students produce the brief derivation that establishes the algebraic equivalence of the two formulas.

Although it may be more convenient for use with a hand calculator, when implemented on a computer the shortcut formula tends to give rise to exactly the sort of numerical problem we have just described. For the values $\sum Y_i^2$ and $n\overline{Y}^2$

TABLE 13.2   Absolute Errors in Calculating the Sample Variance

μ	Original formula (13.18)	Shortcut formula (13.19)
0	0.880×10^{-4}	0.880×10^{-4}
10	0.868×10^{-4}	0.126×10^{0}
10^2	0.553×10^{-4}	0.197×10^{1}
10^3	0.756×10^{-3}	0.410×10^{2}
10^4	0.204×10^{0}	0.302×10^{4}
10^5	0.452×10^{2}	0.733×10^{6}

Source: From **Estimation and Inference in Econometrics** by Russell Davidson and James G. MacKinnon, copyright © 1993 by Oxford University Press, Inc. Used by permission of Oxford University Press, Inc.

will, because they involve squares, often be quite large, even when their difference is fairly small. Thus, the nature of the formula tends to introduce the approximation errors intrinsic to floating-point arithmetic; in the terminology of numerical analysis, the formula is said to be **numerically unstable.**

Davidson and MacKinnon (1993, pp. 27–28) demonstrated the numerical instability of the shortcut formula with a simulation experiment. They generated 1000 normally distributed random numbers with mean μ and variance unity, setting μ equal to 0, 10, 10^2, 10^3, 10^4, and 10^5. For each value of μ they used the 1000 values to compute the sample variance using the two formulas (13.18) and (13.19). Table 13.2 shows how close the formulas come to producing the correct value of the variance which, remember, is exactly 1 by construction.

As μ takes on larger values, the 1000 randomly generated Y_i values scattered around it—and thus the quantities $\sum Y_i^2$ and $n\overline{Y}^2$—take on larger values relative to the variance of unity. For $\mu = 0$, both formulas are extremely accurate in estimating this variance. The original formula (13.18) continues to give a very accurate answer up to $\mu = 10^3 = 1000$. The numerically unstable shortcut formula (13.19), on the other hand, is off by 12.6% even for $\mu = 10$ and becomes grossly inaccurate for larger values of μ.

The lesson of this example is that, even for elementary data analysis, it is important to use professionally written software. We hope that commercially distributed econometrics packages are written by programmers knowledgeable about issues in numerical analysis that bear on the accuracy of floating-point calculations. Unfortunately, it remains an open question how well founded this hope is. McCullough (1999) and McCullough and Vinod (1999) document weaknesses in the numerical reliability of some of the most widely used econometrics packages. In some cases, these weaknesses include errors in the calculation of elementary statistics such as correlations and standard deviations.[6] Applied econometricians are

[6] The estimation results presented in this chapter are obtained using the package TSP. TSP's nonlinear estimation routine is assessed favorably by McCullough (1999).

well advised to pay careful attention to issues of numerical reliability in selecting econometric software.

In the case of estimation problems for which closed-form estimators are unavailable, such as nonlinear regression, and hence for which solutions must be obtained by iteration, the potential for inaccuracies arising from floating-point arithmetic is compounded manyfold. For a sobering account of attempts to replicate published research based on nonlinear estimation, see McCullough and Vinod (2003).

There are, however, measures the applied econometrician can take to mitigate this problem, independent of the software that is used. One is, as we have already emphasized, to use good starting values to reduce the number of iterations. Another is to scale the units of measure of the variables so that they are of similar magnitudes. This decreases the incidence of calculations involving quantities of greatly different magnitudes.

EXAMPLE 4

 mizon57.dat

Consider Mizon's 1957 data as presented in Table 13.1. Detailed variable definitions are given in the exercises at the end of the previous section. The variables used in the estimation of a production function are output Q, capital K, and labor L. The first two are as given in the table. Worker-hours of labor input, on the other hand, must be generated from the remaining variables as

$$L = (LF - U) \times H. \tag{13.20}$$

That is, worker-hours of labor employed in an industry consists of the labor force normally available for work in that industry less those unemployed times the average weekly hours worked by the employed. How does the magnitude of this variable compare with Q and K, and what are the implications for NLS estimation of a production function?

SOLUTION

Whereas Q and K are measured in such a way that their magnitudes are similar, generating L as defined yields a variable larger by a factor of approximately 100. In order to reduce the approximation errors of floating-point arithmetic, it makes sense to redefine L by dividing by this factor, as you have been instructed to do.

The following exercise asks you to check the sensitivity of your NLS software to this data scaling. Although not particularly important for the fairly elementary example we are considering here, in more complex nonlinear estimation problems data scalings can be critical in obtaining convergence and numerically accurate results.

Practitioner's Tip: Floating-point numerics in nonlinear estimation

In nonlinear estimation problems, improve numerical accuracy and the likelihood of convergence by (1) using your background knowledge of related empirical analyses and economic theory to choose good starting values, and (2) scaling variables so that they are of comparable magnitude.

EXERCISES

13.5 🔘 **mizon54.dat mizon60.dat** Repeat your estimations of the CES production function of Exercise 13.4, using the definition (13.20) instead of scaling by the factor 1/100,

(a) assuming an additive disturbance.

(b) assuming a multiplicative disturbance.

In each case, does your estimation converge? If so, how many iterations are required, and how does this compare with what was needed in Exercise 13.4?

13.4   Reparameterization

It is often the case that a statistical model can be written in several different but mathematically equivalent forms. The models are equivalent in that the relationship between the parameters is exactly identifying. We have already encountered examples of this notion of **model reparameterization.**

Dummy Variable Regressions with and without an Intercept One particularly simple example of model reparameterization appeared in our study of dummy variables in Chapter 10. We have seen there that it is possible to distinguish among several categories in the data by including as explanatory variables one fewer dummy variables than there are categories. In the example in Section 10.1, one dummy variable is used to distinguish between two production processes, two dummies for three processes, and so on. In the case of two production processes and a single dummy, the regression is equation (10.50):

$$Y_i = \alpha + \beta D_{2i} + \varepsilon_i,$$

where D_{2i} is assigned the value 0 if output is from process A and 1 if from process B.

One fewer dummy variables is used than there are categories as long as the regression includes an intercept. In a model without an intercept, the same number of dummy variables as categories is required. Defining $D_{3i} \equiv 1 - D_{2i}$, the regression through the origin that is the alternative to the previous model is equation (10.51):

$$Y_i = \beta_2 D_{2i} + \beta_3 D_{3i} + \varepsilon_i.$$

The two models are equivalent in their empirical content; that is, they are just different ways of expressing the same description of the data.

We have found the relationship between the two sets of coefficients to be

$$\beta_2 = \alpha + \beta$$
$$\beta_3 = \alpha.$$

Because this represents a one-to-one correspondence, it is an exactly identifying relationship. This is another way of recognizing the equivalence of the two models—one is a reparameterization of the other. Which parameterization we choose to use in empirical work is a matter of convenience. We have argued that this is normally the model with a single dummy variable and an intercept because the natural hypothesis of interest is that the two production processes have the same mean output. This is easily tested in the first regression as the restriction $\beta = 0$.

The concept of reparameterization is particularly important in nonlinear models because there are often several mathematically equivalent ways of writing such models. Two examples appear in the Introduction to this chapter.

The Mankiw-Romer-Weil Regression   Recall the MRW regression (13.7),

$$\log q_i = \beta_1 + \beta_2 (\log s_i - \log(\delta + n_i)) + \varepsilon_i,$$

which here is written with the restriction $\beta_3 = -\beta_2$ imposed. In terms of the underlying parameters of the Solow-Swan growth model, this is

$$\log q_i = \frac{\log \gamma}{1 - \alpha} + \frac{\alpha}{1 - \alpha} (\log s_i - \log(\delta + n_i)) + \varepsilon_i. \tag{13.21}$$

One regression is a reparameterization of the other because the relationship between the two sets of coefficients is exactly identifying:

$$\beta_1 = \frac{\log \gamma}{1 - \alpha},$$
$$\beta_2 = \frac{\alpha}{1 - \alpha}.$$

Mankiw, Romer, and Weil worked with the first parameterization because it is linear and therefore estimable by OLS. In Example 13 of Chapter 10, this exactly identifying parameter relationship was used to deduce unique implied estimates of γ and α. However, as we note in the introduction to the present chapter, in principle the intrinsically nonlinear parameterization could be estimated by NLS.

The Cobb-Douglas Cost Function   As another example of model reparameterization, recall the two-factor Cobb-Douglas cost function (13.9),

$$\log C_i - \log p_{2i} = \alpha + \beta \log Q_i + \gamma_1 (\log p_{1i} - \log p_{2i}) + \varepsilon_i,$$

which here is written with the linear homogeneity restriction $\gamma_2 = 1 - \gamma_1$ imposed. This can be reparameterized in terms of the parameters of the underlying production function as

$$\log C_i = \alpha + \frac{1}{\alpha_1 + \alpha_2} \log Q_i + \frac{\alpha_1}{\alpha_1 + \alpha_2} (\log p_{1i} - \log p_{2i}) + \varepsilon_i.$$

One model is a reparameterization of the other because the relationship between the two sets of coefficients is exactly identifying. In Chapter 11 we find it convenient to work with the first model because it is linear and therefore estimable by OLS. However, as we note in the introduction to the present chapter, in principle its intrinsically nonlinear reparameterization could be estimated by NLS.

In both these examples one of the parameterizations is intrinsically linear and thus estimable by OLS. Let us turn to an example of the reparameterization of an intrinsically nonlinear model for which no linear version exists.

The CES Production Function   So far we have been working in terms of the following parameterization of the CES production function:

$$Q = \gamma[\delta K^{-\rho} + (1 - \delta)L^{-\rho}]^{-\nu/\rho}. \tag{13.22}$$

This is not the only way of parameterizing it. An alternative parameterization is

$$Q = [\delta_1 K^{-\rho} + \delta_2 L^{-\rho}]^{-\nu/\rho}. \tag{13.23}$$

Both parameterizations involve four coefficients: the first is in terms of γ, ν, δ, and ρ, the second in terms of ν, δ_1, δ_2, and ρ. Going from the first to the second effectively takes the parameter γ inside the parentheses and incorporates it into the new parameters δ_1 and δ_2. In doing this, the implicit restriction that the coefficients on K and L sum to 1 is lost and the restriction $0 < \delta < 1$ specified as part of the first parameterization no longer applies to δ_1 or δ_2.

A model reparameterization is essentially just a change of notation. Consequently, substantive empirical findings should not depend on which parameterization we choose. For example, consider the parameters ν and ρ that enter both CES parameterizations: ν is the degree of returns to scale and ρ the substitution parameter. The estimation results for these features of the production technology should not depend on which parameterization is estimated; they should be **invariant to model reparameterization.**

EXAMPLE 5

 mizon57.dat

Use Mizon's 1957 data to estimate the alternative parameterization of the CES production function, assuming both multiplicative and additive disturbances. How do the results compare with those of the first parameterization?

SOLUTION

An additive disturbance. The CES production function is estimated as

$$Q_i = [\delta_1 K_i^{-\rho} + \delta_2 L_i^{-\rho}]^{-\nu/\rho} + \varepsilon_i. \tag{13.24}$$

NLS yields SSE $= 81397.1$, a loglikelihood function value of $\mathcal{L} = -131.603$, and the following estimates.

Parameter	Estimate	Standard error
ν	1.0208	0.046455
δ_1	0.9935	0.205159
δ_2	0.1542	0.041130
ρ	-0.3441	0.355902

A multiplicative disturbance. This leads to a function that should be estimated as

$$\log Q_i = -\frac{\nu}{\rho} \log \left[\delta_1 K_i^{-\rho} + \delta_2 L_i^{-\rho} \right] + \varepsilon_i. \tag{13.25}$$

NLS yields SSE $= 0.698454$, a loglikelihood value of $\mathcal{L} = 8.38876$, and the following estimates.

Parameter	Estimate	Standard error
ν	0.9723	0.045588
δ_1	0.5573	0.215335
δ_2	0.1758	0.060702
ρ	0.4269	0.407199

For each type of disturbance the values of the SSE and loglikelihood function, and the estimation results for ν and ρ, are very close to, if not identical with, the results for the alternative parameterization presented in Example 3. In this respect, then, we have found the results to be invariant to reparameterization.

EXERCISES

13.6 mizon54.dat mizon60.dat Use Mizon's data for 1954 or 1960 to estimate the reparameterized form (13.23) of the CES production function,

(a) assuming an additive disturbance.

(b) assuming a multiplicative disturbance.

Comparing your results with those of Exercise 13.4, do you find them to be invariant to reparameterization?

13.5 | Identification

The concept of identification is introduced in the context of the linear regression model in Section 10.3, in which examples of over-, exactly, and underidentifying restrictions are given. Model identification is defined, which meant that a unique set of estimates is associated with the minimum of the sum of squares function.

These ideas extend naturally to nonlinear regression. As we will see, identification issues are at least as important in nonlinear models as they are in linear ones.

13.5.1   Coefficient Restrictions

As our discussion of reparameterization suggests, the notion of coefficient restrictions being over-, exactly, or underidentifying applies in nonlinear models just as it does in linear ones. In fact, the conclusions in Table 10.9 continue to apply without modification. It is useful to recapitulate the most important of those conclusions.

Underidentifying restrictions may be neither imposed in estimation nor tested.

Exactly identifying restrictions may be imposed in estimation but, because they do not constrain the ability of a model to fit the data, are not testable. Imposing exactly identifying restrictions in estimation is just what we have called model reparameterizations; that is, rewriting the model in an alternative but mathematically equivalent form.

Overidentifying restrictions may be imposed in estimation and, because doing this constrains the ability of the model to fit the data, they may be tested. We have now encountered several examples of overidentifying restrictions in nonlinear models. In the CES production function, the hypothesis of constant returns to scale is the restriction $\nu = 1$; the hypothesis of a unitary elasticity of substitution is the restriction $\rho = 0$. Both are examples of what in Chapter 10 we call fixed-value restrictions. The restriction $\rho = 0$ is the hypothesis that the CES function specializes to the Cobb-Douglas. An example of a hypothesis that is not a fixed-value restriction is the constant-returns-to-scale restriction $\alpha + \beta = 1$ in the Cobb-Douglas function (13.4).

Just as is true in linear models, because imposing overidentifying restrictions constrains the ability of a model to fit the data, a restricted model should fit the data less well than an unrestricted one. That is, a restricted model should have a larger SSE and a smaller loglikelihood function value than the unrestricted model:

$$SSE_R \geq SSE_U, \tag{13.26a}$$
$$\mathscr{L}_R \leq \mathscr{L}_U. \tag{13.26b}$$

The equalities only hold if the restriction is satisfied exactly in the sample. The first inequality just restates the relationship (10.33) that we have noted much earlier for linear regressions.

Let us consider some examples, beginning with a reminder of how things work in linear regression.

EXAMPLE 6

mizon57.dat

Use Mizon's 1957 data to estimate the Cobb-Douglas production function, imposing constant returns to scale.

SOLUTION

In the Cobb-Douglas production function the hypothesis of constant returns to scale is the coefficient restriction $\alpha + \beta = 1$.

A multiplicative disturbance. As we have seen in Example 2, under a multiplicative disturbance the model is intrinsically linear and so may be estimated, in its unrestricted form, as the loglinear regression

$$\log Q_i = \log \gamma + \beta \log K_i + \alpha \log L_i + \varepsilon_i.$$

We have found there that OLS estimation of this equation using Mizon's 1957 data yields $SSE_U = 0.743489$ and a loglikelihood function value of $\mathscr{L}_U = 7.63894$.

As we have found in Example 6 of Chapter 10, imposing the restriction $\alpha = 1 - \beta$ yields the restricted model

$$\log Q_i - \log L_i = \log \gamma + \beta(\log K_i - \log L_i) + \varepsilon_i.$$

Estimating this with Mizon's 1957 data yields $SSE_R = 0.751876$ and a loglikelihood function value of $\mathscr{L}_R = 7.50432$. These values verify the relationships (13.26), confirming that the restricted model fits the data less well than the unrestricted model.

An additive disturbance. Imposing the restriction $\alpha = 1 - \beta$ yields the restricted model[7]

$$Q_i = \gamma K_i^{\beta} L_i^{1-\beta} + \varepsilon_i.$$

NLS yields $\text{SSE}_R = 85232.1$, a loglikelihood function value of $\mathscr{L}_R = -132.155$, and the estimates $\hat{\gamma} = 1.7318$ and $\hat{\beta} = 0.1427$. Comparing these results with those of Example 2, notice that this SSE is larger than the $\text{SSE}_U = 85002.1$ reported there and the loglikelihood function value is below that of $\mathscr{L}_U = -132.123$. These values verify the relationships (13.26), confirming that the restricted model fits the data less well than the unrestricted model.

EXAMPLE 7

mizon57.dat

Estimate both parameterizations of the CES production function subject to the constant-returns-to-scale restriction that $v = 1$, in each case assuming both an additive and a multiplicative disturbance. Are your estimation results invariant to model reparameterization?

SOLUTION

We continue to use Mizon's 1957 data set.

An additive disturbance. Setting $v = 1$ in the first parameterization (13.16), the model to be estimated is

$$Q_i = \gamma[\delta K_i^{-\rho} + (1 - \delta)L_i^{-\rho}]^{-1/\rho} + \varepsilon_i.$$

NLS yields $\text{SSE} = 82207.0$, a loglikelihood function value of $\mathscr{L} = -131.722$, and the following estimates.

Parameter	Estimate	Standard error
γ	1.7127	0.051361
δ	0.8706	0.044266
ρ	−0.3288	0.368012

Turning to the second parameterization, setting $v = 1$ in (13.24) yields

$$Q_i = [\delta_1 K_i^{-\rho} + \delta_2 L_i^{-\rho}]^{-1/\rho} + \varepsilon_i.$$

NLS yields $\text{SSE} = 82207.0$, a loglikelihood function value of $\mathscr{L} = -131.722$, and the following estimates.

Parameter	Estimate	Standard error
δ_1	1.0390	0.237854
δ_2	0.1545	0.041279
ρ	−0.3287	0.368012

---

[7] Notice that this is not the same thing as the intensive-form model (13.3). In this example, we are starting with the model (13.4) in which the disturbance is specified as additive and imposing constant returns to scale. This is not the same thing as starting with the intensive-form production function and adding a disturbance, as you may wish to verify by estimating the latter.

In both parameterizations the SSEs and loglikelihood function values are identical and the results for ρ very similar, indicating that NLS estimation of the model is invariant to reparameterization.

Recall that the estimation of the unrestricted model in Examples 3 and 5 yields $SSE_U = 81397.1$ and a loglikelihood function value of $\mathscr{L}_U = -131.603$. Comparing these values with those obtained here verifies the relationships (13.26), confirming that the restricted model fits the data less well than the unrestricted model.

A multiplicative disturbance. Setting $\nu = 1$ in the first parameterization (13.17), the model to be estimated is

$$\log Q_i = \log \gamma - \frac{1}{\rho} \log[\delta K_i^{-\rho} + (1-\delta)L_i^{-\rho}] + \varepsilon_i.$$

NLS yields $SSE = 0.711401$, a loglikelihood value of $\mathscr{L} = 8.16836$, and the following estimates.

Parameter	Estimate	Standard error
$\log \gamma$	0.5656	0.045841
δ	0.7535	0.052801
ρ	0.3742	0.358749

Turning to the second parameterization, setting $\nu = 1$ in (13.25) yields

$$\log Q_i = -\frac{1}{\rho} \log[\delta_1 K_i^{-\rho} + \delta_2 L_i^{-\rho}] + \varepsilon_i.$$

NLS yields $SSE = 0.711401$, a loglikelihood value of $\mathscr{L} = 8.16836$, and the following estimates.

Parameter	Estimate	Standard error
δ_1	0.6098	0.159012
δ_2	0.1995	0.037912
ρ	0.3742	0.358750

In both parameterizations the SSEs, loglikelihood function values, and estimates of ρ are identical, as is virtually the case for the standard error of ρ as well. NLS estimation is invariant to reparameterization.

Recall that the estimation of the unrestricted model in Examples 3 and 5 yields $SSE_U = 0.698454$ and a loglikelihood function value of $\mathscr{L}_U = 8.38876$. Comparing these values with those obtained here verifies the relationships (13.26), confirming that the restricted model fits the data less well than the unrestricted model.

EXAMPLE 8

mizon57.dat

Estimate the CES production function subject to the restriction of a unitary elasticity of substitution: $\rho = 0$.

SOLUTION

Under a unitary elasticity of substitution, the CES production function reduces to the Cobb-Douglas. Hence, this question asks us to estimate the Cobb-Douglas production function. This has already been done in Example 2 using Mizon's 1957 data set, and we refer to those results. Note that for the Cobb-Douglas function there is no issue of alternative parameterizations of the model.

An additive disturbance. This yields, in Example 2, SSE = 85002.1 and a loglikelihood function value of $\mathscr{L} = -132.123$. Recall that the estimation of the unrestricted model—the CES—in Examples 3 or 5 yields $SSE_U = 81397.1$ and a loglikelihood function value of $\mathscr{L}_U = -131.603$. Comparing these values verifies the relationships (13.26), confirming that the restricted model fits the data less well than the unrestricted model.

A multiplicative disturbance. This yields, in Example 2, SSE = 0.743489 and a loglikelihood function value of $\mathscr{L} = 7.63894$. Recall that the estimation of the unrestricted model—the CES—in Examples 3 or 5 yields $SSE_U = 0.698454$ and a loglikelihood function value of $\mathscr{L}_U = 8.38876$. Comparing these values verifies the relationships (13.26), confirming that the restricted model fits the data less well than the unrestricted model.

It happens that these examples have been ones in which the coefficient restrictions are linear: $\alpha + \beta = 1$, $\nu = 1$, and $\rho = 0$ are all of the linear form (10.25). Coefficient restrictions may also be nonlinear. In a regression (linear or nonlinear) that includes coefficients β_1 and β_2, say, it may be of interest to consider the possibility that one coefficient is the reciprocal of another,

$$\beta_1 = \frac{1}{\beta_2}, \tag{13.27}$$

that one coefficient is some power of another, such as

$$\beta_1^2 = \beta_2,$$

or that the product of the coefficients is some specified numerical value c_0,

$$\beta_1 \beta_2 = c_0.$$

(The last includes the reciprocal hypothesis (13.27) as a special case.) These are all examples of nonlinear coefficient restrictions in that they are not of the linear form (10.25).

Exactly the same conclusions about identification apply to nonlinear restrictions as apply to linear ones. Most important, exactly identifying restrictions merely constitute a reparameterization of the model that is not testable. Overidentifying restrictions, on the other hand, constrain the ability of the model to fit the data and so are testable. We have not, of course, at this point presented hypothesis testing procedures. This is the subject of Section 13.8.

13.5.2 Model Identification

In addition to the idea of the identification status of coefficient restrictions, we define in Section 10.3 the concept of model identification. A regression model is identified if a unique set of estimates is associated with the minimum of the sum of squares function.

FIGURE 13.2

The model is not
identified: The min-
imum of the sum of
squares function is
not unique.

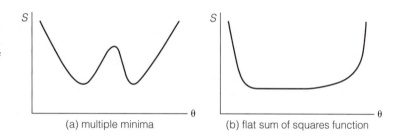

(a) multiple minima   (b) flat sum of squares function

Although we give some examples of this in Section 10.3, they arise from the violation of identifying conditions. Because these identifying conditions—such as the existence of variation in the data or the absence of perfect multicollinearity—are normally satisfied, in practice, model identification is not usually a problem in linear regression models. Solving the K normal equations for K coefficient estimates yields a unique solution.

As we have noted, however, when the normal equations are nonlinear the same number of equations as unknowns does not necessarily yield a unique solution. The sum of squares function for a nonlinear regression problem may not have a unique global minimum. Figure 13.2 shows two ways in which this could happen. Both panels of the figure show a sum of squares function varying with a single parameter θ. In Figure 13.2(a) the sum of squares function has two minima but, in contrast to Figure 13.1, does not have a unique global minimum. In Figure 13.2(b) the sum of squares function does not have a unique minimum because it is flat over a certain range.

Davidson and MacKinnon (1993, p. 49) have given the following example of a model that is not identified, in a manner similar to Figure 13.2(a). Consider

$$Y_i = \beta\gamma + \gamma^2 X_i + \varepsilon_i.$$

Suppose the estimates $[\hat{\beta}\ \hat{\gamma}]$ yield a minimum of the sum of squares function of this model. Then the estimates $[-\hat{\beta}\ -\hat{\gamma}]$ must yield the same minimum because they yield the same predicted values and residuals as the first pair of estimates. There is no objective basis for choosing between these two very different sets of estimates; which of the two minima happens to be located by a nonlinear least squares estimation routine will depend arbitrarily on the starting values and the algorithm used. Notice that this lack of identification is intrinsic to the model and is entirely independent of the data.

For an example like Figure 13.2(b), let us return to the CES production function. In comparing the two parameterizations (13.22) and (13.23), each of which has four coefficients, you may have wondered why we do not consider the five-coefficient model

$$Q = \gamma[\delta_1 K^{-\rho} + \delta_2 L^{-\rho}]^{-\nu/\rho}. \tag{13.28}$$

Clearly this model is more general in that the earlier ones are special cases. The first parameterization (13.22) is the special case of $\delta_1 + \delta_2 = 1$ with, then, the change of notation to δ. The second parameterization (13.23) is the special case of $\gamma = 1$. In estimating the CES production function, should we not begin by estimating this more general model and then testing these restrictions to see if the data support restricting it to the special case?

The parameterization (13.28) is indeed a more general model; it is so general it is not identified! There is an indeterminacy in the estimation of γ, δ_1, and δ_2 that may be seen as follows. Consider any values of these coefficients that minimize the sum of squares function $S(\boldsymbol{\beta})$. Now consider alternative coefficient values that, say, double δ_1 and δ_2 and scale γ by the factor $2^{v/\rho}$. Substituting these into the right-hand side of (13.28) yields

$$2^{v/\rho}\gamma[2\delta_1 K^{-\rho} + 2\delta_2 L^{-\rho}]^{-v/\rho} = \gamma 2^{v/\rho} 2^{-v/\rho}[\delta_1 K^{-\rho} + \delta_2 L^{-\rho}]^{-v/\rho}$$
$$= \gamma[\delta_1 K^{-\rho} + \delta_2 L^{-\rho}]^{-v/\rho},$$

which is just the right-hand side of (13.28) at the initial coefficient values. Hence, both sets of estimates yield the same minimum value of $S(\boldsymbol{\beta})$ and, because there are an infinite number of similar scaling factors that do the same thing (the choice of the value 2 is arbitrary), there are an infinite number of such estimates. This version of the CES production function is not identified.

Identification of the model is achieved by imposing parameter restrictions. The first version of the CES production function we considered, model (13.5), achieves identification by imposing the restriction $\delta_1 + \delta_2 = 1$. By contrast, the function (13.23) achieves identification by imposing the restriction $\gamma = 1$. These restrictions "pin down" the coefficients of the model so that unique estimates correspond to the minimum of the sum of squares function. Because these restrictions serve merely to convert an unidentified model into an identified one, they are not testable. Restrictions such as these that convert unidentified parameters into identified ones are sometimes called **normalizing restrictions.**

What happens if we attempt to estimate an unidentified model? This depends both on the estimation algorithm and the nature of the lack of identification. If the lack of identification is similar to that of Figure 13.2(a), so that the model is locally identified, then the algorithm will typically converge to a point of local identification without, of course, giving any indication that these estimates are not unique. If the lack of identification is like that of Figure 13.2(b), then there are several possibilities. One is that the algorithm may fail to converge. Because there is no way the estimation routine can know that the reason it cannot find unique estimates is that there is no unique minimum of the sum of squares function, the error messages that accompany this failure to converge will typically give no indication that the model is not identified. Even worse, another possibility is that the routine may give the appearance of having converged, perhaps even producing standard errors suggesting that the coefficients have been estimated with some precision, without any indication that the reported estimates are just one set of an infinite number of estimates associated with a common minimum of the sum of squares function.

In these two examples, identification is examined by inspecting the functional forms to see whether the parameterization involves an indeterminacy. Beyond this, there is in general no systematic means of determining whether a nonlinear regression model is identified. If your NLS estimation routine fails to converge—or produces other puzzling error messages alluding cryptically to some mysterious numerical problem—you may be trying to estimate a model that is not identified!

One reason for our emphasis on identification issues is that, in addition to its obvious importance for nonlinear regression, it is a concept that applies much more broadly in all econometric models and to the analysis of data in other disciplines as well.[8] There are some modeling contexts in which there *are* systematic methods for establishing whether a model is identified. The example most familiar to econometricians is the simultaneous equations model, the kind of model mentioned in Section 5.3.3. Because identification is so often treated in the context of that model, there is an unfortunate tendency among many economists—and even econometricians—to think that the topic arises only in connection with it. Our development of identification should have made it clear that this is not the case.

EXERCISES

13.7 mizon54.dat mizon60.dat Use Mizon's data for 1954 or 1960 to estimate the Cobb-Douglas production function with constant returns to scale imposed,

(a) assuming a multiplicative disturbance.

(b) assuming an additive disturbance.

In each case, compare the SSE and loglikelihood function value with those you have obtained in Exercise 13.3. Are the relationships (13.26) verified?

13.8 mizon54.dat mizon60.dat The hypothesis of constant returns to scale is an overidentifying restriction on the CES production function. Use Mizon's data for 1954 or 1960 to do the following.

(a) Assuming an additive disturbance, estimate the parameterizations (13.22) and (13.23), in each case imposing the restriction that $v = 1$. Consider the resulting estimates of ρ and their standard errors, the values of the SSE, and the loglikelihood function values.

i. Are your estimation results invariant to model reparameterization?

ii. Are the relationships (13.26) verified?

(b) Repeat part a, this time assuming a multiplicative disturbance.

(c) What natural source of starting values have you used in these estimations?

13.9 mizon54.dat mizon60.dat In Exercise 13.4 you estimate the CES production function unrestricted; in Exercise 13.3 you effectively impose the restriction $\rho = 0$ by estimating the Cobb-Douglas production function. Compare the SSEs and loglikelihood function values of these restricted and unrestricted models for

(a) an additive disturbance.

(b) a multiplicative disturbance.

Are the relationships (13.26) verified?

13.10 mizon54.dat mizon60.dat Use Mizon's data for 1954 or 1960 to try estimating the unidentified version of the CES production function. What happens? Does your econometric software give any indication that the model is not identified?

[8] For a treatment of identification that takes this broader interdisciplinary perspective, see Manski (1995).

13.6 | Sampling Properties of Nonlinear Least Squares Estimators

So far, we have focused on the practicalities of obtaining NLS estimates, without discussing their sampling properties. In linear regression models we know, from our earlier discussions in Sections 4.3 and 8.3, that OLS estimators possess a number of important properties such as unbiasedness, efficiency, and best linear unbiasedness. What can be said of NLS estimators?

As a review of those earlier discussions reveals, the derivation of the properties of OLS estimators relies critically on the fact that they are closed-form expressions that are linear in the dependent variable Y_i. This makes it possible to manipulate those expressions using mathematical expectations in order to establish, for example, the property of unbiasedness. (Recall the derivation of Result 2.1 in Chapter 2 or the proof of the unbiasedness of $\hat{\beta}$ in Section 4.3.)

In contrast, we have seen that NLS estimators cannot be derived analytically as closed-form expressions. The numerically obtained NLS estimators are nonlinear functions of the dependent variable Y_i. This makes a fundamental difference in how the sampling properties of NLS estimators are investigated and what can be said about them. In particular, NLS estimators *cannot* be shown to be unbiased, efficient, or best linear unbiased. It is not possible to establish any of the properties that, in Chapter 2, we call finite-sample or small-sample properties. This is true, incidentally, not just of NLS estimators, but of the estimators yielded by any estimation principle applied to the nonlinear regression model.

In view of this, what is the justification for NLS as an estimation method? Although it is not possible to say much about the sampling distributions of NLS estimators in finite samples, it turns out that by advanced methods it *is* possible to say quite a lot about their sampling distributions as the sample size becomes large; that is, as $n \to \infty$. This means that NLS estimators may be shown to possess what in Chapter 2 we call large-sample or asymptotic properties. For example, although NLS estimators are not necessarily unbiased, they may be shown to be asymptotically unbiased. Recall this means that the sampling distribution becomes centered over the true parameter value as $n \to \infty$.

Other asymptotic properties may also be established. NLS estimators may be shown to be **consistent.** This means that, in addition to the sampling distribution becoming centered over the population value of the parameter, the sampling distribution collapses about that true value as $n \to \infty$; its variance goes to zero. The sampling distribution of a consistent estimator is illustrated in Figure 13.3. As a concrete example of an estimator whose sampling distribution evolves in a manner similar to that depicted in this figure, consider the estimator $\hat{\sigma}^2$ discussed in Chapter 2. Although biased, both its bias and variance go to zero as $n \to \infty$, as illustrated in Figure 2.3.

Consistency is an enormously important property. Roughly speaking, it means that as more and more data become available it is possible to get better and better estimates. This is typically the minimal property econometricians insist on from an

FIGURE 13.3

The estimator $\hat{\theta}$ is consistent: Its bias and variance go to zero as $n \to \infty$.

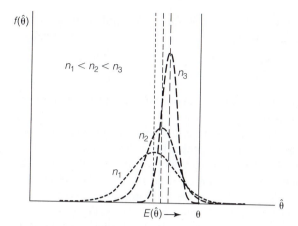

FIGURE 13.3

The estimator $\hat{\theta}$ is consistent: Its bias and variance go to zero as $n \to \infty$.

estimator. If an estimator is *not* consistent the implication is that even if infinite data were available—so even if we had the population—the estimate can still be wrong, clearly an unappealing feature.

Finally, if we add to the specification of the nonlinear regression model the assumption that the disturbance is normally distributed, it may be established that NLS estimators are **asymptotically efficient.** This means that, in the final stages toward its collapse as $n \to \infty$, the sampling distribution of the NLS estimator has the smallest variance among all consistent estimators.

OLS estimators are, of course, just a special case in which NLS is applied to the linear regression model—a special case in which closed-form expressions for the estimators are available. It follows that OLS estimators possess these desirable properties of consistency and asymptotic efficiency. This is not emphasized in our earlier discussion of the properties of OLS because it was at that point premature to introduce these concepts. One by-product of our study of NLS is that it helps motivate the importance of asymptotic results in econometrics.

Although these asymptotic properties serve to justify the use of NLS estimators, it is apparent that the mechanics of applying NLS are not particularly dependent on an understanding of these concepts. You were able to use NLS to estimate nonlinear models such as the CES production function prior to reading this section. It turns out, however, that an appreciation of the fundamentally different foundations underlying statistical inference in nonlinear models is critical for hypothesis testing. This is the theme of Section 13.8.

13.7 Estimating σ^2

So far, our treatment of NLS has focused on the estimation of the K coefficients of the vector $\boldsymbol{\beta}$. There is, of course, an additional parameter of the model that we have so far not considered, the variance σ^2.

Estimation of σ^2 is fairly straightforward, because we can continue to approach this exactly as we have in the past. In the linear regression model, we estimate σ^2 by

$$s^2 = \frac{\text{SSE}}{n-K} = \frac{1}{n-K} \sum_{i=1}^{n} e_i^2,$$

and exactly the same estimator continues to be appropriate. The e_i are now the NLS residuals.

For the reasons we have just discussed in connection with the NLS coefficient estimators, the sampling properties of this estimator are no longer what they were in the case of the linear regression model. Specifically, s^2 can no longer be shown to be unbiased. It can, however, be shown to have desirable asymptotic properties; s^2 is consistent (and therefore, by implication, asymptotically unbiased).

Purely on the basis of asymptotic properties there is no analytical justification for dividing by $n - K$ instead of n. If only asymptotic properties matter, then obviously as $n \to \infty$ the properties of the estimator are the same regardless of whether the divisor is n or $n - K$. For this reason, some NLS routines estimate σ^2 using the alternative formula

$$\hat{\sigma}^2 = \frac{\text{SSE}}{n} = \frac{1}{n} \sum_{i=1}^{n} e_i^2,$$

a special case of which we have examined much earlier in Chapter 2 as equation (2.8). It is apparent that the relationship between the two estimators is

$$\hat{\sigma}^2 = \frac{n-K}{n} s^2, \tag{13.29}$$

so that $\hat{\sigma}^2$ gives a smaller variance estimate than does s^2. This is analogous to the earlier relationship (2.9).

Nevertheless, even though s^2 cannot be shown to be unbiased, it can be shown to be less biased than $\hat{\sigma}^2$; see Davidson and MacKinnon (1993, pp. 166–167). Complementary to this is a body of Monte Carlo evidence supporting the use of s^2 as the estimator with superior properties in finite samples. This is hardly surprising. We know analytically that in linear regression division by $n-K$ improves the finite sample properties of the estimator. It only stands to reason that this should continue to be the case in nonlinear regression.

Implications for Estimated Standard Errors and t Ratios

One of the most important things we use an estimate of σ^2 for is to obtain estimated standard errors for the least squares coefficient estimators. For example, in the simple regression model in Chapter 4 the estimated variance of the slope estimator $\hat{\beta}$ is equation (4.29b):

$$s_{\hat{\beta}}^2 = \frac{s^2}{\sum x_i^2}.$$

Similarly, in the multiple regression model with $K = 3$ in Chapter 8 the estimated variances are given by (8.18), which uses s^2 in the numerator.

Suppose the estimator $\hat{\sigma}^2$ had been used in the numerator instead of s^2. Then, using the simple regression case to illustrate, the slope coefficient variance estimator would instead be

$$\hat{\sigma}_{\hat{\beta}}^2 = \frac{\hat{\sigma}^2}{\sum x_i^2}.$$

It is apparent that the relationship between the two estimators is

$$\hat{\sigma}_{\hat{\beta}}^2 = \frac{n-K}{n} s_{\hat{\beta}}^2.$$

That is, analogous to (13.29), the only difference between them is the factor $(n - K)/n$. Taking square roots, the relationship between the standard errors is

$$\hat{\sigma}_{\hat{\beta}} = \sqrt{\frac{n-K}{n}} s_{\hat{\beta}}.$$

If, in turn, these standard errors are used to form t ratios, the relationship between the two possible definitions of the t ratio is

$$t = \left(\frac{\hat{\beta} - \beta_0}{s_{\hat{\beta}}}\right) = \sqrt{\frac{n-K}{n}} \left(\frac{\hat{\beta} - \beta_0}{\hat{\sigma}_{\hat{\beta}}}\right). \qquad (13.30)$$

Notice that we continue to use the symbol t to denote what it always has in the past—the statistic based on $n - K$ rather than n.

For the reasons we have given, the numerical examples in this chapter report standard errors and t ratios based on s^2 rather than $\hat{\sigma}^2$. Nevertheless, you should be aware that some econometrics packages report statistics based on $\hat{\sigma}^2$, although they often offer an option that uses s^2 instead.

Practitioner's Tip: Degrees-of-freedom corrections in NLS

If you are comparing the output of two NLS routines and find that they produce the same coefficient estimates but different standard errors and t ratios, they are probably using different estimators for σ^2. Check to see if the values are related as follows. To transform statistics based on $\hat{\sigma}^2$ to ones based on s^2, multiply by the following factors.

	Standard error	t ratio
Adjustment factor	$\sqrt{\dfrac{n}{n-K}}$	$\sqrt{\dfrac{n-K}{n}}$

EXERCISES

13.11 Which of the estimators does the NLS routine of your econometric software report as the default estimator for σ^2? Does the command offer an option that uses the other estimator?

13.8   Hypothesis Testing

As always, hypothesis testing involves the testing of a null hypothesis against an alternative. The null hypothesis is that some parameter restriction, or set of restrictions, holds. Coefficient restrictions may be linear or nonlinear. They may be fixed-value restrictions, such as $\nu = 1$ or $\rho = 0$ in the CES production function. Or they may be in the form of some functional relationship between coefficients, such as the constant returns to scale restriction $\alpha + \beta = 1$ in the Cobb-Douglas production function. We may be interested in testing more than one restriction—for example, that $\nu = 1$ and $\rho = 0$ hold simultaneously. Conceptually, then, the task of hypothesis testing in nonlinear regression models is no different from what we have considered in the past, with the exception that the methods we will develop apply to nonlinear coefficient restrictions as well as to linear ones.

Although conceptually the task of hypothesis testing is much as before, the methods for doing this change somewhat from those that are appropriate in the context of linear models. In the linear regression model we have seen that linear restrictions can always be tested with an F test; in the special case of fixed-value restrictions, the F test reduces to the familiar t test. As we have emphasized, these test statistics are based on exact distributional results that arise from the joint features of normality and linearity: normality of the disturbance and linearity of the model and restrictions. The distributional results were exact in that they applied for any sample size. We have seen in Chapter 2 that in the absence of population normality an alternative basis for inference is available—central limit theorems describe the limiting form of sampling distributions as the sample size becomes large.

We have noted that, once we leave the realm of linear regression, it is no longer possible to establish small-sample properties of estimators such as unbiasedness. Instead estimators must be evaluated on the basis of their asymptotic properties. For the same reasons, exact tests are no longer available. Hypothesis tests must be based on asymptotic distributional results yielded by central limit theorems. Because this is true regardless of whether a normal (or, for that matter, any other) form for the population distribution is assumed, we no longer bother to make any such assumption. This is reflected in the specification of the disturbance of the nonlinear regression model (13.1) as i.i.d. rather than n.i.d.

Econometricians use tests based on a variety of testing principles and asymptotic distributional results. This chapter introduces you to the two types of tests most commonly encountered in applied work: the Wald and likelihood ratio tests.

Although the statistical theory underlying inference in nonlinear models is highly technical, applying these tests in practice is often no more difficult than is the case with t and F tests in the linear regression model. Before turning to the mechanics of applying the Wald and likelihood ratio tests, more general aspects of asymptotic testing principles should be discussed.

13.8.1   The Three Classical Testing Principles

In our study of linear regression in Chapters 8 and 10 we learn that, whereas t statistics can be used to test fixed-value restrictions on coefficients, an F test is used for more general sets of linear restrictions. In the special case in which the linear restriction is just a fixed-value restriction, the t and F tests are equivalent in that the F statistic is just the square of the t.

In the same way, in nonlinear regression models the need often arises to test restrictions that are not fixed-value restrictions or may be more than one in number. These restrictions may be linear or nonlinear. A variety of testing principles are used in nonlinear models. The best known of these are the **Wald** principle, the **likelihood ratio** (LR) principle, and the **Lagrange multiplier** (LM) principle. These principles yield test statistics that are denoted by W, LR, and LM. For the reasons we have discussed, exact distributional results are not in general available for these statistics. Instead, the statistical theory on which they are based is asymptotic. In fact all three have the same asymptotic distribution. This is the chi-square distribution with g degrees of freedom, denoted $\chi^2(g)$; g is the number of restrictions under test. That all three statistics have this asymptotic distribution means that, as the sample size becomes very large so that $n \rightarrow \infty$, all three sampling distributions take the form $\chi^2(g)$. Nevertheless, for any sample under study the computed values of the statistics will differ.

Because the three statistics have the same asymptotic distribution, in large samples the choice among them tends to be based on considerations other than their sampling properties. One such consideration is the invariance properties of the statistics. Recall from Section 4.8 that one important example of an invariance property is scale invariance—test statistics should be invariant to changes in units of measure. It turns out that likelihood ratio tests have very strong invariance properties, whereas Wald tests are much weaker; we examine this in detail in Section 13.8.6.

Another consideration is ease of computation because the three statistics have different computational requirements. As we shall see, the Wald statistic is computed on the basis of the estimation of the unrestricted model. Hence, it is often used when the unrestricted model is the easiest one to estimate—for example, when the model is linear but the restrictions are nonlinear, so that the restricted model requires nonlinear estimation. We exploit this feature of the Wald statistic in Section 13.8.5. Likelihood ratio statistics, by contrast, require estimation of both the restricted and unrestricted models and so cannot be computed if NLS fails to converge for either model.

Finally, Lagrange multiplier statistics are based on the estimation of the restricted model and so are often the test of choice when the restricted model is simpler than the unrestricted one. An especially important area of application of LM tests is specification testing, which, as we discuss in Chapter 12, is concerned with determining whether the assumptions on which a model is predicated may be inconsistent with the data. Because it is easier to estimate a model under the null hypothesis that it is correctly specified than under the alternative hypothesis that it is not, the LM princi-

FIGURE 13.4

Under the null hypothesis the *W*, *LR*, and *LM* statistics all have the same χ^2 distribution asymptotically. Computed values of the statistics in the right tail of the distribution constitute evidence against the null.

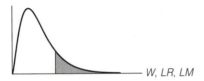

W, LR, LM

ple is often used to derive specification tests. Our discussion of heteroskedasticity in the next chapter offers a good illustration of this. For a survey of the LM principle applied to specification testing authored by one of the major contributors in this area, see Godfrey (1988).

In small samples, additional considerations bear on the use of these statistics, in particular how well their small-sample distributions are approximated by their asymptotic distribution. Most notably, it appears that Wald statistics sometimes have rather poor small-sample properties, in the sense that their χ^2 asymptotic distribution is often not a very close approximation to their true sampling distribution.

These testing principles are widely applicable to a broad range of econometric problems and so are of interest well beyond the present context of nonlinear regression. They apply, for example, to systems of equations. For linear restrictions on certain classes of linear models—including certain systems of regression equations—the three statistics are related by the famous Berndt-Savin inequality (Berndt and Savin 1977; see also Breusch 1979):

$$W \geq LR \geq LM. \tag{13.31}$$

The implication of this numerical relationship is that, for a given hypothesis on a given model, in repeated sampling the Wald statistic will reject the null more often than the LR statistic, which in turn will reject more often than the LM statistic. If we follow classical testing methodology in regarding a Type I error of incorrectly rejecting the null as the most serious testing error, the implication is that LM tests are relatively conservative. The Berndt-Savin inequality does not hold in general if either the model or the restrictions are nonlinear.

Operationally the Wald, LR, and LM tests are similar to *F* tests of linear restrictions; the statistics only take on positive values, and large values constitute evidence against the null. As usual, *large* means in the right tail of the distribution, exceeding a critical value $\chi^2_a(g)$ associated with the level of significance *a*. This is depicted in Figure 13.4.

Virtually all econometric software packages offer options that compute Wald statistics, and likelihood ratio tests are easily calculated even by the novice (given convergence in the NLS estimation of the associated models). Lagrange multiplier statistics, on the other hand, are usually computed using **artificial regressions.** An artificial regression is just the use of an OLS regression as a computational device, as opposed to it constituting the estimation of a model that has some economic interpretation. Artificial regressions are widely employed for a variety of purposes in applied work, but are an advanced topic that cannot be developed systematically in an introductory text. The definitive treatments of artificial regressions are

Davidson and MacKinnon (1993, 2001, 2004) and MacKinnon (1992). However, we encounter in an ad hoc way in Chapter 14 the use of an artificial regression to compute an LM test for heteroskedasticity.

The main purpose of the sections that follow is to show you just how easy it is to use Wald and LR statistics to handle interesting inference problems of the kind that routinely arise in empirical work. Particularly simple to implement are tests of fixed-value restrictions—the restrictions that in the past we have tested with t tests. As we are about to see, the practicalities of doing these tests do not change at all from the way they are done in linear models.

13.8.2 Pseudo-t Tests

In our estimation of nonlinear models we have seen that NLS routines produce estimated standard errors for the coefficients, statistics of the type we have denoted by $s_{\hat{\beta}}$. Following the practice in linear models, it is natural to test fixed-value restrictions such as H_0: $\beta = \beta_0$ using the "t ratio"

$$t = \frac{\hat{\beta} - \beta_0}{s_{\hat{\beta}}}.$$

The reason this is called a t statistic is that, in the classical linear regression model in which the disturbance is assumed to be normally distributed, these t ratios can be shown to follow the Student's t distribution with $n - K$ degrees of freedom. This is a finite-sample distributional result in that it applies, as we have emphasized, for any sample size n.

No such exact distributional result applies in nonlinear models. It is, however, possible to use central limit theorems to establish that the asymptotic distribution is standard normal:

$$t = \frac{\hat{\beta} - \beta_0}{s_{\hat{\beta}}} \sim N(0, 1) \quad \text{asymptotically.} \tag{13.32}$$

As always with asymptotic distributional results, the meaning of this is that, for large samples, the sampling distribution of this statistic should be closely approximated by the standard normal. Just how large the sample must be for this approximation to be a good one depends, as we discuss in Section 2.5.3, on the nature of the population distribution from which the data are drawn.

In finite samples, on the other hand, no analytical result is available on the sampling distribution of the t ratio; it cannot be established that it follows the t or any other determinable distribution exactly. Hence, it is called a **pseudo-t statistic.** Nevertheless, by analogy with the result that would apply in the linear case if the population were normal, it is reasonable to believe that the t distribution will often provide a good approximation to its sampling distribution:

$$t = \frac{\hat{\beta} - \beta_0}{s_{\hat{\beta}}} \sim t(n - K) \quad \text{approximately in finite samples.} \tag{13.33}$$

The basis for this belief is Monte Carlo evidence such as that of Gallant (1975), who studied an example of nonlinear regression and found that this approximation was quite good. Recall that as $n \to \infty$ the t distribution approaches the standard normal, as a comparison of tabulated values of the two distributions confirms. Hence, using this approximation is, as we consider larger and larger sample sizes, consistent with using the asymptotic distribution (13.32).

Recall the distinction of Section 13.7 between the two estimators s^2 and $\hat{\sigma}^2$. As we have seen there, the pseudo-t statistic could be based on either estimator, and some econometrics packages do use $\hat{\sigma}^2$ because the asymptotic distribution (13.32) holds regardless. But because s^2 is a less biased estimator there is reason to expect that the approximation (13.33) should be a better one for pseudo-t statistics based on it. The implication is that when the approximation is used as the basis for hypothesis testing at the a level of significance, we are more likely to in fact incur a probability of Type I error of a if the pseudo-t statistic uses s^2. In the terminology of Section 2.5.3, the use of s^2 is more likely to result in a test of the correct *size*: The empirical size is more likely to conform to the nominal size. For this reason the t statistic based on s^2 is sometimes called the **size-corrected** pseudo-t statistic, the size correction being the factor $\sqrt{(n-K)/n}$ that appears in (13.30).

Of course even with this size correction the result (13.33) remains an approximation that, for small samples in some applications, might not be a good one. The alternative to assuming that the t distribution provides a good approximation to the finite sample distribution of the pseudo-t statistic is to use bootstrapped tests. This again follows the logic originally laid out in Sections 2.5.3 and 2.6.2.

The conclusion of this rather intricate chain of reasoning is almost embarrassingly simple. In the absence of a desire to proceed to bootstrapped tests, applied econometricians use the pseudo-t statistics of NLS exactly as they use the t statistics produced by OLS in linear regression.

Practitioner's Tip: Pseudo-t tests

In nonlinear regression, use pseudo-t statistics just as you would the t statistics in linear regression: Compare the computed value of the statistic to the tabulated value of the t distribution with $n - K$ degrees of freedom.

Let us consider two examples.

EXAMPLE 9

 mizon57.dat

In the CES production function estimated with Mizon's 1957 data, test the hypothesis of constant returns to scale.

SOLUTION

This is the restriction $\nu = 1$. The alternative hypothesis is that this restriction does not hold: $\nu \neq 1$.

An additive disturbance. In Examples 3 and 5, NLS yields $\hat{\nu} = 1.0208$ and $s_{\hat{\nu}} = 0.046455$. The pseudo-t statistic for the hypothesis H_0: $\nu = 1$ is

$$\frac{\hat{\nu} - 1}{s_{\hat{\nu}}} = \frac{1.0208 - 1}{0.046455} = 0.4477.$$

Comparing this with tabulated values of the t distribution with $n - K = 24 - 4 = 20$ degrees of freedom fails to reject the null at conventional significance levels. (For example, $t_{0.025}(20) = 2.086$.) Constant returns to scale is not rejected.

A multiplicative disturbance. In Examples 3 and 5, NLS yields $\hat{\nu} = 0.9723$ and $s_{\hat{\nu}} = 0.045588$. The pseudo-t statistic for the hypothesis $H_0: \nu = 1$ is

$$\frac{\hat{\nu} - 1}{s_{\hat{\nu}}} = \frac{0.9723 - 1}{0.045588} = -0.6076.$$

Again, comparing this with tabulated values of the t distribution with 20 degrees of freedom fails to reject the null at conventional significance levels.

We have found that both versions of the CES production function lead to the same finding—constant returns to scale is not rejected by the data.

EXAMPLE 10

 mizon57.dat

In the CES production function estimated with Mizon's 1957 data, test the hypothesis of a unitary elasticity of substitution.

SOLUTION

This is the restriction $\rho = 0$. The alternative hypothesis is that this restriction does not hold: $\rho \neq 0$.

An additive disturbance. In Examples 3 and 5, NLS yields $\hat{\rho} = -0.3441$ and $s_{\hat{\rho}} = 0.355902$. The pseudo-$t$ statistic for the hypothesis $H_0: \rho = 0$ is

$$\frac{\hat{\rho}}{s_{\hat{\rho}}} = \frac{-0.3441}{0.355902} = -0.9667.$$

Comparing this with tabulated values of the t distribution with $n - K = 24 - 4 = 20$ degrees of freedom fails to reject the null at conventional significance levels. The hypothesis of a unitary elasticity of substitution is not rejected.

A multiplicative disturbance. In Examples 3 and 5, NLS yields $\hat{\rho} = 0.4269$ and $s_{\hat{\rho}} = 0.407196$. The pseudo-$t$ statistic for the hypothesis $H_0: \rho = 0$ is

$$\frac{\hat{\rho}}{s_{\hat{\rho}}} = \frac{0.4269}{0.407196} = 1.0484.$$

Again, comparing this with tabulated values of the t distribution with 20 degrees of freedom fails to reject the null at conventional significance levels.

We have found that both versions of the CES production function lead to the same finding—the hypothesis of a unitary elasticity of substitution, $\sigma = 1/(1+\rho) = 1$, is not rejected by these data. Because under this restriction the CES production function reduces to the Cobb-Douglas, the implication is that these data would be adequately modeled with a Cobb-Douglas production function.

In his original work, Mizon compared several production function specifications estimated with his 1954, 1957, and 1960 data sets, using alternative testing methodologies. Table 13.3 presents his test results for the hypothesis that the CES

TABLE 13.3

Mizon's Test Results for $\rho = 0$ in the CES Production Function

Test statistic	Additive disturbance			Multiplicative disturbance		
	1954	1957	1960	1954	1957	1960
$|t|$	0.52	0.97	0.97	0.90	1.05	0.89
LR^*	0.26	0.84	0.96	0.91	1.22	0.87

Source: Mizon, G.E. (1977) "Inferential Procedures in Nonlinear Models: An Application in a UK Industrial Cross Section Study of Factor Substitution and Returns to Scale," *Econometrica* 45, 1221–1242. Reprinted with permission.

production function specializes to the Cobb-Douglas. The absolute values of his pseudo-t statistics are given in the first row. Notice that the 1957 values are those we have obtained. (The LR^* statistics are reported for future reference in this chapter.)

Fixed value restrictions such as $v = 1$ and $\rho = 0$ are an important class of hypotheses, and so pseudo-t tests are very useful. As we know from the examples of previous chapters, however, broader classes of restrictions are often of interest. Let us turn to more general testing methods.

EXERCISES

13.12 💿 **mizon54.dat mizon60.dat** Refer to your NLS estimation results for the CES production function in Exercise 13.4.

(a) Do a pseudo-t test of the hypothesis of constant returns to scale for the model with
i.   an additive disturbance.
ii. a multiplicative disturbance.

(b) Do a pseudo-t test of the hypothesis of a unitary elasticity of substitution for the model with
i.   an additive disturbance.
ii. a multiplicative disturbance.
How close do you come to reproducing Mizon's t statistics reported in Table 13.3?

13.8.3 Wald Tests

Wald tests generalize pseudo-t tests to handle more complicated restrictions or several restrictions jointly. Like a pseudo-t statistic, the Wald statistic is computed from the estimation of the unrestricted model, so the restricted model need not be estimated. Another similarity is that the Wald statistic makes use of an estimate of σ^2 and either $\hat{\sigma}^2$ or s^2 may be employed. It is useful to distinguish between the two versions of the Wald statistic with the following notation:

W denotes the Wald statistic based on $\hat{\sigma}^2$,

whereas

W^* denotes the size-corrected Wald statistic based on s^2.

Like the earlier relationships (13.29) and (13.30), the two are related by the factor $(n - K)/n$:

$$W^* = \frac{n - K}{n} W. \tag{13.34}$$

For the discussion that follows, it is important that the distinction between the two versions of the statistic be explicit. Theoretical propositions about Wald statistics are usually stated in terms of W, and these propositions do not always hold for its size-corrected version. The Berndt-Savin inequality is an example. At the same time, the fact that s^2 is the less-biased estimator argues in favor of W^* as the basis for inference in applied problems, although some econometrics packages use $\hat{\sigma}^2$ and report W. The numerical examples of this chapter are stated in terms of W^*.

Because the factor $(n - K)/n \to 1$ as $n \to \infty$, the two statistics are asymptotically equivalent. As we have mentioned, their asymptotic distribution is $\chi^2(g)$, so the null hypothesis is rejected if the test statistic exceeds a critical value based on this distribution.

Beyond these comments, we make no attempt to present a general formula for the Wald statistic because it can only be conveniently expressed using matrix algebra. However in some special circumstances it reduces to simpler forms, one of which we encounter when we discuss the relationship between the Wald statistic and the F statistic. In any case, familiarity with the formula is not essential for the applied researcher because the statistic is normally calculated by an option of NLS routines. The option requires, of course, that you specify the restriction(s) to be tested.

Turning to examples, it is instructive to begin with one that contrasts the applicability of the Wald test with the F test in Chapter 10.

EXAMPLE 11

mizon57.dat

In Example 2, the Cobb-Douglas production function is estimated using Mizon's 1957 data. Test the hypothesis of constant returns to scale.

SOLUTION

This is the restriction $\alpha + \beta = 1$.

A multiplicative disturbance. As we have seen in Example 2, under a multiplicative disturbance the model is intrinsically linear and so may be estimated by OLS as a loglinear regression. In principle, it is possible to proceed by specifying the restriction $\alpha + \beta = 1$ in the Wald test option of the OLS routine. However, because both the model and restriction are linear it is preferable to use the exact F testing methodology of Chapter 10. In fact, we examine exactly this testing problem in Examples 6 and 8 of Chapter 10, although using the Cobb-Douglas data set. In Example 2, OLS estimation of the unrestricted loglinear regression with Mizon's data yields $\text{SSE}_U = 0.743489$. In Example 6, the model is estimated with the restriction $\alpha + \beta = 1$ imposed, which yields $\text{SSE}_R = 0.751876$. The computed value of the F statistic is therefore

$$F = \frac{(\text{SSE}_R - \text{SSE}_U)/g}{\text{SSE}_U/(n - K)} = \frac{(0.751876 - 0.743489)/1}{0.743489/(24 - 3)} = 0.237.$$

Comparing this against tabulated values of the $F(1, 21)$ distribution (for example, $F(1, 21) = 4.32$ for a 0.05 level of significance), the hypothesis of constant returns to scale is not rejected.

An additive disturbance. This means that the Cobb-Douglas production function is intrinsically nonlinear and no exact test is available. Instead, we must rely on asymptotic test criteria. Repeating the NLS estimation in Example 2 and using the appropriate option to test the restriction $\alpha + \beta = 1$ yields a computed Wald statistic of $W^* = 0.0565$. Comparing with the $\chi^2(1)$ distribution, the p-value is 0.8121. Constant returns to scale is not rejected.

Understanding How Wald Tests Work

The way a Wald test works is fairly easy to understand intuitively. Consider an arbitrary restriction on the coefficient vector $\boldsymbol{\beta}$ that we denote by

$$h(\boldsymbol{\beta}) = 0. \tag{13.35}$$

This could be linear or nonlinear. For example, in the Cobb-Douglas case we have just considered, the coefficient vector is $\boldsymbol{\beta} = [\gamma \, \alpha \, \beta]$ and the hypothesis of constant returns to scale is the linear restriction

$$h(\boldsymbol{\beta}) = \alpha + \beta - 1 = 0.$$

The Wald test evaluates the restriction (or set of restrictions if $g > 1$) using the coefficient estimates $\hat{\boldsymbol{\beta}}$ obtained from the estimation of the unrestricted model and asks how close $h(\hat{\boldsymbol{\beta}})$ comes to satisfying (13.35).

The way in which the Wald test makes this decision is particularly easy to understand in the case of just $g = 1$ restriction because it does it by computing an estimated standard error for $h(\hat{\boldsymbol{\beta}})$ and forming the pseudo-t statistic

$$\frac{h(\hat{\boldsymbol{\beta}})}{s_{h(\hat{\boldsymbol{\beta}})}}. \tag{13.36}$$

Consider the example of constant returns to scale, for which it is convenient to resurrect the notation $\nu \equiv \alpha + \beta$ of Chapter 7 for the degree of returns to scale. In Example 11, referring to the coefficient estimates reported for the model with an additive disturbance in Example 2, the value of $h(\hat{\boldsymbol{\beta}})$ is

$$h(\hat{\boldsymbol{\beta}}) = \hat{\nu} - 1 = \hat{\alpha} + \hat{\beta} - 1 = 0.863078 + 0.147607 - 1 = 0.010685.$$

The variance of $h(\hat{\boldsymbol{\beta}})$ is, using the laws in Table B.2 (Appendix B),

$$V(h(\hat{\boldsymbol{\beta}})) = V(\hat{\nu} - 1) = V(\hat{\nu}) = V(\hat{\alpha} + \hat{\beta}) = V(\hat{\alpha}) + V(\hat{\beta}) + 2\mathrm{cov}(\hat{\alpha}, \hat{\beta}).$$

Hence, this variance may be estimated by

$$s^2_{h(\hat{\boldsymbol{\beta}})} = s^2_{\hat{\nu}} = s^2_{\hat{\alpha}} + s^2_{\hat{\beta}} + 2s_{\hat{\alpha}, \hat{\beta}},$$

where $s_{\hat{\alpha}, \hat{\beta}}$ is our notation from earlier chapters for the estimated covariance of the random variables $\hat{\alpha}$ and $\hat{\beta}$. The estimated standard errors $s_{\hat{\alpha}}$ and $s_{\hat{\beta}}$ are reported in Example 2. Although not normally included in the presentation of estimation results, the covariance estimate $s_{\hat{\alpha}, \hat{\beta}}$ is also reported in anticipation of its use here.

Substituting these estimates into this formula yields

$$s^2_{h(\hat{\beta})} = s^2_{\hat{v}} = (0.046523)^2 + (0.046187)^2 + 2(-0.0011364) = 0.0020248.$$

Taking the square root of this to obtain a standard error, the pseudo-t statistic (13.36) is

$$t = \frac{h(\hat{\beta})}{s_{h(\hat{\beta})}} = \frac{\hat{v} - 1}{s_{\hat{v}}} = \frac{0.010685}{0.044998} = 0.2375.$$

The Wald statistic is the square of this pseudo-t statistic:

$$W^* = t^2 = (0.2375)^2 = 0.0564,$$

which is the value of the Wald statistic we find in Example 11.

This way of understanding how Wald statistics are computed yields an important insight. The Wald statistic is to the pseudo-t statistic as the F is to the t in linear regression: In the special case of just $g = 1$ restriction the more general statistic is just the square of the simpler one. In fact, the Wald test routines of econometric software usually make this interpretation of the Wald test explicit by reporting, in addition to the value of W^*, the value of $h(\hat{\beta})$ and its standard error—that is, the numerator and denominator of the pseudo-t statistic associated with W^*.

In the special case when the $g = 1$ restriction under test is the hypothesis of a zero coefficient, such as $\rho = 0$ in the CES production function, the standard error produced by the Wald test is just that for the coefficient itself. Hence, the Wald statistic is just the square of the pseudo-t statistic that is reported with the NLS coefficient estimate on your regression output. The following example of Wald tests of fixed-value restrictions confirms this.

EXAMPLE 12

 mizon57.dat

In the CES production function estimated with Mizon's 1957 data, perform individual Wald tests of the restrictions $v = 1$ and $\rho = 0$. How do the results compare with those of Examples 9 and 10?

SOLUTION

Rerunning the NLS estimation of the CES production function (in either parameterization) with additive and multiplicative disturbances, and using the appropriate option to compute Wald tests of each of these restrictions, yields the following Wald statistics.

Restriction	Additive Disturbance		Multiplicative Disturbance	
	W^*	Pseudo-t	W^*	Pseudo-t
$v = 1$	0.2000	0.4477	0.3692	-0.6076
$\rho = 0$	0.9346	-0.9667	1.0991	1.0484

The pseudo-t statistics are reproduced from Examples 9 and 10. Notice that in all cases $W^* = t^2$ and so the tests are equivalent. In no case is the restriction rejected at conventional significance levels.

Wald tests generalize beyond the specifics of Examples 11 and 12 in two ways. First, they apply to nonlinear as well as to linear restrictions; even when $h(\boldsymbol{\beta})$ is nonlinear, Wald test routines are still able to compute an estimated standard error for $h(\hat{\boldsymbol{\beta}})$. This turns out to have important implications; it means that given the estimation of a regression model—linear or nonlinear—it is possible to obtain an estimated standard error for any arbitrary function $h(\boldsymbol{\beta})$ of its coefficients. This may seem like a rather obscure point: Why would this be of any practical interest beyond the role that this standard error plays in the Wald statistic itself? In fact, situations arise all the time in applied work in which it is very useful to be able to obtain a standard error for some function of the estimated coefficients. We see several examples in Section 13.8.5.

The second way in which Wald tests generalize beyond the situations of the above examples is that they apply to more than one restriction. This is another respect in which they are analogous to F tests. Let us consider an example of a Wald test of $g = 2$ restrictions.

EXAMPLE 13

mizon57.dat

In the CES production function estimated with Mizon's 1957 data, test the joint hypotheses of constant returns to scale and a unitary elasticity of substitution.

SOLUTION

These are the joint restrictions $\nu = 1$ and $\rho = 0$. The alternative hypothesis is that either or both of these is false: $\nu \neq 1$ and/or $\rho \neq 0$.

An additive disturbance. Reestimating either parameterization of this version of CES production function, and specifying the joint restrictions $\nu = 1$ and $\rho = 0$ in the Wald test option, yields

$$W^* = 1.0832.$$

Referring to the $\chi^2(2)$ distribution, the p-value is 0.582. The null hypothesis is not rejected at conventional significance levels.

A multiplicative disturbance. Reestimating either parameterization of this version of CES production function, and specifying the joint restrictions $\nu = 1$ and $\rho = 0$ in the Wald test option, yields

$$W^* = 1.2318.$$

Referring to the $\chi^2(2)$ distribution, the p-value is 0.540. The null hypothesis is not rejected at conventional significance levels.

This example is one in which the outcome of the joint test is consistent with those for the restrictions individually—in Examples 9 and 10 we have found that pseudo-t tests do not reject either $\nu = 1$ or $\rho = 0$. In general, however, there is no assurance of this sort of common outcome from testing restrictions individually versus jointly. Just as is true of the relationship between an F test and individual t tests (recall Section 8.5.3), it is possible for seeming inconsistencies to arise between joint and individual tests. As that earlier discussion argues, these are

TABLE 13.4   Wald Tests Using Mizon's 1957 Data

Maintained model	Restriction(s) under test	Wald statistic W^*		Critical value $(a = 0.05)$
		Additive disturbance	Multiplicative disturbance	
CES	$\nu = 1$	0.200	0.369	$\chi^2(1) = 3.84$
	$\rho = 0$	0.935	1.099	$\chi^2(1) = 3.84$
	$\nu = 1, \rho = 0$	1.083	1.232	$\chi^2(2) = 5.99$
Cobb-Douglas	$\alpha + \beta = 1$	0.057	0.237	$\chi^2(1) = 3.84$

seeming rather than real inconsistencies—to ask whether restrictions hold individually is a fundamentally different question from asking whether they hold jointly. This is another respect in which the relationship between a Wald test and individual pseudo-t tests is analogous to that between an F test and individual t tests.

The Wald statistics for the various models and hypotheses we have considered are summarized in Table 13.4.

Relationship between the Wald and F Statistics

We have noted several parallels between the Wald and F tests. Whereas the F test applies to linear restrictions on linear models, the Wald test is used in the more general context of nonlinear models and/or restrictions. Being a general test procedure, the Wald test could in principle be applied when the model and restrictions are linear. The reason this is not in practice done is that there is another test with superior properties: the F test, for which an exact distributional result is available. In this special case, what is the relationship of the Wald statistic and the F statistic?

When the regression and restrictions are linear it may be shown that the Wald statistic based on $\hat{\sigma}^2$ reduces to[9]

$$W = \frac{(\text{SSE}_R - \text{SSE}_U)}{\hat{\sigma}^2} = \frac{n(\text{SSE}_R - \text{SSE}_U)}{\text{SSE}_U}, \quad (13.37)$$

whereas the size-corrected Wald statistic based on s^2 is[10]

$$W^* = \frac{(\text{SSE}_R - \text{SSE}_U)}{s^2} = \frac{(n - K)(\text{SSE}_R - \text{SSE}_U)}{\text{SSE}_U}.$$

Clearly the relationship between the two is

$$W^* = \frac{n - K}{n} W,$$

which verifies (13.34).

[9] This is Evans and Savin (1982, eq. 3.1) or Engle (1984, eq. 26). See also Seber and Wild (1989, p. 231, Example 5.3).

[10] This is Evans and Savin (1982, eq. 4.1).

Comparing this with the F statistic (10.34), the relationship to W is

$$W = \left(\frac{ng}{n - K}\right) F \tag{13.38}$$

whereas the relationship to W^* is

$$W^* = gF.$$

Note in particular that in the case of $g = 1$ restriction, the size-corrected Wald statistic *is* just the F statistic, which makes sense because we know that in this special case both are the square of the t statistic.

In this chapter, we have studied one example of a linear restriction on a linear regression: Constant returns to scale in the loglinear Cobb-Douglas production function. In Example 11 we have found that the F statistic for this hypothesis is $F = 0.237$ and so this is the value for W^* reported in Table 13.4. By contrast, the uncorrected Wald statistic is

$$W = \left(\frac{ng}{n - K}\right) F = \left(\frac{24 \times 1}{24 - 3}\right) 0.237 = 0.271. \tag{13.39}$$

EXERCISES

13.13 mizon54.dat mizon60.dat Returning to the Cobb-Douglas production function that you have estimated previously in Exercises 13.3 and 13.7, use an appropriate testing procedure to test constant returns to scale in the model with

(a) a multiplicative disturbance.

(b) an additive disturbance.

13.14 mizon54.dat mizon60.dat Using Mizon's data for 1954 or 1960, construct a table similar to Table 13.4. Indicate which of the tests reject the null hypothesis at a 5% significance level.

13.8.4 Likelihood Ratio Tests

Likelihood ratio tests permit the testing of the same broad classes of restrictions as Wald tests. They proceed by comparing the loglikelihood function values of the restricted and unrestricted models. We know that imposing restrictions in estimation should always result in at least as small a loglikelihood function value:

$$\mathscr{L}_R \leq \mathscr{L}_U.$$

We have now seen a series of examples involving the CES and Cobb-Douglas production functions that illustrate this, and it is useful to summarize those examples. Table 13.5 shows the loglikelihood function values yielded by Mizon's 1957 data for the CES production function and its various restricted forms, one of which is, of course, the Cobb-Douglas production function. The table lists the models, the restrictions we have considered, and the relevant example numbers. The CES model is the maintained hypothesis in that it is the most general model under study and all

TABLE 13.5   Loglikelihood Function Values $\mathcal{L}$ for Mizon's 1957 Data

Model[a]	Restriction(s)	Additive disturbance	Multiplicative disturbance	Examples
CES	Maintained	−131.603	8.38876	3, 5
CES with CRTS	$v = 1$	−131.722	8.16836	7
Cobb-Douglas	$\rho = 0$	−132.123	7.63894	2, 8
Cobb-Douglas with CRTS	$v = 1, \rho = 0$	−132.155	7.50432	6

[a]CRTS, constant returns to scale.

other models are special cases of it; it is not itself under test as the restricted form of some yet more general model, although of course in the context of some broader analysis it could be.

Intuitively, if the restrictions are consistent with the data, then imposing them in estimation should make little difference in the loglikelihood function values; if the restrictions are not consistent with the data, then the values should be quite different. More formally, it can be shown that the likelihood ratio statistic defined as

$$LR = 2(\mathcal{L}_U - \mathcal{L}_R)$$

has the following distribution under the null hypothesis:

$$LR \sim \chi^2(g) \quad \text{asymptotically.}$$

Hence, just as for a Wald test, the restriction is rejected at the a level of significance if the LR statistic exceeds the tabulated value $\chi_a^2(g)$.

Table 13.6 presents computed values of the likelihood ratio statistic using the loglikelihood values from Table 13.5. They permit the testing of the same individual and joint hypotheses that are examined in Table 13.4. The top portion takes the CES production function as the maintained model and asks whether the restrictions $v = 1$ and $\rho = 0$ are individually or jointly rejected by the data. Comparing the computed values of LR with critical values of the χ^2 distribution indicates that the restrictions are not rejected, suggesting that for these data the Cobb-Douglas production function with constant returns to scale is a reasonable model.

Notice that as we include additional restrictions among those being tested, the LR statistic must increase. Considering either the additive or multiplicative models, as we go from either of the individual restrictions $v = 1$ or $\rho = 0$ to the joint restriction that both hold, the value of $\mathcal{L}$ in Table 13.5 falls and so the value of LR in Table 13.6 must increase. Does this mean that, as we consider more and more restrictions on a model, eventually they must be jointly rejected? No, because the $\chi^2(g)$ distribution against which we are comparing the LR statistic is also changing with the number of restrictions g under test.

The last line of Table 13.6 takes the Cobb-Douglas production function as the maintained model. That is, it takes as given the restriction of a unitary elasticity of substitution, $\rho = 0$, so that the CES specializes to the Cobb-Douglas. Under this

TABLE 13.6   Likelihood Ratio Tests Using Mizon's 1957 Data

Maintained model	Restriction(s) under test	$LR = 2(\mathcal{L}_U - \mathcal{L}_R)$		Critical Value $(a = 0.05)$
		Additive disturbance	Multiplicative disturbance	
CES	$v = 1$	0.238	0.441	$\chi^2(1) = 3.84$
	$\rho = 0$	1.040	1.500	$\chi^2(1) = 3.84$
	$v = 1, \rho = 0$	1.104	1.769	$\chi^2(2) = 5.99$
Cobb-Douglas	$\alpha + \beta = 1$	0.064	0.269	$\chi^2(1) = 3.84$

maintained hypothesis we then ask: Do the data reject constant returns to scale. Again the answer is no.

It is instructive to compare the values of W^* and LR in Tables 13.4 and 13.6. They confirm that, despite the fact that the two statistics have the same asymptotic distribution, their computed values differ. For linear restrictions on linear models the Berndt-Savin inequality (13.31) should hold. The only test of this type that we have considered is for constant returns to scale in the Cobb-Douglas production function with a multiplicative disturbance. Recalling the value of the uncorrected Wald statistic from (13.39) and comparing it with LR indicates that

$$0.271 = W > LR = 0.269,$$

and so the Berndt-Savin inequality is verified. Note that the Berndt-Savin inequality refers to W rather than to its size-corrected version W^*, which in this example does not satisfy the inequality.

All the other test statistics in these tables are for restrictions on nonlinear models, and so there is no reason to expect that they necessarily satisfy the Berndt-Savin inequality. This is illustrated in Table 13.4, in which, multiplying the values of W^* by the appropriate factor to obtain W and comparing this with Table 13.6, the Berndt-Savin inequality *is* sometimes violated. You are asked to do this in Exercise 13.18.

In the present application, the Wald and LR statistics give consistent answers to the questions we are asking. Neither rejects the hypotheses of constant returns to scale and/or a unitary elasticity of substitution, suggesting that these data are satisfactorily described by the Cobb-Douglas production function with constant returns to scale. In general, however, the fact that the statistics take on different values means that for a chosen level of significance they may give different answers to a given question; one test may reject a hypothesis while the other fails to reject. To use Berndt and Savin's (1977) now familiar phrase, there may be conflict among criteria for testing hypotheses.

> ...two researchers employing the same body of data, the same estimation technique ..., the same significance level, but different asymptotically equivalent testing procedures, may reach conflicting decisions with regard to the truth of the null hypothesis. Another disturbing implication is that if the researcher has subjective preferences

regarding the truth of the null hypothesis, he can... judiciously choose the test procedure which is most likely to provide supporting evidence. (Berndt and Savin 1977,
p. 1275)

It turns out that, for linear restrictions on a single linear regression, there is
an even more precise relationship between the Wald and LR statistics than the
Berndt-Savin inequality. The easiest way to develop this is to first consider the
relationship between the LR and F statistics.

Relationship between the LR and F Statistics

Just as, in the special case when the regression model and restrictions are linear,
the Wald and F statistics are related, so too is the LR statistic related to the F.
This may be seen as follows.

Using (13.15) it is possible to reexpress the likelihood ratio statistic in terms
of SSE_U and SSE_R, and ultimately in terms of the F statistic:

$$
\begin{aligned}
LR &= 2(\mathscr{L}_U - \mathscr{L}_R) \\
&= -n \log SSE_U + n \log SSE_R \\
&= n(\log SSE_R - \log SSE_U) \\
&= n \log \left(\frac{SSE_R}{SSE_U} \right) \qquad\qquad (13.40) \\
&= n \log \left(1 + \frac{SSE_R - SSE_U}{SSE_U} \right) \\
&= n \log \left(1 + \frac{g}{n-K} F \right). \qquad\qquad (13.41)
\end{aligned}
$$

For example, in Example 11 we have found that in the loglinear Cobb-Douglas
production function the F statistic for constant returns to scale is $F = 0.237$.
Consequently,

$$
LR = 24 \log \left(1 + \frac{1}{21-3}(0.237) \right) = 0.269,
$$

which is the value of LR in Table 13.6.

Relationship between the LR and Wald Statistics

Because, for linear restrictions on a single linear regression, the Wald and LR statistics are both related to the F statistic, it follows that they are in turn functionally
related. Examining (13.38) and (13.41) it is apparent that this relationship is

$$
LR = n \log \left(1 + \frac{W}{n} \right). \qquad\qquad (13.42)
$$

For example, for constant returns to scale in the loglinear Cobb-Douglas production function the statistics are related by

$$
LR = 24 \log \left(1 + \frac{0.271}{24} \right) = 0.269.
$$

This exact functional equivalence of the two statistics is a stronger result than the Berndt-Savin inequality. It is, of course, consistent with it. This follows from the standard property of logarithms that

$$x > \log(1 + x),$$

which you have encountered previously as equation (6.30) in our discussion of discrete versus continuous growth rates. Examining the right-hand side of (13.42), this inequality implies that

$$\frac{W}{n} > \log\left(1 + \frac{W}{n}\right) = \frac{LR}{n}.$$

Hence,

$$W > LR,$$

the first inequality in the Berndt-Saving inequality (13.31).

Although the functional equivalence (13.42) is a stronger result than the Berndt-Savin inequality, it does not apply as generally. Nevertheless, it can be shown to hold somewhat beyond the present context of linear restrictions on a linear regression; see Stewart (1995).

A Size-Corrected LR Statistic

In our treatment of Wald tests we have distinguished between two versions of the statistic based on the alternative estimators s^2 and $\hat{\sigma}^2$. The size-corrected version W^* is related to the uncorrected version by

$$W^* = \frac{n - K}{n} W. \tag{13.43}$$

Because W^* is based on the less biased estimator s^2, the notion is that the size-correction factor $(n - K)/n$ should improve the approximation to the sampling distribution of the statistic offered by its limiting χ^2 distribution. The hope is therefore that, when this distribution is used as the basis for a hypothesis test at significance level a, we are closer to in fact incurring a probability of Type I error of a. That is, the test is nearer to having the correct size in finite samples.

So far we have made no mention of any similar issues with respect to the likelihood ratio statistic because it does not explicitly depend on any estimate of σ^2. Nevertheless some authors in some modeling contexts apply size-correction factors to the likelihood ratio statistic in an attempt to improve its small-sample properties. Mizon is an example. He adopted the size-corrected statistic[11]

$$LR^* = \frac{n - K - 1 + g/2}{n} LR,$$

Although the derivation of such size-correction factors is a technical matter (see Mizon 1977, p. 1237 and Evans and Savin 1982, p. 742 for brief explanations and

---

[11] This is Evans and Savin (1982, eq. 4.2), with some notational changes.

references), notice that it is very similar to the factor $(n - K)/n$ that we use for the Wald statistic (13.43).

For example, applying this statistic to the $g = 1$ restriction $\rho = 0$ in the CES production function estimated with his 1957 data, Mizon obtained the following values. For the model with an additive disturbance,

$$LR^* = \frac{n - K - 1 + g/2}{n} LR = \frac{24 - 4 - 1 + 1/2}{24} (1.040) = 0.84,$$

whereas for the model with a multiplicative disturbance, by a similar calculation, $LR^* = (19.5/24) \times 1.500 = 1.22$. These are the values of LR^* reported in Table 13.3.

The analytical derivation of improved approximations to the finite-sample distributions of estimators and test statistics is a well-developed, although highly technical, area of econometric theory. Perhaps the definitive survey is Rothenberg (1984). One problem with this approach to improving the properties of asymptotic tests is that the improved procedures are typically specific to very particular modeling contexts. The size-corrected statistic adopted by Mizon cannot, for example, be recommended for routine use in all applications of likelihood ratio tests.

Furthermore this is just one approach to improving the reliability of asymptotic tests—one that, in light of the computing technology now available, may not be the most fruitful in empirical research. The alternative is to use bootstrapping methods and simulate the sampling distribution of the test statistic, as we describe in Section 2.6.2. Indeed, this is a good example of an area in which capital has tended to be substituted for labor in empirical research over the past decade. Instead of the technically difficult analytical derivation of size-corrected statistics, the tendency has been to use computer simulation as the route to improved inference. It seems a safe prediction that this trend will continue and that bootstrapped procedures will increasingly be programmed into econometric software for routine use in applied work.

EXERCISES

13.15 💿 mizon54.dat mizon60.dat Use your estimations from previous exercises to create a table of loglikelihood function values similar to Table 13.5, for either Mizon's 1954 or 1960 data.

13.16 💿 mizon54.dat mizon60.dat Create a table of likelihood ratio statistics similar to Table 13.6, for either Mizon's 1954 or 1960 data. How many of these test statistics reject at a 5% significance level?

13.17 💿 mizon54.dat mizon60.dat Consider the likelihood ratio statistics for the restriction $\rho = 0$ based on Mizon's 1954 or 1960 data. Obtain the size-corrected likelihood ratio statistics LR^*. How close do you come to replicating the values reported by Mizon, as presented in Table 13.3?

13.18 Multiply by the appropriate factor to obtain the values of W associated with the values of W^* presented in Table 13.4. Comparing this with Table 13.6, for which models and restrictions is the Berndt-Savin inequality not satisfied?

13.19 Restate the functional equivalence (13.42) in terms of W^*. Which values in Tables 13.4 and 13.6 should satisfy this relationship? Do they?

13.20 We have seen that, for linear restrictions on a linear regression, the Wald and LR statistics are functionally related to the F statistic. This turns out to be true of the Lagrange multiplier statistic as well, which in this context reduces to[12]

$$LM = \frac{n(\text{SSE}_R - \text{SSE}_U)}{\text{SSE}_R}.$$

Comparing with (13.37), notice that this differs from the Wald statistic only by comparing the difference of the SSEs in the numerator against

SSE$_R$ in the denominator instead of SSE$_U$.

(a) Show that the LM statistic is functionally related to the F statistic according to

$$LM = \frac{ngF}{n - K + gF}.$$

(b) Show that the LM and Wald statistics are functionally related as

$$LM = \frac{W}{1 + W/n}.$$

13.8.5 Further Applications of Wald Statistics

We have seen that when a single restriction $h(\boldsymbol{\beta}) = 0$ is being tested, a Wald test does this by computing an estimated standard error for $h(\hat{\boldsymbol{\beta}})$. This means that given the estimation of a regression model—linear or nonlinear—it is possible to obtain an estimated standard error for any function of its coefficients. A few examples will illustrate the usefulness of this fact.

The Elasticity of Substitution of the CES Production Function

Estimation of the CES production function yields an estimate of the substitution parameter ρ. This is related to the elasticity of substitution σ by

$$\sigma = \frac{1}{1 + \rho}.$$

For Mizon's 1957 data we have found in Example 3 that the implied estimates of σ yielded by the additive and multiplicative models are 1.525 and 0.701.

In applied work we often obtain implied estimates of quantities such as this. But how precise are these point estimates? A standard error would allow us to gauge this.

It is not possible to deduce a standard error for σ from that for ρ because the relationship between the two parameters is nonlinear; the laws of variance in Appendix B, Table B.2, only apply to linear functions. We can, however, exploit the fact that an estimated standard error for a function of coefficients can be obtained numerically as a by-product of computing a Wald statistic.

EXAMPLE 14

 mizon57.dat

Use the ability to perform Wald tests to (a) obtain estimated standard errors for the elasticities of substitution of Example 3 and (b) test the hypothesis that $\sigma = 1$.

---

[12] This is Engle (1984, eq. 27), although note the typographical error in his denominator. See also Seber and Wild (1989, p. 231, Example 5.3).

SOLUTION

Estimating the CES production function as described in Example 3 (or the reparameterization of Example 5) and specifying the restriction $h(\boldsymbol{\beta}) = 1/(1 + \rho) - 1 = 0$ in the Wald test option yield the following results.

An additive disturbance. Example 3 reports an implied estimate of the elasticity of substitution of 1.525. The estimated standard error yielded by the Wald test is 0.8272.[13] The Wald statistic for the restriction $h(\boldsymbol{\beta}) = 1/(1 + \rho) - 1 = 0$ is

$$W^* = 0.4021.$$

Comparing with the $\chi^2(1)$ distribution, the p-value is 0.526. Thus the hypothesis of a unitary elasticity of substitution is not rejected at conventional significance levels.

Notice that, because this is a case of a single restriction ($g = 1$), the Wald statistic is the square of the pseudo-t statistic

$$t = \frac{1.525 - 1}{0.8272} = 0.635.$$

A multiplicative disturbance. Example 3 reports an implied estimate of the elasticity of substitution of 0.701. The estimated standard error yielded by the Wald test is 0.200. The Wald statistic for the restriction $h(\boldsymbol{\beta}) = 1/(1 + \rho) - 1 = 0$ is

$$W^* = 2.2377.$$

Comparing with the $\chi^2(1)$ distribution, the p-value is 0.135. Thus the hypothesis of a unitary elasticity of substitution is not rejected at conventional significance levels.

Notice that, because this is a case of a single restriction ($g = 1$), the Wald statistic is the square of the pseudo-t statistic

$$t = \frac{0.701 - 1}{0.200} = -1.495.$$

This is not the first time we have tested the hypothesis of a unitary elasticity of substitution. In Example 12 we do this directly in terms of ρ, with the hypothesis being the restriction $\rho = 0$. Obviously the two restrictions

$$\rho = 0 \quad \Leftrightarrow \quad \sigma = \frac{1}{1 + \rho} = 1$$

are equivalent statements of the hypothesis in that one holds if and only if the other does; one is just a reparameterization of the other. Thus, it is possible to speak of a reparameterization of restrictions, just as it is possible to speak of the reparameterization of a model.

Although these two expressions of the hypothesis of a unitary elasticity of substitution are mathematically equivalent, it is of some interest to note that they have

---

[13] The standard error for the estimate of $\sigma = 1/(1 + \rho)$ is the same as that for $h(\boldsymbol{\beta}) = 1/(1 + \rho) - 1$. Because the two expressions differ only by the constant -1, their estimators have the same variance.

led to different values of the Wald statistic. Comparing the results of Examples 12 and 14, the values of W^* are as follows.

Restriction	Additive disturbance	Multiplicative disturbance
$\rho = 0$	0.9346	1.0991
$1/(1 + \rho) = 1$	0.4021	2.2377

For a given model, then, it is possible to obtain a different value for the Wald statistic by expressing the restriction in a different, albeit mathematically equivalent, form. In this example, this does not occur to such a degree that the decision changes. Our findings across alternative disturbance specifications and parameterizations of the restriction are uniformly that, at conventional significance levels, a unitary elasticity of substitution is not rejected. Nevertheless, that the Wald statistic is *not* invariant to reparameterization is an important deficiency of this testing principle that we say more about in Section 13.8.6.

The Elasticity of Scale of the Log-Quadratic Cost Function

In Section 8.8 we study the quadratic-in-logs cost function

$$\log C_i = \alpha + \beta \log Q_i + \delta(\log Q_i)^2 + \varepsilon_i. \tag{13.44}$$

This describes how production costs C vary with output Q. In Exercise 8.12 this is estimated using Nerlove's electricity generation data. An expanded version of the function that included factor prices is considered in Exercise 11.14. Regardless of whether or not factor prices are included, we have seen that this cost function has an elasticity of scale of

$$\epsilon = \frac{1}{\beta + 2\delta \log Q}. \tag{13.45}$$

As this formula indicates, the elasticity of scale varies with the output level Q. This is in contrast to a Cobb-Douglas cost function, which does not have a quadratic term (δ is set to zero); its elasticity of scale is constant at all output levels.

The elasticity of scale is another example of a quantity for which it is natural to compute an implied estimate; the precision of this estimate is in turn gauged by a standard error. In this case, however, the estimate of ϵ must be evaluated conditional on some value of Q.

EXAMPLE 15

 nerlove1.dat

Use Nerlove's data set described in the exercises in Section 8.8 to estimate this version of the log-quadratic cost function that does not include factor prices. Estimate using Nerlove's full sample of 145 firms, as is done previously in Exercise 8.12.

To study how returns to scale vary with output, Nerlove split his data into five 29-firm subsamples ordered by output level. Obtain an implied estimate $\hat{\epsilon}$ of the elasticity of scale for each of Nerlove's five subsamples, evaluated at the mean level of output $\overline{Q}$ for each subsample. Use a Wald test routine to, for each subsample, (a) obtain an estimated standard error for $\hat{\epsilon}$ and (b) test the hypothesis of constant returns to scale, $\epsilon = 1$.

TABLE 13.7 Elasticities of Scale for Nerlove's Five Subsamples

Subsample observations	Subsample mean, $\overline{Q}$	Elasticity of scale, $\hat{\epsilon}$	Standard error, $s_{\hat{\epsilon}}$	Wald test of $\epsilon = 1$	
				W^*	p-value
1–29	61.9	1.8224	0.07804	111.05	0.000
30–58	391.9	1.3437	0.02797	150.99	0.000
59–87	1073.8	1.1750	0.03026	33.45	0.000
88–116	2224.7	1.0773	0.03354	5.32	0.021
117–145	6913.0	0.9539	0.03739	1.52	0.217

SOLUTION

Estimation of the cost function using Nerlove's full sample of data yields the estimates $\hat{\beta} = 0.11150$ and $\hat{\delta} = 0.052983$.[14] Substituting these values into equation (13.45) the implied elasticity of scale is

$$\hat{\epsilon} = \frac{1}{0.11150 + 2(0.052983) \log \overline{Q}}.$$

This is evaluated in Table 13.7 for each of the five subsample mean output levels $\overline{Q}$. The finding is that the elasticity of scale declines steadily with output. At low output levels returns to scale appear to be increasing, whereas at the highest output levels returns to scale are roughly constant or perhaps even decreasing. This is, of course, exactly what we usually think of as the typical pattern of returns to scale; recall the discussion in Section 7.1.1.[15]

In addition to this pattern revealed by the point estimates of ϵ, it is useful to have a measure of the precision of these point estimates and a test of whether they are significantly different from 1. This information is produced by the Wald test and is presented in the last three columns of Table 13.7. The estimated standard errors reveal that ϵ has been estimated precisely enough that, for at least the first three subsamples, it is possible to reject the hypothesis of constant returns at conventional significance levels. For the fourth subsample the p-value indicates that $\epsilon = 1$ is rejected at a 5% significance level but not at 1%.

Notice that, because the null hypothesis

$$\epsilon = \frac{1}{\beta + 2\delta \log Q} = 1 \tag{13.46}$$

is just a single restriction ($g = 1$), the Wald statistic is in each case just the square of the pseudo-t statistic

$$\frac{\hat{\epsilon} - 1}{s_{\hat{\epsilon}}}.$$

[14] These are your findings if you answered Exercise 8.12.

[15] Nerlove found that the same pattern emerged using other ways of permitting returns to scale to vary across the subsamples. See Table 11.1.

The empirical evidence suggests, then, that in 1955 much of the U.S. steam-driven electric power generation industry was operating at output levels characterized by increasing returns. Exercise 13.22 asks you to investigate whether this conclusion is robust to using a more realistic specification of the cost function that includes factor prices.

Our examples so far have been ones in which there is some hypothesis that it is of natural interest to test. For the CES production function, this is the restriction of a unitary elasticity of substitution, $\sigma = 1/(1 + \rho) = 1$. For the log-quadratic cost function it is the constant returns restriction (13.46).

In some applications, there may be no natural parameter restriction to test, yet the standard error generated by the Wald test may be of interest in providing a confidence interval.

For example, for the log-quadratic cost function we have found in Section 8.8 that the minimum efficient scale of production is[16]

$$Q^* = \exp\left(\frac{1 - \beta}{2\delta}\right).$$

There is no obvious hypothesis to be tested in connection with this quantity, yet, when it is evaluated, it is of interest to have a measure of the precision of this estimate.

EXAMPLE 16

 nerlove1.dat

Based on the cost function specification (13.44), compute an estimate of the minimum efficient scale of production for Nerlove's data and an associated standard error. How precise is your estimate of this minimum efficient scale?

SOLUTION

Using the coefficient estimates reported in the previous example, an estimate of the minimum efficient scale is[17]

$$\hat{Q}^* = \exp\left(\frac{1 - \hat{\beta}}{2\hat{\delta}}\right) = \exp\left(\frac{1 - 0.11150}{2 \times 0.052983}\right) = 4379.83.$$

For steam-driven electric power generation plants in the United States in the 1950s, the minimum efficient scale of production was approximately 4380 billion kWh. This is the minimum of the average cost curve. However, if this average cost curve is fairly flat over a broad range of production, this estimate will be imprecise. It is therefore not surprising that, using a Wald test routine to generate an estimated standard error by specifying

$$h(\boldsymbol{\beta}) = \exp\left(\frac{1 - \hat{\beta}}{2\hat{\delta}}\right),$$

we obtain the seemingly large value of 1490.65.

---

[16] This is the subject of Exercises 8.13 and 11.14c.

[17] This is your finding if you answered Exercise 8.12c.

The true minimum efficient scale of production should be within approximately two standard deviations of our estimated minimum, with 95% confidence. More precisely, in analogy with the confidence interval bounds (8.20) derived in connection with multiple regression, for $n = 145$ and $K = 3$ a 95% confidence interval is

$$4379.83 \pm 1490.65 \times t_{0.025}(n - K) = 4379.83 \pm 1490.65 \times 1.96.$$

In conclusion, the minimum efficient scale of production falls in the range of 1458 to 7302 billion kWh, with 95% confidence.

Let us consider another application in which, even though there may be no hypothesis to test, it is of interest to be able to get a standard error as a by-product of computing a Wald test statistic.

The Factor Share of Human Capital

Mankiw, Romer, and Weil (1992) developed an augmented version of the Solow-Swan growth model based on the three-factor Cobb-Douglas production function

$$Q = \gamma K^{\alpha} H^{\beta} L^{1-\alpha-\beta}.$$

Here L is raw labor input, and H denotes human capital. As usual in the Cobb-Douglas production function, the exponents have the interpretation as factor shares, and so β is the factor share of human capital.

This leads to the regression that we describe in Chapter 9:

$$\log q_i = \beta_1 + \beta_2 \log s_{ki} + \beta_3 \log(\delta + n_i) + \beta_4 \log s_{hi} + \varepsilon_i. \tag{13.47}$$

The slope coefficients have the following interpretations in terms of the production function parameters:

$$\beta_2 = \frac{\alpha}{1 - \alpha - \beta},$$

$$\beta_3 = \frac{-(\alpha + \beta)}{1 - \alpha - \beta},$$

$$\beta_4 = \frac{\beta}{1 - \alpha - \beta}.$$

The relationship between the two sets of parameters is an overidentifying one that implies the restriction $\beta_2 + \beta_3 + \beta_4 = 0$. Imposing this in the way described in Example 5 in Chapter 10 yields a restricted regression that implies unique estimates of α and β:

$$\alpha = \frac{\beta_2}{1 + \beta_2 + \beta_4},$$

$$\beta = \frac{\beta_4}{1 + \beta_2 + \beta_4}.$$

Estimation of the restricted regression with the Mankiw-Romer-Weil 75-country data set yields the estimates $\hat{\beta}_2 = 0.709$ and $\hat{\beta}_4 = 0.733$ (and therefore an implied

$\hat{\beta}_3 = -1.442$). The unique implied estimates of α and β are therefore $\hat{\alpha} = 0.290$ and $\hat{\beta} = 0.300$.

This estimate of α is about what we expect. We have seen that one of the empirical regularities that originally led Cobb and Douglas to formulate their production function was that historically in the United States capital's factor share had remained remarkably stable at approximately 30%. That we should obtain roughly the same figure from a cross-country regression is not surprising.

The estimate of β is of considerably more interest because factor payments to human capital are not directly observable. National income accounting data tell us the total labor income, but not how this is divided between raw and improved labor.[18] The Mankiw-Romer-Weil results indicate that 30% of national product is paid out to human capital and the residual, $1 - 0.29 - 0.30 = 0.41$ or 41%, goes as a payment to raw labor.

But how precise is this estimate of human capital's factor share? A standard error of, say, 0.1, would correspond to a 95% confidence interval of $0.30 \pm 0.1 \times 1.96$ or $(0.10, 0.50)$. This is a rather broad range—a finding that human capital earns between 10 and 50% of national income is not particularly revealing. Most of us would probably place this factor share somewhere in this range purely on a priori grounds, independent of any consideration of data. We would hope that the data would do better than this.

EXAMPLE 17

mrw.dat

Estimate the augmented Mankiw-Romer-Weil regression (13.47) by OLS in restricted form so that unique estimates of α and β are implied. Use a Wald test routine to obtain a standard error for the factor share of human capital. Present a 95% confidence interval for this factor share.

SOLUTION

The estimation repeats that of Example 5 of Chapter 10 and yields the coefficient estimates cited. Specifying the quantity

$$h(\boldsymbol{\beta}) = \frac{\beta_4}{1 + \beta_2 + \beta_4}$$

in the Wald test option yields an estimated standard error of 0.0400. For $n = 75$ and $K = 4$ a 95% confidence interval is therefore

$$0.300 \pm 0.0400 \times t_{0.025}(n - K) = 0.300 \pm 0.0400 \times 1.96 = (0.222, 0.378).$$

With 95% confidence, human capital earns between 22.2 and 37.8% of national income.

Notice that in this example there is no natural hypothesis to test on β, yet the ability to use a Wald test routine to compute a standard error is still very useful.

---

[18] This is true of official national income accounting statistics. There have been some attempts to rework national accounts to distinguish between physical and human capital, notably Jorgenson and Fraumeni (1995) for the United States.

Output Elasticities in the Cobb-Douglas Cost Function

In Chapter 11 we study the Cobb-Douglas cost function, deriving it from its name-sake production function. Marc Nerlove's application of it to the electric power generation industry involved three factors of production: x_1, labor; x_2, capital; and x_3, fuel. The production function is denoted

$$Q = \alpha_0 x_1^{\alpha_1} x_2^{\alpha_2} x_3^{\alpha_3}.$$

As usual the exponents have interpretations as factor shares or, equivalently as we have seen in Chapter 7, output elasticities.

We have seen that the cost function can be written as a loglinear relationship (11.41):

$$\log C = \alpha + \beta \log Q + \gamma_1 \log p_1 + \gamma_2 \log p_2 + \gamma_3 \log p_3. \tag{13.48}$$

The correspondence between these slope coefficients and the underlying parameters of the production function is given by the equations (11.42), which it is useful to reproduce here:

$$\beta = \frac{1}{\alpha_1 + \alpha_2 + \alpha_3}, \tag{13.49a}$$

$$\gamma_1 = \frac{\alpha_1}{\alpha_1 + \alpha_2 + \alpha_3}, \tag{13.49b}$$

$$\gamma_2 = \frac{\alpha_2}{\alpha_1 + \alpha_2 + \alpha_3}, \tag{13.49c}$$

$$\gamma_3 = \frac{\alpha_3}{\alpha_1 + \alpha_2 + \alpha_3}. \tag{13.49d}$$

The last three of these imply the linear homogeneity restriction

$$\gamma_1 + \gamma_2 + \gamma_3 = 1. \tag{13.50}$$

We have seen that a number of quantities of interest are functions of the slope coefficients. Own-price elasticities are

$$\epsilon_{ii} = \gamma_i - 1$$

and cross-price elasticities are

$$\epsilon_{ij} = \gamma_j \qquad (i \neq j).$$

Because these are linear relationships, obtaining implied standard errors for these elasticities is straightforward. By the properties of variances applied to linear functions (specifically, Corollary B.2.2 of Appendix B) we have that $V(\hat{\epsilon}_{ii}) = V(\hat{\gamma}_i)$ and $V(\hat{\epsilon}_{ij}) = V(\hat{\gamma}_j)$, and so the standard errors of the elasticities are just the standard errors of the $\hat{\gamma}$ estimates yielded by OLS.

In contrast, obtaining standard errors for estimates that are nonlinear functions of the regression coefficients requires the use of a Wald test routine. Consider the output elasticities α_i. Solving the relationships (13.49b)–(13.49d), these are

$$\alpha_1 = \frac{\gamma_1}{\beta}, \qquad \alpha_2 = \frac{\gamma_2}{\beta}, \qquad \alpha_3 = \frac{\gamma_3}{\beta}. \tag{13.51}$$

Thus, implied estimates of the output elasticities are nonlinear functions of the OLS cost function coefficient estimates.

EXAMPLE 18

nerlove.dat

Estimate Nerlove's cost function, imposing linear homogeneity (13.50) as a maintained hypothesis. Compute implied estimates of the output elasticities and obtain standard errors for them.

SOLUTION

Nerlove imposed linear homogeneity by estimating the function (13.48) in the form

$$\log C - \log p_3 = \alpha + \beta \log Q + \gamma_1 (\log p_1 - \log p_3) + \gamma_2 (\log p_2 - \log p_3).$$

The OLS slope estimates are $\hat{\beta} = 0.72069$, $\hat{\gamma}_1 = 0.59291$, $\hat{\gamma}_2 = -0.0073811$, and, by the homogeneity restriction, $\hat{\gamma}_3 = 1 - \hat{\gamma}_1 - \hat{\gamma}_2 = 0.41447$. Substituting these estimates into the expressions (13.51) for the α_i yields the following estimates. The standard errors have been obtained using the Wald test option of the OLS estimation routine.

Output elasticity	Estimated as	Estimate	Standard error
α_1	γ_1/β	0.82270	0.28751
α_2	γ_2/β	-0.01024	0.26467
α_3	$(1 - \gamma_1 - \gamma_2)/\beta$	0.57511	0.13541

The negative output elasticity for capital is, of course, implausible, although the standard error indicates that it is not significantly different from zero. This finding is one that Nerlove gave some attention to, and it is investigated in Exercise 11.10. You are asked to consider it further in Exercise 13.27.

Output elasticities are another example of quantities for which no obvious hypothesis suggests itself, yet for which it is valuable to be able to compute standard errors.

An example of a quantity for which there *is* a natural hypothesis, and which is a nonlinear function of the coefficients, is the elasticity of scale:

$$\epsilon = \frac{1}{\beta}.$$

This expression is derived as the elasticity of scale for the Cobb-Douglas cost function in Chapter 11. You will recognize it as the special case of (13.45) when $\delta = 0$; that is, when cost is not a quadratic function of output. The natural hypothesis of interest is, of course, constant returns to scale:

$$\epsilon = \frac{1}{\beta} = 1. \tag{13.52}$$

EXAMPLE 19

nerlove.dat

Estimate Nerlove's cost function, imposing linear homogeneity (13.50) as a maintained hypothesis. Compute an estimate of the elasticity of scale and its standard error. Do a Wald test of constant returns to scale.

SOLUTION

From Example 18, OLS yields $\hat{\beta} = 0.72069$, for an implied elasticity of scale of $\hat{\epsilon} = 1/\hat{\beta} = 1.3876$. The standard error yielded by a Wald test routine is $s_{\hat{\epsilon}} = 0.03357$. The Wald test statistic for the restriction (13.52) is $W^* = 133.29$. Comparing with the $\chi^2(1)$ distribution, constant returns to scale is rejected.

Notice that, because there is just a single restriction, the Wald statistic is just the square of the pseudo-t statistic

$$t = \frac{\hat{\epsilon} - 1}{s_{\hat{\epsilon}}} = \frac{1.3876 - 1}{0.03357} = 11.54.$$

A Wald test of the nonlinear restriction $1/\beta = 1$ is not the only approach we have taken to test constant returns to scale in this specification of the cost function. The simpler alternative is just a t test of the equivalent linear restriction $\beta = 1$, which is the way it is done in Chapter 11. An OLS estimation of the cost function with linear homogeneity imposed yields not only the point estimate $\hat{\beta} = 0.72069$ previously reported, but also the standard error $s_{\hat{\beta}} = 0.01744.$[19] The t statistic for the hypothesis $\beta = 1$ is therefore

$$t = \frac{\hat{\beta} - 1}{s_{\hat{\beta}}} = \frac{0.72069 - 1}{0.01744} = -16.02,$$

which corresponds to a size-corrected Wald statistic value of

$$W^* = t^2 = 256.63.$$

Hence, we have arrived at two values for the Wald statistic, depending on how the null hypothesis is parameterized.

Restriction	*W**
$\beta = 1$	256.63
$1/\beta = 1$	133.29

Although in this instance the test decision is not affected by the reparameterization of the restriction—in either case constant returns is easily rejected at conventional significance levels—this serves as another illustration of the troubling property of Wald tests that the value of the statistic is not invariant to reparameterization.

EXERCISES

13.21 **mizon54.dat mizon60.dat** Use Mizon's data for 1954 or 1960 to estimate the CES production function, as in Exercise 13.4,

(a) assuming an additive disturbance.

(b) assuming a multiplicative disturbance.

In each case use a Wald test routine to obtain a standard error for the elasticity of substitution and to test the hypothesis $1/(1 + \rho) = 1$. How do the values of your Wald statistics compare with those you obtained for the restriction $\rho = 0$ in

Exercise 13.14? Are your Wald statistics invariant to reparameterization of the restriction?

13.22 **nerlove.dat** Use Nerlove's data to estimate the log-quadratic cost function, including factor prices:

$$\log C = \alpha + \beta \log Q + \delta(\log Q)^2$$
$$+ \gamma_1 \log p_1 + \gamma_2 \log p_2 + \gamma_3 \log p_3.$$

Impose linear homogeneity $\gamma_1 + \gamma_2 + \gamma_3 = 1$ as a

---

[19] These are your estimates if you answered Exercise 11.9a.

maintained hypothesis. For each of Nerlove's five subsamples use a Wald test routine to:

(a) obtain an implied estimate of the elasticity of scale, evaluated at the mean level of output $\overline{Q}$ for each subsample.

(b) obtain an estimated standard error for each estimate.

(c) test the hypothesis of constant returns to scale.

Summarize your results in a table similar to Table 13.7. Does the inclusion of factor prices in the regression substantially alter the pattern of returns to scale that is revealed?

13.23 💿 **nerlove.dat** Using your estimation results from Exercise 13.22, obtain an estimate of the minimum efficient scale of production and an associated standard error. Construct an approximate 95% confidence interval for the minimum efficient scale. Inspecting the data set, how many of Nerlove's 145 firms were operating at output levels below this range?

13.24 💿 **mrw.dat** Repeat the OLS estimation of the augmented Mankiw-Romer-Weil regression (13.47) described in Example 17.

(a) Use your Wald test option to obtain an estimated standard error for α, the factor share of physical capital. Construct a 95% confidence interval for this factor share.

(b) Consider the factor share of raw labor input, $1 - \alpha - \beta$.

i. What is the expression for this factor share in terms of β_2 and β_4, the slope coefficients appearing in the restricted form of (13.47)? Compute a point estimate.

ii. Use your Wald test option to obtain an estimated standard error and 95% confidence interval for this factor share.

13.25 💿 **mrw.dat** As noted in Section 13.1 in the context of the textbook Solow-Swan model, the Mankiw-Romer-Weil regressions are intrinsically nonlinear if they are written explicitly in terms

of the underlying parameters of the production function.

(a) Write the model (13.47) in its intrinsically nonlinear form.

(b) Obtain NLS estimates of α and β by estimating this nonlinear regression. How do these compare with the estimates implied by the restricted linear regression reported in Example 5 of Chapter 10?

(c) How do the reported standard errors for the estimated α and β compare with those obtained using the Wald test option in Exercise 13.24 and in Example 17?

(d) What is the implied factor share of raw labor input? Obtain a standard error for this factor share.

13.26 💿 **nerlove.dat** Estimate Nerlove's cost function (13.48), imposing linear homogeneity in a way alternative to that described in Example 18. Present estimates of the output elasticities and their standard errors in a table similar to that given in that example. Do these results depend on the way in which linear homogeneity is imposed?

13.27 💿 **nerlove.dat** In Example 18 we have found a negative, but statistically insignificant, output elasticity for capital. In light of this result, Nerlove considered a version of the cost function that did not include the rental price of capital:

$$\log C = \alpha + \beta \log Q + \gamma_1 \log p_1 + \gamma_3 \log p_3.$$

This is examined in Exercise 11.10. Estimate this version of the cost function.

(a) Use your estimation results to present estimates of all three output elasticities and their standard errors. Present them in a table similar to that in Example 18.

(b) How does your estimate of the output elasticity of capital compare with that in Example 18, in which the price of capital is included in the regression? Which do you choose as the more plausible estimate?

(c) Present an estimate of the elasticity of scale and its standard error.

13.8.6 Invariance Properties of Test Statistics

Any statistical or econometric analysis involves elements that are arbitrary, such as units of measure. Conclusions drawn from the data should be invariant to such arbitrary incidentals. Let us consider the invariance properties that a test statistic should possess.

Scale Invariance One example of an arbitrary incidental is units of measure. The findings of a data analysis should not depend on how variables happen to be measured. In Section 4.8 we consider the consequences of variable scalings for the least squares estimation of the simple regression model. The most important conclusion of that discussion is that the t statistics for the hypotheses of zero coefficients, $\alpha = 0$ or $\beta = 0$, and the R^2 are unaffected by changes in units of measure. We have said that statistics such as these that are invariant to variable scalings are said to be scale invariant. In Chapter 3, the scale invariance of the correlation coefficient is used to motivate it as an alternative to the covariance as a measure of the relationship between variables.

Invariance to Sample Order Another basic invariance property that is discussed in Section 4.8 is invariance to the labeling of i.i.d. sample drawings. Consider the simplest case of a sample on a single variable Y_i, $i = 1, \ldots, n$, drawn randomly from a population. Clearly, inferences about the population should not depend on the ordering of a given set of drawings—whether, say, the values yielded by the first and second drawings were obtained in the reverse order. The least squares estimator for the population mean μ possesses this invariance property. The sample mean $\overline{Y}$ is

$$\overline{Y} = \frac{1}{n} \sum_{i=1}^{n} Y_i.$$

The value of this statistic does not depend on the ordering of the values in the sum; a reshuffling of the data yields the same value of $\overline{Y}$. Thus the sample mean is invariant to the labeling of the observations.

It is easy to see that *all* least squares estimators possess this invariance property. Any least squares estimator is defined to be associated with the minimum of some sum of squares function. For the nonlinear regression model this is (13.12):

$$S(\boldsymbol{\beta}) = \sum_{i=1}^{n} (Y_i - f_i(\boldsymbol{\beta}))^2.$$

A reshuffling of the data changes the order of the terms in this sum but not the sum itself and hence not the value of $\boldsymbol{\beta}$ that minimizes it. Thus least squares coefficient estimators—and the SSE value associated with the minimum of the $S(\boldsymbol{\beta})$ function—are, in general, invariant to sample order.

Notice that this is only a desirable invariance property for an i.i.d. sample. If the sample is not i.i.d.—say, because it was observed over time and the values in the time series have a temporal dependence—then obviously the ordering of the data is itself important and conveys information in addition to the values of the observations. Inferences drawn from the data will therefore depend on its ordering, and there is no reason to expect that estimators or test statistics should be invariant to sample order.

Invariance to Reparameterization In this chapter we have encountered another respect in which statistical inference should be invariant to an aspect of the analysis that is arbitrary—reparameterization. A model or null hypothesis can often be expressed in several mathematically equivalent forms. Ideally, inferences should be **invariant to reparameterization.**

Yet we have seen that not all testing principles possess this property. In particular, there are two instances in our examples in which the Wald statistic was not invariant to reparameterization of the null hypothesis. The first is the hypothesis of a unitary elasticity of substitution in the CES production function, which can be parameterized as $\rho = 0$ or $1/(1 + \rho) = 1$. As we observe in Section 13.8.5, these alternative expressions of the restriction lead to different values of the Wald statistic.

The second example is the hypothesis of constant returns in the Cobb-Douglas cost function, which can be parameterized as

$$\beta = 1 \quad \text{or} \quad \frac{1}{\beta} = 1. \tag{13.53}$$

As we observe in Section 13.8.5, these alternative expressions of the restriction lead to different values of the Wald statistic.

These findings call for a more systematic consideration of the invariance properties of test statistics.

F Tests

It is useful to begin by rethinking our understanding of these invariance properties in a simpler context—the linear regression model. We have seen in Chapter 10 that the F test provides a means of testing arbitrary sets of linear restrictions and that it subsumes t tests as a special case. What are the invariance properties of the F test?

The F statistic is computed based on the restricted and unrestricted SSEs, so let us start by examining them. In general, the SSE of a regression model—linear or nonlinear—is of the form

$$\text{SSE} = S(\hat{\boldsymbol{\beta}}) = \sum_{i=1}^{n} e_i^2 = \sum_{i=1}^{n} (Y_i - f_i(\hat{\boldsymbol{\beta}}))^2.$$

If the regression is linear, then the function $f_i(\boldsymbol{\beta})$ just takes the form (13.2).

Consider first a reparameterization of the model or null hypothesis. Reparameterizations of the model just involve rewriting $f_i(\boldsymbol{\beta})$ in terms of exactly identifying restrictions. Because they are exactly identifying, these restrictions do not affect the ability of the model to fit the data and the SSE is unaffected. The same is true of reparameterizations of restrictions to be tested: Alternative representations of given overidentifying restrictions yield the same restricted SSE.

The F statistic is

$$F = \frac{(SSE_R - SSE_U)/g}{SSE_U/(n - K)}.$$

Because neither the restricted nor unrestricted SSE is affected by reparameterization of the model or restrictions, the F test is invariant to reparameterization. We have seen some examples of this. In Chapter 10, we have studied two versions of a test for structural change in the linear regression model: the Chow test and a dummy variable version of the same test. One model is a reparameterization of the other, and so we are able to establish that the SSEs in the two versions of the test are the same.

Next consider changes in units of measure. As we have seen in Section 4.8[20] the SSE of a linear regression is only affected by scalings of the dependent variable, which we denote by wY_i. The effect is that the SSE is transformed by the square of this scaling factor: $w^2 SSE$. The key point is that, for any given change w in measurement units, both the restricted and unrestricted SSEs are affected in exactly the same way. The F statistic is therefore

$$F = \frac{(w^2 SSE_R - w^2 SSE_U)/g}{w^2 SSE_U/(n - K)} = \frac{(SSE_R - SSE_U)/g}{SSE_U/(n - K)}.$$

Because the variable scalings cancel, the F statistic is scale invariant. This generalizes our previous conclusion in Section 4.8 that the t statistic in the simple regression model is scale invariant.

The conclusion is that the t and F tests in linear regressions have strong invariance properties; so strong, in fact, that they tend to be taken for granted and are rarely discussed explicitly. Perhaps because familiarity with linear regression has caused them to be taken for granted, it is only fairly recently that applied econometricians have come to appreciate that these invariance properties do *not* necessarily extend to other estimation problems and testing principles. To investigate this, let us begin by considering the asymptotic test that, like the F test, does have strong invariance properties.

Likelihood Ratio Tests

In Section 13.8.4 we have seen that, for a regression model, it is possible to express the likelihood ratio statistic in terms of the SSEs of the restricted and unrestricted regressions. Reproducing (13.40),

$$LR = n \log \left(\frac{SSE_R}{SSE_U} \right).$$

---

[20] Specifically, Exercise 4.29. Although that exercise is in the context of the simple regression model, the same result applies to multiple regression.

The reasoning that the SSEs are invariant to the reparameterization of the model or restrictions holds for nonlinear regressions just as it does for linear ones. Hence, the LR statistic is invariant to reparameterization.

Turning to scale invariance, we have seen that the SSEs are *not* in general invariant to changes in units of measure. For nonlinear models as for linear ones, it continues to be the case that the SSE is unaffected by scalings of the explanatory variables.[21] However, again as in linear models, a scaling factor w applied to the dependent variable changes the SSE by the factor w^2. Because the same factor applies to both the restricted and unrestricted SSEs, their ratio is unaffected:

$$LR = n \log \left(\frac{w^2 \text{SSE}_R}{w^2 \text{SSE}_U} \right) = n \log \left(\frac{\text{SSE}_R}{\text{SSE}_U} \right).$$

The likelihood ratio statistic is scale invariant.

These proofs of the invariance of the LR statistic to data scaling and reparameterization have been done in the context of regression models. It turns out, however, that these invariance properties can be established much more generally. Likelihood ratio tests have very strong invariance properties.

Wald Tests

By contrast, the invariance properties of Wald tests are rather poor. As some of the examples we have studied in this chapter have indicated, Wald tests are not in general invariant to the reparameterization of the model or restrictions. As it happens, they are not even scale invariant.

The noninvariance of Wald tests to reparameterization of the null hypothesis appears to have first been brought to the attention of econometricians by Burgete, Gallant, and Souza (1982). It was subsequently investigated by Gregory and Veall (1985), Lafontaine and White (1986), Breusch and Schmidt (1988), and Phillips and Park (1988).

Perhaps the most dramatic demonstration of this deficiency was provided by Lafontaine and White (1986) in an article provocatively entitled "Obtaining Any Wald Statistic You Want." They considered the restriction $\beta = 1$ on one of the slope coefficients in a linear regression. The least squares estimate of the coefficient is $\hat{\beta} = 1.14$ with standard error $s_{\hat{\beta}} = 0.16$. This hypothesis is, of course, a linear restriction on a linear model that would normally be tested with a t test. However, the restriction can be reparameterized into any of the following nonlinear forms, which are equivalent if $\beta > 0$:

$$\beta^2 = 1, \quad \beta^3 = 1, \quad \beta^4 = 1, \quad \beta^{-1} = 1, \quad \beta^{-2} = 1, \quad \beta^{-3} = 1, \quad \beta^{-4} = 1, \ldots.$$

Note that one way of motivating interest in this hypothesis is that two of these parameterizations, $\beta = 1$ and $1/\beta = 1$, are the alternative expressions (13.53)

---

[21] For example, if you have done Exercises 13.4 and 13.5 you might want to check your output and confirm that the SSE is unaffected by the rescaling of the explanatory variable you consider there.

TABLE 13.8 Wald Statistics for Alternative Parameterizations of the Hypothesis $\beta = 1$

Restriction	Wald statistic	p-value
$\beta^{40} = 1$	0.03	0.855
$\beta^{20} = 1$	0.12	0.733
$\beta^{12} = 1$	0.24	0.626
$\beta^{10} = 1$	0.29	0.589
$\beta^{6} = 1$	0.45	0.502
$\beta^{3} = 1$	0.65	0.420
$\beta^{2} = 1$	0.74	0.390
$\beta = 1$	0.84	0.359
$\beta^{-1} = 1$	1.10	0.294
$\beta^{-2} = 1$	1.26	0.262
$\beta^{-3} = 1$	1.46	0.227
$\beta^{-6} = 1$	2.26	0.133
$\beta^{-10} = 1$	4.24	0.039
$\beta^{-12} = 1$	5.91	0.015
$\beta^{-20} = 1$	24.56	0.000
$\beta^{-40} = 1$	1479.65	0.000

Source: Reprinted from F. Lafontaine and K.J. White, "Obtaining any Wald Statistic You Want," p. 37, *Economics Letters* 21, 35–40. © 1986, with permission from Elsevier.

that we have considered for constant returns to scale in the Cobb-Douglas cost function.

Lafontaine and White computed the Wald statistics for many such nonlinear reparameterizations. Their values for W and the associated p-values are reproduced in Table 13.8. Although most fail to reject the restriction at conventional significance levels (the decision that arises from the simplest parameterization $\beta = 1$) the p-values vary over virtually the entire possible range of 0 to 1 and it is possible to obtain a rejection by choosing a suitably nonlinear parameterization of the hypothesis—hence, their conclusion that, with an appropriate reparameterization, you can "obtain any Wald statistic you want."

Findings such as this led Dagenais and Dufour (1991, 1992) to a comprehensive study of invariance properties. In addition to confirming the noninvariance of Wald tests to reparameterization they showed that they are also not scale invariant: "...simply changing measurement units can lead to vastly different answers. ..." Furthermore, Wald tests are not alone in suffering from these deficiencies. The same is true of a widely used version of the Lagrange multiplier test.

Practitioner's Tip:	**Wald tests have poor invariance properties**
	In your own empirical work, beware of the poor invariance properties of Wald tests. Especially when you are studying highly nonlinear models or restrictions, defer to likelihood ratio tests when both the restricted and unrestricted models can be estimated.

13.9   Conclusions

Economic theory often leads to regression models that are nonlinear in their coefficients, in the restrictions to be tested, or both. Least squares estimation of nonlinear regression models is in principle straightforward, but may in practice be complicated by numerical and identification problems.

When it comes to hypothesis testing, the methods of inference are altered fundamentally from those appropriate in linear regression. For when either the model or restrictions are nonlinear, exact tests are no longer available. Consequently, hypothesis testing must be conducted on the basis of asymptotic distributional results. Table 13.9 emphasizes this by distinguishing among four possibilities. Only when both the model and restrictions are linear is an exact test available—the F test in Chapter 10. When either the model, the restrictions, or both are nonlinear, testing must be based on asymptotic criteria. The most widely used asymptotic test criteria are the Wald, likelihood ratio, and Lagrange multiplier principles. The table does not show t tests explicitly because, as we now understand, these are just special cases of F and Wald tests.

From this perspective, the availability of exact tests in the linear regression model may be seen to be a rather special case. As soon as we leave the rather limited framework of linear restrictions on a single-equation linear regression, exact tests are not normally available and inference requires the use of asymptotic distributional results.[22] This is true not only of nonlinear regression but also of many

TABLE 13.9   Exact versus Asymptotic Tests

| Model | Restrictions | |
	Linear	Nonlinear
Linear	F	Wald, LR, LM
Nonlinear	Wald, LR, LM	Wald, LR, LM

---

[22] As we have seen in Chapter 12, there are rare exceptions in which exact tests are available in broader contexts than single-equation linear regression—notably uniform mixed linear restrictions in multivariate regression.

other types of econometric models including, for example, systems of equations, models with qualitative or limited dependent variables, and, in the next chapter, models with a heteroskedastic disturbance. Hence, the importance of asymptotic methods in econometrics.

The focus of this chapter has been on the use of Wald and likelihood ratio tests. Although in principle both are available to test a given null hypothesis, in practice the choice between them rests on several practical considerations. Wald tests have several deficiencies relative to likelihood ratio tests. First, their finite sample behavior may be poor, in the sense that their true sampling distribution may not be well approximated by their asymptotic χ^2 distribution. Second, they have weak invariance properties. Whereas likelihood ratio tests are invariant to reparameterization and scaling, Wald tests are not. For these reasons applied econometricians usually prefer to report likelihood ratio tests or some other test statistic with good invariance properties such as appropriate variants of the Lagrange multiplier test.

Nevertheless, Wald tests continue to be widely employed in empirical research. At times, computational considerations weigh in their favor. The likelihood ratio test requires the estimation of both the restricted and unrestricted model; if either estimation fails to converge it cannot be computed. The Wald test, on the other hand, requires only the estimation of the unrestricted model and so is particularly attractive when this unrestricted model is linear. When a series of restrictions are to be tested, this can be done with Wald tests using the results of a single model estimation; likelihood ratio tests would require the estimation of each restricted model.

Finally, we have seen a number of examples in which, as a convenient by-product, the Wald test computes an estimated standard error for an arbitrary function of the model coefficients. In situations in which the model is linear and the function nonlinear, there should be no issue of invariance to reparameterization because the function of interest is presumably unambiguous.

14

Heteroskedasticity

So far in this book we have adhered fairly closely to the analysis of regression models satisfying the classical assumptions. In fact, we have engaged in a systematic analysis of only one weakening of the assumptions of the classical normal linear regression model—the previous chapter considered the extension of the least squares estimation principle to intrinsically nonlinear functional forms.

Beyond this, we have offered only a passing treatment of other violations of the classical assumptions. In Section 5.3.2 we have considered briefly qualitative and limited dependent variables, for which the nature of the dependent variable suggests some alternative to normality of the disturbance that can be exploited in estimation. In Section 5.3.3, and in Section 12.5, we have considered the possibility that the equation is part of a system—a violation of the assumption that the single-equation regression model is completely specified.

This chapter considers another possible violation of the classical assumptions: The assumption of a constant disturbance variance across all observations. Recall that the classical normal linear regression model is specified as having a **homoskedastic** disturbance:

$$\varepsilon_i \sim \text{n.i.d.}(0, \sigma^2) \qquad (i = 1, \ldots, n).$$

Here we consider instead the possibility that the disturbance is **heteroskedastic.** In its most general form, this means that the variance may differ across all observations:

$$\varepsilon_i \sim \text{n.i.d.}(0, \sigma_i^2) \qquad (i = 1, \ldots, n).$$

Heteroskedasticity is common in cross-sectional data in which the dependent variable varies greatly in magnitude. We have encountered a number of such data sets in previous chapters. In Nerlove's electricity generation data, for example, costs vary more than a thousandfold from \$82,000 to \$139 million; Figure 3.1 shows that the variability of costs tends to increase with output. In Houthakker's electricity demand data, electricity consumption varies considerably across households; Figure 3.3(a) suggests that its variability may increase systematically with income. In the Mankiw, Romer, and Weil data, we have noted that living standards vary enormously among countries, a stylized fact of economic growth that is emphasized in the introduction to Chapter 9. Figure 3.5(a) suggests that the variability of living standards may increase with the saving rate. We revisit all these applications in this chapter.

Sources of Heteroskedasticity

This chapter considers the treatment of heteroskedastic disturbances in otherwise-classical regressions. Sometimes, however, heteroskedasticity can be accommodated by other aspects of model specification.

For example, in Section 5.3.2 we have seen that qualitative dependent variables give rise to a heteroskedastic disturbance. The appropriate resolution, as we have indicated, is maximum likelihood–based estimators such as probit and logit, which exploit the distribution of the disturbance to yield appropriate estimators. The consequent treatment of heteroskedasticity is an incidental feature of those procedures.

Similarly, sometimes heteroskedasticity can arise from model misspecification, such as the use of an inappropriate functional form. Davidson and MacKinnon (1993, p. 481) give the following simple example. Consider two variables related by a log-log simple regression in which $\alpha = 0$ and $\beta = 1$:

$$\log Y_i = \log X_i + \varepsilon_i, \qquad \varepsilon_i \sim \text{n.i.d.}(0, \sigma^2).$$

By implication, Y_i is generated as follows:

$$Y_i = \exp(\log X_i + \varepsilon_i) = X_i \exp(\varepsilon_i) \approx X_i(1 + \varepsilon_i) = X_i + X_i \varepsilon_i.$$

The approximation will be a good one for a disturbance that takes on relatively small values. It uses the result (6.29) that the log of 1 plus a small number is approximately that small number:[1]

$$\log(1 + \varepsilon_i) \approx \varepsilon_i \quad \Leftrightarrow \quad 1 + \varepsilon_i \approx \exp(\varepsilon_i).$$

Suppose that instead of using a log-log functional form we make the mistake of estimating a linear regression:

$$Y_i = \alpha + \beta X_i + u_i.$$

Because the true relationship between Y_i and X_i is

$$Y_i \approx X_i + X_i \varepsilon_i,$$

it follows that the disturbance $u_i = X_i \varepsilon_i$ is heteroskedastic:

$$V(u_i) = V(X_i \varepsilon_i) = X_i^2 V(\varepsilon_i) = X_i^2 \sigma^2.$$

Thus, the estimation of a misspecified functional form induces heteroskedasticity in the disturbance.

Clearly the proper way of treating heteroskedasticity in instances such as these is through the estimation of a correctly specified population model, as opposed to

---

[1] To go from one approximation to the other, remember the basic property of logarithms that $\exp(\log x) = x$.

a focus on heteroskedasticity per se. In this chapter, then, our concern is not with heteroskedasticity of these kinds. Instead, it is with correctly specified regression models that, other than being applied to heteroskedastic data and so possessing a heteroskedastic disturbance, otherwise satisfy the classical assumptions.

14.1   Consequences for Ordinary Least Squares

As a purely mechanical matter, a heteroskedastic regression can still be estimated by OLS. Consider, for example, the heteroskedastic simple regression

$$Y_i = \alpha + \beta X_i + \varepsilon_i, \qquad \varepsilon_i \sim \text{n.i.d.}(0, \sigma_i^2). \tag{14.1}$$

The OLS slope estimator formula can still be applied:

$$\hat{\beta} = \frac{\sum x_i y_i}{\sum x_i^2}. \tag{14.2}$$

The question is: What are its properties in these circumstances? After all, if OLS continues to possess its desirable properties even under heteroskedasticity, there is no need to consider alternative estimation strategies.

The key considerations bearing on the applicability of least squares to heteroskedastic data are as follows.

The OLS Coefficient Estimators Remain Unbiased.   This can be seen by reviewing the derivation of unbiasedness given in Section 4.3. Inspection reveals that at no point is the homoskedasticity assumption used. This illustrates that, in general, unbiasedness continues to hold even when OLS regression is applied to heteroskedastic data.

The OLS Coefficient Estimators Are No Longer Efficient or BLUE.   In contrast to the robustness of the unbiasedness property to heteroskedasticity, OLS loses its efficiency properties. Intuitively this makes sense: To obtain optimal estimators, the information in the heteroskedastic disturbance must be used. An efficient estimator should place more weight on observations generated by a small variance, and that are therefore more accurately representative of the population regression line, and should place less weight on observations generated by large variances.

The easiest way to see this formally is to suspend disbelief for a moment and suppose that the heteroskedastic variances σ_i^2 are known. It is then possible to derive the efficient estimators that apply.

Although this might seem like a difficult task, it is actually quite easy by using the following trick. Consider transforming the heteroskedastic regression (14.1) into a homoskedastic one by multiplying through by $1/\sigma_i$:

$$\frac{Y_i}{\sigma_i} = \alpha \frac{1}{\sigma_i} + \beta \frac{X_i}{\sigma_i} + \varepsilon_i^*. \tag{14.3}$$

The transformed disturbance is $\varepsilon_i^* \equiv \varepsilon_i / \sigma_i$, which a simple derivation shows to be homoskedastic:

$$V(\varepsilon_i^*) = V\left(\frac{\varepsilon_i}{\sigma_i}\right) = \frac{1}{\sigma_i^2} V(\varepsilon_i) = \frac{1}{\sigma_i^2} \sigma_i^2 = 1.$$

In addition, ε_i^* satisfies all the other classical properties. It has mean zero, because

$$E(\varepsilon_i^*) = E\left(\frac{\varepsilon_i}{\sigma_i}\right) = \frac{E(\varepsilon_i)}{\sigma_i} = 0.$$

It is independent across observations if ε_i is, because

$$\mathrm{cov}(\varepsilon_i^*, \varepsilon_j^*) = E(\varepsilon_i^* \varepsilon_j^*) = E\left(\frac{\varepsilon_i}{\sigma_i} \cdot \frac{\varepsilon_j}{\sigma_j}\right) = \frac{E(\varepsilon_i \varepsilon_j)}{\sigma_i \sigma_j} = 0.$$

Finally, it is normally distributed if ε_i is, because normality transfers across linear transformations.

The transformed disturbance ε_i^* is, therefore, a classical disturbance, although one that happens to have variance 1:

$$\varepsilon_i^* \sim \text{n.i.d.}(0, 1).$$

It follows that the transformed model (14.3) satisfies all the classical assumptions and that the application of least squares must yield estimators that are both efficient and BLUE.

What are these least squares estimators? The transformed model is of the form

$$Y_i^* = \alpha X_{2i} + \beta X_{3i} + \varepsilon_i^*$$

where

$$Y_i^* \equiv \frac{Y_i}{\sigma_i}, \qquad X_{2i} \equiv \frac{1}{\sigma_i}, \qquad X_{3i} \equiv \frac{X_i}{\sigma_i}. \tag{14.4}$$

That is, it is a regression through the origin with two explanatory variables.

Our analysis of regression through the origin in Section 5.2 is done in terms of simple regression, where the model is $Y_i = \beta X_i + \varepsilon_i$. We have seen that, instead of the usual slope formula $\sum x_i y_i / \sum x_i^2$ as in (14.2), the estimator becomes $\hat{\beta} = \sum X_i Y_i / \sum X_i^2$. That is, the appropriate formula replaces deviation-form variables with nondeviation-form ones.

By analogy, it turns out that the appropriate formulas for the two-variable regression through the origin are the slope formulas (8.12), but with variables converted to nondeviation form. Substituting in the definitions (14.4), these estimators are

$$\tilde{\alpha} = \frac{\sum (X_i/\sigma_i)^2 \sum (1/\sigma_i)(Y_i/\sigma_i) - \sum (1/\sigma_i)(X_i/\sigma_i) \sum (X_i/\sigma_i)(Y_i/\sigma_i)}{\sum (1/\sigma_i)^2 \sum (X_i/\sigma_i)^2 - \left[\sum (1/\sigma_i)(X_i/\sigma_i)\right]^2},$$

$$\tilde{\beta} = \frac{\sum (1/\sigma_i)^2 \sum (X_i/\sigma_i)(Y_i/\sigma_i) - \sum (1/\sigma_i)(X_i/\sigma_i) \sum (1/\sigma_i)(Y_i/\sigma_i)}{\sum (1/\sigma_i)^2 \sum (X_i/\sigma_i)^2 - \left[\sum (1/\sigma_i)(X_i/\sigma_i)\right]^2}.$$

The idea of obtaining efficient estimators by transforming a model that does not satisfy the classical assumptions to one that does, and then applying least squares to the transformed model, is called **generalized least squares** (GLS). Thus, these are examples of GLS estimators, which distinguishes them from the *ordinary* least squares estimators such as (14.2) that are yielded by least squares applied to the original (that is, untransformed) model. The GLS idea is, however, one that has much broader applicability than is suggested by this example and is useful in a variety of contexts—not just heteroskedasticity. In the case of heteroskedasticity, GLS is often called **weighted least squares** (WLS) because the effect of $1/\sigma_i$ in the formulas is to give greater weight to sample observations having smaller variances.

Because GLS is the result of applying least squares to a model satisfying the classical assumptions, it must be efficient and BLUE. The point of writing the estimators out explicitly is to see that they involve the heteroskedastic variances; the σ_i, appearing as they do within the summation expressions, do not cancel out of the formulas. This confirms what common sense tells us: Efficient estimators should use the heteroskedasticity in the data, and estimators that fail to do so—specifically, OLS—must be inefficient.

Conventional OLS Hypothesis Testing Is Invalid. The efficiency loss of OLS is not, however, its greatest deficiency. An even more serious problem is that, even though the OLS point estimators continue to be unbiased, the usual estimators for their variances are not. In turn, the standard confidence interval formulas and hypothesis testing procedures, which use these variance estimators, are invalid.

This can be illustrated by continuing to work in terms of the heteroskedastic simple regression (14.1) and the OLS slope estimator (14.2). The variance of the latter is no longer given by the expression (4.26) derived in Chapter 4 because the model is no longer the homoskedastic one that is assumed there. Instead, the correct formula can be obtained by a modification of that earlier derivation; it depends, as you might expect, on the heteroskedastic variances.

$$V(\hat{\beta}) = V\left(\frac{\sum x_i y_i}{\sum x_i^2}\right) = \left(\frac{1}{\sum x_i^2}\right)^2 \sum x_i^2 V(Y_i) = \frac{\sum x_i^2 \sigma_i^2}{\left(\sum x_i^2\right)^2}. \tag{14.5}$$

This may be usefully compared with the earlier derivation of (4.26).

Because the OLS variance estimator $s_{\hat{\beta}}^2$ in Chapter 4 is based on the estimator s^2 for a homoskedastic σ^2, it stands to reason that it does not provide an unbiased estimate of this correct variance:

$$E(s_{\hat{\beta}}^2) \neq V(\hat{\beta}).$$

Thus, the conventional confidence interval and hypothesis testing formulas in Chapter 4, which are based on $s_{\hat{\beta}}^2$, are not reliable. Furthermore, it turns out that it is not possible to say anything in general about the direction or size of this bias. Depending on the model and data, OLS standard errors can either under- or overestimate the correct ones and can be only slightly inaccurate or grossly so.[2]

Responses to Heteroskedasticity

In light of the efficiency loss and erroneous standard errors that arise when OLS is applied to heteroskedastic data, what is to be done?

There are two approaches to treating heteroskedasticity, an older approach, which was the only one available prior to 1980, and a newer approach. The older approach is to implement the GLS idea using an assumed specification for the heteroskedasticity in an attempt to achieve both estimator efficiency and legitimate inference. The problem with this is that the assumed specification for the heteroskedasticity can rarely be anything more than nonverifiable conjecture. If the assumption is incorrect, then all the considerations of specification error that we have emphasized in Chapter 12 come to the fore and we run the risk of obtaining estimators and test statistics that may have no desirable properties whatsoever—not even the unbiasedness that OLS possesses.

This motivates the modern approach to heteroskedasticity, dating from White (1980). He emphasized that, despite its efficiency loss, OLS retains an important desirable property—unbiasedness. This property alone supports the continued use of the OLS coefficient estimators. The real problem is to overcome the inadequacy of the OLS standard errors. White's contribution was to show how to do this.

Because White's approach dominates contemporary applied econometrics, we begin with it. There is still, however, much of pedagogical value to be gained in understanding the traditional approach, and we turn to it in the subsequent section.

14.2   Heteroskedasticity-Robust Tests

White's idea can be illustrated in its greatest simplicity by continuing to consider the OLS slope estimator in a heteroskedastic simple regression, the model (14.1) and estimator (14.2). We have seen that the correct expression for the estimator variance $V(\hat{\beta})$ is given by (14.5). White showed that this can be estimated by replacing the heteroskedastic σ_i^2 with the corresponding squared least squares residuals e_i^2:

$$V(\hat{\beta}) = \frac{\sum x_i^2 \sigma_i^2}{\left(\sum x_i^2\right)^2} \quad \text{can be estimated with} \quad \frac{\sum x_i^2 e_i^2}{\left(\sum x_i^2\right)^2}. \tag{14.6}$$

More significantly, White showed how this simple idea can be generalized to multiple regression and nonlinear regression. In these general contexts, he showed that these estimated standard errors are consistent estimators of the true standard errors

---

[2]   For a simple numerical demonstration of this, see Davidson and MacKinnon (1993, Table 16.1).

and so provide a legitimate basis for inference in large samples.[3] Because the importance of White's formulas is that they provide consistent estimates in the presence of heteroskedasticity, they are called **heteroskedasticity-consistent standard errors.** The idea has been generalized further to the construction of heteroskedasticity-robust Wald statistics for more general linear and nonlinear restrictions.

Because White's formulas are only asymptotically valid, tests based on them are not exact and the usual issues of small-sample accuracy arise. It turns out that their performance in practical applications can often be improved considerably with modifications to White's original formulas. Following the discussion of Section 13.7, one such small-sample modification is to multiply the variance estimator by the factor $n/(n-K)$; in the simple regression context of (14.6) in which there are $K=2$ coefficients, this is the factor $n/(n-2)$. For a discussion of the other finite-sample corrections that have been investigated, with references to the literature, see Davidson and MacKinnon (2004, Sec. 5.5). Which of these corrections is used in practice is probably less important than simply that one be used.

White's approach is now the received methodology for treating heteroskedasticity and so is implemented in virtually all econometric software. We need only give the appropriate option to the OLS or NLS command to have heteroskedasticity-consistent standard errors reported or, in the case of more complex linear or nonlinear restrictions, to have heteroskedasticity-robust Wald statistics computed. Unfortunately many econometrics packages still only report statistics such as (14.6) that do not use small-sample corrections, or, if a correction is being used, do not document it well. This will probably change in the future as our understanding of the comparative performance of these corrections improves. In the meantime, in situations in which it is apparent that your software makes no correction, it is easy to do this yourself manually with the simplest correction factor.

Practitioner's Tip: Size corrections in heteroskedasticity-robust tests

If your software makes no degrees-of-freedom adjustment to its heteroskedasticity-robust statistics, you can do this as follows. Consistent with what we have seen in Chapter 13, to transform unadjusted values to size-corrected ones, multiply by the following factors.

	Standard error	t ratio	Wald statistic
Adjustment factor	$\sqrt{\dfrac{n}{n-K}}$	$\sqrt{\dfrac{n-K}{n}}$	$\dfrac{n-K}{n}$

Notice that this parallels the Practitioner's Tip in Section 13.7.

These adjustment factors are illustrated in the following examples. Let us begin with an example of heteroskedasticity-consistent standard errors in linear regression.

[3] The property of consistency is explained in Section 13.6 of Chapter 13.

EXAMPLE 1

houthak.dat

Exercise 8.7 estimates Houthakker's linear-reciprocal specification for electricity demand,

$$q_i = \beta_1 + \beta_2 m_i + \beta_3 \frac{1}{p_{1i}} + \beta_4 p_{2i} + \beta_5 h_i + \varepsilon_i. \tag{14.7}$$

Recall that q denotes household electricity consumption, m is income, p_1 is the price of electricity, p_2 the price of gas, and h is holdings of heavy electric equipment. How do heteroskedasticity-consistent standard errors, t statistics, and p-values compare with those yielded by OLS?

SOLUTION

The results are summarized as follows. You may wish to verify that the two sets of White standard errors and t statistics are related by the given adjustment factors.

	β_1 (intercept)	β_2 (m)	β_3 (1/p_1)	β_4 (p_2)	β_5 (h)
OLS coefficient estimate	−1507.6	1.917	752.7	1.751	286.5
OLS:					
standard error	498.0	0.182	164.9	34.29	98.69
t statistic	−3.027	10.54	4.565	0.051	2.903
p-value	0.004	0.000	0.000	0.960	0.003
White (unadjusted):					
standard error	458.6	0.201	157.6	31.55	91.61
pseudo-t statistic	−3.288	9.529	4.777	0.055	3.128
p-value	0.002	0.000	0.000	0.956	0.003
White (adjusted):					
standard error	488.6	0.214	167.9	33.62	97.60
pseudo-t statistic	−3.086	8.943	4.483	0.052	2.936
p-value	0.004	0.000	0.000	0.959	0.006

These results show that the substantive conclusions reached about electricity demand in Section 8.6 are not sensitive to any heteroskedasticity in the data. In particular, the significance of variables is not materially affected by the use of heteroskedasticity-robust standard errors; income m, own-price p_1, and holdings of heavy electric equipment h continue to be highly significant, whereas the price of gas p_2 is insignificant. This is true regardless of whether the small-sample adjustment is used.

The t ratios formed with White's standard errors are labeled "pseudo-t statistics" because, in contrast to OLS t statistics under the classical assumptions, they cannot literally be shown to have t distributions in finite samples. Instead, we know only that they are asymptotically N(0, 1). Nevertheless, consistent with the reasoning in Chapter 13, it is reasonable to believe that their unknown finite sample distributions are best approximated as $t(n - K)$, and so this is the distribution used in the calculation of the p-values.

This example illustrates that White's pseudo-t statistics can increase or decrease relative to the OLS ones and may not all change in the same direction.

Our next examples are of heteroskedasticity-robust Wald tests of linear restrictions.

EXAMPLE 2

mrw.dat

Chapter 9 shows that the steady-state solution for living standards of the Solow-Swan growth model takes the form of a multiple regression. A linear restriction on the coefficients of this multiple regression is implied. For the textbook version of the model, this is the restriction $\beta_2 + \beta_3 = 0$ on the regression (9.16),

$$\log q_i = \beta_1 + \beta_2 \log s_i + \beta_3 \log(\delta + n_i) + \varepsilon_i.$$

For the augmented version that introduces human capital, it is the restriction $\beta_2 + \beta_3 + \beta_4 = 0$ on the regression (9.24),

$$\log q_i = \beta_1 + \beta_2 \log s_{ki} + \beta_3 \log(\delta + n_i) + \beta_4 \log s_{hi} + \varepsilon_i.$$

Example 7 in Chapter 10 reproduces Mankiw, Romer, and Weil's F tests of these restrictions. Are their conclusions robust to a treatment of heteroskedasticity?

SOLUTION

The F statistics that follow are reproduced from the earlier example, and their p-values are obtained from the $F(1, n-K)$ distribution. The adjusted Wald statistic is obtained from the unadjusted one by applying the factor $(n-K)/n$, where $K = 3$ for the textbook model, $K = 4$ for the augmented model, and $n = 75$. Their p-values are obtained from the $\chi^2(1)$ distribution. (There is one degree of freedom because there is a single restriction under test.)

Test	Textbook $\beta_2 + \beta_3 = 0$		Augmented $\beta_2 + \beta_3 + \beta_4 = 0$	
	Statistic	p-value	Statistic	p-value
F	1.293	0.259	0.022	0.883
Heteroskedasticity-robust tests:				
Wald (unadjusted)	1.502	0.220	0.033	0.856
Wald (adjusted)	1.442	0.230	0.031	0.860

The treatment of heteroskedasticity does not affect the essential conclusions of the analysis, regardless of whether the finite-sample adjustment is used. Neither restriction is rejected at conventional significance levels, although to the extent that there is evidence against either, it is considerably stronger for the textbook model.

EXAMPLE 3

nerlove1.dat

In Section 11.4 we have studied Marc Nerlove's estimation of the Cobb-Douglas cost function using data on the cost of electricity generation:

$$\log C_i = \alpha + \beta \log Q_i + \gamma_1 \log p_{1i} + \gamma_2 \log p_{2i} + \gamma_3 \log p_{3i} + \varepsilon_i.$$

Here C is cost, Q is electricity generated, and the prices are those of the factor inputs labor, capital, and fuel. The property that a cost function should be homogeneous of degree 1 in factor prices is the hypothesis of linear homogeneity, which is the restriction $\gamma_1 + \gamma_2 + \gamma_3 = 1$. Are the test results for this hypothesis sensitive to treating heteroskedasticity?

SOLUTION

The F statistic for this restriction follows;[4] its p-value is calculated from the $F(1, n - K)$ distribution, where $n = 145$ and $K = 5$. The adjusted Wald statistic is obtained from the unadjusted one by applying the factor $(n - K)/n$. Their p-values are obtained from the $\chi^2(1)$ distribution.

	Linear homogeneity $\gamma_1 + \gamma_2 + \gamma_3 = 1$	
Test	Statistic	p-value
F	0.574	0.450
Heteroskedasticity-robust tests:		
Wald (unadjusted)	0.669	0.414
Wald (adjusted)	0.645	0.422

Regardless of whether the finite-sample adjustment is used, the treatment of heteroskedasticity does not affect the essential conclusions of the analysis, which is that linear homogeneity is not rejected by Nerlove's data.

Finally, let us consider heteroskedasticity-robust Wald statistics in nonlinear regression.

EXAMPLE 4

mizon57.dat

Chapter 13 uses as examples of nonlinear regression the additive- and multiplicative-disturbance forms of the Cobb-Douglas and CES production functions (the multiplicative-disturbance Cobb-Douglas being the loglinear regression that is used in earlier chapters). The hypotheses of interest in these models are, in the CES, the restrictions $v = 1$ (constant returns to scale) and $\rho = 0$ (a unitary elasticity of substitution). Imposing the latter as a maintained hypothesis reduces the CES to the Cobb-Douglas, within which constant returns to scale can be tested as $\alpha + \beta = 1$.
    Wald tests for these restrictions, using Mizon's 1957 data, are summarized in Table 13.4. How do analogous heteroskedasticity-robust statistics compare?

SOLUTION

Table 13.4 reports size-corrected statistics W^*, and so for comparability we limit ourselves to the adjusted heteroskedasticity-robust statistics. The unadjusted ones may, of course, be obtained by multiplying by the reciprocals of the adjustment factors given in the Practitioner's Tip, setting $K = 4$ for the CES function, $K = 3$ for the Cobb-Douglas, and $n = 24$. The appropriate 5% χ^2 critical values are also given in Table 13.4.

---

[4] If you have answered Exercise 11.8, this is what you have obtained.

Maintained model	Restriction(s) under test	Heteroskedasticity-robust Wald statistic W^*	
		Additive disturbance	Multiplicative disturbance
CES	$\nu = 1$	0.340	0.329
	$\rho = 0$	0.742	1.353
	$\nu = 1, \rho = 0$	1.102	1.485
Cobb-Douglas	$\alpha + \beta = 1$	0.112	0.228

Comparing this with the previous results, the substantive conclusions are unchanged. None of these statistics reject at 5%, suggesting that Mizon's 1957 data are adequately described by a constant-returns Cobb-Douglas production function.

The Behrens-Fisher Problem Revisited Again

A nice feature of heteroskedasticity-robust Wald tests is that they can be applied anywhere Wald or F tests can—including specification tests. Suppose, for example, that we wish to perform nonnested tests with data that may be heteroskedastic. The encompassing and J tests in Section 12.3 can be implemented with heteroskedasticity-robust formulas. Indeed, although not indicated at the time, the Milbourne, Otto, and Voss J tests reported in Theory Meets Application 12.3 use heteroskedasticity-consistent standard errors.

As another example, consider testing for structural change. In Chapter 10 we remark on the artificiality of conventional Chow F tests for parameter constancy, which implicitly assume a constant variance over all observations at the same time they test for a shift in the regression coefficients. It is now evident that a simple solution to this version of the Behrens-Fisher problem is to treat a possible shift in the variance by using the dummy variable implementation of the Chow test and computing a heteroskedasticity-robust Wald statistic for the joint significance of the dummy variable terms.

Remarks on Heteroskedasticity-Robust Wald Tests

As Chapter 13 developed in some detail, Wald tests are one of three classical testing principles. (Recall that one purpose in constructing Table 13.4 was so that it could be compared with the likelihood ratio tests for the same restrictions given in Table 13.6.)

Heteroskedasticity-robust Wald statistics are subject to all the qualifications to the use of Wald tests that we have offered there. Specifically, they suffer from the same poor invariance properties as ordinary Wald statistics. Because this is a fatal flaw, Wald tests—whether computed as heteroskedasticity-robust statistics or not—are not recommended for more complex nonlinear restrictions. This is why we have limited ourselves to very simple restrictions in illustrating heteroskedasticity-robust Wald tests in the previous example.

In such situations, what is the alternative? Likelihood ratio tests have much better invariance properties, but there is no such thing as a heteroskedasticity-robust LR test. LR statistics are computed from a comparison of the maximized values of the restricted and unrestricted loglikelihood functions. If these are based on an assumed homoskedastic disturbance, there is no sense in which the LR statistic can then be corrected for heteroskedasticity.[5]

The third classical testing principle is the Lagrange multiplier principle, which is usually implemented with artificial regressions. LM tests have much better invariance properties than Wald tests. And indeed there is an important variant of the usual artificial regression that is heteroskedasticity-robust; see Davidson and MacKinnon (1993, Sec. 11.6). This is the preferred approach to obtaining heteroskedasticity-robust tests of nonlinear restrictions. For a brief description of the artificial regression used to compute heteroskedasticity-robust LM tests, see Wooldridge (2000, pp. 253–255).

Conclusions

This section has shown how to use the heteroskedasticity-robust approach to computing t and Wald statistics that are valid in the presence of heteroskedasticity.

If these formulas are so great, why not use them routinely and abandon the conventional OLS formulas entirely? In cross-sectional data in which the dependent variable takes on values over a broad range and descriptive inspection reveals that heteroskedasticity is likely, increasingly this is the practice. A good example is the exclusive use of heteroskedasticity-robust statistics by Milbourne, Otto, and Voss (2003), as cited in Theory Meets Application 9.1 and 12.3, which is typical of contemporary empirical work in this respect. Often OLS and heteroskedasticity-consistent standard errors are both reported to give an indication of the sensitivity of inferences to the treatment of heteroskedasticity.

But as always in economics (and econometrics), there is no free lunch. Benefits always come at a cost. The cost of the heteroskedasticity-robust approach is that it is only asymptotically valid. By contrast, when the assumptions underlying conventional OLS analysis hold—such as homoskedasticity—it has the advantage of yielding exact tests.

In fact, there is considerable evidence that heteroskedasticity-robust statistics can perform quite poorly in small samples, so that they are best used with larger data sets. When sample sizes are more limited, there may be a case for returning to the older tradition of treating heteroskedasticity—weighted least squares.

---

[5] An LR test could be based on the restricted and unrestricted loglikelihood function values under some specification for the heteroskedasticity, along the lines of the next section, but this is a different matter.

EXERCISES

Use your econometric software to do the following. Indicate whether the heteroskedasticity-robust statistics it produces are unadjusted, adjusted according to the factor we have discussed, or adjusted in some other way.

14.1 ⊙ **houthak.dat** Consider the results for Houthakker's linear-reciprocal demand specification that are reported in Example 1.

(a) Use your software to verify the OLS results.

(b) Redo the estimation, this time giving the appropriate option to obtain heteroskedasticity-consistent standard errors and related statistics. Does your software compute the unadjusted values, the adjusted values, or something else?

14.2 ⊙ **houthak.dat** Use your estimation results from Exercise 14.1 to redo Exercise 8.7. Does the treatment of heteroskedasticity alter the substantive conclusions you reach in that exercise?

14.3 ⊙ **mrw.dat** Can you replicate the results of Example 2?

14.4 ⊙ **nerlove.dat** Can you replicate the results of Example 3?

14.5 ⊙ **mizon57.dat** Can you replicate the results of Example 4?

14.6 ⊙ **marginal productivity conditions** Consider the Chow test you perform in Exercises 10.17 and 10.22. Obtain a heteroskedasticity-robust version of the test. Is your conclusion altered?

14.3   Weighted Least Squares ★

Prior to White's introduction of heteroskedasticity-robust test statistics, econometricians treated heteroskedasticity by working with particular specifications for it.

Our initial discussion of WLS in Section 14.1 is based on the assumption of known heteroskedastic variances σ_i^2. That analysis is, of course, a purely theoretical one made for the purpose of establishing that OLS is inefficient in the presence of heteroskedasticity. In practice, the σ_i^2 would never be known, just as in classical regression the homoskedastic variance σ^2 is never known.

However, the WLS idea can be implemented with less information than this. As perhaps the simplest example, suppose that in the simple regression model (14.1) the heteroskedasticity is proportional to the explanatory variable,

$$\sigma_i^2 = \sigma^2 X_i.$$

This describes the variability of Y as increasing with X, something that in practice might often be the case.

To implement WLS, consider transforming the model by $1/\sqrt{X_i}$,

$$\frac{Y_i}{\sqrt{X_i}} = \alpha \frac{1}{\sqrt{X_i}} + \beta \sqrt{X_i} + \varepsilon_i^*.$$

The transformed disturbance is $\varepsilon_i^* \equiv \varepsilon_i/\sqrt{X_i}$, which a simple derivation shows to be homoskedastic:

$$V(\varepsilon_i^*) = V\left(\frac{\varepsilon_i}{\sqrt{X_i}}\right) = \frac{1}{X_i}V(\varepsilon_i) = \frac{1}{X_i}\sigma^2 X_i = \sigma^2.$$

The transformed model is of the form

$$Y_i^* = \alpha X_{2i} + \beta X_{3i} + \varepsilon_i^*$$

where

$$Y_i^* \equiv \frac{Y_i}{\sqrt{X_i}}, \qquad X_{2i} \equiv \frac{1}{\sqrt{X_i}}, \qquad X_{3i} \equiv \sqrt{X_i}.$$

Similar to the earlier transformed model (14.3), this is a regression through the origin with two explanatory variables; the difference is that this transformation can be done in practice. Because the transformed model satisfies the classical assumptions, least squares will yield estimators with all desirable properties, and the usual t and F tests will be valid. These test statistics are based on the usual variance estimator s^2 appropriate to the regression-through-the-origin case, which estimates σ^2, the homoskedastic variance of ε_i^*.

14.3.1 Heteroskedasticity Known up to a Multiplicative Constant

This WLS idea can be elaborated in increasingly complex ways. The previous reciprocal-square-root transformation can be applied whenever the heteroskedasticity is known up to a multiplicative constant, say

$$\sigma_i^2 = \sigma^2 h_i(\cdot). \qquad (14.8)$$

Here $h_i(\cdot)$ denotes some function of known constants and variables that determine the form of the heteroskedasticity. Exactly what these constants and variables might be will vary from application to application, and so for the moment $h_i(\cdot)$ is left unspecified. The previous implementation of WLS is the special case of $h_i(\cdot) = X_i$.

As long as $h_i(\cdot)$ is completely known, the regression can be transformed by $1/\sqrt{h_i(\cdot)}$,

$$\frac{Y_i}{\sqrt{h_i(\cdot)}} = \alpha \frac{1}{\sqrt{h_i(\cdot)}} + \beta \frac{X_i}{\sqrt{h_i(\cdot)}} + \varepsilon_i^*. \qquad (14.9)$$

As before, ε_i^* can be shown to be homoskedastic, and so this is an estimable classical regression through the origin. Although simple regression has been used for illustration, WLS is applicable to multiple regression in the same way.

As our previous examples suggest, the effect of this transformation is to convert the heteroskedastic disturbance ε_i to the homoskedastic one ε_i^*. But is there any further intuition about why this transformation of the model works as a way of obtaining efficient estimators? The application of least squares to the transformed model has the effect of choosing estimators that minimize the transformed sum of squares

$$S = \sum_{i=1}^{n} \frac{(Y_i - \alpha - \beta X_i)^2}{h_i(\cdot)}.$$

Compared to the OLS sum of squares function (4.12) that does not have $h_i(\cdot)$ in the denominator, this chooses coefficient estimators by *underweighting* the deviations associated with large-variance observations and *overweighting* those associated with small-variance ones. That is, it does exactly what an efficient estimator should do.

An Example of Weighted Least Squares

In what circumstance might the form of the heteroskedasticity be known in this way? Perhaps the best example is when the dependent variable consists of group means, as is the case in Houthakker's study of electricity demand.

EXAMPLE 5

houthak.dat

Houthakker's data was observed across $n = 42$ towns. Consider his linear-reciprocal specification (14.7),

$$q_i = \beta_1 + \beta_2 m_i + \beta_3 \frac{1}{p_{1i}} + \beta_4 p_{2i} + \beta_5 h_i + \varepsilon_i. \tag{14.10}$$

Electricity consumed q, income m, and holdings of heavy electric equipment h were all obtained as household averages in each town. (The last variable is, of course, not to be confused with our notation $h_i(\cdot)$ for the heteroskedastic function.) Thus, a typical observation q_i for town i is an average over the n_i household consumption values q_{ij} $(j = 1, \ldots, n_i)$ in that town,

$$q_i = \frac{1}{n_i} \sum_{j=1}^{n_i} q_{ij}.$$

Hence, even if the electricity consumption of individual households in all towns has a common variance $V(q_{ij}) = \sigma^2$, the variance of q_i is nevertheless

$$V(q_i) = V\left(\frac{1}{n_i} \sum_{j=1}^{n_i} q_{ij} \right) = \frac{\sigma^2}{n_i}.$$

(Recall Result 2.3.) What are the implications of this for the estimation of the demand for electricity?

SOLUTION

This variance describes heteroskedasticity of the form (14.8) in which $h_i(\cdot) = 1/n_i$. Hence, the regression should be transformed by $1/\sqrt{h_i(\cdot)} = \sqrt{n_i}$:

$$q_i \sqrt{n_i} = \beta_1 \sqrt{n_i} + \beta_2 m_i \sqrt{n_i} + \beta_3 \frac{\sqrt{n_i}}{p_{1i}} + \beta_4 p_{2i} \sqrt{n_i} + \beta_5 h_i \sqrt{n_i} + \varepsilon_i^*. \tag{14.11}$$

Houthakker (1951, p. 363) explained this as follows.

In the calculations the figures for each town were weighted by the number of consumers, the theory being that for each consumer the error term . . . is a normal variable. . . . The variance of the error term in the average for a town will then be inversely proportional to the number of consumers.

He reported the following estimation results.

Coefficient	Variable	Estimate	Standard error
β_1	Intercept	-1700	
β_2	m	2.378	0.199
β_3	$1/p_1$	609.2	123.7
β_4	p_2	41.58	20.61
β_5	h	270.1	60.6

A comparison with Example 1 emphasizes the differences in the two approaches. Instead of retaining the OLS coefficient estimates and computing alternative standard errors, here we have obtained both different estimates and standard errors. Indeed, the coefficient on the price of gas p_2 changes dramatically from the previous $\hat{\beta}_4 = 1.751$ to the new $\hat{\beta}_4 = 41.58$, reflecting its relatively large standard error. You are asked to explore the implications of these new estimates in Exercise 14.9.

Further Comments

Although WLS arises from the application of least squares to a transformed model such as (14.11), remember that the model that is fundamentally of interest is the original one (14.10). The transformed model is merely a stepping-stone to obtaining heteroskedasticity-corrected estimation results for the original model and is otherwise of no intrinsic interest. In particular, all economic analysis—such as the derivation and evaluation of elasticities—should be done in terms of the original model. To reinforce this point, Exercise 14.9 below asks you to analyze some elasticities using the WLS results for Houthakker's demand function.

One important qualification relates to the R^2, for which much the same issues arise as was true for regression through the origin. Specifically, the WLS estimators yield, for the original model, no natural decomposition of sample variation on which an R^2 can be based. Although various ad hoc R^2 measures are sometimes computed, there is no universally adopted definition for models estimated by WLS.

Practitioner's Tip: **Goodness-of-fit measures in WLS**

Weighted least squares (including feasible WLS, discussed next) yields no natural decomposition of sample variation analogous to that available for OLS. As with regression through the origin, when reporting WLS results it is probably best to omit any goodness-of-fit measure or to be explicit about which definition is being used.

14.3.2 Feasible Weighted Least Squares

In practice WLS as we have so far presented it has some limitations. Applications in which the nature of the problem suggests a known expression for $h(\cdot)$ are rare; in fact, it is difficult to think of examples other than the one we have given, in which the dependent variable consists of group means. Our initial example of $h(\cdot) = X_i$ might be plausible for simple regression, but in the more typical case of multiple regression there is no similar known specification for the dependence of the heteroskedasticity on the explanatory variables. It is, however, possible to estimate such a specification and then use it in the treatment of the heteroskedasticity, and this is the possibility considered here.

Consider a multiple regression:

$$Y_i = \beta_1 + \beta_2 X_{2i} + \cdots + \beta_K X_{Ki} + \varepsilon_i. \tag{14.12}$$

In general, heteroskedasticity may depend on all the explanatory variables:

$$E(\varepsilon_i^2) = \sigma_i^2 = \sigma^2 h(X_{2i}, X_{3i}, \ldots, X_{Ki}).$$

In specifying the form of this dependence, there is no clear basis for making anything other than the simplest assumption that the argument of $h(\cdot)$ is linear:

$$E(\varepsilon_i^2) = \sigma_i^2 = \sigma^2 h(\gamma_2 X_{2i} + \gamma_3 X_{3i} + \cdots + \gamma_K X_{Ki}). \tag{14.13}$$

In specifying the function $h(\cdot)$, it is necessary to use a functional form that yields only positive values because variances must be positive. A simple way to do this is to specify $h(\cdot)$ as the exponential function,

$$E(\varepsilon_i^2) = \sigma_i^2 = \sigma^2 \exp(\gamma_2 X_{2i} + \gamma_3 X_{3i} + \cdots + \gamma_K X_{Ki}). \tag{14.14}$$

Equivalently,

$$\log \sigma_i^2 = \log \sigma^2 + \gamma_2 X_{2i} + \gamma_3 X_{3i} + \cdots + \gamma_K X_{Ki}.$$

The γ_k are unknown coefficients and must be estimated. Because the σ_i^2 can be measured by the squared OLS residuals e_i^2 obtained from (14.12), the γ_k can be estimated with the regression

$$\log e_i^2 = \gamma_1 + \gamma_2 X_{2i} + \gamma_3 X_{3i} + \cdots + \gamma_K X_{Ki} + \text{disturbance}. \tag{14.15}$$

Let $\hat{h}_i = \exp(\widehat{\log e_i^2})$, where $\widehat{\log e_i^2}$ denotes the predicted values of this regression. These $\hat{h}_i$ can be used to transform the original regression as in (14.9) and implement WLS.

Applying WLS in this way, using an estimated specification for the heteroskedasticity, is called **feasible weighted least squares** (FWLS), or sometimes **estimated weighted least squares.** It has the advantage that any plausible specification for the heteroskedasticity can be used. Although we have illustrated FWLS with the most common practice of using the same set of explanatory variables as appear in the original regression, other variables can be used if there is some a priori reason for believing that this is the pattern of the heteroskedasticity. It is evident that yet other variations on the method are possible. For example, the use of the exponential function in (14.14) is just one way of ensuring a positive variance.

Summary: Feasible Weighted Least Squares

Step 1. Estimate the original model (14.12) by OLS, saving the residuals e_i.

Step 2. Generate $\log e_i^2$ and run the OLS regression (14.15), saving the predicted values. Generate $\hat{h}_i$ by taking the exponential function of these predicted values.

Step 3. Generate the variable $1\big/\sqrt{\hat{h}_i}$ and use it to transform the variables of the original model, as in (14.9). Estimate the transformed model as a regression through the origin.

A common mistake in implementing this procedure is to forget to estimate a regression through the origin in Step 3, with the variable $1\big/\sqrt{\hat{h}_i}$ as one of the regressors.

Further Comments on FWLS

Because the weights are estimated, FWLS has only asymptotic properties; its point estimates are consistent and asymptotically efficient. They cannot be shown to be unbiased. Thus, in going from OLS to FWLS we have traded the unbiasedness of OLS for the asymptotic efficiency of FWLS. We have also, of course, obtained asymptotically valid tests statistics—but so too are White's heteroskedasticity-robust statistics asymptotically valid. Even these desirable properties of FWLS are predicated on the assumption that the heteroskedasticity has been correctly specified; if this is not the case then these desirable properties may be lost.

These considerations help explain why White's alternative approach of using heteroskedasticity-robust statistics, retaining the OLS point estimates, is the dominant empirical strategy in contemporary applied econometrics.

EXERCISES

14.7 Show that the transformed disturbance ε_i^* in (14.9) is homoskedastic.

14.8 Based on the WLS results presented in Example 5, Houthakker reported an income elasticity of demand of $\hat{\eta} = 1.01$ and a price elasticity of -1.04, both evaluated at the point $m = 500$, $p_1 = 0.50$, $p_2 = 8.0$, $h = 0.50$. (These are the elasticity values cited in Exercise 8.7.) Show how Houthakker obtained these values.

14.9 houthak.dat Estimate Houthakker's linear-reciprocal demand specification by WLS, as described in Example 5. The number of consumers in each town, n_i, is contained in the variable num

of the data set, as documented in Section 8.6. How close are you able to come to producing Houthakker's WLS results? (Your results will differ somewhat from his. Remember that you have a far better computer than he did!) Use your results to redo Exercise 8.7a–c.

14.10 houthak.dat Estimate Houthakker's linear-reciprocal demand specification by FWLS. Use your results to redo Exercise 8.7a–c.

14.11 houthak.dat Summarize the alternative approaches to analyzing Houthakker's linear-reciprocal model as follows. List in a table the own-price elasticity and t statistic and the income elasticity obtained

(a) by OLS, as reported in Exercise 8.7.

(b) by OLS with heteroskedasticity-consistent standard errors, as in Exercise 14.2.

(c) by Houthakker's (1951) implementation of WLS, as cited in previous examples and exercises.

(d) in your implementation of WLS in Exercise 14.9.

(e) by FWLS, as in Exercise 14.10.

In all cases cite elasticities evaluated at the point $m = 500$, $p_1 = 0.50$, $p_2 = 8.0$, $h = 0.50$.

14.4   Testing for Heteroskedasticity ★

Given an otherwise correctly specified regression model, how can we tell whether the data are heteroskedastic around the population regression line?

Answering this question is quite important when the choice for treating heteroskedasticity is between OLS and some form of WLS estimation. Because WLS involves all that we have seen—the use of alternative coefficient point estimators and test statistics, all predicated on some assumed specification for the heteroskedasticity—the decision to turn away from OLS is not to be taken lightly. Consequently, when WLS was the standard response to heteroskedasticity, formal tests for heteroskedasticity were ubiquitous in empirical work with cross-sectional data, and many test procedures were developed.

By contrast, if the choice is instead between presenting OLS or heteroskedasticity-consistent standard errors and test statistics, testing for heteroskedasticity becomes less important because it is easy enough—and often quite informative—to present both.

For this reason, testing for heteroskedasticity is less prevalent in applied econometrics than it once was, and in this sense it is a less important topic. It is now common to see empirical work presenting OLS and heteroskedasticity-robust results—or even just the latter—with no formal tests for heteroskedasticity reported.

In this spirit, our discussion of heteroskedasticity testing is limited to a single test—one due to Breusch and Pagan (1979). This test follows naturally from our discussion of WLS; it is among the most widely used tests, and another well-known test due to White (1980) can be viewed as a version of it; and it serves to usefully illustrate some of the testing principles that are highlighted in Chapter 13.

14.4.1   The Breusch-Pagan Test

Consider a potentially heteroskedastic multiple regression, with the heteroskedasticity related to some set of variables $Z_1, Z_2, \ldots, Z_g$:

$$E(\varepsilon_i^2) = \sigma_i^2 = \sigma^2 h(\gamma_1 Z_{1i} + \gamma_2 Z_{2i} + \cdots + \gamma_g Z_{gi}). \qquad (14.16)$$

This is similar to the specification (14.13) in that the function $h(\cdot)$ is left unspecified. The variables $Z_1, \ldots, Z_g$ could be some or all of the regressors of the original model; but the formulation generalizes this to permit the heteroskedasticity to be related to yet other variables.

Regardless of the form of the function $h(\cdot)$, the null hypothesis of homoskedasticity consists of the restrictions

$$H_0: \gamma_1 = \gamma_2 = \cdots = \gamma_g = 0.$$

Breusch and Pagan showed that these restrictions can be tested by running a regression that, in a form suggested by Koenker (1981), is

$$e_i^2 = \gamma_0 + \gamma_1 Z_{1i} + \gamma_2 Z_{2i} + \cdots + \gamma_g Z_{gi} + \text{disturbance}. \tag{14.17}$$

As in our discussion of FWLS, e_i denotes the OLS residuals of the original model, say (14.12). Notice that regression (14.17) differs from the FWLS regression (14.15) because there is no need to ensure positive predicted values. Our interest is purely in knowing whether the potentially heteroskedastic σ_i^2's are systematically related to the Z variables.

If regression (14.17) were a classical regression, H_0 could be tested with an F test. But it is not—the dependent variable e_i^2 is not an observed data series; instead it is constructed from the results of another regression, the OLS estimation of the original model. Consequently, the appropriate test statistic can only be established as having a chi-square distribution asymptotically. This test statistic takes a particularly simple form; it is n times the R^2 from regression (14.17), which we denote by R_e^2,

$$LM = nR_e^2 \sim \chi^2(g).$$

This Breusch-Pagan statistic is denoted LM because they derived it as a Lagrange multiplier test. To implement the test, this statistic is computed and compared against the χ^2 distribution with g degrees of freedom because g is the number of restrictions in H_0. A large R_e^2 will generate a value of the statistic in the right tail of the $\chi^2(g)$ distribution, constituting evidence against the null of homoskedasticity.

Summary: The Breusch-Pagan Test for Heteroskedasticity

Step 1. Estimate the original model by OLS, saving the residuals e_i.

Step 2. Generate e_i^2 and run the OLS regression (14.17) to obtain R_e^2.

Step 3. Compute the test statistic $LM = nR_e^2$ and compare it against the appropriate tabulated value of the $\chi^2(g)$ distribution.

Note, incidentally, that the Breusch-Pagan test can be applied to nonlinear models as easily as to linear ones. The residuals e_i obtained in Step 1 can be NLS residuals, and the explanatory variables of the nonlinear model would be candidates for the Z variables.

EXAMPLE 6

houthak.dat

Consider Houthakker's linear-reciprocal demand specification. Should heteroskedasticity be treated?

SOLUTION

Using the OLS residuals e_i from the estimation of that regression and letting the Z variables be the regressors from that model, the Breusch-Pagan regression (14.17) is

$$e_i^2 = \gamma_0 + \gamma_1 m_i + \gamma_2 \frac{1}{p_{1i}} + \gamma_3 p_{2i} + \gamma_4 h_i + \text{disturbance.}$$

This yields $R_e^2 = 0.132$ and an LM statistic value of

$$LM = nR_e^2 = 42 \times 0.132 = 5.53.$$

Comparing this against $\chi_{0.10}^2(4) = 7.78$, the null of homoskedasticity is not rejected at even a 10% significance level. This suggests that there is little point in treating heteroskedasticity in this model. This conclusion is, of course, consistent with the finding in Example 1 that heteroskedasticity-consistent standard errors are similar to the OLS ones, so that the statistical significance of individual coefficients is not sensitive to heteroskedasticity.

The Breusch-Pagan Test as an Application of the LM Principle

At the level at which we have presented it, the mechanics and intuition of the Breusch-Pagan test are straightforward enough. It is useful, however, to comment on the theory underlying the test as it relates to the testing principles in Chapter 13.

As Section 13.8 explains, Lagrange multiplier tests are based on the estimated restricted model and are usually implemented using artificial regressions. They are especially suitable for use in specification testing, in which typically the null hypothesis is that the model is correctly specified and the alternative hypothesis is that it is misspecified. The model is readily estimated under the null hypothesis; estimation under the alternative, for which it is often desirable to leave the nature of the misspecification as general as possible, may be more problematic.

These considerations are nicely illustrated by heteroskedasticity as a specification error. The natural null hypothesis is of homoskedasticity because the complication of treating heteroskedasticity should only be introduced if the data provide compelling evidence that it is necessary to do so. The natural alternative hypothesis is, therefore, of heteroskedasticity, according to which the assumption of a homoskedastic disturbance constitutes a specification error. In formulating this alternative hypothesis, it is desirable that it be left as general as possible. A test based on an alternative hypothesis that is limited to some special form of heteroskedasticity is not of much interest. Thus, although it is easy enough to estimate the model under the null of homoskedasticity, we prefer not to have to estimate it under the alternative of heteroskedasticity because we prefer to leave this alternative as amorphous as possible.

Thus heteroskedasticity is a situation—typical of specification testing generally—in which it is highly desirable to be able to construct a test based solely on the estimation of the restricted model. This is exactly what the Lagrange multiplier principle allows us to do.

Breusch and Pagan derived their test by recognizing that the heteroskedasticity testing problem was amenable to the LM principle.[6] Notice that their test requires no estimation of a heteroskedastic model; that is, the model need not be estimated under the alternative hypothesis. By taking the LM approach, it is possible to leave the alternative hypothesis specified only very generally; it is not necessary to specify the form of the function $h(\cdot)$ in (14.16). Breusch and Pagan derived the artificial regression needed to implement the LM test; the version (14.17) presented here is one form of that artificial regression.

Heteroskedasticity Tests as General Misspecification Tests

In the introduction to this chapter we note that heteroskedasticity can sometimes arise from model misspecification, so that the appropriate response is to alter the specification rather than compute heteroskedasticity-robust statistics or use WLS. It is useful to end this chapter by returning to this point.

EXAMPLE 7

 houthak.dat

Consider Houthakker's linear-reciprocal specification for electricity demand, and suppose that the Engel curve version of it is estimated. Should heteroskedasticity be treated?

SOLUTION

The Engel curve is just the linear specification

$$q_i = \alpha + \beta m_i + \varepsilon_i.$$

Using the OLS residuals e_i from this regression, and letting $Z_i = m_i$, the Breusch-Pagan regression is

$$e_i^2 = \gamma_0 + \gamma_1 m_i + \text{disturbance}.$$

This yields $R_e^2 = 0.145$ and an LM statistic value of

$$LM = nR_e^2 = 42 \times 0.145 = 6.07.$$

Comparing this against $\chi_{0.05}^2(1) = 3.84$, homoskedasticity is rejected at 5%.

This test decision contrasts, of course, with that of Example 6. Given this new conclusion in favor of heteroskedasticity, is the appropriate response to compute heteroskedasticity-robust statistics for the Engel curve or perhaps to use WLS? Of course not. We know that this Engel curve is misspecified; it omits the relevant regressors that appear in the fully specified demand equation.

In short, heteroskedasticity is a joint feature of the model and the data, and this is why it is appropriate to test for heteroskedasticity in a manner that is model-based, as the Breusch-Pagan test does. Sometimes, therefore, a rejection of homoskedasticity is a rejection of the model.

---

[6] Godfrey (1978) made a related contribution, and so the test is sometimes called the Breusch-Pagan-Godfrey test.

This is not to suggest that heteroskedasticity tests should be used as general misspecification tests; there are other tests designed specifically for this purpose, such as the RESET in Chapter 12. Instead, it is merely to reiterate that rejection of a null hypothesis does not imply the acceptance of the alternative; a null hypothesis can be rejected for many reasons. If we reject the null of homoskedasticity, this may be due to other deficiencies of model specification than heteroskedasticity per se.

EXERCISES ──

14.12 🖬 **houthak.dat** Replicate the Breusch-Pagan test in Example 6.

15

Time Series: Some Basic Concepts

...the element of Time ... is the centre of the chief difficulty of almost every economic problem ...

Alfred Marshall, Principles of Economics, *1890*

A fundamental assumption underlying the econometric methods we have studied so far is that the data are obtained by random sampling, so that successive observations are statistically independent. This is usually a reasonable assumption for cross-sectional data[1]—data observed across "cases" such as individuals, firms, and countries. We have now worked with several cross-sectional data sets. In Section 8.6 we have estimated Houthakker's electricity demand equation using data from 42 British towns. The Arrow, Chenery, Minhas, and Solow marginal productivity conditions in Section 7.4 and the Mankiw, Romer, and Weil regressions in Chapter 9 were estimated with country data. Nerlove's cost function was estimated using data on electricity generating plants. It is reasonable to regard each of these data sets as having been obtained as successive random drawings from the population of towns, countries, or plants, much like drawing numbered balls randomly from a container. As we have discussed in Chapter 2, this is the basis for the specification of the classical disturbance as identically *independently* distributed,

$$\varepsilon_i \sim \text{i.i.d.}(0, \sigma^2). \tag{15.1}$$

The only variation on this classical specification we have so far considered—other than adding the assumption of normality—is the possibility of heteroskedasticity, treated in the preceding chapter.

Although the assumption of random sampling usually makes sense for cross-sectional data, it almost never does when the data are collected over time. Instead,

---

[1]   An exception is when the population is small enough that random sampling cannot reasonably be viewed as being with replacement, so successive drawings are not statistically independent. See Ullah and Breunig (1998).

data observed over time usually involve some degree of **temporal dependence,** often called **serial dependence** or **autocorrelation.** As we have discussed briefly in Chapter 1, the temporal dependence in a time series variable typically arises from several sources: growth in the variable over time, seasonal variation, business cycle fluctuations, and so on. Because temporal dependencies can arise from many sources and take many forms, the statistical analysis of time series data is more complicated than the analysis of cross-sectional data. A comprehensive introduction to time series analysis would require a longer book than this one, with a higher level of analytical difficulty. Hamilton (1994) is the definitive technical reference for some topics, and there are many other good treatments of aspects of time series analysis, some of which we will cite as we go along.

Nevertheless many of the most basic ideas of time series analysis are quite intuitive and can be understood at an elementary level. In part this is so because it turns out to be possible for certain purposes to separate the study of the long-term trend of growing economic variables from the study of their shorter-term cyclical and seasonal components. Growing economic variables are dominated by their trends, and so it is possible to study their long-term behavior in a way that abstracts from short-term fluctuations.

The purpose of this and the following chapters is to introduce you to some basic ideas of time series analysis by emphasizing the modeling of trends in economic data. As a starting point, this chapter introduces some basic concepts that reappear throughout time series analysis.

This chapter and the next two abstract from the complex task of analyzing relationships between variables—the sort of statistical question that Chapters 3–14 addressed for cross-sectional data. Instead, the initial focus is on the simpler problem of analyzing the behavior of a single variable studied in isolation—**univariate** time series analysis. In reverting to first principles in this way, we are taking the approach of Chapter 2, in which methods of statistical inference for a single variable are developed. In Chapter 18 we return to the more difficult task of saying something about relationships between time series variables.

15.1 Introduction

Although our ultimate focus is on the long-term trends in economic time series, this requires that we begin by saying something about short-term fluctuations. The best way to do this is to abstract entirely from the trend and consider time series that fluctuate around a fixed mean.

As examples of time series that might reasonably be interpreted in this way, consider Figure 15.1. Figure 15.1(a) plots the U.S. unemployment rate for the years 1890–1970, one of a number of macroeconomic time series studied by Nelson and Plosser (1982). The average unemployment rate over this period was 7.12%, shown by the horizontal line. Figure 15.1(b) plots the simple monthly return R_t on IBM

FIGURE 15.1

Some time series
variables do not
trend.

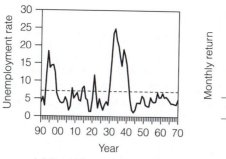

(a) The U.S. unemployment rate,
1890–1970

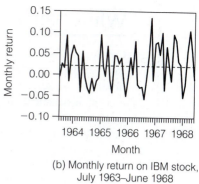

(b) Monthly return on IBM stock,
July 1963–June 1968

stock over the period July 1963 through June 1968, a series studied by Fama (1976) and presented earlier in Table 5.2 in connection with our discussion of the capital asset pricing model in the appendix to Chapter 5. (These data are also used in Chapter 2—see the histogram in Figure 2.14—and briefly in Chapter 6.) The average return was 2.12%, shown by the horizontal line. A similar plot of this series transformed to the continuously compounded form $\log(1 + R_t)$ is given in Figure 2.16.

The two series are similar in that, although both fluctuate considerably, they show no clear tendency to systematically increase or decrease over long historical time periods; neither is a growing variable. It is often reasonable to regard variables such as these as fluctuating around a constant mean, say α, at least over the sample period under study. In such cases the "trend" of the series is just this population mean: $E(Y_t) = \alpha$. The natural estimator of this population mean is the sample mean $\overline{Y}$. As we have indicated, the sample mean of the unemployment rate is $\overline{Y} = 7.12$, that for the IBM return is $\overline{Y} = 0.0212$.

Although similar in their long-term behavior, inspection of the figure suggests that these variables differ somewhat in their short-term behavior—their fluctuations around the mean. Loosely speaking, the IBM returns series seems more "random" than the unemployment rate. In other words, the unemployment rate appears to exhibit more temporal dependence: Periods of high unemployment tend to persist, as in the depression years of the 1890s and the 1930s, as do periods of low unemployment. Some variables are characterized by a higher degree of autocorrelation than others; we learn how to measure this in this chapter.

How can fluctuations such as these be described statistically? Let us begin by formulating the simplest model of how a variable might evolve through time. In fact the model we will study, of white noise around a constant mean, is too simple—it abstracts from both the trending and cyclical behaviors that typify most economic time series. Nevertheless it is for the most part a model we already understand from Chapter 2, and so it provides a convenient vehicle for introducing some new terminology, notation, and ideas.

15.2 White Noise

Consider a time series in which each observation Y_t comes from a common distribution with a mean $E(Y_t) = \alpha$ and variance $V(Y_t) = \sigma^2$, and in which the observations are generated as if by a process of random sampling. In a time series context, a statistical model is called a **stochastic process.** Speaking most generally, a stochastic process is a series of random variables ordered in time. One way of notating this particular stochastic process is

$$Y_t \sim \text{i.i.d.}(\alpha, \sigma^2) \qquad (t = 1, \ldots, n). \tag{15.2}$$

This is, of course, nothing more than the model (2.6) of Chapter 2, with the mean μ relabeled α and the index i changed to a t to emphasize that we now have in mind observations over time.

Just as we have always regarded sample data as being generated by a statistical model, we now regard an observed time series as being generated by a stochastic process. The sample data—the observed time series—is called a **realization** of the process. Thus, the distinction between a stochastic process and a realized time series is the distinction we have made in Chapter 2 between the statistical model and the sample data. And just as before, statistical inference in time series analysis involves using the data to learn about the parameters of the stochastic process.

Because the model (15.2) is, with the notational changes we have identified, the same one we have studied in Chapter 2, the same methods of statistical inference apply: The least squares estimator of α is the sample mean $\overline{Y}$, the population variance σ^2 is estimated by the sample variance s^2 given by the formula (2.7), and so on. These estimators possess the same desirable properties we discuss in Chapter 2, and the same hypothesis testing techniques apply.

Something else we learn in Chapter 2 is that another useful way of notating this model is in terms of a disturbance ε_t:

$$Y_t = \alpha + \varepsilon_t, \quad \varepsilon_t \sim \text{i.i.d.}(0, \sigma^2). \tag{15.3}$$

This is, again, just the model (2.15) with μ relabeled α and i changed to t. In this particularly simple time series model, the trend is just the constant α and variation around this trend is captured by the disturbance ε_t.

In the terminology of time series analysis, a classical disturbance such as this is called **white noise** and the model we have specified is one of **white noise around a constant mean.** The term *white noise* comes from physics, in which white light consists of an equal balance of light of all colors, in contrast to being dominated by light at certain frequencies.

To be precise, there are three slightly different definitions of white noise.

Weak-form white noise specifies that the ε_t are uncorrelated across time, so that they have zero covariance:

$$\text{cov}(\varepsilon_t, \varepsilon_{t-j}) = E(\varepsilon_t \varepsilon_{t-j}) = 0 \qquad \text{for all } t \text{ and } j \neq 0. \tag{15.4}$$

The first equality holds because, from Appendix B, Section B.10.3, when at least one of the random variables has zero mean the covariance is just the expected value of the product. This is called weak-form white noise because it is the least restrictive, or weakest, definition. It is summarized by the notation

$$\varepsilon_t \sim \text{wn}(0, \sigma^2).$$

Independent white noise specifies not just that the ε_t are uncorrelated, but that they are statistically independent, a stronger assumption:

$$\varepsilon_t \sim \text{i.i.d.}(0, \sigma^2). \tag{15.5}$$

This is just the classical disturbance of (15.3). Our study of nonlinear regression in Chapter 13 uses this disturbance specification in a cross-sectional context. Because independence implies zero covariance (but not the reverse—see Appendix B, Section B.10.3) independent white noise implies weak-form white noise.

Gaussian white noise specifies not just that the ε_t are generated by *some* distribution, but that this distribution is normal:

$$\varepsilon_t \sim \text{n.i.d.}(0, \sigma^2). \tag{15.6}$$

The name arises from the fact that the normal distribution is sometimes called the Gaussian distribution. Our study of linear regression in Chapters 4–12 uses this disturbance specification in a cross-sectional context, exploiting the result that in linear models normality yields exact tests. Because it assumes a particular form for the population distribution, this is the strongest white noise specification of all and implies the other two.

We have taken the trouble to state these alternative definitions because, as we will see, white noise disturbances are one of the basic building blocks of time series models. For the methods of time series analysis developed in this book, we need only require that disturbances be of the weak-form type, and so it is this least restrictive definition that we'll have in mind when we specify disturbances as "white noise." Consequently, any time a model involves a disturbance ε_t you can interpret it as being specified as

$$\varepsilon_t \sim \text{wn}(0, \sigma^2).$$

Given a choice of distribution and a value for the variance, it is possible to use the random number generator of a computer to generate a white noise time series. Figure 15.2(a) shows a realization of computer-generated Gaussian white noise for $n = 100$ periods. It is shown around a mean of $\alpha = 1$ and has been obtained by setting the variance to $\sigma^2 = 0.25$. The figure also shows forecasts and associated forecast intervals for out-of-sample periods. We comment on these shortly.

It is of course possible to obtain as many such simulated series as we might like. Imagine that, instead of a single realization of the process, several realizations had been generated simultaneously. For concreteness, think of flipping three coins

FIGURE 15.2

White noise around
a constant mean.

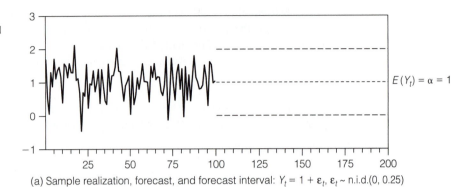

(a) Sample realization, forecast, and forecast interval: $Y_t = 1 + \varepsilon_t$, $\varepsilon_t \sim$ n.i.d.(0, 0.25)

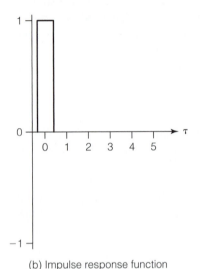

(b) Impulse response function

in each of 100 periods, for each coin assigning the value 1 if it lands heads and −1 if tails. (The resulting series is Bernoulli white noise instead of Gaussian.) Obviously the three series will be different, even though they are generated by the same stochastic process (successive flips of a fair coin).

Such a collection of simultaneously generated time series is called an **ensemble.** The nature of economic data is such that a time series is normally observed only once. Econometricians do not usually have an ensemble to work with. Nevertheless, it is important to keep in mind that the particular time series realization being studied is just one of an infinite number of realizations that could in principle have been generated by the underlying stochastic process. The econometrician's task is to use this single realization to learn about the fundamental forces or laws generating it, these laws being embodied in the specification of the stochastic process.

Learning about these fundamental laws from a single realization assumes that there are some such fundamental laws; that is, that there is some sort of stable structure generating the data. The most important such structure is the idea of stationarity, introduced in Section 15.4.

Impulse Response Function

The are a number of ways of interpreting the pattern of temporal dependence implied by a stochastic process. One is to ask the following question: How does a shock today affect the variable now and in the future? The answer to this question is given by the **impulse response function.**

The impulse response function for white noise is trivially simple. According to the model (15.3) the effect of a shock or impulse ε_t is to change Y_t by exactly the amount of the shock in that period, relative to the value α that Y_t would have taken on in the absence of the shock. This unit-for-unit effect is expressed by saying that the impulse response in this period (that is, $\tau = 0$ periods ahead) is 1.

There is no effect on future values of Y (that is, $\tau > 0$ periods ahead), for two reasons. First, the model does not specify any *direct* link between ε_t and future values of Y. Second, white noise shocks are uncorrelated over time, and so a shock today cannot affect future values of Y *indirectly* by influencing the shocks in those future periods. The absence of these direct or indirect effects means that the impulse response for all future periods $Y_{t+\tau}$ ($\tau = 1, 2, \ldots$) is zero. Another way of expressing this absence of any effect of shocks across time is to say that a white noise process has no memory: Past events have no relevance to what is happening today.

This impulse response function is portrayed in Figure 15.2(b).

Properties of White Noise

These comments on the impulse response function lead naturally to four remarks about a white noise time series.

Shocks are Temporary in Their Effect. Another way of expressing what we have said about the impulse response function is that the effect of a shock dissipates completely within the current period. In this extreme sense shocks are temporary in their effect. In particular, shocks do not affect the mean $E(Y_t) = \alpha$ that is the base from which future values of Y are generated.

The Variable Exhibits Mean Reversion. As a visual inspection of Figure 15.2(a) indicates, the mean $E(Y_t) = \alpha$ can be thought of as a central line around which the observed time series fluctuates. Values of Y cannot wander arbitrarily far from this line for indefinite periods of time. Periods in which shocks happen to be large and Y is far from the line will not persist, because white noise is uncorrelated over time. Instead, they will eventually be followed by periods in which ε_t is small and Y_t is close to the line. In this sense there is a force causing Y to return to its central line—that is, gravitate or revert toward its mean. This is sometimes expressed by saying that the central line serves as an attractor of the variable.

A Shock Does Not Alter Forecasts. Suppose you knew the value of α and were asked to forecast the value of Y in some period in the future. What would be your best guess of this future value? The answer, of course, is α. The best forecast of a white noise series is its mean. This is depicted in Figure 15.2(a), in which $\alpha = 1$ is the forecast for the out-of-sample periods $t = 101, \ldots, 200$.

Notice that this forecast is not affected by today's value of Y. If the most recently available observation on Y is unusually large or small due to an unusually large or small shock ε, this would not lead you to use a value other than α as your forecast of the future. The reason is that, because a white noise disturbance is uncorrelated over time, there is no information in a recent shock that can be used to improve the forecast. In short, a shock does not alter forecasts.

The Forecast Error Variance Is Bounded. The error made in forecasting will be the difference between the value that actually occurs in that future period, Y_t, and your forecast $E(Y_t) = \alpha$:

$$Y_t - E(Y_t) = Y_t - \alpha = \varepsilon_t.$$

The variance of this forecast error is

$$V(Y_t - EY_t) = V(\varepsilon_t) = \sigma^2.$$

This variance may be used to construct a forecast interval. If the white noise is Gaussian, then there is approximately a 95% probability that Y_t falls within two standard deviations of its mean α.[2] Consequently a 95% forecast interval is[3]

$$\alpha \pm 2\sigma.$$

EXAMPLE 1

The white noise series depicted in Figure 15.2(a) is generated using $\alpha = 1$ and the disturbance

$$\varepsilon_t \sim \text{n.i.d.}(0, 0.25).$$

Compute a 95% forecast interval.

SOLUTION

The standard deviation is $\sigma = \sqrt{\sigma^2} = \sqrt{0.25} = 0.5$, and so the forecast interval is

$$\alpha \pm 2\sigma = 1 \pm 2 \times 0.5 = (0, 2).$$

This forecast interval is shown in the figure.

---

[2] Recall that 1.96 is the tabulated value of the standard normal distribution cutting off a tail area of 0.025. Because in practice shocks may not be Gaussian, we may as well round this to 2.

[3] In presenting this formula, we have assumed known values for α and σ. As discussed in Section 5.1, in real-world forecasting problems in which the parameters must be estimated, this forecast interval would have to be modified to reflect the uncertainty in the estimates.

Notice that the forecast error variance σ^2, and hence the interval, is the same for all future periods. It does not matter how far in the future the period in question is; the uncertainty associated with forecasting for next year is the same as that for 20 or 100 years hence. This is, of course, just a special case of Result 5.1 that is established much earlier in Section 5.1.1 for a deterministic trend model in the absence of coefficient uncertainty; here the deterministic trend is just the constant α.

As we have pointed out in that earlier discussion, the implication is that the uncertainty associated with predicting the future does not become larger and larger as we look further and further into the future. This idea is expressed by saying that the forecast error variance is **bounded.** This is, of course, contrary to what should be true of real-world forecasting problems.

Conclusions

In summary, consideration of the impulse response function has revealed the following key properties of a white noise process:

- Shocks are temporary in their effect.

- The variable exhibits mean reversion.

- A shock does not alter forecasts.

- The forecast error variance is bounded.

The impulse response function is one useful way of thinking about certain features of a stochastic process. Other useful tools are the autocovariance and autocorrelation functions, to which we now turn.

15.3 Measuring Temporal Dependence

The model of white noise around a constant mean is a natural first step in discussing stochastic processes. However, an interesting model of time series behavior must permit a degree of temporal dependence in the variable, something white noise does not do.

15.3.1 Autocorrelations

The temporal dependence in a time series variable may be described by its covariances across successive lags: $\text{cov}(Y_t, Y_{t-1})$, $\text{cov}(Y_t, Y_{t-2})$, $\text{cov}(Y_t, Y_{t-3})$, and so on. A convenient way of summarizing these **autocovariances** is by defining the **autocovariance function** at lag j, denoted γ_j:[4]

$$\gamma_j = \text{cov}(Y_t, Y_{t-j}) = E[(Y_t - EY_t)(Y_{t-j} - EY_{t-j})]. \tag{15.7}$$

---

[4] The notation γ_j makes the autocovariance function dependent only on the lag length j but not the time period t. This reflects an implicit assumption that the process is stationary, something we

continued

The autocovariance at lag 0 is just the variance because, from Appendix B, Section B.10.3, the covariance of a random variable with itself is just its variance:

$$\gamma_0 = \text{cov}(Y_t, Y_t) = E[(Y_t - EY_t)(Y_t - EY_t)] = E(Y_t - EY_t)^2 = V(Y_t).$$

The autocovariance function γ_j summarizes the pattern of temporal dependence in a stochastic process. As always, however, covariances are not scale invariant; their value depends on the units in which the variable happens to be measured. It is, therefore, often useful to state this pattern of temporal dependence using the analogous correlations. This **autocorrelation function** (ACF) is denoted ρ_j:

$$
\begin{aligned}
\rho_j &= \text{cor}(Y_t, Y_{t-j}) \\
&= \frac{\text{cov}(Y_t, Y_{t-j})}{\sqrt{V(Y_t)}\sqrt{V(Y_{t-j})}} \qquad \text{by the definition of the correlation;} \\
&= \frac{\text{cov}(Y_t, Y_{t-j})}{V(Y_t)} \qquad \text{assuming a common variance;}^5 \\
&= \frac{\gamma_j}{\gamma_0}.
\end{aligned}
\tag{15.8}
$$

The ACF ρ_j just normalizes the autocovariance function γ_j by dividing by the variance γ_0 to yield a scale-invariant measure of the pattern of temporal dependence.[6] This normalization has the result that the ACF for any stochastic process must equal 1 at lag zero:

$$\rho_0 = \frac{\gamma_0}{\gamma_0} = 1.$$

Because $\rho_0 = 1$ by definition for any stochastic process, the ACF is usually presented only for nonzero lags.

White Noise

As we have seen, white noise does not permit any temporal dependence, and so its autocovariance function is trivially simple:

$$
\gamma_j = \begin{cases} \sigma^2 & \text{at lag } j = 0; \\ 0 & \text{at lag } j \neq 0. \end{cases}
$$

make explicit in the next section. At lag 0, the implication is that the variance is constant, ruling out heteroskedasticity.

[5]   As in the previous footnote, the assumption of a common variance is related to the concept of stationarity, as is discussed further in the next section.

[6]   The term *normalization* is here being used in a different way than in Chapter 13. In Chapter 13, it refers to the elimination of an indeterminacy in parameters that is achieved by imposing identifying restrictions on an otherwise unidentified model. Here it refers to the elimination of a different kind of indeterminacy—the non–scale invariance of the covariance.

That the autocovariances at nonzero lags are zero is, of course, implied by the specification of the model (15.2) that the Y_t are independent. To derive the obvious formally,

$$
\begin{aligned}
\gamma_j &= \mathrm{cov}(Y_t, Y_{t-j}) && (15.9) \\
&= E[(Y_t - EY_t)(Y_{t-j} - EY_{t-j})] && \text{by the definition of the covariance;} \\
&= E[(Y_t - \alpha)(Y_{t-j} - \alpha)] && \text{from the model (15.2);} \\
&= E(\varepsilon_t \varepsilon_{t-j}) && \text{from the model (15.3);} \\
&= 0 && \text{when } j \neq 0, \text{ by white noise (15.4).}
\end{aligned}
$$

Using this result, the autocorrelation function for white noise is

$$
\rho_j = \begin{cases} 1 & \text{at lag } j = 0; \\ 0 & \text{at lag } j \neq 0. \end{cases} \tag{15.10}
$$

Although there is no temporal dependence and so this ACF is, in this sense, uninteresting, it provides a useful benchmark by which to compare the autocorrelation functions of stochastic processes that do permit a temporal dependence.

EXERCISES

15.1 What are the autocovariance and autocorrelation functions of

(a) weak-form white noise?

(b) independent white noise?

(c) Gaussian white noise?

15.3.2 Sample Autocorrelations

The ACF, defined as it is in terms of mathematical expectations, describes the population model—the stochastic process. Given data on an observed time series, it is possible to estimate the autocorrelations ρ_j using the analogous **sample autocorrelations** r_j summarized by the **sample autocorrelation function** (SACF)

$$
r_j = \frac{\hat{\gamma}_j}{\hat{\gamma}_0}. \tag{15.11}
$$

The estimated autocovariances are calculated as

$$
\hat{\gamma}_j = \frac{1}{n} \sum_{t=j+1}^{n} y_t y_{t-j},
$$

where as usual lowercase denotes deviation form: $y_{t-j} \equiv Y_{t-j} - \overline{Y}$. The range of the summation in this formula reflects the fact that, for a sample $t = 1, \ldots, n$, the

FIGURE 15.3

Correlograms and related statistics.

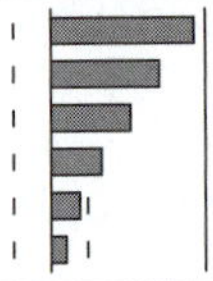

Autocorrelation		AC	Q-Stat	Prob
ı ▓▓▓▓▓	1	0.856	61.595	0.000
ı ▓▓▓▓	2	0.650	97.526	0.000
ı ▓▓▓	3	0.479	117.34	0.000
ı ▓▓	4	0.311	125.77	0.000
ı ▓ı	5	0.175	128.48	0.000
ı ▓ ı	6	0.094	129.28	0.000

(a) Unemployment rate

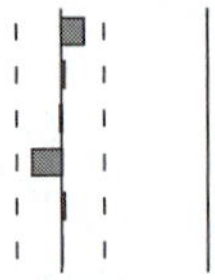

Autocorrelation		AC	Q-Stat	Prob
ı ▪ı	1	0.139	1.2151	0.270
ı ı	2	0.022	1.2470	0.536
ı ı	3	-0.003	1.2474	0.742
ı▪ ı	4	-0.171	3.1883	0.527
ı ı	5	0.021	3.2189	0.666
ı ı	6	0.002	3.2191	0.781

(b) IBM stock return

variable Y_t and its lag Y_{t-j} have only $n - j$ observations in common. Note that at lag $j = 0$ the sample autocovariance reduces to

$$\hat{\gamma}_0 = \frac{1}{n} \sum_{t=1}^{n} y_t^2.$$

With the exception of the minor difference in the divisor, this is the conventional variance estimator (2.7). All the sample autocovariances $\hat{\gamma}_j$ are specified in terms of the common divisor n, so it cancels in the formula for r_j.

The sample autocorrelation r_j is just an application to a time series variable of the sample correlation coefficient (3.4) that we originally studied in Chapter 3. It measures how a time series variable is correlated with its own past history. To illustrate this, Figure 15.3 reports the sample autocorrelations for the unemployment rate and IBM stock return series in Figure 15.1, computed for lags $j = 1, \ldots, 6$.[7] These are shown graphically as well; such a graphical depiction of an autocorrelation function is called a **correlogram.** The figure also reports related statistics, a Q statistic and associated p-value, to be discussed shortly.

An examination of these correlograms leads to some interesting observations. Consider first Fama's IBM returns series in Figure 15.3(b). Its autocorrelations are fairly low. Evidently this series exhibits little time dependence; the rate of return earned in one period has little to do with the rate earned in earlier periods.

Contrast this with the results for the unemployment rate in Figure 15.3(a). Here the sample autocorrelations are much larger, especially at short lags. Evidently there is much greater time dependence in this series, confirming the conclusion we have reached by casual inspection in Figure 15.1.

The Statistical Significance of Sample Autocorrelations

Statements that sample autocorrelations seem "fairly low," with the inference that a series exhibits "little time dependence," contrasted with others being "much larger" and so exhibiting "greater time dependence," are unfortunately rather imprecise. Is there a better way of deciding whether sample autocorrelations indicate time dependence in a series?

[7] The first three sample autocorrelations for IBM were obtained by Fama in his early analysis of this series. See Fama (1976, Table 4.2).

A sample autocorrelation, like any statistic, has a sampling distribution with a variance. It turns out that, if the process is white noise, the variance of this sampling distribution is well estimated as the reciprocal of the sample size: $1/n$. This provides a basis for hypothesis tests and confidence intervals on the autocorrelations: Under the null hypothesis of white noise in which the ACF is zero ($\rho_j = 0$ for $j > 0$), the two-standard-deviation confidence interval $\pm 2/\sqrt{n}$ should include the sample autocorrelations 95% of the time. Consequently, a value of r_j outside these bounds implies a rejection of the hypothesis that $\rho_j = 0$ at that lag.

EXAMPLE 2

np.dat
fama.dat

What are the autocorrelation confidence bounds for the unemployment rate and IBM stock returns series in Figure 15.1?

SOLUTION

Nelson and Plosser's unemployment rate series consists of annual observations for 1890–1970, so the sample size is $n = 81$. The two-standard-deviation confidence interval is therefore

$$\pm \frac{2}{\sqrt{81}} = \pm 0.222.$$

Fama's IBM returns series consists of monthly observations for January 1963 to December 1968, so the sample size is $n = 60$. The two-standard-deviation confidence interval is therefore

$$\pm \frac{2}{\sqrt{60}} = \pm 0.258.$$

These confidence intervals are shown by the dotted lines in the correlograms in Figure 15.3

Inspecting these confidence intervals strengthens our earlier conclusions. The sample autocorrelations for the IBM returns series are inside the bounds, indicating an absence of autocorrelation; the hypothesis $\rho_j = 0$ is not rejected at the indicated lags. The unemployment rate, on the other hand, has several statistically significant autocorrelations, indicating substantial temporal dependence.

EXERCISES

Nelson and Plosser's unemployment rate series is one of fourteen macroeconomic time series that they studied, all of which are available in the file **np.dat**. The variables and their sample periods are as follows.

year	Year	1860–1970
rgnp	Real GNP	1909–1970
ngnp	Nominal GNP	1909–1970
rgnpcap	Real GNP per capita	1909–1970
indprod	Industrial production	1860–1970
emp	Employment	1890–1970
unemp	Unemployment rate	1890–1970
gnpdef	GNP deflator	1889–1970
conpri	Consumer prices	1860–1970
wages	Nominal wages	1900–1970
rwages	Real wages	1900–1970
money	Money stock	1889–1970
velocity	Velocity	1869–1970
irate	Bond yield	1900–1970
stockpri	Common stock prices	1871–1970

In reading these variables into your software, note that they do not span a common sample period.

Fama's stock returns series are given in Table 5.2, and are available in the file **fama.dat**. This file is documented in the exercises at the end of the appendix to Chapter 5.

15.2 💿 **np.dat** Use your econometric software to verify the sample autocorrelations given in Figure 15.3(a) for the unemployment rate.

15.3 💿 **fama.dat**

(a) Use your econometric software to verify the sample autocorrelations given in Figure 15.3(b) for the IBM simple returns.

(b) Autocorrelations, both population and sample, are scale invariant because correlations in general are invariant to linear transformations of the data.[8] Confirm this by obtaining sample autocorrelations for the *gross* returns $1 + R_t$. Are they the same as those for the simple returns R_t?

(c) The scale invariance you have just confirmed refers to linear transformations of the data.

i. Are autocorrelations invariant to *nonlinear* transformations of the data?

ii. Verify your conjecture by considering, not the simple or gross returns, but the continuously compounded returns $\log(1 + R_t)$. How do the sample autocorrelations compare with those in Figure 15.3(b)? In principle, could continuously compounded returns yield a different pattern of temporal dependence than simple returns? Is this true in practice?

15.4 💿 **fama.dat** The file **fama.dat** includes a rate of return series for Xerox. Fama (1976, Table 4.5) reports the following values for the first three sample autocorrelations.

Lag	r_j
1	0.039
2	0.065
3	−0.067

(a) Are you able to reproduce these values using your software?

(b) Compute 95% bounds for these sample autocorrelations. Are any of these autocorrelations statistically significant? In this respect, are the findings similar to or different from those for IBM?

15.3.3 Testing for White Noise

The confidence intervals we have just studied indicate the statistical significance of a sample autocorrelation at a particular lag j. Although this is very useful, it does have a couple of limitations.

First, the null hypothesis is only that $\rho_j = 0$ *at that lag*; autocorrelation may be present at other lags. The hypothesis more likely to be of interest is whether autocorrelation is absent at all lags—the hypothesis that the series is weak-form white noise.

Second, in examining a large number of autocorrelations, some are bound to be statistically significant purely as a matter of chance, even if the series is white noise. Remember that any hypothesis test is conducted at a chosen level of significance, and this level of significance is the probability of Type I error—the mistake of incorrectly rejecting the null. This means that, in repeated applications at, say, 5%,

---

[8] This was established in Example 10 of Chapter 4 for the special case of multiplicative scaling factors. It is easily generalized to linear transformations using the result of Appendix A, Exercise A.3.

on average 5 tests out of every 100 will reject the null even when it is true. In the present context, this means that white noise time series will generate sample autocorrelations exceeding $\pm 2/\sqrt{n}$ approximately 5% of the time. Hence, a small number of statistically significant autocorrelations are not necessarily evidence that a series is not white noise.

Both these issues in the interpretation of sample autocorrelations can be addressed as follows. Instead of testing the autocorrelations individually, we can do a single test of the joint hypothesis

$$H_0: \rho_1 = \rho_2 = \cdots = \rho_k = 0.$$

Here k denotes the maximum lag considered. The alternative hypothesis is that at least one of these autocorrelations is nonzero, so that the series is not white noise.

To test this hypothesis, Box and Pierce (1970) suggested a statistic based on the sample autocorrelations r_j,

$$Q = n \sum_{j=1}^{k} r_j^2.$$

Under the null hypothesis of white noise, this has an asymptotic chi-square distribution with k degrees of freedom. Subsequently Ljung and Box (1978) suggested the modification

$$Q = n(n+2) \sum_{j=1}^{k} \frac{r_j^2}{n-j},$$

which they showed to be better approximated by the χ_k^2 distribution in finite samples. This is the version of the Q statistic we use, referred to as the Box-Pierce-Ljung statistic. These Q statistics are also known as **portmanteau statistics** for autocorrelation.

Because the choice of the maximum lag length k to be used in the calculation of the statistic is somewhat arbitrary, it is common to report the statistic for several values of k.

EXAMPLE 3

Obtain the Box-Pierce-Ljung statistic for the IBM returns series, using maximum lags of $k = 1, \ldots, 6$. For each value of k, perform a hypothesis test to see whether the joint restriction $\rho_1 = \cdots = \rho_k = 0$ is rejected.

SOLUTION

The sample autocorrelations r_j, $j = 1, \ldots, 6$, are reported in Figure 15.3. Using these to calculate the Box-Pierce-Ljung statistic based on $n = 60$, for $k = 1$ the statistic is

$$Q_1 = 60 \times 62 \times \frac{r_1^2}{59} = 1.22,$$

for $k = 2$ the statistic is

$$Q_2 = 60 \times 62 \times \left(\frac{r_1^2}{59} + \frac{r_2^2}{58} \right) = 1.25,$$

and so on. Continuing through $k = 6$, and in each case comparing the computed value of the statistic against the χ^2_k distribution to obtain a p-value, the results are summarized in Figure 15.3(b).

At all lags, these p-values are well in excess of conventional significance levels, indicating that the null hypothesis that returns on IBM were white noise during this period is not rejected.

By contrast, the Q statistics reported in Figure 15.3(a) for the unemployment rate are much larger. The accompanying p-values indicate a rejection at even a 1% significance level at all lags, so the unemployment rate is clearly not white noise.

EXERCISES

15.5 np.dat Use your econometric software to verify the Q statistics given in Figure 15.3(a) for Nelson and Plosser's unemployment rate series.

15.6 fama.dat Use your econometric software to do the following.

(a) Verify the Q statistics given in Figure 15.3(b) for Fama's IBM simple returns.

(b) Obtain Q statistics for the continuously compounded returns $\log(1 + R_t)$. In Exercise 15.3c you found that sample autocorrelations are not materially affected by the use of continuously compounded instead of simple returns. Is this true of the Q statistics as well?

15.7 fama.dat Compute Q statistics for Xerox using $k = 1, 2, 3$, either using your econometric

software or by hand using the sample autocorrelations given in Exercise 15.4. Is the null hypothesis of white noise rejected?

15.8 (a) At lag $j = 1$,
i. what parameter restriction is tested by a comparison of the sample autocorrelation r_1 with its $\pm 2/\sqrt{n}$ confidence bounds?

ii. what parameter restriction is tested by the Box-Pierce-Ljung statistic for $k = 1$?

(b) In light of this correspondence, there should be some approximate relationship between the pseudo-t statistic $r_1/(1/\sqrt{n})$ and the Box-Pierce-Ljung statistic when $k = j = 1$. What is this approximate relationship?

15.3.4 Application: Are Technology Shocks White Noise?

In Chapter 7 we study Robert Solow's (1957) method for obtaining a measure of the level of technology. It was constructed from the rate of technological progress $\Delta \log A$, the Solow residual of growth accounting. The Solow residual is a measure of technical change; that is, of the period-by-period shocks to technology. These are shown in Figure 7.6(a); the index $A(t)$ that they imply appears in Figure 7.6(b).

What are the stochastic properties of these technology shocks? Is technological innovation heavily autocorrelated, so that the economy tends to go through sustained periods of innovation followed by periods of technological stagnation? Or does technological progress occur in unpredictable spurts, so that technical change in one period is largely unrelated to that in past and future periods?

Nelson and Plosser (1982, p. 153, n. 15) studied Solow's technology series and concluded that "The log of Solow's $A(t)$ variable exhibits little autocorrelation in its first differences. ..." This suggests that the growth rate of technology is approximately white noise. The following exercise asks you to verify this finding.[9]

EXERCISES

Solow's $A(t)$ series is shown in the last column of Table 7.2 and is available in the file **solow.dat**. This data set is documented in the exercises at the end of Section 7.3.

15.9 💿 **solow.dat** Generate the log-differences of Solow's $A(t)$ series.

(a) Obtain the SACF and 95% bounds up to ten lags. What do you conclude?

(b) Obtain the Q statistic at lag $k = 10$. What do you conclude from it?

Do you agree with Nelson and Plosser's claim?

15.4   Stationarity and Nonstationarity

For it to be possible to learn something from time series data, it must be that the observations available to us are the realization of some common underlying structure. In this sense, the fruitful analysis of an economic time series requires that the historical episodes available to us be sufficiently similar, so that the analysis of these similar experiences reveals this common structure.[10] This is the essence of the idea of **stationarity.**

Stationarity

Technically, stationarity means that the joint probability distribution governing the observations in a time series remains the same throughout time; in particular, it

---

[9] This finding should be viewed as illustrative rather than definitive. Although the particular series obtained by Solow for his 1909–1949 sample period may have little autocorrelation, there is no suggestion that this is necessarily the case for all sample periods or that the Solow residual may not be correlated with other variables. In fact, it is well established that TFP growth is procyclical, tending to be large during booms and small during recessions; see Hall (1990) and Basu and Fernald (1997).

[10] At the same time, time series observations should be sufficiently *different* that new observations contribute new information; nothing is learned from new data that merely repeat old data. Technically, this is the requirement that a stochastic process be **ergodic.** Ergodicity is a second important structure on time series processes; stationarity and ergodicity together permit the estimation of the parameters of these processes. However, the formal definition of ergodicity is beyond the scope of this book; see Hamilton (1994, pp. 46–47).

FIGURE 15.4

Stationarity: The temporal dependence depends only on the number of lags and not the point in time.

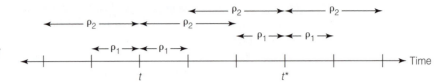

means that the mean is constant and that the temporal dependence between observations at different points in time does not change as time passes. Specifically, in defining the notation γ_j and ρ_j for the autocovariance and autocorrelation functions, it is implicitly assumed that they depend only on the lag length and not the time period—γ_j and ρ_j are functions of j but not of t. This captures the idea that the strength of the temporal dependence between Y_t and Y_{t-j} depends only on the number of periods j between them, not on whether t is 1986, 1991, or 2001. The temporal dependence between 1985 and 1986 is the same as that between 1990 and 1991, and between 2000 and 2001. The temporal dependence between 1984 and 1986 is the same as that between 1989 and 1991, and between 1999 and 2001. And so on.

This idea is depicted in Figure 15.4. It shows two points in time, t and t^*. The strength of the temporal dependence between observations on Y that are j lags apart, as measured by the autocorrelation ρ_j, depends only on the number of lags and not on whether the reference time point is t or t^*. Features of a stochastic process that do not change with the passage of time are said to be **time invariant.**

There are two versions of the concept of stationarity.

Weak-form stationarity specifies that the mean, variance, and autocovariances of the process are time invariant. This is most often called **covariance stationarity.**

Strong-form stationarity specifies not just that the process is covariance stationary, but that *all* features of the joint probability distribution governing $Y_t, Y_{t-1}, Y_{t-2}, \ldots, Y_{t-j}$ are time invariant for all j.

Strong-form stationarity relates to all the features of the joint distribution over time, features that can include aspects of the joint distribution such as skewness and kurtosis in addition to the mean, variance, and autocovariances of the series. Consequently, it is the more restrictive of the two specifications; strong-form stationarity implies covariance stationarity, but not the reverse.

How does the concept of white noise relate to stationarity? Loosely speaking, white noise is stationary. The model (15.3) of white noise around a constant mean has mean α, variance σ^2, and autocovariances zero. None of these properties depends on the time period t; consequently, they are time invariant, and so the process is covariance stationary. You are asked to think about the precise relationship between each of our three definitions of white noise and the two concepts of stationarity in Exercise 15.10.

Symmetry of the Autocovariance and Autocorrelation Functions

Recall that the autocovariances of a stochastic process are defined in equation (15.7):

$$\gamma_j = \text{cov}(Y_t, Y_{t-j}) = E[(Y_t - EY_t)(Y_{t-j} - EY_{t-j})].$$

If a stochastic process is covariance stationary, then these autocovariances depend only on the lag length j and not on t. Consequently, we can shift time t ahead j periods to $t + j$ and write the same autocovariance as

$$\gamma_j = \text{cov}(Y_{t+j}, Y_t) = \text{cov}(Y_t, Y_{t+j}).$$

In other words, the autocovariance function of a stationary process is said to be symmetric:

$$\gamma_j = \text{cov}(Y_t, Y_{t-j}) = \text{cov}(Y_t, Y_{t+j}) = \gamma_{-j}.$$

This symmetry transfers to the autocorrelation function:

$$\rho_j = \frac{\gamma_j}{\gamma_0} = \frac{\gamma_{-j}}{\gamma_0} = \rho_{-j}.$$

If a variable is stationary, the strength of the temporal dependence between Y_t and its value j periods distant is the same whether that value is j periods in the past or j periods in the future.

By contrast, if a variable is nonstationary, its ACF can depend on both t and j and may not be symmetric. This is illustrated in Section 15.8, where the ACF for a certain nonstationary process is derived and shown to depend on both t and j.

Nonstationarity

Perhaps the best way to develop our intuition about the meaning of stationarity is to contrast it with situations in which it is not satisfied.

If the mean, variance, or autocovariances of a stochastic process are not time invariant, then the process is not covariance stationary (and, by implication, not strong-form stationary) and is said to be **nonstationary.** As an example of an economic variable that is clearly nonstationary, Figure 15.5 plots an annual series for U.S. real GNP per capita, 1909–1970, studied by Nelson and Plosser (1982). This series is nonstationary because it trends upward, so that its mean cannot be constant.

Like GNP, many economic variables grow over time. Consequently, methods for studying nonstationary variables are of great importance in economics. As a first step in developing these methods, in the remainder of this chapter it is useful to consider three important examples of nonstationary processes. The first, a special case of a trend stationary process, is nonstationary in its mean; the second, a random walk process, is nonstationary in its variance; and the third, a random walk with drift, is nonstationary in both its mean and variance. In all three cases, the nonstationarity manifests itself by the fact that the variable can move further and further away from its starting point as time goes on.

FIGURE 15.5

Real GNP per capita is an example of a nonstationary variable.

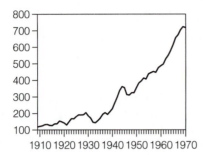

This is not the first time we have encountered these processes; they have been introduced briefly in Chapter 2 and reappeared in various forms in Chapters 3 and 6. We are now in a position to analyze them using the formal tools of time series analysis that we have developed in this chapter: impulse response functions and autocorrelation functions. They are special cases of more general trend and difference stationary stochastic processes that are developed in Chapter 17.

EXERCISES

15.10 Consider our three definitions of white noise.

(a) Is weak-form white noise
i. covariance stationary?
ii. strong-form stationary?

(b) Is independent white noise, as defined by (15.5),

i. covariance stationary?
ii. strong-form stationary?

(c) Is Gaussian white noise, as defined by (15.6),
i. covariance stationary?
ii. strong-form stationary?

15.5 Nonstationarity in the Mean: Trend Stationary Processes

Suppose that Y_t fluctuates around, not a constant mean α, but a time trend:

$$Y_t = \alpha + \beta t + \varepsilon_t. \tag{15.12}$$

As discussed previously, we are for the moment assuming a white noise disturbance:

$$\varepsilon_t \sim \text{wn}(0, \sigma^2).$$

We first consider this example of a deterministic trend model in Chapter 2 as equation (2.32). A simulated realization of such a process is given in Figure 2.15(a).

FIGURE 15.6

White noise around
a deterministic
trend: sample real-
ization, forecast,
and forecast inter-
val, $Y_t = 4.605 +
0.04879t + \varepsilon_t$.

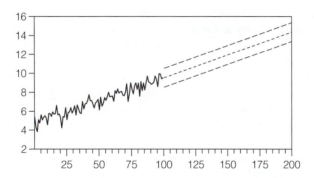

This same realization is reproduced in Figure 15.6; it is generated using the white noise shocks in Figure 15.2(a). The figure shows out-of-sample forecasts and forecast intervals for periods beyond $n = 100$; we comment on these shortly.

The mean of this stochastic process is the deterministic trend

$$E(Y_t) = \alpha + \beta t. \qquad (15.13)$$

Clearly this mean changes with time; it is not time invariant. Consequently, this process is nonstationary. It is said to be trend stationary because the short-run white noise fluctuations ε_t are stationary about the deterministic trend.

A linear time trend is just one example of a deterministic trend. A trend could be quadratic,

$$Y_t = \alpha + \beta t + \delta t^2 + \varepsilon_t, \qquad (15.14)$$

or a higher-order polynomial in time. However, if Y_t is in logarithmic form, then we know from Chapter 6 that a log-lin time trend describes constant growth, suggesting this will often be adequate for studying trend stationary series.

Structural Breaks as a Source of Nonstationarity. Another type of nonstationarity in the mean occurs if the variable fluctuates around a horizontal central line, but this mean undergoes structural shifts. This can be captured with a dummy variable:

$$Y_t = \alpha + \beta D_t + \varepsilon_t. \qquad (15.15)$$

Structural breaks are often important in economics, and so it is frequently necessary to treat them in the deterministic component of time series models. Wars, the Great Depression, the postwar baby boom, and the oil embargo of the early 1970s are oft-cited examples of such structural breaks. Another example is the decline in growth rates experienced by most industrialized countries around 1970; in the absence of an economic explanation for this as-yet-unexplained event, it has to be treated with a dummy variable.

As another example, the unemployment rate is bounded by the values 0 and 1, and so cannot trend indefinitely. It may nevertheless be nonstationary in its mean due to structural breaks. Such a structural break probably took place in the late 1960s for reasons described by Milton Friedman (1977, p. 458).

... the natural rate has clearly been rising in the United States for two major reasons. First, women, teenagers, and part-time workers have been constituting a growing fraction of the labor force. These groups are more mobile in employment than other workers, entering and leaving the labor market, shifting more frequently between jobs. As a result they tend to experience higher average rates of unemployment. Second, unemployment insurance and other forms of assistance to unemployed persons have been made available to more categories of workers and have become more generous in duration and amount. Workers who lose their jobs are under less pressure to look for other work, will tend to wait longer in the hope, generally fulfilled, of being recalled to their former employment, and can be more selective in the alternatives they consider. Further, the availability of unemployment insurance makes it more attractive to enter the labor force in the first place, and so may itself have stimulated both the growth that has occurred in the labor force as a percentage of the population and its changing composition.

Friedman's description of this structural break suggests a model for the unemployment rate much like equation (15.15).

These examples of trend stationary processes have in common the feature that the only portion of the right-hand side that is random is the disturbance ε_t. This means that, regardless of the specific form of the deterministic trend, the variable Y inherits the stochastic behavior of the disturbance. Let us investigate this.

Impulse Response Function: White Noise around a Deterministic Trend

One aspect of the stochastic behavior of the disturbance that is transmitted directly to Y is the impulse response function. In the case of white noise, Y inherits the impulse response function we have discussed: a shock ε_t today has a unit-for-unit effect on Y_t in the current period, but no effect in future periods. Hence, Figure 15.2(b) continues to be a correct depiction of the impulse response function of white noise around a deterministic trend.

Accordingly, the key properties of white noise around a trend mirror those we have discussed for white noise around a constant. These key properties are the following.

Shocks Are Temporary in Their Effect. Another way of expressing what we have said about the impulse response function is that the effect of a shock dissipates completely within the current period. In this extreme sense, shocks are temporary in their effect. In particular, shocks do not affect the mean $E(Y_t) = \alpha + \beta t$ (or whatever the deterministic trend may be, quadratic or otherwise)—that is, the base from which future values of Y are generated.

The Variable Exhibits Mean Reversion. The mean $E(Y_t) = \alpha + \beta t$ may be thought of as a central line around which the observed time series fluctuates, as illustrated by the straight line underlying the simulated series in Figure 2.15(a). The values of Y cannot wander arbitrarily far from this line for indefinite periods of time. Periods in which shocks happen to be large and Y is far from the line will not persist because white noise is uncorrelated. Instead, they will eventually be followed by periods in which ε_t is small and Y_t is close to the line. In this sense, there is a force causing Y to gravitate or revert toward its mean. In the present context, in which this mean is a deterministic trend instead of just a constant, this property is often called **trend reversion.** Another way of expressing this is to say that the deterministic trend serves as an attractor of the series.

A Shock Does Not Alter Forecasts. Suppose a variable is generated by white noise around a linear trend (15.12) and you are asked to forecast its value in some period t in the future. What would be your best guess of this future value? The answer, of course, is $\alpha + \beta t$; the best forecast is just the deterministic trend. This is depicted in Figure 15.6, in which $\alpha + \beta t = 4.605 + 0.04879t$ is the forecast for the out-of-sample periods $t = 101, \ldots, 200$.

EXAMPLE 4	Sometimes it is convenient to index time so that the most recently observed period is $t = 0$ and the forecasts are for periods $t = 1, 2, 3, \ldots$. Consider a time series variable generated as white noise around the linear deterministic trend

$$4.60517 + 0.04879t.$$

Forecast the variable in periods 1, 2, and 3.

SOLUTION   The forecasts are as follows.

Period	Forecast
1	$4.60517 + 0.04879 \times 1 = 4.65396$
2	$4.60517 + 0.04879 \times 2 = 4.70275$
3	$4.60517 + 0.04879 \times 3 = 4.75154$

Notice that, given the trend line used for prediction, forecasts are not affected by the realized values of the series. If the most recently available observation on Y is unusually large or small due to an unusually large or small disturbance ε, this will not lead you to use a value other than the deterministic trend as your forecast of the future. The reason is that, because a white noise disturbance is uncorrelated over time, there is no information in a recent shock that can be used to improve the forecast. In short, a shock does not alter forecasts.

The Forecast Error Variance Is Bounded. The error made in forecasting is the difference between the value that actually occurs in the future period, Y_t, and your forecast $\alpha + \beta t$:

$$Y_t - E(Y_t) = Y_t - \alpha - \beta t = \varepsilon_t.$$

The variance of this forecast error is

$$V(Y_t - EY_t) = V(\varepsilon_t) = \sigma^2. \tag{15.16}$$

This variance may be used to construct a forecast interval around the deterministic trend, as depicted in Figure 15.6. An approximate 95% forecast interval is[11]

$$\alpha + \beta t \pm 2\sigma.$$

EXAMPLE 5

The series depicted in Figure 15.6 is generated using the trend

$$4.605 + 0.04879t$$

and the disturbance

$$\varepsilon_t \sim \text{n.i.d.}(0, 0.25).$$

Compute a 95% forecast interval.

SOLUTION

The standard deviation is $\sigma = 0.5$, and so a two-standard-deviation forecast interval is

$$\alpha + \beta t \pm 2\sigma = 4.605 + 0.04879t \pm (2 \times 0.5) = 4.605 \pm 1 + 0.04879t.$$

This is computed for the periods $t = 101, \ldots, 200$ and is shown in Figure 15.6.

Notice that the forecast error variance σ^2 is the same in all future periods and, consequently, that the forecast interval is of constant width. This is, of course, just Result 5.1, established much earlier in Section 5.1.1 for a deterministic trend model in the absence of coefficient uncertainty. It generalizes the conclusions of Example 1 regarding the special case of white noise around a constant mean. In the terminology introduced there, the forecast error variance is bounded.

Conclusions

In summary, consideration of the impulse response function has revealed the following key properties of the trend stationary process based on white noise:

- Shocks are temporary in their effect.
- The variable exhibits trend reversion.
- A shock does not alter the forecast.
- The forecast error variance is bounded.

These properties mirror those of white noise around a constant mean.

Autocorrelation Function

In addition to inheriting the impulse response function of its disturbance, a trend stationary process also inherits its autocorrelation function. This may be seen as follows.

---

[11] In presenting this formula, we have assumed known values for α, β, and σ. As discussed in Section 5.1, in real-world forecasting problems where the parameters must be estimated, this forecast interval would have to be modified to reflect the uncertainty in the estimates.

The autocovariances for the trend stationary process (15.12) are, following the earlier derivation (15.9),

$$\gamma_j = \text{cov}(Y_t, Y_{t-j})$$
$$= E[(Y_t - EY_t)(Y_{t-j} - EY_{t-j})]$$
$$= E[(Y_t - \alpha - \beta t)(Y_{t-j} - \alpha - \beta(t-j))]$$
$$= E(\varepsilon_t \varepsilon_{t-j}).$$

Because white noise is uncorrelated, these are zero at nonzero lags. The autocorrelation function is just the earlier ACF for white noise $\rho_j = 0$ given by equation (15.10).

This property that a trend stationary process inherits the autocorrelation function of its disturbance generalizes in two ways. First, the form of the deterministic trend does not matter. The derivation uses the linear deterministic trend $E(Y_t) = \alpha + \beta t$; the previous derivation (15.9) is for the special case when the deterministic trend is just the constant mean $E(Y_t) = \alpha$. But it is easy to see that we could have used the quadratic trend (15.14) or one that involves structural shifts such as (15.15) or, for that matter, any other specification for the deterministic trend and still found that

$$\gamma_j = \text{cov}(Y_t, Y_{t-j}) = E(\varepsilon_t \varepsilon_{t-j}).$$

Thus, a trend stationary process inherits the autocorrelation function of its disturbance, regardless of the nature of the deterministic trend.

Second, a trend stationary process inherits the autocorrelation function of its disturbance, regardless of the nature of the disturbance. Suppose that instead of being white noise, ε_t is autocorrelated. It is still the case that $\gamma_j = E(\varepsilon_t \varepsilon_{t-j})$, and so Y_t inherits this pattern of autocorrelation.

Notice that in the model of white noise around a deterministic trend, although Y_t follows a trend and thus exhibits a pattern to its behavior that is partially predictable, it is nevertheless *not* autocorrelated. Autocorrelation is a feature of the stochastic behavior of the variable, not of any deterministic component.

Sample Autocorrelation Function

Although a trend stationary process inherits the ACF of its disturbance, this pattern of temporal dependence will not be correctly revealed by the SACF.

To illustrate this, consider the simulated trend stationary process depicted in Figure 15.6. Because this series is by construction one of white noise around a deterministic trend, we know that its autocorrelations are $\rho_j = 0$, the ACF for white noise given by equation (15.10). Compare this with the sample autocorrelations, which are given in Figure 15.7(a). This correlogram is very different from the theoretical ACF and suggests a quite different pattern of temporal dependence—one of strong correlation at many lags, the correlations declining only gradually.

FIGURE 15.7

The correlogram of a nonstation- ary series typically declines slowly.

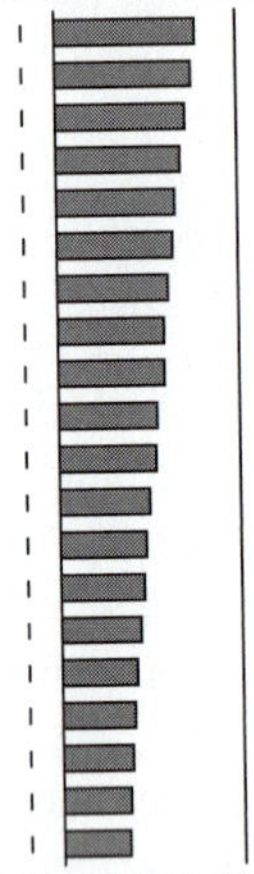

Autocorrelation		AC	Q-Stat	Prob
	1	0.867	77.403	0.000
	2	0.843	151.36	0.000
	3	0.800	218.63	0.000
	4	0.767	281.06	0.000
	5	0.735	339.07	0.000
	6	0.715	394.51	0.000
	7	0.687	446.28	0.000
	8	0.657	494.14	0.000
	9	0.660	543.03	0.000
	10	0.610	585.16	0.000
	11	0.603	626.89	0.000
	12	0.562	663.51	0.000
	13	0.538	697.47	0.000
	14	0.521	729.63	0.000
	15	0.496	759.15	0.000
	16	0.472	786.19	0.000
	17	0.458	811.99	0.000
	18	0.436	835.67	0.000
	19	0.426	858.49	0.000
	20	0.414	880.38	0.000

(a) Simulated trend stationary series

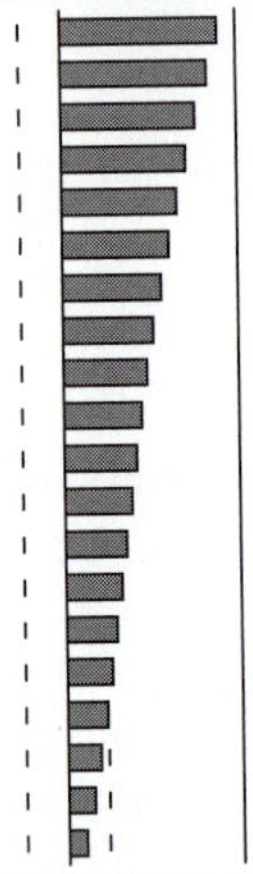

Autocorrelation		AC	Q-Stat	Prob
	1	0.947	58.364	0.000
	2	0.880	109.58	0.000
	3	0.811	153.82	0.000
	4	0.751	192.37	0.000
	5	0.696	226.09	0.000
	6	0.646	255.68	0.000
	7	0.596	281.35	0.000
	8	0.548	303.45	0.000
	9	0.502	322.32	0.000
	10	0.471	339.23	0.000
	11	0.442	354.42	0.000
	12	0.409	367.67	0.000
	13	0.373	378.96	0.000
	14	0.340	388.54	0.000
	15	0.307	396.51	0.000
	16	0.271	402.84	0.000
	17	0.238	407.82	0.000
	18	0.199	411.39	0.000
	19	0.156	413.63	0.000
	20	0.111	414.80	0.000

(b) Log of real GNP per capita

Why is this? At all lags, the variable contains a deterministic trend,

$$Y_t = \alpha + \beta t + \varepsilon_t,$$
$$Y_{t-j} = \alpha + \beta(t - j) + \varepsilon_{t-j}.$$

Hence, Y_t and Y_{t-j} contain a common deterministic trend that, *in the sample*, yields an apparent strong correlation between the variables even though their disturbances are uncorrelated, $E(\varepsilon_t \varepsilon_{t-j}) = 0$. This is just an example of spurious correlation arising from common trends, a phenomenon we discuss in Chapter 3.

The conclusion is an important one: Sample autocorrelations give a correct portrayal of temporal dependence only for stationary series, not for nonstationary ones. The reason is that the SACF uses the sample mean $\overline{Y}$ to estimate the mean of the process. In doing this, it implicitly assumes stationarity and thus that the mean $E(Y_t)$ is constant, therefore missing the trend in the data.

This is not quite the same thing as saying that the SACF of a nonstationary series has no useful interpretation. In the exploratory analysis of time series data, a gradually declining correlogram may be an indicator that the series is nonstationary—although of course this conclusion can often be reached simply by direct inspection of the series.

Practitioner's Tip: **Sample autocorrelations for nonstationary series**

Sample autocorrelations give a correct portrayal of temporal dependence only for stationary series, not for nonstationary ones. A gradually declining correlogram may indicate that a series is nonstationary rather than accurately describing its autocorrelation properties.

This point can be made using real-world data instead of a simulated series. Consider Nelson and Plosser's per capita GNP series in Figure 15.5. Taking logarithms to treat the constant growth trend, the sample autocorrelations are shown in Figure 15.7(b). Notice that they exhibit a pattern of gradual decline very similar to the simulated series. This gradual decline arises, we now understand, from the trend in the series; beyond serving as an indicator of nonstationarity, the correlogram does not usefully describe the temporal dependence in the series.

Detrending Economic Time Series

The obvious question prompted by these examples is: How can a trending time series be analyzed so as to correctly reveal the true nature of its autocorrelation? In the case of trend stationary processes the answer is clear: by studying, not the raw series, but its deviations from trend.

The only way to obtain these deviations is to estimate the trend; this is easily done using least squares regression. The least squares residuals are then the measured deviations from trend—the **detrended** series—from which sample autocorrelations can be computed.

Let us use both our simulated series and Nelson and Plosser's per capita GNP series to illustrate this idea of detrending.

The simulated series is by construction white noise around the deterministic trend $4.605 + 0.04879t$. Suppose, however, that we did not know these population values of the coefficients and instead had to estimate them. Least squares estimation of this trend line yields

$$Y_t = 4.662 + 0.04827t + e_t.$$

A correlogram computed from the residuals e_t is shown in Figure 15.8(a). Notice that this is much more like the theoretical ACF $\rho_j = 0$ given in equation (15.10) than it is like the SACF of the variable in raw form shown in Figure 15.7(a). This is, of course, as it should be if the correlogram is to offer a useful indication of the true nature of the autocorrelation. None of the sample autocorrelations exceed the confidence bounds, and the p-values for the Q statistics fail to reject the hypothesis that the series is generated by a white noise process.

The Nelson-Plosser real GNP per capita series, when we examine the curvature exhibited in Figure 15.5, suggests an underlying process of constant growth that should be treated by estimating the trend in log-lin form:

$$\log Y_t = 6.9842 + 0.0181t + e_t. \tag{15.17}$$

A correlogram computed from the residuals e_t is shown in Figure 15.8(b). In contrast to the simulated series, it shows significant autocorrelation at a number of lags; the Q statistics clearly reject the null hypothesis of white noise. This is, of course, what we expect: GNP exhibits temporal dependence due to, for

FIGURE 15.8

The correlograms of detrended series.

Autocorrelation		AC	Q-Stat	Prob
ı ▌ ı	1	−0.056	0.3251	0.569
ı ı	2	0.023	0.3824	0.826
ı ı	3	0.030	0.4761	0.924
ı ı	4	0.009	0.4838	0.975
ı ▐ ı	5	−0.088	1.3194	0.933
ı ▐ ı	6	−0.081	2.0285	0.917

Autocorrelation		AC	Q-Stat	Prob
ı ▆▆▆▆▆	1	0.865	48.674	0.000
ı ▆▆▆	2	0.650	76.598	0.000
ı ▆▆	3	0.426	88.829	0.000
ı ▆	4	0.242	92.824	0.000
ı ▌ ı	5	0.113	93.707	0.000
ı ▎ ı	6	0.043	93.836	0.000

(a) Simulated trend stationary series   (b) Log of real GNP per capita

example, business cycles. This pattern of autocorrelation is, however, entirely different from that of the raw series in Figure 15.7(b).

These examples of detrending have used least squares to estimate linear trends. However, it is clear that the same idea can be applied to any specification for the deterministic trend: quadratic, one involving a structural break (when the break point is known), or otherwise.

That detrending is an appropriate first step in analyzing trending variables assumes, of course, that they are in fact generated by a trend stationary process. However, a trend stationary model is not the only way in which trending variables can be generated, as we begin to investigate next.

EXERCISES

15.11 ⊙ **np.dat** Nelson and Plosser's real GNP per capita series is available in the file **np.dat**. Use it to do the following.

(a) Obtain the SACF up to 20 lags for the raw series. Does it replicate the correlogram of Figure 15.7(b)?

(b) Detrend the series by estimating a log-lin trend line and saving the residuals. How must time be defined in order to replicate the regression (15.17)?

(c) Obtain the SACF up to six lags for the detrended series. Does it replicate the correlogram of Figure 15.8(b)?

(d) Suppose you detrend the series using a different definition of time. Are the sample autocorrelations of the residuals affected?

15.12 ⊙ **jones.dat** In Chapter 6 we have studied Jones's per capita GDP series, which spanned a longer sample period than the Nelson-Plosser series: 1880–1987. Jones's series may be generated from his real GDP and population data in the file **jones.dat**.

(a) Generate Jones's real GDP per capita series and obtain the SACF up to 20 lags. What interpretation do you attach to this correlogram?

(b) Detrend the series by estimating a log-lin trend line and saving the residuals. How does your trend line compare with the one that is estimated in Example 2 of Chapter 6?

(c) Obtain the SACF up to six lags for the detrended series. What interpretation do you attach to this correlogram? Is the pattern of temporal dependence similar to that revealed by the Nelson-Plosser series or quite different?

15.6 Nonstationarity in the Variance: A Random Walk

Let us consider an example of a stochastic process that has a constant mean, but is nonstationary because its variance is not time invariant. The most important example of such a stochastic process is the **random walk** model

$$Y_t = Y_{t-1} + \varepsilon_t. \tag{15.18}$$

The period-by-period changes in a random walk are white noise,

$$\Delta Y_t = \varepsilon_t.$$

Hence, in contrast to a trend stationary process, which is stationary around a deterministic trend, a random walk is stationary in its differences; it is an example of a **difference stationary** process.

We first encountered the random walk model in Chapter 2. A simulated random walk series is given in Figure 2.15(c). Figure 15.9 shows an ensemble of three simulated random walk time series (the middle series, shown by the solid line, is from Figure 2.15(c)). All begin with the initial value $Y_0 = 4.605$ and are then generated for periods $t = 1$ through $t = 100$ using Gaussian white noise with $\sigma^2 = 0.25$; the middle series (solid line) uses the white noise realization of Figure 15.2. Examining an ensemble serves as a reminder that very different time series realizations can arise from a given stochastic process. Inspecting Figure 15.9 shows that what these realizations have in common is the characteristic meandering or wandering behavior that is the source of the name *random walk*.

The Random Walk Model of Stock Prices

As we discuss briefly in Chapter 2, the classic application of the random walk model is to stock prices. It is noted there that asset prices tend to be roughly lognormally distributed, and so it makes sense to work in terms of the logarithm of the stock price: $Y_t \equiv \log P_t$. The random walk model (15.18) says that (the

FIGURE 15.9

An ensemble of three random walk time series.

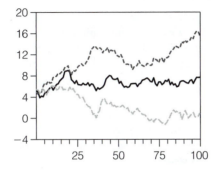

log of) today's price is just (the log of) yesterday's price plus a random shock. Equivalently, the model may be written

$$Y_t - Y_{t-1} = \log P_t - \log P_{t-1} = \varepsilon_t.$$

Recall that $\Delta \log P_t$ is the continuously compounded growth rate of the price—the continuously compounded rate of return. Hence, another way of looking at the random walk model is that it says the rate of return is white noise.

The proposition that a variable is white noise is, of course, capable of being tested empirically, something we learned how to do in Section 15.3.3 using the Q statistic. Example 3 shows that the white noise hypothesis is not rejected for Fama's IBM returns series.[12]

The model as stated is actually a slight oversimplification of the true behavior of stock prices. Over time, the price of most stocks tends to drift upward, so that the mean rate of return is positive instead of zero. For example, we have noted in our discussion of Figure 15.1(b) that the average monthly rate of return for IBM was 2.12%. That is, a more accurate model of stock returns would be one of white noise around a constant mean rather than white noise around zero. This more accurate model—known as a random walk with drift—is studied in the next section. This modification of the model does not alter the implication that stock returns are white noise, and so for the moment we focus on the version of the random walk model in which there is an absence of drift.

There is another important qualification to what we have said. Strictly speaking, the random walk model assumes more about asset prices than is really necessary to capture the idea that returns are unrelated over time. Because ε_t is an i.i.d. disturbance, the random walk model has the implication that the distribution of returns is unchanging over time—a needlessly strong assumption that is not necessary for returns to be unrelated. For this reason, finance theorists use weaker statistical models to describe asset prices—called **fair-game** and **martingale** models—that capture the essentials of the random walk idea without requiring its needlessly strong assumptions. For our purposes, however, these technical distinctions are unimportant, and we shall continue to use the term random walk in the discussion that follows.

The Efficient Markets Hypothesis

What is the basis for believing that stock returns are unrelated over time? The random walk model is the statistical implication of the famous **efficient markets hypothesis,** which says that all available information is fully reflected in securities prices. Because there are different ways of defining just what is meant by "all available information," there are several variants of the efficient markets hypothesis.

---

[12] Exercise 15.7 shows that this is also true of the Xerox series. Although these examples and exercises were done with simple returns, you have found in Exercise 15.6 that the results are not materially affected by the use of continuously compounded returns.

Without getting into the details of these alternative definitions, the basic idea is as follows. A stock's price is determined by the interaction of supply and demand in the market. Purchasers and sellers of the stock make their trading decisions on the basis of information available to them. At least some of these market participants have knowledge of the firm, either by studying its operations or through direct acquaintance as principals, employees, customers, or suppliers of the firm. Hence, the price established in the market reflects this information.

It follows that when the price changes it can only be due to the arrival of new information. New information is by definition a surprise—otherwise it would not be new—and so price changes are unpredictably random, like white noise.

Like all simple but profound ideas, it requires some thought to become comfortable with the random walk model of stock prices. There is a natural tendency to think that it contradicts the common sense that stock prices must depend on real factors such as the future profitability of the firm, market and industry conditions, and the state of the economy. Surely we should make stock selection decisions by studying the details of a firm's operations and finding stocks that seem underpriced in relation to the firm's likely future prospects. The random walk model seems to ignore this common sense.

In fact, there is no contradiction. Certainly it is the case that a firm's stock price reflects its prospects for future profitability; more specifically, some present discounted value of its expected future stream of dividend payments. The point is that in an efficient market all information relevant to gauging this future profitability is already embedded in the price. At the margin, there are no profits to be made from additional research into identifying underpriced stocks. Statistically this is manifested as price changes being purely random. An investor attempting to forecast tomorrow's price cannot do any better than use today's price, which reflects all relevant information; the difference between the two prices is just unpredictable white noise.

This reasoning has important implications for investment practice. One implication is that an investor with no knowledge whatsoever is in just as good a position to forecast future prices as someone who has studied the operations of the firm. Research on the firm is of no advantage because in an efficient market prices already reflect that information.

A second implication is that there is also no point in studying historical patterns in stock prices. The most recently observed price reflects all information relevant to the firm's future prospects and so is the best forecast of the price at any point in the future.[13] Its historical evolution is irrelevant.

---

[13] This assumes that the mean historical return is zero. If the mean historical return is nonzero, then the optimal forecast marks up the most recent observation by this mean historical return. This is made explicit in the next section, where we consider a random walk with drift. However, this does not change the essential conclusion of the random walk model that historical patterns in stock movements are not useful in forecasting future movements.

These implications are important because they conflict with much applied investment practice. Elton and Gruber (1987, pp. 366–368) have summarized the mindset that tends to dominate the investment community.

> Have you ever looked at a chart showing prices of a security or a market index over time? Most people who do start to see patterns. They look at a chart showing the S&P index over time. Suddenly, they notice that the prices were high every seven years. Then they notice that there is an exception to this pattern: in the third period the peak does not occur until the tenth year. They then notice that after each peak the index declines over 30%. With rising excitement, they realize that if they had sold their portfolio every seven years (except in the third cycle where it takes ten years) and bought when the index declines by at least 30%, they would make substantial money. A theory of stock market behavior is born. If the individual is a manager of a mutual fund and vocal, then the theory will likely be discussed in the financial press. The latest copy of *Business Week* will have an article on the seven-year cycle. A reader will learn that the third seven-year cycle takes ten years because the market is tired after its earlier thrusts.
>
> The authors have visited mutual fund managers that managed billion dollar portfolios on the basis of these patterns. One was particularly memorable. The fund had a dozen clerks that plotted the prices through time of the securities the fund owned or were considering owning. In addition, they plotted the values of various market and economic indexes over time. The fund maintained a war room in the shape of a theater. In the war room was installed an extremely efficient procedure for flashing the charts of security prices on a screen in the front of the war room. The fund managers would meet every day and examine the charts of the securities in which they were considering investing. The discussion concerned the patterns they saw. Had the price of a security broken through a price it had not previously obtained? Was the upward movement slowing? Was it at the end of a cycle? Funds were managed by seeing patterns in past price series and buying and selling on that basis.[14]

Given the gulf between the random walk model and much applied investment practice, it is natural to ask what empirical evidence supports the random walk theory. We have already noted that statistical tests, such as our application of the Q statistic to IBM returns in Example 3, typically fail to reject the random walk hypothesis. However, perhaps the most compelling support is not formal statistical testing but, instead, the well-documented failure of actively managed stock portfolios to outperform market indices. The classic guide to personal investment that develops this theme is the book by Malkiel (1999), *A Random Walk down Wall Street*, who finds that

> ...the evidence from several studies is remarkably uniform. Investors have done no better with the average mutual fund than they could have done by purchasing and holding an unmanaged broad stock index. In other words, over long periods of time

---

[14] Copyright ©1987 by John Wiley & Sons, Inc. This material is used by permission of John Wiley & Sons, Inc.

TABLE 15.1   Mutual Funds versus the Market Index: Total Return for the 10 Years Ending 30 June 1998

	Cumulative	Annual Rate
Standard & Poor's 500 Index	+448.88	+18.56
Average general equity fund	+313.05	+15.24

Source: Reprinted from the *Journal of Monetary Economics* 10, C.R. Nelson and C.I. Plosser "Trends and Random Walks in Macroeconomic Times Series," pp. 147–150, © 1982, with permission from Elsevier.

mutual-fund portfolios have not outperformed randomly selected groups of stocks. Although funds may have very good records for certain short time periods, there is generally no consistency to superior performance. (Malkiel 1999, pp. 178–179)

Indeed not only has active management not added value, on average mutual funds have significantly underperformed market indices. Table 15.1 compares returns from the average American general equity fund against those from Standard & Poor's 500-stock index. In the 10-year period ending 30 June 1998 the index yielded an annual return more than three percentage points in excess of the typical fund. Cumulated over the decade, an investor's wealth would have been over one-third greater had it been invested in the unmanaged index.

Recognition that active management does not add value has led to the creation and widespread use of index mutual funds. Unavailable as recently as 1975, according to Malkiel index funds now account for more than $1 trillion of invested capital.

Integrated Variables

With this background on efficient markets to motivate our interest in the random walk model, let us turn to the formal analysis of that model.

Some useful insights into the behavior of a random walk variable can be obtained by expressing it in terms of the history of white noise shocks that have generated it. This is done using the method of recursive substitution, which we first used in Chapter 6.

Because the random walk model (15.18) describes the determination of Y_t at any point in time, it can be lagged back to period $t = 1$:

$$Y_{t-1} = Y_{t-2} + \varepsilon_{t-1}$$

$$Y_{t-2} = Y_{t-3} + \varepsilon_{t-2}$$

$$\vdots$$

$$Y_1 = Y_0 + \varepsilon_1.$$

Think of Y_0 as a presample initial value of the series. From this starting point, the period-by-period white noise shocks $\varepsilon_1, \varepsilon_2, \ldots, \varepsilon_n$ generate the sample observations $Y_1, Y_2, \ldots, Y_n$.

The method of recursive substitution is the repeated substitution of these successive lags into the original model (15.18). Substituting the first, then the second, and so on, yields

$$Y_t = Y_{t-1} + \varepsilon_t$$
$$= Y_{t-2} + \varepsilon_t + \varepsilon_{t-1}$$
$$= Y_{t-3} + \varepsilon_t + \varepsilon_{t-1} + \varepsilon_{t-2}$$
$$\vdots$$
$$= Y_0 + \varepsilon_t + \varepsilon_{t-1} + \varepsilon_{t-2} + \cdots + \varepsilon_1$$
$$= Y_0 + \sum_{j=0}^{t-1} \varepsilon_{t-j}. \tag{15.19}$$

This shows that Y_t at any point in time may be thought of as the historical accumulation of shocks that have occurred up to that point, added to its initial value. Today's stock price, for example, is the total of the day-to-day shocks it has experienced since its initial public offering.

Unlike stocks, many variables have no obvious start date. In this case, the method of recursive substitution can be carried on indefinitely, so that a variable is best thought of as the cumulation of shocks going back into the indefinite past:

$$Y_t = \sum_{j=0}^{\infty} \varepsilon_{t-j}. \tag{15.20}$$

This historical accumulation of shocks is of fundamental importance to a random walk series and differentiates it fundamentally from a trend stationary series. Compare the random walk (15.19) with our model of white noise around a constant mean,

$$Y_t = \alpha + \varepsilon_t. \tag{15.21}$$

The latter is a trend stationary model in the sense that the deterministic trend is the particularly simple one of a horizontal central line α. These two models might seem to indicate that the two variables are similar in their behavior: Both consist of random variation around a horizontal central line. In the case of the random walk (15.19), this central line is the starting value Y_0; in the case of the white noise process, it is the mean α. That their behavior is in fact very different is illustrated by a comparison of Figures 15.2(a) and 15.9. Figure 15.9 showed three random walks; recall that the middle series (solid line) is generated using the same white noise realization as that in Figure 15.2(a). In contrast to the trend stationary series, the random walk evolves in a meandering manner—it can wander arbitrarily far from its initial value.

The reason for this is revealed by the previous expressions. According to equations (15.19) or (15.20), at any time point t the random walk depends on the *entire history* of accumulated shocks via the sum $\sum \varepsilon_{t-j}$. The trend stationary variable (15.21), on the other hand, depends only on the *current* shock ε_t; the history of shocks prior to t is irrelevant.

A random walk is an example of an **integrated** variable. An integrated variable is one that is determined as a function of the sum of historical shocks that generate it. The term comes from calculus, where an integral is the limit of a sum (of discrete areas under a curve), just as equation (15.20) is defined mathematically as the limit of a sum. Let us denote the integrated expression by ST_t,

$$ ST_t \equiv \sum_{j=0}^{t-1} \varepsilon_{t-j} $$

because it is the mathematical representation of the stochastic trend of the difference stationary process. Recall that the term stochastic trend is introduced in Section 2.7 and appears again in Section 6.2.2. It comes from the fact that the disturbance can—indeed, in the long run must—generate a trend in Y, as we see shortly. By contrast, the trend in a trend stationary process is due entirely to its deterministic component, the stochastic disturbance merely generating variation around that deterministic trend.

Although the random walk (15.19) and the model of white noise around a constant mean (15.21) may appear formally similar, especially because Y_0 and α play the similar role of determining a horizontal central line, a random walk is *not* trend stationary. This is because this integrated component—the stochastic trend—is nonstationary, something we will establish momentarily by deriving its variance.

The Mean and Variance of a Random Walk

The interpretation of a random walk as an integrated variable makes it easy to use the laws of mathematical expectation and variance to obtain its mean and variance.

Mean   Treating the initial value Y_0 as a numerical constant, taking the mathematical expectation of equation (15.19) shows that the mean of Y_t is just that initial value:

$$ E(Y_t) = Y_0 + E(\varepsilon_t) + E(\varepsilon_{t-1}) + E(\varepsilon_{t-2}) + \cdots + E(\varepsilon_1) = Y_0. \qquad (15.22) $$

This is the formal basis for the statement that the best forecast of a random walk variable at any point in the future is just its most recently observed value. (We can always regard the most recently observed value as the initial value Y_0, with Y_t then evolving into the future according to the model.) In forecasting a future stock price, we cannot do any better than use today's price.

Of course today's price changes on a day-by-day basis, and so this mean is constantly changing as time evolves. However at a given point in time the most recently observed price Y_0 is a constant that is the base for forecasting into the future. Paradoxically, the mean of a random walk is time invariant, despite the fact that this mean will be different tomorrow.

Variance   The consequence of Y_t being integrated is that there is nothing to prevent it from wandering arbitrarily far from its initial value. This becomes apparent when the variance is examined. Applying the laws of variance to the linear expression (15.19) yields

$$V(Y_t) = V(\varepsilon_t) + V(\varepsilon_{t-1}) + V(\varepsilon_{t-2}) + \cdots + V(\varepsilon_1) = t\sigma^2. \qquad (15.23)$$

That is, the variance becomes larger with time, ultimately becoming infinite as time advances into the indefinite future and $t \to \infty$. The more time passes, the greater the potential that a random walk variable will wander away from its initial value Y_0. Although the best forecast of a stock's price at any point in the future may be today's price, future prices can nevertheless stray arbitrarily far from the currently observed price.

Because the variance of a random walk changes with time, it is not time invariant. Although from the perspective of any given point in time the mean of a random walk is constant, the process is nonstationary due to its variance. In general, integrated variables are nonstationary because, as this special case of a random walk illustrates, the variance changes with time.

Random Walks Often Trend Ex Post

If a variable follows a random walk, its expected change is zero:

$$E(\Delta Y_t) = E(\varepsilon_t) = 0. \qquad (15.24)$$

Thus the variable has no systematic tendency to move predominantly in one direction. Nevertheless, because the variable can wander arbitrarily far from its starting value, a realized random walk time series will often appear to trend. Consider again Figure 15.9. The three series are realizations of the same stochastic process, a random walk based on $\varepsilon_t \sim$ n.i.d.$(0, 0.25)$. They differ only because they use different white noise realizations. Yet the top series trends upward and the bottom series downward. The nonstationarity of the variance manifests itself as a trend in the realized series. To use the terminology of an economist, random walks have the remarkable property that although there is no tendency to trend ex ante, they often exhibit a trend ex post.

Indeed, we can say something even stronger. Not only will a random walk observed over some limited sample period often appear to trend, but in the long run it *must* trend. For as time advances into the indefinite future, the infinite variance means that there is a tendency for the variable to wander ever further away from its starting value. This property can be used to dismiss random walks as appropriate specifications for economic variables that cannot evolve in this way, such as the unemployment rate or interest rates. This point has been made by Cochrane (1991, p. 208):[15]

---

[15] The assertion that interest rates must be stationary is premature. There is an intermediate class of stochastic processes known as **fractionally integrated processes** that can have the property of having an infinite variance, and thus being nonstationary, and yet be mean reverting. Interest rates are sometimes thought to be fractionally integrated. However, fractionally integrated processes are beyond the scope of

continued

... interest rates are almost certainly stationary in levels. Interest rates were about 6% in ancient Babylon; they are about 6% now. The chances of a process with a random walk component displaying this behavior are infinitesimal.

Pitfalls in the Analysis of Random Walk Time Series

The fact that random walks often appear to trend has important implications for data analysis. Suppose you were given a random walk time series such as the top or bottom series in Figure 15.9, but were unaware of the distinction between trend and difference stationary processes. Observing the apparent trend, you might be tempted to analyze the data using the methods appropriate to a trend stationary series; that is, by estimating a linear trend. Such a least squares trend line fitted to the top series yields

$$\hat{Y}_t = 7.39 + \underset{(11.82)}{0.070}\, t, \qquad R^2 = 0.588.$$

One fitted to the bottom series yields

$$\hat{Y}_t = 5.53 - \underset{(-17.10)}{0.064}\, t, \qquad R^2 = 0.749.$$

Furthermore, a mechanical interpretation of the usual regression statistics would appear to support this approach: Both R^2s are substantial and the t ratios (given in parentheses) suggest a statistically significant effect. However, it is clear that these findings are highly misleading; one regression suggests a significant positive dependence on time and the other a significant negative dependence. The difference is just the result of which white noise realization happens to have occurred. Clearly this approach to data analysis tells us nothing about the underlying process that has in fact generated these variables because we know that, by construction, this underlying process has *no* tendency to move predominantly in one direction—that is, there is no trend in the population model.

Practitioner's Tip: **Regression on a time trend**

Least squares regression of a time series variable on a time trend yields R^2 and t statistics that are unreliable. In particular, the t statistic does not have its usual distribution.

This explains why, in the analysis of the Jones (1995) per capita GDP series in Exercise 6.10 of Section 6.2.6, least squares is used only to obtain coefficient point estimates but not for hypothesis testing.

You might wonder whether the misleading findings are not just the chance outcome of the particular random walk series that have been presented in Figure 15.9.

this book. As well, of course, the level of interest rates may trend in the short run due to an acceleration in inflation or undergo structural shifts in response to changes in monetary policy regimes.

How often will random walks appear to be well explained by deterministic trends? Nelson and Kang (1984) examined this in a Monte Carlo study. They found that, for a sample size of $n = 100$ and a nominal 5% significance level, t tests reject the null hypothesis of a zero slope 87% of the time. Furthermore, such regressions typically produce an R^2 of approximately 0.44, appearing to suggest that a substantial portion of the behavior of the variable is explained by a dependence of its mean on time. In fact, of course, *none* of its variation is due to a dependence of its mean on time because, as equation (15.22) reveals, its mean is not a function of time.

In producing an artificially high R^2, least squares is mistakenly attributing much of the variation in the series to the deterministic trend instead of the disturbance. In overstating the importance of the deterministic trend, least squares understates the importance of the disturbance. Nelson and Kang (1984, p. 80) found that "Residuals from a regression of a random walk on time will have a variance that is, on average, only about 14% of the true stochastic variance of the series."

Finally, suppose we attempt to use the residuals from a least squares trend line to study the autocorrelation properties of the series by, say, computing their sample autocorrelations or testing for whether the residuals are white noise. Although this would be appropriate if the series were trend stationary, clearly it tells us nothing about the true autocorrelation properties of the random walk. The residuals from the least squares trend line will tend to be autocorrelated, when we know by construction that the random walk is in fact uncorrelated in its changes. The autocorrelation properties of detrended random walk series have been studied rigorously by Nelson and Kang (1981) in an article entitled "Spurious Periodicity in Inappropriately Detrended Time Series."[16] They found that

> ... inappropriate detrending of time series will tend to produce apparent evidence of periodicity which is not in any meaningful sense a property of the underlying system. ... the dynamics of econometric models estimated from such data may well be wholly or in part an artifact of the trend removal procedure. (1981, p. 742)

The Nelson and Kang findings are an important example of the statistical principle that we first articulated in Section 2.7: Inference is conditional on the model. Statistical techniques that may be useful in one context—in this case, least squares regression estimators applied to trend stationary data—may be of no value when applied to data generated by a different model, in this case a random walk.

Spurious Regression Revisited

There is another respect in which conventional statistical techniques may be misleading when applied to difference stationary series, one that relates to studying relationships between them. Section 3.2.2 cites the famous study of Granger and

---

[16] Nelson and Kang proceeded primarily on the basis of Monte Carlo simulation. Relevant analytical results are provided by Durlauf and Phillips (1988).

FIGURE 15.10

A random walk:
Sample realization
and forecast. The
optimal forecast is
the most recently
observed value.
A shock alters all
future forecasts.

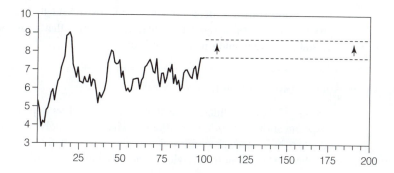

Newbold (1974), who showed that independent random walks are subject to the spurious regression phenomenon—they often seem to be related. Our finding that random walks commonly exhibit trends ex post makes it easy to see the reason for this: The trends will make the series appear to be related. Consider, for example, the upper and lower random walks depicted in Figure 15.9. The sample correlation between them is $r = -0.641$. A regression of one on the other yields a t statistic of -8.27, which, interpreted mechanically, would appear to indicate a highly significant inverse relationship. In reality, of course, the two series are completely unrelated; by construction the period-by-period changes in the variables are statistically independent because the simulations are based on different white noise realizations.

The likelihood of finding spurious correlation between independent random walks is greater the larger the sample size because the longer the variables evolve, the more likely it is that they will wander away from their initial central line, imparting a trend to the realized series. In an important theoretical contribution that paved the way for much subsequent analysis of difference stationary variables, Phillips (1986) formalized this intuition by showing that as $n \rightarrow \infty$ random walks continue to be correlated and the t statistics relating them grow ever larger.[17] That is, contrary to the usual intuition that more data give more reliable results, instead the problems of interpretation of the standard statistics only become worse with the sample size.

Conclusions

The integrated nature of random walks means that their behavior is fundamentally different from trend stationary variables. In contrast to a trend stationary variable, the optimal forecast of a random walk is just its most recently observed value; its historical evolution is irrelevant. It follows that a different most recently observed value changes all forecasts. This is depicted in Figure 15.10, which uses the middle random walk shown in Figure 15.9. A different shock in period 100 shifts all future forecasts. This property is in sharp contrast to what we have seen is true of a trend stationary process based on white noise, where a shock does not alter forecasts.

Because of its fundamentally different behavior, the application to a random walk of a statistical analysis appropriate to a trend stationary variable—detrending

[17] Phillips's analysis was not limited to random walks, but applied to more general classes of integrated processes that we study in Chapter 17.

via the estimation of a deterministic trend—will lead to faulty inferences. The appropriate means of analysis is instead to recognize that a random walk is difference stationary and study it in its differences.

> **Practitioner's Tip: Fluctuations and trends**
>
> The study of short-run fluctuations in economic variables depends on the correct specification of their long-run trends. Mistakenly applying a trend stationary model to a difference stationary series, or the reverse, will lead to flawed conclusions about the short-term behavior of the variable.

These conclusions about a random walk have arisen from an examination of its mean and variance. Other key properties relate to its impulse response function. Before turning to this, it is useful to consider a more general random walk process.

15.7   Nonstationarity in the Mean and Variance: A Random Walk with Drift

There is one important feature of stock prices that the simple random walk model (15.18) fails to capture: Over extended periods stocks usually appreciate in value. This tendency for prices to drift upward may be captured by modifying the random walk model as

$$Y_t = \beta + Y_{t-1} + \varepsilon_t.$$

This is a **random walk with drift;** β is called the drift parameter. In contrast to (15.24), the expected change in the variable is now

$$E(\Delta Y_t) = \beta + E(\varepsilon_t) = \beta,$$

so that the series can gravitate upward (positive drift: $\beta > 0$) or downward (negative drift: $\beta < 0$) over time.

The random walk of the previous section was the special case of $\beta = 0$, which we will refer to as the zero-drift random walk model. Although a zero-drift random walk can exhibit a trend ex post—and indeed in the long run must do so due to its infinite variance—ex ante it is as likely to wander in one direction as the other. By contrast, when a random walk has drift it is more likely to wander in the direction determined by its drift.

As a model of stock prices, a random walk with drift may be reinterpreted as

$$\Delta \log P_t = \beta + \varepsilon_t,$$

so that the stock's rate of return is white noise around a mean β. If $\beta > 0$ then this mean return is positive and the stock price drifts upward over time, the normal

FIGURE 15.11

An ensemble of three drifting random walk time series.

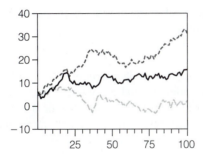

circumstance. For example, in our discussion of Figure 15.1(b) we note that the average monthly return for IBM was $\hat{\beta} = 2.12\%$. Of course, a positive drift does not imply that the price increases in *every* period; a sufficiently large negative shock ε_t could swamp the positive drift, resulting in a price decline and a negative return in that period.

Because white noise around a constant mean is stationary, a random walk with drift is stationary in its differences; like a zero-drift random walk, it is said to be difference stationary.

We first encountered the random walk with drift model in Chapter 2. A simulated series is given in Figure 2.15(b). An ensemble of three drifting random walk time series is shown in Figure 15.11; the middle series, shown by the solid line, is that from Figure 2.15(b). The series have been generated using $Y_0 = 4.605$, $\beta = 0.04879$, and the three white noise realizations used in Figure 15.9. As we have emphasized, the introduction of a drift parameter typically imparts a trend. We say "typically" because, depending on the particular realization of white noise shocks that occurred, it is possible that the drift may not be evident in the realized series. This is illustrated by the bottom series in Figure 15.11, which is generated using the same drift parameter $\beta = 0.04879$ as the other two, but in which this drift is not apparent because of the particular shocks that happen to have occurred.

Testing for an Absence of Drift

Note, then, that it can easily be the case that a zero-drift random walk trends in such a way as to misleadingly suggest the presence of drift; conversely, a nonzero drift may not be evident in the realized series.

Practitioner's Tip: **Random walks and drift**

Simple inspection of a random walk series is not a reliable means of judging whether drift is present.

However, a formal means of testing for the absence of drift is readily available. The random walk with drift model

$$\Delta Y_t = \beta + \varepsilon_t$$

is, despite the change in notation and definition of the variable, nothing more than the model (15.3) of white noise around a constant mean, which is formally the same as the model (2.15) of Chapter 2. Hence, a test of $\beta = 0$, the null hypothesis of zero drift, is just a standard t test using the sample mean, the first and simplest hypothesis test discussed in this book (in Section 2.5).

EXAMPLE 6

 fama.dat

We have found using the Q test that the IBM returns series is serially uncorrelated, so that the stock price behaves as a random walk. Does this random walk exhibit drift?

SOLUTION

The point estimate of the drift parameter is the sample mean return of $\hat{\beta} = 0.0212$. The issue to be addressed is whether this point estimate is significantly different from zero. The calculation of the sample variance of the returns series using the formula (2.7) yields a standard deviation of $s = 0.0474$ and hence an estimated standard error of $s_{\hat{\beta}} = s/\sqrt{n} = 0.0474/\sqrt{60} = 0.00612$. The t statistic (2.23) is, evaluated under the null hypothesis $\beta = 0$,

$$t = \frac{\hat{\beta}}{s_{\hat{\beta}}} = \frac{0.0212}{0.00612} = 3.46.$$

Comparing against the tabulated values of the t distribution with $n - 1 = 59$ degrees of freedom, the hypothesis of an absence of drift is rejected at conventional significance levels. Hence, the IBM stock price behaves as a drifting random walk.[18]

It is important to note that this test procedure is only valid because the disturbance ε_t is white noise—it takes the classical i.i.d. form that we originally discuss in Chapter 2. It is our use of the Q statistic that establishes that the disturbance can reasonably be regarded as being of this form. If this were not the case—had the Q statistic rejected the white noise hypothesis—then this test would be inappropriate. Addressing the question of whether the mean of the variable is nonzero would instead require that the autocorrelation around that mean be treated. A class of models that does this is the subject of Chapter 16.

---

[18] This is the same hypothesis test that we perform in Example 13 of Chapter 2. The slight difference in the numerical values arises because there we use the continuously compounded returns $\log(1 + R_t)$. Throughout the present chapter we follow Fama's (1976) original practice of using the approximation $\log(1 + R_t) \approx R_t$ and working in terms of simple returns. As a comparison of the two examples indicates, the substantive empirical findings are not affected by the definition of returns.

The Integrated Nature of the Process

With this background, let us turn to a formal analysis of a drifting random walk.

A random walk with drift is an integrated process. As before, this is revealed by the method of recursive substitution, which yields, as a generalization of equation (15.19),

$$
\begin{aligned}
Y_t &= Y_{t-1} + \beta + \varepsilon_t \\
&= Y_{t-2} + 2\beta + \varepsilon_t + \varepsilon_{t-1} \\
&= Y_{t-3} + 3\beta + \varepsilon_t + \varepsilon_{t-1} + \varepsilon_{t-2} \\
&\vdots \\
&= \underbrace{Y_0 + \beta t}_{\text{DT}_t} + \underbrace{\sum_{j=0}^{t-1} \varepsilon_{t-j}}_{\text{ST}_t} .
\end{aligned}
$$

(15.25)

As the braces emphasize, this shows that Y_t can be interpreted as the sum of a deterministic trend $\text{DT}_t \equiv Y_0 + \beta t$ and a stochastic trend $\text{ST}_t \equiv \sum \varepsilon_{t-j}$. This generalizes the analogous equation of the earlier zero-drift case: In the special case of $\beta = 0$, this deterministic trend reduces to the earlier Y_0. The stochastic trend, again denoted ST_t, is the same as previously. As before, it reveals that the value a random walk takes on today depends on the sum of the entire history of shocks.

In the previous case of a zero-drift random walk, any trend exhibited by the variable is due entirely to its stochastic trend ST_t. By contrast, the trend exhibited by a random walk with drift is due both to a deterministic component DT_t arising from the drift β and a stochastic component arising from the integrated role of the disturbance, the stochastic trend ST_t.

As a more economical notation for the stochastic trend, we sometimes denote it by v_t:

$$
v_t = \text{ST}_t = \sum_{j=0}^{t-1} \varepsilon_{t-j}.
$$

(15.26)

Interpreting the initial value Y_0 as a constant α, equation (15.25) may be expressed as

$$
Y_t = \alpha + \beta t + v_t.
$$

(15.27)

As in the zero-drift case, this historical accumulation of shocks is of fundamental importance to the series and differentiates it fundamentally from a trend stationary series. Equation (15.27) is especially suited for comparison with our model of a trend stationary process,

$$
Y_t = \alpha + \beta t + \varepsilon_t.
$$

(15.28)

The two equations might seem to indicate that the two variables are similar in their behavior: Both consist of random variation around a linear trend. In the case of the random walk (15.25), this is the variation v_t around the linear trend $Y_0 + \beta t$; in the case of the trend stationary process, it is the variation ε_t around the deterministic trend $\alpha + \beta t$. That their behavior is in fact very different is illustrated by a comparison of Figures 15.6 and 15.11.[19] Figure 15.11 shows three drifting random walks; the middle series (solid line) is generated using the same white noise realization as that of Figure 15.6. In contrast to the trend stationary series, the random walk evolves in a meandering manner—it can wander arbitrarily far from its linear trend.

The reason for this is revealed by expressions (15.25) and (15.28). At any time point t, the random walk depends on the entire history of accumulated shocks via the sum $\sum \varepsilon_{t-j}$. The trend stationary variable, on the other hand, depends only on the current shock ε_t; the history of shocks prior to t is irrelevant. Although the random walk with drift (15.25) and the model of white noise around a linear trend (15.28) may appear formally similar, especially because of the analogous role of the linear trends $Y_0 + \beta t$ and $\alpha + \beta t$, a random walk is *not* trend stationary. This is because the integrated component—the stochastic trend—is nonstationary, something we will establish momentarily by deriving its variance.

One way of seeing this is to note that the stochastic trend v_t is itself a zero-drift random walk. Its first difference is

$$\Delta v_t = v_t - v_{t-1}$$
$$= (\varepsilon_t + \varepsilon_{t-1} + \varepsilon_{t-2} + \cdots + \varepsilon_1) - (\varepsilon_{t-1} + \varepsilon_{t-2} + \varepsilon_{t-3} + \cdots + \varepsilon_1)$$
$$= \varepsilon_t.$$

Hence, using (15.27), another way of stating the random walk with drift model is

$$Y_t = \alpha + \beta t + v_t, \tag{15.29a}$$
$$v_t = v_{t-1} + \varepsilon_t. \tag{15.29b}$$

That is, a random walk with drift can be interpreted as a zero-drift random walk superimposed on a linear trend. The zero-drift random walk v_t has fundamentally different properties from the disturbance ε_t of the trend stationary process, as we now investigate.

The Mean and Variance of a Random Walk with Drift

The interpretation of a random walk with drift as an integrated variable makes it easy to use the laws of mathematical expectation and variance to obtain its mean and variance.

Mean Taking the mathematical expectation of (15.25), the mean is

$$E(Y_t) = Y_0 + \beta t + \sum_{j=0}^{t-1} E(\varepsilon_{t-j}) = Y_0 + \beta t.$$

---

[19] Or, equivalently, Figures 2.15(a) and 2.15(b).

The commonsense meaning of this expression is that, for a stock that is appreciating at rate β on average each period, the best one-period-ahead forecast is $Y_0 + \beta$, the best two-period-ahead forecast is $Y_0 + 2\beta$, and so on. In general the best t-period-ahead forecast is $Y_0 + \beta t$.

EXAMPLE 7   The price of a stock today is $P_0 = 100$, and historically it has increased on average at a continuously compounded annual rate of $\beta = 0.04879$. Forecast the price 1, 2, and 3 years hence.

SOLUTION   By the previous reasoning, future prices are forecast as

$$\widehat{\log P_t} = \log P_0 + \beta t.$$

Using the specified values, this trend line is

$$\log 100 + 0.04879t = 4.60517 + 0.04879t.$$

Substituting in the values $t = 1$, 2, and 3, the forecasts are as follows.

Period	Forecast of $\log P_t$	Implied forecast of P_t
1	$4.60517 + 0.04879 \times 1 = 4.65396$	105.00
2	$4.60517 + 0.04879 \times 2 = 4.70275$	110.25
3	$4.60517 + 0.04879 \times 3 = 4.75154$	115.76

The implied forecasts of P_t are, of course, just the antilogs of the forecasts of $\log P_t$.[20] The forecasted P_t values are just those from our numerical example of an exponential trend given much earlier in Tables 6.1 and 6.2.

It is now apparent why we chose the symbol β for the drift parameter: It plays much the same role in the determination of Y_t as the slope β in the deterministic trend (15.13). Both the random walk with drift and the trend stationary model (15.28) have means that are linear functions of time:

the trend stationary model has mean $\alpha + \beta t$;
the random walk with drift has mean $Y_0 + \beta t$.

In fact, starting from a base of $Y_0 = \alpha$, both models use a common trend to produce the same forecasts, as a comparison of Examples 4 and 7 reveals. However, a key difference between the two processes is that, in the case of the random walk, the base Y_0 that is used to forecast will change from period to period as new observations become available. We elaborate on this shortly.

Variance   A second important difference between the random walk with drift and the trend stationary process is their variances. The trend stationary process has constant variance σ^2 around its linear trend. In contrast, a random walk with drift has variance

$$V(Y_t) = t\sigma^2.$$

[20] Because the antilog is a nonlinear transformation, an improved forecast is given by $\exp(\widehat{\log P_t} + \sigma^2/2)$. This technical complication is neglected in our illustrative examples.

This is obtained by taking the variance of equation (15.25). Because only the last term involving the disturbances ε_{t-j} is random, the variance is the same as that for a random walk without drift.

As before, this expression shows that the variance becomes larger with time, ultimately becoming infinite as time advances into the indefinite future and $t \to \infty$. The more time passes, the greater the potential that a random walk variable wanders further from its linear trend $Y_0 + \beta t$. The implication is that, although both the random walk with drift and the trend stationary process have means given by these linear trends, the random walk with drift does not exhibit trend reversion. Unlike the trend stationary process, it can wander arbitrarily far from its linear trend for indefinite periods of time.

We have noted that in addition to this difference in their variances, there is an important difference in the linear trends of the two processes. Although from the perspective of any given initial time point 0 the trend $Y_0 + \beta t$ is constant, as a base for forecasting this mean is continually shifting. This is illustrated in the following example.

EXAMPLE 8

In Example 7 a one-period-ahead forecast of 105 is calculated. Suppose that the realized value actually occurring in period 1 turns out to be $P_1 = 103$. How does this new information affect your forecasts for periods 2 and 3, using both the trend stationary and drifting random walk models?

SOLUTION

As we have seen in Example 4, for forecasting the trend stationary model uses its mean of

$$\alpha + \beta t = 4.60517 + 0.04879t.$$

This is unaffected by the knowledge that $P_1 = 103$. Hence, the forecasts of $\log P_t$, and those implied for P_t, are the values given in that example.

By contrast, the random walk model uses the most recently observed value as a base for forecasting, which is now $P_1 = 103$. It produces τ-period-ahead forecasts by marking up this base using the mean growth rate $\beta = 0.04879$:

$$\log 103 + 0.04879\tau = 4.63473 + 0.04879\tau.$$

Forecasting $\tau = 1$ and 2 periods ahead from period 1, the forecasts for periods 2 and 3 are as follows.

Period	Forecast of $\log P_t$	Implied forecast of P_t
2	$4.63473 + 0.04879 \times 1 = 4.68352$	108.15
3	$4.63473 + 0.04879 \times 2 = 4.73231$	113.56

Comparing these forecasts with those in Example 7, here the path of forecasts is shifted down. A negative shock in period 1 has resulted in a smaller than expected realization of the variable in that period. This smaller than expected realization constitutes new information that alters the forecasts in all periods.

FIGURE 15.12

A random walk with drift: sample realization and forecast. Random walk forecasts adapt to new information; a shock shifts the forecast trajectory.

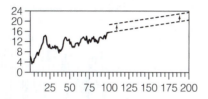

In this way the random walk model uses new realizations of the variable to shift the entire trajectory of forecasts. Because they adapt to new information in this way, random walk forecasts are said to be **adaptive.** This is illustrated in Figure 15.12, which depicts a forecast of the middle random walk shown in Figure 15.11. As in Example 8, forecasts mark up the last observed value of the series using the drift $\beta = 0.04879$. A larger shock in period 100 shifts up this linear forecast trajectory. This figure generalizes the earlier Figure 15.10 to the case of a nonzero drift.

EXERCISES

15.13 **fama.dat** Use the IBM returns series to verify the hypothesis test in Example 6.

15.14 **fama.dat** In Exercise 15.7, you used Q statistics to show that the random walk hypothesis is not rejected for Xerox. Obtain an estimate of the Xerox drift parameter. Is this drift parameter statistically significant?

15.7.1 Application: Is Velocity a Random Walk?

The velocity of circulation of money is the ratio of the volume of transactions relative to the money stock used to facilitate those transactions:

$$V = \frac{PQ}{M}.$$

It indicates the rate at which a typical dollar turns over in exchange.

We first define the concept of velocity in our discussion of the quantity theory of money in Appendix 6A. Figure 6.15 shows a time series for velocity for the United States, 1869–1970, studied by Nelson and Plosser (1982), an update and revision of data constructed by Friedman and Schwartz (1963, Chart 57, Table A-5) for the years 1869–1960. Figure 6.15 is reproduced as Figure 15.13(a); Figure 15.13(b) shows the log-differences of the series.

As we observe in our earlier inspection of this series, velocity declined substantially during this period. It was suggested by Friedman and Schwartz that this might be due to an income effect arising from the increase in living standards over the century.

FIGURE 15.13

The velocity of
money in the United
States, 1869–1970.

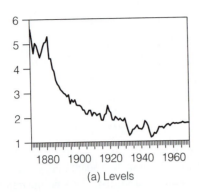

(a) Levels

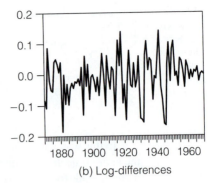

(b) Log-differences

> We are inclined to attribute the secular decline to the associated rise in per capita
> real income, that is, to view the services rendered by money balances as a "luxury"
> of which the amount demanded rises more than in proportion to the rise in income.
> (Friedman and Schwartz, 1963, p. 639)

This conjecture was investigated by Gould and Nelson (1974), who studied
the stochastic properties of the original Friedman-Schwartz data. They found that,
despite its long-term decline, the series could not be distinguished statistically
from a zero-drift random walk. Their analysis made use of the tools of time series
analysis that we have developed.

Let us consider the application of these tools to the updated Nelson-Plosser
series. Table 15.2 reproduces the Nelson-Plosser results for the sample autocorrelations of (1) the logarithms of the raw series, (2) the log-differences, and (3) the
deviations from a logarithmic time trend.

Consider first the variable in its levels, shown in Figure 15.13(a). The plot
reveals that the secular decline in velocity is of a nonlinear form. Inspection of
the log-differences in Figure 15.13(b) reveals an important feature of this nonlinear
decline: The percentage changes in the variable do not trend. This suggests that
the decline in velocity is of a constant-growth form and therefore that we should
work with the variable in its logarithms.

TABLE 15.2   Sample Autocorrelations for the Nelson-Plosser Velocity Series, 1869–1970

	Lag					
	r_1	r_2	r_3	r_4	r_5	r_6
Log-levels	0.96	0.92	0.88	0.85	0.81	0.79
Log-differences	0.11	−0.04	−0.16	−0.15	−0.11	0.11
Deviations from logarithmic trend	0.91	0.81	0.72	0.65	0.59	0.56

Source: Nelson and Plosser (1982, Tables 2, 3, and 4). Copyright ©1982, reprinted with
permission from Elsevier.

The log-levels of the variable will, of course, still be nonstationary, just as the raw series is. This is confirmed by the SACF of these log-levels, reported in the first row of Table 15.2. These autocorrelations are high and decline slowly, much like the SACFs for the simulated trend stationary variable and per capita GNP that we examine in Figure 15.7. As we know from that earlier discussion, this SACF merely reflects the nonstationarity in the series; it is not indicative of the true nature of its temporal dependence.

Obtaining a useful indication of this temporal dependence requires that the trend in the data be treated. There are two ways of doing this: treating the variable as difference stationary and treating it as trend stationary.

Difference Stationarity

Treating velocity as difference stationary, consider the log-differences graphed in Figure 15.13(b). The SACF for these percentage changes is reported in the second column of Table 15.2. These autocorrelations are quite low; all are within the two-standard-deviation confidence bounds, $\pm 2/\sqrt{n} = \pm 2/\sqrt{102} = \pm 0.20$. Gould and Nelson found that Q tests did not reject the hypothesis of white noise, suggesting that velocity is a random walk in its logarithms.

Does this random walk drift? The "secular decline" described by Friedman and Schwartz seems to suggest that it does. But remember that random walks can be deceiving; apparent trends can be the random outcome of the particular shocks that happened to occur. And in fact this is just what Gould and Nelson found. The sample mean of their log-differences was -0.109, indicating an average annual decline in velocity of 1.1%. However, they also found a t statistic of just -1.456, suggesting that this point estimate is not statistically significant. That is, the data do not reject the hypothesis of zero drift.

From this perspective there is no need to explain any systematic downward movement in velocity, either in terms of an income effect or any other explanation, because there is no compelling evidence of any systematic downward movement. The decline in velocity that took place could have arisen as the happenstance outcome of the particular shocks that occurred.

These findings led Gould and Nelson (1974, p. 410) to conclude "...our tests based on the Friedman-Schwartz data do not provide evidence against the hypothesis that changes in velocity are serially uncorrelated" and "...the Friedman-Schwartz velocity series, when considered as a univariate stochastic process, is empirically indistinguishable from a random walk; that is, the simple summation of uncorrelated shocks."

> Another way of phrasing this conclusion is that whatever the determinants of velocity and their individual stochastic structures may be, their combined effect is such that successive changes in velocity are essentially uncorrelated. This would imply that of the past history available at any given date only the current observation is relevant for prediction. We also find that the apparent downward historical "drift" in velocity is not statistically significant. (Gould and Nelson, 1974, p. 405)

Trend Stationarity

These conclusions presuppose that velocity is best viewed as difference stationary, so that first differencing is the appropriate means of removing its trend—of transforming the variable to stationarity. The alternative is to treat it as trend stationary. In this case, the appropriate means of trend removal is not to difference but instead to estimate a deterministic trend and detrend the series by using the residuals.

Of course, the pattern of autocorrelation revealed by the SACF depends on which method of trend removal is used. The last line of Table 15.2 shows the autocorrelations of the least squares residuals from a loglinear trend. They suggest a pattern of substantial autocorrelation, entirely different from the pattern suggested by the second line of the table. Thus if we were to adopt the premise that velocity is trend stationary, we would conclude that there is substantial autocorrelation around the long-term trend that must be explained. This is a quite different conclusion from the Gould-Nelson one that the annual changes in velocity are white noise. At the same time, we know from our discussion of Nelson and Kang (1981, 1984) that if velocity is in fact difference stationary then the serial correlation in its deviations from a deterministic trend are spurious, telling us nothing about the true nature of its temporal dependence.

It is evident that it would be of considerable interest to be able to test formally for difference stationarity versus trend stationarity. At the time they were writing, no test of this kind was available to Gould and Nelson. Such tests have since been developed and are the subject of much of Chapter 17.

EXERCISES

The Nelson-Plosser velocity series is available in the file np.dat.

15.15 np.dat Use these data to obtain, for lags $j = 1, \ldots, 6$,

(a) the SACF of the log-levels.

(b) the SACF of the log-differences.

(c) the SACF of the deviations from a logarithmic time trend.

Are you able to replicate the Nelson-Plosser results, as summarized in Table 15.2?

15.16 np.dat Focusing on the log-differences, Gould and Nelson calculated Q statistics based on lags $k = 12$, 24, and 36 and were unable to reject the hypothesis of white noise. What do you find using the Nelson-Plosser series?

15.17 np.dat Treating the series as a random walk in its logarithms, estimate the drift parameter and test the hypothesis of zero drift. How do your findings compare with those of Gould and Nelson (who used the somewhat shorter Friedman-Schwartz series)?

15.7.2 Application: Is Consumption a Random Walk?

Macroeconomic variables such as aggregate output and investment grow over time and so exhibit an upward trend or drift. In contrast to the random walk model, however, we do not normally expect their period-by-period changes to be uncorrelated.

Instead, these changes usually exhibit some degree of serial dependence: The change in production or investment this period presumably depends somewhat on the change the period before, which in turn depends on the period before that, and so on. Consequently, we do not expect most aggregate variables to evolve as random walks.

In a landmark contribution to macroeconomics, Robert Hall (1978) argued that aggregate consumption is an exception to this intuition. His reasoning was based on the standard models of household consumption behavior accepted by all economists—the life-cycle model of Franco Modigliani and the permanent income model of Milton Friedman (1957).

The essence of the life cycle–permanent income hypothesis is as follows. Households make their consumption and saving decisions as part of a lifetime plan. The goal of this lifetime plan is to smooth consumption relative to income, saving in high-income years in order to maintain consumption in low-income years. If the lifetime path of income were known in advance, consumption could be spread smoothly over all periods. But in practice households live in a world of uncertainty, facing a future income stream that is to some degree random. The best they can do is to form expectations about their future income, consuming today on the basis of those expectations. If expectations were always fulfilled, there would be no need for households to alter their consumption plans. In practice, however, unanticipated events cause households to continually revise their expectations of future income, in turn revising their consumption decisions.

Hall's contribution was to note that because expectations are only revised in response to unanticipated events, so too should consumption decisions. In making this point, Hall was using the idea of rational expectations: Unanticipated events are by definition unforecastable—they are like a white noise disturbance.[21] It should therefore also be the case that changes in consumption are unforecastable. That is, consumption should evolve as a random walk.

Is this prediction borne out empirically? Although in some respects consumption data are consistent with Hall's ideas, formal random walk tests tend to reject the hypothesis. There are a number of possible reasons for this result, both statistical and economic. With respect to statistics, Theory Meets Application 15.1 describes one econometric explanation for why observed consumption data do not follow a random walk. With respect to economics, it is not difficult to think of factors that would prevent households from behaving in accordance with Hall's model. For example, consumption smoothing requires that households be able to borrow and lend freely; yet many households are constrained in their ability to borrow, which limits their ability to smooth consumption to the extent that the life cycle–permanent income model suggests they otherwise would.

Nevertheless Hall's random walk consumption model was among the early important applications of rational expectations in macroeconomics. It demonstrated just how radically our understanding of the determination of economic variables can be altered by the treatment of expectations formation. His model remains an

---

[21] Rational expectations is discussed in Appendix B, Section B.2.3.

THEORY MEETS APPLICATION   15.1

Temporal Aggregation and Hall's Random Walk Model of Consumption

People make their economic decisions at various points in time. These decisions may be taken daily, weekly, monthly, annually, or at some other interval. Most realistically, perhaps decisions are taken irregularly or are best thought of as being made continuously. There is no particular reason to believe that the quarterly or annual sampling interval of the time series data available to econometricians corresponds to the decision interval of economic agents.

It seems plausible that most economic variables evolve as a result of decisions made more frequently than the quarterly or annual intervals at which economic data are typically sampled. When a *stock* variable is sampled less frequently than the decision interval—for example, when the capital stock evolves continuously but is measured only annually—the observed time series is said to be the result of **sampling aggregation.** When a *flow* variable is sampled less frequently than the decision interval—for example, when income is received weekly or monthly but is measured only quarterly—the observed time series is said to be the result of **temporal aggregation.**

In an important early contribution to time series analysis, Working (1960) studied the effect

of this sort of aggregation over time on a random walk. Suppose that a variable is generated as a random walk, but is observed over a longer sampling interval. Consequently, the available measurements on the variable are the result of aggregation over time. Working found that these data do *not* follow a random walk; instead, the aggregation over time induces a serial dependence in the period-by-period changes of the observed series. In short, the aggregation over time of a random walk is not a random walk.

Pursuing Working's insight, Ermini (1988, 1989) and Christiano, Eichenbaum, and Marshall (1991) considered the possibility that the quarterly sampling interval of the consumption data normally used to test Hall's random walk model may exceed the decision interval that people use in making their consumption choices. They showed that the autocorrelation in the period-by-period changes in quarterly consumption data—autocorrelation that would appear to violate the random walk hypothesis—may well be an artifact of temporal aggregation. Hence, this autocorrelation may not constitute a rejection of Hall's model. Ermini's work is considered further in Theory Meets Application 17.1.

important theoretical benchmark that all analyses of aggregate consumption—both theoretical and empirical—now use as their starting point.

EXERCISES

King, Plosser, Stock, and Watson (1991) studied quarterly per capita data on U.S. private GNP, consumption expenditure, and gross private investment. Their data set is in the file **kpsw.dat**. It has been studied previously in Exercise 5.4 and contains the following variables.

quarter	Quarterly period, 1947:1–1988:4
output	Real private GNP per capita.
consump	Real consumption expenditure per capita.
invest	Real private investment per capita.

Let us use the consumption series to investigate Hall's hypothesis.

15.18 🔵 **kpsw.dat** Plot the consumption series in its levels and in its first differences. Based on these plots, do you judge aggregate consumption to be nonstationary in its levels? In its differences?

15.19 🔵 **kpsw.dat** Obtain the SACF of the first differences for lags up to 3 years. How many of the sample autocorrelations fall outside two-standard-deviation confidence bounds?

15.20 🔵 **kpsw.dat** Perform a Q test at lag $k = 12$. What is your conclusion?

15.8 Key Properties of Random Walks

A zero-drift random walk is just a special case of the model with drift, and we have shown that the two models share a common set of essential features: both are difference stationary and both are integrated processes. Consequently, we no longer need consider them separately in summarizing the key features of their stochastic behavior.

Impulse Response Function

The equations (15.19) and (15.25), obtained by recursive substitution, have in common the integrated expression

$$ST_t = \sum_{j=0}^{t-1} \varepsilon_{t-j}. \tag{15.30}$$

This stochastic trend reveals the impulse response function for a random walk. All shocks have a unit-for-unit effect on Y_t, no matter how far in the past they may have occurred. Equivalently, a shock today has a unit-for-unit effect on Y today and in all future periods.

This property is in stark contrast to white noise around a deterministic trend in Section 15.5. There a white noise shock affected the variable only in the current period. Hence, although we have offered both trend stationary processes and random walks as examples of nonstationary processes, the integrated nature of random walks means that they differ fundamentally from trend stationary processes in their key properties. It is useful to emphasize this by summarizing the key properties of random walks.

Shocks Are Permanent in Their Effect. Another way of expressing what we have said about the impulse response function is as follows: Each shock changes the base from which the variable evolves in the future. A larger shock ε_t today changes Y_t today in that amount. Because Y_t is the base from which the random walk evolves in the future, this in turn affects the value of the variable in all future periods. This property is shown in Figure 15.14 for random walks both with and without drift.

FIGURE 15.14

A shock to a ran-
dom walk perma-
nently shifts the
evolution of the
variable.

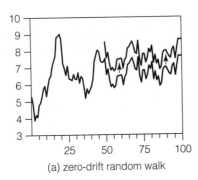

(a) zero-drift random walk

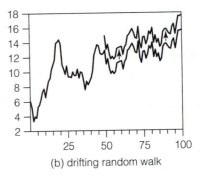

(b) drifting random walk

A larger shock in period 50 shifts the entire future evolution of the variable. In this sense, the effect of a shock does not dissipate over time; it is permanent in its effect.

The Variable Does Not Exhibit Mean Reversion. We have seen that a random walk with drift has mean

$$E(Y_t) = Y_0 + \beta t.$$

Interpreting the initial value Y_0 as a constant and relabeling it α, this is the same as the deterministic trend of the trend stationary process (15.28). However, the variance expression $V(Y_t) = t\sigma^2$ indicates that there is nothing preventing Y from straying arbitrarily far from this linear trend for indefinite periods of time. The cumulation of disturbances given by the integrated expression (15.30) can grow larger and larger as Y evolves through time, enabling it to wander further and further from this trend. In this sense, there is no force causing the variable to gravitate toward its mean. In contrast to a trend stationary process, a random walk does not exhibit mean reversion.

A Shock Alters All Forecasts. That shocks are permanent in their effect has an important implication for forecasting. As we have seen in our discussion of Figures 15.10 and 15.12 (the zero-drift and drifting cases, respectively) and illustrated in Example 7, a shock changes the base for forecasting. It therefore shifts the trajectory of forecasts.

The Forecast Error Variance Is Unbounded. The error made in forecasting is the difference between the value that actually occurs in the future period, Y_t, and the forecast $Y_0 + \beta t$:

$$Y_t - E(Y_t) = Y_t - (Y_0 + \beta t) = \sum_{j=0}^{t-1} \varepsilon_{t-j}.$$

This has variance $t\sigma^2$, the variance of the process itself; as we have seen, the same expression holds in the special case of a zero drift, $\beta = 0$. Hence, in

FIGURE 15.15

Random walks: Sample realization, forecast, and forecast interval. Random walks have unbounded forecast intervals.

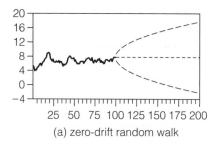

(a) zero-drift random walk

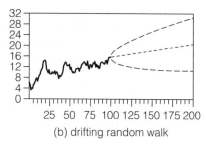

(b) drifting random walk

contrast to a trend stationary process, in which the forecast error variance is constant, a random walk has a forecast error variance that increases with the forecast horizon.

This forecast error variance can be used to construct a forecast interval. However, because the variance increases with the forecast horizon, now this interval widens as the horizon lengthens. A two-standard-deviation forecast interval is $\pm 2\sigma\sqrt{t}$ around the forecast $Y_0 + \beta t$.[22] Hence, in contrast to a trend stationary process in which, by Result 5.1, the forecast interval is of constant width, the following conclusion holds.

Result 15.1   *In the absence of coefficient uncertainty, a random walk has a forecast interval that increases with the square root of the forecast horizon.*

Only for a one-period-ahead forecast are the forecast variance and the associated interval the same as those that apply to a trend stationary process because only for $t = 1$ does the variance $t\sigma^2$ reduce to the earlier forecast error variance σ^2 given in equation (15.16). For forecasts beyond $t = 1$ the uncertainty implied by the random walk model is greater and becomes even greater as the forecast horizon lengthens; in contrast to what we found for trend stationary processes, the forecast error variance for a random walk is unbounded. The unbounded forecast intervals are illustrated in Figure 15.15.

This is a much more realistic portrayal of the uncertainty associated with real-world forecasting problems. Consider forecasting stock prices, and suppose you knew only the current price Y_0 and its historical average return β. Both the trend stationary and random walk models would have you forecast using the linear trend $Y_0 + \beta t$, as we have illustrated in Examples 4 and 7. However, given the theory of efficient markets, which suggests that prices follow a random walk, the forecast interval for the trend stationary model greatly underestimates the uncertainty associated with these forecasts, giving the mistaken impression of a bounded forecast

---

[22] This statement assumes known values for β and σ. In real-world forecasting problems where these parameters must be estimated, this forecast interval has to be modified to reflect the uncertainty in the estimates.

error variance—there is nothing to prevent the actual stock price from straying arbitrarily far from the linear trend. In using the linear trend to forecast, the trend stationary model greatly understates the likelihood of both making and losing a substantial amount of money.

Conclusions

In summary, a consideration of the impulse response function reveals that random walks have the following key properties:

- Shocks are permanent in their effect.
- The variable does not exhibit mean reversion.
- A shock alters all forecasts.
- The forecast error variance is unbounded.

It is useful to emphasize these key properties because they are in stark contrast to those of white noise around a constant mean or trend.

Autocorrelation Function

In addition to yielding the impulse response function, equations (15.19) and (15.25) can also be used to derive the autocorrelation function. To do this, it is easiest to reformulate the summation index in the stochastic trend (15.30) as

$$ST_t = \sum_{i=1}^{t} \varepsilon_i.$$

To derive the autocovariances, for either the zero-drift or drifting cases we have

$$\text{cov}(Y_t, Y_{t-j}) = E[(Y_t - EY_t)(Y_{t-j} - EY_{t-j})]$$

$$= E\left[\left(\sum_{i=1}^{t} \varepsilon_i\right)\left(\sum_{i=1}^{t-j} \varepsilon_i\right)\right]$$

$$= E\left[(\varepsilon_1 + \varepsilon_2 + \cdots + \varepsilon_t)(\varepsilon_1 + \varepsilon_2 + \cdots + \varepsilon_{t-j})\right]$$

$$= (t - j)\sigma^2.$$

The last line follows because the two summation expressions have $t - j$ of the ε_i in common. When the mathematical expectation is applied to the product, only $t - j$ nonzero terms are left, each equal to the variance σ^2. In the special case of $j = 0$, this autocovariance expression reduces to the random walk variance (15.23).

Notice that these autocovariances depend not only on j, the distance in time between the observations Y_t and Y_{t-j}, but also on the time period t itself. This is an example of a situation in which the autocovariances are *not* time invariant and

FIGURE 15.16

The ACF of a random walk has a slow decay.

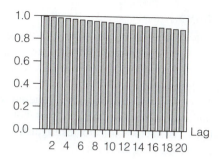

the usual notation γ_j that we define in equation (15.7) is inadequate. This reflects the nonstationarity of a random walk; autocovariances are only time invariant and symmetric for stationary processes, as we have emphasized in our initial treatment of those concepts.

The intuition for this lack of time invariance is perhaps best explained in terms of the autocorrelation function, which can be obtained in the usual way by dividing by the standard deviations:

$$\operatorname{cor}(Y_t, Y_{t-j}) = \frac{\operatorname{cov}(Y_t, Y_{t-j})}{\sqrt{V(Y_t)}\sqrt{V(Y_{t-j})}} = \frac{(t-j)\sigma^2}{\sqrt{t\sigma^2}\sqrt{(t-j)\sigma^2}} = \sqrt{1 - \frac{j}{t}}.$$

What are we to make of this dependence of the autocorrelations on t as well as j? Note first that, for a given lag j, as $t \to \infty$ the autocorrelation approaches 1. Because Y depends on the entire past history of shocks in a way that does not dissipate over time, as $t \to \infty$ it is the case that Y_t and Y_{t-j} come to depend on the same past history. The j shocks that distinguish them come to be of negligible importance relative to the rest of the historical experience on which they depend. Consequently, they are perfectly correlated.

On the other hand, if we consider a given time horizon t and let the distance in time become larger, $j \to \infty$, then the autocorrelation approaches zero. Because Y_t and Y_{t-j} have fewer and fewer shocks in common as $j \to \infty$, they come to be unrelated.

However, the convergence of the autocorrelations to zero as $j \to \infty$ is very slow. At modest lags—when j is small relative to t—the fact that Y_t and Y_{t-j} share a large common history of nondissipating shocks means that they are highly correlated. For example, at time $t = 100$ the previous formula yields an autocorrelation of 0.995 at lag $j = 1$, of 0.990 at lag $j = 2$, and declining to 0.894 at lag $j = 20$. This very slow decay of the ACF is shown in Figure 15.16.

Notice that the ACF of a random walk is entirely different from the ACF of the other nonstationary process we have studied, white noise around a deterministic trend, which we have seen has the ACF of white noise itself, shown in Figure 15.2(b).

Sample Autocorrelations

The sample autocorrelations of a random walk, like their theoretical counterparts, exhibit a gradual decay and in this respect are not misleading in their portrayal of the theoretical ACF. This contrasts with trend stationary processes, in which the SACF does not accurately describe the ACF.

Notice that the SACFs of trend stationary and random walk variables are similar—both decline gradually, reflecting the fact that both are nonstationary. Because of this similarity, it is not possible to distinguish trend and difference stationary processes by inspecting their SACFs.

Practitioner's Tip: **Trend and difference stationarity and the SACF**

Despite being fundamentally different in their properties, trend and difference stationary variables nevertheless often have similar SACFs. Thus, the two types of variables cannot be distinguished on the basis of their sample autocorrelations.

This being the case, as we have already noted, it would clearly be useful to be able to test formally for whether a series is trend or difference stationary; this is pursued in Chapter 17.

15.9   Conclusions

Economic variables exhibit fluctuations and trends. In this chapter we have laid the groundwork for studying these fluctuations and trends by introducing some of the basic ingredients needed to describe them.

Two of these ingredients are the concepts of white noise and stationarity. Loosely speaking, a white noise variable is one that is "purely random"; it is uncorrelated through time and so contains no temporal dependence that can be used in forecasting. Stationarity means that the variable as it evolves through time has been generated by a stable underlying structure—some common set of economic forces—such that we can hope to use the observed realization of the time series to uncover that structure. Even though most economic time series are neither white noise nor stationary, these concepts are important because they play a key role in specifying models of fluctuations and trends.

There are two broad classes of models for trending variables: trend stationary processes and difference stationary processes. In this chapter we have studied special cases of these models based on a white noise disturbance. As an example of a trend stationary process we have studied the model of white noise around a deterministic trend; an example of difference stationary processes are random walks, which are white noise in their first differences. These examples are important because they illustrate the key properties of these two classes of models.

White noise around a trend implies that shocks are temporary in their effect, that the variable is trend reverting, that a shock does not alter forecasts, and that the forecast error variance is bounded. By contrast, difference stationary processes are integrated: shocks are permanent in their effect, variables are not mean reverting, a shock alters the forecast, and forecast error variances are unbounded. These differences in the two types of models are important because it is the second set of properties that seems more typical of economic variables, suggesting that economic variables will often best be modeled as difference stationary.

To model period-by-period changes in economic variables as white noise is, with the exception of a few special cases such as stock prices and perhaps technology, not realistic for most variables. In contrast to the study of cross-sectional data, in which the assumption of a classical disturbance usually makes sense, the analysis of time series data requires that the idea of a white noise disturbance be generalized to one that permits autocorrelated fluctuations. This is the task of the next chapter.

Once this task is complete we can return to the study of trends in growing economic variables. This is the subject of Chapter 17, in which we use the autocorrelated disturbances of Chapter 16 to specify general trend and difference stationary models.

16 *Fluctuations*

This chapter builds on the basic concepts introduced in Chapter 15 by developing models of fluctuations in economic time series. In doing this, we follow our past practice of initially modeling fluctuations around a constant mean, fluctuations that can be summarized by

$$Y_t = \alpha + u_t. \tag{16.1}$$

Here u_t denotes a disturbance that, in contrast to past specifications, may be serially correlated. We began Chapter 15 by studying the special case in which $u_t = \varepsilon_t$, the model of white noise around a constant mean. As we have seen, the concept of white noise is important for a number of reasons. However, few economic variables behave like white noise—stock returns being something of an exception. Instead, most economic variables evolve with some degree of serial dependence, and the first task of this chapter is to develop a class of models, called **autoregressive–moving average processes,** for describing this serial dependence.

However, even having done this, it must nevertheless be concluded that the model (16.1) is inadequate for describing most economic time series—few variables consist merely of fluctuations around some constant mean. Instead, we have noted that most economic variables follow trends and so evolve in a manner that is mean-varying (perhaps also with a changing variance, as in the case of a random walk). We have seen that there are two types of trends: deterministic trends and stochastic trends. The two differ fundamentally in their key properties. In Chapter 17 we use the autoregressive–moving average representation for a serially correlated disturbance to specify general classes of trend and difference stationary processes.

Because the primary role of this chapter is as a bridge to understanding these more general processes, the treatment of short run fluctuations is directed solely to that end and so is a minimal one. Much more can be said, as the references cited throughout the chapter indicate.

16.1 Introduction

There are essentially two ways to formulate models of temporal dependence. The first is to specify that the disturbance u_t is a weighted average of white noise shocks in several time periods. The simplest example of such a **moving average** model is

$$u_t = \varepsilon_t + \theta \varepsilon_{t-1}. \tag{16.2}$$

As in the previous chapter, the disturbance ε_t always denotes white noise:

$$\varepsilon_t \sim \text{wn}(0, \sigma^2).$$

The second way to specify a model of autocorrelation is to note that if a variable is temporally dependent this means that its value today is related to its values in the past. This suggests that u_t be specified to be a function of its own past values. In the simplest case, u_t is a linear function of its value one period previously plus white noise:

$$u_t = \phi u_{t-1} + \varepsilon_t. \tag{16.3}$$

Because this bears some similarity to a regression model in which u_t is regressed on its own lagged value, this specification is said to be **autoregressive.**

The model of fluctuations around a constant mean (16.1), those fluctuations being described by a moving average process such as (16.2) or an autoregressive process like (16.3), can always be restated directly in terms of the observable variable Y and the white noise shock ε, eliminating the disturbance u. In the case of a moving average disturbance, this involves nothing more than substituting the disturbance (16.2) into the model (16.1):

$$Y_t = \alpha + \varepsilon_t + \theta \varepsilon_{t-1}. \tag{16.4}$$

In the case of the autoregressive disturbance (16.3), eliminating u_t is only slightly more complicated:

$$
\begin{aligned}
Y_t &= \alpha + \phi u_{t-1} + \varepsilon_t & \text{substituting (16.3) into (16.1)} \\
&= \alpha + \phi(Y_{t-1} - \alpha) + \varepsilon_t & \text{using the lagged model (16.1)} \\
&= \alpha(1 - \phi) + \phi Y_{t-1} + \varepsilon_t. & \tag{16.5}
\end{aligned}
$$

Defining the symbol $\phi_0 \equiv \alpha(1 - \phi)$, this can be rewritten as

$$Y_t = \phi_0 + \phi Y_{t-1} + \varepsilon_t. \tag{16.6}$$

This is an autoregressive process stated directly in terms of the observable variable Y_t.

In other words, it does not matter whether we think of Y_t as being generated by a constant plus a disturbance u_t, that disturbance behaving according to an autoregressive or moving average process, or as being specified directly in terms of these processes, eliminating the notation u_t. In fact, many treatments of these models take the latter approach. However, our interest lies in generalizing the model (16.1) to mean-varying behavior; in the case of deterministic trends, for example, in Chapter 17 we consider models such as

$$Y_t = \alpha + \beta t + u_t.$$

Because the study of trending variables is our ultimate objective, it is natural to begin by stating these models in their constant-plus-disturbance form.

16.1.1 Deterministic versus Stochastic Difference Equations and the Role of White Noise

Notice that both the moving average and autoregressive models use white noise. There is now an important distinction between the disturbance u_t and the underlying white noise shock ε_t that generates it. This is the basis for the comment in the previous chapter that white noise is a basic building block of all time series models. A white noise shock ε_t is sometimes called an **innovation,** because it is these shocks that are the source of randomness determining how the variable innovates, or changes, over time.

To illustrate the predicament of attempting to proceed without any concept of white noise, consider the autoregressive model (16.3). The innovation ε_t introduces a source of randomness into the process; without it, u_t, and in turn Y_t, would be deterministic rather than stochastic. If we had just specified u_t to be generated as $u_t = \phi u_{t-1}$, the implication would be that it follows a smooth time path that, with knowledge of the parameter ϕ, is perfectly predictable. This would translate into deterministic behavior for Y_t; the derivation leading to (16.6) would reduce to

$$Y_t = \phi_0 + \phi Y_{t-1}. \tag{16.7}$$

In mathematics, an equation that involves a variable at different points in time is called a **difference equation.** Because this equation includes no random shocks, it is an example of a **deterministic difference equation.** It turns out that the behavior of a difference equation depends on its **characteristic roots.** Equation (16.7) has a single root z, the solution to

$$1 - \phi z = 0,$$

which is

$$z = \frac{1}{\phi}.$$

Thus, the parameter ϕ governs the behavior of the variable through its determination of the root. For example, the special case of $\phi = 1$ corresponds to $z = 1$ and so is said to be the case of a **unit root.**

The main limitation of using deterministic difference equations to describe the evolution of economic variables is that they do not permit the erratic variation that we observe in actual time series data. This can be illustrated by considering two cases for ϕ.

The stable case: $|\phi| < 1 \Leftrightarrow |z| > 1$. If $|\phi| < 1$, the variable described by (16.7) evolves in a manner that is **stable,** converging in the long run to an equilibrium value: that is, a value that repeats itself every period.[1] Let this equilibrium value be denoted by Y^*. It must itself satisfy the difference equation (16.7):

$$Y^* = \phi_0 + \phi Y^*.$$

Solving for Y^* we have

$$Y^* = \frac{\phi_0}{1 - \phi} = \frac{\alpha(1 - \phi)}{1 - \phi} = \alpha. \tag{16.8}$$

Hence, the constant α in the constant-plus-disturbance form (16.1) of the autoregressive model has the interpretation as the equilibrium value to which the variable would converge in the absence of shocks. This interpretation of α holds under other specifications of the disturbance u_t, as long as any autoregressive component is stable. If u_t were instead generated by our moving average process, the expression (16.4) makes it easy to see that, after just two periods without shocks ($\varepsilon_t = \varepsilon_{t-1} = 0$), the variable would take on its equilibrium value α. Thus in this instance the "long-run" prevails very quickly.

When a difference equation includes shocks, and so is a **stochastic difference equation** instead of a deterministic one, the shocks prevent the variable from settling down to its equilibrium value. Consequently the long run equilibrium never actually obtains, just as is no doubt true in real-world economies. Nevertheless, the fact that the stability of the model is a force driving the variable toward an equilibrium value is an important feature of the model, and the interpretation of the constant-plus-disturbance model (16.1) as one of short run fluctuations around a long run equilibrium is a useful one. The parameter α also has the interpretation as the expected value of Y, as we verify shortly.

An unstable case: $\phi > 1 \Leftrightarrow z < 1$. What if the stability condition is not satisfied? As a numerical example, let $\phi_0 = 0$ and $\phi = 1.05$ in the deterministic difference equation (16.7), and suppose the process starts at the initial value $Y_0 = 100$. Then Y_t follows the constant-growth exponential trend of 5% per period given in Table 6.1 and illustrated in Figure 6.3. Without the underlying source of randomness provided by white noise innovations, there is no erratic variation around this trend.

These examples help illustrate why random shocks are an essential ingredient in describing economic phenomena. The time series variables we observe in practice do not converge to constant values or follow smooth trends. Instead, they exhibit an element of erratic variation, and so to properly describe them white noise innovations must be included in our models. These white noise innovations generate autocorrelated fluctuations via moving average or autoregressive mechanisms.

---

[1] If you have studied difference equations you will be aware that the pattern of convergence depends on ϕ. If $0 < \phi < 1$, the path is smooth; if $-1 < \phi < 0$, it is oscillatory. For an introduction to the use of deterministic difference equations in economics, see Chiang (1984).

The Stability Condition and Stationarity

Noting the link between the unstable autoregressive process and the constant growth model in Section 6.2 is useful for another reason. It leads us to observe that the autoregressive process is only stationary when the stability condition $|\phi| < 1$ is satisfied; otherwise it is nonstationary.

To see this, consider the behavior of the variable when the stability condition is not satisfied. When $\phi > 1$—the unstable case just discussed—an autoregressive process follows a random growth trajectory instead of fluctuating around a constant mean; it is therefore nonstationary because its mean is not constant. In the razor's-edge case of $\phi = 1$ the disturbance (16.3) reduces to the random walk

$$u_t = u_{t-1} + \varepsilon_t.$$

Setting $\phi = 1$ in equation (16.5), this in turn translates into random walk behavior for Y_t,

$$Y_t = Y_{t-1} + \varepsilon_t.$$

This is the zero-drift random walk model (15.18) that we have studied in Section 15.6 of the previous chapter. As we have seen there, this is nonstationary because it has a stochastic trend—its variance changes over time.

A stochastic difference equation is a stochastic process. Because the stability condition for the associated deterministic difference equation is also a stationarity condition for the stochastic process, comprehensive introductions to time series analysis sometimes begin with a treatment of deterministic difference equations, developing fully the relationship between the stationarity of the stochastic process and the roots of the deterministic difference equation; notable examples are Hamilton (1994) and Enders (1995). Although our own discussion will fall well short of such a comprehensive treatment, we will return to examine in more detail the dependence of the stationarity properties of our models on the autoregressive parameter ϕ. Because setting the root $z = 1$ in an autoregressive model yields a random walk, the hypothesis that a variable has a stochastic trend is sometimes called the **unit root hypothesis.** In Chapter 17 we develop a test of the hypothesis that a time series has a stochastic trend; such tests are also called tests for a unit root.

16.1.2 The Frisch-Slutsky Rocking Horse Model

Using stochastically shocked difference equations to describe fluctuations and trends is all very well as a set of statistical concepts, but does it have anything to do with economics?

Economists have for many years debated the best way of describing fluctuations and trends in economic variables. In a famous 1933 article entitled "Propagation Problems and Impulse Problems in Dynamic Economics"—and drawing on a 1927 paper by Eugen Slutsky (1880–1948), "The Summation of Random Causes as the Source of Cyclic Processes" (subsequently published as Slutsky 1937)—Ragnar Frisch (1895–1973) argued that the framework of stochastically shocked difference

FIGURE 16.1

Which is actual
GDP per person
and which are data
simulated by a
model? (*Source:* From
Macroeconomics 1st
edition by FARMER
(Fig. 1.10, p. 17). ©
1999. Reprinted with
permission of South-
Western, a division
of Thomson Learning:
www.thomsonrights.
com. Fax 800 730-
2215.)

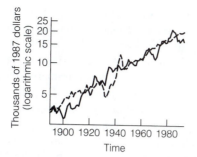

equations is a natural one for describing economic variables. He likened the economy to a rocking horse that is repeatedly pushed, an analogy he attributed to a 1907
paper by Knut Wicksell (1851–1926). If the rocking horse is pushed just once it
rocks a few times, but then settles down. Only if it is pushed repeatedly does the
rocking continue. The oscillations depend on the size and frequency of the shocks
as well as the construction of the horse. Although the motion of the rocking horse
depends critically on the shocks, in appearance the two will be very different.

The pushes Frisch called impulses–our white noise innovations. These are
propagated into serially correlated fluctuations according to the construction of
the horse, just as white noise innovations are propagated into serially correlated
fluctuations by the moving average or autoregressive models we have described. If
the impulses were to end the rocking horse would gradually come to a stop, just
as the variable described by the model (16.1) would settle at its equilibrium value
α. Frisch argued that the economy can only be understood by understanding both
these impulse and propagation mechanisms.

Dramatic support for Frisch's idea was provided by Adelman and Adelman
(1959), who simulated one of the earliest macroeconometric forecasting models, the Klein and Goldberger (1955) model. The Klein-Goldberger model, like
any macroeconometric model, was essentially a system of estimated difference
equations. Adelman and Adelman found that when this system was simulated with
random shocks it produced fluctuations very similar to those actually observed in
macroeconomic variables.

As a simple way of illustrating this point, Farmer (1999a) generated a simulated
stochastic time series and plotted it against the historical series for U.S. per capita
GDP. His plot is reproduced as Figure 16.1.

> . . . ask yourself which of the lines is real data and which is artificial data simulated
> by an economic model. If you think about it, you will realize that the [dashed] line
> is real data because only that line dips in the 1930s (the Great Depression) and rises
> in 1945 (the end of World War II). But if you didn't know anything about economic
> history, you would be unable to tell which was real. In this sense the model that sim-
> ulated the artificial series is a good model of the real world. (Farmer, 1999a, p. 16)

In part because of the Adelman and Adelman findings, stochastic difference
equations are now the standard framework for studying economic dynamics. Macro-

economists differ mainly in their views about the importance of alternative impulse and propagation mechanisms. Indeed, debates about the construction of the rocking horse and the nature of the shocks to which it is subject are at the center of contemporary controversies in macroeconomics. With respect to impulse mechanisms, some economists believe shocks originate primarily on the real side of the economy associated with production and investment. The real business cycle school mentioned in Section 7.3.2, which attributes special importance to the technological innovations described by the Solow residual, is an especially important stream within this view. Representative of this school, Prescott (1986b, p. 29) has suggested that "technology shocks account for more than half the fluctuations in the postwar period, with a best point estimate near 75 percent ...," a view that has since been much debated.[2] Other macroeconomists attribute importance to shocks originating in the monetary and financial sectors. For a classic argument in favor of some role for monetary factors, deeply influential at the time, see Lucas (1977). Yet other economists might assign some role to changes in consumer tastes or to psychological factors. J. M. Keynes (1883–1946), in his landmark 1936 book *The General Theory of Employment, Interest, and Money*, expressed the view that "waves of optimistic and pessimistic sentiment" periodically sweep the business community, and that this is an important source of business cycle impulses (p. 154). In characteristically flamboyant fashion Keynes referred to these "waves of irrational psychology" as the **animal spirits** of investors (1936, 162), a phrase that has since entered the popular lexicon of economics. Animal spirits continue to be of interest to some macroeconomists as a possible source of business cycle impulses; see, for example, the references to animal spirits in Farmer (1999a) or, at a more advanced level, Farmer (1999b).

For our purposes the specifics of these controversies are less important than that they all fall under Frisch's framework. It turns out that quite simple autoregressive and moving average models, combined with the ideas of deterministic and stochastic trends, can provide remarkably good descriptions of observed macroeconomic time series. In this chapter our focus is on understanding how moving average and autoregressive processes can be used to describe fluctuations around a constant mean. In Chapter 17 we turn to adapting these processes to describing fluctuations in trending variables.

16.2   Moving Average Processes

Repeating equations (16.1) and (16.2), the simplest model of moving average fluctuations around a constant α is

$$Y_t = \alpha + u_t, \tag{16.9a}$$
$$u_t = \varepsilon_t + \theta\varepsilon_{t-1}. \tag{16.9b}$$

This disturbance specification, involving as it does just a single lagged inno-

[2] For an assessment of this debate, see Aiyagari (1994).

vation, is called a moving average of order 1, abbreviated MA(1). In general, we can average over any number of lags going q periods into the past, which specifies a moving average of order q, abbreviated MA(q):

$$u_t = \varepsilon_t + \theta_1 \varepsilon_{t-1} + \theta_2 \varepsilon_{t-2} + \cdots + \theta_q \varepsilon_{t-q}. \tag{16.10}$$

Moving average processes are important in economics because this tends to be the kind of autocorrelation that arises from the aggregation of data, both over agents, such as households and firms, and over time. An important example is given in Theory Meets Application 15.1 in the previous chapter, which describes how the time-aggregation in available consumption data relative to the household decision period can induce autocorrelation that leads to a rejection of Hall's random walk model. As we have noted, this is an application of the famous finding by Holbrook Working (1895–1985) that the aggregation over time of a random walk is not a random walk. It is now possible to remark further that what Working showed in his 1960 article is that the pattern of autocorrelation induced by the aggregation over time of a random walk is of a moving average form.

As well, differencing a variable tends to induce a moving average. As a simple example, consider white noise around a constant mean,

$$Y_t = \gamma + \varepsilon_t.$$

Its first differences are

$$\Delta Y_t = \varepsilon_t - \varepsilon_{t-1}.$$

This is the MA(1) model (16.9) with $\alpha = 0$ and $\theta = 1$. Thus the changes in white noise are not themselves white noise; they are autocorrelated according to a moving average.

To give some idea of the nature of the autocorrelation yielded by a moving average process, Figure 16.2 shows simulated MA(1) series based on $\alpha = 1$ and $\theta = 0.6$ in Figure 16.2(a) and $\theta = -0.6$ in (b). The white noise innovation used to generate these simulations is the realization used in Figure 15.2(a). Notice that, particularly in Figure 16.2(a), there is a pattern of serial dependence evident in the MA series that is not present in the white noise. However, for a given model, in

FIGURE 16.2

Representative MA(1) realizations.

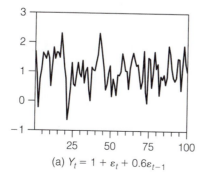

(a) $Y_t = 1 + \varepsilon_t + 0.6\varepsilon_{t-1}$

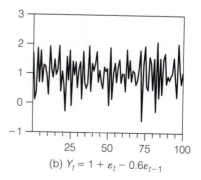

(b) $Y_t = 1 + \varepsilon_t - 0.6\varepsilon_{t-1}$

this case MA(1), the appearance of that serial correlation can be quite different depending on the value of the parameter θ.

The properties of a moving average process can be studied using the tools in Chapter 15. We begin by examining the impulse response function and then turn to the mean and variance of the process. The autocorrelation function is derived in the appendix to this chapter.

Impulse Response Function

According to a moving average model, how does a shock today affect the variable now and in the future? Substituting (16.9b) into (16.9a) to reproduce (16.4), Y_t is generated as

$$Y_t = \alpha + \varepsilon_t + \theta\varepsilon_{t-1}.$$

According to this equation, a shock ε_t has a unit-for-unit effect on Y_t in the same period; that is, the current-period impulse response is 1. In the next period, the shock ε_t will have effect θ on Y_{t+1}. In periods beyond $t + 1$, the effect will be zero.

Generalizing this reasoning, the impulse response function for an MA(q) process consists of its coefficients $1, \theta_1, \theta_2, \ldots, \theta_q$. The implication is that the effect of a shock is temporary, lasting for only q periods into the future. Another way of expressing this idea is to say that an MA(q) process has a memory of q periods; shocks occurring as far back as q periods previously have an effect on events today, but not ones earlier than that.

This impulse response function for an MA(1) process is illustrated in Figure 16.3 for the two parameter values $\theta = 0.6$ and $\theta = -0.6$ used in the simulations of Figure 16.2. These may be usefully contrasted with the impulse response function for white noise, shown in Figure 15.2(b).

FIGURE 16.3

The impulse response function of an MA(1) process.

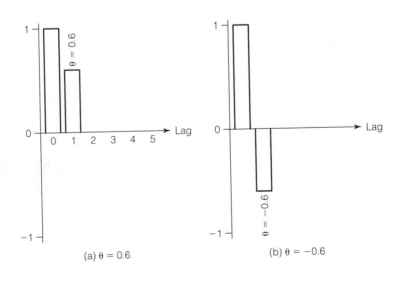

(a) $\theta = 0.6$

(b) $\theta = -0.6$

The Mean and Variance of an MA Process

Deriving the mean and variance of a moving average process requires nothing more than the application of the laws of expectation and variance of Appendix B.

Mean Regardless of the number of lags involved, the mean of the MA(q) disturbance (16.10) is

$$E(u_t) = E(\varepsilon_t) + \theta_1 E(\varepsilon_{t-1}) + \theta_2 E(\varepsilon_{t-2}) + \cdots + \theta_q E(\varepsilon_{t-q}) = 0$$

because the white noise innovation ε_t has zero mean. This confirms that u_t is a zero-mean disturbance and that the constant α is in turn the mean of Y_t:

$$E(Y_t) = \alpha + E(u_t) = \alpha.$$

These means are constant; they do not change with time. This is illustrated in Figure 16.2, where both series fluctuate around their mean of $\alpha = 1$.

Variance The variance of an MA(q) process is

$$
\begin{aligned}
V(Y_t) &= V(u_t) \\
&= V(\varepsilon_t) + \theta_1^2 V(\varepsilon_{t-1}) + \theta_2^2 V(\varepsilon_{t-2}) + \cdots + \theta_q^2 V(\varepsilon_{t-q}) \\
&= (1 + \theta_1^2 + \theta_2^2 + \cdots + \theta_q^2)\sigma^2.
\end{aligned}
\tag{16.11}
$$

Although it depends on the specified order q of the model, this variance does not change with time.

EXAMPLE 1 | What are the variances of the MA(1) variables shown in Figure 16.2?

SOLUTION | When $q = 1$ the variance expression (16.11) reduces to $V(Y_t) = (1 + \theta_1^2)\sigma^2$. Both realizations shown in Figure 16.2 are generated using white noise with variance $\sigma^2 = 0.25$. The series in Figure 16.2(a) uses $\theta_1 = 0.6$, so its variance is

$$V(Y_t) = (1 + \theta_1^2)\sigma^2 = (1 + 0.6^2)0.25 = 0.34.$$

The series in Figure 16.2(b) uses $\theta_1 = -0.6$, which yields the same variance.

In conclusion, a moving average process fluctuates around its mean $E(Y_t) = \alpha$ with a constant variance. The pattern of the time-dependence in these fluctuations is described by the autocorrelation function, which is derived in the appendix to this chapter. The key point about this autocorrelation function is that it too is time invariant. Consequently, moving average processes are stationary. In contrast to autoregressive processes, this does not require that any restrictions be placed on the coefficients.

How good are MA models at describing temporal dependence in a variable? A famous result known as **Wold's theorem** suggests that a covariance stationary process can be approximated by a moving average of adequate order—that is, with a large enough lag length q. The qualification "adequate order" is key. Potentially it might be necessary to include many lags to adequately describe a variable, resulting in an excessive number of parameters. As a step toward models requiring fewer parameters, let us turn to the second way of describing temporal dependence.

16.3   Autoregressive Processes

The second way of specifying a model of autocorrelated fluctuations is to use an autoregressive process. Repeating equations (16.1) and (16.3), the simplest model of autoregressive fluctuations around a constant α is

$$Y_t = \alpha + u_t, \qquad (16.12a)$$

$$u_t = \phi u_{t-1} + \varepsilon_t. \qquad (16.12b)$$

Because this disturbance specification involves just a single lag, it is called an autoregressive process of order 1, abbreviated AR(1).

It turns out that stationary AR(1) processes do a surprisingly good job of describing the fluctuations in many economic variables, including real GDP growth, interest rates and international interest rate differentials, and real exchange rates.[3] It is fair to say that the AR(1) is the workhorse model of economic fluctuations in applied studies.

This is not to suggest, of course, that it is always adequate. The same idea can be generalized to p time lags, which specifies an autoregressive process of order p, abbreviated AR(p):

$$u_t = \phi_1 u_{t-1} + \phi_2 u_{t-2} + \cdots + \phi_p u_{t-p} + \varepsilon_t. \qquad (16.13)$$

For example, AR(2) processes generate cyclical fluctuations that are more typical of business cycle phenomena.

In an manner analogous to (16.6), an AR(p) model is often stated directly in terms of the observable variable Y:

$$Y_t = \phi_0 + \phi_1 Y_{t-1} + \phi_2 Y_{t-2} + \cdots + \phi_p Y_{t-p} + \varepsilon_t. \qquad (16.14)$$

We have seen that an AR(1) process is stationary if $|\phi| < 1$ or, equivalently, if its characteristic root z satisfies $z > 1$. For an AR(p) process, the analogous stationarity condition involves restrictions on all the coefficients ϕ_j, $j = 1, \ldots, p$, or, equivalently, on the roots of the associated difference equation. The technical expression of this stationarity condition is that these roots must lie "outside the complex unit circle." However, for our purposes an understanding of the precise meaning of this phrase is less important than a general appreciation that, in contrast to moving average processes, autoregressive processes are only stationary for certain parameter values.

To give some idea of the nature of the temporal dependence yielded by an autoregressive process, Figure 16.4 shows simulated AR(1) series based on $\alpha = 1$

---

[3] The concept of a real exchange rate is defined in Exercises 6.34 and 8.9 and discussed further in Section 18.4.3.

FIGURE 16.4

Representative
AR(1) realizations.

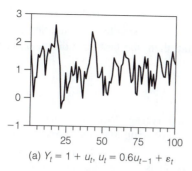

(a) $Y_t = 1 + u_t$, $u_t = 0.6u_{t-1} + \varepsilon_t$

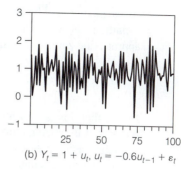

(b) $Y_t = 1 + u_t$, $u_t = -0.6u_{t-1} + \varepsilon_t$

and $\phi = 0.6$ in Figure 16.4(a) and $\phi = -0.6$ in (b). The white noise innovation used to generate these simulations is the realization used in Figure 15.2(a). Notice that, particularly in Figure 16.4(a), there is a pattern of serial dependence evident in the AR series that is not present in the white noise, a pattern that can be quite different depending on the value of ϕ. The pattern of serial dependence is also somewhat different from the MA(1) series shown in Figure 16.2, which was generated using the same white noise realization.

The properties of an autoregressive process can be studied using the tools we have developed. We begin by examining the impulse response function and then turn to the mean and variance of the process. The autocorrelation function is derived in the appendix to this chapter. The key properties of autoregressive processes can be understood by studying the AR(1) model, and so the derivations that follow are limited to the special case of $p = 1$.

Impulse Response Function

In deriving the effect of a shock today on current and future values of the variable, it is useful to begin by observing that an autoregressive specification implies that Y_t is the cumulation of the past history of innovations $\varepsilon_t, \varepsilon_{t-1}, \varepsilon_{t-2}, \ldots$. This can be seen by applying the method of recursive substitution to successive lags of the AR(1) disturbance (16.12b):

$$
\begin{aligned}
u_t &= \phi u_{t-1} + \varepsilon_t \\
&= \phi^2 u_{t-2} + \varepsilon_t + \phi \varepsilon_{t-1} \\
&= \phi^3 u_{t-3} + \varepsilon_t + \phi \varepsilon_{t-1} + \phi^2 \varepsilon_{t-2} \\
&= \phi^4 u_{t-4} + \varepsilon_t + \phi \varepsilon_{t-1} + \phi^2 \varepsilon_{t-2} + \phi^3 \varepsilon_{t-3} \\
&\vdots
\end{aligned}
$$

At this point the pattern is clear. Going s periods into the past, u_t is generated as

$$
u_t = \phi^{s+1} u_{t-s-1} + \sum_{j=0}^{s} \phi^j \varepsilon_{t-j}.
$$

As we go infinitely far into the past, $s \to \infty$. If the parameter ϕ satisfies the stability condition $|\phi| < 1$, then ϕ^{s+1} gets smaller and smaller as $s \to \infty$, eventually approaching zero. In the limit, then, the first term disappears and the expression is

$$u_t = \sum_{j=0}^{\infty} \phi^j \varepsilon_{t-j}. \qquad (16.15)$$

Notice that this is of a moving average form, but one that goes infinitely far into the past. It is called the **infinite moving average representation** for u_t. In general, stationary autoregressive processes of any order p can be restated in an equivalent infinite moving average form. Thus, the specification of a variable as following an AR process has the implication that it is generated by the full history of shocks going back into the infinite past; equivalently, it has infinite memory.

One reason the infinite moving average representation is important is because it allows us to see the impulse response function. The observed variable Y_t is generated as

$$Y_t = \alpha + u_t = \alpha + \sum_{j=0}^{\infty} \phi^j \varepsilon_{t-j}.$$

The dependence of Y_t on the history of shocks is in accordance with a particular pattern of weights; these weights are the impulse response function. The current period shock has effect $\phi^0 \varepsilon_t = \varepsilon_t$, the shock one period previously has effect $\phi^1 \varepsilon_{t-1} = \phi \varepsilon_{t-1}$, the shock two periods previously has effect $\phi^2 \varepsilon_{t-2}$, and so on. Consequently, a one-unit shock today has one-unit effect today, a ϕ-unit effect next period, a ϕ^2-unit effect the period after that, and so on. This impulse response function is illustrated in Figure 16.5 for the two parameter values $\phi = 0.6$ and $\phi = -0.6$ used in the simulations of Figure 16.4. It may be usefully contrasted

FIGURE 16.5

The impulse response function of an AR(1) process.

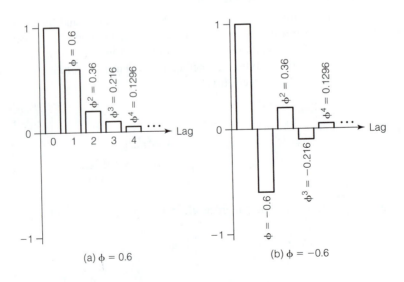

(a) $\phi = 0.6$

(b) $\phi = -0.6$

with the impulse response of a moving average in Figure 16.3 and with that of white noise in Figure 15.2(b).

As the figure makes clear, under the stability condition $|\phi| < 1$ the impulse response weights $1, \phi, \phi^2, \phi^3, \ldots$ follow a geometrically declining pattern. Thus, it is the recent shocks that are the most important in their effect. The further back in time we go, the less important are the shocks that took place then for events today. As we go infinitely far back in time, the weight ϕ^j approaches zero. This means that the influence of any past shock dissipates over time, eventually becoming negligible. In this sense, shocks are temporary in their effect. Notice that in this terminology a stochastic process can have infinite memory, yet be affected only temporarily by shocks.

The Mean and Variance of an AR Process

In addition to yielding the impulse response function, the infinite moving average representation has another important use. Applying the laws of expectation and variance in Appendix B, the mean, variance, and autocorrelation function of the process can be derived.

Mean Because the infinite moving average representation is linear in the ε_{t-j}, the laws of mathematical expectation applied to linear functions can be used to confirm that the disturbance u_t has zero mean:

$$E(u_t) = \sum_{j=0}^{\infty} \phi^j E(\varepsilon_{t-j}) = 0.$$

Hence Y_t has mean α:

$$E(Y_t) = \alpha + E(u_t) = \alpha.$$

Because these means do not depend on the time period t, the mean of an AR(1) process is time invariant. This is shown in Figure 16.4, in which the two series fluctuate around their means of $\alpha = 1$.

Variance Similarly the laws of variance applied to linear functions establish that the variance of u_t, and therefore of Y_t, is

$$V(Y_t) = V(u_t)$$

$$= \sum_{j=0}^{\infty} (\phi^j)^2 V(\varepsilon_{t-j})$$

$$= \sigma^2 \sum_{j=0}^{\infty} (\phi^2)^j \qquad \text{because all } \varepsilon_{t-j} \text{ have common variance } \sigma^2$$

$$= \frac{\sigma^2}{1 - \phi^2}. \qquad\qquad (16.16)$$

The last step follows from the geometric series result that, for any constant b satisfying $|b| < 1$,[4]

$$\sum_{j=0}^{\infty} b^j = \frac{1}{1-b}.$$ (16.17)

Because $V(Y_t)$ does not depend on the time period t, the variance of an AR(1) process is time invariant.

EXAMPLE 2 | What are the variances of the AR(1) variables shown in Figure 16.4?

SOLUTION   Both realizations shown in the figure are generated using white noise with variance $\sigma^2 = 0.25$. The series in Figure 16.4(a) uses $\phi = 0.6$, so its variance is

$$V(Y_t) = \frac{\sigma^2}{1-\phi^2} = \frac{0.25}{1-0.6^2} = 0.391.$$

The series in Figure 16.4(b) uses $\theta_1 = -0.6$, which yields the same variance.

In conclusion, the mean and variance of an AR(1) process with $|\phi| < 1$ are time invariant. The appendix to this chapter shows that this is also true of the autocorrelation function. Consequently, an AR(1) process is stationary, as long as the stability condition $|\phi| < 1$ is satisfied. Because stationarity hinges on the condition $|\phi| < 1$, we call this the **stationarity condition** for an AR(1) process. In the same way, in general AR(p) processes are stationary as long as suitable stability conditions hold.

EXERCISES

The derivation of the mean and variance of an AR(1) process we have presented is directed at showing that the stability condition $|\phi| < 1$ implies that the mean and variance are constant. This contributes to the general conclusion that the stability condition implies stationarity. However, if we begin with the knowledge that a stable AR(1) process is stationary, there is an easier way of deriving its mean and variance.

16.1 Consider a stable AR(1) process

$$Y_t = \phi_0 + \phi Y_{t-1} + \varepsilon_t, \quad \varepsilon_t \sim \text{wn}(0, \sigma^2).$$

Given the knowledge that Y_t is stationary and therefore has a constant variance, so that $E(Y_t) = E(Y_{t-1})$ and $V(Y_t) = V(Y_{t-1})$, do the following.

(a) Show that $E(Y_t) = \alpha$. (You may use the notation $\phi_0 \equiv \alpha(1 - \phi)$ given in equations (16.5) and (16.6).)

(b) Derive $V(Y_t)$.

---

[4]   We have used this geometric series result previously in Appendix 6A.

16.4   The Stationarity Condition

The role of the stationarity condition in an AR process leads us naturally to ask: What happens if it is not satisfied? This question suggests itself particularly in view of our ultimate interest in modeling nonstationary variables. Our conclusion is that, with one important exception, nonstationary AR processes are not a useful means of modeling nonstationary variables. However, it is necessary to consider the various cases to understand why this is true.

16.4.1   Violation of the Stationarity Condition in an AR(1) Process

We have seen that the stationarity condition $|\phi| < 1$ implies a geometrically declining impulse response function for an AR(1) process, so that the effect of a shock decays over time. The commonsense interpretation of this property is that "the past is less important than the present." In considering the implications of a violation of this condition, there are two cases to examine: $|\phi| > 1$ and $|\phi| = 1$.

1. *Nonstationarity when $|\phi| > 1$.* Setting aside the first term $\phi^{s+1}u_{t-s-1}$, the infinite moving average representation for an AR(1) process makes no special assumption about ϕ and so continues to be valid even if $|\phi| > 1$. However, in this case the impulse response weights $1, \phi, \phi^2, \phi^3, \ldots$ *increase* geometrically instead of decaying. This has the implausible implication that shocks are more important the further back in time we go or "the past is more important than the present." No one believes that a shock of a given size that took place 1000 years ago is more important for events today than one that occurred last week.

   Another way of seeing the implausibility of this case is to simulate an AR(1) process under this assumption. It is useful to consider two cases: $\phi > 1$ and $\phi < -1$.

   (a) Nonstationarity when $\phi > 1$. Consider the AR(1) process (16.6), setting $\phi_0 = 0$ and $\phi = 1.05$:

   $$Y_t = 1.05 Y_{t-1} + \varepsilon_t.$$

   Figure 16.6(a) shows such a simulated series, generated using an initial value of $Y_0 = 100$.[5] Also plotted is the deterministic constant growth series that would be generated in the absence of random shocks, reproduced from Figure 6.3.

---

[5] The simulation uses the white noise innovation of Figure 15.2, amplified to have variance $\sigma^2 = 25$. The amplified variance makes it possible to see that in the long run the stochastic series diverges from the deterministic trend.

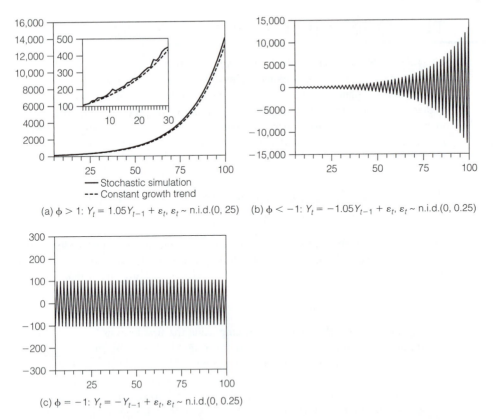

(a) φ > 1: $Y_t = 1.05Y_{t-1} + \varepsilon_t, \varepsilon_t \sim$ n.i.d.(0, 25)   (b) φ < −1: $Y_t = -1.05Y_{t-1} + \varepsilon_t, \varepsilon_t \sim$ n.i.d.(0, 0.25)

— Stochastic simulation
--- Constant growth trend

(c) φ = −1: $Y_t = -Y_{t-1} + \varepsilon_t, \varepsilon_t \sim$ n.i.d.(0, 0.25)

FIGURE 16.6 With the exception of the unit root case φ = 1, nonstationary autoregressive processes are not a useful way of describing economic time series.

In the early periods of its evolution, the stochastic series exhibits some erratic variation because there is little accumulated history of shocks compared to recent shocks. This erratic variation is displayed in the magnification of the early portion of the curve inserted into Figure 16.6(a). As time goes on, however, the accumulated history of past shocks comes to dominate the series, recent shocks being insignificant in comparison. The result is that the trajectory becomes smooth. Note, however, that this smooth trajectory does *not* correspond to the deterministic 5% exponential trend generated by the constant growth model. The fact that the stochastically simulated series is dominated by the historical accumulation of shocks means that it departs from the deterministic growth path.

Over time, then, the appearance of the stochastic series changes fundamentally. It begins by displaying erratic variation, but gradually this disappears. The series is said to be nonstationary in a manner that is **nonhomogeneous.**

Such a pattern is not, of course, what we observe in real data. Instead, economic variables continue to exhibit substantial erratic variation as time passes. Consequently, we must conclude that an AR(1) model with $\phi > 1$ is not a useful way of describing economic time series. This is perhaps surprising because the deterministic version of this model—the constant growth model—*is* useful, as we have seen in Chapter 6. Evidently we must seek other means of introducing stochastic elements into the constant growth model in order to create a stochastic version of that model, a quest we pursue in the next chapter.

(b) Nonstationarity when $\phi < -1$. Consider setting $\phi_0 = 0$ and $\phi = -1.05$ in the AR(1) process (16.6),

$$Y_t = -1.05Y_{t-1} + \varepsilon_t.$$

Figure 16.6(b) shows such a simulated series, generated using an initial value of $Y_0 = 100$ and the white noise realization of Figure 15.2. It shows an oscillatory trajectory with increasing variance. Once again this is not what we observe in practice, and it must be concluded that an AR(1) model with $\phi < -1$ is not a useful way of describing economic time series.

2. *Nonstationarity when $|\phi| = 1$.* How about the razor's-edge case of $|\phi| = 1$? It is useful to examine both the cases of $\phi = 1$ and $\phi = -1$.

(a) Nonstationarity when $\phi = 1$. This is the case of a random walk; notice that the infinite moving average representation (16.15) reduces to the stochastic trend (15.20) of the previous chapter. As we have seen, this model is of considerable practical importance. Examples of random walks—both with and without drift—are simulated in Chapters 2 and 15. Inspecting these earlier simulations, it is apparent that a random walk is nonstationary in a manner that "looks the same" throughout time; it is nonstationary in a manner that is **homogeneous.**

(b) Nonstationarity when $\phi = -1$. Such a process is simulated in Figure 16.6(c) using, once again, a starting value of $Y_0 = 100$ and the white noise innovation of Figure 15.2. Now the variable oscillates wildly from period to period, although not with increasing variance as in Figure 16.6(b). Once again it is evident that economic variables do not behave in this way, and so this is not a useful model for describing economic time series.

Conclusions

The stationarity condition $|\phi| < 1$ has the commonsense interpretation that "the past is less important than the present." If instead $|\phi| > 1$, then the implication is that "the past is more important than the present," which is implausible for economic processes—it implies a nonhomogeneous form of nonstationarity. The razor's-edge case of $|\phi| = 1$ has the interpretation that "the past and the present are equally important." The case of $\phi = -1$ is implausible, but the alternative of $\phi = 1$ is of considerable practical interest.

In conclusion, for the most part nonstationary versions of autoregressive processes do not offer useful descriptions of economic data. The one exception is the unit root case of $\phi = 1$.

16.4.2 Fire, the Wheel, and Double-Entry Bookkeeping

The unit root case $\phi = 1$ is of interest because it is the only nonstationary AR process that offers the promise of describing nonstationary economic variables. Its implication that shocks are permanent in their effect contrasts with the implication of the stationary case that shocks are transitory.

The notion that some shocks can permanently influence a variable, changing its value in all future periods, may strike you as odd because it is no doubt the case that many economic shocks are merely transitory in their effect. It is natural to think of most shocks as having a large initial effect on the economy, but one that either terminates after a few periods like an MA process or peters out gradually over time like the decaying influence of an AR process. To develop our sense of how the unit root case might apply to economics, let us consider some examples of transitory versus permanent shocks.

Monetary Policy as an Example of a Transitory Shock

As an example of a shock that economists have traditionally regarded as transitory, consider monetary policy. Suppose a central bank decides to increase the money supply, say through an open market operation in which it purchases securities. By paying for the purchase with checks drawn on itself, the central bank creates additional reserve deposits held by the commercial banks. These new reserves induce a chain of new loan and deposit creation throughout the commercial banking system, the new deposits constituting the increase in the money supply. Economists have long understood that the accompanying loan creation temporarily (during the period while the new loans are being made) lowers interest rates and finances investment spending.[6] Hence, monetary policy temporarily affects interest rates and capital formation. However, these effects dissipate over time as the new loan and deposit creation comes to an end and the money stock reaches its new level, much like the impulse response weights in an AR process. Interest rates return to the level that would otherwise have prevailed, determined by the normal borrowing

---

[6] This understanding originated with Henry Thornton (1760–1815), a London banker who described what we now call "the transmissions mechanism for a monetary impulse" 2 centuries ago. See Makinen (1977).

and lending activity in financial markets, and the effect of the temporarily altered flow of investment spending on the economy's total stock of capital is negligible.

It is for these reasons that macroeconomists have traditionally regarded monetary policy as temporary rather than permanent in its effect. The temporary effects of monetary policy lead some economists to include it among a set of demand management tools that might be used to stabilize the economy over the business cycle.[7] The absence of a permanent effect, on the other hand, means that most do not view it as a tool that can usefully contribute to, say, economic growth.[8] Indeed, there is a strong tradition in macroeconomics that regards money as **neutral** in the long run. A monetary shock that took place last month may be important for events today; one that took place 20 years ago is not. The past is less important than the present.

Technical Change as an Example of a Permanent Shock

In contrast to a temporary shock such as monetary policy, for what sort of economic shock might it be true that "the past and present are equally important"?

Consider the creation of new ideas. The discovery of fire and the invention of the wheel continue to be of significance to modern economies, undiminished by the passage of thousands of years. Similarly, more recent inventions such as electricity, the telephone, radio and television, flight, the automobile, computers, and the Internet promise to be of permanent value to humankind, making life better into the indefinite future in a way that would not otherwise have been possible.

New ideas are not necessarily in the form of a tangible product: Many are of a "software" rather than "hardware" nature. Pure knowledge is of this type—Sir Isaac Newton's invention of calculus was an essential prelude to vast scientific advance. New ideas can also take the form of better ways of doing things—Henry Ford's introduction of the production line into large-scale manufacturing was a fundamental reorganization of the means of production. Similarly, the invention of double-entry bookkeeping made possible the financial control of business enterprise, providing the foundation for modern accounting and management information systems that in turn have made possible the modern large-scale production and distribution of goods. Some innovations are of a social nature; the widespread introduction of public school systems a century ago has been the source of enormous human capital formation, providing the educated workforce essential to the operation of a modern economy and further technological advance. These are all examples of "software" innovations that promise to be of permanent value, little different economically from the "hardware" innovations of fire and the wheel.

---

[7] Of course not all economists advocate the use of monetary policy for countercyclical purposes. For the classic statement of the contrary view see Friedman (1968).

[8] We are speaking here of monetary policy as we have defined it. Obviously, the more basic function of government in maintaining sound currency—that is, not debasing the currency through inflation—is important for the long-term health of an economy.

Of course, not all new ideas are permanent in their significance. The kerosene lamp was an important invention when it was first introduced, providing an enormous improvement over candlelight, and continued to be in widespread use in rural areas until only a couple of generations ago. But it is of no significance today, having in turn been supplanted by new forms of illumination.

Most ideas are like the kerosene lamp: They are useful for awhile, but are eventually overtaken by even better ideas. Thus, like monetary policy, they are transitory rather than permanent in their effect. They are like shocks to an AR process in which the stationarity condition $|\phi| < 1$ holds, decaying gradually in their influence so that "the past is less important than the present."

A few ideas, however, are like fire, the wheel, and double-entry bookkeeping: Their influence is permanent rather than transitory. They are like shocks to an AR process in which there is a unit root, so that "the past and the present are equally important."

16.5   Key Properties of Moving Average and Autoregressive Processes

Having developed an appreciation of the importance of the stationarity condition by considering situations in which it is violated, let us return to ones in which it is satisfied. We have seen that in some respects MA and stationary AR processes differ. Nevertheless, the temporal dependence they imply has a number of common properties, and it is useful to emphasize these.

Shocks Are Temporary in Their Effect. An inspection of the impulse response functions shows this to be the case. It is most obviously true of MA models; a shock to an MA(q) process has an effect for q periods following but not beyond. For a stationary AR process, a shock has effects into the indefinite future, but according to a declining set of impulse response coefficients, so that the effect of a shock eventually becomes negligible. In this sense, the effect is temporary.

The Variable Exhibits Mean Reversion. Like the model of white noise around a constant mean, MA and stationary AR models describe variation around a constant mean. The difference is that now this variation is autocorrelated. However, like white noise around a constant mean, the variable cannot wander arbitrarily far from its mean for indefinite periods of time. Instead, the mean represents a central line to which the series tends to revert. That is, MA and stationary AR processes exhibit mean reversion.

A Shock Does Not Alter the Long-Term Forecast. Suppose a variable evolves according to an MA or stationary AR process. How should future values be forecasted? The answer depends on whether we are forecasting over the short term or the long term.

FIGURE 16.7

Stylized forecast intervals for AR or MA processes.

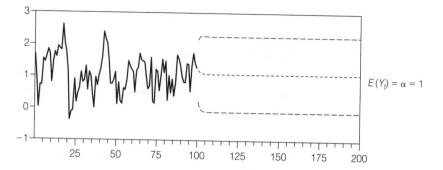

In the long run, the forecast is the mean. Because both MA and stationary AR processes exhibit mean reversion and have the feature that shocks are temporary in their effect, a current shock affects Y in the short run but not in the long run. Consequently, in the long run the best forecast of Y is just its mean α. In this respect, the implications for forecasting are no different from when the variation around that mean is white noise.

In the short run, autocorrelation can be used to improve forecasts. When a variable fluctuates in a way that is partly predictable, that knowledge can be used in short-term forecasting. That is, when MA or AR processes are used to describe the short-run variation in a variable, it is possible to use this pattern of autocorrelation to improve short-term forecasts over just using the mean. This is illustrated in Figure 16.7, in which the forecasts take several periods to converge to the mean of $\alpha = 1$. (Although the figure shows monotonic convergence to the long-term forecast, this is because the simulation uses an AR(1) disturbance. A higher-order AR process could yield cyclic convergence to the long-term forecast.) This figure may be usefully contrasted with the case of white noise around a constant mean in Figure 15.2(a), in which there is no autocorrelation that can be exploited in short-term forecasting.

For example, suppose the variable of interest is the unemployment rate and an estimated MA or AR model describes its historical movement over several business cycle episodes. Suppose further that you wish to use this model to forecast for the quarters immediately ahead and that at present the economy is at the peak of a business cycle. The model will use the historical pattern of fluctuations in the unemployment rate to forecast.

As we go further into the future, knowledge of the short-term behavior of the variable becomes less and less useful in forecasting. Knowing that the economy is currently at the peak of a business cycle may be useful for forecasting unemployment in the next year or two, but is unlikely to be of any value in forecasting it 10 years hence. Consequently, in the long run it is not possible to use the short-term autocorrelation in the variable to improve forecasts, and the best long-term forecast is just the mean α.

Another way of expressing this idea is to say that a shock does not alter the long-term forecast. A larger value observed for Y_t today may change our forecasts in the periods immediately ahead because those future values depend on the current value in the way described by the autocorrelated MA or AR process. But because the effect of the shock is temporary, it does not affect the long-term forecast, which continues to be α. In this respect MA and stationary AR models differ fundamentally from random walks, in which a shock does alter the long-term forecast.

The Forecast Error Variance Is Bounded   In the long run, the optimal forecast is the mean α and the forecast error is

$$Y_t - E(Y_t) = Y_t - \alpha = u_t.$$

Because this forecast error is just the disturbance u_t, it has constant variance given by the appropriate expression of the associated AR or MA model. Let this variance be denoted σ_u^2,

$$V(Y_t - EY_t) = V(u_t) = \sigma_u^2.$$

For example, if u_t is MA(q) then σ_u^2 is given by (16.11); if u_t is AR(1) then σ_u^2 is given by (16.16).

This is the forecast error variance associated with the long-term forecast α. It may be used to construct a forecast interval around α, as depicted in Figure 16.7.[9] The important point about σ_u^2 is that it does not depend on t. Therefore, long-term forecast intervals are of a fixed width around the long-term forecast of α.

Result 16.1	*In the absence of coefficient uncertainty, MA and stable AR processes have fixed-width long-term forecast intervals.*

In the short run, the forecast intervals are narrower, as Figure 16.7 indicates. Knowledge of the immediate past, as captured by an AR or MA model, improves the precision of forecasts. But in the long run, forecast error variances are bounded.

Conclusions

In summary, a consideration of the impulse response functions has revealed the following key properties of MA and stationary AR processes:

- Shocks are temporary in their effect.
- The variable exhibits mean reversion.
- A shock does not alter the long-term forecast.
- The forecast error variance is bounded.

In their key properties, therefore, these models are much like white noise. They differ from white noise in permitting temporal dependence, a temporal dependence that can be exploited in short-term forecasting.

We have emphasized these common properties of MA and stationary AR processes because they continue to hold when these processes are combined, a class of models to which we now turn.

---

[9]   This discussion assumes known values for α and the parameters of the disturbance. Of course in real-world forecasting problems in which these parameters must be estimated, this forecast interval will have to be modified to reflect the uncertainty in the estimates.

16.6   Autoregressive–Moving Average Processes

Although both moving average and autoregressive processes provide ways of describing the autocorrelation in time series variables, using just one approach or the other often necessitates an excessive number of parameters to adequately model a variable. The number of parameters can often be dramatically reduced by combining them into an autoregressive–moving average (ARMA) model.

If Y_t fluctuates around a constant α,

$$Y_t = \alpha + u_t, \tag{16.18a}$$

then an ARMA(p, q) specification for the disturbance u_t is

$$u_t - \phi_1 u_{t-1} - \cdots - \phi_q u_{t-p} = \varepsilon_t + \theta_1 \varepsilon_{t-1} + \cdots + \theta_q \varepsilon_{t-q}. \tag{16.18b}$$

As before, p and q denote the maximum lags in the autoregressive and moving average components. In the special case where the $\phi_j = 0$, so that there is no autoregressive component, this reduces to the MA(q) disturbance (16.10). Alternatively, if the $\theta_j = 0$ so that there is no moving average component, it reduces to the AR(p) process (16.13). As before, stationarity of the ARMA model requires certain restrictions on the roots of its AR component.

In many presentations of ARMA modeling, the model is stated directly in terms of the observable variable Y_t,

$$Y_t - \phi_0 - \phi_1 Y_{t-1} - \cdots - \phi_q Y_{t-p} = \varepsilon_t + \theta_1 \varepsilon_{t-1} + \cdots + \theta_q \varepsilon_{t-q}. \tag{16.19}$$

Under the appropriate coefficient restrictions, this reduces to the various special cases we have encountered: in the MA(1) case, equation (16.4); in the AR(1) case, equation (16.6); and, in the AR(p) case, equation (16.14). As previously, we have chosen to state the model in its constant-plus-disturbance form (16.18) in anticipation of generalizing the constant to deterministic and stochastic trends.

In combining the AR and MA approaches to modeling autocorrelation, ARMA models continue to possess the key properties of these processes: shocks are temporary in their effect, the variable exhibits mean reversion, a shock does not alter the long run forecast, and the forecast error variance is bounded.

16.6.1   The Box-Jenkins Methodology

A well-established methodology exists for estimating ARMA models. This methodology was first unified in a coherent form by Box and Jenkins (1970) and so is often called the **Box-Jenkins methodology.** It consists of three steps: model identification, estimation, and diagnostic checking.

1.   **Model identification.** If the ARMA model is to be estimated, what lag lengths should be used? Model identification refers to the preliminary use of

data analysis tools such as the correlogram to conjecture plausible orders for p and q.[10]

2. **Estimation.** Based on chosen lag lengths p and q, techniques are available for estimating ARMA models. These techniques have been implemented in most econometrics packages. For data for which it is judged appropriate to set $q = 0$, so that there is no MA component, the estimation of the $AR(p)$ model involves nothing more than the estimation of equation (16.14) as a least squares regression.

3. **Diagnostic checking.** Does the estimated model satisfactorily describe the variable it is intended to represent? Does it successfully capture the predictable behavior of the variable, in effect transforming it to white noise? The techniques of model evaluation—which draw in part on the tools of specification testing and model choice developed in Chapter 12—can be used to assess the adequacy of the estimated ARMA model. If it is judged unsatisfactory, the researcher returns to the model identification stage to consider alternative lag orders.

There are many good expositions of the Box-Jenkins methodology. Their 1970 book (or its subsequent 1976 or 1994 editions) remains a valuable reference. For a more recent treatment in the context of a broader introduction to time series analysis, see Enders (1995, Chap. 2). Some econometrics texts include discussions of the Box-Jenkins methodology, among them Diebold (2004), Griffiths, Hill, and Judge (1993, Chap. 20), Johnston and DiNardo (1997, Chap. 7), Maddala (2001, Chap. 13), and Pindyck and Rubinfeld (1991, Chaps. 16–19).

Perhaps the most important remark to offer on the Box-Jenkins methodology is that it is largely an exercise in atheoretical statistical analysis. Although MA behavior is sometimes suggested by data transformations such as aggregation or differencing, and economic models sometimes predict AR behavior, in general the scope for economic theory to be brought to bear on the specification of the ARMA model is limited. In particular, economics usually has nothing to say about the choice of the lag lengths p and q. Similarly, economic theory does not normally suggest testable restrictions on the coefficients of ARMA models.[11]

In part because of this, for our purposes an acquaintance with the application of the Box-Jenkins methodology is less important than a general appreciation that ARMA models provide the statistical framework for describing the short-run

---

[10] This use of the term *identification* is an entirely different one from the concept of *econometric identification* that we introduce in Section 10.3 and study further in Chapter 13.

[11] This remark applies to the use of ARMA models in *univariate* time series analysis—the modeling of a single variable studied in isolation. The spirit of the Box-Jenkins methodology generalizes to *multivariate* time series analysis—the modeling of the joint behavior of several time series—and is implemented in the form of **vector autoregressive** (VAR) models, which are discussed in Chapter 18. Here economic theory sometimes suggests testable hypotheses in the form of **causality restrictions** among variables. However, this is a topic beyond the scope of this book.

temporal dependence in time series variables. With this appreciation, we can turn from the modeling of short-run fluctuations to the modeling of long-run trends, the subject of the next chapter.

Appendix   # Autocorrelation Functions for Moving Average and Autoregressive Processes

As we have seen in Section 15.3, the ACF of a stochastic process is a valuable way of summarizing its pattern of serial dependence.

In Section 16.1, the means and variances of AR and MA processes are derived. Here we turn to the autocorrelation functions of these models. We find that, just as is true of the means and variances, the ACFs are time invariant. Hence, MA and AR processes (the latter with coefficients appropriately restricted) are stationary.

Obtaining an ACF requires that we begin with the autocovariance function, defined by equation (15.7):

$$\gamma_j = \text{cov}(Y_t, Y_{t-j}) = E[(Y_t - EY_t)(Y_{t-j} - EY_{t-j})].$$

The ACF is then defined by

$$\rho_j = \frac{\gamma_j}{\gamma_0}.$$

As with the mean and variance, deriving the autocovariance function involves applying the laws of expectation and variance of Appendix B.

Moving Average Processes

Let us derive the autocorrelation function for the MA(1) process (16.9). As a special case of the more general expression (16.11), the variance is

$$\gamma_0 = V(Y_t) = V(\varepsilon_t) + \theta^2 V(\varepsilon_{t-1}) = (1 + \theta^2)\sigma^2.$$

At lag $j = 1$ the autocovariance is

$$\begin{aligned}
\gamma_1 &= \text{cov}(Y_t, Y_{t-1}) \\
&= E[(Y_t - EY_t)(Y_{t-1} - EY_{t-1})] \\
&= E[(Y_t - \alpha)(Y_{t-1} - \alpha)] \\
&= E(u_t u_{t-1}) \\
&= E[(\varepsilon_t + \theta\varepsilon_{t-1})(\varepsilon_{t-1} + \theta\varepsilon_{t-2})] \\
&= E(\varepsilon_t \varepsilon_{t-1} + \theta\varepsilon_t \varepsilon_{t-2} + \theta\varepsilon_{t-1}^2 + \theta\varepsilon_{t-1}\varepsilon_{t-2}) \\
&= \theta E(\varepsilon_{t-1}^2) \\
&= \theta\sigma^2.
\end{aligned}$$

The penultimate step holds because ε_t is white noise and therefore uncorrelated over time. Consequently, ε in different time periods have zero covariance: $E(\varepsilon_t \varepsilon_{t-j}) = 0$ for all $j \neq 0$.

The autocorrelation at this lag is therefore

$$\rho_1 = \frac{\gamma_1}{\gamma_0} = \frac{\theta\sigma^2}{(1+\theta^2)\sigma^2} = \frac{\theta}{1+\theta^2}.$$

Notice that for any value of θ this must be fractional, so the requirement that a correlation be in the range $-1 < \rho < 1$ is satisfied.

In a similar manner, at lag $j = 2$ the autocovariance is

$$
\begin{aligned}
\gamma_2 &= \operatorname{cov}(Y_t, Y_{t-2}) \\
&= E[(Y_t - EY_t)(Y_{t-2} - EY_{t-2})] \\
&= E[(Y_t - \alpha)(Y_{t-2} - \alpha)] \\
&= E[(\varepsilon_t + \theta\varepsilon_{t-1})(\varepsilon_{t-2} + \theta\varepsilon_{t-3})] \\
&= 0.
\end{aligned}
$$

Hence, for an MA(1) process, at lag $j > 1$ it is the case that Y_t and Y_{t-j} have no shocks in common, and so their covariance is zero:

$$\gamma_j = 0 \quad \text{for } j > 1.$$

Consequently, the ACF for an MA(1) model is very simple:

$$
\rho_j = \frac{\gamma_j}{\gamma_0} =
\begin{cases}
1 & \text{at lag } j = 0 \\
\dfrac{\theta}{1+\theta^2} & \text{at lag } j = 1 \\
0 & \text{at lag } j > 1.
\end{cases}
$$

Notice that this ACF is time invariant: It depends only the lag length j and not on the time period t.

This time invariance of the ACF extends to MA(q) processes generally, establishing that MA processes are stationary. In general the ACF of an MA(q) process cuts off after lag q. This is another way of seeing the conclusion that came from our examination of the impulse response function: An MA(q) process has a memory of q periods.

Autoregressive Processes

In deriving the ACF of an AR process, it is helpful to work with the simplest case of an AR(1). In Section 16.3 we have seen that an AR process has an infinite MA representation; for an AR(1) model, this is equation (16.15). It tells us that

$$Y_t - E(Y_t) = \sum_{j=0}^{\infty} \phi^i \varepsilon_{t-j} = \varepsilon_t + \phi\varepsilon_{t-1} + \phi^2\varepsilon_{t-2} + \phi^3\varepsilon_{t-3} + \cdots.$$

Hence, the autocovariance function $\gamma_j = E[(Y_t - EY_t)(Y_{t-j} - EY_{t-j})]$ may be evaluated as

$$\gamma_j = E[(\varepsilon_t + \phi\varepsilon_{t-1} + \phi^2\varepsilon_{t-2} + \phi^3\varepsilon_{t-3} + \cdots + \phi^i\varepsilon_{t-j} + \phi^{j+1}\varepsilon_{t-j-1} + \cdots)$$
$$\times (\varepsilon_{t-j} + \phi\varepsilon_{t-j-1} + \phi^2\varepsilon_{t-j-2} + \phi^3\varepsilon_{t-j-3} + \cdots)].$$

This seemingly complex expression turns out to be quite easy to evaluate. Remember that, just as in the previous MA derivation, because ε_t is white noise and therefore uncorrelated over time, the ε in different time periods have zero covariance: $E(\varepsilon_t\varepsilon_{t-j}) = 0$ for all $j \neq 0$. Consequently in multiplying out the product and taking the mathematical expectation of the resulting sum, the only nonzero terms will be those for cross-products involving the same lag:

$$\gamma_j = \phi^j E(\varepsilon_{t-j}^2) + \phi^{j+2} E(\varepsilon_{t-j-1}^2) + \phi^{j+4} E(\varepsilon_{t-j-2}^2) + \cdots$$
$$= \phi^j \sigma^2 (1 + \phi^2 + \phi^4 + \phi^6 + \cdots)$$
$$= \sigma^2 \phi^j \sum_{i=0}^{\infty} (\phi^2)^i$$
$$= \frac{\sigma^2 \phi^j}{1 - \phi^2} \quad \text{by the geometric series result (16.17).}$$

The geometric series result (16.17) only holds for $-1 < \phi < 1$, and so this expression only applies when the AR(1) process is stationary. Notice that at lag $j = 0$ the expression reduces to $\gamma_0 = \sigma^2/(1 - \phi^2)$, which is just the variance expression (16.16), as it should be.

Dividing the covariance function γ_j by this variance γ_0 yields the ACF:

$$\rho_j = \frac{\gamma_j}{\gamma_0} = \phi^j. \tag{16.20}$$

This shows that the pattern of temporal dependence described by an AR(1) process is of a simple form; in fact, the ACF of an AR(1) process is the same as its impulse response function. At one lag the autocorrelation is ϕ, at two lags ϕ^2, and three lags ϕ^3, and so on. If ϕ is positive, these autocorrelations are always positive; a large value for Y_t in this period tends to be followed by large values in subsequent periods. In this case, the coefficient satisfies $0 < \phi < 1$ and so the autocorrelations decline geometrically, as shown in Figure 16.5(a) for $\phi = 0.6$. If, on the other hand, ϕ is negative, then a large value for Y_t this period tends to be followed by a small one next period. Values an even number of periods apart are positively correlated; values an odd number of periods apart are negatively correlated. Under the stability requirement $-1 < \phi < 0$, these alternating autocorrelations decline geometrically. This is shown in Figure 16.5(b) for $\phi = -0.6$.

This diminishing pattern of temporal dependence makes sense. In terms of their infinite MA representations, Y_t and Y_{t-j} both depend on the entire past history of shocks. As j gets larger so that Y_t and Y_{t-j} are further apart in time, they have less of their past history in common and so the correlation between them weakens.

Notice that the ACF (16.20) is time invariant: It depends only the lag length j and not on the time period t. This time invariance of the ACF extends to AR(p) processes generally, as long as the appropriate stationarity conditions are satisfied. The ACF of an AR(p) process decays, eventually becoming negligible. As in the special case of an AR(1), shocks are said to be temporary in their effect, yet the process has infinite memory.

17 Trends

ARMA models offer a very flexible framework for modeling fluctuations in economic variables. As formulated in the previous chapter, however, they describe only fluctuations around a constant mean. As we have emphasized repeatedly, many variables do not consist simply of variation around some horizontal line. Instead, many economic variables grow over time and so follow trends.

The key tool in modeling trending variables is one we have introduced in Chapter 6—the constant growth model. There, however, it is motivated in terms of offering a good descriptive fit to the trend of many growing variables. We have given only a cursory introduction to the distinction between deterministic and stochastic trends. We also have given only offhand treatment to the modeling of fluctuations around the trend using the only tool at our disposal at the time, a white noise disturbance that does not permit autocorrelated fluctuations.

The time has now come to marry the ARMA approach to modeling fluctuations with the constant growth model of trends. In Chapter 15, we reemphasize that there are two types of trends: the deterministic trends of trend stationary processes and the stochastic trends of difference stationary ones. We have shown that the two types of processes differ fundamentally in their key features. In this chapter, we use ARMA models of serial correlation to specify general classes of trend and difference stationary models. This culminates in a test for the presence of a stochastic trend that allows us to distinguish between them. Let us begin with a recapitulation of the constant growth model.

17.1 The Constant Growth Model Revisited

In Section 6.2.1 we study the constant growth model. In its discrete-time form, the model specifies a variable Y as evolving through time according to

$$Y_t = (1 + g)Y_{t-1}. \tag{17.1}$$

We have seen that g has the interpretation as the growth rate. Some values generated by this model for $t = 1, 2, 3, \ldots$ are given in Table 6.1 and Figure 6.3, based on a growth rate of 5% ($g = 0.05$) and the initial value $Y_0 = 100$.

Specified in these terms, the constant growth model is deterministic. There is no element of randomness in the model. Given knowledge of the initial value Y_0 and the growth rate g, the time path of Y is perfectly predictable. Let us remind ourselves of some of the key features of this deterministic time path.

By the method of recursive substitution, we have found that a convenient way of summarizing the determination of Y_t at any time point t is in terms of the "solution"

$$Y_t = Y_0(1+g)^t. \tag{17.2}$$

It is this solution that is the basis for our observation that, although the evolution of Y_t is nonlinear, it is linear in its logarithms:

$$\log Y_t = \log Y_0 + \log(1+g)t = \alpha + \beta t. \tag{17.3}$$

That is, $\log Y_t$ follows a deterministic time trend. As we have seen, the slope coefficient β has the interpretation as a continuous growth rate. For example, if Y_t grows at a discrete rate of $g = 0.05$, then this is equivalent to a continuously compounded growth rate of $\beta = \log(1+g) = \log 1.05 \approx 0.04879$.

Another interpretation of the model is to lag this linear function and subtract, yielding

$$\log Y_t - \log Y_{t-1} = \beta t - \beta(t-1)$$

or

$$\Delta \log Y_t = \beta. \tag{17.4}$$

The log-differences of the series—multiplied by 100, the percentage changes (in continuously compounded form)—equal the constant growth rate β. That is, each period Y_t changes by a constant percentage amount.

These two interpretations are mathematically equivalent expressions of the same behavior. One implies the other. Instead of starting with (17.3) and deriving (17.4) by differencing, as we have done, we could start with the latter and use the method of recursive substitution to observe that

$$\begin{aligned} \log Y_t &= \beta + \log Y_{t-1} \\ &= \beta + (\beta + \log Y_{t-2}) \\ &= 2\beta + (\beta + \log Y_{t-3}) \\ &\vdots \\ &= \beta t + \log Y_0. \end{aligned} \tag{17.5}$$

This just reproduces the linear relationship (17.3).

Consider a series that evolves deterministically according to the constant growth model, such as the values of Y_t given in Table 6.1. Is it better to think of these values as, in their logarithms, being a linear function of time, as described by (17.3), or is it better to think of them as growing at a constant percentage rate, as described by (17.4)? The answer, of course, is that it does not matter. These are just two ways of thinking about the same thing; they are mathematically equivalent interpretations of the constant growth model (17.1).

17.1.1   Introducing Stochastic Elements into the Constant Growth Model

The deterministic constant growth model is mainly useful in economic theory as a way of specifying exogenous growth processes. We use it in Chapter 9 as the specification for population growth, equation (9.2), in the Solow-Swan growth model, and in the appendix to that chapter as the specification for technological progress. As Ragnar Frisch emphasized so long ago, however, economic variables do not evolve according to smooth deterministic trends; if they did there would be no role for econometric analysis. Observed time series data are generated in part by random factors.

In considering how random factors might be introduced into the constant growth model, notice that there are only three equations that serve as candidates for the introduction of a disturbance: the original constant growth equation (17.1), the solution (17.2) (or its loglinear version (17.3)), and the log-differences (17.4). Let us consider each of these.

An Approach That Does Not Work

One idea that might occur to us is to add an ARMA disturbance to equation (17.1):

$$Y_t = (1 + g)Y_{t-1} + u_t.$$

In fact we have already studied a model very similar to this. If we consider the special case in which u_t is white noise, then this is an AR(1) process such as we studied in Chapter 16,

$$Y_t = \phi Y_{t-1} + \varepsilon_t.$$

However, it is one in which the stationarity condition $|\phi| < 1$ is violated because $\phi = 1 + g > 1$ for a positive growth rate g. The implication of this violation, as we have seen in Section 16.4, is the implausible one that the further back in time we go, the more important are shocks that took place then for events today. Simulation of such a process in Figure 16.6(a) reveals a pattern of nonstationarity that we have found to be nonhomogeneous. On this basis, we conclude that such models are not a useful means of describing trending economic variables. These implications are unchanged even if we permit an autocorrelated disturbance u_t.

If this method of introducing a disturbance into the constant growth model does not work, why bother considering it? Because it reiterates the important lesson of the previous chapter: Autoregressive processes in which $|\phi| > 1$ are not a useful means of describing growing economic variables. Instead, we must consider other possibilities.

A Deterministic Trend

A more promising approach to introducing stochastic elements into the constant growth model is to add an ARMA disturbance u_t to the deterministic trend (17.3),

$$\log Y_t = \alpha + \beta t + u_t. \tag{17.6}$$

This says that the observations $\log Y_t$ are generated as random variables around this deterministic trend. In general, this short-run variation can reflect many influences and take many forms, so all it is appropriate to assume is that u_t follows some stationary ARMA process. Thus specified, this is a trend stationary model: The fluctuations u_t are stationary around the deterministic trend $\alpha + \beta t$.

In our preliminary discussion of this model in Chapter 6 we proceed on the basis of the specification that $u_t = \varepsilon_t$, a classical (what we now call a white noise) disturbance. This gives us the log-lin regression model (6.21). The obvious approach to estimating that model is the one we take in Chapter 6: applying least squares as we would to any regression model.

How should this change now that the disturbance is recognized as potentially being autocorrelated? The trend stationary specification suggests an obvious approach to modeling the short-run fluctuations in the series around its deterministic trend: Just estimate the trend by least squares, exactly as in Chapter 6, and use the residuals e_t as measures of u_t. The autocorrelation in these least squares residuals can then be described using the ARMA techniques of Chapter 16.

In other words, if a variable is trend stationary, then it is natural to proceed by detrending it and then using the Box-Jenkins methodology to model the fluctuations around its deterministic trend. You may find it surprising that the deterministic trend in a trend stationary variable can be legitimately estimated by least squares without explicitly treating the autocorrelation in the disturbance; this is the result of a famous theorem by Grenander and Rosenblatt (1957). It is analogous to our finding in Chapter 14 that least squares coefficient estimators are unbiased even in the presence of heteroskedasticity.

Practitioner's Tip: **Trend stationary time series**

The appropriate means of studying a trend stationary variable is to estimate the deterministic trend as a least squares regression and then analyze the autocorrelation in the least squares residuals.

EXAMPLE 1

Consider Jones's real GDP per capita series in the exercises in Section 6.2.6. Assuming the series to be trend stationary, and with the advanced understanding of time series analysis that you now possess, how should the trend be studied?

SOLUTION

The deterministic trend should be estimated as a least squares regression, exactly as is done in Exercise 6.10 (and in Example 2 of that chapter).

A Stochastic Trend

Another approach to introducing stochastic elements into the constant growth model is to return to our original specification of that model, equation (17.1), and make the growth rate g a random variable. Because $\beta \equiv 1 + g$, this is equivalent to adding a disturbance to (17.4),

$$\Delta \log Y_t = \beta + u_t. \tag{17.7}$$

This says that the period-by-period percentage changes $\Delta \log Y_t$ vary randomly around a mean growth rate β. Instead of the *constant growth* model (17.1) that gives rise to the deterministic trend (17.3), this specifies *random growth* and a stochastic trend. That the mean growth rate β is a constant carries the implication that, although the percentage changes $\Delta \log Y_t$ vary from period to period (sometimes being large, sometimes small, sometimes negative), they do not systematically increase or decrease over time. In saying that u_t follows some stationary ARMA process we are allowing these period-by-period growth rates to be autocorrelated. Thus specified, this is a difference stationary model; although the variable $\log Y_t$ is nonstationary in its levels because it is growing, it is stationary in its differences.

Our preliminary discussion of stochastic trends in Chapter 6 is stated in terms of the special case in which $u_t = \varepsilon_t$, a model that in Chapter 15 we study as a random walk with drift. There we show that random walks are examples of integrated variables: They are determined as the sum of their history of shocks. In the same way, it can be shown that it is an implication of the model (17.7) that $\log Y_t$ is determined as the sum of its history of shocks and so is integrated, something we examine in more detail later in this chapter. That is, the model (17.7) generalizes our previous concept of an integrated process to one that permits autocorrelation in the period-by-period changes.

Practitioner's Tip: Difference stationary time series

The appropriate means of studying a difference stationary variable is to detrend it by differencing and then analyze the autocorrelation in the differenced series.

The model (17.7) describes a variable that requires just a single differencing to be stationary. Such a variable is said to be **integrated of order 1,** denoted I(1). Random walks are special cases of I(1) variables in which the first differences are white noise and therefore serially uncorrelated. Notice that the concepts of integrated variables, difference stationarity, and stochastic trends are inextricably linked. An integrated variable is difference stationary and contains a stochastic trend.

The notation I(1) suggests that integration of higher orders is possible. An I(2) variable is one that must be differenced twice to achieve stationarity, an I(3) variable one that must be differenced three times, and so on. In general, a variable that must be differenced d times to be stationary is denoted I(d). For reasons that become apparent as we proceed, it is the I(1) case that is of the greatest practical interest and so the focus of most of our discussion. Higher orders of integration are considered in Section 17.4.

There is another way of thinking about an I(1) process. In Chapter 16 we have seen that the constant-plus-ARMA-disturbance model (16.18) can be restated as an ARMA model directly in terms of Y_t, equation (16.19). In the same way, the model (17.7) can be restated as an ARMA model in the differences $\Delta \log Y_t$,

$$\Delta \log Y_t - \phi_0 - \phi_1 \Delta \log Y_{t-1} - \cdots - \phi_q \Delta \log Y_{t-p}$$
$$= \varepsilon_t + \theta_1 \varepsilon_{t-1} + \cdots + \theta_q \varepsilon_{t-q}. \tag{17.8}$$

That is, we are using an ARMA model to describe fluctuations in, not the level of the variable as in the previous chapter, but its period-by-period percentage changes. In this formulation, the drift parameter β is embedded in the intercept ϕ_0. Such models are called **autoregressive *integrated* moving average** (ARIMA) models—that is, ARMA models for an integrated process. They are fully specified by the orders p and q of the autoregressive and moving average components and by the order of integration d, and so in general are denoted ARIMA(p, d, q). The model (17.8) for the I(1) case is an ARIMA$(p, 1, q)$.

EXAMPLE 2

Although the terminology of integrated processes, unit roots, and stochastic trends is recent, the realization among some researchers that economic variables may be modeled in this way is not. Orcutt (1948) was among the first to recognize the value of what we now call I(1) models. In studying annual U.S. macroeconomic time series for the period 1919–1932, he found that many series were well described by[1]

$$\Delta \log Y_t = 0.3 \Delta \log Y_{t-1} + e_t.$$

How does this model relate to the stochastic trend models we have discussed?

SOLUTION

This is an ARIMA model in first differences (so $d = 1$) in which the intercept ϕ_0 is zero, there is no moving average component (so $q = 0$), and there is a first-order autoregressive component (so $p = 1$). One way of expressing the model is in terms of equation (17.7),

$$\Delta \log Y_t = \beta + u_t,$$

with the disturbance u_t specified as AR(1),

$$u_t = \phi u_{t-1} + \varepsilon_t.$$

The equivalence of this with the ARIMA(1,1,0) formulation may be seen by substituting the latter equation into the former,

$$\Delta \log Y_t = \beta + u_t$$
$$= \beta + \phi u_{t-1} + \varepsilon_t$$

[1] Consistent with our treatment of regression, estimated models are stated in terms of the residuals e_t instead of the disturbance ε_t.

$$= \beta + \phi(\Delta \log Y_{t-1} - \beta) + \varepsilon_t$$
$$= \beta(1 - \phi) + \phi \Delta \log Y_{t-1} + \varepsilon_t$$
$$= \phi_0 + \phi \Delta \log Y_{t-1} + \varepsilon_t.$$

Orcutt's model is the special case in which $\phi_0 = \beta(1 - \phi) = 0$, the implication being that the drift β is zero. A zero drift is surprising in view of the fact that most macroeconomic variables exhibit positive growth rates. However, Orcutt was working with data over a fairly brief sample period—just 14 years—and perhaps over such a short time span a zero drift was a reasonable approximation.

EXAMPLE 3

Watson (1986, p. 59) used quarterly data on U.S. GNP over the years 1949–1984 to estimate the model

$$\Delta \log Y_t = 0.005 + 0.406 \Delta \log Y_{t-1} + e_t.$$

How does this relate to the models we have discussed?

SOLUTION

This is the same ARIMA(1,1,0) model estimated by Orcutt almost 40 years earlier, with the exception that an intercept is now included. Notice that, despite the inclusion of the intercept, the difference in sample period, the use of quarterly instead of annual data, and the change in available estimation technology, the estimate of the autocorrelation parameter is very similar: $\hat{\phi} = 0.406$ instead of Orcutt's value of 0.3.

From the derivation in Example 2, the drift parameter may be deduced as $\beta = \phi_0/(1 - \phi)$. Consequently, the intercept estimate of $\hat{\phi}_0 = 0.005$ implies an estimated drift of $\hat{\beta} = 0.005/(1 - 0.406) = 0.00842$. This has the interpretation as the average quarterly growth rate over this period. Multiplying by 4, the implied estimate of the average annual growth rate is 3.4%.

EXAMPLE 4

Stock and Watson (1988, p. 154) used quarterly data on U.S. GNP for the period 1947:2–1985:4 to estimate the model

$$\Delta \log Y_t = 0.008 + e_t + 0.3e_{t-1}.$$

How does this relate to the models we have discussed?

SOLUTION

This is the model (17.7) in which the disturbance is MA(1). There is no AR component. Consequently, this is an ARIMA(0,1,1) model. The drift estimate of $\hat{\beta} = 0.008$ has the interpretation as the average quarterly growth rate over this period. Multiplying by 4, the implied estimate of the average annual growth rate is 3.2%, very similar to the 3.4% estimate obtained from the ARIMA(1,1,0) model in Example 3, which is based on a slightly different sample period.

THEORY MEETS APPLICATION   17.1

Temporal Aggregation and the Random Walk Model of Consumption Revisited

Theory Meets Application 15.1 cites the analysis of Working (1960), who showed that the aggregation over time of a random walk induces autocorrelation in the period-by-period changes of the constructed variable. In other words, the temporal aggregation of a random walk is not itself a random walk.

Working further showed that the autocorrelation induced by temporal aggregation takes a very specific form: The period-by-period changes in the constructed variable are MA(1), so that the variable is ARIMA(0,1,1):

$$\Delta Y_t = \beta + \varepsilon_t + \theta \varepsilon_{t-1}.$$

Furthermore he established that the autocorrelation coefficient θ must be positive.

Motivated by these ideas, Ermini (1989) found that this model does indeed provide a good fit to quarterly consumption data. Using U.S. real consumption per capita, 1947:1–1985:4, he estimated the following ARIMA(0,1,1) model (*t* statistics are given in parentheses):

$$\Delta C_t = \underset{(0.02)}{0.06} + e_t + \underset{(2.67)}{0.211} e_{t-1}.$$

Notice that the coefficient estimate $\hat{\theta} = 0.211$ is positive and statistically significant. Ermini found that alternative ARIMA models, including ones with autoregressive terms or higher-order moving averages, did not offer a significant improvement in describing these data. This suggests that quarterly consumption data may well be the temporal aggregation of an underlying random walk series generated by weekly or monthly household spending decisions, consistent with Hall's theory.

Conclusions

There are two ways of describing economic variables that grow randomly: trend stationary processes and difference stationary processes. These two ways of introducing stochastic elements into the constant growth model are not mathematically equivalent. To describe a variable as varying randomly around a deterministic trend, as in (17.6), is not the same thing as saying that its percentage changes vary randomly around a constant mean, as in (17.7). We first demonstrate this in Chapter 2, in which the simulations in Figure 2.15 show that a series constructed as a deterministic trend plus disturbance looks quite different from one generated as a stochastic trend. The reason for this, as we have studied rigorously in Chapter 15 using white noise rather than autocorrelated disturbances, is that the two models differ fundamentally in their key properties. Section 17.2 extends that analysis to trend and difference stationary processes based on autocorrelated disturbances.

17.1.2 Logarithms or Levels?

The constant growth model, because it describes exponential growth, leads us to work in terms of the logarithm of the variable. Let us revisit briefly just how this compares with working in the raw or untransformed levels of the variable.

Banerjee, Dolado, Galbraith, and Hendry (1993, pp. 28–32) illustrated the issues at stake by considering U.K. net national product, 1872–1975, although the same points could be made by examining most growing macroeconomic variables. Figure 17.1(a) shows the variable in its untransformed levels and (b) shows it in its logarithms. Focusing on Figure 17.1(a), clearly a linear trend fitted to the raw series,

$$Y_t = \alpha + \beta t + u_t,$$

fails to capture the curvature associated with exponential growth. To describe this curvature, a researcher intent on working in terms of the untransformed series would have to fit, at a minimum, a quadratic trend such as

$$Y_t = \alpha + \beta t + \delta t^2 + u_t.$$

As Figure 17.1(b) makes clear, a more appealing alternative is to work in log-levels and fit a loglinear trend,

$$\log Y_t = \alpha + \beta t + u_t.$$

This approach is preferable for a couple of reasons. First, casual inspection suggests that it offers as good a fit to the secular trend as the quadratic model—yet it uses fewer parameters to do so. Note in particular that adding a quadratic term to the loglinear model does very little, if anything, to improve the model's ability to describe the trend in the data. Second, its link to the constant growth model means that the loglinear equation has a clear economic meaning, β having the interpretation as the continuous growth rate.

Differences-in-Logs versus Differences-in-Levels

So far we have phrased our comparison in terms of alternative trend stationary models. Consider instead the changes in the series. Figure 17.1(c) shows the raw differences ΔY_t, and (d) shows the log-differences $\Delta \log Y_t$. The raw differences ΔY_t have two interesting features. First, they do not seem to vary around a constant mean; instead, the size of the changes tends to drift upward over time. This suggests that a model of the form

$$\Delta Y_t = \beta + u_t \tag{17.9}$$

will be inadequate. The second interesting feature of the raw differences is that there appears to be a trend in the variance over time—it tends to become larger. That is, with the data in this form the variance does not seem to be time invariant.

Another way of seeing the inadequacy of the differences-in-levels model (17.9) is as follows. If it were correct, it would imply that the absolute changes in the variable fluctuate around the fixed mean β. As the variable grows, in its levels taking on larger and larger magnitudes, the implication would be that changes in the variable become smaller and smaller relative to its absolute magnitude. In the long run, the series would converge to a constant growth exponential curve. This is, of course, not what we observe of actual time series variables.

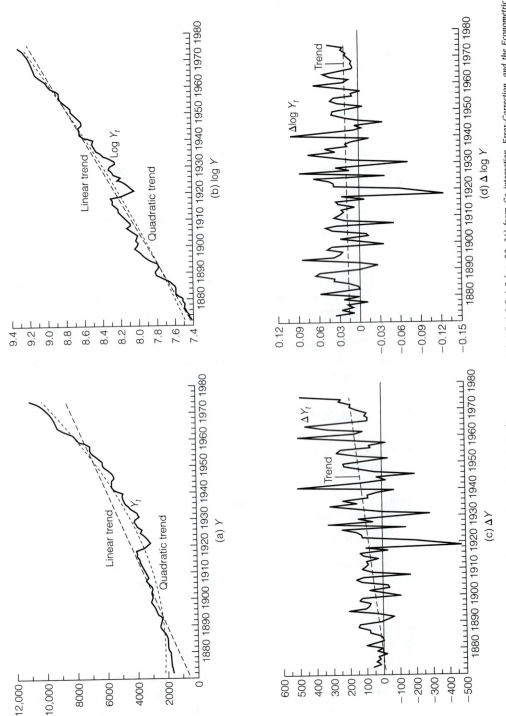

FIGURE 17.1 U.K. real net national product, 1872–1975. (*Source:* Figures 1.6, 1.7, 1.8 & 1.9 (pp. 29–31) from *Co-integration, Error-Correction, and the Econometric Analysis of Non-Stationary Data* by Banerjee, A. et al. (1993). Reprinted by permission of Oxford University Press.)

These issues disappear when we work in terms of log-differences. Figure 17.1(d) suggests that the series $\Delta \log Y$ varies systematically in neither its mean nor its variance, so that the model

$$\Delta \log Y_t = \beta + u_t$$

offers a description of the series that appears to be adequate in these respects. It allows absolute changes to grow with the magnitude of the variable.

Conclusions

When a variable grows over time there is a compelling case for working in terms of its logarithm. Growth often occurs in such a way that absolute changes in the variable tend to increase over time, but percentage changes do not. This means that the variable is more likely to be trend or difference stationary in its logarithms than in its untransformed levels.

This is not to say that variables should never be studied in their levels; in some circumstances, this may well be appropriate, especially for nontrending variables. It does explain, however, why econometricians almost routinely work in terms of the logarithms of trending variables.

> **Practitioner's Tip: Logarithms or levels?**
>
> Growing variables should normally be modeled in their logarithms.

In light of this, we henceforth often let logarithmic transformations be implicit rather than carrying the notation *log* through expressions. Variables will be understood to be in log form in situations in which this is appropriate. For example, when we refer to differences ΔY_t as percentage changes, it will be understood that Y is in log form.

17.2   Trend and Difference Stationary Processes

We have seen that there are two useful ways of introducing an autocorrelated disturbance u_t into the constant growth model so as to create a stochastic version of that model: trend and difference stationary processes.

The prototypical trend stationary process is

$$Y_t = \alpha + \beta t + u_t. \tag{17.10}$$

Chapter 16 is largely devoted to the special case in which $\beta = 0$; there the ARMA approach to modeling autocorrelation in u_t is developed. Two other

FIGURE 17.2

A trend stationary
process: sample,
forecast, and fore-
cast interval.

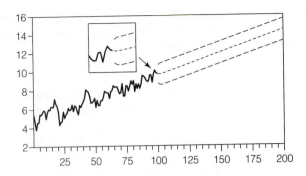

special cases are studied in Chapter 15. Section 15.5 considers the case in which fluctuations around the trend are white noise, so $u_t = \varepsilon_t$. Section 15.2 considers the further specialization of white noise around a constant mean, so $\beta = 0$, which is our first example of a stochastic process. We have noted as well that other types of trend stationary processes could be based on alternative specifications of the deterministic trend, say a quadratic trend or one involving dummy variables to capture structural breaks.

The prototypical difference stationary process is the I(1) model

$$\Delta Y_t = \beta + u_t. \tag{17.11}$$

In Chapter 15 we have studied the special case of a random walk, in which the period-by-period changes are white noise: $u_t = \varepsilon_t$. Both the drifting ($\beta \neq 0$) and zero-drift cases are considered.

Now that the ARMA specification for autocorrelation in u_t allows us to generalize the earlier models of Chapter 15, it is useful to revisit what we have said in that chapter about the key features of trend and difference stationary processes. These key features follow naturally from our remarks in the last two chapters.

17.2.1 Key Properties of Trend Stationary Processes

A trend stationary process like (17.10) is depicted in Figure 17.2. This series is generated by adding the AR(1) realization of Figures 16.4(a) to the trend 4.605 + 0.04879t, the same deterministic trend we use for illustrative purposes in Section 15.5. The result may be usefully contrasted with Figure 15.6, which shows white noise around that trend.

Generalizing from the earlier findings of Chapter 15, which are based on white noise, trend stationary processes inherit, in their stochastic behavior, the features of their ARMA disturbance. In particular, the autocovariance and autocorrelation functions are those for the ARMA process itself. However, as we have seen in the earlier analysis, this pattern of autocorrelation will not be correctly revealed by the sample autocorrelation function computed from the raw time series; the deterministic trend generates a spurious correlation in the sample autocorrelations. The result is that the correlogram typically shows a slow decay of the sample autocorrelations; the only useful interpretation of this slow decay is as an indicator of the nonstationarity associated with the trend, not as a depiction of the true nature of the temporal dependence in the series. As we have seen, to analyze the autocorrelation in a trend stationary series, the appropriate procedure is to detrend it by estimating the deterministic trend as a least squares regression and then apply the Box-Jenkins methodology to the residuals.

Impulse Response Function

Another feature of a trend stationary process that transmits directly from the disturbance is the impulse response function. We have seen this in Section 15.5 for the case of a white noise disturbance. Similarly, when u_t is generated by an ARMA process, the impulse response function for Y is that of this ARMA disturbance. Drawing on our study of ARMA processes in Chapter 16, this has the following implications.

Shocks Are Temporary in Their Effect The effect of a shock ε_t to the ARMA disturbance u_t in (17.10) dissipates over time and so is temporary in its effect. The nature of this temporary effect depends on the ARMA disturbance, which propagates the shock. An MA(q) disturbance has a memory of q periods, after which the effects of the shock cease. A disturbance with an AR component has infinite memory, but eventually the effects of the shock dissipate and become negligible. Shocks do not affect the mean of the series—the deterministic trend—that is the base from which future values of Y are generated.

The Variable Exhibits Trend Reversion The deterministic trend is a central line around which the observed time series fluctuates, as suggested by the simulated series of Figure 17.2. The fluctuations around the trend are governed by the ARMA disturbance, which permits autocorrelation. Nevertheless, values of Y cannot wander arbitrarily far from this line for indefinite periods of time. In this sense, there is a force causing Y to gravitate toward its trend—the trend is an attractor of the variable—so that the variable exhibits trend reversion.

A Shock Does Not Alter the Long-Term Forecast Suppose you knew the deterministic trend and the ARMA specification for u_t and were asked to forecast Y in some future period. What would be your best guess of this future value? The answer depends on the forecast horizon; that is, whether we are forecasting over the short term or the long term.

In the long run, the forecast is the deterministic trend. Because trend stationary variables exhibit trend reversion and shocks are temporary in their effect, in the long run forecasts converge to the trend. Indeed, as Stock (1994, p. 2747) has remarked, "... an intuitively appealing definition of the trend component of a series is that its long-run forecast *is* its trend."

In the short run, autocorrelation in the disturbance can be used to improve forecasts. Intuitively, when a variable fluctuates in a way that is partly predictable, that knowledge can be used in forecasting. This is shown in Figure 17.2, in which the forecasts take a number of periods to converge to the trend. (Although the figure shows monotonic convergence to the long-term forecast, this is because the simulation uses an AR(1) disturbance. A higher-order AR process could yield cyclic convergence to the long run forecast.)

It follows that a shock alters the short-term forecast: A shock ε to Y today affects the variable in the immediate future and therefore forecasts of it via the auto-correlation captured by the ARMA process. This effect lasts q periods in the case of an MA(q) disturbance; it lasts into the indefinite future for a disturbance with an AR component, but eventually becomes negligible as the impulse response dissipates.

However, "eventually" can often be a very short period of time—in Figure 17.2 it takes only a few periods for the forecast to converge to the trend. Thus, the auto-correlation in a variable's short-run fluctuations may be useful in forecasting only a few periods ahead and become irrelevant very quickly. The long run over which the forecast converges to the trend may occur at quite short time horizons.

The Forecast Error Variance Is Bounded In the long run, the optimal forecast is the mean $\alpha + \beta t$, and the forecast error is

$$Y_t - E(Y_t) = Y_t - \alpha - \beta t = u_t.$$

Because this forecast error is just the disturbance u_t, it has constant variance given by the appropriate expression of the associated AR or MA model. Let this variance be denoted σ_u^2,

$$V(Y_t - EY_t) = V(u_t) = \sigma_u^2.$$

For example, if u_t is MA(q), then σ_u^2 is equation (16.11); if u_t is AR(1), then σ_u^2 is equation (16.16).

This is the forecast error variance associated with the long-term forecast $\alpha + \beta t$. It may be used to construct a forecast interval around this deterministic trend, as depicted in Figure 17.2, which generalizes the previous Figure 16.7. The important point about σ_u^2 is that it does not depend on t. Therefore, long-term forecast intervals are of a fixed width around the long-term forecast $\alpha + \beta t$.[2]

Result 17.1 *In the absence of coefficient uncertainty, trend stationary processes have fixed-width long-term forecast intervals.*

---

[2] This discussion assumes known values for the parameters of the deterministic trend and the disturbance. Of course, in real-world forecasting problems in which these parameters must be estimated, this forecast interval would have to be modified to reflect the uncertainty in the estimates. In an interesting contribution, Sampson (1991) notes that when parameter uncertainty is taken into account, forecast error variances are *unbounded* for trend stationary processes, and so in this respect they are not fundamentally different from difference stationary processes. This is, of course, a conclusion we reach in our introductory treatment of forecasting in Section 5.1. But as we argue there, in the hypothetical case in which parameters are known, forecast uncertainty should nevertheless be unbounded, arguing in favor of difference stationarity as the more plausible specification.

In the short run, the forecast intervals are narrower, as Figure 17.2 indicates. Knowledge of the immediate past, as captured by the ARMA model, improves the precision of forecasts. But in the long run, forecast error variances are bounded.

Conclusions

In summary, trend stationary processes have the following key properties:

- Shocks are temporary in their effect.
- The variable exhibits trend reversion.
- A shock does not alter the long-term forecast.
- The forecast error variance is bounded.

These just generalize our findings of the previous chapter, which deals with ARMA variation around a constant mean, to the present context of variation around a deterministic trend. As well, these conclusions parallel similar findings for white noise variation around a constant mean or a deterministic trend, discussed in Chapter 15.

These key properties have been established by working in terms of a linear trend $\alpha+\beta t$ as the specification for the deterministic trend around which the variable fluctuates. It should be clear, however, that these conclusions are not contingent on this choice. They would hold for *any* choice of deterministic trend: quadratic, subject to structural breaks, or otherwise. These key properties are generic to all trend stationary processes.

17.2.2 Key Properties of Difference Stationary Processes

Turning to difference stationarity, examples of I(1) processes such as the prototypical model (17.11) are depicted in Figure 17.3; both the drifting and nondrifting cases are portrayed. The two series are generated using an initial value of $Y_0 = 4.605$ and the AR(1) realization in Figure 16.4(a); the drifting series uses a drift of $\beta = 0.04879$. The AR(1) realization is, in turn, generated from the same white noise realization used in many of our examples of the last two chapters,

FIGURE 17.3

An I(1) process: sample realization, forecast, and forecast interval.

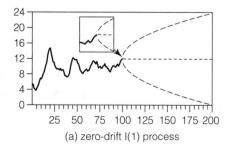

(a) zero-drift I(1) process

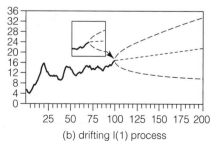

(b) drifting I(1) process

in particular that used to generate the random walk realizations of Figure 15.15. Comparing the I(1) processes of Figure 17.3 with those earlier random walks, it is apparent that the I(1) series are essentially modified and smoothed versions of the random walks. This modification and smoothing comes from the variance and autocorrelation of the AR(1) process.

The appropriate means of analyzing an I(1) series is with an ARIMA model; that is, by applying the Box-Jenkins methodology to the variable in its differences. Examples of estimated ARIMA models are given in Examples 2–4.

As in the case of a trend stationary process, computing the sample autocorrelation function from the levels of the series yields a misleading picture of the true nature of its autocorrelation. Instead, the sample autocorrelations of its first differences would be an important tool at the initial model identification step of the Box-Jenkins methodology.

The Integrated Nature of Difference Stationary Processes

Just as in the derivations of the integrated expressions (15.19) and (15.25) for zero-drift and drifting random walks, the method of recursive substitution may be used to verify that a difference stationary process is integrated:

$$
\begin{aligned}
Y_t &= \beta + Y_{t-1} + u_t \\
&= \beta + (\beta + Y_{t-2} + u_{t-1}) + u_t \\
&= 2\beta + (\beta + Y_{t-3} + u_{t-2}) + u_{t-1} + u_t \\
&\;\;\vdots \\
&= \beta t + Y_0 + \sum_{j=0}^{t-1} u_{t-j}.
\end{aligned}
\tag{17.12}
$$

This is, of course, the same as the earlier derivation (15.25) in the special case when u_t is white noise: $u_t = \varepsilon_t$.

Letting the stochastic component be denoted by v_t and interpreting Y_0 to be a presample constant α, this I(1) variable may therefore be written

$$
Y_t = \alpha + \beta t + v_t.
\tag{17.13}
$$

It depends on the integrated expression

$$
v_t = \sum_{j=0}^{t-1} u_{t-j},
$$

which is analogous to the earlier expression (15.26). The difference is that now the disturbance u_t is generated, not as white noise, but by a stationary ARMA process as a function of current and past shocks. Consequently, the impulse response function—the effect now and in the future of any shock ε_t today—will depend on the parameters of this ARMA process.

One way of interpreting the I(1) model is to note that the integrated expression v_t is itself a zero-drift I(1) process; its first difference is

$$\Delta v_t = v_t - v_{t-1}$$
$$= (u_t + u_{t-1} + u_{t-2} + \cdots + u_1) - (u_{t-1} + u_{t-2} + u_{t-3} + \cdots + u_1)$$
$$= u_t.$$

By assumption, this is zero-mean stationary. Hence, another way of stating the I(1) model is

$$Y_t = \alpha + \beta t + v_t, \tag{17.14a}$$
$$v_t = v_{t-1} + u_t. \tag{17.14b}$$

That is, the prototypical I(1) variable can be interpreted as zero-drift I(1) noise superimposed on a linear trend. This is analogous to the result in Chapter 15 that a random walk with drift can be interpreted as a zero-drift random walk superimposed on a linear trend, as represented by the model (15.29).

Let us use these expressions to evaluate the mean and variance of Y_t.

Mean In Chapter 16 we show that an ARMA disturbance has mean zero: $E(u_t) = 0$. Taking the mathematical expectation of (17.12) and regarding the initial value Y_0 as a numerical constant, the mean of Y_t is therefore

$$E(Y_t) = Y_0 + \beta t + \sum_{j=0}^{t-1} E(u_{t-j}) = Y_0 + \beta t.$$

In forecasting, Y_0 may be reinterpreted as the most recent observation on the variable. The implication is that the optimal long-term forecast simply extrapolates from this most recent value along the trend line, marking it up by the amount β each period.

Variance Taking the variance of (17.12), in principle the variance of Y_t may be evaluated as

$$V(Y_t) = V\left(\sum_{j=0}^{t-1} u_{t-j} \right).$$

However, in contrast to the analogous derivation (15.23) for a random walk, now the u_{t-j} in this sum are correlated. The variance of the sum therefore depends not only on the variances $V(u_{t-j})$, but also on the covariances, and so it will in general be a complex expression that depends in turn on the ARMA specification of u_t. Consequently, without developing more advanced notational devices, it is not possible to present a convenient expression for this variance.

However, this is not important for our purposes. It turns out that the autocorrelation in u_t does not change the basic result that we have derived in the random walk case: The variance depends on time t, becoming larger as time advances. For this reason, I(1) processes, just like the special case of random walks, are non-stationary even when they have zero drift—because their variances are not time invariant. And like random walks, these variances become infinite as time advances into the indefinite future.

Key Properties

With these remarks on the mean and variance, it is evident that the integrated nature of Y_t implies the following key properties.

Shocks Are Permanent in Their Effect Any shock ε_t contributes to the disturbance u_t and hence, according to the model specification (17.11), to the change from the previous value Y_{t-1} to the current value Y_t. This new value is the base from which the future evolution of the variable takes place. Consequently, any shock ε_t shifts this base, changing all future values of the variable. In this sense, shocks are permanent in their effect.[3]

The Variable Does Not Exhibit Trend Reversion Although the mean of Y_t is the linear trend $Y_0 + \beta t$, the fact that the variance $V(Y_t)$ increases with time means that the variable can wander arbitrarily far from this trend. There is no force causing the series to gravitate toward any central line. In contrast to a trend stationary process, an integrated process does not exhibit trend reversion.

A Shock Alters the Long-Term Forecast Suppose you knew the drift parameter β and the ARMA specification for u_t and were asked to forecast Y in some future period. What would be your best guess of this future value? The answer depends on the forecast horizon; that is, whether we are forecasting over the short term or the long term.

In the long run, the forecast is the trend. As we have remarked, the optimal long-term t-period-ahead forecast is the trend $Y_0 + \beta t$, where Y_0 is interpreted as the most recent observation on Y.

In the short run, autocorrelation in the disturbance can be used to improve forecasts. Recent observations on Y can be used to forecast the values of u that will occur in the periods ahead, enabling us to improve forecasts of future Y over just using the trend $Y_0 + \beta t$. In Figure 17.3, it takes a few periods for the forecasts to converge to the trends.

It follows that a shock alters the short-term forecast; a shock ε to Y today affects the variable in the immediate future, and therefore forecasts of it, via the

---

[3] Although shocks are permanent in their effect, that effect is not unit for unit, as it was in the case of a random walk. Instead, the effect of a shock ε_t today on the long-term forecast depends on the parameters of the ARMA process governing u_t and will be somewhere between the extremes of zero (the long-term effect of a shock on a trend stationary process) and one (the unit-for-unit effect that holds for a random walk). For an observed time series that is modeled as difference stationary, it is therefore of interest to ask: How big is the effect of a shock on the long-term forecast of the variable? For classic applications of this idea in macroeconomics, see Campbell and Mankiw (1987) and Cochrane (1988).

autocorrelation captured by the ARMA process. This effect lasts q periods in the case of an MA(q) disturbance; it lasts into the indefinite future for a disturbance with an AR component, but eventually becomes negligible as the impulse response dissipates. Notice that, in this respect, a difference stationary process does not differ from a trend stationary one.

What is more surprising is that, when a variable is integrated, the fact that shocks are permanent in their effect has an important implication for forecasting in the long run as well. By changing the base from which the variable evolves in the future—the most recently observed value Y_0—a shock alters the forecasts in all future periods.

The Forecast Error Variance Is Unbounded. The error made in long-term forecasting is the difference between the value that actually occurs in that future period, Y_t, and the long-term forecast $Y_0 + \beta t$:

$$Y_t - E(Y_t) = Y_t - Y_0 - \beta t = \sum_{j=0}^{t-1} u_{t-j}.$$

Hence, the forecast error variance is the variance of the process itself. As we have remarked, this variance is a function of time t and so, like a random walk but in contrast to a trend stationary processes, an I(1) variable has a forecast error variance that increases with the forecast horizon.

This forecast error variance can be used to construct a forecast interval. Because the variance increases with the forecast horizon, this interval widens as the horizon lengthens. It turns out that, just as in Result 15.1 for a random walk, we have:

Result 17.2   *In the absence of coefficient uncertainty, an I(1) variable has a forecast interval that increases with the square root of the forecast horizon.*

These unbounded forecast intervals are depicted in Figure 17.3. They contrast with the bounded intervals of trend stationary processes.[4]

[4]   As the statement of the result indicates, known parameter values are assumed. As we have seen in Section 5.1, in real-world forecasting problems where parameters must be estimated, results such as these must be modified to reflect the uncertainty in the estimates. Sampson (1991) showed that, when parameter uncertainty is taken into account, both trend and difference stationary models have the property that forecast error variances increase with the *square* of the forecast horizon, while forecast intervals increase linearly. (We establish these results in an elementary way for a deterministic trend model in Section 5.1.) Hence, both classes of models have unbounded forecast intervals (although for a given forecast horizon the forecast interval of the difference stationary process is wider).

Even so, as we suggest in Section 5.1, even in the hypothetical case in which parameters are known, it might be argued that forecast uncertainty should be unbounded. If we accept this view, difference stationarity becomes the more plausible specification.

Conclusions

In summary, difference stationary processes have the following key properties:

- Shocks are permanent in their effect.
- The variable does not exhibit trend reversion.
- A shock alters the long-term forecast.
- The forecast error variance is unbounded.

This just generalizes our previous conclusions about random walks reached in Chapter 15. They contrast with the key properties of trend stationary processes.

17.2.3 The Beveridge-Nelson Decomposition

Trend and difference stationary models combine the ARMA model of stationary fluctuations in Chapter 16 with the deterministic and stochastic trends introduced in Chapter 15. In this way, trend and difference stationary models describe both the long-run or permanent behavior in the variable as captured by the trend and the short-run or transitory behavior, the fluctuations or cycles superimposed on this trend. We can think of any variable as being the sum of these two components, say

$$Y_t = Y_t^P + Y_t^T. \tag{17.15}$$

Here Y_t^P denotes the permanent component in the variable and Y_t^T the transitory component. In terms of our earliest musings about time series components in Chapter 1, this is just alternative notation for the trend and cyclical components that we denote by T_t and C_t in equation (1.1).

In the case of trend stationary processes, the distinction between these two components is conceptually straightforward. Considering the prototypical model

$$Y_t = \alpha + \beta t + u_t,$$

the permanent variation is due to the deterministic trend, so that $Y_t^P = \alpha + \beta t$, whereas the transitory variation is due to the stationary fluctuations around this trend described by the disturbance, so $Y_t^T = u_t$. From our discussion of forecasting with trend stationary processes, the optimal long-term forecast is the permanent component Y_t^P, whereas short-term forecasts modify this to take into account any autocorrelation in the transitory component Y_t^T.

When a variable is difference stationary, on the other hand, the distinction between its permanent and transitory components is less obvious. If a variable is integrated, what is its "long-run" versus its "short-run" behavior? What is trend and what is cycle?

The answer to this question was provided by Beveridge and Nelson (1981), who showed that any I(1) variable can be decomposed into permanent and transitory components, as in equation (17.15). The transitory component Y_t^T is stationary, whereas the permanent component Y_t^P evolves as a random walk. In other words, the Beveridge-Nelson decomposition shows that any I(1) variable can be interpreted as a random walk plus stationary noise.

Consider the permanent component Y_t^P. Letting β denote its drift and ξ_t its white noise disturbance, its random walk specification may be denoted

$$Y_t^P = \beta + Y_{t-1}^P + \xi_t, \qquad \xi_t \sim \text{wn}(0, \sigma^2). \tag{17.16}$$

It is this permanent random walk component that provides the basis for long-term forecasts of Y_t, those forecasts being altered period by period by the permanent shocks ξ_t. The transitory component Y_t^T, being stationary, does not affect long-term forecasts, although to the extent that it exhibits autocorrelation it is relevant to short-term forecasting.

Recall that, as in the derivation of equation (15.25), a random walk can always be cumulated using the method of recursive substitution. Hence, the permanent component of an I(1) variable can be written as a deterministic trend DT_t plus a stochastic trend ST_t:

$$Y_t^P = DT_t + ST_t.$$

This contrasts with a trend stationary process, in which the permanent component Y_t^P is purely deterministic, involving no stochastic component. In terms of the white noise disturbance ξ_t of (17.16), the stochastic trend is

$$ST_t = \sum_{j=0}^{t-1} \xi_{t-j}.$$

This stochastic trend is itself a zero-drift random walk. Consequently, for an I(1) variable the permanent component Y_t^P does not revert to its deterministic trend DT_t, a property that is transmitted to the variable Y_t itself.

Substituting this expression for Y_t^P into equation (17.15), in total an I(1) variable may be decomposed as

$$Y_t = DT_t + \underbrace{ST_t + Y_t^T}_{v_t}, \tag{17.17}$$

As the brace emphasizes, the total stochastic variation v_t in an I(1) variable is due to two components: the nonstationary stochastic trend ST_t and the stationary transitory component Y_t^T.

$$v_t = ST_t + Y_t^T$$

By contrast, as we have seen, the stochastic variation in a trend stationary series is due entirely to the stationary transitory component Y_t^T. The opposite contrast is with the random walk (15.25), in which the stochastic variation is due entirely to the stochastic trend: $v_t = ST_t$, as indicated by equation (15.26).

The Beveridge-Nelson Decomposition of an ARIMA(0, 1, 1)

Let us illustrate the Beveridge-Nelson decomposition for a particular difference stationary model, an ARIMA(0,1,1). This is the prototypical I(1) process

$$\Delta Y_t = \beta + u_t, \tag{17.18}$$

in which the disturbance u_t is MA(1),

$$u_t = \varepsilon_t + \theta\varepsilon_{t-1}.$$

As examples of the application of this model, Example 4 cites Stock and Watson's (1988) model for GNP, and Theory Meets Application 17.1 cites Ermini's (1989) model for real consumption per capita.

Applying recursive substitution to the first equation reproduces equation (17.12),

$$Y_t = Y_0 + \beta t + \sum_{j=0}^{t-1} u_{t-j}.$$

Recognizing the deterministic trend $DT_t = Y_0 + \beta t$, this confirms that this I(1) variable may be interpreted as the sum of deterministic and stochastic components,

$$Y_t = DT_t + v_t,$$

as in equation (17.17).

Our development of the Beveridge-Nelson decomposition leads us to expect that the stochastic component v_t is the sum of a nonstationary stochastic trend ST_t and a stationary transitory component Y_t^T. This may be confirmed by using the MA(1) specification for u_t to examine this stochastic component more carefully.

$$
\begin{aligned}
v_t &= \sum_{j=0}^{t-1} u_{t-j} \\
&= \sum_{j=0}^{t-1} (\varepsilon_{t-j} + \theta\varepsilon_{t-j-1}) \\
&= (\varepsilon_t + \varepsilon_{t-1} + \cdots + \varepsilon_1) + \theta(\varepsilon_{t-1} + \varepsilon_{t-2} + \cdots + \varepsilon_1 + \varepsilon_0) \\
&= \underbrace{(1+\theta)\sum_{j=0}^{t-1} \varepsilon_{t-j}}_{ST_t} \underbrace{-\theta\varepsilon_t}_{Y_t^T}
\end{aligned}
$$

In rewriting the third line as the fourth, we have used the fact that the presample initial value Y_0 is treated as nonstochastic, implying that there is no shock in that period: $\varepsilon_0 = 0$.

As the braces indicate, the stochastic component of Y_t has been written in a form that can be interpreted as the sum of a stochastic trend ST_t and a transitory component Y_t^T. Notice that in the special case of $\theta = 0$ where the MA(1) disturbance reduces to white noise, so that $u_t = \varepsilon_t$, this expression reduces to equation (15.26), the stochastic trend of a random walk given in Chapter 15. In this case, the stochastic component consists only of the stochastic trend ST_t; there is no transitory component Y_t^T because the disturbance u_t is not autocorrelated.

The permanent component is the sum of the deterministic and stochastic trends,

$$Y_t^P = DT_t + ST_t = Y_0 + \beta t + (1 + \theta) \sum_{j=0}^{t-1} \varepsilon_{t-j}.$$

Notice that if we define a disturbance $\xi_t = (1 + \theta)\varepsilon_t$ then Y_t^P can be written as the random walk

$$Y_t^P = \beta + Y_{t-1}^P + \xi_t \qquad\qquad\qquad (17.19)$$

because the former equation can be obtained from the latter by recursive substitution. This is, of course, just the random walk (17.16), confirming that in the decomposition (17.15),

$$Y_t = Y_t^P + Y_t^T,$$

the permanent component Y_t^P follows a random walk. In the present case of an ARIMA(0,1,1), the transitory component happens to be white noise, $Y_t^T = -\theta \varepsilon_t$, although this would not in general be the case for other ARIMA(p, 1, q) processes.

Comparison with the Case of a Pure Random Walk

It is instructive to compare the Beveridge-Nelson decomposition for an I(1) variable with the special case that obtains when the process is a pure random walk, so that the disturbance in the prototypical model (17.11) is white noise: $u_t = \varepsilon_t$. This corresponds to setting $\theta = 0$ in the MA(1) disturbance, and the expression for the permanent component Y_t^P reduces to

$$Y_t^P = Y_0 + \beta t + \sum_{j=0}^{t-1} \varepsilon_{t-j}.$$

This reproduces the earlier expression (15.25) derived for a random walk in Chapter 15. Because, as we have previously concluded, the transitory component Y_t^T is zero, a random walk has only a permanent component,

$$Y_t = Y_t^P = DT_t + ST_t.$$

Of course, the variable can be reexpressed equivalently in its explicit random walk representation (17.19), in which $\xi_t = (1 + \theta)\varepsilon_t = \varepsilon_t$ when $\theta = 0$.

Thus, a random walk is a special case of an I(1) process that consists entirely of trend and no cycle. This trend is the total of the deterministic trend DT_t and the stochastic trend ST_t. In contrast, I(1) processes in general include, in addition to these permanent components, a transitory component Y_t^T. Shocks to a random walk affect it only through its permanent component, because there is no transitory component, and so they are permanent in their effect. In contrast, a shock ε_t to an I(1) process affects it through both its permanent and transitory components, and so it is partially permanent in its effect and partially transitory. To the extent that the effect of the shock is permanent, it alters long-term forecasts; to the extent that it is transitory, this is relevant to short-term forecasting.

In conclusion, although shocks to a random walk are entirely permanent in their effect, this property does not extend to I(1) processes generally, in which the relative effects of a shock on the permanent and transitory components is an empirical matter. A shock to an I(1) process can be largely transitory. As Cochrane (1991, p. 206) has put it, "... unit roots need have nothing to do with persistence."

Comparison with the Unobserved Components Decomposition

The Beveridge-Nelson decomposition is not the only way of decomposing an integrated series into long- and short-run components. A competing decomposition is the unobserved components approach of Harvey (1985) and Clark (1987). It turns out that the two approaches give rather different answers to the question of what is trend and what is cycle. The relationship between the two decompositions has been studied by Morley, Nelson, and Zivot (2003, p. 235), who apply them to GDP:

> The decomposition of real GDP into trend and cycle is of considerable practical importance, but two widely used methods yield starkly different results. The unobserved component approach ... implies a very smooth trend and a cycle that is large in amplitude and highly persistent. In contrast, the approach of Beveridge and Nelson implies that much of the variation in GDP is variation in trend, whereas the cycle component is small and noisy.

The implication is that "The Beveridge-Nelson decomposition implies that a stochastic trend accounts for most of the variation in output, whereas the unobserved-components implies cyclical variation is dominant. Which is correct has broad implications for the relative importance of real versus nominal shocks" (2003, p. 235).

These authors show that the unobserved components approach is a special case of the Beveridge-Nelson decomposition, a special case that corresponds to a testable parameter restriction. This restriction is rejected for U.S. GDP, suggesting that the more general Beveridge-Nelson decomposition is the appropriate one.

17.2.4   Comparing Trend and Difference Stationary Processes

With the understanding of the properties of trend and difference stationary processes that we have now developed, we should ask: Which type of model is most likely to be appropriate to economics?

Most econometricians believe that the properties of difference stationary processes make them the compelling choice. A class of models in which shocks can be permanent in their effect and alter long-term forecasts, there is no tendency to revert to a deterministic trend, and forecast uncertainty is unbounded seems a more plausible description of the behavior of economic variables than a class of models in which these properties are not possible.

Furthermore, we know that in some instances economic theory predicts difference stationarity. The theory of efficient markets predicts that stock prices follow a random walk. Robert Hall's rational expectations version of the life cycle–permanent income hypothesis predicts—at least as a theoretical benchmark—that consumption is a random walk. Technology shocks are a plausible source of unit root behavior. And, as discussed in the appendix to Chapter 9, theories of endogenous growth predict that variables will be integrated.

However, the adoption of the view that many variables are best thought of as difference stationary is relatively recent because only in recent decades have econometricians come to fully understand the differences in the two types of models. For many years economists tended to think of economic variables as evolving in a trend stationary manner, largely because—as we have seen in our study of the constant growth model in Chapter 6—linear or loglinear deterministic trends often provide a good descriptive fit to growing variables.

The choice of model is, of course, of fundamental significance to our understanding of economics and the study of time series data. We know from Nelson and Kang (1984) and Durlauf and Phillips (1988) that if a difference stationary variable is mistakenly analyzed as trend stationary the conclusions will be entirely spurious: Zero-drift processes will often generate series that appear to have deterministic trends, and apparent short-run fluctuations in the variable will be an artifact of the incorrect detrending procedure.

Although the key features of difference stationary processes seem to argue in their favor, model choice should never be done on purely a priori grounds. Instead, we should ask whether the data support the model specification. Given an economic time series, how can we decide whether it is reasonable to model it as difference stationary?

17.3 Testing for Stochastic Trends

Is the modeling of economic variables as integrated processes supported empirically? Consider, for example, a variable such as the per capita GNP series in Figure 15.5. Because this variable is growing, the difference stationary approach suggests that it be modeled in its logarithms as I(1) with drift:

$$\Delta Y_t = \beta + u_t. \tag{17.20}$$

The trend stationary approach, on the other hand, uses the model

$$Y_t = \alpha + \beta t + v_t. \tag{17.21}$$

Here u_t and v_t denote stationary disturbances; the use of distinct symbols serves to emphasize that, in using one or the other of these models to describe an economic variable, there is no suggestion that the same disturbance will apply in both cases.[5] Do the data provide evidence on the basis of which one model is preferred to the other?

Although our task is one of model choice, these two alternatives are not on an equal footing. For the reasons we have discussed, a priori considerations suggest that difference stationarity will most often be the natural way of describing economic variables. Accordingly, the framework of hypothesis testing is the obvious one to apply, and the presence of a stochastic trend is the natural null hypothesis. Only when strong evidence leads us to reject this null should we turn to the alternative of a trend stationary model.

A test of the null hypothesis of difference stationarity against the alternative of trend stationarity was first formulated by Dickey and Fuller (1979). Their test was first applied to economic data by Nelson and Plosser (1982), who found that the Dickey-Fuller test failed to reject the hypothesis of difference stationarity for most macroeconomic time series. Because prior to that time economists had tended to think of time series variables in trend stationary terms, the Nelson-Plosser finding revolutionized empirical macroeconomics in the years that followed, a revolution that continues to this day.

As we have seen, difference stationarity implies a unit characteristic root $z = 1$. Hence, tests for the presence of a stochastic trend are known as **tests for a unit root.** Because trend and difference stationary processes each come in several versions—for example, drift or no drift in the case of difference stationary processes, and constant plus disturbance or trend plus disturbance in the case of trend stationary processes—unit root tests in turn come in several versions. Let us begin by considering the most commonly applied version of the Dickey-Fuller test.

17.3.1   The Dickey-Fuller Test: Intercept and Trend

Consider the models (17.20) and (17.21), the two models we have described as the prototypical difference and trend stationary processes.

To test the null hypothesis of difference stationarity against the alternative of trend stationarity we need (to adopt the terminology of Chapter 12) an encompassing or artificial compound model; that is, a model that includes these alternatives as special cases. The encompassing model should have the property that the parameter restrictions that hold under the null and alternative hypotheses reduce it to difference and trend stationarity.

As such an encompassing model, Dickey and Fuller (1979) proposed the regression

$$Y_t = \beta_0 + \beta_1 t + \phi Y_{t-1} + u_t.$$

---

[5]   The choice of the symbol v_t to denote a stationary disturbance may seem odd, given that it has previously been used to denote an integrated process. However, this choice is not coincidental; its purpose will become clear in Section 17.3.2.

The null hypothesis is the unit root restriction $\phi = 1$ and the alternative is that $\phi < 1$. Let us consider the sense in which these restrictions reduce the regression to difference and trend stationarity.

In the special case of $\phi = 1$, the Dickey-Fuller regression reduces to

$$\Delta Y_t = \beta_0 + \beta_1 t + u_t.$$

This is a generalization of the difference stationary process (17.20). You might argue that if we literally want to specify model (17.20) as the null hypothesis we should test the joint restrictions $\phi = 1$, $\beta_1 = 0$, and indeed some variants of the Dickey-Fuller test do this. However, the economic issue of interest is whether the series contains a stochastic trend, and this is fully reflected in the unit root restriction $\phi = 1$; with this restriction, this equation provides for integrated behavior in the variable. In other words, even if it were the case that $\beta_1 \neq 0$, we would not want to reject the null that the variable contains a stochastic trend.[6]

How about the alternative hypothesis that $\phi < 1$? The disturbance u_t of the Dickey-Fuller regression is a stationary ARMA process describing the autocorrelation in Y_t. When $-1 < \phi < 1$ the term ϕY_{t-1} simply becomes part of this description of the autocorrelation in Y_t around the deterministic trend $\beta_0 + \beta_1 t$. That is, when $-1 < \phi < 1$ the Dickey-Fuller regression reduces to a trend stationary process. Recall from Section 16.4 that a parameter in the range $\phi \leq -1$ implies implausible nonstationary behavior, and so we rule out values of ϕ in this range a priori. Consequently, the alternative hypothesis may simply be stated as $\phi < 1$, the understanding being that we are not entertaining any possibility that $\phi \leq -1$. For similar reasons—the nonhomogeneous nonstationary behavior that we discussed most recently in Section 17.1.1—the Dickey-Fuller test also rules out a priori any possibility that $\phi > 1$.

It is in this sense that the restrictions $\phi = 1$ and $\phi < 1$ reduce the Dickey-Fuller regression to difference and trend stationarity, respectively. Consequently, running the regression and testing $H_0: \phi = 1$ versus $H_A: \phi < 1$ permits a test of the null hypothesis of difference stationarity against the alternative of trend stationarity.

In practice, a slightly different form of the Dickey-Fuller regression is usually estimated, one that simplifies the calculation of the test statistic. Consider subtracting Y_{t-1} from both sides of the regression:

$$\Delta Y_t = \beta_0 + \beta_1 t + \rho Y_{t-1} + u_t. \tag{17.22}$$

We have defined the symbol $\rho \equiv \phi - 1$. In terms of this regression, the null hypothesis is $\rho = 0$, the alternative is $\rho < 0$, and the test statistic is the usual t ratio for ρ:

$$t = \frac{\hat{\rho}}{s_{\hat{\rho}}}. \tag{17.23}$$

---

[6] There are other ways of rationalizing a test of ϕ alone. It can be argued that we are simply ruling out a priori the possibility that $\beta_1 \neq 0$ when $\phi = 1$, so that the latter restriction is all that needs to be tested. This was the reasoning offered by Nelson and Plosser (1982, n. 8). The relationship between ϕ and β_1 is investigated in more detail in the next section.

TABLE 17.1   Critical Values for Augmented Dickey-Fuller Unit Root Tests

Sample size	Intercept, no trend			Intercept and trend		
n	0.01	0.05	0.10	0.01	0.05	0.10
25	−3.75	−2.99	−2.64	−4.38	−3.60	−3.24
50	−3.59	−2.93	−2.60	−4.16	−3.50	−3.18
100	−3.50	−2.90	−2.59	−4.05	−3.45	−3.15
∞	−3.42	−2.86	−2.57	−3.96	−3.41	−3.13

Source: Adapted from Fuller (1976, Table 8.5.2, p. 373), as revised in Fuller (1996, Table 10.A.2, p. 642). Copyright ©1976 and 1996 by John Wiley & Sons, Inc. This material is used by permission of John Wiley & Sons, Inc.

Thus formulated, the unit root test statistic is just the standard t ratio printed out by any regression package.

The most important issue that arises in implementing unit root tests is that, although this test statistic is standard enough, its distribution is not. Because Y_t is nonstationary, the usual distribution theory that applies in regression analysis when the classical assumptions are satisfied no longer holds: the "t statistic" for $\rho = 0$ does not in fact have a t distribution. Instead the appropriate critical values were tabulated by Fuller (1976) and are summarized in Table 17.1. The table is divided into two sections: "intercept, no trend" and "intercept and trend." We are presently considering the case in which the regression includes an intercept and trend. We turn to the intercept, no trend case in Section 17.3.3.

EXAMPLE 5

 np.dat

One series studied by Nelson and Plosser was the velocity of circulation of money for the years 1869–1970. We examine these data in Figures 6.15 and 15.13, and in Section 15.7.1 we replicate the finding of Gould and Nelson (1974) that velocity is a zero-drift random walk. However, this finding is premised on the maintained hypothesis that the series is difference stationary. Is this premise warranted?

SOLUTION

When Gould and Nelson were writing, unit root tests were not available, and so they had little choice but to take difference stationarity as a maintained hypothesis. The Dickey-Fuller test makes this hypothesis testable.

The result for the Dickey-Fuller regression is

$$\Delta Y_t = 0.0520 - 0.0003t - \underset{(0.0355)}{0.0590}\, Y_{t-1} + e_t.$$

Following the treatment in Section 15.7.1, velocity Y_t is in log form. Because the series is for 102 years, after generating the lagged variable the regression is estimated with a sample size of $n = 101$.

The test statistic is $t = \hat{\rho}/s_{\hat{\rho}} = -0.0590/0.0355 = -1.66$. Because the alternative hypothesis is the one-sided restriction $\rho < 0$, we reject for values of the test statistic *less than* the tabulated values in Table 17.1. For example, for a 10% significance level and a sample of size $n = 100$ the rejection region is $t < -3.15$. Because the computed value of the statistic is not in this rejection region, the null hypothesis of a unit root is not rejected. The conclusion is that velocity can be treated as containing a stochastic trend rather than as being trend stationary.

That the data support modeling velocity as difference stationary is typical of the Nelson-Plosser findings. For only a single variable—the unemployment rate—was the unit root hypothesis rejected.

Treating Autocorrelation: The Augmented Dickey-Fuller Regression

There is one further aspect of the implementation of Dickey-Fuller tests that must be considered. The disturbance u_t describes fluctuations that are, in general, autocorrelated. In order for the tabulated Dickey-Fuller distribution to be accurate, it is necessary that this autocorrelation be treated. The easiest way to do this is to add lags of the dependent variable as explanatory variables, estimating an **augmented Dickey-Fuller** (ADF) regression:

$$\Delta Y_t = \beta_0 + \beta_1 t + \rho Y_{t-1} + \rho_1 \Delta Y_{t-1} + \cdots + \rho_k \Delta Y_{t-k} + \varepsilon_t.$$

Velocity was the only variable studied by Nelson and Plosser in which they judged this unnecessary, so that $k = 0$ lags were used. Let us use another variable to illustrate an ADF regression.

EXAMPLE 6

 np.dat

Consider Nelson and Plosser's per capita GNP series shown in Figure 15.5. They estimated an ADF regression with $k = 1$ lag,[7]

$$\Delta Y_t = 1.1339 + 0.0035t - \underset{(0.0598)}{0.1822}\ Y_{t-1} + 0.4097 \Delta Y_{t-1} + e_t.$$

For the usual constant growth reasons, Y_t is in log form. The data are for the years 1909–1970, so after defining the lagged variables the sample size is $n = 60$. Perform a Dickey-Fuller test.

SOLUTION

The test statistic is $t = -0.1822/0.0598 = -3.05$. For a 10% significance level and a sample size of $n = 50$, Table 17.1 indicates a rejection region of $t < -3.18$. Consequently, the null hypothesis of a unit root is not rejected at conventional significance levels.

Determining the Lag Order

The goal in choosing a lag order k is to capture the autocorrelation in the series so that the regression disturbance ε_t is approximately white noise—in other words,

---

[7] You may find it interesting to locate the Nelson and Plosser article and compare it with our discussion. If you do, you will find that our definition of k differs from theirs. In their notation, this is a regression in which $k = 2$.

so that we are estimating a regression with an approximately classical disturbance. For annual data, this lag order may often be quite short, as the two examples we have given illustrate. For quarterly or monthly data, on the other hand, that lag order will probably be at least 4 or 12.

The choice of lag order is an issue of model specification, and so all the considerations of specification testing and model choice that have been discussed in Chapter 12 are relevant. Fundamentally, a balance must be struck between the benefits of including additional lags and the costs of having to estimate their coefficients. Recall that in our discussions of the effect of specification error on estimators in Section 8.9 and Chapter 12, too few parameters tended to introduce bias into estimators, whereas too many introduced an efficiency loss. In the present context where it is the properties of the Dickey-Fuller test statistic that are in question, rather than an estimator, the issues are nevertheless similar. Too few lags in the augmented Dickey-Fuller regression introduces a size distortion, so that the actual size may be quite different from the nominal one; in this sense, test decisions are unreliable. Too many lags, on the other hand, weakens the power of the test, so that it has a relatively low probability of rejecting the null of a unit root when it is appropriate to do so.[8] This means that a stationary or trend-stationary variable that is strongly autocorrelated, such as an AR(1) process with $|\phi|$ close to 1, may easily be mistaken as having a unit root. Consistent with the discussion in Chapter 12, there are two approaches to determining lag order: model choice and specification testing.

Model Choice   The model choice approach asks which lag length is best. As we emphasize in Section 12.4, different selection criteria make this trade-off in different ways, imposing different penalties for additional lags.[9]

The values yielded by any model selection criterion across different model specifications can only be meaningfully compared if those different specifications are estimated from a common data sample. This is obvious enough in the cross-sectional contexts of the discussion in Chapter 12, but is easily forgotten in a time series context. Consequently, we offer the following Practitioner's Tip.

Practitioner's Tip: **Lag length and model choice**

If you take the model choice approach to selecting the augmenting lag length, be sure to estimate ADF regressions of different lag lengths with a *common* data sample (i.e., the same number of observations); otherwise, the information criterion values are not comparable.

---

[8]   Recall that the concepts of size distortion and power are defined in Section 2.5.1.

[9]   In many time series contexts the preferred selection criterion is the Bayesian information criterion (BIC) of Schwartz (1978). As the sample size becomes large, the BIC selects the correct lag length. It is said to be consistent—a different use of this term from the property of estimator consistency (Chapter 13). This property is not possessed by many other selection criteria, including the Akaike information criterion (AIC). The BIC imposes a heavier penalty for additional parameters than does the AIC (Chapter 12). Although consistent, the BIC underselects the augmentation lag order in finite

continued

Specification Testing   The alternative approach is to test. Consistent with the general-to-specific testing paradigm, it is best to begin with a relatively long lag length. Perhaps surprisingly in view of the nonstandard sampling behavior of the unit root t statistic, it turns out that the t statistics on the augmenting lags have sampling distributions that are well approximated by the usual t distribution. Hence, beginning with a lag order k that is on the generous side, standard t tests can be used to eliminate insignificant lags, paring k down to as modest a value as seems warranted by the data.

This general-to-specific strategy has been endorsed by Hall (1994), who found that it compared favorably with the alternative of a specific-to-general strategy in which we begin with a small k, increasing it successively until an insignificant lag is encountered.

The two approaches to determining lag length were compared by Ng and Perron (1995). Recall that in Section 8.9 we conclude that, in a regression model, the bias arising from too few regressors is a more serious problem than the efficiency loss arising from too many, and on this basis we recommend in favor of erring on the side of more generously parameterized models. In the same spirit, Ng and Perron concluded that size distortions arising from too few lags are a more serious problem than the power loss that arises from too many. They also found that information criteria "... tend to select truncation lags that are too small. ..." These considerations led them to recommend the testing approach to determining lag length: "... a t or an F test for the significance of lags will have an advantage over information-based rules such as the AIC, because the former produces tests with more robust size properties..." (Ng and Perron 1995, p. 277).

In taking a general-to-specific approach to testing for lag length, the question arises of the maximum lag length to begin with. One consideration, as we have indicated, is the frequency of the data: annual versus quarterly or monthly. In addition, Schwert (1989) suggested a guideline that links the initial truncation lag to the sample size n.

Practitioner's Tip: **Testing for lag length**

If you take the testing approach to selecting the augmenting lag length, use a general-to-specific strategy that begins with an initial lag length of

$$k_{\max} = \text{int}\left[12 \times \left(\frac{n}{100} \right)^{1/4} \right].$$

Here int[·] indicates that the argument, which will typically be noninteger, is to be truncated to its integer value.

Phillips–Perron Tests

Introducing augmenting lags on the dependent variable is not the only way of treating autocorrelation in the Dickey-Fuller regression. Phillips and Perron (1988) showed how instead to modify the formula for the unit root test statistic (17.23) to

samples. The AIC chooses at least as high a lag order, reducing the probability of size distortions at the expense of increasing the probability of power loss. In the context of unit root testing size distortion may be a more serious problem than power loss, arguing in favor of the AIC.

take autocorrelation into account. Their test statistic is computed by many econometrics packages and is widely employed in applied work.

The advantage of the ADF test is that it requires nothing more than an OLS regression and so can be implemented with any statistical package. By contrast, the Phillips-Perron test requires preprogrammed software. As well, ADF tests seem to perform at least as well in practice as Phillips-Perron tests. Consequently, the treatment here has been limited to the ADF procedure.

Further Comments

The Nelson and Plosser view that most nonstationary economic variables are probably best described as difference stationary, although novel at the time, now dominates macroeconometrics. This is not to say, of course, that it is entirely uncontroversial; for a taste of the ongoing debate over the stochastic properties of GDP, see Murray and Nelson (2000).

To the extent that controversy continues to exist over unit root testing, that controversy is both methodological and empirical. On the methodological side, the Dickey-Fuller test is now just one of many unit root tests that have been developed, and a great deal of ink has been spilled over the comparative properties of alternative procedures. Maddala and Kim (1998, p. 145) provide a good survey of this literature, going so far as to suggest that "... it is time now to completely discard the ADF and PP [Phillips-Perron] tests ..." in view of the development of procedures with superior size and power properties. Even so, the Dickey-Fuller test continues to be widely applied, and an understanding of it offers important insights into the basic nature of unit root testing, to which much of the rest of this chapter is devoted.

On the empirical side, any time that alternative test procedures are applied to many economic variables—as unit root tests have now been—the results are bound to be mixed, and this is certainly true of unit root testing in economics. Nevertheless, at an early stage of the debate Stock and Watson (1988, p. 152), speaking specifically of GNP, offered an assessment that still seems accurate today.

> ... the preponderance of evidence currently suggests that the integrated model provides the best approximation of U.S. GNP. This is not to say that U.S. GNP is an integrated process, for this can never be learned with certainty by examining a finite time series; nor is it to say that future research using new techniques or more data could not change this assessment. But, given currently available statistical techniques, modelling GNP as an integrated process seems to provide a good approximation to its long run properties.

It is precisely because of the methodological and empirical controversies surrounding unit root testing that we have emphasized the key properties of difference stationary processes as providing an a priori basis for regarding them as the natural specification for economic variables. Once we accept this premise, unit root testing per se loses much of its interest. Instead, attention turns to questions that are ultimately of more interest to economists, questions about relationships between variables. Rather than focusing on the *univariate* behavior of variables, it becomes more interesting to ask how the structure of integrated processes can be exploited in the study of *multivariate* relationships. This is the subject of the next chapter.

Having said this, enough issues arise in the use of unit root tests that we should spend some time investigating them in more detail. We begin with a deeper look at the Dickey-Fuller test.

EXERCISES

Nelson and Plosser's data are available in the file **np.dat**, which is documented in the exercises at the end of Section 15.3.2.

17.1 np.dat Use their series on velocity to answer the following. Remember to begin by converting the series to logarithmic form.

(a) Are you able to replicate the Dickey-Fuller test statistic reported in Example 5?

(b) Try introducing some augmenting lags into the regression. Do the results support Nelson and Plosser's restriction of the regression to one without lags? If you think they may not, is the outcome of the unit root test affected by your preferred choice of lag length?

17.2 np.dat Use their series on real GNP per capita to answer the following. Remember to begin by converting the series to logarithmic form.

(a) Are you able to replicate the Dickey-Fuller test statistic reported in Example 6?

(b) Try introducing some additional augmenting lags into the regression. Do the results support Nelson and Plosser's restriction of the regression

to one with a single lag? If you think they may not, is the outcome of the unit root test affected by your preferred choice of lag length?

17.3 np.dat Choose one of the other Nelson-Plosser series. Consult their 1982 journal article, locating in their Table 5 the ADF test result for your chosen variable.

(a) Using the augmenting lag length they suggest, are you able to replicate their value for the Dickey-Fuller statistic? (See footnote 7 for a tip on understanding their notation for the lag length.)

(b) Try introducing some additional augmenting lags into the regression. Do the results support Nelson and Plosser's choice of lag length? If you think they may not, is the outcome of the unit root test affected by your preferred choice of lag length?

17.4 jones.dat In Chapter 6 we study the GDP per capita series of Jones (1995), available in the file **jones.dat**. We use it to make the point that, in its logarithms, the series is well described by a linear trend. Even so, is the hypothesis of difference stationarity rejected for this series? Justify your choice of augmenting lag length.

17.3.2 Deriving the Dickey-Fuller Regression

Our introduction to the mechanics of ADF tests has presented the Dickey-Fuller regression in a somewhat ad hoc manner: We simply wrote down the regression, advancing it as a primitive concept. It is useful to examine more carefully just how it nests the trend and difference stationary models.

The Trend Stationary Model This is the prototypical model

$$Y_t = \alpha + \beta t + v_t. \tag{17.24a}$$

Here v_t is assumed to follow some stationary ARMA process of the form (16.18b). It turns out that such a stationary ARMA process can be reparameterized as[10]

$$v_t = \phi v_{t-1} + u_t, \quad |\phi| < 1, \tag{17.24b}$$

where u_t is in turn a stationary disturbance. This stationary disturbance is, in general, autocorrelated: u_t would only be white noise in the special case where v_t happened to be AR(1). Thus, v_t can in general be thought of as being of an AR(1) form, albeit one in which the disturbance is autocorrelated. It will become apparent shortly why it is useful to think of v_t in these terms.

The Difference Stationary Model This is the prototypical model

$$\Delta Y_t = \beta + u_t, \tag{17.25}$$

where u_t follows some stationary ARMA process. (For the moment do not be concerned about the choice of the common symbol u_t in these last two formulas. The reason for this choice will become evident momentarily.) We have seen earlier in this chapter that an I(1) variable can be interpreted as I(1) noise superimposed on a deterministic trend. This is expressed by the model (17.14), which we restate here as

$$Y_t = \alpha + \beta t + v_t, \tag{17.26a}$$
$$v_t = v_{t-1} + u_t. \tag{17.26b}$$

Because v_t is integrated, the variable does not revert to this deterministic trend, in contrast to what is true of the trend stationary model (17.24).

The Encompassing Model Comparing the models (17.24) and (17.26), the conclusion is that both the trend and difference stationary processes imply models of the form

$$Y_t = \alpha + \beta t + v_t.$$

They differ in the specification of the disturbance. The trend stationary model assumes the stationary disturbance (17.24b). The difference stationary model instead assumes the integrated disturbance (17.26b). Thus, the two models are encompassed by the common model

$$Y_t = \alpha + \beta t + v_t, \tag{17.27a}$$
$$v_t = \phi v_{t-1} + u_t. \tag{17.27b}$$

They are distinguished by the value of ϕ. The difference stationary model (17.26) is the special case of $\phi = 1$. The trend stationary model (17.24) is the special case

---

[10] The technical details of this reparameterization are given in Hamilton (1994, p. 437).

of $\phi < 1$ (ruling out a priori any possibility that $\phi > 1$ or $\phi \leq -1$, which we know to be implausible for economic data).

Hence, a test of the unit root hypothesis is a test of $\phi = 1$ against $\phi < 1$. But what should be estimated in order to perform this test? Using the common model (17.27),

$$
\begin{aligned}
Y_t &= \alpha + \beta t + v_t \\
&= \alpha + \beta t + \phi v_{t-1} + u_t \\
&= \alpha + \beta t + \phi(Y_{t-1} - \alpha - \beta(t-1)) + u_t \\
&= \underbrace{\alpha(1-\phi) + \phi\beta}_{\beta_0} + \underbrace{\beta(1-\phi)}_{\beta_1} t + \phi Y_{t-1} + u_t.
\end{aligned} \tag{17.28}
$$

With the indicated reparameterization, and subtracting Y_{t-1} from both sides, this is the Dickey-Fuller regression (17.22):

$$
\Delta Y_t = \beta_0 + \beta_1 t + \rho Y_{t-1} + u_t.
$$

This derivation of the Dickey-Fuller regression shows that the coefficients β_0 and β_1 have important interpretations in terms of the parameters of the underlying trend and difference stationary processes. Most important, under the unit root restriction $\phi = 1$ these coefficients reduce to $\beta_0 = \beta$ and $\beta_1 = 0$, confirming that the regression reduces to the difference stationary model. Hence, when we test the hypothesis $\phi = 1$ (or, equivalently, $\rho = 0$) we are implicitly also setting these coefficients to these values.

Understanding where the Dickey-Fuller regression comes from is important because it shows us how to modify the unit root test when other trend and difference stationary processes are of interest. Let us consider the most important such case.

17.3.3 The Dickey-Fuller Test: Intercept, No Trend

The Dickey-Fuller test as we have presented it tests what we have called the prototypical trend and difference stationary models. In some applications, however, it is not these prototypical models that are of interest. For nontrending variables the choice may be between describing the variable as variation around a constant,

$$
Y_t = \alpha + v_t,
$$

and as I(1) without drift,

$$
\Delta Y_t = u_t.
$$

For example, these might be the choices for describing nominal or real exchange rates or perhaps (over a limited sample period) unemployment or interest rates. These models are, of course, the special cases of the prototypical models in which $\beta = 0$.

As our study of trend and difference stationary processes has revealed, these modifications of the prototypical models are essentially variations on the specification of the underlying deterministic trend (to which the variable may or may not revert). The models here are of variation around a horizontal central line: In the first, the trend stationary model, the variable reverts to the central line α; in the second, the difference stationary model, there is no tendency to revert to the horizontal line determined by the initial value Y_0. By contrast, in the prototypical models the presence or absence of mean-reverting behavior concerns a linear trend rather than a horizontal line.

Consider, for example, Nelson and Plosser's unemployment rate series shown in Figure 15.1(a). It does not trend, suggesting that it is best viewed as variation around a horizontal central line. Because unemployment is usually thought of as gravitating to a "natural rate," we would expect it to exhibit mean-reverting behavior, suggesting the first of the two models. Even so, in principle, the series shown in Figure 15.1(a) can be the realization of a zero-drift I(1) process. How can we choose between these two models?

Because alternative trend and difference stationary models imply different underlying deterministic trends—horizontal, linear, or otherwise—these variations in the models lead to variations in the deterministic component of the Dickey-Fuller regression. Most notably, the time trend is sometimes dropped, so the regression is

$$\Delta Y_t = \beta_0 + \rho Y_{t-1} + u_t. \tag{17.29}$$

In this "intercept, no trend" case, it turns out that it is the trend and difference stationary models that are being tested. Establishing this requires a reworking of the derivations that applied in the case of the prototypical models, a reworking that is the subject of this section.

In yet another version, the Dickey-Fuller regression without either intercept or trend is sometimes discussed,

$$\Delta Y_t = \rho Y_{t-1} + u_t.$$

As may become apparent as we examine the intercept, no trend case, it is difficult to think of any practical application in which this model would be appropriate, and so we neglect it in favor of the versions that are important in empirical work.

Deriving the Dickey-Fuller Regression
As before, we proceed by specifying the trend and difference stationary models in a form that suggests an encompassing model.

The Trend Stationary Model If Y_t follows a stationary ARMA process, it may be specified as

$$Y_t = \alpha + v_t, \tag{17.30a}$$

where v_t is a stationary ARMA disturbance such as (16.18b) or, using the notation (17.24b),

$$v_t = \phi v_{t-1} + u_t, \quad |\phi| < 1. \tag{17.30b}$$

In this model the "trend" is, of course, not really a trend at all, but just the constant α. This model is nothing more than the stationary ARMA model (16.18) developed in the previous chapter.

The Difference Stationary Model An I(1) process without drift is

$$\Delta Y_t = u_t,$$

where u_t is a stationary ARMA process. Because this is just the special case of the prototypical I(1) model in which $\beta = 0$, it may be restated as

$$Y_t = \alpha + v_t, \tag{17.31a}$$
$$v_t = v_{t-1} + u_t. \tag{17.31b}$$

This just sets $\beta = 0$ in the model (17.26). The interpretation is that a zero-drift I(1) variable can be regarded as being generated by an integrated disturbance attached to a constant. Because the disturbance is integrated, the variable does not revert to this horizontal central line, in contrast to the stationary ARMA model (17.30).

The Encompassing Model Comparing the models (17.30) and (17.31), the conclusion is that both the trend and difference stationary processes imply models of the form

$$Y_t = \alpha + v_t.$$

They differ in the specification of the disturbance. The trend stationary model assumes the stationary disturbance (17.30b). The difference stationary model instead assumes the integrated disturbance (17.31b). Thus, the two models are encompassed by the common model

$$Y_t = \alpha + v_t, \tag{17.32a}$$
$$v_t = \phi v_{t-1} + u_t. \tag{17.32b}$$

They are distinguished by the value of ϕ. The difference stationary model (17.31) is the special case of $\phi = 1$. The trend stationary model (17.30) is the special case of $\phi < 1$.

Hence, a test of the unit root hypothesis is a test of $\phi = 1$ against $\phi < 1$. But what should be estimated in order to perform this test? Using the common model (17.32),

$$
\begin{aligned}
Y_t &= \alpha + v_t \\
&= \alpha + \phi v_{t-1} + u_t \\
&= \alpha + \phi(Y_{t-1} - \alpha) + u_t \\
&= \underbrace{\alpha(1 - \phi)}_{\beta_0} + \phi Y_{t-1} + u_t.
\end{aligned}
\tag{17.33}
$$

With the indicated reparameterization, and subtracting Y_{t-1} from both sides, this is the Dickey-Fuller regression without a time trend, equation (17.29):

$$\Delta Y_t = \beta_0 + \rho Y_{t-1} + u_t.$$

This derivation shows that the coefficient β_0 has an important interpretation in terms of the parameters of the underlying trend and difference stationary processes. Under the unit root restriction $\phi = 1$, this coefficient reduces to $\beta_0 = 0$, confirming that the regression reduces to the difference stationary model. Hence, when we test the hypothesis $\phi = 1$ (or, equivalently, $\rho = 0$) we are implicitly also setting $\beta_0 = 0$ under the null hypothesis.

EXAMPLE 7

 np.dat

Consider Nelson and Plosser's unemployment rate series shown in Figure 15.1(a). Because it does not trend, it is natural to formulate the choice between trend and difference stationarity in terms of the two previous models. Furthermore, as we have reasoned, it should exhibit mean reverting behavior, suggesting that the unit root hypothesis should be rejected. Is this the finding?

SOLUTION

Nelson and Plosser used $k = 3$ lags in their ADF regression for this variable. An intercept, no trend regression with this lag length yields an ADF statistic of -3.69. The data are for the period 1890–1970; after $k = 3$ lags on first differences, the sample size is $n = 77$. Comparing this against the appropriate tabulated values in Table 17.1, the unit root hypothesis is rejected at even a 1% significance level.

Hence, the outcome of the ADF test is consistent with the intuition that the unemployment rate should be mean-reverting. This was the only variable of the 14 studied by Nelson and Plosser that had this property.

EXERCISES _____

17.5 np.dat Replicate the ADF statistic reported in Example 7. How sensitive is the rejection of the unit root hypothesis to alternative augmenting lag lengths?

17.6 np.dat Nelson and Plosser analyzed all their variables using an intercept and trend ADF regression, and hence this was the version of the regression they estimated for the unemployment rate. Estimate this version of the ADF regression. Nelson and Plosser reported an ADF statistic of -3.55. How close do you come to replicating this value?

17.3.4 Which Version Should We Choose?

Two versions of the Dickey-Fuller regression have now been derived. Both are a test of the unit root null hypothesis $\rho = 0$ against the alternative $\rho < 0$. They differ in their specification of the trend—that is, of the deterministic terms of the regression. Let us call these two versions Version 1 and Version 2. Version 1 includes an intercept denoted β_0, but does not include a trend. Version 2 includes both an intercept and trend and so has deterministic terms of the linear form $\beta_0 + \beta_1 t$.

Because our development of the theory underlying these two versions has been quite extended, this is a topic in which it is easy to lose the forest for the trees. Let us therefore summarize the essentials the two versions of the Dickey-Fuller test.

Version 1: Intercept, no trend. The Dickey-Fuller regression is

$$\Delta Y_t = \beta_0 + \rho Y_{t-1} + u_t. \tag{17.34}$$

The restriction $\rho = 0$ is the null hypothesis that a zero-drift I(1) process is the appropriate model,

$$\Delta Y_t = u_t. \tag{17.35}$$

The alternative hypothesis $\rho < 0$ is of stationarity, the model (17.30):

$$Y_t = \alpha + v_t.$$

Version 2: Intercept and trend. The Dickey-Fuller regression is

$$\Delta Y_t = \beta_0 + \beta_1 t + \rho Y_{t-1} + u_t. \tag{17.36}$$

The restriction $\rho = 0$ is the null hypothesis that a drifting I(1) process is the appropriate model,

$$\Delta Y_t = \beta + u_t. \tag{17.37}$$

The alternative hypothesis $\rho < 0$ is of linear trend stationarity:

$$Y_t = \alpha + \beta t + v_t.$$

Summarized in this way, one aspect of these tests may seem puzzling. In both versions of the test the unit root restriction $\rho = 0$ does not literally reduce the Dickey-Fuller regression to the model that is asserted to hold as the null hypothesis. Indeed, imposing $\rho = 0$ on Version 1 of the regression reduces it not to (17.35) but to (17.37), the null of Version 2. Similarly, imposing $\rho = 0$ on Version 2 of the regression does not literally reduce it to (17.37), the model that is asserted to hold under the null; instead it seems to suggest that under the null ΔY_t follows a "trending drift."

This has often been the source of confusion in the interpretation of Dickey-Fuller tests in applied work and may lead you to wonder whether the model that is asserted to hold under the null hypothesis is in fact the one we are testing when we test the restriction $\rho = 0$. When we run Version 1 and test $\rho = 0$, are we not testing the null hypothesis of a drifting I(1) process, the model (17.37), rather than that of a zero-drift I(1) model (17.35)? Similarly, when we run Version 2 and test $\rho = 0$, are we not testing the null hypothesis of an I(1) process with a trending drift rather than that of a drifting I(1) model (17.37)?

Clarifying this issue is one reason we have given careful attention to deriving the two versions of the Dickey-Fuller regression as encompassing models. The fully parameterized forms (17.33) and (17.28) of the regressions reveal that the restriction $\rho = \phi - 1 = 0$ does reduce each version to the correct model under the null hypothesis; for in each case setting $\phi = 1$ implies an additional restriction. Considering Version 1, an inspection of the primitive form (17.33) and the notation

$$\beta_0 = \alpha(1 - \phi)$$

indicates that the restriction $\rho = \phi - 1 = 0$ implies the additional restriction $\beta_0 = 0$. In Version 2, an inspection of the primitive form (17.28) and the notation

$$\beta_1 = \beta(1 - \phi)$$

indicates that the restriction $\rho = \phi - 1 = 0$ implies the additional restriction $\beta_1 = 0$. In testing $\rho = 0$ in each case, then, the additional restriction that reduces the regression to the correct model under the null hypothesis is implicit.[11]

One way of thinking about this is as follows. The choice of a Version 1 ADF regression involves a maintained hypothesis of mean stationarity—that is, of an absence of drift/trend. After all, if there is some possibility that the series may be nonstationary in its mean, then Version 2 should be run instead. Consequently, in implementing Version 1 we have already precluded the possibility of a drift/trend in the series a priori, so that the drifting I(1) process (17.37) has automatically been rejected from consideration. It is precisely because researchers are often unwilling to adopt this maintained hypothesis—to rule out a priori the possibility of any drift/trend—that Version 2 is the more commonly used test. Nelson and Plosser, for example, used Version 2 tests for all their series, even the unemployment rate.

17.3.5 What Exactly Are We Testing for When We Test for a Unit Root, and Why Do We Care?

With these comments on the mechanics of ADF tests as background, it is useful to develop further our intuitive understanding of the meaning of these tests.

As we have seen many times throughout this book, any hypothesis test is a test of a parameter restriction. The null hypothesis is that the restriction holds, the alternative hypothesis is that it does not. The Dickey-Fuller unit root test (in either of its versions) tests $H_0: \phi = 1$ (or, equivalently, $\rho \equiv \phi - 1 = 0$) against $H_A: \phi < 1$ (or, equivalently, $\rho \equiv \phi - 1 < 0$). But when we run a Dickey-Fuller regression to "test for a unit root" in a time series, what exactly are we testing for?

These alternative versions of the Dickey-Fuller regression help clarify the answer to this question.

Practitioner's Tip: The interpretation of unit root tests

Fundamentally, a unit root test is a test for the presence of a stochastic trend.

That is, the null hypothesis is that the series contains a stochastic trend and the alternative hypothesis is that it does not.

---

[11] Indeed, in their original work Dickey and Fuller also presented simulated sampling distributions for F tests of the joint restrictions $\rho = \beta_0 = 0$ (in Version 1) and $\rho = \beta_1 = 0$ (in Version 2). However, the t tests that we have presented are much more widely used in practice than these joint tests.

Rejection of the null hypothesis in favor of the alternative has the implication that the series is trend stationary and so may be studied as variation around a deterministic trend. That is, least squares detrending is the appropriate means of transforming the data to stationarity.

Of course, if it is a Version 1 test that has been run (the intercept, no trend case), then it is a maintained hypothesis under either H_0 or H_A that the series is stationary in its mean. In this case, the deterministic trend is the trivial one of the constant α. If the unit root hypothesis is rejected, the series can be modeled as an ARMA process in its levels using the Box-Jenkins methodology, as discussed in the previous chapter; no detrending is necessary.

Failure to reject the null hypothesis suggests that the series is difference stationary: It should be modeled as stationary in its differences using an ARIMA model. Least squares detrending is inappropriate. Suggested as well are the key properties of a stochastic trend: Shocks are permanent in their effect, the variable does not exhibit trend reversion, a shock alters long-term forecasts, and the forecast error variance is unbounded.

Notice that a failure to reject the presence of a stochastic trend carries no necessary implication of an absence of a deterministic trend. On the contrary, as the representations (17.26) and (17.31) reiterate, stochastic trend models always contain an implicit deterministic trend, although in the case of the zero-drift model (17.31) this trend is the trivial one of a horizontal central line. The issue is not whether a deterministic trend is present but whether the series reverts to it. Failure to reject the unit root null indicates that the series is not trend reverting, due to the presence of a stochastic trend.

It is useful to emphasize these points because discussions of unit root tests are often riddled with confusing assertions about the interpretation of these tests. In particular it is useful to note what unit root tests are *not*.

Unit Root Tests Are* Not, in General, Tests of Nonstationarity*** That is, it is not the case that the null hypothesis is that the series is nonstationary and the alternative that it is stationary. In Version 2, the series is nonstationary under both the null and alternative.

Having said this, unit root tests do have this interpretation in some circumstances. Specifically, in Version 1 of the Dickey-Fuller test when the regression contains no trend, the series is nonstationary under the null hypothesis (where the model is a zero-drift random walk, which is nonstationary in its variance), yet stationary under the alternative (where an ARMA model would apply). In general, however, it is incorrect to characterize unit root tests as tests for stationarity or nonstationarity. If we must interpret unit root tests in terms of the concept of stationarity, it is perhaps best to say that a unit root test is a test of the null hypothesis that the series is difference stationary against the alternative that it is trend stationary, with the understanding that in Version 1 this "trend" is horizontal.

Unit Root Tests Are Not Tests for a Random Walk. That is, it is not the case that the null hypothesis is that the series follows a random walk and the alternative that it does not. In neither of Versions 1 or 2 is the series a random walk under the null hypothesis (and certainly not under the alternative).[12]

A random walk is the special case of the I(1) models (17.35) and (17.37), the zero-drift and drift cases, respectively, in which the disturbance is white noise: $u_t = \varepsilon_t$. Autocorrelation in the period-by-period changes in a variable is a separate matter from whether it has a unit root. A series can contain a stochastic trend, yet not be a random walk. Random walks have a unit root, but unit root processes are not random walks if their first differences are autocorrelated. One implication of this is that unit root tests are of no value in testing the efficient markets hypothesis, a point emphasized by Campbell, Lo, and MacKinlay (1997, pp. 64–65).

If the question of interest is whether a series is a random walk, one way to examine this is to test whether its first differences are autocorrelated. We have seen in Chapter 15 how to use the Box-Pierce-Ljung statistic to test whether a series is autocorrelated.

17.4 Higher Orders of Integration

So far in our study of stochastic trends our focus has been limited to variables that are I(1). However, higher orders of integration are possible.

17.4.1 Introduction

To motivate this in terms of a practical problem, think of the price level P_t and let $Y_t = \log P_t$. Then, ΔY_t is the growth rate of the price level, the inflation rate. Suppose that the inflation rate is positive, so that the price level is increasing over time and is therefore nonstationary. We may distinguish between the following possibilities. In using the term *price level* in the discussion that follows, we take it to be in log form: $Y_t = \log P_t$.

The Price Level Is I(1). If the price level is increasing, but in such a way that the inflation rate neither systematically increases nor decreases over time, then Y_t is I(1); a single differencing (yielding the inflation rate) transforms Y_t to stationarity. This is described by our I(1) model

$$\Delta Y_t = \beta + u_t. \tag{17.38}$$

---

[12] Having said this, it is perhaps useful to add a further clarification. As we have seen in our discussion of the Beveridge-Nelson decomposition, any I(1) process can be decomposed as the sum of a random walk plus stationary noise. It is the random walk component that embodies the stochastic trend that distinguishes the series from being trend stationary. Hence, a test for a unit root *can* correctly be interpreted as a test for a random walk *component* in the series. But this is different from a test that the series is a random walk.

As in the past, u_t denotes a zero-mean stationary disturbance. The drift parameter β is therefore the mean inflation rate, $E(\Delta \log P_t) = \beta$, and the actual inflation rate fluctuates in a stationary manner around this mean.

But what if the inflation rate is not stationary? Suppose that instead the inflation rate drifts upward over time. This is what happens during periods of hyperinflation. In Chapter 6, we examine some of Philip Cagan's data for the European hyperinflations that followed the world wars of the twentieth century. Figure 6.6 shows data for Hungary in 1945–1946, Figure 6.13 for Germany in 1921–1923, and Figure 6.14 for Poland in 1922–1924. These figures plot the log of the price level over the course of each hyperinflationary episode. (The last two figures also plot the money stock, which is not relevant for the present discussion.)

The log-differences of these price indices are shown in Figure 17.4(a), (b), and (c).[13] Consistent with this defining feature of hyperinflations, in all three countries the inflation rate tended to increase over the course of the hyperinflation. Hence, the model of a stationary inflation rate—an I(1) price level—is unsatisfactory. Instead we should consider the next possibility.

The Price Level Is I(2)   If the inflation rate is increasing, but by amounts that are not themselves systematically increasing or decreasing, then a single differencing of the inflation rate (a twice-differencing of the price level) will yield a stationary series. The appropriate model is

$$\Delta^2 Y_t = \beta + u_t.$$

The meaning of the left-hand side is[14]

$$
\begin{aligned}
\Delta^2 Y_t &= \Delta(\Delta Y_t) \\
&= (Y_t - Y_{t-1}) - (Y_{t-1} - Y_{t-2}) \\
&= Y_t - 2Y_{t-1} + Y_{t-2}.
\end{aligned}
$$

These second differences of the price levels are shown in Figure 17.4(d), (e), and (f).

These diagrams indicate that, in the cases of Germany and Poland, this second order of differencing appears to transform the price level to stationarity, at least in its mean.[15] Although the changes in these inflation rates certainly fluctuate over time, they do so in a way that does not seem to trend upward or downward over

---

[13] These panels plot Cagan's original series for $\Delta \log P_t$, which he chose to calculate using common rather than natural logarithms. Hence, the vertical axis is not directly interpretable as the monthly percentage change.

[14] Notice that, for levels of differencing higher than the first, absolute rather than percentage changes are used. That is, $\Delta^2 Y_t \equiv \Delta(\Delta \log P_t)$ instead of $\Delta \log(\Delta \log P_t)$. The latter usually cannot be computed because a differenced series ΔY_t typically includes some negative values, for which logarithms are not defined.

[15] The twice-differenced series does not appear to be stationary in its variance, but that is a separate matter that we do not attempt to address here.

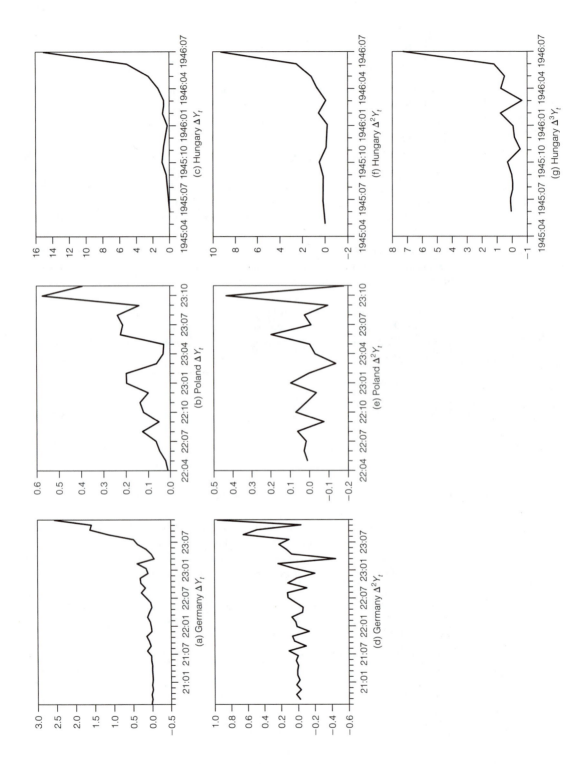

FIGURE 17.4 Orders of differencing of the logarithm of the price level in three European hyperinflations.

time. The price level is said to be **integrated of order 2,** or I(2), and we need not consider any further differencing of the German and Polish price levels.

For the Hungarian hyperinflation, on the other hand, even the twice-differenced series appears to be drifting upward, suggesting that the I(2) model is inadequate. This suggests the following possibility.

The Price Level Is I(3) Suppose that the inflation rate is increasing, by amounts that are increasing. If the differences in these increasing amounts do not trend, a suitable model is

$$\Delta^3 Y_t = \beta + u_t.$$

That is, if a third order of differencing is required to transform the price level to stationarity, it is said to be **integrated of order 3,** or I(3).

Figure 17.4(g) shows the third difference of the Hungarian price series. Any strong tendency in these third differences to increase over time is primarily associated with the last observation, and so perhaps it might be argued that it can be treated as I(3). At least as plausibly, however, we might argue that one more level of differencing is required, so that the Hungarian price level is I(4).

At this point, however, the intuitive meaning of different orders of integration is clear, and so we do not bother to inspect additional levels of differencing. Instead, let us consider more formal ways of distinguishing orders of integration.

17.4.2 Testing the Order of Integration

Although the inspection of graphs of alternative orders of differencing is a useful first step in reaching conclusions about the order of integration of a series, formal tests are available. In fact, it is apparent that we can just use the ADF test applied to the appropriately differenced series. Consider, for example, a test of the null hypothesis that a series is I(2). An I(2) series is I(1) in its first differences, so the I(2) hypothesis is equivalent to the hypothesis that ΔY_t is I(1):

$$Y_t \sim I(2) \Leftrightarrow \Delta Y_t \sim I(1).$$

Consider a standard ADF regression which, in its Version 1 of no trend, tests the null of I(1) against stationarity:

$$\Delta Y_t = \beta_0 + \rho Y_{t-1} + \sum_j \rho_j \Delta Y_{t-j} + \varepsilon_t.$$

Replacing Y_t by ΔY_t in this regression tests the null that $\Delta Y_t \sim I(1)$, equivalent to $Y_t \sim I(2)$:

$$\Delta^2 Y_t = \beta_0 + \rho \Delta Y_{t-1} + \sum_j \rho_j \Delta^2 Y_{t-j} + \varepsilon_t.$$

The alternative hypothesis is that the order of integration is less than $d = 2$.

EXAMPLE 8

germany.dat
poland.dat

Our inspection of Figure 17.4(a) and (d) for the German and Figure 17.4(b) and (e) for the Polish data suggests that for both countries log P_t must be twice-differenced to attain stationarity in the mean—once is not enough. Test formally whether this is the case by testing whether these series are I(2). (For future reference in Chapter 18, for the German data use the subsample ending in July (rather than November) 1923. This has been studied previously in Exercise 6.27, where the work of Taylor 1991 was replicated.)

SOLUTION

A test of the null that the price level log P_t is I(2) is just a test of whether the inflation rate $\Delta \log P_t$ is I(1). Estimating the ADF regression in $\Delta^2 Y_t$ for Cagan's data where $Y_t = \log P_t$, it is useful to consider a range of augmenting lag lengths in order to confirm that our findings are not sensitive to any one choice. The ADF statistic is, as before, the t statistic on $\hat{\rho}$.

Lags	Germany	Poland
0	−2.22	−1.98
1	−1.76	−0.29
2	−0.93	−0.13
3	−0.89	0.72
4	−0.76	0.36

After differencing, the German and Polish samples include $n = 34$ and $n = 19$ observations, respectively; the sample size on which these ADF statistics are based is reduced by the number of lags. Comparing with the ADF critical values for $n = 25$ in Table 17.1, we find that for both countries the unit root hypothesis is not rejected. This conclusion is not sensitive to the choice of lag length. Hence, we conclude that the price levels in these hyperinflationary episodes may be described as I(2), as opposed to I(1).

Clearly this idea can be extended to higher orders of integration. To test the null of I(3), for example, we make use of the fact that

$$Y_t \sim I(3) \Leftrightarrow \Delta^2 Y_t \sim I(1).$$

The ADF regression is

$$\Delta^3 Y_t = \beta_0 + \rho \Delta^2 Y_{t-1} + \sum_j \rho_j \Delta^3 Y_{t-j} + \varepsilon_t.$$

In testing for higher orders of integration in this way, it is important to be clear about the precise nature of the null and alternative hypotheses. In Example 8 we test the null hypothesis of I(2)—in technical jargon, that there are "two unit roots." The alternative hypothesis is that there are fewer than two unit roots; that is, that the series is either I(1) (a single unit root) or stationary (no unit roots). A rejection of this null would presumably lead to a second-stage test of the null hypothesis of

I(1)—a standard ADF test—in order to test whether the series contains a single unit root.[16]

The null of I(2) takes as a maintained hypothesis that there are not more than two unit roots; that is, that no more than two orders of differencing are required to achieve stationarity. If this maintained hypothesis is inappropriate—as judged by, say, a preliminary visual inspection of alternative orders of differencing similar to Figure 17.4—then we should start with a higher order of integration as the null hypothesis. Notice that, consistent with the general-to-specific methodology advocated in Chapter 12, the optimal testing strategy is to start with the highest plausible order of integration as the initially adopted maintained hypothesis and work downward from there.

Multiple Unit Roots Are Unusual

The point of our hyperinflation example is to emphasize that orders of integration greater than 2 should be unusual in economic data and, consequently, that it will often be unnecessary to start with anything higher than this as an initial maintained hypothesis. Even I(2) variables should be uncommon. As we remark in our initial analysis of Cagan's data in Chapter 6, hyperinflations are extraordinary economic events, quite atypical of economic phenomena generally. The Hungarian hyperinflation was the most extreme of these extraordinary events in history. Growing growth rates are usually not sustainable in the economic world. Consequently, when economic variables grow they usually do so in a way that is well approximated by a constant growth rate. This is especially true of the real variables (as distinct from nominal or monetary ones) such as output, employment, and productivity that economists are most often interested in studying. Because the I(1) model is just a stochastic version of the constant growth model—the point of the opening sections of this chapter—it should be adequate for the study of most nonstationary variables.

EXERCISES _____

Cagan's German and Polish hyperinflation data are available in the files **germany.dat** and **poland.dat**. These files are documented in the preface to Exercise 6.27 at the end of Appendix 6A. (If you use the German data in answering the following questions, use the subsample ending in July 1923 that is used in Example 8.)

17.7 🌐 **germany.dat poland.dat** Choosing either the German or Polish data, verify the ADF test statistics reported in Example 8.

17.8 🌐 **germany.dat poland.dat** The ADF test statistics reported in Example 8 are based on Version 1 Dickey-Fuller regressions. Choosing either the Ger-

_____

[16] When the test of I(1) is arrived at as part of such a sequential procedure, it turns out that there are implications for the form of the Dickey-Fuller regression. The primary reference is Dickey and Pantula (1987); textbook treatments include Enders (1995, pp. 227–228) and, at a more technical level, Banerjee, Dolado, Galbraith, and Hendry (1993, pp. 119–120).

man or Polish data, try using a Version 2 regression instead. Is the substantive conclusion of the test affected?

17.9 germany.dat poland.dat The tests reported in Example 8 take as a maintained hypothesis that the German and Polish series are integrated of order no greater than 2. Suppose a null of I(3) had instead been adopted. Choosing one of the countries, perform a test of this null hypothesis using the same augmenting lag lengths as in Example 8. What are your findings?

17.4.3 Order of Integration and Degree of Implicit Trend

When an integrated process has a nonzero drift, the drift gives rise to an implicit deterministic trend. This is demonstrated most recently in Section 17.2.2, in which the I(1) model (17.25),

$$\Delta Y_t = \beta + u_t,$$

is accumulated using recursive substitution and reexpressed in the form (17.13),

$$Y_t = \alpha + \beta t + v_t, \tag{17.39}$$

where $v_t = \sum_{j=0}^{t-1} u_{t-j}$. Thus, Y_t has the implicit linear trend $\alpha + \beta t$, albeit one that is buried in integrated noise.

A linear trend is a polynomial of degree 1 in time. In general, a polynomial in a variable x is a function of x that takes the form

$$f(x) = \sum_{i=0}^{k} b_i x^i = b_0 + b_1 x + b_2 x^2 + b_3 x^3 + \cdots + b_k x^k.$$

The coefficients b_i are the parameters of the polynomial. The largest power k is called the **degree** of the polynomial. If the argument of the function is time t and the polynomial is of degree $k = 1$, then the function is a linear trend:

$$b_0 + b_1 t.$$

A second-degree polynomial is a quadratic trend,

$$b_0 + b_1 t + b_2 t^2;$$

a third-degree polynomial is a cubic trend,

$$b_0 + b_1 t + b_2 t^2 + b_3 t^3;$$

and so on.

Notice that an I(1) process with drift has an implicit trend that is a polynomial of degree 1 in time. It turns out that, in general, an I(d) process with drift has an implicit trend that is a polynomial of degree d in time.

To illustrate this for the case of $d = 2$, consider an I(2) process with drift,

$$\Delta^2 Y_t = \beta + u_t,$$

or, equivalently,

$$\Delta(\Delta Y_t) = \beta + u_t.$$

Because ΔY_t plays exactly the same role here that Y_t does in the I(1) derivation, this process can be accumulated using recursive substitution just as before. The result is analogous to (17.39),

$$\Delta Y_t = \alpha + \beta t + v_t.$$

Similar to the previous model, α denotes a presample initial value of the series ΔY_t and $v_t = \sum_{j=0}^{t-1} u_{t-j}$. This says that, if Y_t is I(2), then ΔY_t follows a linear trend buried in integrated noise.

This may in turn be accumulated using recursive substitution:

$$
\begin{aligned}
Y_t &= Y_{t-1} + \alpha + \beta t + v_t \\
&= Y_{t-2} + 2\alpha + \beta[t + (t-1)] + v_t + v_{t-1} \\
&= Y_{t-3} + 3\alpha + \beta[t + (t-1) + (t-2)] + v_t + v_{t-1} + v_{t-2} \\
&\;\;\vdots \\
&= Y_0 + \alpha t + \beta[t + (t-1) + (t-2) + \cdots + 3 + 2 + 1] + \sum_{j=0}^{t-1} v_{t-j} \\
&= Y_0 + \alpha t + \beta \frac{t(t+1)}{2} + \sum_{j=0}^{t-1} v_{t-j} \text{ because } 1 + 2 + 3 + \cdots + t = \frac{t(t+1)}{2} \\
&= Y_0 + (\alpha + \beta/2)t + (\beta/2)t^2 + w_t.
\end{aligned}
$$

The last line defines the integrated disturbance $w_t = \sum_{j=0}^{t-1} v_{t-j}$. Relabeling appropriately reveals an implicit quadratic trend,

$$Y_t = b_0 + b_1 t + b_2 t^2 + w_t.$$

In conclusion, an I(2) model with drift has an implicit deterministic trend that is a polynomial of degree 2. As in the I(1) case, the fact that w_t is an integrated disturbance means that the variable does not revert to this trend. Notice that w_t is I(2) because it must be twice-differenced to obtain the original stationary disturbance u_t. Hence, just as an I(1) variable can be interpreted as a linear trend buried in I(1) noise, an I(2) variable can be interpreted as a quadratic trend buried in I(2) noise. In general, an I(d) variable is I(d) noise superimposed on a polynomial of order d in time.

EXERCISES

17.10 A simple way of seeing the correspondence between order of integration and degree of trend is to note that differencing of order d eliminates a deterministic trend of that degree.

(a) Consider the linear trend

$$Y_t = b_0 + b_1 t.$$

Show that a single differencing ΔY_t eliminates the trend.

(b) Consider the quadratic trend

$$Y_t = b_0 + b_1 t + b_2 t^2.$$

Show that twice-differencing $\Delta^2 Y_t$ eliminates the trend.

(c) Consider the cubic trend

$$Y_t = b_0 + b_1 t + b_2 t^2 + b_3 t^3.$$

Show that thrice-differencing $\Delta^3 Y_t$ eliminates the trend.

18 *Cointegration*

At the least sophisticated level of economic theory lies the belief that certain pairs of economic variables should not diverge from one another by too great an extent, at least in the long-run. Thus, such variables may drift apart in the short-run or according to seasonal factors, but if they continue to be too far apart in the long-run, then economic forces, such as a market mechanism or government intervention, will begin to bring them together again.

C. W. J. Granger, "Developments in the Study of Cointegrated Economic Variables," 1991

In the last three chapters we have studied the univariate behavior of time series variables. This has given us the tools we need to turn at last to the study of the interaction of economic variables over time.

18.1 Long-Run Relationships between Variables

One of the basic distinctions that has come out of our discussion of univariate time series is the distinction between short-run and long-run behavior. Outside the context of a specific model, the concepts of short- and long-run are, of course, amorphous, and that is why we have devoted some effort to formulating models in which the distinction is clear. The long-run behavior of a variable is reflected in its permanent component, the trend; the short-run behavior is reflected in its transitory component.

Modeling the Short and Long Run

Short- and long-run behavior is captured differently by the different models we have studied. In an ARMA model such as equation (16.1),

$$Y_t = \alpha + u_t, \tag{18.1}$$

785

where the disturbance u_t follows a stable autoregressive moving average model of the kind we specify in Chapter 16, the long-run behavior of the variable is reflected in its constant mean α. As we have seen, α has the interpretation as the equilibrium value to which Y would converge were the shocks driving u_t to terminate. In the presence of shocks, the variable fluctuates around this long-run equilibrium, those fluctuations constituting its short-run behavior. The precise nature of the fluctuations depends, as we have seen, on the parameter values of the ARMA process and its lag lengths p and q.

Of course the economy may never actually attain equilibrium—just as a rocking horse will never settle down if it is repeatedly pushed—and so Y_t may well never take on the value α, nor would we have any way of knowing if it did. Even so, with data on Y_t we can perform statistical inference on this parameter; for example, α can be estimated using $\overline{Y}$.

As a generalization of the constant plus disturbance model, we have considered trend stationary models such as the prototypical model

$$Y_t = \alpha + \beta t + u_t. \tag{18.2}$$

Here the long-run behavior is associated with the deterministic trend $\alpha + \beta t$ and the short-run behavior with the stationary fluctuations u_t around this trend.

Finally, in a difference stationary model such as

$$\Delta Y_t = \beta + u_t$$

the distinction between short- and long-run behavior is given by the Beveridge-Nelson decomposition. Long-run behavior is determined by a random walk component which, like any random walk, can be interpreted as consisting of deterministic plus stochastic trends, the former arising from the drift β. Short-run behavior is associated with a stationary transitory component.

Relationships between Time Series Variables

Our study of relationships between time series variables will similarly hinge on this distinction between short-run fluctuations and long-run trends. Variables can be related in either or both the short and long run. Consider two variables Y_{1t} and Y_{2t}, both of which evolve over time. It could be the case that they are unrelated in any way—in either the short or long run. Or their short-run fluctuations could be linked, but in a way that ends up not being important for their long-run behavior, so that in the long run they are unrelated. Conversely, the variables could be linked in the long run, but in a way that does not involve any strong association in their short-run fluctuations. Finally, the variables could be linked in both the short and long run.

It is apparent that the analysis of the short- and long-run interaction between economic variables is in principle a complicated matter, as indeed it can be in practice. For precisely this reason, we take the same strategy in simplifying this task that we did in our study of univariate time series: We focus on the long run. There are several reasons why this strategy makes sense. First, long-run relationships between variables often dominate any short-run interaction to an extent that makes the latter relatively unimportant. Consequently, it is sometimes possible to study long-run relationships between economic variables in a way that allows us to neglect—in the sense of not having to model explicitly—their short-run interaction. One of the most important goals of this chapter is to formulate this idea precisely. Second, economic theory often has more to say about relationships between variables in the long run than in the short run. This is because economic theory makes key use of the concept of an equilibrium—economic forces work so as to cause variables to take on certain relationships to one another. However, as our discussion of the constant plus disturbance model (18.1) has reminded us, adjustments to equilibrium take time and are probably never entirely complete before new shocks hit the economy. Consequently, the equilibrium relationships predicted by theory are often only manifested in the long run. Formulating the notion of the long run in terms of the trends of economic time series suggests that equilibrium relationships between economic variables will often be relationships between their trends.

Implications of Univariate Behavior for the Study of Joint Behavior

Our study of the univariate behavior of variables has given us some ideas that are important in discussing joint behavior. In particular, we have seen that there are two fundamentally different types of trends: the deterministic trends of trend stationary processes and the stochastic trends of difference stationary ones. The main reason we have taken the time to develop these concepts is that, because equilibrium relationships between variables are often relationships between their trends, the treatment of trends is of critical importance in studying relationships between economic variables.

In beginning to think about the joint behavior of economic variables, it is useful to distinguish among a number of possibilities involving their univariate behavior. The following discussion is phrased in terms of just two variables, but it will be easy to see how the ideas generalize to more than two variables.

18.2 Relationships between Variables

18.2.1 When Variables Are Stationary

First let us suppose that two variables X and Y are stationary and therefore can be modeled individually using the Box-Jenkins ARMA techniques in Chapter 16. As we have just recapitulated in our discussion of the model (18.1), all this means is that the variables fluctuate around fixed means, these fluctuations being described by the autoregressive and moving average components of their univariate ARMA models.

Short-Run Behavior The simplest approach to describing the joint behavior of Y with X is to begin with an AR(p) model (16.14) for Y and add X in current and lagged form:

$$Y_t = \phi_0 + \phi_1 Y_{t-1} + \cdots + \phi_p Y_{t-p} + \gamma_0 X_t$$
$$+ \gamma_1 X_{t-1} + \cdots + \gamma_q X_{t-q} + \varepsilon_t. \tag{18.3}$$

This is called an **autoregressive distributed lag** (ADL) model with lags p and q, denoted ADL(p, q). If other variables in addition to X were under study, they could be introduced in a similar manner. In this way Y_t is described as being determined not only by its own past values, but also by the current and past values of other variables. Because an ADL model has no moving average component, it can be estimated as a least squares regression, as long as X_t is exogenous.

Long-Run Behavior It is useful to investigate the long-run properties of ADL models by considering the special case of a single lag on each variable, an ADL(1,1):

$$Y_t = \phi_0 + \phi_1 Y_{t-1} + \gamma_0 X_t + \gamma_1 X_{t-1} + \varepsilon_t. \tag{18.4}$$

Given the assumption that X is stationary, the stability condition for this model is the same as that for an AR(1) process: $|\phi_1| < 1$. As long as this is satisfied, in the absence of shocks these variables will converge to long-run equilibrium values X^* and Y^*, values that must themselves satisfy the ADL equation:

$$Y^* = \phi_0 + \phi_1 Y^* + \gamma_0 X^* + \gamma_1 X^*.$$

Solving for the equilibrium value Y^* in terms of X^* yields

$$Y^* = \frac{\phi_0}{1 - \phi_1} + \frac{\gamma_0 + \gamma_1}{1 - \phi_1} X^* = \lambda_0 + \lambda_1 X^*. \tag{18.5}$$

We have defined the symbols

$$\lambda_0 = \frac{\phi_0}{1 - \phi_1}, \qquad \lambda_1 = \frac{\gamma_0 + \gamma_1}{1 - \phi_1}.$$

The intercept λ_0 is just the expression (16.8), the equilibrium value of an AR(1) process that we derive in Section 16.1.1. Hence, this equilibrium solution generalizes that earlier result: It shows that, when Y depends on another variable X, its equilibrium value will depend on the equilibrium value of X. A change in the equilibrium value of X will affect the equilibrium value of Y in the amount

$$\frac{\partial Y^*}{\partial X^*} = \lambda_1 = \frac{\gamma_0 + \gamma_1}{1 - \phi_1}.$$

This is called the **long-run multiplier.** If X and Y are in log form, this is the elasticity of one equilibrium value with respect to the other.

In summary, when an ADL model is used to describe stationary variables, the variables implicitly fluctuate around constant long-run equilibrium values that are linked by the parameters of the ADL model.

Systems Approaches

In using a single equation to describe the interaction of variables, the ADL approach treats them asymmetrically; one variable must be assigned the role of dependent variable. More sophisticated approaches to studying the joint behavior of time series variables avoid this asymmetry by using systems of equations.

One such approach is a generalization of the Box-Jenkins methodology to groups of variables—called **multivariate** or **vector ARMA** models. The AR and MA components of these multiequation models describe the short-run interaction between the variables—how movements in one are linked to prior, current, and future movements in others.

However, it turns out that the MA component of vector ARMA models can be difficult to estimate. In practice, econometricians use equation systems that involve only an autoregressive component, known as a **vector autoregression** (VAR). In the simplest case of two variables Y_{1t} and Y_{2t} with just a single lag on each, a typical VAR system is[1]

$$Y_{1t} = \phi_{10} + \phi_{11}Y_{1,t-1} + \phi_{12}Y_{2,t-1} + \varepsilon_{1t} \tag{18.6a}$$

$$Y_{2t} = \phi_{20} + \phi_{21}Y_{1,t-1} + \phi_{22}Y_{2,t-1} + \varepsilon_{2t}. \tag{18.6b}$$

It is easy to see how this would generalize to more variables and lags.

Notice that an ADL regression is very similar to one equation taken from a VAR system; with the obvious changes in notation, the ADL(1,1) model (18.4) is almost the same as equations (18.6a). The only difference is that a VAR does not include contemporaneous variables on the right-hand side; Y_{2t} does not appear in equation (18.6a), nor does Y_{1t} appear in (18.6b). The reason is that the contemporaneous effect between Y_{1t} and Y_{2t} is captured by the correlation between the equation disturbances ε_{1t} and ε_{2t}, a correlation that is treated in the system estimation of the VAR.

Despite this minor difference, much of what is true of ADL regressions also holds for VARs. In particular, the variables implicitly fluctuate around constant long-run equilibrium values that are linked by the parameters of the VAR. As well, an important reparameterization discussed in Sections 18.7 and 18.8 applies similarly to both models, as we shall see. Consequently, much of the important intuition about studying relationships between time series variables can be developed by phrasing our discussion in terms of ADL models.

Further Remarks

Regardless of whether we take the single-equation ADL approach to describing time series relationships or the VAR systems approach, all the same issues of specification, estimation, and diagnostic checking arise just as they do for univariate

---

[1] If the variables have drifts, structural breaks, or seasonal elements, a VAR system can include other deterministic components in addition to the intercepts, in particular time trends and dummy variables. In omitting time trends, this VAR implicitly assumes that the variables are nondrifting. A VAR with time trends, suitable for drifting variables, is analyzed in Section 18.8.

ARMA models. And just as in the univariate case, much can be said about this—as evidenced by the chapters devoted to these topics in many books.

Nevertheless, these issues are of peripheral interest for our purposes. For, just as in the univariate case, economic theory usually has little to say about the modeling of these short-run fluctuations: The choice of appropriate lag lengths is an empirical matter. Economic theory also typically offers little in the way of testable parameter restrictions on such models.[2] For example, it is difficult to think of an economic theory that suggests an overidentifying restriction on the value of a long-run multiplier relating stationary variables, such as λ_1 in the equilibrium condition (18.5), however interesting an estimate of such a multiplier might be in some applications.

As we have noted, the long-run behavior of stationary variables is represented by their means. Because economic theory usually does not make predictions about the relationships between the means of stationary variables, this long-run "interaction" is relatively uninteresting. In practice, the main interest of these models to economists is to exploit short-run behavior in forecasting; our ability to forecast a variable over the short term may depend critically on its short-run linkages to other variables.

In conclusion, when variables are stationary their interesting behavior, from an economist's point of view, is usually in their short-run interaction. However, the modeling of these short-run interactions is usually an atheoretical exercise. Instead of focusing on this, it makes more sense to turn to situations in which dynamic behavior is manifested in a way that economic theory may have more to say about—long-run equilibrium relationships among nonstationary variables.

18.2.2 When Variables Are Trend Stationary

To consider relationships between variables that are trend stationary, consider two such variables:

$$Y_t = \alpha + \beta t + u_{1t}$$
$$X_t = \gamma + \delta t + u_{2t}.$$

Although their deterministic trends constitute what we might regard as interesting long-run behavior, with respect to the interaction of these variables it is nevertheless the case that much of what we have said about stationary variables continues to apply.

As a preliminary remark, let us begin by noting that, just as with variables stationary around a constant mean, we can speak meaningfully about short-run interactions between trend stationary variables; the short-run fluctuations captured by the ARMA disturbances u_{1t} and u_{2t} may be related. Abstracting from the deterministic trends of the variables, it may be possible to study these short-run interactions.

---

[2] The main exception is hypotheses concerning temporal precedence among the variables—called **Granger causality**—which are sometimes tested in VAR models.

Long-Run Behavior The problem arises when we try to study long-run relationships between variables that we have chosen to model as trend stationary because there is no way of dealing with the problem of spurious correlation. Notice that these equations reproduce the pair of equations (3.6) that we consider in our earliest discussion of spurious correlation in Chapter 3. That white noise disturbances have been replaced by ones that permit autocorrelation does not affect the essential points about spurious correlation that we made there.

Remember that a great many variables grow over time in a way that, at least at a descriptive level, might be modeled as trend stationary, and conventional regression or correlation analysis will often appear to indicate that such variables are related. Yule (1926) illustrated this with the correlation between the proportion of Church of England marriages relative to all marriages and the mortality rate in England and Wales (as discussed in Section 3.1.3). Hendry (1980) illustrated it with a regression of the price level on cumulative rainfall (as discussed in Section 3.2.2). We illustrated it (beginning in Section 3.1.3) with the high correlations that relate the populations of Canada, the United Kingdom, and the United States. When such variables are modeled as trend stationary, there is no way of distinguishing spurious relationships from real ones.

Short-Run Behavior For this reason it would be quite inappropriate to estimate unmodified ADL or VAR models such as (18.3) or (18.6) using trend stationary variables—just as it would be inappropriate to estimate a univariate ARMA model with nonstationary data. It *would* be possible to study their short-run interaction by detrending each variable and estimating an ADL model with the residuals—just as it would be possible to study the short-run fluctuations in an individual series by detrending it and analyzing the residuals, as we have remarked in our preliminary discussion of trend stationary processes in Section 17.1. Remarkably, it turns out that detrending the variables is equivalent to introducing a time trend into the ADL model in the original variables, say[3]

$$Y_t = \phi_0 + \beta t + \phi_1 Y_{t-1} + \gamma_0 X_t + \gamma_1 X_{t-1} + \varepsilon_t.$$

Although this is fine purely for the purpose of studying short-run interactions—as long as the variables truly are trend stationary—this approach does not address the problem of spurious correlation in the long run. The modified ADL model offers no insight into the presence or absence of any long-run relationship between the variables.

If the variables are *not* trend stationary, then, of course, this modified ADL regression is subject to all the standard lessons of Nelson and Kang (1981, 1984). The model is not a useful description of the short-run interaction between the variables because their short-run behavior is the spurious outcome of the inappropriate detrending procedure.

---

[3] The equivalence of the inclusion of a time trend in a regression to detrending each series individually is a special case of an important theoretical result known as the Frisch-Waugh-Lovell theorem. A thorough development of the Frisch-Waugh-Lovell theorem, with applications in a variety of contexts, may be found in Davidson and MacKinnon (1993).

18.2.3 When Variables Are Difference Stationary

In contrast, when nonstationary variables are modeled as integrated processes, a methodology is available for studying their long-run interaction that provides a test for spurious relationships.

Long-Run Behavior Consider two variables that are I(1). Being I(1), their behavior exhibits the features characteristic of this type of process: Their stochastic trends give rise to a meandering behavior that does not exhibit trend reversion. What does it mean for two such variables to nevertheless possess an equilibrium relationship? As the opening quotation from Granger (1991, p. 65) suggests, the two variables exhibit an equilibrium relationship if, despite their meandering behavior, they are unable to wander apart indefinitely, to "... diverge from one another by too great an extent, at least in the long run." Although "... such variables may drift apart in the short-run ... if they continue to be too far apart in the long-run, then economic forces ... will begin to bring them together again." A more formal statement of this intuition is that two I(1) variables possess an equilibrium relationship if, despite their univariate nonstationary behavior, they move together in a manner that is stationary. Two variables that possess an equilibrium relationship defined in this way are said to be **cointegrated.**

Hence, when time series variables are difference stationary there is a natural definition of an equilibrium relationship, in contrast to what is true when variables are trend stationary. This definition, in turn, makes possible a formal statistical test for cointegration, the focus of this chapter. This test enables us to distinguish spurious relationships from genuine ones. An important feature of the technique is that it turns out not to require an explicit modeling of the short-run fluctuations in variables (although some treatment of those short-run dynamics may be desirable to improve the properties of the test, as we will see).

Short-Run Behavior Suppose that two variables are I(1) but are not cointegrated: They have no long-run relationship. They may nevertheless be related in the short run. Their short-run fluctuations are described by their first differences, which must be stationary if the variables are I(1). The interactions in these short-run fluctuations may therefore be described by an ADL model in first differences,

$$\Delta Y_t = \phi_0 + \phi_1 \Delta Y_{t-1} + \cdots + \phi_p \Delta Y_{t-p}$$
$$+ \gamma_0 \Delta X_t + \gamma_1 \Delta X_{t-1} + \cdots + \gamma_q \Delta X_{t-q} + \varepsilon_t. \tag{18.7}$$

This generalizes the AR model in first differences; that is, it drops the MA component from the ARIMA($p, 1, q$) model (17.9) and introduces a distributed lag on the other variable X_t. Similarly, a researcher taking a systems approach could estimate a VAR such as (18.6) in first differences:

$$\Delta Y_{1t} = \phi_{10} + \phi_{11} \Delta Y_{1,t-1} + \phi_{12} \Delta Y_{2,t-1} + \varepsilon_{1t} \tag{18.8a}$$
$$\Delta Y_{2t} = \phi_{20} + \phi_{21} \Delta Y_{1,t-1} + \phi_{22} \Delta Y_{2,t-1} + \varepsilon_{2t}. \tag{18.8b}$$

Although such models can be estimated, it is important to understand that they describe only short-run interactions. Furthermore, if the variables *are* cointegrated, these models are not satisfactory because they ignore the long-run relationship between the variables. This point is developed further in Section 18.8.

Most of this chapter is concerned with using the idea of cointegration to study long-run relationships between variables. Toward the end of the chapter, in Sections 18.7 and 18.8, we discuss the kinds of models that econometricians use to integrate the concept of cointegration with the study of short-run fluctuations.

18.3   The Arithmetic of Integrated Processes

An important first step in understanding cointegration and how to test for it is to understand the effect of combining integrated series.

Consider two I(1) variables Y_{1t} and Y_{2t}. According to our concept of cointegration, they move together if they can be combined in a manner that is stationary. Mathematically, such a combination is the linear combination

$$a_1 Y_{1t} + a_2 Y_{2t}, \tag{18.9}$$

where a_1 and a_2 are constants. Formally, then, two variables are cointegrated if, despite their univariate I(1) behavior, such a linear combination is stationary:

$$a_1 Y_{1t} + a_2 Y_{2t} \sim \text{stationary.}$$

Consider, for example, the ensemble of I(1) realizations shown in Figures 15.9 or 15.11. Because they are wandering apart stochastically, this definition cannot be satisfied, and they are not cointegrated.

This suggests that it is useful to introduce our study of cointegration by considering more generally the results of combining series of various orders of integration. Consider the general situation in which Y_{1t} and Y_{2t} may be stationary or I(1), I(2), and so on, not necessarily of the same order. The linear combination (18.9) includes simply adding the series (the special case when $a_1 = a_2 = 1$) or subtracting them (the special case when $a_1 = 1$ and $a_2 = -1$). What is the order of integration of the resulting series? It is useful to distinguish two cases.

When the orders of integration differ, the higher one dominates. If a stationary series is added to (or subtracted from) one that is I(1), the resulting series is I(1). If an I(1) series is combined with one that is I(2), the result is I(2). In general, if we have two series that are I(d_1) and I(d_2), with $d_1 < d_2$, then a linear combination of the two is integrated of order d_2.

When the orders of integration are the same, a linear combination has order of integration no greater than that of the original series. When two series are I(d), combining them will usually yield a series that is also I(d). The exception—of central interest to us—is when the stochastic trends "cancel," leaving a linear combination of a lower order of integration than the original series. It is when variables move together in this way that they are said to be cointegrated. Because, as we have seen in Chapter 17, orders of integration of 2 or higher are unusual, the special case of cointegration most often of relevance in economics is when a linear combination of I(1) variables is stationary.

Many macroeconomic variables bear certain accounting, definitional, or behavioral relationships to one another. It follows that the arithmetic of integrated processes imposes a certain structure on many macroeconomic relationships. Let us consider some examples.

Accounting and Definitional Relationships

We have encountered the idea of linear combinations of variables earlier in this book in our treatment of multicollinearity in Chapter 8. (Compare the linear combination (18.9) with equation (8.29).) Indeed, in some respects the arithmetic of integrated processes is the stochastic generalization of the concept of linear dependence among variables that is important in that discussion, and so it is useful to illustrate it with many of the same examples we use in Section 8.7.1.

National Income Accounting Identities. Variables from national income accounts are constructed according to certain accounting identities. For example, GDP is defined to be the total of consumption, investment, and government expenditure, plus exports less imports:

$$Y = C + I + G + X - M.$$

Suppose that the expenditure categories on the right-hand side are all I(1) or perhaps some mix of I(1) and stationary series. Then, by the arithmetic of integrated processes, GDP can be at most I(1). It cannot be I(2). Similarly, if GDP is judged to be I(1), the arithmetic of integrated processes implies that not all of the right-hand side variables can be stationary.

Multiplicative Definitions Are Additive in Logarithms. We have, many times, used the property that multiplicative relationships between variables are additive in logarithms. The arithmetic of integrated processes imposes a certain structure on such linear-in-logs definitional relationships. Here are three examples.

Per Unit Quantities. Economists often work with variables defined as ratios of other variables. Consider series on output Q_t, labor input L_t, and labor productivity q_t, in which the latter is defined as

$$q_t = \frac{Q_t}{L_t}.$$

In their logarithms, these variables are related by

$$\log q_t = \log Q_t - \log L_t. \tag{18.10}$$

Now suppose that output Q_t and labor L_t grow such that they are I(1) in their log-levels, as is the case if their percentage changes are stationary. As we have seen in previous chapters beginning with our discussion of the constant growth model in Chapter 6, growth of this kind is typical of many economic variables. By the arithmetic of integrated processes, it follows that the logarithm of labor productivity $\log q_t$, being an aggregation of I(1) series, must be either I(1) or stationary. It cannot be I(2).

The case in which the difference between two I(1) variables is stationarity is, as we have indicated, of special interest; it will be the subject of our initial treatment of cointegration in the next section.

Nominal and Real Quantities.   Another application of these principles is to the relationship between nominal and real quantities. Consider a series on some variable Y_t measured in nominal (dollar) terms and some price index P_t having base 100. Then, a real series y_t is obtained by using the price index to deflate the nominal series:

$$y_t = \frac{Y_t}{P_t/100}.$$

In their logarithms these variables are related by

$$\log y_t = \log Y_t - \log P_t + \log 100. \tag{18.11}$$

Now suppose that Y_t and P_t exhibit roughly constant growth so that they are I(1) in their logarithms. By the arithmetic of integrated processes, $\log y_t$ must be either I(1) or stationary. It cannot be I(2).

This example illustrates that numerical constants such as $\log 100$ do not affect the arithmetic of integrated processes.

Money, National Income, and the Velocity of Circulation of Money.   The quantity theory of money is often summarized by the equation of exchange

$$M_t V_t = P_t Q_t.$$

Here M is the quantity of money in circulation, PQ is nominal gross national income (the product of the price level P and real gross national income Q), and V is the velocity of circulation of money. Because money M and gross national income PQ are both observable variables, a series on V may be calculated as

$$V_t = \frac{P_t Q_t}{M_t}.$$

Taking logarithms of this relationship yields

$$\log V_t = \log(P_t Q_t) - \log M_t. \tag{18.12}$$

Now suppose that $P_t Q_t$ and M_t exhibit roughly constant growth such that they are I(1) in their logarithms. By the arithmetic of integrated processes, $\log V_t$ must be either I(1) or stationary. It cannot be I(2).

Recall that Gould and Nelson (1974) found that the Friedman-Schwartz series for $\log V_t$ was a random walk, and therefore I(1). If $\log(P_t Q_t)$ and $\log M_t$ are each I(1)—a plausible assumption—then it follows that these variables cannot be cointegrated.

Identities between Growth Rates

When variables are related multiplicatively, we have seen in Appendix 6B that their growth rates are related additively. Hence, the arithmetic of integrated processes imposes a structure on such growth rates. The three examples we have just considered may be extended to make this point.

Per Unit Quantities.   Let us return to the example of labor productivity $q = Q/L$. Taking logarithms and time-derivatives (see Example 12 in Appendix 6B, in particular equation (6.50a)) the instantaneous growth rates of these variables are related by

$$\frac{\dot{q}}{q} = \frac{\dot{Q}}{Q} - \frac{\dot{L}}{L}.$$

We have seen as well in Appendix 6B that, when it comes to studying observed time series Q_t, L_t, and q_t on these variables, the same identity relates their continuous growth rates computed as log-differences:

$$\Delta \log q_t = \Delta \log Q_t - \Delta \log L_t.$$

This parallels the linear dependence in their log-levels given by equation (18.10).

By the arithmetic of integrated processes, the order of integration of the left-hand-side growth rate cannot exceed the orders of integration of the right-hand-side ones. For example, suppose that output Q_t and labor L_t grow such that they are I(1) in their log-levels. Then, the log-differences $\Delta \log Q_t$ and $\Delta \log L_t$ must be stationary. It follows that the growth rate of labor productivity $\Delta \log q_t$, being an aggregation of stationary series, must in turn be stationary. It cannot be I(1).

Nominal and Real Quantities.   In the same way, an identity relates the growth rates of nominal and real variables and the price level,

$$\Delta \log y_t = \Delta \log Y_t - \Delta \log P_t.$$

This parallels the linear dependence in their log-levels given by equation (18.11). The order of integration of the left-hand-side growth rate cannot exceed the orders of integration of the right-hand-side ones.

Money, National Income, and the Velocity of Circulation of Money.   Similarly, an identity relates the growth rates of velocity, nominal income, and the money stock,

$$\Delta \log V_t = \Delta \log(PQ_t) - \Delta \log M_t.$$

This parallels the linear dependence in their log-levels given by equation (18.12). The order of integration of the left-hand-side growth rate cannot exceed the orders of integration of the right-hand-side ones.

For example, recall that Gould and Nelson (1974) found that $\Delta \log V_t$ was white noise and therefore stationary. It follows that $\Delta \log(P Q_t)$ and $\Delta \log M_t$ must themselves be stationary or, if nonstationary, then cointegrated.

The Fisher Identity

Another relationship much like these is the Fisher identity between real and nominal interest rates and inflation, which is derived in Example 19 of Chapter 6. This constructs an ex post real rate of return as

real rate of return r_t = nominal rate of return i_t − inflation rate.

Recall from the discussion in Section 15.6 that real interest rates do not appear to be I(1) because we do not observe them wandering arbitrarily far from their initial values over long historical time periods. Suppose as well that over some sample period the inflation rate is judged to be I(1), as would be the case during a hyperinflation when the inflation rate is accelerating. Then it follows from the arithmetic of integrated processes that the nominal interest rate i_t must also be I(1); it would be logically inconsistent to model it as stationary. Another way of expressing this is to say that the treatment of real interest rates as stationary implies the belief that, in periods of hyperinflation, nominal rates are cointegrated with inflation.

Balanced and Unbalanced Regressions

Because the arithmetic of integrated processes often imposes a structure on functional relationships between variables, it can have implications for the specification of regression equations, in particular the mixing of integrated and stationary variables.

For example, it would be difficult to know what to make of a simple regression in which one variable is stationary and the other is I(1); a regression in which, say, the stationary growth rates in one variable are explained by the nonstationary levels of another or vice versa. Regressions like this are said to be **unbalanced;** more precisely,

> An unbalanced equation is one in which the regressand is not of the same order of integration as the regressors or any linear combination of the regressors. A requirement in order to obtain a meaningful estimation with integrated variables is balance in the orders of integration of the variables on the left-hand side and right-hand side of the regression equation. (Maddala and Kim, 1998, p. 251)

These remarks apply to regressions that are meant to describe economic relationships and so have an economic interpretation. There may be exceptions when regressions are instead computational devices for obtaining test statistics. As a simple example, consider the Version 1 Dickey-Fuller regression (17.29),

$$\Delta Y_t = \beta_0 + \rho Y_{t-1} + v_t.$$

If Y_t is I(1), then the dependent variable ΔY_t is stationary while the explanatory variable Y_{t-1} is I(1). This is unbalanced. Even so,

> The mere fact that a regression is unbalanced may not be a matter for concern; for example, ADF statistics are computed from models that, in this terminology, are unbalanced. They are nevertheless valid tools for inference as long as the correct critical values are used. (Banerjee, Dolado, Galbraith, and Hendry, 1993, p. 166)

Notice, however, that under the null hypothesis of a unit root the restriction $\rho = 0$ reduces the Dickey-Fuller regression to a balanced one. Thus, the Dickey-Fuller test can be thought of as a test for a balanced regression.

Practitioner's Tip: Beware of unbalanced regressions

In estimating time series regressions that are intended to have an economic interpretation, be suspicious of specifications that involve an unbalanced mixture of orders of integration.

With this appreciation of the importance of the integration properties of variables for studying relationships between economic time series, let us now focus on the concept of cointegration.

18.4   Cointegration

We have defined cointegration as a situation in which two I(d) variables are combined and their linear combination is integrated of order less than d. For our purposes, this formal definition is more general than we need. It includes higher orders of integration—two I(2) series that, when combined, are I(1), are cointegrated. However, as we have noted, few nonstationary economic time series are integrated of order 2 or higher; most integrated series are I(1). Hence, we phrase our discussion in terms of I(1) series that, when combined, are stationary.

That the idea of cointegration is the natural way of making precise the notion that time series variables move together in equilibrium is best illustrated with an example.

18.4.1   Application: The Great Ratios of Macroeconomics and the Cointegrating Restrictions of Balanced Growth

Klein and Kosobud (1961) observed that although many macroeconomic variables follow trends, they nevertheless move together in such a way that their ratios do not trend. For example, if C denotes aggregate consumption expenditure and

FIGURE 18.1

U.S. private out-
put, consumption,
and investment,
1949:1–1988:4.

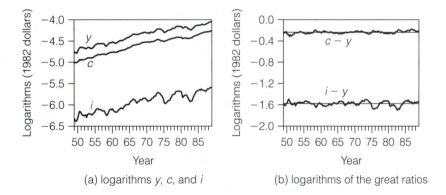

(a) logarithms *y*, *c*, and *i*   (b) logarithms of the great ratios

Y denotes output, then each of these variables grows over time and is therefore
nonstationary. However, consumption as a proportion of output, the ratio C/Y,
although it certainly fluctuates over time, does not trend. After all, suppose that
the proportion of output devoted to consumption were to systematically increase
over time; then eventually all production would be consumed, leaving nothing
for the maintenance of the capital stock. Similarly, suppose that there were a
continual trend decline in this ratio; then eventually nothing would be consumed.
Both extremes are, of course, implausible.

This property is illustrated in Section 5.2.3 with the work of King, Plosser,
Stock, and Watson (1991), who studied quarterly per capita data on U.S. private
GNP (Y), consumption expenditure (C), and gross private investment (I), for the
period 1949:1–1988:4. They began by plotting these series in log form, reproduced
here as Figure 18.1(a). The figure uses lowercase symbols to denote logarithms:

$$y = \log Y, \quad c = \log C, \quad i = \log I.$$

As we expect, all three series trend upward over time in a way that is roughly
linear in the logarithms of the variables, suggesting an underlying process of
approximately constant growth. Superimposed on these long-run trends is a considerable degree of short-run fluctuation, although the variables differ in this respect.
Consumption fluctuates less than output because people act—as individuals and
therefore also in the aggregate—to smooth consumption relative to income. This
difference is picked up by the other key category of aggregate expenditure, investment, which is much more volatile than the other two variables.

Having made the observation that these variables are nonstationary in their
levels, let us turn to an examination of C and I as proportions of Y:

$$\frac{C}{Y}, \quad \frac{I}{Y}.$$

Similar arguments apply to I/Y as we have already made with respect to C/Y.
Although investment as a proportion of output fluctuates in the short run, it should
do so in a way that does not exhibit any trend in the long run. After all, if I were to

account for a larger and larger proportion of Y over time, eventually all production would be reinvested as an addition to the capital stock and none would be left for consumption, use by the government, or export. Similarly, if I were to account for a smaller and smaller proportion of Y over time, eventually there would be no investment and the capital stock could not be maintained, let alone expanded. Again, both extremes are implausible.

Because the levels of the variables were plotted in log form, consider the logarithms of the ratios:

$$\log\left(\frac{C}{Y}\right) = \log C - \log Y = c - y, \qquad \log\left(\frac{I}{Y}\right) = \log I - \log Y = i - y.$$

That is, these log-ratios are just the differences between the log-levels depicted in Figure 18.1(a); they are plotted in Figure 18.1(b).[4] Notice that it is indeed the case that the ratios do not trend; instead they fluctuate around the horizontal lines given by their sample means, suggesting that they may be adequately described by a stationary process such as model (18.1).

As we have discussed in Section 5.2.3 and Appendix 6B, proportions such as C/Y and I/Y are examples of what Klein and Kosobud called **great ratios;** although the numerators and denominators may grow, they should do so in a way that is *balanced*. That is, the growth rates should on average be the same over long periods, so that the ratios do not trend. The implication is that the ratios should be stationary even though the numerators and denominators are not.

Statistical Analysis

With this descriptive examination of the KPSW data as background, let us ask what can be said of a more formal statistical nature about these variables. In parallel with the two graphs in Figure 18.1, two kinds of questions can be asked about the variables Y, C, and I: questions about their univariate behavior and questions about their interaction over time.

Univariate Behavior The key question about the univariate behavior of these variables concerns their trends. In particular, are the trends exhibited in Figure 18.1(a) best described as deterministic or stochastic? We already know how to answer this question—by using the unit root tests in Chapter 17.

EXAMPLE 1

kpsw.dat

Use ADF tests to test for the presence of a unit root in each of y, c, and i. KPSW concluded that these series can reasonably be characterized as possessing stochastic trends. Do you agree?

SOLUTION

Our casual inspection of these series in Figure 18.1 indicates that they trend; this is consistent with our general background knowledge that macroeconomic variables

---

[4] Figure 18.1 is a logarithmic version of Figure 5.3. It is similar to King, Plosser, Stock, and Watson (1991, Fig. 1).

such as these grow at positive average growth rates. This suggests that Version 2 of the ADF test, in which a trend is included, is the appropriate form of the ADF regression. Recall that in this version of the test the null hypothesis is that the variable is I(1) with drift, and the alternative is that it is stationary around a linear trend. These are the hypotheses of natural interest.

Following KPSW (1987), and in view of the data being quarterly consider implementing the ADF regression with an augmenting lag length of $k = 4$. The ADF statistics are as follows.

Variable	ADF statistic
y	-2.63
c	-2.19
i	-3.56

Comparing these statistics with the critical values of Table 17.1 (using the intercept and trend case and a sample size of $n = 160$), in the case of y and c the null hypothesis of a stochastic trend is not rejected at conventional significance levels. In the case of investment i, it is rejected at 5% but not at 1%. Hence, the KPSW conclusion that these variables can reasonably be thought of as following stochastic trends is supported.

The conclusion that these variables may be modeled as I(1) has implications for the study of their relationship over time, to which we now turn.

The Interaction of Variables over Time   The second kind of question that can be posed about these variables concerns their interaction over time. Are they related in some way?

One possibility is that they are related in their short-run behavior, that the quarterly fluctuations of the three variables exhibited in Figure 18.1 are interrelated. No doubt it is the case that, for example, investment decisions by the business sector affect production and that seasonal and business cycle variation in production, and hence national income, affects consumption decisions by households. However, as we have argued, short-run interactions are likely to be complex, especially because they may involve simultaneous relationships in which causality flows in both directions: National income affects consumption spending, but consumer demand affects production; business investment determines the demand for capital goods and therefore influences production, but production decisions also affect investment needs. It is precisely because of the complexity of these short-run interactions that we have argued for an initial strategy of abstracting from them in favor of a focus on the long run.

A long-run relationship is the manifestation of economic equilibrium, an equilibrium from which the variables may depart in the short run. Is there any statistical evidence that there are economic forces at work causing these variables to revert toward some sort of equilibrium?

We have seen that there is such a long-run relationship: C/Y and I/Y are great ratios. Consequently, their differences-in-logarithms plotted in Figure 18.1(b),

$$\log C - \log Y = c - y, \qquad \log I - \log Y = i - y,$$

should be stationary. Notice that we have described a situation in which, although the variables y, c, and i are each I(1), certain linear combinations of them should be stationary. That is, we have described a situation in which the existence of a long-run equilibrium relationship between variables implies that they should be cointegrated.

How can we test statistically whether these pairs of variables are cointegrated? From the arithmetic of integrated processes, if two variables are I(1) their difference must be either I(1) or stationary. If the difference is I(1), then it contains a stochastic trend and the variables tend to drift apart over time; there is no force keeping them together. If there is a force keeping them together, then the difference should be stationary. Hence, the hypothesis of balanced growth implies that the difference should not contain a stochastic trend.

Interpreted in these terms, it is easy to test the null hypothesis that growth is not balanced against the alternative that it is because we already know how to test for the presence of a stochastic trend.

EXAMPLE 2

 kpsw.dat

Use an ADF test to test for the presence of stochastic trends in the differences $c - y$ and $i - y$. Do the findings support the hypothesis of balanced growth?

SOLUTION

KPSW ran Version 2 ADF regressions on these differences using five augmenting lags. They obtained the following ADF statistics.

Variable	ADF statistic
$c - y$	-4.21
$i - y$	-3.99

Comparing these with the critical values of Table 17.1 (using the intercept and trend case, and for a sample size $n = 160$), these statistics reject the null hypothesis that stochastic trends are present in these differences. That is, the data reject the null hypothesis of an absence of balanced growth in favor of the alternative that growth is balanced. This suggests that economic forces are at work keeping the variable pairs (c, y) and (i, y) together in the long run.

Further Comments

It can be helpful to contrast this with the case in which two I(1) variables are not cointegrated. Suppose that the difference

$$\log C - \log Y$$

is I(1) instead of stationary. (Remember from the arithmetic of integrated processes that a combination of I(d) variables is integrated of order no greater than d, so this difference cannot be I(2).) The implication is that, in addition to the variables individually meandering through time according to their stochastic trends, their difference also meanders with a stochastic trend. That is, there is nothing to prevent the variables from wandering arbitrarily far from one another, just as two random walks will, in general, wander away from one another over time. There is no equilibrium relationship between the variables causing them to move together.

By contrast, when there is such an equilibrium relationship there is a limit to the extent to which the variables can wander away from one another. They may well depart from their equilibrium relationship in the short run because it takes time for equilibrium forces to assert themselves. But eventually these equilibrium tendencies dominate, causing the variables to revert toward their long-run relationship. The linear combination of the variables associated with this equilibrium—in our current example, the difference $\log C - \log Y$—must be stationary.

EXERCISES

The KPSW series for real per capita output, consumption, and investment are available in the file **kpsw.dat** and have been used previously in Sections 5.2.3 (Exercise 5.4) and 15.7.2. The file has the following format.

quarter	Quarterly period, 1947:1–1988:4
output	Real private GNP per capita
consump	Real consumption expenditure per capita
invest	Real private investment per capita

KPSW used the sample 1949:1–1988:4 in their analysis, employing the available presample observations as initial observations in regressions containing lags. Thus, ADF regressions involving augmenting lags are based on a sample of size $n = 160$.

18.1 💿 **kpsw.dat** Generate the logarithms of these variables. Plot these logarithms and the differences $c - y$ and $i - y$, producing your own version of Figure 18.1, in order to satisfy yourself that our descriptive inspection of that figure is correct in its portrayal of the essential features of these data.

18.2 💿 **kpsw.dat** *The univariate behavior of these series.*

(a) Run Version 2 ADF regressions on the series y, c, and i, using an augmenting lag length of 4. Are you able to replicate the ADF statistics given in Example 1?

(b) Explore the effect of alternative lag lengths on these statistics. Are the conclusions about the univariate behavior of these variables sensitive to the choice of augmenting lag length?

(c) Section 15.7.2 discussed Robert Hall's theory that the rational expectations version of the life cycle–permanent income model predicts that consumption should follow a random walk. Are your unit root tests on c consistent with Hall's view?

18.3 💿 **kpsw.dat** *The interaction of these series.* Consider the differences $c - y$ and $i - y$.

(a) Run Version 2 ADF regressions as described in Example 2. Are you able to replicate the ADF statistics reported there? (You may find it interesting to locate KPSW's discussion of their analysis, 1991, p. 825, and compare it with your findings.)

(b) Our inspection of Figure 18.1(b) indicates that the differences $c - y$ and $i - y$ do not exhibit trends. Consequently, the presence of a stochastic trend in these differences could reasonably be tested using Version 1 of the ADF regression, which tests the null hypothesis of I(1) without drift against the alternative of stationarity. Are our conclusions about the hypothesis of balanced growth sensitive to this alternative version of the test?

18.4 💿 **kpsw.dat** If c and i both have long-run relationships with y, they must have a long-run relationship with one another. Are c and i cointegrated? Report the results of both Version 1 and 2 tests, justifying your choice of lag length in each case.

18.5 Whether for a single firm or for the economy as a whole, production, sales, and inventory investment are related by an accounting identity. Letting Q_t and S_t denote production and sales over the period and I_t the end-of-period stock of inventories,

the identity may be expressed as

$$Q_t = S_t + \Delta I_t.$$

The interpretation of this definition is that, if production exceeds sales, inventory stocks will accumulate and the flow of inventory investment will be positive over the period: $\Delta I_t > 0$. If sales exceed production, then inventories decumulate and inventory investment is negative: $\Delta I_t < 0$.

Suppose that production and sales are both I(1) and are cointegrated. What does this imply about the stochastic properties of:

(a) inventory investment ΔI_t?

(b) inventory stocks I_t?

18.4.2 The Common Trends Interpretation of Cointegration

One useful way of understanding cointegration is to recognize that cointegrated variables share common stochastic trends. This may be seen as follows. Consider two I(1) variables Y_{1t} and Y_{2t}. By the Beveridge-Nelson decomposition, each is the sum of permanent and transitory components:

$$Y_{1t} = Y_{1t}^P + Y_{1t}^T$$
$$Y_{2t} = Y_{2t}^P + Y_{2t}^T.$$

Recall that the permanent components evolve as random walks, whereas the transitory components are stationary.

If Y_{1t} and Y_{2t} are cointegrated, this means that a linear combination of them is stationary:

$$a_1 Y_{1t} + a_2 Y_{2t} \sim \text{stationary}.$$

Substituting in the decompositions,

$$a_1(Y_{1t}^P + Y_{1t}^T) + a_2(Y_{2t}^P + Y_{2t}^T) = (a_1 Y_{1t}^P + a_2 Y_{2t}^P) + (a_1 Y_{1t}^T + a_2 Y_{2t}^T) \sim \text{stationary}.$$

Because the transitory components are stationary, their linear combination $a_1 Y_{1t}^T + a_2 Y_{2t}^T$ must be stationary. For the expression as a whole to be stationary, it must therefore be the case that the linear combination of the permanent components is stationary:

$$a_1 Y_{1t}^P + a_2 Y_{2t}^P \sim \text{stationary}.$$

In other words, the random walk permanent components must be cointegrated. Equivalently, they differ from one another only by a multiplicative constant and stationary noise,

$$Y_{1t}^{P} = \lambda Y_{2t}^{P} + \text{stationary noise,}$$

where $\lambda \equiv -a_2/a_1$. In essence, then, cointegrated variables share a common random walk permanent component. Because the key feature governing the behavior of this random walk component is its stochastic trend, this is expressed by saying that cointegrated variables have a **common stochastic trend.**

Implications of the Common Trends Interpretation

The common trends interpretation of cointegration has an important implication: If variables do not have common stochastic trends they cannot be cointegrated. There are a number of reasons why this might be. It could be because they do not have stochastic trends; that is, they are not integrated variables, as would be the case if they are stationary or trend stationary. Or it could be because the variables do have stochastic trends, but not common ones; this must be the case if the orders of integration differ. It is useful to delineate these possibilities.

Stationary Variables Cannot Be Cointegrated. If variables follow stationary ARMA models such as (18.1), then a linear combination of them must be stationary and so the formal definition of cointegration would appear to be satisfied. In this sense, the variables are trivially cointegrated. Nevertheless, they do not share a common stochastic trend because they do not have stochastic trends. Thus they cannot move together in the long run according to the real meaning of cointegration. It may be that their short-run fluctuations around their constant means are linked, but this is another matter.

Trend Stationary Variables Cannot Be Cointegrated. In the same way, if variables are stationary around deterministic trends, as in the trend stationary model (18.2), then they cannot share a common stochastic trend. Thus, they cannot have a long-run equilibrium relationship as defined by the concept of cointegration. Their deterministic trends may give them the appearance of being related, but there is no statistical methodology for distinguishing true long-run relationships from spurious ones.

These conclusions reiterate the remarks of the opening section of this chapter regarding stationary and trend stationary variables. As those remarks suggest, an absence of cointegration does not imply that such variables cannot be related in the short run. Cointegration deals only with long-run relationships between variables.

Variables Having Different Orders of Integration Cannot Be Cointegrated. If variables have different orders of integration, so too must their permanent components. Consequently, they cannot have common stochastic trends. The different orders of integration must cause the variables to depart from one another in the long run. There can be no equilibrium force bringing them together.

18.4.3 Application: Purchasing Power Parity

The cointegrating restrictions of balanced growth relate variable pairs. However, sometimes equilibrium relationships involve more than just two variables. This is usefully illustrated by purchasing power parity (PPP), a hypothesized relationship between currency exchange rates and country price levels.

Real and Nominal Exchange Rates

In international economics, there is an important distinction between **nominal** and **real exchange rates.** A nominal exchange rate e_n is the rate at which *currencies* are traded. This is the exchange rate that is quoted in the newspaper and that applies when you buy foreign currency to travel abroad. For example, if $1.00 buys £ 0.50 then the nominal exchange rate is e_n = £0.50 per dollar. This is of course equivalent to taking the reciprocal and quoting the rate as $2.00 per pound sterling. As defined, so that we are looking at the exchange rate from the point of view of dollars being the domestic currency, if e_n increases we say that the domestic currency has **appreciated** in value—each dollar buys more pounds. If the nominal exchange rate decreases, the domestic currency is said to have **depreciated.**

By contrast, the real exchange rate e_r is the rate at which *goods* are exchanged. It is also known as the **terms of trade.** This is not quoted in the newspaper, but is the exchange rate that is usually of most interest to economists because it governs the demands for imports and exports. The real exchange rate is defined as

$$e_r = e_n \times \frac{P_d}{P_f}. \tag{18.13}$$

Here P_d denotes the domestic price level (the domestic price of a bundle of goods in dollars) and P_f is the foreign price level (the price of the same bundle of goods in Britain, in pounds sterling). The real exchange rate tells us the rate at which domestic goods can be traded for foreign goods. For example, suppose that the domestic price of a Big Mac is $2.00 but in Britain it is £1.50. If the currencies trade at a rate of e_n = 0.5, the implication is that Big Macs trade at a rate of

$$e_r = 0.5 \times \frac{2.00}{1.5} = \frac{2}{3}.$$

This says that, at prevailing prices and the nominal exchange rate, you would have to give up three Big Macs domestically in order to buy two in Britain. Real exchange rates are essentially this idea, but computed on the basis of price levels generally rather than a particular good such as Big Macs.

But suppose a situation such as we have just described prevails. There is an incentive for sharp goods traders to engage in arbitrage, selling Big Macs at the

relatively high price that exists in Britain, exchanging pounds for dollars, and buying Big Macs at the relatively low domestic price. In doing this, they would be
trading Big Macs at the real exchange rate of 2 for 3. They could then transport
these domestically acquired Big Macs to Britain and repeat the process, ultimately
amassing huge Big Mac fortunes. As many people attempt to enrich themselves
in this way, the demand to exchange pounds for dollars will cause the nominal exchange rate e_n to appreciate; the dollar will come to trade for more than
just £0.5. According to the definition, this will in turn cause the real exchange
rate to appreciate, so that three domestic Big Macs will trade for more than just
two British Big Macs. These forces will continue to operate until profitable arbitrage opportunities are eliminated and Big Macs trade one for one; that is, the
real exchange rate is $e_r = 1$. The idea that, if goods fail to trade one for one,
forces should be set in motion to cause them to do so, is called the **law of
one price.**

Substituting $e_r = 1$ into the definition and solving for the nominal exchange rate,

$$e_n = \frac{P_f}{P_d} = \frac{1.5}{2} = \frac{3}{4}.$$

That is, the nominal exchange rate must appreciate so that a dollar buys £0.75
instead of just £0.5. In general, if goods are to trade one for one, it must be that
the nominal exchange rate is determined by relative price levels.

Qualifications

There are two important qualifications to the reasoning we have just presented. First,
many goods are not homogeneous storable goods like oil or grain that are readily
arbitraged. Instead, many goods are like Big Macs; they have an important service
component that is location-specific and so is not transportable. The prevalence of
such **nontradable goods** limits the scope for arbitrage, and so it is possible for
real exchange rates to deviate substantially from 1 for extended periods of time.

Second, real exchange rates are based on country price levels, not the single
commodity that we have used for illustrative purposes. Country price levels are
measured by price indices, such as consumer or wholesale price indices, or GDP
deflators. However, the baskets of goods and services on which these price indices
are based have little uniformity across countries—the "market basket" used by one
country's statistical agency may be quite different from that used by another. The
implication is that, although real exchange rates should gravitate to some value, just
what that value will be depends arbitrarily on the definition of the price indices; it
will not necessarily be $e_r = 1$.

These properties are illustrated in Figure 18.2, which plots data collected by
Lothian and Taylor (1996) on the dollar-sterling and franc-sterling real exchange
rates over the periods 1791–1990 and 1805–1990, respectively. Both rates appear
to exhibit mean reversion; they do not wander arbitrarily far from their starting
values, confirming that eventually the forces of arbitrage assert themselves. Indeed,
the terms of trade were little different in 1990 from what they were 2 centuries
earlier. However, it is also evident that the value to which these series revert is not

FIGURE 18.2

Dollar-sterling and
franc-sterling real
exchange rates.

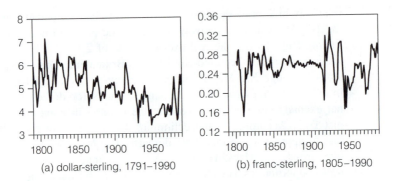

(a) dollar-sterling, 1791–1990   (b) franc-sterling, 1805–1990

1; instead, they fluctuate around arbitrary values determined by the different baskets on which the price indices are based. Finally, although the series appear to exhibit mean reversion, deviations from their "central lines"—the horizontal line your eye imposes on the graph—are substantial and can persist for extended periods.

Purchasing Power Parity

In view of these remarks, what should be true of the relationship among the observed variables e_n, P_d, and P_f? Taking the logarithm of the definition (18.13),

$$\log e_r = \log e_n + \log P_d - \log P_f. \tag{18.14}$$

According to the theory we have just described, real exchange rates are mean-reverting and so the left-hand side should be stationary. By contrast, price levels and the nominal exchange rate may be, and typically are, I(1); there is nothing preventing them from wandering away from any initial value. However, this wandering is not unrestricted; it must satisfy the relationship (18.14)—the linear combination on the right-hand side must be stationary. In other words, there is a cointegrating relationship among e_n, P_d, and P_f, in their logarithms.

Another way of looking at this is that, given the stationarity of the real exchange rate, any nonstationarity in the nominal exchange rate must be generated by nonstationarity in the price levels. In this sense, in the long run the nominal exchange rate is determined by relative price levels, or purchasing power, across countries so as to equalize the terms of trade, despite the fact that in the short run the relationship is very loose. It is this long-run determination of nominal exchange rates by relative price levels that is called **purchasing power parity.**

Testing Purchasing Power Parity

The obvious test of purchasing power parity is to test for a unit root in the real exchange rate. If purchasing power parity does not hold, then the I(1) behavior of the right-hand-side variables of equation (18.14) should translate into I(1) behavior of the left-hand side, so that there is no cointegrating relationship. In this case, the null hypothesis of a unit root in the real exchange rate should not be rejected. By

TABLE 18.1   Lothian and Taylor's Tests of Purchasing Power Parity

	ADF statistics	
	Dollar-Sterling	**Franc-Sterling**
Intercept, no trend	−3.47	−4.85
Intercept and trend	−4.36	−4.83

Source: Adapted from Lothian and Taylor (1996, Table 1).

contrast, if the unit root hypothesis is rejected, this suggests that the real exchange rate is stationary and there is a cointegrating relationship, supporting PPP.

Table 18.1 reproduces the ADF statistics reported by Lothian and Taylor (1996) for unit root tests on their real exchange rate series. In light of the theoretical background we have sketched, Version 1 tests might seem to be the natural choice: If real exchange rates are stationary, the theory suggests they are stationary without trend. Even so, if PPP fails and real exchange rates are integrated variables, nothing rules out the possibility of drift, suggesting the use of Version 2 tests. Consequently Lothian and Taylor report both tests for both real exchange rate series.

Comparing their ADF statistics with the critical values in Table 17.1, in all cases the unit root hypothesis is rejected. Hence, the purchasing power parity hypothesis of a cointegrating relationship between price levels and nominal exchange rates is supported.

EXERCISES

The Lothian-Taylor data are available in the file **ppp.dat**. The variables are as follows.

year	Year	1791–1990
usdstg	Dollar-sterling nominal exchange rate	1791–1990
ffstg	Franc-sterling nominal exchange rate	1803–1990
frwpi	Wholesale price index for France	1803–1990
ukwpi	Wholesale price index for the United Kingdom	1791–1990
uswpi	Wholesale price index for the United States	1791–1990

18.6 ⊙ **ppp.dat** Inspect this data file, noting that ffstg and frwpi are assigned the value 0 prior to 1803.

(a) Examining the more recent values for the exchange rates and drawing on your own general knowledge of currency values (or perhaps by checking the newspaper), is the dollar-sterling rate expressed as pounds per dollar or dollars per pound? Is the franc-sterling rate expressed as francs per pound or pounds per franc?

(b) Using the nominal exchange rates as defined, generate corresponding real rates according to the definition (18.13). Graph these real rates. Are you able to reproduce Figure 18.2?

(c) Taking the logarithms of your real exchange rates, test the purchasing power parity hypothesis by performing ADF tests. Experiment with augmenting lag lengths in the range of $k = 0$ to $k = 5$, and try both Version 1 and 2 tests. How close are you able to come to replicating the results reported by

Lothian and Taylor, as reproduced in Table 18.1? Are your test conclusions sensitive to the choice of lag length or the inclusion of a time trend?

18.7 🔵 **ppp.dat** Cointegration testing presumes that series are nonstationary in a manner that is integrated. Returning to the individual series on the nominal exchange rates and price levels, choose the series related to either the dollar-sterling or franc-sterling real rates and do the following.

(a) Plot the nominal exchange rates and whole-sale price indices. Do you judge them to be non-stationary?

(b) Use ADF tests to test for a unit root in the logarithms of these series. Justify your choice of lag length and your decision whether to include a time

trend. Do your test results support the treatment of these series as I(1)?

18.8 Purchasing power parity is the hypothesis that real exchange rates are stationary. Our discussion has been phrased in terms of all three variables on the right-hand side of

$$\log e_r = \log e_n + \log P_d - \log P_f$$

being I(1).

(a) Suppose that only two of the three right-hand-side variables are I(1), the third being stationary. Can PPP still hold?

(b) Suppose that only one of the three right-hand-side variables is I(1), the other two being stationary. Can PPP still hold?

18.4.4 Do Cointegration Tests Detect Spurious Correlation?

In the applications we have considered, cointegration tests reject the null hypothesis of an absence of an equilibrium relationship, thus supporting purchasing power parity and the cointegrating restrictions of balanced growth. In testing economic theories of long-run equilibrium, it is important that the problem of spurious correlation be overcome. That is, we wish to avoid being misled into interpreting variables as being related simply because they trend. Do cointegration tests detect cases of spurious correlation?

One example of spurious correlation given in our earliest treatment of that topic in Chapter 3 is country populations. In Section 3.1.3 we note the very high correlations that relate the populations of Canada, the United Kingdom, and United States, correlations that are high because the populations of all three countries trend upward. Yet we reason that it is implausible that the populations of these countries somehow cause one another. Although the three populations trend upward, there is no underlying force requiring them to move together; in the long run, there is nothing preventing them from moving in an entirely unrelated manner.

The implication of this reasoning is that populations are not great ratio–type quantities. Letting the populations of two countries be denoted Y_{1t} and Y_{2t}, there is no reason to expect that the ratio Y_{1t}/Y_{2t} is necessarily stable over time. That is, there is no reason to expect

$$\log Y_{1t} - \log Y_{2t} \sim \text{stationary}.$$

If this reasoning is sound, a unit root test should fail to reject the presence of a unit root in these log-deviations.

The ADF statistics for the log-deviations of the data of Table 3.3, based on a Dickey-Fuller regression with intercept and trend and $k = 3$ augmenting lags, are as follows.

Countries	ADF statistic
Canada–United Kingdom	−3.12
Canada–United States	−2.40
United Kingdom–United States	−2.82

Comparing these against the critical values in Table 17.1, these values do not reject the unit root null. This suggests that, despite their high correlations, the populations of these countries are not governed by any equilibrium relationship causing them to move together, consistent with our a priori reasoning.

The absence of a long-run equilibrium relationship does not necessarily imply the absence of a short-run relationship. It is possible, for example, that World War II affected the in- and out-migration of these countries, and their birth and death rates, in related ways at that time and therefore their populations. But evidently such short-run relationships are of a transitory rather than permanent nature.

EXERCISES

The three-country population data in Table 3.3 is available in the file **pop.dat**. Use this to do the following.

18.9 **pop.dat** The ADF statistics just reported are based on an augmenting lag length of $k = 3$. How sensitive are they to the choice of alternative lag lengths? What choice of k do you advocate for each of the country pairs?

18.10 **pop.dat** Cointegration testing presumes that series are integrated. Perform ADF tests on the log population series individually, justifying your choice of lag length. Do your test results support the treatment of these series as difference stationary?

18.4.5 The Cointegrating Vector

According to our definition (18.9), two I(1) variables are cointegrated if a linear combination of them is stationary,

$$a_1 Y_{1t} + a_2 Y_{2t} \sim \text{stationary}. \tag{18.15}$$

In mathematics a list of values is called a **vector;** the set of coefficients $[a_1, a_2]$ is called the **cointegrating vector.** For example, consider the cointegrating restriction of balanced growth on consumption and output. Here, one variable is the log of consumption, $Y_{1t} = \log C_t = c_t$, and the other is the log of output, $Y_{2t} = \log Y_t = y_t$. Balanced growth requires that the log-ratio $c_t - y_t$ be stationary, so in this case the cointegrating vector is $[1, -1]$. Similarly, consider purchasing power parity, which predicts that the log of the real exchange rate should be stationary,

$$\log e_n + \log P_d - \log P_f \sim \text{stationary.}$$

The cointegrating vector is $[1, 1, -1]$—extending the definition in the obvious way to more than two variables.

Normalization

Notice that cointegrating vectors are only unique up to a multiplicative constant. That is, the cointegrating vector can be multiplied by any value without changing its meaning. The cointegrating vector for the balanced growth restriction could have been equivalently specified as $[2, -2]$, $[5, -5]$, $[0.1, -0.1]$, $[-1, 1]$, and so on. However, the simplest way to express a cointegrating vector is to define it so that at least one of the coefficients is set equal to 1, as we have in the preceding two applications. This is expressed by saying that the cointegrating vector is **normalized** on one of the variables. Making this normalization explicit, we can reexpress the definition (18.15) as

$$Y_{1t} - \lambda Y_{2t} \sim \text{stationary,}$$

where $\lambda \equiv -a_2/a_1$.

A stationary series can have a nonzero mean: Two variables can move together in a long-run equilibrium relationship even if their values are separated by some fixed constant. This nonzero mean can be recognized explicitly in the cointegrating vector by including an intercept. Generalizing the definition (18.15) in this way, two variables are cointegrated if

$$a_0 + a_1 Y_{1t} + a_2 Y_{2t} \sim \text{stationary.}$$

Normalizing on Y_{1t}, this is

$$Y_{1t} - \lambda_0 - \lambda_1 Y_{2t} \sim \text{stationary,} \tag{18.16}$$

where $\lambda_0 \equiv -a_0/a_1$ and $\lambda_1 \equiv -a_2/a_1$.

Especially in its normalized form, the linear combination has a natural interpretation as the **equilibrium error** of the cointegrating relationship. The expression $\lambda_0 + \lambda_1 Y_{2t}$ is the value of Y_{1t} that would be generated in the long run on the basis of its cointegrating relationship with Y_{2t}. The deviation $Y_{1t} - (\lambda_0 + \lambda_1 Y_{2t})$ measures the short-run departures from this equilibrium.

Cointegrating Vectors Are Unique

Two variables are governed by at most one long-run relationship. There cannot be several cointegrating relationships between them. In other words, given a normalization, the cointegrating vector is unique.

This may be confirmed formally as follows. Consider two variables X_t and Y_t that are I(1) and cointegrated,

$$Y_t + \lambda_1 X_t \sim \text{stationary.}$$

Now suppose it is possible for there to be another cointegrating relationship between them,

$$Y_t + \lambda_2 X_t \sim \text{stationary.}$$

Because both linear combinations are stationary, the difference between them must be stationary. (Remember that by the arithmetic of integrated processes, taking a linear combination cannot increase the order of integration beyond that of the variables individually, so a linear combination of stationary variables cannot be I(1).) Therefore,

$$(Y_t - \lambda_1 X_t) - (Y_t - \lambda_2 X_t) = (\lambda_2 - \lambda_1)X_t \sim \text{stationary.}$$

But here there is a contradiction. By assumption, X_t is I(1), and so a multiple of it cannot be stationary unless that multiple is zero. Thus, the only possibility is that $\lambda_1 = \lambda_2$, and the cointegrating vector is unique.

18.5 The Engle-Granger Test for Cointegration

In contrast to the examples we have considered so far, in many applications the cointegrating vector is not known a priori and must instead be estimated. This may be done by rearranging the normalized cointegrating relationship (18.16) as a regression equation,

$$Y_t = \lambda_0 + \lambda_1 X_t + u_t. \tag{18.17}$$

Here u_t denotes a stationary disturbance, and the variables are denoted X_t and Y_t in order to return to conventional regression notation.

When the cointegrating vector is known a priori, it is usually stated without an intercept because a priori considerations usually do not suggest an intercept value. This is the case in both the examples of the cointegrating restrictions of balanced growth and purchasing power parity. By contrast, when the cointegrating vector must be estimated it is natural to include an intercept in order that u_t may be defined to be a zero-mean stationary disturbance.

18.5.1 Estimating the Cointegrating Regression

The obvious way of estimating this regression is with least squares. However, notice that cointegrating regressions do *not* satisfy the assumptions of the classical linear regression model: The variables Y_t and X_t are I(1) time series, not the outcome of a classical random sampling experiment. Consequently, OLS does not necessarily have all the desirable properties that we established for a classical regression model.

Remarkably, when the regression is truly a cointegrating relationship the asymptotic properties of OLS are in some respects superior to those that apply in the classical case; OLS is said to be **superconsistent,** an important result established by Stock (1987). Intuitively, the I(1) behavior of the variables permits an even better estimation of the regression coefficients than is true when the data are stationary.

Unfortunately this intuition does not extend to small-sample properties: OLS is in general biased, and the bias can be fairly large, especially when the R^2 is low. As well, least squares is not efficient because, in estimating only the cointegrating relationship, it does not use information in the variables' short-run behavior. How these considerations might be addressed is an issue we return to in Section 18.7.

These remarks on the properties of OLS as applied to a cointegrating regression—in particular, Stock's superconsistency result—presume, of course, that the regression is in fact a cointegrating relationship. A regression estimated with non-stationary variables that are *not* cointegrated is just a spurious regression. As such, it may well possess the classic features of spurious regressions that we originally discuss in Chapter 3, such as large t and R^2 statistics. The regression is nevertheless not a meaningful one, in terms of describing any genuine economic relationship.

Consequently, testing for cointegration continues to be of interest when the cointegrating vector has been estimated, just as it is when the cointegrating vector is known a priori. When we estimate what we believe to be a cointegrating relationship, how can we be confident that it is not a spurious regression?

Testing for Cointegration Using a Cointegrating Regression

To test for cointegration when the cointegrating vector must be estimated, we simply use the residuals from the cointegrating regression in place of an observed equilibrium error. Cointegration testing therefore proceeds in two steps.

Step 1. **Estimation of the cointegrating regression.** Let the estimated cointegrating regression be denoted

$$Y_t = \hat{\lambda}_0 + \hat{\lambda}_1 X_t + e_t.$$

The least squares residuals e_t are a measure of the equilibrium error $Y_t - \lambda_0 - \lambda_1 X_t$.

Step 2. **An ADF test based on the residuals.** With the residuals e_t, we can proceed much as we did when the cointegrating vector was known. If the relationship is indeed a cointegrating one, the residuals e_t should be stationary. If the relationship is not cointegrating, the regression is spurious and the disturbance, being a linear combination of I(1) variables, should be I(1), so the residuals e_t should have a unit root.

Hence, we can test the null hypothesis of an absence of cointegration by running an ADF test on the residuals. The Dickey-Fuller regression is of the form

$$e_t = \phi e_{t-1} + \text{disturbance}.$$

Notice that the regression is usually estimated without an intercept because least squares residuals have zero mean by construction. In implementation, the regression is typically modified in the usual ways: e_{t-1} is subtracted from both sides in order to state the unit root null as $\rho = \phi - 1 = 0$, and lags on the dependent variable are introduced to treat autocorrelation,

$$\Delta e_t = \rho e_{t-1} + \text{lagged } \Delta e_t + \text{disturbance}. \tag{18.18}$$

TABLE 18.2   Critical Values for Engle-Granger Cointegration Tests[a]

Number of variables	Intercept, no trend			Intercept and trend		
K	0.01	0.05	0.10	0.01	0.05	0.10
2	−3.90	−3.34	−3.04	−4.32	−3.78	−3.50
3	−4.29	−3.74	−3.45	−4.66	−4.12	−3.84
4	−4.64	−4.10	−3.81	−4.97	−4.43	−4.15
5	−4.96	−4.42	−4.13	−5.25	−4.72	−4.43
6	−5.25	−4.71	−4.42	−5.52	−4.98	−4.70

Source: From *Estimation and Inference in Economics* by Russell Davidson and James G. MacKinnon, copyright © 1993 by Oxford University Press, Inc. Used by permission of Oxford University Press, Inc.

[a] Cointegrating regression includes an intercept and perhaps a trend.

As previously, conventional t tests on the augmenting lags can be used to determine an appropriate lag order.

Just as before, the ADF statistic is the t statistic for the restriction $\rho = 0$; this restriction is the null hypothesis of an absence of cointegration. This hypothesis is rejected in favor of the alternative that $\rho < 0$ for sufficiently small values of the statistic.

There is, however, one important difference in the implementation of the test. The ADF regression is now based on an estimated series—the residuals arising from the estimation of the cointegrating vector in step 1—instead of a known cointegrating vector and an observed equilibrium error. Consequently, the ADF critical values in Table 17.1 are no longer valid. Davidson and MacKinnon (1993, Table 20.2) tabulated revised critical values, which are summarized in Table 18.2. (These critical values are revisions to widely cited ones by Phillips and Ouliaris 1990.) Referring to the table, at present we are dealing with the case in which the cointegrating regression includes an intercept but no trend. The intercept and trend case is discussed in Section 18.5.3.

This two-step procedure is called the Engle-Granger test for cointegration. Let us consider an example.

18.5.2 Application: The Monetary Dynamics of Hyperinflation

Appendix 6A in Chapter 6 develops Phillip Cagan's (1956) model of real money demand under hyperinflation. The purpose of the model is to describe people's tendency to economize on their real money holdings in response to the rapid depreciation

TABLE 18.3   Taylor's Engle-Granger Cointegration Tests

| | OLS cointegrating regression | | |
Country	Semielasticity	R^2	ADF statistic
Germany	−2.211	0.60	−2.612
Poland	−1.219	0.75	−2.453

Source: Taylor (1991, Table 3).

in the value of money that occurs during hyperinflations. Cagan's model specifies the logarithm of real money holdings to be a function of expected inflation,

$$m_t - p_t = \alpha + \beta(p_{t+1}^e - p_t) + \varepsilon_t. \tag{18.19}$$

We have here adopted the notational convention of using lowercase symbols to denote variables in logarithms: $m_t \equiv \log M_t$ and $p_t \equiv \log P_t$.

Taylor (1991) estimated Cagan's model by replacing expected inflation in the coming period, $p_{t+1}^e - p_t$, with the most recently observed rate of inflation, $\Delta p_t = p_t - p_{t-1}$:

$$m_t - p_t = \alpha + \beta \Delta p_t + \varepsilon_t. \tag{18.20}$$

In Appendix 6A we argue that this is one plausible, albeit very simple, way of treating expectations formation. Taylor, however, justified his regression in a more sophisticated way as the cointegrating regression implied by the Cagan model. The appendix at the end of this chapter outlines his reasoning.

Let us focus here on whether Taylor's regression does indeed describe a cointegrating relationship. The two steps of the Engle-Granger test are implemented as follows.

Step 1. **Estimation of the cointegrating regression.** Taylor estimated his regression using data for several European hyperinflations of the early 1920s. His results are summarized in Table 6.7, and those for two hyperinflations—Germany in 1922–1923 and Poland in 1923–1924—were replicated in Exercise 6.27. Table 18.3 reproduces Taylor's key results for these two countries: the slope estimate, interpreted as the semielasticity of real money demand with respect to inflation, and the regression R^2.

Step 2. **An ADF test based on the residuals.** The second step of the Engle-Granger procedure is to do a unit root test on the residuals from the first step. Taylor ran Dickey-Fuller regressions of the form

$$\Delta e_t = \phi_0 + \rho e_{t-1} + \text{disturbance}.$$

As indicated, no augmenting lags were used and, in contrast to the most common practice, an intercept was included. However, typically the intercept estimate will be close to zero and will not make an important difference to the ADF statistic.

Taylor's ADF statistics for the German and Polish hyperinflations are reported in the last column of Table 18.3. They have been computed from the residuals of an intercept, no trend first-stage regression. Comparing the ADF statistics with the relevant critical values from Table 18.2, the null hypothesis is *not* rejected at conventional significance levels. The evidence therefore does not suggest that Cagan's series are cointegrated, and in this respect his model of money demand under hyperinflation—or at least Taylor's implementation of it—is not supported.

There are many reasons why the prediction of a theory may not be borne out in the data. One is that the theory is inadequate and in need of revision, but there are other possibilities as well. In this case, perhaps the most obvious one is that hyperinflationary episodes are by their nature short-lived. The German data studied by Taylor ran from September 1920 through July 1923 and the Polish data from April 1922 through November 1923—just 33 and 20 months, respectively. Over such a short time period it may be unrealistic to expect the forces of long-run equilibrium to manifest themselves to an extent that results in the rejection of the null hypothesis that there are no such forces at work.

It is a generic problem of time series analysis that data limitations tend to represent more of a constraint on what can be learned than is true with cross-sectional data. In cross-sectional data sets on individuals, households, or firms, thousands of observations may be available. By contrast, the time series available to economists often have fewer than 100 observations or, if more, are typically monthly or quarterly series for which it may be necessary to treat seasonality. Furthermore, the longer the span of an economic time series the more likely the economy will have undergone structural changes that must be treated. These limitations mean that the use of time series data to distinguish between competing hypotheses is often a challenging task.

18.5.3   Further Remarks on the Engle-Granger Test

Our treatment of the Engle-Granger test leads naturally to a number of additional remarks.

Choice of the Null Hypothesis

The Engle-Granger test—a term that we now use loosely to include the test based on a known cointegrating vector, so that a first-stage regression is unnecessary—tests the null hypothesis of a unit root. Thus, the null hypothesis is the absence of cointegration. Because the economic theory in question—balanced growth, purchasing power parity, Cagan's money demand model, or otherwise—predicts a cointegrating relationship, the Engle-Granger methodology takes as the null hypothesis that the theory is *false*. This is only rejected in favor of the alternative hypothesis—that the theory is *true*—in the face of compelling evidence.

Notice that this is the opposite of the traditional assignment of null and alternative hypothesis, as described in our discussion of the falsificationist view of the philosophy of science in Section 2.8. Usually economic theory predicts a parameter restriction, and that parameter restriction is taken as the null hypothesis. The task of empirical analysis is to see whether the data reject the parameter restriction, falsifying the theory.

Throughout this book, we have encountered many examples of this methodological paradigm. For example, in the appendix to Chapter 5 we have seen that the capital asset pricing model predicts a zero intercept. In Chapter 9 we have seen that the Solow-Swan growth model predicts the restriction $\beta_2 + \beta_3 = 0$ on the loglinear solution for living standards, the regression (9.16). Similarly, the Solow-Swan model augmented to include human capital predicts the restriction $\beta_2 + \beta_3 + \beta_4 = 0$ on the regression (9.24). In Chapter 11 we have seen that the theory underlying the Cobb-Douglas cost function implies the linear homogeneity restriction $\gamma_1 + \gamma_2 = 0$ on the two-factor cost function (11.26). And so on.

The Engle-Granger procedure, by contrast, turns this traditional methodology on its head, taking as the null hypothesis a parameter restriction corresponding to an absence of cointegration—the unit root restriction. It then examines whether the data reject this restriction.

Depending on our point of view, this may or may not be a problem. We may, after all, simply not subscribe to the falsificationist view of the philosophy of science and regard it as quite appropriate that a theory only be viewed as supported if there is compelling evidence against the null that it is false. The problem with this perspective is that the rejection of a null hypothesis never implies the acceptance of the alternative. There are many reasons why a parameter restriction might be false; the formally stated alternative hypothesis is just that suggested by the theoretical framework at hand. This is why the rejection of the null hypothesis is never regarded as "proving" or establishing the "truth" of the alternative; it is only in a loose sense evidence consistent with the alternative hypothesis.

For these reasons, there has been some interest in formulating tests in which cointegration is the null hypothesis, consistent with the falsificationist paradigm. When the cointegrating vector is known a priori, this is just a univariate unit root test in which stationarity is the null hypothesis and unit root behavior the alternative. A number of such tests have been developed, perhaps the best known being that of Kwiatkowski, Phillips, Schmidt, and Shin (1992), although Maddala and Kim (1998, p. 145) recommend against the use of this particular test.

When the cointegrating vector must be estimated, the literature is more obscure; see Maddala and Kim (1998, Sec. 6.4) for an assessment. We know little about the properties of these tests and in practice they have seen little use.

The substantive outcome of empirical testing may well hinge on the initial assignment of the null and alternative hypotheses. The specification of a null hypothesis reflects the adoption of certain a priori beliefs, beliefs that are only rejected in light of compelling evidence. A test in which cointegration is the null could easily reverse the findings of an Engle-Granger test in an application such as the Cagan hyperinflation model. It is entirely possible that the data do not reject the null of no cointegrating relationship—the result of the Taylor's Engle-Granger tests—and yet, when the hypotheses are reversed, neither do the data reject the null of a cointegrating relationship.

A Time Trend in the Cointegrating Regression

Cointegration means that variables share a common stochastic trend and so concerns only their stochastic component. It does not concern the deterministic components of the variables, for which a number of possibilities exist.

Consider two I(1) variables Y_{1t} and Y_{2t} with drifts β_1 and β_2:

$$\Delta Y_{1t} = \beta_1 + u_{1t} \tag{18.21a}$$

$$\Delta Y_{2t} = \beta_2 + u_{2t}. \tag{18.21b}$$

They may be viewed as zero-drift I(1) noise superimposed on linear trends, as in equation (17.14a):

$$Y_{1t} = \alpha_1 + \beta_1 t + v_{1t}$$

$$Y_{2t} = \alpha_2 + \beta_2 t + v_{2t}.$$

Now suppose that Y_{1t} and Y_{2t} are cointegrated. This means that their zero-drift I(1) components are related such that

$$v_{1t} - \lambda v_{2t} \sim \text{stationary}. \tag{18.22}$$

Substituting in the previous representations,

$$(Y_{1t} - \alpha_1 - \beta_1 t) - \lambda(Y_{2t} - \alpha_2 - \beta_2 t) \sim \text{stationary}.$$

Rearranging yields a cointegrating relationship of the form

$$Y_{1t} - (\alpha_1 - \lambda\alpha_2) - (\beta_1 - \lambda\beta_2)t - \lambda Y_{2t} \sim \text{stationary}.$$

Defining the notation λ_0, λ_1, and λ_2, this may be expressed as

$$Y_{1t} - \lambda_0 - \lambda_1 t - \lambda_2 Y_{2t} \sim \text{stationary}. \tag{18.23}$$

That is, when either or both variables have drift, the cointegrating regression can include a time trend; the coefficient $\lambda_1 \equiv \beta_1 - \lambda\beta_2$ is in general nonzero. This broadens the definition of cointegration from the previous definition (18.16), which implicitly treats variables as nondrifting. According to this broader definition, variables can move apart deterministically yet still be cointegrated because they share common stochastic trends. In other words, it is possible for variables to move apart deterministically at the same time that they move together stochastically.

In special cases, it is possible that the time trend may disappear from the cointegrating relationship, even when the variables drift. Consider the cointegrating restrictions of balanced growth. In a great ratio such as the average propensity to consume C/Y the numerator and denominator each grow, and so if modeled as I(1) in their logarithms they have positive drifts β_1 and β_2, as in (18.21). Being a great ratio the APC is constant in the long run, and so these growth rates must be the same: $\beta_1 = \beta_2$. Furthermore, the cointegrating relationship associated with the linear combination

$$\log C_t - \log Y_t = c_t - y_t = Y_{1t} - Y_{2t}$$

implies $\lambda = 1$ in (18.22). Consequently, the coefficient λ_1 in (18.23) reduces to

$$\lambda_1 = \beta_1 - \lambda\beta_2 = \beta_1 - \beta_2 = 0,$$

and the trend term disappears. This is why it is not necessary to include a time trend in our analysis of the cointegrating restrictions of balanced growth, even though the variables in question drift.

In general, however, this rather special set of circumstances will not hold. Consequently, when at least one of the variables drifts, cointegrating regressions often include a time trend. This affects the critical values for the Engle-Granger test, as indicated in Table 18.2. Notice that it is only the cointegrating regression that includes a time trend, *not* the second-step ADF test on the residuals, which is still of the form (18.18).

Practitioner's Tip: **A time trend in the cointegrating regression**

When any of the variables may have nonzero drift, the cointegrating regression should normally include a time trend.

Limitations of the Engle-Granger Test

The Engle-Granger test uses the residuals of an OLS regression; it is the best known of several **residual-based tests** for cointegration. As such, it relies on an arbitrary assignment of the dependent variable—an arbitrary choice of normalization. Renormalizing the cointegrating vector on another variable—selecting it as the dependent variable—will generate a different residual series that may yield a different unit root test result. Yet the conclusion about whether variables are cointegrated should not depend on an arbitrary choice of normalization.

This problem with the Engle-Granger procedure—indeed, with all residual-based tests—is solved by more sophisticated approaches to cointegration testing. Instead of describing time series relationships using a single equation, these approaches use systems of equations that treat variables symmetrically—these are the VAR models mentioned in Section 18.2. More is said about these models in the next section.

By far the best known of these approaches, due to Johansen (1988, 1995), uses the maximum likelihood method of estimation. Both because it uses VAR systems and because it uses maximum likelihood, the Johansen cointegration testing methodology is beyond the scope of this book. There are now several good textbook treatments; for applied introductions see Enders (1995, Chap. 6), Harris (1995, Chap. 5), and Johnston and DiNardo (1997, Chap. 9).

In addition to using Engle-Granger tests, Taylor (1991) applied the Johansen methodology to Cagan's inflation and real money demand series, obtaining somewhat more encouraging evidence of cointegration for some hyperinflationary episodes. These findings were further strengthened by Engsted (1993), who modified Taylor's analysis to incorporate rational expectations.

Conclusions

Despite these qualifications and the availability of alternative tests, the Engle-Granger test is important for several reasons. First, despite its deficiencies it has been widely used in applied work. Second, it is important pedagogically as a natural first step in understanding the intuition behind testing for cointegration.

EXERCISES

Cagan's German and Polish hyperinflation data are available in the files **germany.dat** and **poland.dat**. These files are documented in the exercises at the end of Appendix 6A.

The following exercises ask you to investigate aspects of the cointegrating regression implied by the Cagan model. The first exercise asks you to verify that, when estimated with Cagan's German or Polish data, the regression is balanced. The second asks you to replicate Taylor's Engle-Granger cointegration tests, and to examine their sensitivity to some variations in the analysis. If you choose to work with the German data, recall that Taylor used the subsample ending in July (rather than November) 1923.

18.11 💿 **germany.dat poland.dat** In Section 17.4 of the previous chapter, the Δp_t series for the German and Polish hyperinflations are studied. The outcome of that analysis is that these inflation rates can be described as I(1).

(a) For Cagan's regression to be balanced—that is, for it to potentially represent a cointegrating relationship—what must be the order of integration of the dependent variable $m_t - p_t$?

(b) Suppose it is found that the order of integration is something different than in part a. Is there any point in doing an Engle-Granger test based on Taylor's regression?

(c) Choosing either the German or Polish series on real money holdings, perform an ADF test. Justify your choice of lag length. Justify as well your decision whether to include a trend in the ADF regression. (*Hint:* Reason based on an inspection of Figure 6.16.) Is the null hypothesis that the series is I(1) rejected?

(d) Is your conclusion sensitive to your decision whether to include a trend?

18.12 💿 **germany.dat poland.dat** Choosing either the German or Polish data, perform the two steps of the Engle-Granger test.

(a) Estimate Taylor's regression, saving the residuals for use in the second step. Are you able to reproduce the semielasticity and R^2 given in Table 18.3? (This regression repeats one originally done in Exercise 6.27.)

(b) Use the residuals of this regression to perform an Engle-Granger test for cointegration, as implemented by Taylor. What choice of augmenting lag length enables you to reproduce Taylor's ADF statistic, as reported in Table 18.3? Do you agree with Taylor's choice of lag length?

(c) Taylor included an intercept in his ADF regressions. We have asserted that the estimated intercept will typically be close to zero and that the ADF statistic will not usually be sensitive to the inclusion of the intercept. Is this the case in your regression?

(d) Suppose you alter Taylor's regression by including a time trend and then recompute the ADF statistic using these new residuals. Comparing this against the appropriate critical values from Table 18.2, is your conclusion about the hypothesis of cointegration affected by this modification of the procedure?

(e) Suppose you reverse the dependent and explanatory variables in the first-stage regression and do an Engle-Granger test using the new residual series. Is the conclusion about cointegration sensitive to this arbitrary choice of normalization?

18.6 Testing Restrictions on the Cointegrating Vector

Because cointegrating regressions do not satisfy the assumptions of the classical normal linear regression model, and despite the superconsistency of the OLS point estimates that nevertheless holds, other aspects of conventional least squares regression analysis as developed in Chapters 4–10 are not in general valid.

Most important, the t and F statistics do not in general have their usual distributions and so cannot be used in the standard way to test linear restrictions. The reason for this lies not so much with the nonstationarity of the variables as with two other aspects of the cointegrating regression.

Autocorrelation in the disturbance. The disturbance u_t is stationary (as long, of course, as the regression is indeed a cointegrating one and is not spurious). However, it is not white noise; that is, it is not the classical disturbance assumed in Chapters 4–10. Instead u_t is in general autocorrelated. Although this autocorrelation does not get in the way of using OLS to get good point estimates of the coefficients in the cointegrating vector (at least asymptotically—Stock's superconsistency result), it does result in the standard t and F test statistics not having their usual t and F distributions.

In this respect, autocorrelation in a regression disturbance has the same effect as heteroskedasticity. Recall that in Chapter 14 we have found that heteroskedasticity makes the standard least squares test statistics invalid.

Simultaneity and exogeneity. In Section 5.3.3 we discuss the distinction between endogenous and exogenous variables and the problems that arise with conventional least squares regression analysis when endogenous variables (variables determined simultaneously with the dependent variable) are used as regressors. As we show there, the regression disturbance must logically be correlated with the right-hand-side endogenous variables. This leads to the same sort of coefficient biases that, in Section 8.9.1, we have seen arise from the omission of relevant regressors.

That conclusion is reached in the context of the analysis of cross-sectional data obtained by randomly sampling; more formally, it is predicated on what we now call stationary data. By contrast, when the regression is a cointegrating one relating nonstationary time series, simultaneity is not a problem for the asymptotic properties of OLS point estimates. This is the essence of Stock's superconsistency result. It can, however, be a problem with other aspects of the least squares estimators, in particular the sampling distributions of test statistics, and the standard distributional results no longer hold.

In conclusion, there are two reasons why the usual t and F tests are invalid for cointegrating regressions: autocorrelation and simultaneity. The general means of resolving these problems are beyond the scope of this book and, in any case, are the subject of ongoing research, so that new developments are likely. One approach—see Wooldridge (2000, pp. 590–591) for a brief introductory treatment—is to modify the cointegrating regression in an attempt to address them. Another is to perform hypothesis tests, not within a single-equation analysis but instead within VAR systems of the kind discussed in Section 18.8.

An Interesting Special Case

Although it is not possible here to consider generally applicable methods for testing linear restrictions on cointegrating vectors, it is worth noting that there may be special cases in which neither autocorrelation nor simultaneity are important problems, and so standard t and F tests are legitimate.[5]

As an example of an application that might plausibly be of this type, consider our use in the early chapters of this book of the Cobb-Douglas (1928) data on output, capital, and labor for the U.S. manufacturing sector, 1899–1922. This is used in Chapter 8 to estimate a Cobb-Douglas production function as a loglinear regression,

$$\log Q_t = \beta_1 + \beta_2 \log K_t + \beta_3 \log L_t + \varepsilon_t. \tag{18.24}$$

We have found that the slope estimates are sensible factor shares and are statistically significant and, in Chapter 10, that an F test does not reject the hypothesis of constant returns to scale, the restriction $\beta_2 + \beta_3 = 1$. This, in turn, justified our use in Chapter 7 of the labor-intensive version of this production function as an example of simple regression.

Although seemingly innocent and straightforward at the time, our application of these methods to these data may now be seen to have been brazenly cavalier, for these are time series data that, because production and factor inputs in an economy tend to grow over time, are bound to be nonstationary. If we regard them as I(1), the production function must be interpreted as a hypothesized cointegrating relationship. In light of what we have said, it is surprising that conventional t and F tests seem to work so well in terms of yielding plausible answers to the hypotheses they have been used to test.

---

[5] This special case is analyzed rigorously by Hamilton (1994, pp. 602–603).

Why might the use of the standard test procedures be appropriate in this application? Consider the two problems we have identified.

Autocorrelation in the disturbance. If a production function is interpreted as a cointegrating relationship, economic reasoning tells us something about the nature of this relationship that has implications for what we might expect to be true about the disturbance. Specifically, production this period is determined by factor inputs *this period,* not by factor inputs in previous periods. This is why a production function specifies production today as depending on current factor inputs, not on factor inputs in the past as well. This suggests that there are no such lagged omitted influences that would result in an autocorrelated disturbance. Although the series Q_t, K_t, and L_t are no doubt themselves heavily autocorrelated—as must be the case if they are I(1)—the cointegrating relationship among them may be white noise, not just stationary.

Simultaneity and exogeneity. Are choices about capital and labor inputs made simultaneously with decisions about output, so that all three are the endogenous outcome of the same decision process? Or is it better to think of capital and labor as evolving exogenously, output then being generated by the production function as the only endogenous variable of the three-variable system?

If the unit of observation is the individual firm, it is certainly the first view that is the appropriate one. Firms make decisions about factor inputs jointly with their production decisions, so that all three variables are endogenous. This has important implications for the estimation of production functions using firm-level data: In a loglinear Cobb-Douglas production function the explanatory variables $\log K$ and $\log L$ are endogenous just as $\log Q$ is, and least squares will suffer from simultaneous equations bias. This is especially important for cross-sectional data collected by random sampling; there is no superconsistency result and least squares point estimates are biased even asymptotically. Indeed, an important motivation for the cost function approach to production analysis that we develop in Chapter 11 is that it works in terms of estimated relationships (the cost function or its associated system of factor demands) in which the explanatory variables (factor prices) are exogenous if firms are competitive price-takers. Although not emphasized in that chapter, resolving simultaneity problems is one of the most important reasons for exploiting the duality of production and cost in the analysis of cross-sectional data.

If, on the other hand, the unit of observation is not the firm but is, instead, the economy as a whole or some large component of it such as the manufacturing sector, then the second view may be more reasonable: Factor inputs evolve historically in a way that is predetermined at a point in time and therefore may be treated as exogenous.

In conclusion, a production function estimated from aggregate time series may be an example of the special case in which t and F tests have the same legitimacy that they do in classical regression. Of course, this should not be asserted solely on the basis of a priori reasoning. To the extent that it is possible to do so, we should see whether the data are consistent with this view. The following exercises give you an opportunity to do this.

EXERCISES

The Cobb-Douglas data are available in the file **cobbdoug.dat**, which is documented in the exercises at the end of Section 7.2. Our ability to study the issues just discussed is limited by the fact that, in this book, we have not developed tests for exogeneity. As well, the Cobb-Douglas data consist of just 24 annual observations, and there is a limit to what can be learned from such short time series. Consequently, the goals of the following exercises are fairly modest; you are asked to examine whether the Cobb-Douglas production function can reasonably be regarded as a cointegrating relationship and whether the regression disturbance is autocorrelated.

18.13 💿 **cobbdoug.dat** If the loglinear production function (18.24) is to be interpreted as a cointe-

grating relationship, the series $\log Q_t$, $\log K_t$, and $\log L_t$ must be integrated. Perform unit root tests on these series, justifying (a) the version of the Dickey-Fuller regression you choose, and (b) your choice of augmenting lag length. Do you find that these series can be treated as difference stationary?

18.14 💿 **cobbdoug.dat** Given the premise that the series are I(1), perform an Engle-Granger test to determine whether the loglinear production function (18.24) can reasonably be regarded as a cointegrating regression. Justify your choice of augmenting lag length in the second step of the Engle-Granger procedure.

18.15 💿 **cobbdoug.dat** Is the disturbance white noise? Apply a Box-Pierce-Ljung Q test to the residuals of the cointegrating regression.[6]

18.7   Error Correction Models

Cointegration concerns long-run relationships between variables. As we have seen, an important feature of the concept is that it is possible to estimate cointegrating vectors and test for the absence of cointegration without having to model explicitly the short-run fluctuations in the variables.

Even so, variables that have long-run equilibrium relationships typically interact in the short run as well. Intuitively, then, the long-run cointegrating relationship

---

[6] When the series of interest is not an observed time series but instead consists of residuals from an estimated relationship, there are alternatives to the Box-Pierce-Ljung test. The best known of these is the famous **Durbin-Watson test.** Prior to the rise of nonstationary time series methods the Durbin-Watson test—and accompanying techniques known as Cochrane-Orcutt and Prais-Winsten transformations of time series regressions—were a mainstay of econometrics textbooks. For a critique of the habitual use of such methods, see Mizon (1995). As Davidson (2000) has put it, the Durbin-Watson statistic "... does not really deserve the role of primary diagnostic still accorded to it for reasons of habit and tradition." For further comments on the obsolescence of the Durbin-Watson test, see Davidson and MacKinnon (2004, Sec. 7.7).

must be embedded within a more general model that also describes short-run variation. In this section and the next, we describe this more general model, called an **error correction model** (ECM).

In our discussion of modeling the interaction of stationary variables, we discuss the autoregressive distributed lag model (18.3). In the simplest case in which just a single lag on each variable is all that is needed to yield a white noise disturbance, this is

$$Y_t = \phi_0 + \phi_1 Y_{t-1} + \gamma_0 X_t + \gamma_1 X_{t-1} + \varepsilon_t. \tag{18.25}$$

We remarked that, in the case of I(1) variables that are not cointegrated, it is not appropriate to estimate such an ADL model *in levels* because the variables have no long-run relationship. Any apparent relationship suggested by such an estimated model would be a spurious one. However, if the variables are related in the short run they may legitimately be described by an ADL model *in first differences*. In the simplest case of just a single difference on each variable, this is

$$\Delta Y_t = \phi_0 + \gamma_0 \Delta X_t + \varepsilon_t. \tag{18.26}$$

Of course, in general as many lags on each difference may be included as are necessary to yield a white noise disturbance, as in equation (18.7).

18.7.1   The Error Correction Form of the Autoregressive Distributed Lag Model

When I(1) variables *are* cointegrated, on the other hand, the existence of a long-run relationship means that their short- and long-run interactions *can* be described by the ADL model (18.25) in levels.[7] In this case, it turns out that a certain alternative form of the model is especially instructive. Let us derive this alternative form, the ECM.

Begin by recalling that, in the absence of shocks, the ADL model (18.25) implies a certain long-run relationship between the variables. Let us consider the simplest case of I(1) variables without drift, so that the cointegrating relationship does not include a time trend. An absence of shocks means that the variables reproduce themselves period after period: $Y_t = Y_{t-1}$ and $X_t = X_{t-1}$. Consequently, the equilibrium condition is the same as in the stationary case (18.5),

$$Y^* = \frac{\phi_0}{1 - \phi_1} + \frac{\gamma_0 + \gamma_1}{1 - \phi_1} X^* = \lambda_0 + \lambda_1 X^*. \tag{18.27}$$

---

[7] As in the stationary case, appropriate exogeneity assumptions must be made on X_t. In a time series context, there is a distinction between **weak exogeneity** and **strong exogeneity,** and the appropriate estimation strategy depends on which assumption is valid. Because our interest here is less in the specifics of estimating the ADL model than in using it as a prelude to VAR models, we sidestep these technical issues. For a good introductory treatment that delineates the various possibilities, see Stock and Watson (2003, Chap. 13).

Because this is the long-run relationship between the variables, it must be what the cointegrating relationship reduces to in the absence of shocks.

That is, the cointegrating relationship is

$$Y_t - \lambda_0 - \lambda_1 X_t \sim \text{stationary.}$$

Now let us return to the ADL model itself, equation (18.25). Like any regression model, it may be reparameterized in a number of ways. Consider subtracting Y_{t-1} from both sides, and adding and subtracting $\gamma_0 X_{t-1}$ from the right-hand side. The result may be rearranged as

$$\Delta Y_t = (\phi_1 - 1)\left[Y_{t-1} - \frac{\phi_0}{1 - \phi_1} - \frac{\gamma_0 + \gamma_1}{1 - \phi_1}X_{t-1}\right] + \gamma_0 \Delta X_t + \varepsilon_t.$$

Recognizing the term inside the square parentheses as the equilibrium error of the cointegrating relationship and defining $\psi = \phi_1 - 1$, this is

$$\Delta Y_t = \psi[Y_{t-1} - \lambda_0 - \lambda_1 X_{t-1}] + \gamma_0 \Delta X_t + \varepsilon_t. \tag{18.28}$$

This is the ADL model in error correction form. The name comes from the interpretation that changes ΔY_t are in part a response or "correction" to the equilibrium error of the previous period—deviations from the cointegrating relationship.

The speed of this response is determined by the speed of adjustment parameter $\psi = \phi_1 - 1$. Notice that, under the stability condition $|\phi_1| < 1$, this speed of adjustment parameter is negative. If at time $t - 1$, the variable Y is above its equilibrium value as given by the cointegrating relationship with X, then the equilibrium error is positive,

$$Y_{t-1} - \lambda_0 - \lambda_1 X_{t-1} > 0.$$

The response is that Y falls in the next period: $\Delta Y_t < 0$. Similarly, if at time $t - 1$ the variable Y is below its equilibrium value, then the equilibrium error is negative,

$$Y_{t-1} - \lambda_0 - \lambda_1 X_{t-1} < 0.$$

The response is that Y increases in the next period: $\Delta Y_t > 0$.

The ECM can also be written

$$\Delta Y_t = \phi_0 + (\phi_1 - 1)\left[Y_{t-1} - \frac{\gamma_0 + \gamma_1}{1 - \phi_1}X_{t-1}\right] + \gamma_0 \Delta X_t + \varepsilon_t$$

$$= \phi_0 + \psi[Y_{t-1} - \lambda_1 X_{t-1}] + \gamma_0 \Delta X_t + \varepsilon_t.$$

That is, intercepts in the error correction term and in the regression itself are not separately identified. If the ECM is expressed with an intercept, one should not be included in the equilibrium error, and vice versa.

That an ADL model can be reparameterized as an ECM is not contingent on the lag lengths in the ADL. Had we started with the general ADL(p, q) model (18.3) instead of an ADL(1,1), a similar derivation would still yield an ECM, although with cointegrating coefficients λ_0 and λ_1 suitably redefined in terms of the coefficients of the ADL(p, q).

In the special case in which there is no long-run relationship, changes in Y_t do not occur in response to any deviation from a cointegrating relationship. Consequently, the speed of adjustment coefficient ψ is zero and the ECM reduces to the ADL in first differences (18.26),

$$\Delta Y_t = \phi_0 + \gamma_0 \Delta X_t + \varepsilon_t.$$

This explains why, regardless of the number of lags that may be included, this model is by itself inadequate for describing variables that are cointegrated. Although it describes the interaction of their short-run changes, it fails to recognize the long-run relationship between their levels by failing to include the equilibrium error. This constitutes an omission of a relevant regressor (to use the terminology in Section 8.9.1) and therefore an important specification error.

Notice that although it is acceptable to study a cointegrating relationship ignoring short-run interactions in the variables—the approach adopted whenever a cointegrating regression is estimated—it is not acceptable to do the opposite: Estimate short-run relationships without taking into account a long-run relationship.[8]

In situations in which the cointegrating vector is known a priori, this can be used to advantage in estimating the ECM. Using known values for λ_0 and λ_1 in (18.28) improves the efficiency of estimation of the remaining parameters. The obvious approach to estimation is, therefore, to estimate the ECM directly; this uses the a priori knowledge of the cointegrating vector in a way that estimation of the original ADL model (18.25) would not.

Estimation When the Cointegrating Vector Is Unknown

When the cointegrating vector is unknown and must be estimated, several approaches to estimation are possible.

One is to not estimate the ECM at all but instead to estimate the ADL. The relationship between the parameters of the two models is exactly identifying, so point estimates of the parameters of the ECM can be deduced. It is the parameters of the ECM that are usually of economic interest; for example, the long-run multiplier λ_1 and the speed of adjustment parameter ψ. However, not all the relationships between the two sets of parameters are linear, and so this approach does not provide a means of obtaining all the standard errors that are potentially of interest.

If estimates of only certain parameters are required, then the task may be simplified. If it is only the cointegrating vector that is of interest—such as the long-run multiplier λ_1—then we know that this can be obtained from the estimation of

---

[8] To say that it is acceptable to estimate cointegrating relationships ignoring short-run interactions is not to say that there is no cost to doing so. In Section 18.5.1, we remark that OLS estimation of cointegrating vectors has good asymptotic properties—Stock's (1987) superconsistency result—but can have rather poor small-sample ones. The small-sample properties can be improved by estimating the cointegrating relationship within a more general model that also treats the short-run behavior of the variables; that is, that treats the influences omitted from the cointegrating regression. This makes ECMs all the more interesting.

the cointegrating relationship alone, without regard to the ADL model in either of its forms. Of course, as we have remarked, the small-sample properties of these estimates may be at issue.

If the speed of adjustment parameter ψ is of primary interest, we can estimate

$$\Delta Y_t = \phi_0 + \psi Y_{t-1} + \delta X_{t-1} + \gamma_0 \Delta X_t + \varepsilon_t,$$

where we have defined $\delta = -\psi \lambda_1$. This yields the same estimate of ψ (and its standard error) that will be obtained indirectly from the ADL model (18.25) using the definition $\psi = \phi_1 - 1$ because one regression is just an exactly identifying reparameterization of the other. For the same reason, the same estimates will be yielded by nonlinear least squares estimation of the ECM (18.28) itself, an approach that has the advantage of yielding a direct estimate of λ_1.

However, the best-known method for estimating all the parameters of the ECM in a way that does not require nonlinear least squares is the **Engle-Granger two-step procedure,** due to Engle and Granger (1987).[9] The method makes use of the fact that typically if variables are cointegrated the researcher will have begun as a *first step* by estimating the cointegrating relationship as an OLS regression, say

$$Y_t = \hat{\lambda}_0 + \hat{\lambda}_1 X_t + e_t.$$

The OLS residuals serve as a measure of the equilibrium error and may be substituted into the error correction term in estimating the ECM as a *second step,*

$$\Delta Y_t = \phi_0 + \psi e_{t-1} + \gamma_0 \Delta X_t + \varepsilon_t.$$

This Engle-Granger two-step procedure has been widely applied in empirical work. Its main competitor is the systems approach to cointegration, to which we turn next.

EXERCISES

18.16 Starting with the ADL model (18.25), derive the ECM, showing your steps carefully.

18.8

The Error Correction Form of a Vector Autoregression

An especially important aspect of ECM's is that, because an ADL regression is very similar to one equation from a VAR, everything that we have said about ECMs applies equally to VARs. In particular, a VAR system has an ECM representation.

As we have seen, the form of a cointegrating equation depends on whether the variables drift. Drifting variables give rise, in general, to a cointegrating equation

---

[9] This is not to be confused with the two steps of the Engle-Granger test for cointegration.

that includes a time trend. Consequently, the form of a VAR and its associated ECM depend on whether the variables drift, and we must distinguish between the two cases of nondrifting and drifting variables.

18.8.1 Case 1: Nondrifting Variables

Consider two I(1) variables without drift. Setting $\beta_1 = \beta_2 = 0$ in (18.21), their univariate behavior is specified by

$$\Delta Y_{1t} = u_{1t} \tag{18.29a}$$

$$\Delta Y_{2t} = u_{2t}. \tag{18.29b}$$

Their bivariate behavior is described by a VAR, which we will illustrate with the simplest situation of the two-variable system (18.6) in which only a single lag on each variable is needed to obtain white noise disturbances:

$$Y_{1t} = \phi_{10} + \phi_{11} Y_{1,t-1} + \phi_{12} Y_{2,t-1} + \varepsilon_{1t} \tag{18.30a}$$

$$Y_{2t} = \phi_{20} + \phi_{21} Y_{1,t-1} + \phi_{22} Y_{2,t-1} + \varepsilon_{2t}. \tag{18.30b}$$

In practice additional lags might be needed, but this is not important for what follows.

The Cointegrating Restrictions

In the absence of shocks, the stationary disturbances of (18.29) are zero, $u_{1t} = u_{2t} = 0$, and in long-run equilibrium the variables remain constant:

$$\Delta Y_{1t} = 0 \quad \Leftrightarrow \quad Y_{1t} = Y_{1,t-1},$$

$$\Delta Y_{2t} = 0 \quad \Leftrightarrow \quad Y_{2t} = Y_{2,t-1}.$$

Let us denote these long-run equilibrium values by Y_1^* and Y_2^*.

In the absence of shocks, the equations of the VAR generate equilibrium relationships analogous to (18.27) for the ADL model:

$$Y_1^* = \frac{\phi_{10}}{1 - \phi_{11}} + \frac{\phi_{12}}{1 - \phi_{11}} Y_2^*$$

$$Y_1^* = -\frac{\phi_{20}}{\phi_{21}} + \frac{1 - \phi_{22}}{\phi_{21}} Y_2^*.$$

In both cases, we have normalized on Y_1^* in order to indicate that both are cointegrating relationships of the form (18.16),

$$Y_1^* - \lambda_0 - \lambda_1 Y_2^*.$$

The two equations are not, however, *independent* cointegrating relationships, because two variables can be related by at most one long-run relationship. Instead, the two equations must be different expressions of the same cointegrating relationship.

In other words, cointegration imposes parameter restrictions on the VAR system, which in this case are

$$\frac{\phi_{10}}{1 - \phi_{11}} = -\frac{\phi_{20}}{\phi_{21}} \quad (= \lambda_0) \tag{18.31a}$$

$$\frac{\phi_{12}}{1 - \phi_{11}} = \frac{1 - \phi_{22}}{\phi_{21}} \quad (= \lambda_1). \tag{18.31b}$$

This reveals a key insight of the VAR/ECM approach: The parameter restrictions on a VAR system implied by cointegration provide a route to cointegration testing that serves as an alternative to the residual-based approach. It is this insight that is exploited by the Johansen methodology, mentioned in Section 18.5.3.

Reparameterization to Obtain the ECM

These restrictions may be used to reparameterize the VAR in its ECM form,

$$\Delta Y_{1t} = \psi_1[Y_{1,t-1} - \lambda_0 - \lambda_1 Y_{2,t-1}] + \varepsilon_{1t} \tag{18.32a}$$

$$\Delta Y_{2t} = \psi_2[Y_{1,t-1} - \lambda_0 - \lambda_1 Y_{2,t-1}] + \varepsilon_{2t}. \tag{18.32b}$$

The speed-of-adjustment parameters are

$$\psi_1 = \phi_{11} - 1 \tag{18.33a}$$

$$\psi_2 = \phi_{21}. \tag{18.33b}$$

In other words, the ECM is a restatement of the VAR that incorporates the restrictions implied by cointegration. Exercise 18.17 asks you to verify this reparameterization.

The economic interpretation of the equations of the ECM is similar to that of the ECM (18.28) of the ADL model. The expression in parentheses is the equilibrium error. The same equilibrium error appears in both equations: There is only a single long-run relationship to which the variables respond in the short run. However, the speed-of-adjustment coefficients ψ_1 and ψ_2 are different, so each variable responds differently to a given departure from equilibrium. Under the stationarity restriction $|\phi_{11}| < 1$, the speed-of-adjustment parameter in the first equation is negative, $\psi_1 < 0$, indicating that Y_{1t} declines when it is above its equilibrium value.

If the cointegrating relationship is satisfied so that the equilibrium error is zero, the two equations of the ECM reduce to the univariate zero-drift processes (18.29).[10]

If there is no long-run relationship between the variables, then their short-run behavior is not in part an adjustment to the long-run equilibrium, and the speed-of-adjustment coefficients are zero: $\psi_1 = \psi_2 = 0$. In this case, the error correction terms disappear and the ECM reduces to a VAR in first differences, in this instance

---

[10] Remember that in general the VAR and ECM would include additional lags on the right-hand-side variables, generating autocorrelation that is captured in the disturbances u_{1t} and u_{2t} of the I(1) processes (18.29).

a special case of the model (18.8). When there is a cointegrating relationship, on the other hand, a VAR in first differences such as (18.8) is misspecified because it omits the error correction terms.

The ECM (18.32) has an intercept in the cointegrating equation, the coefficient λ_0, but not in the equations of the ECM itself. Hence, it is described as the "intercept in the cointegrating equation, but not in the model equations" version of the ECM.[11]

This characterization may seem arbitrary because it is evident that the model can be restated with intercepts in the ECM equations instead of the cointegrating equation:

$$\Delta Y_{1t} = \phi_{10} + \psi_1[Y_{1,t-1} - \lambda_1 Y_{2,t-1}] + \varepsilon_{1t} \tag{18.34a}$$

$$\Delta Y_{2t} = \phi_{20} + \psi_2[Y_{1,t-1} - \lambda_1 Y_{2,t-1}] + \varepsilon_{2t}. \tag{18.34b}$$

However, this fails to make explicit the underlying parameter interpretations $\phi_{10} = -\psi_1\lambda_0$ and $\phi_{20} = -\psi_2\lambda_0$ and hence fails to impose the implicit restriction

$$\frac{\phi_{10}}{\phi_{20}} = \frac{\psi_1}{\psi_2}.$$

The ECM with "intercept in the cointegrating equation but not in the model equations" form (18.32) imposes this restriction.

Practitioner's Tip: The ECM for nondrifting variables

When none of the variables drift, the "intercept in the cointegrating equation, but not in the model equations" version of the ECM is the natural specification.

18.8.2 Case 2: Drifting Variables

Let us consider the generalization of the previous analysis to the case of drifting variables.

Drifting I(1) variables are specified as in (18.21),

$$\Delta Y_{1t} = \beta_1 + u_{1t} \tag{18.35a}$$

$$\Delta Y_{2t} = \beta_2 + u_{2t}. \tag{18.35b}$$

Their bivariate behavior is described by a VAR, which we continue to illustrate with the simplest situation of a single lag on each variable. Now, however, the fact that drifts can lead the variables to move apart deterministically means that a properly specified VAR includes time trends:

$$Y_{1t} = \phi_{10} + b_1 t + \phi_{11} Y_{1,t-1} + \phi_{12} Y_{2,t-1} + \varepsilon_{1t} \tag{18.36a}$$

$$Y_{2t} = \phi_{20} + b_2 t + \phi_{21} Y_{1,t-1} + \phi_{22} Y_{2,t-1} + \varepsilon_{2t}. \tag{18.36b}$$

The need for these time trends will become clear as we derive the ECM.

---

[11] That is, it is version H_1^* of the taxonomy given by Johansen (1995, p. 81, eq. (5.16)).

The Cointegrating Restrictions

In the absence of shocks, the stationary disturbances of the I(1) processes (18.35) are zero, $u_{1t} = u_{2t} = 0$, and in long-run equilibrium the variables grow at constant rates given by their drifts:

$$\Delta Y_{1t} = \beta_1 \quad \Leftrightarrow \quad Y_{1t} = \beta_1 + Y_{1,t-1},$$
$$\Delta Y_{2t} = \beta_2 \quad \Leftrightarrow \quad Y_{2t} = \beta_2 + Y_{2,t-1}.$$

Substituting these into the VAR, in the absence of shocks the variables are related deterministically at time t by

$$Y_{1t} = \phi_{10} + b_1 t + \phi_{11}(Y_{1t} - \beta_1) + \phi_{12}(Y_{2t} - \beta_2)$$
$$Y_{2t} = \phi_{20} + b_2 t + \phi_{21}(Y_{1t} - \beta_1) + \phi_{22}(Y_{2t} - \beta_2).$$

Solving each equation for Y_{1t} yields

$$Y_{1t} = \frac{\phi_{10} - \phi_{11}\beta_1 - \phi_{12}\beta_2}{1 - \phi_{11}} + \frac{b_1}{1 - \phi_{11}} t + \frac{\phi_{12}}{1 - \phi_{11}} Y_{2t}$$
$$Y_{1t} = -\frac{\phi_{20} - \phi_{21}\beta_1 - \phi_{22}\beta_2}{\phi_{21}} - \frac{b_2}{\phi_{21}} t + \frac{1 - \phi_{22}}{\phi_{21}} Y_{2t}.$$

Each solution has been normalized on Y_{1t} in order to indicate that both are cointegrating relationships of the form (18.23),

$$Y_{1t} - \lambda_0 - \lambda_1 t - \lambda_2 Y_{2t}.$$

The two equations are not, however, *independent* cointegrating relationships because two variables can be related by at most one long-run relationship. Instead, the two equations must be different expressions of the same cointegrating relationship. In other words, cointegration imposes parameter restrictions on the VAR system, which in this case are

$$\frac{\phi_{10} - \phi_{11}\beta_1 - \phi_{12}\beta_2}{1 - \phi_{11}} = -\frac{\phi_{20} - \phi_{21}\beta_1 - \phi_{22}\beta_2}{\phi_{21}} \qquad (= \lambda_0), \qquad (18.37a)$$

$$\frac{b_1}{1 - \phi_{11}} = -\frac{b_2}{\phi_{21}} \qquad (= \lambda_1), \qquad (18.37b)$$

$$\frac{\phi_{12}}{1 - \phi_{11}} = \frac{1 - \phi_{22}}{\phi_{21}} \qquad (= \lambda_2). \qquad (18.37c)$$

Reparameterization to Obtain the ECM

These restrictions may be used to reparameterize the VAR in its ECM form,

$$\Delta Y_{1t} = \beta_1 + \psi_1[Y_{1,t-1} - \lambda_0 - \lambda_1(t - 1) - \lambda_2 Y_{2,t-1}] + \varepsilon_{1t} \qquad (18.38a)$$
$$\Delta Y_{2t} = \beta_2 + \psi_2[Y_{1,t-1} - \lambda_0 - \lambda_1(t - 1) - \lambda_2 Y_{2,t-1}] + \varepsilon_{2t}. \qquad (18.38b)$$

The speed-of-adjustment parameters are, as before, given by (18.33). This is described as the "linear trend in the cointegrating equation, intercepts in the model equations" version of the ECM.[12] Exercise 18.18 asks you to verify this reparameterization.

The economic interpretation of this ECM is similar to the previous one. The equilibrium error appears in both equations, each variable responding to a given departure from equilibrium according to the speed-of-adjustment parameters ψ_1 and ψ_2. If the cointegrating relationship is satisfied so that the equilibrium error is zero, the two equations of the ECM reduce to the univariate processes (18.35).

As before, if there is no long-run relationship between the variables, then their short-run behavior is not in part an adjustment to long-run equilibrium and the speed-of-adjustment coefficients are zero: $\psi_1 = \psi_2 = 0$. In this case, the error correction terms disappear and the ECM reduces to a VAR in first differences. When there is a cointegrating relationship, on the other hand, a VAR in first differences is misspecified because it omits the error correction terms.

Practitioner's Tip: **The ECM for drifting variables**

When some of the variables may drift, the "intercept and trend in the cointegrating equation, intercepts in the model equations" version of the ECM is the natural specification.

18.8.3 The Two Relevant Forms of the Error Correction Model in Practice

In general we can conceive of several alternative combinations of intercept and trend in the cointegrating equation and the equations of the ECM; Johansen (1995, Sec. 5.7) delineates five possibilities. Our analysis suggests, however, that only two of these are relevant in practice, a point made by Franses (2001) and summarized in the two previous Practitioner's Tips. When all variables have zero drifts the ECM (18.32) is the appropriate one; this corresponds to Franses (2001, eq. (12)). When at least some variables drift, it is the more general ECM (18.38) that applies; this corresponds to Franses (2001, eq. (13)). These are Johansen (1995, p. 81, eqs. (5.16), (5.14)). Because, in practical applications, some variables usually drift—or at least this often cannot be ruled out a priori—it is the more general model (18.38) that is the natural default.

In special cases, this more general model may simplify. Specifically, we have seen that in an application such as the cointegrating restrictions of balanced growth in which variables have common growth rates, the time trend may disappear from the cointegrating equation even though the variables drift. The appropriate ECM therefore sets $\lambda_1 = 0$ in (18.38) so that the time trends disappear, leaving intercepts in the cointegrating equation and the equations of the ECM. This is the "intercept in

---

[12] That is, it is version H^* of the taxonomy given by Johansen (1995, p. 81, eq. (5.14)).

the cointegrating equation, intercepts in the model equations" version of the ECM, corresponding to Johansen (1995, eq. (5.15)). However, such special circumstances cannot be assumed to hold in general.[13]

EXERCISES

18.17 Verify the reparameterization of the VAR into the ECM in the nondrifting case.

(a) Start with the ECM (18.32) and substitute in the appropriate expressions for the cointegrating coefficients (18.31) and the speed-of-adjustment parameters (18.33) to obtain the VAR (18.30).

(b) Do you agree that the system (18.34) is a correct alternative reparameterization?

18.18 ⨍ Verify the reparameterization of the VAR into the ECM in the drifting case.

(a) Start with the ECM (18.38) and substitute in the appropriate expressions for the cointegrating coefficients (18.37) and the speed-of-adjustment parameters (18.33) to obtain the slope coefficients of the VAR (18.36).

(b) The constants in your equations have not simplified to the VAR intercepts because the drift parameters β_1 and β_2 are implicitly defined in terms of the VAR parameters.

i. For each of your equations, give the restriction that must hold for the constant terms to reduce to the VAR intercept.

ii. Show how these two restrictions can be solved simultaneously to obtain expressions for β_1 and β_2 in terms of the VAR parameters.

(c) The coefficient λ_1 of the cointegrating vector is defined in terms of the VAR parameters by equation (18.37b). Recall that λ_1 also has an interpretation in terms of the drift parameters; from (18.23) this is

$$\lambda_1 = \beta_1 - \lambda\beta_2,$$

where λ is an arbitrarily chosen symbol used to denote a normalized cointegrating coefficient. By implication, λ must be implicitly defined in terms of the VAR parameters. Obtain an expression for λ in terms of

i. the parameters of the first equation of the VAR.

ii. the parameters of the second equation of the VAR.

Ultimately λ must be uniquely defined. Are your two expressions consistent? (*Hint:* Consult equation (18.37c).)

18.9 Cointegrating Rank

Thus far our discussion has been of single cointegrating relationships between variables. For example, purchasing power parity predicts a single cointegrating relationship between the nominal exchange rate e_n and the domestic and foreign

---

[13] The widely used econometrics package EViews implements all five of Johansen's specifications in its cointegration test command. Our two relevant forms for the ECM correspond to Options 2 and 4 of that command; the special case in which the time trend disappears is Option 3. EViews presents Option 3 as the default ECM specification, a peculiarity noted by Franses (2001). Our analysis suggests that Option 4 is the natural default.

TABLE 18.4   Cointegrating Rank

Number of variables, K	Number of distinct cointegrating relationships (cointegrating rank), r	Number of independent stochastic trends, $K - r$
2	0	2
	1	1
3	0	3
	1	2
	2	1
$\vdots$	$\vdots$	$\vdots$
K	0	K
	1	$K - 1$
	2	$K - 2$
	$\vdots$	$\vdots$
	$K - 1$	1

price levels P_d and P_f. However, in general, when we study the interactions among a number of variables there can be more than one long-run relationship among them. The number of cointegrating relationships is called the **cointegrating rank.** Let us denote the cointegrating rank by r. Among K variables, there can be between $r = 0$ and $r = K - 1$ long-run relationships. It is useful to illustrate this by considering some values for K. Our conclusions are summarized in Table 18.4.

Two Variables: $K = 2$. If the interaction of just two variables is being studied, there either is or is not a long-run relationship between them; either $r = 0$ or $r = 1$. If there is no long-run relationship the variables are not cointegrated; each is driven by a distinct stochastic trend, so there are $K - r = 2 - 0 = 2$ stochastic trends at work. If there *is* a long-run relationship, then the variables are cointegrated. By the common trends interpretation of cointegration, they are driven by one $(K - r = 2 - 1 = 1)$ common stochastic trend.

It is not possible to have more than one long-run relationship between two variables. The maximum cointegrating rank is $r = K - 1 = 2 - 1 = 1$.

Three Variables: $K = 3$. In the case of three variables, potentially these interact with one another in the long run in a number of ways. There could be no long-run relationships, so that $r = 0$ and the variables are driven by $K - r = 3 - 0 = 3$ distinct stochastic trends. Or there could be a single cointegrating relationship ($r = 1$) between just two or all three of the variables. Finally, among $K = 3$ variables there could be more than one long-run relationship. Let us illustrate these situations with some examples.

EXAMPLE 3

Consider the three macroeconomic variables real consumption C_t, real output Y_t, and the price level P_t. Suppose all three are I(1). What long-run relationships are likely to hold?

SOLUTION

By the cointegrating restrictions of balanced growth, C_t and Y_t should be cointegrated (at least in their logarithms). However, there is no reason why either or both of these would have a long-run equilibrium relationship with the price level; in the long run, real variables are determined independently of nominal variables. Consequently, there is just $r = 1$ cointegrating relationship among these $K = 3$ variables. The three variables are jointly driven by $K - r = 3 - 1 = 2$ distinct stochastic trends, one being the common stochastic trend driving the cointegrated variables and the other the trend driving prices.

Sometimes long-run relationships involve more than just variable pairs. Purchasing power parity is an example.

EXAMPLE 4

Consider the nominal exchange rate r_n, the domestic price level P_d, and the foreign price level P_f. Suppose all are I(1). What long-run relationships are likely to hold?

SOLUTION

Purchasing power parity is a single long-run relationship that involves all three variables. Beyond this, there are no additional long-run relationships; there is no reason, for example, why price levels in different countries evolve in a cointegrating manner because in the long run they are determined by independent monetary policies. Hence, the cointegrating rank is $r = 1$. There are $K - r = 3 - 1 = 2$ distinct stochastic trends. It is arbitrary which two variables we think of as being driven by these stochastic trends, the third then being driven by the long-run relationship with the other two.

Finally, sometimes there is more than one long-run relationship.

EXAMPLE 5

Consider the three macroeconomic variables consumption C_t, investment I_t, and output Y_t. Suppose all are I(1). What long-run relationships are likely to hold?

SOLUTION

By the cointegrating relationships of balanced growth, the variable pairs (C_t, Y_t) and (I_t, Y_t) should be cointegrated in their logarithms. Thus, there are $r = 2$ cointegrating relationships. Notice that, if C_t and I_t each have long-run equilibrium relationships with Y_t, by implication they must themselves have a long-run relationship. That is, if C/Y and I/Y are stable great ratios, then so too must be

$$\frac{C_t}{Y_t} \times \frac{Y_t}{I_t} = \frac{C_t}{I_t}.$$

In other words, C_t and I_t must be cointegrated. However this "third" cointegrating relationship follows automatically from the other two; it is not a distinct or "independent" relationship. Among $K = 3$ variables, there can be at most $K - 1 = 2$ distinct cointegrating relationships; this is the maximum cointegrating rank. In this case, the variables are driven by a single ($K - r = 3 - 2 = 1$) stochastic trend—the stochastic trend driving Y_t must be the same one driving C_t and I_t, given their long-run equilibrium relationships.

With this background let us turn to the general case.

An Arbitrary Number of Variables: K. Generalizing from these examples, for K variables the cointegrating rank is between $r = 0$ and $r = K - 1$. The maximum cointegrating rank is one fewer than the number of variables; it is not possible for K variables to be related by more than $K - 1$ equilibrium relationships.

The number of distinct stochastic trends is $K - r$. In the absence of any equilibrium relationships (so $r = 0$), the K variables are unrelated in the long run and so each evolves according to its own stochastic trend; trivially, these are $K - r = K - 0 = K$ in number. When long-run relationships are present, on the other hand, the common trends interpretation of cointegration tells us that some variables share common stochastic trends, reducing the total number of distinct ones. In the extreme case of maximum cointegrating rank where the K variables have $r = K - 1$ cointegrating relationships, all variables are ultimately driven by one common stochastic trend: $K - r = K - (K - 1) = 1$.

18.10   Conclusions and Further Reading

This chapter has introduced methods for studying relationships between time series variables. It has emphasized that doing this requires distinguishing between long- and short-run behavior, this distinction being made precise by the concept of cointegration. One reason cointegration is important is that it permits the study of long-run relationships in a way that solves the spurious regressions problem. And remarkably, it does this in a way that permits the least squares estimation of these long-run relationships even in the presence of simultaneity—Stock's superconsistency result. By contrast, the estimation of short-run effects requires either appropriate exogeneity assumptions or some treatment of simultaneity, consistent with the development of these ideas in earlier chapters.

The key concept in the study of long- and short-run economic phenomena is the ECM. The practical importance of the ECM is established by the **Granger representation theorem,** due to Engle and Granger (1987), which proves that if I(1) variables are cointegrated they have an ECM representation. Engle and Granger were jointly awarded the 2003 Nobel Prize in Economics, the Nobel Committee citing them "for methods of analyzing economic time series. . . ." Johansen's (1988,

1995) contribution was to show how the representation theorem can be exploited within the VAR framework.

Building toward this treatment of temporal relationships between economic variables has been the primary focus of our development of time series methods in Chapters 15–18. Consequently, a number of important topics have been given short shrift or not discussed at all. Here are some of the more important ones.

Reduced Form, Recursive, and Structural VARs   In practice econometricians use several variants of VAR systems, some of which permit a role for contemporaneous right-hand-side variables. For an accessible survey of the use of different kinds of VARs in macroeconomic policy analysis and forecasting, see Stock and Watson (2001). In their terminology, we have discussed only **reduced form VARs.**

Short-Run Dynamics   In focusing on long-run relationships, only incidental coverage has been given of how econometricians study economic behavior in the short run. Much more can be said about this, both in the univariate context of Chapters 16 and 17 and in the multivariate context of the present chapter. For example, impulse response functions can be used not only in the univariate context of earlier chapters, but also in studying how a shock affects all the variables in a VAR system. Again, see Stock and Watson (2001).

Seasonality   Our treatment of time series analysis has abstracted from the important reality that economic data often exhibit significant seasonal variation. Thus, we have implicitly been assuming that data are annual or that seasonal variation is negligible. But in practice, of course, economic data are often quarterly or monthly, with variation that includes an important seasonal component. And, as we indicate in our earliest mention of seasonality in Section 1.1.3, contemporary practice is to model seasonality explicitly in a manner that is incorporated with the modeling of other sources of variation rather than through a preliminary deseasonalization of the series. Although it is not possible to pursue these methods in any detail, this topic follows naturally enough from others we have studied, such as dummy variables and the Beveridge-Nelson decomposition, that an introduction to these issues is given in Appendix 18B to this chapter.

Structural Breaks   Chapter 10 shows how to use dummy variables to capture structural shifts or breaks in economic relationships. But beyond mentioning structural breaks briefly in Chapter 15 as a possible source of nonstationarity, nothing more has been said about them. This is a significant omission, because structural breaks are often endemic to time series data. They can arise both from changes in technology or people's behavior, such as an unexplained decline in productivity growth or an increase in female labor force participation, and changes in government policy, such as a change in tax policy or altered monetary policy.

Structural breaks can be of critical importance in studying time series data. A structural break in a trend stationary process can cause it to "look like" a difference stationary one, so that in the presence of structural breaks unit root tests will fail to reject the unit root hypothesis too often. This point was first emphasized in a famous paper by Perron (1989) entitled "The Great Crash, the Oil Price Shock, and the Unit Root Hypothesis," in which he showed that the finding of a unit root in GDP can be the artifact of failing to treat structural breaks such as the Great Depression or the 1970s oil embargo. In the same way, structural breaks introduce size distortions into standard cointegration tests, causing them to be misleading.

Conditional Heteroskedasticity An important feature of many financial series is that they go through occasional periods of high volatility associated with, say, financial crises, interspersed with extended periods of comparative stability. Thus, not only are the returns stochastic, but so too is the volatility of those returns: The returns are heteroskedastic over time in such a way that the heteroskedasticity is autocorrelated. One way of thinking about this autocorrelated heteroskedasticity is that the variance today is conditional on the variance in recent periods, and so the clustering of volatility is called **conditional heteroskedasticity.**

Econometricians use two types of models to study series exhibiting clustered volatility: the **autoregressive conditional heteroskedasticity** (ARCH) model of Engle (1982) and the **generalized autoregressive conditional heteroskedasticity** (GARCH) model of Bollerslev (1986). An enormous number of empirical studies apply these techniques. The literature is nicely introduced by Bera and Higgins (1993) and Engle (2001).

Appendix 18A   Cointegration and the Cagan Model

Phillip Cagan's (1956) model of money demand under hyperinflation specifies the logarithm of real money holdings to be a function of expected inflation,

$$m_t - p_t = \alpha + \beta(p_{t+1}^e - p_t) + \varepsilon_t. \tag{18.39}$$

Taylor (1991) estimated Cagan's model by replacing expected inflation in the coming period, $p_{t+1}^e - p_t$, with the most recently observed rate of inflation, $\Delta p_t = p_t - p_{t-1}$:

$$m_t - p_t = \alpha + \beta \Delta p_t + \varepsilon_t. \tag{18.40}$$

Taylor derived this as the cointegrating regression implied by the Cagan model. His derivation draws on the arithmetic of integrated processes and so is of some interest to consider.

The expected rate of inflation $p_{t+1}^e - p_t$ is a forecast of the rate that will actually occur in the next period, Δp_{t+1}. The mistake that is made in forecasting is the forecast error

$$v_{t+1} \equiv \Delta p_{t+1} - (p_{t+1}^e - p_t).$$

What can be said about this forecast error? The most important feature that makes sense is that it should *not* trend, either deterministically or stochastically. It should not be the case that the mistakes people make in forecasting grow systematically larger over time; for the same reason, neither should the variance. That is, the forecast error v_t should be *stationary*.[14]

Consider substituting this forecast error into the Cagan model (18.39) and inverting to solve for future inflation Δp_{t+1}:

$$\Delta p_{t+1} = -\frac{\alpha}{\beta} + \frac{1}{\beta}(m_t - p_t) + u_{t+1}.$$

The disturbance is $u_{t+1} \equiv v_{t+1} - \varepsilon_t/\beta$. Because this composite disturbance is a linear combination of stationary series, it is itself stationary.

The left-hand-side variable Δp_{t+1} is the inflation rate, which we have found in Chapter 17 to be I(1) for the German and Polish data. Hence, its first difference $\Delta^2 p_{t+1}$ is stationary. Consider subtracting Δp_t from both sides of the relationship:

$$\Delta^2 p_{t+1} = -\frac{\alpha}{\beta} + \frac{1}{\beta}(m_t - p_t) - \Delta p_t + u_{t+1}.$$

Now, because $m_t - p_t$ and Δp_t are both I(1) and $\Delta^2 p_{t+1}$ and u_{t+1} are both stationary, this equation describes a linear combination of I(1) variables that is stationary. Multiplying this linear combination through by $-\beta$, it may be reexpressed as

$$(m_t - p_t) - \alpha - \beta \Delta p_t \sim \text{stationary}.$$

Equivalently, this is Taylor's cointegrating regression (18.40) that is estimated in step 1 of the cointegration analysis of Section 18.5.2.

Taylor's conclusion is that the statistical implication of Cagan's hyperinflation model is that real money holdings $m_t - p_t$ and inflation Δp_t should be cointegrated. Furthermore, the cointegrating vector $[1, -\alpha, -\beta]$ includes the parameters of interest in the Cagan model—specifically, the semielasticity β. Remember that the intuition of Cagan's model is that real money demand should fall in response to higher inflation. Hence, the cointegrating relationship between these variables should be inverse; that is, β should be negative. This was in fact the finding, as reported in Table 18.3.

Appendix 18B   Seasonality

Many time series variables are measured more often than once a year. Macroeconomic data such as GDP, employment, and prices are normally available quarterly or, in some cases, even monthly. Financial variables such as interest rates, foreign exchange rates, and stock prices are observed almost continuously, although they may be recorded for analysis on, say, a daily, weekly, or monthly basis.

Variation with the seasons is often an important part of the behavior of such variables. We recognize this in our earliest musings about economic time series

[14] This is a weaker assumption than the hypothesis of rational expectations, which assumes not just that forecast errors are stationary but that they are white noise. The rational expectations hypothesis is discussed in Appendix B, Section B.2.3. Engsted (1993) extended Taylor's analysis to incorporate the stronger assumption of rational expectations.

in Chapter 1, where equation (1.1) divided a variable Y_t into trend, cyclical, and seasonal components:

$$Y_t = T_t + C_t + S_t. \tag{18.41}$$

For many years, there was a tradition among economists of abstracting from seasonal variation in the study of the trend and cyclical components of economic variables. This was done by removing the seasonal component through a univariate seasonal adjustment of the variable and studying the resulting deseasonalized series, as we describe briefly in Section 1.1.3. The idea was that, because seasonality is a noneconomic phenomenon, this component of the series should be removed in order to study the behavior of the variable that is attributable purely to economic forces. This approach was so widely accepted that many macroeconomic variables were published by statistical agencies in seasonally adjusted form and were often unavailable in their original unadjusted form. This practice continues to this day.

More recently, however, the tendency has been to question this tradition and instead to explicitly model the seasonal component of a variable jointly with its trend and cyclical components. One impetus to this change is the insights into the interaction of the trend and cyclical components that have been provided by difference stationary models. Recall that in Chapter 17 the Beveridge-Nelson decomposition of an I(1) variable has permanent and transitory components, the permanent component consisting of deterministic and stochastic trends:

$$Y_t = \underbrace{DT_t + ST_t}_{Y_t^P} + Y_t^T.$$

In terms of the earlier notation (18.41), the permanent component Y_t^P is the trend T_t and the transitory component Y_t^T is the cycle C_t.

As we have emphasized, one of the most important lessons of the difference stationary approach is that the trend consists of both deterministic and stochastic components, a subtlety that is lost on the trend stationary approach. Consequently, the econometric modeling of economic variables must treat trend and cycle jointly rather than viewing them as independent influences that can be separated for study in the way that the trend stationary approach, and a naive interpretation of the decomposition (18.41), might suggest. As Nelson and Kang (1981, 1984) showed, attempting to study the fluctuations in an economic variable by first eliminating its long-run behavior through a preliminary deterministic detrending will fundamentally misspecify its short-run behavior.

These insights suggest that much the same may be true of the seasonal component S_t. The stochastic behavior of seasonality may interact with the stochastic trend and transitory components in a way that makes treating seasonality as a separately modelable independent influence quite inappropriate. Attempting to eliminate the seasonal component through a preliminary deseasonalization may be just as misguided as a preliminary detrending. Good introductions to this view, certainly

THEORY MEETS APPLICATION   18.1

Money, the Economy, and Seasonality

The quantity of money in circulation tends to be procyclical, rising at the peak of the business cycle and falling during recessions. Economists have long debated the direction of causality in this relationship. Because increases in the money supply take place through new loan creation that involves a temporary decline in interest rates and an increase in business investment, which in turn may stimulate economic activity generally, one possibility is that the direction of causality flows from money to national income. This view goes back to at least Fisher (1920). As we have seen in Section 16.1.2, monetary shocks have long been regarded as a possible impulse mechanism within the Frisch-Slutsky paradigm. In a similar vein, Section 16.4.2 cites monetary policy as an example of a transitory shock. This view was supported by the landmark book of Friedman and Schwartz (1963), who carefully documented the tendency of money to lead economic activity.

In a classic contribution to monetary economics, Tobin (1970) argued that the inference that the Friedman-Schwartz evidence supports the money-causes-income hypothesis is an example of the fallacy of *post hoc ergo propter hoc* (Latin for "after this, therefore because of this"). He suggested instead that procyclical variation in money could arise as the passive response of people's money-holding practices to economic activity, so that causality flows in the other direction: An economic boom leads people to hold more money to facilitate the larger number of transactions taking place, and a recession leads to the opposite. Tobin

constructed a model in which this occurs in such a way that the demand for money leads income. This idea was incorporated into a real business cycle model by King and Plosser (1984), in which procyclical money can occur in an economy in which the impulses driving the business cycle originate on the real side. For a textbook treatment of a Tobin-type mechanism, see Champ and Freeman (2001, Chap. 9).

The subtleties of the money-income relationship make it difficult to distinguish between these two hypotheses empirically. In an innovative study, Barsky and Miron (1989) used the seasonal behavior of money to do this. They found that quarterly growth in money is strongly related to quarterly growth in output. In the fourth quarter, for example, Christmas consumption spending stimulates economic activity, and the money supply increases as the banking system accommodates people's demand for money to use in their purchases. Note that this seasonal causality must be from output to money; no one believes that the Christmas boom is caused by the increase in the money supply.

The Barsky-Miron analysis is important evidence favoring the Tobin hypothesis. At least as important as the light it sheds on the money-income debate, their study makes the point that the seasonal behavior of economic variables can sometimes provide important insights into economic questions that have nothing to do with seasonality.

now the dominant one among econometricians, are Miron (1994) and, at a more technical level, Ghysels (1994). Miron (1996) surveys important research on reformulating the econometric study of macroeconomic phenomena so as to model seasonal variation jointly with the other time series components.

Treating Seasonality

If seasonality is not to be treated through univariate seasonal adjustment but instead is to be incorporated explicitly into econometric models, how is this to be done? There are three ways of modeling seasonality.

Deterministic seasonality. We have seen in Chapter 10 that dummy variables are often used to describe seasonality. For example, with quarterly data four dummies could be defined and the variable Y_t specified as

$$Y_t = \alpha_1 D_{1t} + \alpha_2 D_{2t} + \alpha_3 D_{3t} + \alpha_4 D_{4t} + u_t.$$

This is, of course, equivalent to using three dummies and an intercept. The same idea can be used in more complicated models involving trends or cointegrating relationships. The implication of this specification is that the variable evolves according to the ARMA disturbance u_t around a mean that shifts with the seasons. Seasonality is deterministic in that it does not affect the autocorrelation function of the variable. Recall that the ACF of a variable is determined by its stochastic component, not by any deterministic component. Consequently, Y_t simply inherits the ACF of the disturbance u_t; this is unaffected by the pattern of seasonality as reflected in the dummy coefficients α_k.

The optimal forecast of the variable in quarter k is its mean α_k plus, in the short run, any predictable component of u_t. This specification will be appropriate in situations in which the influence of the seasons is unchanged from year to year; for example, when the effect of Christmas on fourth quarter retail sales relative to their average level is the same year after year.

Seasonal integration. An alternative specification for seasonality is that the variable evolves in an I(1) manner from year to year in any given season, say

$$Y_t = Y_{t-4} + u_t.$$

A drift coefficient could be included if the variable is growing systematically. This seasonality is stochastic, in that it affects the ACF. If the disturbance were white noise, $u_t = \varepsilon_t$, then Y_t would be autocorrelated only at every fourth lag, so that the ACF is nonzero only at the "seasonal frequency." In general, the ARMA disturbance u_t introduces autocorrelation at nonseasonal frequencies, but the ACF will nevertheless have peaks at the seasonal frequency.

Under this specification, the optimal forecast for this quarter is the value in the same quarter the year before, plus any other predictable influences captured by the autocorrelation in u_t. In forecasting sales this Christmas, a retailer begins by asking "What happened this time last year?"—a forecasting technique that may well correspond to the informal predictions of many people in business and government.

THEORY MEETS APPLICATION   **18.2**

Inventories, Production Smoothing, and Seasonality

As we have discussed in Theory Meets Application 3.1, fluctuations in inventory stocks are an important component of GDP fluctuations over the business cycle. Firms' inventory holding behavior has therefore long been of interest to economists.

There are many reasons why firms hold inventories. One that has been intensively studied is the idea of **production smoothing:** When firms face fluctuating sales, production costs may be minimized by smoothing production relative to sales, the difference being met by inventory accumulation or decumulation. For example, a toy manufacturer may produce at a fairly constant rate throughout the year, building up inventories to meet Christmas sales.

There are other reasons why firms hold inventories. A clothing store has inventories of garments because shoppers want to see a range of colors, fabrics, and styles. Its inventory stocks are a **factor of production,** like labor or capital more generally.

Production smoothing does not depend on uncertainty; even if Christmas sales were perfectly predictable, it would still be optimal to produce in anticipation of that demand. By contrast, uncertainty with respect to future sales makes it desirable to use inventories to meet random demand. That is, there is also a **buffer stock** motive for inventory holding.

How important is production smoothing relative to other motives? Miron and Zeldes (1988) pointed out that, because seasonal fluctuations in sales are largely predictable, if production smoothing is important there should be a strong seasonal component to inventory holding. Firms should use seasons of weak demand to build up their inventories, drawing them down to meet demand in seasons when sales are strong.

Remarkably, they found that this is not the case. Instead, most firms produce "just in time" to meet sales, apparently not finding it profitable to use predictable seasonal demand to smooth production. This suggests that production smoothing is not an important motive for inventory holding and that economists' efforts to understand inventory fluctuations in terms of production smoothing are misplaced. Instead, we must look to other reasons, such as their role as a factor of production or as buffer stocks, to understand the important role that inventory accumulation and decumulation play in the business cycle.

Why is production smoothing not important? Remember that inventory holding is expensive. Inventories must be financed and insured. As well, they must be stored so as to be protected from spoilage, damage, and theft; this storage is costly. Apparently, these costs outweigh any benefits of production smoothing for most firms.

The finding that production smoothing is not an important motive for inventory holding is consistent with the relative volatilities of production and sales over the business cycle. In Theory Meets Application 3.1 we note that inventory stocks are procyclical, accumulating in boom periods when production exceeds sales and decumulating in recessions when sales exceed production. This means that production is more volatile than sales, so that at the level of the economy as a whole production is not being smoothed relative to sales.

Stationary seasonality. A third possibility is that seasonal variation is stationary, so that the usual stationary AR and MA models hold at the seasonal frequency; modifying equations (16.4) and (16.6), the simplest examples are

$$Y_t = \phi_0 + \phi Y_{t-4} + \varepsilon_t \quad (|\phi| < 1) \qquad \text{and} \qquad Y_t = \alpha + \varepsilon_t + \theta \varepsilon_{t-4}.$$

Because these processes are stationary, they have a constant mean; unlike the other specifications, the mean does not shift from season to season. The long-term quarterly forecast does not, therefore, depend on the season—in the long run the forecast for Christmas is the same as for any other quarter. Because it is difficult to think of examples in which this would be a plausible description of seasonality, it is not one that sees much use. Furthermore, in situations in which it might be applicable the implications for modeling are no different from those for autocorrelation from any other source. The researcher should simply estimate an appropriately specified ARMA model because autocorrelation due to seasonality is not qualitatively different from any other kind of stationary temporal dependence.

The main choice in modeling seasonality is therefore between deterministic seasonality and seasonal integration. The difference is analogous to the difference between deterministic and stochastic trends in modeling the trend in a series. Recall that the Dickey-Fuller test is of the null hypothesis of I(1) against the alternative of trend stationarity. As a generalization of this, Hylleberg, Engle, Granger, and Yoo (1990) developed a test of the null of seasonal integration against the alternative of deterministic seasonality. Their procedure has since been widely applied. One example is Beaulieu and Miron (1993), who found that seasonal integration is often rejected. This led Miron (1994, 1996) to advocate deterministic seasonality as a satisfactory specification for many purposes. For a dissenting view, see Hylleberg (1994).

A

Laws of Summation and Deviation Form

A.1 Laws of Summation

Consider a variable X for which we have a series of observations X_i $(i = 1, \ldots, n)$. The total of the X_i values arises so frequently in algebraic expressions that it is useful to have notation to represent it. The conventional means of denoting the sum of the X_i is with **summation notation:**

$$\sum_{i=1}^{n} X_i \equiv X_1 + X_2 + \cdots + X_n.$$

The following three elementary rules apply to the use of summation notation in manipulating algebraic expressions.

Law A.1   *Any multiplicative factor that is not indexed, and is therefore common to each term, may be factored out of the summation:*

$$\sum_{i=1}^{n} a X_i = a \sum_{i=1}^{n} X_i.$$

Proof:

$$\sum_{i=1}^{n} a X_i = a X_1 + a X_2 + \cdots + a X_n = a(X_1 + X_2 + \cdots + X_n) = a \sum_{i=1}^{n} X_i. \quad \square$$

Law A.2   *If a common (i.e., nonindexed) term is added n times, the result is simply n times that term:*

$$\sum_{i=1}^{n} a = na.$$

Proof:

$$\sum_{i=1}^{n} a = \underbrace{a + a + \cdots + a}_{n \text{ times}} = na$$

$\square$

Law A.3   *When a summation sign is applied to an expression that is itself a sum of terms, the summation may be applied to each of the terms individually:*

$$\sum_{i=1}^{n}(X_i + Y_i) = \sum_{i=1}^{n} X_i + \sum_{i=1}^{n} Y_i.$$

Proof:

$$\sum_{i=1}^{n}(X_i + Y_i) = (X_1 + Y_1) + (X_2 + Y_2) + \cdots + (X_n + Y_n)$$

$$= (X_1 + X_2 + \cdots + X_n) + (Y_1 + Y_2 + \cdots + Y_n)$$

$$= \sum_{i=1}^{n} X_i + \sum_{i=1}^{n} Y_i$$

$\square$

EXERCISES

In each of the following exercises indicate clearly which laws you use in establishing the result.

A.1 Suppose the variable Z_i is a linear function of X_i: $Z_i = a + bX_i$.

(a) Establish how their averages $\overline{Z}$ and $\overline{X}$ are related.

(b) Consider the special case in which $Z_i = bX_i$. Indicate how the averages $\overline{Z}$ and $\overline{X}$ are related, explaining how this follows as a special case of your general result in part a.

(c) Consider the special case in which $Z_i = a + X_i$. Indicate how the averages $\overline{Z}$ and $\overline{X}$ are related, explaining how this follows as a special case of your general result in part a.

A.2 Consider a variable Z_i that is a linear combination of the variables X_i and Y_i: $Z_i = aX_i + bY_i$.

(a) Establish how $\sum Z_i$ is related to $\sum X_i$ and $\sum Y_i$. Indicate clearly the laws of summation you have used in your derivation.

(b) Establish how $\overline{Z}$ is related to $\overline{X}$ and $\overline{Y}$.

A.2   Laws of Deviation Form

If a variable X_i is transformed by subtracting its mean $\overline{X}$ from all observations, the resulting deviations from the mean are called its *deviation form*:

$$x_i = X_i - \overline{X} \qquad (i = 1, \ldots, n).$$

Deviation-form notation is extremely useful in econometrics because, as a result of satisfying the following rules, it simplifies many expressions and derivations.

Law A.4   *The sum of any variable in deviation form is identically equal to zero:*

$$\sum_{i=1}^{n} x_i = 0.$$

Proof:

$$\sum_{i=1}^{n} x_i = \sum_{i=1}^{n} (X_i - \overline{X}) = \sum_{i=1}^{n} X_i - n\overline{X} = \sum_{i=1}^{n} X_i - \sum_{i=1}^{n} X_i = 0 \qquad \square$$

Law A.5   *Defining a second variable Y_i with deviation form y_i, it is the case that*

$$\sum_{i=1}^{n} x_i y_i = \sum_{i=1}^{n} x_i Y_i.$$

Proof:

$$\sum_{i=1}^{n} x_i y_i = \sum_{i=1}^{n} x_i (Y_i - \overline{Y}) = \sum_{i=1}^{n} x_i Y_i - \overline{Y} \sum_{i=1}^{n} x_i = \sum_{i=1}^{n} x_i Y_i \qquad \square$$

The last step uses Law A.4.

Law A.5 says that, in an expression of the form $\sum x_i y_i$, it is always possible to switch one of the two variables from deviation to raw form. Note, however, that it is *not* legitimate to switch both variables to raw form. That is, $\sum x_i y_i \neq \sum X_i Y_i$, as you will confirm in Exercise A.6. As a corollary in which Y_i is set equal to X_i, it follows that $\sum x_i^2 \neq \sum X_i^2$.

EXERCISES

Establish the following properties of deviation-form notation.

A.3 Suppose the variable Z_i is a linear function of X_i: $Z_i = a + bX_i$.

(a) How are their deviation forms z_i and x_i related? (*Hint:* Use the result from Exercise A.1.)

(b) Consider the special case in which $Z_i = bX_i$. Indicate how the deviation forms z_i and x_i are related, explaining how this follows as a special case of your general result in part a.

(c) Consider the special case in which $Z_i = a + X_i$. Indicate how the deviation forms z_i and x_i are related, explaining how this follows as a special case of your general result in part a.

A.4 A variable's sample variance s^2 is given by equation (2.7). Suppose the variable Z_i is a linear function of X_i: $Z_i = a + bX_i$. Use the result in

Exercise A.3 to establish the relationship between s_Z^2 and s_X^2.

A.5 Consider a variable Z_i that is a linear combination of the variables X_i and Y_i: $Z_i = aX_i + bY_i$.

(a) Use the result in Exercise A.2 to show how the deviation forms z_i, x_i, and y_i are related.

(b) Derive an expression for z_i^2 in terms of x_i and y_i.

(c) Show how the sample variance s_Z^2 is related to the sample variances s_X^2 and s_Y^2 and the sample covariance s_{XY}.

A.6 Show that $\displaystyle\sum_{i=1}^{n} x_i y_i = \sum_{i=1}^{n} X_i Y_i - n\overline{XY}$.

A.7 Show that $\displaystyle\sum_{i=1}^{n} x_i^2 = \sum_{i=1}^{n} X_i^2 - n\overline{X}^2$.

A.8 Given the result in Exercise A.7, what conclusion can be drawn concerning

(a) the relative magnitudes of the quantities $\sum X_i^2$ and $n\overline{X}^2$?

(b) the relative magnitudes of $\sum x_i^2$ and $\sum X_i^2$?

B

Distribution Theory

Methods of statistical inference make routine use of the concepts of a random variable, a probability distribution, mathematical expectation, and several laws governing the use of expected values and variances. This appendix reviews these important ideas.

B.1 Random Variables and Probability Distributions

A **random variable** is a rule that assigns a numerical value to each outcome of a random experiment. As perhaps the simplest example imaginable, consider the experiment of flipping a coin. The possible outcomes are a head (H) or a tail (T); a list of all possible outcomes of such a random experiment is called the **sample space.** If we assign the value 1 to a head and 0 to a tail, we have defined a random variable. Let us call it Y. The probabilities associated with Y may be summarized in a table; if the coin is fair, they are:

y	$f(y)$
0	1/2
1	1/2

or, using a formula:

$$f(y) = \frac{1}{2}, \qquad y = 0, 1. \tag{B.1}$$

Note that the lowercase symbol y is used to denote the particular values taken on by the random variable; the function $f(y)$ is used to denote the associated probabilities. These two pieces of information fully characterize a random variable and are called its **probability distribution.** On any single running of the experiment only one of the particular y values can occur; this is called the **realization** of the random variable.

More generally, if the coin is not necessarily fair but lands heads with probability π $(0 < \pi < 1)$, then the probability distribution is given by:

y	$f(y)$
0	$1 - \pi$
1	π

or in terms of a formula:

$$f(y) = \pi^y (1 - \pi)^{1-y}, \qquad y = 0, 1. \tag{B.2}$$

This is called the **Bernoulli distribution** after the Swiss mathematician Jacob Bernoulli (1654–1705), who was the first to study it in detail. A random experiment in which there are just two possible outcomes, such as flipping a coin, is called a Bernoulli trial. It is often convenient to think of the two outcomes as success and failure.

It is evident that the behavior of a Bernoulli random variable is completely characterized by the value of π because this fully determines the distribution. For example, knowledge that $\pi = 1/2$ yields the probabilities (B.1) for each possible value of the random variable. π is an example of a **parameter** of a distribution; parameters are simply key features of a distribution that, in common with the specified form of the distribution (in this case Bernoulli), fully describe the behavior of the random variable. The Bernoulli distribution has just the single parameter π. Other distributions are more complicated and have more than one parameter. Let us turn to such an example.

As a slightly more complicated random experiment, consider flipping a coin three times. The sample space consists of the eight possible outcomes HHH, HHT, HTH, THH, HTT, THT, TTH, TTT. If the coin is fair, each outcome has probability 1/8. As an example of a random variable defined on this sample space, let Y denote the number of heads. This random variable can take on only four values which, along with their respective probabilities, may be summarized as:

y	$f(y)$	
0	1/8	
1	3/8	(B.3)
2	3/8	
3	1/8	

This probability distribution could also be expressed graphically or as a formula. The formula is

$$f(y) = \frac{3!}{y!(3-y)!} \frac{1}{8}, \qquad y = 0, 1, 2, 3. \tag{B.4}$$

The exclamation symbol ! denotes a **factorial** (3! is read "three factorial"), which is defined as follows: $n! \equiv n(n-1)(n-2) \cdots 1$. For example, $3! = 3 \cdot 2 \cdot 1 = 6$.[1] You should verify that substitution of the y values into this formula yields the probabilities of the table.

---

[1] By definition $0! = 1$.

This example is a special case of the **binomial distribution,** which has the formula

$$f(y) = \frac{n!}{y!(n-y)!} \pi^y (1-\pi)^{n-y}, \qquad y = 0, 1, 2, \ldots n. \qquad (\text{B.5})$$

A binomial random variable has the interpretation as the number of successes in n independent Bernoulli trials, where π is the probability of success on any single trial; n and π are the parameters of the distribution. In the case in which Y is the number of heads in three flips of a fair coin, the values of these parameters are $n = 3$ and $\pi = 1/2$. Note that by substituting these values into (B.5) the binomial formula reduces to (B.4). In the special case of just a single trial, so that $n = 1$, observe that the binomial formula reduces to the Bernoulli distribution (B.2).

The Bernoulli and binomial distributions are examples of **discrete** probability distributions: The random variable takes on a countable number of values. This is in contrast to a **continuous** random variable, which takes on an infinite number of possible values in some continuous range. Consider, for example, the amount of time it will take you to solve Exercise B.1. Because time is measured continuously, this is a random value between zero and infinity. (Its realization will hopefully turn out to be close to the former!) Many economic variables are continuous or involve such fine gradations of measure that they are best thought of as continuous: length of time unemployed, quantity produced, price, GNP, and so on.

Although a discrete random variable takes on a countable number of values, it is possible for these to be infinite in number. Perhaps the simplest example is the **geometric distribution,** which gives the probability that the first success comes on the yth Bernoulli trial. That is, consider a series of Bernoulli trials in which the probability of a success on any one trial is π; let Y denote the trial on which the first success is encountered, and let $f(y)$ be the distribution of this random variable. The probability that the first success occurs on the first trial is π: $f(1) = \pi$. The probability that the first success occurs on the second trial is $f(2) = (1 - \pi)\pi$, which is the probability of a failure followed by a success. The probability of two failures followed by a success is $f(3) = (1 - \pi)^2 \pi$. And so on. It is evident that the pattern is:

y	$f(y)$
1	$\pi(1 - \pi)^0$
2	$\pi(1 - \pi)^1$
3	$\pi(1 - \pi)^2$
4	$\pi(1 - \pi)^3$
$\vdots$	$\vdots$

or, expressing the distribution as a formula,

$$f(y) = \pi(1 - \pi)^{y-1}, \qquad y = 1, 2, 3, \ldots . \qquad (\text{B.6})$$

Figure B.1 depicts the distribution for $\pi = 1/6$.

This random variable takes on an infinite number of possible values because we could conceivably go on running Bernoulli trials indefinitely without encountering

FIGURE B.1

The geometric distribution for $\pi = \frac{1}{6}$.

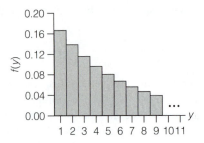

a success. It is called the geometric distribution because the probabilities $f(y)$ represent a geometric progression. By the properties of a geometric series, it may be confirmed that the probabilities in this distribution sum to 1:[2]

$$
\sum_{y} f(y) = \sum_{y=1}^{\infty} \pi(1 - \pi)^{y-1}
$$

$$
= \pi[(1 - \pi)^0 + (1 - \pi)^1 + (1 - \pi)^2 + \cdots] \tag{B.7}
$$

$$
= \pi \frac{1}{1 - (1 - \pi)} = 1.
$$

The geometric distribution is a special case of the **negative binomial** distribution, which gives the probability that the kth success occurs on trial y; the geometric distribution sets $k = 1$.

Continuous Distributions

Because a continuous random variable takes on values in a continuous range, its distribution cannot be expressed in tabular form and instead must be expressed as a formula. The formula for a continuous distribution is called a **probability density function** (pdf); that for a discrete distribution is called a **probability mass function** (pmf). The Bernoulli, binomial, and geometric distributions given by formulas (B.2), (B.5), and (B.6) are examples of pmf s. As an example of a pdf, consider the **continuous uniform distribution** graphed in Figure B.2(a); its formula is:

$$
f(y) = \frac{1}{\theta_1 - \theta_0}, \qquad \theta_0 \le y \le \theta_1. \tag{B.8}
$$

It is apparent that this distribution has two parameters; these are the values θ_0 and θ_1, which specify the range of Y. Outside this range, the pdf is, by definition, zero.

The continuous uniform distribution serves to illustrate the properties of density functions in relation to those of mass functions. First, just as the probabilities yielded by any pmf must be nonnegative, so too it is required of a pdf that $f(y) \ge 0$. However, note that, unlike a pmf, a pdf does not yield probabilities by direct

---

[2] Consider a geometric series in b: $1 + b + b^2 + b^3 + \cdots$. If $-1 < b < 1$, this series converges to $1/(1 - b)$. In (B.7), $b = 1 - \pi$, which, because π is a probability, satisfies $0 < b < 1$.

FIGURE B.2

The continuous uniform distribution.

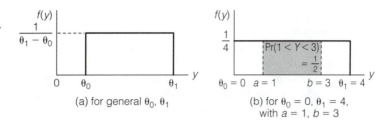

(a) for general θ_0, θ_1

(b) for $\theta_0 = 0$, $\theta_1 = 4$, with $a = 1$, $b = 3$

substitution; indeed, the probability that a continuous random variable yields a realization equal to any particular value is defined as zero. (The probability that it will take you exactly 5 minutes to complete Exercise B.1, as opposed to 5 minutes plus or minus some arbitrarily small amount of time, is zero.) Instead, a pdf may be used to find the probability that the random variable takes on values in some range. Graphically, this probability is the area under the pdf associated with that range. Mathematically, the area is given by an integral,

$$\Pr(a < Y < b) = \int_a^b f(y)\mathrm{d}y.$$

EXAMPLE 1

Consider the continuous uniform distribution with $\theta_0 = 0$ and $\theta_1 = 4$, as depicted in Figure B.2(b). Find the probability that $1 < Y < 3$.

SOLUTION

Examining Figure B.2(b), it is evident that $P(1 < Y < 3) = 1/2$. Integral calculus may be applied to obtain the same conclusion:

$$\Pr(1 < Y < 3) = \int_1^3 \frac{1}{4 - 0}\mathrm{d}y = \frac{y}{4}\Big|_1^3 = \frac{3}{4} - \frac{1}{4} = \frac{1}{2}.$$

Finally, just as a pmf has probabilities that sum to one, the area under a pdf must be equal to one:

$$\int_{-\infty}^{\infty} f(y)\mathrm{d}y = 1.$$

This means simply that it is certain that the random variable must take on a value somewhere within its range. For example, in the case of the continuous uniform distribution (B.8), Y must take on a value somewhere between θ_0 and θ_1 with probability 1:

$$\Pr(\theta_0 < Y < \theta_1) = \int_{\theta_0}^{\theta_1} \frac{1}{\theta_1 - \theta_0}\mathrm{d}y = \frac{y}{\theta_1 - \theta_0}\Big|_{\theta_0}^{\theta_1} = \frac{\theta_1}{\theta_1 - \theta_0} - \frac{\theta_0}{\theta_1 - \theta_0} = 1.$$

Although the continuous uniform distribution is useful in illustrating the properties of pdfs, it does not play a significant role in econometrics. A much more important example of a pdf is the **normal distribution,** which has the formula (2.2) given in Chapter 2. The normal distribution is another example of a distribution

having two parameters; these are denoted by μ and σ^2. They have the interpretations as the mean and variance of the random variable, concepts that are developed
in the following sections. If Y follows a normal distribution with mean μ and
variance σ^2, this is summarized by the notation $Y \sim N(\mu, \sigma^2)$. The special case of
$\mu = 0$ and $\sigma^2 = 1$ is called the **standard normal distribution:** $Y \sim N(0, 1)$.

The formula for the normal distribution is difficult to integrate. For this reason,
and because it is so frequently used, probabilities associated with the standard
normal distribution are tabulated. Other examples of continuous distributions that
have been tabulated are the t, F, and chi-square distributions. All are very heavily
used in applied econometrics.

Because the pdfs relevant to econometrics have been tabulated (or can easily
be integrated numerically by econometric software), the integration of continuous distributions in order to obtain probabilities is not, for our purposes, of great
practical interest. Of far greater importance is the role that integration plays in
defining the concepts of mathematical expectation and variance and establishing
rules associated with these concepts.

EXERCISES

B.1 Consider the experiment of flipping a fair coin
three times. Let us define a different random variable on the sample space from that used in this
section: Let Y take on the value 1 if all flips come
up the same, and 0 otherwise.

(a) Is this a discrete or continuous random variable?

(b) Express the probability distribution both as a
table and as a formula.

(c) This random variable is an example of one of
those discussed in this section. Which is it?

B.2 If a die is rolled repeatedly, what is the probability that the first six appears on the fourth role?

B.2   Mathematical Expectation

The **mean** or **expected value** of a random variable is the average value that occurs
in repeated runnings of the experiment. To illustrate, let us return to the example
of the number of heads in three flips of a coin. The sample space and associated
values of Y are as follows.

HHH HHT HTH THH HTT THT TTH TTT
3   2   1   0

The average value of Y that will occur in repetitions of the experiment is therefore

$$\frac{0+1+1+1+2+2+2+3}{8} = 0 \cdot \frac{1}{8} + 1 \cdot \frac{3}{8} + 2 \cdot \frac{3}{8} + 3 \cdot \frac{1}{8} = \frac{3}{2}.$$

Notice that this "average value" need not be a value that can actually occur as
a realization of the random variable. Comparing with the probability distribution

(B.3), it is apparent that the expected value of a discrete random variable is a probability weighted average of the form

$$\sum_{y} yf(y);$$

that is, a weighted average of the y values in which the weights are the respective probabilities $f(y)$ given by the pmf. The expected value is a measure of the center of the distribution; This is why it is also called the mean of the distribution, in analogy with the sample mean, which is the average value of a variable.

For a continuous random variable, the expected value is defined analogously in terms of its pdf; instead of summing over all y values, it is necessary to integrate over the full range of y, which is in general $-\infty$ to $+\infty$.

Definition B.1   *The* mathematical expectation *of a random variable Y is*

$$E(Y) = \begin{cases} \sum_{y} yf(y) & \text{if Y is discrete} \\ \int_{-\infty}^{\infty} yf(y)\mathrm{d}y & \text{if Y is continuous.} \end{cases}$$

The term *mathematical expectation* is used to emphasize the distinction between this mathematically precise concept of expectation and the "psychological" or "subjective" expectation that a person forms of the future. As an interesting aside, the problem often arises in economics of treating the role of subjective expectations; an economic model might, for example, specify interest rates as being influenced by agents' expectations of future inflation, expectations that must be formed in the face of uncertainty about the future. As we discuss in Section 1.2.5, economic models capture uncertainty through the introduction of random elements. Any such stochastic economic model implies probability distributions for the endogenous variables of the model. The technique of **rational expectations** models agents' subjective expectations as being equal to the mathematical expectations of the variables computed on the basis of these implied distributions. This equating of subjective and mathematical expectations, once controversial, is now the received methodology for the modeling of expectations formation in stochastic economic models. It had its earliest application in the field of finance, whence it spread to the rest of economics, because, as we see in Appendix C, it is natural to model the expected return on an investment as the mean of the distribution of that random return. In the next section, the rational expectations idea is illustrated in an analysis of the efficiency of barter versus monetary exchange.

We will make very heavy use of the notation $E(\cdot)$ for the mathematical expectation of a random variable. Particularly when the mean is a parameter of the distribution, however, it is convenient to use the even briefer notation μ. An example is the normal distribution, where $\mu = E(Y)$ is, as we have noted in examining the pdf (2.30), a parameter of the distribution. This use of the symbol

μ is, however, purely a matter of convenience, and in other contexts it might not be used. An example is the Bernoulli distribution.

EXAMPLE 2

Consider the Bernoulli distribution

$$f(y) = \pi^y (1 - \pi)^{1-y}, \qquad y = 0, 1.$$

Find the expected value of Y.

SOLUTION

The Bernoulli distribution is discrete. Applying the relevant definition,

$$E(Y) = \sum_y yf(y) = 0 \cdot (1 - \pi) + 1 \cdot \pi = \pi.$$

Hence, in our specification of the Bernoulli distribution we have chosen to use the symbol π to denote the mean of the distribution.

The formula for the expected value of a discrete random variable applies even if the random variable takes on an infinite number of values. For example, the mean of the geometric distribution (B.6) is[3]

$$E(Y) = \sum_y yf(y) = \sum_{y=1}^{\infty} y\pi(1 - \pi)^{y-1} = \frac{1}{\pi}. \tag{B.9}$$

Suppose, for instance, that the probability of success on any one trial is $\pi = 1/6$, as in Figure B.1. Then, on average, the first success occurs on the sixth trial; $E(Y) = 1/\pi = 1/(1/6) = 6$.

In the Bernoulli distribution, like the normal distribution, the mean $E(Y)$ is a parameter of the distribution. However, this is not necessarily the case for all distributions. An example is the uniform distribution.

EXAMPLE 3

Consider the continuous uniform distribution (B.8). Find the expected value of Y.

SOLUTION

Applying the definition of $E(Y)$ for a continuous distribution,

$$E(Y) = \int_{-\infty}^{\infty} yf(y)dy = \int_{\theta_0}^{\theta_1} y\frac{1}{\theta_1 - \theta_0}dy = \frac{y^2}{2}\frac{1}{\theta_1 - \theta_0}\Big|_{\theta_0}^{\theta_1}$$

$$= \frac{\theta_1^2 - \theta_0^2}{2(\theta_1 - \theta_0)} = \frac{(\theta_1 - \theta_0)(\theta_1 + \theta_0)}{2(\theta_1 - \theta_0)} = \frac{\theta_0 + \theta_1}{2}.$$

The expected value of a continuous uniform random variable is simply the average of its bounds.

Thus, although the mean of the continuous uniform distribution is a function of its parameters, neither parameter corresponds to its mean.

[3]   The proof uses the power series result that, for $-1 < b < 1$, $\sum_{y=1}^{\infty} yb^y = b/(1 - b)^2$. See Exercise B.4.

Expected Value of a Constant

As a final comment, it is worth noting that the expected value of a quantity that is *not* random is simply that quantity. That is, if X is nonrandom, then $E(X) = X$. Relating this to Definition B.1, X takes on just one value X with certainty, all other values with probability zero. Consequently, $E(X) = \sum_x xf(x) = X \cdot 1 = X$.

An expected value $E(Y) = \mu$ is, of course, itself some constant numerical value. It therefore follows that $E(EY) = E(\mu) = \mu$; that is, the expected value of an expected value is just that expected value.

EXERCISES

B.3 Find the expected value of the random variable Y in Exercise B.1. What is the probability that this expected value occurs as a realization of Y?

B.4 Use the property of a power series given in footnote 3 to establish (B.9).

B.2.1 Application: Ranking Random Alternatives

Random variables and their mathematical expectations play an important role in economic models involving uncertainty. In this section and the next, we illustrate this with two examples. Both are adapted from Champ and Freeman (2001). The first is an example of using mathematical expectations to rank alternative gambles. The second is a model of barter versus monetary exchange.

Economics is often said to be the science of choice. But often choices must be made in the face of uncertainty about the future. How do people make choices between alternatives when outcomes are random? One possibility is that alternatives are ranked according to expected outcomes, where these expectations are formed according to our concept of mathematical expectation. Consider the following example, adapted from Champ and Freeman (2001, pp. 228–229, Ex. 12.1).

EXAMPLE 4

Suppose that you are the sole shareholder of a savings and loan (S&L) with deposits of $1,200,000 and assets of $1,000,000. Because it is an incorporated enterprise, your liability in the S&L is limited to your investment (if it fails, you do not need to make up losses to depositors).

Suppose you may reinvest your assets into one, but only one, of the following projects before the examiners audit your books.

Project A: pays a certain return of 7%.
Project B: has a 50% chance of a 21% net return and
                    a 50% chance of a net return of −21%.
Project C: has a 10% chance of doubling your assets
                    and a 90% chance of losing everything.

Rank these projects according to how much they will benefit you personally.

SOLUTION

At present, the net worth of the S&L is negative: Assets − Liabilities = −$200,000. You will benefit only if the net worth can be made positive; however, you are not personally responsible for making up a negative net worth to depositors.

Project A pays a certain return of 7%, but this would still leave the net worth negative:

Net worth = $1.07 \times \$1,000,000 - \$1,200,000 = -\$130,000$.

Consequently, your personal benefit is zero.

Project B has a 50% chance of a 21% return, which would yield a positive net worth, and a 50% chance of a 21% loss, which would result in your net worth still being negative and your personal benefit being zero. Your expected personal benefit is

$0.5 \cdot (1.21 \times \$1,000,000 - \$1,200,000) + 0.5 \cdot (0) = \$5,000$.

Project C has a 10% chance of doubling your assets, which would yield a positive net worth, and a 90% chance of losing everything, which would result in your personal benefit being zero. Your expected personal benefit is

$0.1 \cdot (2 \times \$1,000,000 - \$1,200,000) + 0.9 \cdot (0) = \$80,000$.

On the basis of these expected personal benefits of 0, $5,000, and $80,000, your first choice is Project C, followed by B, with Project A the least favored. The conclusion is that under these circumstances it is in the interests of S&L ownership to invest in the riskiest project in which there is the greatest chance of loss of depositors' funds.

In treating choices among random alternatives as being made by comparing mathematical expectations, we have assumed that people care only about the means of the probability distributions they face. The implicit assumption about people's preferences is that they are **risk neutral:** People pay no attention to other features of the distributions such as their dispersion. In many situations, this may be unrealistic. People are more likely to be **risk averse;** if two gambles have the same expected return but different dispersions, so that one is riskier than the other, the less risky one is preferred. In Appendix C we develop in detail the modern theory of finance that is based on the belief that people are risk averse in making investment decisions. People are assumed to evaluate investment alternatives by taking into account not only the expected return on investments but also their risk. As a measure of risk we use, at least in the first instance, the variance, a concept introduced in Section B.4.

EXERCISES

B.5 Consider the three projects in Example 4.[4] Continue to assume that S&L ownership is risk neutral.

(a) How would your ranking change if the assets of the S&L were $1,200,000?

[4] Like Example 4 this exercise is taken from Champ and Freeman (2001, pp. 229, Ex. 12.1). This material is reprinted with the permission of Cambridge University Press.

(b) How would your ranking change if the assets of the S&L were $2,000,000?

(c) If you had the chance to abscond with $100,000 at the cost of losing ownership in the S&L, would you do it (setting aside questions of morality)? How does your answer depend on the net worth of the S&L?

(d) If S&Ls are covered by government deposit insurance, why should the government take an active role in closing down failed S&Ls as soon as they can be discovered? Answer with references to the examples in this exercise.

B.2.2 Application: Barter versus Monetary Exchange

Our second example using the concept of mathematical expectation to analyze economic uncertainty is a model of barter versus monetary exchange. The model is originally due to Freeman (1989). An accessible nontechnical treatment may be found in Champ and Freeman (2001, Chap. 2).

Why do we use money to facilitate the exchange of goods instead of obtaining them directly through barter? Common sense tells us that the answer lies in the number of goods that may be traded. Barter may be a satisfactory means of trade for a primitive economy in which the number of goods is small. This is because, when there are only a few goods, it is fairly easy to find someone else who both wants the commodity you have and has what you want—in Stanley Jevons's (1875) famous phrase, for a "double coincidence of wants" to occur. In an economy of any sophistication, on the other hand, the number of goods is such that it is very time consuming to find another trader for whom the double coincidence of wants is satisfied. Money eliminates this cost of barter.

How can this common sense be formalized? A model attempting to describe the benefits of monetary versus barter exchange requires two features. The first is the existence of many goods and many traders. The second is some element of the passage of time because the "store of value" function of money is intrinsic to its serving as a medium of exchange. In describing a model of this type, Champ and Freeman (2001, pp. 34–35) offer the following allegory.[5]

> Consider a model economy ... in which there are J different types of goods. Each person is endowed with ... one type of good when young and with nothing when old. Equal numbers of the young are endowed with each type of good. When young, individuals wish to consume the type of good with which they are endowed. When old, they will wish to consume one of the other types of goods. However, young people do not know what type of good they will want to consume when old.
>
> There exists a fixed stock of M units of fiat money, which is also costlessly stored. In the first period, the stock of fiat money is owned by the initial old. To allow an alternative to fiat money, we assume that goods can be stored costlessly over time.

---

[5] Reprinted with the permission of Cambridge University Press.

People live on a large number of spatially separated islands. Everyone on a given island has the same endowments and tastes. Hence, all young people on a given island will be endowed with the same type of good. For example, a large number of islands will have young people endowed with good 1 when young and similarly for the remaining goods. When old, all the people on a given island will again desire to consume the same type of good, a good with which they were not endowed.

People who want to trade must travel in a group to a trading area, where a group from one island is matched at random with a group from another island seeking to trade. When the people from a pair of islands meet, they can reveal to each other the type of good they are carrying and the type of good they want. If the groups agree to trade, they do so and go home. If they do not both wish to trade, they split and are each matched again with some other island. We assume that islands searching for trading partners can choose to search among the young or the old.

Exchange is costly in the following way. Each time a group from one island is matched with a group from another island, each person in the group loses α units of utility. This represents the bother of searching for a suitable trading partner.

There are two ways, then, that a young person in this economy can provide for consumption in old age. One is through monetary exchange, when the right match occurs (with another island in which the old seek the good with which this young person has been endowed), by trading the good for the money of the old. This money is then carried into old age, to be spent on the needed consumption good when, again, the right match occurs. The second route by which the needs of the old may be satisfied is through barter, by holding the unconsumed portion of the endowment to old age and at that time trading it directly for the needed consumption good when a match occurs for which the double coincidence of wants is satisfied.

Let us consider each of these in turn, beginning with barter. As an agent seeking to trade by barter, you must wait for the right random match to occur. How long are you likely to have to wait? A successful match will be one in which agents of the other island both want the particular good that you have and have what you want in return. Consider an economy of just $J = 3$ goods, as illustrated in Table B.1. The agents of any other island with which you are matched will have a pattern of endowments and desires corresponding to one of the asterisks in this table. (The diagonal entries are not possibilities because our description of the model has ruled out agents consuming in old age the good with which they were endowed in youth.) There are, then, $J^2 - J$ possibilities, only one of which satisfies the double coincidence of wants. Thus, any one random match is a Bernoulli trial in which the probability of success is $\pi = 1/(J^2 - J)$. In the case of $J = 3$, for example, $\pi = 1/6$.

Returning to our original question, how long are you likely to have to wait for a successful match? The probability that the first success comes on the yth trial is, as we have seen in Section B.1, given by the geometric distribution (B.6). On average, agents in this economy wait until trial $E(Y)$ for the double coincidence of wants to be satisfied. From the result (B.9) of the previous section, this mean

TABLE B.1

Endowments and Desired Goods ($J = 3$)

Good desired	Endowment		
	a	b	c
a		*	*
b	*		*
c	*	*	

Source: Champ and Freeman (2001, Figure 2.1). Reprinted with the permission of Cambridge University Press.

FIGURE B.3

Rational expectations: Under uncertainty, your best guess is the mathematical expectation.

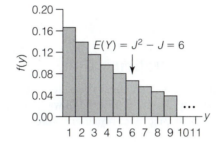

of the geometric distribution is

$$E(Y) = \frac{1}{\pi} = J^2 - J.$$

For $J = 3$ goods, on average agents will wait until the sixth match to be able to trade by barter. This is their best guess as to how long they will have to wait. The hypothesis of rational expectations says that sensible agents will use this mathematical expectation in forming their psychological expectations concerning the cost of barter. Figure B.3 depicts this by indicating the mean of the distribution given in Figure B.1. Because each match involves a utility loss of α, you expect that barter will involve a utility loss of $\alpha(J^2 - J)$.

How does this compare with the alternative of monetary exchange? Unlike barter, which involves just a single trade of goods for goods, monetary exchange involves two steps: (1) a trade of the endowment good for money, followed by (2) a second trade of money for the good desired in old age. At the first step, the probability of any one trial resulting in a match with an island on which the old seek your particular good is $\pi = 1/J$. Again applying the mean of the geometric distribution (B.9), your best guess is that you will have to wait $1/\pi = J$ matches for this to happen. At the second step, the probability that any one trial successfully matches you with the goods you want to buy is also $\pi = 1/J$, and again you expect to wait J times for this to occur. In total, then, the expected cost of monetary exchange is $2\alpha J$.

How do the costs of the two modes of exchange compare? For $J > 3$ goods, these results allow us to conclude that

$$\text{Expected cost of barter} = \alpha(J^2 - J) > 2\alpha J$$

$$= \text{Expected cost of monetary exchange.}$$

This formalizes our commonsense intuition that, for all but the most primitive economies, the use of money offers an efficiency over barter.

EXERCISES _____

B.6 Graph the cost of barter versus monetary exchange for $J = 2$ through $J = 5$.

B.2.3 Rational Expectations

Notice how these examples use mathematical expectations to model agents' behavior in the face of uncertainty. John Muth (1961) was the first to formulate an economic model in which mathematical expectations were used to model subjective expectations.

Of course behaving in this way could turn out to be a mistake, in the sense that events might unfold in such a way that the agent would have been better off making a different decision. It happens all the time that with the benefit of hindsight we would have done things differently. An agent operating in an economy with many goods who nevertheless chooses to trade by barter might just happen to quickly encounter others for whom the double coincidence of wants is satisfied. Ex post the cost of barter could turn out to be low on occasion. But the probability of this happening is very small. The hypothesis of rational expectations does not say that agents are always right or that they do not make decisions that, in retrospect, they may regret. It just says that sensible agents will use their knowledge of the economic environment to assess the risks they face in a rational manner.

This approach assumes that agents have some idea of the probabilities associated with the range of possible events that may occur. If the agents in our model of monetary versus barter exchange had no understanding of their economic environment and consequently had no idea of the probability of successfully matching under the two modes of exchange, it would not be possible to use a mathematical expectation to treat their subjective expectations. Indeed, in the 1920s the economist Frank Knight distinguished between situations of *risk*, which he defined as those in which agents were capable of assigning probabilities, and those of *uncertainty*, in which agents' knowledge of their environment was so limited that probabilities could not be assigned. However, Knight's distinction is today primarily of historical interest. Most economists regard economic decisions as typically being taken in contexts in which agents have a fair understanding of the probability distributions they face.

As just one example, consider business cycle phenomena. How should we model the effect on an agent's behavior of the possibility that, say, a recession next year will lead to a spell of unemployment?

> Even to begin to think about decision problems of this general form, one needs to imagine a fairly precise view of the future in the mind of this agent. Where does he get this view, and how can an observer infer what it is?...
>
> John Muth (1961) proposed to resolve this problem by identifying agents' subjective probabilities with observed frequencies of the events to be forecast, or with the "true" probabilities, calling the assumed coincidence of subjective and "true" probabilities *rational expectations*. Evidently, this hypothesis will not be of value in understanding psychotic behavior. Neither will it be applicable in situations in which one cannot guess which, if any, observable frequencies are relevant: situations which Knight called "uncertainty." It will *most* likely be useful in situations in which the probabilities of interest concern a fairly well defined recurrent event, situations of "risk" in Knight's terminology. In situations of risk, the hypothesis of rational behavior on the part of agents will have usable content, so that behavior may be explainable in terms of economic theory. In such situations, expectations are rational in Muth's sense.. . .
>
> Insofar as business cycles can be viewed as repeated instances of essentially similar events, it will be reasonable to treat agents as reacting to cyclical changes as "risk," or to assume their expectations are *rational*, that they have fairly stable arrangements for collecting and processing information, and that they utilize this information in forecasting the future in a stable way, free of systematic and easily correctable biases. (Lucas 1977, pp. 14–15)

Recessions are not, then, on-off events of which agents have no experience. Quite the contrary, economic agents have typically lived through periods of boom and bust in the past. This is just one small part of the generally risky environment in which they live, and it is a risk they are able to gauge. They may be modeled as having the ability to assess the risk of future unemployment and to incorporate this assessment into their plans.

B.3   Expected Value of a Function

Often one random variable is defined in terms of another, say $Y = g(X)$, where $g(\cdot)$ denotes the functional relationship between the two. (It is to be emphasized that $g(\cdot)$ does *not* denote a pmf or pdf). Obviously, the distributional properties of Y, including its mean, will be determined by the distribution of X and the nature of the function $g(\cdot)$. The following example is helpful in understanding such relationships.

EXAMPLE 5   Let X denote the number of heads in three flips of a coin. Define two new random variables $Y = g(X) = 1 + 2X$ and $Z = h(X) = X^2$. Find the probability distributions of Y and Z and use these to compute $E(Y)$ and $E(Z)$.

SOLUTION

The following table reproduces the pmf of X from (B.3) and computes the associated values of Y and Z.

x	$f(x)$	$y = g(x) = 1 + 2x$	$z = h(x) = x^2$
0	1/8	1	0
1	3/8	3	1
2	3/8	5	4
3	1/8	7	9

What are the probabilities associated with Y and Z? Clearly, they are the same as those given by $f(x)$ because Y takes on the value, say, 1 if and only if $X = 0$, and so on. Consequently, the expected values may be computed as

$$E(Y) = E[g(X)] = \sum_x g(x) f(x) = 1 \cdot \frac{1}{8} + 3 \cdot \frac{3}{8} + 5 \cdot \frac{3}{8} + 7 \cdot \frac{1}{8} = 4,$$

$$E(Z) = E[h(X)] = \sum_x h(x) f(x) = 0 \cdot \frac{1}{8} + 1 \cdot \frac{3}{8} + 4 \cdot \frac{3}{8} + 9 \cdot \frac{1}{8} = 3.$$

For a continuously distributed random variable, the expected value of a function is defined analogously in terms of an integral. In general, then, the following result is apparent.

Result B.1

The mathematical expectation of a function $g(X)$, where the random variable X has probability distribution $f(x)$, is

$$E[g(X)] = \begin{cases} \displaystyle\sum_x g(x) f(x) & \text{if } X \text{ is discrete} \\ \displaystyle\int_{-\infty}^{\infty} g(x) f(x) \, dx & \text{if } X \text{ is continuous.} \end{cases}$$

EXAMPLE 6

Let X follow a Bernoulli distribution. In Example 2, it is found that $E(X) = \pi$. Find $E(X^2)$.

SOLUTION

The Bernoulli distribution is given by (B.2) and is discrete. Applying the relevant definition,

$$E(X^2) = \sum_x x^2 f(x) = 0^2 (1 - \pi) + 1^2 \pi = \pi.$$

Hence, for the Bernoulli distribution, $E(X) = E(X^2) = \pi$.

When a new random variable Y is defined as a function $g(X)$, is there any dependable relationship between its expected value $E(Y)$ and $E(X)$? In general, the answer is no. In particular, note that in general the expected value of a function is *not* the function of the expected value; that is, $E[h(X)] \neq h(EX)$. This is illustrated in both Examples 5 and 6, where the function $h(X) = X^2$ was considered. In Example 5, it is found that $E[h(X)] = E(X^2) = 3$, which is clearly *not* equal to $h(EX) = h(3/2) = (3/2)^2 = 9/4$. Similarly, Example 6 shows that, for the Bernoulli distribution, $E(X^2) = \pi \neq \pi^2 = (EX)^2$.

There is, however, one important class of functions for which it is the case that the expected value of the function *is* the function of the expected value: These are linear functions, which take the form $g(X) = a + bX$. This is our first law of mathematical expectation.

Law B.1	*For a linear function $a + bX$ of a random variable X, where a and b are constants, it is the case that* $$E(a + bX) = a + bE(X).$$ *In other words, the expected value of a linear function is the linear function of the expected value.*

Proof:

Applying the definition of $E[g(X)]$ for a discrete random variable, and making use of the laws of summation,[6] yields

$$E(a + bX) = \sum_x (a + bx) f(x) = a \sum_x f(x) + b \sum_x x f(x) = a + bE(X).$$

The last step uses the fact that the probabilities in any pmf sum to 1: $\sum_x f(x) = 1$.

□

This proof is for the discrete case. An identical proof for the continuous case is obtained essentially by replacing the summation signs with integrals; this will continue to be true for all the other proofs of this appendix. Hence, the laws of mathematical expectation and variance apply regardless of whether the random variable is discrete or continuous.

EXAMPLE 7

The function $g(X) = 1 + 2X$ considered in Example 5 is a linear function in which $a = 1$ and $b = 2$. Confirm that Law B.1 holds.

SOLUTION

In Example 5, we find that $E[g(X)] = E(1 + 2X) = 4$. Recall that $E(X) = 3/2$, so $g(EX) = 1 + 2E(X) = 1 + 2(3/2) = 4$. This illustrates that the expected value of a linear function is the linear function of the expected value.

The constants a and b may, of course, take on any numerical values. Two useful special cases are obtained by considering the values $a = 0$ and $b = 1$. First, setting $a = 0$ yields the function $g(X) = bX$; Law B.1 allows us to conclude the following.

---

[6] The laws of summation are presented in Appendix A.

COROLLARY B.1.1. $E(bX) = bE(X)$.
That is, the expected value of a constant times a random variable is the constant times the expected value.

Second, setting $b = 1$ yields the function $g(X) = a + X$, giving us the following result.

COROLLARY B.1.2. $E(a + X) = a + E(X)$.
That is, the expected value of a constant added to a random variable is the constant plus the expected value.

EXERCISES

B.7 Let X take on the values -1, 0, and 1 with equal probability, and consider the function $Y = g(X) = X^2$. Compute $E(X)$ and $E(Y)$.

B.8 Let X be continuously uniformly distributed with $\theta_0 = 0$ and $\theta_1 = 1$. Compute $E(X^2)$.

B.4   Variance

In defining the expected value we have seen that it serves as a measure of the center of the distribution. Another feature of the behavior of a random variable that is typically of interest is its dispersion, the most common measure of which is the **variance.**

Definition B.2   *The* variance *of a random variable X is* $V(X) = E(X - EX)^2$.

Just as it is often useful to employ the symbol μ as shorthand notation for the expected value, so too the symbol σ^2 is often used as alternative notation for the variance. The units of measure of σ^2 are the square of the units in which X is defined. In situations in which it is desirable to have a measure of dispersion defined in the same units as the random variable, the **standard deviation** $\sigma = \sqrt{V(X)}$ is used.

From the definition $E[(X - EX)^2]$, it is apparent that the variance is essentially the mathematical expectation of a certain function of X, that function being of the form $g(X) = (X - \mu)^2$. Hence, it may be evaluated using the rules of the previous section. Because the function is nonlinear, Law B.1 does not apply. Instead, we must revert to the more fundamental Result B.1.

EXAMPLE 8 | Let X be the number of heads in three flips of a coin. Find $V(X)$.

SOLUTION

Applying Definition B.2 for the discrete case, and making use of our previous knowledge about this random variable, yields

$$V(X) = E(X - EX)^2 = \sum_x (x - \mu)^2 f(x)$$

$$= \left(0 - \frac{3}{2}\right)^2 \frac{1}{8} + \left(1 - \frac{3}{2}\right)^2 \frac{3}{8} + \left(2 - \frac{3}{2}\right)^2 \frac{3}{8} + \left(3 - \frac{3}{2}\right)^2 \frac{1}{8} = \frac{3}{4}.$$

It may be shown[7] that an alternative expression for the variance, equivalent to that of Definition B.2, is

$$V(X) = E(X^2) - (EX)^2. \tag{B.10}$$

EXAMPLE 9 | Find the variance of the Bernoulli distribution.

SOLUTION

Letting X denote a Bernoulli random variable, we have found in Examples 2 and 6 that $E(X) = E(X^2) = \pi$. Hence, applying (B.10),

$$V(X) = E(X^2) - (EX)^2 = \pi - \pi^2 = \pi(1 - \pi).$$

Because the variance is essentially a weighted sum of squares, as indicated by Example 8, it must be positive. It then follows that, for any random variable, $E(X^2) > (EX)^2$. This confirms our previous conclusion that, due to the nonlinear nature of the function $g(X) = X^2$, in general $E(X^2) \neq (EX)^2$.

EXERCISES

B.9 Let X be the number of heads in three flips of a coin. Compute the variance using the alternative formula (B.10).

B.10 Let X be Bernoulli. Compute its variance using Definition B.2.

B.11 Let X be continuously uniformly distributed

with $\theta_0 = 0$ and $\theta_1 = 1$. Compute its variance using

(a) Definition B.2.

(b) the alternative variance formula (B.10). (*Hint:* Use your answer to Exercise B.8.)

B.5   Variance of a Function

Just as we considered the expected value of a function of a random variable, so too can we consider the variance of such a function. As usual, it is helpful to begin with an example.

[7] The equivalence is proven in Example 17.

EXAMPLE 10

Returning to our previous example of X as the number of heads in three flips of a coin, consider again the linear function $Y = g(X) = 1 + 2X$. Find the variance of this function.

SOLUTION

The variance of Y is $V(Y) = E(Y - EY)^2$; in terms of $Y = g(X)$ this is

$$V[g(X)] = E\{g(X) - E[g(X)]\}^2, \tag{B.11}$$

which is simply the expected value of the function $\{g(X) - E[g(X)]\}^2$. Although this expression may seem complicated, it is nevertheless just a function of X and so may be evaluated using Result B.1. Using our previous finding that $E(Y) = E[g(X)] = 4$, and applying the formula appropriate to the discrete case, the result is

$$V[g(X)] = E\{g(X) - E[g(X)]\}^2 = \sum_x \{g(x) - E[g(x)]\}^2 f(x)$$

$$= (1-4)^2 \frac{1}{8} + (3-4)^2 \frac{3}{8} + (5-4)^2 \frac{3}{8} + (7-4)^2 \frac{1}{8} = 3.$$

Just as is true of the expected value, in general it is *not* the case that the variance of a function is the function of the variance; that is, $V[g(X)] \neq g(V(X))$. Such a relationship is absent even for linear functions, as the example illustrates: $V[g(X)] = 3 \neq 1 + 2V(X) = 1 + 2(3/4) = 5/2$. Is there any relationship between the variance of a function of a random variable and the variance of the random variable itself? For linear functions, the following law holds.

Law B.2

In obtaining the variance of a linear function, additive constants are irrelevant and multiplicative constants must be squared:

$$V(a + bX) = b^2 V(X).$$

Proof:

Begin by applying the general expression (B.11), which is always true, to the particular function $g(X) = a + bX$:

$$V(a + bX) = E[a + bX - E(a + bX)]^2$$
$$= E[a + bX - (a + bEX)]^2$$
$$= E[b(X - EX)]^2$$
$$= b^2 E(X - EX)^2$$
$$= b^2 V(X). \qquad \square$$

Note that the numerical values of our example satisfy this relationship: For $g(X) = 1 + 2X$, where we have previously found that $V(1 + 2X) = 3$, it is the case that $b^2 V(X) = 2^2(3/4) = 3$.

Law B.2 holds for any numerical constants a and b. It is again useful to note the special cases of $a = 0$ and $b = 1$. First, setting $a = 0$, the general law allows us to conclude the following.

COROLLARY B.2.1. $V(bX) = b^2 V(X)$.
That is, the variance of a constant times a random variable is the square of the constant times the variance.

Second, setting $b = 1$ gives the following result.

COROLLARY B.2.2. $V(a + X) = V(X)$.
That is, additive constants are irrelevant to the variance.

In combination with Corollary B.1.2 that $E(a + X) = a + E(X)$, the implication is that additive constants shift the mean of a random variable but do not affect its dispersion about that mean.

EXERCISES

B.12 Redo Example 10 using the alternative variance formula (B.10) to obtain $V(Y)$.

B.13 If X is the number of heads in three flips of a fair coin, find the variance of the function $Z = h(X) = X^2$.

B.6   Standardized Random Variables

Imagine some random variable X with mean $\mu = E(X)$ and variance $\sigma^2 = V(X)$. No particular assumptions are made about this random variable; it may have any distribution, either discrete or continuous. Now consider a certain function of this random variable, one that subtracts the mean and divides by the standard deviation:

$$\frac{X - \mu}{\sigma} = \frac{1}{\sigma}X - \frac{\mu}{\sigma}.$$

This function is called a **standardizing transformation** because it transforms X to a random variable with mean 0 and variance 1. This is easily seen using Laws B.1 and B.2 because the standardizing transformation is a linear function $a + bX$ with $a = -\mu/\sigma$ and $b = 1/\sigma$. Hence,

$$E\left(\frac{X - \mu}{\sigma}\right) = \frac{1}{\sigma}E(X) - \frac{\mu}{\sigma} = \frac{\mu}{\sigma} - \frac{\mu}{\sigma} = 0,$$

$$V\left(\frac{X - \mu}{\sigma}\right) = \left(\frac{1}{\sigma}\right)^2 V(X) = \frac{1}{\sigma^2}\sigma^2 = 1.$$

You have most likely encountered the concept of a standardized random variable in connection with the normal distribution, where the standardizing transformation converts a $N(\mu, \sigma^2)$ random variable into one having a standard normal distribution $N(0, 1)$. This in turn makes possible the use of standard normal tables to obtain probabilities for normally distributed random variables with arbitrary μ and σ^2. The application of Laws B.1 and B.2 demonstrates that the concept of standardization is not limited to the normal distribution.

B.7   Bivariate Distributions

So far our focus has been on a random variable X (or some function $g(X)$ of it) studied in isolation; its probability distribution $f(x)$ is called a **univariate** distribution. Most often, however, our interest lies in the relationship between variables. The interaction of X with another random variable Y is described by their **bivariate** distribution, which is denoted $f(x, y)$. Exactly as for a univariate distribution, in the discrete case, $f(x, y)$ tells us the probabilities associated with various pairs of (x, y) values; in the continuous case, integration of $f(x, y)$ yields the probability that X and Y take on values in certain ranges.

EXAMPLE 11   Consider the sample space associated with three flips of a coin. Let us define the following two random variables on this sample space: X is the number of heads and Y is assigned the value 1 if all flips are the same and 0 otherwise. Find the bivariate distribution of X and Y.

SOLUTION   Because this bivariate distribution is discrete, it may be expressed as a table. You should satisfy yourself that the probabilities $f(x, y)$ are as follows. (You have obtained the univariate probabilities $f_Y(y)$ in Exercise B.1.)

y \ x	0	1	2	3	$f_Y(y)$
0	0	3/8	3/8	0	6/8
1	1/8	0	0	1/8	2/8
$f_X(x)$	1/8	3/8	3/8	1/8	

The univariate distributions are given in the margins of the table. They are now denoted $f_X(x)$ and $f_Y(y)$ in order to emphasize the distinction between the two; for example, $f_X(1) = 3/8$ whereas $f_Y(1) = 2/8$. Their inclusion in the margins reflects the fact that the univariate probabilities $f_Y(y)$ may be obtained by summing across the columns of the table (that is, over the x values), and those for $f_X(x)$ by summing down the rows of the table (that is, over the y values). For this reason the univariate distributions are also called the **marginal distributions.** In general, marginal distributions may be obtained in this way; this applies as well when the distributions are expressed as formulas.

Result B.2 *The univariate distribution of X may be obtained as*

$$f_X(x) = \begin{cases} \displaystyle\sum_y f(x, y) & \text{when X and Y are discrete} \\ \displaystyle\int_{-\infty}^{\infty} f(x, y)dy & \text{when X and Y are continuous,} \end{cases}$$

and analogously for the univariate distribution of Y.

EXAMPLE 12

Consider a random experiment consisting of four flips of a fair coin. Let X be the number of heads obtained on the first three flips; let Z take on the value 1 if the fourth flip is a head, 0 if a tail. It may be shown that the formula for the bivariate distribution is

$$f(x, z) = \frac{3}{8x!(3 - x)!}, \qquad x = 0, 1, 2, 3, \quad z = 0, 1. \tag{B.12}$$

Find the formulas for the univariate distributions.

SOLUTION

Applying Result B.2 for the discrete case, the marginal distribution of X is

$$f_X(x) = \sum_z f(x, z) = \sum_{z=0, 1} \frac{3}{8x!(3 - x)!}$$

$$= 2\left(\frac{3}{8x!(3 - x)!}\right) = \frac{3}{4x!(3 - x)!}. \tag{B.13}$$

This is the binomial formula (B.5) for $n = 3$ trials with $\pi = 1/2$; that is, equation (B.4). The marginal distribution of Z is

$$f_Z(z) = \sum_x f(x, z) = \sum_{x=0,1,2,3} \frac{3}{8x!(3 - x)!}$$

$$= \frac{3}{8}\left(\frac{1}{0!(3 - 0)!} + \frac{1}{1!(3 - 1)!}\right.$$

$$\left. + \frac{1}{2!(3 - 2)!} + \frac{1}{3!(3 - 3)!}\right) = \frac{1}{2}. \tag{B.14}$$

This is, of course, simply (B.1).

EXERCISES _____

B.14 For Example 12,

(a) present the bivariate distribution in tabular form. Obtain the marginal probabilities by summing across the rows and columns.

(b) use the formulas derived for $f_X(x)$ and $f_Z(z)$

to verify the marginal probabilities found in part a.

B.15 Let X be a random variable that takes on the values -1, 0, and 1 with equal probability, and define $Y = X^2$. Present the bivariate and marginal distributions of X and Y in tabular form.

B.8   Conditional Distributions and Expectation

Suppose we are given information about one random variable. For example, imagine that in Example 11, in which a coin is flipped three times, we are told that the outcome is $Y = 1$. This means that one of the outcomes HHH or TTT has occurred. How does this knowledge affect the probabilities that should be assigned to the other random variable X? Given the knowledge that all flips have turned out the same, it cannot be the case that $X = 1$ or 2; hence the probability that $X = 1$ or 2 *conditional* on $Y = 1$ is zero:

$$\Pr(X = 1|Y = 1) = f_{X|Y}(1|1) = 0,$$
$$\Pr(X = 2|Y = 1) = f_{X|Y}(2|1) = 0.$$

The realizations $X = 0$ (the outcome is TTT) and $X = 3$ (the outcome is HHH) have equal probability:

$$\Pr(X = 0|Y = 1) = f_{X|Y}(0|1) = 1/2,$$
$$\Pr(X = 3|Y = 1) = f_{X|Y}(3|1) = 1/2.$$

Note, then, that the **conditional distributions** $f_{X|Y}(x|y)$ and $f_{Y|X}(y|x)$ differ from the marginal distributions $f_X(x)$ and $f_Y(y)$: Knowledge about one random variable changes the probabilities assigned to the other. In general, the conditional distribution may be obtained from the bivariate and univariate distributions as follows.

Result B.3   *The distribution of X conditional on Y is given by*

$$f_{X|Y}(x|y) = \frac{f(x, y)}{f_Y(y)},$$ (B.15)

and analogously for $f_{Y|X}(y|x)$.

This result holds irrespective of whether the variables are discrete or continuous. It is applied in the next section in an example of the derivation of formulas for conditional distributions. For the moment, let us use it to obtain conditional probabilities for the current example.

EXAMPLE 13 | For Example 11, find the probabilities associated with Y conditional on $X = 0$.

SOLUTION | Using (B.15) we have

$$\Pr(Y = 0|X = 0) = f_{Y|X}(0|0) = \frac{f(0, 0)}{f_X(0)} = \frac{0}{1/8} = 0,$$
$$\Pr(Y = 1|X = 0) = f_{Y|X}(1|0) = \frac{f(0, 1)}{f_X(0)} = \frac{1/8}{1/8} = 1.$$

In other words, if it is known that no heads have occurred, it must be the case that the outcome of the experiment is TTT; it follows that $Y = 1$ with probability 1.

Just as knowledge about one random variable affects our assignment of probabilities to the other, so too does it affect the calculation of its expected value. Recall that the *unconditional* expectation of X is

$$E(X) = \sum_x x f_X(x) = 0 \cdot \frac{1}{8} + 1 \cdot \frac{3}{8} + 2 \cdot \frac{3}{8} + 3 \cdot \frac{1}{8} = \frac{3}{2}.$$

Given the information that $Y = 1$, on the other hand, the expected value of X should be computed using the conditional probabilities; the resulting **conditional expectation** is

$$E(X|Y = 1) = \sum_x x f_{X|Y}(x|1) = 0 \cdot \frac{1}{2} + 1 \cdot 0 + 2 \cdot 0 + 3 \cdot \frac{1}{2} = \frac{3}{2}.$$

Although the expected value turns out to be the same in this instance, the change in the relevant probabilities means that in general a conditional expectation may differ from an unconditional one. This is confirmed by the following example.

EXAMPLE 14 | Find the expected value of Y conditional on the knowledge that $X = 0$. Compare it with the unconditional expectation of Y.

SOLUTION | From Example 13, we know the probabilities associated with the conditional distribution $f_{Y|X}(y|0)$. Hence,

$$E(Y|X = 0) = \sum_y y f_{Y|X}(y|0) = 0 \cdot 0 + 1 \cdot 1 = 1.$$

That is, because the information that $X = 0$ tells us that $Y = 1$ with certainty, its expected value conditional on this information is 1. In contrast, in the absence of this information the *unconditional* expectation is

$$E(Y) = \sum_y y f_Y(y) = 0 \cdot \frac{6}{8} + 1 \cdot \frac{2}{8} = \frac{1}{4},$$

as you have found in Exercise B.3.

These examples suggest the following general result.

Result B.4 | *The mathematical expectation of X conditional on Y is given by*

$$E(X|Y) = \begin{cases} \displaystyle\sum_x x f_{X|Y}(x|y) & \text{when } X \text{ and } Y \text{ are discrete} \\[2mm] \displaystyle\int_{-\infty}^{\infty} x f_{X|Y}(x|y)dx & \text{when } X \text{ and } Y \text{ are continuous,} \end{cases}$$

and analogously for $E(Y|X)$.

EXERCISES

B.16 For Example 11, use Result B.3 to obtain the probabilities associated with

(a) $f_{X|Y}(x|1)$.

(b) $f_{X|Y}(x|0)$.

(c) $f_{Y|X}(y|1)$.

Present your answers for the conditional distribution $f_{X|Y}(x|y)$ in a table.

B.17 Use the probabilities in Exercise B.16 to find

(a) $E(X|Y = 0)$.

(b) $E(Y|X = 1)$.

In each case how does the conditional expectation compare with the unconditional expectation?

B.9 Statistical Independence

Are there circumstances in which information about one random variable does not affect the probabilities assigned to another? In other words, can it be the case that the conditional distribution is the same as the marginal distribution: $f_{X|Y}(x, y) = f_X(x)$? Consider the following example.

EXAMPLE 15

Consider Example 12, in which a fair coin is flipped four times: X is the number of heads obtained on the first three flips and $Z = 1$ if the fourth flip is a head and 0 if a tail. Find the formulas for the conditional distributions $f_{X|Z}(x|z)$ and $f_{Z|X}(z|x)$, and compare them with the marginal distributions $f_X(x)$ and $f_Z(z)$.

SOLUTION

Applying Result B.3 to the bivariate distribution (B.12) and the derived univariate distributions (B.13) and (B.14) yields

$$f_{X|Z}(x|z) = \frac{f(x, z)}{f_Z(z)} = \frac{3/(8x!(3-x)!)}{1/2} = \frac{3}{4x!(3-x)!},$$

which is the marginal distribution $f_X(x)$. Similarly,

$$f_{Z|X}(z|x) = \frac{f(x, z)}{f_X(x)} = \frac{3/(8x!(3-x)!)}{3/(4x!(3-x)!)} = \frac{1}{2},$$

which is the marginal distribution $f_Z(z)$.

Hence, this is one case in which conditional distributions equal marginal distributions: Information about one random variable does not affect the probabilities relevant to the other. What is the key feature of this example? It is that the number of heads X on the first three flips are unrelated to, or *independent of*, the outcome Z of the fourth flip. This provides us with a very precise concept of what it means for one random variable to be independent of another; this concept is called **statistical independence**.

Definition B.3 *Two random variables X and Y are* statistically independent *if*

$$f_{X|Y}(x|y) = f_X(x) \tag{B.16}$$

or, equivalently,

$$f(x, y) = f_X(x) f_Y(y). \tag{B.17}$$

The equivalence of the two definitions follows by rearranging (B.15) and noting that, when (B.16) is satisfied,

$$f(x, y) = f_{X|Y}(x|y) f_Y(y) = f_X(x) f_Y(y).$$

That is, two random variables are statistically independent if their bivariate distribution is the product of their univariate distributions. This is illustrated in the previous example, where $f(x, z) = f_X(x) f_Z(z)$. Of course, if (B.16) is satisfied, it follows automatically that the converse $f_{Y|X}(y|x) = f_Y(y)$ holds because, starting with (B.15),

$$f_{Y|X}(y|x) = \frac{f(x, y)}{f_X(x)} = \frac{f_X(x) f_Y(y)}{f_X(x)} = f_Y(y).$$

By contrast, consider Example 11 in which X is the number of heads in three flips and $Y = 1$ if all three flips are the same and 0 otherwise. Intuitively it is clear that these two random variables are related; this is reflected in our finding (in the previous section) that, in this instance, $f_{X|Y}(x|y) \neq f_X(x)$, so that X and Y are statistically *dependent*. Equivalently, it may be observed from the bivariate distribution given in Example 11 that $f(x, y) \neq f_X(x) f_Y(y)$; the joint probabilities $f(x, y)$ in the body of the table are *not* the products of the respective marginal probabilities.

An important implication of statistical independence is the equality of conditional and unconditional expectations because substituting (B.16) into Result B.4 shows that

$$E(X|Y) = \sum_x x f_{X|Y}(x|y) = \sum_x x f_X(x) = E(X).$$

In contrast, for the random variables in Example 11, where X and Y are dependent, we have found in Example 14 (and Exercise B.17) that $E(Y|X) \neq E(Y)$, so that conditional expectations differ from unconditional ones.

Although statistical independence implies the equality of conditional and unconditional expectations, it is important to note that the converse is not true. It is possible that, say, $E(X|Y) = E(X)$, and yet the two random variables are not independent. In fact, this too is illustrated by the random variables in Example 11 because despite their dependence it has been found in the previous section that $E(X|Y) = E(X)$.

EXERCISES

B.18 In the tabular representation you obtained for $f(x, z)$ in Exercise B.14, are the joint probabilities the products of the respective marginal probabilities?

B.19 Consider an experiment consisting of four flips of a fair coin. Let $Y = 1$ if the first three flips are the same and 0 otherwise, and let $Z = 1$ if the fourth flip is a head and 0 if a tail.

(a) Propose a formula for the bivariate distribution $f(y, z)$. (*Hint:* Use your answer to Exercise B.1.)

(b) Use your formula to present the bivariate distribution in tabular form. Add across the rows and columns to obtain the marginal probabilities.

(c) Are the joint probabilities the products of the marginal probabilities?

B.10   Functions of Two Random Variables

Consider two random variables X and Y having bivariate distribution $f(x, y)$. Any function $g(\cdot)$ of X and Y defines a new random variable, say $Z = g(X, Y)$, which in turn has some distribution with a mean and variance. It is therefore possible to speak of the expected value $E[g(X, Y)]$ and the variance $V[g(X, Y)]$. How do these relate to the bivariate distribution $f(x, y)$ and to the expected values and variances of X and Y individually?

To explore these questions, let us begin with the basic result from which all else will follow. In analogy with Result B.1,

Result B.5   *The mathematical expectation of a function $g(X, Y)$, where X and Y have bivariate probability distribution $f(x, y)$, is*

$$E[g(X, Y)] = \begin{cases} \displaystyle\sum_x \sum_y g(x, y) f(x, y) & \text{if } X \text{ and } Y \text{ are discrete} \\ \displaystyle\int_{-\infty}^{\infty} \int_{-\infty}^{\infty} g(x, y) f(x, y)\,dx\,dy & \text{if } X \text{ and } Y \text{ are continuous.} \end{cases}$$

EXAMPLE 16 | For Example 11, find $E(X + Y)$ and $E(XY)$.

SOLUTION

Applying Result B.5 to these two functions using the discrete bivariate distribution given in Example 11 yields:

$$E(X + Y) = \sum_{x=0,1,2,3} \sum_{y=0,1} (x + y) f(x, y)$$

$$= (0 + 0)0 + (0 + 1)\frac{1}{8} + (1 + 0)\frac{3}{8} + (1 + 1)0$$

$$+ (2 + 0)\frac{3}{8} + (2 + 1)0 + (3 + 0)0 + (3 + 1)\frac{1}{8} = \frac{7}{4},$$

$$E(XY) = \sum_{x=0,1,2,3} \sum_{y=0,1} xyf(x, y)$$

$$= (0 \cdot 0)0 + (0 \cdot 1)\frac{1}{8} + (1 \cdot 0)\frac{3}{8} + (1 \cdot 1)0$$

$$+ (2 \cdot 0)\frac{3}{8} + (2 \cdot 1)0 + (3 \cdot 0)0 + (3 \cdot 1)\frac{1}{8} = \frac{3}{8}.$$

The next sections apply Result B.5 to three functions that are of special interest:

1. $g(X, Y) = aX + bY$, which is a linear combination of the variables.
2. $g(X, Y) = XY$, which is the product of the variables.
3. $g(X, Y) = (X - EX)(Y - EY)$, which is related to the concept of the *covariance*.

EXERCISES

B.20 Compute $E(X+Z)$ and $E(XZ)$ for the bivariate distribution in Example 12.

B.21 Compute $E(XY)$ for the random variables in Exercise B.15.

B.10.1 Expectation of a Linear Combination

In Section B.3 we have found that although $E[g(X)] \neq g(EX)$, so that in general it is not the case that the expected value of a function is the function of the expected value, the special case of a linear function does possess this property.

A similar property holds in the case of several random variables, as the following law states. A linear function of several variables is called a **linear combination.**

Law B.3   *The expected value of a linear combination of random variables is the linear combination of the expected values:*

$$E(aX + bY) = aE(X) + bE(Y).$$

Proof:
Starting with Result B.5 and applying the laws of summation,

$$E(aX + bY) = \sum_x \sum_y (ax + by)f(x, y)$$

$$= \sum_x \sum_y axf(x, y) + \sum_x \sum_y byf(x, y)$$

$$= a \sum_x x \sum_y f(x, y) + b \sum_y y \sum_x f(x, y)$$

$$= a \sum_x xf(x) + b \sum_y yf(y)$$

$$= aE(X) + bE(Y). \qquad \square$$

It is to be emphasized that in establishing this law no special assumptions have been made about the nature of $f(x, y)$; we have not, for example, assumed statistical independence. We have chosen to provide the proof for the discrete case; as usual, the analogous proof for continuously distributed variables may be obtained essentially by substituting integrals for summations.

As in the past, it is useful to note how the general result specializes for particular values of a and b, in this case $a = b = 1$.

COROLLARY B.3.1. $E(X + Y) = E(X) + E(Y)$.
That is, the expected value of a sum is the sum of the expected values.

For example, for the coin-flipping problem Example 11, we have found in Section B.2 that $E(X) = 3/2$ and $E(Y) = 1/4$ whereas in Example 16 we have found $E(X + Y) = 7/4$. Note that these values satisfy the corollary.

As another application of Law B.3, consider the following.

EXAMPLE 17

In Section B.4 it has been asserted that the alternative variance formula $V(X) = E(X^2) - (EX)^2$ given by equation (B.10) is equivalent to the formula in Definition B.2. Use Law B.3 to establish this equivalence.

SOLUTION

Starting with the original formula in Definition B.2,

$$V(X) = E(X - \mu)^2 = E(X^2 - 2\mu X - \mu^2)$$
$$= E(X^2) - 2\mu E(X) - \mu^2 = E(X^2) - \mu^2.$$

The penultimate step applies Law B.3 (as well as Law B.1).

Law B.3 generalizes to an arbitrary number of random variables. In general, a linear combination of n random variables X_i takes the form $\sum_{i=1}^{n} a_i X_i$, and it is the case that

$$E\left(\sum_{i=1}^{n} a_i X_i\right) = \sum_{i=1}^{n} a_i E(X_i). \tag{B.18}$$

The following example illustrates the use of this generalization of Law B.3.

EXAMPLE 18

Consider a series of n Bernoulli trials X_i ($i = 1, \ldots, n$). Each trial takes on the value 1 (a success) with probability π, and the value 0 (a failure) with probability $1 - \pi$, and so has the pmf given by equation (B.2). Let the random variable Y denote the number of successes in these n trials. What is (a) the form of the distribution of Y, (b) the relationship between Y and the individual trials X_i, and (c) the expected value of Y?

SOLUTION

From the discussion in Section B.1 we know that the number of successes in n Bernoulli trials is the definition of a binomial random variable. Hence, Y has the pmf given by (B.5).

The functional relationship between Y and the X_i is $Y = \sum X_i$ (for example, if all trials are failures, then the number of successes is $Y = \sum X_i = \sum 0 = 0$). This is a special case of the linear combination (B.18) in which the $a_i = 1$.

Finally, in Example 2 we have found that $E(X_i) = \pi$; applying (B.18) yields

$$E(Y) = E\left(\sum_{i=1}^{n} X_i\right) = \sum_{i=1}^{n} E(X_i) = \sum_{i=1}^{n} \pi = n\pi.$$

This establishes that the binomial distribution has mean $n\pi$.

B.10.2 Expectation of a Product

In general, the expected value of a product $E(XY)$ must be computed from first principles according to Result B.5 in the way illustrated, for the discrete case, in Example 16. If the conditional and marginal expectations have already been computed, however, then $E(XY)$ is easily obtained, as indicated by the following result.

Result B.6 $E(XY) = E(X|Y)E(Y)$.

Proof:

Starting with Result B.5 and making use of (B.15) yields

$$E(XY) = \sum_x \sum_y xy f(x, y) = \sum_x \sum_y xy f_{X|Y}(x|y) f_Y(y)$$

$$= \sum_x x f_{X|Y}(x|y) \sum_y y f_Y(y) = E(X|Y) \cdot E(Y). \qquad \square$$

Note that it is not, in general, the case that $E(XY) = E(X)E(Y)$, although this can occur in special circumstances.

Result B.7   *If $E(X|Y) = E(X)$ (or, equivalently, $E(Y|X) = E(Y)$), then*

$$E(XY) = E(X) \cdot E(Y).$$

One set of circumstances that could give rise to $E(XY) = E(X)E(Y)$ is statistical independence because we have seen that independence implies the equality of conditional and marginal expectations. As stressed in that discussion, however, independence is not a necessary condition for $E(X|Y) = E(X)$ and so is certainly not a necessary condition for Result B.7 to hold. In turn, it follows that $E(XY) = E(X)E(Y)$ does not imply statistical independence. This is illustrated by the coin-flipping problem Example 11, which we have seen is an example of statistically dependent random variables. Nevertheless, we have found in Example 16 that

$E(XY) = 3/8$ which, drawing on the values $E(X) = 3/2$ and $E(Y) = 1/4$ obtained in that problem, happens to satisfy $E(XY) = 3/8 = (3/2)(1/4) = E(X)E(Y)$.

B.10.3 Covariance

Just as it is useful to have summary measures of the center and dispersion of a univariate distribution, so too it is useful to have a measure summarizing the nature of the interaction between bivariately distributed variables. One such measure is the **covariance,** denoted $\text{cov}(X, Y)$ or σ_{XY}, which is defined as follows.

Definition B.4   *The* covariance *between two random variables is*

$$\sigma_{XY} = E[(X - EX)(Y - EY)].$$

The covariance may be evaluated using Result B.5. It takes on values in the range $-\infty < \sigma_{XY} < \infty$; the implication of $\sigma_{XY} > 0$ is that the variables are directly related and $\sigma_{XY} < 0$ that they vary inversely. It is apparent from the definition that the covariance is symmetric: $\text{cov}(X, Y) = \text{cov}(Y, X)$. Note as well that the covariance of a random variable with itself is simply the variance: $\text{cov}(X, X) = E(X - EX)(X - EX) = E(X - EX)^2$, which must, as we know, be positive. An alternative expression for the covariance is given by the following result.

Result B.8   *An equivalent definition of the covariance is* $\sigma_{XY} = E(XY) - E(X)E(Y)$.

Proof:

Beginning with Definition B.4 and applying Law B.3 yields

$$\begin{aligned}
\sigma_{XY} &= E(X - \mu_X)(Y - \mu_Y) \\
&= E(XY - \mu_X Y - \mu_Y X + \mu_X \mu_Y) \\
&= E(XY) - \mu_X E(Y) - \mu_Y E(X) + \mu_X \mu_Y \\
&= E(XY) - \mu_X \mu_Y. \qquad \qquad \square
\end{aligned}$$

As a special case it follows immediately that, if one of the random variables (let us call it ε) has zero mean, then the covariance is simply the expected value of the product:

$$\text{cov}(X, \varepsilon) = E(X\varepsilon) - E(X)E(\varepsilon) = E(X\varepsilon) - E(X) \cdot 0 = E(X\varepsilon).$$

Note that according to this alternative definition the covariance of a random variable with itself is $E(XX) - E(X)E(X) = E(X^2) - (EX)^2$, which is simply the alternative expression for the variance given by (B.10). As well, the covariance of a random variable with a nonrandom constant, say a, is always zero:

$$\text{cov}(X, a) = E(aX) - E(a)E(X) = aE(X) - aE(X) = 0.$$

Using Result B.7, it follows immediately from the alternative definition that, if the two random variables are statistically independent,

$$\text{cov}(X, Y) = E(XY) - E(X)E(Y) = E(X)E(Y) - E(X)E(Y) = 0.$$

This proves the following.

Result B.9   *If X and Y are statistically independent, then $\sigma_{XY} = 0$.*

It is to be emphasized that although statistical independence implies zero covariance, the converse is not true; $\sigma_{XY} = 0$ does *not* imply statistical independence. This is illustrated by the random variables in Example 11, for which we have seen that $E(XY) = E(X)E(Y)$, but for which the bivariate distribution does not factor into the product of the marginals.

One feature that limits the usefulness of the covariance as a measure of the strength of the relationship between variables is that its value depends on the units in which the variables are measured. Specifically, suppose that the variables X and Y are measured in, say, dollars, and we initially compute $\text{cov}(X, Y)$ on this basis. Now suppose the variables are redefined using other units represented by vX and wY; the numerical constants v and w are called **scaling factors.** For example, if the variables are now measured in dimes, then $v = w = 10$. The effect on the covariance is given by the following result.

Result B.10 $\text{cov}(vX, wY) = vw\,\text{cov}(X, Y)$.

Proof:

$$\begin{aligned}
\text{cov}(vX, wY) &= E[(vX - E(vX))(wY - E(wY))] \\
&= E[vw(X - EX)(Y - EY)] \\
&= vw\,E[(X - EX)(Y - EY)] \\
&= vw\,\text{cov}(X, Y)
\end{aligned}$$

$\square$

This indicates that measuring in dimes rather than dollars increases the value of the covariance by a factor of $vw = 100$. Thus, the covariance may be made arbitrarily large or small by redefining the units of measure. This in turn means that the magnitude of the covariance—that it is, say, 5, or any other particular value—carries with it little intuitive meaning concerning the strength of the relationship between the variables. It would be preferable to have an alternative measure that is invariant to variable scaling.

EXERCISES

B.22 Compute the covariance for the random variables in Exercise B.15.

B.23 Consider a change in the units of measure that is in the form of additive constants $v+X$ and $w+Y$. Establish whether the covariance is affected.

884 APPENDIX B Distribution Theory

B.10.4 Correlation

A measure of the relationship between random variables that rectifies this deficiency of the covariance is the **correlation,** denoted ρ or $cor(X, Y)$.

Definition B.5   *The* correlation *between X and Y is* $\rho = \dfrac{\sigma_{XY}}{\sigma_X \sigma_Y}$.

It may be shown that the correlation takes on values in the range $-1 < \rho < 1$; because σ_X and σ_Y must be positive, it has the same sign as the covariance. As well, clearly $\rho = 0$ if and only if $\sigma_{XY} = 0$. Because the covariance is symmetric, so too is the correlation: $cor(X, Y) = cor(Y, X)$. To establish its invariance to positive scaling constants v and w, note that

$$cor(vX, wY) = \frac{cov(vX, wY)}{\sqrt{V(vX)V(wY)}} = \frac{vw\, cov(X, Y)}{vw\sqrt{V(X)V(Y)}} = \frac{\sigma_{XY}}{\sigma_X \sigma_Y} = cor(X, Y).$$

The second step uses Result B.10 and, in the denominator, Corollary B.2.2. The invariance of the correlation to variable scalings, even when *different* scalings are applied to each variable, means that it is a **dimensionless** or **scale invariant** quantity, like an elasticity.

This property means that the correlation is more useful than the covariance as an indicator of the strength of the relationship between variables. The use of either for this purpose must, however, be qualified by our finding that a zero covariance or correlation does *not* imply statistical independence. Indeed, it is possible to construct examples in which variables are exactly functionally dependent, so that knowledge of one variable implies exact knowledge of the value of the other, and yet $\rho = 0$. The following is such an example.

EXAMPLE 19   Consider a random variable X that takes on the values -1, 0, and 1 with equal probability and a second random variable defined as $Y = X^2$. Present in tabular form the bivariate and marginal distributions of X and Y and compute their correlation. Are they statistically independent?

SOLUTION   The distributions are summarized by

x $\quad$ y	-1	0	1	$f_Y(y)$
0	0	$1/3$	0	$1/3$
1	$1/3$	0	$1/3$	$2/3$
$f_X(x)$	$1/3$	$1/3$	$1/3$	

Applying Definition B.1 for the discrete case to the marginal distributions in the usual way, the expected values are $E(X) = 0$ and $E(Y) = 2/3$. Applying

Result B.5 to the bivariate distribution yields $E(XY) = 0$. Hence, the covariance is $\sigma_{XY} = E(XY) - E(X)E(Y) = 0 - 0 \cdot 2/3 = 0$; the correlation must therefore also equal zero. However, the random variables are *not* statistically independent because the bivariate probabilities in the body of the table are not the products of the respective marginal probabilities.

How is it that one variable can be exactly functionally related to another, yet the two have zero correlation? The answer is that ρ provides a measure only of the strength of the *linear* relationship between variables; a value close to zero indicates the absence of a linear relationship and a value close to 1 (or -1) a strong direct (or inverse) linear relationship. Example 19 is one in which, although a linear relationship is absent, there is a strong (in fact, precise) *nonlinear* relationship between the variables.

Indeed, an exact linear relationship always gives rise to $|\rho| = 1$. To see this, let $Y = a + bX$ and note that:[8]

$$\text{cor}(X, Y) = \frac{\text{cov}(X, a + bX)}{\sqrt{V(X)V(a + bX)}} = \frac{b\,\text{cov}(X, X)}{\sqrt{V(X)b^2V(X)}} = \frac{bV(X)}{|b|V(X)} = \frac{b}{|b|} = \pm 1.$$

The second step uses Result B.10 and, in the denominator, Law B.2.

An important special case in which $\sigma_{XY} = \rho = 0$ *does* imply statistical independence is the normal distribution. The univariate normal distribution is given by (2.2); the formula $f(x, y)$ for the bivariate normal is

$$\frac{1}{2\pi\sigma_X\sigma_Y\sqrt{1 - \rho^2}}$$

$$\times e^{\frac{-1}{2(1 - \rho^2)}\left[\left(\frac{x - \mu_X}{\sigma_X}\right)^2 - 2\rho\frac{x - \mu_X}{\sigma_X}\frac{y - \mu_Y}{\sigma_Y} + \left(\frac{y - \mu_Y}{\sigma_Y}\right)^2\right]}.$$

$$\text{(B.19)}$$

Note that the bivariate normal distribution depends on five parameters: the univariate means and standard deviations μ_X, μ_Y, σ_X, and σ_Y and the correlation (or, equivalently, the covariance) describing the interaction of the two random variables. Although the formula (B.19) has been written in terms of ρ it can of course be written equivalently in terms of σ_{XY} by substituting in Definition B.5.

Exercise B.25 asks you to use the univariate and bivariate densities to show that, for normally distributed random variables, $\rho = 0$ implies statistical independence.

EXERCISES

B.24 Show that the correlation has the interpretation as the covariance between *standardized* random variables.

B.25 Show that if $\rho = 0$ the bivariate normal distribution (B.19) factors into the product of the univariate densities: $f(x, y) = f_X(x)f_Y(y)$.

---

[8]   Recall you have shown in Exercise B.23 that the covariance is invariant to variable transformations involving additive constants.

B.11

Variance of a Linear Combination

Law B.3 establishes that $E(aX + bY) = aE(X) + bE(Y)$. Let us now turn to the variance of such linear combinations.

Law B.4 $V(aX + bY) = a^2\sigma_X^2 + b^2\sigma_Y^2 + 2ab\sigma_{XY}.$

Proof:

Applying Definition B.2 and Law B.3 yields

$$V(aX + bY) = E[(aX + bY) - E(aX + bY)]^2$$
$$= E[a(X - EX) + b(Y - EY)]^2$$
$$= E[a^2(X - \mu_X)^2 + b^2(Y - \mu_Y)^2 + 2ab(X - \mu_X)(Y - \mu_Y)]$$
$$= a^2 E(X - \mu_X)^2 + b^2 E(Y - \mu_Y)^2 + 2abE(X - \mu_X)(Y - \mu_Y)$$
$$= a^2\sigma_X^2 + b^2\sigma_Y^2 + 2ab\sigma_{XY}. \qquad \square$$

Law B.4 says that the variance of a linear combination of random variables depends, as we expect, on the variances of the random variables individually and on the constants a and b of the linear combination. In addition, however, the variance of the combination depends on the manner in which the random variables *covary*: Positive covariation increases the variance of the total (assuming a and b are both positive), whereas negative covariation serves to reduce the total variance.

It is helpful to understand this in terms of an example. Suppose that X denotes the random percentage return on Ford stock over the next year, and Y denotes the random return on GM stock and that you invest \$500 in Ford and \$300 in GM. Law B.3 indicates that your expected dollar return on this portfolio of assets is $E(500X + 300Y) = 500E(X) + 300E(Y)$; that is, that the expected return on the total depends on the individual returns and the relative investments in each. Law B.4 tells us about the risk of this portfolio, as measured by the variance; it indicates that $V(500X + 300Y) = 500^2\sigma_X + 300^2\sigma_Y + 2 \cdot 500 \cdot 300\sigma_{XY}$, so that the risk of the portfolio depends not only on the variances of the individual returns but on how the two returns covary. For example, it seems likely that the returns on GM and Ford stock will covary positively because both are in the same industry and therefore will be subject to common industrywide influences such as business cycle effects. Thus, when one stock does well the other will also tend to do well. If so, this contributes to the overall risk of the portfolio.

Suppose that instead of investing in GM you invest in, say, an auto parts rebuilder. This firm may not tend to do well in periods of prosperity when consumers are buying new cars and Ford's profits are high, but may do well during recessions when consumers spend to maintain their existing vehicles. In this case, the return on the two investments will tend to covary negatively, reducing the variance of the portfolio. In fact, it is possible that the variance of the portfolio can actually be less than that of either of the investments individually. The common-sense meaning of Law B.4 is that it is possible to reduce risk by "not putting all your eggs in one basket." This diversification effect is studied in much more detail in Appendix C.

From Law B.4, it is evident that if the returns on the investments are unrelated, then the risk of the portfolio will depend only on the individual asset risks and the investment amounts. This is formalized in the following corollary.

COROLLARY B.4.1. If $\sigma_{XY} = 0$, then $V(aX + bY) = a^2\sigma_X^2 + b^2\sigma_Y^2$.

Finally, as usual, it is useful to note specializations of the general result that apply for particular numerical constants, in this case $a = b = 1$.

COROLLARY B.4.2. $V(X + Y) = \begin{cases} \sigma_X^2 + \sigma_Y^2 + 2\sigma_{XY} & \text{in general} \\ \sigma_X^2 + \sigma_Y^2 & \text{if } \sigma_{XY} = 0. \end{cases}$

As is true of Law B.3, a generalization of Law B.4 applies to a linear combination of an arbitrary number of random variables. Specifically,

$$V\left(\sum_{i=1}^{n} a_i X_i\right) = \sum_{i=1}^{n} a_i^2 \sigma_i^2 + 2 \sum_{i=1}^{n-1} \sum_{j=i+1}^{n} a_i a_j \sigma_{ij}. \tag{B.20}$$

The last term uses the notation $\sigma_{ij} = \text{cov}(X_i, X_j)$. The implication is that the risk of an n-asset portfolio depends on the n variances σ_i^2 plus the $n(n-1)/2$ distinct pairwise covariances σ_{ij} $(i, j = 1, \ldots, n; i \neq j)$. These variance-covariance parameters may be summarized as follows.

$$\begin{matrix} \sigma_1^2 & \sigma_{12} & \sigma_{13} & \cdots & \sigma_{1n} \\ & \sigma_2^2 & \sigma_{23} & \cdots & \sigma_{2n} \\ & & \sigma_3^2 & \cdots & \sigma_{3n} \\ & & & \ddots & \vdots \\ & & & & \sigma_n^2 \end{matrix}$$

The generalizations (B.18) and (B.20) are mathematical expectations and variances defined on a **multivariate** distribution that might be denoted $f(x_1, x_2, \ldots, x_n)$. A bivariate distribution is the special case of $n = 2$ random variables. Bivariate and multivariate distributions are also called **joint** distributions. In the case of multivariate normal random variables, the distribution is fully characterized by the variances and covariances along with, of course, the n variable means $\mu_i = E(X_i)$.

In the special case where the X_i are mutually independent (or, a weaker requirement, where $\sigma_{ij} = 0$ for all i, j) equation (B.20) specializes to

$$V\left(\sum_{i=1}^{n} a_i X_i\right) = \sum_{i=1}^{n} a_i^2 \sigma_i^2. \tag{B.21}$$

Consider the following example in which the $a_i = 1$.

EXAMPLE 20

(Continuation of EXAMPLE 18) As in Example 18, let $Y = \sum X_i$ be the sum of n Bernoulli trials. It is established in Example 18 that Y has a binomial distribution with mean $E(Y) = n\pi$. Find the variance of Y.

SOLUTION

In Example 9, we have found that if X_i is Bernoulli then $V(X_i) = \pi(1 - \pi)$. Since the trials are independent, (B.21) applies:

$$V\left(\sum_{i=1}^{n} X_i\right) = \sum_{i=1}^{n} V(X_i) = \sum_{i=1}^{n} \pi(1 - \pi) = n\pi(1 - \pi).$$

This establishes that a binomial random variable has variance $n\pi(1 - \pi)$.

EXERCISES

B.26 Show that, if $\sigma_{XY} = 0$, then $V(X - Y) = V(X + Y)$.

TABLE B.2   Laws of Expectation and Variance

Law		Corollary	
B.1	$E(a + bX) = a + bE(X)$	**B.1.1**	$E(bX) = bE(X)$
		B.1.2	$E(a + X) = a + E(X)$
B.2	$V(a + bX) = b^2 V(X)$	**B.2.1**	$V(bX) = b^2 V(X)$
		B.2.2	$V(a + X) = V(X)$
B.3	$E(aX + bY) =$ $aE(X) + bE(Y)$	**B.3.1**	$E(X + Y) = E(X) + E(Y)$
B.4	$V(aX + bY) =$ $a^2\sigma_X^2 + b^2\sigma_Y^2 + 2ab\sigma_{XY}$	**B.4.1**	$V(aX + bY) =$ $a^2\sigma_X^2 + b^2\sigma_Y^2$ if $\sigma_{XY} = 0$
		B.4.2	$V(X + Y) =$ $\begin{cases} \sigma_X^2 + \sigma_Y^2 + 2\sigma_{XY} & \text{in general} \\ \sigma_X^2 + \sigma_Y^2 & \text{if } \sigma_{XY} = 0 \end{cases}$

B.12 Laws of Expectation and Variance: Summary

The laws of expectation and variance that we have derived in this appendix are summarized in Table B.2. As their use in this book indicates, they are applied repeatedly in econometric derivations. As well, they play an important role in the economic modeling of uncertainty. One example is the field of finance, in which the randomness of asset returns is central. This is illustrated in Appendix C, in which we find that the laws of expectation and variance are a key ingredient in the foundations of modern financial theory.

The laws of expectation and variance are paralleled by analogous laws of *sample* means and variances. These are presented in the appendix of Chapter 3 and are summarized in Table 3.5. A comparison of Tables B.2 and 3.5 serves to usefully contrast the two sets of laws.

References

Abramovitz, M. (1950) *Inventories and Business Cycles* (New York: National Bureau of Economic Research).

Adelman, I., and F.L. Adelman (1959) "The Dynamic Properties of the Klein-Goldberger Model," *Econometrica* 27, 596–625. Reprinted in the American Economic Association *Readings in Business Cycles*, ed. by R. Gordon and L. Klein (Homewood, IL: Irwin, 1965).

Aghion, P., and P. Howitt (1998) *Endogenous Growth Theory* (Cambridge, MA: MIT Press).

Aigner, D.J. (1971) *Basic Econometrics* (Englewood Cliffs, NJ: Prentice-Hall).

Aitchison, J., and J.A.C. Brown (1957) *The Lognormal Distribution* (Cambridge, UK: Cambridge University Press).

Aiyagari, S.R. (1994) "On the Contribution of Technology Shocks to Business Cycles," Federal Reserve Bank of Minneapolis *Quarterly Review* 18 (Winter), 22–34.

Akaike, H. (1974) "A New Look at Statistical Model Identification," *IEEE Transactions on Automatic Control* AC-19, 716–723.

Allais, M. (1947) *Économie et Intérêt* (Paris: Impremerie Nationale).

Alston, J.M., Foster, K.A., and R.D. Green (1994) "Estimating Elasticities with the Linear Approximate Almost Ideal Demand System: Some Monte Carlo Results," *Review of Economics and Statistics* 76, 351–356.

Amemiya, T. (1980) "Selection of Regressors," *International Economic Review* 21, 331–354.

Amemiya, T. (1983) "Nonlinear Regression Models" in *Handbook of Econometrics*, Vol. I, ed. by Z. Griliches and M.D. Intriligator (Amsterdam: North-Holland).

Anderson, G. (1994) "Simple Tests of Distributional Form," *Journal of Econometrics* 62, 265–276.

Angrist, J.D., and A.B. Krueger (1991) "Does Compulsory School Attendance Affect Schooling and Earnings?" *Quarterly Journal of Economics* 106, 979–1014.

Arrow, K.J., Chenery, H.B., Minhas, B.S., and R.M. Solow (1961) "Capital-Labor Substitution and Economic Efficiency," *Review of Economics and Statistics* 43, 225–250. Reprinted in *Economic Statistics and Econometrics*, ed. by A. Zellner (Boston: Little, Brown, 1968).

Atkeson, A., Chari, V.V., and P.J. Kehoe (1999) "Taxing Capital Income: A Bad Idea," Federal Reserve Bank of Minneapolis *Quarterly Review* 23 (Summer), 3–17.

Auerbach, A.S., and L.S. Kotlikoff (1998) *Macroeconomics: An Integrated Approach*, 2nd ed. (Cambridge, MA: MIT Press).

Banerjee, A., Dolado, J.J., Galbraith, J.W., and D.F. Hendry (1993) *Co-integration, Error-Correction, and the Econometric Analysis of Non-stationary Data* (Oxford: Oxford University Press).

Banks, J., Blundell, R., and A. Lewbel (1997) "Quadratic Engel Curves and Consumer Demand," *Review of Economics and Statistics* 79, 527–539.

Barro, R.J. (1974) "Are Government Bonds Net Wealth?" *Journal of Political Economy* 82, 1095–1118.

Barro, R., and X. Sala-i-Martin (1995) *Economic Growth* (New York: McGraw-Hill).

Barsky, R.B., and J.A. Miron (1989) "The Seasonal Cycle and the Business Cycle," *Journal of Political Economy* 97, 503–535.

Basu, S., and J.G. Fernald (1997) "Returns to Scale in U.S. Production: Estimates and Implications," *Journal of Political Economy* 105, 249–283.

Basu, S., and J.G. Fernald (2002) "Aggregate Productivity and Aggregate Technology," *European Economic Review* 46, 963–991.

Beaulieu, J.J., and J.A. Miron (1993) "Seasonal Unit Roots and Deterministic Seasonals in Aggregate U.S. Data," *Journal of Econometrics* 55, 305–328.

Beaulieu, M.-C., Dufour, J.-M., and L. Khalaf (2003) "Testing Black's CAPM with Possibly

Non-Gaussian Errors: An Exact Simulation-Based Approach," paper given at the conference on *Simulation-Based and Finite Sample Inference in Finance*, Quebec City, May 2003.

Belsley, D., Kuh, E., and R.E. Welsch (1980) *Regression Diagnostics* (New York: Wiley).

Bera, A.K., and M.L. Higgins (1993) "ARCH Models: Properties, Estimation, and Testing," *Journal of Economic Surveys* 7, 305–366. Reprinted in *Surveys in Econometrics*, ed. by L. Oxley, D.A.R. George, C.J. Roberts, and S. Sayer (Oxford: Blackwell, 1995).

Berndt, E.R. (1991) *The Practice of Econometrics: Classic and Contemporary* (Reading, MA: Addison-Wesley).

Berndt, E.R., and N.E. Savin (1977) "Conflict among Criteria for Testing Hypotheses in the Multivariate Linear Regression Model," *Econometrica* 45, 1263–1278.

Beveridge, S., and C.R. Nelson (1981) "A New Approach to Decomposition of Economic Time Series into Permanent and Transitory Components with Particular Attention to Measurement of the Business Cycle," *Journal of Monetary Economics* 7, 151–174.

Black, F. (1972) "Capital Market Equilibrium with Restricted Borrowing," *Journal of Business* 45, 444–454.

Black, F., Jensen, M., and M. Scholes (1972) "The Capital Asset Pricing Model: Some Empirical Tests," in *Studies in the Theory of Capital Markets*, ed. by M. Jensen (New York: Praeger).

Blanchard, O.J., and S. Fischer (1989) *Lectures on Macroeconomics* (Cambridge, MA: MIT Press).

Blinder, A.S. (1981) "Retail Inventory Behavior and Business Fluctuations," *Brookings Papers on Economic Activity*, 443–505.

Bodie, Z., Kane, A., and A.J. Marcus (1989) *Investments* (Homewood, IL: Irwin).

Bollerslev, T. (1986) "Generalized Autoregressive Conditional Heteroskedasticity," *Journal of Econometrics* 31, 307–327.

Boskin, M.J., Dulberger, E.R., Gordon, R.J., Griliches, Z., and D.W. Jorgenson (1998) "Consumer Prices, the Consumer Price Index, and the Cost of Living," *Journal of Economic Perspectives* 12, 3–26.

Bound, J., Jaeger, D.A., and R.M. Baker (1995) "Problems with Instrumental Variables Estimation When the Correlation between the Instruments and the Endogenous Explanatory Variable Is Weak," *Journal of the American Statistical Association* 90, 443–450.

Box, G.E.P. (1976) "Science and Statistics," *Journal of the American Statistical Association* 71, 791–799.

Box, G.E.P., and G.M. Jenkins (1970, revised ed. 1976) *Times Series Analysis: Forecasting and Control* (San Francisco: Holden-Day).

Box, G.E.P., Jenkins, G.M., and G. Reinsel (1994) *Times Series Analysis: Forecasting and Control*, 3rd ed. (Englewood Cliffs, NJ: Prentice-Hall).

Box, G., and D. Pierce (1970) "Distribution of Autocorrelations in Autoregressive Moving Average Time Series Models," *Journal of the American Statistical Association* 65, 1509–1526.

Breusch, T.S. (1979) "Conflict among Criteria for Testing Hypotheses: Extensions and Comments," *Econometrica* 47, 203–207.

Breusch, T.S., and A.R. Pagan (1979) "A Simple Test for Heteroskedasticity and Random Coefficient Variation," *Econometrica* 47, 1287–1294.

Breusch, T.S., and P. Schmidt (1988) "Alternative Forms of the

Wald Test: How Long Is a Piece of String?" *Communications in Statistics, Theory and Methods* 17, 2789–2795.

Browning, M. (1983) "Necessary and Sufficient Conditions for Conditional Cost Functions," *Econometrica* 51, 851–856.

Burgete, W.J., Gallant, A.R., and G. Souza (1982) "On Unification of Asymptotic Theory of Nonlinear Econometric Models," *Econometric Reviews* 1, 151–190.

Buse, A. (1994) "Evaluating the Linearized Almost Ideal Demand System," *American Journal of Agricultural Economics* 76, 781–793.

Cabral, L.M.B., and J. Mata (2003) "On the Evolution of the Firm Size Distribution: Facts and Theory," *American Economic Review* 95, 1075–1090.

Cagan, P. (1956) "The Monetary Dynamics of Hyperinflation," in *Studies in the Quantity Theory of Money*, ed. by M. Friedman (Chicago: University of Chicago Press).

Cagan, P. (1987) "Hyperinflation," in *The New Palgrave: A Dictionary of Economics*, ed. by J. Eatwell, M. Milgate, and P. Newman (New York: Norton).

Cameron, A.C., and P.K. Trivedi (1998) *Regression Analysis of Count Data* (New York: Cambridge University Press).

Cameron, A.C., and P.K. Trivedi (2001) "Essentials of Count Data Regression," in *A Companion to Theoretical Econometrics*, ed. by B.H. Baltagi (Oxford: Blackwell).

Campbell, J.Y., Lo, A.W., and A.C. MacKinlay (1997) *The Econometrics of Financial Markets* (Princeton, NJ: Princeton University Press).

Campbell, J.Y., and N.G. Mankiw (1987) "Are Output Fluctuations Transitory?" *Quarterly Journal of Economics* 102, 857–880.

Card, D. (1999) "The Causal Effect of Education on Earnings," in the *Handbook of Labor Economics*, Vol. IIIA, ed. by O. Ashenfelter and D. Card (Amsterdam: North-Holland).

Cass, D. (1965) "Optimum Growth in an Aggregative Model of Capital Accumulation," *Review of Economic Studies* 32, 233–240.

Chakraborty, I. (1999) "Living Standard and Economic Growth: A Fresh Look at the Relationship through the Nonparametric Approach," *Journal of Quantitative Economics* 15, 39–66.

Chalfant, J.A. (1987) "A Globally Flexible, Almost Ideal Demand System," *Journal of Business and Economic Statistics* 5, 233–242.

Chambers, R.G. (1988) *Applied Production Analysis—A Dual Approach* (Cambridge, UK: Cambridge University Press).

Champ, B., and S. Freeman (2001) *Modeling Monetary Economies*, 2nd ed. (Cambridge, UK: Cambridge University Press).

Chiang, A.C. (1984) *Fundamental Methods of Mathematical Economics*, 3rd ed. (New York: McGraw-Hill).

Chow, G.C. (1960) "Tests of the Equality between Subsets of Coefficients in Two Linear Regressions," *Econometrica* 28, 591–605.

Christensen, L.R., and W.H. Greene (1976) "Economies of Scale in U.S. Electric Power Generation," *Journal of Political Economy* 84, 655–676.

Christensen, L.R., Jorgenson, D.W., and L.J. Lau (1973) "Transcendental Logarithmic Production Frontiers," *Review of Economics and Statistics* 55, 28–45.

Christiano, L.J., Eichenbaum, M., and D. Marshall (1991) "The Permanent Income Hypothesis Revisited," *Econometrica* 59, 397–423.

Clark, P.K. (1987) "The Cyclical Component of U.S. Economic Activity," *Quarterly Journal of Economics* 102, 797–814.

Cobb, C.W., and P.H. Douglas (1928) "A Theory of Production," *American Economic Review* 18 (Supplement), 139–165.

Cochrane, J.H. (1988) "How Big Is the Random Walk in GNP?" *Journal of Political Economy* 96, 893–920.

Cochrane, J.H. (1991) "Comment," in *NBER Macroeconomics Annual 1991*, 201–210.

Cooley, T.F., and E.C. Prescott (1995) "Economic Growth and Business Cycles," in *Business Cycle Theory*, ed. by T.F. Cooley (Princeton, NJ: Princeton University Press).

Copeland, T.E., and J.F. Weston (1988) *Financial Theory and Corporate Policy*, 3rd ed. (Reading, MA: Addison-Wesley).

Dagenais, M.G., and J.-M. Dufour (1991) "Invariance, Nonlinear Models, and Asymptotic Tests," *Econometrica* 59, 1601–1615.

Dagenais, M.G., and J.-M. Dufour (1992) "On the Lack of Invariance of Some Asymptotic Tests to Rescaling," *Economics Letters* 38, 251–257.

Davidson, J. (2000) *Econometric Theory* (Oxford: Blackwell).

Davidson, R., and J.G. MacKinnon (1981) "Several Tests for Model Specification in the Presence of Alternative Hypotheses," *Econometrica* 49, 781–793.

Davidson, R., and J.G. MacKinnon (1993) *Estimation and Inference in Econometrics* (Oxford: Oxford University Press).

Davidson, R., and J.G. MacKinnon (2001) "Artificial Regressions," in *A Companion to Theoretical Econometrics*, ed. by B. Baltagi (Oxford: Blackwell Publishers).

Davidson, R., and J.G. MacKinnon (2004) *Econometric Theory and Methods* (Oxford: Oxford University Press).

Davison, A.C., and D.V. Hinkley (1997) *Bootstrap Methods and Their Application* (Cambridge, UK: Cambridge University Press).

Deaton, A. (1986) "Demand Analysis," in *Handbook of Econometrics*, Vol. III, ed. by Z. Griliches and M.D. Intriligator (Amsterdam: North-Holland).

Deaton, A., and J. Muellbauer (1980a) "An Almost Ideal Demand System," *American Economic Review* 70, 312–326.

Deaton, A., and J. Muellbauer (1980b) *Economics and Consumer Behavior* (Cambridge, UK: Cambridge University Press).

Deb, P., and M. Sefton (1996) "The Distribution of a Lagrange Multiplier Test of Normality," *Economics Letters* 51, 123–130.

Diamond, P.A. (1965) "National Debt in a Neoclassical Growth Model," *American Economic Review* 55, 1126–1150.

Dickey, D.A., and W.A. Fuller (1979) "Distribution of the Estimators for Autoregressive Time Series with a Unit Root," *Journal of the American Statistical Association* 74, 1057–1072.

Dickey, D.A., and S.G. Pantula (1987) "Determining the Order of Differencing in Autoregressive Processes," *Journal of Business and Economic Statistics* 15, 455–61.

Diebold, F.X (2004) *Elements of Forecasting*, 3rd ed. (Cincinnati, OH: Thomson/South-Western).

Diewert, W.E. (1971) "An Application of the Shephard Duality Theorem: A Generalized Leontief Production Function," *Journal of Political Economy* 79, 481–507.

Diewert, W.E. (1974) "Applications of Duality Theory," in *Frontiers of Quantitative Economics*, ed. by M.D. Intriligator and D.A. Kendrick (Amsterdam: North-Holland).

Diewert, W.E., and T.J. Wales (1987) "Flexible Functional Forms and Global Curvature Conditions," *Econometrica* 55, 43–68.

Dubin, J.A. (1985) *Consumer Durable Choice and the Demand for Electricity* (Amsterdam: North-Holland).

Dubin, J.A., and D.L. McFadden (1984) "An Econometric Analysis of Residential Electricity Appliance Holdings and Consumption," *Econometrica* 52, 345–362.

Dufour, J.-M. (2003) "Identification, Weak Instruments and Statistical Inference in Econometrics," *Canadian Journal of Economics* 36, 767–808.

Dufour, J.-M., and L. Khalaf (2003) "Finite-Sample Simulation-Based Tests in Seemingly Unrelated Regressions," in *Computer-Aided Econometrics*, ed. by D.E.A. Giles (New York: Marcel Dekker).

Dumas, B., and B. Allaz (1996) *Financial Securities: Market Equilibrium and Pricing Methods* (London: Chapman and Hall).

Durlauf, S.N., and P.C.B. Phillips (1988) "Trends versus Random Walks in Time Series Analysis," *Econometrica* 56, 1333–1354.

Durlauf, S.N., and D.T. Quah (1999) "The New Empirics of Economic Growth" in *Handbook of Macroeconomics*, Vol. IA, ed. by J.B. Taylor and M. Woodford (Amsterdam: North-Holland).

Efron, B., and R.J. Tibshirani (1993) *An Introduction to the Bootstrap* (New York: Chapman & Hall).

Elton, E.J., and M.J. Gruber (1987) *Modern Portfolio Theory and Investment Analysis* (New York: Wiley).

Enders, W. (1995) *Applied Econometric Time Series* (New York: Wiley).

Engle, R.F. (1982) "Autoregressive Conditional Heteroskedasticity with Estimates of the Variance of

United Kingdom Inflation," *Econometrica* 50, 987–1007.

Engle, R.F. (1984) "Wald, Likelihood Ratio, and Lagrange Multiplier Tests in Econometrics" in *Handbook of Econometrics*, Vol. II, ed. by Z. Griliches and M.D. Intriligator (Amsterdam: North-Holland).

Engle, R.F. (2001) "GARCH 101: The Use of ARCH/GARCH Models in Applied Econometrics," *Journal of Economic Perspectives* 15, 157–168.

Engle, R.F., and C.W.J. Granger (1987) "Cointegration and Error Correction: Representation, Estimation, and Testing," *Econometrica* 55, 251–276.

Engsted, T. (1993) "Cointegration and Cagan's Model of Hyperinflation under Rational Expectations," *Journal of Money, Credit, and Banking* 25, 350–360.

Ermini, L. (1988) "Temporal Aggregation and Hall's Model of Consumption Behaviour," *Applied Economics* 20, 1317–1320.

Ermini, L. (1989) "Some New Evidence on the Timing of Consumption Decisions and on Their Generating Process," *Review of Economics and Statistics* 71, 643–650.

Evans, G.B.A., and N.E. Savin (1982) "Conflict among the Criteria Revisited: The *W*, *LR*, and *LM* Tests," *Econometrica* 50, 737–748.

Fama, E.F. (1976) *Foundations of Finance* (New York: Basic Books).

Farmer, R.E.A. (1999a) *Macroeconomics* (Cincinnati, OH: South-Western).

Farmer, R.E.A. (1999b) *The Macroeconomics of Self-Fulfilling Prophecies*, 2nd ed. (Cambridge, MA: MIT Press).

Fatás, A. (2000) "Endogenous Growth and Stochastic Trends," *Journal of Monetary Economics* 45, 107–128.

Feldstein, M.S. (1967) "Alternative Methods of Estimating a CES Production Function for Britain," *Economica* 34, 384–394.

Fisher, I. (1920) *Stabilizing the Dollar: A Plan to Stabilize the General Price Level without Fixing Individual Prices* (New York: Macmillan).

Fisher, L., and J.H. Lorie (1970) "Some Studies of the Variability of Returns on Investments in Common Stocks," *Journal of Business* 43, 99–134.

Foley, D.K., and T.R. Michl (1999) *Growth and Distribution* (Cambridge, MA: Harvard University Press).

Franses, P.H. (2001) "How to Deal with Intercept and Trend in Practical Cointegration Analysis?" *Applied Economics* 33, 577–579.

Freedman, D.A. (1983) "A Note on Screening Regression Equations," *American Statistician* 37, 152–155.

Freeman, S. (1989) "Fiat Money as a Medium of Exchange," *International Economic Review* 30, 137–151.

Friedman, M. (1953) "The Methodology of Positive Economics," in *Essays in Positive Economics*, ed. by M. Friedman (Chicago: University of Chicago Press).

Friedman, M. (1957) *A Theory of the Consumption Function* (Princeton, NJ: Princeton University Press).

Friedman, M. (1968) "The Role of Monetary Policy," *American Economic Review* 58, 1–17.

Friedman, M. (1977) "Nobel Lecture: Inflation and Unemployment," *Journal of Political Economy* 85, 451–472.

Friedman, M. (1987) "Quantity Theory of Money" in *The New Palgrave: A Dictionary of Economics*, ed. by J. Eatwell, M. Milgate, and P. Newman (New York: Norton).

Friedman, M. (1992) "Do Old Fallacies Ever Die?" *Journal of Economic Literature* 30, 2129–2132.

Friedman, M., and A.J. Schwartz (1963) *A Monetary History of the United States, 1867–1960* (Princeton, NJ: Princeton University Press for the National Bureau of Economic Research).

Frisch, R. (1933) "Propagation Problems and Impulse Problems in Dynamic Economics," in *Economic Essays in Honor of Gustav Cassel* (London: George Allen and Unwin, Ltd.). Reprinted in the American Economic Association *Readings in Business Cycles*, ed. by R. Gordon and L. Klein (Homewood, IL: Irwin, 1965).

Fuchs, V.R. (1963) "Capital-Labor Substitution: A Note," *Review of Economics and Statistics* 45, 436–438.

Fuller, W.A. (1976) *Introduction to Statistical Time Series* (New York: Wiley).

Fuller, W.A. (1996) *Introduction to Statistical Time Series*, 2nd ed. (New York: Wiley).

Gali, J., Gertler, M., and J.D. López-Salido (2001) "European Inflation Dynamics," *European Economic Review* 45, 1237–1270.

Gallant, A.R. (1975) "Nonlinear Regression," *American Statistician* 29, 73–81.

Ghysels, E. (1994) "On the Economics and Econometrics of Seasonality," in *Advances in Econometrics: Sixth World Congress of the Econometric Society*, Vol. I, ed. by C.A. Sims (Cambridge, UK: Cambridge University Press).

Gibbons, M.R., Ross, S., and J. Shanken (1989) "A Test of the Efficiency of a Given Portfolio," *Econometrica* 57, 1121–1152. Reprinted in *Asset Pricing Theory and Tests*, ed. by R.R. Grauer (London: Elgar, 2003).

Giles, D.E.A. (1982) "The Interpretation of Dummy Variables in Semilogarithmic Equations," *Economics Letters* 10, 77–79.

Giles, J.A., and D.E.A. Giles (1993) "Pre-Test Estimation and Testing in Econometrics: Recent Developments" *Journal of Economic Surveys* 7, 145–197. Reprinted in *Surveys in Econometrics*, ed. by L. Oxley, D.A.R. George, C.J. Roberts, and S. Sayer (Oxford: Blackwell, 1995).

Godfrey, L.G. (1978) "Testing for Multiplicative Heteroskedasticity," *Journal of Econometrics* 8, 227–236.

Godfrey, L.G. (1988) *Misspecification Tests in Econometrics* (Cambridge, UK: Cambridge University Press).

Gould, J.P., and C.R. Nelson (1974) "The Stochastic Structure of the Velocity of Money," *American Economic Review* 64, 405–418.

Granger, C.W.J. (1991) "Developments in the Study of Cointegrated Economic Variables," in *Long-Run Economic Relationships*, ed. by R.F. Engle and C.W.J. Granger (Oxford: Oxford University Press).

Granger, C.W.J., King, M.L., and H. White (1995) "Comments on Testing Economic Theories and the Use of Model Selection Criteria," *Journal of Econometrics* 67, 173–187.

Granger, C.W.J, and P. Newbold (1974) "Spurious Regressions in Econometrics," *Journal of Econometrics* 2, 111–120.

Grauer, R.R. (2003) "Introduction" in *Asset Pricing Theory and Tests*, ed. by R.R. Grauer (London: Elgar).

Greene, W.H. (2003) *Econometric Analysis*, 5th ed. (Upper Saddle River, NJ: Prentice-Hall).

Gregory, A.W., and M.R. Veall (1985) "Formulating Wald Tests of Nonlinear Restrictions," *Econometrica* 53, 1465–1467.

Grenander, U., and M. Rosenblatt (1957) *Statistical Analysis of Stationary Time Series* (New York: Wiley).

Griffiths, W.E., Hill, R.C., and G.G. Judge (1993) *Learning and Practicing Econometrics* (New York: Wiley).

Griliches, Z. (1976) "Wages of Very Young Men," *Journal of Political Economy* 84, S69–S85.

Griliches, Z. (1977) "Estimating the Returns to Schooling: Some Econometric Problems," *Econometrica* 45, 1–22.

Gruber, M.H. (1998) *Improving Efficiency by Shrinkage: The James-Stein and Ridge Regression Estimators* (New York: Dekker).

Hall, A. (1994) "Testing for a Unit Root in Time Series with Pretest Data-Based Model Selection," *Journal of Business and Economic Statistics* 12, 461–470.

Hall, R.E. (1978) "Stochastic Implications of the Life Cycle-Permanent Income Hypothesis: Theory and Evidence," *Journal of Political Economy* 86, 971–987.

Hall, R.E. (1990) "Invariance Properties of Solow's Productivity Residual," in *Growth/Productivity/Employment: Essays to Celebrate Bob Solow's Birthday*, ed. by P. Diamond (Cambridge, MA: MIT Press).

Halvorsen, R., and R. Palmquist (1980) "The Interpretation of Dummy Variables in Semilogarithmic Equations," *American Economic Review* 70, 474–475.

Hamilton, J.D. (1994) *Time Series Analysis* (Princeton, NJ: Princeton University Press).

Hanushek, E.A., and J.M. Quigley (1978) "Implicit Investment Profiles and Intertemporal Adjustment of Relative Wages," *American Economic Review* 68, 67–79.

Harris, R.I.D. (1995) *Using Cointegration Analysis in Econo-*

metric Modelling (London: Prentice Hall/Harvester Wheatsheaf).

Hart, P.E. (1987) "Lognormal Distribution," in The New Palgrave: A Dictionary of Economics, ed. by J. Eatwell, M. Milgate, and P. Newman (New York: Norton).

Hart, P.E., and S.J. Prais (1956) "The Analysis of Business Concentration: A Statistical Approach," Journal of the Royal Statistical Society, Series A, 119, 150–191.

Harvey, A.C. (1985) "Trends and Cycles in Macroeconomic Time Series," Journal of Business and Economic Statistics 3, 216–227.

Harvey, C.R. (1991) "The World Price of Covariance Risk," Journal of Finance 46, 111–158.

Hayashi, F. (2000) Econometrics (Princeton, NJ: Princeton University Press).

Hendry, D.F. (1980) "Econometrics—Alchemy or Science?" Economica 47, 387–406. Reprinted in D.F. Hendry, Econometrics: Alchemy or Science? Essays in Econometric Methodology (Oxford: Blackwell, 1993).

Hendry, D.F. (2000) Econometrics: Alchemy or Science? Essays in Econometric Methodology, new ed. (Oxford: Oxford University Press).

Heston, A., Summers, R., and B. Aten (2002) Penn World Table Version 6.1, Center for International Comparisons at the University of Pennsylvania (CICUP), October 2002.

Hogan, W.P. (1958) "Technical Progress and Production Functions," Review of Economics and Statistics 40, 407–411.

Hoover, K.D., and S.J. Perez (1999) "Data Mining Reconsidered: Encompassing and the General-to-Specific Approach to Specification Search," Econometrics Journal 2, 1–25.

Horowitz, J. (2001) "The Bootstrap" in Handbook of Economet-

rics, Vol. V, ed. by J.J. Heckman and E. Leamer (Amsterdam: North-Holland).

Houthakker, H.S. (1951) "Some Calculations on Electricity Consumption in Great Britain," Journal of the Royal Statistical Society, Series A, 114, 359–371.

Houthakker, H.S., and P.J. Williamson (1996) The Economics of Financial Markets (New York: Oxford University Press).

Hylleberg, S.(1994) "The Economics of Seasonal Cycles: A Comment," in Advances in Econometrics: Sixth World Congress of the Econometric Society, Vol. I, ed. by C.A. Sims (Cambridge, UK: Cambridge University Press).

Hylleberg, S., Engle, R., Granger, C.W.J., and B.S. Yoo (1990) "Seasonal Integration and Cointegration," Journal of Econometrics 44, 215–338.

Jagannathan, R., and E.R. McGrattan (1995) "The CAPM Debate" Federal Reserve Bank of Minneapolis Quarterly Review 19 (Fall), 2–17.

Jarque, C.M., and A.K. Bera (1980) "Efficient Tests for Normality, Heteroskedasticity and Serial Independence of Regression Residuals," Economics Letters 6, 255–259.

Jarque, C.M., and A.K. Bera (1987) "A Test for Normality of Observations and Regression Residuals," International Statistical Review 55, 163–172.

Jeong, J., and G.S. Maddala (1993) "A Perspective on Application of Bootstrap Methods in Econometrics," in Handbook of Statistics, Vol. 11, ed. by G.S. Maddala, C.R. Rao, and H.D. Vinod (Amsterdam: North-Holland).

Jevons, W.S. (1875) Money and the Mechanism of Exchange (London: Appleton).

Johansen, S. (1988) "Statistical Analysis of Cointegrating Vectors,"

Journal of Economic Dynamics and Control 12, 231–254.

Johansen, S. (1995) Likelihood-Based Inference in Cointegrated Vector Autoregressive Models (Oxford: Oxford University Press).

Johnston, J., and J. DiNardo (1997) Econometric Methods, 4th ed. (New York: McGraw-Hill).

Jones, C.I. (1995) "Time Series Tests of Endogenous Growth Models," Quarterly Journal of Economics 110, 495–525.

Jones, C.I. (2002) Introduction to Economic Growth, 2nd ed. (New York: Norton).

Jorgenson, D.W. (1986) "Econometric Methods for Modeling Producer Behavior," in Handbook of Econometrics, Vol. III, ed. by Z. Griliches and M.D. Intriligator (Amsterdam: North-Holland).

Jorgenson, D.W., and B.M. Fraumeni (1995) "The Accumulation of Human and Nonhuman Capital, 1948–1984," in Productivity, Volume 1: Postwar U.S. Economic Growth, ed. by D.W. Jorgenson (Cambridge, MA: MIT Press).

Judge, G.G., Griffiths, W.E., Hill, R.C., Lütkepohl, H., and T.-C. Lee (1985) The Theory and Practice of Econometrics, 2nd ed. (New York: Wiley).

Judge, G.G., Hill, R.C., Griffiths, W.E., Lütkepohl, H., and T.-C. Lee (1988) Introduction to the Theory and Practice of Econometrics (New York: Wiley).

Kennedy, P.E. (1981) "Estimation with Correctly Interpreted Dummy Variables in Semilogarithmic Equations," American Economic Review 70, 801.

Kennedy, P.E. (1985) "Interpreting Dummy Variables," Review of Economics and Statistics 67, 174–175.

Kennedy, P.E. (1998) A Guide to Econometrics, 4th ed. (Cambridge, MA: MIT Press).

Keynes, J.M. (1936) *The General Theory of Employment, Interest, and Money* (London: Macmillan).

King, R.G., and C.I. Plosser (1984) "Money, Credit, and Prices in a Real Business Cycle," *American Economic Review* 74, 363–380.

King, R.G., Plosser, C.I., Stock, J.H., and M.W. Watson (1987) "Stochastic Trends and Economic Fluctuations," NBER Working Paper No. 2229. National Bureau of Economic Research, New York.

King, R.G., Plosser, C.I., Stock, J.H., and M.W. Watson (1991) "Stochastic Trends and Economic Fluctuations," *American Economic Review* 81, 819–840.

Klein, L.R. (1962) *An Introduction to Econometrics* (Englewood Cliffs, NJ: Prentice-Hall).

Klein, L.R., and A.S. Goldberger (1955) *An Econometric Model of the United States, 1929–52* (Amsterdam: North-Holland).

Klein, L.R., and R.F. Kosobud (1961) "Some Econometrics of Growth: Great Ratios of Economics," *Quarterly Journal of Economics* 75, 173–198.

Kmenta, J. (1986) *Elements of Econometrics*, 2nd ed. (New York: Macmillan).

Knowles, S., and P.D. Owen (1995) "Health Capital and Cross-Country Variation in Income per Capita in the Mankiw-Romer-Weil Model," *Economics Letters* 48, 99–106.

Knowles, S., and P.D. Owen (1997) "Education and Health in an Effective-Labour Empirical Growth Model," *Economic Record* 73, 314–328.

Knuth, D.E. (1997) *Seminumerical Algorithms*, Vol. 2 of *The Art of Computer Programming* (Reading, MA: Addison-Wesley).

Koenker, R. (1981) "A Note on Studentizing a Test for Heteroskedasticity," *Journal of Econometrics* 17, 107–112.

Koopmans, T.C. (1965) "On the Concept of Optimal Economic Growth," in *The Econometric Approach to Development Planning* (Amsterdam: North-Holland).

Kuznets, S. (1946) *National Product since 1867* (New York: National Bureau of Economic Research).

Kwiatkowski, D., Phillips, P.C.B., Schmidt, P., and Y. Shin (1992) "Testing the Null Hypothesis of Stationarity against the Alternative of a Unit Root," *Journal of Econometrics* 54, 159–178.

Lafontaine, F., and K.J. White (1986) "Obtaining Any Wald Statistic You Want," *Economics Letters* 21, 35–40.

Laidler, D.E.W. (1993) *The Demand for Money*, 4th ed. (New York: Harper-Collins).

Latinen, K. (1978) "Why Is Demand Homogeneity So Often Rejected?" *Economics Letters* 1, 187–191.

Lau, S.-H.P. (1997) "Using Stochastic Growth Models to Understand Unit Roots and Breaking Trends," *Journal of Economic Dynamics and Control* 21, 1645–1667.

Lau, S.-H.P. (1999) "I(0) In, Integration and Cointegration Out: Time Series Properties of Endogenous Growth Models," *Journal of Econometrics* 93, 1–24.

Lawrence, R.J. (1988) "Applications in Economics and Business," in *Lognormal Distributions: Theory and Applications*, ed. by E.L. Crow and K. Shimizu (New York: Dekker).

Layard, P.R.G., and A.A. Walters (1978) *Microeconomic Theory* (New York: McGraw-Hill).

Leser, C.E.V. (1963) "Forms of Engel Functions," *Econometrica* 31, 694–703.

Levy, H., and M. Sarnat (1984) *Portfolio and Investment Selection: Theory and Practice* (Englewood Cliffs, NJ: Prentice-Hall).

Lewbel, A. (1991) "The Rank of Demand Systems: Theory and Non-Parametric Estimation," *Econometrica* 59, 711–730.

Lintner, J. (1965) "The Valuation of Risk Assets and the Selection of Risky Investments in Stock Portfolios and Capital Budgets," *Review of Economics and Statistics* 47, 13–37.

Lipsey, R.G., and K. Carlaw (2000) "What Does Total Factor Productivity Measure?" *International Productivity Monitor* 1, 31–40.

Ljung, G., and G. Box (1978) "On a Measure of Lack of Fit in Time Series Models," *Biometrika* 65, 297–303.

Long, J.S. (1997) *Regression Models for Categorical and Limited Dependent Variables* (Thousand Oaks, CA: Sage Publications).

Lothian, J.R., and M.P. Taylor (1996) "Real Exchange Rate Behavior: The Recent Float from the Perspective of the Past Two Centuries," *Journal of Political Economy* 104, 488–509.

Lovell, M.C. (1983) "Data Mining," *Review of Economics and Statistics* 65, 1–12.

Lucas, R.E., Jr. (1976) "Econometric Policy Evaluation: A Critique," in *The Phillips Curve and Labor Markets*, ed. by K. Brunner and A.H. Meltzer, *Carnegie-Rochester Conference Series on Public Policy* 1, 19–46. Reprinted in R.E. Lucas, Jr., *Studies in Business-Cycle Theory* (Cambridge, MA: MIT Press, 1981).

Lucas, R.E., Jr. (1977) "Understanding Business Cycles" in *Stabilization of the Domestic and International Economy*, ed. by K. Brunner and A.H. Meltzer, *Carnegie-Rochester Conference Series on Public Policy* 5, 7–29.

Reprinted in R.E. Lucas, Jr. *Studies in Business-Cycle Theory* (Cambridge, MA: MIT Press, 1983), and in F.E. Kydland, *Business Cycle Theory* (Aldershot, UK: Elgar, 1995).

Lucas, R.E., Jr. (1988) "On the Mechanics of Economic Development," *Journal of Monetary Economics* 22, 3–42.

Lucas, R.E., Jr. (2003) "Macroeconomic Priorities," *American Economic Review* 93, 1–14.

MacKinlay, A.C. (1987) "On Multivariate Tests of the CAPM," *Journal of Financial Economics* 18, 341–371.

MacKinnon, J.G. (1992) "Model Specification Tests and Artificial Regressions," *Journal of Economic Literature* 30, 102–146.

MacKinnon, J.G. (2002) "Presidential Address: Bootstrap Inference in Econometrics," *Canadian Journal of Economics* 35, 615–645.

Maddala, G.S. (1983) *Limited Dependent and Qualitative Variables in Econometrics* (Cambridge, UK: Cambridge University Press).

Maddala, G.S. (2001) *Introduction to Econometrics*, 3rd ed. (New York: Wiley)

Maddala, G.S., and I.-M. Kim (1998) *Unit Roots, Cointegration, and Structural Change* (Cambridge, UK: Cambridge University Press).

Maddison, A. (1982) *Phases of Capitalist Development* (Oxford: Oxford University Press).

Maddison, A. (1989) *The World Economy in the 20th Century* (Paris: OECD).

Makinen, G.E. (1977) *Money, the Price Level, and Interest Rates—An Introduction to Monetary Theory* (Englewood Cliffs, NJ: Prentice-Hall).

Malinvaud, E. (1970) *Statistical Methods of Econometrics* (Amsterdam: North-Holland).

Malkiel, B.G. (1996) *A Random Walk down Wall Street*, 6th ed. (New York: Norton).

Malkiel, B.G. (1999) *A Random Walk down Wall Street*, 7th ed. (New York: Norton)

Malkiel, B. (2003) "The Efficient Market Hypothesis and Its Critics," *Journal of Economic Perspectives* 17, 59–82.

Mankiw, N.G., Romer, D., and D.N. Weil (1992) "A Contribution to the Empirics of Economic Growth," *Quarterly Journal of Economics* 107, 407–437.

Manski, C.F. (1995) *Identification Problems in the Social Sciences* (Cambridge, MA: Harvard University Press).

Markowitz, H.M. (1952) "Portfolio Selection," *Journal of Finance* 7, 77–91.

Markowitz, H.M. (1959) *Portfolio Selection: Efficient Diversification of Investments* (New York: Wiley).

Marshall, A. (1890) *Principles of Economics* (London: Macmillan).

McCullough, B.D. (1999) "Econometric Software Reliability: EViews, LIMDEP, SHAZAM, and TSP," *Journal of Applied Econometrics* 14, 191–202.

McCullough, B.D., and H.D. Vinod (1999) "The Numerical Reliability of Econometric Software," *Journal of Economic Literature* 37, 633–665.

McCullough, B.D., and H.D. Vinod (2003) "Verifying the Solution from a Nonlinear Solver: A Case Study," *American Economic Review* 93, 873–892.

McGrattan, E.R., and J.A. Schmitz, Jr. (1999) "Explaining Cross-Country Income Differences," in *Handbook of Macroeconomics*, Vol. IA, ed. by J.B. Taylor and M. Woodford (Amsterdam: North-Holland).

Milbourne, R., Otto, G., and G. Voss (2003) "Public Investment and Economic Growth," *Applied Economics* 35, 527–540.

Miller, M.H., and C.W. Upton (1974) *Macroeconomics: A Neoclassical Introduction* (Chicago: University of Chicago Press).

Mills, J.A., and K. Prasad (1992) "A Comparison of Model Selection Criteria," *Econometric Reviews* 11, 201–233.

Mincer, J. (1974) *Schooling, Experience and Earnings* (New York: Columbia University Press for the National Bureau of Economic Research).

Miron, J.A. (1994) "The Economics of Seasonal Cycles," in *Advances in Econometrics: Sixth World Congress of the Econometric Society*, Vol. I, ed. by C.A. Sims (Cambridge, UK: Cambridge University Press).

Miron, J.A. (1996) *The Economics of Seasonal Cycles* (Cambridge, MA: MIT Press).

Miron, J.A., and S.P. Zeldes (1988) "Seasonality, Cost Shocks, and the Production Smoothing Model of Inventories," *Econometrica* 56, 877–908.

Mizon, G.E. (1977) "Inferential Procedures in Nonlinear Models: An Application in a UK Industrial Cross Section Study of Factor Substitution and Returns to Scale," *Econometrica* 45, 1221–1242.

Mizon, G.E. (1984) "The Encompassing Approach in Econometrics," in *Quantitative Economics and Econometric Analysis*, ed. by K.F. Wallis and D.F. Hendry (Oxford: Blackwell).

Mizon, G.E. (1995) "A Simple Message for Autocorrelation Correctors: Don't," *Journal of Econometrics* 69, 267–288.

Mizon, G.E., and J.-M. Richard (1986) "The Encompassing Principle and Its Application to Testing

Non-Nested Hypotheses," *Econometrica* 54, 657–678.

Morley, J.C., Nelson, C.R., and E. Zivot (2003) "Why Are Beveridge-Nelson and Unobserved Components Decompositions of GDP So Different?" *Review of Economics and Statistics* 85, 235–243.

Mossin, J. (1966) "Equilibrium in a Capital Asset Market," *Econometrica* 34, 768–783.

Murray, C.J., and C.R. Nelson (2000) "The Uncertain Trend in U.S. GDP," *Journal of Monetary Economics* 46, 79–95.

Muth, J. (1961) "Rational Expectations and the Theory of Price Movements," *Econometrica* 29, 315–335.

Nelson, C.R., and H. Kang (1981) "Spurious Periodicity in Inappropriately Detrended Time Series," *Econometrica* 49, 741–751.

Nelson, C.R., and H. Kang (1984) "Pitfalls in the Use of Time as an Explanatory Variable in Regression," *Journal of Business and Economic Statistics* 2, 73–82.

Nelson, C.R., and C.I. Plosser (1982) "Trends and Random Walks in Macroeconomic Time Series," *Journal of Monetary Economics* 10, 139–162.

Nerlove, M. (1963) "Returns to Scale in Electricity Supply," in *Measurement in Economics: Studies in Mathematical Economics and Econometrics in Memory of Yehuda Grunfeld*, ed. by C.F. Christ (Stanford, CA: Stanford University Press). Reprinted in *Economic Statistics and Econometrics*, ed. by A. Zellner (Boston: Little, Brown, 1968).

Ng, S., and P. Perron (1995) "Unit Root Tests in ARMA Models with Data-Dependent Methods for the Selection of the Truncation Lag," *Journal of the American Economic Association* 90, 268–281.

Nonneman, W., and P. Vanhoudt (1996) "A Further Augmen-

tation of the Solow Model and the Empirics of Economic Growth for OECD Countries," *Quarterly Journal of Economics* 111, 943–953.

Orcutt, G.H. (1948) "A Study of the Autoregressive Nature of the Time Series used for Tinbergen's Model of the Economic System of the United States, 1919–1932," *Journal of the Royal Statistical Society*, Series B, 10, 1–45.

Osberg, L. (2000) "Poverty in Canada and the United States: Measurement, Trends, and Implications," *Canadian Journal of Economics* 33, 847–877.

Osberg, L., and K. Xu (2000) "International Comparisons of Poverty Intensity: Index Decomposition and Bootstrap Inference," *Journal of Human Resources* 35, 51–81.

Pagan, A. (1996) "The Econometrics of Financial Markets," *Journal of Empirical Finance* 3, 15–102.

Parkin, M. (1998) "Unemployment, Inflation, and Monetary Policy," *Canadian Journal of Economics* 31, 1003–1032.

Perron, P. (1989) "The Great Crash, the Oil Price Shock, and the Unit Root Hypothesis," *Econometrica* 57, 1361–1401.

Phillips, A.W. (1958) "The Relation between Unemployment and the Rate of Change of Money Wage Rates in the United Kingdom, 1861–1957," *Economica* 25, 283–299.

Phillips, P.C.B. (1986) "Understanding Spurious Regressions in Econometrics," *Journal of Econometrics* 33, 311–340.

Phillips, P.C.B., and S. Ouliaris (1990) "Asymptotic Properties of Residual Based Tests for Cointegration," *Econometrica* 58, 165–193.

Phillips, P.C.B., and J.Y. Park (1988) "On the Formulation of Wald Tests of Nonlinear Restrictions," *Econometrica* 56, 1065–1083.

Phillips, P.C.B., and P. Perron (1988) "Testing for a Unit Root in Time Series Regression," *Biometrika* 75, 335–346.

Pindyck, R.S., and D.L. Rubinfeld (1991) *Econometric Models and Economic Forecasts*, 3rd ed. (New York: McGraw-Hill).

Poincaré, H. (1905) *La Science et l'Hypothèse*, translated into English as *Science and Hypothesis* (London: Walter Scott Publishing).

Poirier, D.J. (1995) *Intermediate Statistics and Econometrics: A Comparative Approach* (Cambridge, MA: MIT Press).

Pollak, R. (1969) "Conditional Demand Functions and the Implications of Separability," *Quarterly Journal of Economics* 83, 70–78.

Poole, W. (1978) *Money and the Economy: A Monetarist View* (Reading, MA: Addison-Wesley).

Prais, S.J., and H.S. Houthakker (1955, abridged impression 1971) *The Analysis of Family Budgets* (Cambridge, UK: Cambridge University Press).

Prescott, E.C. (1986a) "Theory Ahead of Business Cycle Measurement," Federal Reserve Bank of Minneapolis *Quarterly Review* 10 (Fall), 9–22.

Prescott, E.C. (1986b) "Response to a Skeptic," Federal Reserve Bank of Minneapolis *Quarterly Review* 10 (Fall), 28–33.

Psacharopoulos, G. (1994) "Returns to Investment in Education: A Global Update," *World Development* 22, 1325–1343.

Pyatt, G., and R. Stone (1964) *Capital, Output and Employment 1948–60, A Programme for Growth*, Vol. 4 (London: Chapman and Hall).

Quah, D. (1993) "Galton's Fallacy and Tests of the Convergence Hypothesis," *Scandinavian Journal of Economics* 95, 427–443.

Quandt, R.E. (1983) "Computational Problems and Methods" in *Handbook of Econometrics*,

Vol. I, ed. by Z. Griliches and M.D. Intriligator (Amsterdam: North-Holland).

Ramsey, F.P. (1928) "A Mathematical Theory of Saving," *Economic Journal* 38, 543–559.

Ramsey, J.B. (1969) "Tests for Specification Error in Classical Linear Least Squares Regression Analysis," *Journal of the Royal Statistical Society*, Series B, 31, 250–271.

Roll, R. (1977) "A Critique of the Asset Pricing Theory's Tests; Part I: On Past and Potential Testability of the Theory," *Journal of Financial Economics* 4, 129–176.

Romer, D. (2001) *Advanced Macroeconomics*, 2nd ed. (New York: McGraw-Hill).

Ross, S.A. (1987) "Finance" in *The New Palgrave: A Dictionary of Economics*, ed. by J. Eatwell, M. Milgate, and P. Newman (New York: Norton).

Rothenberg, T.J. (1984) "Approximating the Distributions of Econometric Estimators and Test Statistics," in *Handbook of Econometrics*, Vol. II, ed. by Z. Griliches and M.D. Intriligator (Amsterdam: North-Holland).

Russell, B. (1945) *A History of Western Philosophy* (New York: Simon & Schuster).

Ruttan, V.W. (2001) *Technology, Growth, and Development* (Oxford: Oxford University Press).

Ryan, D.L., and T.J. Wales (1999) "Flexible and Semiflexible Consumer Demands with Quadratic Engel Curves," *Review of Economics and Statistics* 81, 277–287.

Sachs, J.D., and F.B. Larrain (1993) *Macroeconomics in the Global Economy* (Englewood Cliffs, NJ: Prentice Hall).

Sala-i-Martin, X. (1996) "Regional Cohesion: Evidence and Theories of Regional Growth and Convergence," *European Economic Review* 40, 1325–1352.

Sampson, M. (1991) "The Effect of Parameter Uncertainty on Forecast Variances and Confidence Intervals for Unit-Root and Trend Stationary Time-Series Models," *Journal of Applied Econometrics* 6, 67–76.

Samuelson, P.A. (1958) "An Exact Consumption-Loan Model of Interest with or without the Social Contrivance of Money," *Journal of Political Economy* 66, 467–482.

Sarlo, C. (1998) "Do the Poor Have More Children?" *Fraser Forum*, February 1998, 24–25.

Schultze, C.L. (2003) "The Consumer Price Index: Conceptual Issues and Practical Suggestions," *Journal of Economic Perspectives* 17, 3–22.

Schwartz, G. (1978) "Estimating the Dimension of a Model," *Annals of Statistics* 6, 461–464.

Schwert, G.W. (1989) "Tests for Unit Roots: A Monte Carlo Investigation," *Journal of Business and Economic Statistics* 7, 147–160.

Scitovsky, T. (1976) *The Joyless Economy* (New York: Oxford University Press).

Seber, G.A.F., and C.J. Wild (1989) *Nonlinear Regression* (New York: Wiley).

Sen, A.K. (1976) "Poverty: An Ordinal Approach to Measurement," *Econometrica* 44, 219–231.

Sharpe, W.F. (1964) "Capital Asset Prices: A Theory of Market Equilibrium under Conditions of Risk," *Journal of Finance* 19, 425–442.

Sharpe, W.F. (1985) *Investments*, 3rd ed. (Englewood Cliffs, NJ: Prentice-Hall).

Shephard, R.W. (1953) *Cost and Production Functions* (Princeton, NJ: Princeton University Press).

Slutsky, E.E. (1937) "The Summation of Random Causes as a Source of Cyclic Processes," *Econometrica* 5, 105–146.

Solnik, B. (1974) "Why Not Diversify Internationally Rather than Domestically?" *Financial Analysts Journal*, July/August, 48–54.

Solow, R.M. (1956) "A Contribution to the Theory of Economic Growth," *Quarterly Journal of Economics* 70, 65–94.

Solow, R.M. (1957) "Technical Change and the Aggregate Production Function," *Review of Economics and Statistics* 39, 312–320. Reprinted in *Economic Statistics and Econometrics*, ed. by A. Zellner (Boston: Little, Brown, 1968); in *Readings in Macroeconomics*, 2nd ed., ed. by M.G. Mueller (Hinsdale, IL: Dryden, 1971); in *Business Cycle Theory*, ed. by F.E. Kydland (Aldershot, UK: Elgar, 1995); and in *Real Business Cycles—A Reader*, ed. by J.E. Hartley, K.D. Hoover, and K.D. Salyer (London: Routledge, 1998).

Solow, R.M. (1970) *Growth Theory—An Exposition* (Oxford: Clarendon Press).

Stamp, J. (1929) *Some Economic Factors in Modern Life* (London: King and Son).

Stewart, K.G. (1995) "The Functional Equivalence of the W, LR, and LM Statistics," *Economics Letters* 49, 109–112.

Stewart, K.G. (1997) "Exact Testing in Multivariate Regression," *Econometric Reviews* 16, 321–352.

Stewart, K.G., and J.C.H. Jones (1998) "Hedonics and Demand Analysis: The Implicit Demand for Player Attributes," *Economic Inquiry* 36, 192–202.

Stigler, G.J. (1987) *The Theory of Price*, 4th ed. (New York: Macmillan).

Stock, J.H. (1987) "Asymptotic Properties of Least-Squares Estimators of Co-integrating Vectors," *Econometrica* 55, 1035–1056.

Stock, J.H. (1994) "Unit Roots, Structural Breaks, and Trends," in *Handbook of Econometrics*, Vol. IV, ed. by R.F. Engle and D.L. McFadden (Amsterdam: North-Holland).

Stock, J.H., and M.W. Watson (1988) "Variable Trends in Economic Time Series," *Journal of Economic Perspectives* 2, 147–174.

Stock, J.H., and M.W. Watson (1999) "Business Cycle Fluctuations in US Macroeconomic Time Series," in *Handbook of Macroeconomics*, Vol. IA, ed. by J.B. Taylor and M. Woodford (Amsterdam: North-Holland).

Stock, J.H., and M.W. Watson (2001) "Vector Autoregressions," *Journal of Economic Perspectives* 15, 101–115.

Stock, J.H., and M.W. Watson (2003) *Introduction to Econometrics* (New York: Addison-Wesley).

Stock, J.H., Wright, J.H., and M. Yogo (2002) "A Survey of Weak Instruments and Weak Identification in Generalized Method of Moments," *Journal of Business and Economic Statistics* 20, 518–529.

Suits, D.B. (1984) "Dummy Variables: Mechanics vs. Interpretation," *Review of Economics and Statistics* 66, 177–180.

Summers, R., and A. Heston (1988) "A New Set of International Comparisons of Real Product and Price Levels for 130 Countries, 1950–85," *Review of Income and Wealth* 34, 1–26.

Summers, R., and A. Heston (1991) "The Penn World Table (Mark 5): An Expanded Set of International Comparisons, 1950–1988," *Quarterly Journal of Economics* 106, 327–368.

Swan, T.W. (1956) "Economic Growth and Capital Accumulation," *Economic Record* 32, 334–361.

Taylor, M.P. (1991) "The Hyperinflation Model of Money Demand Revisited," *Journal of Money, Credit, and Banking* 23, 327–351.

Temple, J. (1998) "Equipment Investment and the Solow Model," *Oxford Economic Papers* 50, 39–62.

Theil, H. (1971) *Principles of Econometrics* (New York: Wiley).

Thomas, R.L. (1987) *Applied Demand Analysis* (London: Longman).

Tobin, J. (1958a) "Estimation of Relationships for Limited Dependent Variables," *Econometrica* 26, 24–36.

Tobin, J. (1958b) "Liquidity Preference as Behavior Towards Risk," *Review of Economic Studies* 25, 65–86.

Tobin, J. (1970) "Money and Income: Post Hoc Ergo Propter Hoc," *Quarterly Journal of Economics* 84, 301–317.

Topel, R. (1999) "Labor Markets and the Macroeconomy," in *Handbook of Labor Economics*, Vol. IIIC, ed. by O. Ashenfelter and D. Card (Amsterdam: North-Holland).

Ullah, A., and R. Bruenig (1998) "Econometric Analysis in Complex Surveys," in *Handbook of Applied Economic Statistics*, ed. by A. Ullah and D.E.A. Giles (New York: Dekker).

Urzúa, C.M. (1996) "On the Correct Use of Omnibus Tests for Normality," *Economics Letters* 53, 247–251.

Varian, H.R. (1992) *Microeconomic Analysis*, 3rd ed. (New York: Norton).

Varian, H.R. (1996) *Intermediate Microeconomics*, 4th ed. (New York: Norton).

Veall, M.R. (1998) "Applications of the Bootstrap in Econometrics and Economic Statistics," in *Handbook of Applied Economic Statistics*, ed. by A. Ullah and D.E.A. Giles (New York: Dekker).

Wagner, W.H., and S.C. Lau (1971) "The Effect of Diversification on Risk," *Financial Analysts Journal* 27, 48–53.

Watson, M.H. (1986) "Univariate Detrending Methods with Stochastic Trends," *Journal of Monetary Economics* 18, 49–75.

White, H. (1980) "A Heteroskedasticity-Consistent Covariance Matrix and a Direct Test for Heteroskedasticity," *Econometrica* 48, 817–838.

White, H. (2000) "A Reality Check for Data Snooping," *Econometrica* 68, 1097–1126.

Winkelmann, R. (2000) *Econometric Analysis of Count Data*, 3rd ed. (Berlin: Springer-Verlag).

Wooldridge, J.M. (2000) *Introductory Econometrics: A Modern Approach* (Cincinnati, OH: South-Western)

Wooldridge, J.M. (2001) *Econometric Analysis of Cross Section and Panel Data* (Cambridge, MA: MIT Press).

Working, H. (1943) "Statistical Laws of Family Expenditure," *Journal of the American Statistical Association* 38, 43–56.

Working, H. (1960) "Note on the Correlation of First Differences of Averages in a Random-Chain," *Econometrica* 28, 916–918.

Young, A. (1995) "The Tyranny of Numbers: Confronting the Statistical Realities of the East Asian Growth Experience," *Quarterly Journal of Economics* 110, 641–680.

Yule, G.U. (1926) "Why Do We Sometimes Get Nonsense-Correlations between Time-Series?—A Study in Sampling and the Nature of Time-Series," *Journal of the Royal Statistical Society* 89, 1–64. Reprinted in *The Foundations of Econometrics*, ed. by D.F. Hendry and M.S. Morgan (New York: Cambridge University Press, 1995).

Zellner, A. (1987) "Bayesian Inference" in *The New Palgrave: A Dictionary of Economics*, ed. by J. Eatwell, M. Milgate, and P. Newman (New York: Norton).

Index

Page numbers beginning with C are references to Appendix C, which is provided as the file appendc.pdf on the CD packaged with this book. Items within footnotes have "n" next to the page number.